Flowers
A Guide for Your Garden

*Translated from the Italian and revised by Henry Cocker
(edited by Michael Sonino)*

Ippolito Pizzetti and Henry Cocker, A.H.R.H.S.

Flowers

A GUIDE FOR YOUR GARDEN

*Being a Selective Anthology of Flowering Shrubs,
Herbaceous Perennials, Bulbs, and Annuals,
Familiar and Unfamiliar, Rare and Popular,
with Historical, Mythological, and Cultural Particulars*

Illustrated with 297 colourplates selected
from early-18th- and 19th-century botanical periodicals

VOLUME TWO

Harry N. Abrams, Inc., Publishers, New York

Frontispiece: *Platycodon grandiflorus* var. *mariesii*
From Curtis's Botanical Magazine, 1794

Nai Y. Chang, *Vice-President, Design and Production*
John L. Hochmann, *Executive Editor*
Margaret L. Kaplan, *Managing Editor*
Julia Fahey, *Copy Editor*
Barbara Lyons, *Director, Photo Department, Rights and Reproductions*
Nancy D. Rosen, *Index*
Christy S. Nettles, *Book Design*

Italian edition edited by Orietta Garzanti
Black-and-white illustrations by Orietta Garzanti, Carla della Beffa,
and Gabriele Gossner

Library of Congress Cataloging in Publication Data

Pizzetti, Ippolito.
 Flowers: a guide for your garden.

 Translation of Il libro dei fiori.
 Bibliography: p.
 1. Flowers. 2. Flower gardening. I. Cocker,
Henry, joint author. II. Title.
SB406.P5913   635.9   73-7526
ISBN 0-8109-0127-7

Copyright 1968 in Italy by Garzanti Editore, Milan
Library of Congress Catalogue Card Number: 73-7526
Published by Harry N. Abrams, Incorporated, New York, 1975
All rights reserved. No part of the contents of this books may be
reproduced without the written permission of the publishers
Printed and bound in Italy

CONTENTS VOLUME I

Editor's Foreword and Acknowledgements • xv
Introduction by Henry Cocker • xix

$\mathcal{A}$BELIA • 1; ABUTILON • 2; ACACIA ("*Mimosa*") • 4; ACHILLEA (*Yarrow*) • 12; ACIDANTHERA [BICOLOR] • 19; ACONITUM (*Monkshood* or *Aconite*) • 20; ACTINIDIA • 25; ADONIS (also see ANEMONE and PULSATILLA) • 27; AESCULUS (*Horse-Chestnut*) • 30; *African Daisy* (see ARCTOTIS, DIMORPHOTHECA, GAZANIA, GERBERA, and VENIDIUM); AGAPANTHUS (*Lily-of-the-Nile*) • 31; AGERATUM • 35; ALLIUM • 36; *Almond* (see PRUNUS); ALONSOA • 39; ALSTROEMERIA (*Peruvian Lily*) • 41; ALTHAEA (*Hollyhock*) • 43; ALYSSUM (also see LOBULARIA) • 48; AMARANTHUS (*Amaranth*: also see GOMPHRENA) • 51; AMARYLLIS (also see HIPPEASTRUM) • 52; AMYGDALUS (see PRUNUS); ANCHUSA (*Bugloss*) • 54; *Andromeda* (see PIERIS); ANEMONE (also see ADONIS and PULSATILLA) • 56; ANTHEMIS (*Camomile*) • 66; ANTIRRHINUM (*Snapdragon*) • 67; *Apricot* (see PRUNUS); AQUILEGIA (*Columbine*) • 72; ARABIS • 79; ARCTOTIS • 82; ARMERIA (*Thrift*) • 85; ASCLEPIAS (*Milkweed*) • 87; ASTER (also see CALLISTEPHUS) • 90; ASTILBE (also see SPIRAEA) • 98; AUBRIETA • 102; AURICULA (see PRIMULA); *Autumn Crocus* (see COLCHICUM); *Azalea* (see RHODODENDRON)

$\mathcal{B}$*aby's Breath* (see GYPSOPHILA); *Bachelor's Button* (see CENTAUREA); *Balloon Flower* (see PLATYCODON); *Balsam* (see IMPATIENS); *Barberry* (see BERBERIS); *Barberton Daisy* (see GERBERA); *Beard Tongue* (see PENSTEMON); *Beauty Bush* (see KOLKWITZIA); *Bee Balm* (see MONARDA); BEGONIA • 103; *Bell-Flower* (see CAMPANULA); BELLIS • 112; BERBERIS (*Barberry*) • 117; BIGNONIA [CAPREOLATA] (*Trumpet-Flower*) • 126; *Bindweed* (see CONVOLVULUS); *Black-Eyed Susan* (see RUDBECKIA); *Bladder Nut* (see STAPHYLEA); *Bleeding Heart* (see DICENTRA); BLETILLA • 129; *Bluebell* (see CAMPANULA, CLEMATIS, PHACELIA, and SCILLA); *Bottle-Brush Flower* (see CALLISTEMON); BOUGAINVILLEA • 130; *Brazilian Spider Flower* (see TIBOUCHINA); *Broom* (see CYTISUS and GENISTA); BUDDLEIA (*Butterfly Bush*) • 132; *Bugloss* (see ANCHUSA: also see ECHIUM); *Buttercup* (see RANUNCULUS); *Butterfly Bush* (see BUDDLEIA); *Butterfly Weed* (see ASCLEPIAS)

$\mathcal{C}$ALCEOLARIA (*Slipper Flower*) • 139; CALENDULA (*Marigold*) • 144; *California Poppy* (see ESCHSCHOLZIA); *California Tree Poppy* (see ROMNEYA); *Calla* (see ZANTEDESCHIA); *Calliopsis* (see COREOPSIS); CALLISTEMON (*Bottle-Brush Flower*) • 146; CALLISTEPHUS [CHINENSIS]

(*China Aster*: also see ASTER)•148; CALLUNA [VULGARIS] (*Heather*: also see ERICA)•153; CALONYCTION (*Moonflower*)•157; CAMELLIA•159; *Camomile* (see ANTHEMIS); CAMPANULA (*Bell-Flower*)•174; *Campion* (see LYCHNIS); CAMPSIS (*Trumpet Vine*)•182; *Candytuft* (see IBERIS); CANNA•186; CAPPARIS (*Caper*)•188; *Carnation* (see DIANTHUS); CARYOPTERIS•191; CASSIA (*Senna*)•193; *Catchfly* (see LYCHNIS and SILENE); *Catnip* (see NEPETA); CEANOTHUS•195; CELOSIA [ARGENTEA] (*Cockscomb*)•203; CENTAUREA (*Cornflower* or *Bachelor's Button*)•204; CERASTIUM (*Snow-in-Summer*)•209; CERATOSTIGMA (*Plumbago*)•210; CESTRUM•214; CHAENOMELES (*Quince*: also see CYDONIA)•216; *Cherry* (see PRUNUS); CHEIRANTHUS (*Wallflower*)•221; *China Aster* (see CALLISTEPHUS); *Chinese Lantern* (see PHYSALIS); CHIONODOXA•224; *Christmas Rose* (see HELLEBORUS); CHRYSANTHEMUM•225; *Cineraria* (see SENECIO); *Cinquefoil* (see POTENTILLA); CISTUS (*Rock Rose*)•244; CLARKIA•252; CLEMATIS•253; CLEOME (*Spider Flower*)•270; CLERODENDRUM ("*Hydrangea*")•272; COBAEA•276; *Cockscomb* (see CELOSIA); COLCHICUM (*Autumn Crocus* or *Meadow Saffron*)•278; COLEUS•283; *Columbine* (see AQUILEGIA); *Cone Flower* (see ECHINACEA and RUDBECKIA); CONVALLARIA (*Lily of the Valley*)•285; CONVOLVULUS (*Bindweed* or *Morning Glory*)•287; *Coral Bells* (see HEUCHERA); COREOPSIS•295; *Cornflower* (see CENTAUREA); CORNUS (*Dogwood*)•300; CORYLOPSIS•308; COSMOS•309; COTONEASTER•312; *Cowslip* (see PRIMULA); *Crabapple* (see MALUS); *Crape Myrtle* (see LAGERSTROEMIA); CRATAEGUS (*Hawthorn*)•322; CROCUS (also see COLCHICUM)•330; CUPHEA•338; CYCLAMEN•339; CYDONIA [OBLONGA] (*Quince*: also see CHAENOMELES)•346; *Cypress Vine* (see QUAMOCLIT); CYTISUS (*Broom*: also see GENISTA)•348

*D*affodil (see NARCISSUS); DAHLIA•355; *Daisy* (see BELLIS, CHRYSANTHEMUM, FELICIA, and OLEARIA); DAPHNE•364; DATURA•369; *Daylily* (see HEMEROCALLIS); DELPHINIUM (*Larkspur*)•376; DESMODIUM•387; DEUTZIA•389; DIANTHUS (*Carnation, Pink,* and *Sweet William*)•394; DICENTRA (*Bleeding Heart* and *Dutchman's Breeches*)•405; DIERVILLA (also see WEIGELA)•409; DIGITALIS (*Foxglove*)•411; DIMORPHOTHECA (*Namaqualand Daisy* or *Cape Marigold*)•415; *Dogwood* (see CORNUS); DOLICHOS•419; DORONICUM (*Leopard's Bane*)•421; DRACOCEPHALUM (see PHYSOSTEGIA); *Dutchman's Breeches* (see DICENTRA)

*E*CHINACEA (*Cone Flower*: also see RUDBECKIA)•422; ECHINOPS (*Globe Thistle*)•425; ECHIUM•427; *Edelweiss* (see LEONTOPODIUM); EDGEWORTHIA [PAPYRIFERA] (*Paper Tree*)•429; ELSHOLTZIA•430; ENKIANTHUS•431; EPIMEDIUM•434; ERANTHIS (*Winter Aconite*)•437; EREMURUS (*Foxtail Lily*)•438; ERICA (*Heather* or *Heath*: also see

CALLUNA VULGARIS)·441; ERINUS [ALPINUS]·451; ERYNGIUM (*Sea Holly*)·452; ESCHSCHOLZIA (*California Poppy*)·455; *Evening Primrose* (see OENOTHERA); EXOCHORDA·458

*F*ELICIA·459; *Fig Marigold* (see MESEMBRYANTHEMUM); *Fire Thorn* (see PYRACANTHA); *Flax* (see LINUM); *Forget-Me-Not* (see MYOSOTIS); FORSYTHIA·463; FOTHERGILLA·468; *Four O'Clock* (see MIRABILIS); *Foxglove* (see DIGITALIS); *Foxtail Lily* (see EREMURUS); FREESIA·469; FRITILLARIA·471; FUCHSIA·473; *Funkia* (see HOSTA); *Furze* (see ULEX)

*G*AILLARDIA·491; GALANTHUS (*Snowdrop*: also see LEUCOJUM)·494; GARDENIA·495; GAZANIA (*African Daisy*)·502; GENISTA (*Broom*: also see CYTISUS)·506; GENTIANA (*Gentian*)·512; GERANIUM (also see PELARGONIUM)·519; GERBERA (*African Daisy*)·524; GERMANDER (see TEUCRIUM); GEUM·526; GLADIOLUS (*Gladiola*)·529; *Globe Amaranth* (see GOMPHRENA); *Globe Flower* (see TROLLIUS); *Globe Thistle* (see ECHINOPS); GLORIOSA (*Glory Lily*)·538; *Gloxinia* (see SINNINGIA: also see INCARVILLEA); GODETIA·539; *Golden Chain* (see LABURNUM); *Goldenrod* (see SOLIDAGO); GOMPHRENA (*Globe Amaranth*: also see AMARANTHUS)·542; *Gorse* (see ULEX); *Grape Hyacinth* (see MUSCARI); *Gromwell* (see LITHOSPERMUM); *Groundsel* (see SENECIO); GYPSOPHILA (*Baby's Breath*)·543

*H*ALESIA·546; HAMAMELIS (*Witch-Hazel*)·548; *Hardy Gloxinia* (see INCARVILLEA); *Hawthorn* (see CRATAEGUS); *Heather* (see ERICA and CALLUNA VULGARIS); HELENIUM (*Sneezeweed*)·551; HELIANTHEMUM (*Rock Rose*)·555; HELIANTHUS (*Sunflower*)·557; HELICHRYSUM (*Strawflower*)·565; HELIOPSIS·569; HELIOTROPIUM (*Heliotrope*)·572; HELLEBORUS (*Hellebore*, or *Christmas* or *Lenten Rose*)·575; HEMEROCALLIS (*Daylily*)·580; HEPATICA (*Liverwort*)·586; HEUCHERA (*Coral Bells*)·589; HIBISCUS (*Mallow*)·590; HIPPEASTRUM (*"Amaryllis"*)·601; HOHERIA·605; *Hollyhock* (see ALTHAEA); *Honesty* (see LUNARIA); *Honeysuckle* (see LONICERA); *Horse-Chestnut* (see AESCULUS); *Hortensia* (see HYDRANGEA); HOSTA (*Funkia* or *Plantain Lily*)·608; *Houseleek* (see SEMPERVIVUM); HUNNEMANNIA [FUMARIIFOLIA] (*Mexican Tulip-Poppy*)·612; HYACINTHUS (*Hyacinth*: also see MUSCARI)·614; HYDRANGEA (*Hortensia*: also see CLERODENDRUM)·622; HYPERICUM (*Rose of Sharon*)·633

*I*BERIS (*Candytuft*)·638; IMPATIENS (*Impatience, Balsam*)·643;

INCARVILLEA (*Hardy Gloxinia*)·651; INDIGOFERA (*Indigo*)·654; IPOMOEA (*Morning Glory*)·656; IRIS·668; IXIA·683

*J*acob's Ladder (see POLEMONIUM); JASMINUM (*Jasmine*: also see TRACHELOSPERMUM)·684; *Jerusalem Sage* (see PHLOMIS); *Jonquil* (see NARCISSUS)

*K*ALMIA (*Mountain Laurel*)·694; KERRIA [JAPONICA]·700; KIRENGSHOMA [PALMATA]·704; KNIPHOFIA (*"Tritoma"* or *Red-Hot Poker*)·705; KOLKWITZIA [AMABILIS] (*Beauty Bush*)·710

*L*ABURNUM (*Golden Chain*)·712; LAGERSTROEMIA (*Crape Myrtle*)· 716; LANTANA·720; *Larkspur* (see DELPHINIUM); LATHYRUS (*Sweet Pea*)·723; LAVANDULA (*Lavender*)·730; LAVATERA (*Mallow*)·736; *Leadwort* (see PLUMBAGO); *Lenten Rose* (see HELLEBORUS); LEONOTIS· 739; LEONTOPODIUM (*Edelweiss*)·740; *Leopard's Bane* (see DORONICUM); LEPTOSPERMUM·742; LEUCOJUM (*Snowflake*)·745; LIATRIS (*Snakeroot*)·746; *Lilac* (see SYRINGA); LILIUM (*Lily*: also see AGAPANTHUS, AMARYLLIS, CONVALLARIA, EREMURUS, GLORIOSA, HEMEROCALLIS, HIPPEASTRUM, and HOSTA)·749; *Lily-of-the-Nile* (see AGAPANTHUS); *Lily of the Valley* (see CONVALLARIA); LIMONIUM (*"Statice"*)·770; LINARIA (*Toadflax*)·772; LINUM (*Flax*)·776; LITHOSPERMUM (*Gromwell* or *Puccoon*)·781; *Liverwort* (see HEPATICA); LOBELIA·784; LOBULARIA (*Sweet Alyssum*: also see ALYSSUM)·790; LONICERA (*Honeysuckle*)·792; *Love-in-a-Mist* (see NIGELLA); LUNARIA (*Honesty*)·805; LUPINUS (*Lupine*)·806; LYCHNIS (*Catchfly* or *Campion*)·813

CONTENTS VOLUME II

Seed, Bulb, and Plant Sources • 1397
Selected Books for Further Reading • 1401
Biographical Particulars of Botanical Authorities • 1409
Illustrated Glossary • 1428
Index • 1433

*M*AGNOLIA·818; *Mallow* (see LAVATERA: also see HIBISCUS); MALUS (*Crabapple*)·829; MANDEVILLA·838; *Marigold* (see TAGETES: also see CALENDULA and MESEMBRYANTHEMUM); MATTHIOLA (*Stock*) · 840; MAURANDIA·844; *Meadow Saffron* (see COLCHICUM); MECONOPSIS (*Poppywort*)·847; MENTZELIA·852; MESEMBRYANTHEMUM (*Fig*

Marigold)•854; *Mexican Tulip-Poppy* (see HUNNEMANNIA); *Mignonette* (see RESEDA); *Milkweed* (see ASCLEPIAS); MIMOSA (also see ACACIA • 858; MIMULUS (*Monkey Flower*) • 860; MIRABILIS (*Four O'Clock*)•864; *Mock Orange* (see PHILADELPHUS); MONARDA (*Bee Balm* or *Oswego Tea*) • 868; *Monkey Flower* (see MIMULUS); *Monkshood* (see ACONITUM); *Montbretia* (see TRITONIA); *Moonflower* (see CALONYCTION); *Morning Glory* (see IPOMOEA: also see CONVOLVULUS); *Mountain Laurel* (see KALMIA); *Mullein* (see VERBASCUM); MUSCARI (*Grape Hyacinth*) • 870; MYOSOTIS (*Forget-Me-Not*) • 873; MYRTUS (*Myrtle*: also see LAGERSTROEMIA, LEPTOSPERMUM, and VINCA) • 877

*N*amaqualand Daisy (see DIMORPHOTHECA and VENIDIUM); NARCISSUS (*Daffodil* or *Jonquil*)•880; *Nasturtium* (see TROPAEOLUM); NEMESIA•891; NEMOPHILA•893; NEPETA (*Catnip*)•896; NERIUM (*"Oleander"*)•898; NICOTIANA•904; NIGELLA (*Love-in-a-Mist*)•910

*O*ENOTHERA (*Evening Primrose*)•912; *Oleander* (see NERIUM); OLEARIA (*Tree Daisy*)•917; ORNITHOGALUM (*Star of Bethlehem*)•919; OSMANTHUS (*Sweet Olive*)•922; *Oswego Tea* (see MONARDA); OXALIS (*Wood Sorrel*)•924

*P*AEONIA (*Peony*)•929; *Pansy* (see VIOLA); PAPAVER (*Poppy*)•942; *Paper Tree* (see EDGEWORTHIA); *Pasque Flower* (see PULSATILLA); PASSIFLORA (*Passion Flower*)•952; *Peach* (see PRUNUS); PELARGONIUM (*"Geranium"*)•959; PENSTEMON (*Beard Tongue*)•976; *Periwinkle* (see VINCA); *Peruvian Lily* (see ALSTROEMERIA); PETUNIA•982; PHACELIA•988; PHILADELPHUS (*"Syringa"* or *Mock Orange*)•991; PHLOMIS (*Jerusalem Sage*)•998; PHLOX•999; PHYGELIUS•1007; PHYSALIS (*Chinese Lantern*)•1009; PHYSOSTEGIA [VIRGINIANA] (*"Dracocephalum"*)•1013; PIERIS (*Andromeda*)•1015; *Pink* (see DIANTHUS); *Plantain Lily* (see HOSTA); PLATYCODON [GRANDIFLORUS] (*Balloon Flower*)•1017; *Plum* (see PRUNUS); PLUMBAGO (*Leadwort*: also see CERATOSTIGMA)•1020; POLEMONIUM (*Jacob's Ladder*)•1024; POLYANTHES [TUBEROSA] (*Tuberose*)•1026; *Polyanthus* (see PRIMULA); *Pomegranate* (see PUNICA); PONCIRUS [TRIFOLIATA]•1028; *Poppy* (see PAPAVER: also see ESCHSCHOLZIA, HUNNEMANNIA, MECONOPSIS, and ROMNEYA); *Poppywort* (see MECONOPSIS); *Pot Marigold* (see CALENDULA); PORTULACA•1030; POTENTILLA (*Cinquefoil*)•1033; PRIMULA (*Primrose, Auricula, Cowslip,* and *Polyanthus*)•1038; PRUNUS•1054; *Puccoon* (see LITHOSPERMUM); PULSATILLA (*"Anemone"* or *Pasque Flower*: also see ANEMONE)•1071; PUNICA (*Pomegranate*)•1073; PYRACANTHA (*Fire Thorn*)•1080; *Pyrethrum* (see CHRYSANTHEMUM)

*Q*UAMOCLIT (*Cypress Vine*)·1083; *Quince* (see CYDONIA: also see CHAENOMELES)

*R*agwort (see SENECIO); RANUNCULUS (*Buttercup*)·1085; *Red-Hot Poker* (see KNIPHOFIA); RESEDA (*Mignonette*)·1090; RHODODENDRON (including *Azalea*)·1091; RHODOTYPOS [KERRIODES]· 1123; *Rock Rose* (see CISTUS and HELIANTHEMUM); ROMNEYA (*California Tree Poppy*)·1124; ROSA (*Rose*)·1126; *Rose of Sharon* (see HYPERICUM: also see HIBISCUS); RUDBECKIA (*Black-Eyed Susan* or *Cone Flower*: also see ECHINACEA)·1173

*S*AGE (see SALVIA: also see PHLOMIS); SALPIGLOSSIS [SINUATA]· 1179; SALVIA (*Sage*)·1180; SANVITALIA·1188; SAPONARIA (*Soapwort*)· 1190; SAXIFRAGA (*Saxifrage*)·1193; SCABIOSA·1202; SCHIZANTHUS· 1206; SCILLA (*Squill* or *Bluebell*)·1210; *Sea Holly* (see ERYNGIUM); SEDUM (*Stonecrop*)·1212; SEMPERVIVUM (*Houseleek*)·1215; SENECIO (*Cineraria, Groundsel,* or *Ragwort*)·1218; *Senna* (see CASSIA); SILENE (*Catchfly*)·1225; SINNINGIA (*Gloxinia*)·1228; *Slipper Flower* (see CALCEOLARIA); *Snakeroot* (see LIATRIS); *Snapdragon* (see ANTIRRHINUM); *Sneezeweed* (see HELENIUM); *Snowdrop* (see GALANTHUS); *Snowflake* (see LEUCOJUM); *Snow-in-Summer* (see CERASTIUM); *Soapwort* (see SAPONARIA); SOLANUM·1231; SOLIDAGO (*Goldenrod*)·1235; SOPHORA· 1237; *Sorbaria* (see SPIRAEA); SPARTIUM [JUNCEUM]·1240; SPECULARIA·1241; *Speedwell* (see VERONICA); *Spider Flower* (see CLEOME); SPIRAEA (also see ASTILBE)·1243; *Squill* (see SCILLA); STAPHYLEA (*Bladder Nut*)·1253; *Star Jasmine* (see TRACHELOSPERMUM); *Star of Bethlehem* (see ORNITHOGALUM); *Statice* (see LIMONIUM); STERNBERGIA [LUTEA] (*Winter Daffodil*)·1254; *Stock* (see MATTHIOLA); *Stonecrop* (see SEDUM); *Strawflower* (see HELICHRYSUM); STYRAX·1256; *Sunflower* (see HELIANTHUS); *Sweet Alyssum* (see LOBULARIA); *Sweet Olive* (see OSMANTHUS); *Sweet Pea* (see LATHYRUS); *Sweet William* (see DIANTHUS); SYRINGA (*Lilac*: also see PHILADELPHUS)·1258

*T*AGETES (*Marigold*)·1268; TAMARIX (*Tamarisk*)·1274; TECOMA (*Trumpet Creeper*)·1276; TEUCRIUM (*Germander*)·1279; THALICTRUM (*Meadow Rue*)·1282; *Thrift* (see ARMERIA); THUNBERGIA·1284; TIBOUCHINA [SEMIDECANDRA] (*Brazilian Spider Flower*)·1288; TIGRIDIA (*Tiger Flower*)·1290; TITHONIA·1292; *Toadflax* (see LINARIA); TORENIA (*Wishbone Flower*)·1293; TRACHELOSPERMUM (*Star Jasmine*)·1295; *Tree Daisy* (see OLEARIA);

Tritoma (see KNIPHOFIA); TRITONIA (*"Montbretia"*)·1297; TROLLIUS (*Globe Flower*)·1300; TROPAEOLUM (*"Nasturtium"*)·1302; *Trumpet Creeper* (see TECOMA); *Trumpet Flower* (see BIGNONIA); *Trumpet Vine* (see BIGNONIA and CAMPSIS); *Tuberose* (see POLYANTHES); TULIPA (TULIP)·1310

*U*LEX (*Furze* or *Gorse*)·1331; URSINIA·1333

*V*ALERIANA (*Valerian*: also see POLEMONIUM)·1336; VENIDIUM (*Namaqualand Daisy*)·1337; VERBASCUM (*Mullein*)·1338; VERBENA (*Vervain*)·1341; VERONICA (*Speedwell*)·1348; VIBURNUM·1352; VINCA (*"Myrtle"* and *Periwinkle*)·1361; VIOLA (*Violet* and *Pansy*)·1365; VISCARIA (see LYCHNIS); VITEX·1376

*W*allflower (see CHEIRANTHUS); WEIGELA (also see DIERVILLA)·1377; *Windflower* (see ANEMONE); *Winter Aconite* (see ERANTHIS); *Winter Daffodil* (see STERNBERGIA); *Wishbone Flower* (see TORENIA); WISTARIA (*Wisteria*)·1383; *Witch Alder* (see FOTHERGILLA); *Witch-Hazel* (see HAMAMELIS); *Wood Sorrel* (see OXALIS)

*Y*arrow (see ACHILLEA)

*Z*ANTEDESCHIA (*"Calla"*)·1388; ZINNIA·1393

Kalmia

(Mountain Laurel, Sheep Laurel, Lambkill, Swamp Laurel, or Calico Bush)
Family: Ericaceae
Hardy or half-hardy evergreen or deciduous shrubs
Position: partial shade (in south) or full sun (in north)
Propagation: seed, air layering, or cuttings
Cultivation easy
Poisonous

Kalmia hirsuta

Kalmia is one of the most beautiful genera of the family Ericaceae. It was named by Linnaeus in honour of one of his pupils, Peter Kalm (1716–1771), a Finnish botanist who, during a journey in America, became one of the first Europeans to study the genus. He was also the first to discover the plant's poisonous properties when some sheep belonging to his expedition nearly died after eating leaves of *Kalmia angustifolia*. He noted that the sheep were saved by being dosed with "gunpowder and other medicines". (It is with good reason that one of the common names of kalmia is Lambkill. The foliage can also be deadly to horses.) In regions where kalmias grow wild, the prudent beekeeper will always test some of his new honey before selling it. It is even said that the flesh of partridges can be poisonous if the birds have eaten kalmia seeds, but such an assertion is probably an exaggeration. It is true, however, that some American Indians used to extract a deadly poison from a distillation of young kalmia leaves.

Although potentially so poisonous, kalmias are also very beautiful. Kalm himself wrote that when nearly all other trees and shrubs have lost their foliage, kalmias brightened the woods with their green leaves, and that when in flower their beauty surpassed the majority of all other native plants; the unusual form of the individual blooms being similar to that of an ancient Greek drinking cup, or kylix. John Ruskin, who was said to be familiar with every beautiful object, used silversmiths' terminology to describe them, likening the interior of the blooms to "beaten silver, with the petals struck by the stamens instead of with a hammer".

Contrary to general belief, kalmias were not discovered and introduced into Europe by Kalm, but by Mark Catesby, who noticed them during travels in the Carolina colonies and brought seeds and plants to England in 1726, subsequently describing them in his *Natural History of Carolina*. Catesby was not successful in cultivating them. Another grower, Peter Collinson, was more fortunate,

Kalmia latifolia
From *Curtis's Botanical Magazine*,
1791, plate 175

and in 1740 he succeeded in producing flowering specimens from plants he received from Virginia in 1736.

There are eight species of kalmia distributed in an area extending from North America to Cuba. In its native habitat, *Kalmia latifolia* often attains the proportions of a tree up to 30 ft. high, with a trunk nearly 3 ft. in diameter; in gardens, however, the plants normally reach a height of 15 ft. The wood, particularly that from the base of the trunk and from the roots, is remarkably fine-grained; it is easy to work when freshly cut, but hard and heavy when seasoned. The American Indians, and after them the first American colonists, used the wood for making spoons, pipes, and shovel handles; in fact, this species is often called Spoon-Wood or Spoon-Tree. Today, toy makers are showing some interest in the use of the wood.

Cultivation. In the garden kalmias should be planted like rhododendrons, as both require a similar environment: an acid non-alkaline (non-calcareous), humus-rich soil, with a damp atmosphere, plenty of moisture at the roots (particularly in summer), and semi-shade; but while rhododendrons will thrive in quite dense shade, kalmias flower poorly, with the plants losing their very pleasing compact habit if the shade is too intense. Kalmias are also tolerant of considerable moisture at their roots, as demonstrated by the conditions of their natural habitat, swampy, damp woods. They must always be grown in an acid soil. For those who have a garden with only alkaline (calcareous) soil, the only successful methods of cultivating kalmias are to grow them either in large tubs filled with a compost composed of equal parts of leafsoil and peat, with a small amount of sand to ensure good drainage, or in specially prepared beds containing the same compost. Watering will also have to be done with non-alkaline (non-calcareous) water. In the north and in mountainous areas, kalmias can also be grown in full sun.

Kalmias can be propagated from soft-wood cuttings taken in spring and inserted in a mixture of sand and peat under plastic or a glass bell-jar, but the percentage of success is generally low. Reproduction may also be effected by means of air layering or ground layering, but this is a very slow process and not very sure. The best method of propagation is from seed, but much time and patience is required to collect the seed from strongly coloured forms, as seedlings tend to produce plants with paler-coloured blooms. In the spring, seed can be sown in pans or flats filled with peat in an unheated greenhouse or coldframe. Pot-grown specimens of kalmia are easy subjects to force into bloom in early spring, and during recent years they have become increasingly popular in flower shops.

If the above-mentioned details of kalmia cultivation appear excessively gloomy and arduous, the grower will in any case be amply rewarded by results. The beauty of a kalmia in bloom is so great that the United States at one time almost selected it as its national flower.

Kalmia latifolia is, however, the official flower of the State of Connecticut, and, in that state and many others, is a "protected" plant (it is illegal to cut the branches or lift specimens found growing in the wild).

Kalmia angustifolia L.

(Sheep Laurel, Lambkill, Dwarf Laurel, or Wicky)
Evergreen shrub
Flowering period: June–July
Height: up to 4½ ft.
Zone 1 southwards

Native to eastern North America, from Newfoundland and Hudson Bay to Georgia. Flourishes in fresh, moist, generally acid soils. It forms an erect shrub up to nearly 5 ft. high; open in habit, with opposite short-stalked elongated-lanceolate leaves, 1–2 ins. long, $\frac{1}{4}$–$\frac{3}{4}$ in. wide, light green on the upper surface, paler green beneath. The leaves tend to droop during the coldest days in winter. The flowers are borne in dense compact axillary corymbs produced on the previous season's growth. The corolla is $\frac{1}{3}$ in. wide and a lovely shade of purple-red. This is a species particularly suitable for wet soils. The foliage is very poisonous, especially to cattle. There are several varieties:

> var. *candida* Fern., white-flowered
> var. *ovata* Pursh., conspicuous for its ovate or oval foliage
> var. *pumila* Bosse. (syn. var. *nana*), a dwarf only 12–16 ins. high
> var. *rosea*, with pale-purple blooms
> var. *rubra* Lodd. (syn. var. *hirsuta* Voss.), with reddish flowers

Kalmia cuneata Michx.

Deciduous or semi-evergreen shrub
Flowering period: June
Height: up to 10 ft.
Zone 7 southwards

Native to North and South Carolina. A deciduous or semi-evergreen shrub up to 9–10 ft. high, with an erect, rather sparse habit; the young growths are reddish, slender, and wide-spreading. Leaves alternate, stalkless, cuneate, narrowly oval, 1–2 ins. long, $\frac{1}{4}$–$\frac{1}{2}$ in. wide, pointed, dark green on the upper surface, lighter beneath with a few scattered hairs. Flowers borne in groups of 2–6 on the previous season's growth: white, suffused pink internally; cup-shaped, $\frac{3}{4}$ in. wide, with thread-like 1-in.-long hairy stalks.

Kalmia hirsuta Walt. (syn. *Kalmiella hirsuta*)

Evergreen shrub
Flowering period: June
Height: 1–2 ft.
Zone 8 southwards

Native from southern Virginia to Florida. An evergreen species up to 2 ft. high with very slender hairy stems and an erect habit. Leaves alternate, nearly stalkless, oblong or lanceolate, pointed, $\frac{1}{4}$–$\frac{1}{2}$ in. long, vivid green and bristly. Flowers axillary, solitary, with slender hairy stalks, and grouped into lateral corymbs; each bloom $\frac{1}{2}$ in. wide, saucer-shaped, light purple-pink. A conspicuous species for its bristly appearance; an attractive plant but probably the least hardy.

Kalmia latifolia L.

(Mountain Laurel, American Laurel, or Calico Bush)
Evergreen shrub
Flowering period: June–July
Height: up to 15 ft.
Zone 4 southwards

Native to Eastern North America: in Canada from New Brunswick to Ontario, and in the United States from northern Indiana and the

Kalmia angustifolia

Kalmia polifolia

(Swamp Laurel
or Pale Laurel)
Evergreen shrub
Flowering period: May–June
Height: up to 2 ft.
Zone 5 southwards

eastern coastal states as far south as Florida and Louisiana; often found in mountainous areas. This is certainly the most beautiful species of the genus and one of the most attractive of all flowering evergreen shrubs. When not in bloom it has the general appearance and dimensions of one of the larger rhododendrons. Its natural habitat is in woody, moist positions in an acid, sandy, peaty, humus-rich soil, and at higher altitudes it is often established in large isolated groups in grassland. Leaves alternate, leathery, glabrous, rich dark green, oval or oval-lanceolate, up to 5 ins. long and 2 ins. wide, tapering at the apex and at the base; yellowish green on the undersurface; leaf stalks up to 1 in. long. The flowers are borne in large compact terminal corymbs on the previous season's growth, and each corymb can be up to 5 ins. in diameter. The individual flowers are 1 in. wide, saucer-shaped, with the colour varying from pinkish white to a lovely deep rose-pink. Their beauty is greatly increased by the white stamens and the dark-brown anthers. The foliage is poisonous to animals, particularly sheep and goats, but as such animals are not normally kept in home gardens the danger is more academic than actual, although the poisonous aspect should be borne in mind where there are children. *Kalmia latifolia* deserves to be much more widely planted, especially in Europe, and on a scale similar to that at Boston's Arnold Arboretum, which provides a superb floral display for the city every June. There are numerous varieties:

var. *alba* Bosse., white-flowered

var. *fuscata* Rehd., with a purple-maroon stripe inside the flowers

var. *laevipes* Fern., from the coastal plains of the southeastern United States

var. *myrtifolia* Bosse. (syn. var. *nana* and var. *minor*), with minute myrtle-like foliage, dark green, 1–2 ins. long, and forming a slow-growing dense dwarf shrub

var. *obtusata* Rehd., compact, slow-growing; foliage composed of elliptic or ovate leaves blunted at either end, 2–3 ins. long

var. *polypetala* Nichols. (syn. var. *monstruosa* Mouillef.), with the corolla divided into five narrow feathery petals

var. *rubra* Sweet (syn. var. *pavartii* and var. *André*) with dark-pink flowers

Kalmia polifolia Wang. (syn. *Kalmia glauca*)
Native to North America, where it is found in swampy districts. It is a spreading dwarf evergreen somewhat straggly shrub when grown under its natural conditions, but in drier conditions that are still cool, fresh, and moist, it will assume a more erect and compact habit. Leaves from oval to linear-oblong, obtuse, leathery, with slightly recurved margins; 1–1½ ins. long, rich dark green above and glau-

cous white on the undersurface; minutely stalked, in groups of 2–3. Flowers borne in terminal corymbs up to 1½ ins. wide, each bloom ½ in. in diameter with five rather wide petals of a delightful pale-purple-pink shade and from bell- to funnel-shaped. The var. *rosmarinifolia* Rehd. (syn. *Kalmia glauca* var. *rosmarinifolia*) has much narrower more linear leaves, with the margins more recurved and a green undersurface.

Kerria japonica

(JAPANESE ROSE, GLOBE FLOWER, OR JEW'S MALLOW)
Family: Rosaceae
Hardy deciduous shrub
Flowering period: Apr.–May
Height: normally up to 8 ft.
Position: sun or partial shade
Propagation: seed, cuttings, or division
Cultivation very easy
Zone 4 southwards

Kerria japonica D.C. (syn. *Corchorus japonicus*)
Native to western and central China. Some authorities maintain that *Kerria japonica* was introduced into Europe as long ago as 1700, but the assertion is open to doubt and not researchable. Kacmpfcr described it in 1712, under its Japanese name of *Jamma* or *Yamma Buki,* and in 1784 Thunberg included it in his *Flora Japonica.* The first definite records of its introduction are, however, dated 1805, when William Kerr sent plants of the double-flowered form from China to Kew Gardens. Although its specific name *japonica* refers to Japan, the plant is, in fact, native only to western and central China, where it was found growing wild in 1900 by Augustine Henry and E. H. Wilson. It is, however, very widely grown in Japan.

Because the first double-flowered plants introduced were seedless, classification and identification were difficult and Thunberg at first assigned the plant to the genus *Corchorus.* Owing to this mistake the plant was commonly referred to as Jew's Mallow because Jews were in the habit of eating the leaves of *Corchorus* in salads. In 1817, De Candolle assigned *Kerria* to its correct family and named it after its introducer, William Kerr. When, in 1835, the typical single-flowered form eventually reached Europe it was possible to prove unequivocal-

Kerria japonica var. *pleniflora*
From *Curtis's Botanical Magazine*,
1810, plate 1296

ly that it belonged to the family Rosaceae. (*Corchorus* is an annual belonging to the family Tiliaceae, and the species *C. capsularis* yields jute. The so-called Jew's Mallow is the species *Corchorus olitorius* from India. The old mistake in nomenclature still persists, however, especially in Europe, and there are still nurserymen who catalogue *Kerria* as *Corchorus*.)

Kerria japonica forms a monotypic genus; that is, it is the sole species. Once it became established in Europe it spread with amazing rapidity, particularly in British gardens, and for many years it has also been a relatively common plant in the United States. By the year 1810, only five years after its introduction to England—and while in some quarters it was still being grown as a greenhouse plant—*Kerria japonica* had already found a place in London gardens. On the authority of the Abbé Romani of Padua, it seems that by 1820 a great many Italian amateurs were also growing the double-flowered form in their gardens. However, the single-flowered form is more attractive, and can be utilized with greater freedom in the average garden without creating any jarring effects.

Kerria japonica is a deciduous shrub with green, shiny stems. Initially, its development in width is greater than its height owing to the abundance of suckers that appear all round the base of the plant, thus making lateral development extremely rapid, so much so that it can even become invasive in restricted areas (as it does in my small garden near Venice). The leaves are simple, alternate, oval-lanceolate, acuminate, dentated, 1–2 ins. long on the longer, flowering stems but up to twice that size on the younger, flowerless stems. The foliage is lightish green and the flowers are a vivid golden yellow and produced in the greatest profusion. The blooms are single, solitary, terminal, stalked, up to 2 ins. in diameter, with 5 large petals. The calyx is persistent and divided into 5 lobes.

Kerria japonica is one of the most valuable and easily grown of the early-flowering shrubs, generally blooming shortly after forsythias, but earlier in mild climates. A pleasing feature of the plant is that it generally continues to produce a few scattered flowers throughout the summer. And in autumn still another attraction is provided by the lovely yellow assumed by the leaves before they fall. In winter the plant is pleasing for the fresh green of its slender, interlacing, twiggy branches. It is generally believed that the minute, imitation flower buds modelled by the Japanese for floating in their cups of *sake* are actually made from the pith found in the centre of kerria stems.

Kerria japonica has still another curious, interesting, and unusual characteristic. It sometimes forgets to be a shrub and decides to become a climber. This occurs when old specimens of kerria, growing at the base of tall windbreaks or screens of evergreens, extend their stems into the taller plants and gradually grow to a remarkable height. I have frequently seen this effect in European gardens (even in such an unlikely place as the centre of Milan), and have noted that the kerria stems will extend up to 15–20 ft. and will produce flowers even at their extremity.

Single-flowered *Kerria japonica*

Cultivation. In excessively cold zones where the winter temperature is liable to fall below 0°F., there is a chance that the younger, sappy growths may be killed down to ground level, while the tips of the older stems may become frosted. Otherwise, *Kerria japonica* is generally considered to be a completely hardy plant. In the north it is best to plant it in full sun, while in the south excellent results can also be obtained in semi-shade. In zones where there is an abundance of hot sunshine the flowers will retain a better colour in partial shade. The best planting times are spring and autumn, and while no regular pruning is necessary a light pruning is beneficial in June so the plants will keep their good shape. Dead, weak, or badly formed growths should be removed during the winter. The best effects are obtained by planting in large, isolated groups, and *Kerria japonica* is also an excellent subject for making an informal hedge. In all normal, fertile garden soils the plant is so vigorous and robust that fertilizing is rarely required, but in poor soils a top dressing of well-decomposed stable manure or leafsoil will be beneficial.

Although propagation can be effected by means of soft or semi-woody cuttings, or from seed, propagation by division, using the prolifically produced suckers, is the most practical method of multiplication. There are numerous forms and varieties, such as:

> var. *argentea-variegata,* single yellow flowers; small foliage margined white

var. *aureo-variegata*, single yellow flowers; leaves margined yellow

var. *aureo-vittata*, single yellow flowers; stems striped yellow

var. *grandiflora*, a particularly vigorous larger flowered form

var. *picta*, a slow grower and poor flowerer; leaves margined white

var. *pleniflora*, a very vigorous form with double yellow flowers

Kirengshoma palmata

(YELLOW WAXBELLS)
Family: Saxifragaceae
Half-hardy herbaceous perennial
Flowering period: Aug.–Oct.
Height: up to 3 ft.
Position: partial or complete shade
Propagation: division or seed
Cultivation fairly easy

Kirengeshoma palmata Yatabe (See page 706 for colourplate)
Native to Japan. A monotypic genus consisting of only one species with no varieties. A very lovely half-hardy perennial that deserves to be much more widely cultivated. Apart from the elegance, grace, and charm of its waxy-textured flowers, it is of particular value for its late-flowering habit at the end of summer, with the blooms remaining attractive until autumn, well after the Michaelmas Daisies have finished. On the Continent it is little known, but it can always be found in British gardens owned by connoisseurs of choice plants. In the United States it appears to be even less well known and is completely ignored by some of the most authoritative text-books.

Kirengeshoma palmata has attractive thin-textured light-green dentated palmate foliage, and is a well-proportioned plant up to 3 ft. high. The stems are dark green and, well above the foliage, bear terminal and axillary groups of large pendulous bright-yellow bell-shaped flowers with a waxy appearance. They are long lasting, and I have achieved some delightful effects by planting it with another taller very late-flowering herbaceous perennial, *Vernonia crinita* Raf., whose purple-red flowers make a superb contrast with the yellow kirengeshoma.

Kirengeshoma palmata requires the same environment as rhododendrons—shade and a moist, acid, humus-rich soil—making them ideal subjects for planting together so that the kirengeshoma blooms make the rhododendrons more attractive at a period when the latter are without bloom. Kirengeshomas also do well when planted in the vicinity of water.

Although the plants start into growth somewhat late in the spring, in the north there is some risk of new growth being damaged by late frosts, so they should always be planted in a sheltered position. Although they require shade, they also need plenty of air and space around them. Propagation can be effected by means of seed sown in spring, in an unheated greenhouse or coldframe, or by careful division in spring or autumn.

Kniphofia

(RED-HOT POKER, TRITOMA, FLAME FLOWER, TORCH LILY, OR POKER PLANT)
Family: Liliaceae
Tender or half-hardy evergreen herbaceous perennials
Position: sun
Propagation: division or seed
Cultivation easy
Useful for cutting

For a great many years kniphofias have been among the most cherished and most popular of all herbaceous perennials in European and American gardens; the only restriction on their even greater employment in beds, borders, or informal groupings is their somewhat limited degree of hardiness. They are all native to warm and even tropical areas such as Central and Southern Africa, Ethiopia, Madagascar, etc. Frequently, but erroneously, they are referred to as tritomas, under which name certain species of kniphofia achieved so much popularity as Red-hot Pokers in old-fashioned gardens. Today, the majority of kniphofias cultivated are hybrids with a much wider range of colours and, collectively, with a longer flowering period than the original species.

The genus *Kniphofia* was named by the German botanist Konrad Moench in 1794, in honour of Johann Hieronymus Kniphof, professor of medicine and botanist at Erfurt, who lived between 1704 and 1765. (Moench was the author of a folio volume containing coloured illustrations of the genus.) There are about sixty to seventy known species. The first introduced into Europe was *Kniphofia uvaria,* in 1704; the popular *Kniphofia caulescens* was not introduced until 1862.

Kniphofias are particularly suited to seaside localities, where the climate is generally milder, as well as to other areas near water,

Kirengeshoma palmata
From *Curtis's Botanical Magazine*,
1904, plate 7944

such as the margins of a pond or the banks of a stream, where they lend an exotic effect without looking out of place as would be the case with roses, geraniums, poppies, or stocks. They also look well with agapanthus, daylilies, and other similar plants with long strap-shaped arching foliage.

Cultivation. Kniphofias have great lateral development and therefore require an abundance of space. After flowering has finished it is generally necessary to thin out some of the outer leaves, which can even become invasive or untidy in appearance, as they spread out horizontally over the soil surface all around the parent plant. Kniphofias are essentially warm-climate plants, but they will survive a considerable amount of frost if their bases are given winter protection—using a mulch of dried ferns, dead leaves, peat, wood ashes, etc. The foliage is evergreen and should not be cut off in autumn as this also helps to protect the plants. However, their outdoor cultivation cannot be advised in zones where the winter temperature is apt to fall to 0°F. for long periods, or where the soil surface freezes to such a depth that the fleshy roots become frozen. To fully appreciate the beauty of the magnificent richly coloured flower spikes, kniphofias should be planted in such a way that the inflorescences are seen against the blue sky or against some shrubs with light-coloured foliage. In any case they require a warm, open, moderately dry, sunny position preferably in deep but well-drained heavy clayey soil, either acid or alkaline (calcareous); although good results can be obtained in lighter soil if the stratum is deep. In either case, an abundance of water is necessary during hot summer weather, and applications of organic fertilizer are advisable, either in liquid form or as a top dressing or mulch. The flowers can be effectively used for arranging in vases—especially when combined with light-coloured foliage such as that of *Cornus siberica spaethii*—but the flowers are not long lasting.

The plants hybridize with the greatest ease and it is difficult to raise new true-to-the-parent stock from seed. If sown from seed, the plants will bloom the second year. The best time for sowing seed is as soon as it is ripe, or in early spring; and it should be sown in pots, flats, or pans in coldframes or in an unheated greenhouse. Propagation can also be very easily effected by division—preferably in spring—using either the young side growths or actually splitting apart the original plant.

Flowering period: July–Aug.
Height: 3 ft.

Kniphofia burchellii Kunth.
Native to South Africa. Leaves acuminate, basal, up to 2 ft. 4 ins. long and 1 in. wide. Flowers brilliant yellow on tall spikes (racemes) up to 3 ft. high, flowering in July–Aug.; individual flowers drooping and tube-shaped.

Kniphofia caulescens Baker (syn. *Tritoma caulescens*)
Native to South Africa. Leaves an attractive shade of steel-blue; long, slender, pointed, recurved, and arising from an almost woody central stem or trunk 6 ins. high and almost as wide. The inflorescence is borne at the summit of a tall rigid erect stem 4½ ft. high, and is composed of a cylindrical mass of individual tubular pendulous flowers 1 in. long. The blooms are a beautiful shade of pink gradually suffused into greenish-yellow.

Flowering period: Aug.–Sept.
Height: 4½ ft.

Kniphofia foliosa Hochst. (syn. *Tritoma foliosa*)
Native to Ethiopia. Leaves produced directly from the base of the plant to form a close compact tuft of vegetation. They are lanceolate, pointed, 2–2½ ft. long, 1½–2 ins. wide, brilliant green, bending at an angle about half-way along their length, with the top pointed part inclined downwards. The floral stems are up to 6 ft. high, vigorous and robust, bearing at their summit a 12-in.-high raceme composed of a mass of bright-yellow-and-orange tubular pendulous flowers.

Flowering period: Aug.
Height: up to 6 ft.

Kniphofia galpinii Baker (syn. *Tritoma galpinii*)
Native to South Africa. One of the smallest species, with miniature inflorescences particularly suitable for cutting. It is also one of the least hardy of the genus. Leaves green and identical in form to those of *Kniphofia uvaria,* but on a smaller scale. The flower spikes bear small flame-coloured blooms.

Flowering period: July–Sept.
Height: 2½ ft.

Kniphofia macowanii Baker (syn. *Tritoma rigidissima, Tritoma maroccana*)
Native to South Africa. Leaves erect, linear, rigid, 2 ft. long, with 3–5 conspicuous veins on either side of the midrib. The 4-in.-long flowers are borne in dense compact racemes on slender stems up to 3 ft. high, varying in colour from brilliant yellow to orange-red. The var. *corallina,* which is a hybrid of *Kniphofia uvaria* and *Kniphofia macowanii,* bears spikes of coral-red flowers in July; and the var. *media macowanii* is another earlier-flowering hybrid.

Flowering period: July–Aug.
Height: 3 ft.

Kniphofia rufa Baker
Native to South Africa. Leaves 1½ ft. long and nearly 1 in. wide. Flowers borne on rigid stems in dense inflorescences; yellow when fully expanded, with the upper half-opened buds tinged red. The protruding stamens are conspicuous.

Flowering period: June–Sept.
Height: 2 ft.

Kniphofia tuckii Baker
Native to South Africa. Leaves 1½ ft. long, ¾ in. wide. The ½-in.-long flowers are borne in clusters 6 ins. long on erect stems and their colour is yellow-tinged red.

Flowering period: June–July
Height: 2 ft.

Flowering period: July
Height: 3 ft.

Kniphofia uvaria Hook. (syn. *Kniphofia aloides* Moench, *Kniphofia hybrida*, *Tritoma uvaria*)

Native to South Africa. Generally found to be the hardiest of all the species. Leaves borne directly from the base of the plant; lanceolate, pointed, up to 3 ft. long and 1 in. wide. Each leaf bends at an angle about half-way along its length, with the top pointed part inclining downwards; sometimes they curve so that their tips touch the ground. The flower stems are erect and rigid, with the inflorescence in the form of a dense cylindrical spike 8–10 ins. long and $2\frac{1}{2}$ ins. wide at the tip of the stem. This spike of bloom is composed of numerous small semi-pendulous closely packed orange-scarlet cylindrical flowers with prominent protruding stamens. The lowest flowers of the spike open first, while those above open in succession, but always from the base upwards. The evergreen foliage should not be removed in the autumn. There are numerous attractive varieties:

> var. *grandis* Hort. (syn. *Tritoma grandis*), with enormous floral spikes up to 6 ft. high and slightly earlier-flowering
> var. *maxima* Baker (syn. *Tritoma grandiflora* Hort.), taller than the species, with wider inflorescences and bigger flowers
> var. *nobilis* Baker (syn. *Tritoma nobilis*), an even larger-proportioned variety with flower stems up to 7 ft. high and individual flowers $1\frac{1}{2}$ ins. long

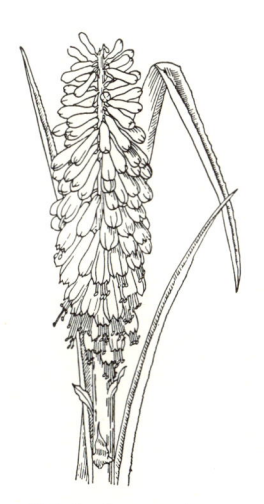

Kniphofia uvaria    *Kniphofia caulescens*    *Kniphofia foliosa*

Kniphofia Hybrids

The most beautiful of all, however, are the hybrids derived from the above-mentioned species and varieties. Among the modern kniphofia hybrids—which are such an improvement on the original species—those developed by Max Leichtlin are of exceptional beauty. They are very numerous, of various dimensions, and with a flowering period extending from June to September. Here is a selection of the most interesting:

August Gold	golden-yellow	4½ ft.	Aug.–Sept.
Autumn Queen	vivid bronze & yellowish green	4 ft.	Aug.–Sept.
Bee's Lemon	yellow and green	3 ft.	June–July
Gold Else	golden-yellow	2 ft.	Aug.–Sept.
John Benary	orange-red	4 ft.	Aug.–Sept.
July Glow	apricot-yellow	2½ ft.	June–July
Lord Roberts	vivid red	3 ft.	July–Aug.
Maid of Orleans	straw-yellow becoming ivory-white	3½ ft.	June–Sept.
Mount Etna	scarlet	4½ ft.	Aug.–Sept.
Royal Standard	red & yellow	3½ ft.	June–July
Sir C. K. Butler	rosy pink & yellow	3 ft.	June–July
Springtime	cream & orange	3 ft.	July–Aug.
Yellow Hammer	yellow	3 ft.	July–Sept.

Many lovely vividly coloured planting effects can be created with these hybrids, but one of the most striking is to combine the unusual colour and long-flowering habit of Maid of Orleans with blue delphiniums.

Kolkwitzia amabilis

(BEAUTY BUSH)
Family: Caprifoliaceae
Hardy deciduous shrub
Flowering period: May–June
Height: up to 10 ft.
Position: sun or partial shade
Propagation: seed or cuttings
Cultivation very easy
Useful for cutting
Zone 4 southwards

Kolkwitzia amabilis Grabner.
Native to China, at altitudes of up to 10,000 ft., and very hardy. Aptly named Beauty Bush, this flowering shrub deserves to be as widely grown as forsythia. Relatively popular in the United States, in Europe it has recently attracted the attention of professional flower growers, and branches in bloom are now beginning to appear in

Kolkwitzia amabilis
From *Curtis's Botanical Magazine*,
1914, plate 8563

flower shops. *Kolkwitzia amabilis* is a beautiful deciduous shrub well-suited for growing in large isolated groups, for planting as a single specimen, or for making an informal hedge. It has relatively modest proportions, with a dense, compact, much-branched, somewhat contorted, twiggy habit. It is particularly easy to cultivate in any normal fertile garden soil, either acid or alkaline (calcareous), and requires no pruning except for the removal of dead or weak growths. The leaves are attractive and conspicuous; dark green, slightly wrinkled, opposite, ovate, shallowly dentated, up to 3 ins. in length and 2 ins. wide, long-pointed with the point curiously twisted, and with a prominent network of veins covering the surface. The foliage is also slightly hairy or bristly. The 3-in.-wide inflorescence is made up of numerous small corymbs of bell-shaped flowers; each floweret $\frac{1}{2}$ in. long and $\frac{1}{2}$ in. wide at the mouth, pale pink with a yellow throat, and borne on short hairy stalks. The abundantly produced fruits are dry, covered with stiff brown hairs, with the persistent elongated calyx protruding $\frac{1}{3}$ in. Var. *rosea* has darker-pink flowers.

Kolkwitzia amabilis was introduced into Europe by the botanist E. H. Wilson in 1901, and flowered for the first time in 1910 in the famous nursery of John Gould Veitch in England. The somewhat difficult generic name was given in honour of R. Kolkwitz, a German professor of botany. The popular name Beauty Bush may be somewhat pretentious, but it is certainly well-merited.

Propagation can be effected by means of seed sown at any time during spring, summer, or autumn, in pots, flats, or pans in an unheated greenhouse or in coldframes; by means of soft-wood cuttings in spring, or from cuttings of half-ripened wood in July–August in coldframes.

Laburnum

(GOLDEN CHAIN, GOLDEN RAIN, OR BEAN TREE)
Family: Leguminosae
Hardy deciduous shrubs or trees
Position: sun or partial shade
Propagation: seed, grafting, or cuttings
Cultivation very easy
Poisonous

The genus *Laburnum* is small, with only three species, two of which are large shrubs or small trees, while the other is practically unknown to modern gardens (*Laburnum caramanicum* Benth. & Hook., a shrub with erect terminal inflorescences of yellow flowers, native to Greece and Asia Minor). There are, however, numerous forms, varieties, and hybrids, including one of the most remarkable of all flowering plants found in nature, *Laburnum* x *adami* Kirch.

Laburnums have leaves divided into three leaflets and pendulous inflorescences which are similar in form to wisterias (except in the case of *Laburnum caramanicum*). They are particularly effective when planted against a dark background of conifers or some other evergreen tree or shrub, so that the flowers can be seen and the full significance of the popular name Golden Rain can be appreciated. In Europe, certain districts in the Dolomite and Apennine mountains are a glorious sight in early summer when entire forests or scattered groups of indigenous laburnums are in full bloom.

Seeds of laburnum are enclosed in small pods, similar to the culinary pea, which are produced in great abundance. Like the entire plant, however, they are deadly poisonous if eaten because they contain the alkaloid cytisine, which even in small doses can have deadly results and adequate precautions should be taken so that children do not put them in their mouths. At one time cytisine was used in the treatment of nervous disorders, but because of its dangerously toxic properties it is no longer used in modern medicine. The laburnum foliage is also poisonous to goats and horses, but, curiously enough, it can be eaten with impunity by deer. Rabbits and hares are very fond of the bark, and can cause serious damage to the plants.

The timber of old specimens is highly valued for its dark colour and long-lasting properties; it is, in fact, similar to ebony, for which it is sometimes substituted, and on the Continent laburnum is often known as False Ebony.

Cultivation. The cultivation of laburnums is simple and easy. In the north or at high altitudes they prefer a fresh, moist soil in a sunny position; but in very hot, excessively sunny climates it is best to plant them in partial shade as there is some risk of the foliage being scorched. Large specimens require support (or protection) in districts where windstorms are common. No pruning is required and propagation of the species from seed is easy. Sow in either autumn or spring in nursery beds outside; the varieties, however, must be propagated by grafting or from soft-wood or semi-hard cuttings.

Nurserymen and gardeners have taken full advantage of the ease with which young laburnums can be cultivated, and of the large number of seeds produced, using young plants as stock onto which varieties (and forms) and other leguminous plants (in particular cytisus) are grafted. Laburnums begin to bloom when quite small, thus making them excellent subjects for pot culture or for use as temporary house plants in late winter. From early in the new year most florists stock pot-grown plants in bloom, and there are few more attractive subjects for indoor decoration at that dull season.

Laburnum alpinum
From *Curtis's Botanical Magazine*,
1791, plate 176

(Purple Laburnum)
Small deciduous tree
Flowering period: June–July
Height: up to 20 ft.
Zone 6 southwards

Laburnum x *adami* Kirch. (syn. *Laburnocytisus* x *adami* C.K.S.)
This remarkable plant, which botanists prefer to call *Laburnocytisus*, is a genuine freak of nature which has only been repeated on two other occasions (a tomato plant with *Solanum nigrum*, and *Mespilus germanica* with a crataegus). It is, in fact, a hybrid produced by grafting instead of by pollination. *Laburnum* x *adami* is a small tree with pendulous inflorescences which on the same plant can be either yellow, purple, or bicoloured (yellow suffused with purple). It was created in 1825 by Jean Louis Adam, at Vitry, near Paris, by grafting *Cytisus purpureus* onto *Laburnum anagyroides*. Shortly afterwards, one of the branches bore flowers with a yellowish-purple tint, that is, intermediate in colour between the yellow laburnum and the purple cytisus, and the plant was named *Laburnum* x *adami*. Later, after new plants came into commercial distribution, the remarkable effects of this botanic marriage began to manifest themselves. The plants began to produce branches bearing flowers resembling both parents as well as the bicoloured blooms, with the result that each tree had branches with three different types of flowers. This strange characteristic has been maintained ever since, so that even today every tree of *Laburnum* x *adami* exhibits this tendency. The possibility of this type of graft-hybrid was at one time doubted by scientists, but they have now accepted the fact and refer to the results as *chimaeras*, explaining that the plants have a mixture of the parents in the tissues of their branches, rather than an orthodox fusion as in the case of hybrids raised from seed. In the present instance, the result is an attractive and interesting laburnum, a small deciduous tree up to 20 ft. high, flowering in June–July with yellow and purple flowers.

(Scotch Laburnum)
Small deciduous tree
Flowering period: June
Height: up to 30 ft.
Zone 4 southwards

Laburnum alpinum Berch. & Presl.
Native to Southern and Central Europe, and, although grown in Great Britain for more than three hundred years, is not indigenous to that country. At one time it was much confused with *Laburnum anagyroides*, but it is a superior garden plant, earlier-flowering, with larger foliage and longer inflorescences. Leaves dark green, trifoliate; leaflets up to 4 ins. long, oval. Inflorescences in the form of pendulous racemes 15 ins. long, bearing masses of golden-yellow $\frac{3}{4}$-in.-long slightly fragrant individual flowers. There are numerous varieties:

> var. *autumnale*, which flowers for a second time in autumn
> var. *grandiflorum*, with wider foliage and larger flowers
> var. *pendulum*, with pendulous, weeping branches

There is also a very old variety with the curious name *Latest and Longest*; this still remains one of the best of all laburnums for planting in gardens.

Laburnum anagyroides Medicus (syn. *Laburnum vulgare* Presl.)
Native to Southern and Central Europe. Not indigenous to the British Isles, although widely planted there for many years, and generally believed to be one of the earliest hardy exotic flowering shrubs to be introduced into England. Has in the past often been confused with *Laburnum alpinum,* which is a superior plant for garden purposes. It is a small deciduous tree up to 20 ft. high with long-stalked trifoliate leaves; leaflets obovate, up to 3 ins. long, and downy on the undersurface. The pendulous inflorescences are racemes up to 10 ins. long with masses of golden-yellow flowers, each $\frac{3}{4}$ in. long, borne on slender $\frac{1}{2}$-in.-long stalks. There are numerous varieties:

    var. *aureum* Rehd., with beautiful golden foliage
    var. *autumnale,* which blooms for a second time in autumn
    var. *pendulum,* with pendulous branches of great elegance
    var. *pyramidalis,* of erect pyramidal habit
    var. *quercifolium,* with the leaflets lobed like oak leaves, and sometimes five in number instead of the usual three. Also, the leaf stalk is frequently winged, making this an unusual and attractive form
    var. *semperflorens,* flowering again in late summer

(Common Laburnum)
Large deciduous shrub or small tree
Flowering period: May–June
Height: up to 20 ft.
Zone 4 southwards

Laburnum x *vossii* (see *Laburnum* x *watereri*)

Laburnum x *watereri* Hort. (syn. *Laburnum* x *vossii*)
A small deciduous tree of hybrid origin *(Laburnum alpinum* x *Laburnum anagyroides).* This is a natural hybrid, generally considered to be the best of all the laburnums for the length of its pendulous racemes. Its general characteristics and appearance are intermediate between the two parents.

Small deciduous tree
Flowering period: May–June
Height: up to 25 ft.
Zone 6 southwards

Lagerstroemia

(CRAPE, OR CREPE, MYRTLE)
Family: Lythraceae
Half-hardy or tender deciduous trees or shrubs
Position: sun
Propagation: seed or cuttings
Cultivation easy

Lagerstroemia is not an attractive or euphonic name, but Linnaeus, like many other botanists of a kind and generous nature, had the habit of naming plants and genera after his friends, in this case, Magnus von Lagerstroem (1696–1759), whose botanical fame was due to his friendship with Linnaeus. (If Italy had possessed a greater number of celebrated botanists there would probably now be in existence such genera as *Cavouria, Verdia, Goldonia, Manzonia, Garibaldia, Donizettia,* etc., but, as it is, such imaginary generic names must remain only dreams.)

In 1759 the first lagerstroemia introduced into Europe was the species *L. indica* (Crape Myrtle). In Europe the plants are grown exclusively for ornament, but in India they have considerable economic importance, especially for their timber, which is very fine-grained and has the advantage of never being attacked by insects; an important factor in latitudes where termites are a real scourge. The wood is brownish red, and, apart from its value in cabinet-making, it is (or was) used in the construction of large packing cases, small bridges, and railway sleeping-cars.

The genus *Lagerstroemia* comprises about thirty species distributed over an area including Southern and Eastern Asia, New Guinea, and Australia. They are widely grown in the warmer parts of Europe, and much planted in Florida and California. In districts suited to their successful cultivation, Crape Myrtles are justifiably considered to be the most spectacular of all summer-flowering deciduous shrubs; while the autumn colouring of their foliage is equal to that of maple, dogwood, or sumac. They must, however, have a long, hot, moderately dry summer, which not only favours abundant flowering on the new season's growths, but also, through a thorough ripening of the wood, enables the plants to withstand even severe winter cold.

Lagerstroemia indica can be successfully grown outside in any district which has long, hot summers with an abundance of brilliant sunshine. They are essentially sun-lovers and will thrive in the hottest positions, even in poor and dry soils, as demonstrated by their wide use as street trees in many Southern European towns, where the only cultural care they receive is summary (annual pruning at the end of winter), and where they withstand a polluted atmosphere as well as the violent radiation of an almost subtropical sun reflected from cement sidewalks and paved streets. Drastic pruning (cutting back the previous season's growths to within 2–3 buds or eyes from the point where they depart from the main branches) is essential to obtain the maximum extravagant mass of bloom produced on the new growths from the end of July until September. The plants are extraordinarily long-lived, several hundred years being quite a common occurrence in Southern European gardens, where specimens attain a height of up to 25 ft. with a diameter of similar proportions. Plants of such size can also be seen in the United States. In winter they will tolerate temperatures as low as $-10°$ F. without any protection, providing that the wood is not sappy and has received a thorough ripening the previous summer. Young plants are somewhat less hardy than old, woody, well-established specimens. Although *L. indica* is hardy, it cannot be recommended for northern districts where the summers are cloudy, wet, and cool; nor would it, or the other species, do well at high altitudes. Like so many other plants of this type, Crape Myrtles suffer from lack of summer heat rather than from winter cold. Even when not in bloom, and without their foliage, the plants have a certain attraction or fascination, with their often contorted, somewhat futuristic branches and glabrous, maroon-coloured, peeling bark. In gardens it is a very great mistake to grow them as standards (a method which must be followed when they are planted as street trees). If allowed to develop naturally, as bushes, an almost limitless number of basal growths will be produced. Each will develop into a definite trunk up to 1 ft. in diameter, which will allow the plant to attain an attractive, rounded, symmetrical habit that is seen to best effect when the plants are grown as isolated, individual specimens.

Cultivation. Although Crape Myrtles (especially *L. indica*) will withstand the rigorous conditions referred to above, plus long periods of drought, they will, of course, give better results if given more congenial treatment. Ideally they prefer a deep heavy soil, preferably slightly alkaline (calcareous), containing plenty of humus, and a top dressing or mulching with leafsoil or well-rotted manure each spring. Periodic applications of a liquid organic fertilizer during the growing period will also be beneficial. Good drainage, an abundance of sun, and summer heat are essential. As previously mentioned, severe pruning is necessary at the end of winter. The new flowering growths—square in cross-section—can reach a length of 5 ft. in a few months.

Propagation is easily effected by means of seed sown in a warm greenhouse in spring, from soft-wood cuttings taken in April–May and rooted in a heated greenhouse or under transparent plastic or a glass bell-jar, or by means of semi-woody cuttings taken in August and inserted in sandy soil in coldframes.

Lagerstroemia indica L. (Crape Myrtle)
Flowering period: Aug.–Oct.
Height: up to 25 ft.
Zone 6 southwards

Native to Japan, Korea, China, Indo-China, and northern Australia. This is the species most frequently cultivated in gardens, with smooth, glabrous stems and maroon bark. Leaves somewhat small, 1–3 ins. long, stalkless or very short-stalked, elongated-elliptic, abruptly pointed, with silky hairs on the midrib of the undersurface. Flowers borne in large terminal racemes up to 10 ins. high; individual blooms up to $1\frac{1}{2}$ ins. wide; colour reddish carmine-pink. There are several forms, such as:

> var. *alba,* with pure-white flowers. This is a plant of almost incredible grace, charm, elegance, and beauty, especially for the lace-like appearance of the flowers.

Lagerstroemia indica
From *Curtis's Botanical Magazine*,
1798, plate 405

var. *purpurea,* with purple flowers
var. *rubra,* with rich ruby-red blooms

There are also numerous forms with pale- to dark-pink flowers.

Lagerstroemia speciosa Pers. (syn. *Munchausia speciosa, Lagerstroemia flos-reginae*)
(Queen's Flower)
Flowering period: Aug.–Sept.
Height: up to 50 ft.
Zone 9 southwards

Native to a vast area extending from India to Australia. Leaves elliptic or elongated-lanceolate, obtuse, up to 10 ins. long. Flowers up to 3 ins. in diameter, borne in large spectacular racemes, purple towards evening, but pinkish earlier in the day. Much less hardy than the preceding *Lagerstroemia indica*.

Lagerstroemia subcostata L.
Flowering period: July–Aug.
Height: up to 20 ft.
Zone 9 southwards

Native to China and Taiwan, where it develops into a tree up to 60 ft. high, although in gardens it rarely exceeds a height of 20 ft. Leaves ovate, acuminate, wedge-shaped at the base. Inflorescences tall, terminal, with pyramidal panicles up to 9 ins. high composed of masses of white-and-pink flowers. This, too, is much more tender than *Lagerstroemia indica,* but it merits cultivation in warm localities not only for its attractive blooms but also for its superb autumn colouring.

Lantana

(RED OR YELLOW SAGE)
Family: *Verbenaceae*
Tender deciduous shrubs
Position: sun
Propagation: seed or cuttings
Cultivation easy
Slightly fragrant

A useful, easily grown, brilliantly coloured group of non-hardy tender shrubs. Some have an almost trailing habit, while others are semi-climbers; both have the greatest value for temporary outdoor use from early summer until autumn in any temperate climate, but they are not tolerant of frost. In sheltered positions or frost-free localities in Southern Europe, Texas, Florida, California, and other places with a Mediterranean climate, they can be planted permanently outside with, if necessary, some light winter protection. They are also excellent subjects for pot culture. The flowering period is extremely long, and if a sufficiently high temperature is maintained the plants remain more or less permanently in bloom. Leaves are rough-surfaced, dentated, dark green; inflorescence a terminal raceme similar to that of verbenas. The stems can be spiny, smooth, or hairy. After the flowers are finished an abundant crop of fleshy fruits is produced and it is a common sight to see plants bearing flowers and fruits simultaneously. There are about fifty known species, mostly native to tropical and subtropical America. They are rarely found wild in the Old World.

Cultivation. A few lantanas have been cultivated in Europe since the nineteenth century, at first exclusively in greenhouses; later, they came into popular use as summer bedding subjects, and they are also used as temporary house plants and are excellent for growing in large receptacles on terraces, where their profuse flowering habit is much appreciated. In the north, however, they must be removed to greenhouses or some other frost-free location for the winter. They tolerate being cut or pruned into almost any size or form, although such unnatural treatment spoils the graceful but sometimes rampant habit of species such as *Lantana Camara*. The plants are very adaptable to training, either as trailers or climbers. *Lantana Camara,* in particular, will assume the character of a climbing shrub if planted against a sunny wall and trained over a wooden trellis, where its long spreading branches will rapidly form a dense screen of flowers and foliage for the duration of the summer. On the other hand, *Lantana sellowiana,* with its more prostrate and less expansive character, is excellent for planting in large rock-gardens, at the top of walls, in the pockets of dry walls, by the side of stone steps, on terraces, or in large pots, where its semi-trailing recumbent habit will be emphasized. Plants used as temporary seasonable subjects in outdoor summer beds can be dug up in late autumn, energetically pruned, potted, and moved to a frost-free location for the winter (a temperature of 45°–50°F. is sufficient), where they should be allowed to enter a semi-dormant state and should be given only a minimum amount of water. In the spring new growth will begin and the plants can be planted outside again. Lantanas love a hot, sunny position—an essential requirement in the north—but in really hot, brilliantly sunny localities in the south they will also give good results in partial shade. They are not particular about soil, although the position must be well drained. During the summer they need plenty of water and will appreciate occasional applications of liquid fertilizer. It is something of a surprise that so few species and varieties have become established as good garden plants.

Propagation can be effected by means of seed sown in a warm greenhouse in February–March and if well-cared-for and grown on in pots the plants will bloom by the end of summer. Otherwise, propagation can be effected by means of soft cuttings taken in spring, inserted in

Lantana Camara

pots of sand or sandy peat in a warm greenhouse at a temperature of not less than 75°F., and then potted individually when rooted. Good results are also obtained from cuttings of half-ripened wood taken in August and inserted in frames, or in pots in an unheated greenhouse. If lantanas are to be used on an extensive scale, it is advisable to always have a stock of young plants, as the older ones tend to flower less and less, becoming excessively woody, gaunt, and lacking a good supply of vigorous young growths.

Lantana Camara L. (syn. *Lantana aculeata*)

(Mountain Sage of Jamaica)
Flowering period: June–Oct.
Height: up to 6 ft.
Zone 9 southwards as a permanent outdoor plant;
Zone 4 southwards as a seasonable (summer) outdoor plant

Native to tropical America and extending northwards as far as Texas and even North Carolina. Originally discovered in Brazil by the botanist William Pison and—among all tropical and subtropical plants—one of the most suitable for cultivating in United States and European gardens, where it flowers profusely and continuously. In its natural habitat the plant can attain a height of 10 ft., generally with very spiny stems, hence the original specific name of *aculeata*—from the Latin *aculeatus* (prickly)—given it by Linnaeus. It is so widely distributed and multiplies so easily that it is often considered an invasive weed for the harm it can cause other plants. In gardens, however, it is generally of more modest proportions, forming a shrub with occasional curved spines on the branches. The foliage is brilliant green when young, darker with age, dentated, rough-surfaced to the touch, oval or heart-shaped, and 3–6 ins. long. The inflorescence is a corymb composed of a mass of minute flowers $\frac{1}{3}$ in. wide; the entire flattish corymb having a diameter of about 2 ins. and borne on a stalk longer than the leaf stalks. The inflorescences are terminal and axillary. The colour of the flowers varies according to the form, the variety, and the age of the inflorescence. This colour variation is so marked that an inflorescence can change its hue in the course of a single day; the Germans in fact call it *Wandelröschen*, which literally means "changeable little rose", and in Italy it is known as the "aurora plant". Basically the flowers are yellow in the bud stage and when they first open, after which they change to orange, and finally to red. It is nearly always possible to find all three colours simultaneously on the same branch, or even on the same inflorescence. In one form, often catalogued as var. *flava,* the flowers remain a rich vivid yellow. Both the flowers and the leaves have a somewhat acrid fragrance which some people find unpleasant, but it is not always easily detected. The seed-bearing fruits are also attractive and appear in profusion immediately after the flowers have finished. They are fleshy, rounded, and about the size of peppercorns, green at first, but turning to dark metallic blue when ripe. It is a common sight to see branches laden simultaneously with flowers of three different tints and fruits of two colours. Among the numerous forms and varieties the following are of special interest:

var. *crocea,* flowers at first sulphur-yellow, later changing to saffron-yellow

var. *mista,* distinguishable for the greater number of spines on its stems, and for the flowers which change colour with age: externally from yellow to brick-red, and internally from yellow to orange

var. *mutabilis,* as the name suggests, even more variable in colour—outer flowers white, passing to yellow, pink, and lilac, with the centre yellow

var. *nivea,* the outer flowers white, with a tendency to pale bluish towards the centre

var. *sanguinea,* flowers at first saffron-yellow, changing later to bright red

(Weeping or Trailing Lantana)
Flowering period: June–Oct.
Height: up to 3 ft.
Zone 9 southwards as a permanent outdoor plant;
Zone 4 southwards as a seasonable (summer) outdoor plant

Lantana sellowiana Link & Otto (syn. *Lantana delicatissima, Lantana montevidensis*)

Native to South America. A relatively small shrub with semi-prostrate stems and a semi-pendulous almost trailing habit. Leaves small, oval, 1 in. long, closely dentated. Flowers a delightful shade of lilac-pink, borne in 1½-in.-wide flattish corymbs. Rather less hardy than the preceding but equally free-flowering, more or less continuously while the temperature remains sufficiently high. The blooms are fragrant and the plant is excellent for cultivating in large pots, boxes, or tubs, and hanging baskets.

Lathyrus

Lathyrus sativus

(Sweet Pea)
Family: Leguminosae
Annual or perennial hardy herbaceous or tuberous-rooted climbers
Position: sun or partial shade
Propagation: seed or division
Cultivation easy
Fragrant
Useful for cutting

Soon after *Lathyrus odoratus* left its home in Sicily in the seventeenth century and travelled to England, it rapidly established itself as one of the most popular plants in European and American gardens for the colour and fragrance of its flowers; but when many years later it returned home, it spoke another language, and few recognized it as the same plant that had departed so many years previously. The detailed story is summarized as follows. In 1699, when Queen Anne reigned in Great Britain, a certain Father Francisco Cupani sent a few seeds of *Lathyrus odoratus* from Palermo to his friend Doctor Uvedale, a surgeon who lived near London (and whose garden was still in existence until a few years ago; as a child I often played there, but now the site is occupied by a supermarket, although a nearby thoroughfare has been named Uvedale Road in memory of the worthy doctor).

Uvedale was an enthusiastic amateur gardener, noted as "an avid collector and introducer of many exotic plants and flowers". No more was heard of these seeds for about twenty years, when suddenly there appeared in the London flower market a new plant with the habit of a small climber, bearing strongly scented red and purple flowers. It was promptly christened Sweet Pea. The name has remained, but little else has survived which bears any resemblance to the original Sicilian species.

Today's Sweet Peas are grown by professional florists in greenhouses and sold in winter at high prices. But what a delusion when one buys a bunch—hoping to be regaled with the traditionally delicious fragrance—and finds them almost completely without perfume. Industrialized, Sweet Peas have also become sterilized and aseptic. To restore a little equity in our gardens one should buy Sweet Pea seeds from the best firms and, when the plants begin to bloom, carefully control each one, immediately discarding without pity all those with scentless flowers, no matter how beautiful they may be. Seed can then be collected from the remainder and the gardener will gradually obtain a strain of Sweet Peas worthy of the name.

In one of his books, H. L. V. Fletcher briefly but clearly traces the history of the catastrophe of "The-Great-Lament-Of-The-Sweet-Peas-Which-Lost-Their-Perfume." In England in the year 1800, fragrant Sweet Peas in five different colours had been obtained. Towards the end of the century, Henry Eckford succeeded in enlarging the size of the flowers and increasing their range of colours, thus paving the way for the giant-flowered types. One of these, var. *Primadonna*, gave birth to a family with frilled petals in the year 1901; one was named Countess Spencer, from which has derived the modern strain of Spencer Sweet Peas with frilled petals. At this point began the escalation in favour of bigger flowers, bizarre forms, and a vastly increased range of tints, but, as Fletcher notes, the more pleasing the flowers became to the eye, the more they lost the power to please the nose. Not only did this loss concern the intensity of perfume, but also its quality, and the original typical fragrance vanished completely. Charles Unwin, one of the major Sweet Pea hybridists of our times, who has done everything possible to defend his work and that of his colleagues, wrote that some years ago he

Lathyrus tingitanus

Lathyrus tuberosus

Lathyrus vernus

received the gift of some Sweet Pea seeds from an almost forgotten English village. The flowers were small and not very attractive in colour, but their fragrance was marvellous and, after an entire lifetime dedicated to Sweet Peas, Unwin admitted that, "until that moment I never fully realized why Sweet Peas were so named". Unfortunately, neither in England nor on the Continent is it now possible to find seed of the original fragrant Sweet Peas. Possibly they *do* exist in some hidden out-of-the-way garden, and it would be a fascinating occupation to seek them out. According to Unwin, the most fragrant are those coloured blue, lavender, mauve, and white; while the orange, pink, and salmon ones are the least scented. But Wilson and Bell maintain exactly the opposite.

To increase the probability of having at least some fragrance in our Sweet Pea flowers, the plants should be cultivated in the simplest possible manner, in rows, without practising all those surgical operations so dear to the experts (removal of lateral growths, reducing the number of buds, cutting off the tendrils, etc.).

Lathyrus odoratus is also famous for the part it played in the study of genetics and Mendelism. It was, in fact, the most important plant used by Father Gregor Mendel, whose experiments founded the basis of the modern science of heredity. (Born in 1822 of Austro-Silesian parents, early in his life he entered the Augustinian monastery at Brünn [Brno], where he carried out his experiments. In 1865 he published the results, but it was not until 1900, sixteen years after his death, that the full significance of his work was appreciated.)

So far we have confined our remarks to *Lathyrus odoratus,* the Sweet Pea, but the genus is so numerous, and comprises so many plants of economic value to mankind, that its decorative value forms only a part of its importance. *Lathyrus aphaca, Lathyrus paluster,* and *Lathyrus pratensis* provide excellent forage for cattle. *Lathyrus ochroleucus* figured largely in the diet of the Chippewa Indians, the Indian tribes of Nebraska ate the entire pod of *Lathyrus ornatus* just as we eat scarlet runner beans while the Indians of New Mexico ate the pods of *Lathyrus polymorphus.* On the Continent several hybrid forms are eaten complete with the pod (and therefore called *mangetout* in France) and are considered a delicacy. In Italy, Spain, Turkey, and France *Lathyrus cicera* and its var. *sativus* were at one time widely cultivated for eating in the green state and also used dried for preparing a flour, but it is now much less used on account of its possibly harmful effects to both man and beast. It contains the alkaloid lathyrin, which, if absorbed over a long period (particularly in cold, damp climates), can produce symptoms of paralysis in the lower limbs which, in advanced cases, can cause difficulty in walking (although some authorities are of the opinion that the phenomenon is due to a fungus found in the plant rather than to its content of lathyrin). Flour made from *Lathyrus cicera* has also been used to

Lathyrus odoratus
From *Curtis's Botanical Magazine*,
1788, plate 60

adulterate true pea flour—not a serious matter in itself, but potentially dangerous in view of the above-mentioned poisonous properties of *Lathyrus cicera*. *Lathyrus tuberosus* is another edible species; the tubers having a high sugar content and a flavour similar to that of chestnuts. The pleasantly fragrant blooms make it a worthwhile plant for the garden; in fact, in the sixteenth century the flowers were used for the distillation of a popular scent, later superseded by *Lathyrus odoratus*. Finally, it is interesting to note that some Indians of the Pacific Northwest brew a type of coffee from the dried seeds of *Lathyrus vestitus*. (The common, or garden, edible pea—*Pisum sativum*—is not an ornamental plant.)

The genus comprises between one hundred and two hundred species, but authorities are not in agreement about the exact number. Its area of distribution extends throughout Northern Europe—excluding the coldest zones, Asia, the Americas, and the mountains of tropical Africa, but always in temperate climates.

Cultivation. In their natural habitat, lathyrus thrive generally in cool pasture-land, thin woods, along river banks, ditches, hilly and mountainous areas up to 6,000 feet, and sea-shores. They always require freshness, good drainage, and a soil rich in humus. In city gardens where the climate is hot and dry, Sweet Peas are not always a success; they are still less satisfactory when grown in receptacles on a hot terrace. In a city garden that receives fresh air and good light (in other words, one that is cool and fresh), the plants will give excellent results. Not all experts agree on the ideal soil for Sweet Peas: Wilson and Bell advise a very alkaline (calcareous) soil; while both Plenzat and Parey indicate a mildly acid or neutral soil. Personally, I favour the latter theory, with a soil of pH 6–7.50. From April onwards it is beneficial to mulch the plants with a 2–3-in.-deep layer of peat or leafsoil to conserve moisture and to keep the roots cool and fresh. If the plants are to be grown in rows, a deep (18–20 ins.), well-dug trench should be prepared, preferably some months before planting (the previous autumn is a good time for this). Fertilizing and enriching the soil is accomplished by placing a generous layer (4–5 ins.) of well-composted manure at the bottom of the trench and covering it with soil to the surface (if the trench is prepared the previous autumn, fresh manure may be used). If natural (or dried) manure is not available, excellent results can be obtained by using organic material such as peat mixed with dried blood, or with a ureaform fertilizer, seaweed, spent hops from a brewery, or sewage sludge (such as Milorganite). Seed is generally sown in March–April, directly into the trench, about 2 ins. apart and 1 in. deep. Some people find it more convenient to sow in small pots (1–2 seeds per pot) in January or February, and then set out the seedlings in April. In Mediterranean and southern climates it is possible to sow seed directly in the soil in late summer and have flowering plants soon after Christmas. As soon as the young plants begin to develop, adequate support must be provided for them to climb upon. For British gardeners the most appropriate, almost legendary, support is that provided by hazel branches, which are so well furnished with masses of small twiggy growths. However, nylon netting or chicken wire is equally successful (if not as aesthetic). We will not discourage the reader with details of the complicated operations adopted by those who grow their flowers for exhibition purposes rather than for garden display or for providing cut flowers for the home. There are, however, a few rules which should be observed: all dead blooms, complete with stalks, should be removed immediately, to prevent the formation of unwanted seed which curtails the length of the plants' flowering period; during May–July, because Sweet Pea plants like a change of diet, the following substances should be used alternately —dried blood, liquid fertilizer made from horse or chicken manure mixed with a little bone meal and wood ash, or any of the specially prepared organic fertilizers available on the market. We will leave disbudding, the removal of lateral growths, and the cutting of tendrils to the more fanatic professionals. Another rule worth following is to rotate the position where Sweet Peas are to be grown and not grow them in the same position two years running. Sometimes the seeds have an attraction for mice and birds but this inconvenience can be avoided by immersing the seeds for a few minutes in a solution of red lead and paraffin (kerosene) before sowing. Mothballs sown in with the seeds will also discourage predators.

Lathyrus latifolius

Lathyrus grandiflorus L.
Native to Southern Europe. A hardy herbaceous climbing perennial up to 6 ft. high. Leaves typical of the annual Sweet Pea. Flowers abundantly produced in large compact groups similar in size and shape to the older type of Sweet Pea, with fuchsia-pink blooms. A most useful and easily grown permanent plant for walls, etc. It is long-lived, requires no attention (apart from some support during its growing season), and it is very ornamental.

(Everlasting Pea)
Herbaceous perennial climber
Flowering period: June–July
Height: 6 ft.

Lathyrus latifolius L.
Native to Southern Europe. A vigorous herbaceous, climbing perennial up to 9 ft. high. Leaves dark green, oval or elliptic. The long-stalked inflorescences are composed of multi-flowered sprays of attractive typical Sweet-Pea-like flowers of a delightful shade of pink. An interesting free-flowering and decorative plant that requires no special attention and is ideal for training over summer-houses, walls, porches, or trellises in warm, sunny climates. This plant deserves to be much more widely cultivated. Even in England, where conditions are certainly not ideal for this type of Mediterranean plant, it is a great success. There are two beautiful varieties—var. *roseus,* with rich pink flowers, and var. *Snow Queen,* with white flowers.

(Perennial Pea
or Everlasting Pea)
Herbaceous perennial climber
Flowering period: June–Aug.
Height: up to 9 ft.

Herbaceous perennial
Flowering period: May–June
Height: 18 ins.

Lathyrus luteus L. (syn. *Orobus luteus*)
Native to Europe. A hardy herbaceous perennial only 18 ins. high, and of particular interest for its yellow flowers—a colour rarely found among the perennial lathyrus. Leaves dark green, 1¼–2 ins. long and divided into 4–5 pairs of small leaflets. The plant has a low spreading habit and in May–June produces an abundance of miniature pea-like flowers of considerable attraction in a mixed border. The var. *aureus* has yellow-and-brown flowers.

(Sweet Pea)
Annual climber
Flowering period: May–Aug.
Height: up to 9 ft.

Lathyrus odoratus L.
Native to Sicily. The original species is a somewhat hairy plant generally found growing in wild inaccessible places. Its habit is either trailing or climbing; with oval leaves and 1-in.-long flowers that are dark red and purple and intensely fragrant. It is the parent of the hundreds of varieties of today's Sweet Peas, but is now rarely cultivated in gardens. Modern Sweet Peas are the most exquisite of all climbing annuals, with lovely graceful flowers in superb colours, sometimes slightly scented, and marvellous for cutting. Although widely cultivated and much appreciated in gardens, some people have found cause for complaint because of the brevity of the flowering period—relatively short in comparison with many other annuals—and because of the necessity for staking. Today, however, both of these problems have been solved: the first through the introduction of the tall Galaxy strain, which has all the characteristics and beauty of the ordinary Sweet Peas, but flowers continuously for several months if the dead flowers are removed daily so that seed is not allowed to form. This new strain also has longer flower stems and more individual flowers per stem. The problem of staking has been solved by the introduction of dwarf Sweet Peas such as:

Lathyrus odoratus

    var. *Americana*, a strain 2 ft. high with long-stemmed flowers
    var. *Bijou*, 12–16 ins. high with flower stems sufficiently long for cutting
    var. *Knee Hi*, 3 ft. high and continuous-flowering

(Pride of California or Campo Pea)
Semi-shrubby perennial
Flowering period: June–July
Height: up to 6–7 ft.

Lathyrus splendens L.
Native to southern California. An interesting and attractive semi-shrubby perennial much neglected by European gardeners. Leaves oval-oblong, 1 in. in length, borne in up to five pairs. Flowers carried on robust stems, 6–12 in a group, variable in colour from pink to violet or reddish-purple, each 1 in. wide. Seed pods up to 3 ins. long, smooth-surfaced, and beaked at the end.

(Tangier Scarlet Pea)
Half-hardy annual
Flowering period: Apr.–June
Height: up to 5–6 ft.

Lathyrus tingitanus L.
Native to the Mediterranean regions. A lovely annual species introduced into gardens in 1680, but in northern countries it has never become popular or widely grown, probably because of its doubtful

hardiness and habit of flowering early when there may still be risk of late frost. For southern gardens, however, it is a desirable plant. Leaves narrow, lanceolate, pointed. The long slender flower stems bear clusters of large red and purple blooms. The var. *roseus* has pink flowers.

Lathyrus tuberosus L.

(Tuberous Pea)
*Tuberous-rooted perennial
Flowering period: June–Aug.
Height: 3 ft.*

Native to Europe. A tuberous-rooted perennial species with vigorous, even invasive roots that make it a difficult plant to eradicate once established. Sometimes used for culinary purposes, the tubers taste like those of *Helianthus tuberosus* (Jerusalem artichoke). Because of its invasive character, it should be used with caution in the garden, but the brilliant-pink scented flowers are very attractive and the light-green elliptic foliage arranged in pairs is pleasing. It is a plant to grow under semi-wild natural conditions, where it can spread, climb, or trail unchecked.

Lavandula

(LAVENDER)
Family: Labiatae
Half-hardy or tender evergreen shrubs
Position: full sun
Propagation: cuttings or seed
Cultivation easy
Fragrant
Useful for cutting

The genus *Lavandula* is typically Mediterranean for several reasons: its grey-green or olive-green foliage; its fragrance, which blends so well with other Mediterranean plants such as rosemary, sage, myrtle, and lemons; its love of sunshine; and its ability to thrive in alkaline (calcareous) arid soils among rocks and stones. Several species are, however, also excellent garden plants in a temperate climate, where they can be persuaded to forget their wild, carefree, natural habitat and can be adapted into being grown as hedges and other restricted (and prosaic) forms and uses. Others refuse to forsake their birthright of heat and brilliant sunshine and, although tolerating garden conditions, insist on a frost-free climate.

The name *Lavandula* is derived from the Latin *lavare* (to wash), which alludes to the ancient custom of scenting water for the toilette with oil of lavender or a few lavender flowers. There are about twenty-five species diffused throughout the Mediterranean regions, the

Lavandula dentata
From *Curtis's Botanical Magazine*,
1798, plate 400

Canary Islands, and India. They are shrubby or sub-shrubby evergreen plants with entire or divided leaves. The inflorescences take the form of spikes, sometimes branched, composed of minute blue-, lilac-, or violet-coloured flowers; in the case of the numerous varieties and forms, the range of colours is extended to purple, pink, and white. All are fragrant, in both flower and foliage, but the perfume has not always the same intensity and is not always as agreeable as that of the common lavender (*Lavandula Spica*).

Lavender has been cultivated since Classical Antiquity, not for its decorative properties but for its extensive medicinal and domestic uses, many of which still survive today. In fact, in large gardens certain species are grown in the flower garden for their beauty, while the same plants are cultivated in the vegetable or herb garden for household use. The dried flowers are still esteemed for the fragrance they impart to linen, and clothing. Above all, lavender is widely used—in particular, *Lavandula vera*—not only for oil of lavender, but also for the well-known lavender water or lavender cologne. This may be prepared as follows:

> 2 ounces freshly picked lavender flowers (gathered in the early morning before the sun has dried the dew that clings to them)
> 1 pint alcohol (a good grade of non-grain alcohol for external use—such as rubbing alcohol—may be used)

Steep the flowers in the alcohol in a tightly covered jar or bottle. Expose to direct sunlight for at least 2 hours every day for 2 weeks. After this time, carefully filter (or strain through 5 layers of cheesecloth or muslin) and bottle in tightly stoppered small bottles.

Lavandula Stoechas

A pleasant recipe for sachets to place among linens, lingerie, clothing, etc., can be made as follows:

> 8 ounces freshly picked lavender flowers (see above), dried for 1 week in a warm, dark, dry, well-ventilated place
> $\frac{1}{2}$ ounce each dried thyme and mint leaves
> $\frac{1}{4}$ ounce each whole cloves, cumin seed, and carnation petals
> $\frac{1}{4}$ ounce powdered orris root (may be purchased at a drugstore or chemist's)
> 1 ounce coarse (Kosher or sea-) salt

Mix all ingredients well and sew into small gauze or chiffon bags.

Lavandula latifolia renders a volatile oil of inferior quality, similar in composition to oil of turpentine and with a slightly rancid odour. It is used as a medium for painting on porcelain, in the manufacture of paint, and occasionally in perfumery. In medicine today the use of lavender is practically confined to its aromatic properties, but until the end of the last century it was prescribed for its believed sedative or anaesthetic properties, which include a lowering of body temperature and slowing the heartbeat—factors that favoured its substitution by more reliable drugs. At one time it was even used to cure paralysis and stuttering, but no records remain to show with what success. Finally, one author affirms that the essential oil of lavender can be used to exterminate vermin.

In mild climates, lavender is an excellent shrub for hedge-making; although, because of the necessity for clipping, and because the plants must be grown so close together, flowering is much reduced. Such hedges are, however, of rapid and vigorous growth, attractive to look at, and a delight for their fragrance. H. L. V. Fletcher (in *The Fragrant Garden*) rightly advises that, to exploit the true beauty of the plant, lavender should be allowed to grow and develop completely naturally, in an informal manner.

Cultivation. Lavender cultivation is extremely easy. It requires a dry, not-too-fertile, alkaline (calcareous), heavy soil containing plenty of humus, and a warm, sunny position. The plants are tolerant of clipping and even severe pruning—essential requirements in more northern gardens where the tips of the branches are liable to be frost-nipped. In really cold areas the stems may be severely affected by frost, and the base of the plant should be protected with a mulch of straw, peat, wood ashes, leafsoil, etc. Propagation of the species is easy from seed sown in a warm greenhouse in spring. In the case of forms, hybrids, and varieties it is, of course, necessary to propagate only by cuttings to ensure faithful reproduction of such special characteristics as the colour of the flowers, etc. Soft cuttings can be taken in spring, and inserted in sand or sandy soil in a greenhouse or under transparent plastic or glass bell-jars. They are quick to root, especially if treated with one of the commercial hormone products available for this purpose. Propagation from semi-woody cuttings can be effected in autumn or early spring in coldframes, and these cuttings should also be treated with one of the above-mentioned hormone products. When all risk of frost has passed, the young plants can be set out in rows, and for the first year periodically topped to prevent flowering and to encourage the formation of well-branched bushy specimens. Commercially grown plants are allowed to bloom when two to four years old and they continue to produce flower spikes on an economically viable scale for four to six years, after which they should be destroyed. In gardens, however, they are long-lived plants, and old specimens develop a definite woody trunk. The best time to gather the inflorescences is before the flowers are fully expanded, on cloudless mornings, and while the spikes are still slightly damp from the dew.

Flowering period: Apr.–May
Height: up to 3 ft.
Zone 8 southwards

Lavandula dentata L.
Native to Italy, Spain, Malta, Morocco, and Algeria, where it is found in rocky, siliceous soils. Leaves opposite, narrow, tomentose,

silver-grey, aromatic, and the margins deeply but finely dentated. Flower spikes are composed of pale-violet-coloured flowers with darker-violet ovate bracts. In a frost-free climate the plants will bloom practically continuously, but in cooler zones the flowering period is restricted to early summer.

Lavandula latifolia Vill.
Native to the Mediterranean regions. Less common than *Lavandula Spica*, which it resembles, but of a more herbaceous and less shrubby character, with wider-leaved foliage. Also less hardy and not so fragrant.

Flowering period: June–July
Height: 2–2½ ft.
Zone 8 southwards

Lavandula multifida L. (syn. *Lavandula pinnata*)
Native to Madeira, introduced into England in 1777. Forms a shrub about the same size as *Lavandula dentata*. The leaves are very attractive—pinnate, silvery or almost white—but not fragrant. The flower spikes are larger than those of *Lavandula dentata* and deep violet.

Flowering period: Feb.–Apr.
Height: 2–3 ft.
Zone 8 southwards

Lavandula Spica Cav. (syn. *Lavandula officinalis* Chaix.)
Native to and very common throughout the Mediterranean regions. A bushy evergreen shrub up to 4½–5 ft. high with erect stems which are square when the plant is young. The entire plant is covered with a fine down, which gives it a characteristic silver-grey appearance. Leaves opposite, linear, 1½–2 ins. long and ⅓ in. wide, with recurved margins. Flowers borne at the top of slender erect stems up to 18 ins. long, arranged in whorls and crowded in dense spikes up to 2 ins. long. Corolla tubular at the base, pale grey-blue, two-lipped at the mouth. Calyx tubular, of a deeper tint than the corolla. A beautiful plant that has been cultivated in gardens for centuries and, apart from its fragrance, is much appreciated for the flowers that appear when few other shrubs are in bloom. When the flower spikes are cut and dried their fragrance will endure for many years. Both the leaves and the flowers have a similar perfume, but the scent of the flowers is stronger and more agreeable. There are numerous attractive varieties:

(Common Lavender)
Flowering period: June–July
Height: 4½–5 ft.
Zone 5 southwards

- var. *Atropurpurea* (syn. var. *Hidcote*), very compact, particularly free-flowering, dark violet, and only 12–16 ins. high
- var. *Grappenhall*, a particularly vigorous form
- var. *Munstead Dwarf*, of dwarf compact habit and with darker flowers
- var. *Rosea*, flowers pale lilac-pink
- var. *Twickel Purple*, purple flowers, with a very compact habit

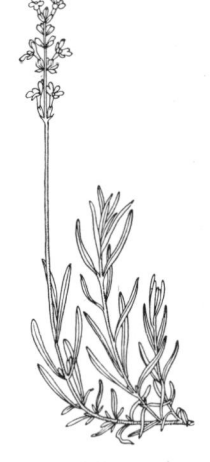

Lavandula Spica

Lavandula multifida
From *Curtis's Botanical Magazine*,
1798, plate 401

Lavandula Stoechas L.   (French Lavender)
Flowering period: Mar.–May
Height: 1½–2½ ft.
Zone 9 southwards

Native to the Mediterranean regions. Forms a grey tomentose shrub with stalkless linear leaves about $\frac{1}{3}$ in. long, very narrow, and joined to the stems at the point of the nodes; soft, greenish grey, and covered on both surfaces with dense velvety white hairs. Flower spikes quadrangular and compact with a tuft of purple bracts overhanging the darker-purple flowers. The flower spikes are borne on tall leafy stems and the tuft of large purple bracts at the summit makes this one of the easiest species to identify. The perfume is also different from that of other lavenders, more reminiscent of rosemary and so strong that it is almost unpleasant.

Lavandula vera D.C.
Flowering period: June–July
Height: 4½–5 ft.
Zone 6 southwards

Native to the Mediterranean regions. At one time this plant was not recognized as a distinct species from *Lavandula Spica,* which it closely resembles. The nineteenth-century Swiss botanist Augustin De Candolle separated the two, and gave *Lavandula vera* its present name. (He explained the most important differences as follows: leaves linear or narrowly oblong and never becoming wedge-shaped or spatulate as is frequent in *Lavandula Spica,* and greener in colour and less wide.) *Lavandula vera* is also superior for its yield of lavender oil. There is a white-flowered form, var. *alba*; and a dwarf form, var. *nana. Lavandula vera* is sometimes known as Dutch Lavender.

Lavatera

(LAVATER OR MALLOW)
Family: Malvaceae
Annuals or herbaceous perennials
Position: sun
Propagation: seed
Cultivation easy

Lavateras are mostly summer-flowering plants, several of which are widely cultivated in European and American gardens. Their native habitat includes the Mediterranean regions, the Canary Islands, Australia, Central Asia, and California. The genus was named in honour of the famous Lavater brothers of Zurich, seventeenth-century Swiss naturalists and physicians. Although the genus contains about twenty-five species, relatively few are in general cultivation, although the four mentioned here are first-class garden plants. (An-

Lavatera trimestris
From *Curtis's Botanical Magazine*,
1790, plate 109

other species, *Lavatera olbia* L., native to Southern Europe, is similar to the species *L. arborea*, but it is an inferior plant.) The perennial species *L. arborea* and *L. assurgentiflora* are large rampant plants more suited to the wild or informal garden than to beds, and should be grown in bold masses. The annual species *L. trimestris* and its varieties are more modestly proportioned and can effectively be used for a summer display in borders. In all cases they are plants which associate particularly well with lawns and grassland, and the dominant colour of their flowers is some shade of pink.

Cultivation. Same for all the species normally grown in gardens: seed can be sown directly in the flowering positions in April–May, subsequently thinning out the seedlings to about 18 ins. apart. Like all the Malvaceae, germination is rapid, a matter of 8–10 days. They are plants with no demands about soil, so long as it is not too wet and cold or too compact. The perennial species are quite hardy, but not always long-lived; it is sometimes advisable to replant younger specimens every few years. They are sun lovers and should be grown only in warm, well-lighted positions, preferably in a sheltered site, as the very tall types can be easily disturbed by wind because of their somewhat restricted root system—a factor that also makes them difficult plants to move or even to transplant when young.

Lavatera arborea L.

Native to Southern Europe. A vigorous semi-herbaceous plant which, as its specific name suggests, can assume the proportions of a small tree, with a trunk up to 4 ins. in diameter at its base. It is particularly successful in its native habitat, and in gardens in seaside localities in rather poor soil. The leaves are large, velvety, slightly undulated, vaguely palmate, and shallowly divided into seven rounded segments, with the entire leaf measuring up to 8 ins. in diameter and covered with silky hairs on its upper surface. The undersurface is greyish and slightly woolly. The flowers are purple-pink veined with darker purple, 4 ins. in diameter, and borne in terminal racemes. Because of its large dimensions it is a plant to group behind smaller plants and looks its best in an informal country setting. The var. *variegata* is particularly attractive for its variegated foliage with irregular markings of dark and light green, greyish, or cream-white, with variegation more pronounced on adult plants than on younger specimens. This form must, however, be propagated from cuttings and not from seed.

(Tree Mallow)
Semi-herbaceous perennial or biennial
Flowering period: Apr.–July
Height: up to 10 ft.

Lavatera assurgentiflora L.

Native to the offshore islands of southern California. A large herbaceous perennial or sub-shrub. It has never become widely known in the cooler parts of Europe because it is not hardy at temperatures lower than those prevailing in southern California. It is a beautiful fast-growing species, and, where climatic conditions are suitable,

(Californian Windbreak)
Herbaceous perennial or sub-shrub
Flowering period: May–Aug.
Height: up to 12 ft.

makes an excellent informal hedge. Plants raised from seed flower the first year. Leaves up to 6 ins. wide, with 5–7 coarsely dentated lobes. Flowers purple, 2 ins. in diameter, axillary, in clusters of up to four.

Herbaceous perennial
Flowering period: June–Sept.
Height: up to 4½ ft.

Lavatera thuringiaca L.
Native to the Mediterranean regions and Asia. One of the smaller herbaceous perennial species; basal leaves roughly triangular, with three-lobed superior leaves. Flowers light red, axillary, up to 2 ins. wide. A particularly useful plant for mass plantings and for creating quick results when a large area needs to be covered with colour and green vegetation. Under such conditions it will naturalize rapidly.

Annual
Flowering period: May–July
Height: up to 4½ ft.

Lavatera trimestris L. (syn. *Lavatera rosea*)
Native to the Mediterranean regions. An annual species of the easiest cultivation and probably the most widely cultivated of all lavateras. Leaves alternate, somewhat glabrous, dark green, with the lower ones kidney-shaped, and the higher ones vaguely triangular and three-lobed. Flowers pale pink veined purple, up to 4 ins. in diameter. There is a lovely white-flowered form, var. *alba*; and var. *splendens*, which is an improved form of the original species.

Leonotis

(LION'S TAIL OR LION'S EAR)
Family: Labiatae
Semi-shrubby tender herbaceous perennial
Position: full sun
Propagation: seed or cuttings
Cultivation easy

A flower dedicated to the lion. The species *Leonotis leonurus* is known as Lion's Tail in various languages, although the name, of Greek origin, signifies lion's ear, from *leon* (lion) and *ous, otos* (ear). Whichever is correct, tail or ear, it is still difficult to find any real similarity between one or the other. As the genus is native to Southern and Central Africa, it would not be too unreasonable to point out that the colour of the king of beasts and that of the scarlet-orange *Leonotis leonurus* have a certain similarity, both blending very well with their natural environment. The species here described has a most curious form—which may or may not always be admired—but it has the distinction of being unusual, and in flower it is certainly arresting.

Although the genus includes numerous species, only *Leonotis leonurus* is in general cultivation, and the shape of its inflorescence is as droll as its name. In a mild Mediterranean or Californian climate, the plant can be established permanently outside, where it will assume the proportions of a small shrub. But as it will not tolerate frost, it must be taken inside for the winter if grown in northern countries; an easy matter if cultivated as a pot plant, for which purpose it is well suited. In districts where only slight winter frost is experienced, the plants can be left outside, treated as rather tender herbaceous perennials, and given the protection of a straw, peat, or compost mulch. Apart from its attractive appearance and brilliant colour, it is a useful subject because of its late-blooming habit (at a period when so many other plants have finished) and it can be used to prolong the display of colour in beds or borders.

Cultivation. Leonotis leonurus will thrive in any normal, fertile, rather dry soil in a hot, sunny position. After flowering has ended the plants must be severely pruned, leaving only 3–4 eyes (or buds), as the inflorescences are produced on the new season's growths. Propagation can be effected from seed sown in a warm greenhouse in January–February, or by means of soft cuttings taken in the spring and rooted in a warm greenhouse.

Leonotis leonurus

Leonotis leonurus R. Br.
Native to Southern Africa. The inflorescence is carried on tall rigid stems and is arranged in the form of layers, one above the other, which completely encircle the stem. A well-developed specimen may produce 10–12 of these strata or layers of flowers which, individually, are elongated funnel-shaped, two-lipped at the mouth, with the lower lip divided into three lobes; and having an intense vivid orange-scarlet colour. The leaves are opposite, narrow, elongated-oblong, dentated, and 2–4 ins. in length.

(Lion's Tail)
Flowering period: Aug.–Oct.
Height: up to 4½ ft.
Zone 9 southwards

Leontopodium

(EDELWEISS)
Family: Compositae
Herbaceous perennials
Position: sun or semi-shade
Propagation: seed
Cultivation easy
Useful for cutting and drying

As we have already noted, *Leonotis* (Lion's Ear or Lion's Tail) is so-named because of some real or fancied resemblance to a lion or its natural colouring. *Leontopodium*, however, is known to the French as *Pied de Lion* (lion's foot). This literal translation of *Leontopodium* shows that it was taken from the Greek, *leon* (lion) and *pous, podos* (foot), a name apparently given to the plant because some botanist found a similarity between the shape of the flower and a lion's paw. However, the name is totally inappropriate for this alpine plant, native to Europe and Asia. The common Italian name, *Stella Alpina* (alpine star), is much more suitable. In German- and English-speaking countries it is known as "Edelweiss" (noble white), a name that originated in the Tyrol.

Although the various edelweiss have a certain aesthetic and evocative attraction when in bloom, it is not easy to understand why the best-known species, *Leontopodium alpinum*, has such a popular appeal. Possibly it captured people's fancy because in its native habitat the plant is often found growing in inaccessible crannies high in the Alps, and gathering it offers a dangerous challenge to the would-be collector. Every summer there are reports of people falling to their death while attempting to collect edelweiss flowers: useless tragedies, since *Leontopodium alpinum* can be grown with the greatest ease in any garden or on any terrace. All one requires is an earthenware flower-pot, some ordinary garden soil, and a packet of seed which costs only a few pennies. If sown in early spring, the plants will bloom the same year. With the minimum effort plants can also be successfully cultivated in the rock-garden, in dry walls, and in the interstices of stone steps or flagstone paving. Edelweiss has also become popular because the thrifty, tourist-minded Swiss have exploited it mercilessly, adopting it as an "official" emblem for anything remotely connected with the Alps—we see it on ribbons, badges, crockery, wearing apparel, and any kind of souvenir connected with Switzerland or its national holidays. Genuine dried flowers are also attached to postcards (protected by a sheet of cellophane) and sold by the thousands to tourists, but it is doubtful if these blooms have ever seen a mountain, and they were probably grown to order by some nursery. Such banal uses of the plant have robbed it of its almost mystical legendary aura.

Like so many plants with glaucous, grey, or silvery foliage, edelweiss is an excellent subject for highly alkaline (calcareous) soils. In Alpine localities the plant is appreciated not only for its aesthetic aspects, but local people consider it to possess valuable medicinal properties (in the Tyrol, for instance, the plant is used to alleviate abdominal cramps and stomach aches). It is a plant that will tolerate intense cold, and in its native habitat it is found at a height of up to 15,000 ft. Although perennial, edelweiss can be more conveniently treated as an annual when grown in gardens. Although the plants are sun-lovers at high altitudes, they will give better results at low altitudes in partial shade.

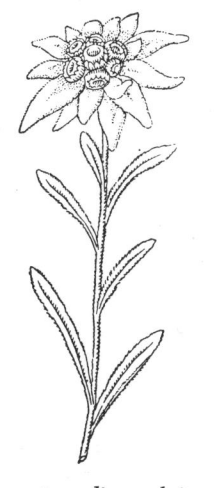

Leontopodium alpinum

Leontopodium alpinum Cass.   (Edelweiss)
Native to the mountains of Europe, particularly the Alps and the Apennines and the Maritime Alps. Generally found on dry, rocky, steeply sloping ground. Leaves silvery, grey-green, lanceolate. Flowers minute, yellow, surrounded by a star-shaped greyish-white woolly involucre. Very hardy and found up to a height of 15,000 ft. in exposed sunny positions.

Flowering period: July–Sept., according to altitude
Height: 4–6 ins.

Leontopodium haplophylloides L. (syn. *Leontopodium aloysiodorum*)
Native to China. The British have given this species the name of Lemon-scented Edelweiss because the foliage has a strong lemon perfume. Flowers greyish green.

Flowering period: June–July
Height: 6 ins.

Leontopodium nivale L.
Native to the Balkans. A dwarf species only 3–4 ins. high, with pure-white flowers in May. Also found wild in Italy in the central Apennines.

Flowering period: May–June
Height: 3–4 ins.

Leptospermum

(SOUTH SEA MYRTLE OR TEA TREE)
Family: Myrtaceae
Half-hardy or tender evergreen shrubs
Position: full sun
Propagation: seed or cuttings
Cultivation easy

An important and lovely genus of flowering evergreen shrubs whose wider use in gardens is only limited by their non-hardy nature. There are thirty species and numerous varieties, all native to Australia, New Zealand, and Malaya. They are large shrubs, or even small trees, with minute leaves of various colours. In size and shape the small five-petalled flowers are reminiscent of myrtle blooms, their colours including white and attractive shades of pink and carmine. The name is of Greek origin and is derived from *leptos* (fine, small) and *sperma* (seed), as the plants have very fine, almost dust-like, seed.

Leptospermums are only completely suitable for warm climates, such as California or the Riviera, where the winter temperature does not fall much below freezing point, and they are particularly suited to seaside localities. Their range of climatic tolerance can be extended northwards to districts where temperatures as low as 20°F. are experienced, but only if planted in warm, sheltered corners and given adequate protection around the trunks and at the base. However, like so many plants of this type, their ability to withstand cold depends largely on numerous other factors such as a hot sunny summer to ripen and mature the wood, the size and age of the plant, and the prevailing wind. In the Lake District of northern Italy, for many years I successfully grew a collection of about a dozen species and several varieties, and during their flowering period in early summer they were a glorious sight. Several species and varieties have proved to be hardy in southern England and in the Scilly Isles off Cornwall; while species such as *L. laevigatum* and *L. scoparium* are widely planted in California. *L. laevigatum* has proved to be of value for growing on dunes as a binder and conserver of shifting sands, while *L. scoparium* is a feature in San Francisco's Golden Gate Park. They are plants with few demands, requiring a well-drained, even dry, rather poor soil in a hot, sunny position. They are equally successful in acid or alkaline (calcareous) soils. Propagation can be effected by means of seed sown in a warm greenhouse in spring, or by cuttings of half-ripened wood in August.

Flowering period: June–July
Height: 9 ft.
Zone 8 southwards

Leptospermum flavescens Smith
Native to Australia and Tasmania. In 1828 this plant was illustrated in Robert Sweet's monumental *Flora Australasica* and labelled *Leptospermum obovatum*. The specimen used for the model was obtained from a nursery near London. This is a white-flowered species of great beauty. The leaves are $\frac{5}{8}$ in. long and $\frac{1}{4}$ in. wide, obovate, wedge-shaped at the base; flowers almost stalkless, $\frac{5}{8}$ in. wide, solitary, axillary.

Flowering period: June–July
Height: up to 30 ft.
Zone 9 southwards

Leptospermum laevigatum F. Muell.
Native to Australia. A species more frequently grown in the southern parts of the United States than in European gardens. A small tree in its native habitat, but more shrub-like under cultivation. Leaves prolific, 1 in. long, $\frac{1}{2}$ in. wide. Flowers white, $\frac{3}{4}$ in. in diameter.

Flowering period: June–July
Height: up to 18 ft.
Zone 9 southwards

Leptospermum scoparium Forst.
Native to Australia and New Zealand. This species together with its varieties forms the elite of the genus. It is a rounded, very twiggy, compact evergreen shrub, attaining a height of about 18 ft., although it begins to bloom when a quarter of that size. The prolific flowers are white. The var. *nichollsii* is a remarkable and beautiful form, with vivid carmine-red flowers. This variety was introduced from New Zealand in 1908 by Captain Dorrien-Smith and established in his famous garden at Tresco Abbey in the Scilly Isles. The foliage has a distinctive reddish-purple tinge. The var. *Red Damask* has dark-red

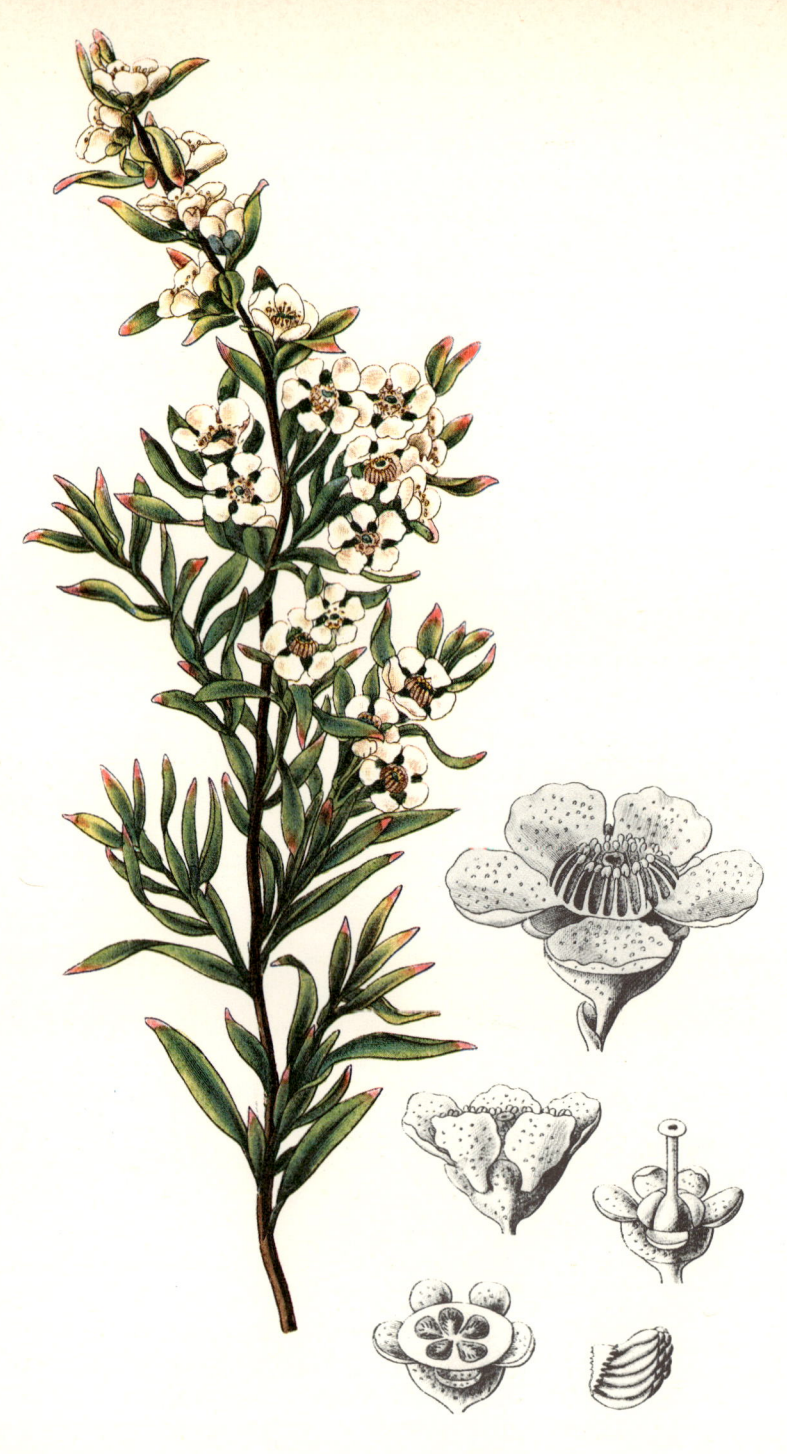

Leptospermum flavescens
From *Curtis's Botanical Magazine*,
1826, plate 2695

double flowers, while the var. *boscaweni* has pink-and-white blooms. Other interesting varieties are:

- var. *eximium*, often claimed to be the most beautiful of all, with $\frac{3}{4}$-in.-wide flowers of the purest white. Introduced by Comber from Tasmania and given an award of merit by the Royal Horticultural Society in 1938
- var. *juniperinum*, with much narrower foliage, and a semi-pendulous habit in the case of the young growths
- var. *prostratum*, a mountain form and the hardiest of all; almost prostrate in habit but with erect branches; ovate leaves and white flowers

Leucojum

(SNOWFLAKE)
Family: Amaryllidaceae
Hardy perennial bulbs
Position: partial shade
Propagation: division or seed
Cultivation easy

Superficially, flowers of the genus *Leucojum* are so similar to those of *Galanthus* (Snowdrops) that they are often confused with each other. To the non-botanist the difference is not always obvious, as it depends on the form of the perianth: in *Leucojum* the six segments of the perianth are of equal length, while in *Galanthus* the external perianths are longer than the three internal ones. Leucojums are also larger more vigorous plants, with taller flower stems and a longer flowering period. The genus comprises eleven species, all native to the Mediterranean regions and the Continent. The name is of Greek origin—*leukos* (white)—and refers to the colour of the flowers. Originally, however, the name was *Leucoeion* (white eye).

Leucojums are small hardy bulbous plants which occupy so little space and involve so little care and maintenance that it should not be difficult to find a corner for them in any garden. They are ideal for naturalizing in grass, or for planting in groups near shrubs or at the base of a tree; but they should always be grown in partial shade. Once established they can be left undisturbed for many years. Some species flower in late winter, some in the spring, and some in autumn. If a mixture of the various types is planted together a succession of flowers can be assured for many months.

Cultivation. Leucojums are easy to cultivate. The bulbs require a well-drained, cool, fresh, moderately moist, and not-too-heavy soil rich in well-decomposed organic matter such as peat and leafsoil. The winter- and spring-flowering types can be planted in early autumn, while those that bloom in the autumn must be planted in July–August. It is necessary to remove them from the soil only for the purpose of multiplication, which is done by dividing the dormant bulbs. Leucojums can also be propagated from seed sown in the open in spring.

Leucojum aestivum L.
Native to Europe. Generally found in moist meadow lands. The small pendulous flowers have white petals marked with green and are borne two together on erect stems 16 ins. high. The leaves are linear and very narrow. A species which insists on a cool, fresh climate.

Flowering period: Apr.–May
Height: 16 ins.

Leucojum autumnale L.
Native to the Mediterranean regions. Generally found in rather arid zones. Less tall than the preceding. Leaves linear and almost thread-like and not fully developed at the flowering period. The small pendulous flowers are white, but very slightly flushed pinkish at the base of the petals. If naturalized in the vicinity of shrubs such as cornus, enkianthus, viburnum, or fothergilla (all noted for the autumn colouring of their foliage), some very lovely effects can be obtained through the combination of autumnal hues and the luminous white of the bell-shaped leucojum flowers.

Flowering period: Sept.–Nov.
Height: 5 ins.

Leucojum vernum L. (See page 748 for colourplate)
Native to Europe. Frequently found in woods, pasture-land, and hedgerows. A particularly easy robust little hardy bulb which produces a profusion of graceful little bell-shaped pendulous pure-white flowers marked with green and pale yellow at the tip of each petal. Essentially a plant for naturalizing in grass; if planted in a formal manner or cultivated in receptacles, the blooms lose much of their elegance and grace.

Flowering period: Feb.–Mar.
Height: 12–14 ins.

Liatris

(SNAKEROOT, BLAZING STAR, OR KANSAS FEATHER)
Family: Compositae
Hardy herbaceous perennials

Position: sun or partial shade
Propagation: seed or division
Cultivation easy
Useful for cutting

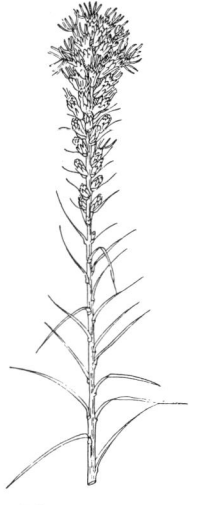

Of the sixteen species belonging to the genus *Liatris* (syn. *Lacinaria*), one, *Liatris spicata*, has recently been "discovered" by florists and exploited as a high-quality cut flower. Many of those on sale in European florists' shops are imported from Holland, where commercial growers have succeeded in producing very tall flower spikes out of season by cultivating the plants in greenhouses. The long purple-red spikes are long-lasting in water and, although not actually beautiful, are decorative, cheerful, and eagerly bought by the public at high prices. They are also excellent for drying and frequently used in winter for the composition of dried-flower arrangements.

Liatris are native to North America, where they are not particularly esteemed, but they are valuable garden plants and are appreciated for their late-flowering habit. The general appearance of the tall rigid colourful flower spikes has, not unjustifiably, been likened to an artist's paint brush. They are hardy herbaceous perennials of the easiest cultivation and have few demands. They thrive in poor, heavy, but well-drained soil, and in the north enjoy full sun, but in the south better results will be obtained by planting in semi-shade.

Propagation is easy from seed sown outside in spring or by division of old plants in spring. The great variety of common names for liatris (mostly of American origin) is evidence of their popularity. One wonders, however, why so many of these common names are associated with snakes, devils, and colic. The origin of the genus name is unknown.

Liatris spicata

(Grassleaved Liatris)
Flowering period: Aug.–Oct.
Height: up to $2\frac{3}{4}$ ft.

Liatris graminifolia Pursh.
Native to the eastern United States. An attractive herbaceous perennial with semi-tuberous roots. Leaves thin, narrow, and grass-like, up to 9 ins. long. The inflorescence is a top-shaped spike of purple flowers borne on rigid stems nearly 3 ft. high; the minute individual blooms are massed together on the terminal spike. A plant particularly suited for sandy arid soils, or for planting in dry walls.

(Prairie Button Snakeroot or Kansas Gay-Feather)
Flowering period: July–Aug.
Height: up to nearly 4 ft.

Liatris pycnostachya Michx.
Native to the central United States. Taller than the preceding, with flower stems up to nearly 4 ft. high. The terminal inflorescences are slightly looser in form than *L. graminifolia*, with the individual red flowers spaced wider apart. The stems are also less rigid, and the leaves are narrowly lance-shaped, becoming stiffer at the tips.

Leucojum vernum
From *Curtis's Botanical Magazine*,
1788, plate 46

(Rattlesnake Master
or Blue Blazing Star)
Flowering period: July–Aug.
Height: up to 5 ft.

Liatris scariosa L.
Native to the central and southern United States. Leaves narrowly oblong, flower stem up to 5 ft. high and slightly hairy. The terminal inflorescence is about 1 in. in diameter and composed of purple-blue flowers. There is also a var. *alba* with white flowers.

(Gay Feather, Prairie Pine, or Devil's Bit)
Flowering period: Aug.–Oct.
Height: up to 3 ft.

Liatris spicata Willd.
Native to the eastern and southern United States. The most decorative species, with linear-lanceolate foliage 12 ins. long at the base of the plant, while the numerous stem leaves are much smaller. The flower stems are up to 3 ft. high, the terminal half bearing the compact small-flowered purple-red inflorescence which is so useful for cutting. An excellent subject for planting in large masses in a rather dry soil.

(Blazing Star or Colicroot)
Flowering period: July–Aug.
Height: 2 ft.

Liatris squarrosa Michx.
Native to the eastern United States, extending westwards to Texas. Foliage narrow, linear, 6 ins. long. Flower stems up to 2 ft. high, bearing terminal inflorescences of reddish-purple flowers.

Lilium

(LILY)
Family: Liliaceae
Hardy or tender perennial bulbs
Position: sun or partial shade
Propagation: seed, scales, or division
Cultivation fairly easy
Fragrant in most cases
Useful for cutting

The association between lilies and purity is one of remote antiquity, and possibly only a few of the women who answer to the euphonious and Mozartean name of Susanna realize that it is of Biblical origin (from Shushan or Shushannah) and that in Hebrew the name also signified a lily. The word meant purity, as well, as evidenced in the Apocryphal tale of Susanna and the Elders; an allegory of virtue, since the parable and the name of the heroine can be interpreted in several aspects. Thus, many women of ancient Israel rejoiced in the double-meaning name of Susanna.

As a popular flower in ancient Jewish civilisation, the lily is frequently mentioned in the Old Testament. For instance, when the Israelites turn from pagan backsliding and cleave to Jehovah once again, the Lord blesses them and says: "I will be as the dew unto Israel: he shall grow as the lily . . ." (Hosea 14:5). The splendour of the flower is exalted in the New Testament, and Jesus speaks of them thus: "Consider the lilies of the field,* how they grow: they toil not, neither do they spin: . . . even Solomon in all his glory was not arrayed like one of these" (Matthew 6: 28–29).

The iconographic history of lilies is a long one, and one of the loveliest and earliest representations of the flower can be seen in a fresco discovered in a villa at Amnisos, Crete, which dates from the Minoan Period III, about 1580 B.C. Assyrian bas-reliefs often employ lily motifs, and we know from the Book of Kings that the columns of Solomon's Temple were adorned with "lily work". These are but a few instances; the art and architecture of the ancient world being replete with lily motifs.

With the diffusion of Christianity, the dignity of the symbolic lily was somewhat overshadowed by sentimentality. It became the sign of chastity and virtue—"fragrant and white as a lily"; "pure and immaculate as a lily"; "chaste and spotless as a lily"—and so on, *ad nauseam*. Overly pious commentators and scholars emasculated the frankly sensuous Song of Songs, and interpreted the lover as "the beloved bridegroom [Christ] of the Church, who for us descended to this vale and became a lily, springing from a poor and humble virgin."

The lily soon became closely associated with the Virgin Mary, one of the many instances where an attribute of a pagan deity (Aphrodite, Hera, the Triple Hecate) was adopted for Christ's Mother. Through its association with the Virgin it also became a symbol of virgin martyrs and also of numerous saints, including Dominic, Anthony of Padua, and, of course, St. Joseph, "the most chaste spouse".

As an important Christian symbol and emblem, it naturally assumed a leading role in religious art. Renaissance artists skilfully depicted lilies in paintings of the Annunciation and in portraits of the above-mentioned saints (and many others, too), and it often figured largely in canvases and panels of the Virgin and Child. One of the chief flowers in Catholic iconography, it is also one of the prime hagiographic floral symbols, and it appears so often that it would take volumes to list its varying aspects. For instance, the patron saint of Mantua, Aloysius Gonzaga, is locally venerated as a protector of youthful virtue, and the Mantuans celebrate his feast day in a festival known as Lily Day.

With the decline in quality of religious art, especially in Italy, a veritable orgy of painted lilies was launched, and by the nineteenth

---

* It has recently been established that the flower is actually *Anemone coronaria* and not a lily. See page 58 in *Anemone* section.

Lilium chalcedonicum

century countless third-rate altarpieces and polychromed plaster saints bristled with a plethora of lilies. The protagonists of Assumptions, Ascensions, and Glorifications struggle amid avalanches of these flowers.

In Italy, lily flowers of wax and cloth are still created by the deft hands of orphans in many convents. These simulacra are destined as altar decorations or as votive offerings for the saints. Also, in most Catholic countries lilies are still carried by small children at Confirmation and First Communion, and lilies are strewn in countless religious processions. In fact, the heavy fragrance of the lily sometimes injected a perfervid note to overly pious practices, and the symbol of purity often introduced an alarmingly sensuous aspect into the chastity of worship. Flaubert's Madame Bovary, for example, is overcome by a "mystic lassitude" from the perfume exhaled by flowers in a religious fête: it would not be assuming too much to hazard a guess that the flowers were lilies.

After these cloying examples, it is with a certain relief that one returns to Classical Antiquity, where the lily symbol appears in a more vigorous and earthy guise. The lily was dedicated to the goddess Hera, spouse of Zeus. Legend has it that when Zeus fathered Hercules on the mortal Alcmene, he wished his son to partake more fully of divinity. To accomplish this, he caused the baby to be brought to Hera as she slept, and had the infant hero placed at her breast. In his greediness, the powerful Hercules bit the goddess's nipple, and, awakening in horrified surprise, she thrust him from her in pain and shock. As she fled, the milk from her breast gushed across the heavens and formed the Milky Way. But a few drops of Hera's milk also fell to earth, and from them sprang the first lilies.

In contrast to the lily's associations with purity and chastity there is an amusing Roman legend that doubtless originated in some decadent and tarnished era. When Venus rose from the sea-foam she was stricken with jealous envy at the whiteness and beauty of a lily that she espied. Seeing in the flower a rival to her own fairness the goddess of love spitefully caused a huge and monstrous pistil to spring from the lily's snow-white chalice. This myth accounts for the lily sometimes being given as an attribute of Venus and the satyrs—personifications of lustful ardour.

The French have loved lilies from the time of Charlemagne, who commanded them to be planted in his garden. But regarding the heraldic *fleur-de-lis*, some caution is necessary, because it appears that it may not have been a lily at all, but rather an iris.

Finally, it can be noted that in both Christian and pagan popular tradition, the significance of the lily as a fertility symbol occasionally coincides. St. Anthony of Padua as the protector of marriages is also, by not-so-oblique association, the patron of procreation; even today during Greek marriages the priest places on the bride's head

Lilium Black Dragon

Lilium speciosum var. *album*
From *Paxton's Magazine of Botany*,
1841, plate 127

a crown of lilies garnished with ears of wheat, as a symbol of purity and abundance. Lilies are also a symbol of death, and at one time lilies were placed on the graves of young innocents.

The name of genus *Lilium* originates from a corruption of the original Greek word *leirion* used by Theophrastus for the Madonna Lily. The number of lily species varies from forty to one hundred according to the estimates of different authorities. The genus is indigenous to a vast area extending throughout north temperate zones of both hemispheres, and the area of distribution stretches through Europe and Asia across the Bering Strait, and from Vancouver eastwards across North America.

The lily has no true medicinal value, although at one time it was considered to possess certain pharmaceutical virtues. It was no doubt its great popularity that endowed it with healing powers, and in the Middle Ages it was credited with magical properties as well. A medieval commentator advised: "When the cunning serpent so filled with endless malice spits forth its deadly poison, spreading a dreadful death through secret wounds into the innermost parts of the body, it is opportune to treat the victim with a potion of lily bulbs pounded in a mortar and mixed with Falernian wine." The lily was prescribed for a thousand and one sicknesses by one of the Elizabethan herbalists, who recommended a decoction of pounded "roots" cooked in wine for the treatment of pestilential fevers. He also prescribed an unguent containing lily "root" as helpful in cases of ringworm; for cleaning wounds, burns, and sores; and even for making the hair grow. Folk medicine demonstrates a certain reticence in prescribing lily-based nostrums, which is fortunate, because *Lilium Martagon,* the European species with the greatest medicinal properties, is becoming increasingly rare and is in danger of extinction, and a wider use of the plant would certainly hasten its complete disappearance. Oil extracted from the fresh bulb or from the petals of both *Lilium Martagon* and *Lilium candidum* was at one time used in the treatment of burns and blisters and other afflictions of the skin, while a decoction for internal use was said to be useful in relieving rheumatic and arthritic symptoms.

Cultivation. The cultivation of lilies is not difficult. In general, they require a light but substantial soil; and heavy, clayey, excessively damp, dry, or sandy soils are to be avoided. Most species need an acid soil, with the exceptions of *Lilium candidum* and *Lilium chalcedonicum,* which prefer a heavy alkaline (calcareous) soil. (Concerning lilies' preference or dislike of an alkaline or calcareous soil, further details are given for each species where necessary.) Lilies prosper in a well-drained location and, like all bulbous plants, dislike fresh manure. The ground where lilies are to be grown should be dug thoroughly and deeply, and fertilized with manure at least two to three years old, or with some other organic fertilizer such as dried blood, urea, hoof-and-horn, bone meal, compost, sludge, etc. The best planting positions are those facing east and west; while excessive sun or excessive shade both are harmful. The plants should have their bulbs and roots well-shaded with low-growing permanent plantings of heather, cistus, or some other light perennial (or even low annual) ground cover, which must, however, allow the sun to reach the stems and flowers. During the period of active growth, periodic applications of a liquid organic fertilizer will be beneficial (dosage and frequency in accordance with the manufacturer's instructions). Nearly all lilies are hardy, in fact, they prefer cold to heat; the most important exceptions to this are *Lilium longiflorum, Lilium japonicum, Lilium brownii,* and *Lilium formosanum,* none of which tolerate frost. Lily bulbs can be planted permanently and left undisturbed for five to six years or longer, replanting them only if the bulbs have multiplied excessively or when it is desired to propagate them by division. Old established groups of vigorous bulbs tend to impoverish the soil, and eventually replanting becomes a necessity. The best planting times are spring or late autumn when the bulbs are dormant (spring in the north, where the soil begins to freeze early). *Lilium candidum* is an exception to this rule, as the bulbs never enter a completely dormant state and should be planted in late summer (some of the basal foliage is almost evergreen). Lily bulbs should not be planted too deeply and should be only slightly covered with soil; in general, a layer of 1–2 ins. from the topmost tip of the bulb to the soil surface is sufficient. In soils where drainage is poor, or not completely effective, a handful of very coarse sand or fine gravel should be placed beneath, around, and above the bulb to prevent an accumulation of excess moisture.

Lilies are eminently suitable for cultivation in large pots or other receptacles, either in the garden, on terraces, or in courtyards. The soil for this purpose should be composed of ordinary fertile garden soil mixed with an equal part of peat, to which has been added a sprinkling of granulated charcoal, to keep the soil sweet, and a small quantity of well-composted manure. One may well question the often-quoted (and often misquoted, too) line from Shakespeare (Sonnet XCIV): "Lilies that fester smell far worse than weeds." Although many interpretations could be advanced to explain this statement, the most logical and probable is that European lilies are often attacked by a rapacious insect, *Crioceris merdigera*. The orange-coloured larvae of this beetle can in a short time completely devour a lily's foliage and flower buds, and as they thrive in their own excreta they create a putrid mess of any plant they infest. (Fortunately, they are not present in all districts, and are less frequent in the north.) The best method of combating these pests is to examine suspected plants daily and, if possible, destroy the larvae by hand, at the same time killing any of the adults, small vermilion beetles.

Lilium longiflorum

In the case of large plantings, the pests can be controlled by using such insecticides as the pyrethrum-based preparations.

It is fairly easy to propagate lilies from seed, although the process is long and tedious and is generally only employed in the case of raising new hybrids. The seed for these should be sown in pans, flats, boxes, or trays as soon as it is ripe, using a soil mixture composed of equal parts of finely sifted sand, peat, and leafsoil, covering the seed only lightly with a fine layer of sand. As germination often takes several months, the containers can be kept in coldframes, even during the winter. When the seedlings are large enough to handle they can be pricked out into beds where the bulbs will gradually develop, but in most cases it takes four to six years before they bloom. Propagation is much easier and quicker using the young bulbs that form around the parent bulb, which can be detached during the plant's dormant period. Another efficient method of propagation is by means of the bulbils, which in numerous species are freely produced in the leaf axils; these can be detached in late summer and placed in trays containing the same compost as that indicated for sowing seed, gently pushing the bulbil into the soil surface but not covering it with soil. On a commercial basis, lilies are mostly propagated by detaching scales, together with a fragment of the bulb where the scale is attached, from the outer surface of mature bulbs. The scales are inserted upright in flats, boxes, and trays, placed in nursery beds or coldframes, and planted in sand or a medium such as vermiculite. Young plants will soon develop and new bulbs will form, reaching flowering size in three to four years according to the variety.

Lilium Hybrids

Contrary to the system followed in this book when describing other genera, lilies of hybrid origin are here dealt with before the species. The reason for this innovation is that lilium hybrids are of such importance, so easily grown, so readily available, so varied in size, shape, and colour, and so extensive in their flowering period and adaptability that a representative collection of these remarkable bulbs is generally sufficient to satisfy the ambitions of even the most avid lily collector. As a result, he no longer needs to concern himself with the cultivation of the frequently more capricious species. (There are, of course, also many perfectly easily cultivated species of the greatest beauty, which will be discussed later.) The modern hybrid lilies are superb subjects for cultivating in pots on a roof garden, terrace, or balcony, and many of them are excellent for forcing into bloom out of season.

The reasons for the importance of lily hybrids are many, and the fact that the hybrids have revolutionized lily cultivation is a matter of the greatest gardening significance in many countries. For centuries, no attempts were made to cross the wild species. This was partly because of insufficient interest, but it was due more to the world-wide distribution of lily species and the great variation in their flowering times; both factors made pollen transportation a real problem. Now, with modern systems of refrigerated storage and rapid air transport, these difficulties have been eliminated. Perhaps the most important factor of all, however, is that, while wild lily species are difficult to cross with each other, the hybrids are exceptionally easy to cross, not only with each other but also with their parents, the true species. All these factors have started a virtual avalanche of new hybrid lilies and even new lily strains. The major part of this amazing development of lilies is due to the enthusiasm of Jan de Graaff, a Dutchman, established in the United States, who comes from a long line of famous breeders and bulb growers. In his extensive lily nursery in Oregon he has developed and made available to gardeners more new varieties than any other hybridizer in the world, and he has grown more than eight million lily bulbs. His creations have been awarded every possible honour and prize in every major nation, and for the future still more remarkable hybrids are expected. When I last met Jan de Graaff he stated, "We are about as far along with lilies as my great-grandfather was with tulips and narcissus a hundred years ago." The full story of this remarkable adventure is brilliantly told in the *Book of Lilies* by F. F. Rockwell, Esther C. Grayson, and Jan de Graaff. A fascinating account of De Graaff lilies was also published in the *Reader's Digest* of August 1965. Among the vast number of lily hybrids, we have chosen a brief selection to give some idea of the range of colours, appearance, and flowering period (see opposite page). With regard to origin and parentage, the horticultural classification of both hybrids and species is as follows:

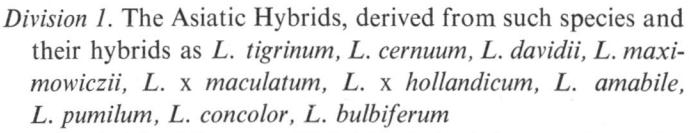

Lilium Corsage

> *Division 1.* The Asiatic Hybrids, derived from such species and their hybrids as *L. tigrinum, L. cernuum, L. davidii, L. maximowiczii, L.* x *maculatum, L.* x *hollandicum, L. amabile, L. pumilum, L. concolor, L. bulbiferum*
> *Division 2.* The Martagon Hybrids, derived from such species and their hybrids as *L. Martagon, L. hansonii,* Backhouse Hybrids, Paisley Hybrids
> *Division 3.* The Candidum Hybrids, derived from *L. candidum, L. chalcedonicum, L.* x *testaceum,* etc.
> *Division 4.* The American Hybrids, derived from hybrids of such American species as Bellingham Hybrids, hybrid Shuksan, hybrid Buttercup
> *Division 5.* The Longiflorum Hybrids, derived from such species and their hybrids as *L. longiflorum, L. formosanum, L. formolongi*
> *Division 6.* The Trumpet Hybrids, derived from such species

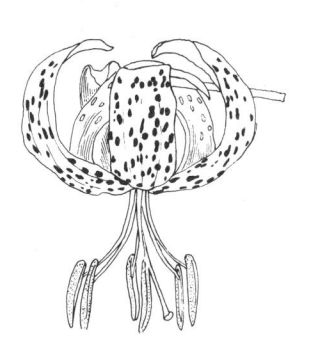

Lilium Shuksan

Lilium regale

and their hybrids as *L. henryi,* Aurelian Hybrids, and other trumpet lilies derived from Asiatic species

Division 7. The Oriental Hybrids, including hybrids of *L. auratum, L. speciosum, L. japonicum, L. rubellum,* and the crosses of these with *L. henryi*

Division 8. Containing those hybrids not included in the other divisions

Division 9. Containing all the true species and their botanical forms

Achievement (Div. 2) Ivory-white pendent flowers 3 ins. in diameter; 8–10 flowers per stem. Height $3\frac{1}{2}$ ft. June flowering

Allegra (Div. 7) White-and-apple-green flat flowers with recurved petals, 8 ins. in diameter; 8–10 flowers per stem. Height about 5 ft. August flowering

Black Dragon (Div. 6) White-and-purple-brown trumpet-shaped flowers 6 ins. in diameter; 12 flowers per stem. Height $4\frac{1}{2}$ ft. July flowering

Cinnabar (Div. 1) Maroon-red upright flowers 5 ins. in diameter; 10 or more per stem. Height $2\frac{1}{2}$ ft. June flowering

Corsage (Div. 1) Ivory-and-pink outward-facing flowers 3 ins. in diameter; 5–6 per stem. Height 4 ft. July flowering

Crimson Beauty (Div. 7) White-and-crimson flattish bowl-shaped flowers 10 ins. in diameter; 10–12 per stem. Height $4\frac{1}{2}$ ft. August flowering

Damson (Div. 6) Fuchsia-pink trumpet-shaped flowers 5 ins. in diameter; 8–10 flowers per stem. Height $4\frac{1}{2}$ ft. June–July flowering

Discovery (Div. 1) Lilac-pink crimson-spotted outward-facing flowers with curved petals, 4 ins. in diameter; 16 flowers per stem. Height $3\frac{1}{4}$ ft. July flowering

Empress of India (Div. 7) White-gold-and-maroon outward-facing flowers 10 ins. in diameter; 10 per stem. Height $4\frac{1}{2}$ ft. July–August flowering

Enchantment (Div. 1) Nasturtium-red upright flowers 6 ins. in diameter; 16 or more per stem. Height $3\frac{1}{4}$ ft. May–June flowering

Fireflame (Div. 1) Crimson-red outward-facing flat flowers 11 ins. in diameter; 8–10 flowers per stem. Height 3 ft. May–June flowering

Gaylights (Div. 2) Bronze-pink pendent flowers 3 ins. in diameter; up to 30 flowers per stem. Height $4\frac{1}{2}$ ft. May–June flowering

Good Hope (Div. 6) Golden-yellow flattish bowl-shaped flowers with recurved petals, 6 ins. in diameter; 6–8 flowers per stem. Height $4\frac{1}{2}$ ft. July–August flowering

Green Dragon (Div. 6) Chartreuse-green trumpet-shaped flowers 6 ins. in diameter; 12 per stem. Height 6 ft. July flowering

Honeydew (Div. 6) Greenish-yellow trumpet-shaped flowers 6 ins. in diameter; 15 flowers per stem. Height $4\frac{1}{2}$ ft. June–July flowering

Prosperity (Div. 1) Lemon-yellow outward-facing flowers 5 ins. in diameter; 5–6 flowers per stem. Height $3\frac{1}{4}$ ft. June flowering

Prince Charming (Div. 1) Lilac-red black-spotted upright flowers 5 ins. in diameter; 8 or more flowers per stem. Height $2\frac{1}{2}$ ft. July flowering

Shuksan (Div. 4) Orange and orange-black-spotted pendulous flowers 6 ins. in diameter; 16 flowers per stem. Height $4\frac{1}{2}$ ft. June–July flowering

Sonata (Div. 2) Orange-and-pink pendent flowers with curved petals 5 ins. in diameter; 8–10 flowers per stem. Height $4\frac{1}{2}$ ft. July flowering

Stardust (Div. 6) Silver-white-and-orange flat bowl-shaped flowers 7 ins. in diameter; 18–20 flowers per stem. Height 4 ft. July–August flowering

Sunday Best (Div. 7) Silver-crimson-red-and-gold outward-facing flowers 9 ins. in diameter; 8–10 flowers per stem. Height $4\frac{1}{2}$ ft. July–August flowering

Lilium candidum

Lilium Species (Division 9)

Lilium amabile Palibin
Native to Korea. A species very easily raised from seed and one of the easiest lilies to cultivate. Tolerant of alkaline (calcareous) soil, prefers semi-shade, and excellent for naturalizing in light woodland conditions. Leaves narrow, lanceolate, borne at irregular intervals along the stem; height 3 ft. Flowers orange-red, of medium size, and spotted with black on the recurved petals. Anthers chocolate-brown. Scent not pleasant. Eight or more flowers per stem.

Flowering period: July
Height: 3 ft.
Unpleasantly scented

Lilium auratum Lindl.
Native to Japan. The most famous of all Japanese lilies and appropriately referred to as the queen of lilies. It is certainly most spectacular and has an intensely strong perfume. Widely cultivated commercially for the sale of cut bloom. The flower stems are purple-green and bear up to thirty flowers per stem, although in gardens the number is generally about ten. Individual blooms are 8 ins. in diameter or even larger, widely funnel-shaped, with petals not curved back, and of a thick, almost fleshy texture. In colour they are white, with irregular yellow and crimson markings. Leaves narrow,

(Golden-rayed Lily of Japan)
Flowering period: July–Aug.
Height: up to 6 ft.
Strongly scented

lanceolate, and irregularly placed on the flower stem, which can be up to 6 ft. high. An excellent lily for pot culture or for planting permanently in well-drained soil, with the base of the plant in shade and the stem and flower in full sun; an effect easily achieved by cultivating the bulbs among a light ground cover, or low shrubs such as dwarf lavender, erica, cistus, etc. *Lilium auratum* is not suitable for alkaline (calcareous) soil. There are numerous magnificent varieties:

> var. *pictum*, with the flowers more abundantly marked with crimson
> var. *platyphyllum*, with larger flowers less marked with crimson
> var. *virginale*, with white-and-pale-yellow flowers

Flowering period: June–July
Height: up to 3 ft.

Lilium bolanderi S. Wats.
Native to California. Height up to 3 ft., leaves basal, grouped close together, greenish blue in colour. The stems bear 1–4 smallish reddish-purple flowers spotted darker red internally.

Flowering period: July
Height: 3 ft.
Scented

Lilium brownii E. H. Wilson
Native to China. One of the first Chinese lilies to be introduced into Europe, probably in 1835. One of the most beautiful species, with large trumpet-shaped flowers of perfect form. Petals waxy textured, white inside, purple-mahogany outside; slightly scented, generally with four flowers per stem. Leaves dark, glossy green, lanceolate, arranged at irregular intervals on the stem. It is a species that rarely produces seed, is not hardy in very cold localities, and not suitable for alkaline (calcareous) soils.

Flowering period: June–July
Height: 2½–3 ft.

Lilium bulbiferum L.
Native to Western and Central Europe. This species and its varieties comprise a variable group of lilies with orange-coloured upright flowers borne in clusters on rigid stems. Linnaeus mentioned seven different forms. The plant is sometimes referred to as *Lilium croceum* or *Lilium aurantiacum*. Certain forms bear minute bulbils in their leaf axils, and these offer a good method of propagation. The colour is intense, and in 1543 the famous German botanist Leonhard Fuchs described the flowers as being "fire-red". This is a lily which appreciates sun, although, as usual, the bulb and roots must be in shade in a cool, moist soil. Some particularly good varieties are:

> var. *chaixii*, from the Maritime Alps; less tall and with fewer flowers per stem. Petals orange-yellow tipped orange-red and spotted reddish purple
> var. *croceum*, the best form for planting in gardens, native to the central Alps; 4½ ft. high, and with clusters of 7–8 flowers per stem, each bloom 4½ ins. in diameter and light orange in colour

Lilium bulbiferum

Lilium candidum L. *(Madonna Lily or Annunciation Lily)*
Flowering period: June–July
Height: up to 6 ft.
Strongly scented

Native to the Balkans and Middle East. The best-known and most beloved of all lilies by the old-fashioned gardener. Very widely cultivated in even the most modest garden, but becoming increasingly rare in its native habitat. Intensely and deliciously fragrant. Height up to 5–6 ft.; each rigid erect stem bearing numerous pure-white trumpet-shaped flowers with conspicuous golden anthers. Stem leaves lanceolate, arranged in an irregular random manner. The basal leaves appear in late summer and are more or less evergreen. For this reason the best planting time is late July–August, after flowering is finished, when the bulbs are as near dormant as possible. (Like all lilies, but much more so in this particular case, the bulbs are never completely dormant like those of tulips, for instance, and a few basal roots are nearly always active. This should be kept in mind when handling lilies.) The bulbs of *Lilium candidum* should not be planted deeply; the top of the bulb should be only 1–2 ins. below soil level. They are tolerant of alkaline (calcareous) soil, but they rarely produce seeds.

Lilium chalcedonicum L. *Flowering period: May–June*
Height: up to 4 ft.

Native to Greece. One of the Martagon-type lilies and one of the most intensely coloured species. Each flower stem bears up to ten vivid mandarin-red pendulous blooms with thick recurved waxy petals. Leaves linear, green, edged with silver, and produced exclusively on the lower part of the flower stem. Prefers an alkaline (calcareous) soil and is one of the few lilies that prefers a hot, dry, sunny position.

Lilium croceum (see *Lilium bulbiferum* var. *croceum*)

Lilium dauricum Ker-Gawl. *Flowering period: June–July*
Height: up to 3 ft.

Native to Siberia. A somewhat dwarf species rarely attaining a height of 3 ft. in gardens; in its native state little more than 2 ft. Flowers upright, orange-red, marked with darker orange spots; up to 5 ins. in diameter and cup-shaped. A very hardy species and sun-loving in the north. Because of its susceptibility to virus disease, the original species has now generally been superseded by hybrid varieties. Of particular beauty is var. *luteum*, with dark-yellow flowers.

Lilium davidii Duchartre *Flowering period: July–Aug.*
Height: up to 6 ft.

Native to China. One of the most beautiful Chinese lilies and an appropriate memorial to the famous Père Armand David who collected this and so many other superb plants from China. Each flower stem bears up to twenty orange-red semi-pendulous flowers marked with very dark orange-red spots. Leaves narrow, linear, and prolific, with a conspicuous small tuft of white hairs at the base. One of the

Lilium speciosum var. *rubrum*
From *Paxton's Magazine of Botany*,
1838, plate 1

easiest lilies to cultivate if planted in a cool, fresh soil; making sure the roots are shaded and the actual plant is in full sun. Two particularly good varieties are:

> var. *Maxwell*, a hybrid from Canada (*Lilium davidii* x *Lilium davidii* var. *willmottiae*), with orange-red pendulous flowers in July–August. Height up to 6 ft.
>
> var. *willmottiae*, with up to forty individual flowers per stem; dark orange-red spotted flowers in July–August. Height 6 ft. or more.

Lilium formosanum Wallace

Flowering period: July–Aug.
Height: up to 6 ft.
Scented

Native to Taiwan. Not hardy in cold climates. A remarkably beautiful lily which can be treated as an annual. It will, in fact, flower 9 months after seed has been sown in a warm greenhouse. Each stem bears four or more long, white, scented, wide-mouthed, trumpet-shaped horizontal flowers 6 ins. long. Externally suffused crimson-purple. Leaves linear, narrow, dark green, stem-borne. Sometimes wrongly referred to as *Lilium longiflorum* var. *formosum* or *Lilium philippinense* var. *formosanum*. Widely cultivated commercially for the sale of cut blooms and for forcing into flower out of season.

Lilium giganteum Wall. (syn. *Cardiocrinum giganteum*)

Flowering period: June–July
Height: up to 10 ft.
Scented

Native to the Himalayas, northeast Burma and southeast Tibet. A truly phenomenal species, which when in bloom reaches a height of up to 10 ft. According to modern nomenclature it belongs to the genus *Cardiocrinum*, but gardeners (who are such conservative people) still refer to it as *Lilium*, and for the sake of convenience it is here included in that genus. Curiously enough, if the plant had never been placed in the genus *Lilium* probably no one would have thought of it as a lily because in appearance it is so very different, although botanically it is closely related to the liliums (the genus *Cardiocrinum* consists of only three species). Masses of this gigantic "lily" growing wild in the Himalayas, among specimens of *Rhododendron arboreum* with the dimensions of real trees, provided one of the most remarkable sights I saw when I visited that area. This was one of the favourite plants of the late Captain Neil McEacharn, founder of the well-known Villa Taranto Botanic Gardens, at Pallanza on Lake Maggiore in Italy, which now belongs to the Italian Government and is open to the public. When he bought a large quantity of bulbs I planted them in a semi-shady wood of birches, robinias, sweet chestnuts, and *Rhododendron arboreum*. They proved to be an immediate success, flowering with such freedom and producing so many seeds that they soon naturalized over a wide area. However, seven years are necessary for a bulb to reach flowering size when raised from seed. *Lilium giganteum* is hardy, and its bulb is the size of a small football. It is essentially a woodland plant that is not tolerant of alkaline (calcareous) soil. The plants are gross feeders and require an abundance of a nitrogen-rich organic fertilizer. They should not be grown in hot, dry, sunny positions in light, sandy soils. The monumental flower stems, up to 10 ft. high and 4 ins. in diameter, bear up to twenty trumpet-shaped slightly pendulous individual blooms that are 8 ins. long. They are pure white outside and inside, but with red markings at the base. The plants bear vivid shiny green leaves that are large, cordate, basal, 12 ins. wide, while the stem leaves are fewer and smaller. The large erect seed cases, up to 3–4 ins. long, are also decorative, and the manner in which the vast number of large flat seeds are packed into their cases is something to cause real wonder and admiration.

Flowering period: July
Height: up to 6–7 ft.

Lilium henryi Baker

Native to China. One of the most easily cultivated of all lilies and, once established, it will generally naturalize through the rapid increase of its bulbs. Suitable for either acid or alkaline (calcareous) soils. Stems purple-brown, tall, arching, with each stem normally carrying about twenty individual flowers (although as many as seventy flowers have been recorded). Flowers are pale orange in colour, with the Martagon-type form, and are borne on long stalks, either singly or two or three together, pendulous, with recurved petals and long prominent stamens. Diameter of each flower about $3\frac{1}{2}$ ins. Magnificent for cutting and a joy to arrange. Leaves abundant, the lower ones lanceolate, upper ones ovate. Introduced by Augustine Henry. The var. *citrinum* has lemon-yellow flowers.

Flowering period: June–July
Height: about $2\frac{1}{2}$ ft.

Lilium x hollandicum

Of hybrid origin (believed to be the result of a cross between *Lilium bulbiferum* and *Lilium elegans*). Often referred to in trade catalogues as *Lilium umbellatum*. The name, *L.* x *hollandicum*, actually refers to a group of lilies varying in colour from yellow to orange-red, several of which have been given specific names. The flower stems are robust, up to $2\frac{1}{2}$ ft. high, while flowers are upright, cup-shaped, and borne several together. Leaves abundantly produced on the stems. This group is easy to cultivate, very decorative, and requires more sun than most lilies. Some of the best varieties are:

    var. *Erectum*, orange-red
    var. *Golden Fleece*, golden-yellow
    var. *Moonlight*, pale yellow
    var. *Vermilion Brilliant*, brilliant vermilion-scarlet

Flowering period: July
Height: up to 6 ft.

Lilium humboldtii Roezl & Leichtlin

Native to the Sierra Nevada Mountains in California. A fine species with stems up to 6 ft. high bearing fifteen or more large $3\frac{1}{2}$-in-long orange-red pendulous flowers spotted with maroon or dark purple, but variable in colour. Leaves stem-borne in whorls. Definitely a semi-shade-loving species and suitable for either acid or alkaline (calcareous) soils.

Lilium japonicum Wall.
Native to Japan. As one of the aristocrats of the genus, with an air of grace, refinement, and elegance, it is, appropriately enough, capricious. Often better cultivated in pots than in the open ground and not hardy in cold localities. The large trumpet-shaped flowers are an exquisite shade of pink, 5 ins. long, and equally large at the mouth. Up to five flowers per stem, beautifully shaped and waxy textured with slightly recurved petals and long conspicuous stamens bearing orange-brown anthers. Leaves few, dark green, narrow, lanceolate, 6 ins. long. Requires a semi-shady position in a soil rich in organic matter.

Flowering period: June–July
Height: 3 ft.
Scented

Lilium kelloggii Purdy
Native to the Pacific Coast of the United States. Brownish stems 3–4 ft. high, clothed with lanceolate foliage. Flowers pinkish, spotted red, 2 ins. long, and of Martagon-type form with recurved petals.

Flowering period: July
Height: up to 4 ft.

Lilium leucanthum Baker
Native to Hupeh province of central China; originally collected by Augustine Henry, who sent bulbs to Kew, where it was judged to be one of the most beautiful of all the tall trumpet-flowered lilies, comparable to the superb *Lilium sulphureum*, but with the advantage of being hardier. The erect flower stems, up to 4 ft. high, bear four or more funnel-shaped blooms 5 ins. long. Flowers are cream-white, externally suffused at the base with pale yellow; each petal marked with a long narrow greenish stripe. Fragrant. This original species is now rare in gardens, and may even be lost to cultivation, but its place has been taken by the equally beautiful var. *centifolium*, with stems up to 8–9 ft. high. (This species is thus often referred to as *Lilium centifolium*.) It was discovered in 1914 by Reginald Farrer, who gives an account of it in his enthralling book *On the Eaves of the World*. The tall rigid stems bear up to eighteen narrowly trumpet-shaped large flowers that are white inside and suffused yellow at the throat, while outside the blooms are flushed green and pinkish purple. The anthers are brownish red and the petals slightly recurved. Foliage profuse, linear-lanceolate. It is tolerant of alkaline (calcareous) soil and requires a warm, sunny position but with the bulb and roots in shade.

Flowering period: July–Aug.
Height: up to 9 ft.
Scented

Lilium longiflorum Thunb.
Native to Japan. Like *L. speciosum, L. auratum,* and *L. candidum,* it is important for the commercial cultivation of its flowers, but is only

(Easter Lily)
Flowering period: June–July
Height: up to 3 ft.
Scented

hardy in mild localities. It is one of the most beautiful species, with 4–5 trumpet-shaped 6-in.-long white flowers per stem. Leaves numerous, irregularly placed on the stems, lanceolate in form. Perfume very slight. An easy lily to raise from seed and will often bloom within a year from the date of sowing—commercially an important point, as it is often more expedient to propagate new bulbs than care for the old ones, which unfortunately are very liable to a virus disease that is not transmissible through the seeds. There are numerous named varieties, all improvements on the species, and some of the best are: *L. Croft, L. Estate, L. Eximium, L. Holland's Glory, L. Slocum's Ace,* and *L. White Queen.* The var. *Lilium Eximium* is the well-known Easter Lily.

Lilium Martagon L.

(Turk's Cap Lily)
Flowering period: June
Height: 4½ ft.
Unpleasantly scented

Native to Europe, Turkistan, Siberia, and Mongolia. Although a species, *Lilium Martagon* also represents an entire type, or class, of lilies because of its numerous forms and varieties and because it has been so widely used as a parent for crosses between the original species and other lilies. Its distinctive appearance also serves as a convenient form of comparison when describing the appearance of other lilies. The true *Lilium Martagon* is tolerant of alkaline (calcareous) soil and rarely exceeds a height of 4½ ft. in the wild. It is found mostly in light woodlands, although it has been found at altitudes of 6,000 ft. or more in full sun in alpine meadows. The flower stem is strong and rigid, greenish purple, and bears a large number of medium-sized waxy textured individual pendulous blooms in diverse shades of purple spotted with a darker tint. The scent is strong and not agreeable. The shape of the flowers has been likened to the typical Turk's cap and it is thus known as Turk's Cap Lily. The leaves are oval-lanceolate, borne in whorls. An excellent lily for naturalizing, but when used as a prominent feature of a garden the various forms and varieties are more effective. Two of the best varieties are:

Lilium Martagon

    var. *album*, white flowers with yellow anthers; height 4½ ft., with up to thirty flowers per stem
    var. *cattaniae*, wine-purple flowers; height 6 ft. Native to Dalmatia and sometimes referred to as *Lilium dalmaticum*

Some others are:

    var. *Backhouse Hybrids*, a very floriferous strain, with yellow, orange, and orange-pink flowers
    var. *Dalhansonii*, flowers dark reddish maroon, heavily spotted
    var. x *Marhan*, orange flowers spotted reddish brown, with the petals less recurved than in the species

Lilium michauxii Poiret (Carolina Lily)
Native to the southeastern United States. Flower stems up to 2½ ft. high, bearing orange-red purple-spotted pendulous flowers 3–5 ins. long. Leaves lanceolate, blue-green, in whorls of about seven. In shape the flowers have the typical Turk's cap, Martagon form.

Flowering period: Aug.
Height: up to 2½ ft.

Lilium nepalense D. Don
Native to Nepal. A fairly tall species up to 5 ft. high with dark-purple stems bearing a few scattered leaves. Flowers pendulous, large, greenish yellow, suffused purple in the throat, and fragrant. A beautiful and unusual species and quite hardy, growing naturally in Nepal at a height of up to 8,000 ft.

Flowering period: June–July
Height: up to 5 ft.
Scented

Lilium ochraceum Woodcock (syn. *Lilium primulinum*)
Native to western China and northern Burma. A peculiar and strangely beautiful Asiatic species apparently now lost to commercial cultivation, although still grown by some private collectors. Long before World War II, I established a large group of these lilies in the Villa Taranto Botanic Gardens, the first to be grown in Italy. On behalf of the founder of the gardens, Captain Neil McEacharn, a collection of blooms, together with flowers of *Lilium sulphureum*, was exhibited at a Rome flower show. They caused a sensation, since neither flower had previously been seen in Italy, and each was awarded a gold medal.
Lilium ochraceum reaches a height of up to 9 ft., with purple-green stems bearing seven or more large greenish-yellow pendulous blooms with fleshy recurved petals heavily marked with purple-red spots. Very late-flowering, September–October or even later, and quite hardy. Leaves dark green, broadly lanceolate, and irregularly borne on the stems. It is a variable species and at least three different forms have been recorded.

Flowering period: Sept.–Nov.
Height: up to 9 ft.
Scented

Lilium pardalinum Kellogg (Leopard Lily)
Native to California. A very easily cultivated North American species particularly suited to damp sites. Flower stems up to 8 ft. high, bearing numerous Turk's cap type of pendulous blooms. Colour reddish orange, with crimson at the tips of the petals, and the entire flower is generously leopard-spotted with dark crimson-brown. Diameter of flower up to 4 ins., but it is a variable species so far as size and colour are concerned. Agreeably scented. Leaves arranged in whorls; linear or lanceolate. Suitable for sun or shade, but must have a damp, but not waterlogged, position.

Flowering period: July
Height: up to 8 ft.
Scented

Lilium parvum L. (Sierra Lily)
Native to the Pacific Coast of the United States from Oregon to California. A tall attractive lily found growing wild in its native habitat.

Flowering period: July
Height: 5 ft.

Height up to 5 ft., bearing small trumpet-shaped orange or yellow flowers spotted dark purple at the base; 1½ ins. long, nearly erect. The var. *crocatum* is almost without spots.

(Coral Lily)
Flowering period: June–July
Height: 2 ft.

Lilium pumilum D. C.
Native to northern China, Mongolia, and Manchuria. Sometimes referred to as *Lilium tenuifolium*. A dwarf Martagon-flowered type up to 2 ft. high, with pendulous 2-in.-wide vivid scarlet flowers sometimes spotted at the tips of the recurved petals. There are several good varieties:

    var. *Golden Gleam,* golden yellow
    var. *Red Star,* red
    var. *Yellow Bunting,* yellow

Flowering period: June
Height: 3 ft.
Unpleasantly scented

Lilium pyrenaicum L.
Native to the Pyrenees and northern Spain. A yellow-flowered Turk's cap type of lily with stems up to 3 ft. high with up to twelve greenish-yellow dark-spotted pendulous flowers with tightly recurved petals. Unpleasantly scented (by some described as fox-like) but a particularly easy species for cultivating, and excellent for naturalizing. Leaves narrowly lanceolate and prolific. The var. *rubrum* is more attractive, with 2-in.-long reddish-orange maroon-spotted flowers.

(Royal Lily)
Flowering period: June
Height: up to 6 ft.
Scented

Lilium regale E. H. Wilson
Native to central China. Discovered by E. H. Wilson in western Szechwan province. A species of relatively recent introduction but already as widely grown and as well known as *Lilium candidum*. Undoubtedly one of the finest of the trumpet-flowered type, and of the easiest cultivation. It is tolerant of alkaline (calcareous) soil, easily raised from seed—flowering the second year—and of a robustly vigorous habit. Widely cultivated commercially for cut blooms. Happier in full sun than most lilies, although in a hot climate shade for the roots is essential. The 6-ft.-high flower stems bear up to thirty large funnel-shaped blooms 5 ins. long, pure white internally with a yellow throat, externally white suffused maroon and dark pink at the base. Petals slightly recurved at the tips; mouth wide. Fragrant. Leaves numerous, linear, scattered.

(Chaparral Lily)
Flowering period: June–July
Height: up to 6 ft.
Scented

Lilium rubescens S. Wats.
Native to the Pacific Coast of the United States from Oregon to California. Height up to 6 ft. with erect stems bearing 2-in.-long lavender-pink upright flowers which vary in colour according to age. This is, in fact, one of the most beautiful species, and on the same flower stem it is possible to see three colour changes: the newly opened waxy textured white flowers, those fully expanded in a lovely shade of pink, and the almost purple older flowers. The blooms are

tubular, with a wide flat star-like mouth. Unfortunately not an easy lily to cultivate and prefers partial shade. It has a certain similarity to *Lilium washingtonianum*, but its flowers are more upright.

Lilium sargentiae E. H. Wilson

Flowering period: July
Height: up to 6 ft.
Scented

Native to western China. A valuable late-flowering species superficially similar to *Lilium regale* and, like that lily, also discovered and introduced into the West by E. H. Wilson. Stems up to 6 ft. high bearing up to ten 6-in.-long trumpet-shaped white flowers, which externally are a dark purple-mahogany, with wider mouths than those of *Lilium regale*. Bulbils are produced in the axils of the somewhat broader foliage, which is linear-oblong and dark green. It is a little later-flowering than *L. regale*, rather less hardy, and not so easy to cultivate. Fragrant.

Lilium speciosum E. H. Wilson

Flowering period: June–Aug.
Height: 3–4½ ft.
Scented

Native to Japan. Height up to 6 ft. in the wild, while in gardens usually only about half that height. Has for many years been one of the most popular lilies for gardens and the florist. Stems are rigid, bearing numerous well-spaced pendulous flowers 4 ins. long on long stalks; petals recurved, with undulated edges, and thick and waxy in texture; very prominent stamens. The basic colour is white but the flowers are densely zoned with pink and crimson markings. A very beautiful species with a long flowering period from June to August. Prefers a sunny position but is not happy in alkaline (calcareous) soils. Leaves linear, dark green, but not prolific. There are several good varieties:

>   var. *album*, of exceptional beauty with pure-white flowers
>   var. *magnificum*, with the coloured markings more extensive and more vivid
>   var. *rubrum*, coloured zones red and crimson-scarlet

Lilium sulphureum Baker (syn. *Lilium myriophyllum*)

Flowering period: Aug.–Sept.
Height: up to 8½ ft.
Scented

Native to northern China, the Yunnan province in southwestern China, north Burma. When describing lilies, one is tempted to use adjectives such as superb, beautiful, magnificent, etc., until they become monotonous, leaving no adequate superlatives to describe so noble a species as *Lilium sulphureum*, probably the best of them all, but for some inexplicable reason difficult to obtain commercially. In northern Italy, at the Villa Taranto Botanic Gardens on Lake Maggiore, I established an enormous bed of these lilies in full sun, using a dwarf evergreen cistus to provide the necessary shade for the roots and bulbs. The 8½-ft.-high flower stems each bear up to fifteen large funnel-shaped blooms that are 10 ins. or more in length and 8 ins. wide at the mouth, quite the largest of all lily blooms. The colour is sulphur-yellow, suffused with pink, chocolate-brown, and green outside; with paler-yellow colouring inside, while the throat is suffused with dark yellow. Very strongly and agreeably scented. Leaves numerous, up to 8 ins. long, linear-lanceolate, with bulbils produced in their axils that provide a good means of propagation. For the first time in Europe, the specimens at Villa Taranto also produced fertile seed.

(Turk's Cap Lily of America, Swamp Lily, or Wild Tiger Lily)
Flowering period: July
Height: up to 8 ft.

Lilium superbum L.
Native to the eastern United States. Another Turk's cap Martagon-type lily with flower stems up to 8 ft. high bearing pendulous, 4-in.-wide, dark-spotted, orange-red flowers, with petal tips recurved. An excellent lily for damp positions and a superb species which well merits its specific name.

Native to North America, it was one of the earliest exotic lilies to be introduced into Europe. It was known to Linnaeus and painted by Redouté. It is easy to cultivate but does not do well in alkaline (calcareous) soil. Large bulbs will produce flower stems with as many as forty individual blooms. Leaves lanceolate, borne in whorls on the stems. Requires semi-shade at the roots, with the upper part of the plant in full sun. Can almost be treated as a bog plant, although in such a position the actual bulb should be planted in a slightly raised mound to avoid contact with an excess of water while allowing the roots to receive an abundance of moisture.

(Nankin Lily)
Flowering period: June–July
Height: up to 10 ft.

Lilium x *testaceum* Lindl.
Of hybrid origin (*Lilium candidum* x *Lilium chalcedonicum*), and believed to be the oldest lily hybrid for which official records are available. Height up to nearly 10 ft. under the most favourable conditions, although 6–8 ft. is a more normal dimension in gardens. The rigid purple-green stems bear up to twelve large apricot-yellow flowers which are fragrant, pendulous, mostly unspotted, with the tips of the petals recurved. Leaves thick-textured, small, lanceolate, silvery margined, and prolific. Requires a sunny position and is tolerant of alkaline (calcareous) soil. Seed is not produced, so propagation can be effected only by vegetative means. *Lilium* x *testaceum* has for very many years been one of the most popular garden lilies, particularly esteemed for the unusual orange reddish-yellow colour of its flowers; a tint not exactly duplicated in any other lily.

(Tiger Lily)
Flowering period: July–Sept.
Height: up to 5½ ft.
Scented

Lilium tigrinum L.
Native to China and Japan. The specific name well describes the colour of the flowers, which are bright orange-red freely marked with nearly black spots. One of the best-known garden lilies and appreciative of a warm sunny position; but not a good lily for alkaline (calcareous) soils, and it does not normally produce seeds. Stems robust, rigid, often more than 5 ft. high, clothed with numerous

cobweb-like white hairs. Each flower stem bears up to twenty-five individual 5-in.-wide pendent flowers with strongly recurved petals. Leaves numerous, linear-lanceolate, with bulbils borne in the leaf axils. There are several excellent varieties such as:

- var. *flaviflorum*, with lemon-yellow flowers spotted purple
- var. *flore-pleno*, with double flowers
- var. *fortunei*, stems covered with a dense white wool
- var. *splendens*, a more vigorous later-flowering form with richer-coloured flowers

Lilium washingtonianum Kellogg

(Washington Lily)
Flowering period: July
Height: up to 6 ft.
Scented

Native to the Pacific Coast of the United States from Oregon to California. A magnificent species in its native habitat, but a lily with a bad reputation among growers, because it is generally considered to be difficult to cultivate. Height up to 6 ft., with the rigid stems bearing fragrant, horizontal, white-and-purple-spotted, tubular-shaped, 4-in.-long flowers with a wide, flat mouth. The var. *purpureum* is a more vigorous form with purple-pink flowers; and there is also a lovely pure-white form.

Limonium

(STATICE OR SEA LAVENDER)
Family: Plumbaginaceae
Hardy herbaceous perennials or annuals
Position: sun
Propagation: seed, division, or root cuttings
Cultivation easy
Some species useful for cutting and drying

As defined by Linnaeus, the genus *Statice* included plants of the genera now known as *Armeria* and *Limonium;* but the genera *Armeria, Limonium,* and *Statice* are, in fact, botanically distinct one from the other. The name *Statice* has now become ambiguous and is therefore no longer used. The genus *Limonium* (syn. *Statice*) comprises an invaluable group of plants for the garden and also for providing excellent flowers for drying. They are either annuals or perennials of graceful habit, characterized by delicate inflorescences composed of small paper-textured flowers in vivid colours. Because of the lightness of the branching sprays of bloom, the perennial types

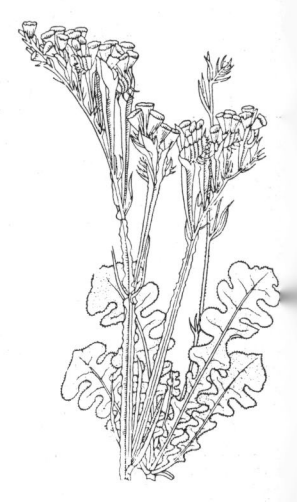

Limonium sinuatum

are even better than the popular gypsophilas for use in flower arrangements. Limoniums require a well-drained light soil which is fertile but not excessively rich, and they are thus particularly suitable for seaside localities. The genus is native to Continental Europe, the Mediterranean regions, and Asia.

Propagation of the perennial species can be effected from seed sown in July in coldframes or in seed beds, or by division in spring. Another method is by root cuttings in autumn or spring, inserted in pots, flats, boxes, or trays of pure sand or very sandy soil. Propagation of the annual species is by means of seed sown in a greenhouse in February–March, in coldframes in March, or outdoors in April.

Herbaceous perennial
Flowering period: June–Sept.
Height: up to 2 ft.
Useful for cutting

Limonium latifolium Kuntze (syn. *Statice latifolia*)
Native to southern Russia and Bulgaria. The most popular perennial species for general garden planting. Bright, cobwebby masses of deep lavender-blue flowers in the form of a large branching inflorescence on stems up to 2 ft. high. The basal leaves form a large rosette of evergreen foliage and are rounded-triangular in shape, up to 6 ins. long. The best species for cutting and drying. The var. *violetta* has dark-blue flowers; var. *album* is white.

Annual
Flowering period: May–July
Height: 1 ft.
Useful for cutting

Limonium sinuatum Mill. (syn. *Statice sinuata*)
Native to the Mediterranean regions. The most popular species cultivated as an annual for summer blooming in beds and borders in the garden, and for drying for winter use indoors. There are many hybrid forms with vivid flowers in shades of blue, white, pink, red, yellow, violet, etc. The inflorescences are in the form of much-branched dense panicles. Leaves up to 8 ins. long, oval or harp-shaped.

Annual
Flowering period: June–Sept.
Height: 18 ins.
Useful for cutting

Limonium suworowii Mill. (syn. *Statice suworowii*)
Native to Central Asia. A striking and extremely effective species. The densely flowered candle-like spikes of pink flowers are of great value for flower arrangements. The form of the inflorescence has given rise to the sometimes used, but incorrect, name of *Statice candelabrum*.

Annual
Flowering period: July–Aug.
Height: 1 ft.

Limonium tataricum Mill. (syn. *Statice tatarica*)
Native to the Caucasus Mountains. A rather dwarf species which can be effectively used in small beds, narrow borders, and the rock-garden. The inflorescence in the form of a corymb bears masses of minute brilliant pink and white flowers on rigid stems. Leaves oval, widest at the ends, up to 6 ins. long.

Herbaceous perennial
Flowering period: June–Sept.
Height: 10–12 ins.

Limonium vulgare Mill. (syn. *Statice limonium*)
Native to Europe, generally in seaside localities. A beautiful little plant with oblong foliage 4–6 ins. long, and masses of minute lilac-

purple flowers throughout the summer. Gives best results in a moist soil in an open sunny position. The corymbs of bloom are excellent for cutting and drying for use in miniature dried-flower arrangements.

Linaria

(TOADFLAX)
Family: Scrophulariaceae
Hardy herbaceous perennials or annuals
Position: sun or partial shade
Propagation: seed or division
Cultivation very easy

Like many other plants belonging to the family Scrophulariaceae, linarias are neither spectacular nor ostentatious, but they do possess a grace, elegance, and charm which is often more appealing than certain other more flamboyant but coarser flowers. They are small plants which occupy little space in the garden, with blooms similar to a miniature snapdragon. Their flowering season is very long, and a corner devoted to them will rarely lack colour from April to September.

Some of the species belonging to this genus—which has an area of distribution extending from Europe to North Africa and the Mediterranean regions—are ideal for the rock-garden or for planting in dry walls; others are useful for cultivating as cut bloom, and some are excellent for beds and borders. According to some authorities a few of the species have been reclassified into the genus *Cymbalaria* (here given as a synonym).

Linarias do not present any cultivation problems; the plants merely require a well-drained light soil in an open sunny position, but care must be taken that they do not become smothered by larger neighbouring plants. *Linaria Cymbalaria* also thrives in a damp position in partial shade.

Propagation of the perennial species should be done in spring either by division or from seed sown in pots in an unheated greenhouse or coldframe. The annual species should be sown in March–April in the positions where they are to flower.

Linaria vulgaris has some medicinal value as an astringent, hepatic, and detergent.

Linaria purpurea
From *Curtis's Botanical Magazine*,
1789, plate 99

Linaria alpina
From *Curtis's Botanical Magazine*,
1792, plate 207

Linaria alpina Mill.
Native to the Alps and Apennines. Generally found in dry, stony localities and therefore a valuable little plant for the rock-garden and for planting in dry walls, etc. Habit almost completely prostrate and trailing. The minute grey-green foliage makes a mat of vegetation against which the 3-in.-long spikes of bloom—intense vivid purple with orange-yellow throats—make a delightful contrast. The pink-flowered var. *rosea* is equally attractive. This is a species which requires a sunny position in poor, sandy, light, stony soil.

Herbaceous perennial
Flowering period: May–Sept.
Height: almost prostrate

Linaria bipartita L.
Native to Portugal and North Africa. Habit erect, compact, and bushy, with small narrow pointed leaves. The inflorescence is a spike up to 6 ins. long; purple-violet, marked orange on the edge of the corolla. A most effective plant when grown in bold masses in a light soil in a warm, moderately dry sunny position. The var. *alba* is white-flowered, while the var. *splendida* has blooms of a rich intense purple.

Annual
Flowering period: May–Sept.
Height: 15 ins.

Linaria Cymbalaria Mill. (syn. *Cymbalaria muralis*)
Native to Europe and very widely diffused, being a common sight in old walls, stone steps, paving, and even at the top of church steeples and other towers. Although it will thrive in quite damp semi-shady positions, it will also prosper in dry, sunny localities in the poorest of soils. The plant is completely glabrous with small alternate leaves similar in shape to a miniature ivy leaf, with the lobes rounded. It forms a dense prostrate or trailing mat of vegetation which will rapidly cover the soil surface, the face of a wall, or rocks. Can also be effectively grown in hanging baskets or in pots placed on columns or pedestals. *Linaria Cymbalaria* is quite distinct from other species, being of great value for its foliage. Its flowers are about $\frac{1}{3}$ in. long, pale blue, with the internal upper part of the corolla yellowish. When trailing over a surface where there is sufficient moisture it readily roots at the nodes, thus making propagation very easy. There are also white- and pink-flowered forms.

(Kenilworth Ivy, Colosseum Ivy, Aaron's Beard, or Climbing Sailor)
Herbaceous perennial
Flowering period: May–Sept.
Height: up to 6 ins.

Linaria dalmatica Mill.
Native to Southeastern Europe. One of the tallest species. A herbaceous perennial of erect expansive habit with an abundance of oblong-lanceolate glaucous-green foliage. The inflorescence is an erect spike, pointed like that of a small snapdragon, but narrower and with the flowers more widely spaced. The blooms are golden-yellow marked with orange, making it a beautiful plant for a vivid splash of colour in an informal or wild part of the garden.

Herbaceous perennial
Flowering period: May–Sept.
Height: up to 4 ft.

Annual
Flowering period: Apr.–Aug.
Height: up to 18 ins.

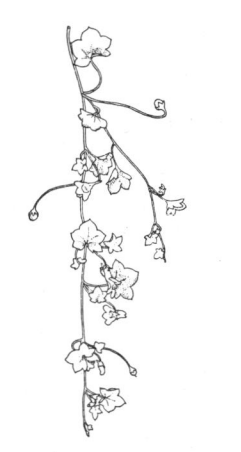

Linaria Cymbalaria

Herbaceous perennial
Flowering period: June–Sept.
Height: up to 2 ft.

Herbaceous perennial
Flowering period: May–Sept.
Height: up to 18 ins.

(Butter-and-Eggs or Wild Toadflax)
Herbaceous perennial
Flowering period: June–Sept.
Height: up to 18 ins.

Linaria maroccana Hook. f.

Native to Morocco and certainly the most beautiful of the annual linarias. Parent of numerous interesting and fascinating garden hybrids. The 18-in.-high slender branched stems are covered with small narrow glaucous-green pointed leaves. The inflorescences are erect compact spikes composed of numerous violet-purple flowers marked pale yellow at the throat. Seed sown in its flowering position in March will be in bloom by the end of April and the plants will continue to flower until late summer. The following are some of the best hybrids:

> var. *alba,* with pure-white flowers
> var. *excelsior* (syn. *Linaria excelsior*), a variable strain 1 ft. high with pink, blue, yellow, or purple flowers. There is also an improved strain available commercially under the name of *Linaria excelsior Hybrids,* with a still wider range of colours including violet, sky-blue, rose-pink, and orange
> var. *Fairy Bouquet,* with variably coloured larger flowers, but only 9 ins. high
> var. *rosea,* pink-flowered

Linaria purpurea Mill.

Native to Europe. Generally found in light woodlands in poor, stony soil. A tall glabrous plant with a glaucous appearance and a woody base from which arise numerous single or branched stems. The basal leaves are verticillate, linear, small; those borne on the upper parts opposite, widely spaced, and lanceolate. Inflorescences erect and composed of short-stalked elongated racemes of individual flowers with incurved spurs. They are violet-blue marked white at the throat. Requires a fairly light dry soil in a sunny position. Very easily raised from seed sown directly in the flowering position in March–April. The var. *Canon West,* with pink-and-orange flowers, is one of the most popular varieties in English gardens, and is particularly beautiful. It is excellent for planting in dry walls, in the same manner that one often sees snapdragons planted.

Linaria repens Mill.

Native to Europe. A prostrate stoloniferous plant which expands rapidly by means of roots formed at the nodes, and quickly provides a dense expanse of vegetation. Leaves minute, lanceolate, stem-borne in small erect compact groups. The inflorescences are erect branched spikes composed of numerous tiny white flowers veined with blue. Excellent for naturalizing on slopes and for the rock-garden.

Linaria vulgaris Mill.

Native to Europe and so widely diffused that it can become an invasive weed (but a very attractive one). In general appearance, the blooms resemble miniature snapdragons. Leaves minute, linear, or narrowly lanceolate, glaucous green. The 18-in.-high inflorescences are erect and compact; composed of numerous small gold-and-yellow flowers with spurs slightly longer than the corolla. It is excellent for cutting, and thrives in even the poorest soils.

Linum

(FLAX)
Family: Linaceae
Hardy or non-hardy annual, perennial, or woody-based herbaceous plants
Position: sun
Propagation: seed or division
Cultivation easy

Linums are not showy plants, and for that reason are frequently neglected in gardens. Their delicate, ephemeral flowers have nothing in common with the bright, hearty zinnias and marigolds—those flowers so profusely planted in round, square, elliptic, or even heart-shaped beds which meet the eye at every turn during the summer months. Linum flowers are fragile and thin-textured, and even the plants are ruffled and tousled by the slightest puff of wind. The blooms last for only one day, but are produced in such profusion that the plants appear to be continuously in flower, but never with the abundance of ageratums or alyssums. The charm of linum flowers lies in their grace and delicacy, which even compensates for their lack of fragrance.

The genus is very extensive—at least two hundred species dispersed throughout subtropical and temperate zones in all parts of the world—and includes annuals, herbaceous perennials, and semi-shrubby perennials. Relatively few have any ornamental value for the garden, but those that are grown in gardens are delightful. One species, *Linum usitatissimum,* has been cultivated for thousands of years for its economic value as the source of fine linen. In tombs more than forty centuries old, mummified pharaohs have been found shrouded in linen woven from flax. Linum was known to the Egyptians, Chinese, Greeks, Peruvians, Spanish, Welsh, Germans, and Romans, not only for its fibre-producing properties, but also for the valuable oil extracted from the seeds. Today, however, with the greater use of cotton and synthetic fibres, the golden age of linen is declining.

Linum grandiflorum
From *Curtis's Botanical Magazine*,
1856, plate 4956

Until about the middle of the nineteenth century, linum represented the most widely cultivated textile fibre in Europe. Until just before World War I, 20,000–25,000 acres were cultivated in the fertile Lombardy Plain in Italy, while today its cultivation there has almost ceased. Even in Belgium, where the famous Flanders linen is produced, cultivation fell from 170,000 acres to 60,000 acres between 1876 and 1912. Today it has risen to 110,000 acres, where it remains stationary because the high cost of production has made pure linen a luxury article. In the Soviet Union, however, production is still believed to be high. Apart from its value as a source of fibre, oil produced from the seed of certain species is still widely used in industry. It serves in the manufacture of paints, inks, soap, and linoleum, although even for these purposes its use is declining as more and more synthetic chemical substances are introduced, and linoleum is being replaced by vinyl and other plastics. (The name linoleum was derived from *Linum,* as it was manufactured from oxidized linseed oil.)

In folk medicine linum is used as a demulcent and emollient, and is often added to cough medicines, while linseed oil is of value in the treatment of burns and scalds.

Cultivation. The cultivation of the various species offers no difficulties. They all need an open, sunny, warm position in a not-too-rich soil, which does not require any special preparation. The annual garden species are particularly tolerant of hot and dry conditions. Seed can be sown in March–April in the position where it is to bloom: preferably in large informal groups, either isolated or in a mixed border. They are also suitable for terrace cultivation in pots, boxes, or other receptacles. In localities with a mild climate and long summers, successive sowings can be made until May–June to further prolong the flowering period.

The perennial species, whose natural habitat is generally at higher altitudes, need a cooler atmosphere without an excess of hot sun. They are ideal for the rock-garden and prefer a light, sandy, well-drained, cool soil in an open position. Seed can be sown in March–April, in flats in an unheated greenhouse or coldframe, and the young plants should be pricked out and grown on in small pots until ready for bedding out. Propagation can also be effected by means of division in spring, or from cuttings taken in August and inserted in sandy soil in coldframes. It is advisable to always have a few young plants in reserve because, although hardy, there is a risk of losing older specimens during a particularly severe winter.

Linum alpinum L.
Native to Europe, from the Pyrenees to the Alps and particularly in the alkaline (calcareous) soils of alpine meadows. The stems are semi-prostrate, with minute foliage densely arranged at the base. Flowers relatively large, sparse, and of a good shade of blue.

Linum alpinum

Herbaceous perennial
Flowering period: June–Aug.
Height: 6 ins.

Herbaceous perennial
Flowering period: May–June
Height: 12–18 ins.

Linum austriacum L.
Native to Southern Europe, the Austrian Alps, the Caucasus Mountains, Asia Minor, and parts of Asia. Generally found in stony alkaline (calcareous) soils. Leaves linear, pointed, $\frac{1}{2}$ in. long. Flowers violet-blue, $\frac{3}{4}$ in. in diameter, with conspicuous yellow stamens in the centre.

Semi-woody perennial
Flowering period: June–July
Height: up to 1 ft.

Linum campanulatum L.
Native to the Mediterranean regions. A 6–12-in.-high herbaceous perennial with the base of the stems woody, angled, and almost shrub-like in old specimens. Leaves elongated-oval, shallowly dentated, glabrous. Flowers a rich golden-yellow, with the petals slightly striped orange, and with a diameter of $1\frac{1}{2}$ ins.

(Golden Flax)
Semi-woody perennial
Flowering period: May–Aug.
Height: 1–2 ft.

Linum flavum L.
Native to Southeastern Europe and central and eastern U.S.S.R. A perennial up to 2 ft. high with semi-woody erect stems rising from a woody semi-shrubby base. Leaves linear-lanceolate. Flowers golden-yellow, $\frac{3}{4}$ in. in diameter, borne at the ends of the much-branched stems.

(Flowering Flax)
Annual
Flowering period: June–Sept.
Height: 12–15 ins.

Linum grandiflorum Desf. (syn. Linum rubrum)
Native to North Africa. The best-known and most widely cultivated annual species. Habit erect, much-branched, smooth. Leaves very numerous, alternate, elongated-lanceolate. Flowers up to nearly 2 ins. wide, borne at the ends of thread-like stems, colour variable from pink to red. There are several improved and more vividly coloured varieties:

- var. *coeruleum*, sky-blue
- var. *coccineum*, with scarlet flowers
- var. *kermesinum*, crimson
- var. *rubrum*, ruby-red
- var. *Venetian Red*, a recent introduction with very large carmine-red flowers of a particularly attractive tint

Herbaceous perennial
Flowering period: June–Aug.
Height: 10–18 ins.

Linum narbonense L.
Native to the Mediterranean regions. A herbaceous perennial with smooth, slightly glaucous, alternate, linear-lanceolate, pointed foliage. Flowers $1\frac{1}{2}$ ins. wide, sky-blue with a white eye, borne on very thin stalks. The vars. *Heavenly Blue* and *Six Hills* are particularly attractive.

Herbaceous perennial
Flowering period: May–June
Height: 12–18 ins.

Linum perenne L.
Native to Europe from southern Germany to Switzerland. A smooth, much-branched herbaceous perennial. Leaves very small, alternate,

Linum austriacum
From *Curtis's Botanical Magazine*,
1808, plate 1086

linear, pointed. Flowers 1 in. wide, a beautiful sky-blue, and borne at the ends of thread-like stalks. Will bloom the first year from seed sown in March. There is a white-flowered form, var. *alba*.

(Common Flax)
Annual
Flowering period: Apr.–May
Height: 2–3 ft.

Linum usitatissimum L.
Original habitat uncertain, probably Asia, but now naturalized in parts of Southern Europe and North Africa. As mentioned above, the source of flax for linen and linseed oil. Of no value as an ornamental garden plant but interesting for its historical and economic associations. An annual plant with a deeply penetrating tap-root. Stems branched, erect, slender, up to 3 ft. high, with small grey-green narrow leaves. Flowers about $\frac{1}{2}$ in. wide, pale blue or white, with the petals veined in dark blue. Has a certain attraction if grown massed in an informal semi-wild part of the garden.

Lithospermum

(GROMWELL OR PUCCOON)
Family: Boraginaceae
Hardy or half-hardy evergreen sub-shrubs,
herbaceous perennials, or annuals
Position: sun or partial shade
Propagation: seed, cuttings, or division
Cultivation not always easy

Referring to the colour of *Lithospermum purpureo-caeruleum*, the Swiss nurseryman Henry Correvon remarked that the flowers have one of the most intense and most beautiful blues of any May-blooming plant. The majority of the species normally used in gardens are of greater significance for their beautiful shades of blue than for their general appearance. The relatively small flowers have a most curious appearance, with the apparent aspect of stone, and one is tempted to think that the generic name—composed of two Greek words, *lithos* (stone) and *sperma* (seed)—would be more appropriate to the flower than to the hardness of the seeds. The genus—which includes herbaceous perennials, some with a woody, almost shrubby appearance, and a few annuals—comprises sixty to seventy species distributed throughout North and South America, Eurasia, and, above all, the Mediterranean regions. Some botanists have transferred certain species into the two new genera *Lithodora* and *Moltkia*, but it is doubtful if this new nomenclature will ever find favour with gardeners.

The flowers are borne in the leaf axils and extend through white, yellow, blue, and violet-purple. Although not recognized as having any medicinal value, *Lithospermum officinalis* was at one time largely used in folk medicine as a diuretic and—following the Doctrine of Signatures, the old belief that a plant, flower, or seed could be used as a cure for an illness or disease with which it had some visible characteristic in common—the small, hard, shiny, stone-like seeds were at one time used in the treatment of gall-stones. *Lithospermum tinctorium,* however, is still used as a colouring agent for such oleaginous compounds as ointments, pomades, and hair oil.

Cultivation. Lithospermums thrive in most soils, but being woodland plants they need a good percentage of humus and leafsoil, and *Lithospermum diffusum* will not tolerate alkaline (calcareous) soil. Seed can be sown in pots from April to June in an unheated greenhouse or coldframe, growing the young plants on in small pots until they are ready for planting out. Propagation can also be effected by division in the spring, or by means of soft cuttings taken in spring and rooted under glass, or in August from cuttings of half-ripened growths rooted in coldframes.

Lithospermum canescens L.
(Orange Puccoon)
Herbaceous perennial
Flowering period: May–June
Height: 12–18 ins.

Native to the southeastern United States. An 18-in.-high, hairy-stemmed herbaceous perennial with narrowly oblong foliage. Flowers stalkless, ½ in. long, rich orange-yellow, and borne in terminal and axillary clusters in May–June.

Lithospermum diffusum Lag. (syn. *Lithospermum prostratum*)
Evergreen sub-shrub
or herbaceous perennial
Flowering period: May–June
Height: 6–8 ins.

Native to Spain, the South of France, Morocco, and Algeria. This small evergreen widely cultivated species is the aristocrat of the genus, but it is not always easy to grow and it does not do well in an alkaline (calcareous) soil. Although hardy in most temperate climates, it is liable to suffer if the winter temperature falls below 15°F. In habit it is a small, almost prostrate, widely spreading, somewhat woody-based plant which forms a dense mat of dark-green vegetation. The spreading stems, covered with fine hairs, can reach a length of 2½ ft.; they are abundantly clothed with alternate narrow dark-green leaves ⅔ in. long, which are hairy on the upper surface and lighter green on the undersurface. The attractive, freely produced small flowers are an intense vivid blue. (The var. *Heavenly Blue* is even more beautiful, with flowers described exactly by its name, while the var. *Grace Ward* has larger flowers of a lighter colour.) In English gardens, where choice plants are genuinely appreciated, this species and its varieties are generally grown in a mixture of peat and leafsoil in the rock-garden or in an unheated greenhouse in terra-cotta pans or wide pots.

(Yellow Puccoon)
Herbaceous perennial
Flowering period: Apr.–July
Height: 1–2 ft.

Lithospermum incisum L.
Native to central and western North America. A 2-ft.-high much-branched herbaceous perennial with very narrow leaves. The vivid-yellow flowers are about 1 in. long and appear much earlier than those of the majority of lithospermums. It is an effective plant when grown in a cool, airy position in an informal setting.

Lithospermum purpureo-caeruleum

Herbaceous perennial
Flowering period: Apr.–Aug.
Height: 6–18 ins.

Lithospermum purpureo-caeruleum L.
Native to Central and Southern Europe, the Black Sea area, and Asia Minor. Generally found at the base of hedges or under groups of shrubs, and always in an alkaline (calcareous) soil; natural conditions which should be reproduced for its successful cultivation in gardens. In the north and at high altitudes it can be grown in full sun; but in the south it should be treated as a woodland subject. It is an attractive plant with such lovely coloured flowers that a little extra trouble in finding the exact locality it prefers will be fully repaid. In the bud stage the flowers are dark purple-red, changing to a stupendous blue when fully open. This colour change is brought about by a chemical reaction in the petals when certain acids contained therein become alkaline. The plant has a silky surface, with dark-green lanceolate foliage. The base is quite woody and produces numerous slender stems; those bearing flowers are erect, while the others are spreading, stoloniferous, and root-forming at the nodes. The plants like a rather dry sandy soil containing plenty of humus.

Herbaceous perennial
Flowering period: Dec.–Apr.
Height: 1–2 ft.

Lithospermum rosmarinifolium Tenore
Native to Southern Europe. A not-too-hardy herbaceous perennial more suited to a Mediterranean climate, it is a very beautiful plant

with—as suggested by its specific name—foliage similar to that of rosemary: about 2 ins. long, oblong-lanceolate, with slightly recurved margins, dark green above, silky-white beneath. The flowers are borne in terminal racemes; the corolla is funnel-shaped and of an intense vivid blue. Requires a rather dry, sunny, warm position in a not-too-rich alkaline (calcareous) soil.

Lobelia

Family: Campanulaceae or, by some authorities, Lobeliaceae
Annual or half-hardy or tender perennial herbaceous plants
Position: sun or partial shade
Propagation: seed, division, or cuttings
Cultivation easy
Poisonous

Lobelias are loved and known by all; but this, of course, refers to the blue-flowered varieties of *Lobelia Erinus,* because when one says "lobelia" it is automatically assumed that reference is being made to this dwarf species grown as an annual and not to one of the tall red-flowered perennial lobelias. To many, lobelias are synonymous with the colour blue in the same manner that the mention of gentians and delphiniums immediately evokes that colour. Lobelias certainly give our gardens some of the most desirable shades of true blue among herbaceous plants.
Lobelia Erinus is also a generous plant, continuously producing its welcome blooms throughout late spring, summer, and early autumn. Apart from its popular use as an edging plant, it is also very effective when grown in an informal manner, more or less at random, with an odd group appearing here and there either by itself or mixed with other plants. The semi-trailing forms are spectacular when grown in hanging baskets or large pots, or planted in walls and allowed to freely produce their miniature cascades of bloom.
The genus *Lobelia* was named by Plumier in honour of Matthias de l'Obel (1538–1616), who was known as Lobelius. *Lobelia cardinalis,* red-flowered and beautiful, but less graceful than the species *L. Erinus,* was imported into Europe in 1626 and flowered for the first time in Italy in the garden of Cardinal Barberini in Rome.
The various species of lobelia are not solely decorative. In folk medicine the root of *Lobelia laxiflora* was considered to have diuretic and anti-asthmatic properties; while, in official materia medica, the

authoritative *Potter's Cyclopaedia of Botanical Drugs and Preparations,* published in 1932, referring to *Lobelia inflata,* states that it is "extensively employed and is regarded as one of the most valuable remedies ever discovered. . . chiefly used as an emetic."

The various preparations based on *Lobelia inflata* are very poisonous if wrongly used, and should only be employed when prescribed by a doctor. The chief constituents are lobeline, a poisonous volatile oily alkaloid, lobelic acid which forms crystallizable salts, and lobelacin. For the extraction of these substances, *Lobelia inflata* is widely cultivated commercially in Europe and in the United States; where, despite the plant's poisonous properties, certain Indian tribes dried the leaves and smoked them like tobacco, hence the common name of Indian Tobacco. (The specific name *inflata* refers to the minute inflated seed-bearing capsules.) Another of the lobelias with the ominous name of *Lobelia syphilitica* was once used to treat that disease. The species was introduced into Europe in 1665 and so named by Linnaeus. *Lobelia succulenta* is eaten as a vegetable by the Javanese, generally with rice, and is one of the few comestible species; unlike the majority of the others, it is not poisonous.

The genus is a numerous one; systematic botanists being divided in opinion between the existence of two hundred and three hundred sixty-five different species. They are widely diffused throughout the temperate areas of Asia, Australia, and North and South America. Europe has only two species, *Lobelia dortmanna* and *Lobelia lurens.*

Cultivation. Lobelias require a cool, moist, rich soil preferably with a good proportion of leafsoil—a sunny position in the north, partial shade in the south. The annual types, or those cultivated as annuals (some are not hardy and will not tolerate frost), have seed so fine that it should not be covered, but just lightly pressed into the soil surface. The soil should be composed of finely sieved sand, peat, and leafsoil in equal proportions. The seed can be sown in January–February in a warm greenhouse; or in March–April in an unheated greenhouse, subsequently pricking out the seedlings into flats, boxes, or trays, and then potting them into small fibre (or peat) pots; eventually they can be planted out in their flowering position in May–June. Propagation can also be done effectively by cuttings taken at any time and inserted in pots, flats, or boxes of sandy soil in a greenhouse, then potting them into small individual pots when well rooted. It will generally be possible to take the cuttings with a fragment of root attached. If the cuttings are taken in late summer the plants can be kept in a warm greenhouse during the winter, where they will continue to bloom, and provide vigorous, well-advanced young plants for early spring planting after all risk of frost has passed. This method is particularly recommended in the case of *Lobelia Erinus* which, although invariably grown as an annual, is actually perennial.

Lobelia tenuior
From *Paxton's Magazine of Botany*,
1842, plate 101

The perennial species also require a cool, moist, fresh soil which is fertile, well-drained, and sandy rather than heavy and compact. They thrive in a sunny position if there is an abundance of moisture at the roots, and actually prefer sun in the north; but in hot and very sunny climates, better results will be obtained by planting in semi-shade. They are only moderately hardy in areas where frost is experienced and plants should be given the winter protection of a light mulch of dead leaves. In districts where severe cold is of long duration such a covering may not prove effective (unless the ground is well snow-covered) and the plants should be removed to a greenhouse or well-protected coldframe, where they can remain for the winter in pots, flats, trays, or boxes. The most hardy of the herbaceous species is *L. syphilitica,* and it is one of the most attractive. Propagation can be effected by division in spring (the only method in the case of hybrid forms), or from seed sown in a greenhouse in spring or early summer in the same manner as the annual types.

Lobelia cardinalis   *Lobelia Erinus*

(Cardinal Flower)
Herbaceous perennial
Flowering period: July–Oct.
Height: up to 2¾ ft.

Lobelia cardinalis L. (syn. *Rapuntium cardinale*)
Native to eastern North America. A quite hardy herbaceous perennial up to 2¾ ft. high when in bloom. With flowers of a true vivid red, it is one of the most intensely coloured of all herbaceous plants. Leaves lanceolate, up to 5 ins. long, and stalkless, or nearly so; they are coarsely dentated, and borne on the erect flower stems, those at the base of the plant being larger and forming rosettes. Flower stems strong and rigid, bearing masses of 1½-in.-long brilliant scarlet flowers with a conspicuous lower lip. Although in its native habitat it grows in partial shade, spectacular results can be obtained in full

sun if the plant is well watered (partial shade, however, is recommended below Zone 8). Often confused with *Lobelia fulgens,* which is similar but with wine-red foliage. There is also a white-flowered form, and the var. *Russian Princess* has pink flowers.

Lobelia Erinus L. (syn. *Lobelia heterophylla, Lobelia gracilis, Lobelia bicolor*)

Annual
Flowering period: May–Sept.
Height: 2–4 ins.

Native to South Africa. Often and appropriately known as the Edging Lobelia. A non-hardy compact dwarf annual (perennial in its natural habitat) of rapid growth. There are, however, many taller forms, and others with a pendulous or trailing habit. One of the most popular of all dwarf summer-flowering plants for small beds and for pot cultivation, with a very long flowering season. The minute blooms are produced in the greatest profusion and are an intense vivid blue. Foliage minute, dentated, dark green, oval in the case of the basal leaves, $\frac{1}{3}$ in. long; but linear, narrow, and pointed on the graceful little flower stems. First introduced to gardens in 1752; there are now many beautiful hybrids and forms with flowers dark or light blue, red, violet, pinkish, or white, some on stems $\frac{2}{3}$ in. long, with the three lower petals each $\frac{1}{8}$ in. wide and joined at the base, forming a conspicuous broad lip.

Some of the best varieties are:

- var. *Aubretia Shades,* height 6 ins. A blend of very compact varieties in shades of light and dark blue, purple, red, violet, and white
- var. *Blue Cascade,* with a trailing habit and Cambridge-blue flowers
- var. *Blue Stone,* height 6 ins. Clear blue without the characteristic white eye
- var. *Crystal Palace,* the oldest variety and still one of the best. Height 6 ins. Dark-blue flowers with a white eye and red-bronze-green foliage
- var. *Rosamund,* rounded compact plants. Height 6 ins. Wine-red flowers
- var. *Sapphire,* trailing habit and dark-blue flowers
- var. *White Lady,* height 6 ins. Pure-white flowers

Lobelia fulgens Willd.

Herbaceous perennial
Flowering period: May–Sept.
Height: up to 3 ft.

Native to North America. Very similar to *Lobelia cardinalis* but with wine-red instead of green foliage, which makes a remarkable contrast with the vivid scarlet flowers. The flower stems are also more robust and the lower petals are more pronounced, forming a pendulous lip to the blooms. Not hardy. There are several good varieties such as:

- var. *Queen Victoria,* with purple-red foliage and crimson flowers

    var. *The Bishop,* bronze-red foliage and scarlet flowers
    var. *Jack MacMasters,* a hybrid with *Lobelia syphilitica;* violet-blue flowers and dark purple-red foliage
    var. *Purple Emperor,* purple flowers and green foliage

(Indian Tobacco)
Annual
Flowering period: June–Sept.
Height: up to 3 ft.

Lobelia inflata L.
Native to the United States. Not one of the most decorative for garden purposes but of extraordinary medicinal value. The minute pale-blue flowers are produced on slender spikes borne on the strong hairy erect stems. Leaves lanceolate, dentated, alternate, up to 3 ins. long, stalkless, with small white glands at their edges.

Herbaceous perennial
Flowering period: Aug.–Oct.
Height: up to 5 ft.

Lobelia laxiflora L.
Native to Mexico. A hairy herbaceous perennial up to 5 ft. high with narrowly oval dentated foliage. Flowers a striking contrast of red and yellow, $1\frac{1}{2}$ ins. long, with conspicuous protruding stamens. Not hardy. Excellent for pot culture.

Herbaceous perennial
Flowering period: June–Sept.
Height: 12–18 ins.

Lobelia syphilitica L.
Native to the eastern United States. A very beautiful hardy herbaceous perennial with the pleasing habit of reproducing itself from self-sown seed and appearing spontaneously in the most unexpected positions. Prefers a cool, moist soil in semi-shade (can take full sun from Zone 7 northwards). Leaves bright green, narrowly oblong, 3–4 ins. long, forming a dense basal rosette. Inflorescence an erect rigid spike up to 18 ins. high bearing a profusion of lovely sky-blue flowers 1 in. long and similar in form and shape to those of *Lobelia cardinalis,* with which it makes a remarkably effective contrast. There is also an attractive white-flowered form.

Annual
Flowering period: June–Sept.
Height: up to 18 ins.

Lobelia tenuior L. (syn. *Lobelia ramosa*)
Native to Australia. A half-hardy annual best described as a giant form of *Lobelia Erinus,* which it resembles in shape, flower, and general habit but on a larger scale and rather less compact. Leaves light green, divided, each segment narrowly linear. Flowers vivid blue, up to 1 in. long—with an enlarged conspicuous basal petal—produced in such abundance from June to September that they completely hide the plant. An excellent species for cultivating in large pots or tubs and for use in greenhouses in winter.

Herbaceous perennial
Flowering period: June–Sept.
Height: up to $4\frac{1}{2}$ ft.

Lobelia tupa L.
Native to Chile. A non-hardy herbaceous perennial of imposing aspect. A beautiful species with tall erect leafy flower stems bearing brick-red flowers from June to September. Particularly suitable for

coastal districts and for warm positions where it is desired to create an exotic tropical effect. The entire plant is covered with woolly hairs. Inflorescence a long spike up to 2 ft. high bearing individual flowers $1\frac{1}{2}$ ins. long, with the petals united to form a single large pendulous lip. The large attractive leaves borne on the stems are 10 ins. long and 4 ins. wide, while the basal foliage is twice that size. They are of a velvety texture, greenish white in colour.

Lobularia

(SWEET ALYSSUM OR SNOWDRIFT)
(*Also see* ALYSSUM)
Family: Cruciferae
Annual or tender herbaceous perennial
Flowering period: spring to autumn
Height: 3–8 ins.
Position: sun
Propagation: seed
Cultivation very easy
Fragrant

The annual *Lobularia*, better known as *Alyssum maritimum*, is generally sold by seedsmen under the name of Sweet Alyssum, or just Alyssum. Everybody is quite happy with this arrangement (except the botanists) until the less-well-informed gardener asks for "Alyssum", when he really means the yellow-flowered perennial *Alyssum saxatile,* and is given seed of the mauve or white annual Sweet Alyssum. The botanist is thus vindicated; Sweet Alyssum is *Lobularia maritima.*

Once established in the garden, *Lobularia maritima* will never leave it. About ten years ago I grew a few plants in a bed at the edge of a gravel path; every year since, there has appeared a profusion of self-sown seedlings (actually sown in the gravel), which flourish to perfection and seed themselves again the following season.

The flowering season is very long, normally from April–May until the first frost, even longer in warmer climates. The colour can vary from white through all shades of mauve and violet to pinkish; while the delicious honey-like fragrance deserves to have been given to a taller plant so that it could be better appreciated. (This problem of bringing the blossoms to nose-level can be overcome by planting a few specimens in dry walls, or in some other raised position.) Although as common as couch grass, Sweet Alyssum never becomes monotonous; its quietly modest aspect is unsophisticated and it never tries to obtrude. Its general form has not been greatly changed by the hybridists, although its colour range has been slightly extended.

The genus *Lobularia* comprises five species, mostly native to the Mediterranean regions, but only the one species *(L. maritima)* is cultivated in gardens.

Cultivation. Lobularia maritima is so easy to cultivate and is so undemanding that detailed cultural instructions are almost superfluous. It requires a rather dry very sunny position in a well-drained not-too-heavy soil. Seed can be sown in its flowering position in March–April (earlier in southern climes); or in pots, boxes, flats, or trays in February–March in an unheated greenhouse or coldframe; the seedlings should be planted out in April. If in late summer largish plants show signs of exhaustion through abundant and continuous flowering, they can be cut back to within half their length and given an application of a liquid organic fertilizer. They will soon send out new growth and bloom again until autumn.

Lobularia maritima Desv. (syn. *Alyssum maritimum*)
A dwarf semi-trailing much-branched little annual. The slender branches extend parallel over the soil surface, with the tips and lateral growths curving upwards. The leaves are minute, linear-lanceolate, silvery-olive green, up to $\frac{3}{4}$ in. long. The original species has fragrant white flowers borne in compact, terminal umbels 3–4 ins. high and $\frac{3}{4}$ in. wide; every lateral growth produces another terminal inflorescence. Ripe seed is produced at the base of the fully developed inflorescences while the upper part is still in full bloom. This original species is now rarely grown, being superseded by improved hybrid forms which have the same general characteristics but with a wider range of colours. In very sunny dry positions and in poor soils the plants develop a more dwarf and more compact habit than those grown in partial shade and in richer soil. Sometimes the plant is judged to be a perennial, and technically this assessment is correct in the case of isolated plants growing under particularly favourable conditions; but for practical gardening purposes it is considered an annual and is treated as such. (The yellow-flowered *Alyssum saxatile* is definitely a perennial.) One authority recalled that in error he once sowed *Lobularia maritima* among roses, but with very happy results as the scent of the blooms was intensified, and the two subjects grew together in perfect harmony. This is a combination I have frequently and deliberately used in hot and sunny climates to provide a ground cover among rose bushes—which, although sun-lovers, appreciate some shade over their roots. The same system can be effectively employed among dahlias, gladioli, hollyhocks, and many other plants that do not bear a profusion of basal foliage. Sweet Alyssum is, in fact, an excellent ground cover; it prevents the growth of weeds, conserves moisture, maintains a cooler soil, and, above all, it does not have to be resown every year. It is also effective when planted in walls, among paving, in the rock-garden, in stone steps,

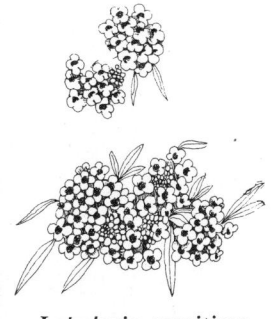

Lobularia maritima

and even in large balls of sphagnum moss in wire baskets suspended from any overhead support. There are many forms and varieties:

> var. *Benthamii,* in cultivation since 1812, with a dwarf compact habit, 6–8 ins. high
> var. *Giganteum,* a taller form with broader foliage
> var. *Königsteppich,* dark violet, 3 ins. high
> var. *Little Dorrit,* white-flowered, 4 ins. high
> var. *Rosie O'Day,* pinkish lilac, 3 ins. high, flowers eight weeks after sowing
> var. *Schneeteppich,* particularly pure-white flowers, $3\frac{1}{2}$ ins. high
> var. *Variegatus,* with white-edged leaves
> var. *Violet Queen,* rich violet, 5 ins. high

Lonicera

(HONEYSUCKLE)
Family: *Caprifoliaceae*
Hardy or half-hardy evergreen or deciduous shrubs, or climbers
Position: sun or partial or complete shade
Propagation: seed, cuttings, grafting, or layering
Cultivation easy
In some cases useful for cutting

Charles Darwin's grandfather, Erasmus, who lived between 1731 and 1802, was a curiously eccentric individual, according to the *Encyclopaedia Britannica.* A transitory but important figure, he was a follower of English Deism, a typical child of eighteenth-century English materialism, and a believer in theories later advanced by Lamarck, Pavlov, and (naturally) those of his grandson. He produced a good deal of rather mediocre prose and also concocted some excessively turgid verse. Among the latter efforts was a lengthy poem, "The Botanic Garden" (1792), which apparently had considerable success. Several lines were dedicated to the genus *Lonicera:*

Lonicera fragrantissima

> Fair Lonicera prints the dewy lawn,
> And decks with brighter blush the vermeil dawn;
> Winds round the shadowy rocks, and pansied vales,
> And scents with sweeter breath the summer gales.
> With artless grace and native ease she charms,
> And bears the horn of plenty in her arms.
> *Five* rival swains their tender cares unfold,
> And watch with eye askance the treasured gold.

Thus daintily couched in hyberbole, the poet alludes to the honeysuckle's habit of growing over everything, and the "swains" (obviously neighbouring plants) nervously await the next move of its twining growths. (Doctor Johnson was, of course, far more blunt, and once referred to "honeysuckle-like wives, who generally destroy the support over which they so tenderly entwine".)

Charles Darwin affirmed that honeysuckle can climb to the top of a young oak with a trunk 5 ins. in diameter, coiling around it so tightly that the vine makes a deep indentation in the bark of the tree. During the nineteenth century, this tight-coiling characteristic was exploited for making "artistically contorted" canes and walking sticks. For the moment, however, we are more concerned with the decorative value of the most common of all honeysuckles, *Lonicera Caprifolium,* which has so many virtues that it is desired in every garden. It is beautiful in late spring—with flowers emitting the fragrance of spring itself—and still beautiful at the end of summer when, after the flowers have faded, it gladdens the eye with cheerful red berries.

Honeysuckles are plants within the reach of all. They attained the zenith of their popularity during the nineteenth century, when there was hardly a garden without some type of honeysuckle-covered arbour, summer-house, or gazebo (where, in the scented half-light, poetically amorous meetings and assignations flourished).

We do not know for certain when honeysuckle was first introduced into gardens. We do know, however, that the Earl of Lincoln grew *Lonicera Periclymenum* in his garden at Holborn before 1286. Towards the end of the seventeenth century, when the fashion for formal gardens began, Flemish merchants introduced two varieties into England, *Lonicera Periclymenum* var. *belgica* and var. *serotina*. Having a more pliable character than the species, these varieties were more suited for training over summer-houses and "follies", in accordance with the whims of landscape architects of those times. (The fashion for formal gardens also fostered the establishment of other species and varieties now lost to cultivation.) *Lonicera* x *italica* (a hybrid raised by crossing *Lonicera Caprifolium* with *Lonicera etrusca*) was in cultivation in England in 1730. It was later transported to America, where it became naturalized, and then, still later, owing to one of those frequent vagaries of nomenclature so common in the world of botany, it was reintroduced into Europe under the name of *Lonicera* x *americana*. *Lonicera japonica* was discovered in Japan, but was actually introduced into Japan from China by William Kerr in 1806. In 1860, Robert Fortune subsequently sent it to Europe from Japan together with the var. *aureo-reticulata*. It was an immediate success throughout the whole Continent.

The most fragrant honeysuckles are not necessarily the most beautiful, and, in fact, the scentless varieties are the most spectacular.

Lonicera Periclymenum

Although admitting that this is the case, one is tempted to refrain from saying so because, as the British garden-book author Alice M. Coats so rightly states, "a honeysuckle without perfume is like a man without a shadow". It would be delightful if this inconsistency could be rectified by combining beauty and fragrance by planting both the spectacular and the scented types side by side. Among the most beautiful scentless honeysuckles is *Lonicera sempervirens,* which was brought from North America and cultivated in England by John Tradescant in 1656. In Budapest, in the Hungarian Royal Horticultural Society Garden, it became one parent of an even more beautiful scentless hybrid, *Lonicera* x *tellmanniana,* first put into commerce in 1927.

The climbing types, however, represent only one section of the genus and many of the species are interesting and beautiful shrubs. In England, Gerard cultivated the shrubby species, *L. Xylosteum,* and Parkinson grew *Lonicera coerulea.* In 1845, Robert Fortune introduced two lovely Chinese species (both strongly fragrant), *Lonicera standishii* and *Lonicera fragrantissima.* Then, in 1908, E. H. Wilson introduced the small-leaved shrubby evergreen *Lonicera nitida,* which has neither attractive flowers nor fragrance, but instead has decorative violet-coloured translucent fruits. This species soon became extremely popular for use as hedges, a purpose for which it is almost perfect in country gardens; however, it is not always a success in the polluted atmosphere of large cities.

The genus *Lonicera* comprises about 180 species with a distribution extending throughout the Northern Hemisphere, especially the wooded hilly regions of Central and Eastern Asia where loniceras grow wild up to an altitude of 12,000 ft.

Linnaeus named the genus in honour of the German naturalist Adam Lonitzer (1528–1586). The older generic names were thus eliminated from official botanic nomenclature but not from popular usage. They are the Latin *Caprifolium*—so-named because goats *(capri)* were apparently fond of grazing on the plant, not because the plant could climb like a goat—and the Greek *Periclymenon,* which was derived from *periklan* (to interlace, entwine).

Among the European species, *Lonicera Caprifolium* and *Lonicera Periclymenum* both contain salicylic acid (among other properties, this substance is noted as a preservative and an antiseptic), and they were often employed in folk medicine. The fruits of *Lonicera Xylosteum* contain xylostein, a substance used as a purgative by Alpine peasants. Regarding the exotic species, Reginald Farrar mentions one native to Tibet (probably *Lonicera angustifolia*), the fruits of which were widely relished by the local inhabitants. When some American missionaries added the berries to cakes or made them into jams and jellies, they experienced some rather peculiar though not unpleasant reactions. (It is possible that these berries possess hal-

Lonicera sempervirens
From *Curtis's Botanical Magazine*,
1804, plate 781

lucinogenic or stimulating properties, but the equivocal nature of the description of the missionaries' "rapturous" reactions leads one to wonder whether it was the berries' exquisite flavour or their psychological effects that were being rhapsodized over.) The natives of the Kamchatka Peninsula in northeastern Siberia eat the large cherry-like fruits of *Lonicera coerulea* out of hand, and they are apparently also delicious when made into a conserve. The U.S. Department of Agriculture recommends the fruits of *Lonicera involucrata* and *Lonicera ciliosa* for their edibility, but, as yet, these two species have not been grown on a commercial scale.

Cultivation. Most books affirm that honeysuckles are of the easiest cultivation, thriving in any soil; but this is only true up to a certain point: where soil and climate are too dry, honeysuckles become an easy prey to insect pests and produce ugly, contorted, and sparse vegetation, with the vines having more bends and nodes than leaves. In his superb book *Climbing Plants for Walls and Gardens* (Heinemann, London, 1967), Brigadier E. Lucas Phillips very wisely reminds his readers that honeysuckles are woodland plants, requiring a cool fresh position in a humus-rich soil. The correct treatment afforded to clematis is also valid in the cultivation of honeysuckle; that is, the base of the plant in shade, with the above-ground part in full sun. In any case, a glance at honeysuckles in their natural habitat will fully confirm the efficacy of such a system and will demonstrate the type of habitat preferred. From time to time, they manifest a tendency to die back—in such cases the plants should be energetically pruned, even down to ground level, after which they will send forth new growth. This dying back is a characteristic of the genus and not a disease. Some species have a tendency to lose their basal foliage. To avoid this inconvenience, it is well to establish round their base some dwarf annual plants that will provide shade and keep the soil surface cool, moist, and fresh. In the south, and in very hot and dry localities, it is a mistake to plant climbing honeysuckle against sunny walls, since they will absorb and radiate heat that is not agreeable to the plant (the same is true for bignonia, bougainvillea, etc.), and the ideal planting position is facing northeast. Honeysuckles require abundant watering during hot, dry weather, and heavy pruning is not necessary if the vines are periodically thinned out, and put into some kind of order by training, by the removal of dead, weak, or badly formed growths, and by the cutting back of the lateral growths after they have flowered.

Propagation does not present any difficulty. If raised from seed, obviously the slowest method, the seed can be sown in spring or autumn outside or in coldframes (except in the case of the non-hardy species, the seed of which should be sown in a warm greenhouse). One of the quickest methods of propagation is layering; while the best results are obtained by propagation from soft-wood cuttings

Lonicera x *tellemanniana*

under glass, in spring, or by means of semi-woody cuttings, in cold-frames, in late summer. Treating the cuttings with a root-forming hormone product is helpful.

For growing honeysuckle in tubs or other large receptacles, the following soil mixture is advised: 1 part ordinary garden soil, 1 part leafsoil, 1 part peat, $\frac{1}{4}$ part sand, $\frac{1}{2}$ part well-decomposed manure, and a handful of bone meal (or dried blood) to every wheelbarrow full of compost.

Evergreen climber
Flowering period: July–Sept.
Height: up to 15 ft.
Zone 7 southwards

Lonicera alseuosmoides Graebn.
Native to China. Introduced into Europe by E. H. Wilson in 1904. A vigorous, hardy, rampant evergreen climber with slender glabrous stems. Leaves oblong, 2 ins. long, $\frac{1}{3}$ in. wide, dark green. Inflorescence in the form of a small panicle, borne at the terminals of the current season's growth, and also in the leaf axils along the branches. Individual flowers funnel-shaped, $\frac{1}{2}$ in. long, yellow outside, purple inside. Fruit globose, $\frac{1}{4}$ in. in diameter, black and covered with purple bloom, growing together in compact bunches, and of considerable ornamental value in autumn. One of the small number of evergreen climbers that will thrive in shade and, judging from the specimens I have grown, of rapid development. However, it is not hardy in very cold climates.

Deciduous shrub
Flowering period: May–June
Height: up to 10 ft.
Zone 4 southwards

Lonicera x *bella* Zabel
Of hybrid origin (*Lonicera morrowii* x *Lonicera tatarica*). Leaves heart-shaped or oblong, 2 ins. long. Flowers white, fading to pink, and then to yellow. Fruits brilliant red in autumn, borne in the greatest profusion. An upright deciduous shrub of spreading habit which is effective when planted in a bold group.

(Common Woodbine
or Italian Honeysuckle)
Deciduous climber
Flowering period: May–July
Height: up to 20 ft.
Very fragrant
Zone 4 southwards

Lonicera Caprifolium L.
Native to Europe. The common and beloved Woodbine of the English countryside. A hardy deciduous rampant climber. Leaves oval, 2–4 ins. long, up to 1 in. wide; glaucous on either surface. The higher leaves on each stem are stalkless, in pairs; joined at their base, they form a type of miniature cup. It is from this cup, or leaf axil, that the flower stalks are produced, bearing whorls of tubular, 2-in.-long fragrant flowers; yellowish white tinted pink and two-lipped at the mouth. Fruits orange-scarlet, translucent. The flowering period begins from late spring onwards, but varies in accordance with local climate. Prefers semi-shade and a moderately moist soil.

Deciduous shrub
Flowering period: May–June
Height: up to 12 ft.
Zone 4 southwards

Lonicera chrysantha Turczan.
Native to Siberia, northern China, and Japan. A very attractive fast-growing, compact, and easily cultivated hardy deciduous shrub. Leaves oval, pointed, 2–4 ins. long and half as wide. Flowers $\frac{3}{4}$

in. long, borne in pairs in the leaf axils of the previous season's growth; pale yellow and prolifically produced. Fruits coral-red, translucent, and highly ornamental in autumn. A beautiful shrub in flower and in fruit. Characteristically, as with other shrubby honeysuckles, the young stems are hollow.

Lonicera dioica L. (Small Honeysuckle or Small Woodbine)
Native to eastern North America. A wide-spreading, elegant, hardy deciduous shrub with glabrous elongated-oval leaves up to 4 ins. long and half as wide, long-pointed at both ends, with the undersurface very glaucous (they produce an effect of remarkable beauty when set in motion by a breeze). Flowers yellow, slightly suffused with purple, borne in the stalkless leaf axils, $\frac{3}{4}$ in. long. Fruits red. Old specimens will sometimes develop a semi-climbing habit if given the encouragement of some support.

Deciduous shrub
Flowering period: May–June
Height: up to 10 ft.
Zone 3 southwards

Lonicera etrusca Santi.
Native to the Mediterranean region. A vigorous semi-evergreen climber with conspicuous reddish-purple young vegetation. Leaves opposite, oval, $1\frac{1}{2}$–3 ins. long and nearly half as wide, and glaucous. Short-stalked lower leaves, while those at the ends of the branches are stalkless and joined to the branch at their base. Flowers yellow, suffused red, fragrant, and borne in terminal and axillary groups of three; each flower $1\frac{3}{4}$ ins. long, tubular, conspicuously two-lipped at the mouth. Fruits red. One of the most beautiful species for its rich colouring and for the abundance of its flowers and fruits, but hardy only in a mild climate. A particularly fine form is the var. *superba*, with larger panicles of bloom.

Semi-evergreen climber
Flowering period: May–July
Height: up to 20 ft.
Scented
Zone 9 southwards

Lonicera flava Sims (Yellow Honeysuckle)
Native to the United States from North Carolina to Oklahoma, and reputed to be the most beautiful of the American honeysuckles but rarely found in European gardens. A wide-spreading deciduous climber with 3-in.-long elliptic leaves that are blue-green on the undersurface and borne in pairs, the upper two or three pairs joined at the base. The $1\frac{1}{4}$-in.-long flowers are tubular, fragrant, and vivid orange-yellow, borne in two or three whorls, one above the other, on terminal inflorescences. Not a common plant even in its natural habitat, and plants offered for sale under the name *L. flava* are often either *Lonicera prolifera* or *Lonicera glaucescens*, both similar but inferior to *L. flava*.

Deciduous climber
Flowering period: May–June
Height: up to 10 ft.
Scented
Zone 4 southwards

Lonicera fragrantissima Lind. & Pax.
Native to China, and introduced into European gardens by Robert Fortune in 1845. A semi-evergreen hardy shrub with leathery oval leaves 1–2 ins. long and $\frac{3}{4}$–1 in. wide, with pointed, dentated edges,

Semi-evergreen shrub
Flowering period: Dec.–Mar.
Height: up to 8–9 ft.
Strongly scented
Zone 4 southwards

dark green above, glaucous beneath. Flowering period in a mild climate is from December onwards, but is generally at its maximum in February–March. Flowers in pairs in the leaf axils; creamy white, $\frac{1}{3}$ in. long, strongly and deliciously scented. Although tolerant of sun, it will thrive and bloom in complete shade. A valuable shrub for its early-flowering habit, strong fragrance, attractive foliage, and brilliant-red fruits produced in early summer. Similar to, and sometimes confused with, *Lonicera standishii,* but better than the last-named.

Evergreen climber
Flowering period: June–July
Height: up to 75 ft.
Scented
Zone 9 southwards

Lonicera hildebrandiana Collett & Hemsl.

Native to Southeast Asia and southern China. A very vigorous, even rampant, fast-growing climber; evergreen in a mild climate and only hardy in localities with a mild winter, such as the Riviera, Florida, California, Cornwall, etc. Leaves oval, pointed, 3–6 ins. long, $1\frac{1}{2}$–3 ins. wide, dark green above, lighter in colour beneath. Inflorescence in the form of racemes produced in the leaf axils, always in pairs. Flowers fragrant, each individual bloom 3–6 ins. long; creamy white at first, later changing to orange; tubular in shape, divided at the mouth into bilobed lips with a diameter of $2\frac{3}{4}$ ins. Fruits reddish black, 1 in. long. Discovered by Sir Henry Collett in 1888. Apart from its spectacular beauty, it is also of botanical interest as the species with the largest leaves, flowers, and fruits. Requires a hot, very sunny, not too damp position. It is one of the least-known of the honeysuckles.

(Rough Woodbine)
Deciduous climber
Flowering period: June–July
Height: up to 12 ft.
Zone 4 southwards

Lonicera hirsuta Eaton

Native to the northeastern United States. A very hardy slender climber up to about 12 ft. high. Leaves ovate, 2–4 ins. long, covered with hairy down on either surface; those towards the ends of the branches fused together at the base; the lower ones stalked. Flowers 1 in. long, orange-yellow, borne several together in whorls, one above the other, on terminal and axillary spikes. The corolla tube is swollen at the base, while the mouth of the flower is two-lipped.

(Twinberry)
Deciduous shrub
Flowering period: May–June
Height: 3 ft.
Zone 2 southwards

Lonicera involucrata Banks

Native to western North America. A small upright deciduous shrub with square, not rounded, branches; leaves oval-elliptic, 3–5 ins. long. Flowers $\frac{1}{2}$ in. long with two conspicuous basal bracts; yellow suffused with red. Fruits black, shiny. The dwarf var. *humilis* is only 2 ft. high.

(Japanese Honeysuckle)
Evergreen or semi-evergreen climber
Flowering period: June
Height: up to 30 ft.
Zone 8 southwards

Lonicera japonica Thunb.

Native to Japan, China, and Korea. A very vigorous moderately hardy evergreen or semi-evergreen climber up to 30 ft. high. Not hardy in exceptionally cold areas unless planted in a warm sheltered position (where it can become so rampant that it will smother any nearby plant and can even become a nuisance). Stems hollow and hairy; leaves oval, 2–4 ins. long, $1\frac{1}{4}$–2 ins. wide, with undulated edges, and slightly downy on both surfaces. Flowers sweetly scented, borne in pairs in the leaf axils of the new season's growths; $1\frac{1}{2}$ ins. long, two-lipped; the $\frac{3}{4}$-in.-long flower stalks bear two conspicuous but small bracts near their base. Colour of flowers at first white, later becoming orange-yellow. Fruits opaque black. First introduced into Europe in 1806. There are several varieties, the most interesting of which are:

> var. *aureo-reticulata* Nich. (syn. *Lonicera brachypoda reticulata*). Leaves 2 ins. long, variegated green and yellow, with the veins a vivid yellow colour. Less hardy than *L. japonica* and less free-flowering, but attractive for its coloured foliage.
>
> var. *flexuosa* Nich. (syn. *Lonicera flexuosa*). A form with purple-red stems and smooth leaves with purple-tinted veins. Flowers light red outside, white inside.
>
> var. *halliana* Nich. (syn. *Lonicera flexuosa halliana*). Leaves woolly on either surface. Flowers white.

Lonicera korolkowii Stapf.

Deciduous shrub
Flowering period: May–June
Height: up to 12 ft.
Zone 4 southwards

Native to Turkistan. First grown in Europe by A. Lavallée, at Segrez, France, but first identified at Boston's Arnold Arboretum in 1893. A graceful, wide-spreading hardy deciduous shrub of an attractive pale-grey hue in all its parts. Leaves ovate, narrower at the base, pointed, up to $1\frac{1}{2}$ ins. long, pale glaucous-grey, downy on the undersurface, stalks $\frac{1}{4}$ in. long. Flowers pale pink, borne in pairs from the leaf axils on short lateral branches, $\frac{2}{3}$ in. long, two-lipped. Fruits red.

Lonicera maackii Max.

Deciduous shrub
Flowering period: May–June
Height: up to 15 ft.
Scented
Zone 4 southwards

Native to Manchuria and China. A hardy deciduous shrub with a wide, spreading habit and more or less flat horizontal branches; an arrangement that effectively displays the masses of intensely scarlet translucent fruits which are abundantly produced in late summer. Leaves oval, pointed, dark green, $1\frac{1}{2}$–3 ins. long and about half as wide. Flowers slightly fragrant, borne in pairs along the entire length of the upper part of the branches. Individual blooms nearly 1 in. long, tubular, two-lipped. Introduced by Wilson in 1900, and certainly one of the most beautiful shrubby honeysuckles I have grown.

Lonicera morrowii A. Gray

Deciduous shrub
Flowering period: May–June
Height: up to 8 ft.
Zone 3 southwards

Native to Japan. A robust deciduous shrub of open, spreading habit. Leaves ovate, up to $2\frac{1}{2}$ ins. long and half as wide; tapering at the base and slender-pointed; dull green above, grey and downy on the undersurface. Flowers creamy white gradually changing to yellowish cream; borne in pairs on short twiggy growths from the leaf axils; tubular, two-lipped, about 1 in. long. Fruits dark red to yellow, the same plant bearing fruits of different shades.

Evergreen shrub
Flowering period: June–July
Height: up to 12 ft.
Scented
Zone 6 southwards

Lonicera nitida Wilson (on the Continent more frequently known as *Chamaecerasus nitida*)
Native to China (western Szechwan and the Yunnan provinces, where it grows in mountainous areas up to 7,000 ft. above sea level). A hardy small-leaved evergreen shrub of dense very leafy compact habit. One of the finest evergreens for making small hedges. Young growths a purple-green tint. Mature leaves dark green, shiny, almost leathery in texture, ovate, blunt at the tips; ½ in. long, minutely stalked. Tiny, ¼-in.-long, inconspicuous, creamy white, fragrant flowers produced in pairs in the leaf axils. Fruits globose, translucent, purple-blue, ¼ in. in diameter. Introduced into the West by Wilson in 1908. A really beautiful and useful ornamental evergreen that can be allowed to develop naturally in an informal manner, or pruned and clipped to any desired shape or size. Much more attractive than box (buxus) or privet (ligustrum), and of rapid growth. The branches are also excellent for arranging in vases with cut flowers. I have found it suitable for positions in either sun or complete shade, but it prefers a cool, moderately moist soil, either acid or alkaline (calcareous). Closely related botanically to *Lonicera pileata,* which it resembles. Neither can be recommended for planting in the badly polluted atmosphere of large cities where smog is frequently experienced.

(Woodbine, Twisted Eglantine, or Honeysuckle)
Deciduous climber
Flowering period: June–Sept.
Height: up to 20 ft.
Scented
Zone 4 southwards

Lonicera Periclymenum L.
Native to Europe, the Caucasus Mountains, and Asia Minor. This is the common honeysuckle of the English countryside. A rampant, vigorous deciduous climber, very hardy and easily cultivated, which likes to ramble over other shrubs and is thus frequently found in a wild state in hedgerows. A plant for which the British have a most particular regard and affection. Flowers deliciously fragrant. Leaves oval, pointed, 1–2½ ins. long, green above, glaucous green beneath. Flowers yellowish white suffused pink and red, with the proportion of each colour greatly varying from plant to plant. Inflorescence in the form of a compact terminal whorl borne on a long stem, making it excellent for cutting. Individual flowers 2 ins. long, tubular, two-lipped, with recurved petals. Fruits red, decorative, but poisonous.

Evergreen shrub
Flowering period: Apr.–May
Height: up to 18 ins.
Scented
Zone 6 southwards

Lonicera pileata Oliver (on the Continent more frequently known as *Chamaecerasus pileata*)
Native to China. Discovered and imported by Henry in 1900. A small

Lonicera japonica
From Gaetano Savi's *Flora italiana* . . .
(plate 103), Pisa, 1818

hardy evergreen shrub with the neat compact habit regarded as excellent for making small hedges. Similar to, and botanically allied to, *Lonicera nitida,* but of smaller proportions. Young growths purple-green and hirsute. Mature leaves oblong-ovate, blunt at the tips, about ¾ in. long, shiny dark green borne on minute stalks. The foliage is so prolific that the individual leaves are often only ½ in. apart on the stems. Flowers ivory-white, inconspicuous, ¼ in. long, axillary, and produced in pairs. Fruits translucent, violet-blue, ⅕ in. in diameter.

(Trumpet Honeysuckle or Coral Honeysuckle)
Evergreen climber
Flowering period: June–July
Height: up to 24 ft.
Zone 3 southwards

Lonicera sempervirens L.

Native to the United States, from Massachusetts to Florida and Texas. A robust and reasonably hardy fast-growing climber; evergreen in mild climates. Will thrive in partial or complete shade. Young vegetation glaucous. Leaves oval, 1½–3 ins. long, ¾–2 ins. wide, dark bluish green. Flowers scentless but of an intensely rich orange-scarlet outside, yellow inside, 2 ins. long, tubular, borne in groups of whorls with six individual flowers in each whorl; the whole inflorescence forms a terminal spike with a long stalk on the previous season's growth. First introduced into Europe in 1656.

Semi-evergreen shrub
Flowering period: Nov.–April
Height: up to 8–9 ft.
Scented
Zone 4 southwards

Lonicera standishii Carr.

Native to China. Like *Lonicera fragrantissima,* which it resembles, introduced by Fortune in 1845. A hardy evergreen shrub in a mild climate but only semi-evergreen where the winters are cold. Branches have a conspicuously peeling bark. Habit loose and open, somewhat irregular in shape. Leaves oblong, 2–4½ ins. long, ¾–2 ins. wide, slenderly pointed. Very early-flowering, from November intermittently until April (according to climate). Flowers borne in pairs in the leaf axils; creamy white and intensely fragrant; rather squat in form and only ⅓ in. long. The fruits mature in summer and are brilliant translucent red and are borne in joined pairs. Although hardy, this species should be planted in a sheltered position to afford winter protection to the flowers.

(Tartarian Honeysuckle, Bush Honeysuckle, or Garden Fly Honeysuckle)
Deciduous shrub
Flowering period: May–June
Height: up to 10 ft.
Zone 3 southwards

Lonicera tatarica L.

Native to a vast region from Russia to Central Asia. Introduced into European gardens in 1752. It rapidly became so well-established that it naturalized itself and is now the most common of the shrubby honeysuckles, not only in Europe but also in the United States. It is a vigorous deciduous plant up to 10 ft. high with oblong foliage, heart-shaped at the base, pointed, length 2–3 ins. and about half as wide, but on the extremities of the flowering branches considerably smaller; green on the upper surface, glaucous beneath. Flowers white or pale pink, in pairs, two-lipped, 1 in. long. Fruits globose, bright red. There are several forms and varieties, some with more richly coloured flowers. Where a hardy easily cultivated ornamental shrub is required for naturalizing, any of the following varieties have much to recommend them:

    var. *alba,* white-flowered
    var. *latifolia* (syn. var. *speciosa,* var. *splendens*), with dark pinkish-red flowers
    var. *nana,* with a dwarf compact habit
    var. *siberica* (syn. var. *rubra*), with larger dark-pink flowers up to $3\frac{1}{2}$ ins. long

Lonicera x *tellemanniana*
Of hybrid origin *(Lonicera tragophylla* x *Lonicera sempervirens)*. A superb deciduous climber raised at the Hungarian Royal Horticultural Society's School in Budapest and put on sale in 1927 by the Berlin firm of Späth. First seen in bloom in London in June 1931, when exhibited by Sir William Lawrence, and immediately given the coveted award of merit by the Royal Horticultural Society. At the Villa Taranto Botanic Gardens on Lake Maggiore in northern Italy, I grew specimens equally well in complete shade and partial sun, but found that the plants require a cool, reasonably moist soil. It is a lovely honeysuckle with all the good qualities except one: it has no fragrance. Leaves elliptical-ovate, $2-3\frac{1}{2}$ ins. long and about half as wide. Inflorescence a terminal cluster of 6–12 flowers borne on the previous season's growth. The individual blooms have a slender tubular form, 2 ins. long and 1 in. wide at their two-lipped mouth. Colour a lovely shade of yellow suffused bronze-red. Fruits scarlet-red.

Deciduous climber
Flowering period: June–July
Height: up to 20 ft.
Zone 4 southwards

Lonicera thibetica Bureau & Franch.
Native to Tibet. A distinctive, charming, hardy deciduous shrub up to 5–6 ft. high and often 10 feet in diameter, with a pleasing rounded form. Young growth is greenish purple, the mature branches have peeling bark. Leaves generally in groups of three, elongated-oblong, pointed, up to 1 in. long and $\frac{1}{3}$ in. wide; upper surface shiny dark green, undersurface densely covered with white down. Flowers in pairs formed in the leaf axils of the new growths, up to six together, $\frac{1}{3}$ in. wide, lilac-coloured and lilac-scented. Fruits oval, $\frac{1}{4}$ in. long, red.

Deciduous shrub
Flowering period: May–June
Height: up to 6 ft.
Scented
Zone 4 southwards

Lonicera Xylosteum L.
Native to Europe. A deciduous shrub of compact bushy habit; young growths hairy or woolly. Leaves obovate, up to $2\frac{1}{2}$ ins. long, downy on either surface. Flowers ivory-white, occasionally suffused red, borne in pairs, two-lipped, $\frac{2}{3}$ in. long. Fruits red, and very decorative in autumn.

(European Fly Honeysuckle)
Deciduous shrub
Flowering period: May–June
Height: up to 10 ft.
Zone 4 southwards

Deciduous climber
Flowering period: June
Height: up to 15 ft.
Zone 7 southwards

Lonicera yunnanensis Franch.
Native to the Yunnan province of China. A trailing dwarf species which, with support, can be trained to climb up to 15 ft. Stems very slender and glabrous. Leaves narrowly oval, up to 3 ins. long and 1 in. wide; glabrous on the upper surface, glaucous and downy beneath, those towards the ends of the stems united at their base and stalkless. Flowers yellow, 1 in. long, borne in compact terminal whorls.

Lunaria

(HONESTY, SATIN FLOWER, MOON WORT, SILVER SHILLING, OR ST. PETER'S PENCE)
Family: Cruciferae
Annual, biennial, or herbaceous perennials
Position: semi-shade
Propagation: seed
Cultivation easy
Useful for cutting

The name of this genus—from the adjective "lunar", pertaining to the moon—derives from the form and colour of the silvery white membrane-like transparent disc (about the size and shape of an old-fashioned British penny piece) which bears the seeds. These curious seed cases, or pods (silicles), are freely borne on tall stiff stems which can be cut and dried for indoor decoration. If carefully handled they will last for years.

There are only three species distributed between Central Europe and Southeastern Europe. They first became popular in medieval gardens, more for their decorative seed cases than for their flowers, which, however, are attractively coloured and certainly not to be deprecated. Lunarias reached their maximum popularity in the nineteenth century, when all types of dried flowers, leaves, seeds, and even wax fruits, were so popular in the Victorian drawing-room. Occasionally, and with the greatest patience, these small moon-like seed-bearing cases were hand-painted with designs. Thus embellished, they certainly helped to brighten the dull winter days of many English homes.

In their natural habitat, lunarias are woodland plants and should therefore be planted in half or even complete shade. They are more suited to large park-like areas and extensive gardens (where they can be grown in big informal masses) than to small beds or borders.

Lunaria annua

Two species are in general cultivation, *L. annua* and *L. rediviva*; the first is an annual or biennial, while the second is a perennial. They are hardy, and have no particular demands, thriving in any normal fertile garden soil which is cool, moist, and fresh. Seed can be sown in spring, preferably in the position where the plants are to bloom, because once grown they are not easily or successfully transplanted.

Lunaria annua L. (syn. *Lunaria biennis*)
Native to Europe. Conveniently grown as an annual but really a biennial, sometimes even living for three years. If sown early in the season, it will bloom and produce its round flat moon-like silicles (seed cases) the same year. Flowers reddish-violet, 1 in. wide, scented; leaves dark green, dentated, and somewhat coarse in appearance. The disc-like flat silicles are $1\frac{1}{2}$ ins. in diameter, and when cut and dried are much appreciated for indoor use. There is also a white-flowered form.

Annual or biennial
Flowering period: April–May
Height: $1–2\frac{1}{2}$ ft.

Lunaria rediviva L.
Native to Europe. Similar to the preceding but perennial, with less effective large oval silicles. The flowers appear the second year after sowing, and are violet-coloured and violet-scented, particularly at night.

Perennial
Flowering period: May–July
Height: $1\frac{1}{2}–2$ ft.
Scented

Lupinus

(LUPINE)
Family: Leguminosae
Hardy annuals and herbaceous perennials, or tender evergreen shrubs
Position: sun
Propagation: seed, division, or cuttings
Cultivation not always easy
Useful for cutting

Lupinus albus.

The famous French nurseryman Vilmorin devotes eight or nine pages to lupines and illustrates sixteen species—eloquent testimony to their popularity in France. By contrast, Italian botanical sources do not even mention them, and it is the exception rather than the rule to see them in Italian gardens. Lupines are, however, widely grown in Great Britain, Germany, and, in particular, in the United States (which is as it should be, considering that the majority of the species are native to eastern North America, where in certain climatically favourable zones lupines grow so profusely that thousands upon thousands blaze with blue-and-white splendour).

Not all districts, however, are suited to the cultivation of lupines, and even the magnificent modern hybrids can be capricious if conditions are not exactly to their liking. Lupines require an abundance of sun and a liberal supply of water during their growing season; but they cannot tolerate an alkaline (calcareous) soil, and it can often kill them off. Thus, when growing lupines in the garden one should always remember—no lime but plenty of sun and water.

What might be considered a defect, or an undesirable characteristic, in perennial lupines, is their somewhat gaunt and angular habit, with hard, rigid stems and inflorescences as straight as a candle. In spite of their wide range of vivid colours, they do not always easily blend with other plants and it must be confessed that after flowering the plants are anything but elegant or attractive for many weeks. This point is a strong argument in favour of growing them in nursery beds, or in some not-too-visible part of the garden, where they can be visited during their period of glory, and where they can be cultivated exclusively for use as cut blooms, a purpose for which they are ideal. The plants are also much more effective when massed. Curiously enough, when cut and arranged in vases, the tall spikes lose their rigidity and contort themselves into all kinds of fascinating twists and turns as if seeking to escape and return to the garden. The colours of the flowers are superb, with a limitless range of tints which seem to be even more varied and more effective at twilight.

The cultivation of lupines goes back to the most ancient times, but they were not always cultivated as ornamental plants. According to some authorities their cultivation extends back to 4000 B.C. Lupine seeds have been found in tombs of the Pharaohs, and we know for certain that as early as 2000 B.C. the Egyptians grew *Lupinus termis* for food, boiling the seeds (which resemble lima beans) in water to eliminate their bitter taste and to loosen their tough outer skin. Other species cultivated in Antiquity were *Lupinus angustifolius,* and the white-seeded *Lupinus graecus,* and *Lupinus albus.* The seeds of the last-named, after having soaked in water for a lengthy period and then dried, were considered a delicacy and were commonly sold in the streets of ancient Rome (in the same way that sunflower seeds are sold in Russia and certain Continental countries). These delicacies were also distributed gratis by victorious generals when welcomed home by cheering crowds, by vote-seekers to public office, and by the authorities on national holidays. In Italy, until a few years ago (before the age of bubble gum), itinerant vendors on tricycles could be seen stationed outside schools selling what were probably the identical type of lupine seeds relished by ancient Romans two

Lupinus arboreus

thousand years ago. Packed in cans or jars, they frequently appear in the "Italian food sections" of American supermarkets.

At present, the most widely cultivated species is *Lupinus luteus,* native throughout the Mediterranean regions, and largely grown as a food crop in Central Europe and in Russia. At one time it was cultivated only as green manure for enriching the soil, but following repeated selection several improved species have been obtained; these are generally grown in sandy soils, and they serve numerous purposes. Seed is generally sown in autumn and the plants are harvested in early summer, yielding a crop of seed rich in nitrogenous materials (up to 45 percent) and also containing a good percentage of oil (up to $11\frac{1}{2}$ percent). They are used in place of chicory in coffee substitutes, or ground into meal and blended with oat, pea, and bean flours and used in bread and other baked goods. The green plants are also employed as cattle fodder. Generally the seed is sown after wheat has been harvested, as inter-cropping, to exploit the land to its maximum. Like all other Leguminosae, when ploughed into the soil the plants also improve its quality because of the nitrogen they manufacture.

Lupines contain alkaloids, chemically similar to sparteine, in the form of lupinine, lupanine, and lupinic acid; together with organic acids such as cholesterin. The continuous consumption of lupine seed can eventually cause a condition known as lupinosis, a type of jaundice accompanied by a high temperature. It is believed that lupinine may be useful in medicine as a substitute for insulin in the treatment of diabetes.

Lupinus polyphyllus, chief parent of the most beautiful of all the hybrid garden lupines, was introduced into Europe from North America in 1826. Its fame began in 1911 due to the patient work of George Russell, an English gardener who for many years devoted his life to the hybridization and selection of lupines until eventually he produced the famous strain that bears his name. His work involved the use of numerous species as parents, in particular *Lupinus laxiflorus, Lupinus lepidus, Lupinus nootkatensis, Lupinus mutabilis, Lupinus leucophyllus,* and *Lupinus polyphyllus.* The final results are a strain with larger individual flowers, bigger spikes of bloom, and better-shaped inflorescences; but their real glory lies in their remarkable colours which have so changed the appearance of our flower beds and herbaceous borders. Some are of one colour, some of two shades of the same colour, while others are bicoloured with a mixture of contrasting hues.

Certain plants have the ability of turning their flowers so that they constantly face the sun, and follow its course from sunrise to sunset. Lupines, however, go even further, and if one has forgotten one's watch they can be used as a rudimentary timekeeper; throughout the day the leaves constantly follow the course of the sun, even when the weather is cloudy. Therefore, with a little practice, by observing their position it is possible to approximately estimate the position of the sun and thereby tell the time.

There are many lupine species, anywhere from one hundred to three hundred according to the various botanists who have classified them. As already mentioned, they are nearly all American, native to an area extending from the southern part of the Northern Hemisphere as far south as northern Chile, flourishing generally in warm to temperate climates or in the mountainous areas of the tropics. There are only a few European or Asiatic species, principally: *Lupinus angustifolius, Lupinus hirsutus, Lupinus albus,* and *Lupinus luteus.* The name of the genus *Lupinus* derives from Greek and not from Latin as might be supposed; moreover, the name has nothing to do with *lupi* (wolves), and refers more likely to *lype* (which signifies pain, sadness, bitterness). The plant was so named for two reasons: because the seeds have a bitter flavour if eaten raw, and because the seeds were considered a food of the poor and miserable. The genus was named by J. P. de Tournefort.

Cultivation. We have already referred to the potential difficulty in the cultivation of lupines (because they are lime-haters). In actual fact, however, it is not that the plants themselves are difficult; the difficulty lies in finding garden conditions that are favourable to the plants' development.

Light, sandy, silica-rich soils are most suited to lupines—being even better than peaty, acid soils—in a sunny but ventilated position, with water in abundance. They should always, however, be in a neutral and never alkaline (calcareous) soil. Lupines are particularly suited to seaside locations.

Seed of the perennial species can be sown in July, pricking out the seedlings individually into small fibre (or peat) pots and then planting them the following spring; they take a year to reach flowering size. A new dwarf strain of the famous Russell Hybrids has recently appeared on the market—if sown in an unheated greenhouse or coldframe in March it will bloom the same season. Another difficulty in the cultivation of lupines is that they do not like being moved or having their roots disturbed in any manner, so seed must either be sown in the plants' flowering position, or in small fibre (or peat) pots (or pricked out into such pots when still tiny, before the tap-root begins to form). If it is desired to propagate certain plants of a particular colour from seed, the matter becomes more complicated, as flowers from self-sown seed appear in a widely random range of colours. Once planted, and having reached flowering size so that the desired colour can be selected, it is not easy to move the plants because of the long tap-root which penetrates deeply into the soil and which, if broken, seriously damages the plant. To overcome this problem, the seedlings should be continuously repotted and then

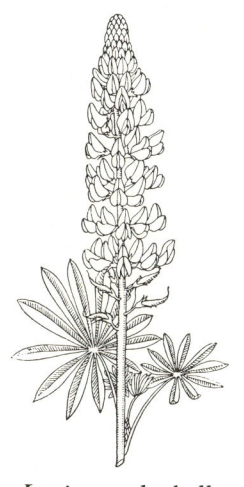

Lupinus polyphyllus

Lupinus mutabilis
From *Curtis's Botanical Magazine*,
1826, plate 2682

cultivated in large pots until they reach flowering size. The colour of the blooms thus determined, they can then be planted out, taking the greatest care not to break the root ball. To avoid so much trouble it is easier to propagate from cuttings, which can be taken from the new growth in spring, if possible with a fragment of root from the parent plant. Propagation by division is another method; it is best done in early autumn, but in this case the problem of root damage is always present. The seed of annual lupines should be sown in its flowering position in April, or in small fibre (or peat) pots (two seeds per pot) in an unheated greenhouse or coldframe in March. The seedlings should be subsequently planted out complete with their pots to avoid disturbing the roots.

(Tree Lupine)
Evergreen shrub
Flowering period: May–Aug.
Height: up to 9 ft.
Scented
Zone 9 southwards

Lupinus arboreus Sims
Native to California. A tender evergreen shrub up to 9 ft. high and 6 ft. in diameter. Of rapid vigorous growth and of the greatest beauty when in full bloom. An ideal plant for warm, dry climates (and seaside localities) in full sun. Leaves digitate, generally with nine glaucous-green leaflets each up to 2 ins. long and about a third as wide—oval-lanceolate, pointed. Inflorescence an erect terminal raceme up to 10 ins. high, composed of numerous small pale-yellow typically lupine-like scented flowers. If dead blooms are regularly removed to prevent the formation of seed, the flowering period will last from May to August. In a rich soil the plants will thrive but their life will be relatively brief (five to six years). They will, however, flourish and live far longer in light, moderately poor soil. There are forms with white, blue, or purple flowers.

Annual
Flowering period: July–Sept.
Height: up to 3 ft.

Lupinus hartwegii Lindl.
Native to Mexico. A delightful annual species with a branching habit. Leaves dark green, divided into 7–9 leaflets, rather hairy. Inflorescence a compact spike of vivid-blue flowers flushed pink on the standard (the erect petal at the rear of the flower). There are numerous forms with white, sky-blue, or dark-red flowers. The var. *nanus* is a dwarf and grows to only 18 ins. high.

Annual
Flowering period: May–June
Height: up to 2 ft.
Strongly scented

Lupinus luteus L.
Native to Europe. A hardy annual species up to 2 ft. high with small digitate dark-green leaves divided into 8–9 lanceolate hairy segments. Inflorescences on erect stems in the form of rigid spikes 10 ins. high, composed of dense masses of strongly scented yellow flowers.

Annual
Flowering period: May–June
Height: 3–4½ ft.
Scented

Lupinus mutabilis L.
Native to South America. A much-branched hardy tall annual species up to 4½ ft. high. Leaves glaucous green, digitate, divided into long thin segments with long stalks. Inflorescence an erect spike up to 18

ins. high, very decorative, composed of numerous large widely spaced sweetly scented white flowers with the rear erect petal (the standard) often flushed blue and with yellow markings, but the colour can vary. A beautiful plant worthy of wider cultivation. There are several varieties of equal beauty, including:

> var. *cruckshanksii* (syn. *Lupinus cruckshanksii*) with vivid-blue flowers suffused white, yellow, or purple
> var. *roseus,* pink-flowered
> var. *versicolor,* with blue flowers which deepen in colour with age

Lupinus nanus Dougl.
Native to California. An attractive free-flowering small species, little more than 1 ft. in height. Stems much branched, bearing light-green foliage, hairy, and divided into 5–7 segments. Freely produced inflorescences in the form of short spikes of relatively large blue flowers, the standard bearing a white spot dotted purple. Particularly effective when massed.

Annual
Flowering period: May–June
Height: 12–15 ins.

Lupinus perennis L.
Native to the eastern United States, where it is a common wild flower with the picturesque common name of Quaker Bonnet. A hardy herbaceous perennial up to 2 ft. high, hairy in all its parts. Flowers variable in colour, from blue to nearly white. Requires a rather dry light sandy soil, and can be of considerable value in poor soils in seaside localities.

(Quaker Bonnet)
Herbaceous perennial
Flowering period: June–July
Height: 1–2 ft.

Lupinus polyphyllus Lindl.
Native to North America. A hardy herbaceous perennial of vigorous habit and an excellent garden plant. Digitate leaves, large, dark green, and much divided, forming a mass of basal vegetation. Vigorous, robust, erect flower stems with the top half bearing a large spike-shaped inflorescence composed of a mass of blue or blue-and-white flowers. A quarter-century ago this was a very popular plant for herbaceous borders and beds, but with the introduction of the spectacular Russell Hybrids the original species is rarely cultivated.

Herbaceous perennial
Flowering period: June–July
Height: up to 5 ft.
Fragrant
Useful for cutting

Lupinus Russell Hybrids
The origin and history of these remarkable hybrids is given above. All bloom within the period late May–early July, and their average height is $2\frac{1}{2}$–3 ft. When raised from seed the plants take about a year to reach flowering size. In the gardening world the name of George Russell has become immortal, and some of the best of his hybrids are:

Alice Parrett, pale cream   Betty Astell, pink

Billy Wright, dark pink & white
Charmaine, orange-salmon
Commando, mauve & yellow
Daydream, pink & yellow
Eleanor Richards, yellow & orange
George Russell, pink & yellow
Josephine, blue & gold
Maud Tippets, orange-red
Susan of York, yellow & red
Blue Jacket, dark blue & yellow
City of York, light & dark red
Cynthia Knight, violet & white
Dusky Minstrel, plum-red & yellow
Firedrake, orange-pink & gold
Heatherglow, purple & bronze
Lilac Time, pink & mauve
Melody, carmine-red & ivory
Torchlight, apricot & yellow

These hybrids can only be propagated by vegetative means (division or cuttings) as they do not breed true from seed. It is, however, possible to buy true-to-name young plants.

Lychnis

(CAMPION OR CATCHFLY)
(*Also see* SILENE)
Family: Caryophyllaceae
Hardy or tender annuals or herbaceous perennials
Position: sun
Propagation: seed or division
Cultivation easy

Lychnis is another genus whose nomenclature the botanists, with their continuous but officially legitimate reclassifications, have succeeded in rendering confused and complicated. According to these scientific enthusiasts, the genus *Lychnis* should be divided into three separate genera: *Melandrium, Viscaria,* and *Agrostemma,* which are given here as synonyms after the name of each species referred to. The name *Lychnis* derives from the Greek and means "lamp", possibly because of the flame-coloured flowers of some species, although the blooms much resemble miniature single pinks (dianthus) and, in fact, they belong to the same family.

The genus comprises about thirty-five species of annuals and herbaceous perennials native to Europe and Asiatic Russia, several of which are renowned for their vividly coloured blooms and long-flowering habit. They thrive in any fertile soil, are completely hardy, and love the sun; but in very hot climates they should be planted in semi-shade. The perennial species can be propagated by seed or division. Seed can be sown in March–April in pans in a greenhouse or frame;

the seedlings should be pricked out into flats, boxes, or trays and subsequently transferred into small pots prior to planting out permanently in spring or autumn. From spring-sown seed it is generally possible to obtain late-summer-flowering plants. Division of established plants is best done in cold climates in the spring, but in mild localities it can also be done in autumn. Seed of the annual lychnis should be sown in spring in its flowering position.

Lychnis chalcedonica L. (Scarlet Lychnis, Jerusalem Cross, Maltese Cross or Scarlet Lightning)
Herbaceous perennial
Flowering period: May–July
Height: up to 2½ ft.

Native to northern Russia and Siberia but sometimes found naturalized in Europe. One of the most decorative of the species and cultivated in gardens for hundreds of years. Leaves oval, rough-surfaced, stalkless. Flowers vivid scarlet with the petals arranged in the form of a Maltese cross about 1 in. wide and borne in dense terminal groups on stems up to 2½ ft. high. There are pink- and white-flowered forms, and also double red and double white varieties, but these are rare.

Lychnis Coeli-rosa Desr. (syn. *Agrostemma Coeli-rosa*) (Rose of Heaven)
Annual
Flowering period: May–July
Height: 12 ins.

Native to Eastern Europe, generally found in rather dry stony soils. The typical species has pink or purple-pink flowers ⅔ in. in diameter and has been grown in gardens since 1713. From this species a group of very beautiful garden hybrids has evolved which are ideal for beds, borders, and pot culture. They are often sold under the name of *Lychnis oculata* or *Viscaria oculata,* and generally as a mixture, with abundant pink, scarlet, blue, violet, or white flowers. These are about 1 ft. high but there is also a dwarf strain only 6 ins. high:

    var. *Tom Thumb Blue Gem,* blue
    var. *Tom Thumb Innocence,* white
    var. *Tom Thumb Rosy Gem,* pink

Lychnis coronaria Desr. (syn. *Agrostemma coronaria*) (Mullein Pink, Dusty Miller, or Rose Campion)
Herbaceous perennial
Flowering period: May–July
Height: up to 2 ft.

Native to Southern Europe. A perennial species with a white woolly appearance owing to its dense covering of silvery hairs. Leaves elongated, oblong, and soft-surfaced. Flowers an intense vivid pink or pinkish crimson, 1 in. in diameter, with rounded petals. There are various forms with white or pale-pink flowers. A very common and very easily grown plant effective for its foliage and flowers.

Lychnis coronata Thunb. (syn. *Lychnis grandiflora, Lychnis bungeana*) *Annual*
Flowering period: June–Sept.
Height: 18 ins.

Native to China and Japan, introduced into Europe in 1744. Normally grown as an annual and not hardy, but actually a biennial. Seed sown in early spring will produce flowering plants the same season. An erect glabrous plant with stalkless ovate foliage forming a dense mass of basal vegetation. The flowers are borne in an open spreading inflorescence carried by rigid stems 18 ins. high. The

Lychnis coronaria
From *Curtis's Botanical Magazine*,
1787, plate 24

colour is variable, from brick-red to pale pink; each flower 2 ins. wide with incised petals. There are two very beautiful varieties:

> var. *sieboldii* (syn. *Lychnis sieboldii*), with large white flowers
> var. *speciosa* (syn. *Lychnis japonica speciosa*), more bushy in habit, with narrower leaves and larger scarlet flowers

Lychnis Viscaria 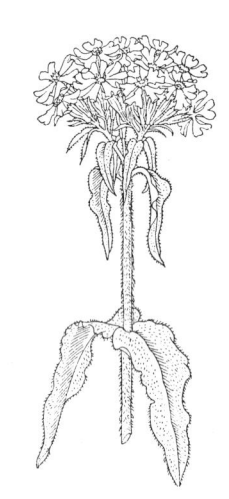   *Lychnis chalcedonica*    *Lychnis coronata*

Lychnis Flos-cuculi L. (syn. *Agrostemma Flos-cuculi*)
Native to Europe and Western Asia. Slightly hairy erect stems up to 18 ins. high and slightly sticky towards the top. Leaves narrowly lanceolate, stalkless in the case of those that are stem borne. Flowers pink (rarely white) in loose panicles, the petals divided for half their length into four narrow segments, giving the blooms their typical "ragged" appearance. There is also a double-flowered form.

(Cuckoo Flower or Ragged Robin)
Herbaceous perennial
Flowering period: Apr.–July
Height: 12–18 ins.

Lychnis Flos-Jovis L. (syn. *Agrostemma Flos-Jovis*)
Native to Southern Europe, growing particularly in the lower mountainous regions in poor stony soil. Both the stems and the foliage are covered with white woolly hair. Leaves oblong, stalkless. Flowers reddish purple, $\frac{1}{2}$ in. wide and borne in dense umbels.

(Flower of Jove)
Herbaceous perennial
Flowering period: Apr.–June
Height: up to 2 ft.

Lychnis x *Haageana*
A perennial of hybrid origin (*Lychnis fulgens* Fisch. x *Lychnis coronata* Thunb., var. *sieboldii*). Flowers in shades of red, orange, or crimson, 2 ins. in diameter, in groups of two or three, with bilobed petals. The entire plant is slightly hairy and is not hardy. It requires a rather dry soil and, in the south, partial shade.

Herbaceous perennial
Flowering period: June–July
Height: 1 ft.

Lychnis Flos-Jovis
From *Curtis's Botanical Magazine*,
1798, plate 398

Lychnis pyrenaica L.
Native to the Pyrenees. A dwarf alpine species excellent for the rock-garden, but not tolerant of hot and dry conditions at low altitudes. Basal foliage spatulate, $1\frac{1}{2}$ ins. long, stem leaves heart-shaped. Flowers solitary, long-stalked, $\frac{1}{4}$ in. wide, pink.

Herbaceous perennial
Flowering period: June
Height: 4 ins.

Lychnis Viscaria L. (syn. *Viscaria viscosa*)
Native to Southern Europe and to Asia. The tops of the stems are sticky enough (as the common name indicates) to trap any small fly that lights upon them. Leaves narrow, long and tapering, with a shiny surface. Flowers pinkish red, borne in elongated panicles, and with the tips of the petals notched. The var. *splendens plena* with double flowers is particularly attractive.

(German Catchfly)
Herbaceous perennial
Flowering period: May–July
Height: 18 ins.

Magnolia

Family: Magnoliaceae
Hardy deciduous or half-hardy evergreen shrubs or trees
Position: partial shade or sun
Propagation: seed, cuttings, grafts, or layers
Cultivation easy
Fragrant
Useful for cutting

Magnolia macrophylla

In this book we have been concerned with shrubs rather than trees, but it would be wronging many fine magnolias if we considered them shrubs. A considerable proportion of the genus does include some of the most noble trees, deserving a volume all to themselves. Yet, we cannot ignore the genus completely, since many species have the proportions of shrubs—some small, some large, and some that can be classified as either large shrubs or small trees—all of which have a legitimate place in these pages. Our enthusiasm for the genus may tempt us to refer to some species that definitely are trees. W. J. Bean, in his monumental work *Trees and Shrubs Hardy in the British Isles,* unequivocally states, "In one respect magnolias are the most splendid of all hardy trees, for in the size of their individual flowers they are easily first; the evergreen species, too, have some of the largest leaves of all evergreen trees hardy with us. . . . Perhaps no group of exotic trees gives more distinction to a garden than a comprehensive collection of Magnolias. There is not one that is not worthy of cultivation."

Magnolia x *soulangiana*

Traces of the genus *Magnolia* can be found in the most remote prehistoric eras. Geological finds have revealed the existence of more than eighty species of magnolia in fossilized form dating back five million years. Today we know only about eighty living species, fifty of which are native to the East, from Japan and the eastern Himalayas south to Java, and about twenty-five are native to the New World, western Ontario, the eastern United States, Mexico, Venezuela, and the Antilles. Strangely enough, no natural hybrids have ever been found, although garden hybrids are plentiful. There are about thirty species now in general cultivation; the majority will tolerate even such severe cold as that experienced in Great Britain, Germany, northern Italy, and much of the United States. The American species were the first magnolias to be discovered; *Magnolia virginiana* was first sent to Bishop Compton in England by John Banister in 1688; while the same species reached the Pavia and, Pisa botanic gardens in 1760. Cobbett writes that the perfume of *Magnolia virginiana* flowers was "the most delicious imaginable, far superior to that of roses, and equal in intensity to that of jasmine and tuberoses, but much more delicious." The other early American arrival in Europe, now very widely planted, was *Magnolia grandiflora*. According to Catesby, it bloomed in England in 1737. In its native habitat, this noble tree reaches a height of 100 ft. and, although such proportions are rarely attained in European gardens, many truly monumental specimens can be found in Southern Europe and, in northern Italy. According to legend, North American Indians refused to sleep under a flowering *Magnolia grandiflora* tree because of the intensity of its flowers' scent; there also is a belief that a single flower kept in a closed bedroom at night can be fatal to the sleeping occupant.

The first Asiatic species to reach Europe was *Magnolia denudata,* introduced into England from China about 1789 by Sir Joseph Banks. This species was cultivated in China since the seventh century, both in temple and palace gardens as well as in pots. According to John Claudius Loudon, a fine blooming pot-grown specimen was so highly esteemed that it was considered a fitting gift to the Emperor himself. *Magnolia liliflora* is the smallest shrub of the genus and was imported from Japan in 1790 by Carl Peter Thunberg, quickly becoming widely diffused in Europe. By crossing *Magnolia denudata* with *Magnolia liliflora* in 1826, Soulange-Bodin obtained the hybrid *Magnolia* x *soulangiana*. *Magnolia salicifolia* was introduced into England in 1906; *Magnolia stellata* was discovered in 1862 by Richard Oldham, but was only introduced into Europe in 1878, by the firm of Veitch; both are native to Japan.

The genus *Magnolia* was so named by Plumier in honour of Pierre Magnol (1638–1715), author of *Botanicum Montpeliensis* (1676) and of *Prodromus Historia Generalis Plantarum* (1689). Wilson and Bell furnished the most detailed particulars about the fragrance of magnolia flowers. *Magnolia stellata* has a perfume of "melon and honey mixed with Easter lilies", a scent also transmitted to its forms and varieties such as Waterlily, Royal Star, var. *rosea,* and var. *rubra.* The most fragrant, although not the most agreeable, is *Magnolia kobus* with "an orange and pineapple aroma sweetened by a trace of lily"; *Magnolia denudata* has a similar but weaker perfume. The bark and foliage of magnolias has a pleasing but slightly pungent fragrance when bruised, as do the superficial roots. *Magnolia liliflora* flowers also have a unique scent similar to raspberries. *Magnolia virginiana* blooms vary in fragrance from plant to plant; some are almost scentless, while others combine the fragrance of gardenias and lilies. *Magnolia grandiflora* has an indisputably lemon scent, *Magnolia macrophylla* blooms are sweetly fragrant, as are those of the late-flowering *Magnolia sieboldii*. One exceptionally strongly scented small evergreen shrub is sometimes offered by nurserymen as *Magnolia fuscata*; actually this plant belongs to another genus entirely and is *Michelia fuscata* (syn. *Michelia fico*). This *Michelia* is one of the most strongly scented of all flowering shrubs, with a fruity perfume recalling the old-fashioned sweets, pear-drops.

Cultivation. Magnolias require a deep substantial soil that retains moisture but that is at the same time well-drained. The soil should be of a peaty leafsoil texture rich in organic matter and slightly acid in a partially shaded position. *Magnolia virginiana* especially requires a rather damp position. All species will benefit greatly from an annual mulching or top dressing composed of equal parts of peat, leafsoil, and composted manure. Species can be propagated from seed sown as soon as it is ripe, outside in nursery beds or in boxes. Owing to the seeds' oily nature, they do not keep well unless stored in slightly moist moss or peat. Propagation from seed is, however, a terribly slow process and advisable only for those who have a long life expectancy. Propagation by semi-woody cuttings treated with a root-forming hormone product, in frames in late summer, is moderately successful. But the most efficient methods are air layering, ground layering, and grafting onto young plants of *Magnolia kobus* or *Magnolia liliflora* raised from seed. Most deciduous magnolias bloom before the leaves appear, but late-flowering species flower simultaneously with the appearance of the young foliage. The branches of all species are superb for cutting and the flowers will last well in water.

Magnolia acuminata L. (Cucumber Tree)
Deciduous tree
Flowering period: Apr.–May
Height: up to 100 ft.
Zone 5 southwards

Native to eastern North America. A real tree up to 100 ft. high, forming a trunk 12 ft. in circumference. Leaves up to 10 ins. long and half as wide, oval-oblong, bright green, pointed, rounded at the base, undersurface downy. Flowers are among the least interesting of all magnolias, greenish yellow with the 2–3-in.-long petals arranged in two circlets of three each. The fruits, however, are very

Magnolia denudata
From *Curtis's Botanical Magazine*,
1814, plate 1621

beautiful, up to 4 ins. long, cucumber-shaped, green when young but ripening to a lovely dark red and bearing many seeds. There is a var. *variegata* with the leaves irregularly splashed golden-yellow.

Magnolia campbellii Hook. f.
Native to the Himalayas, found at a height of up to 3,500 ft. Leaves up to 10 ins. long, oval, tapering at either end. Flowers cup-shaped, each petal up to 5 ins. long, colour varying from pink to crimson. One of the most beautiful of all deciduous magnolias and the parent of some superb hybrids. Not hardy in cold regions.

Deciduous tree
Flowering period: Mar.–Apr.
Height: up to 150 ft.
Zone 9 southwards

Magnolia dawsoniana Rehd. & Wils.
Native to China. A deciduous small tree or very large shrub. Of almost incredible beauty for its flowers in March–April. The actual colour is difficult to define: the Royal Horticultural Society's official colour chart classifies it as "Spiraea Red" in the bud stage, fading to delicate pale pink when fully open. The insides of the petals are pure white. When fully expanded, each flower has a diameter of 10 ins. It is completely hardy, with a compact erect habit that makes it ideal for the smaller garden. Leaves 6 ins. long, half as wide, leathery, bright green. This magnolia is different from all other species, but, unfortunately, it is rare both in the wild and in cultivation, and it does not bloom when young. Fruits orange-scarlet when ripe. Given an award of merit by the Royal Horticultural Society in 1939. Introduced into England in 1919, where it flowered for the first time in 1937. This species was named in honour of J. Dawson, a former superintendent of the Arnold Arboretum in Boston, and principal assistant to Professor Sargent at the time of the Arboretum's formation.

Deciduous small tree
Flowering period: Mar.–Apr.
Height: up to 30 ft.
Zone 5 southwards

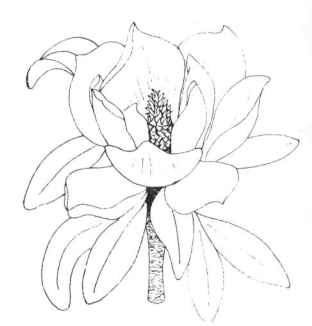

Magnolia grandiflora

Magnolia delavayi Franch.
Native to China. Introduced by E. H. Wilson in 1899. An evergreen small tree or very large shrub with long-stalked, oval foliage up to 14 ins. long and half as wide; dull grey-green on the upper surface, glaucous beneath. With the possible exception of *Rhododendron sinogrande,* this magnolia has the largest leaves of any evergreen tree or shrub cultivated in temperate-zone gardens. It is not suitable for excessively cold regions or for very windy, exposed positions. Flowers 6–8 ins. in diameter, cup-shaped, cream-white, fragrant, in May–June. Fruits cone-shaped, $4\frac{1}{2}$ ins. long. An excellent magnolia for alkaline (calcareous) soils, similar to the tree-like evergreen *Magnolia grandiflora.*

Evergreen small tree
Flowering period: May–June
Height: up to 30 ft.
Zone 7 southwards

Magnolia denudata Desr. (syn. *Magnolia conspicua, Magnolia Yulan*)
Native to China. One of the most beautiful of all early-flowering deciduous trees and reputed to have been cultivated by the Chinese

(Yulan)
Deciduous small tree
Flowering period: Mar.–Apr.
Height: up to 30 ft.
Zone 4 southwards

for more than a thousand years. It is one of the most popular of all magnolias in European and North American gardens. Maximum height about 30 ft. In its natural habitat, it has the form of a rounded small tree but in gardens it often assumes the habit of a very large shrub. Leaves 4–6 ins. long, half as wide, oval. Flowers cup-shaped, white, with 3-in.-long petals. Fruits 5 ins. long and decorative when ripe. Although completely hardy, its early-flowering habit renders the flowers liable to damage in localities where late spring frosts are experienced.

Deciduous small tree
Flowering period: May–June
Height: up to 45 ft.
Zone 4 southwards

Magnolia fraseri Walter (syn. *Magnolia auriculata* Lam.)
Native to the southeastern United States. A wide-spreading, deciduous small tree with an open habit and a height up to 45 ft. Originally discovered by William Bartram in 1776, but named in honour of John Fraser who introduced the species into England in 1786 (together with many other North American plants during the period 1780–1810). Leaves up to 6 ins. long, half as wide, long-stalked, light green, pointed, obovate, borne in groups or clusters at the branches' extremities, and with two long auricles (or ear-like lobes) at their base; this characteristic is shared by only two other species, *M. macrophylla* and *M. pyramidata*. Flowers 8 ins. in diameter, with a strong not always pleasing scent; light yellow fading to ivory-white, borne in May–June when the branches are already in leaf. Fruits pink, 5 ins. long, cone-shaped. Seeds scarlet.

(Bull Bay, Evergreen Magnolia, or Big-leaved Magnolia)
Evergreen tree
Flowering period: spring–autumn
Height: up to 100 ft.
Zone 7 southwards

Magnolia grandiflora L. (syn. *Magnolia foetida*)
Native to the southern United States. Introduced into Europe early in the eighteenth century and undoubtedly the finest of all hardy evergreen flowering trees. The enormous lemon-scented white blossoms are produced more or less continuously from late spring until autumn; globular in shape, up to 10 ins. in diameter when fully expanded. The beautiful foliage is always attractive, ovate in form, up to 10 ins. long, pointed, leathery and tough-textured, dark shiny green above, with the undersurface covered in a thick rust-coloured down. The fruits are also of great beauty, up to 4 ins. long, roughly egg-shaped, with brilliant scarlet-red seeds. As it is a very large tree, it is beyond the scope of this work, although this brief mention is essential. There are numerous forms and varieties. Excellent for alkaline (calcareous) soils.

Deciduous small tree
Flowering period: April
Height: up to 30 ft.
Zone 4 southwards

Magnolia kobus D.C.
Native to Japan. This is the hardiest magnolia and the easiest to cultivate, thriving even in complete shade and in alkaline (calcareous) soils. Forms a small deciduous tree or a very large shrub up to 30 ft. high, but it does not bloom until it reaches a considerable size. The white flowers are much smaller than those of other tree magnolias,

only 3–3½ ins. in diameter, but they are borne in such abundance that they cover the plant completely in April. The pink fruits are among the most attractive of all magnolia fruits, especially when the scarlet seeds begin to emerge. Leaves up to 5 ins. long, ovate. The var. *borealis* is an even more attractive plant, with larger proportions and larger cream-white flowers.

Magnolia x *lennei* Van Houtte

Deciduous shrub
Flowering period: April
Height: up to 20 ft.
Zone 5 southwards

Of hybrid origin. Forms a very large spreading shrub-like small tree. The origin of this attractive deciduous magnolia is something of a mystery, and there is reason to suspect that it was first raised in Italy. The late W. J. Bean explains the origin of *Magnolia* x *lennei* as follows in his *Trees and Shrubs Hardy in the British Isles*: "This remarkable magnolia is said to have originated accidentally in Lombardy, where it was noticed by an Erfurt nurseryman named Tupf in 1850, and by him introduced to Germany. It was figured by Van Houtte in *Flore des Serres* (fig. 1693) and named in honour of M. Lenné, a royal gardener in Berlin." It is certainly one of the best deciduous hybrid magnolias and is considered to be a hybrid from the same parents as *Magnolia* x *soulangiana* (that is, *Magnolia denudata* x *Magnolia liliflora*). The leaves are 8 ins. long and 4½ ins. wide; the flowers have broad fleshy petals that form a large globular bloom 5 ins. high, with each petal of a similar width; pinkish purple externally, white internally. A few flowers are also produced in autumn.

Magnolia *liliflora* Desr. (syn. *Magnolia purpurea*)

Deciduous shrub
Flowering period: Apr.–June
Height: up to 12 ft.
Zone 5 southwards

Native to China. Introduced into Europe in 1790. A large deciduous shrub with a loose open habit. Leaves 4–8 ins. long and about half as wide, pointed, dark green. Flowering period longer than most magnolias, often prolonged from April to June, when the plants are in leaf, while a second less abundant flowering generally occurs in early autumn. Individual blooms upright, narrow; petals 3–4 ins. long and about 1½ ins. wide. Irregular in colour but white inside, reddish purple shading to white outside. There are several attractive varieties:

- var. *nigra,* a more compact habit, larger and longer flowers, and a very dark purple externally
- var. *purpurea,* a larger-flowered form, with petals dark purple at the base shading to pinkish purple towards the tips

Magnolia *macrophylla* Michx.

Deciduous tree
Flowering period: Apr.–May
Height: up to 60 ft.
Zone 7 southwards

Native to the southeastern United States, but rare and found only in restricted areas. A large deciduous tree which, as W. J. Bean remarks, "is one of the most interesting of the world's trees." The leaves are the largest of all species, up to 3 ft. long and 1 ft. wide,

Magnolia liliflora var. *purpurea*
From *Curtis's Botanical Magazine*,
1797, plate 390

auriculate at the base. Flowers cream-white with a pinkish-mauve mark at the base of each petal, up to 16 ins. in diameter, fragrant. Fruits are the size and shape of a large egg, pink, and very ornamental when the coral-tinted seeds begin to emerge. In all respects, this is a beautiful, unusual tree, easy to cultivate and hardy in its adult stage, but young plants are liable to be damaged by hard frost. Numerous very fine specimens can be found in European gardens, although, unfortunately, inferior large-leaved magnolias are sometimes offered for sale in place of the true species. The real plant is easily distinguised when in leaf by the conspicuous auricules (lobes) at the base of the leaves.

Magnolia stellata   *Magnolia sieboldii*   *Magnolia obovata*

Magnolia obovata Thunb. (syn. *Magnolia hypoleuca* Sieb. & Zucc.) Native to Japan. One of the most beautiful hardy flowering trees, and widely planted in European and North American gardens. Height up to 100 ft. Leaves 18 ins. long and half as wide; flowers 8 ins. in diameter, strongly scented, cream-white. Introduced into Europe in 1884. The ripe fruits are particularly attractive, vivid red, cone-shaped, 8 ins. high, 3 ins. wide.

Deciduous tree
Flowering period: Apr.–May
Height: up to 100 ft.
Zone 4 southwards

Magnolia salicifolia Maxim.
Native to Mount Hakkoda in Japan. Introduced into Europe in 1906; flowered for the first time at Kew in 1911. A small deciduous tree with an erect compact habit, but in gardens it frequently takes the form of a very large shrub. Of particular interest for the strong lemon scent of the bark when bruised. Leaves lanceolate, 2–5 ins. long and $\frac{3}{4}$–$1\frac{1}{4}$ ins. wide. Flowers white, 4 ins. in diameter, with six petals, three of which are longer than the others. Very hardy and of the easiest cultivation.

Deciduous small tree
Flowering period: April
Height: up to 30 ft.
Zone 4 southwards

(Oyama Magnolia)
Deciduous shrub
Flowering period: May
Height: up to 10 ft.
Zone 5 southwards

Magnolia sieboldii K. Koch (syn. *Magnolia parviflora* Sieb. & Zucc.) Native to Japan and Korea. Introduced into Europe in 1893. A slender-branched deciduous shrub of relatively small proportions; generally about 10 ft. high in gardens and with a similar diameter. A late-flowering species of remarkable floral beauty. Leaves oblong, up to 6 ins. in length, dark green above, glaucous beneath. Long-stemmed cup-shaped flowers, very fragrant, semi-pendulous, 3–4 ins. in diameter, white with a mass of crimson stamens in the centre that make a splash of colour $1\frac{1}{2}$ ins. wide. The carmine fruits with their vivid scarlet seeds are also of great beauty and very freely produced. Requires an acid soil in a semi-shady cool position.

(Lily Tree)
Large deciduous shrub
Flowering period: April
Height: up to 20 ft.
Zone 3 southwards

Magnolia x *soulangiana* Soulange-Bodin
Of hybrid origin (*Magnolia denudata* x *Magnolia liliflora*). A very large deciduous shrub of spreading but shapely habit. Together with its varieties, this is the most popular and most widely planted deciduous magnolia in gardens. Raised by Soulange-Bodin at Fromont, near Paris; bloomed for the first time in 1826. Leaves up to 6 ins. long, narrowing towards the point. Flowers very large, cup-shaped, white inside, petals reddish purple on the outside and darker at the base; superb for cutting for indoor use, and a particularly easy magnolia to cultivate. Among the numerous varieties, the following deserve special mention:

> var. *alba,* white flowers and a more compact erect habit
> var. *alexandrina,* purple-red flowers
> var. *amabilis,* violet-pink and white flowers
> var. *lennei,* see *Magnolia* x *lennei*
> var. *nigra,* see *Magnolia liliflora* var. *nigra*
> var. *rustica rubra,* one of the best of the *soulangiana* hybrids with a particularly vigorous habit; very large flowers, white inside, pinkish purple outside

(Star Magnolia)
Deciduous shrub
Flowering period: Mar.–Apr.
Height: up to 15 ft.
Zone 5 southwards

Magnolia stellata Maxim. (syn. *Magnolia halleana*)
One of the most popular garden magnolias, much valued for its small compact habit and generous flowering in March–April. Believed to be native to Japan; certainly found growing wild in the woods around Mount Fuji. Suspected to be of hybrid origin because of the remarkable variation in general appearance occurring among plants raised from seed. Actually, it is impossible to propagate this species from seed with any certainty, and for this reason propagation is generally by grafting onto seedlings of *Magnolia kobus* or by air layers. Introduced into European gardens in 1878, where it rapidly became popular. The true type forms a much-branched deciduous shrub of compact habit; up to 15 ft. high, with characteristically aromatic bark. Leaves narrow, up to $3\frac{1}{2}$ ins. long. Flowers slightly fragrant, small, white, star-like, and profusely produced, with a greater number of petals

than any other magnolia, generally 12–18. There is a beautiful pale pink var. *rosea* and a darker pink var. *rubra*. Certainly the most useful magnolia for small gardens and even for pot culture. Begins to bloom when young, even when only 10–12 ins. high. Prefers an acid soil rich in organic matter and a cool position in semi-shade.

Magnolia x *thompsoniana* Sargent
Believed to be of hybrid origin, possibly *Magnolia virginiana* x *Magnolia tripetala*. Originally found by a Mr. Thompson in his London nursery in 1808. Useful for its late flowering, but a somewhat unprepossessing deciduous shrub of loose open unbranched habit, producing growths up to 2–3 ft. in length in a single season. Foliage up to 10 ins. long; otherwise, similar to the leaves of *Magnolia virginiana* and very glaucous on the undersurface. Flowers cream-white with petals 3–4 ins. long.

Deciduous shrub
Flowering period: May-June
Height: up to 15 ft.
Zone 5 southwards

Magnolia tripetala L. (syn. *Magnolia umbrella*)
Native to eastern North America. The peculiar specific synonym *umbrella* refers to the radiating disposition of the leaves at the ends of the branches. Forms a large deciduous tree up to 40 ft. high with many wide-spreading branches. Leaves 1–2 ft. long and half as wide. Flowers cream-white with petals 4–5 ins. long, strongly but not pleasantly scented. It is generally considered to be the most decorative of all magnolias for its fruits, which I have often measured as 6 ins. long, cone-shaped, bright pinkish red, with scarlet seeds. Introduced in 1752.

(Umbrella Tree)
Deciduous tree
Flowering period: May-June
Height: up to 40 ft.
Zone 4 southwards

Magnolia x *veitchii* Bean
Of hybrid origin (*Magnolia campbellii* x *Magnolia denudata*). A large deciduous tree up to 30 ft. high and probably the most beautiful of all the tree-like hybrid deciduous hardy magnolias. Leaves obovate, 6–12 ins. long. Stupendous flowers in March–April, before the leaves, with a diameter of 10 ins. in an exquisite shade of pink. The fruits are also attractive and interesting for their carmine colouring and for their curious contorted shapes, no two of which are alike. Of very vigorous and rapid growth.

Deciduous tree
Flowering period: Mar.–Apr.
Height: up to 30 ft.
Zone 6 southwards

Magnolia virginiana L. (syn. *Magnolia glauca*)
Native to the eastern United States from Massachusetts to Florida, frequently found in swampy, boggy areas, hence Swamp Laurel. A compact-growing small evergreen tree or large shrub of great charm. Leaves oval, $2\frac{1}{2}$–$3\frac{1}{2}$ ins. long and half as wide; dark green above, glaucous, almost blue-white on the undersurface. Flowers globose, 3 ins. in diameter, cream-white, sweetly scented. A first-class garden plant for its pleasing appearance and fragrant flowers. Interesting for its one-time use in folk medicine, when its bark was used in the treatment of rheumatism and malaria, and as a stimulant.

(Sweet Bay, Beaver Tree, White Bay, Swamp Bay, or Swamp Laurel)
Evergreen shrub
Flowering period: May
Height: up to 15 ft. in gardens
Zone 4 southwards

Deciduous shrub
Flowering period: May–June
Height: up to 20 ft.
Zone 6 southwards

Magnolia wilsonii Rehd.
Native to China. Introduced by E. H. Wilson in 1908. A large deciduous shrub up to 20 ft. high. Leaves narrowly oval, pointed, up to 6 ins. long and half as wide; dull green above, velvety beneath and clothed with brownish wool similar to that found on the undersurface of many *Magnolia grandiflora* leaves. Flowers white, 4 ins. wide, cup-shaped, pendulous, fragrant, with a cluster of beautiful red stamens in the centre. Fruits purple-pink, seeds scarlet. Generally acknowledged to be one of Wilson's most beautiful introductions. Prefers a semi-shady, cool, fairly moist position.

Malus

(CRAB-APPLE)
Family: Rosaceae
Hardy deciduous shrubs or small trees
Position: sun or partial shade
Propagation: seed, grafting, or cuttings
Cultivation easy
Useful for cutting

Malus x *lemoinei*.

The fruiting edible apple (malus) is wholly admirable, beautiful in flower and decorative when branches are laden with ripe fruit. (Apple blossoms are so popular that they are a frequently reproduced motif on wallpaper, fabric, china, glassware, and even enamelled saucepans.) The flowering or crab-apples offer even more since these plants are among the most beautiful of all spring-flowering trees and shrubs, outdoing even the famous Japanese flowering cherries. Not only are they beautiful in bloom, they are equally attractive in autumn when they produce their prolific crops of brightly coloured ornamental fruits which in many cases are edible. These flowering crabs are, in fact, wild apple species and one, *Malus pumila* (syn. *Malus communis*), is one parent of the cultivated garden apples. The ornamental character of both the flowers and fruits makes the flowering crabs dual-purpose shrubs and trees of great garden value.

The genus comprises about thirty species of small deciduous trees or large shrubs with a habitat that includes the temperate regions of Europe to North America and Asia. There are also numerous garden hybrids and varieties. At one time the genus *Malus* also included those plants now classified under the genus *Pyrus,* the wild pears—more tree-like in form than *Malus*. The two sections are now definitely divided, and the difference between the two is both practical and botanical. It has never been possible to cross-pollinate the two groups and, because of this phenomenon—"rejection"—it is very difficult to intergraft plants of the genera *Pyrus* and *Malus*.

Crab-apples contain a high percentage of malic acid and can be used to make delicious jelly. Verjuice was also at one time prepared from crab-apples as well as from green grapes. They were also served in hot drinks and punches (wassails) and were well-known to Shakespeare:

> When roasted crabs hiss in the bowl,
> Then nightly sings the staring owl.
> *(Love's Labour's Lost)*
>
> And sometimes lurk I in a gossip's bowl
> In very likeness of a roasted crab.
> *(A Midsummer-Night's Dream)*

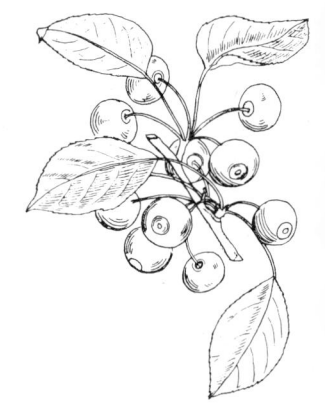

As regards cultivation and propagation, the species can be grown from seed easily, but because the species and varieties so readily hybridize with each other it is not possible to guarantee that the seedlings will always reproduce the characteristics of their parents. Seed can be sown outdoors in pots, boxes, pans, or flats. The best method of propagation and the one generally used by commercial growers, is to graft the more desirable species and varieties onto the particularly vigorous more common species and varieties, always using young plants raised from seed as stock. Crab-apples can also be propagated by hard-wood cuttings taken after the leaves have fallen and placed outside in unheated frames.

General cultivation of crab-apples is very easy. In the north they give best results planted in full sun. In very hot districts, however, better results are obtained if they are established in partial shade. This not only benefits the plants, but it also prolongs the flowering season. Crab-apples require a deep, cool, moderately moist soil rich in humus and organic matter, with a mulching or top dressing every spring. The plants are equally satisfactory in acid or alkaline (calcareous) soils, and are fast growing. No pruning is necessary apart from the removal of dead, badly formed, or unwanted branches. Specimens grown as shrubs are more attractive and longer-lived than those cultivated as standards.

Fruits of *Malus baccata*

Malus angustifolia Mich. (syn. *Pyrus angustifolia*)
Native to eastern North America, from New Jersey southwards to Florida. A small semi-evergreen tree up to about 25 ft. high. Dark shiny green dentated leaves, oblong to lanceolate, 3 ins. long and half as wide, but smaller on the flowering branches. Flowers borne in groups of four, pale pink or nearly white, stalked, $1\frac{1}{4}$ ins. long, and violet-scented. Fruits greenish yellow, $\frac{3}{4}$ in. wide, with a sharp acid flavour. Introduced into European gardens in 1750.

(Southern Crab-Apple)
Flowering period: April
Height: up to 25 ft.
Zone 5 southwards

Flowering period: April
Height: up to 25–30 ft.
Zone 4 southwards

Malus x arnoldiana Sargent
Of hybrid origin (*Malus floribunda* x *Malus baccata*). A natural hybrid found in the Arnold Arboretum in Boston in 1915. Has a very graceful deciduous habit with semi-pendulous branches. Foliage similar to that of *Malus floribunda* but larger. Flowers 1½ ins. wide, ruby-red changing to pink. Fruits egg-shaped, ¾ in. long, at first pale yellow, red when mature.

(Siberian Crab)
Flowering period: April
Height: up to 40 ft.
Zone 3 southwards

Malus baccata Borkh. (syn. *Pyrus baccata*)
Native to Siberia, northern China, and the Himalayas. Introduced into Kew in 1784. A large deciduous shrub or small tree with a wide-spreading head of semi-pendulous branches. Leaves 1½–3 ins. long, half as wide, oval. White flowers in April borne in umbels; individual blooms 1½ ins. wide. Fruit globular, ⅔ in. in diameter, vivid red. One of the most ornamental of all small flowering garden trees; particularly beautiful in autumn after the leaves have fallen, when the branches bear the large cherry-like fruits. These fruits make an excellent jelly.

(American Crab, Sweet Crab, or Garland Crab)
Flowering period: May–June
Height: up to 30 ft.
Zone 4 southwards

Malus coronaria Miller (syn. *Pyrus coronaria*)
Native to the eastern United States; introduced into Europe in 1724. A vigorous small deciduous tree that generally retains the proportions of a large shrub in gardens, with a wide spreading open habit. Leaves ovate, sometimes lobed, 2–3 ins. long, 2 ins. wide. Flowers white suffused pink, deliciously scented, nearly 2 ins. in diameter, and borne in clusters of 4–6. Fruits orange-shaped, yellowish green, 1 in. in diameter.

(Eley Crab)
Flowering period: April
Height: up to 20 ft.
Zone 4 southwards

Malus x eleyi C. K. Schneid. (syn. *Pyrus* x *eleyi*)
Of hybrid origin (*Malus niedzwetzkyana* x *Malus spectabilis*). A large deciduous shrub or small tree. One of the most beautiful crab-apples. Leaves light reddish purple, ovate, 1½–3 ins. long and half as wide. Flowers borne in clusters, each bloom 1¼ ins. wide, wine-coloured. Fruits purple-red, conical, 1 in. long. Two other hybrid crab-apples of the same parentage can also be conveniently discussed here.

Malus x *aldenhamensis*. In general aspect similar to *Malus* x *eleyi* but with orange-shaped fruits, dentated foliage, and slightly smaller. Raised by the Hon. Vicary Gibbs, at Aldenham in England.

Malus x *lemoinei*. Raised at Nancy in France by the firm of Lemoine and given the coveted award of merit by the Royal Horticultural Society in 1928. Generally considered to be the most beautiful of all the hybrid deciduous crabs, and, in my opinion, the most beautiful of all flowering shrubs. Fast-growing and equally happy in acid or alkaline (calcareous) soils. In general habit and appearance it resembles *Malus* x *eleyi*, but everything about the plant is extra: its dark bronze-purple foliage, its rich carmine-crimson 2-in. flowers

Malus florentina
From *Curtis's Botanical Magazine*,
1895, plate 7423

borne in groups of 5–6, its delicate fragrance, and its prolific production of bloom, followed in autumn by masses of small wine-red edible crab-apples.

(Showy Crab)
Flowering period: May–June
Height: up to 30 ft.
Zone 4 southwards

Malus floribunda Sieb. (syn. *Pyrus floribunda*)
Native to Japan, introduced into Europe in 1862, and one of the best species. Height up to 25–30 ft., with a wide rounded head of branches giving the plant the appearance of a very large shrub rather than a small tree. Deciduous. Leaves ovate, dentated, $1\frac{1}{2}$–$2\frac{3}{4}$ ins. long and half as wide, dull green. Flowers red in bud, pink when fully open, $1\frac{1}{2}$ ins. wide, and borne in clusters. Fruit round, yellow, $\frac{2}{3}$ in. in diameter. The var. *atrosanguinea* has richer-coloured flowers and more vivid green foliage, while the var. *Excellens Thiel* is a weeping form with more modest proportions.

Flowering period: May–June
Height: up to 20 ft.
Zone 5 southwards

Malus florentina C. K. Schneid. (syn. *Pyrus crataegifolia*)
Native to North Italy but very rare in both its wild and cultivated state. A large deciduous shrub or small tree of rounded habit. The dark-green leaves are similar to those of hawthorn. Flowers white, in bunches of 5–7 in the form of a corymb, each bloom $\frac{2}{3}$ in. in diameter. Fruits oval, about $\frac{1}{2}$ in. long, yellow ripening to a rich red. A beautiful hardy plant, thriving at Kew from plants introduced from Florence in 1886. In autumn the foliage assumes magnificent orange-scarlet shades.

Flowering period: April
Height: up to 20 ft.
Zone 4 southwards

Malus halliana Koehne (syn. *Pyrus halliana*)
Native to the western part of Szechwan province in China. Introduced from Japan into the United States in 1863 by Dr. G. R. Hall, for whom it was named. A large shrub, 15–20 ft. high, with the young growths purplish. Leaves ovate, up to 3 ins. long and half as wide, dentated, pointed, glabrous, dark shiny green suffused purple at the midrib. Flowers in clusters of up to seven, each bloom $1\frac{1}{2}$ ins. in diameter, stalked, dark pink. Fruits purple, the size and shape of a pea.

(Prairie Crab or Iowa Crab)
Flowering period: May–June
Height: up to 25 ft.
Zone 4 southwards

Malus ionensis Brit. (syn. *Pyrus coronaria ionensis*)
Native to the central United States. Closely related to and resembling *Malus coronaria*, although the branches are downy. Leaves oval, up to 4 ins. long and half as wide, undersurface woolly. Flowers pinkish white, $1\frac{1}{2}$ ins. in diameter, borne 4–6 in corymbs. Fruits yellowish green, $1\frac{1}{4}$ ins. wide. There is a beautiful double-flowered var. *coronaria plena,* strongly scented with the perfume of violets, whose correct name is *Malus ionensis* var. *plena;* in the United States popularly known as Bechtel's Crab, as it was originally put on the market by the nursery firm Bechtel of Stanton, Illinois, in 1891. It is June-flowering, a lovely shade of pale pink, with individual blooms $2\frac{1}{2}$ ins. in

diameter. A variety sometimes known as *Malus coronaria* var. *Kaido* (which should actually be called *Malus x micromalus*) is, in fact, a hybrid of *Malus spectabilis*. It is a lovely erect-branched small tree with pink and white flowers.

Malus niedzwetzkyana Diech

Flowering period: April
Height: up to 30 ft.
Zone 3 southwards

Introduced from Siberia by Dr. Diech of Zossen, Germany, and first cultivated in England in 1894. The late W. J. Bean doubted that it was a true species and suggested that it was a form of *Malus pumila*. (This opinion is supported by the fact that when curator of Kew he raised a number of plants from seed and they showed great variation in the leaf and fruit colour.) The typical form of *Malus niedzwetzkyana* is, however, particularly interesting. It makes a large deciduous shrub with oval dentated leaves up to $4\frac{1}{2}$ ins. long and $2\frac{3}{4}$ ins. wide. The stalk and centre vein are red, while the leaf blade has a reddish tinge when young becoming purple-red with age. The flowers are dark purple-red, $2\frac{3}{4}$ ins. in diameter, and are borne in clusters. Fruits conical, 2 ins. long, dark wine-red. I have grown several of the typical form and have always been intrigued to note that the red colouring permeates the interior of the wood and also the flesh of the fruits (which make a beautifully coloured jelly). There are several varieties including the lovely var. *pendula* (syn. *Elise Rathke*) with semi-pendulous spreading branches and sweetly flavoured large fruits; and var. *Veitch's Scarlet* with particularly vividly coloured fruits.

Malus niedzwetzkyana

Malus prunifolia Borkh. (syn. *Pyrus prunifolia*)

Flowering period: April
Height: up to 20 ft.
Zone 4 southwards

Possibly native to Siberia and to China, but the matter is open to doubt and some authorities suggest it may be of hybrid origin, resulting from a cross between *Malus baccata* and *Malus pumila*. According to William Aiton (curator of Kew, and editor of *Hortus kewensis*, 1789) it was first cultivated in England in 1758. A large deciduous shrub with ovate leaves 2–4 ins. long and half as wide, irregularly dentated. Flowers white, $1\frac{1}{2}$ ins. in diameter, borne in umbels of 6–10. Fruits round, 1 in. wide, yellowish red. The var. *dulcis* and the var. *edulis* have greenish-yellow fruits; the var. *lutea* has golden-yellow fruits. There is also a pendulous variety, var. *pendula*. The var. *rinki* (syn. *Malus ringo, Pyrus ringo*), under which name it is illustrated in the *Botanical Magazine* (pl. 8265), is described by W. J. Bean as "probably the handsomest of our yellow-fruited hardy trees. They have an apple-like flavour and are quite pleasant eating." It is certainly a beautiful small tree. E. H. Wilson believed it to be a native of China, but it was originally introduced into Europe from Japan about 1850 by Von Siebold. It has pale-pink flowers borne on long pendent branches in April.

Malus spectabilis
From *Curtis's Botanical Magazine*,
1796, plate 267

Malus pumila Mill. (syn. *Pyrus malus, Malus communis*)   (Wild Apple)
Native to Western Europe and Northern Asia. A small deciduous tree up to 40 ft. high, but in gardens generally not more than 15–18 ft. Of no particular ornamental value but of great scientific and botanical interest as the parent of the cultivated apple. Among its many hybrids are also to be found some of the best of the ornamental crab-apples. Develops a rounded head of semi-pendulous branches; leaves oval, up to $2\frac{3}{4}$ ins. long. Flowers pinkish white, borne in corymbs. Fruit red or reddish yellow, globose. Among the forms of special interest, mention should be made of the var. *paradisiaca,* a dwarf form and the plant normally used for the grafting of eating apples. Among the ornamental *Malus* hybrids that owe their origin in part to *Malus pumila* through a series of complicated crosses, several have already been mentioned (where both parents are known). There remain, however, several beautiful hybrids whose origin is obscure, although one parent is certainly *Malus pumila.* Among these the following deserve special mention:

Flowering period: Apr.–May
Height: up to 18 ft.
Zone 3 southwards

Malus x *John Downie.* This is the most beautiful of all crab-apples for its colourful fruits. The miniature conical apples are $1\frac{1}{2}$ ins. long and a mixture of intense gradations of orange and scarlet. White flowers in late spring.

Malus x *Dartmouth.* This produces prolific quantities of large plum-shaped fruits covered with a purple-red bloom.

Malus x *purpurea* Rehd. (syn. *Pyrus purpurea*)
A cross between *Malus niedzwetzkyana* and *Malus floribunda* var. *atrosanguinea.* Leaves $3\frac{1}{2}$–$4\frac{1}{2}$ ins. long, lobed, purple-red. One of the most beautiful crab-apples with ruby-red flowers when in bud opening to a fine reddish purple, $1\frac{1}{4}$ ins. in diameter, borne in groups of 6–7. Fruits globose, cherry-like, dark wine-red. The var. *pendula* has completely straight pendulous branches.

Flowering period: April
Height: up to 20 ft.
Zone 5 southwards

Malus rivularis Roemer (syn. *Malus fusca, Pyrus fusca*)   (Oregon Crab)
Native to western North America. A slender-branched deciduous small tree or large shrub. Leaves not always the same shape, varying from ovate to oblong-lanceolate and frequently three-lobed, but with a maximum length of about 4 ins.; dentated, pointed, hairy on either surface. Flowers borne in corymbs of 6–12, $\frac{3}{4}$ in. in diameter, pale pink or white. Fruits egg-shaped, greenish yellow, $\frac{3}{4}$ in. long. Recorded by John Claudius Loudon as having been introduced into Europe in 1836.

Flowering period: April
Height: up to 30 ft.
Zone 3 southwards

Malus sargentii Rehd. (syn. *Pyrus sargentii*)
Native to Japan. One of the most ornamental of the smaller crabs, with a pleasing bushy habit. Leaves oval, 2–3 ins. long, lobed, dentated. Flowers white, 1 in. in diameter, borne in groups of 5–6. Orange-

Flowering period: Apr.–May
Height: up to 8 ft.
Zone 4 southwards

shaped vivid red fruits about $\frac{1}{3}$ in. in diameter. Originally sent to Kew by Professor Sargent in 1908.

Flowering period: May
Height: up to 25 ft.
Zone 4 southwards

Malus x *scheideckeri* Zabel (syn. *Pyrus* x *scheideckeri*)
Of hybrid origin, *Malus floribunda* x *Malus spectabilis* (?). A large deciduous shrub or small tree with rigid erect branches. Leaves ovate, dentated, shiny green, 2–3 ins. long. Flowers semi-double, pale pink, $1\frac{1}{2}$ ins. wide, borne in umbels of 6–10. Fruits globose, yellow. Of very vigorous growth and prolific in flowering. New growths in excess of 4 ft. long are made in one season, with blooms produced along nearly the entire length, thus making it a superb subject for cutting.

(Toringo Crab)
Flowering period: April
Height: up to 15 ft.
Zone 4 southwards

Malus sieboldii Rehd. (syn. *Pyrus sieboldii*)
Native to Japan. A large shrub with curving or semi-pendulous branches. Leaves variable in shape, from narrow-oval to ovate and sometimes lobed; dark dull green, up to 3 ins. long, dentated. Flowers also variable in colour from light to dark pink, $\frac{1}{3}$ in. wide, borne in clusters of 3–6. Fruits pea-shaped, reddish yellow.

Flowering period: April
Height: up to 25 ft.
Zone 4 southwards

Malus spectabilis Borkh. (syn. *Pyrus spectabilis*)
Native to China. Its exact date of introduction into the West is not known, but the species was cultivated by Dr. Fothergill in 1780. Although one of the most beautiful crabs in flower, the fruits are not decorative. Forms a large rounded shrub or small tree with a width that eventually equals its height. Leaves oval, up to $3\frac{1}{2}$ ins. long and $2\frac{1}{2}$ ins. wide, glossy green. Flowers reddish pink when young, pale pink when fully expanded, 2 ins. in diameter. Fruit globose, yellow. There is an excellent double-flowered form, var. *plena*.

Flowering period: April
Height: up to 25 ft.
Zone 4 southwards

Malus theifera Rehd. (syn. *Pyrus theifera, Malus hupehensis*)
Native to western and central China and to Assam. Introduced into Europe by E. H. Wilson in 1900. A small deciduous tree of rigid erect habit. Leaves ovate, pointed, up to 4 ins. long and about half as wide, and of a dark brilliant green. Flowers scented, white flushed with pink, $1\frac{1}{2}$ ins. in diameter, and borne in groups of 3–7. Fruits globose, greenish yellow suffused red, $\frac{1}{3}$ in. in diameter. A very hardy and very attractive species. The inhabitants of central China use the leaves to make a kind of tea, hence the specific name *M. theifera*.

Flowering period: May
Height: up to 25 ft.
Zone 4 southwards

Malus toringoides Hughes (syn. *Pyrus toringoides*)
Native to the western part of Szechwan province in China. A small deciduous tree with an elegant open habit; young growths downy, later becoming glabrous. Leaves lanceolate, lobed, pointed, up to 4 ins. long and half as wide. Flowers cream-white, 1 in. in diameter, borne 6–8 in corymbs. Fruits pear-shaped, $\frac{1}{2}$ in. wide, yellow suf-

fused scarlet. Introduced to Europe by E. H. Wilson in 1904 and one of the best crabs for its brilliantly coloured fruits in autumn.

Malus trilobata C. K. Schneid. (syn. *Pyrus triloba, Eriolobus trilobata*)
Native to Syria. Rare and infrequently grown in gardens. A small deciduous tree of interest for its much-divided foliage. Leaves up to 4 ins. in length and breadth, deeply trilobed, the central lobe again trilobed while the two lateral lobes are bilobed. Flowers white, $1\frac{3}{4}$ ins. wide, borne in terminal corymbs. Fruits pear-shaped, $\frac{3}{4}$ in. wide, reddish yellow. The foliage's trilobate form gives the plant an almost maple-like appearance.

Flowering period: Apr.–May
Height: up to 20 ft.
Zone 4 southwards

Malus zumi Rehd. (syn. *Pyrus zumi*)
Native to Japan. A small pyramidal deciduous tree. Leaves oblong, up to $3\frac{1}{2}$ ins. long and $1\frac{1}{2}$ ins. wide. In the bud stage the flowers are pink, opening to white, $1\frac{1}{2}$ ins. in diameter, borne in clusters of 4–7. Fruits globose, crimson-red, $\frac{1}{2}$ in. wide. Introduced to North America by Charles Sargent in 1892 and grown particularly successfully at the Arnold Arboretum in Boston. Introduced into Kew in 1905.

Flowering period: May
Height: up to 20 ft.
Zone 4 southwards

Mandevilla

Family: *Apocynaceae*
Tender deciduous shrubs or climbers
Position: sun
Propagation: seed or cuttings
Cultivation fairly easy
Fragrant

Mandevilla suaveolens Lindl. (syn. *M. laxa, Echites funiformis*)
This South American genus was named by Lindley for H. J. Mandeville, the British minister at Buenos Aires in 1837, the year the first plants were introduced into England. The genus is fairly numerous, with at least fifty species of shrubs and climbers native to Argentina, Brazil, Mexico, and the West Indies; curiously enough only two—both climbers—have become established as garden plants, and of these only one is really well known (*Mandevilla suaveolens*). Their non-hardy character has impeded their wider diffusion in northern countries, where they make excellent greenhouse climbers. In Mediterranean climates and in the southern United States, *Mandevilla suaveolens* is widely cultivated outdoors.
Mandevillas are long-stemmed semi-woody climbers with masses of slender soft-wooded glabrous lateral growths. Like other members

(Chilean Jasmine)
Deciduous perennial climber
Flowering period: July–Aug.
Height: up to 30 ft.
Zone 9 southwards
Fragrant

Mandevilla suaveolens
From *Curtis's Botanical Magazine*,
1840, plate 3797

of the family Apocynaceae (such as *Nerium oleander*), these exude a white latex-like sap when cut. The large white five-lobed tubular flowers are 2 ins. long, $1\frac{1}{2}$ ins. wide at the mouth, very agreeably scented, and borne up to eight together in a somewhat open long-stalked loose corymb produced in the leaf axils. Leaves opposite, heart-shaped with a long drawn-out point; up to $3\frac{1}{2}$ ins. long and up to 2 ins. wide. The seeds are borne in long narrow pods up to 16 ins. long and $\frac{1}{4}$ in. wide, which, when produced in pendulous bunches, are of considerable interest and decorative value.

Cultivation. In a warm climate, the cultivation of mandevillas is not difficult. They require an ordinary fertile garden soil mixed with about a quarter part leafsoil and a quarter part peat, with a sprinkling of rather coarse sand to ensure good drainage. At planting time add a good spadeful of well-composted manure for each plant. They are essentially sun lovers and require a hot and moderately dry position, preferably against a wall. The plants are not self-supporting and must be provided with wires, a wooden trellis, or large-holed wire or plastic mesh on which the long thin growths can cling and climb. In districts where the winter temperature drops to about 28°F. for short periods, the plants can be established permanently outside. Where the temperature falls as low as 20–22°F., the plants can still be planted outside in a sheltered position if the base of the stem is wrapped with straw and some plastic material to keep the straw dry; the soil surface above the roots should also be protected with a thick mulch of peat, leaves, or manure, etc. Where temperatures below 20°F. are experienced, the plants must be cultivated in large receptacles and taken to a greenhouse in late autumn, or actually cultivated in a greenhouse. A light pruning should be given after flowering has finished. Propagation is by seed sown in a warm greenhouse in spring, from soft cuttings rooted in sand under transparent plastic or a glass bell-jar in a warm greenhouse, or from cuttings of half-ripened wood taken in July and inserted in frames.

Matthiola

(STOCK)
Family: Cruciferae
Hardy herbaceous semi-woody perennials, biennials, or annuals
Height: 1–3 ft., according to type
Position: sun
Propagation: seed or cuttings
Cultivation easy
Fragrant

The third scene of Act IV in *A Winter's Tale* seems to provide a mine of quotable garden lore. Shakespeare, whose store of knowledge seems inexhaustible, here gives a beautifully written account of Elizabethan horticultural practices. We have drawn upon this scene elsewhere, and will here do so again:

> POLIXENES. Shepherdess,—
> A fair one are you,—well you fit our ages
> With flowers of winter.
> PERDITA. Sir, the year growing ancient,
> Not yet on summer's death, nor on the birth
> Of trembling winter, the fairest flowers o' the season
> Are our carnations, and streak'd gillyvors,
> Which some call nature's bastards: of that kind
> Our rustic garden's barren, and I care not
> To get slips of them.
> POLIXENES. Wherefore, gentle maiden,
> Do you neglect them?
> PERDITA. For I have heard it said
> There is an art which in their piedness shares
> With great creating nature.
> POLIXENES. Say there be;
> Yet nature is made better by no mean
> But nature makes that mean: so, over that art,
> Which you say adds to nature, is an art
> That nature makes. . . .
> Then make your garden rich in gillyvors,
> And do not call them bastards.
> PERDITA. I'll not put
> The dibble in earth to set one slip of them;
> No more than, were I painted, I would wish
> This youth should say, 'twere well, and only therefore.
> Desire to breed by me. Here's flowers for you.

These lines clearly reveal that by the end of the sixteenth century the English were already expert gardeners, familiar with hybridization and selection. Here, too, we see that stocks ("gillyvors") were cultivated in their various bicoloured forms. Perdita, however, seems to scorn the "streak'd gillyvors" because they seem to be more the result of "art" (artifice) than nature. (I, for one, tend to agree with her, for bicoloured and double-flowered stocks are indeed suitable in only the most formal of gardens.)

The genus *Matthiola* (or *Mathiola*) was named in honour of Pietro Andrea Matthioli (1500–1577), an Italian botanist and writer on plants. The common name of *Matthiola incana,* gillyflower, is apparently either a dialect form of "July Flower", or an anglicization of the old French *girolfle* (in which latter case, it would refer to the clove-gillyflower—*Dianthus caryophyllus*).

Double-flowered matthiola

Single-flowered matthiola

Matthiola sinuata
From *Curtis's Botanical Magazine*,
1900, plate 7703

Many people who own a small weekend house in the country or by the shore often complain they never know what to plant in the garden. There are many solutions to such a problem; wherever there is a corner with even the minimum of soil, such plants as *Lobularia maritima, Alyssum saxatile, Cheiranthus, Argemone mexicana, Glaucium flavum,* and, above all, *Matthiola incana* can be established. Single-flowered stocks are ideal for a bank, the edge of a wood or orchard, or any semi-wild position where the plants can be allowed complete freedom to grow, spread, and seed themselves at will. Near the house, at the edge of the vegetable garden, at some corner where fragrance is desired, and in all those odd corners where the evening breeze can waft a fragrant perfume towards open windows at twilight, the so-called Night-scented Stock (*Matthiola bicornis*) can be sown. Wilson and Bell state that during the day *Matthiola bicornis* has a sad, forlorn aspect; the flowers droop and the petals fold like hands hiding some secret treasure. But when daylight fades the flowers open to form a cross of wide pale-lilac petals and their treasure is released—a rich, strong fragrance combining the scent of lilies and honey. The annual forms of *Matthiola incana* are also more fragrant at night than during the day. Their lily-carnation scent masks a deep-down but recognizably horsy odour, a characteristic also shared by wallflowers.

(Night-scented or Evening Stock)
Annual or biennial
Flowering period: May–June
Height: up to 15 ins.

Matthiola bicornis Sibth. & Smith
Native to Greece. A much-branched rather low bushy and expansive annual or biennial with short-stalked linear or lanceolate leaves up to 3 ins. long. Flowers strongly and deliciously fragrant at dusk and during the night; they are borne rather widely spaced in racemes, each flower ¾ in. wide, lavender-pink or pale mauve. The seed pods bear twin horns, hence the specific name. Seed should be sown in its flowering position from March onwards, according to climate and zone.

(Gillyflower or Brompton Stock)
Perennial
Flowering period: Mar.–June
Height: 1½–3 ft.

Matthiola incana R. Br.
Native to Southern Europe, Asia Minor, North Africa, and the Canary Islands. Typical to the Mediterranean regions, where the perennial woody-stemmed herbaceous plants often establish themselves in cracks and crannies in rocks, reaching a height of up to 3 ft. and living up to 5–6 years. The entire plant is tomentose and covered with minute downy hairs. The stems and branches are rigid, vertical, and bear spikes of fragrant pinkish-violet or purple flowers. Leaves greyish green, felt-textured, up to 4 ins. long, and narrowly oblong in shape. The original species was in cultivation early in the sixteenth century, while the double-flowered form was introduced into Europe in 1570. The old original forms are rarely cultivated today, their place having been taken by numerous hybrid strains and

forms, which are generally grown as biennials. For sake of convenience they are divided into three sections: Brompton Stocks, Intermediate Stocks, and Ten-Week Stocks.

Brompton Stocks. These are generally cultivated as biennials, sowing the seed in frames in July–August and planting the young plants out in autumn for flowering the following spring or early summer.

Intermediate Stocks. The best of these is the East Lothian Strain, sown in early spring for autumn flowering and treated as annuals; or sown in autumn for spring flowering and treated as biennials.

Ten-Week Stocks. Cultivated as annuals from seed sown in spring in frames or in a greenhouse for summer flowering.

There are single- and double-flowered forms in each section, but it is the double-flowered types that are most widely grown. Each type has a very wide range of colours and all are fragrant.

Matthiola sinuata R. Br. (Sea Stock)
Native to the northern shores of the Mediterranean, Asia Minor, and Algeria. A perennial or biennial species with much-branched stems; the entire plant is covered with silky hairs. Leaves thick-textured with the margins conspicuously edged with grey, dentated; those at the base undulated. Flowers borne in erect racemes, each bloom 1 in. wide, white suffused blue or lilac, fragrant.

Perennial or biennial
Flowering period: May–July
Height: 10–20 ins.

Maurandia

Family: Scrophulariaceae
Tender climbing perennials often grown as annuals
Height: up to 10 ft., according to the species
Position: sun
Propagation: seed or cuttings
Cultivation fairly easy

A genus of delightful little non-hardy deciduous perennial climbers that do well where space is limited and where the more rampant climbing plants would be out of place. In a warm climate they can be allowed to develop their natural perennial character, while in districts where winters are cold, they can be easily and successfully treated as annuals. If seed is sown in a warm greenhouse in February–March the plants will bloom with the greatest profusion during summer and autumn. They are also suitable for permanent planting in an unheated greenhouse where the flowering period will be extended throughout winter.

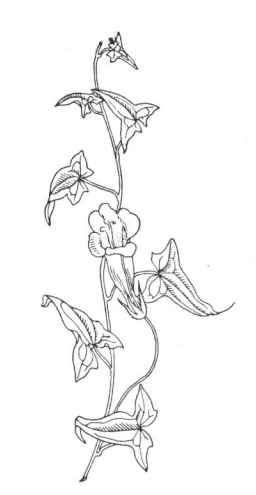

The genus *Maurandia* is closely related to the genus *Antirrhinum* (snapdragons), an obvious affinity when the flowers are closely examined, although in the case of the maurandias the mouth is not closed. They are very similar to climbing antirrhinums, with an especially graceful form. There are about ten species, all native to an area extending from Mexico northwards to Arizona. The name *Maurandia* is believed to be derived from a certain Da Maurandy, at one time a professor of botany in Cartagena in Spain, but there are no extant records of his date of birth or death. Others maintain that the genus was named for Catharina Pancratia Maurandy, said to be an eighteenth-century student of botany, but whose biographical particulars are as vague as those of the Spanish professor.

Cultivation. Maurandias love sun and warmth, and dislike excessive moisture, especially in the seedling stage. Seed should therefore be sown in a porous sandy soil in pots, flats, or trays with perfect drainage. An appropriate soil mixture for sowing and for potting the seedlings can be prepared as follows:

> 3 parts ordinary garden soil
> 2 parts leafsoil
> 1 part peat
> 1 part sand

Maurandia barclaiana

The seed is extremely fine and should be covered only with a light dusting of finely sifted compost, watering only with a very fine spray or mist. For successful germination and for growing the seedlings on, the night temperature should not fall below 55°F.; this temperature in many cases permits sowing in an unheated greenhouse or in coldframes in spring. When the seedlings are large enough to handle they can be potted individually in $2-2\frac{1}{2}$-in. pots, using the same soil mixture, but with the addition of a small quantity of some organic fertilizer. As the plants develop they should be provided with small stakes on which to climb. When about 5 ins. high they can be planted out in their flowering positions, immediately providing enough support for the long slender growths. Wire or plastic mesh or a wooden trellis is ideal for this purpose, especially if placed against a wall. After planting, water only sparingly. When the plants are about 2 ft. high and ready to begin flowering, periodic applications of organic liquid fertilizer are advisable.

Flowering period: July–Sept.
Height: up to 10 ft.

Maurandia barclaiana Lindl.
Native to Mexico. A much-branched slender twining climber. The triangular long-pointed $1\frac{1}{2}$-in.-long leaves have very extended stalks that will twist round the plant's support. Flowers $1\frac{1}{4}-1\frac{3}{4}$ ins. long, tubular, violet-purple. A beautiful graceful plant, attractive for its flowers and foliage. There are several varieties:

    var. *alba*, white-flowered

Maurandia scandens
From *Curtis's Botanical Magazine*,
1799, plate 460

var. *atropurpurea,* dark purple
var. *rosea,* with rose-pink flowers

Flowering period: July–Aug.
Height: up to 6–8 ft.

Maurandia erubescens A. Gray (syn. *Lophospermum erubescens*)
Native to Mexico. A slender climber with triangular light-green foliage up to 4 ins. long and covered with slightly sticky hairs. Flowers reddish pink, up to 3 ins. long, tubular, and very attractive.

Flowering period: July–Sept.
Height: up to 10–12 ft.

Maurandia scandens A. Gray (syn. *Maurandia semperflorens*)
Native to Mexico. A semi-shrubby perennial climber. Leaves arrow-shaped, smooth, about 3 ins. long. Flowers tubular, 1 in. long, brilliant purple, and particularly long-lasting.

Meconopsis

(POPPYWORT)
Family: Papaveraceae
Hardy annual, biennial, monocarpic, or perennial herbaceous plants
Position: shade in the south, half-shade in the north
Propagation: seed or division
Cultivation rather difficult

This is a genus of exquisitely beautiful plants. Unfortunately, they are as difficult to grow as they are beautiful. Their greatest enemies are heat and a dry atmosphere, making their cultivation in the south even more difficult. Only one species, *Meconopsis cambrica,* the Welsh Poppy native to Great Britain, can be considered an easy or popular plant. The others, above all *Meconopsis betonicifolia,* the legendary blue poppy of the Himalayas which could be of such value in our gardens, are a real challenge to any gardener's skill. My attempts with this temperamental blue-flowered beauty in sunny Italy have never been really satisfactory; however, after seeing the plant thriving in the cool, fresh atmosphere high in the Himalayas, I can well appreciate its preference. For those who have an alpine garden or a northern garden with a cool, fresh, well-lighted situation, meconopsis is worth trying. If successful, the grower will be rewarded with flowers of remarkable colouring and more than ordinary beauty.

The genus comprises about forty-five species of herbaceous perennials, biennials, and annuals, together with several that are monocarpic—they live for 3–4 years, bloom, produce seed, and then die. In general appearance, meconopsis resemble poppies, a similarity confirmed in the Greek origin of the name—*mekon* (poppy) and *opsis* (aspect)—but their cultivation is entirely different and is more similar to primula cultivation. Meconopsis require a well-drained soil rich in humus and decomposed vegetable matter, a cool, fresh, moist atmosphere, an abundance of moisture at the roots, and shade from hot sunshine. Propagation from seed can be easy, but as the seed rapidly loses its viability it is essential that it is sown soon after maturity in late summer. The best sowing medium is a compost made up of equal parts of peat, sand, fibrous loam, and leafsoil. The flats, pans, or pots of freshly sown seed should be kept in a temperature of 65°F. Seedlings can be pricked out into trays or boxes and later potted on individually into small pots. The seedlings develop rapidly, vigorously, and without difficulty, thriving throughout autumn and winter, either outdoors or in coldframes. Development should continue in a satisfactory manner during the following spring, when the plants can be planted out in their flowering positions. If climatic conditions are to their liking, all will be well and the plants will grow, prosper, and bloom. However, if the late spring and early summer temperature is too high and the air too dry, the plants will show signs of distress immediately; growth slows down, eventually stops, and they will gradually wither and die. Their successful cultivation depends on providing them with living conditions exactly similar to those found in their natural habitat. In the case of well-established perennial species, propagation can also be effected by division in early spring.

Meconopsis aculeata Royle
Native to the Himalayas. Introduced into Europe in 1864. A biennial species with slightly hairy grey-green foliage divided into lobes of irregular shape. Stems erect, bearing groups of purple-blue flowers 3 ins. in diameter.

Biennial
Flowering period: May–June
Height: 18 ins.

Meconopsis betonicifolia Franch. (syn. *Meconopsis baileyi*)
Native to the Himalayas, Tibet, and to the Yunnan province of China. Introduced into Europe in 1924 by the famous botanical explorer, Captain Kingdon-Ward. This is the most beautiful and most desirable of the species. Flowers are an intense sky-blue, 2–3 ins. in diameter, with petals that have a texture similar to silk taffeta. When the flowers are moved by the slightest breeze, their colour is iridescent and changes like shot silk, contrasting spectacularly with the incredible mass of golden-yellow stamens in the centre. Leaves are basal, borne in the form of a large rosette and are hairy like the stems. This is a monocarpic species that dies after flowering, generally 2–3 years after seed has been sown. Often seedlings attempt to bloom during their first year, but it is advisable to remove these premature flower buds immediately to ensure larger and better flowers the

(Himalayan Blue Poppy)
Monocarpic
Flowering period: May–June
Height: up to 3 ft.

Meconopsis simplicifolia
From *Curtis's Botanical Magazine*,
1911, plate 8364

following season. Seed is freely produced and, under ideal conditions, the plant will naturalize itself.

Meconopsis betonicifolia

Meconopsis cambrica Vig.
Native to Great Britain and Western Europe and the easiest species to cultivate. Once a group has been established in the garden the plants will naturalize freely by means of self-sown seedlings. Leaves grey-green. Flowers large, solitary, poppy-like, orange, borne on erect rigid stems. There is also a yellow-flowered variety, and a double-flowered form, var. *flore pleno*.

(Welsh Poppy)
Perennial
Flowering period: May–June
Height: 12–15 ins.

Meconopsis dhwojii Franch.
A lovely biennial species native to Nepal. Introduced into Europe in 1931. Leaves deeply lobed, hairy, arranged in a basal rosette. Flowers borne on tall erect branching stems; nearly 3 ins. in diameter and a lovely shade of yellow.

Biennial
Flowering period: May–June
Height: 2–2½ ft.

Meconopsis grandis Prain
Native to Nepal and Tibet. A perennial species with oval-oblong entire leaves. Flowers solitary, a beautiful shiny purple, borne on stems up to 2½ ft. high.

Perennial
Flowering period: May–June
Height: 2½ ft.

Meconopsis heterophylla Benth. (syn. *Papaver heterophyllum, Stylomecon heterophylla*)
Native to western North America. By some authorities considered a member of the genus *Stylomecon* (given here as a synonym). A lovely annual, sometimes biennial, plant with greyish-green deeply cut foliage up to 6 ins. long. Flowers freely and abundantly produced on tall branching stems. The blooms are long-stalked, 2 ins. in diameter, brick-red in colour, with a maroon-red mark at the base of each of the four satin-textured petals making a fine contrast with the central mass of golden stamens.

(Wind Poppy)
Annual
Flowering period: May–June
Height: up to 2 ft.

Biennial
Flowering period: May–June
Height: 3 ft.

Meconopsis horridula Maxim. (syn. *Meconopsis prattii, Meconopsis rudis, Meconopsis racemosa, Meconopsis rigidiuscula*)
Native to Central Asia. Introduced into Europe in 1904. A biennial species with long narrow irregularly lobed yellowish-green foliage covered with prickly hairs. Flowers borne on a long spike bearing numerous blooms $2\frac{1}{2}$ ins. wide and purple or wine-red in colour.

(Lampshade Meconopsis)
Biennial
Flowering period: May–June
Height: 2–2¼ ft.

Meconopsis integrifolia Franch. (syn. *Cathcartia integrifolia*)
Native to China and Tibet. Introduced into Europe in 1904. A biennial with the foliage arranged in a basal rosette. Leaves narrow, long, pointed. Stems erect, very vigorous, and hairy, bearing very large 6-in.-wide clear yellow cup-shaped flowers that have earned the plant the most appropriate common name of Lampshade Meconopsis. A species of very great beauty.

(Satin Poppy)
Monocarpic
Flowering period: May–June
Height: up to 6 ft.

Meconopsis napaulensis D.C. (syn. *Meconopsis wallichii, Meconopsis nepalensis*)
Native to Central Asia. Introduced into Europe in 1852. A monocarpic species with flowers that vary in colour from purple-red to dark blue. Petals with a lovely silk-like sheen. Leaves deeply cut and covered with reddish-maroon hairs.

Perennial
Flowering period: May–June
Height: 16 ins.

Meconopsis quintuplinervia Prain
Native to Tibet and China. An unusual, conspicuous species with bronze-coloured foliage that is hairy, rough, and wrinkled on the surface, and forms a basal rosette of vegetation. Stems erect, bearing solitary vivid lavender-blue pendulous flowers.

Monocarpic
Flowering period: May–June
Height: 5½ ft.

Meconopsis regia Don
Native to Nepal. Introduced into Europe in 1852. A monocarpic species with narrow hairy leaves up to 2 ft. in length and arranged in a large basal rosette that is highly decorative. From the centre of this rosette emerge tall rigid stems up to $5\frac{1}{2}$ ft. high bearing spikes of yellow flowers 3 ins. in diameter, and of a truly spectacular beauty.

Monocarpic
Flowering period: May–June
Height: 2½ ft.

Meconopsis x *sheldonii*
Of hybrid origin (*Meconopsis betonicifolia* x *Meconopsis grandis*). A magnificent hybrid that has inherited the superb very large dark-blue flowers of its parents.

Annual
Flowering period: May–June
Height: 18 ins.

Meconopsis simplicifolia Don
Native to Central Asia. Introduced into European gardens in 1848. The plants form a dense mass of basal vegetation with lanceolate dentated hairy leaves from which arise erect rigid stems bearing blue or violet-blue solitary pendulous flowers $2\frac{3}{4}$ ins. wide. It is one of the easier annual species and, if an appropriate position can be found for it in the garden, it creates a delightful effect.

Meconopsis superba King & Prain
Native to Tibet. A magnificent biennial species worthy of its specific name. The large oval leaves form a big basal rosette of vegetation from which arise erect vigorous leafy stems bearing white 6-in.-wide flowers in loose inflorescences. A spectacular plant that can sometimes be naturalized.

Biennial
Flowering period: May–June
Height: 3 ft.

Meconopsis wallichii (see *Meconopsis napaulensis*)

Mentzelia

(BARTONIA)
Family: Loasaceae
Hardy or half-hardy annuals, biennials, herbaceous perennials, or shrubs
Position: sun
Propagation: seed
Cultivation fairly easy
Useful for cutting

This genus, which some prefer to call *Bartonia*, was named for the German botanist Christian Mentzel (1622–1701). It comprises about fifty annual, biennial, perennial, or shrubby species native to California and Texas. The annual and biennial species are excellent for growing in pots or other large containers, for bedding, for the rock-garden, for dry walls, and for terrace gardens. They love sun, warmth, and a fairly dry not-too-rich soil. The flowering period is long with the blooms produced in profusion, and the plants are easy to cultivate.

Mentzelia stems are frequently greenish white and hairy. The foliage is either alternate or opposite and deeply lobed. The flowers are solitary, five-petalled, with numerous conspicuous stamens reminiscent of a hypericum and borne in terminal racemes. Propagation is easily effected from seed sown in a warm greenhouse in February–March, or in the flowering position in the open in April. Germination is slow, often a matter of 2–3 weeks, after which growth is rapid and the first flowers can be expected ten weeks after the sowing date. The flowering period lasts up to three months. *Mentzelia* requires a warm, sunny, fairly dry position in a light, preferably sandy, well-drained soil.

Mentzelia bartonioides Torr. & Gray
Native to California. An annual species about 15 ins. high that at one time was known as *Eucnide bartonioides*. Leaves hairy, dentated, lobed. Throughout summer, it bears a profusion of large golden-

Annual or biennial
Flowering period: July–Sept.
Height: 15 ins.

Mentzelia lindleyi
From *Curtis's Botanical Magazine*,
1838, plate 3649

yellow flowers, five-petalled, and widely expanded to show a conspicuous mass of long yellow stamens in the centre.

Mentzelia decapetala Torr. & Gray (syn. *Bartonia decapetala, Mentzelia ornata*)

(Prairie Lily or Gumbo Lily)
Biennial
Flowering period: July–Sept.
Height: 12 ins.

Native to Texas. A biennial species up to 12 ins. high with much-divided leaves. Flowers fragrant, white or pale yellow, up to 5 ins. in diameter, with a mass of protruding stamens. The blooms do not open until dusk, when the scent is particularly strong.

Mentzelia laevicaulis Torr. & Gray

(Blazing Star)
Perennial
Flowering period: July–Sept.
Height: up to 3 ft.

Native to California. A vigorous robust perennial species up to 3 ft. high. Leaves narrow, up to 8 ins. long, dentated, with undulated margins. Flowers up to 4 ins. in diameter, pale yellow with pointed petals. A beautiful and effective garden plant.

Mentzelia lindleyi Torr. & Gray (syn. *Mentzelia aurea, Bartonia aurea*)

Annual
Flowering period: July–Sept.
Height: up to 12 ins.

Native to California. An annual species up to 12 ins. high. Leaves narrow, dark green, shallowly lobed, making a beautiful contrast with the large saucer-shaped golden-yellow flowers up to $2\frac{1}{2}$ ins. in diameter. Flowers are also very strongly scented.

Mesembryanthemum

(Fig Marigold)
Family: Mesembryanthemaceae (or Aizoaceae)
Annuals or tender herbaceous perennials or sub-shrubs
Position: full sun
Propagation: seed or cuttings
Cultivation easy

At one time the genus *Mesembryanthemum* contained about two thousand species, mostly native to South Africa. During recent years, however, botanists have divided them into many separate genera such as *Aptenia, Carpanthea, Carpobrotus, Cryophytum, Dorotheanthus, Faucaria, Lampranthus, Prenia*, etc. This reclassification has been so drastic that all the popular annual garden mesembryanthemums have been absorbed into the newly created genera. The splitting up of such a vast genus was botanically inevitable, and for the experts it has many advantages. To the practical gardener,

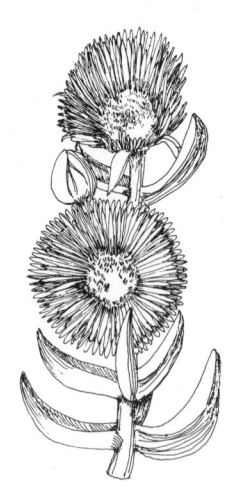

Mesembryanthemum (Carpobrotus) acinacifor

however, and the amateur gardener in particular, such segregation is both confusing and frustrating; we have thus retained the old names here and given the new nomenclature as synonyms.

None of the mesembryanthemums are hardy, a factor that has restricted their cultivation to areas with a South African climate (the Mediterranean, Florida, southern California, etc.). The annual species can be much more widely cultivated, and two or three species should be included among our most popular summer-flowering annuals; but to be really successful they need a long hot dry season.

In general, mesembryanthemums are easy to cultivate. Many have semi-succulent fleshy leaves and thrive with only a minimum of water. The first species were probably introduced into Europe towards the end of the seventeenth century; and in regions with a climate similar to their native habitat, several of the perennial species have practically naturalized themselves. They thrive in the poorest soils, are of rapid, expansive development, form a magnificent ground cover, and will flourish with the minimum attention, flowering profusely and beautifully (particularly the species *M. acinaciforme* and *M. edule*). They are evergreen and of the greatest value for planting in sandy soils where practically nothing else will grow. In discussing such a vast genus, obviously we can mention only a few species, but the following are those most frequently found in gardens.

Mesembryanthemum propagation is very easy. The perennial species may be increased by cuttings or division during almost any season except winter. Cuttings root with ease if inserted in sandy soil and kept fairly dry. The annual species should be sown in a warm greenhouse in March–April, pricking out the seedlings into pans, applying very little water, and then growing them on in small individual pots until they can be planted out in May–June. In the south, seed may be sown earlier, in frames or even in the open.

Herbaceous perennial
Flowering period: Apr.–June
Height: 10–12 ins.

Mesembryanthemum acinaciforme L. (syn. *Carpobrotus acinaciformis*)

Native to South Africa, but now naturalized in many other countries. Stems prostrate and articulated, up to 6 ft. long, but never rising more than 10–12 ins. above the soil; frequently forming new roots at the nodes. Leaves fleshy, glabrous, up to 3 ins. long, sickle-shaped. Flowers amaranth-red with yellow stamens, up to 5 ins. in diameter, of a rounded star shape, and opening only on sunny days.

Semi-shrubby herbaceous perennial
Flowering period: July–Sept.
Height: up to 1½ ft.

Mesembryanthemum aurantiacum L.

Native to South Africa. Herbaceous perennial with a woody base. Leaves fleshy, glaucous green, narrow, angled, up to 2 ins. long. Flowers golden-orange, 2 ins. in diameter, solitary on long stems with numerous rows of very small petals. A particularly effective, easily grown species.

Mesembryanthemum tricolor
From *Paxton's Magazine of Botany*,
1842, plate 219

(Livingstone Daisy)
Annual
Flowering period: June–Aug.
Height: 2–3 ins.

Mesembryanthemum criniflorum L. (syn. *Dorotheanthus bellidiflorus*)
Native to South Africa. Popularly known as Livingstone daisy in memory of the great African explorer Dr. Livingstone. A non-hardy, almost prostrate, mat-forming annual that prefers a poor, hot, dry soil in a sunny position. In a soil too rich the plants will grow larger but will flower less. Leaves minute, oval, succulent, bright green. Flowers daisy-like, 1–1½ ins. in diameter, very short-stalked, and produced in such abundance in summer that the plant is completely hidden under a carpet of colour. For brilliance, intensity, and variety of hues there are few equal to these remarkable blooms. Flowers are single, with many very narrow petals and a colour range including white, carmine, pink, apricot, salmon, orange, violet, purple, red, and yellow; sometimes they have a white zone in the centre and they always have a darker eye. The flowers remain closed when there is no sunshine.

(Ice Plant)
Annual
Flowering period: June–Aug.
Height: 4–6 ins.

Mesembryanthemum crystallinum L. (syn. *Cryophytum crystallinum*)
Native to South Africa and the Mediterranean regions. A dwarf, non-hardy annual. This is a most curious and interesting little plant cultivated for its attractive foliage more than for its flowers. Habit prostrate, spreading, not more than 6 ins. high. Flowers daisy-like with many narrow petals, single, white or pale pink, borne immediately above the foliage. Leaves pale green, small, oval, succulent, with undulated margins and the entire surface covered with crystal-like pustules, giving the whole plant the appearance of having been sprinkled with broken ice. Requires a hot, dry, sunny position in a poor soil. If given too much water or a too rich soil, the ice-like vesicles are formed with less frequency. Excellent for the rock-garden, narrow borders, etc., as well as for pot culture. When the sun shines on the plant a remarkable effect is obtained from the reflections from the pustules.

(Hottentot Fig)
Herbaceous perennial
Flowering period: Apr.–July
Height: 10–12 ins.

Mesembryanthemum edule L. (syn. *Carpobrotus edulis*)
Native to South Africa. In general appearance very similar to *Mesembryanthemum acinaciforme*, but the flowers are yellow instead of red and sometimes suffused purplish. Also unlike the species *M. acinaciforme*, the foliage is not widened at its ends.

Herbaceous perennial
Flowering period: Apr.–June
Height: 8–12 ins.

Mesembryanthemum roseum L. (syn. *Lampranthus roseum*)
Native to South Africa. A very popular perennial species in gardens on the French and Italian Rivieras and one of the more hardy species, even tolerating one or two degrees of frost for brief periods. Height 8–12 ins., forming a dense carpet, and excellent for use as a ground cover in hot, dry, sunny positions. Flowers bright pink, up to 1½ ins. in diameter, with a long flowering period. Leaves needle-like, small, fleshy. The narrow petals of the daisy-like blooms have a shiny, enamelled aspect, while the central disc is yellow.

Mesembryanthemum tricolor Willd. (syn. *Erepsia mutabilis, Mesembryanthemum pyropaeum, Dorotheanthus gramineus*)

Native to South Africa. A dwarf, non-hardy annual not more than 4 ins. high with a compact habit. Minute, cylindrical, succulent, dark-green leaves that are hidden during summer by masses of vividly coloured, single, daisy-like flowers on minute stems. Each bloom is 1½ ins. in diameter and comes in white, pink, or red with the central zone a contrasting shade of blue, crimson, or white. Requires the hottest and driest position possible in full sun. Also excellent for pot culture.

Annual
Flowering period: June–Aug.
Height: 4 ins.

Mimosa

(Also see ACACIA)
Family: Leguminosae (or Mimosaceae)
Non-hardy trees, deciduous shrubs, or sub-shrubby perennials
Position: sun
Propagation: seed
Cultivation easy

Mimosa pudica

> But none ever trembled and panted with bliss
> In the garden, the field, or the wilderness,
> Like a doe in the noontide with love's sweet want,
> As the companionless Sensitive Plant.
>
> Shelley, "The Sensitive Plant"

> Weak with nice sense the chaste mimosa stands,
> From each rude touch withdraws her timid hands.
>
> Erasmus Darwin, "The Botanic Garden"

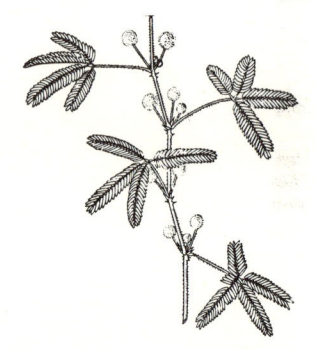

As already noted, the popular yellow-flowered flower-shop "mimosa" is actually an acacia. The genus *Mimosa* is large and comprehensive, comprising about 250 species of herbaceous perennials, shrubs, and even trees. The majority are native to tropical America and are therefore of greater use in tropical gardens than in temperate zones of Europe or the United States. There are only two species that are normally cultivated in northern gardens; both are small deciduous shrubs and neither is hardy. One, *Mimosa pudica* (popularly called the Sensitive Plant), is generally cultivated as an annual, frequently in pots, and it is one of the most remarkable plants found in nature. We have already referred to *Desmodium gyrans*, the Telegraph Plant, capable of certain movements in response to outside stimuli; but *Mimosa pudica* is even more remarkable, and capable of more spectacular motion. If touched, the feathery pairs of minute individual leaflets immediately fold together, and the leaf stalk lowers itself to a pendulous or nearly prostrate position leaving only the bare stalk and stem visible and giving the entire plant the appearance of being dead and withered. The energy and complicated mechanism that would cause such a large plant to collapse completely in a matter of seconds is remarkable; especially so when the collapse is only temporary and reverses itself a few minutes later. *Mimosa pudica* is always ready at the slightest touch to repeat the entire performance for an unlimited number of times. The phenomenon is so perfect and precise that if the minute leaflets are touched individually they will react one pair at a time, or even one-half a pair; the reaction will gradually extend along the entire length of the leaf as each minute segment is touched (there are up to forty segments in a single leaf). If violently agitated the entire plant reacts at once. Another curious feature is that the degree of sensitivity is more acute at a temperature of about 80°F. At higher or lower temperatures the plant reacts more slowly—below about 60°F. or above 100°F. This tends to confirm the theory that the plant's sensitive action is actually a form of defence against grazing animals, which would not feed at night—when the temperature is lower—or during the hottest part of the day—when the temperature is at its maximum. *Mimosa pudica* is easily raised from seed and grown as a pot plant. I always sow mine in March–April in an unheated greenhouse. By early August the plants are well-developed and in bloom. I use a soil mixture composed of 1 part ordinary garden soil, $\frac{1}{2}$ part peat, $\frac{1}{2}$ part leafsoil, and a small quantity of coarse sand. Obviously such an unusual plant has a particular fascination for children, and a small pot-grown specimen given as a gift provides a welcome change from toy moon rockets or jet aircraft.

The other fairly common garden species is *Mimosa spegazzinii*, a non-hardy deciduous shrub up to 8 ft. high. In frost-free localities it can be planted permanently in the open in a hot, sunny, moderately dry position; in colder areas it is generally grown as a pot plant for outdoor decoration from May to September and removed to a greenhouse for the winter. This, too, can be propagated from seed sown in spring in a warm greenhouse, using the same soil mixture as suggested for *Mimosa pudica*.

(Sensitive Plant or Humble Plant)
Sub-shrubby perennial (frequently grown as an annual)
Flowering period: July–Sept.
Height: up to $4\frac{1}{4}$ ft.

Mimosa pudica L.
Native to Brazil. A non-hardy semi-woody perennial of much-branched erect habit; stems slightly spiny. If planted permanently, it can reach a height of up to $4\frac{1}{2}$ ft., but when cultivated as a pot plant and treated as an annual, it generally reaches about 18 ins. Inflorescence a small globose head about $\frac{2}{3}$ in. in diameter composed of a compact mass of minute lavender-pink flowers of con-

siderable attraction. Leaves graceful, fern-like, bright green, bipinnate, up to 4 ins. long and 3 ins. wide. Each leaf is divided into as many as forty minute oval leaflets arranged in pairs. When the plant is touched the leaflets fold together and the leaf stalk droops to a pendulous position. Leaflets and leaf stalk return to their normal condition after a brief interval.

Mimosa spegazzinii Pir.
Native to Argentina. An attractive non-hardy deciduous shrub. If climate does not permit outdoor cultivation, it can be grown as a pot plant and placed outside during summer. Graceful much-divided foliage; small pink globose inflorescences in summer.

Deciduous spiny shrub
Flowering period: July–Sept.
Height: up to 6–8 ft.
Zone 10

Mimulus

(MONKEY FLOWER OR MUSK)
Family: Scrophulariaceae
Annuals, non-hardy herbaceous perennials, or small tender shrubs
Propagation: seed, cuttings, or division
Cultivation easy

The genus *Mimulus* is remarkable on several counts, especially since there are types to satisfy every fancy and environment. The natural distribution of those species normally cultivated in gardens is restricted to North and South America, but among eighty known species, there are prostrate herbaceous perennials, several annuals, and a few shrubs. Cultivation conditions vary also; some thrive in almost aquatic settings in nearly complete shade, while others require a hot, dry, sunny position. None, however, are hardy enough to tolerate long periods of frost; but many make excellent pot plants and can even serve as temporary house plants. Also interesting are the never-ending, often heated, sometimes ridiculous discussions concerning the supposed musk-like perfume of *Mimulus moschatus*. Some sources feel that the scented form of this species never existed; others maintain that it is actually the public that has lost its ability to smell the fragrance. It has been more or less definitely established that from 1919–1920 *Mimulus moschatus* did lose its perfume in most parts of the world and has since never regained it. No reason for this strange loss has ever been discovered. Even the name of the genus is unusual, deriving from the Latin *mimus* (a mimic), in reference to the often grotesque appearance of mimulus flowers, which resemble Roman and Greek theatrical masks. Popularly,

Mimulus cardinalis
From *Curtis's Botanical Magazine*,
1837, plate 3560

they are thought to resemble monkey faces. Those species not native to North or South America are indigenous to Asia and Australia. Cultural details and methods of propagation are so variable that they are given here individually for each species.

Mimulus brevipes Benth.
Native to California. A lovely large-flowered annual species with masses of 2-in.-long canary-yellow blooms. Will tolerate more sun than most mimulus, although in hot climates it should be grown in partial shade. Requires an abundance of moisture during the summer. Propagate from seed sown in a warm greenhouse in spring or from cuttings rooted in frames or in a greenhouse at any time during the summer.

Annual
Flowering period: July–Sept.
Height: 12–15 ins.

Mimulus cardinalis Douglas
Native to North America. A showy herbaceous perennial with crimson-scarlet snapdragon-like flowers. Excellent for beds and borders in a semi-shady position. Leaves opposite, oval, dentated, with conspicuous veins. Propagated by seed sown in a warm greenhouse in spring, by division of old plants in spring, from cuttings of young growths rooted in a greenhouse in May, or from cuttings of half-ripened growths rooted in frames during summer. When sowing mimulus seed (which is very fine and powder-like), do not cover it, but press it lightly into the soil with some flat object such as the bottom of a glass. The plants require a good fertile soil rich in decomposed organic matter and constantly moist, particularly in summer.

Herbaceous perennial
Flowering period: June–July
Height: up to 2¾ ft.

Mimulus cupreus Regel
Native to Chile. Herbaceous perennial with large coppery-orange flowers; the parent of a great many brilliantly coloured perennial garden hybrids. Some of the best are:

> Bees' Dazzler, brilliant scarlet
> Leopold, flowers yellow marked with orange
> Plumtree, a lovely shade of pink
> Queen's Prize, pink and yellow
> Red Emperor, crimson
> Whitecroft Scarlet, vermilion-scarlet

All these forms have a height of about 12 ins. and a very long flowering season. They give best results in a semi-shady position and require a moist soil. All must be propagated from cuttings or by division in spring if they are to be grown true to colour. Like most other mimulus they will not survive frost.

Herbaceous perennial
Flowering period: June–Sept.
Height: 12–15 ins.

Mimulus glutinosus Wendl. (syn. *Diplacus glutinosus* Nutt.)
Native to California. A small attractive evergreen shrub suitable for outdoor cultivation in a mild climate such as that found on the

Evergreen shrub
Flowering period: July–Sept.
Height: up to 3½ ft.
Zone 10 southwards

Riviera or in California or Florida. Particularly suitable for seaside localities, and also excellent when cultivated as a pot plant. Bears large salmon-yellow flowers throughout the summer. The foliage is dark green, small, oval, and sticky to the touch. The var. *puniceus* has crimson flowers. The original species may be propagated from seed sown in a warm greenhouse in spring, and both species and variety can be propagated by cuttings of half-ripened wood taken in July–August and rooted in frames. The plants require a fairly dry warm soil and a sunny position.

Herbaceous perennial
Flowering period: June–Sept.
Height: 18 ins.

Mimulus lewisii Pursh.
Native to British Columbia. Similar to *Mimulus cardinalis* but shorter and with pink flowers freely spotted with maroon. Propagation and cultural details as for *Mimulus cardinalis*.

Herbaceous perennial
Flowering period: May–Sept.
Height: 12 ins.

Mimulus luteus L.
Native to Chile. This species and its varieties have become naturalized in Europe and other parts of the world with a warm climate. Rounded-ovate leaves with parallel veins; the stem leaves smaller than the basal foliage and frequently quite narrow. Both the species and its forms need more moisture than most other species, and they will even thrive in very shallow water. Their long free-flowering period makes them particularly useful plants where the required cultural conditions can be provided. Some of the best varieties are:

> var. *duplex* (Hose-in-Hose), so-called because the flower structure gives the impression of one flower inside another. Yellow with bronze markings
> var. *guttatus* (syn. *Mimulus langsdorfii*), yellow blooms spotted with purple-brown or dark red
> var. *maculatus*, flowers yellow spotted with red

Mimulus luteus

The propagation of *Mimulus luteus* and its varieties is the same as for *Mimulus cardinalis*; as usual, in the case of varieties, the only certain method of obtaining true-to-colour reproduction is by means of cuttings or division rather than from seed. *Mimulus luteus* can also be grown from seed as an annual if sown in early spring in a warm greenhouse. The plants require a soil rich in humus and well-decomposed organic matter.

(Musk)
Perennial,
usually grown as an annual
Flowering period: June–Sept.
Height: 6–8ins.

Mimulus moschatus Douglas
Native to North America, and like *Mimulus luteus* often found naturalized in other temperate-zone countries. As already mentioned, this is the musk-scented mimulus that has lost its fragrance. Prostrate habit, with a rapidly expanding creeping form. Small yellow flowers are produced in the greatest profusion. Leaves opposite, dentated,

elongated-oval. Thrives in a damp position in complete shade, but it can also be grown in full sun if given plenty of water. Propagation is by seed sown in a warm greenhouse in early spring, or by breaking off fragments from the parent plant with a small piece of root and rooting them in a greenhouse or frame at any time during the summer. Although generally grown as an annual, *Mimulus moschatus* is actually a perennial in mild climates and it even makes excellent ground cover.

Mimulus primuloides L.
Native to the mountainous areas of the northwestern United States. A mat-forming dwarf perennial species that spreads rapidly by means of stolons, forming roots at every node. Flowers rich brilliant yellow, solitary, ¾ in. long, occasionally spotted reddish brown. Requires cool, moist conditions.

Herbaceous perennial
Flowering period: June–Sept.
Height: up to 4 ins.

Mimulus ringens L.
Native to North America. A tall herbaceous perennial with magnificent violet-coloured flowers freely produced throughout the summer. Has a much-branched habit and narrowly oblong leaves up to 4 ins. long. Excellent for naturalizing, but requires a very damp position. There is also a rare white-flowered form.

Herbaceous perennial
Flowering period: July–Sept.
Height: 2½–3½ ft.

Mirabilis

(FOUR-O'CLOCK OR MARVEL OF PERU)
Family: Nyctaginaceae
Tender tuberous-rooted herbaceous perennials often grown as annuals
Position: sun
Propagation: seed or division
Cultivation easy
Fragrant

At one time this genus was called *Admirabilis*; later its name was changed by Linnaeus to *Mirabilis*, taken from the Latin word *mirabilis* (admirable, wonderful). The name was chosen no doubt because of several curious habits of the plants rather than the actual beauty of its flowers. A single plant can bear different coloured blooms, and the custom of not opening until about 4 o'clock is another curious feature. In the hotter, sunnier south, opening time occurs even later, and the plants are evening- and night-flowering. The delightful French

Mirabilis Jalapa
From *Curtis's Botanical Magazine*,
1797, plate 371

popular name is *Belle de Nuit*, while the Italians call the plants *Bella di Notte*; the more prosaic British are content with Four-o'Clocks (with the advent of official Daylight Saving or Summer Time in Europe, this should now be Five-o'Clocks). The flowers do not have a corolla or petals but consist of a solitary, brilliantly coloured elongated calyx, identical in shape to a corolla, and scented. In its early stages this unusual calyx is enclosed in an involucre of small leaves. Of greater interest to the entomologist than to the botanist is the plant's attraction to night-flying moths who find the scent quite irresistible. If collectors of lepidoptera desire a rich harvest, all they have to do is to place their specially prepared traps near some mirabilis plants.

Mirabilis have been grown in Old World gardens since 1540, when they were first imported into Europe from the Peruvian Andes; they were never really popular plants, possibly because they are too easy to cultivate and often thought of as weeds, or considered too common for serious present-day gardening. In England they are often classified as "old-fashioned" flowers, which seems to suggest that at one time they were more popular and possibly even had a moment of fame. They have, however, achieved notoriety in another area. They were of great value to Correns in his experiments dealing with heredity, and later they were used as guinea-pigs in research work on the verification of the laws of genetics. In medicine, the name *Mirabilis Jalapa* is linked to an equivocal mistake. For a long time it was believed that the purgative jalap was obtained from the roots of that plant. Actually, the roots of *Mirabilis Jalapa* are far more violent in their cathartic action, more so than those of *Ipomoea purga,* from which the true jalap is extracted. The only substances now obtained from mirabilis have no medicinal value; in Japan a cosmetic is obtained from the powdered seeds, while in China the flowers are soaked in water to obtain a crimson dye used to colour gelatine made from seaweed, which would otherwise have the unappetizing colour of a dead fish.

Admirers of mirabilis can generally find some odd corner in the garden where it is effective and appreciated. It is more suited to informal rural gardens than to the neat, tidy garden; it also looks better grouped here and there, in a courtyard, at the side of a gate or door, or at the edge of a field or orchard rather than confined to formal beds or borders. It is an excellent subject for cultivating in large receptacles such as tubs, barrels, urns, or big pots, etc. Unfortunately, most of the commercially available seed comes as a mixture and does not always include the best colours. To obtain some of the really delightful colours, plants should be propagated only by means of the tubers (not from seed). The foliage certainly cannot be considered attractive; in fact, the leaves are definitely ugly and coarse. The plant compensates for this with the delicious fragrance of its flowers which, like the colour, varies from plant to plant. Only those with the most intense fragrance should be propagated. The perfume is so attractive after sundown that a row of plants located near an open window, or even a single pot plant, will give intense pleasure. In Europe such refinements are not always considered, but in the East the actual position of plants in the garden is a matter of prime importance.

Cultivation. Mirabilis are easy, generous plants without any unusual demands, growing and flowering almost anywhere. I have even seen them flourishing in almost pure sand in seaside localities and on hot, dry, windy terraces. They do, however, give best results when given an abundance of water in summer. The secret of growing really good plants on a terrace lies in giving them a generous supply of liquid organic fertilizer during their growth period and in planting the little tubers in new soil each season. The dormant tubers should be planted in spring as soon as they show signs of vegetation, arranging them on a layer of ordinary garden soil mixed with an equal proportion of well-composted manure and covering them with 2–3 ins. of sandy soil. The tubers can be used for up to five consecutive seasons. After this, it is advisable to propagate new plants raised from seed sown in March–April in an unheated greenhouse, or earlier in a heated greenhouse, placing 2–3 seeds in a small fibre pot. When the seedlings are large enough, and when the weather is suitable, they can be set out in the plants' flowering position. Mirabilis can also be successfully grown as annuals each year. In a warmer climate, the seed can be sown directly in the open ground in March–April (in April–May in colder localities). Seedlings will also appear spontaneously from self-sown seed, and these give excellent results if carefully thinned so that there is a distance of at least 8–10 ins. between each plant. For terrace plants, it is a mistake to attempt the cultivation of mirabilis in too-small receptacles; a minimum size of 12–15 ins. in diameter, 18 ins. in depth, and 15 ins. in length is required for a single vigorous plant. They prefer a compost of ordinary garden soil, sand, and plenty of well-composted organic matter. They like a moist atmosphere, plenty of light, and an abundance of water during hot weather. In mild localities, the tubers can be left in the ground during winter, but they are not hardy, and if the soil is liable to freeze in depth the small black tubers should be lifted and stored in moist peat or sand in a frost-free place until the following season.

(Four-o'Clock or Marvel of Peru)
Flowering period: June–Sept.
Height: 1½–3 ft.

Mirabilis Jalapa L. (syn. *Nyctago Jalapa, Nyctago hortensis*)
Native to Central America and to Peru. The most popular garden species. Tuberous, erect herbaceous plant, much-branched, the many nodes giving the branches a notched appearance. Leaves opposite, pale green, smooth, thin-textured, stalked, oval, pointed at the apex, and heart-shaped at the base. Flowers in terminal clusters of 3–6,

up to 2 ins. long and 1 in. wide, tubular or trumpet-shaped when fully expanded, opening in the late afternoon. The colours are exceptionally vivid and include crimson, red, scarlet, white, pink, yellow, etc.; either self-coloured, mottled, or bicoloured. Fragrant.

Mirabilis longiflora L. (syn. *Nyctago longiflora*)
Native to Mexico, Arizona, and Texas. Less known in gardens than the preceding but a better plant. Habit erect, branched, slightly sticky in all its parts, and wide-spreading. Leaves opposite, short-stalked or stalkless, light green, heart-shaped, pointed. Flowers very fragrant, opening in the late afternoon; narrowly tubular, up to 6 ins. long, wider at the mouth. Colour variable from pink to pinkish mauve or nearly white. Very free-flowering. Stamens and anthers yellow and very conspicuous. The var. *violacea* has violet blooms. Roots tuberous.

(Mexican Jalap)
Flowering period: June–Sept.
Height: 3 ft.

Monarda

(BEE BALM, OSWEGO TEA, HORSEMINT, OR BERGAMOT)
Family: Labiatae
Hardy herbaceous perennials or annuals
Position: partial shade or shade
Propagation: seed or division
Cultivation very easy
Aromatic

This genus of North American plants was named in honour of Nicholas Monardes (1493–1588), a Spanish physician who published an important book on American flora in 1571. Monardas are closely related to the culinary mint, and all have aromatic foliage. There are seventeen species, including perennial and annual types; several of these also have vividly coloured and decorative "flowers", although it is often the bracts rather than the true flowers that are so ornamental. They are somewhat coarse in appearance and can become quite rampant or even invasive in positions they find congenial, rapidly extending by self-sown seed and by their vigorous lateral growths. Monardas are particularly effective when massed and grown in an informal manner, especially when planted near water, by the side of a stream or the edge of a pond. The plants thrive in any ordinary garden soil that is cool, fresh, deep, and moist, and they are quite hardy. Propagation is very easy by division in spring or from seed sown outside in March–April.

Monarda didyma
From *Curtis's Botanical Magazine*,
1791, plate 145

Monarda citriodora Cerv. (Lemon Mint)
Annual
Flowering period: July–Sept.
Height: 1 ft.

Native to the United States, in an area extending from Illinois through Nebraska to Texas. An annual species up to 12 ins. high; leaves narrowly oblong, dentated, emitting a delicious lemon fragrance when rubbed or crushed. Flowers terminal, borne on erect stems which—as is the case with all monardas—are square; the colour is pale pink or whitish pink; individual blooms two-lipped, borne in a loosely formed, rounded inflorescence.

Monarda didyma L. (Oswego Tea, Bee Balm, or Red Balm)
Herbaceous perennial
Flowering period: June–July
Height: up to 2½ ft.

Native to North America, particularly the eastern states. A perennial species which with its numerous varieties constitutes the most popular garden monarda. A vigorous and robust plant with opposite, elongated, acute, dentated foliage rounded at the base; colour brilliant green. It is very free-flowering, with whorls of bright scarlet two-lipped longish flowers borne at the ends of rigid erect square stems. The bracts below the flowers are of a similar colour. The dried leaves are said to provide an excellent infusion known as Oswego or Pennsylvania Tea. Among the numerous varieties the following are all of considerable attraction:

    var. *alba*, white-flowered
    var. *Burgundy*, purple-blue
    var. *Cambridge Scarlet*, scarlet
    var. *Croftway Pink*, one of the best with brilliant pink blooms
    var. *Mrs. Perry*, crimson-red
    var. *violacea*, purple-red

Monarda fistulosa L. (Wild Bergamot)
Herbaceous perennial
Flowering period: May–July
Height: up to 3 ft.

Native to eastern North America. A vigorous, aromatic herbaceous perennial species up to 3 ft. high, with narrowly oval 6-in.-long leaves. Inflorescence a terminal whorl composed of narrow elongated flowers that vary in colour from pale pink to red; the surrounding bracts are generally light purple. A most useful and easily grown plant for the herbaceous border or for growing massed in semi-wild conditions.

Muscari

(GRAPE HYACINTH)
Family: Liliaceae
Hardy or half-hardy perennial bulbs
Flowering period: Feb.–Apr.

Position: sun or shade
Propagation: division or seed
Cultivation very easy
Fragrant

Muscari are modest, graceful bulbous plants whose flowers are a welcome prelude to spring. They are native to continental Europe, the Mediterranean regions, and Asia Minor; and are found growing mostly in grasslands, thin woodlands, at the base of hedges, etc. The majority of species are very similar, with linear lanceolate leaves; the inflorescences are in the form of small racemes, have globose or oval individual flowers and are generally some shade of blue, although there are also white- and yellow-flowered varieties. The best-known and most widely cultivated species in gardens is *Muscari botryoides*. Muscari are very hardy, perfect for naturalizing in grass, at the base of large trees, among flowering shrubs, in the rock-garden, or even in window boxes. Once planted they multiply rapidly and their intensely blue flowers are particularly pleasing against a background of green grass. Some delightful combinations can be achieved by planting blue muscari around a group of yellow forsythias, or by planting them near some pale-pink prunus.

Cultivation. Easy. Simply plant the small bulbs in early autumn and then leave them alone for several years. They need to be dug up only to divide the dormant bulbs or if they form too dense a mass. Muscari thrive in any normal soil, in sun or shade, but they prefer a cool, moist site rather than a dry, hot, arid one. Besides division, propagation may also be effected from seed sown in pots, outside, in late summer or in spring.

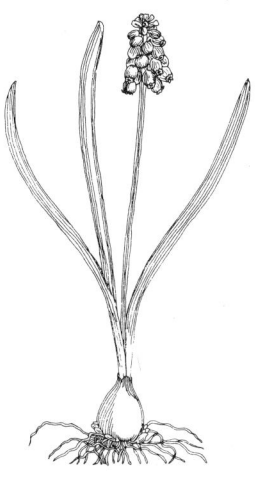

Muscari racemosum

Flowering period: Mar.–Apr.
Height: 8 ins.

Muscari armeniacum L.
Native to Asia Minor. An elegant, graceful species that has been the origin of many garden hybrids, all ideal for naturalizing in grass. The original species has dense racemes of beautiful, dark-blue flowers with the petal tips marked white, and borne on rigid stems. They are slightly scented. Propagation is very easy by division of the dormant bulbs. The following are some of the best forms:

> Cantab, dwarf, with pale-blue flowers
> Heavenly Blue, similar to the type, but more intensely coloured
> Early Giant, similar to Heavenly Blue but earlier flowering

In each case the leaves are long, narrow, and dark green. They often appear the previous autumn, but they never seem to suffer from the winter cold.

(Starch Hyacinth)
Flowering period: Feb.–Mar.
Height: 4–6 ins.

Muscari botryoides Mill.
Native to Europe. One of the first bulbs to bloom in spring. Not so robust as the preceding, and not so tall, but a very lovely plant

Muscari botryoides
From *Curtis's Botanical Magazine*,
1791, plate 157

with pale-blue globular flowers borne on small, dense racemes. The leaves are few, shorter than the flower stems, linear, and channelled towards the centre. A species particularly suited to the rock-garden or for pot culture. There is a lovely rather rare white-flowered var. *Pearls of Spain*.

(Yellow Grape Hyacinth)
Flowering period: April
Height: up to 9 ins.

Muscari macrocarpum Sweet
Native to the Aegean Islands. The most beautiful of the yellow-flowered species. Leaves strap-shaped and much wider than in other muscari. Flower stems up to 9 ins. high bearing an inflorescence of intensely yellow bell-shaped pendulous flowers with brown edges; their fleshy texture gives them a waxy appearance. Cannot be considered hardy where the soil is frozen in depth in winter.

(Musk-scented Muscari)
Flowering period: Mar.–Apr.
Height: 5–8 ins.

Muscari moschatum Willd.
Native to Asia Minor. Foliage grass-like but fleshy, linear, channelled, up to $\frac{2}{3}$ in. wide. Yellowish-green flowers are strongly musk-scented and are borne in racemes carried on 8-in.-high stems. The flower tube is narrow with a wider star-like mouth.

Flowering period: Feb.–Mar.
Height: 8 ins.

Muscari racemosum L.
Native to Europe where it is an attractive common plant. It is also one of the most robust and easily grown species; however, it does not have the decorative value of the species *M. armeniacum* or *M. botryoides,* and it is more suited to naturalizing in semi-wild parts of the garden. Flowers small, slightly fragrant, dark blue with the petal tips marked white; shape ovoid with a narrower mouth. Leaves narrow, dark green, channelled.

Myosotis

(FORGET-ME-NOT)
Family: Boraginaceae
Hardy herbaceous annuals, biennials, or perennials
Position: sun or partial shade
Propagation: seed or division
Cultivation easy

In spite of many crosses and frequent hybridization, myosotis still retains its modesty and air of rural simplicity; mankind, however, has devoted itself to inventing stories and legends about these plants which, for the most part, are nauseatingly sentimental. The most pleasing and simplest story has for its protagonists the forget-me-not and God, who, according to the German tradition of this legend, is an old, very dignified, melancholy figure (somewhat like Wotan in Act III of *Siegfried*). After much work distributing names among all the animals, plants, flowers, and objects, a small voice cried out "Forget me not, O Lord," and God replied, "Forget-me-not shall be your name." Another story is about two children who always played together and loved each other deeply and truly. One day, when the boy had grown up, he set out to seek his fortune in the world. On parting, the two friends promised each other that whenever they found one of the little blue flowers so characteristic of the woods where they played, they would pick it as a reminder of the one who was absent. After many years, when both were old, they met at the edge of a wood; neither recognized the other, but seeing one of the blue flowers they both bent down to pick it, their hands touching. . . . From then on, the flower was called Forget-me-not. After such over-sentimentality, it is interesting to note that the name of genus *Myosotis* is of Greek origin, *mys* (mouse) and *ous, otos* (ear), signifying mouse ear. It must be confessed, however, that the fancied similarity between a myosotis leaf and a mouse's ear is less real than apparent. The genus comprises about fifty species, native to Europe, Asia, America, South Africa, Australia, and New Zealand.

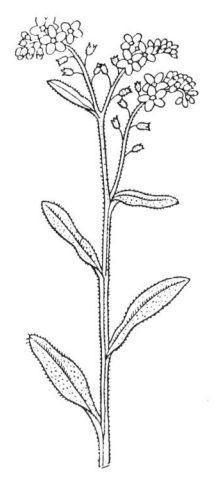

Cultivation. The majority of garden forget-me-nots are hybrids, derived mostly from *Myosotis sylvestris*. They require a fairly moist soil and are particularly happy at the edges of ponds and streams. Those hybrids used for bedding or for edging require abundant watering. One of the most effective uses for the annual dwarf varieties is as a ground cover in tulip beds, where they make a most appropriate background and prolong the beds' own flowering period. Particularly delightful effects can be created by associating yellow tulips with blue forget-me-nots, or planting pink ones with white tulips. (The young forget-me-not plants must be planted before the tulip bulbs, thus avoiding the bare appearance of the beds before the bulbs start into growth.) Annual and biennial forget-me-nots can be sown in June or July in frames or in nursery beds, planting the seedlings out in their flowering positions in autumn. The perennial forget-me-nots are easily propagated by division at any time except during winter; or propagate by cuttings that will root with the greatest ease in spring. Perennial forget-me-nots can also be propagated from seed sown in spring, outdoors in pots or in frames. In either case, seed should be sown in a compost containing at least half organic material such as peat or leafsoil.

Myosotis alpestris

Myosotis alpestris Schmidt (syn. *Myosotis rupicola*)
Native to Europe. A perennial species found growing wild in thin woodlands and alpine meadows. The entire plant is densely covered

Herbaceous perennial
Flowering period: Apr.–Aug.
Height: about 2–6 ins.
Position: sun or half-shade
Slightly scented

with fine hairs. Stems erect, much-branched. Inflorescence a dense compact raceme. Leaves oblong, stalkless. The flowers are slightly scented, sky-blue, occasionally white. The var. *stricta* has very thin erect stems; the var. *aurea* has golden-yellow foliage.

(Field Forget-me-not)
Annual or biennial
Flowering period: Mar.–July
Height: 8–12 ins.
Position: sun or half-shade

Myosotis arvensis Lam.

Native to Europe and Asia. An annual or biennial species generally found in fields and grasslands. Stems much-branched, hairy; leaves oblong, stalkless, obtuse. Very similar to *Myosotis alpestris* but with the individual flowers more widely spaced on the racemes and the calyx deeply divided into five lobes of equal size. Flowers blue or white. A species that thrives in poor soils.

Herbaceous perennial
Flowering period: Apr.–May
Height: 10–12 ins.
Position: partial shade

Myosotis azorica H. C. Wats.

Native to the Azores. A dwarf perennial species, hairy in all its parts; leaves oblong, obtuse. Inflorescence a dense raceme, calyx divided into five parts, habit erect. Flowers fairly large, indigo-blue with a white mark at the throat. Suitable for damp soils in a shady position. The var. *coelestina* has sky-blue flowers.

Herbaceous perennial
Flowering period: June–July
Height: 1½–2 ins.
Position: sun
Cultivation difficult

Myosotis caespitosa Schultz

Native to Central Europe, where it is found in very damp localities. One of the smallest of the perennial species and a difficult plant to cultivate in gardens, especially at low altitudes. Requires a sunny position without excessive heat. The entire plant is covered with fine dense hairs. Stems erect, leaves linear-oblong. Inflorescence an obtuse raceme with the basal flowers bearing minute leaf-like bracts. Flowers small, light blue.

Herbaceous perennial
or biennial
Flowering period: Mar.–Apr.
Height: 6–8 ins.
Position: sun or partial shade

Myosotis dissitiflora Baker

Native to Switzerland. A perennial or biennial species covered with minute erect hairs. Leaves wide, spatulate-oblong, acute. Inflorescences on longer and more extended racemes than in the other species, with larger blue flowers.

(Water Forget-me-not)
Herbaceous perennial
or biennial
Flowering period: Mar.–Apr.
Height: 8–9 ins.
Position: partial
or complete shade

Myosotis palustris Hill (syn. *Myosotis scorpioides*)

Native to Europe and Asia. A perennial or biennial species found in very damp positions near streams, ponds, and at the edges of ditches. Stems stoloniferous, very narrow, and root-forming at the nodes. Leaves oblong-lanceolate, nearly stalkless. Inflorescence a raceme bearing only a few intensely blue flowers with yellow eyes. Very common in the wild state. In gardens requires shade and a wet soil.

Perennial or biennial
Flowering period: Mar.–May
Height: 12–18 ins.
Position: sun or partial shade

Myosotis sylvatica Hoffm. (syn. *Myosotis alpina, Myosotis oblonga*)

Native to Europe. A perennial or biennial species, compact and bushy, with thin pointed leaves that are soft and slightly woolly surfaced.

Myosotis dissitiflora
From *Curtis's Botanical Magazine*,
1898, plate 7589

Inflorescence made up of tiny groups of vivid blue small scented flowers. The chief parent of the popular garden forget-me-nots which bloom continuously from spring until early summer. The original species is common in light woodlands in rather dry soils; but the garden hybrids require a rather moist soil rich in humus and are tolerant of sun or shade. Some of the best of these are:

    Alba, 8–10 ins., white-flowered
    Blue Ball, 6–8 ins., with indigo-blue flowers
    Rose Pink, about 7 ins., with pink flowers
    Ultramarine, 6 ins., with dark-blue flowers

Myrtus

(MYRTLE)
(*Also see* VINCA)
Family: Myrtaceae
Tender or half-hardy evergreen shrubs
Position: sun
Propagation: seed or cuttings
Cultivation easy
Aromatic

Myrtus communis is the only species of the genus *Myrtus* found growing wild in Europe, although it may not be a true native and there is good reason to suspect that it was imported from Iran or Afghanistan centuries ago. Now, however, it is one of the characteristic plants which form the basis of the famous Mediterranean *maquis* (a thick heath-like growth of small trees, shrubs, and underbrush). It is also a plant steeped in Classical and mythological tradition. It was much-loved by the Greeks, and the Romans, especially, held it in high esteem. Myrtles were often associated with the goddess of love, Venus, and bushes were also planted around temples of Quirinus (with Mars and Jupiter, one of the three tutelary deities of the Roman State). Virgil speaks of Venus's fair myrtle, and in the *Odes* of Horace (Book I, xxxviii) we have:

    Plainer myrtle pleases me
      Thus outstretched beneath my vine,
    Myrtle more becoming thee,
      Waiting with thy master's wine,

Poets were traditionally crowned with wreaths of myrtle (as victors were crowned with laurel), and the plant was often apostrophized in song and story. Also, Pliny the Elder asserts that roast pork is made even more tasty when dished up with a sauce of myrtle berries, and the berries were often employed in making a wine that was highly thought of for hundreds of years. According to an ancient Middle Eastern legend, Adam took a branch of myrtle with him when he was expelled from Eden, and kept the sprig as a reminder of his sinless existence in the Garden. The Egyptians adorned themselves with myrtle garlands on festal occasions; even today in many Old World countries myrtle retains its association with happy memories, and a sprig of myrtle is often used in wedding bouquets.

Myrtle flowers are modest but particularly graceful. The foliage of *Myrtus communis* has an unmistakable and delightful fragrance, and a cologne called Acqua Angelica is distilled from its leaves; they have also been used to make a type of tea.

The genus comprises about one hundred species, with an unusually wide area of distribution; in the Northern Hemisphere extending from Southern Europe to Asia, and in the Southern Hemisphere, from New Zealand to South America. They are warm-climate plants and even the hardiest will tolerate only a few degrees of frost, thus making their outdoor cultivation in the north or at high altitudes difficult. Myrtles are particularly successful in seaside localities and are tolerant of alkaline (calcareous) soils. *Myrtus communis,* in particular, is excellent for hedges that are aromatic, free-flowering, evergreen, and attractive in autumn when in fruit. The plants can be kept cut to any size or left to develop in an informal manner. They appreciate a well-drained fertile soil in a hot, sunny, fairly dry position. Propagation can be from seed sown in a greenhouse in spring, by soft cuttings started in spring in a heated greenhouse, or from cuttings of half-ripened wood taken in July and started in frames. All species normally grown in gardens also make excellent pot plants.

Myrtus bullata Soland.
Native to New Zealand. A most attractive, distinct, different species with larger, almost circular foliage of leathery texture and reddish brown in colour. The leaf surface has the appearance of being blistered because of its corrugations. Flowers white with purple calyx. At the Royal Botanic Gardens at Kew, it flowered for the first time in 1854.

Flowering period: July–Aug.
Height: up to 15 ft.
Zone 10

Myrtus communis L.
Native to the Mediterranean regions, Southern Europe, and Asia. An evergreen shrub that can reach a height of up to 12 ft., although in gardens it is generally smaller, with a rounded compact habit; however, very old specimens can attain the proportions of a small tree. The foliage is small, opposite, oval or oval-lanceolate, leathery,

(True Myrtle)
Flowering period: July–Sept.
Height: up to 12 ft.
Zone 9 southwards

with a dark-green, shiny surface. Leaves have a characteristic pleasing aroma when crushed. The flowers are small, solitary, axillary, cream-white, and fragrant; in autumn appear the fleshy, lovely dark blue-black berries, rendering the branches most attractive. The var. *tarentina* (Tarentum Myrtle) has smaller leaves and white fruits. Recognizable myrtle twigs have been found in Roman tombs two thousand years old.

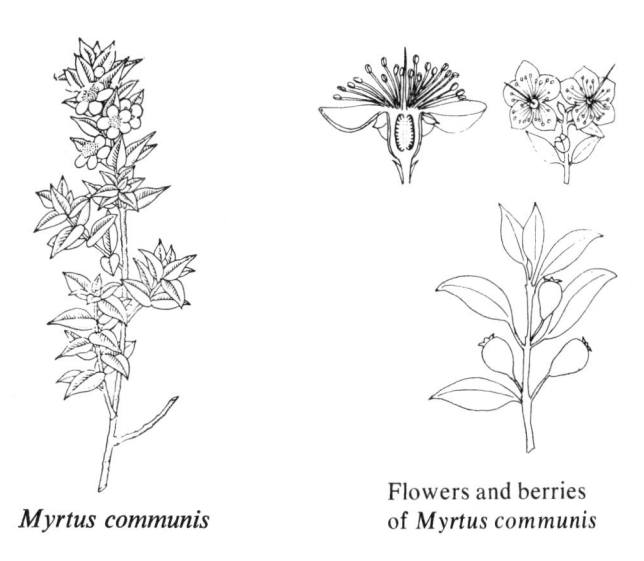

Myrtus communis

Flowers and berries of *Myrtus communis*

Flowering period: July–Aug.
Height: nearly prostrate
Zone 8 southwards

Myrtus nummularia Poiret
Native to South America and to the Falkland Islands. This species is completely different from all others. It forms a prostrate evergreen shrub that develops into a dense carpet of vegetation never more than a few inches high. Leaves small, oval, up to $\frac{1}{4}$ in. long, brilliant dark green, glabrous on either surface, with recurved edges. Flowers white, up to $\frac{1}{3}$ in. in diameter, freely produced, with prominent stamens. Fruit a $\frac{1}{4}$-in.-long pink berry. This species has been known to botanists for many years. Charles Darwin collected it in Tierra del Fuego in 1833 during the historic voyage of the *Beagle*. So far it has failed to become popular or widely planted, although it is the most hardy of the myrtles and therefore excellent to use as a carpeting plant, for the rock-garden, or for planting in walls. Always needs a damp position.

(Chilean Guava)
Flowering period: July–Aug.
Height: up to 8–9 ft.
Zone 10

Myrtus ugni Molina (syn. *Ugni molinae, Eugenia ugni*)
Native to Chile. A large evergreen shrub with leather-textured shiny ovate foliage similar to the typical myrtle but greyish white on the undersurface. Flowers small, pale pink, five-petalled. Fruits in the form of a reddish-purple berry about $\frac{1}{2}$ in. wide, very juicy, edible, and with an agreeable flavour.

Narcissus

(Daffodil, Jonquil, and Narcissus)
Family: Amaryllidaceae
Hardy and tender perennial bulbs
Position: sun or partial shade
Propagation: seed or division of dormant bulbs
Cultivation very easy
Fragrant
Useful for cutting
Poisonous

Double-flowered
Narcissus pseudo-narcissus

> O Proserpina!
> For the flowers now that frighted thou let'st fall
> From Dis's waggon! daffodils
> That come before the swallow dares, and take
> The winds of March with beauty. . . .
>   (Shakespeare, *The Winter's Tale,* Act IV, Scene 3)

The reader who expects to read here something of the fables concerning the mythical Narcissus will be disillusioned. The flower of this name has nothing to do with that neurotic, self-loving youth. According to Pliny the Elder, Plutarch, and many other Classical writers, the name of the genus *Narcissus* derives from the Greek *narkan*, which means to stupefy (the word narcotic is derived from the same root), because it was thought that both the scent of narcissus flowers and the substances contained in them possessed narcotic properties. In Antiquity the flower was often associated with Avernus, a sort of limbo or forecourt to the Underworld, where the dead first arrived—and from where a return to earth was still possible—before the final crossing of Lethe on the journey down to Hades or Elysium. Thus, to the pre-Classical Greeks, Avernus signified a stage that was not as final as death, a strange borderland that lay on the fringes of consciousness and unconsciousness (a state of being for which narcotics often provide the key). This association with the limbo-like Avernus was not due solely to the narcotic properties of the narcissus but also to the rather deathly, almost lunar pallor of the flowers. There are further Classical connexions with the Underworld. When Persephone was abducted by Hades she was gathering poppies, violets, and narcissi; and it was at the moment that she plucked the narcissus that Hades burst forth and carried her to his domain. The Greeks also dedicated the flower to Hecate, Queen of the Underworld, and to Demeter, Persephone's mother and goddess of fertility.

Narcissus Tazetta

The mythological aspects of the narcissus were not always associated with the valley of the shadow, however. Garlands of the flower were often used to adorn statues of Dionysus, and, according to some mythographers, narcissi were favoured by Aphrodite, who, to make herself even more beautiful in the eyes of Paris, appeared before him surrounded by a veritable sea of narcissi. Poetic allusions to narcissi—associating the flower with Persephone or, in the case of Theocritus, with Europa, as well as with that pallid youth, Narcissus—are so numerous that it would be a great effort to cite them all, and a still greater effort to read them. It is sufficient to recall such names as Virgil, Ovid, Sophocles, and Shakespeare.

The true medicinal values or virtues of the plant are slight. Bulbs of the European species *N. Jonquilla, N. Tazetta, N. poeticus,* and *N. Pseudo-narcissus* have been used in folk medicine for what were believed to be their purgative, dermal, and depurative actions. The essential substance contained in these bulbs is narcissine, a substance so poisonous that even minute doses of 8–10 gr. can be fatal. The poison reacts on the nervous system and causes inflammation of the stomach lining. In 1587 yellow and white narcissi were mentioned in a German herbarium, which prescribed an infusion made from the bulbs with honey as a poultice to alleviate gout.

In the perfume districts, such as Grasse and Cannes in France, as well as centres in the Near East and China and other Far Eastern countries, narcissi are cultivated for the extraction of a perfume. The most useful species for this purpose are *N. Jonquilla, N. Pseudo-narcissus,* and *N. poeticus.* About 1,500 lbs. of flowers are necessary to provide $2\frac{1}{2}$ lbs. of essence.

In 1629, John Parkinson referred to the var. *Van Sion*, imported into England by a Flemish merchant, and mentions that at that time ninety-four varieties of narcissus were cultivated in English gardens. By the eighteenth century, the number had further increased through the importation of new varieties and the raising of new hybrids, all causing great confusion in the botanical world. Even now there is controversy about the number of narcissus species; some authorities recognize only nine species, others as many as forty. One thing is certain, however; the narcissus, like the tulip and lily, is a flower that is still evolving, with the continuous introduction of new forms and types with different aspects and new colours, while new uses are constantly being found for the different types.

The genus is diffused throughout Europe, in the southern regions in particular, North Africa, and Asia Minor. Only one species, *Narcissus Tazetta,* extends into the Orient, passing through Iran and into China and Japan. However, there is some doubt if the species is a true native to those countries; it may have escaped from the gardens of Portuguese settlers in the colonies where it was widely cultivated.

Narcissus triandus var. *albus*

Narcissus Jonquilla
From *Curtis's Botanical Magazine*,
1787, plate 15

Wilson and Bell take up more than ten pages of their book, *The Fragrant Year,* to give extremely useful information concerning narcissus perfume. They note that all narcissus blooms are to a greater or lesser degree fragrant. Those not scented constitute rare exceptions. Concerning the perfume of *Narcissus Pseudo-narcissus,* Fletcher writes that the trumpet types of narcissus have a fragrance difficult to describe. It is not sweet like that of lilies, nor aromatic like many herbs, and it is doubtful if anybody would appreciate it bottled, since it is not that kind of fragrance, but it is strong, agreeable, almost earthy, and garden-like. The same author notes that the older varieties are the most strongly scented, and the types with the smallest cup or trumpet have the most pronounced perfume (such as the *Jonquilla* and *Tazetta* types).

Cultivation. The narcissi (except for the *Tazetta* group) are hardy bulbs of the easiest cultivation; they are easier than tulips and hyacinths, and more suitable for permanent planting under natural conditions, such as in rough grass, among deciduous shrubs, or in thin woodlands. When cultivated in gardens, the bulbs can be left undisturbed for 4–5 years or more; they should be removed from the soil only for division and multiplication, as they increase so rapidly. Narcissi thrive in almost any well-drained, fertile, not-too-compact soil. They should be planted in areas where they will not be disturbed during the bulbs' long dormant period in summer. The best planting time is September, and certainly not later than mid-October because root action begins early.

Propagation is by division of the dormant bulbs, so freely produced at the sides of the parent bulb; or from seed sown as soon as it is ripe, in pots, pans, or flats, outside or in frames. Only the species, however, will breed true from seed. Germination is generally very slow, sometimes taking up to two years; while another two years are necessary before the young bulbs will reach flowering size, although these periods vary according to the species. Narcissi are excellent for growing in receptacles and for forcing, in the same manner as tulips and hyacinths (see pages 619 and 1319).

Narcissi are so numerous and so varied in form that when describing them it is necessary to divide them into eight groups or sections:

Bulbocodium group
Cyclamineus group
Jonquilla group
Poeticus group
Tazetta group
Triandrus group
Autumn-flowering group

Each group has its species, forms, varieties, and garden hybrids, and each group has its own particular characteristics. Practically the only point they have in common is they are mostly hardy bulbs; for the rest, their differences in size, habit, flowering period, and general appearance are vast and varied, although their predominant colours are white and yellow.

Bulbocodium group. These are minute narcissi that have the curious common name Hoop Petticoat narcissus because the shape of the miniature flower resembles the crinoline petticoats of many years ago. There are only two species, but several varieties.

Cyclamineus group. Only one species, but several varieties that are the gems of the genus, with minute cyclamen-like flowers.

Jonquilla group. This group contains the most strongly scented narcissi, and includes about half a dozen species together with numerous varieties. The flowers are borne in groups.

Poeticus group. The so-called Poet's Narcissus with a very wide natural habitat extending from Spain to Greece and including the Alps and Pyrenees. Variable in form and the parent of numerous hybrids.

Tazetta group. A group of miniature narcissi with their flowers borne in bunches. Has a wider distribution than any other group, extending from Spain through the Mediterranean regions, passing through Asia Minor, Iran, and Kashmir into China and Japan. This wide distribution has created many geographical forms (at least fifty-four have been recorded). There is a certain amount of discussion about whether they constitute separate species or not. There are also many garden hybrids. They are all sweetly scented and include some of the best varieties for forcing into bloom for sale as cut flowers. They are also excellent for forcing for indoor flowering. They are divided into three sub-sections: *bicolor,* with the petals white and the central cup or corona orange or yellow; *alba,* with the petals and central cup or corona white; and *lutea,* with the petals and central cup or corona both yellow.

Triandrus group. This includes some of the most graceful of the smaller species and hybrids. Excellent for forcing in pots and for the rock-garden. Their chief characteristic is their pendulous flowers, borne either singly or in groups, with recurved petals; the leaves are small, narrow, filiform. All prefer a sunny position in very well-drained, light soil.

Trumpet group. The largest group, containing a vast number of species, forms, varieties, and hybrids, all of which have a more or less elongated trumpet in place of the saucer-shaped corona or cup. Borne singly on erect stems. Included in this group are the typical familiar large-flowered daffodils of our gardens. They are of the easiest cultivation, superb for naturalizing, and they increase very rapidly. They prefer a cool, moderately moist soil in partial shade; except in northern localities where they prefer full sun. Sometimes there are complaints that bulbs fail to bloom. This may be caused by

Narcissus cyclamineus

excessive shade or from not dividing and replanting old groups of bulbs that are suffocating one another; but in most cases the cause is due to the leaves being cut down while still green, instead of allowing them to mature and die back naturally.

Autumn-flowering group. It may be a surprise to some people that there are autumn-flowering narcissus, but there are several such species of considerable beauty and certainly of the greatest interest. They require a warm, sunny position and are better suited to the south. In more northern gardens the short coolish summers do not permit them to develop and bloom satisfactorily. They all have central trumpets much less developed than the spring-flowering narcissus, and they are sweetly scented. The bulbs are less hardy and not suitable to cold zones where the soil is liable to freeze in depth.

Flowering period: Jan.–Mar.
Height: 2½–3 ins.
Position: sun

Narcissus asturiensis L. (*Trumpet* group)
Native to the mountainous regions of Spain. Sometimes referred to as *Narcissus minimum,* a most appropriate name because they are trumpet-flowered narcissus in miniature, with a height of only 2½–3 ins. The blooms are dark golden-yellow with the edges of the trumpet dentated; leaves minute and grass-like. Very early-flowering and should, therefore, be planted in a position that is protected from rough weather. The bulbs require a particularly well-drained soil.

(Petticoat Narcissus
or Hoop Petticoat Narcissus)
Flowering period: Apr.–May
Height: 6–8 ins.
Position: sun or partial shade

Narcissus Bulbocodium L. (*Bulbocodium* group)
Native to Southern Europe. Foliage small, almost thread-like; flowers funnel-shaped with a diameter of about 1–1¼ ins. at the mouth; yellow, solitary, borne on thin, graceful stems up to 6–8 ins. high. Perfect for naturalizing on a large scale in grass, between trees and shrubs, etc.; excellent also for growing in pans. The var. *citrinus* has lemon-yellow flowers.

Flowering period: Feb.–Apr.
Height: 8 ins.
Position: sun

Narcissus canaliculatus L. (*Tazetta* group)
Generally considered to be a dwarf form of *Narcissus Tazetta*. Has all the characteristics of that species (which see), but is later-flowering. Corona yellow and petals white. The strongly scented flowers are in groups of up to six per stem. Ideal for the rock-garden and for forcing in pots.

Flowering period: March
Height: 4–6 ins.
Position: sun

Narcissus cantabricus L. (*Bulbocodium* group)
Native to southern France, Spain, and North Africa. Thread-like foliage; flowers funnel-shaped, often 2–3 per stem, snow-white, with almost transparent petals and with very conspicuous stamens.

Flowering period: Feb.–Mar.
Height: 4–6 ins.
Position: semi-shade

Narcissus cyclamineus (*Cyclamineus* group)
Native to Spain and Portugal, and the only species of the group. One of the most beautiful and most original of the miniature narcissi.

Narcissus Bulbocodium
From *Curtis's Botanical Magazine*,
1789, plate 88

Narcissus poeticus
From *Curtis's Botanical Magazine*,
1792, plate 193

Foliage minute, grass-like; flowers vivid yellow and, as indicated by the specific name, similar in form to a wild cyclamen, but with the corolla narrower and tubular; also the petals are completely recurved, which—with imaginative fantasy worthy of a Baroque poet—a great botanical expert compared to "the laid-back ears of an angry horse", a description which is most appropriate, although the length of the flower is only 1 in. An excellent species for naturalizing, and for cultivation in pots for indoor display. Prefers a cool, shady, moist position. Not frost-tolerant.

Flowering period: Sept.–Oct.
Height: 8–10 ins.
Position: sun

Narcissus elegans Spach. (syn. *Narcissus autumnalis*) (*Autumn-flowering* group)
Native to Algeria, southern Italy, and the Mediterranean islands. Foliage linear and flat, channelled, $\frac{1}{4}$ in. wide, up to 10 ins. long, appears with the flowers. The erect stems bear one or more blooms 2 ins. in diameter, with the central corona almost flat; pale orange, with the petals greenish white, widely spaced, thin-textured, and undulated. Not hardy in northern gardens.

(Jonquil or Daffodil)
Flowering period: March
Height: 12 ins.
Position: sun

Narcissus Jonquilla L. (*Jonquilla* group)
Native to Spain, Portugal, North Africa, and the Balearic Islands, but also found growing wild in various parts of Southern Europe, escaping from gardens and naturalizing itself here and there. This is certainly the narcissus with the strongest, most pleasing fragrance. The flowers are golden-yellow, small, saucer-shaped, and borne in groups of up to six on erect, slender stems. The leaves are very narrow, up to 12 ins. long, less than $\frac{1}{4}$ in. wide, elegant, and semi-cylindrical like rush leaves.

(Poet's Narcissus)
Flowering period: Apr.–May
Height: 6–8 ins.
Position: partial shade

Narcissus poeticus L. (*Poeticus* group)
Native to Southern Europe. Flowers solitary on tall erect stems; very fragrant, with white petals, and with the edges of the flattish corona reddish scarlet and orange. The latest to bloom of the spring-flowering narcissi, often remaining in bloom until May. The small-flowered var. *verbenensis*, with star-like blooms, has a particularly intense perfume; while the var. *recurvus*, with recurved petals and a particularly colourful central corona, is especially popular in English gardens. It is often called Pheasant's Eye narcissus because the centre of the bloom has a certain similarity to a pheasant's eye. This is an even later-flowering variety, with an abundance of robust tall erect glaucous-green foliage. Both the species and the varieties prefer a fresh, rather moist semi-shady position.

(Trumpet Narcissus, Daffodil, or Lent Lily)
Flowering period: Feb.–Mar.
Height: 10–15 ins.
Position: sun or partial shade

Narcissus Pseudo-narcissus L. (*Trumpet* group)
Native to Europe. The original species is rarely found in gardens, but its many forms and hybrids constitute the largest and most

widely cultivated group of narcissi, including the popular daffodils. All are conspicuous for their large flowers and central trumpet. The foliage is abundant, channelled, linear, rather wide, glaucous green. Each flower stem bears a solitary bloom, with the central trumpet lobed or ruffled at the edges. The blooms can be bicoloured or with the petals and central trumpet the same colour. The flowering period can vary from February to April according to the locality and variety; one form is known in England as Lent Lily because it blooms at that period. It is impossible to list the vast number of garden hybrids of *Narcissus Pseudo-narcissus*, with their many forms, sizes, and colours. They vary from 10–15 ins., and the predominant colours are shades of yellow, cream, and white; although strenuous efforts are being made to increase the colour range of the pink-flowered varieties. The following is a brief but representative selection of the most widely grown varieties:

Yellow-flowered Varieties

> Burgemeester Gouverneur, very large, golden-yellow
> Dutch Master, golden-yellow with the central trumpet dentated
> Garron, primrose-yellow, very large and very vigorous
> Golden Harvest, golden-yellow, one of the most popular and one of the best for forcing
> King Alfred, golden-yellow, early-flowering
> Moonrise, lemon-yellow, wide central trumpet
> Mulatto, sulphur-yellow with the central trumpet white internally
> Unsurpassable, large, golden-yellow flowers

Bicoloured Varieties

> Celebrity, cream-white with yellow trumpet
> Foresight, milk-white with yellow trumpet
> Oklahoma, white with dark golden-yellow trumpet
> Queen of Bicolors, white with canary-yellow trumpet
> World's Favourite, white with pale-yellow trumpet

White-flowered Varieties

> Angel's Wings, large silver-white flowers
> Beersheba, the best white narcissus, excellent for naturalizing
> Mount Hood, pure white with cream-white trumpet
> Mrs. E. H. Krelage, snow-white with ivory-white trumpet

Pink-flowered Varieties

> Mrs. R. O. Backhouse, ivory-white with dark-pink trumpet
> Pink Isle, white with pink trumpet
> Rose Caprice, white with pink trumpet suffused green at the base

> Salmon Trout, the best of the pink narcissus; white with salmon-pink trumpet
>
> Toscanini, white with trumpet ivory-white and reverse of the petals apricot-pink

Double-flowered Varieties

> Indian Chief, sulphur-yellow striped orange
>
> Inglescombe, primrose-yellow
>
> Irene Copeland, white and cream-white
>
> Mary Copeland, cream-white with some of the central petals lemon and orange
>
> Texas, yellow and orange
>
> Valencia, yellow and orange

Flowering period: March
Height: 5–7 ins.
Position: sun

Narcissus rupicola L. (*Jonquilla* group)
Native to Spain and Portugal. Narrow glaucous-green foliage; erect and up to 7 ins. high. Flowers solitary, 1 in. in diameter, vivid yellow, strongly scented; slightly concave saucer-shaped with 6 lobes. Excellent for naturalizing and tolerant of dry sunny soils.

(Polyanthus Narcissus or Paper White Narcissus)
Flowering period: Jan.–Mar., according to zone
Height: 12–18 ins.
Position: sun

Narcissus Tazetta L. (*Tazetta* group)
Native to Europe and Asia. Prolific, dark-green, erect, often twisted foliage up to 18 ins. high. Flowers white, scented, as many as 10 on a single stalk, up to $1\frac{1}{2}$ ins. in diameter, saucer-shaped. Very early-flowering, in mild localities often beginning in late autumn or at the beginning of the year, a characteristic that calls for a protected position sheltered from bad weather and cold winds. They are non-hardy and require a moist fertile soil. Two famous old varieties are particularly adapted to forcing into bloom for winter or late-fall flowering.

> Paper White, white and strongly scented
>
> Soleil d'Or, golden-yellow, strongly and deliciously fragrant

(Angel's Tears)
Flowering period: Mar.–Apr.
Height: up to 10–11 ins.
Position: sun

Narcissus triandrus var. *albus* L. (*Triandrus* group)
Native to Spain. Legend has it that the common name, Angel's Tears, refers to a guide named Angel employed by the famous botanical collector Peter Barr. One day while accompanying his employer on a plant-hunting expedition in the mountains of Spain, and after a particularly tiring and fruitless day, Angel sat down and burst into tears. A few moments later there appeared at his feet a group of *Narcissus triandus* var. *albus*, with pendulous, globose teardrop-like flowers. It is a graceful, elegant little narcissus with up to six individual blooms per stem, white or cream-white. Leaves relatively long and thin. There are numerous attractive garden hybrids.

Flowering period: Oct.–Nov.
Height: 6–8 ins.
Position: sun

Narcissus viridiflorus Schousb. (*Autumn-flowering* group)
Native to Gibraltar, southern Spain, and Morocco. The question is often asked about narcissus, "Is there a green-coloured species?"

Narcissus Pseudo-narcissus
From *Curtis's Botanical Magazine*,
1788, plate 51

This narcissus provides the answer, the flowers being dull olive-green; up to 2 ins. in diameter. They are borne from 1 to 4 per stem, with narrow, twisted, widely spaced petals, giving the flower a six-pointed-star-like appearance. Corolla shallow, six-lobed. Leaves filiform.

Flowering period: Nov.–Apr.
Height: 6 ins.
Position: sun

Narcissus watieri Baker (*Jonquilla* group)
Native to North Africa and the Atlas Mountains. A large-flowered pure-white species and one of the most beautiful. Individual blooms $1\frac{1}{2}$ ins. in diameter, flatly saucer-shaped, but without perfume. Leaves narrow, linear, erect, glaucous, up to 6 ins. high. Flowering period November–April; therefore it should be given a warm sunny position in a moderately dry soil. Not suitable for growing in cold northern climates.

Nemesia

Family: Scrophulariaceae
Annuals or perennial herbaceous plants
Position: sun
Cultivation easy

Nemesia strumosa

A South African genus. Several annual nemesia species are grown in European and American gardens for the intensely vivid colouring of their flowers. They are of the easiest cultivation and will add greatly to the colour of herbaceous borders, beds, window boxes, large pots, etc. If planted early and then cut back after the first flowering in June, the plants will bloom again and extend their flowering period until early autumn.

Towards the end of the nineteenth century, *Nemesia strumosa* was one of the great garden introductions; it is therefore of relatively recent introduction but poor in history or legend. It was also one of the forerunners of the subsequent flood of South African genera, such as *Dimorphotheca, Ursinia, Venidium*, etc., which are now so much a feature of our gardens. It is certainly one of the most attractive for its graceful, compact habit and lovely colours.

If the plant is new to gardens, the name is of great antiquity and was used by Dioscorides to define either *Linaria* (toadflax) or *Antirrhinum* (snapdragon). The genus was founded by Etienne-Pierre Ventenat in 1803, when the Empress Joséphine's plant collection at Malmaison was being classified and catalogued, but we do not know how the plants or seeds were introduced into Europe. There are about fifty species; a few are native to tropical Africa, while the remainder are indigenous to South Africa. The best species, *Nemesia strumosa*, can be found growing wild in all its stupendous colours only fifty miles from Cape Town.

Nemesias thrive in any normal fertile garden soil, but, like most South African plants, they require a hot, sunny, fairly dry position. Seed can be sown at any time between February and April in a warm greenhouse; in April–May in frames; or, in warm localities, directly into its flowering position in May. Seed can also be sown in a greenhouse in September–November, growing on the young plants in pots until they are ready for planting out and actually in flower, in April–May; but they are not tolerant of frost. After spring-sown seed has germinated in a greenhouse, the seedlings can be pricked out into boxes or trays and later individually potted into small fibre pots which should be planted outside as soon as the weather is suitably warm. During their period under glass, the young plants should be given plenty of air, only a moderate amount of water, and never at any time coddled. Seed takes 2–3 weeks to germinate. As previously mentioned, a second flowering will be obtained if the plants are cut back to about half their height when the first flowering has finished; but after this operation, the plants should be given an application of a liquid organic fertilizer. Nemesias associate particularly well with snapdragons, and some lovely and remarkably colourful effects can be obtained by growing the dwarfer nemesias against a background of the taller snapdragons.

Nemesia floribunda Lehm. (syn. *Nemesia affinis*)

Annual
Flowering period: July–Aug.
Height: 8–12 ins.

Native to South Africa. Glabrous at the base, with the upper part of the plant slightly hairy. Stems slender, much-branched, erect. Leaves opposite, those at the base oval, dentated, stalked; the stem leaves linear and only briefly stalked. Inflorescences in the form of rather loose terminal racemes. Individual flowers are small, numerous, and short-stalked. The calyx is divided into five segments, while the corolla is irregularly tubular-shaped, slender, with the mouth divided into two lips, the upper lip trilobed, with the central lobe bent backwards and elongated; the lower lip is entire or slightly dentated with two small protuberances on the upper part. Corolla milk-white inside, outside it is marked and striped pale violet.

Nemesia lilacina Benth.

Annual
Flowering period: July–Aug.
Height: 12–15 ins.

Native to tropical Southwest Africa. A much-branched, woolly, glandulous plant with elongated-lanceolate dentated foliage. Upper lip of the flowers lilac striped purple; lower lip yellowish. Spur short and whitish.

Annual
Flowering period: June–Aug.
Height: 10–15 ins.

Nemesia strumosa Benth.
Native to South Africa. An erect much-branched but compact plant covered with minute hairs on the upper part of the stem. Basal leaves elongated-spatulate, entire; stem leaves elongated-lanceolate, dentated. Flowers borne in racemes 2–4 ins. long, individual blooms about 1 in. in diameter and extremely variable in colour, ranging through shades of white, yellow, orange, scarlet, carmine, etc. There are various garden hybrids and strains such as:

> var. *compacta*, 8 ins. high, of which the var. *Feuerkönig*, scarlet-red, and the var. *Orange Prince*, vivid orange, are particularly attractive
>
> var. *grandiflora* (syn. *Nemesia strumosa* var. *suttonii*), 12 ins. high

Through a series of crosses between *Nemesia strumosa* and *Nemesia versicolor*, some lovely hybrids in various shades of blue have been obtained.

Nemophila

(BABY BLUE EYES)
Family: Hydrophyllaceae
Annuals
Position: sun in the north, partial shade in the south
Propagation: seed
Cultivation easy

The genus *Nemophila* is—as indicated by its Greek name, from *nemos* (grove) and *philein* (to love)—a "lover of woods", and therefore it ought to be cultivated in half-shade where it will be protected from fierce sunshine. However, in the case of the two most popular species (*N. maculata* and *N. menziesii*), personal experience has convinced me that complete success can also be obtained in full sun, where, although the plants develop a dwarfer and more compact habit, they flower more profusely. This is another example of how unwise it is to be dogmatic in gardening matters, and further proves that personal experience is frequently of greater value than traditional or expert advice, often too intent on set rules.

The nemophilas are fairly recent introductions to European gardens; *Nemophila phacelioides* in 1822, *Nemophila insignis* in 1832, *Nemo-*

phila menziesii in 1834, and *Nemophila maculata* in 1848. The dwarf species are excellent for small beds, for edging, for the rock-garden, for pots and window boxes, for dry walls, or for planting in the interstices of paving or in stone steps, etc. They like a cool, fresh, fertile soil moderately moist and rich in organic matter such as well-decomposed leafsoil, but they are very easy subjects with few demands.

The genus was created in 1882 by Bentham and Nuttall and consists of 11–18 species—botanists are not in agreement about the exact number. There are also about fifty forms and varieties. All are native to the United States, particularly California, Texas, and Arkansas.

Seed can be sown directly into the flowering position in March–April. Germination takes about two weeks and the first flowers can be expected 7–8 weeks after sowing. The dwarf species are excellent for use as an annual ground cover.

Nemophila aurita Benth. (syn. *Pholistoma auritum*)
(Fiesta Flower)
Annual climber
Flowering period: June–July
Height: up to 6 ft.

Native to the Pacific Coast of the United States, and, in particular, to California. A trailing or climbing much-branched annual with slender prickly stems. Leaves mostly alternate, small, hairy and much divided into lanceolate segments with conspicuous teeth at the edges. Flowers lavender-blue or violet, $1\frac{1}{4}$ ins. wide, borne in terminal clusters forming loose open racemes. An effective and unusual climbing annual that requires a warm, sunny position in the north, but partial shade in the south.

Nemophila maculata Benth.
(Five Spot)
Annual
Flowering period: June–Sept.
Height: up to 10 ins.

Native to California where it is found growing wild in the Sierra Nevada Mountains. A dwarf, branching, spreading little plant with erect, somewhat succulent lateral growths. Leaves opposite, light green, 5–9-lobed. Flowers flattish bell-shaped, up to 2 ins. wide, white but slightly veined purple with a dark purple spot at the tip of each of the rounded petals; a characteristic which has given the plants their common name, Five Spot. In the var. *purpurea* the petals are profusely marbled purple; while the var. *grandiflora* is larger flowered, and the var. *albida* is white.

Nemophila menziesii Hook. & Arn. (syn. *Nemophila insignis, Nemophila atomaria, Nemophila modesta, Nemophila pedunculata*)
(Baby Blue Eyes or California Bluebell)
Annual
Flowering period: July–Sept.
Height: 6–8 ins.

Native to California and Oregon. This species and its many forms and varieties is the most widely grown garden nemophila. The plants are dwarf, with a dense but spreading and erect habit. Leaves opposite or alternate, pinnatified with 5–9 segments, brilliant green, sometimes slightly marked or marbled with white. Flower stems axillary, longer than the leaves; flowers solitary, broad and flattish

Nemophila menziesii
From *Paxton's Magazine of Botany*,
1836, plate 151

saucer-shaped, with five slightly overlapping petals; the colour is a lovely sky-blue shading to white towards the centre. Diameter of individual blooms up to 1½ ins. The colour of the type plant is, however, somewhat variable with both darker and paler forms, sometimes with the petals slightly suffused with darker colour gradations. In fact, no less than nineteen different subspecies and botanically recognized varieties have been recorded. The var. *discoidalis*, for instance, has a large purple eye. The following are among the most interesting varieties:

>   var. *alba*, pure white flowers
>   var. *argentea*, white flowers striped violet-mauve
>   var. *elegans*, white flowers with a chocolate-coloured centre
>   var. *marginata*, light-blue flowers edged with white
>   var. *oculata*, white with a purple centre
>   var. *purpurea-rubra*, wine-coloured flowers
>   var. *vittata*, flowers almost black with the petals edged white

Nepeta

(CATMINT OR CATNIP)
Family: Labiatae
Half-hardy or hardy herbaceous perennials
Position: sun or partial shade
Propagation: division, cuttings, or seed
Cultivation easy
Aromatic

One particular plant belonging to this genus is much appreciated for its evergreen, silver-green foliage and attractive, lavender-blue flowers. It would be difficult to find an English garden without at least one plant of the so-called Catmint, while it is also planted in effective masses, used to form small hedges or divisions, or employed for edging paths and roads. This useful and attractive little plant is inevitably but erroneously known as *Nepeta mussinii*. Actually it is a hybrid raised by a Dutch nurseryman named Faassen and its correct name is *Nepeta mussinii* x *faassenii*. The true *Nepeta mussinii* is a plant of little interest or decorative value and is rarely found outside botanic gardens.

The genus is native to Europe, Iran, the Caucasus, and the Himalayas. Its name probably derives from the ancient city of Nepi (called

Nepeta cataria

Nepete by the Etruscans), where it is believed that nepetas once grew wild in great profusion. In gardens it is hardy in all except very cold localities, and even if frost should kill the branches, the plant will generally revegetate from the base in spring.

Nepetas thrive in any normal fertile garden soil, being equally happy in full sun or partial shade. Propagation is easy by division in spring or autumn (preferably spring in the north); or by means of soft cuttings taken in July and inserted into sand or very sandy soil or a substance such as perlite and started in a greenhouse or in closed frames. To ensure a good supply of young shoots suitable for making soft cuttings, one or two established plants can be cut back to the ground in June and they will rapidly form new growths. Propagation can also be effected from seed sown in a warm greenhouse in February, in an unheated greenhouse in March–April, or in the open in April–May.

Flowering period: July–Sept.
Height: up to 2½ ft.

Nepeta cataria L.

Native to Europe. A plant of no particular ornamental value in the garden, but at one time it was cultivated for its medicinal properties as a carminative agent, tonic, diaphoretic, and refrigerant. Also useful in the treatment of colds as it induces perspiration. Leaves long-stalked, cordate-ovate, pointed, dentated, light green on the upper surface (which is rather crinkled), whitish beneath. The stems are also covered with a whitish down and this, together with the white undersurface of the leaves, has given rise to the old English saying "as white as nep"; "nep" being a common name of this species. It is also known as Catmint because of its extraordinary attraction for cats (they prefer the dry to the fresh foliage). Flowers tubular, two-lipped, and wider at the mouth; colour white or pale blue, and arranged in short, much-branched, spike-like inflorescences. The entire plant has a characteristic mint-like fragrance. The var. *citriodora* is interesting for its lemon-scented foliage.

Flowering period: July–Sept.
Height: up to 2 ft.

Nepeta x *faassenii*

Generally referred to as *Nepeta mussinii*, but it is actually of hybrid origin (*Nepeta mussinii* x *Nepeta nepetella*). A semi-evergreen, semi-shrubby herbaceous perennial; completely evergreen in a mild climate. Strongly aromatic. Leaves silver-grey, densely clothing the stems, lance-shaped, $\frac{2}{3}$ in. long, about half as wide. Flowers are prolific, small, tubular, in groups of three in small erect corymbs; lavender-blue, two-lipped, and very long-lasting. The plant is sterile and does not produce seeds. To maintain a good, compact shape, the plants should be thoroughly cut back in late summer.

Flowering period: June–Sept.
Height: up to 2 ft.

Nepeta nervosa L.

Native to Kashmir. A lovely species with brilliant green, lanceolate foliage, with the undersurface a lighter colour; 1½ ins. long, half as wide. Flowers violet-blue, borne in dense, cylindrical spikes on much-branched stems, with a long flowering period. A really first-class garden plant and given a high award by the Royal Horticultural Society.

Nerium

(OLEANDER OR ROSE BAY)
Family: Apocynaceae
Tender, non-hardy evergreen shrubs or small trees
Position: sun
Propagation: cuttings, seed, air layers, or grafting
Cultivation easy
Fragrant
Poisonous

The old saying "familiarity breeds contempt" could not be more aptly demonstrated than by the way oleanders are treated in Southern Europe. As natives to the Mediterranean regions, the plants are of the easiest cultivation in countries of that area, and they are consequently abused, ill-treated, and more or less ignored. Their lot seems to be destined to the precincts of railway stations, outside bars and cafés, the more squalid areas of public beaches, neglected terraces, etc.; all positions that rob these superb, noble, flowering evergreens of all their dignity and charm. There are, of course, notable exceptions where specimens are well-planted and properly cared for, providing truly magnificent effects with their handsome foliage and profusely produced brilliantly coloured blooms with their range of colours extending from yellow to blood-red and crimson. When grown in large masses or as isolated specimens, with a diameter of perhaps 12–15 ft., there are few more impressive flowering evergreen garden shrubs, but they should be allowed to develop naturally without cutting or pruning, and above all they should never be grown as standards. In favourable climates, they make spectacular hedge plants and, as they thrive in alkaline (calcareous) soils, they offer an excellent alternative in positions where the soil is too alkaline (calcareous) for the cultivation of azaleas. Oleanders are remarkably good-natured and do not ask for a lot of attention, even giving excellent results in large tubs; but they do require an abundance of water during summer and they respond gratefully to periodic applications of liquid fertilizer during the growing season. It is un-

Nerium Oleander (double-flowered variety)
From Gaetano Savi's *Flora italiana* . . .
(plate 9), Pisa, 1818

fortunate that they cannot be grown on the same scale as rhododendrons, but there is a limit to the amount of cold the plants will tolerate and it is wise not to attempt their outdoor cultivation where the winter temperature falls to about 17°F. for any length of time, unless some particularly warm and sheltered corner can be found for them. Some extra warmth can be gained by protecting the stems and roots with straw, salt hay, dead leaves, peat, or manure, although oleanders also suffer from continuous cold winds. They are real sun-lovers, and thrive where summers are long and hot.

Apart from their native habitat in the Mediterranean, oleanders are also indigenous to Iran, India, and Japan. In the Atlas Mountains they can be found growing at a height of 6,000 ft. Their generosity and good nature also extends to a rapid recovery if they should be slightly frozen during winter. Plants that seem 90 percent dead at the beginning of spring, with all their leaves scorched and brown, will produce new foliage and completely recover by early summer with a few weeks of hot sunny weather. Their degree of hardiness is closely related to the amount of sun received during their growing season. It is easier to cultivate oleanders outside during their flowering period from June to August if the plants are grown in large receptacles and placed outside from May–June until October–November. In the north, oleander cultivation is a real problem, not only because of the cold, but also because of the lack of sunshine, and in England they are only used in the seaside localities of the south and west, or they are grown as wall plants in sheltered positions. In southern regions of the United States they are widely planted and are extremely popular. When growing oleanders it should always be remembered that the white latex or sap that is exuded whenever the plants are damaged or a leaf is removed is very poisonous and that the entire plant is toxic.

The genus *Nerium* was known to the Greeks, but it is believed that still more ancient civilizations were familiar with the plant. Many think that the "rose growing by the brook of the field" found in the Apocrypha's Ecclesiasticus (39:13), and the branches of the "willows of the brook" of Leviticus (23:40) were the oleanders that are frequently found growing along the banks of the River Jordan. We do not know when the plants were introduced into Europe, but in England John Gerard had a white and red variety in his garden in 1596. John Parkinson also grew plants that he raised from seed sent to him from Spain by John More; in 1629, these particular plants had a diameter at the base of their trunk "equal to the thickness of the thumb of a robust man", and by 1640 they had reached the size of "the wrist of an average man".

The name *Nerium* was given to oleanders by Linnaeus in 1735 and is of Greek origin: *neros* signifies water, with obvious allusion to the swampy regions where the plants grow wild. Almost two millennia earlier, Pliny the Elder had used the same name and expressed regret at being unable to find an original Latin name for the plants. In Italy and France the oleander is often known as St. Joseph's Flower, possibly through a connexion with an episode related in one of the Apocryphal Gospels. According to this legend, when St. Joseph was seeking the hand of Mary he and a band of other suitors went to the Temple to plead their suit before the High Priest. After calling upon God for Divine guidance, the High Priest told all the men to place their staffs on the altar. When Joseph came forward and placed his staff among the others it immediately burst into leaf and flower. It thus became clear to the High Priest that among the assembled company it was Joseph alone who was worthy to become Mary's spouse, and he united them in matrimony. (However, it is unclear why popular belief should have subsequently ascribed a staff of oleander wood to St. Joseph.)

There are generally considered to be only two species of oleander, although some authorities give the number as three. Others maintain that *Nerium odorum* (syn. *Nerium indicum*) is not a true species but only the Asiatic form of *Nerium oleander*. Plants in Crete are said to have reached such proportions that the wood was used as building timber. Generally, however, the plants have the dimensions of large shrubs, often with stout woody stems.

Oleanders have always been known as poisonous and medicinal plants. Theophrastus mentions a plant called *Oenothera*, but gives a description of it that exactly corresponds to oleander—from previous experience we note that not too much attention should be paid to the names used by the ancients. He even specified that soaking the roots of this plant in wine gave it a better and more sprightly character. Dioscorides stated that the poison in the leaves could be used as an antivenin for snake bite. The Rev. William Turner (c. 1510–1568, physician to the Duke of Somerset) was fully conscious of the toxicity of the plant and advised its use only in cases of extreme emergency, commenting that he had seen the plants in various parts of Italy, but was not enthusiastic about importing them into England "because in every respect externally it resembled a beautiful Pharisee, while internally it was a rapacious wolf and an assassin". However, more than a thousand years before Turner, Apuleius and his contemporaries knew the oleander as a poisonous plant. And the hero of *The Golden Ass*, after being transformed into an ass and desperately seeking the special rosebush that would help him regain his original form, was momentarily fooled by the likeness of oleander flowers to roses. He was about to eat the oleander when he recognized his error and remembered that oleander flowers are an instant and deadly poison to asses. The Florentines at one time called the oleander *ammazzalasino* (donkey killer), but we do not know through what experience or from whom they obtained this information.

The poisonous principle of oleanders is found in all parts of the plant, but it is particularly virulent in the leaves and bark. Proof of its deadliness can be seen in the white specks that appear in the mouth and on the tongue of the person who has chewed the leaves, and in the quick death of animals which have eaten the plant. Two dramatic instances of oleander poisoning are related by Loiseleur Deslonchamps: in 1796 some French soldiers in Corsica died immediately after eating some meat skewered and cooked on a stick of oleander; during the war in North Africa, some soldiers slept on pallets made from oleander branches, and the majority of the men either died or were seriously poisoned. Today we know that the fresh and dried leaves, the bark, seeds, and flowers all contain in a greater or less measure two alkaloids, two glucosides, tannic substances, sugar, oils, and resin. Oleander poisoning is characterized by gastric disturbances such as vomiting, colic, diarrhoea, as well as by fever, dizziness, slowness and irregularity of heartbeat, loss of consciousness, and finally death through heart failure. Immediate measures to be taken in cases of such poisoning are use of a stomach pump, doses of tannic liquids, opium and atropine, but above all the immediate intervention of qualified medical assistance.

In Libya, where oleander is a very common plant in the damp coastal regions, the natives make poultices of chopped-up leaves to bring abscesses to a head; an ointment is also made for the cure of scabies. In India and in some Mediterranean countries the plant is associated with and used at funerals.

Single-flowered
Nerium Oleander

Cultivation. Oleander cultivation does not present any difficulties. In climates where warm sunny summers ripen the wood, plants will, as we have said, survive short periods of frost. In areas that experience lower temperatures, plants should be grown in large receptacles, placed outside during the summer and removed to well-lighted winter quarters where the temperature does not fall below about 40°F. Normally, the plants thrive in quite poor soils, although it is advisable to give them a fertile, deeply dug soil in gardens. If grown in pots or tubs, the receptacles should be deeper than they are wide, since the roots are very long and deeply penetrating. During winter, oleanders require little water, but from spring to autumn they need an abundance of moisture at their roots. In all cases they like an open position in full sun. Young plants grown in containers require repotting every year; while very large specimens can be kept in the same receptacles almost indefinitely if given generous applications of liquid organic fertilizer and plenty of water. No regular pruning is necessary, but young plants should be topped to ensure bushy, well-branched specimens, while old plants should be periodically cleaned of weak, dead, or misshapen growths. If they develop a too-straggly, weak, or ill-formed appearance, they should be cut down almost to ground level in late spring or early summer, and they will soon produce new basal growth.

Propagation can be effected in various ways. Seed sown in a warm greenhouse in spring is one method, but it gives no assurance of the flower colour of the seedlings. Probably the best method is by cuttings, which if taken in summer and inserted in moist sand in a greenhouse root very easily. Another good method is to insert the cutting through a cork-stoppered bottle filled with water and leave it in a sunny position, removing and potting the cutting when roots have formed. When varieties with particularly good colours are desired, air or ground layering or grafting may be accomplished during June or July.

(Sweet Oleander)
Flowering period: June–Sept.
Height: up to 10 ft.
Zone 10

Nerium odorum Soland. (syn. *Nerium indicum*)
Native to Iran, India, and Japan. An evergreen shrub with a less vigorous habit than *Nerium oleander*. It has an erect form with linear-lanceolate leaves borne in groups of three. Flowers are pink, 2 ins. in diameter, single, fragrant, and borne in masses of up to eighty individual blooms.

(Common Oleander)
Flowering period: June–Aug.
Height: up to 25 ft.
Zone 9 southwards

Nerium oleander L. (syn. *Nerium laurifolium* Lam.)
Native to the Mediterranean regions, the Orient, and most tropical and subtropical areas of the Old World. A large evergreen shrub or small tree with narrow coriaceous lanceolate leaves up to 8 ins. long; dark green above, paler on the undersurface, borne in groups of two or three. The flowers are borne in terminal cymes; single, generally white or pink, up to $2\frac{1}{2}$ ins. in diameter. The corolla tube is cylindrical at its base, while the throat is bell-shaped. There are many single- and double-flowered forms and varieties with a colour range including lovely shades of yellow, apricot, reddish orange, white, pink, carmine, cream, crimson, dark wine-red, reddish purple, ruby-red, and

even bicoloured flowers. Very few of these have official names and they are sold generally by colour, but var. *loddigesii* specifies a type with flowers variegated in white, pink, red, while vars. *album, atropurpureum,* and *roseum* indicate the colours by their names. Var. *Sister Agnes* is pure white, var. *Cardinal* is one of the best reds, and var. *Mrs. Swanson* is a lovely double pink.

Nicotiana

Family: Solaneaceae
Tender herbaceous perennials, annuals, or semi-shrubby perennials
Position: sun or partial shade
Propagation: seed
Cultivation easy
Fragrant
Poisonous

The genus *Nicotiana* offers enough species and varieties to satisfy every taste. There are annuals, perennials, and sub-shrubs that vary in height from 1 to 10 ft., and are either day- or night-flowering. They are slightly, moderately, or strongly fragrant, all are of the easiest cultivation and beautiful in leaf and flower. There is a good range of colours from which to select, and the annuals are excellent garden plants for a wide range of climates.

Apart from the decorative garden forms, the best-known species is *Nicotiana tabacum,* whose leaves provide smoking tobacco. The first Europeans to know of this species were the Spaniards. When Columbus's crew touched at Hispaniola in 1492, they saw the natives smoking the dried leaves. The same species was later found in abundance on the island of Tobago (whence the island's present name) at the time of Hernando Cortes's conquest of Mexico in 1518. It seems likely that seed was imported into Spain from Mexico by Francisco Hernandez; while Sir Francis Drake imported it into England from Virginia in 1586. It was, however, Sir Walter Raleigh who introduced tobacco smoking to the English court.

The name *Nicotiana* owes its origin to Jean Nicot (1530–1600), a gentleman of Nîmes, France, who went to Portugal as French ambassador and was introduced to tobacco at the Portuguese court in 1560; he subsequently sent seeds of the plant to Catherine de Médicis at the French court. But the real propagandist for tobacco was Sir Walter Raleigh, whose portrait graces a popular brand of

American cigarettes which bear his name. The species *Nicotiana tabacum* and *Nicotiana rustica* are the most important commercially and medically, but much that is bad and little that is good can be said about either, and for medicinal purposes neither is now much used. All parts of the plant contain substances that are dangerously poisonous; they also contain nicotine, which is the most poisonous substance of all, and even if absorbed in quite moderate doses it can cause rapid and fatal results. In many cases, physicians and other research workers whose work involves the internal use of nicotine in living tissue have been so impressed by its potency, speed, and drastically poisonous properties that they have abandoned its use. On the other hand, extracts of tobacco have proved to be of the greatest value as insecticides and as destroyers of parasites that attack humans as well as animals. Above all, however, the preparations are useful in horticulture and agriculture, especially for the extermination of aphids and other harmful insects; although these products are almost pure water in comparison to the much more dangerous synthetic chemical insecticides now so widely and indiscriminately used, often with fatal results to birds, useful insects, fish, and even valuable crops. Nonetheless, the tobacco extracts still remain deadly poisonous and should either be banned from private gardens or used with great care by qualified operators.

The genus *Nicotiana* is large, comprising at least sixty species of herbaceous perennials, annuals, and woody shrub-like types of plants; many that are widely cultivated in European and American gardens bear very beautiful fragrant blooms. Their native habitat is almost exclusively confined to tropical or subtropical America; but a few species are found in Australia and some of the Pacific Islands.

Cultivation. Nicotiana plants are not difficult to cultivate, but they are not hardy and will not tolerate frost. They need warmth and sunshine, especially when young, when their growth is very fast. Seed is of rapid germination, generally within a week of sowing if the temperature is between 68–80°F., and therefore it should never be sown too early in cold localities. The soil should be well-soaked with liquid fertilizer before seed is sown because nicotianas, like many other tropical or subtropical plants, need plenty of food as soon as the roots are formed. Seed can be sown in flats, boxes, pans, seed beds, or frames according to the temperature. In warm climates sowing can be made outside in April–May, while in colder climates it is better to sow in a warm greenhouse in March–April, when the seedlings can be pricked out individually into small fibre pots and then be planted into their flowering positions when they have reached a reasonable size. In the case of the popular garden hybrids of *Nicotiana* x *sanderae* and *Nicotiana alata,* it is best to sow directly into the flowering positions as soon as the outdoor shade temper-

Nicotiana tabacum

ature reaches 65–68°F. Actually, when any of these hybrids are cultivated in a bed or border, it is rarely necessary to sow seed again as many self-sown seedlings generally appear on or near the vicinity of the original growing site. All nicotianas are gross feeders and, while they will grow in poorer soils, they give far better results if an abundance of organic fertilizer is dug into the soil before planting or sowing. As the plants develop, periodic applications of liquid fertilizer will repay with generous dividends. In the north nicotianas should be grown in full sun, while in the south the garden hybrids will also give good results in partial shade.

Nicotiana alata Link & Otto (syn. *Nicotiana affinis*)
Native to southeastern Brazil, Uruguay, Paraguay, and Argentina. In gardens this herbaceous perennial is generally grown as an annual in its various hybrid forms. The basal leaves are wide and large, up to 4 ins. long, stalkless, while the stem leaves are lanceolate. Stems much-branched, bearing loose, open racemes of fragrant, pinkish-white flowers, tubular in shape with the mouth up to 2 ins. in diameter, and a pale yellowish colour, with the reverse of the five petals light violet. The hybrids, however, can be white, pink, crimson, lilac, cream, or greenish white in colour. The flowering season is very long and in warm climates, or if cultivated in receptacles that can be moved to a warm place in autumn, will extend well into early winter. Some of the best hybrids are:

*Perennial
generally grown as an annual
Flowering period: June–Oct.
Height: 2½–5½ ft.
Fragrant*

 Crimson Bedder, only 15 ins. high, excellent for beds, with lovely crimson flowers
 Lime Green, 2 ft. high, with greenish-yellow flowers
 Dwarf White Bedder, 15–18 ins. high, with white flowers that remain open during the day

Nicotiana glauca R. Gran.
Native to Argentina, Paraguay, and Bolivia. A perennial often grown as an annual, but old, well-established plants often assume the form of small shrubs with a definitely woody stem densely covered with fine hairs at the base, while the upper part and the young growths are glabrous. It is an excellent subject for establishing against hot, dry, sunny walls, where growths up to 9 ft. long are produced. The basal foliage is spatulate, obtuse, glaucous blue-green, smooth-surfaced, long-stalked; while the stem leaves are more heart-shaped or oval-lanceolate and slightly undulated with conspicuous veins. The flowers are borne in inflorescences made up of terminal corymbs; the individual blooms pendulous, up to 1½ ins. long, widest at the mouth, yellow and roughly funnel-shaped. It is a handsome, stately plant, but not hardy; in warm climates it is esteemed for its attractive foliage. The var. *macrantha* has larger, white flowers; while the var. *undulata* is much taller and with almost ruffled leaves.

*Semi-shrubby perennial
Flowering period: Aug.–Oct.
Height: up to 9 ft.*

Nicotiana noctiflora
From *Curtis's Botanical Magazine*,
1827, plate 2785

Nicotiana langsdorfii Wein.
Native to Brazil and Chile. A much-branched annual with hairy stems; basal foliage oval, obtuse, undulated; stem leaves lanceolate, pointed. Flowers greenish yellow and borne in pendulous clusters, tubular, and more curious than beautiful.

Annual
Flowering period: July–Aug.
Height: up to 4½ ft.

Nicotiana longiflora Cav.
Native to Texas, Argentina, and Chile. A perennial generally grown as an annual; with the ends of the stems much-branched. Basal leaves rosette-forming, oval, obtuse, undulated, 10–12 ins. long; stem leaves lanceolate or elongated heart-shaped, pointed. Flowers borne in terminal corymbs; narrowly tubular, the tube 4–5 ins. long, with the mouth widely saucer-shaped. Colour light violet or violet-green outside, white inside. A most attractive plant for the mixed border.

Herbaceous perennial
generally grown as an annual
Flowering period: July–Aug.
Height: up to 3 ft.

Nicotiana noctiflora Link & Otto
Native to Argentina and Chile. A sticky-surfaced herbaceous perennial of slender, branched habit and densely covered with very fine hairs. Leaves narrowly oblong or lanceolate, undulated; those borne on the stems stalkless, linear, pointed. Inflorescence a terminal raceme of horizontal, stalked, tubular flowers with the mouth saucer-shaped; colour greenish purple outside, white inside; very fragrant.

Herbaceous perennial
Flowering period: July–Sept.
Height: 2–3 ft.
Very fragrant

Nicotiana x *sanderae* Hort.
A hybrid obtained by crossing *Nicotiana alata* with *Nicotiana forgetiana,* raised in 1903 by the English firm of Sander & Sons. Basal foliage large, spatulate, undulated; stem leaves elongated-lanceolate. Together with its various forms, it is one of the most attractive of hybrid garden nicotianas. The type plant has clusters of flowers up to nearly 4 ins. long; tubular, yellowish green suffused pink with a wide, carmine-pink mouth. Fragrant. The various forms and varieties extend the colour range to dark crimson, light and dark reddish pink, and pale rose.

Annual
Flowering period: July–Oct.
Height: 2–3 ft.

Nicotiana suaveolens Lehm.
Native to Australia. An annual or biennial species with an erect branched shrubby habit. Leaves robust, sticky, elongated-lanceolate, hairy. Inflorescence a terminal raceme bearing fragrant 2-in.-long pendulous flowers, pale green outside, reddish yellow inside, with the mouth 1 in. in diameter. The var. *variegata* has foliage marbled and edged white; var. *macrantha* has larger, white flowers (syn. *Nicotiana fragrans*); var. *undulata* has larger, undulated foliage. *Nicotiana suaveolens* and its varieties all prefer partial shade when grown in hot sunny climates.

Annual or biennial
Flowering period: July–Aug.
Height: 1–2 ft.
Fragrant

*Perennial
generally grown as an annual
Flowering period: July–Sept.
Height: 4½ ft.
Fragrant*

Nicotiana sylvestris Speg.
Native to Argentina. A perennial frequently grown in gardens as an annual. Habit erect, branched; leaves rough-surfaced, dark green, oblong; basal leaves rosette-forming; stem leaves stalkless, widely oval or lyre-shaped. Individual flowers up to 3½ ins. long, borne in terminal corymbs, white, scented, with the mouth 1½ ins. in diameter, and day-flowering if the sun is not too strong.

*(Tobacco Plant)
Annual or biennial
Flowering period: July–Sept.
Height: 4–6 ft.*

Nicotiana tabacum L.
Native to tropical America. A vigorous herbaceous plant sometimes grown as an annual, but under frost-free conditions actually living for several seasons, forming an almost-woody basal stem. This is the species cultivated for the production of tobacco. Leaves are light green, often up to 1½ ft. long near the base of the plant, but decreasing in size towards the top. In shape they are oblong or lanceolate and sharply pointed. The inflorescence is a terminal corymb of pink or red flowers each about 2 ins. long and funnel-shaped. There are several varieties worthy of garden cultivation:

> var. *angustifolia,* with narrow leaves and available in forms with slight variation of flower colour
> var. *atropurpurea grandiflora,* with large reddish-purple flowers
> var. *macrophylla,* with very large foliage and brilliant-red flowers

All of these are plants of considerable development, requiring at least a distance of 3 ft. between plants.

Nicotiana alta, Dwarf White Bedder hybrid

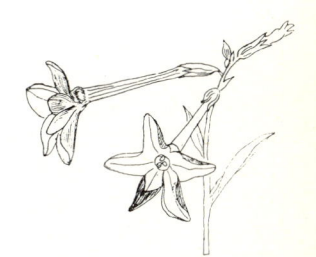

Nicotiana x *sanderae*

*Perennial
generally grown as an annual
Flowering period: July–Sept.
Height: up to 10 ft.*

Nicotiana tomentosa Cav.
Native to Brazil and Peru. A glabrous, grey-green perennial grown chiefly for its attractive foliage. The leaves are long-stalked, oval, sharply pointed, up to 8 ins. long and half as wide, and of a most

attractive colour. The flowers are borne in corymbs, each bloom up to 1½ ins. long, at first greenish yellow, becoming pinkish yellow. Can easily be grown from seed and treated as an annual, but flowers may not be produced the first year if the weather is not sufficiently hot. The var. *variegata* has the leaves mottled white.

Nigella

(LOVE-IN-A-MIST, FENNEL FLOWER, DEVIL-IN-A-BUSH, JACK-IN-PRISON, JACK-IN-THE-GREEN, OR LADY-IN-THE-BOWER)
Family: Ranunculaceae
Annual

These attractive annuals are from the Mediterranean regions and Western Asia. The only representatives cultivated in gardens today are the numerous hybrid forms of *Nigella damascena,* which are valued not only for their curiously formed colourful inflorescences, but also for their decorative seed vessels that are often cut, dried, and used in the composition of dried-flower arrangements.

The genus comprises about a dozen species, the most attractive of which are *Nigella damascena, Nigella arvensis,* and *Nigella sativa.* When seen growing wild, often in vast expanses, they provide a delightful effect with their predominately sky-blue flowers. The jet-black seeds are of irregular shape, and rather like minute coal chippings. It is from the black colour of the seeds that the genus takes its Latin name, *niger* (black).

Nigellas have been known since ancient times; the plants were mentioned by Dioscorides and Theophrastus, and later there is mention of them in one of Charlemagne's treatises. But none of these commentators referred to their decorative qualities, and they did not become popular as ornamental garden plants until the seventeenth century. Nigella plants contain an alkaloid, damasceine, which has narcotic properties, and they were first known for their medicinal use as a stimulant, as a febrifuge, and as a resolvent substance. At the present time, seeds of *Nigella sativa,* with their strawberry fragrance and flavour, are used in the preparation of certain liqueurs and for flavouring soft drinks, sweets, and ice cream. They were at one time extensively used for culinary purposes and an old book notes that years ago it was the habit to sprinkle the seeds on bread; also, when aromatic substances were scarce, the seeds were used to add flavour to cooked foods.

Cultivation. Nigellas will thrive in any soil, even the poorest, as long as it contains a proportion of lime. They require an open, sunny position in moderately dry porous soil. Seed can be sown in its flowering position in April, thinning out the seedlings to about 6–8 ins. apart. In mild localities seed can also be sown in autumn, but in either case the long slender tap-roots make transplanting a difficult matter. Once nigellas have been grown on a certain site, they will generally reappear spontaneously in successive years from self-sown seed. Their seed is easy to store, retaining its viability for at least two years. Flowering plants can be expected 8–10 weeks after sowing. In a hot climate the flowering period is not long, only a matter of 4–6 weeks, but this defect can be rectified by successive sowings every 15–20 days.

Nigella damascena

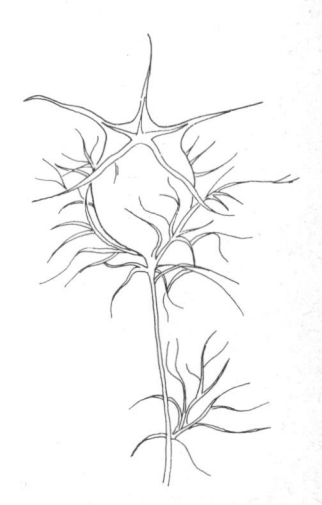

Seed vessel of
Nigella damascena

Flowering period: May–July
Height: 15–18 ins.
Position: sun
Propagation: seed
Cultivation easy

Nigella damascena L.
Native to Asia Minor and naturalized in many parts of Southern Europe. An annual species with much-branching erect stems and long, deeply penetrating yellowish tap-roots. Leaves finely and much-divided into lace-like segments, alternate. Flowers solitary, terminal, generally blue but occasionally white or pale pink; $1\frac{1}{2}$ ins. in diameter, five-petalled, and surrounded by a collar of thin, almost thread-like bracts that have so caught garden-lovers' imagination over a period of years that the plant has collected a lengthy assortment of vivid popular names, a selection of which is given above. The plants are of the easiest cultivation and naturalize freely from self-sown seed, but they cannot be satisfactorily transplanted. The original species is rarely grown, having been replaced by numerous strains of hybrid origin such as:

>Miss Jekyll, with deep sky-blue flowers surrounded by delicate feathery foliage

Persian Jewels, comprising a mixture of blue, pink, white, carmine, mauve, and violet flowers
Altpreussen, with indigo-blue flowers

All the above are excellent for cutting and last well in water.

Oenothera

(EVENING PRIMROSE OR SUNDROPS)
Family: Onagraceae
Hardy herbaceous perennials, annuals, or biennials
Position: semi-shade
Propagation: seed, division, or cuttings
Cultivation very easy

Oenothera biennis

The name *Oenothera* derives from the Greek *oinos* (wine) and *thera* (hunt or chase). It is thought to be the name given by Theophrastus to a plant of the genus *Epilobium*. The roots of this plant were supposed to have an aroma of wine; an infusion prepared from them apparently had the power to soothe the most ferocious animal, and it was also used as an antitoxin. Other sources indicate that another infusion from the same plant was used at ancient banquets to induce thirst, thus stimulating a desire to drink wine. However, the etymology of the name has nothing to do with the present-day oenotheras, because all of the plants of this genus are native to North and South America, with the exception of a single species indigenous to Tasmania; thus, their introduction into Europe and the Mediterranean regions could not have taken place prior to the discovery of America.

In the garden, oenotheras are used almost exclusively for ornamental purposes. A notable exception to this is *Oenothera biennis,* naturalized in Europe since 1614, known by varied and picturesque names such as Donkey Weed, Gardener's Bacon, St. Anthony's Ham, and cultivated in Germany and France for its edible roots that are said to have a nutty flavour similar but inferior in quality to rampion *(Campanula rapunculus)*. These fleshy roots are eaten boiled or raw in salads or served with a dressing of mustard, olive oil, pepper, and salt. The flowers of this species rarely open before 6 or 7 o'clock in the evening and for that reason the plant is popularly known as Evening Primrose (during dull, cloudy weather, however, the flowers may also open earlier). The blooms also have a singular manner of opening: the sections of the calyx begin to open at the base, exposing the corolla, while the summit of the flower is kept closed by the

Oenothera fruticosa

Oenothera rosea

minute hooks or claws at the top of the calyx; after about a quarter of an hour the flower appears to gain sufficient strength to open at the top as well and it will expand quite rapidly for about five minutes, when there is another pause as if the plant were waiting to gain sufficient strength before opening completely. There are several other species which are also night-flowering.

One of the genus *Oenothera*, like *Mirabilis* (Four-o'Clocks), played a vital and fundamental part in the history and story of plant genetics. In 1886, the Dutchman De Vries noticed that in a field of naturalized North American oenotheras growing near Amsterdam, several plants bore different characteristics from others of the same species. These plants (of the species *O. lamarckiana*) permitted De Vries to study the phenomenon of mutation.

The genus *Oenothera* was named by Linnaeus in 1735, and at the present time comprises 20 to 200 species, according to the method by which they are classified. Not all oenotheras are fragrant and those that do have perfume are mostly night-flowering. The scent of *Oenothera caespitosa* is excellent; "a mixture of lemon and jasmine" (Wilson and Bell). *Oenothera lamarckiana* has a strong fragrance of lilies and lemon that permeates the air for several yards. Other scented species are *O. odorata, O. biennis,* and *O. speciosa.*

Cultivation. The fact that many species of oenothera have become naturalized in various parts of the world is proof that they are easy subjects to cultivate. The annual species flower better in a poor stony soil; in a rich soil the plants will be more robust but less freely flowering, of a paler colour, and not so long-lasting. Perennial species generally flower poorly the first year after planting. The biennial and perennial species are quite hardy, although *Oenothera rosea* and *Oenothera caespitosa* require some protection in districts where winters are very severe. *Oenothera caespitosa* is liable to be killed off by excessive moisture during winter months, and it should be planted in rather dry, well-drained soils. The species *O. fruticosa, O. missourensis,* and *O. tetragona* thrive in a soil containing a good proportion of peat and sand, but they are all very easy to raise and are not choosey about soil.

Seed of the annual species should be sown in March–April in frames and the seedlings transplanted out into their flowering positions in May. Seed of biennial species can be sown in frames in July–August, pricking out the seedlings into coldframes where they should remain over the winter, planting them out in their flowering positions the following spring. The perennial species can be propagated from seed sown in spring, by division in spring or autumn, or from cuttings taken in May and rooted under glass. *Oenothera caespitosa* is somewhat more difficult to propagate by vegetative means and those plants to be propagated should be removed from the soil in September–October, divided, potted, and kept in coldframes during the winter, giving them very little water until March, when they can be planted out.

Oenothera biennis L. (syn. *Onagra biennis*)　(Evening Primrose)
Native to North America and widely naturalized in Europe. A hardy biennial that will often bloom the first year after sowing. When established in a favourable position, it will naturalize and reproduce from self-sown seed. Leaves basal, rosette-forming, long, narrow, pointed, profuse, light green in colour with a glaucous tendency. Flower stems up to 6–7 ft. high, bearing a spike of widely spaced lemon-yellow flowers 2½ ins. wide and very decorative, but not opening until evening. Requires a position in semi-shade and a fairly moist soil. The var. *grandiflora* has more attractive lobed and deeply cut foliage, with larger strongly scented flowers marked externally with red.

Biennial
Flowering period: June–Sept.
Height: up to 7 ft.
Fragrant
Night-flowering

Oenothera bistorta Nutt.
Native to California. This is slightly different from the other species as the flowers have a corolla marked dark purple at the base. An elegant and attractive annual with an abundance of inch-wide flowers borne on leafy and slightly hairy stems. The colour is a rich dark yellow. Foliage small, basal, rosette-forming, narrow, pointed, dentated. The var. *veitchiana* (syn. *Oenothera veitchiana*) is an improvement on the type.

Annual
Flowering period: June–July
Height: 12 ins.

Oenothera caespitosa Nutt. (syn. *Pachylophus caespitosa*)
Native to North America. An almost prostrate dwarf perennial forming a dense cushion of vegetation. Flowers 3 ins. in diameter, at first white, gradually changing to pinkish; delicately scented and attached almost directly onto the stems. Leaves narrow, dentated, prostrate, covered with soft hairs, and arranged in closely formed groups. Perennial, but not long-lived, it is more satisfactory when grown as a biennial. It will not tolerate excessive moisture.

Herbaceous perennial
Flowering period: May–Aug.
Height: 10 ins.
Fragrant
Night-flowering

Oenothera fruticosa L.
Native to the eastern United States. The most attractive of the herbaceous perennial species for beds and borders. Flowering is prolific and long-lasting, with lovely lemon-yellow blooms 1½ ins. in diameter borne on rigid, leafy slender stems in terminal groups. Foliage small, narrow, pointed, slightly dentated. There are several excellent varieties such as var. *major,* var. *William Cuthbertson,* and var. *Yellow River.*

Herbaceous perennial
Flowering period: June–Aug.
Height: up to 2 ft.

Oenothera hookeri L.
Native to the mountainous regions of California. A biennial species with glaucous-grey foliage up to 9 ins. long, lanceolate or elongated-

Biennial
Flowering period: June–Aug.
Height: up to 5 ft.

oval, pointed. Flower buds slightly pinkish, opening to spectacular 4-in.-wide yellow blooms.

Biennial
Flowering period: June–Sept.
Height: up to 4 ft.
Fragrant
Night-flowering

Oenothera lamarckiana Hort.
A beautiful biennial of hybrid origin that has produced many other lovely varieties. Can best be described as a dwarfish form of *Oenothera biennis*, only with much larger flowers and bigger leaves, which are wide and crinkled. Stems reddish; flower buds hairy. The best of its progeny are var. *Afterglow* (syn. *Oenothera rubricalyx*) and var. *johnsonii*, with particularly large sweetly scented flowers which have a red calyx.

(Missouri Primrose)
Herbaceous perennial
Flowering period: June–Sept.
Height: 6 ins.

Oenothera missourensis Sims
Native to the central United States. An almost prostrate herbaceous perennial and one of the most popular of all oenotheras. Given an award of merit by the Royal Horticultural Society in 1935. A truly beautiful hardy plant with trailing stems up to 2 ft. long. Established specimens form a dense carpet of vegetation. Excellent for the rock-garden, for pockets in dry walls, for use as a ground cover, or for planting along the edges of wide gravel paths or courtyards (a practice I employ in my own garden). The beautiful freely produced flowers are 4 ins. in diameter, sulphur-yellow, saucer-shaped, and borne on 6-in. stems. The flowering period is very long, until the end of September or later, but each flower lasts for only a day. Leaves bright green, long and narrow, tapering at each end. The stems are reddish, while on the same plant the buds can be entirely green outside or spotted with red. The flowers are followed by curiously formed large seed vessels up to 3 ins. long and bearing four large flat wings.

Perennial
Flowering period: June–Aug.
Height: up to 2 ft.

Oenothera perennis L.
Native to the eastern United States, where it is sometimes known as *Oenothera pumila* or *Oenothera pusilla*. Maximum height up to 2 ft., but begins to bloom when only a few inches high. A perennial with green lanceolate foliage, not dentated at the edges. Flowers bright yellow, prolific, 1 in. in diameter. A very common weed in its native habitat.

Perennial,
usually cultivated as a biennial
Flowering period: July–Sept.
Height: 12–18 ins.
Night-flowering

Oenothera rosea Ait. (syn. *Hartmannia rosea*)
Native to Texas and the central United States. Only moderately hardy, perennial, and generally grown in gardens as a biennial. Leaves oval, dentated, pointed. Flowers produced in profusion, reddish pink, $\frac{2}{3}$ in. in diameter, opening at dusk. Requires a more sunny position than the majority of oenotheras. It is an excellent plant for pot culture.

Oenothera missourensis
From *Curtis's Botanical Magazine*,
1813, plate 1592

Herbaceous perennial
Flowering period: June–Aug.
Height: 12–18 ins.
Fragrant

Oenothera speciosa Nutt.
Native to the central United States and sometimes included in the genus *Hartmannia*. Herbaceous perennial with large fragrant saucer-shaped flowers up to 2½ ins. in diameter. Flowers initially white with a pale-green centre, gradually changing to pink. Leaves small, elongated, narrow, dark green.

Herbaceous perennial
Flowering period: June–Sept.
Height: 12–18 ins.

Oenothera tetragona Cav. (syn. *Oenothera youngii*)
Native to the United States. A small graceful perennial with a very long flowering period. Much-branched, erect habit. Flowers much smaller than those of most species but of a magnificent, rich dark yellow. Leaves shiny-surfaced, glaucous green. The var. *fraseri* (syn. *Oenothera glauca* Michx.) is similar to the type but more vigorous, with flowers 1 in. in diameter and of an even more intense yellow.

Herbaceous perennial
Flowering period: June–Aug.
Height: up to 12 ins.

Oenothera trichocalyx (syn. *Onagra trichocalyx*)
Native to the United States. Leaves narrowly lanceolate, 2 ins. long, dentated, and slightly undulated. Flowers white, 2 ins. in diameter, borne on stems up to 1 ft. high that are covered with silky hairs.

Olearia

(DAISY BUSH OR TREE DAISY)
Family: Compositae
Tender evergreen shrubs
Position: sun
Propagation: seed or cuttings
Cultivation easy
Fragrant

Olearia gunniana

The olearias could be summarily described as shrubs with olive-like leaves; in fact, it is thought that the name derives from *olea* (olive), although some authorities attribute its origin to J. G. Olearius, a botanist who lived in 1600. The flowers are mostly cream-white and closely resemble those of perennial asters or Michaelmas Daisies. They are certainly the most decorative of all shrubs belonging to the family Compositae and are particularly suited to seaside localities. They are sun lovers, easy to cultivate, and require a sandy but robust soil. The genus *Olearia* comprises more than one hundred species native to Australia and New Zealand. *Olearia gunniana*, with white flowers and a yellow centre, was introduced into European gardens in 1848.

In 1929, during one of his expeditions to Tasmania, the botanical explorer H. F. Comber discovered specimens with pink, mauve, purple, and blue flowers; he immediately sent seed back to the Royal Botanic Gardens at Kew, where I was fortunate enough to be entrusted with the first plants to bloom in Europe. Today these lovely forms are available commercially under the name of *Olearia gunniana* var. *splendens*. *Olearia semidentata* was first introduced into Europe by Major A. A .Dorrien-Smith who established it in his unique garden at Tresco Abbey in the Scilly Isles; it is now one of the most widely diffused species in the south of England, where it has become quite a common plant.

Olearias are evergreen shrubs with variously coloured flowers and are excellent garden plants in warm climates. Leaves are generally alternate, occasionally opposite, mostly tomentose on the undersurface, frequently rigid and leathery. The aster-like flowers are variable in size, either solitary or borne in compact corymbs. Apart from *Olearia haastii*, which is relatively hardy, olearias are best in a mild climate, although they will tolerate a few degrees of frost if they are in good condition and planted in a sheltered position. They are not lovers of alkaline (calcareous) soil and give much better results in acid soils that are light, sandy, and contain a good percentage of organic matter such as peat or leafsoil. Although they are sun-lovers, it is advisable to plant them in partial shade in very hot southern gardens. Propagation is easy by means of seed sown in an unheated greenhouse or coldframe in spring, or from cuttings of half-ripened wood taken in July and inserted in sandy soil in frames.

Olearia gunniana Hook. f.

Flowering period: June–July
Height: up to 9 ft.
Zone 9 southwards

Native to Tasmania; introduced into Europe in 1848. A much-branched evergreen shrub up to 9 ft. high with opaque-green obovate leaves, whitish on the undersurface, dentated, up to $1\frac{1}{2}$ ins. long, blunt at the tips. Young growths are densely covered with a layer of white felt-like down. Flowers similar to a miniature daisy, white with a yellow eye, up to $1\frac{1}{2}$ ins. in diameter. As already mentioned, there are some lovely coloured forms that flower profusely in early summer and are collectively known as var. *splendens*. These shrubs can be grown in the open only in a warm climate and cannot be considered hardy. They can, however, be cultivated in large pots and placed outside from spring to autumn, removing them to an unheated greenhouse for the winter.

Olearia haastii Hook. f.

Flowering period: July–Aug.
Height: up to 8 ft.
Zone 8 southwards

Native to New Zealand where it can be found at altitudes of up to 6,000 ft. This is the only really hardy species. Even if killed back to ground level by frost, it will generally revegetate the following spring and rapidly grow back to its normal 8-ft. height. An evergreen shrub of compact rounded habit with thick, leathery, dark-green oval leaves up to 1 in. long; shiny on the upper surface, densely covered with white down beneath. Flowers white, fragrant, very numerous, in axillary corymbs; individual blooms about $\frac{1}{3}$ in. wide, with the entire inflorescence up to 3 ins. in diameter and held well above the foliage, creating a most pleasing effect in July–August, when so few other shrubs are in bloom. The plant will tolerate being clipped or cut and can be used to make unusual and attractive hedges. The scent of the flowers is likened by some to the fragrance of hawthorn (May).

Flowering period: July–Aug.
Height: up to 9 ft.
Zone 9 southwards

Olearia semidentata Decne. (syn. *Eurybia semidentata*)
Native to the Chatham Islands. A beautiful and unusual evergreen shrub up to 9 ft. high with elongated-lanceolate pointed foliage up to 3 ins. long; upper surface dark green and wrinkled, the underside covered with silver-white down. Flowers terminal, solitary, 2 ins. in diameter, and a lovely shade of lilac-mauve with the centre dark violet or purple. Prefers a light, stony, well-drained soil.

Ornithogalum

(CHINCHERINCHEE OR STAR OF BETHLEHEM)
Family: Liliaceae
Hardy and half-hardy perennial bulbs
Position: full sun
Propagation: division of dormant bulbs or seed
Cultivation easy

Ornithogalum nutans

Ornithogalum umbellatum

The genus *Ornithogalum* has achieved fame through the wide use of the species *O. thyrsoides* as cut bloom. Its popularity is due largely to the long-lasting properties of the flowers and to the ease with which they can be exported from their native habitat in South Africa. They are also attractive and decorative. The genus comprises about one hundred species, some native to South Africa, a few indigenous to Europe and the Mediterranean regions and some native to South America. They are bulbous plants, of rather limited ornamental value, but curious for the strange colouring of their flowers, a mixture of white and green. The peculiar common name of Chincherinchee *(O. thyrsoides)* is said to have originated from the characteristic squeaky sound produced by the smooth flower stems when they rub against one another in the wind, or when they are packed in bunches or in baskets for shipping.

Ornithogalum arabicum
From *Curtis's Botanical Magazine*,
1804, plate 728

Other species in general cultivation are *O. arabicum, O. umbellatum,* and *O. nutans,* while the remainder are practically unknown in gardens. The European species are more or less hardy, although *Ornithogalum arabicum* is hardy only in a mild climate. The South African species will not tolerate frost and in northern gardens they must be treated like gladioli, removed from the soil in autumn and replanted every spring. Cultivation is easy. The plants are sun-lovers and have no special demands about soil so long as it is light, porous, preferably sandy, and fertile. Propagation can readily be effected by means of seed sown in a warm greenhouse in spring, but 2–3 years are necessary to obtain flowering-size bulbs. Propagation can also be effected by division of the dormant bulbs, which increase very rapidly.

Flowering period: May–June
Height: 18 ins.
Fragrant

Ornithogalum arabicum L.
Native to the Mediterranean regions. Frequently found in grasslands in coastal zones. The bulbs are oviform, about the size of a walnut. Leaves linear, glaucous green, longer than the flower stem. Flowers borne in a raceme composed of up to twelve pearl-white flowers with a black centre, and agreeably scented. There are six petals, and each bloom is about 1 in. in diameter. In warm climates the flowering is profuse, but much less in colder districts. The bulbs will not tolerate frost.

(Star of Bethlehem)
Flowering period: Mar.–Apr.
Height: 8–18 ins.

Ornithogalum nutans L.
Native to Europe and Asia Minor. A popular species in England where it is much appreciated for its graceful pendulous flowers borne in racemes on rigid stems up to 12 ins. high. The flowers are green outside, with a white margin, and white inside; 3–12 per stem. Leaves light green, up to 18 ins. long and $\frac{1}{2}$ in. wide. Bulbs oval, 1 in. wide.

(Chincherinchee)
Flowering period: July–Aug.
Height: 2–2½ ft.
Useful for cutting

Ornithogalum thyrsoides Jasq.
Native to South Africa. The most popular species and the most widely grown for cut bloom. Individual flowers bell-shaped, white with a maroon centre, and borne 12–30 in a dense raceme on tall erect robust stems up to 2½ ft. high. Leaves up to 12 ins. long and 2 ins. wide; bright green, with slightly hairy margins. Bulbs globose, 1½ ins. wide. Not hardy. The var. *aureum* is slightly less tall and has lovely orange-yellow flowers. In northern gardens can be cultivated in the same manner as gladioli.

(Summer Snowflake or Sleepy Dick)
Flowering period: Apr.–June
Height: 12–18 ins.

Ornithogalum umbellatum L.
Native to the Mediterranean regions. In France known as *Dame des onze heures* (Eleven-o'Clock Lady) because the flowers do not open until late in the morning, closing again in the evening. Individual blooms white striped with green, star-like, 12–20 borne in

clusters on stems up to 8 ins. high. Leaves up to 18 ins. long, $\frac{1}{2}$ in. wide, often with white marks on the surface. Bulbs round, 1 in. in diameter. In warm country gardens such as those in California, etc., the plants naturalize rapidly and can even become invasive. In the United States its late-flowering habit has earned it the common name Sleepy Dick; while for some strange reason in Italy it is known as Chicken's Milk (*latte di gallina*).

Osmanthus

(SWEET OLIVE, FRAGRANT OLIVE, OR TEA OLIVE)
Family: Oleaceae
Half-hardy or hardy evergreen shrubs or small trees
Position: sun or partial shade
Propagation: seed, cuttings, or air layers
Cultivation easy
Intensely fragrant

Osmanthus fragrans offers us what is probably the most intense and most exquisite perfume to be found among garden plants. It is certainly familiar to all who have gardens in temperate climates, and to those who frequent the Riviera, California, Florida, or other southern climes. The plant with this remarkable fragrance is sometimes called *Olea fragrans*, but its correct name is *Osmanthus fragrans*. The intensity of its delicious fragrance fully compensates for the insignificant minute (but not by any means ugly) flowers, cream-white or brilliant orange in colour and borne in small bunches hidden in the evergreen leaf axils. As an extra bonus, this penetrating perfume is offered twice a year, in spring and again in late summer. All osmanthus are fragrant, as confirmed in the generic name, of Greek origin, *osme* (perfume) and *anthos* (flower). The genus is closely related to the olive, and it produces fruits that are small oval drupes, dark blue or violet in colour, similar in shape to little olives; particularly so in the case of *Osmanthus delavayi* which is exceptionally prolific in its seed production. Osmanthus are particularly suited to Mediterranean-type climates, although, with the exception of one species indigenous to the southeastern United States (*Osmanthus americanus*), they are all native to the Orient. They are slow-growing and consequently expensive, but they are very long-lived and large specimens are of great market value. There are about ten species, mostly native to China and Japan, but their nomenclature is confused. They are evergreen with opposite leaves, vigorous, easy to cultivate, require no pruning and little special attention. The plants are hardy

Osmanthus fragrans

but not suitable for planting at high altitudes or where the winters are exceptionally cold and where there is little warm sun to ripen the wood. Osmanthus like a deep soil rich in organic matter, and benefit from an annual spring top dressing. Propagation can be effected from seed sown in frames in spring, by means of cuttings taken from half-ripened wood in July and inserted in frames, or by air layering during June–July.

(Devil Wood)
Flowering period: May–June
Height: up to 40 ft.
Zone 7 southwards

Osmanthus americanus L.
Native to the United States, particularly from Virginia to Florida. An evergreen tree up to 40 ft. high with narrowly oval 4–6-in.-long foliage, shiny green on the upper surface, paler beneath, not dentated at the edges. Flowers small, fragrant, greenish white.

Flowering period: June–Aug.
Height: up to 30 ft.
Zone 6 southwards

Osmanthus Aquifolium Sieb. & Zucc. (syn. *Osmanthus ilicifolius* Mouill.)
Native to Japan. Introduced into Europe in 1856 by Thomas Lobb. A tree up to 30 ft. high in its native habitat, but in gardens it generally forms a very large shrub that often develops a definite trunk. It is the most decorative species of the genus and one of the most attractive of all evergreen shrubs, with foliage very similar to that of holly but easily distinguishable by its opposite leaves (holly leaves are alternate). The flowers are minute, pure white, $\frac{1}{8}$ in. in diameter, borne several together in axillary clusters. Fruits oblong-oval, dark blue. Leaves ovate, up to $2\frac{1}{2}$ ins. long and $1\frac{1}{2}$ ins. wide, dark shiny green above, paler on the undersurface. One curious characteristic is that the foliage on the upper branches is without spines, while that on the lower branches is spiny at its edges; a phenomenon suggesting that nature has provided a defence for those leaves within reach of grazing animals. An even more curious feature is that cuttings taken from the spineless branches produce plants that remain entirely without spines, possibly one of the few and very rare oversights of nature! To distinguish one type of plant from another, the spineless form is referred to as var. *myrtifolius*. This form is also more spreading in habit and does not reach the same height as the type. In climates suited to its cultivation, *Osmanthus Aquifolium* can also be used to make impressive and attractive hedges, the spineless form being particularly suited for this purpose. There is also an interesting form with the leaves variegated in green and cream-white, var. *variegata*. Another interesting variety is var. *purpureus*, where the young leaves and new growths are dark blackish purple. This form is also much hardier than the type. It was first raised in 1880 at Kew.

Flowering period: Apr.–May
Height: up to 10 ft.
Zone 7 southwards

Osmanthus delavayi Franch. (syn. *Siphonosmanthus delavayi* Stapf.)
Native to China. Grown for the first time in Europe by Maurice de Vilmorin, from seed sent from China by the Jesuit Jean-Marie (Père)

Delavay, to whom we are indebted for many beautiful plants such as *Paeonia delavayi, Incarvillea delavayi, Rhododendron delavayi,* etc. It is a shrub of modest proportions and completely different to the large tree-like osmanthus; so much so that some botanists have reclassified it into another genus (here given as the synonym). The branches are rigid, expansive, and amply covered with small coriaceous leaves up to 1 in. long, dark green in colour. The flowers are intensely fragrant, pure white, and prolific. It is relatively hardy and the most suitable osmanthus for small gardens.

Osmanthus forrestii Rehder
Native to the Yunnan province of China. An evergreen shrub with the young growths a distinctive greyish yellow. Leaves hard and stiff-textured, dark green, ovate-lanceolate, generally dentated or spiny, up to 8 ins. long and $2\frac{1}{2}$ ins. wide. Flowers very pale yellow, deliciously scented, $\frac{3}{8}$ in. wide at the mouth, four-lobed, and borne several together in dense clusters in the leaf axils. Fruits egg-shaped, $\frac{1}{2}$ in. long, dark purple-blue.

Flowering period: Aug.–Sept.
Height: up to 20 ft.
Zone 7 southwards

Osmanthus fragrans Lour. (syn. *Olea fragrans* Thunb.)
Native to China and Japan. A very large shrub or small tree with a massive trunk. Leaves large, oval, up to $3\frac{1}{2}$ ins. long and half as wide; rather light green, leathery, prolific; the entire mass of branches forms a rounded head of dense vegetation. Flowers minute, cream-white, intensely fragrant, and produced twice a year, first in spring and then again in late summer and autumn. In China, the flowers are used to add fragrance to tea. The var. *aurantiacus* Makino is particularly beautiful, with brilliant orange-coloured flowers, but it is slightly less fragrant.

Flowering period: Apr.–May
Height: up to 25 ft.
Zone 7 southwards

Oxalis

(WOOD SORREL OR ROSE SHAMROCK)
Family: *Oxalidaceae*
Half-hardy or tender herbaceous perennials, bulbs, or tubers
Position: sun
Propagation: seed or division
Cultivation very easy

Before admitting oxalis to the garden it is necessary to issue the challenge "friend or foe". Some oxalis are definitely welcome as well-behaved, exquisitely beautiful guests, but others are invasive and

Oxalis rosea
From *Curtis's Botanical Magazine*,
1815, plate 1712

abuse our hospitality immediately by attempting to take complete possession of the garden. Their eradication is almost impossible without sterilizing the soil or using a total weed-killer. One of the worst offenders is *Oxalis corniculata*, the perennial yellow wood sorrel, about 1 in. high with small reddish clover-like leaves and small bright-yellow flowers; this pest thrives at the roadside, in walls, in courtyards, among paving stones and in gravel, and, if one is unlucky, in lawns. Even the beautiful yellow-flowered *Oxalis cernua* and the lovely pink *Oxalis rosea* can become nuisances if they find conditions too congenial and if allowed to stray beyond definite limits; but it would be a pity to exclude them completely as they are both so very attractive.

The genus is vast, with at least six hundred species attributed to it, and with a distribution that includes Europe, South Africa, Mexico, Chile, Brazil, and much of South America. The name is of Greek origin, *oxys* (sharp), and refers to the acid flavour of the foliage. The common weed, *Oxalis Acetosella*, contains oxalic acid and when boiled in milk or water produces an infusion that has been used as a diuretic, and is reputed to be of use in febrile diseases, urinary affections, catarrh, and haemorrhages. One curious characteristic of this species is its supposed ability to forecast the weather. In rural areas in England and Europe local people consult the plant for this purpose, having noted that the clover-like leaves that always close towards nightfall (in the same manner as clover), also close at the approach of a storm, and if the leaves remain closed during the entire day it is a sure sign of rain. Another curious characteristic is that it bears a number of flowers that never open, although they do produce seeds through self-pollination (and consequently are known as cleistogamous flowers).

Cultivation. The fact that so many oxalis are fast-growing invasive weeds is clear indication that they are often too easy to cultivate. Their greatest enemy is cold and, as the majority are plants from temperate zones, they will not tolerate long periods of severe frost unless, in the case of the bulbous types, the bulbs are planted deeply enough to escape the frost. The only really hardy species is *Oxalis Acetosella*, a woodland plant and one of the first of early spring flowers. The other species are sun lovers, thriving in either acid or alkaline (calcareous) soils that must be light, porous, and warm. Propagation can be effected by division of the roots in spring, or, in the case of the bulbous types, division of the small bulbs. The plants can also be raised from seed sown in pots in spring in greenhouses or frames.

Oxalis adenophylla Gillies (syn. *Oxalis bustillosii*)
Native to Chile. A stemless herbaceous plant with tuberous roots. Leaves numerous on 6-in.-long stalks forming a dense rosette; each

Tuberous
Flowering period: Apr.–June
Height: up to 6 ins.

leaf divided into about twenty segments or leaflets, narrowly obcordate, glaucous green. Flowers generally solitary, bell-shaped, 1 in. long, lilac-pink veined pinkish red. A plant attractive for its blooms and foliage; excellent for cultivating in pots or other containers, but it is not really hardy.

(Bermuda Buttercup)
Bulbous
Flowering period: Mar.–May
Height: up to 9 ins.

Oxalis cernua Thunb. (syn. *Bulboxalis cernuus*)
Native to South Africa but widely naturalized in the Mediterranean regions, and other warm places where it can even become an invasive weed. A non-hardy bulbous stemless herbaceous plant with numerous leaves composed of 3–6 obcordate segments about $\frac{1}{8}$ in. wide; light green and marked dark purple. The semi-pendulous bell-shaped flowers are borne on erect stems up to 9 ins. high, 3–9 per stem, and a lovely shade of bright yellow. When grown in large masses the plant produces a really beautiful effect. There is a rare double-flowered form.

Oxalis enneaphylla    *Oxalis deppei*

Bulbous
Flowering period: Apr.–May
Height: up to 10 ins.

Oxalis deppei Lodd. (syn. *Ionoxalis deppei*)
Native to Mexico. A small black bulb producing leaf stalks 6–8 ins. high, bearing leaves composed of 4–10 obovate glabrous leaflets marked with dark-red spots. Inflorescence a loosely formed umbel borne on a stem longer than the leaf stalks and composed of up to twelve individual flowers variable in colour from red to purple-violet. Moderately hardy but not resistant to prolonged periods of severe frost. Sometimes cultivated as a pot plant for indoor use. In its native habitat it is occasionally grown for its edible bulbs.

Bulbous
Flowering period: Apr.–June
Height: up to 4 ins.
Fragrant

Oxalis enneaphylla Cav.
Native to the Falkland Islands. A stemless bulbous species with numerous glaucous-green leaves borne on stalks up to $3\frac{1}{2}$ ins. high,

closely and compactly arranged, obcordate, each leaf divided into 9–20 leaflets nearly $\frac{1}{2}$ in. long and radiating out from the centre. Bulbs made up of fleshy scales. Flowers fragrant, $\frac{2}{3}$ in. in diameter, solitary, on stalks up to 4 ins. long, white veined with violet, widely bell-shaped. The var. *rosea* has beautiful pink flowers. Both are excellent for pot culture.

Oxalis floribunda L. (syn. *Oxalis lasiandra*)
Native to Mexico and Brazil. A stemless bulbous herbaceous plant; the flower and leaf stalks rising directly from the soil surface. Not completely hardy. Leaves brilliant green divided into 3–5 obcordate segments, up to 3 ins. long, on slender stalks up to 10 ins. high and slightly hairy. Inflorescence a rather loosely formed umbel composed of up to twelve individual flowers $\frac{1}{3}$ in. in diameter, pink with a darker centre. Requires a warm, dry, sunny position. Propagation by means of the small bulbs which form round the parent bulb. Once established, this plant resents disturbance.

Bulbous
Flowering period: May–Aug.
Height: up to 10 ins.

Oxalis rosea Feuill.
Native to Chile. A graceful and elegant small stemless herbaceous perennial. Best in mild climates where it naturalizes with such ease that it can rapidly become an invasive weed. The clover-like foliage is borne on erect reddish stems up to 4 ins. high and each leaf is divided into three obcordate segments; bright green with the undersurface reddish. The inflorescence is borne on stems slightly longer than the leaf stems in the form of a three-branched cyme. The $\frac{2}{3}$-in.-wide individual flowers are an attractive pink veined reddish pink. A beautiful plant for massing, thriving in sun or partial shade.

Herbaceous perennial
Flowering period: Apr.–June
Height: up to 4 ins.

Oxalis variabilis Jacq. (syn. *Oxalis grandiflora*)
Native to South Africa. A robust, vigorous stemless plant with a large oval bulb producing about twenty leaves which form a rosette of vegetation. The leaves are borne on stalks up to 6 ins. high and are composed of three slightly fleshy obcordate leaflets with wedge-shaped bases, often purple-tinted on the undersurface. Flowers solitary, borne on 6-in. stems, variable in colour from pale pink to red, $\frac{2}{3}$ in. wide, yellowish at the base of the petals. Flowering period very long, in mild climates lasting from July until December. Moderately hardy. The var. *rubra* (syn. *Oxalis speciosa, Oxalis purpurea*) is particularly beautiful and often grown indoors as a pot plant for its foliage and its dark-pink or red flowers. The var. *alba* has white flowers and is earlier-flowering.

Herbaceous perennial
Flowering period: July–Sept.
Height: 6 ins.

Oxalis violacea L.
Native to the United States, from Florida to the Rocky Mountains; generally found in woody localities. A herbaceous perennial with

(Purple Wood Sorrel)
Herbaceous perennial
Flowering period: May–June
Height: up to 5 ins.

the foliage divided into three segments, each segment notched at its tip. Flowers pinkish purple or pink, in cymes of 3–7 borne on slender stalks rising directly from the soil. An attractive plant for naturalizing in semi-wild shady positions where the soil is rich in humus.

Paeonia

(Peony or Paeony)
Family: Ranunculaceae
Herbaceous perennials or deciduous shrubs
Position: full sun (partial shade below Zone 8)
Propagation: division, grafting, or air layering
Cultivation easy
Useful for cutting

Among plants, peonies are the masterpieces of the Chinese, for in China the blooms have (or used to have) a place in everyday life, in customs, ceremonies and ritual, and in history. It is difficult for me to convey the enthusiasm I have for these spectacular flowers, or to describe the emotion I experienced when I found my first wild peony in bloom in Southern Italy. It was an unforgettable event, and my enthusiasm has been shared by many others before me. In the case of tree peonies, however, the question of excessive cost has always restricted their wider use and appreciation. The American author Richardson Wright made an accurate and shrewd statement when he remarked that the fastest way towards financial ruin is to have a personal propensity for indulgence in tree peonies; but Coats, whose passion for peonies must be as keen as mine, added: "It is worthwhile selling everything one possesses to buy paeonies, and to dig up everything else in the garden to make room for them."

There are indications that tree peonies have been costly ever since their first introduction into garden cultivation because even in China they were grown only by the rich. In a poem by Po Chu-i (772–846), there is a passage describing the sale of peonies in the market in which he quotes the following prices: "100 pieces of damask for the most beautiful flowers; 5 pieces of silk for the more common types. A poor man passing by commented: 'a bunch of dark red flowers would pay the taxes on ten poor people's houses.'"

Parey attributes thirty-three species to the genus, while other authorities place the number at anything from fifteen to twenty-five. They are diffused throughout Europe, Asia, and the Pacific Coast

Paeonia peregrina

areas of North America, although the sole American species, *Paeonia brownii,* is of little interest. In 1884 John Gilbert Baker divided peonies into herbaceous types—where the disc is never wrapped around or overlaying the base of the carpels—and shrubby or woody types—where the disc does wrap round or overlay the base of the carpels. For horticultural purposes, the division is still valid at the present time and it is used here.

The history of peonies follows two separate branches; the Western species *Paeonia officinalis,* whose chief importance is that of a medicinal plant, and the Asiatic species, which in European and American gardens are cultivated exclusively for decorative purposes. Among the herbaceous peonies—and apart from the hybrids of the European *Paeonia officinalis*—it is only *Paeonia lactiflora,* native to China, which in its hybrid forms has become widely cultivated in our gardens; the remaining species are grown only by enthusiastic specialists.

Paeonia lactiflora has been grown in China since the fifth century B.C. It was named *Paeonia albiflora* by Pallas in 1788, but since he had already described it under the name *Paeonia lactiflora,* the older name takes precedence. It seems to have been introduced into European garden cultivation in 1820; since then more than three thousand hybrids have been raised.

The cultivation of the tree peony, *Paeonia suffruticosa* (syn. *Paeonia moutan*), began in Asia some years after that of the herbaceous *Paeonia lactiflora*. Some reference books record that the first wild plants were found about fifteen hundred years ago, but the first varieties date back to about the seventh century A.D., when the emperors of the Tang dynasty ascended the throne. From that time on, *Paeonia suffruticosa* became the fashionable rage in China and its price soared. Poets sang its praises, it was protected by the emperors, it was painted on walls and on silk and fine papers, and it gradually became an almost obligatory motif in the decoration of imperial palaces. Epigraphists composed material of an almost religious fervour to describe the peonies grown in the imperial gardens. This enthusiastic admiration for the flowers even survived political revolutions and disturbances. Honoured by titles such as Queen of Flowers and A Hundred Ounces of Gold (their original price), peonies were the first plants to be established in the gardens of the Tang emperors. When the Emperor Yung-Lo of the Ming dynasty transferred the court to Peking, he ordered an annual pilgrimage to observe the flowering of *Paeonia moutan,* and this custom was faithfully followed until the nineteenth century.

The Chinese developed more than three hundred varieties of tree peonies, with flowers in various shades of white, purple, pink, amaranth-red, yellow, and violet-blue, as well as numerous intermediate gradations. They probably also developed striped and

Paeonia suffruticosa (double-flowered variety)
From *The Botanical Register*,
1831, plate 1456

bicoloured forms, but, unlike gardeners of later centuries who highly esteemed auriculas and carnations with striped flowers, the Chinese eliminated the striped peonies. The shrubs were trained (and perhaps are still being trained in present-day China) in a thousand different ways; cultivated fanwise, in the form of large globes, as miniature trees, or as espaliers, etc. Robert Fortune, the great traveller and botanical explorer, observed and collected peonies in China during the nineteenth century:

> The gardens devoted to tree-paeony culture in China were many; the soil was not rich, but well cultivated, and lighter than that of the surrounding countryside devoted to the cultivation of cotton. In the gardens of the mandarins one frequently saw paeony plants of extraordinary size. On the outskirts of Shanghai there was a specimen which produced 300–400 flowers annually. The owner lavished the same care upon it which was found among the most fanatic tulip specialist; during its entire flowering period the plant was protected from the sun with shading, while in front of this stupendous example there was a chair on which the many visitors could sit to fully enjoy the spectacle of its blooms. For many hours every day the old mandarin himself could be seen sitting there; and between his pipe and his tea his eyes caressed his favourite tree paeony. It was in fact a magnificent display, well worthy of the adoration of the old amateur, to whom one might wish a hundred years of life so that he could continue to sit under his canopy and enjoy such a beautiful sight.

Long before the actual plants were introduced, tree peonies were known in Europe through the descriptions of missionaries and by examples depicted in Chinese art. Sir Joseph Banks tried to import them from Canton, but all the plants died during the long and dangerous voyage. Dr. Duncan of the East India Company brought a live plant to Kew Gardens in 1789, but it was short-lived. In 1794 the ship *Triton* reached London with seven tree peonies on board; one for the King, two for Sir Joseph Banks, and four for another gentleman. The ship, however, had experienced a slow and difficult voyage, losing its mainmast in the Channel, and the plants were in poor condition; two died, but the other five survived and it is believed that they included pink and single- and double-flowered varieties. Ten years later, the ship *Hope* arrived in England with a consignment of plants sent from Canton by William Kerr. Among these there were some tree peonies so different from the others that several botanists believed them to be another species, naming them *Paeonia papaveracea* because the seed capsules resembled those of a poppy. The flowers were white or flesh-pink, almost single, with a purple mark on each petal. Sir Abraham Hume, the recipient, later

Double-flowered *Paeonia lactiflora*

received another plant with mauve-pink flowers; and there the situation remained for many years, notwithstanding repeated efforts to import new varieties. Meanwhile, live plants of tree peonies had reached France, and, with the limited quantity available, gardeners began placing them on the market. During this time in Paris the plants sold at prices ranging from 1,500 francs to 100 louis d'or (2,000 francs) each. In 1814 there was a real peony mania in France, but enthusiasts had to be content with the limited number of plants available.

The first attempts at hybridizing herbaceous peonies with tree peonies were made in England, at Arley, in 1830, but the results were due to chance rather than to the use of a proper technique. In 1834, Robert Fortune was sent to China by the Royal Horticultural Society to procure new peonies, either herbaceous or woody, and if possible to discover the legendary blue peony, whose actual existence was doubted. Fortune quickly appreciated that every zone or district of China had its own particular varieties, with little exchange taking place between one district and another. Varieties found, for instance, in Shanghai were not available in Canton, and vice versa. The new plants Fortune eventually procured came from a small nursery on the outskirts of Shanghai, where propagation was effected by grafting choice varieties onto the roots of wild peonies. The resulting plants were cultivated to produce a single enormous flower, and were then discarded. The most highly esteemed were the so-called yellow varieties, with white flowers suffused yellow at the centre; there was also a wisteria-coloured variety, a black-flowered variety, one very dark maroon, and a double purple variety with enormous flowers. Fortune believed the double purple was actually the legendary blue-flowered peony with a thousand petals, said to grow only in the Emperor's garden. Altogether, Fortune collected between thirty and forty varieties, most of which safely reached England.

Phillipp Franz van Siebold also brought a vast collection of tree peonies to Europe from Japan, where the plants had been grown since the eighth century. This collection was said to have been gathered from the old imperial gardens in Yedo (Tokyo) and Miyako (Kyoto), and included varieties vastly different to those from China, being mostly single and semi-double forms.

In 1880, the Jesuit missionary Jean-Marie (Père) Delavay sent seeds of *Paeonia lutea* and *Paeonia delavayi* to the Natural History Museum of Paris; here *Paeonia lutea* flowered in 1891 and *Paeonia delavayi* bloomed in 1892. In 1936, in southeastern Tibet, Ludlow and Sheriff found a variety of *Paeonia lutea* far superior to the type and named it *Paeonia ludlowii*. The flowers were much larger, and erect rather than pendent.

Thus, at the beginning of the twentieth century, there was available a sufficiently large number of species for hybridists to begin work, and Lemoine immediately began by crossing the varieties of *Paeonia suffruticosa* with *Paeonia lutea*, adding to the range of colours such tints as yellow, peach, and flame. Unfortunately, many varieties inherited from *Paeonia lutea* a characteristic weak stem with enormous flowers which, if not bundled up like mummies and given adequate support, threatened to weigh down and ruin the entire plant. Lemoine's masterpiece was named Souvenir de Maxime Cornu, in honour of the director of the Jardin des Plantes in Paris. Until the beginning of the twentieth century, the only *Paeonia suffruticosa* in cultivation were garden hybrids of Oriental origin; spontaneous progenitors had never been found, not even on the hill in China called Mountain of Peonies (Mou-tan-Shan), which, according to tradition, was rich in wild peonies. Finally, in 1910, William Purdom found a dark-red peony on the slopes of a mountain in southern Kansu province. In 1914, Reginald Farrer also found a wild variety—with white flowers marked maroon—near a village on the Black River, but he was unable to obtain seed of this specimen. It was not until 1926 that Dr. J. F. Rock sent to the Arnold Arboretum in Boston seed that corresponded to Farrer's description and which was classified as a wild variety.

Europe's *Paeonia officinalis,* although possessing little real medicinal value, has played an important part in the horrible mixtures and potions brewed by sorceresses and witches. This particular species is deeply rooted in mythology; Theophrastus noted that the name *Paeonia* was derived from Paeon, a disciple of Aesculapius, who with a poultice that included *Paeonia officinalis* healed Hades of a wound inflicted by Hercules. Theophrastus also relates that the same plant was used to cure Ares of the wounds he received from Diomedes. Pliny also referred to the plant in his writings. In Greek *Paeonia officinalis* was known as Gift of God, not only because of the many healing powers attributed to it, but also because it was believed that it could drive away evil spirits and prevent storms. Traditionally, for the plant to conserve all its virtues, it was necessary to gather it furtively at dusk, taking great care not to be seen by the green woodpecker who, as noted by Pliny the Elder, would attack the gatherer and peck out his eyes ("Si Picus Martius videat, tuendo in oculos impetum faciat").

In *De Virtutibus Herbarum,* Apuleius wrote that the peony was a powerful specific against madness, while M. Floridus, in his *De Viribus Herbarum,* recommended the use of peonies against infantile epilepsy—some centuries ago it was a common sight to see children wearing a piece of peony root around their neck as a preventative talisman. Hippocrates and Galen were convinced of its healing virtues and recommended it in the treatment of epilepsy, eclampsia, or insanity, as a curative for blisters, as a remedy for obstinate and persistent coughs and catarrh, and for relieving insomnia and nightmares. Furthermore, peasants of the Alpine regions believed

Paeonia suffruticosa (semi-double-flowered variety)
From *Curtis's Botanical Magazine*
1820, plate 2175

(and perhaps still believe today) that the seeds of *Paeonia officinalis* help ease the discomfort of teething.

Present-day knowledge confirms that the essential drug is contained in the flower petals—which should be gathered when fully expanded and dried in the shade—as well as in the seeds and tuberous roots. The alkaloid paeonin is found in all parts of the plant and its chief use is as a sedative. An infusion prepared from the seeds has emetic and purgative action but it should be remembered that, like all of the Ranunculaceae, the peony contains poisonous principles and should be used with great prudence as it can cause severe gastric disturbances.

Apart from their decorative and medicinal uses, peonies are of little value for other purposes. In times of famine the roots of *Paeonia officinalis* have been cooked and eaten, notwithstanding the grave risk of poisoning; but it has been recorded that the Tartars ate *Paeonia lactiflora* roots without any unpleasant after-effects, and for that reason the species was named *Paeonia edulis* by Salisbury. Finally, it should be noted that in certain parts of Japan a dish reported to be delicious is prepared from the flowers of *Paeonia suffruticosa*.

Paeonia officinalis has a curiously unpleasant odour, but the flowers of *Paeonia lactiflora* and many of its modern hybrids have a rose-like fragrance, particularly the French hybrids Adolphe Rousseau, Martin Cahuzac, and M. Jules Elie; and Kelway's Glorious, Baroness Schroeder, Mrs. Franklin D. Roosevelt, Georgina Shayler, Walter Faxon, Myrtle Gentry, Big Ben, Philippe Rivoire, Laura Desert, and Old Siwash, all of which are early-flowering. Scented, late-flowering varieties are: Dr. J. H. Neelsy, Flower Girl, Siloam, Auton's Pride, and Eloise. Somewhat less beautiful, but exceptionally fragrant are the varieties Belle Chinoise and Sistie. Wilson and Bell maintain that all the tree peonies and their hybrids are fragrant, but my own personal experience does not confirm this. Those that are fragrant for certain include Roman Gold, Alice Harding, L'Esperance, Mine d'Or, Souvenir de Maxime Cornu, Chromatella, La Lorraine, Sang Lorraine, Surprise; while among those imported from Japan we can include Asahi-Minato (White Port), Saigyo-Sakura (Sakura Cherry), and Shikoden (Palace of Violet Light).

Cultivation. The cultivation of herbaceous peonies is very easy. They thrive in practically any soil, generously manured in advance and preferably not too light in texture. They require a position in full sun, but cultivation in partial shade is advisable in very hot, southerly climates. Peonies are completely hardy and do not mind severe frost, but they do resent root disturbance, and after planting or replanting it is not unusual for the plants to stop flowering for several years thereafter. Care should be taken not to plant the roots too deeply, with the eyes not more than $1\frac{1}{2}$ ins. below the soil surface.

Paeonia officinalis

Double-flowered
Paeonia officinalis

If properly cared for and well grown, the plants can be left undisturbed for up to twelve years, after which time one can, if desired, lift and divide them. The original planting should allow plenty of room for expansion with a space of up to 2–3 ft. between the plants. Fertilizing, preferably with well-composted manure, is best done in the autumn, while a top dressing of organic matter at the beginning of summer is beneficial.

Propagation is by division in autumn and each of the divided sections should have at least two eyes (three or more is preferable). In the case of old specimens, propagation can also be effected by means of the suckers—or side growths—that appear all round the parent plant in autumn. These can either be planted in their permanent positions or grown on for a year or so in pots. Propagation from seed is possible, but terribly slow, 7–8 years being necessary for the seedlings to reach flowering size; this is a method normally employed only for raising new varieties. Seed can be sown in boxes, frames, or in the open ground—with the site kept covered with a thin layer of dead leaves—in a shady position. The best time for sowing is as soon as the seed is ripe. Germination is slow and capricious, sometimes not until the second year after sowing.

Paeonia suffruticosa—and tree peonies in general—are also hardy, but, as the plants have a habit of starting into growth very early, there is a risk in some localities of the young growths being harmed by late frosts. The plants can be grown either in the open ground or in large tubs or other receptacles, using a soil mixture containing equal amounts of ordinary garden soil, leafsoil, and peat, plus a little coarse sand. During their growing season periodic applications of liquid fertilizer are very beneficial. Propagation can be effected by division (in the case of really large specimens with numerous stems), by grafting, and by air layering. The Chinese, who are still the greatest experts of peony propagation, generally root graft the variety to be propagated; Robert Fortune closely followed this operation in China and described it in detail:

> At the beginning of October gather together under a porch or shed a quantity of tuberous roots of herbaceous paeonies onto which the selected tree paeony growths are to be grafted. The largest roots of the herbaceous paeonies are divided so that each section has the thickness of a finger and will serve to receive a graft. Place all the sections on a table, collect the growths which are to be grafted onto the roots. These growths should be 1–2 ins. long, and be taken from the tips of the current season's vegetation. Cut the base of the graft to form a small wedge and insert it in the top of the piece of tuberous root, firmly tying it with raffia and then wrapping the entire union in a layer of clay. When a certain number of roots have

Paeonia tenuifolia
From *Curtis's Botanical Magazine*,
1806, plate 926

thus been grafted they can be planted outside, in a shady position, 18 ins. apart, taking care that the position where the graft has been made is above the soil surface.

To grow tree peonies from seed takes even longer than growing herbaceous peonies, and 10–12 years is necessary to obtain flowering plants. For those who wish to try, seed should be sown in autumn, in a mixture of peat and leafsoil, in a frame or seed bed in a shady position. The seedlings should be potted individually and grown on in pots for 2–3 years, during which period they should not be exposed to frost.

When tree peonies have finished flowering the plants often enter a period of lethargy during which the leaves droop or even fall and the stems remain bare. No harm is done the peonies if some shallow-rooted summer-flowering annuals of modest proportions are planted among them, such as impatiens, alyssum, or sanvitalia, all of which will give good results in light shade.

Deciduous shrub
Flowering period: May–June
Height: up to 6 ft.
Zone 5 southwards

Paeonia delavayi Franch.
Native to China. A fast-growing shrub, around the base of which many lateral growths are produced. Leaves bipinnate, 6–18 ins. long, dark green on the upper surface, glaucous beneath, segments lanceolate and pointed. Flowers single, terminal, growing in groups of 1–3 on rigid stems; they are cup-shaped, slightly pendulous, $2\frac{1}{2}$–4 ins. in diameter. The petals are blood-red and the anthers are yellow. Botanically, it is closely related to *Paeonia lutea,* although the flower colour easily distinguishes it. The var. *alba* has milk-white flowers. In districts where late frosts can be expected this is a more satisfactory peony than *Paeonia suffruticosa.*

Herbaceous perennial
Flowering period: June–July
Height: up to $2\frac{1}{2}$ ft.
Fragrant

Paeonia lactiflora Steud. (syn. *Paeonia albiflora, Paeonia sinensis*)
Native to Siberia, Mongolia, China, and Japan. Leaves lanceolate, 3–4 ins. long. Flowers borne on long rigid stems, white, scented, 4 ins. in diameter, with numerous yellow stamens at the centre. Important as the species that has produced the many garden hybrids known as Chinese Peonies, probably the most widely grown group of peonies and well-known for their late-flowering habit of long duration. The blooms have a diameter of up to 6 ins. Some of the best hybrids are:

> Adolphe Rousseau, double, purple-red
> Albatron, double, white
> Canary, double, yellow and cream
> Cherry Hill, double, cherry-red
> Le Cygne, double, greenish white
> Eva, single, crimson-pink
> Felix Crousse, double, crimson

Martin Cahuzac, double, purple
Pink Delight, single, pale pink
Sarah Bernhardt, double, apple-blossom pink
Solange, double, orange-salmon
Victoria, single, dark crimson

Paeonia lactiflora can also be successfully grown in wooden tubs or other large receptacles having a diameter not less than 2 ft. It should be remembered that the tuberous roots resent disturbance and once planted should not be disturbed again for several years.

Paeonia lutea Franch. (syn. *Paeonia delavayi* var. *lutea*)
Native to the Yunnan province of China. Foliage leathery, 12–16 ins. long, dark green on the upper surface, glaucous beneath, divided into three segments, each of which has deeply dentated edges and very conspicuous veins. Flowers single or semi-double, $3\frac{1}{2}$ ins. in diameter, golden-yellow with a crimson mark at the base of the crinkled petals.

Deciduous shrub
Flowering period: May–June
Height: $1\frac{1}{2}$ ft.
Zone 5 southwards

Paeonia lutea

Paeonia delavayi

Paeonia mlokosewitschi Lomak.
Native to the Caucasus. Attractive blue-green foliage, divided into numerous obovate, pointed segments. Flowers single, $4-4\frac{1}{2}$ ins. in diameter; primrose-yellow with golden-yellow stamens in the centre. In late summer the seed cases split open to reveal blue-black seeds.

Herbaceous perennial
Flowering period: Apr.–May
Height: $1\frac{1}{2}$ ft.

Paeonia officinalis L. (syn. *Paeonia fulgida* Sabine)
Native to Europe. One of the most widely grown garden peonies in its hybrid forms. Leaves 6–8 ins. long, dark green on the upper surface, paler beneath, and divided into numerous oblong-lanceolate segments 1 in. wide; the basal foliage is often entire. The original species has single, 2-in.-wide flowers of a fine crimson tint. The

Herbaceous perennial
Flowering period: Apr.–May
Height: $2\frac{1}{2}$ ft.

following varieties have double flowers up to 6 ins. in diameter or more:

    var. *alba plena,* white
    var. *rosea plena,* pink
    var. *rubra plena,* ruby-red

Herbaceous perennial
Flowering period: Apr.–May
Height: up to 2½ ft.

Paeonia peregrina Mill.
Native to Europe. Foliage glabrous, dark green on the upper surface, paler green beneath. Flowers crimson, single, and so similar to *Paeonia officinalis* that some botanists consider it to be a form.

Herbaceous perennial
Flowering period: Apr.–May
Height: 15 ins.

Paeonia russi Biv.
Native to Sicily, Corsica, and Sardinia. A species of considerable beauty for its single reddish-pink flowers, nearly 5 ins. in diameter, with rounded overlapping petals and yellow stamens. Leaves up to 5 ins. long, entire, pointed at both ends, green on the upper surface, glaucous beneath, with conspicuous veins.

(Tree Peony or Moutan Peony)
Deciduous shrub
Flowering period: May–June
Height: up to 5½ ft.
Zone 4 southwards

Paeonia suffruticosa Andr. (syn. *Paeonia moutan* Sims, *Paeonia arborea* Don)
Native to China, Tibet, and Bhutan. A shrub of considerable proportions which in its native habitat can reach a height of up to 10 ft. There is little doubt that this species, along with its many hybrid forms, constitutes the most spectacular of all exotic flowering shrubs cultivated in European and American gardens. Habit rigid, erect, and much-branched. Foliage glabrous, bipinnate, up to 18 ins. long, dark green, while the basal leaves are often entire. The flowers of the original species are single, up to 6 ins. in diameter, purplish pink. However, in today's gardens they have largely been superseded by the stupendous single, semi-double, and double forms with their enormous 12-in.-wide blooms. These also come in a range of colours extending through gradations of pink, crimson, yellow, carmine, white, purple, and violet, often with the petals striped in contrasting hues or suffused with different colours. The specific name *moutan* derives from Mütang, the mythical Chinese flower emperor. Peony enthusiasts frequently import the plants by air direct from Japanese growers, with excellent results.

(Fringed Peony)
Herbaceous perennial
Flowering period: May–June
Height: 18 ins.

Paeonia tenuifolia L.
Native to the Caucasus. Appropriately known as the Fringed Peony because of its finely divided fringed fennel-like foliage. Flowers are cup-shaped, up to 3 ins. in diameter, a rich dark crimson, with a mass of yellow stamens in the centre. The colour is, however, variable and reddish-purple forms can be found. The plants rapidly increase by wide-spreading roots and basal growths.

Papaver

(POPPY)
(*Also see* ESCHSCHOLZIA *and* MECONOPSIS)
Family: Papaveraceae
Herbaceous perennials and annuals
Position: sun
Propagation: division, seed, or root cuttings
Cultivation easy
Useful for cutting

The cultivation of poppies dates back to remotest antiquity. The flower, its seeds, and the sap of certain species provided most of the ancient world with an important religious symbol, a palatable foodstuff, and a narcotic that was both beneficial—because it was one of the first effective total anaesthetics—and harmful—because it is a mind- and body-destroying drug. As the colour of some species is reminiscent of fresh blood, and since certain pale-coloured poppies were the source of a substance that produced either a state of visionary ecstasy or blank nepenthe, it was only logical that this flower should become the locus of many myths in many cultures.
To the Mediterranean peoples, poppies are closely linked to the east through their ancient association with Cybele, the Near Eastern goddess of fertility and nature, and through that deity to her Greek and Roman counterparts, Demeter and Ceres. The chief attributes of these two divinities are sheaves of wheat and poppies, which, because of their colour and their profusely produced seeds, became a symbol for life and fertility. The poppy flower had another, darker, symbolic aspect for the ancients, one signifying sleep and death: therefore it became sacred to the Roman god Morpheus. And some Classical writers even averred that the poppy (as well as the narcissus) was one of the flowers gathered by Demeter's daughter, Persephone, at the very moment she was abducted by Hades and spirited away to the Underworld (thus heralding winter and the seasonal death of growing things).
Although poppies played a relatively small part in Christian iconography and symbolism, the flower became tremendously popular in the late nineteenth and early twentieth century in the art and writings of the Symbolists and the Decadents, and also as a major design element in Art Nouveau. Poems, novellas, and novels celebrated its narcotic and sleep-inducing powers, as well as its beauty; and paintings, drawings, and posters proliferated with *femmes fatales* crowned with poppies, clutching poppies, or crushing poppies into potion-filled chalices.
The First World War banished this over-perfumed preciosity in art

Papaver orientale
From *Curtis's Botanical Magazine*,
1788, plate 57

and literature, and the poppy assumed a new role; still, however, death-devoted. The well-known poem that begins "In Flanders' fields the poppies blow," and ends with the lines "If ye break faith with us who die / We shall not sleep, though poppies grow / in Flanders' fields," inspired the artificial poppies which are still given out to those who contribute to various veterans' organizations on or around Memorial or Veterans Day.

Yet, even today, the poppy still qualifies as a symbol of death because of the terrible effects wrought by the opium poppy, the baleful (and beautiful) *Papaver somniferum,* the Poppy of Sleep. The opium extract, heroin, has become one of the major factors in world-wide crime and the terror of urban life. (But we must not forget that in the nineteenth century opium-based nostrums such as laudanum were sold as freely and as openly as aspirin is sold today, and many thousands of perfectly respectable souls were thus made hopeless—though unwitting—addicts.)

The genus *Papaver* comprises about one hundred species, for the most part diffused throughout the Mediterranean regions, eastwards to Armenia and ancient Persia, with a few species native to the Orient, and one each in South Africa and Australia. Poppies have also become naturalized in most parts of western North America, particularly in the warmer zones. Several species are also found in the Alps, even at an altitude of 9,000 feet.

Concerning poppies, one of the most famous nurserymen, the Swiss Correvon, wrote:

> Poppies are annuals which require a poor, dry soil which is light and which lies in full sun. They grow among crops (to which they cause no harm) in arid, hungry land, and for that reason nobody likes to see them on his property. The flowers, of such vivid and brilliant hues and among the most colourful of our indigenous flora, are unfortunately very ephemeral. To enjoy them as cut flowers, pick them in the bud stage and place them immediately in water, after which one can see the petals swell and expand—throwing off the calyx which encloses them like a no longer needed cloak—and begin to unfurl while still crumpled.

The ephemeral character of poppies is not noticeable in large gardens but their short-lived flowering does preclude their cultivation on terraces and it can cause a certain penury of colour in small gardens where space has to be exploited to the maximum. Some garden owners—who are not necessarily gardeners or even garden lovers—do, however, object to the adverse ratio between poppies' flowering and non-flowering periods. Some people wish to grow only those plants with a practical, material value, which will live with little

Seed capsules of poppie

Papaver somniferum,

water in soil that is never cultivated or fertilized, do not require pricking out or transplanting, and remain continuously in flower. They choose a plant much in the same manner they would choose a washing machine: maximum efficiency, fully automatic, minimum water and power consumption. Judged by such standards, poppies should be rated zero, and they are not for people who classify plants in such a manner. However, the shortcomings of poppies are real and admissible, especially in the case of city parks where the maintenance problems are complex and difficult, and where economics must be considered. But the attitude that animates the gardener who loves his plants as well as his garden is completely different. An excellent statement concerning the cultivation of poppies serves as a perfect example of this. Towards the end of last century, the Reverend W. Wilks, creator of the Shirley Poppy hybrid race of *Papaver rhoeas,* wrote an account of his discovery and work, which he summarized as follows:

> In 1880 I noticed in an abandoned corner of my garden a group of the common red poppy, *Papaver rhoeas,* among which was a solitary flower with petals slightly margined in white. I marked the flower and saved the seed, which the following year produced about two hundred plants, four or five of which had white-edged petals. The best of these were marked, their seed saved, and the same process of selection and elimination was repeated for several years; with the subsequent flowers having an increasingly large area of white on the petals and correspondingly smaller areas of red until a pale pink form was obtained, followed by a plant with white flowers. Next I began the long process of changing the centres of the flowers from black to yellow, and then to white, until I finally succeeded in obtaining a group of plants with petals ranging in colour from brilliant red to pure white, with all the intermediate shades of pink plus an extensive selection with margined and suffused petals; all the flowers having yellow or white stamens, anthers, and pollen, and a white centre.

With legitimate pride Wilks concludes his account with the remark that "it is interesting to note that all the gardens of the world, whether they be rich or poor, are ornamented by direct descendents of the single seed capsule cultivated in the vicarage garden at Shirley during the August of 1880." From this true story it is evident that to create a strain of flowers which are today famous throughout the world, Wilks possessed the two virtues essential for those who wish to have a garden worthy of the name: observation and patience.

Many substances are obtained from various species of *Papaver*. The best-known of these (apart from opium) is the edible poppy seed produced by both *Papaver rhoeas* and *Papaver somniferum.* This

Papaver nudicaule
From *Curtis's Botanical Magazine*,
1814, plate 1633

slate-blue seed is an important food crop in many Central and Eastern European countries, as well as the Netherlands (which, according to some authorities, produces the best edible poppy seed). The whole seeds are used as a flavoursome garnish for breads, rolls, crackers, and biscuits, and when ground or crushed they provide a delicious ingredient for many sweet baked goods, especially those originating in German-speaking countries, Hungary, and the Slavic nations. The most deservedly famous of these delicacies include the Austro-German *Mohnkuchen* and *Mohntorten* and the Austro-Hungarian *Mohnstrudel*.

Less well-known to British and Americans, but an equally important product, is poppy-seed oil, extracted from the seeds of *Papaver somniferum*, the highest yields being obtained from the var. *setigerum*, forma *inapertum* (unopened). Why the capsule should be closed is interesting. Normally the ovaries of poppies develop a capsule richly filled with seeds (with Carthusian patience Gravius is reported to have succeeded in counting 32,000 seeds in a single capsule), and the seeds are dispersed by means of small valves situated beneath the capsule's upper edge. These valves are hygroscopic, i.e., responding to an increase of humidity in the air by contracting and closing. During dry weather the valves open, and when the ripe capsule is shaken by a breeze the minute seeds escape. In the above-mentioned form *inapertum*, however, the capsule is without openings—or the valves are atrophied—and the seeds are not dispersed. At first pressing, good quality seeds give 30–40 percent of virgin oil (*huile blanche d'oeillette*), a limpid, slightly yellowish fluid, "bland and pleasant to the taste, with an almost imperceptible odour" according to the *Encyclopaedia Britannica*. In more ingenuous times than the present, this oil was used to adulterate olive oil, but it was a completely innocuous adulteration, more beneficial than harmful, since poppy-seed oil is rich in nitrogenous elements and phosphoric acids. Strangely enough, poppy seeds do not contain even a trace of the terrible toxic narcotic substances present in the latex (sap), contained in the stems, leaves, and pods. The cultivation of *Papaver somniferum* for the extraction of oil is chiefly practised in northern France, Belgium, and Holland. In Near Eastern countries a decoction from the seed of *Papaver rhoeas* is employed as a tonic for horses, and also an eye lotion for domestic animals. Finally, the flower petals were used in the Far East in the manufacture of ink, a practice still followed in remote localities.

Papaver somniferum, however, is of much greater importance for the medicinal uses of its derivatives, not only in folk medicine, but also in official materia medica. There are about twenty principles extracted from its latex (which provides opium); nearly all are alkaloids, the most important being morphine, thebaine, codeine, papaverine, and narcotine. According to their action they can roughly be divided

Double-flowered hybrid poppy

into two groups; those which are analgesic, with narcotic effects, and those that do not possess such characteristics, such as papaverine and thebaine. Codeine is frequently used for alleviating persistent coughs, papaverine for afflictions concerning the circulation or the blood, and morphine as pain killer; the effects of morphine have been described as creating "paralysis of the nervous system, preceded by a transient sense of exaltation, followed by a progressive suspension of all the functions dependent upon it."

One of the principal reasons for the wide cultivation of *Papaver somniferum* in the Near and Far East is opium production, not only as a raw material for pharmaceutical purposes but also as a narcotic drug. In Iran and in India opium is chiefly taken orally, either in liquid form or as a pill. In China, before the advent of Mao Tse-tung, it was smoked. The chief opium producers and exporters are Lebanon, Turkey, Iran, India, Burma, Thailand and Laos. But in history, opium and China are linked together in a sad and bloody union. In many countries, including the United States, the cultivation of *Papaver somniferum* is forbidden by law.

Cultivation. With the exception of some Alpine species, poppy cultivation does not present any difficulties. It should be remembered, however, that as the majority have long tap-roots they do not transplant easily. Seed should be sown in small fibre pots which can be planted directly into the soil when the young plants are large enough. The seed is exceptionally fine and must be sown very, very thinly, mixing it with twice its amount of fine dry sand before sowing to ensure wider and more even spacing. In most cases a considerable amount of thinning out will be necessary after germination. When practical, the best method of cultivation is to sow in the open ground in the position where the plants are to flower. This system of drastically thinning out the seedlings is particularly suitable for poppies grown as annuals; 8–10 ins. apart in the case of *Papaver rhoeas* and its hybrids, 10–12 ins. in the case of *Papaver bracteatum,* while plants of *Papaver orientale* should have at least 18–24 ins. between them. Rather poor, dryish soils are better than rich, damp soils.

Many poppies are true annuals, or if not actually annuals give better results if treated as such. Plants of *Papaver nudicaule,* however, are more satisfactory when two years old. However, the perennial *Papaver orientale* is very long-lived and should be disturbed as little as possible, although the best method of propagating the many lovely varieties of this spectacular poppy is by root cuttings placed in boxes of sand or sandy soil in early autumn. Because of the relatively brief flowering period (especially in hot climates), it is advisable to make successive sowings of the annual types at intervals of 20–25 days to ensure a succession of bloom. The flowering period can also be prolonged by regularly removing the seed capsules when the petals fall. Seed should be sown in either spring or autumn. Annual poppies naturalize freely by means of self-sown seed if the surrounding soil is not overly cultivated. *Papaver bracteatum* can be propagated by seed sown in July or in March, by division in autumn, or from root cuttings in the same manner as *Papaver orientale*. Both *Papaver bracteatum* and *Papaver orientale* are particularly suitable for alkaline (calcareous) soils.

To prolong the flowering period of poppies when they are used as cut blooms, some people advise cutting the flowers in early morning, and while they are still in the bud stage, and placing the stems in boiling water for a few seconds, or searing them over a flame.

(Alpine Poppy)
Herbaceous perennial
Flowering period: May–Aug.
Height: 6–8 ins.

Papaver alpinum L.

Native to the mountainous zones of Europe, generally found among rocks of a calcareous nature. Forms a close-growing, compact little plant with glaucous, smooth, short-stalked leaves all appearing from the basal rosettes; leaves are 4–5 ins. long, lobed, with the lobes divided into numerous segments. Flower stems up to 8 ins. high bearing miniature poppy flowers that vary in colour from white to golden-yellow (the sub-species *P. burseri* is white, the sub-species *P. kerneri* is yellow; these forms are mostly geographical in origin, *P. kerneri* being found at a height of up to 7,500 ft.). *Papaver alpinum* has a reputation, not completely justified, for being difficult; germination of the seed is somewhat capricious and, for practical reasons, it is not always possible to sow directly in the permanent position, and the plants are frequently lost through transplanting. This difficulty can be alleviated by watering the plants with a solution containing one of the root-forming hormone products the day before and the day after replanting. As previously mentioned, it is also advisable to sow and grow the young plants on in pots. *Papaver alpinum* does, in fact, make an excellent pot plant and this delightful little gem merits a little extra attention.

Herbaceous perennial
Flowering period: May–June
Height: up to 3 ft.

Papaver bracteatum Lindl.

Native to Armenia, Asia Minor, and western and southern Iran. In general appearance very similar to *Papaver orientale,* with thick, deeply penetrating tap-roots. The entire plant is covered with silky hairs. Flowers up to 5 ins. in diameter, variable in colour from dark scarlet-red to rich blood-red with a black mark at the base of the petals, and with two large leafy bracts below each flower. Leaves up to 12 ins. long and 4 ins. wide; very deeply segmented with the segments opposite and dentated.

Annual
Flowering period: June–Aug.
Height: up to 2 ft.

Papaver californicum L.

Native to California. A lovely erect annual with segmented feathery foliage. Flowers 2 ins. in diameter, brick-red, and pinkish green at the centre; seed capsules top-shaped.

Papaver glaucum L.   (Tulip Poppy)
Annual
Flowering period: May–June
Height: 18 ins.

Native to an area extending from Syria to Iran. Introduced into European gardens in 1891. Leaves obovate, greyish green, the lobes obliquely triangular. The stems are smooth, branched, and bear beautiful tulip-shaped flowers on long stalks. The flowers are up to 4 ins. in diameter, intense scarlet-red with a black centre. Seed capsules smooth, oval. A most attractive annual species that is very free-flowering and worthy of wider cultivation. Seed can be sown directly into the flowering position in spring.

Papaver nudicaule L.   (Iceland Poppy)
Herbaceous perennial
Flowering period: June–Sept.
Height: 12–15 ins.

Native to the Arctic regions. A hardy evergreen species from which many lovely hybrid forms have been derived. Although strictly a perennial, it is more satisfactory in gardens if treated as a biennial. This is certainly the most useful and most popular of all poppies for cutting; the colours of its flowers include such tints as yellow, orange, pink, white, salmon, reddish, and the plants have a much longer flowering period than any other poppy. The plants form a dense basal rosette of vegetation composed of hairy, rather dark-green, deeply cut leaves. The flowers are borne on slender but stiff and rigid leafless stems up to 15 ins. high; they are sweetly scented, up to 3 ins. in diameter, and last well in water. Their form is rather deeply saucer-shaped, and there are also double-flowered types. Some of the best commercial varieties are:

    var. *album,* white
    var. *aurantiacum,* golden-yellow
    var. *coccineum,* reddish
    var. *croceum,* yellow
    var. *striatum,* striped
    var. *sulphureum,* sulphur-yellow

If grown as a mixture many interesting intermediate colours are also available. The plants are easily raised from seed preferably sown in June, in seed beds or frames or in small pots; the plants should be grown on until the early autumn and then planted in their flowering positions. In view of their intolerance to root disturbance, better results will always be obtained from pot-grown plants. They require an open, sunny position in a light, very well-drained soil; their greatest enemy during autumn and winter is excessive moisture, which can cause the plants to rot at their base.

Papaver orientale L.   (Oriental Poppy)
Herbaceous perennial
Flowering period: May–July
Height: 2–3½ ft.

Native to the southern Mediterranean regions, Armenia, the southern Caucasus, and Iran. A vigorous, easily cultivated, even rampant, hardy herbaceous perennial, all parts of which are densely covered with silky hairs. Flowers 6 ins. or more in diameter on tall, mostly leafless stems which are often slightly bent or curved. Colour dark brick-red, with or without a black mark at the base of the petals. Similar to *Papaver bracteatum* (with which it has been crossed to produce some fine hybrids), one of the chief differences being the absence of the leafy bracts below the flowers. Roots are as thick as one's thumb, and are deeply penetrating. Below are some of the most attractive varieties, mostly with flowers considerably larger than the type:

    var. *atrosanguinea maxima,* gigantic, dark crimson-red flowers
    var. *Duke of Teck,* brilliant crimson-scarlet
    var. *E. A. Bowles,* crinkled petals; apricot, changing to pink
    var. *Ethel Swete,* cherry-pink
    var. *Goliath,* one of the largest, scarlet
    var. *Jenny Mawson,* salmon-pink
    var. *King George,* scarlet with fringed petals
    var. *Lord Lambourne,* one of the most beautiful, with deeply fringed petals, rich orange-scarlet, closely resembling parrot tulips
    var. *Marguerite,* silver-lilac
    var. *Mrs. Perry,* salmon-pink; generally considered to be one of the most beautiful
    var. *Olympia,* double, orange-scarlet
    var. *Orange Queen,* rich orange
    var. *Perry's White,* white with a crimson centre
    var. *Wunderkind,* carmine-pink

A lovely and interesting dwarf variety only 15 ins. high is var. *Thora Perry,* with smallish, cup-shaped, pure white flowers.

Papaver rhoeas   *Papaver alpinum*

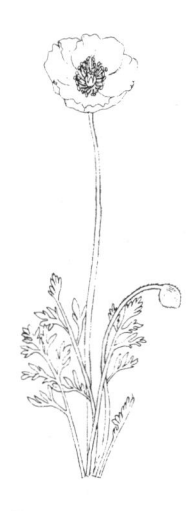

Papaver rhoeas L. (Corn Poppy or Common Red Poppy)
Native to vast areas of Europe and Asia, and also naturalized in parts of the United States. Stems erect, slender, covered with minute silky hairs. Seed capsules glabrous. Leaves elongated, divided into narrow, lanceolate, pointed segments, darkish green in colour. The flowers, which can reach 3 ins. in diameter, are a typical blood-red colour and were immortalized as the Flanders poppies of the First World War. The petals are unequal in size, two large and two small; and the centre of the flower is black. When the buds first open, the petals have a characteristic crinkled appearance like minute pieces of crushed silk, and when the flower is fully expanded the edges are ruffled. There are 25–30 recognized forms, varieties, and geographical types, together with many horticultural or garden varieties, the most famous and most attractive of which are the Shirley Poppies previously referred to. Among the natural forms the following deserve mention:

Annual
Flowering period: June–Sept.
Height: 1–3 ft.

> var. *hookeri*, a bushy form with a shrubby habit up to $3\frac{1}{2}$ ft. high with flowers $3\frac{1}{2}$ ins. wide and variable in colour from pale pink to deep crimson
>
> var. *japonicum*, introduced from Japan in 1893, with smaller, more double, many-petalled flowers
>
> var. *ranunculiflorum*, double-flowered, often with variegated petals
>
> var. *umbrosum*, introduced by Vilmorin in 1891 from Attica; a dwarf type with darker coloured petals and a black centre

Passiflora

(PASSION FLOWER OR GRANADILLA)
Family: Passifloraceae
Tender or half-hardy evergreen or deciduous perennial climbers
Position: sun
Propagation: seed or cuttings
Cultivation easy

One of the most beautiful and mysterious flowers with which the New World endowed the Old is the passion flower. Possibly the most spectacular species of genus *Passiflora* is the common *Passiflora caerulea*, widely grown in gardens on the Riviera and in the southern United States. Although often classified as "tender", it is a robust and vigorous climber and will revegetate with great energy in late spring even if cut down by frost (nonetheless, it is not hardy in gardens

Passiflora van volxemii

Fruit of *Passiflora incarnata*

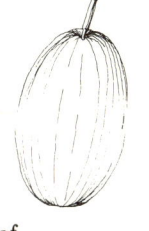

Fruit of *Passiflora quadrangularia*

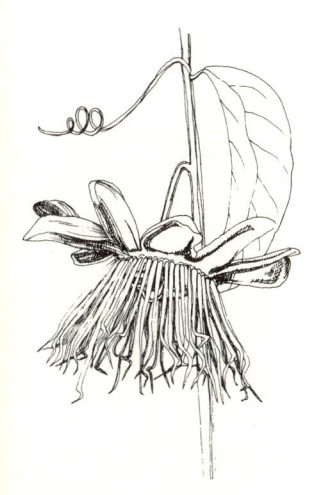

Passiflora quadrangularis

above Zone 7). *Passiflora caerulea* is often sold as a house plant, and will bloom and flourish in an 8-in. pot. (It is a very good temporary indoor subject; and an excellent house plant because it gives best results in a not-too-rich soil and prefers to have its roots restricted. Other fascinating species are *P. incarnata, P. edulis, P. quadrangularis, P. pinnatistipula, P. van volxemii,* and *P. mollissima,* all of which are discussed here.)

The story of the introduction of the passion flower into Europe is this: In the year 1610, the Roman theologian Giacomo Bosio received a visit from an Augustine friar named Emmanuele Villegas, who had recently returned from Mexico. Villegas presented Bosio with a drawing of a flower so unusual and marvellous that Bosio discussed it in the treatise he wrote on the Cross of Calvary, citing it as "the most extraordinary representation of the Cross Triumphant ever discovered in field or forest. The flower contains within itself not only the Saviour's Cross but also the symbols of His Passion." The Spanish colonists in Mexico and South America called it "the Flower of the Five Wounds", and believed it to be a divinely created sign to convert the pagans of the New World. From this drawing, as well as others that soon reached Europe from New Spain, some Bolognese Dominicans prepared an engraving of the flower. The illustration that appeared in Bosio's treatise was rather stylized, and emphasized symbolic features of the flower instead of presenting a scientifically accurate representation. Bosio described it thus:

> The external petals are white in Peru, but those flowers which are found in New Spain have white petals suffused with pink. The filaments which surmount them resemble a fringe spattered with blood, thus seeming to represent the flail with which Christ was scourged. The column at which He was scourged rises from the centre of the flower, the three nails with which He was nailed to the Cross are above it, and the column is surrounded by the Crown of Thorns. At the flower's exact centre, emanating from the base of the column, there is a yellow zone bearing five blood-coloured marks symbolic of the Five Wounds inflicted on Our Lord. The colour of the column, the nails, and the crown is light green. Surrounding these elements is a kind of violet-coloured nimbus composed of 72 filaments that correspond—according to tradition—to the number of spines in the Crown of Thorns. The plant's numerous and attractive leaves are shaped like a lance-head, and remind us of the Lance of Longinus which pierced the Saviour's side. Their undersurface is marked with flecks of white which symbolize Judas' thirty pieces of silver.

It is evident from this romanticized description that the drawing Bosio employed depicted *Passiflora incarnata,* which finally reached Europe

Passiflora caerulea
From *Curtis's Botanical Magazine*,
1787, plate 28

Passiflora coccinea

Passiflora racemosa

in 1622, a dozen years after the publication of his work. There are no references to the European cultivation of *Passiflora caerulea* prior to 1699, when it was recorded that the Duchess of Beaufort grew it.

When Linnaeus named the genus in 1735 the number of species imported into Europe was considerable, but they were cultivated mostly in greenhouses. The genus reached the height of its popularity during the second half of last century. The passion flower even became the theme of a popular song during the 1920s; a type of fame few other plants have achieved, apart from roses and Gracie Fields's *Biggest Aspidistra in the World* in its "old art pot".

Cultivation. The plants are not especially difficult to grow in a sufficiently warm climate. In areas where temperatures fall below freezing for long periods, they may be grown in large tubs or pots and removed to an unheated greenhouse (or sun parlour) during the winter. Certain species (*P. caerulea* and *P. incarnata*) can tolerate some frost, and if they are killed back to ground level there is a good chance that they will revegetate in late spring if the frost has not penetrated to the roots. All require the same type of soil—one that is not too rich, otherwise there will be an abundance of foliage and few flowers. Where the soil is naturally rich it can be made more suitable for them by adding a percentage of stones or gravel. Root pruning also induces better flowering and some growers surround the roots with an underground barrier of bricks 18 ins. deep and about 18–24 ins. from the stem.

Considerable patience is necessary when growing passion flowers since newly planted specimens often do not flower until two or three years after planting. During the winter, the most robust of the new growths should be pruned back a third of their length, leaving only four buds. Long lateral growths should be pruned even more severely, while the short thin growths should not be pruned, as it is these that will bear the new season's blooms. The plants must be provided with some support on which to climb, such as wire or plastic netting tacked against a wall. In all cases, passion flowers require sun and a warm, well-drained soil.

Propagation can be effected from seed or by cuttings. Seed should be sown in a heated greenhouse in spring and the young plants grown on in pots for at least two years before planting outside. Soft cuttings from the new season's growths can be taken in June–July and rooted in sand in a heated greenhouse, but they are not easy to root. When rooted they should be potted and treated as young plants raised from seed. In either case plenty of ventilation is necessary as passion flowers resent a stagnant atmosphere. When the young plants begin to produce vigorous growths they should be topped to induce more robust basal growth. A suitable soil mixture for pot-grown plants can be prepared as follows: 4 parts ordinary garden soil, 2 parts leafsoil, 1 part well-composted manure (or dried manure), and sufficient coarse sand to make the mixture porous.

Passiflora x allardii

Deciduous climber
Flowering period: July–Aug.
Height: up to 20 ft.

Of hybrid origin. Raised at the Cambridge Botanic Garden by crossing *Passiflora caerulea* var. *Constance Elliott* with *Passiflora quadrangularis*. A vigorous deciduous climber that can be successfully cultivated outside in a hot, sunny position, not subject to more than a few degrees below 32°F. The large three-lobed leaves are attractive and the typical passiflora-shaped flowers are a mixture of pink and dark blue.

Passiflora caerulea L.

(Blue Passion Flower)
Evergreen climber
Flowering period: July–Sept.
Height: up to 18 ft.

Native to Brazil. Introduced into European gardens in 1699. A climbing shrub with a very vigorous habit. Hardy and evergreen in localities where the winter temperatures do not go below freezing for more than a few hours. Where frost is experienced the plant will lose its foliage and the younger growths may be killed, but new growths will generally be made from the base in spring. Self-supporting by means of its numerous tendrils. Leaves palmate, 5–7-lobed, 4–7 ins. wide; individual segments oblong, green on the upper surface, glaucous beneath. Flowers axillary, borne on long slender stalks, 4 ins. in diameter and a mixture of blue, purple, and white; agreeably scented. The unusual shape of the round flat flowers with their conspicuous sepals, petals, stigmas, anthers, and central corona, together with the hand-shaped leaves and whip-like tendrils, have all contributed to the common name passion flower. The fruits have the size and shape of a small egg, bright orange in colour when ripe. Blooms are produced more or less continuously from July to September if the plant is in a warm, sunny position. The very lovely var. *Constance Elliott* has ivory-white flowers.

Fruits of *Passiflora edulis*

Passiflora coccinea Aubl.

Evergreen climber
Flowering period: July–Aug.
Height: up to 18 ft.

Native to tropical America. An evergreen climber only suitable for frost-free localities. A particularly beautiful species which in northern districts is often grown as a cool greenhouse climber. Can also be effectively cultivated in large receptacles which are placed outside during the summer months, but it should never be subjected to temperatures lower than 60°F. Leaves oval-acuminate, dentated; flowers slightly different from those of the typical passion flower, with wide rich-red lacquer-surfaced petals and a central crown that is less pronounced.

Passiflora edulis Sims

(Purple Granadilla or Passion Fruit)
Semi-evergreen climber
Flowering period: July–Sept.
Height: up to 20 ft.

Native to South America. A vigorous, even rampant, deciduous or semi-evergreen climber that is hardy only in the mildest localities.

In general appearance and habit very similar to *Passiflora caerulea*, but the fragrant flowers are white suffused purple and the edible violet-blue fruits are much larger. In warm countries it is cultivated for the production of these fruits which have a delicious orange-coloured and orange-flavoured pulp.

Passiflora incarnata L.

(Maypop or May Apple)
Semi-evergreen climber
Flowering period: July–Sept.
Height: up to 28 ft.

Native to the eastern United States, from Maryland to Florida and westwards to Texas. The most hardy species, it is a vigorous woody climber which reaches considerable heights by means of its coiled tendrils. Leaves alternate, deeply divided into 3–5 finely dentated lobes. Flowers solitary, borne from the leaf axils, up to 2 ins. wide, calyx tubular, opening to a cup-shaped bloom with five narrow lobes. The central crown is double, purple or purple-pink. Five whitish petals arise from the throat of the calyx. The edible fruits are fragrant, egg-shaped, about 2 ins. long, and contain a great number of seeds.

Passiflora laurifolia L.

(Yellow Granadilla, Water Lemon, or Jamaica Honeysuckle)
Evergreen climber
Flowering period: July–Aug.
Height: up to 20 ft.

Native to tropical America. A tender vigorous evergreen climber with entire leaves. Flowers up to 4 ins. in diameter, white speckled red; the central crown white and violet. Fruits edible, up to 3 ins. long, yellow. The specific name alludes to a similarity in shape between the foliage of *Laurus nobilis* (bay) and this species.

Passiflora manicata L.

Evergreen climber
Flowering period: July–Aug.
Height: up to 30 ft.

Native to northwestern areas of South America. A very vigorous evergreen climber only hardy in mild climates. Leaves divided into three oval, dentated lobes. Although the yellowish-green fruits are inedible, the plant is widely planted in gardens in such localities as southern California for its exceptionally decorative scarlet-and-blue flowers.

Passiflora mollissima H. B. K. (syn. *Tacsonia mollissima*)

Evergreen climber
Flowering period: July–Sept.
Height: up to 25 ft.

Native to Colombia. Similar in habit and form to *Passiflora caerulea* but of larger proportions, climbing up to 25 ft. or more. The lovely pink flowers are freely produced during the hottest part of the summer. This is definitely a plant for gardens in hot climates.

Passiflora pinnatistipula L. (syn. *Tacsonia pinnatistipula*)

Evergreen climber
Flowering period: July–Oct.
Height: up to 30 ft.

Native to Chile. A beautiful pink-flowered species only suitable for greenhouse cultivation if it cannot be planted outside in a warm almost subtropical climate. Leaves dark green, deeply divided into three elongated lobes. The flowering period is more prolonged than in most passion flowers, often until October. Fruits globose and not very palatable.

Passiflora pinnatistipula
From *Paxton's Magazine of Botany*,
1834, plate 249

(Granadilla)
Evergreen climber
Flowering period: July–Sept.
Height: up to 25 ft.

Passiflora quadrangularis L.
Native to South America. A tropical species which in European or American gardens can be grown outside only in completely frost-free localities where even the winter temperature does not fall below 50°F. A vigorous evergreen climber with entire leaves. Flowers fragrant, similar in shape and form to those of *Passiflora caerulea*, but made up of a mixture of red, white, and violet shades and appearing during the hottest part of the summer. Fruits very large, edible; the pulp is used for flavouring and for preparing the sweet granadilla syrup.

Evergreen climber
Flowering period: July–Sept.
Height: up to 25 ft.

Passiflora racemosa Brot. (syn. *Passiflora princeps*)
Native to Brazil. A vigorous tropical species with red, white, and purple flowers. Only suitable for growing in the hottest positions outside and generally considered a greenhouse subject. Fruits greenish yellow, not palatable.

Evergreen climber
Flowering period: Sept.–Oct.
Height: up to 30 ft.

Passiflora van volxemii Hook. (syn. *Passiflora antioquiensis*)
Native to Colombia. An evergreen species with superb crimson flowers in late summer and early autumn; one of the largest passion flowers, with blooms up to 5 ins. in diameter. Can be grown outside in a warm sunny position where there is no risk of winter frost. Leaves entire, elongated-lanceolate.

Pelargonium

(PELARGONIUM, GERANIUM, OR STORK'S BILL GERANIUM)
(*Also see* GERANIUM)
Family: Geraniaceae
Evergreen or deciduous perennials (often grown as annuals), sometimes semi-woody or succulent
Position: sun or partial shade
Propagation: seed or cuttings
Cultivation easy
Often aromatic

In many countries, particularly in Europe, the name *Pelargonium* is almost exclusively reserved for the species *P. macranthum* (syn. *Pelargonium grandiflorum, Pelargonium regale*), a plant popularly and simply known as Pelargonium or Regal Pelargonium. Also on the Continent the same plant is commonly known as Florist's Pelargonium, Butterfly Pelargonium, or Leopold Pelargonium.
If one wishes to buy plants of *Pelargonium zonale*—in its hybrid form

the most popular species—it is best to make a deliberate botanical mistake and ask for "geraniums", even though geraniums are an entirely different genus of hardy herbaceous perennial or annual plants. There is a good chance that if one asked for *Pelargonium zonale* the answer would be, "Sorry, we only sell geraniums", while if one did ask for a true *Geranium* one would inevitably be offered one of the pelargoniums. This confusion in nomenclature is further aggravated and perpetuated with the pendulous so-called ivy-leaved geraniums, whose correct name is *Pelargonium peltatum.*

Pelargoniums, however, are not limited to so-called "geraniums". They constitute a vast genus—unfortunately not hardy—which, where the climate permits, could easily create an entire garden; many are also excellent pot plants for indoor cultivation. They have an infinite range of sizes, forms, and colours, often with fragrant flowers and colourful perfumed foliage. The majority of these plants are the result of years of patient work by British, American, and German hybridists. Although we obstinately continue to call pelargoniums geraniums, the two are quite distinct, although both belong to the family Geraniaceae. Geranium flowers are generally regular in form, while pelargonium flowers are generally irregular in shape, with the two upper petals different to the others in size, shape, and, very often, in colour. Furthermore, the genus *Pelargonium* has a definitely more restricted area of diffusion than the genus *Geranium,* and is almost exclusively indigenous to warm climates and to sub-tropical South Africa. Only a few *Pelargonium* species are native to Asia Minor, New Zealand, and Australia.

Destiny occasionally plays tricks on plants the same way it does on people. The name *Geranium* derives from the Greek *geranos* (crane) because of the similarity between the long seed vessel and a crane's beak; whereas *Pelargonium* derives from the Greek *pelargos* (stork) for the same reason. As the beak of a crane and the beak of a stork are not unlike, even the origin of the two names tends to cause confusion.

The first pelargonium to reach Europe was probably *Pelargonium zonale*. Plants were sent to Holland from South Africa in 1609 by the Governor of Cape Colony. In 1652 the Dutch East India Company established a trading post at Table Bay that in time developed into a colony, and from here various pelargonium species were imported into Europe. In 1732 Dillenius published his *Hortus Elthamensis*, which contained drawings and descriptions of several of these African "geraniums", while others were illustrated in J. Burman's *Rariorum Africanorum Plantarium* (published in Amsterdam in 1738). But the most intense period for the importation of pelargoniums was between the end of the eighteenth century and the beginning of the nineteenth, when the passing of the Cape Colony into British possession coincided with the boom for greenhouse plants in Great Britain.

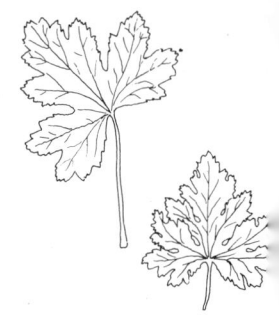

Leaves of Pelargoneum graveolens

Also during this period the first monograph on the family Geraniaceae was published (in 1802) with splendid coloured engravings.

Pelargoniums reached the summit of their success during the Victorian era, and remained on the crest of the wave until 1914-1918, when, because of the war, the cultivation of ornamental plants in greenhouses was banned (because of the fuel shortage) in England. But by the beginning of the 1950s, interest in these plants was rekindled and in 1958 the most up-to-date and complete book on the genus was published—*Pelargoniums, Including the Popular Geraniums* by Derek Clifford (Blandford, London)—and it has been freely consulted in the preparation of this section. In 1952 the Geranium Society was founded in London. In 1964 it was renamed the British Pelargonium and Geranium Society and it now publishes a quarterly bulletin and an annual yearbook for growers.

Commercial pelargonium cultivation began very early in England, when Robert Sweet published his famous treatise and Colville & Co. did so much to popularize the many species and hybrids to which he referred. In France, the firms of Lemoine in Nancy and Bruant in Poitiers became greatly interested in pelargonium culture and were instrumental in introducing numerous new varieties between 1840 and 1900. In Germany, Bürger in Halberstadt and later Faiss in Stockholm also followed the fashion, the latter introducing the variety *P. ostergruss;* while in Switzerland other varieties were introduced by Gubler.

In several countries with warm climates pelargoniums are grown for the extraction of their perfume. The first species to be used for this purpose in England were those imported by the Duchess of Beaufort in 1700. These were the so-called rose-pink (or -scented) geraniums and included the species *P. odoratissimum, P. capitatum, P. radula,* and *P. graveolens.* This industry flourished in the warm coastal districts of France and Spain; and later in Algeria, the Belgian Congo, and other tropical and subtropical countries. The essential oil is contained chiefly in the leaves, but is also found in all the green parts of the plant. The main constituent of the essence is geraniol, which possesses strong bactericidal properties and is widely used in the pharmaceutical industry. The essence is obtained by distillation: one ton of green material produces about two and a half pounds of essence; while two and a half acres of land generally produce between twenty and thirty-five tons of green material. In Europe the crop production generally lasts for one year, while in Algeria the crop production can continue from four to eight years, according to the nature of the soil. It is often possible to harvest two or three crops each year.

The various species and varieties of pelargoniums with scented foliage have a richer and more varied range of perfumes than any other genus—a selection of these pelargoniums is listed at the end of this section. These fragrant-leaved pelargoniums were much in vogue during the Victorian era and, referring to their popularity, Sacheverell Sitwell wrote:

> The rarer species include *Pelargonium fragrans,* with a scent of pines; *Pelargonium clorinda,* sweetly scented; *Pelargonium limoneum* and *Pelargonium crispum,* both lemon-scented; *Pelargonium odoratissimum,* with the fragrance of apples; the species *scabrum* and *tomentosum,* peppermint-scented; *Pelargonium radula* with rose-like fragrance. In fact, everybody who collects these plants is astounded by their range of perfume. Some are also beautiful, and even spectacular in bloom, with shades of white, crimson, pink, or brick-red; while others are almost nonflowering. The texture and shape of the leaves also shows enormous variation, from soft to hairy and from finely dissected to heart-shaped. The actual range of perfumes is almost indescribable and includes the fragrance of: lemon, pine, nutmeg, cinnamon, hazelnut, almond, orange, rose, apple, musk, violet, lavender, balsam, peppermint.

"Aromas which have previously escaped the novice," write Wilson and Bell, "can often be discovered by those who have been growing the plants for years. Not all are sufficiently sensitive to note the presence of apricot, ginger, cocoa and strawberry perfumes." As Wilson and Bell have so rightly stated, not everybody is aware of these scents (Wilson and Bell are both non-smokers—and smoking is a habit which often destroys or impairs one's sense of smell). While most readers could identify the apple-like scent of *Pelargonium odoratissimum,* few probably have a sufficiently acute sense of smell to identify the scent with that of *old* apples.

Cultivation. In their native habitat pelargoniums are able to withstand long periods of drought and therefore can tolerate dry conditions under cultivation. Plants show no signs of distress even if watered only at lengthy intervals. *Pelargonium zonale* ("geraniums") are excellent subjects for summer bedding in the garden, but are equally successful grown as pot plants, especially in wet climates where pot cultivation makes it easier to control the amount of water they receive. The many hybrid forms of *Pelargonium zonale* are magnificent subjects for cultivating in very large receptacles such as big stone or terra-cotta tubs or urns, and are also most satisfactory in window boxes. They do not require a lot of soil and seem to like having their roots confined, but they resent actual root disturbance. The purely botanical species—as well as those with scented foliage—are certainly more satisfactory when cultivated in pots. The scented-foliage types can be conveniently used as temporary house plants since they do not object to some shade or diffused light; in fact, in southerly climates, the majority dislike too much hot sunshine. The

Pelargonium domesticum
From an original watercolour by Giovanna Casartelli, 1968

exquisite little dwarf forms of *Pelargonium zonale,* often with beautifully coloured foliage, are also ideal for pot culture.

There is a widely held opinion that pelargoniums do not require a rich soil, and it is true that they do not need such rich additives as manure. They do, however, appreciate and generously respond to periodic applications of liquid organic fertilizer. A suitable compost for pelargoniums grown in receptacles, judging from personal experience, is as follows:

    2 parts fibrous loam
    1 part coarse sand
    1 part peat
    1 part leafsoil
    a sprinkling of bone meal, dried blood, or hoof-and-horn

The ideal pH for pelargoniums is between 6 and 7.

The best time for planting pelargoniums in the garden varies according to the locality, but it should always be put off until all risk of frost has passed. The varieties of *Pelargonium peltatum* (ivy-leaved geraniums) should be planted so that the stems can hang downwards over a wall or balcony, positions where the growths can reach to a length of 6 ft. or more; they can also be trained upwards, against a wall or on some kind of wooden, plastic, or wire armature or trellis, but they will need a good deal of tying. They are also very effective grown in hanging baskets. *Pelargonium zonale* rarely need support unless they are trained as standards, a system very popular some years ago, and certainly most effective, but much less employed now because of the work involved.

Immediately after planting outside it is wise to remove the flower buds, as this will help the plants become more quickly established. During the flowering season, dead blooms, complete with their stalks, should be regularly removed; they will snap off with the greatest ease close to the main stem. Dead or yellowish foliage should also be periodically removed. Plants that tend to develop too much in height, without producing plenty of bushy lateral growths, should be topped. Some people advise removing the plants from the soil in late autumn, cutting back both roots and stems, and potting the plants, keeping them in a greenhouse or in some well-lighted, well-ventilated, frost-free place until planting time the following spring. Taking into consideration the number of casualties which occur, the work involved does not really justify such a procedure, especially as it is so easy to propagate new plants from cuttings or seed. Even buying new plants each season involves a relatively modest outlay. A common mistake in the cultivation of pot-grown pelargoniums is to use excessively large pots. A medium-sized plant will be quite happy in a 5-in. pot; while larger plants can be kept in pots 7–8 ins. in diameter. Repotting should be done every year in late spring. In England,

Semi-double-flowered vari[ety]
of *Pelargonium peltatum*

Pelargonium crispum

Germany, Scandinavia, and the United States pot-grown specimens of *Pelargonium zonale* hybrids are widely used in the house, where they remain in bloom throughout the winter. Under such conditions a temperature of 60–65°F. is ideal, but the pots should be placed in a well-lighted position which will receive at least six hours of direct sunlight every day. Those varieties with single or semi-double flowers give better results than the double-flowered forms.

On the Continent some gardeners actually prefer to plant pelargoniums in their pots, placing them in beds for summer display by simply burying the pots in the soil. From the excellent results observed, this system appears a good one, especially in cool, wet climates, as it apparently keeps the root ball drier and more compact while at the same time allowing some of the more vigorous roots to escape from the pots and penetrate the surrounding soil.

For pelargonium cultivation in a greenhouse the ideal temperature is 50–60°F. Ventilation is of the greatest importance as the plants dislike a stuffy, stagnant atmosphere, and even during the hottest months the greenhouse temperature should never exceed 90°F. Thus, shading of the greenhouse will be necessary in summer, either with whitewash or some type of sunblind. Hygiene is also a vital factor in the cultivation of pelargoniums and at least once a year the greenhouse should be emptied, thoroughly washed, cleaned, and disinfected. The plants and pots should also be kept scrupulously clean and free from insect pests, spraying them every 10–15 days with one of the commercial insecticides, preferably one with a pyrethrum base. The use of sterilized soil is also a wise precaution. Many Continental growers are now having considerable trouble with a fungus disease that produces yellow spots on the foliage. It is proving extremely difficult to deal with, in spite of sterilization of soil, pots, and greenhouses. Fortunately the disease is not transmitted through the seeds, but is carried and perpetuated through cuttings.

Propagation of pelargoniums can be effected by means of seed or cuttings. A few years ago the only method of reproducing named varieties of the popular garden "geraniums" was by cuttings, a method successfully used ever since "geranium" culture became popular. Now, however, it is possible to propagate from seed named varieties guaranteed to breed true to colour; these seeds rapidly produce really magnificent, healthy free-flowering bushy plants that can actually be treated as annuals. They are of American origin and are more fully described under the heading *Pelargonium zonale*. The best time to take cuttings of "geraniums" is late summer. Each cutting should be long enough to have 3 nodes (usually about 4–5 ins.) and a sharp, clean, slightly oblique cut should be made just below the bottom node. Cut off all the leaves, complete with stalks, with the exception of the top tuft. One of the best rooting mediums is the granular white substance sold under various trade names such

Three types of pelargonium flowers

Pelargonium peltatum
From *Curtis's Botanical Magazine*,
1787, plate 20

as perlite or Agrolite (it was not developed as a horticultural product but has been borrowed by gardeners from the building trade). Ordinary river or builder's sand is also a satisfactory rooting medium. Each of the cuttings should be inserted in small individual pots placed in groups in a larger pot, tray, pan, or flat filled with the previously moistened rooting medium, and placed in a sheltered shaded position such as a coldframe, greenhouse, or, if the climate is mild, even in a sheltered part of the garden. Very little water should be given and roots are generally formed within 10–15 days. When a good root supply has developed, the rooted cuttings must be potted immediately into a more substantial compost as the rooting mediums contain no plant food, and if left in them the plants would soon die unless watered with a solution of liquid plant food such as used in hydroponic culture. The young plants must, of course, be kept in a greenhouse during the winter and repotted two or three times as they develop so that they will be large enough for early summer planting. The scented-leaved pelargoniums and the ivy-leaved "geraniums" can be propagated in the same way. The purely botanical species can be raised from seed sown in a warm greenhouse in late or early spring, or by means of cuttings taken any time between June and August.

Note: The varieties, forms, and hybrids listed under the various species that follow represent merely a fraction of the hundreds, even thousands, that may be found in specialists' catalogues at the present time. We would advise the pelargonium fancier to turn to the various lists issued every year by these growers and seedsmen in order to obtain the widest possible range of pelargoniums.

Evergreen perennial
Flowering period: May–July
Height: 12–15 ins.

Pelargonium acetosum Ait.
Native to South Africa. Foliage grey-green, almost glaucous. Habit stiff, rigid, and erect with a height of up to 15 ins. The pink flowers are elegant and graceful and are freely produced from May to July.

(Pelargonium, Royal Pelargonium,
Lady Washington Geranium, or Show or Fancy Geranium)
Woody evergreen perennial
Flowering period: May–Sept.
Height: up to 5 ft.

Pelargonium domesticum Hort. (syn. *Pelargonium* x *macranthum, Pelargonium grandiflorum, Pelargonium regale*)
The pelargoniums grown under this name are all of hybrid origin, the results of crosses between *Pelargonium cucullatum* Ait., *Pelargonium angulosum* Ait., and *Pelargonium grandiflorum* Willd. The common name Royal or Regal Pelargonium was given the plant because a great number of these hybrids were cultivated at the Royal Gardens at Sandringham in England. The name first appeared in an 1877 catalogue published by the once-famous English firm of Cannels. They have an erect but not very compact form, with woody stems and, in the case of large specimens, they are almost shrub-like. They are mostly cultivated outdoors during the summer months. Leaves are stiff-textured, glabrous, dentated, three-lobed, but often

only shallowly so, with the edges undulated; the form is irregularly triangular, and the width about 3 ins. Inflorescence an umbel very variable in size, composed of numerous butterfly-shaped individual flowers either of one colour or bicoloured. Although frequently referred to as Butterfly Pelargoniums, the flowers have also been compared to those of azaleas. The flowering period is very long, at least from May to September. Some particularly good varieties are:

    var. *Flame,* fiery-red
    var. *Harlequin,* pink and red
    var. *Madrilène,* intense lilac
    var. *Morocco,* rich violet
    var. *Pansy,* purple-red
    var. *Pinocchio,* with white petals bordered red
    var. *Rosy Dawn,* pinkish white
    var. *Smile,* bright pink
    var. *Thea,* salmon-orange

Pelargonium echinatum Curtis   (Sweetheart Geranium)
Native to South Africa. A curious and attractive deciduous species, often called the cactus or prickly geranium because of the soft curved spines on the fleshy, almost succulent, stems. Also known as the Sweetheart Geranium because of the heart-shaped red spot that occurs on one of the upper white petals. The lower petals are white suffused with a reddish purple variable in its intensity. Leaves 5–7-lobed, up to 1½ ins. wide, dentated, green on the upper surface, covered with whitish felt or down beneath.

Deciduous perennial
Flowering period: May–Sept.
Height: 12–15 ins.

Pelargonium grandiflorum (see *Pelargonium domesticum*)

Pelargonium x *hortorum* (see *Pelargonium zonale*)

Pelargonium peltatum Ait. (syn. *Geranium peltatum*)   (Ivy-leaved Geranium)
Native to South Africa. Introduced into European gardens in 1701. An evergreen species with graceful slender stems bearing many nodes, and with a prostrate, trailing, or pendulous habit according to the manner in which it is cultivated. Excellent for hanging baskets, wall brackets, window boxes, terraces, balconies, large receptacles, etc., or for growing against a trellis or netting. It is certainly one of the most decorative of the popular "geraniums" and widely used throughout warmer regions either as a temporary summer-flowering plant, or, where climate permits, as a permanent outdoor subject. It is seen to best effect when hanging from the top of a high wall. The flowering period is very long (from March to November, in frost-free zones, where the climatic conditions are ideal). Leaves

Evergreen, trailing,
or climbing perennial
Flowering period: Mar.–Nov.
Height: up to 6 ft.

glabrous, rather fleshy, five-lobed, and similar to ivy (hedera) foliage. Inflorescence pinkish, borne at the ends of fairly long stalks in the form of a somewhat loose umbel up to 4 ins. in diameter; individual flowers up to 2–2½ ins. wide. In the single-flowered types the lower petals are more numerous than those at the top of the flower. There is also a form known as var. *semiedera*, having all the characteristics of the type but with a more compact bushy form without the long trailing growths and with larger inflorescences. Among the many varieties of *Pelargonium peltatum* the following can be particularly recommended:

>var. *Amethyst*, double, amethyst flowers
>var. *Galilee*, double, vivid pink, and particularly free-flowering for a long period
>var. *Gardenia*, very double, white
>var. *Gloire d'Orléans*, double, flesh-pink
>var. *Lord Dickinson*, double, scarlet-red
>var. *The Pearl*, semi-double, pinkish white
>var. *Souv. Mme. Amelia*, double, deep-violet flowers
>var. *Zazy*, double, violet

(Oak-leaved Geranium)
Semi-woody evergreen perennial
Flowering period: June–Sept.
Height: up to 4 ft.

Pelargonium quercifolium Ait.
Native to South Africa. A much-branched shrubby plant with short-stalked hairy foliage; heart-shaped at the base, edges undulated, and with a shape similar to that of an oak leaf because of its scalloped contour. Inflorescence composed of 3–5 purple or pinkish flowers. The foliage often bears a conspicuous dark-purple spot.

Evergreen perennial
Flowering period: May–June
Height: 10–15 ins.

Pelargonium quinquelobatum Willd.
Native to South Africa. A beautiful but rare species with curious and unusual greenish flowers suffused red. Leaves divided into five lobes. More suited to pot culture than to outdoor cultivation. Height 10–15 ins., flowering period May–June.

Pelargonium regale (see *Pelargonium domesticum*)

Evergreen perennial
Flowering period: May–June
Height: 6 ins.

Pelargonium stipulatum Ait.
Native to South Africa. A fascinating little dwarf species only 6 ins. high and conspicuous for its mimosa-yellow flowers.

Tuberous-rooted evergreen perennial
Flowering period: May–June
Height: 10–15 ins.

Pelargonium triste Ait.
Native to South Africa. A tuberous-rooted species with attractive foliage similar in appearance to carrot leaves. Flowers dark maroon and spotted; agreeably scented after dusk, appearing during the period May–June. Leaves pinnate.

Pelargonium tricolor    *Pelargonium radula*

Pelargonium tricolor Curtis
Native to South Africa. A fascinating species for its tricoloured blooms, each flower having vivid red, black, and white petals. Leaves elongated, irregularly scalloped.

Evergreen perennial
Flowering period: May–June
Height: 15–18 ins.

Pelargonium zonale L'Her.
Native to South Africa. Larger specimens develop a definitely open, erect shrubby habit, rigid in shape, and eventually forming a woody base. Young leaves light green; young growths succulent. The foliage is long-stalked, up to 5 ins., rounded or heart-shaped, lobed, with ruffled edges, and generally with a much darker horseshoe-shaped zone in the centre of the upper surface. Inflorescence an umbel borne on a 6-in. stalk and composed of many individual blooms 2–2½ ins. in diameter that are variable in colour from scarlet to crimson and white. Diameter of entire inflorescence up to 6½ ins., even larger in the hybrid forms. Grown under favourable permanent conditions, old plants can reach a height of up to 6 ft., while those cultivated in pots normally have a maximum height of up to 2 ft. The true, original species is now rare in cultivation, having been superseded by the many hybrid forms and varieties with larger flowers and a much greater range of colours. These hybrids, the first of which were introduced into European gardens in 1710, for the sake of convenience are grouped together under the name of *Pelargonium* x *hortorum,* and for the most part they derive from crosses between *Pelargonium zonale* and *Pelargonium inquinans*. They are probably the most widely cultivated plants in the world, and it would be difficult to find a person who has not at some time possessed or seen a pot of these so-called "geraniums". There are double- and single-flowered forms and types with variously coloured zones in the centre of the foliage, ranging through such tints as gold, silver, red, yellow, white, pink, etc. They all have a strong, pungent odour which is sometimes com-

(Zonal or Horseshoe Geranium or Fish Geranium)
Semi-woody evergreen perennial
Flowering period: almost perpet
Height: up to 6 ft.

Pelargonium zonale

pared to that of fish and, in fact, one of their numerous common names is Fish Geranium. They are grown as pot plants on terraces, balconies, in courtyards, gardens, and on the patio. They are also widely used for summer bedding, and often serve as house plants since they do not need an excess of sunlight in hot southern climates. Among the best varieties the following deserve special mention:

> var. *Clarona,* single, scarlet-red
> var. *Favourite,* very double, pure white flowers
> var. *Lioness,* single, violet
> var. *Lucia,* single, old rose
> var. *Meteor,* double, scarlet-red
> var. *Paul Crampel,* the best-known and one of the oldest; a vigorous, single-flowered, scarlet-red variety
> var. *Queen Sofia,* double, salmon-pink
> var. *Rainbow,* single, brilliant pink
> var. *Sultan,* semi-double, salmon-pink
> var. *Volcano,* single, ruby-red

Miniature Varieties

There is also a beautiful race of miniature or dwarf *Pelargonium zonale* with a maximum height of 8 ins., and frequently much less. They are particularly generous in flowering and have highly decorative foliage. These lovely little plants are best suited to pot culture; some of the most attractive are:

> var. *Caligula,* height 6 ins. Leaves dark green, flowers double, scarlet.
> var. *Claudius,* height 6–8 ins. A plant of small dimensions with dark-green, almost black, foliage and large white flowers suffused pink.
> var. *Nero,* height 6 ins.; compact habit with red stems. Leaves dark green, almost black with a brilliant flame-like red mark in the centre. Flowers bright red.
> var. *Silver Kewense,* height 4 ins.; compact bushy habit with cream-white foliage marked with green. Crimson flowers make a delightful contrast with the elegant little leaves.
> var. *Tiberius,* height 6–8 ins. Leaves greenish black, flowers red.
> var. *Timothy Clifford,* height 6–8 ins. Leaves dark green with a darker green mark. Flowers double, pink.

Another section or group of *Pelargonium zonale* hybrids are known as Tricolour Types. These are among the most wonderful geraniums. Their leaves are particoloured like a tartan, and, although called tricolours, they are often, in fact, quadricoloured. The leaf colour is so variable, even on the same plant, that precise, detailed descriptions are practically impossible. Some of the most fascinating are:

A leaf of
Pelargonium tomentosum

H. Cox, colour of leaves basically pale gold, erratically marked with zones of purple, red, cream, and green. Flowers single, pink, deepening to darker pink in the centre.

Lass O'Gaurie (sometimes known as *Carse O'Gowrie*) similar to *H. Cox* but with the basic colour silver instead of gold.

Miss Burdett-Coutts, a remarkable and beautiful plant with silvery green leaves suffused pinkish carmine and vermilion-red flowers. Slow-growing and very compact.

Skies of Italy, one of the most popular, with maple-like leaves splashed with orange and crimson and edged with creamy white. Flowers single, vermilion.

Sophie Dumaresque, leaves similar to *H. Cox,* but with red and vermilion single flowers and a maximum height of 8–10 ins.

Silver-leaved Varieties

Caroline Schmidt, height 8–10 ins. Leaves variegated silver-white. Flowers red.

Chelsea Gem, height 8 ins. Leaves green variegated silver-cream. Flowers double, fuchsia-red.

Mme. Stalleron, height 8 ins. A non-flowering curious variety with beautiful silver-and-green variegated leaves.

Princess Alexandra, light-green foliage with silver margins. Flowers double, mauve.

Bronze- and Gold-leaved and Other Varieties

Black Cox, leaves vivid dark green widely zoned with black, beneath which can be seen a pale butterfly mark. Flowers single, pale pink, darker at the centre.

Crystal Palace Gem, golden leaves with green, butterfly-like markings. Flowers single, pink.

Distinction, very dark green with a darker circular ring. Flowers single, red and pink.

Freak of Nature, an astonishing variety; very rare and prized by collectors. Leaves apple-green bearing white butterfly markings; stems pure white. Flowers single, pink.

Happy Thought, leaves dark green with a gold butterfly-shaped mark. Flowers single, crimson.

Maréchal MacMahon, leaves dark gold with rich reddish-bronze zone. Flowers single, vermilion.

Verona, leaves pale gold without any zone; flowers single, fuchsia-pink, darker veined at the centre.

A New Race That Can Be Raised from Seed

During recent years a new race of *Pelargonium zonale* has been created, developed, and placed on the market. The result is that geraniums can now be treated as annuals, sowing the seed in a warm greenhouse (or even a sunny enclosed porch) in January, or in an

Variously shaped leaves of *Pelargonium zonale* hybri

unheated greenhouse or coldframe in March–April. Plants raised from the heated greenhouse (or indoors) in January will bloom in July; those sown at the later date will bloom in September. The plants are robust, vigorous, healthy, and bushy, and prolific and continuous in their flowering. If desired they can also be wintered-over in a greenhouse, or taken indoors like the normal *Pelargonium zonale*. They can also be used for bedding or for pot culture. Further propagation by means of cuttings is possible. Seed germinates at a temperature of 68–70°F., and the seedlings can be first pricked out and then grown on in pots. Although they have a naturally bushy habit, it is as well to top the young plants when about 6–8 ins. high if they do not manifest basal growths. The first variety offered to the public was var. *Nittany Lion,* with magnificent crimson-scarlet inflorescences, forming superb, bushy plants up to $2\frac{1}{2}$ ft. high and 15 ins. in diameter and of the easiest cultivation. I had a fine batch that remained in bloom until November. When taken indoors, the plants continued to bloom throughout the winter. Now, however, there is an even better strain known as Carefree hybrids. These give a germination of 95–100 percent and have extended the colour range to scarlet, dark pink, pale pink, white; and white with the petals edged pink, salmon, crimson, or red. The named varieties are guaranteed to flower true to name and colour. The first flowers can be expected about 4 months after sowing. Germination takes 4–5 days in a warm greenhouse.

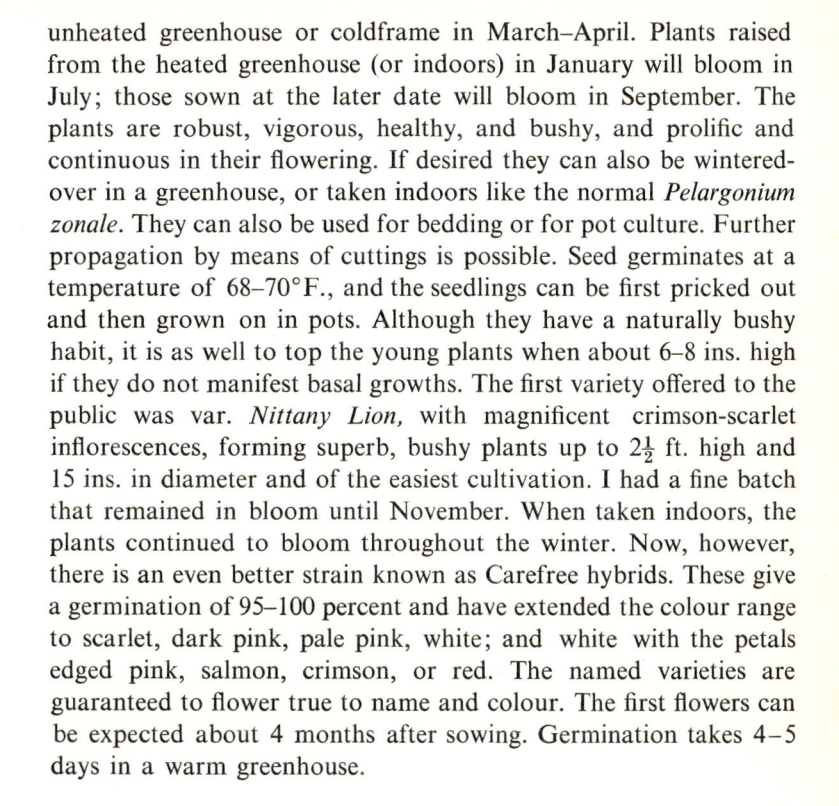

Leaf of *Pelargonium* var. *Lady Plymouth*

Irene Strain
Recently much interest has been shown in this new strain of *P. zonale*. It is rapidly gaining popularity in the United States and Europe for its exceptionally healthy foliage, prolific and early flowering, and good range of colours. These plants have an excellent bushy, compact but well-branched habit. The strain, which originated from a single seedling of crossbred hybrids, was first introduced by the American Dave Adgate.

Pelargonium Species and Varieties with Scented Foliage
These are all evergreen types particularly suited to pot cultivation, and they make excellent house plants if placed in a south window where they can receive maximum sunlight. As mentioned above, the range of fragrance is vast and surprising, although in most cases the flowers are of secondary importance. Apart from their fragrance, the leaves are often ornamental in their form and shape. All the species are native to South Africa, while the varieties are of hybrid origin.

Pelargonium odoratissimum Ait. Of compact habit with soft velvety foliage with an apple-like fragrance. Flowers white.

Pelargonium crispum Ait. Erect columnar habit like a miniature cypress. Leaves lemon-scented; flowers pale lavender. The var. *variegatum* has beautiful cream-and-green variegated foliage.

Pelargonium abrotanifolium Jacq. Leaves with the form and fragrance of *Artemesia Abrotanum*.

Pelargonium limoneum Sweet. A vigorous robust plant with palmate pale-green dentated leaves which are strongly lemon-scented. Flowers pink.

Pelargonium radula Ait. Deeply divided pinnate leaves; rough and hairy surface above, soft and woolly beneath, with a strong rose-like fragrance. Flowers small, pale purple.

Pelargonium graveolens Ait. Heart-shaped foliage, lobed, very dentated, with a strong rose scent. Flowers small, mauve-pink.

Pelargonium capitatum Ait. Rose-scented leaves and small pink flowers.

Pelargonium tomentosum Jacq. Compact habit, peppermint-scented foliage. Small pink flowers.

Pelargonium var. *Clorinda*. Rose-scented foliage and large purple flowers.

Pelargonium var. *Endsleigh*. Leaves with a pepper-like aroma. Flowers attractive, lavender.

Pelargonium var. *Fair Helen*. Dwarf compact habit; dark-green, oak-like leaves with a strong pungent odour. Flowers purple.

Pelargonium var. *Attar of Roses*. A dwarf compact variety with small rose-scented foliage. Small mauve-pink flowers.

Pelargonium var. *filicifolium*. One of the most beautiful varieties with much-divided elegant foliage which is quite fern-like and with a pungent aroma. Small purple flowers.

Pelargonium var. *fragrans*. Silver-grey velvety foliage with a nutmeg-like fragrance. Small white flowers.

Pelargonium var. *Lady Plymouth*. Very serrated foliage variegated in cream and white and rose-scented. Pale-pink flowers.

Pelargonium var. *Prince of Orange*. Orange-scented foliage and pale-pink flowers.

Pelargonium var. *citrodifolium* (syn. var. *Queen of Lemons*). Lemon-scented leaves and pale-pink flowers.

Some of these scented-leaved varieties may be used to add a delicate flavour and aroma to cakes and jellies. The rose-scented varieties are the most widely employed for this purpose; however, if one wishes, any of the others that strike one's gastronomic fancy might also be used, providing the scent is not too overpowering or unsuitable (this, of course, would be a matter of personal taste).

To flavour a cake, one should take a clean leaf (do not use one that

Pelargonium echinatum
From *Curtis's Botanical Magazine*,
1795, plate 309

has been sprayed with an insecticide) and place it at the bottom of a buttered and floured cake tin just before pouring in the cake batter. After the cake is baked and has been turned out onto a cooling rack, carefully pull off the leaf and discard it. The best type of cake for this purpose is a pound cake, although a sponge or angel cake might also prove suitable.

For jellies it is best to use a neutral-tasting fruit, such as apple, since a single leaf will perfume an entire jar and would therefore mask the delicate flavour of strawberry and raspberry and provide unpleasant competition with a strong flavour such as grape. Merely place a small, clean, unsprayed leaf in each sterilized glass or jar before pouring in the hot jelly. Jelly thus flavoured provides a marvellous accompaniment to roast meat or fowl.

Penstemon

or PENTSTEMON
(BEARD TONGUE)
Family: Scrophulariaceae
Semi-hardy or tender herbaceous perennials,
sometimes cultivated as annuals or small shrubs
Position: sun
Propagation: seed, cuttings, or division
Cultivation easy
Useful for cutting

The genus *Penstemon* belongs to the family Scrophulariaceae and—with the exception of one Asiatic species—all of the up to three hundred species are native to North and South America, more or less occupying a place similar in the New World to that of digitalis (foxglove) in the Old World.

Penstemons were introduced into European gardens relatively late; the species *P. hirsutus* in 1758, *P. barbatus* in 1794, and the others during the first half of the nineteenth century. Only a relatively small percentage of the known species have become popular garden subjects, and those that have found acceptance are mostly of hybrid origin, constituting some of our most useful and decorative summer-flowering perennials. Penstemons are of doubtful hardiness and are most frequently grown as temporary summer-flowering bedding plants—a very simple matter as they are so easily propagated from soft-wood cuttings taken in September.

At one time penstemons were considered members of the genus *Chelone;* they were assigned their present genus by Mitchell because of their common characteristic of possessing one sterile stamen among the normal five. This single sterile stamen is often bearded. They make first-class bee-attracting plants. The name *Penstemon* derives from the Greek, *pente* (five) and *stemon* (thread), and it is often variously spelled *Penstemon, Pentstemon,* or *Pentastemon.* In Europe *Penstemon* seems to be preferred, while in the United States *Pentstemon* is favoured. The genus comprises about 250–300 species, although botanists are not in complete agreement about the exact number and some place the total at 148. Their distribution is confined mainly to either side of the Rocky Mountains in the United States, and Mexico, while some species are indigenous to Central America to within 15° of the equator, a fact which explains why those species are not hardy in northern gardens. A few species extend as far north as Canada.

Apart from *Penstemon grandiflorus,* whose roots were used by the Kiowa Indians to prepare a remedy for toothaches, penstemons have no economic (or pharmacopoeial) value, aside from their being extremely decorative and ornamental. Penstemons in their natural habitat prefer a relatively elevated but generally warm position. The position chosen in the garden should be warm and sunny, but at the same time open and aerated. In the case of the smaller permanent species, better results will be obtained by planting on sloping ground rather than on the level, and they are excellent for the rock-garden. The soil should be light but fertile, slightly alkaline (calcareous), and, above all, well drained. Heavy compact soils can be made more acceptable by the addition of coarse sand—as much as they dislike cold, penstemons detest a waterlogged position even more. Herbaceous penstemons which are nearly hardy, or penstemons growing in localities almost sufficiently mild for their permanent outdoor cultivation, will give better results if left outside and protected during the winter than if removed to a greenhouse or coldframe. Where there is no chance of the more delicate species—such as *P. heterophyllus*—surviving the winter outside, the plants should be dug up in late autumn, placed in pots or boxes, and wintered over in a cool greenhouse, frost-free coldframe, or some other appropriate place. The plants should be cut back to ground level and only slight watering will be necessary; weather permitting, they should be given plenty of ventilation. Plants left outside—with the protection of a layer of peat, straw, salt hay, leaves, or manure—should also be cut back to ground level, and even after quite severe frost there is always a good chance that new growth will appear in late spring.

Propagation of herbaceous penstemons by means of cuttings is so easy that it is no loss if the parent plant does die during the winter. If soft cuttings are taken in September, inserted in pots of sand and placed in an unheated greenhouse or coldframe, I have always found that they all will root within a matter of about twenty days. The rooted cuttings can then be potted individually and kept in an unheated greenhouse or coldframe until planting time the following spring. The shrubby species should be propagated by cuttings made from half-ripened wood in July–August and rooted in coldframes, where they can remain until spring, when they should be potted or planted out into their permanent positions. The herbaceous penstemons can also be propagated from seed sown in a warm greenhouse in February, and the seedlings potted on, finally planting them out in May. Shrubby penstemons can also be raised from seed sown in pots or coldframes in June–July. In either case, the species can be propagated from seeds or cuttings, while the hybrids can be propagated only from cuttings if named varieties are wanted.

Penstemon barbatus Nutt. (syn. *Chelone barbata*)
Native to North America. A plant of open habit with erect branching stems. Leaves narrow, glaucous green, linear, long-pointed. The inflorescences have the form of rather loose, open spikes and are composed of two-lipped, inch-long, coral-red tubular flowers, with a beard on the lower lip, as suggested by the common name of Beard Tongue. Thrives in any fertile well-drained soil, including that which is alkaline (calcareous). Propagation is extremely easy by means of soft cuttings inserted in pots or coldframes at any time during late summer, when rooting is rapid and sure. In gardens the typical type plant is now largely replaced by varieties of hybrid origin, among which are the following: var. *Pink Beauty;* var. *Rose Elf,* 18 ins. high with up to ten flowers per spike and remaining in bloom from June to September; var. *torreyi,* with brilliant scarlet flowers which are conspicuous, and unusual for not having a beard; var. *salmonea,* salmon-pink; and var. *coccineus,* scarlet.

Herbaceous perennial
Flowering period: June–Oct.
Height: up to 2½ ft.

Penstemon Cobaea Nutt.
Native to North America. This species is important as the parent of the popular large-flowered garden hybrids classified under the name *Penstemon gloxinioides*. The original species is now grown only infrequently, having been superseded by its progeny. The abundantly produced individual blooms are smaller than those of the well-known hybrids, variable in colour from purple to white, and, when grown in large masses, they create an attractive effect. They are also excellent for cutting. Leaves lanceolate, acute, brilliant green.

Herbaceous perennial
Flowering period: June–Oct.
Height: up to 2 ft.

Penstemon cordifolius Benth.
Native to California. Discovered by David Douglas in 1831. A small evergreen shrub with a somewhat open habit and suitable only for the mildest climates such as that of southern California. Leaves heart-shaped, dentated, pointed, ¾–2 ins. long, dark green and shiny surfaced. Inflorescences in the form of pyramidal terminal panicles

Small evergreen shrub
Flowering period: June–Sept.
Height: up to 2 ft.
Zone 9 southwards

Penstemon Cobaea
From *Paxton's Magazine of Botany,*
1838, plate 243

up to 12 ins. high composed of numerous 1-in.-long, individual tubular flowers, brilliant red in colour; the lower lip is three-lobed, the upper lip two-lobed. This is an excellent plant for growing against a wall, where its rather loose habit lends itself to training and where it will find the warmth and shelter it requires.

Penstemon gloxinioides

Herbaceous perennial
Flowering period: June–Sept.
Height: up to 2½ ft.

Under this name are grouped the popular large-flowered garden penstemon hybrids, raised mostly from crosses between *Penstemon Cobaea* and *Penstemon hartwegii*. They have a shrubby erect habit and, in the case of old plants, the base of the stem becomes quite woody. Leaves very numerous, brilliant green, lanceolate, acute, 4½–6 ins. long, 1–2½ ins. wide. The inflorescences are tall, rather open spikes bearing numerous large individual tubular blooms which, as the specific name suggests, have a certain similarity to gloxinia blooms, although they are longer and narrower and with a mouth up to 1½ ins. wide. They are, in fact, more similar to the digitalis, or foxglove, flowers. The blooms are striking, effective, and long-lasting; if the dead flower spikes are regularly removed, the flowering period will extend from June until the cold weather arrives in autumn. They are ideal for massing in beds or borders and are excellent for cutting. They have no special demands concerning cultivation if given a fertile soil in a sunny position. The dominant colours are red, pink, purple, mauve, white, with many variations. There are a great many available, a selection of which follows:

 Alice Hindley, pale blue and pink
 Firebird, crimson
 Myddleton Gem, crimson
 Newberry, purple-blue
 Southgate Gem, red
 White Bedder, white

Penstemon hartwegii

Penstemon hartwegii Benth.

Herbaceous perennial
Flowering period: May–Oct.
Height: up to 2½ ft.

Native to Mexico. An almost-hardy herbaceous perennial which can be grown outside permanently in all but very cold areas where long periods of frost are experienced. Even then, the plants will generally resprout from the base if they have been covered with a thick mulch of dead leaves or salt hay the previous autumn. The plants can, however, be easily propagated from soft cuttings taken in August–September and over-wintered in coldframes or unheated greenhouses. Crossed with *Penstemon Cobaea,* this species has produced several attractive hybrids, none of which, however, has exceeded the exceptional attractiveness of *Penstemon hartwegii* itself. Leaves dark green, narrow, elongated, narrowly pointed, up to 5½ ins. long, ⅔ in. wide, and slightly curved towards the base. Flowers very numerous in groups of 4–6, on tall slender erect stems of particular grace and charm; I have counted up to fifty individual blooms on a single stem. The colour is a splendid ruby-red, with the throat striped red at its base and white at the top. The corolla is two-lipped, with the lower lip divided into three and the upper lip divided into two lobes. This plant should find a place in every garden, not only for its beauty but also for its ease of cultivation. Its hybrids are classified into the group known as *Penstemon gloxinioides.*

Herbaceous perennial
Flowering period: May–Sept.
Height: up to 3 ft.

Penstemon heterophyllus Lindl.
Native to California. Introduced into Europe in 1828. A lovely species with graceful slender stems bearing opposite, linear foliage 1 in. long and rather less than $\frac{1}{4}$ in. wide; glabrous. Inflorescence a fairly loose erect spike of individual tubular flowers, of an unusual shade of brilliant electric-blue rarely equalled in any other plant. Flowering period very long if the dead flower spikes are regularly removed. Not hardy. A particularly beautiful variety is var. *Blue Gem,* with gentian-blue flowers.

Semi-woody
herbaceous perennial
Flowering period: July–Oct.
Height: up to 3 ft.

Penstemon isophyllus Rabs.
Native to Mexico. Introduced into Europe in 1908. A semi-woody herbaceous perennial suitable for cultivation outdoors only in frost-free climates; although, like so many of the herbaceous penstemons, the below-ground part of the plant will often survive quite severe winters if well covered with a mulch of dead leaves in late autumn. Leaves opposite, oval-elliptic, 1–$2\frac{1}{2}$ ins. long, up to 2 ins. wide; generally acute, rather fleshy, dark green on the upper surface, glaucous beneath. Inflorescences in racemes 10–12 ins. long and 6–8 ins. wide, composed of fairly widely spaced, scarlet-red, tubular flowers, two-lipped, the upper lip two-lobed, the lower lip three-lobed. An excellent plant for alkaline (calcareous) soils.

Small evergreen shrub
Flowering period: Apr.–July
Height: up to 12 ins.
Zone 6 southwards

Penstemon menziesii Hook.
Native to the northwestern United States. An attractive little hardy evergreen shrub which varies considerably in form. In its native habitat of the Rocky Mountains it assumes a dwarf, semi-prostrate, wide-spreading trailing habit; when cultivated in gardens—the climate being warmer and general growing conditions more favourable—the plant develops considerably more in height, even up to 1 ft. Leaves rigid, opposite, obovate, dark green, up to $\frac{2}{3}$ in. long. Flower stems erect, bearing 2–6 tubular, two-lipped blooms—the upper lip two-lobed, the lower lip three-lobed—of a lovely purple tint. The individual flowers are up to $1\frac{1}{4}$ ins. long and give the impression of being exceptionally large in proportion to the size of the plant. An ideal subject for the rock-garden or for cultivating in large shallow receptacles where it will be more likely to retain its characteristic of a prostrate dwarf plant. Like so many mountainous

plants, it requires some protection from excessively hot sunshine when grown at lower altitudes, and it does not like continuous heat.

Penstemon scouleri Douglas (syn. *Penstemon menziesii* var. *scouleri*)
Native to North America. Introduced into Europe in 1828. By some authorities considered to be a variety of *Penstemon menziesii*, which it much resembles, and not a true species. In its native habitat this is a prostrate semi-shrubby dwarf plant; it will assume a taller aspect when cultivated in gardens. A most attractive little plant with pink flowers, similar to *Penstemon menziesii* and requiring the same cultural conditions.

Small evergreen shrub
Flowering period: May–June
Height: up to 12 ins.
Zone 6 southwards

Penstemon utahensis Eastwood
Native to North America. A vigorous, robust herbaceous perennial with a pleasing erect habit. Stems and leaves slightly reddish green. Hardier than the Californian and Mexican species, but not tolerant of severe cold. Leaves lanceolate, acute, $2\frac{3}{4}$– 4 ins. long, up to 1 in. wide. In general aspect similar to *Penstemon hartwegii* but slightly less tall and with 1-in.-long, mauvish-blue flowers. A lovely subject for massing.

Herbaceous perennial
Flowering period: June–Sept.
Height: up to 2 ft.

Petunia

Family: Solanaceae
Tender perennials, invariably cultivated as annuals
Height: 8 ins.–3 ft., according to type and method of cultivation
Position: sun
Propagation: seed or cuttings
Cultivation easy
Fragrant

The name of the genus *Petunia* was coined by Antoine Laurent Jussieu, who Latinized *petun,* a word used by the Brazilian natives for *Nicotiana,* a plant very similar in appearance to the petunia and belonging to the same family. In fact, the foliage of petunias, although on a much smaller scale, has the same characteristics as that of the nicotiana, or tobacco plant. (The discoverer of genus *Nicotiana,* however, was Commerson, who found it growing at the edges of virgin forests in the New World.)

The genus *Petunia* comprises about twenty-five species native to the eastern part of Central and South America down to Brazil. Only two are of any real horticultural interest: *Petunia violacea,* which

Petunia hybrida grandiflora
From *Paxton's Magazine of Botany*,
1835, plate 173

Lindley called *Petunia phoenicea* when he introduced it into Europe, probably because the violet-purple colour of the flowers reminded him of the royal purple of the Phoenicians; and *Petunia nyctaginiflora* (*Petunia axillaris*). These two species are the parents of all the modern hybrid petunias now grown in our gardens. These hybrids so dominate the scene that it is necessary to mention only a few of the non-hybrids, which occasionally but rarely are cultivated outside of botanic gardens.

The first to introduce new hybrid petunias into our gardens were the British, French, Belgian, and German horticulturists; these plants were later to be followed by a wealth of superb American hybrids, and the first double-flowered forms were introduced in 1849.

In their natural habitat petunias are perennial, often living for many years and forming a quite woody basal stem. In frost-free localities they can occasionally be seen established in old walls in the same manner as mature specimens of snapdragons or wallflowers. (For about fifteen years I kept a petunia plant in a large pot containing a lemon tree, which was moved every winter to an unheated greenhouse. The petunia stems trailed over the sides of the pot and bloomed throughout the summer and into the autumn.) Normally, however, petunias are grown in the garden as summer-flowering annuals, and there are few more successful plants for bedding. They are much-branched herbaceous plants with sticky foliage covered with fine hairs. The leaves are borne along the entire length of the trailing slender stems and can be either alternate or opposite. They are soft-surfaced and entire. The tube-shaped flowers are solitary, terminal and axillary, and, in the hybrid forms, embrace almost every colour in the spectrum (although there is as yet no really good rich yellow variety). They have a delicate but most agreeable fragrance, particularly strong at night, and they attract every type of nocturnal moth. For general garden purposes they are among the most widely diffused of all popular plants and are also widely planted in window boxes and large receptacles. The wide-spreading trailing types are seen at their best in hanging baskets, in the rock-garden, at the top of walls, alongside rustic steps, at the edges of balconies or terraces; all positions where the plants can develop to form cascades of colour. In the formal garden, however, the "cascade" types are not always suitable, and more satisfactory results are obtained from the small-flowered compact types. It is a mistake to mix the various types and it is also unwise to use the very large- or double-flowered forms in localities subject to severe and heavy rain, as the fragile blooms can be easily ruined in summer storms.

During recent years so many forms, types, and varieties have been introduced that it is possible to find petunias suitable for every use. There are even types that flourish in 6-in. pots on a windowsill, while the seed of others can be sown broadcast and naturalized in an

Double-flowered hybrid petunia

informal manner over large areas. A few petunia plants along a fence, at the side of a gate, at the foot of a pillar or column, in the corner of a wall, or even ramping over a heap of garden refuse, always create a mass of joyful colour—often unexpected and therefore more welcome.

The vast number of forms and types can often puzzle the amateur, who is likely to become confused by the wealth of material offered in seedsmen's catalogues, but the most satisfactory types are those classified as: Dwarf Multiflora Hybrids, Large-flowered Hybrids, Large-flowered Compact, Pendulous or Balcony, Double, and Fringed. Unfortunately, however, these classifications are not always international, and with the continuous introduction of new varieties there is an increasing tendency for the different types to lose their definition of habit and to merge one into another.

Cultivation. At one time petunias could be considered among the easiest of all summer-flowering annuals. This is still true if one is content to cultivate the older typical types and varieties. When, however, the more highly specialized, very modern forms and varieties are cultivated, one is more likely to encounter difficulty. These forms have been so crossed, hybridized, selected, and groomed that they have become temperamental, delicate, and capricious; characteristics which any living object develops when it is excessively "improved" or highly over-bred. The flower colours will certainly be more brilliant and more varied, the profusion of blooms will be greater, but, as usual, nature takes her revenge and the resulting plants will often prove to be less resistant to disease and bad weather, with little of the stamina and robustness so characteristic of the older types. I have also noted that the ultra-modern forms to a large extent have lost their perennial character and are now true annuals. These observations do not apply only to petunias, but also to numerous other plants, annuals in particular, so much so that seedsmen now often advise their customers not to discard the smaller, weaker seedlings when pricking out as these weaklings may produce the best colours or largest blooms—a kind of survival of the fittest in reverse. Petunias are, however, still easy to cultivate, even if a little extra care is now required. Probably their greatest enemy is excess moisture; while too rich a soil is also harmful. Self-sown seedlings that spring up on dry, stony paths are often more healthy than seedlings raised with care and attention, resulting in too much coddling. The young plants can, in fact, be killed by kindness.

Seed can be sown in flats, pots, pans, trays, or boxes at any time from January onwards in a heated greenhouse. The seedlings should be pricked out, potted individually, and grown on until planting time in April or May, depending on the locality and climate. It should be remembered that the young plants are not hardy and can be damaged by frost, but they should never be given too much heat and they need an abundance of ventilation. If seed is to be sown in an unheated greenhouse, porch, or coldframe, it is advisable to wait until March. At a temperature of about 60°F. germination takes place 14–15 days after sowing. Perfect drainage is essential when sowing and potting. The seed, which is often as fine as dust, should not be covered, but lightly pressed into the soil. Regarding a suitable compost for sowing, pricking out, and potting, the following mixtures can be recommended:

Compost for sowing:
1 part leafsoil
1 part peat
$\frac{1}{4}$ part sand
$\frac{1}{4}$ part fibrous loam or ordinary garden soil

Compost for pricking out:
$\frac{1}{2}$ part fibrous loam or ordinary garden soil
1 part leafsoil
$\frac{1}{4}$ part peat
$\frac{1}{4}$ part sand
a sprinkling of dried blood

Compost for potting:
2 parts fibrous loam or ordinary garden soil
1 part leafsoil
1 part well-rotted manure (or dried manure)
$\frac{1}{4}$ part sand
$\frac{1}{4}$ part peat
a sprinkling of bone meal
a sprinkling of dried blood

Petunias require an open, sunny situation in a well-drained soil. In the south they will also give good results in partial shade, but they should never be planted beneath trees or overhanging branches.

Petunia axillaris Lam. (syn. *Nicotiana axillaris, Petunia nyctaginiflora*)
Native to Argentina. One of the parents of modern garden petunia hybrids. Erect stems up to 2 ft. high; leaves relatively large, oval, and covered with sticky hairs. Flowers are a dull white, strongly scented, especially at night, and $1\frac{1}{2}$–2 ins. in diameter.

Flowering period: June–Sept.
Height: up to 2 ft.
Very fragrant

Petunia inflata R. E. Fries.
Native to Argentina and Paraguay. In general appearance very similar to *Petunia violacea*, but with smaller more linear foliage and with an inflated, swollen corolla tube.

Flowering period: June–Sept.
Height: 15–18 ins.

Petunia integrifolia (see *Petunia violacea*)

Petunia nyctaginiflora (see *Petunia axillaris*)

Petunia parviflora Juss.

Flowering period: June–Sept.
Height: 18 ins.

Native to Central and South America. An elegant little plant with graceful slender stems up to 18 ins. long. Leaves very small, and covered with soft, silky hairs. As indicated by the specific name, the flowers are also small, not more than $\frac{1}{2}$ in. in diameter, light purple, and quite effective when massed.

Flowering period: June–Sept.
Height: 12 ins.

Petunia violacea Lindl. (syn. *Petunia integrifolia*)

Native to Argentina. Another of the important parents in the evolution of modern hybrid petunias. Slender prostrate stems about 12 ins. long. Leaves short-stalked, oval, and, like the stems, rather sticky. Flowers $1\frac{1}{2}$ ins. long, pinkish red or reddish violet and attractive when massed.

Petunia Hybrids

A name of convenience under which are grouped all the present-day hybrid garden petunias resulting from crosses between the species *P. axillaris* and *P. violacea*. These are sticky-leaved annuals or perennials grown as annuals, from 6–24 ins. high. Flowers funnel-shaped, the tube broader than in *Petunia axillaris* and the mouth wider than in *Petunia violacea*. Compact form, spreading or trailing according to the type, with a vast range of colours and flower shape and form. These various types are classified as follows:

Small-flowered, Dwarf, Compact. In catalogues generally referred to as *Petunia hybrida nana compacta*. Height 8–10 ins. Very free-flowering and resistant to rain and bad weather. Excellent for massing, either in mixed colours or in beds of one colour.

Petunia nana compacta,
Star Trophy hybrid

Large-flowered Hybrids. In catalogues this is generally referred to as *Petunia hybrida grandiflora*. Very free-flowering, with blooms twice the size of the preceding. Can develop a height and width of up to 2 ft. and therefore not suitable for windy or exposed sites.

Large-flowered Petunias with Ruffled Petals. This is *Petunia hybrida grandiflora fimbriata* in the catalogues. Height up to 18 ins. and more suitable for large receptacles than for bedding. Flowers with ruffled and often fringed petals, but delicate and liable to be damaged by severe rainstorms or strong winds.

Giant-flowered. This is *Petunia grandiflora superbissima* in the catalogues. Height up to $2\frac{1}{2}$ ft. or more, with enormous heavily ruffled flowers; the corolla mottled, striped, or veined in contrasting colours. Most suited to cultivation in large pots with a diameter of at least 8 ins.; they require staking. They also require a richer soil than other petunias and benefit from applications of liquid, organic fertilizer. Although the flowers are large, the plants produce fewer in number than the smaller types.

Double-flowered
Petunia hybrida fimbriata

Large-flowered, Dwarf, Compact. This is *Petunia nana compacta grandiflora* in the catalogues. Height 8–12 ins. Flowers with entire but ruffled petals. Plants much-branched but compact. Blooms large and held well above the foliage, with a general habit that is neat and bushy.

Large-flowered, Dwarf, Fringed. This is *Petunia grandiflora fimbriata nana* in the catalogues. Height 8–12 ins. Well-branched from the base, free-flowering, and particularly suited to pot cultivation.

Giant-flowered, Dwarf. This is *Petunia grandiflora superbissima nana* in the catalogues. Height 10–12 ins. Less free-flowering than the tall, giant-flowered class but requires the same cultural treatment, although staking and tying is not necessary. Indicated for cultivation in pots.

Hanging or Balcony Petunias. This is *Petunia hybrida pendula* in the catalogues. These form long slender growths of a pendulous or trailing habit. Suitable for growing in pots or other receptacles raised above the ground. Also suitable for hanging baskets, window boxes, or for planting on top of walls. Free-flowering with medium-sized blooms. A particularly good strain is *Petunia longissima pendula.*

Double-flowered Petunias. This is *Petunia flora plena* in the catalogues. There are large- and small-flowered types of double-flowered petunias, varying in height from 10–18 ins. Excellent for pot culture and with a very long flowering period. Not tolerant of bad weather which can soak the flowers with water, beat them down, and spoil their appearance.

All the above-mentioned types are available in a wide range of colours.

Petunia grandifloria fimbriata

Phacelia

Family: Hydrophyllaceae
Tender herbaceous perennials or annuals
Height: 10 ins. to 3 ft., according to the species
Position: sun or partial shade
Propagation: seed
Cultivation easy

A genus of 114 species native to the southwestern United States, in particular Texas, New Mexico, and California. These herbaceous perennials or annuals are not spectacular, but are much appreciated for the intense blue of their flowers. They are easy to cultivate and blend well with other plants in beds, borders, etc., and their somewhat loose habit makes them excellent for growing in window boxes or in large receptacles on terraces. They can also be successfully used as a ground cover and for massing, when their vivid colouring and profuse and prolonged flowering is seen to best effect.

The annual species and their varieties are the most widely used in gardens; they are easy to grow but require warmth. Full sun is essential in the north, but good results can also be obtained in partial shade in the south. The soil must be very well drained and, in the case of the annual types (or perennial species cultivated as annuals), light in texture and fairly sandy. Propagation is by means of seed sown directly in the flowering positions in late spring or in an unheated greenhouse in March; prick out the seedlings into flats or boxes and then grow them on individually in small pots, planting them out in May at a distance of 10–12 ins. apart. This latter method will produce earlier-flowering specimens. In warm southern climates the seed can also be sown in autumn for still earlier flowering, but it should be remembered that the plants are not hardy and will not tolerate frost.

Annual
Flowering period: July–Sept.
Height: 10–12 ins.

Phacelia campanularia Gray
Native to California. The most popular species, with a shapely low habit. Leaves ovate, small, greyish green tinted reddish, and during the flowering period almost hidden by the profusion of bloom. Stems and stalks reddish brown. Flowers brilliant blue, darker internally than externally, bell-shaped.

(Wild Heliotrope or Fiddleneck)
Annual
Flowering period: July–Sept.
Height: 2–3 ft.

Phacelia tanacetifolia Benth. (syn. *Phacelia tripinnata*)
Native to California. An annual species and considerably taller than the preceding. The flowers are much favoured by bees and the plant is thus frequently cultivated by bee-keepers. Leaves alternate, pinnate, lobed, and dentated. Flowers borne in dense racemes that are recurved into twisted spikes. Individual blooms lilac-blue or lavender.

Annual
Flowering period: July–Sept.
Height: up to 2 ft.

Phacelia viscida L. (syn. *Eutoca viscida*)
Native to California. Leaves light green, heart-shaped or oval, pointed, dentated, and covered with viscous hairs. Flowers brilliant gentian-blue, 1 in. in diameter, and borne in spikes. The inside of the flowers is particularly interesting, with a central white eye veined with blue, producing a net-like or lacy appearance that is enhanced by the white anthers. When bruised the foliage has a characteristic but not unpleasant perfume. Another curious feature of this highly decorative free-flowering annual is that when a young

Phacelia campanularia
From *Curtis's Botanical Magazine*,
1884, plate 6735

plant is transferred from a warm greenhouse to cooler conditions outdoors the leaf hairs assume a reddish tinge. There is also a white-flowered var. *alba.*

(Californian Bluebell)
Annual
Flowering period: July–Sept.
Height: up to 18 ins.

Phacelia Whitlavia L. (syn. *Phacelia grandiflora, Whitlavia grandiflora*) Native to southern California. A beautiful much-branched annual species. Leaves small, oval, dentated, pointed. Flowers purple or purple-blue, bell-shaped, in racemes; individual blooms 1 in. long, bell-shaped with a spreading mouth, and in general appearance not unlike a bluebell, hence the common name. There are several varieties:

> var. *alba,* completely white flowers
> var. *gloxinioides,* white with a blue centre

Philadelphus

(SYRINGA OR MOCK ORANGE)
(*Also see* SYRINGA)
Family: Saxifragaceae
Hardy deciduous (rarely evergreen) shrubs
Position: sun or partial shade
Propagation: seed or cuttings
Cultivation very easy
Useful for cutting
Fragrant in many cases

The genus *Philadelphus* has a remarkable history and a fascinating development. It has been the cause of incredible confusion so far as its official and colloquial nomenclature is concerned and even its natural distribution is ambiguous. Its classification still bothers the botanists because of the lack of distinctively defined characteristics between one species and another, a problem further aggravated by the ease with which the plants hybridize to produce vast numbers of garden forms and varieties that are now more widely cultivated than the true species.

Their natural habitat is mainly North America, although some species are native to Asia Minor, Southeastern Europe, and China. *Philadelphus coronarius* is occasionally found growing wild in northern Mediterranean areas, but there is some doubt as to whether it is a true native to countries such as Italy, or whether it became naturalized through its profusely produced seed. We do not know for certain why Linnaeus named this lovely deliciously scented shrub *Philadelphus* (from the Greek, meaning "brotherly love"). This genus was born under an unlucky star so far as names are concerned, and it has always been plagued by misunderstandings. The British call it Mock Orange, the Germans, False Jasmine; but worse follows. In Lower Bavaria, rural German dialects have horribly corrupted jasmine to *Scheissamin,* and those who know the significance of the word *scheiss* also know that it means the very opposite of a fragrant flower. The trials of the plant's various names do not end there, however; even from remote times philadelphus has been confused with *Syringa* (lilac) and in England it is often commonly known as syringa (in France *seringat*). One of the reasons for this particular confusion is that the stems of both plants are hollow or filled with soft pith (long ago, the Turks used philadelphus branches to make pipe stems, and one source states that they were also used to make a kind of whistle, which in Germany was known as *pfeifenstrauch*). Also, *Philadelphus coronarius* and lilac were introduced into Europe simultaneously, in 1562, by Ogier Ghiselin de Busbecq, when he returned to Vienna from Turkey, where he had been the Habsburg Empire's Ambassador to the court of Suleiman the Magnificent. With good Catholic practicality the Tuscans named *Philadelphus coronarius* Angel Flower, probably the most appropriate of all the plant's common names; while in their local dialect the Venetians call the flowers *tientibon,* which can roughly be translated as "remain beautiful", possibly a sarcastic allusion to the flowers' annoying habit of dropping their petals so soon after the branches have been cut and thus quickly losing their attraction.

Philadelphus are worth growing not only for the grace and purity of their flowers but also for their often subtle and exquisite fragrance. However, care should be taken to choose the scented varieties, the best of which are hybrids of *Philadelphus coronarius,* whose perfume can even be too strong for some people. John Gerard, the famous herbalist, wrote about the fragrance of philadelphus 350 years ago: "They have a pleasant sweete smell, but in my judgement troubling and molesting the head in a very strange manner. I once gathered the flowers and laid them in my chamber window, which smelled more strongly after they had laid together a few howers, but with such a pontick and unacquainted savor that they awakened me from sleepe, so that I could not take rest till I had cast them out of my chamber." The perfume industry cultivates philadelphus on an industrial scale. In the Orient, where the plant has found a place in domestic economy, the flowers—like those of *Jasminum*—are used to add fragrance to tea, and the foliage adds a refreshing, cucumber-like flavour to summer drinks. The scent of philadelphus has also played a significant part in the language of flowers as the symbol of memory, because "when one inhales the penetrating perfume, it seems to accompany and remain with one for a very long time."

Philadelphus coronarius was originally imported from Asia Minor,

Philadelphus coronarius
From *Curtis's Botanical Magazine*,
1797, plate 391

and the plant soon became naturalized in various parts of Europe. Its garden cultivation was initiated in the seventeenth century in widely separate localities, from Lisbon to Naples and from Stockholm to St. Petersburg. For more than a century *Philadelphus coronarius* remained the sole parent of the garden varieties, producing forms without fragrance as well as forms with different degrees of fragrance. The early eighteenth century saw the importation into Europe of various American species, but it was not until the nineteenth century that the real boom in overseas philadelphus began, with *Philadelphus pubescens* introduced in 1811, followed by *Philadelphus coulteri* in 1840, and *Philadelphus microphyllus* in 1883—the last-named eventually playing a very important part in the creation of new hybrids.

The genus comprises forty to fifty species diffused from Southern Europe to the Caucasus and the Himalayas, in North and Central America along the eastern coast, from British Columbia to California along the Pacific side, and also extending to Mexico and the southern regions of South America. The majority are deciduous shrubs—although in Central America there are several evergreen species—with pithy stems and either perennially or biennially peeling bark. The leaves are opposite and entire or dentated. The flowers are generally white—although some have the base of the petals suffused mauve or pinkish—either with or without fragrance, and are borne in groups of 1–3, forming racemes carrying up to eleven flowers.

Although they have the disadvantage of being deciduous (which in winter leaves the plants with a skeleton of brownish-barked stems), their naked branches do possess a certain attraction. The bare stems also allow sun and light to reach the base of the shrub, where masses of violets, hepaticas, winter aconite, epimediums, lily of the valley, etc., can be effectively planted. Thus, for these early-spring effects, no garden should really be without a philadelphus or two.

Cultivation. The genus *Philadelphus* includes some very hardy shrubs that can be cultivated in practically any climate, particularly *Philadelphus pekinensis* and the hybrids of *Philadelphus coronarius*. They thrive in any normal garden soil and love the sun, but they will also give good results in semi-shade. They are tolerant of dry conditions and are rarely attacked by insect pests or disease. Propagation is exceptionally easy from seed, although as the plants hybridize so easily this is not always a sure method of true reproduction. Propagation from cuttings of half-ripened wood in July–August in cold-frames is also very easy; while the choicer varieties can also be propagated by air layering. Since the flowers are borne on the previous season's growth, pruning must be done immediately after flowering has finished so that a good supply of new growth will be produced and mature for the flowering season the following year.

It is not easy to give a comprehensive list of the numerous species and varieties available on the market, but the following is a reasonably representative selection of the most attractive.

Flowering period: May–Aug.
Height: up to 10 ft.
Slightly fragrant
Zone 7 southwards

Philadelphus argyrocalyx Wooton

Native to New Mexico. Introduced into Europe in 1922. A shrub of modest dimensions with gracefully curving slender branches. Leaves oval-elliptic, up to $1\frac{1}{2}$ ins. long; light green and densely covered with soft hairs on the undersurface. Flowers solitary or in groups of 2–3, purest white, with a diameter of about $3\frac{1}{4}$ ins. Closely resembles *Philadelphus microphyllus,* but the flowers are larger and the calyx is covered with silvery down, a characteristic that gives the plant its specific name. It is of particular value and interest in gardens because it will remain in bloom as late as August.

(Common Mock Orange)
Flowering period: May–June
Height: up to 12 ft.
Very fragrant
Zone 3 southwards

Philadelphus coronarius L.

Native to Southeastern Europe and Asia Minor. A shrub of erect, compact, rather rigid habit. The dark maroon bark peels from the stems every two years, curling into little rolls. Young growth smooth or slightly hairy. Leaves elongated-ovate, pointed, $1\frac{1}{2}$–$3\frac{1}{4}$ ins. long, smooth on the upper surface, slightly hairy along the veins on the undersurface; edges irregularly and widely dentated. Very free-flowering individual blooms rather small, with a diameter of up to $1\frac{1}{4}$ ins., grouped in terminal racemes. There are many varieties mostly of hybrid origin, some of the most interesting of which are:

> var. *flore pleno,* with more or less double flowers
> var. *foliis argenteis marginatis,* with the leaves margined white
> var. *foliis aureis,* leaves golden-yellow
> var. *nanus,* only 3 ft. high, but rarely flowers

Flowering period: June–July
Height: up to 12 ft.
Fragrant
Zone 5 southwards

Philadelphus gordonianus Lindl.

Native to North America, from British Columbia to California. Discovered by David Douglas about 150 years ago and reputed to have provided arrow shafts for the American Indians. A shrub of medium proportions. Leaves ovate-oblong, up to $3\frac{1}{2}$ ins. long and 2 ins. wide, pointed, tapering at the base, coarsely dentated. Flowers fragrant, up to 2 ins. in diameter, white, borne 7–9 in dense racemes. A very attractive species.

Flowering period: June
Height: up to $7\frac{1}{2}$ ft.
Zone 6 southwards

Philadelphus hirsutus Nutt.

Native to the southwestern United States. Branches pendent, with a silky surface becoming reddish brown with age. Leaves elongated-ovate, pointed, conspicuously dentated, brilliant green changing to reddish brown in autumn, hairy on either surface but more so beneath. Flowers cream-white, $1\frac{1}{4}$ ins. in diameter, in groups of 1–3.

Philadelphus inodorus L. *(English Dogwood)*
Flowering period: June
Height: up to 6 ft.
Zone 5 southwards

Native to the southeastern United States. A shrub with smooth young growths which, in the second year, change to maroon-brown, and with peeling bark. Leaves oval-elliptic, up to 2 ins. long, pointed, entire or with widely spaced dentations; base rounded; upper surface smooth, dark green, and shiny, with the undersurface smooth but hairy along the veins. Flowers borne in groups of 1–3 at the tips of short lateral twigs. Petals rounded, pure white. Not as free-flowering as some but a very attractive species, although because of its penury in blooming it is not recommended for small gardens. The var. *grandiflorus* has bell-shaped flowers borne in groups of three.

Philadelphus lewisii Pursh.
Flowering period: June–July
Height: up to 12 ft.
Zone 4 southwards

Native to the northwestern United States and the state flower of Idaho. Long, smooth, maroon- or yellowish-maroon-coloured stems. Leaves elongated-ovate, up to 4 ins. long, dentated, brilliant green on the upper surface. Flowers pure white, borne 5–9 in dense, compact racemes; very fragrant. Habit pendulous and graceful. Introduced into cultivation in 1823, and considered to be one of the most attractive and free-flowering species.

Philadelphus microphyllus Gray
Flowering period: June
Height: up to 4½ ft.
Very fragrant
Zone 5 southwards

Native to the southwestern United States. A small graceful shrub of rather compact habit and slender branches. Leaves only ¾ in. long, dark green and shiny above, glaucous and hairy beneath. Flowers mostly solitary, terminal, 1 in. wide, white, very fragrant.

Philadelphus pekinensis Ruprecht
Flowering period: June
Height: up to 6 ft.
Zone 4 southwards

Native to northern China, Mongolia and Korea. A smallish shrub with the young growths glabrous, and the bark peeling from the older branches. Leaves ovate-lanceolate, up to 3⅓ ins. long and 2 ins. wide, dentated, pointed, glabrous; stalks and veins on the undersurface darkish purple. Flowers 1 in. in diameter, cream-yellow, scented, borne 5–9 (occasionally more) in racemes. Not one of the most spectacular philadelphus but interesting for the yellowish colouring of its flowers and for its purple leaf stalks.

Philadelphus pubescens Loisel.
Flowering period: June
Height: up to 18 ft.
Zone 6 southwards

Native to the southwestern United States. Of vigorous, rapid growth and erect, rigid habit. Young growths green and smooth; branches ash-grey with bark that does not peel. Leaves widely ovate, 2–4 ins. long with widely spaced dentations, smooth and vivid green on the upper surface, densely hairy beneath; heart-shaped at the base. Flowers prolific, partially hidden by the foliage, borne 5–11 in racemes, cream-white, 1½ ins. in diameter. One of the most robust and vigorous species, particularly suited to large parks or gardens where there is an abundance of space. Some authorities consider it to be scentless, while others claim it has a slight perfume, but as it hybridizes so easily there are probably hybrid forms with and without scent.

Philadelphus Belle Etoile

Philadelphus Hybrids
>Boule d'Argent, dwarf, free-flowering with pure white double or semi-double blooms 1½ ins. wide, slightly scented (Lemoine 1893).
>Voie Lactée, flowers single, 2 ins. wide, white, slightly fragrant, petals with slightly recurved margins (Lemoine 1910).
>Norma, pale-green leaves up to 5 ins. long; prolific flowers borne in groups of 1–3, single or semi-double, white, slightly scented (Lemoine 1910).
>Rosace, flowers flattish, generally single, cream-white, with a fairly strong scent (Lemoine 1904).
>Lemoinei Erectus, with stems that at first are straight and erect but curve with age; leaves rather small, dark green; flowers prolific, single, borne in groups of 3–5, strongly scented, 1¼ ins. wide.
>Belle Etoile, flowers borne in groups of 3–9 in terminal racemes, milk-white with a purplish mark at the centre, fragrant, with the perimeter of the flower almost square and the petals slightly fringed (Lemoine 1930).
>Burkwoodii, small shrub with flowers in groups of 3–5; white single flowers with a central pinkish-mauve mark, scented.
>Mexicana var. coulteri, native to Mexico, vigorous, free-flowering form, maximum height 6 ft.; flowers single, cream-white, purple mark at base of each petal. Very fragrant (also known as *Philadelphus coulteri* or Rose Syringa).

Virginal, best of double-flowered hybrids but slow-growing; peeling brownish bark, leaves dark green on the upper surface, flowers bowl-shaped, very double, white, borne 5–7 in racemes.

Albâtre, prolific flowers, semi-double, white, 1½ ins. in diameter, borne in groups of 5, intensely fragrant.

Phlomis

(JERUSALEM SAGE)
Family: Labiatae
Hardy herbaceous perennials, sometimes tuberous-rooted, or half-hardy evergreen shrubs
Position: full sun
Propagation: seed, cuttings, or division
Cultivation easy

Phlomis tuberosa

Where there is a hot, dry, sunny corner a beautiful effect can be created with a well-developed specimen of *Phlomis fruticosa*, the best species of the genus, whose attractive yellow flowers make a pleasing contrast with its grey-green foliage. It is also an excellent subject for seaside localities, and ideal for planting in a border devoted to grey-leaved plants. Apart from their attractive foliage, phlomis are notable for their tubular flowers borne in inflorescences which greatly resemble those of the stinging nettle *(Urtica dioica)*; that is, in whorls on rigid erect stems, although in the case of phlomis the inflorescences are much larger and more decorative. In most cases, the flowers are some shade of yellow, but there are also white- and purple-flowered species. They require a warm well-drained soil in an open sunny position and are tolerant of even strongly alkaline (calcareous) soils. Phlomis are hardy in all localities except those with exceptionally cold winters. They were first introduced into European gardens towards the end of the sixteenth century. The genus comprises about a dozen species, but they have never attracted the attention of hybridists and there are no garden hybrids. Botanically, phlomis are related to the common herb sage.

Phlomis have an area of distribution which includes Southern Europe, North Africa, Asia Minor, and the Himalayas. Propagation of the shrubby species is by seed sown in a warm greenhouse in spring, or in coldframes from cuttings of half-ripened wood taken in July. The herbaceous species can be propagated from seed sown in a warm greenhouse in spring or by division of mature plants in spring or autumn. Another method is to propagate from soft cuttings taken early in the summer and rooted under a glass bell-jar or transparent plastic or in a warm greenhouse.

Herbaceous perennial
Flowering period: June–July
Height: up to 2 ft.

Phlomis cashmeriana Royle
Native to Kashmir, as indicated by its specific name. A very handsome species with woolly stems and leaves. Excellent for herbaceous borders or individual beds. Inflorescences in the form of whorls of lilac-purple flowers.

(Jerusalem Sage)
Evergreen shrub
Flowering period: July–Aug.
Height: up to 2 ft.
Zone 8 southwards

Phlomis fruticosa L.
Native to the Mediterranean regions, where it is found in dry, sunny, stony areas. A much-branched dwarf evergreen shrub with pleasing glaucous-green hairy foliage and with flowers of a particularly attractive shade of yellow. These are arranged in whorls on erect stems and remain in bloom throughout the summer. Particularly suited to seaside localities. The leaves are oval-elliptic or nearly heart-shaped, rounded at the base, rough-surfaced, and up to 4 ins. long. Each inflorescence bears up to 30 individual flowers.

Tuberous-rooted
herbaceous perennial
Flowering period: June–July
Height: up to 4½ ft.

Phlomis tuberosa L.
Native to Southern Europe. A tuberous-rooted herbaceous perennial. Leaves larger than in most species, heart-shaped or oval-obtuse, with undulated edges. The purple-pink flowers are borne 30–40 together in whorls that are conspicuous and attractive.

Phlox

Family: Polemoniaceae
Annuals or hardy and half-hardy herbaceous perennials
Position: sun or partial shade
Propagation: seed, division, or cuttings
Cultivation easy
Fragrant in some cases and useful for cutting

Phlox divaricata

I once read that a garden without phlox is inconceivable. I am in complete agreement with this assertion; and not only in gardens—providing, of course, that they are not in overly dry localities—but also on terraces and in window boxes, where it would be almost a crime not to cultivate a few dwarf perennial and annual phlox (always remembering that in warm southern climates they require a certain amount

Phlox paniculata
From *Paxton's Magazine of Botany*,
1834, plate 268

of shade). Even the herbaceous perennial phlox can be grown on a terrace if sufficiently deep receptacles with adequate drainage are provided—at least 18 ins. deep and 12 ins. wide.

Phlox fully merit their Greek name which signifies "flame" (in Italy they were at one time known as *Fiamme*). The name was used by Theophrastus for another flame-coloured flower; he could certainly not have known the present-day phlox, which are American in origin. The finest examples of phlox reached Europe during the eighteenth century; *Phlox maculata* in 1740, *Phlox divaricata* in 1746, *Phlox paniculata* in 1752, *Phlox pilosa* in 1759, and *Phlox drummondii* in 1835.

With the exception of a single Siberian species, the genus comprises about fifty species all native to America, where they are indigenous throughout the northern temperate zones. They are mostly found in thin woods and pastures, while some inhabit mountainous or sandy localities in the same manner as the European lychnis, to which phlox were at one time linked. In certain localities of North America phlox occupy a position similar to that occupied by lychnis in Europe, although lychnis have never been so exploited and developed as phlox. *Phlox paniculata* and *Phlox drummondii* are slightly, moderately, or intensely fragrant according to the variety. In the case of *Phlox paniculata,* the scent is particularly delicious, but in all cases the perfume is difficult to define or to compare to other flowers, having a distinct characteristic of its own. Except for the dwarf, prostrate, and trailing types, phlox are superb subjects for cutting.

Cultivation. With the exception of some dwarf alpine species, phlox love a cool moist soil, rich but not too compact. They do not mind the cold, but are not happy in excessive heat and during hot weather they require an abundance of water. In the case of *Phlox paniculata*—the best of the tall herbaceous perennial phlox—best results will be obtained by lifting, dividing, and replanting at least every three years, in either autumn or spring (preferably spring in the north). The plants should be cut down to ground level at the beginning of winter. The many garden hybrids of *Phlox paniculata* bloom at a particularly useful moment in June, when so many spring flowers have finished and before the bulk of summer flowers have started. The flowering period will be very long if the old flower stems are cut back after they have finished. The perennial types can be propagated by division or soft cuttings in spring, or from seed; although this latter method is generally reserved for the raising of new varieties, since seedlings of the popular garden hybrids would not breed true from seed. The best time to sow seed is early autumn, outside, or as soon as the seed is ripe: then the percentage of germination is usually high, although phlox seed is capricious, often requiring a year or more to germinate. Cuttings should be taken very early in the year from old plants that have been potted and forced into growth in a coldframe or greenhouse, and the resulting plants will bloom the same year. Each cutting should be 2–3 ins. long and should be inserted in sand or in very sandy soil, in pots, trays, flats, or boxes, in a warm greenhouse, keeping them shaded until rooted. They will be ready for planting in their flowering positions in April–May. In the case of established plants, if very large inflorescences are desired the number of flower stems should be limited to 5–6.

Annual phlox are of the easiest cultivation and very widely grown. Seed can be sown directly into its flowering position in April, thinning out the seedlings to about 6–8 ins. apart. Seed can also be sown earlier in coldframes or in an unheated greenhouse, the seedlings grown on individually in small pots for planting out in May, when they will be well-developed and showing their first flower buds. Annual phlox are excellent for growing in large pots, where their graceful, rather trailing, spreading habit is particularly effective when the plants spill over the rim of the pot. One old gardener in Regent's Park advised that such plants should be grown in a compost made up of

> 1 part fibrous loam
> 1 part soil previously used for rooting cuttings or sowing seeds
> 2 parts well-decomposed leafsoil
> a small quantity of non-alkaline (non-calcareous) sand

The dwarf, prostrate, and trailing perennial phlox—useful as alpine plants or for planting in walls—can be propagated by division in late summer or early autumn, preferably potting the divided pieces and over-wintering them in coldframes; or else propagated in spring in districts where the spring weather is warm and the season early. The species can also be propagated from seed sown in pots outdoors during the summer, or from soft cuttings taken in spring and rooted in pots of sandy soil in an unheated greenhouse or coldframe.

Phlox adsurgens Torr

Evergreen herbaceous perennial
Flowering period: May
Height: almost prostrate

Native to the United States from northern California to Oregon. A dwarf evergreen perennial of nearly prostrate habit with stems about 12 ins. long. Leaves shiny, elliptic, 1 in. long. The pink or whitish-pink flowers are 1 in. in diameter, and are borne in loosely formed corymbs. Not hardy in cold localities and suited only to acid, non-alkaline (non-calcareous) soils.

Phlox amoena Sims (syn. *Phlox walteri, Phlox involucrata* Wood)

Herbaceous perennial
Flowering period: Apr.–May
Height: 6–8 ins.

Native to the southeastern United States from Virginia to Kentucky, where it is found in rather arid soils. Stems at first prostrate, becoming more erect as they develop; hairy or downy. Leaves very numerous, broadly lanceolate, 2 ins. long, mostly basal in the form of a rosette, fewer on the stems, either obtuse or round-pointed. Individual flowers ¾ in. in diameter, purple-pink or pinkish white, and borne in compact terminal groups. This plant is sometimes referred to as *Phlox* x *procumbens*.

(Sand Phlox)
Prostrate evergreen perennial
Flowering period: Apr.
Height: 3–4 ins.

Phlox bifida Beck
Native to the central United States. Earlier-flowering than *Phlox subulata*, which it much resembles, but conspicuous for its petals which are deeply notched at the tips. Colour of the flowers variable from pink to pale mauve and white. Found in a sandy rocky terrain.

(Wild Sweet William or Blue Phlox)
Herbaceous perennial
Flowering period: May–June
Height: 10–18 ins.
Slightly fragrant

Phlox divaricata L. (syn. *Phlox canadensis* Sweet)
Native to the eastern United States and Canada. A slender-stemmed slightly hairy herbaceous perennial with linear-oblong or oval-lanceolate foliage up to 2 ins. long. Rapidly increases by means of the spreading non-flowering growths that root at the nodes. Flower stems erect, up to 10–18 ins. high. Flowers 1 in. in diameter, mauve, grouped in small terminal cymes, and of great elegance and charm with a slight fragrance. The var. *alba* is white-flowered; while the var. *laphamii* is violet-blue.

(Annual Phlox, Texan Pride, or Drummond Phlox)
Annual
Flowering period: June–Sept.
Height: 8–18 ins.
Fragrant
Useful for cutting

Phlox drummondii Hook.
Native to Texas, where it is found mostly in sandy soils. A much-branched annual, slightly hairy, with alternate, lanceolate or elongated-oblong, pointed foliage. Inflorescence a flattish, rather wide cyme; individual flowers up to 1 in. in diameter with widely ovate petals. The typical species varies in colour from purple-pink to pinkish red, with the colouring more intense in the centre but variable and often of an intense crimson. There are many forms and varieties with different dimensions and a very wide range of colours which does not yet, however, include a good yellow. The garden varieties are generally divided into two groups:

> var. *rotundata* Voss., with wide entire petals which give the flowers a rounded circular form
> var. *stellaris* Voss., with narrow, fringed, or divided petals which give the flower a star-like aspect

owers of
lox drummondii cuspidata

To the first group belong varieties such as var. *heynholdii*, var. *beffei*, var. *formosa*, var. *grandiflora*, var. *hortensiaeflora*, var. *verbenaeflora*, together with dwarf, medium high, and double-flowered forms. To the second group belong varieties such as var. *fimbriata*, var. *cuspidata*, var. *stellata*, with flowers in various forms and sizes.

Herbaceous perennial
Flowering period: June–July
Height: up to 2¾ ft.
Slightly fragrant
Useful for cutting

Phlox maculata L. (syn. *Phlox pyramidalis* Smith)
Native to the eastern zones of the United States. Herbaceous perennial, more slender and less tall than *Phlox paniculata*, which it otherwise much resembles, although unlike the latter its stems are

Phlox drummondii
From *Paxton's Magazine of Botany*,
1835, plate 221

Phlox subulata
From *Curtis's Botanical Magazine*,
1798, plate 411

marked purple. Leaves smooth and rather thick. Inflorescence similar to that of *Phlox paniculata*, but smaller and with dark-violet flowers. Requires a very moist position.

Phlox paniculata L. (syn. *Phlox decussata* Hort.)
Native to western and southern Pennsylvania. A hardy erect herbaceous perennial, glabrous in all its parts. Leaves thin-textured, oblong-lanceolate, pointed, more slender towards the base, up to 6 ins. long. Inflorescence a large terminal panicle densely packed with individual five-lobed pinkish-purple flowers. The superb modern garden hybrids are the results of crosses between this species and *Phlox maculata*. These hybrids are among the most beautiful hardy herbaceous perennials that can be grown in the garden and they are esteemed for their wide range of brilliant colours which includes all shades of red, purple, salmon, mauve, violet, pink, crimson, etc., often with a central eye of a different contrasting colour. These stupendous panicles of bloom can reach a height of up to 10–12 ins. each. Many of the older hybrids are still widely grown and some of the best are:

(Summer Perennial Phlox or Garden Phlox)
Herbaceous perennial
Flowering period: June–Sept.
Height: up to 3–4 ft.
Fragrant
Useful for cutting

>   Frau Ant. Buchner, pure white
>   Le Mahdi, violet-blue
>   Purple King, purple
>   Mars, orange-pink with a crimson eye
>   Leo Schlageter, scarlet with a darker eye

The more modern Seymons-Jeune Strain are, however, a vast improvement: with larger flowers, better form, and more vivid colours. This new race was created by Captain Seymons-Jeune, brother of Lady Hanbury, owner of the famous La Mortola Botanic Gardens near Ventimiglia in Italy. Some of the best of these are:

>   Dorothy Hanbury Forbes, pink
>   Cecil Hanbury, orange-salmon with scarlet eye
>   Border Gem, violet
>   Harewood, carmine
>   Balmoral, lavender-pink with darker eye
>   Olive Wells Durrant, pink with carmine eye

Phlox pilosa L.
Native to North America, from Ontario southwards to Texas and Florida. An erect slender-stemmed generally hairy herbaceous perennial with small linear or linear-lanceolate pointed leaves. Flowers very numerous, with entire petals, purple-pink or white, and borne in loose widely spaced cymes.

(Prairie Phlox)
Herbaceous perennial
Flowering period: Apr.–May
Height: 18 ins.

Almost prostrate herbaceous perennial
Flowering period: Apr.–May
Height: 6 ins.

Phlox stolonifera Sims (syn. *Phlox reptans* Michx.)
Native to the United States, in Pennsylvania, Kentucky, and Georgia. A hardy herbaceous perennial of rather weak and slender habit; hairy, only 6 ins. high, and trailing; freely rooting at the nodes and eventually wide-spreading. The flower stems are taller, up to 10–12 ins. high. Leaves oval or obovate, widely obtuse. Inflorescence a loose cyme of violet or purple flowers with entire petals. The var. *verna* has pink flowers with a dark-purple throat, and the var. *Blue Ridge* has sky-blue flowers of great beauty and was given a high award by the Royal Horticultural Society in 1951.

(Ground Pink or Moss Pink)
Prostrate evergreen perennial
Flowering period: Apr.–May
Height: 2–4 ins.

Phlox subulata L. (syn. *Phlox setacea* L.)
Native to the United States, from New York State to Florida. Generally found in dry meadow-lands and easy to naturalize. There are various forms, all prostrate and cushion-forming. The plants are generally pubescent, with the minute leaves grouped in fascias (except on the flower stems), linear or linear-lanceolate, pointed. Flowers up to $\frac{3}{4}$ in. in diameter, completely covering the entire plant in lovely shades of brilliant sky-blue, pink, purple, or white, and borne in small groups. A graceful, elegant little plant for the rock-garden, walls, paving, steps, etc., and also useful as a ground cover. Some of the best varieties are:

> var. *Atropurpurea*, wine-red
> var. *Fairy*, mauve
> var. *G. F. Wilson*, pale lavender
> var. *Sensation*, reddish pink
> var. *Temiscaming*, reddish purple

Phygelius

(CAPE FUCHSIA OR CAPE FIGWORT)
Family: *Scrophulariaceae*
Half-hardy sub-shrubs or woody-stemmed herbaceous perennials
Position: *full sun in the north, partial shade in the south*
Propagation: *seed, cuttings, or division*
Cultivation easy

In many gardens phygelius plants have failed to obtain the attention they deserve, and when they are grown the selection is generally confined to a single species, *Phygelius capensis*. This neglect is unjustified as they are elegant plants with very beautiful generally red pendulous flowers, and although of South African origin they are hardy in European and North American gardens, except in excessively cold localities. But even if the above-ground part of the plant is killed by frost, new growths will generally be produced from the base in late spring. The name of genus *Phygelius* derives from the Greek *phyga* (escape or flight) and *helios* (sun), and indicates the plants' preference for partial shade. However, only in very hot sunny localities do the plants desire to "escape" from the sun, and in northern gardens they can be successfully grown in full sun; but in the south they certainly give better results in partial shade. Phygelius require a fairly moist soil, preferably acid or neutral, which is fertile and rich in organic matter such as peat or leafsoil. Propagation can be effected from seed sown in a warm greenhouse in spring, by soft cuttings taken in early summer and inserted in sand or sandy soil under a glass bell-jar or transparent plastic, or by division of established plants in spring.

Phygelius aequalis Harv.

Flowering period: July–Oct.
Height: up to 3 ft.

Native to South Africa. A plant of remarkable beauty and a precious gem for the connoisseur, but rarely seen in cultivation. On September 15, 1936, Lady Byng of Vimy exhibited some flowering plants at a Royal Horticultural Society show in London, where they were given the high and much-coveted award of merit. It is a sub-shrub with square stems, the bases of which are woody while the tops have a herbaceous character. Leaves opposite, relatively large, and rigid. The inflorescence is composed of pendulous, brilliant salmon-scarlet flowers, which remain in bloom from July to October.

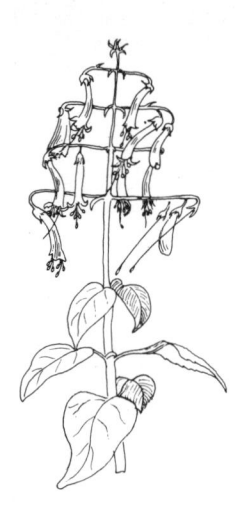

Phygelius capensis

Flowering period: July–Oct.
Height: up to 6 ft.

Phygelius capensis E. Mey.
Native to South Africa. The best-known and most widely grown species. In a warm climate it forms a definite woody shrub up to 6 ft. high; but in colder zones the plant assumes the character of a herbaceous perennial, and during a severe winter will more or less die back to ground level until the following spring, when vigorous new growths appear. Leaves oval-lanceolate, dark green, glabrous. The tubular crimson-scarlet flowers last from July to October and are borne in candelabra-like panicles on erect stems.

Physalis

(CHINESE LANTERN, CAPE GOOSEBERRY, OR HUSK TOMATO)
Family: Solanaceae
Annuals or tender or hardy herbaceous perennials
Position: sun or partial shade
Propagation: seed or division
Cultivation very easy
Seed capsules useful for cutting and drying

Towards Christmas, especially on the Continent, the windows of fruit shops are often decorated with curious shiny yellow, orange, or red little cherry-like fruits. While still on the plant the fruits are enveloped in a bladder-like involucre; when open, this folds back to expose the fruit and forms a crown or halo like a dry leaf in appearance. This decorative little fruit has a galaxy of common names such as Cape Gooseberry, Winter Cherry, Ground Cherry, Strawberry Tomato, Bladder Cherry, Chinese Lantern; but it is neither a cherry, gooseberry, nor a tomato. Its botanical name is *Physalis* and in some species the fruits are edible and are often used to make an excellent jam. In Italy, a most delicious seasonal confection is prepared from the fruits. With the involucre pulled back to form a twisted topknot, the fruits are dipped into bittersweet chocolate and sold in exclusive shops. As no preserving process is used, these sweets are very perishable and must be consumed within a few days of their purchase. For the enthusiastic home cook the process could probably be duplicated by using a very good brand of bittersweet chocolate enriched with some vanilla. Melt the chocolate over warm water (not too hot and *never* boiling or simmering) and dip each fruit until it is coated up to the first $\frac{1}{4}$ in. of the involucre. Then place on a buttered surface to cool. Store in a cool place, and eat them within the week. (The involucre, by the way, is merely employed as a "handle" and is not meant to be eaten.) The involucre is often as attractive as the fruit, frequently of brilliant colour and exquisite design like a miniature lantern. The plant stems, complete with "lanterns", are often cut in late summer, dried, and used for indoor winter decoration, either by themselves or combined in dried-flower arrangements. All physalis fruits are contained in some type of bladder-like involucre, but only those of the species *P. alkekengi*, its var. *franchetii*, and *P. peruviana* have ornamental value. The best species with edible fruits are *P. pubescens*, *P. peruviana*, and *P. edulis*.

Several species are native to America and Canada and are more or less naturalized in parts of Europe. The perennial species, beautiful as they are, can actually naturalize with such abandon that they tend to become invasive and a possible menace, increasing at an amazing rate by means of the long cord-like white rhizomatous roots. Those species normally grown in gardens are cultivated either for their edible fruits or for the decorative appearance of their seed capsules, as the actual flowers have little ornamental value and the plant itself is not particularly attractive. The name *Physalis* derives from the Greek *physallis* (bladder) and was given to the genus because of the thin-textured blister-like membrane that encases the fruit. The plants are herbaceous perennials or annuals native to hot and temperate climates. Of the one hundred or so known species, the majority are of American origin, while the remainder are Asiatic or European. They have an erect or trailing habit according to the species and bloom in early summer, but the flowers are insignificant. In autumn it is fascinating to observe the ripening and then gradual disintegration of the seed capsules. First the thin membraneous-like skin of the "lantern" decomposes, leaving only the skeleton composed of its veins and framework like a miniature filigree cage, exposing the ripe fruit inside. Eventually, this too decomposes and the ripe fruit falls to the ground where its seed disperses.

Physalis have been well known for centuries. Saint Hildegarde described *Physalis alkekengi* in her *Physica* in the twelfth century; while in 1551 Hieronymus Bock figured it in his *Kreüterbuch*. *Physalis pubescens* was illustrated by Dillenius in 1774 in his disquisition on the plants in the garden of Sherard at Eltham in England. The species *P. peruviana* was illustrated and described in 1715 by Morison, also in England; while later John Sims wrote, "This plant originated in Peru or Chile, but is cultivated at the Cape of Good Hope, in various regions of the West Indies, and especially in the British Colonies of New South Wales, and provides a most common fruit; being eaten in tarts, puddings, and conserves."

The calyx, fruit stalks, and foliage of physalis contain a bitter glucoside, physalin, which in ancient times was used for the treatment of gallstones, rheumatism, gout, as a sedative and febrifuge, and in cases of urinary disorders.

Cultivation. Physalis will thrive almost anywhere, although they prefer a well-drained, alkaline (calcareous) soil in an open sunny position. The plants will, however, also give good results in semi-shade, especially in the south, where they will also tolerate damper soils. In the case of the annual species, propagation can be effected by means of seed sown in a warm greenhouse in spring, pricking out and growing on the seedlings so that they can be planted outside in May. The perennial species can also be raised from seed in the same manner, but are generally propagated by division of the prolific roots in either spring or autumn.

Physalis alkekengi   Fruits of *Physalis alkengi*

(Bladder Cherry, Winter Cherry, or Chinese Lantern)
Herbaceous perennial
Flowering period: July
Height: up to 3 ft.

Physalis alkekengi L.
Originally native to an area extending from Southern Europe to Japan but now naturalized in many parts of the world, including the United States and Northern Europe. The entire plant is very slightly hairy or completely glabrous. Leaves elongated-oval, up to 3 ins. long. Flowers pale yellowish white, inconspicuous. The involucre containing the fruit can be up to 3 ins. in diameter, and it is highly ornamental when it assumes its brilliant orange-red colouring. Botanically, this Chinese Lantern is a grossly inflated calyx. The fruits are small red berries resembling miniature tomatoes. It is a herbaceous perennial, completely dying back to the ground in late autumn, while the vigorous, rampant, invasive roots send up new growths each spring with increasing vigour. By some authorities the var. *franchetii* is considered to be a separate species, but here we follow L. H. Bailey who considers it a variety of *Physalis alkekengi*, from which it differs only in its larger proportions. This variety was introduced into England from Japan by James P. Veitch and described for the first time in 1879 by Franchet, a botanist at the Jardin des Plantes

in Paris, as a form of *Physalis alkekengi*. It is now the most widely cultivated form and the most frequently found in flower shops because of its very large vividly coloured "lanterns". There is also a dwarf variety only 8 ins. high which can even be grown in large receptacles.

Physalis ixocarpa L. (Tomatillo)
Native to Mexico. An interesting, attractive annual species but not hardy. Leaves elongated-oval, up to 3 ins. long, dentated. Flowers yellowish, $\frac{3}{4}$ in. in diameter, with five black spots at the throat. The fruits are mauvish blue with a sticky surface and are enclosed in an inflated involucre with conspicuous purple veins.

Annual
Flowering period: June–July
Height: up to 4 ft.

Physalis peruviana L. (syn. *Physalis edulis*) (Cape Gooseberry)
Native to the tropics. One of the best species for a supply of edible fruits and particularly suited to the south as it is late-flowering, with the fruits ripening in autumn. A non-hardy perennial up to 3 ft. high with heart-shaped hairy foliage. Flowers yellowish, with the internal zone of the throat marked purple; wide-mouthed. Involucre long-pointed; fruit yellow, pleasant to the taste, but less sweet than that of *Physalis pubescens*.

Herbaceous perennial
Flowering period: July
Height: up to 3 ft.

Physalis pruinosa Jacq. (Strawberry Tomato)
Native to North America. A vigorous dwarf hardy annual species; stems wide-spreading, erect, angular, and covered with soft grey hairs. Leaves elongated-oval, up to 4 ins. long, dentated. Flowers a rather dirty yellow. Fruits yellowish green, edible. Involucre hairy but not decorative.

Annual
Flowering period: June
Height: up to 1 ft.

Physalis pubescens L. (Ground Cherry)
Native to South America. As indicated by its specific name the entire plant is densely tomentose and hairy. Flowers yellowish, small, marked with five violet spots; anthers also violet. Fruits yellow or yellowish green, enclosed in an inflated involucre of the same colour. It was at one time widely cultivated for its edible fruits, but it has now escaped and naturalized itself widely over large areas, especially in northern Mediterranean countries, where, according to some Continental botanists, it is perennial, although Bailey gives it as an annual. In any case, it invariably reappears each year from self-sown seed. The English common name Ground Cherry is most appropriate as the fruits do resemble small cherries, although the plant has a dwarf trailing, spreading habit. The fruits are very palatable, sweet but agreeably and slightly acid; they mature early, and, if the weather is good, they will remain on the ground in their involucre for 3–4 weeks without rotting. If gathered and dried, the stems with their "lanterns" and fruits will survive the winter. Considerable

Annual
Flowering period: June
Height: 8 ins.

space is necessary when cultivating this species as under favourable conditions the prostrate trailing growths can extend as much as 5 ft. in every direction.

Physostegia virginiana

(OBEDIENT PLANT OR FALSE DRAGONHEAD)
Family: Labiatae
Hardy herbaceous perennials

At one time *Physostegia* formed part of the much larger genus *Dracocephalum* (Dragonhead), which has on several occasions lost various species to other separate independent genera. A trace of its former alliance can be found in the plant's popular English name, False Dragonhead. The name *Physostegia*, however, derives from the Greek *physon* (inflated) and *stege* (covering), with allusion to the inflated form of the calyx.

Physostegia is a small genus native to North America, with only one species, together with its several varieties, in general garden cultivation. This is *Physostegia virginiana*, much appreciated for its long flowering period and interesting for a most curious characteristic. For some unknown reason the individual blooms on the tall flower spikes will remain in whatever position they are poked, twisted, or turned, a characteristic that has resulted in the common name of Obedient Plant.

Physostegias are hardy herbaceous perennials that can be grown in any normal fertile garden soil, either acid or alkaline (calcareous), which does not become excessively dry during the summer. The plants are sun-lovers but will also tolerate a position in partial shade, and they can be left undisturbed for many years. Propagation is best accomplished by division of established plants in spring or autumn; or it can be effected from seed sown in spring in nursery beds, in coldframes, or in pots in an unheated greenhouse. The seedlings will often bloom the same year.

Flowering period: June–Aug.
Height: 18–24 ins.
Position: sun or partial shade
Propagation: seed or division
Cultivation very easy
Useful for cutting

Physostegia virginiana Benth. (syn. *Dracocephalum virginianum*)
Native to Virginia. A hardy herbaceous perennial with elongated arching narrow foliage 4–6 ins. long, pointed, conspicuously dentated, stalkless. The stems are square, and the top third is occupied by a much-branched erect inflorescence in the form of a large spike up to 6 ins. long, composed of groups of tubular flowers 1 in. long and $\frac{1}{3}$ in. wide with a wide mouth, with the stamens attached to the upper

Physostegia virginiana
From *Paxton's Magazine of Botany*,
1838, plate 173

petal. When the flower dies the conspicuous green sepal remains, and in the centre a fairly large seed is formed. The typical species has lovely fuchsia-red flowers; while the var. *alba* has brilliant pure-white blooms. The var. *Vivid* has particularly intense pinkish-red flowers. There are also dwarf forms such as var. *nana*, only 12–15 ins. high with pink flowers.

Pieris

(ANDROMEDA)
Family: Ericaceae
Hardy evergreen shrubs
Position: partial shade
Propagation: seed, cuttings, or air layers
Cultivation easy

Some species of genus *Pieris* were previously included in the genus *Andromeda*, which is now divided into three different genera, *Pieris*, *Leucothoe*, and *Zenobia*. Of these, it is the pieris that are of most value as garden plants. One species, *Pieris forrestii*, produces pure-white flowers on its scarlet-red young growths in early spring, offering a spectacle of exceptional beauty. The other species are also very decorative and deserve a prominent place in the garden.

The genus comprises ten species, native to North America, the Himalayas, China, and Japan, that have been cultivated in gardens since the early eighteenth century. As members of the family Ericaceae they need to be cultivated in the same manner as rhododendrons, requiring an acid, completely alkaline-free (non-calcareous) soil rich in well-decomposed organic matter such as peat and leafsoil. Like rhododendron, pieris loves to have its roots in a cool and moist location, and it thrives in partial shade, particularly in the south. It is, however, hardy and will tolerate more sun at high altitudes in the cooler north. Pieris are very handsome evergreen shrubs with a neat compact habit and require no pruning. They are excellent for planting in light woods, and, since their roots remain confined to a limited space forming a compact mass of rootlets similar to azaleas, they are also suitable for pot or tub culture. Propagation can be effected by means of seed sown outside in spring, from cuttings of half-ripened wood taken in July and inserted in a mixture of sand and peat in coldframes, or by air layers in summer.

Pieris floribunda Benth. & Hook. (syn. *Andromeda floribunda*)
Native to the southeastern United States. A beautiful slow-growing compact evergreen shrub of modest proportions. Ideal for planting in woodlands, in a shady courtyard, or in beds or borders protected from intense sun. Well-cultivated plants retain their branches and dark glossy green foliage down to ground level. The inflorescences are in the form of erect terminal panicles up to 6 ins. high, and the individual pendulous flowers are small, pitcher-shaped, and pure white. This is one of the most desirable hardy flowering evergreen shrubs for locations where shade and an acid soil are available. There is a fine specimen in the Wisley Gardens of the Royal Horticultural Society, 15 ft. in diameter and 6 ft. high; when in full bloom it is a remarkable sight.

Flowering period: Mar.–Apr.
Height: up to 6 ft.
Zone 5 southwards

Pieris formosa D. Don (syn. *Andromeda formosa*)
Native to the Himalayas and found at a height of up to 9,000 ft. This is probably the most beautiful species of the genus, similar to *P. floribunda* and retaining the same compact habit, but later-flowering and with a much larger development. The inflorescences and individual flowers are also larger. Leaves coriaceous, oblong-lanceolate, pointed at each end, $1\frac{1}{4}$–$3\frac{1}{2}$ ins. long, up to $\frac{2}{3}$ in. wide, dentated; brilliant dark green on the upper surface, pale green beneath. Flowers borne in terminal panicles, white, pendulous, and pitcher-shaped.

(Mountain Fetter Bush)
Flowering period: Apr.–May
Height: up to 18 ft.
Zone 6 southwards

Pieris forrestii Harrow (syn. *Pieris formosa* var. *forrestii* Airy-Shaw)
Native to Burma and the Yunnan province of China. A superb plant of relatively recent introduction, with the typical habit, flowers, and general characteristics of *Pieris formosa*, but with the addition of beautiful scarlet-red growths appearing in early spring at the same time as the white flowers.

Flowering period: Apr.–May
Height: up to 9 ft.
Zone 6 southwards

Pieris japonica

Pieris floribunda

(Andromeda)
Flowering period: Mar.–Apr.
Height: up to 10 ft.
Zone 5 southwards

Pieris japonica D. Don (syn. *Andromeda japonica*)
Native to Japan. A distinct species with a more pendulous and less rigid habit and with an earlier flowering season, often beginning in early March. Narrowly oval leathery foliage; flowers similar to those of lily of the valley and borne in terminal clusters of slender pendulous racemes up to 6 ins. long. *Pieris japonica* was given the Royal Horticultural Society's award of merit as far back as 1882. There is also a var. *variegata* with foliage prettily variegated in cream-white and green.

Flowering period: Apr.–May
Height: up to 6 ft.
Zone 7 southwards

Pieris taiwanensis Hayata
Native to Taiwan and found up to an altitude of 10,000 ft. or more. Introduced by E. H. Wilson in 1918; the first flowering plants to be shown in public were those exhibited by Lord Headford in March 1922. Has the typical evergreen compact habit of most andromedas, but the young growths are greenish yellow and glabrous. An interesting characteristic of the plant is that, when raised from seed and cultivated in an unheated greenhouse, it will flower within two years. Leaves oval, tapering at either end, up to 5 ins. long and 1 in. wide; leathery, dark shiny green above, lighter beneath, glabrous. Inflorescences produced in groups in the form of terminal racemes up to 6 ins. long. Individual flowers pitcher-shaped, white, $\frac{1}{4}$ in. wide, with five reflexed lobes at the contracted mouth.

Platycodon grandiflorus

(BALLOON FLOWER OR CHINESE OR JAPANESE BELLFLOWER)
Family: Campanulaceae
Hardy herbaceous perennials
Flowering period: July–Aug.
Height: 1–3 ft.
Position: sun
Propagation: seed or division
Cultivation easy

It is only since 1830 that platycodons have constituted a separate genus. In 1776 they were included by Nikolaus J. Jacquin among the campanulas (some Continental commercial growers still call them campanulas). Later they were transferred by Schrader to the genus *Wahlenbergia*; then, in 1830, De Candolle created the new genus *Platycodon* for them: *platys* from the Greek for wide, and *kodon* for bell, referring to the characteristic widely bell-shaped corolla. The British and Americans call the plants Balloon Flowers because of the unusual shape of the flower buds, which actually do resemble small balloons.

There still exists some doubt whether the genus consists of only the single species *Platycodon grandiflorus*; this species has an extensive area of distribution throughout the Far East, including China, Manchuria, Siberia, Japan, and Korea.

One seventeenth-century Italian author, evidently possessed of a greater enthusiasm for rhetoric than for gardening, apostrophized the plant thus: "and you, at the back, who with false modesty try to hide, tell me of the Great Wall of China which protects the vast Chinese Empire from the marauding Tartars; from the Magyar gypsies, and the Armenian mercenaries; and recount—with the voice of Zephyr who frolics among the flower beds—the legends of the East and the ballads of the Alps." These "Chinese Campanulas" are, however, not so very modest, reaching a height of up to 3 ft. with individual blooms 3 ins. in diameter.

Cultivation. Platycodons require a good deep fibrous loam which is moist but very well drained, giving poor results in very sandy or excessively heavy compact soils. Staking is advisable before the plants reach flowering size, as once the stems fall it is difficult to straighten them without their breaking. In autumn, the current season's growth should not be cut off but should be allowed to die down naturally, as in the case of bulbs. Propagation can be effected by division in spring or from seed. The latter method is preferred, as established plants resent disturbance and their fleshy roots can be easily damaged. Seed can be sown from April to July in seed beds, in frames, or in boxes, in a peaty soil, taking the greatest care not to damage the small roots when the seedlings are planted out in autumn or in the following spring. The plants like an open sunny position.

Platycodon grandiflorus D. C.
Native to China and Japan. Recommended highly for borders, and, in the case of the dwarf varieties, for individual beds. They are resistant to frost, easy to grow, and easy to raise from seed. They are fast-growing plants, with a deeply penetrating fleshy white tap-root that sends up numerous erect leafy flower stems 3 ft. high in the type plant. The var. *mariesii*, introduced into England from Japan by Maries, is only half that height and is the form most widely cultivated in gardens. The flower stems are branched towards their extremities, each branch bearing a large terminal flower which when fully expanded has the form of a wide shallow bell with a conspicuous widely lobed mouth. When damaged, the stems and leaves emit a milky sap. The foliage is light green on the upper surface and glaucous green beneath; dentated, stalkless, elongated-acuminate, with margins that tend to curl inwards. Although the genus is

Platycodon grandiflorus var. *mariesii*
From *Curtis's Botanical Magazine*,
1794, plate 252

probably monotypic, with only one species, there are many forms and varieties in cultivation in gardens:

Double- or Semi-double-flowered Varieties:
- var. *Capri*, medium height, dark-blue flowers
- var. *Cloche Bleu*, sea-blue
- var. *Globe Azuré*, sky-blue
- var. *multiflora*, pale blue
- var. *Seidenball*, lilac-purple
- var. *vineta*, dark blue

Single-flowered Varieties:
- var. *album*, white
- var. *autumnale*, a late-flowering blue variety
- var. *Die Fée*, large sky-blue flowers
- var. *japonicum*, with a bushy habit and flowers up to 3 ins. wide, with the external and internal petals alternating with one another, giving the impression of a ten-pointed star. First placed on the market in France in 1895
- var. *mariesii*, with a neat compact habit and a maximum height of 12–15 ins. Leaves thicker textured than in the type. Flowers variable in colour from purple to white
- var. *rosea*, pale-pink flowers
- var. *striatum*, blue or white flowers striped darker blue

Plumbago

(LEADWORT)
(*Also see* CERATOSTIGMA)
Family: Plumbaginaceae
Tender herbaceous perennials, woody climbers, or annuals
Position: sun
Propagation: seed, cuttings, or division
Cultivation easy

There is considerable doubt concerning the origin of the name of the genus *Plumbago* and the experts are not all of the same opinion. Some compare the flower colour of *Plumbago capensis* to the colour of lead *(plumbum)*; while others, with a rather ingenuous air, refer to "some other old tradition". The text of one old English reference book states that the real origin of the name may possibly be found in an ancient belief which attributes to the plant the virtue of curing an eye ailment known as "plumbus". Still another explanation suggests that chewing the roots of *Plumbago capensis* produces a beneficial effect that relieves toothache, but which at the same time stains the teeth the colour of lead.

The genus comprises about ten species diffused throughout tropical and subtropical countries. Probably the best known is the South African *Plumbago capensis* (if we exclude the popular so-called *Plumbago larpentae* which is really *Ceratostigma plumbaginoides*).

Cultivation. None of the plumbagos can be considered hardy and none will tolerate frost. In the north, *Plumbago capensis* is frequently cultivated in large pots, passing the winter in a cool greenhouse or some other well-lighted and well-ventilated location where the temperature does not fall below 40–45°F.—in company with lemons in pots, lantanas, daturas, and similar tender plants—and should be transferred to the garden for the summer months. In warm climates, however, where the minimum winter temperature remains a few degrees above freezing, the plant can be left permanently outside in a warm sheltered position; either in a large receptacle or planted against a sunny wall, where it will remain in bloom until late autumn. If there should be risk of frost during an unusually cold spell, the plant can be protected with a layer of leaves, peat, or straw at its base; severely pruning the above-ground part and covering the stems with canvas, sacking, or straw. In spring, basal growths will appear soon again and any remaining branches that may have been frost-killed can also be pruned. Pruning does, in fact, induce better flowering and should be energetically carried out in spring as the flowers appear on the new season's vegetation. The lovely blue inflorescences are intolerant of rain and storms, but as the plant is so free-flowering a fresh supply of bloom will soon appear when the weather improves. *Plumbago capensis* is also an excellent climber of modest proportions for growing on a terrace or balcony, where it will continue to bloom throughout the summer and, if associated with yellow or orange marigolds or lantanas or with pink phlox or pink pelargoniums, some delightful effects can be obtained. *Plumbago capensis* will thrive in any normal fertile garden soil, but it must have perfect drainage. During their period of active growth the plants will benefit from periodic applications of liquid organic fertilizer. Permanent plants outside can also be fertilized with well-composted manure.

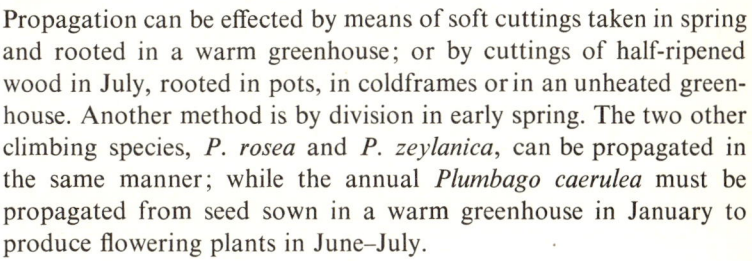

Propagation can be effected by means of soft cuttings taken in spring and rooted in a warm greenhouse; or by cuttings of half-ripened wood in July, rooted in pots, in coldframes or in an unheated greenhouse. Another method is by division in early spring. The two other climbing species, *P. rosea* and *P. zeylanica*, can be propagated in the same manner; while the annual *Plumbago caerulea* must be propagated from seed sown in a warm greenhouse in January to produce flowering plants in June–July.

Plumbago rosea

Plumbago capensis Thunb.   (Leadwort)
Native to South Africa—hence the specific name *capensis* from the Cape of Good Hope. The most widely cultivated species in European and American gardens and greenhouses. Stems long, woody, semi-climbing but not self-attaching. Leaves entire, oblong or oblong-spatulate, smooth, and light green. Inflorescences in the form of umbels at the ends of the branches, and composed of sky-blue flowers with numerous darker blue anthers. Calyx hairy. Individual blooms saucer-shaped at the mouth, $\frac{3}{4}$ in. in diameter. In gardens in southern California the plant reaches a height of up to 18 ft., but grown outside in Europe a maximum height of 10 ft. is more normal, even under the most favourable conditions. Although *Plumbago capensis* is so widely grown as a wall plant or semi-climber, it has a loose open habit with the newer growths almost pendulous, thus requiring adequate support and careful tying. It cannot be treated as a true climber or vine. The var. *alba* has attractive white flowers.

Evergreen perennial semi-climber
Flowering period: June–Oct.
Height: up to 10–18 ft.

Plumbago caerulea H.B.K.
Native to Peru, and therefore only suitable for growing in warm climates. Seed sown in a warm greenhouse in January will provide flowering plants in June–July for summer bedding or for pot culture. Requires a warm soil in a hot sunny position. Leaves rhomboid in form, entire, glabrous, rather pointed at each end; leaf stalks winged. Inflorescences in the form of terminal spikes with intense violet-purple individual flowers. The general appearance of the plant is erect and much-branched.

Annual
Flowering period: July–Sept.
Height: 12–18 ins.

Plumbago rosea L. (syn. *Plumbago indica, Plumbago sanguinea*)
Native to Southern Asia. It is a pity that this lovely pinkish-red plumbago is relatively rare commercially, and not in general cultivation as well, as it can make such a striking contrast to the blue of *Plumbago capensis*. A semi-climber of modest proportions which needs support and careful tying; excellent for use as an indoor pot plant or for outside use in summer, but not hardy. Grown in a greenhouse or in an apartment, the flowering period is prolonged well into winter if a well-lighted, warm, but well-ventilated position can be provided. Leaves oval, up to 4 ins. long. Flowers 1 in. long, borne in small groups on a small pyramidal inflorescence. The colour varies from pinkish red to reddish purple, but the var. *coccinea* has larger scarlet blooms.

Perennial semi-climber
Flowering period: June–Oct.
Height: up to 3 ft.

Plumbago zeylanica L.
Native to tropical Africa and tropical Asia. A semi-climbing shrubby plant with a dense very branched habit. Leaves ovate, 2–3 ins. long, with the base ones clasping the stem. Flowers white, smaller than those of *Plumbago capensis*, but similar in shape and grouped in an umbel

Perennial semi-climber
Flowering period: June–Aug.
Height: up to 10 ft.

Plumbago capensis
From *Curtis's Botanical Magazine*,
1819, plate 2110

which is also smaller than that of *P. capensis*. It is also less hardy than *P. capensis*, but makes an excellent pot plant as it begins to flower while still quite small. Requires a hot sunny position.

Polemonium

(JACOB'S LADDER OR GREEK VALERIAN)
Family: Polemoniaceae
Hardy, half-hardy, or tender herbaceous perennials
Position: sun or partial shade
Propagation: seed or division
Cultivation easy

Polemoniums have lately caught the public's fancy. Their pinnate foliage, so orderly and precisely arranged along long stems, recalls the Biblical ladder dreamed of by Jacob (Genesis 28:12). For this reason polemoniums, particularly *Polemonium coeruleum*—the most widely cultivated species—were given the name Jacob's Ladder.

The genus consists of about thirty species, with a vast area of distribution including Europe, Asia, and North America. All are easily grown mostly hardy herbaceous perennials with bell-shaped flowers borne in groups on branching stems in early summer. Their dominant colour is a lovely shade of blue not easily found among herbaceous perennials suitable for beds and borders. As for other summer-flowering perennials, if the plants are cut down to almost ground level after the first flowering has finished a second crop of bloom will generally be produced in late summer or early autumn.

To be fully appreciated, polemoniums are best grown in bold groups. They are particularly effective massed on a lawn, in the mixed border, in individual beds, or as edging plants along a road or wide path. They will thrive in any normal fertile garden soil that is neither excessively damp nor too dry. In the north they can be planted in full sun, but in southern climates they prefer partial shade and more moisture at their roots. Propagation can be effected by division in spring or autumn; or from seed sown outside in seed beds or boxes in the spring. The origin of the name is curious, deriving from the Greek *polemos* (war); Pliny the Elder recorded that two kings actually went to war in a dispute about which of them first discovered the plant.

Polemonium carneum L.
Native to the western United States, particularly California and Oregon. One of the less typical species because of its salmon-pink or

Flowering period: June–July
Height: 2 ft.

Polemonium coeruleum
From *The Botanical Register*,
1830, plate 1303

flesh-coloured clusters of flowers instead of the more common blue, although as they fade the blooms do assume a purple tinge. They are about 1½ ins. in diameter and are borne in clusters. The plant is also less hardy than the better-known European species, *Polemonium coeruleum*. It has a loose open branching habit with a height up to 2 ft. The lance-shaped leaflets are 1½ ins. in length.

Polemonium coeruleum L.
Native to Europe, where it is found growing at altitudes up to 8,000 ft., generally in fresh and moist alpine meadows. It is also found wild in mountainous regions of Asia, including the Himalayas. Habit bushy and compact. The stems are hollow and covered with minute hairs. Leaves pinnate; the leaflets are in opposite pairs and arranged in a conspicuously precise manner resembling a ladder, with a single leaflet at the tip. Flowers arranged in loose panicles; individual blooms 1½ ins. wide and a lovely shade of blue. There is also a white-flowered var. *album*, and a var. *himalayanum* with darker blue flowers.

Flowering period: June–July
Height: 2½ ft.

Polemonium confertum Gray
Native to Colorado. The smallest species of the genus, not more than 10 ins. high and often several inches less. Less hardy than the preceding. Excellent for individual beds and for edging. The intensely sky-blue flowers are borne in terminal inflorescences and are most effective. Leaflets small, narrow.

(Skunkweed)
Flowering period: June–July
Height: 10 ins.

Polemonium pauciflorum Wats.
Native to Mexico. An unusual species for its attractive yellow flowers, but hardy only in temperate climates and not tolerant of frost.

Flowering period: June–July
Height: 1½ ft.

Polianthes tuberosa

(Tuberose)
Family: Amaryllidaceae
Tender tuberous-rooted herbaceous perennials
Flowering period: summer
Height: 2–3 ft. (when in bloom)
Position: sun
Propagation: division
Cultivation easy
Very fragrant
Useful for cutting

The tuberose is essentially a florist's flower, always available at any season, either from plants that have bloomed naturally or from those

Polianthes tuberosa

which have been forced to flower. The name is well suited to the blooms and is of Greek derivation; *polios* (white) and *anthos* (flower). Only one species is cultivated, together with one variety.

Polianthes (not to be confused with polyanthus) are native to Mexico, although it seems doubtful if the actual tuberose has been found in a wild state. As cut bloom they require no introduction, and, although their fragrance is enjoyed by many, some find it too sweet and sickly, even repellent in a closed room. Outdoors, however, an occasional trace of the perfume carried on a passing breeze can be most pleasant. Tuberoses are not really garden plants, and they are best as cut bloom, for which purpose they are best grown either in the nursery, in a section of the garden devoted to the cultivation of cut bloom for the house, or even in a bed in the vegetable garden. When cut, they are superb either by themselves or arranged with some small-flowered lilies such as *Lilium henryi*. They are long-lasting indoors, but tend to pollute their water to a remarkable extent, making daily changes necessary. A curious feature in the flowering habit of *Polianthes tuberosa* is the erratic manner in which blooms are produced. For instance, in a bed of five hundred bulbs, all planted at the same time and all of the same age, some will produce their flower spikes in July, others will wait until August, and the remainder will defer their flowering period until autumn. It is essential to plant tubers of flowering size which have not previously bloomed. When a tuber has flowered once it will not bloom again and should be discarded.

Propagation can be easily effected using the young tubers produced round the parent tuber, but they require at least four years to reach flowering size and it is advisable to have a bed of 1-, 2-, 3-, and 4-year-old tubers always under cultivation—unless one buys new flowering-sized tubers each year.

Polianthes tuberosa L.

An easily grown tuberous plant requiring the same cultural methods used for gladioli; that is, plant in spring and then (for young tubers not mature enough to flower) remove from the soil, dry, and store during the winter. In general appearance, the plant has a mass of basal foliage, pale green, long, narrow and very dense, with a height of 8–10 ins. The strong erect flower stems can reach a height of up to 3 ft., although $2-2\frac{1}{2}$ ft. is more normal. It is approximately the top third of the stem which bears the pure-white, waxy textured raceme of blooms. The unopened buds are slightly tinted with pink. The long clean stems are a delight to cut, and require no support and never droop. A point to remember when planting in late spring or early summer is that the tubers should be pushed individually into the loose soil surface, so that the tip is very slightly above the level of the soil surface. Generally, the double-flowered var. *Pearl* is cultivated in gardens and for commercial purposes. The true species has single flowers of a more tubular shape with an even stronger perfume (and personally I consider it more graceful). Tuberoses require a hot sunny well-drained position, but they are not hardy. They have no demands about soil so long as it is fertile and well-dug.

The name tuberose is something of an enigma. The plants have nothing to do with roses, although the blooms of var. *Pearl* could possibly be compared in shape to a small double polyantha-type rose. Tuberose is more likely a corruption of the word "tuberous" (tuber-like), referring to the plant's tuberous root-stock.

Poncirus trifoliata

(HARDY OR TRIFOLIATE ORANGE)
Family: Rutaceae
Hardy deciduous or semi-evergreen shrubs
Flowering period: Apr.–May
Height: up to 20 ft.
Position: sun or partial shade
Propagation: seed or cuttings
Cultivation easy
Fragrant
Zone 5 southwards

Poncirus trifoliata Rafin. (syn. *Aegle sepiaria* D. C., *Citrus trifoliata* L.) A monotypic genus from China and Korea of which the species *P. trifoliata* is the sole representative. The name *Poncirus* derives from the French *poncire*, a type of citrus. The plant is closely related to the orange; but it is hardy, easy to grow, and very attractive at all seasons because of its unusual and decorative features. It is one of those really complete plants, always beautiful and with many different practical uses.

Poncirus trifoliata is a large deciduous or semi-evergreen very spiny shrub; it is quite hardy, but whether it is deciduous or evergreen depends upon the severity of the winter weather. The leaves are few but attractive and are divided into 3–5 obovate segments, the central segment up to $2\frac{1}{2}$ ins. long, the others smaller. The white flowers appear in April–May (often on leafless stems) in the axils of the large spines, thus making it rather hazardous to enjoy the delightful lemon-scented fragrance at close quarters. The blooms are single, up to 2 ins. in diameter, with 4–5 obovate concave petals. The really formidable spines are 2 ins. long, stiff, straight, and sharply pointed. The fruits are produced in the greatest profusion in late summer and autumn; they are green at first, later becoming orange-yellow, with a diameter of 2 ins. These fruits are highly ornamental, frequently remaining on the plant until mid-winter. They closely resemble small oranges, but unfortunately they are useless for eating (although it is possible to make a palatable conserve by cooking the fruits with an equal amount of sugar). The plant makes an excellent defensive hedge through which no large animal can pass. Such a hedge will tolerate being cut to any size, although cutting or pruning deprives the plant of many of its flowers and fruits. Specimens left to develop naturally will form very large shrubs with a pleasing rounded symmetrical form up to 10 ft. or more in diameter and 15 ft. high, retaining their many interlaced crooked and angular branches down to ground level. The stems are smooth with a green bark, thus making the plant attractive even if it loses its foliage. In English and Continental gardens, plants frequently tolerate temperatures as low as 0°F. without injury.

As so often happens when a plant is easy to cultivate and easy to propagate from seed, it is often neglected, although *Poncirus trifoliata* deserves a place in every garden. That discerning authority, the late W. J. Bean, writing in his *Trees and Shrubs Hardy in the British Isles*, states that "this species is one of the most striking of all Chinese plants." It has certainly always given me the greatest satisfaction and I have obtained the best results when planting it in a hot sunny position; it is also successful in partial shade in the south. It will thrive in any soil that is fertile, well drained, and deep. The plant's only negative quality lies in its vicious spines which could make it dangerous for young children.

The ease with which *Poncirus trifoliata* can be propagated from seed sown in spring, and its hardiness, has resulted in it being used as a stock onto which choicer citrus plants can be successfully grafted. A hybrid between *Poncirus trifoliata* and the common orange resulted in a plant called the Citrange.

Poncirus trifoliata

Portulaca

(Sun Plant, Rose Moss, Wax Pink, or Sun Moss)
Family: Portulaceae
Tender fleshy-stemmed herbaceous perennials and annuals
Position: full sun
Propagation: seed or cuttings
Cultivation very easy

There are more than one hundred species of the genus *Portulaca* diffused throughout tropical, subtropical, and temperate climates. They are dwarf herbaceous perennials or annuals, often with a prostrate wide-spreading habit, with fleshy stems and foliage, and flowers that open only during sunny weather; a factor precluding, or at least reducing, their use as decorative garden plants in localities with dull, sunless weather. They are of the easiest cultivation, preferring a light, sandy, not-too-rich soil that is warm and well drained and a sunny open position; but they are not hardy.
Portulacas are excellent for seaside localities, where they can often be seen thriving almost on the beaches. Although they will thrive in the poorest soils (in the case of self-sown seedlings even among stones at the roadside), they respond to a moderate amount of fertilizer, particularly fertilizers rich in phosphorus, which induces more prolific and better-coloured flowers.
Only two species are normally found in gardens: *Portulaca grandiflora*, probably the most brilliantly coloured and most attractive of all dwarf prostrate annuals; and *Portulaca oleracea*, one of the most pernicious, fast-growing, invasive, odious weeds with which the gardener has to contend. It is native to the United States and fortunately a seasonable annual easily destroyed; it appears chiefly during the hot summer months and is especially troublesome in southern climates where it can be a menace. Even this obnoxious plant does, however, have certain uses. Its minute yellow flowers are insignificant, but observed impartially and objectively the small, obtuse, fleshy, opaque-red or reddish-green foliage is not unattractive, and with its vigorous, rapid growth the plant can be good for covering steep slopes, sand dunes, positions menaced with erosion, or used as a ground cover where there is insufficient soil depth for other plants. But it should never be allowed in the garden proper. In some countries selected forms of *Portulaca oleracea* (purslane) are relished in salads or cooked briefly in butter.
Portulaca grandiflora is native to Argentina and the more arid plains and open country in Brazil. In 1829, William J. Hooker, referring to

Double-flowered hybrid
Portulaca grandiflora

it in the *Botanical Magazine,* wrote that the plant was discovered in Argentina by Dr. Gillies in a light sandy soil in various areas between the Rio del Saladillo and the western frontier of the pampas; and at the foothills of the mountains in the vicinity of Mendoza. He described the western bank of the Rio Desaguardero, where the plants grew in great profusion, colouring the ground in a rich purple, with a splash of orange here and there provided by an orange-flowered variety that grew among the others.

Like gazanias, arctotis, and other plants found in warm climates growing in dry sandy soils, portulacas are ideal subjects for arid gardens either on the coast or inland. They can be used effectively in the rock-garden, for edging, for small beds, or as a ground cover among roses. But the brilliant colouring of the large flowers is seen to best effect when the plants are scattered here and there in groups of irregular size, preferably over an undulating or irregularly formed surface, when the splashes of scintillating hues look as if handfuls of precious gems had been strewn over the ground. The double- and giant-flowered forms are also excellent for large pots.

Cultivation. As cultivated in gardens, *Portulaca grandiflora* is an easily grown annual, although if left undisturbed under warm, favourable conditions, the plants may be perennial for limited periods. As clearly demonstrated by the self-sown seedlings which frequently appear, seed can be sown in autumn or spring in the positions where the plants are to bloom. In the north, however, it is better to sow only in spring when the soil begins to warm. To gain time in localities where spring is late, seed can be sown in a greenhouse or coldframe in February–March; pricking out the seedlings into boxes or small pots. At a temperature of about 60°F. germination takes place within 14–15 days. Planting out should be done in May, preferably in the evening, as portulacas are not always easy subjects to transplant, and if the weather is very sunny the young plants should be shaded for a day or so. Portulacas will not tolerate even the slightest frost.

(Garden Portulaca or Sun Moss)
Annual (in gardens)
Flowering period: June–Sept.
Height: prostrate to 2–3 ins.

Portulaca grandiflora Hook.
Native to Argentina and Brazil. A herbaceous perennial of short duration; in gardens normally grown as an annual. Forms a dwarf rather bushy plant up to 16 ins. wide. Stems and leaves fleshy and very sappy. Flowers of the original species orange or purple. Those cultivated in gardens are of hybrid origin, with flowers up to $1\frac{1}{2}$ ins. in diameter and with a colour range extending through every shade of yellow, white, pink, crimson, purple, orange, scarlet, apricot, etc., with mottled and striped flowers, single and double forms, and giant-flowered hybrids. It is not easy to purchase seed of individual

Portulaca grandiflora
From *The Botanical Register*,
1843, plate 34

varieties or colours and that which is offered is nearly always a mixture, but the following named varieties do exist:

    var. *albiflora,* pure white
    var. *bedmannii,* white striped purple
    var. *caryophyllus,* red striped white
    var. *splendens,* purple-red
    var. *tellusonii,* scarlet
    var. *sulphurea* and *thorburnii,* dark yellow

Since the plants so easily hybridize, it is not easy to produce seed true to colour or to raise named varieties. If it should be necessary to propagate any specially desired colour this can be done by means of cuttings; an easy matter as any young growth will rapidly root if placed in sand under a glass bell-jar or transparent plastic.

Portulaca oleracea L.

(Purslane or Pussley)
Annual
Flowering period: July–Sept.
Height: prostrate to 6 ins.

Native to the United States. A non-hardy annual with wide-spreading reddish fleshy stems and foliage. Leaves spatulate, up to 2 ins. long but very variable in size. Flowers minute, brilliant yellow. In gardens a dangerous and persistent weed, rapidly spreading from seed and by means of the nodes that root easily. The var. *sativa* is sometimes used in salads and is commonly called purslane or pussley.

Potentilla

(Cinquefoil)
Family: Rosaceae
Hardy herbaceous perennials or small deciduous shrubs
Position: sun or partial shade
Propagation: seed or division (herbaceous species); seed or cuttings (shrubby species)
Cultivation easy

Frequently one meets people with names extraordinarily inappropriate to their physical appearance and personality, such as a scrawny Hercules, an eighty-year-old Baby, or a deformed Angel. The same thing happens to many plants, since certain botanists often snatch at an obscure characteristic of a plant to provide its name. Such a situation occurred in the case of the name of the genus *Potentilla,* which to anyone unfamiliar with it would bring to mind a plant of large proportions—a powerful, potent plant should be indicated by the Latin word *potens.* Instead potentillas are delicate, graceful, modest little flowers occupying only a small space in our garden. Indeed, all the potency of potentillas lies in the medicinal virtues that the plant was believed to possess in ancient times.

Although not spectacular or gaudy, potentillas are extremely elegant and attractive, with an exceptionally long flowering period in the case of the shrubby types. When in bloom, potentilla flowers much resemble those of geum, and their brilliant colours, ease of cultivation, and adaptability make them ideal plants for beds, borders, and the rock-garden.

The genus comprises at least three hundred species, of which the majority are hardy herbaceous perennials; while there is also a good proportion of small hardy deciduous shrubs. The genus is native to China, the Himalayas, Siberia, and Europe. Relatively few of the plants are of garden value, although those that are used include some of our most esteemed plants. Their foliage and flowers have often been likened to those of the strawberry. All the blooms are small, with some shade of yellow as the dominant colour, although there are also plenty of scarlets, pinks, and reds. The leaves are divided into three or five segments, and their characteristic shape is used frequently in heraldry. The fruits are small dry achenes (a thin-walled dry fruit that does not split open when ripe).

As already mentioned, potentillas once had considerable medicinal importance. An infusion of the leaves of *Potentilla anserina* was used as a tonic, while an extract prepared from the roots of *Potentilla x Tormentilla-formosa* was at one time considered to be one of the finest astringents, and was even used to combat cholera. A lotion from the same species was used in the treatment of ulcers, and an infusion made from the leaves of *Potentilla reptans* was used as an astringent and febrifuge.

Cultivation. Potentillas are easy to cultivate. They need a cool, deep, moderately moist soil, either acid or alkaline (calcareous). In the south they thrive in full sun or partial shade, while in the north they should only be planted in open sunny positions. The shrubby types are more tolerant of dry conditions than the herbaceous varieties.

Propagation of the herbaceous types is by division in autumn or spring; or, in the case of the species, from seed sown in spring, either outside or in pots or frames. The shrubby species can also be propagated in spring from seed sown in pots in coldframes or in an unheated greenhouse. The shrubby species and varieties can also be propagated from cuttings of half-ripened wood taken in July–August and inserted in sandy soil in frames.

Potentilla fruticosa

Potentilla atrosanguinea Wall.
Native to the Himalayas. A hardy herbaceous perennial and principal parent of the best of our modern herbaceous potentillas. Leaves similar to those of a strawberry plant, large, trifoliate, deeply dentated, dark green, up to $4\frac{1}{2}$ ins. long, with the three segments widely spaced. The foliage is abundant at the base of the plant and on the

Herbaceous perennial
Flowering period: June–Aug.
Height: up to 2 ft.

flower stems. The original species has single reddish-purple 1-in.-wide flowers with the appearance of a minute single rose. The petals are close together and even overlapping. The flowers are borne in terminal clusters on the central flower stem and also at the ends of the lateral shoots. Some of the best varieties are given below. All have a flowering period from June to August and have an average height of $1\frac{3}{4}$ to 2 ft.

> var. *aurea plena,* yellow, double
> var. *California,* semi-double, golden-yellow
> var. *Etna,* a compact variety only 18 ins. high, with silver-green leaves and dark-crimson flowers
> var. *Gibson's Scarlet,* the most popular, with single blood-red flowers
> var. *Mons. Rouillard,* crimson-red, double, marked with orange
> var. *Wm. Rollisson,* vermilion and yellow, semi-double
> var. *Yellow Queen,* vivid yellow, single

Deciduous shrub
Flowering period: June–Sept.
Height: up to 18 ins.
Zone 2 southwards

Potentilla x *davurica* Nestler (syn. *Potentilla glabra*)

Native to China and Siberia. Introduced in 1822. A hardy dwarf deciduous shrub of very compact habit, often wider than it is high. Branches slender, graceful, and semi-pendulous. Leaves 1 in. long, oval, pointed, glabrous, composed of 5 ovate leaflets. Flowers single, white, $1\frac{1}{4}$ ins. wide, solitary, and very similar to a strawberry flower. When in bloom the plant is most pleasing and is a valuable small shrub for the rock-garden, for small beds, for edging, etc. Of slow growth and prefers a warm dry position.

Deciduous shrub
Flowering period: May–Sept.
Height: up to $2\frac{1}{2}$–3 ft.
Zone 2 southwards

Potentilla *fruticosa* L.

Native to Northern Europe, northern Asia, and North America. A very hardy deciduous shrub of erect habit up to about 3 ft. high, although several of its many forms and varieties are more dwarf. It is a moderately fast-growing compact plant, much-branched and with a rounded form. In the case of young plants, the width is often greater than the height. Bark a conspicuous light reddish brown. Leaves pinnate, divided into five segments; entire leaf up to $1\frac{1}{2}$ ins. long, but often much smaller. Leaflets linear, up to 1 in. long, pointed. Flowers single, vivid yellow, 1–$1\frac{1}{2}$ ins. in diameter. *Potentilla fruticosa* and its varieties are beautiful little shrubs with a flowering period rarely equalled by any other shrub. They begin to produce their profusion of attractive little blooms in late May and remain in bloom until September, thus providing colour when few other shrubs are in flower. They are of the easiest cultivation and prefer an open sunny position. Some of the best forms and varieties are given below:

> var. *beesii* (syn. *Potentilla nana argentea*), golden flowers and silver foliage, 18 ins.

Potentilla reptans
From *Paxton's Magazine of Botany*,
1839, plate 149

    var. *Elizabeth,* a dome-shaped bush 2½ ft. high, which from late spring to autumn is covered with canary-yellow flowers
    var. *farreri,* height 2 ft., of spreading habit, with large yellow flowers. One of the best varieties
    var. *friedrichensii* (syn. *Potentilla friedrichensii*), of German origin *(Potentilla fruticosa* x *Potentilla* x *davurica),* pale-yellow flowers and grey-green foliage, 6 ft.
    var. *Katherine Dykes,* height 4½ ft., primrose-yellow flowers
    var. *Longacre,* a dense mat-forming dwarf variety with yellow flowers
    var. *mandshurica,* height 12–15 ins., spreading habit, with grey-green foliage, purple-barked stems, and white flowers
    var. *Tangerine,* height 16 ins. with copper-orange blooms

Herbaceous perennial
Flowering period: June–Aug.
Height: up to 2 ft.

Potentilla nepalensis Hook. (syn. *Potentilla formosa*)
Native to the Himalayas. In general appearance similar to *Potentilla atrosanguinea* but with glaucous-green foliage and a more open spreading habit. Brilliant cherry-red flowers from June to August on graceful branching stems. The var. *Miss Willmot* is particularly attractive, only 9 ins. high with vivid carmine flowers; while the var. *Roxana,* 18 ins. high, has orange-red blooms.

Herbaceous perennial
Flowering period: July–Aug.
Height: 2–3 ins.

Potentilla nitida L.
Native to Europe. A beautiful little herbaceous species with minute silvery foliage which forms a spreading cushion of attractive vegetation. Ideal for the rock-garden. Requires a dry sunny position in a well-drained light soil; completely hardy. Flowers pale pink throughout the summer, each bloom ⅔ in. in diameter.

Herbaceous perennial
Flowering period: June–July
Height: 1½–2 ft.

Potentilla recta L.
Native to Europe. A hardy herbaceous perennial with the typical large potentilla foliage, very abundant and dark green both at the base of the plant and on the flower stems. The latter are very stiff, large, rigid, and much-branched. Inflorescence a terminal spray composed of yellow flowers 1 in. wide. The var. *sulphurea* has paler flowers and the var. *warrenii* is darker yellow.

Herbaceous perennial
Flowering period: June–Aug.
Height: 1½–2 ins.

Potentilla reptans L.
Native to Europe. Prostrate, mat-forming hardy herbaceous perennial. Height 1½–2 ins., but even less in dry sunny positions. Can be invasive, spreading rapidly by its creeping stolons which travel great distances and root into the soil at every node to form new plants. It is, however, attractive, with palmate leaves 1 in. wide, each of the five lobes deeply dentated and vivid green. Flowers rich yellow, single, ¾ in. wide.

Primula

(Primrose, Auricula, Cowslip, Oxlip, or Polyanthus)
Family: Primulaceae
Tender or hardy herbaceous perennials or annuals
Position: partial shade (may take full sun at high altitudes or in northern climates)
Propagation: seed or division
Cultivation easy
In some cases fragrant

Were I a Medieval knight I would have blazoned on my standard, my shield, and my sword a line of Robert Frost: "Slave to a springtime passion for the earth"; but thank heaven knights errant no longer exist. This great passion is always with me at every season, but it is particularly strong in spring. Every year, while streams and brooks run with newly thawed icy water, and while there are still patches of snow here and there on the grass, fields of yellow flowers carpet the banks of torrents cut into the hillsides, appear in scattered groups on mountain slopes, and illuminate the grassy banks and woodland thickets along the roadside—these splashes of yellow are the first blooms of *Primula vulgaris,* the common primrose. Very soon afterwards, or possibly at the same time, other species appear in rapid succession; *Primula veris,* the Cowslip, and *Primula elatior,* the Oxlip. A little later, and a bit further afield, on higher ground and in sunless corners where winter still lingers, we find the real jewels of the genus: *Primula glutinosa, Primula farinosa, Primula minima, Primula allionii, Primula palinuri.* These are secret little plants, hidden in rocky crevices, in shady valleys, relatively rare, a glimpse of which well merits hours of walking. We also must not forget *Primula Auricula.* Nowadays it is mainly grown by the enthusiast but last century it was extensively cultivated in every English garden. It was one of the most interesting and popular pot plants of Victorian times, generally finding a place of honour on the windowsill of even the humblest house or cottage. Just as other plants—such as dianthus with its many types and forms—are employed for diverse purposes, so can primulas be utilized in many different ways; for the rock-garden, for naturalizing in meadow or parkland, in the bog-garden, for beds and borders, as ground cover in woods, and even in the greenhouse—which is only a stepping-stone to their use as house plants (a purpose for which *Primula obconica* in particular is grown by the thousands on a commercial scale).

The garden cultivation of primulas started at an early date, initially by transferring a few wild plants dug up from the local countryside to the garden. Their alleged medicinal properties also provided an

Primula bulleyana

ulterior motive for bringing them into the home, especially in the case of *Primula veris*. John Parkinson wrote that if the sap of the plant was rubbed on the face it would remove blemishes, and that it was an excellent cure for headaches—a belief also held by other writers. There is a small volume published in 1768 at Leghorn entitled *Virtù della Brettonica* (Virtues of the Brettonica)—Brettonica being one of the common names by which *Primula veris* was known—in which are enumerated the many supposed curative virtues of this plant: to stop weeping, to dissolve gallstones, for soothing red eyes, for curing ear-aches and stomach-aches, for use in alleviating high fever, for eliminating painful coughs and aiding breathing, for healing wounds and broken heads, and for defective eyesight; thus confirming the old French saying: "Qui a du bugle et du sanicle fait au chirurgien le nicle" ("He who possesses ajugas and primulas has no need of a doctor"). In 1812, Thomas Hill in his *Family Herbal* maintained that if the juice was snuffed up through the nostrils it would cure headaches. In ancient days, the roots and leaves of *Primula vulgaris* were used as an astringent, antispasmodic, and vermifuge. It was also considered important in the treatment of muscular rheumatism, paralysis, and gout, but is now rarely used. Primulas are not poisonous plants; on the contrary, certain country people in Europe eat the young leaves of *Primula vulgaris* in salads. However, a good many people are strongly allergic to an oil contained in many of the primulas, particularly *Primula obconica,* the leaves of which can cause hives, erythema, and inflammation of the eyes; such sufferers are advised to use gloves when handling the plants.

Various species of primula were already well known at the beginning of the eighteenth century, but their real exploitation as flowering plants for the garden did not begin until the beginning of the nineteenth century, with the importation of exotic Asian species. The British were the main importers, growers, and subsequent distributors, since the English climate and countryside, with its cool, fresh meadow lands and frequent fogs and mists, is particularly adapted to the cultural requirements of these plants. The abundance of water in rivers, streams, canals, and ponds also favours the cultivation of those species whose native habitat is the edge of swamps or marshes; while the peaty soil of many English localities is ideal since relatively few species are tolerant of an alkaline (calcareous) soil. In dry, southern climates primula cultivation is much more difficult, while the alpine species rarely take to hot, arid soils and climates.

Before considering the cultivation of primulas in detail, a few words concerning their fragrance should be set forth. *Primula veris* has an apple-like perfume—some say apricot-like—which is enhanced in certain hybrids. The *Colossal* and *Giant* strains of polyanthus may or may not have scent, but the blue- and red-flowered varieties are the least scented. *Primula vulgaris* is slightly fragrant, and some

Primula elatior

Primula palinuri
From *Curtis's Botanical Magazine*,
1835, plate 3414

Primula marginata

Primula japonica

perfume can be noted in the species *P. auriculata, P. involucrata, P. marginata, P. alpicola, P. viscosa, P. helodoxa,* and *P. bulleyana.* The flowers of *Primula sikkimensis* and *Primula florindae* have quite a strong fruity perfume.

Primula is a vast genus, with four to five hundred species, according to the opinions of various botanists. They are mostly plants from cold and temperate climates of the Northern Hemisphere, although with such a large genus there are, of course, exceptions, including *Primula magellanica* from South America, a couple of species found in Java, and a few found in mountainous regions in Africa. Their real home, however, is the Orient. In the Himalayas alone there are about eighty species, while a good half the total known number of Oriental species are native to Japan and China. Some primulas are found almost at sea level, such as the Italian *Primula palinuri,* found at Salerno, but they are much more frequently indigenous to hills and mountains, even up to altitudes of 10,000 ft.

Cultivation. The cultivation of primulas calls for enthusiasm and patience, but even those virtues will not prevail in excessively hot, dry, arid climates, or in excessively alkaline (calcareous) soils. Primulas are, however, easy to grow when the conditions are to their liking. Taking all such considerations into account, probably the easiest is *Primula obconica*—if one has a greenhouse or lives in a frost-free locality. In general, primulas prefer a neutral or slightly acid soil, and it is always easier to add lime than it is to eliminate it. The plants like a damp, humid atmosphere which is never stagnant. Except in the cases of bog-loving species, they require a well-drained porous soil which is also moist. In the majority of cases they prefer partial shade.

With such a vast, varied, and cosmopolitan genus it is not possible to generalize about propagation, although certain broad principles can be defined. Where necessary, more detailed particulars are given for the individual species. Practically all hardy primulas can be easily propagated from seed sown in spring, summer, or autumn in pots, flats, or pans of light soil composed of equal proportions of peat, leafsoil, and sand. The seeds are very fine and the soil should be passed through a small-mesh sieve. Gently press the seed into the soil and cover with a dusting of the same compost, more finely sifted, or with a dusting of very finely powdered sphagnum moss. The pots can be placed in an unheated greenhouse or coldframe. Germination can vary from 15–20 days to nearly a year, according to the species and the freshness of the seed. Some of the alpine species will not germinate unless the seed has been exposed to several weeks of winter frost. During this waiting period the pots should be kept shaded and moderately moist. The seedlings can be pricked out into pans, flats, or boxes, and should be replanted into larger boxes or potted or planted out into nursery beds until large enough for permanent planting. Seed of the non-hardy species is generally sown between June and July in a warm greenhouse and the seedlings grown on in pots. Hardy primulas can also be easily propagated by division, a much quicker method but one which produces fewer new plants. This can be done in late summer or autumn, or even in early spring, but spring division may spoil the flowering period. *Primula denticulata* and its varieties can also be propagated by means of root cuttings at almost any time except winter. At all times care must be taken that the young plants are not attacked by slugs or snails, two pests which have a great liking for primulas.

Primula acaulis (see *Primula vulgaris*)

Primula aurantiaca W.W. Sm.

Hardy perennial
Flowering period: June–July
Height: 12 ins.

Native to the Yunnan province of China. Height up to 12 ins., foliage basal, rosette-forming, large, oblong, dentated. Flowers small but of a marvellous golden-red, $\frac{1}{2}$ in. long, in terminal whorls. The leaf stalks are winged and the entire leaf is up to 8 ins. long.

Primula Auricula L.

(Auricula)
Hardy perennial
Flowering period: Apr.–May
Height: up to 8 ins.

Native to mountainous areas of Central and Southern Europe up to an altitude of 6,000 ft., among alkaline (calcareous) rocks. A dwarf species 6–8 ins. high with rather fleshy, ovate or nearly rounded, slightly dentated evergreen leaves, 2–4 ins. long; more or less covered with a white powdery bloom on the surface. Inflorescence an umbel bearing up to twenty dark-yellow flowers. There are numerous beautiful hybrids such as:

> Jean Walker, mauve flowers with cream-coloured eyes, 6–8 ins. high, fragrant
> Blue Velvet, dark velvet-blue with white eye, 4 ins. high
> Dusty Miller, strongly scented yellow flowers, foliage almost white with a farinose surface, 6 ins.
> Red Dusty Miller, identical to the preceding but with red flowers

These lovely auriculas require an alkaline (calcareous) soil which is heavy rather than light, but well-drained. Although hardy, they are liable to suffer from stagnant water which may collect around the collar of the plant when there is a sudden thaw. They also dislike abrupt changes of temperature and hot or dry wind. In their native habitat the original species are protected by a deep covering of winter snow. Choice varieties give better results when grown in pots and over-wintered in coldframes or in an unheated greenhouse; but at all times these require abundant ventilation and, during the summer, shading from strong sunlight unless grown at high altitudes. They want only moderate watering when the soil is really dry or when the

Primula Auricula

foliage begins to show signs of drooping. Repotting is necessary every 2–3 years and should be done in spring after flowering; during the other years an annual top dressing is sufficient in early spring. Propagation is by division, and the best time is late summer, although in a mild climate it can be postponed until autumn. If seedlings are required in spring, seed should be sown during December–March. Otherwise seed can be sown at any time between April and July, when the seed will probably not germinate until the following season, although germination can be erratic and may take place within 15–20 days. In all cases the seed should be sown in pots, pans or flats, outside, or in an unheated, shaded greenhouse. The first flowering is in April–May, but the plants generally bloom again in early autumn.

Hardy perennial
Flowering period: May–June
Height: up to 6 ins.

Primula auriculata Lam.
Native to Asia Minor and Iran. Leaves evergreen, glabrous, lanceolate, 5–6 ins. long. Inflorescence an umbel bearing numerous individual reddish-purple flowers, $\frac{3}{4}$–1 in. wide.

Hardy perennial
Flowering period: May-June
Height: up to 2 ft.

Primula beesiana Forr.
Native to China. A very vigorous large-growing species with basal, obovate, 6-in.-long, rosette-forming foliage. Flowers borne in whorls, one above another, on tall rigid stems up to 2 ft. high; velvet-textured and a fine shade of purple-red. Requires a very damp soil and is ideal for planting near a stream or pond.

Hardy perennial
Flowering period: May–June
Height: up to 2½ ft.

Primula bulleyana Forr.
Native to China. A large, vigorous, hardy herbaceous perennial with big basal leaves forming a dense mass of vegetation. The leaves are ovate, dentated, and thick-textured. One of the best species for naturalizing. Inflorescence composed of whorls of orange- and apricot-coloured flowers on tall erect stems, scented. Has been crossed with *Primula beesiana* to produce a strain of variously coloured hybrids.

Primula cachmiriana (see *Primula denticulata* var. *cachmiriana*)

Herbaceous perennial
Flowering period: Apr.–May
Height: up to 18 ins.

Primula capitata Hook.
Native to the Himalayas. Of rigid habit with basal widely lanceolate dentated leaves up to 5 ins. long with the undersurface greyish. A beautiful species with the inflorescence in the form of a globose head composed of minute violet-coloured flowers with silver-white calyces and borne in a compact flattish mass at the tops of slender erect stems covered with a white farinose powder.

Primula chionantha Balf. f. & Farr.
Native to China. Foliage oblong-lanceolate, up to 10 ins. long, tapering towards the base, winged leaf stalk; undersurface of foliage covered with a yellowish powder. Inflorescence an umbel bearing white 1-in.-wide scented flowers on a slender 18-in.-high stem.

Hardy perennial
Flowering period: May–June
Height: up to 18 ins.

Primula clusiana Tausch.
Native to the Austrian Alps. A dwarf alpine species with shiny elongated-oval pointed leaves, 2–3 ins. long; basal, rosette-forming. Flowers lilac-pink with a white eye, borne in clusters of 2–6 in umbels.

Hardy perennial
Flowering period: April
Height: 6 ins.

Primula cortusoides L.
Native to western Siberia. Leaves form a basal rosette, soft-textured, ovate or heart-shaped with ruffled edges, dark green, lobed, up to 4 ins. long. Inflorescence a terminal cyme of semi-pendulous wine-red flowers carried on slender stems 10–12 ins. high.

Hardy perennial
Flowering period: May–June
Height: up to 12 ins.

Primula denticulata W.W. Sm.
Native to the Himalayas. One of the most widely cultivated and most beautiful of all the hardy primulas; conspicuous for the unusual shape of its inflorescences. Of the easiest cultivation in a semi-shady, moist position. The oblong light-green dentated leaves are covered with a white mealy powder; they are up to 5 ins. long and form a large basal rosette of vegetation. From the centre of this rise vigorous erect flower stems about 1 ft. high, bearing inflorescences in the form of globose balls up to 2 ins. in diameter composed of a great number of small individual flowers closely packed together in an umbel. Colour variable, from lavender to purple or purple-crimson. The plants are easily propagated from seed, but to perpetuate the colour of the most desirable forms, propagation should be by division or from root cuttings. Some of the best varieties are:

Hardy perennial
Flowering period: May
Height: up to 15 ins.

    var. *alba*, white
    var. *Bengal Rose*, ruby-red
    var. *cachmiriana*, purple
    var. *Prichard's Ruby*, ruby-red
    var. *rubra*, magenta-red

Primula denticulata

Primula elatior Hill
Native to Europe, the Caucasus, and Iran. A common European species similar to *Primula veris* but with larger flowers. Leaves 2–4 ins. long with the shape and size of the common yellow primrose; inflorescence an umbel composed of numerous pendulous yellow or orange-red flowers on stems 6–8 ins. high. This species, together with *Primula veris* and *Primula vulgaris,* has produced the modern race of superb, large, and vividly coloured Polyanthus-type garden primulas. These are among the most robust of all primulas, ideal for beds, bor-

(Oxlip)
Hardy perennial
Flowering period: Apr.–May
Height: up to 8 ins.

Primula cortusoides
From *Curtis's Botanical Magazine*,
1798, plate 399

ders, window boxes, etc. They produce an abundance of flowers in early spring and often continue to bloom until early summer; they are also of the easiest cultivation, will tolerate a drier soil than the majority of primulas, and can be propagated by division in July. Propagation can also be effected from seed sown in July–August, outside in seed beds or in frames. The individual blooms are often 2 ins. in diameter and are borne many together in large globose masses at the ends of erect vigorous stems up to 10 ins. high. The colour range includes shades of white, cream, yellow, pink, crimson, and many gradations of blue. A particularly beautiful variety is var. *Garryarde Guinevere* with purple foliage and pink flowers.

Primula farinosa L. (Bird's Eye Primrose)
Native to Europe, including Great Britain, where it is known as Bird's Eye Primula because the minute flowers resemble a bird's eye. Leaves up to 6 ins. long, white on the undersurface and dusted with a farinose powder, broadly lanceolate, basal. Inflorescence an umbel bearing many individual flowers, $\frac{1}{3}$ in. in diameter, pinkish purple with a white or pale-yellow eye.

Hardy perennial
Flowering period: May–June
Height: up to 9 ins.

Primula florindae Kingd.-Ward
Native to Tibet. One of the largest species of the genus with a height of up to 3–4 ft. when in bloom. Discovered by the famous botanical explorer Captain Kingdon-Ward and named in honour of his wife. A truly noble plant with broadly heart-shaped foliage up to 8 ins. wide. Habit robust and vigorous but requires a very wet soil, even thriving in shallow water. Tall erect flower stems bearing clusters of sulphur-yellow, powdery, fragrant pendulous flowers.

Hardy perennial
Flowering period: June–July
Height: up to 4 ft.
Scented

Primula frondosa Janka.
Native to Bulgaria. A beautiful little species of robust and vigorous habit and very easy to grow; excellent for naturalizing. Height up to 5 ins., leaves basal, thin-textured, obovate, dentated, undersurface white mealy powdered. The masses of minute lilac-pink flowers have yellow eyes and are borne on miniature branching stems.

Hardy perennial
Flowering period: Apr.–May
Height: 5 ins.

Primula helodoxa Forr.
Native to Burma and the Yunnan province of China. A vigorous species requiring very wet soil. Large basal leaves, dentated, long and narrow, pointed. Whorls of golden-yellow semi-pendulous flowers in tiers on rigid stems.

Hardy perennial
Flowering period: June–July
Height: up to 2 ft.

Primula japonica A. Gray
Native to Japan. One of the most beautiful of the Candelabra group of primulas, with tall erect rigid flower stems up to $2\frac{1}{2}$ ft. high bearing a candelabrum-like inflorescence made up of layers or tiers of large

Hardy perennial
Flowering period: May–July
Height: up to $2\frac{1}{2}$ ft.

flowers in whorls. Colour variable from white to pink and reddish purple. Forms a basal mass of large, dentated, widely lanceolate, light-green leaves up to 6 ins. long. One of the best for naturalizing, but requires a moist soil. Has produced many lovely hybrids such as:

> Millar's Crimson, crimson-purple
> Postford White, ivory-white
> Splendens, crimson-red

Hardy perennial
Flowering period: Feb.–Mar.
Height: 3 ins.

Primula juliae Kusnez.
Native to the Caucasus. Very early-flowering and, together with its numerous hybrids, is a lovely subject for cultivating in pots in cold-frames or an unheated greenhouse, where it will begin to bloom in December–January. Height 3 ins., leaves small, dark green, forming a dense prostrate mat of vegetation which makes a perfect background to the profusion of lilac-purple flowers borne on minute stems. Some of the best hybrids are:

> Alba, white, 4 ins.
> Betty Green, crimson, 6 ins.
> Dorothy, pale yellow, 4 ins.
> E. R. Janes, cherry-red, 4 ins.
> Jewel, one of the most beautiful with large crimson-purple flowers, 4 ins.
> Kinlough Beauty, lilac-mauve, 3 ins.
> Pam, red, 4 ins.
> Wanda, purple-red, $4\frac{1}{2}$ ins.

(Fairy Primrose)
Non-hardy perennial
generally grown as an annual
Flowering period: Jan.–Apr.
Height: up to 18 ins.
Scented

Primula malacoides Franch.
Native to China. A non-hardy species generally grown in pots as an annual for indoor use. Known as the Fairy Primrose because of the light, airy, graceful appearance of both foliage and flowers. The plants form a compact basal mass of thin-textured, pale green, ovate, pointed, deeply dentated foliage with ruffled edges. Inflorescence a loose, open umbel borne on a graceful slender stem up to 18 ins. high. Individual flowers arranged in whorls and very numerous, $\frac{1}{2}$ in. in diameter, pale lavender, and delicately perfumed. A well-grown plant will simultaneously produce a number of these elegant flower stems. The many hybrids have extended the range of tints to other colours and some of the best are:

> Cherry Glow, cherry-red
> Fimbriata, mauve-pink with fringed petals
> Rosea, pink
> Royal Rose, carmine-pink
> Snow Queen, white
> Tyrian Rose, deep pink

Primula malacoides

Propagation is by means of seed sown in a warm greenhouse in May–

June. The seedlings can be pricked out into boxes or trays and subsequently potted into small individual pots, with periodic repotting until they reach their flowering size. They are not hardy, but they are not tropical plants and should be kept outside in frames while the weather is mild.

Primula marginata Curt.
Native to the Alps and other mountainous districts of Europe. A hardy evergreen species. Leaves up to 4 ins. long, rosette-forming, and very attractive with their silver-white margins, oblong in shape and often covered with a white mealy powder. Inflorescence an umbel bearing several slightly scented lavender-blue flowers 1 in. in diameter. The var. *Linder Pope* has larger violet blooms and wider foliage.

Hardy perennial
Flowering period: May
Height: 4–5 ins.

Primula obconica Hance.
Native to China. A non-hardy species generally grown in pots as an annual, but it can also be used for bedding purposes during the summer and autumn as it is a robust, vigorous plant. When handling this species for the first time great care should be taken to determine if one is subject to the painful and even dangerous skin irritation produced by contact with the leaves. Most people are naturally immune, but others are susceptible to a toxic substance secreted by the leaf hairs. Leaves ovate-oblong, up to 6 ins. in diameter, dark green, and frequently with ruffled edges. Inflorescence a large umbel up to 7 ins. in diameter borne on a rigid stem 6–8 ins. tall, well above the foliage, giving the entire plant a height of up to about 1 ft. in the case of well-developed specimens, which can bear several flower stems. Each of the large globose umbels is composed of numerous loosely arranged individual flowers each up to 2 ins. in diameter, reddish pink in colour. The numerous hybrid forms have, however, extended the colour range to white, pale pink, crimson-mauve, and purple. Some of the best are:

Non-hardy perennial generally grown as an annual
Flowering period: Jan.–Apr.
Height: up to 12 ins.

 Alba, white
 Appleblossom, flowers pale pink at first, changing to dark pink
 Atrosanguinea, dark red
 Peach Blossom, orange-salmon
 Salmon Pink, pink
 True Blue, lavender-blue

Propagation is by means of seed sown in a greenhouse in June–July. The seedlings can be pricked out into flats, boxes, or trays and subsequently potted into small individual pots, with periodic reporting. When they reach their flowering size, periodic applications of liquid organic fertilizer should be given. Although not hardy, the plants resent being coddled and throughout their development they should be kept outside in coldframes while the weather remains mild.

Primula obconica

Hardy perennial
Flowering period: Mar.–Apr.
Height: up to 5 ins.

Primula palinuri Petagna.
Native to Southern Italy. A very beautiful, almost prostrate, rosette-forming evergreen species of spreading habit. Found growing among the coastal rocks and cliffs at an altitude of about 600 ft. immediately above the sea coast. It is closely related to *Primula Auricula,* but with larger dentated foliage, up to 6 ins. long and 3 ins. wide, ovate. Inflorescence a many-flowered umbel bearing a cluster of semi-pendulous yellow flowers on a rigid stem.

Hardy perennial
Flowering period: June–Aug.
Height: 10–12 ins.

Primula parryi Gray
Native to the Rocky Mountains. Leaves elongated-oblong, up to 8 ins. in length, tapering at the base, and with winged stalks. Free-flowering, the inflorescence an umbel bearing blooms 1 in. in diameter, purple with a yellow centre.

(Polyanthus)
Hardy perennial
Flowering period: Apr.–May
Height: up to 12 ins.

Primula Polyantha
A name used to include a group of hybrid primulas mostly derived from crosses between the species *P. elatior*, *P. veris*, and *P. vulgaris*, producing the popular garden Polyanthus, here described under *Primula elatior.*

Hardy perennial
Flowering period: May–July
Height: up to 3 ft.

Primula pulverulenta Duthie
Native to China. One of the best of the Chinese species for garden cultivation and a plant of great beauty. The basal rosette of vegetation is composed of narrow 12-in.-long leaves (even larger in some cases) with dentated margins. Flower stems up to 3 ft. high, covered with white powder, bearing inflorescences in the form of successive whorls of semi-pendulous bell-shaped flowers, wine-red in colour with a darker eye. Has produced many lovely hybrids such as:

   Aileen Aroon, vivid red
   Bartley Strain, with flowers in shades of pink
   Lady Thursby, pink with yellow eye
   Red Hugh, crimson

Hardy perennial
Flowering period: March
Height: 3–4 ins.

Primula rosea Royle
Native to the Himalayas. One of the smallest but most vividly coloured and attractive species, which in March or April provides splashes of intense colour with its bright pink flowers borne several together in loosely formed umbels. The small slightly dentated smooth leaves have a reddish tint when young. Requires a very damp position. A curious characteristic of the plant is the rapidity with which the seeds ripen, a matter of only a few weeks after flowering has finished.

Hardy perennial
Flowering period: May–June
Height: up to 8 ins.

Primula secundiflora Franch.
Native to China. Leaves 2–3 ins. long, obovate, covered with white bloom and dusted with a white floury powder on their undersurface

when young. Flowers in umbels, dark violet-purple, $\frac{3}{4}$ in. wide, and borne as a one-sided inflorescence.

Primula sieboldii Morr.
Native to Japan. An unusual species with basal foliage in the form of a loose, open rosette. The leaves are heart-shaped, up to 3 ins. in diameter, dark green, soft-textured, and completely covered with minute hairs. Inflorescences borne on erect slender stems in the form of many-flowered umbels composed of small lilac or purple-pink fragrant flowers with dentated petals. There are numerous hybrids:

Hardy perennial
Flowering period: May–June
Height: up to 9 ins.

    Alba, white
    Croix de Malte, blue
    Elsie Berger, dark pink
    Queen Victoria, white with reverse of petals lavender
    Rosea-alba, pinkish white

Primula sikkimensis Hook.
Native to Burma, Sikkim, Tibet, Bhutan, Nepal, and the Yunnan province of China. In its native habitat can be found growing in vast extensive masses at a height of 15,000 ft., always in very damp positions. An excellent garden plant of easy cultivation, with fragrant, bell-shaped, pendulous yellow blooms borne in clusters at the top of rigid erect stems. The basal foliage forms a compact rosette with oblong erect leaves, 5 ins. long, 2 ins. wide, which are of real ornamental value.

Hardy perennial
Flowering period: May–June
Height: up to 2 ft.

Primula sinensis Sabine (syn. *Primula chinensis, Primula stellata*)
Native to China. A non-hardy species generally grown in pots as an annual. Forms a basal mass of large, dark-green, thick-textured, lobed, dentated, hairy, rounded leaves from among which rise strong, rigid flower stems 8–10 ins. high. Each stem bears an inflorescence in the form of a series of whorls, one above the other, composed of numerous individual star-like flowers up to $1\frac{1}{2}$ ins. in diameter. The original species is pale pink but the garden varieties are in a wide range of beautiful shades, some of the best of which are:

(Chinese Primrose)
Non-hardy perennial generally grown as an annual
Flowering period: Jan.–Apr.
Height: up to 10 ins.

    var. *Alba,* white
    var. *Dazzler,* orange-scarlet
    var. *Pink Beauty,* pink
    var. *Royal Blue,* dark blue
    var. *Ruby Queen,* dark red

Propagation is by seed sown in a warm greenhouse in May. The seedlings can be pricked out into boxes, or trays, and later potted into small individual pots, with periodic repottings until they reach their flowering size. Although they are not hardy, they should not be coddled, and, once potted, they should be grown outside in frames, while the weather remains mild.

Primula stellata (see *Primula sinensis*)

Hardy perennial
Flowering period: May
Height: up to 12 ins.

Primula veitchii Duthie (syn. *Primula polyneura*)
Native to China. Foliage rounded, 4 ins. in diameter, long-stalked, conspicuously silver-white on the undersurface. Pinkish-red flowers freely produced in umbels on slender stems about 9–10 ins. high.

(Cowslip)
Hardy perennial
Flowering period: Apr.–May
Height: up to 8 ins.

Primula veris L. (syn. *Primula officinalis*)
Native to Western Europe and Western Asia. A dwarf species abundant in cool, fresh meadows and thin woodlands. The foliage forms a basal rosette of rugose ovate leaves. Inflorescence an umbel bearing many small semi-pendulous orange or yellow fragrant flowers on stems 6–7 ins. high. Excellent for naturalizing.

Hardy perennial
Flowering period: May–June
Height: up to 8 ins.

Primula viscosa All. (syn. *Primula latifolia*)
Native to the mountainous regions of Europe. A very hardy evergreen species. Prostrate, mat-forming habit with small yellowish-green oval foliage. Inflorescence an umbel of violet-red flowers $\frac{1}{2}$ in. in diameter, lightly fragrant. The entire plant has a slightly sticky surface and the leaves emit an unpleasant odour when crushed.

(Common or English Primrose)
Hardy perennial
Flowering period: Feb.–May
Height: up to 6 ins.

Primula vulgaris Huds. (syn. *Primula acaulis*)
Native to Europe. One of the best known of all wild flowers and held in affection by flower-lovers in Western and Southern Europe for its welcome carpet of yellow bloom in early spring, often in February if the weather is mild. Forms an almost prostrate mass of dark-green rugose leaves. When in bloom the plants have a height of up to 4–5 ins. A magnificent subject for naturalizing in shady or semi-shady positions. A hardy herbaceous perennial with leaf and flower stalks produced from a central point just below ground level, and with pale-yellow, solitary flowers. Botanically there are two distinct types, each with its reproductive organs arranged in a different manner to make more certain the necessary cross-pollination by as many different types of insect as possible. Unfortunately, however, this rarely occurs and relatively few plants produce seeds because there are not many pollinating insects in circulation so early in the season. The plants also reproduce and multiply by natural division. This failure to produce seeds is mentioned by Shakespeare in *The Winter's Tale* (Act IV, scene 4):

Primula vulgaris

> Pale primroses,
> That die unmarried, ere they can behold
> Bright Phoebus in his strength, a malady
> Most incident to maids.

The common primrose is the parent of many beautiful garden hybrids, both single- and double-flowered, with a wide range of colours.

>Alba Plena, double white, 4 ins.
>Bon Accord Gem, double lilac-pink, 4 ins.
>Blue Queen, various shades of blue, 4 ins.
>Garryarde Victory, wine flowers with reddish-green leaves, 4 ins.
>Lilacina Plena, double lavender, 4 ins.
>Marie Crousse, reddish mauve with petals edged white, 4 ins.
>Our Pat, lilac-blue with bronze foliage, 4 ins.
>Snow Cushion, white flowers and very dwarf, 2 ins.

Primula winteri Wats. (syn. *Primula edgeworthii*)

Hardy perennial
Flowering period: Feb.–Mar
Height: 6 ins.

Native to the Himalayas. One of the most beautiful and unusual of the hardy primulas. The large grey-green leaves (which some people have been unkind enough to call cabbage-like) form a flat rosette of vegetation in the centre of which there appears in March a mass of lavender-pink flowers on stems 6 ins. high. Requires a fairly moist position in semi-shade and prefers coolness to heat.

Classification. Botanically, all the above species are classified into seven sections. This classification also has some bearing on their cultivation, and is as follows.

Auriculata Section. Hardy herbaceous perennials mostly suited to the rock-garden, to narrow borders, or to growing in pots, etc. Characterized by their evergreen, often mealy surfaced, rather fleshy leaves, and in many cases with a preference for alkaline (calcareous), gritty soils: *Primula Auricula, P. marginata, P. pubescens, P. glaucescens, P. allionii, P. palinuri, P. viscosa, P. auriculata, P. pedemontana.*

Candelabra Section. Hardy herbaceous perennials completely dormant in winter and not evergreen. They have a long flowering season because the blooms are borne in tiers, or layers, one above the other, arranged in circles around a tall rigid stem, rather similar, as the name suggests, to the form of a candelabrum. The lower circle of flowers opens first and those above follow in succession. They are all moisture lovers and require semi- or complete shade in a soil rich in humus and preferably non-alkaline (non-calcareous). Excellent for woodland gardens. Where conditions are really favourable, many of them will naturalize from self-sown seed: *Primula anisodora, P. aurantiaca, P. beesiana, P. bulleyana, P. cockburniana, P. helodoxa, P. japonica, P. pulverulenta.*

Farinosae Section. Hardy dwarf herbaceous perennials with an almost prostrate mass of very small leaves. All require a moist, cool position in semi- or complete shade. Inflorescence generally in the form of an

Primula sinensis
From *Curtis's Botanical Magazine*,
1825, plate 2564

umbel, with the flowers in groups: *Primula frondosa, P. rosea, P. farinosa, P. involucrata.*
Sikkimensis Section. Tall, hardy, moisture-loving herbaceous perennials. Flowers are all pendulous, bell-shaped, and borne in clusters at the tops of tall, erect stems: *Primula florindae, P. sikkimensis, P. alpicola.*
Vernalis Section. This section comprises the common wild yellow-flowered hardy primula and its many forms and varieties. All woodland or meadow plants requiring a cool, moderately moist fertile soil rich in organic matter: *Primula vulgaris, P. juliae.*
Miscellaneous Hardy Primulas of Minor Sections. Primula capitata, P. denticulata, P. nutans, P. veris, P. winteri, P. cortusoides, P. elatior, P. sieboldii.
Non-hardy Primulas. This section includes three important species cultivated almost exclusively as pot plants for indoor and greenhouse decoration. They are also sometimes used for summer bedding as they do not require great heat: *Primula obconica, P. sinensis, P. malacoides.*

Primula veris

Prunus

Family: Rosaceae
Hardy deciduous or half-hardy evergreen trees or shrubs
Position: sun or shade according to the species
Propagation: seed, cuttings, or grafting
Cultivation easy
In numerous cases fragrant
Useful for cutting

In the case of this vast genus, lack of space compels us to forego our usual discursive investigation into the history and development of these plants. They include plants which have accompanied mankind on his long climb from one civilization to another, providing a source of food since even the fruits of the wild species are edible; later their medicinal value was appreciated, and eventually they became some of our most cherished ornamental flowering trees and shrubs; but the full story is too long and involved for this work.
The genus *Prunus* contains the important almond, peach, cherry, plum, and apricot; trees whose various forms, varieties, and hybrids are valued for their fruits and their blooms. The genus also contains some of our best evergreen shrubs, the so-called Portuguese Laurel

and Cherry Laurel. To the uninitiated the fact that all these belong to the same genus, *Prunus*, may be something of a surprise.

We cannot do more than mention a few of the many myths and legends that have grown up around these trees and shrubs. The almond, so beautiful with its exciting white or pale-pink flowers, always justifies the hope for spring. To many civilizations it was considered sacred. The Old Testament spoke of it symbolically: "And Moses laid up the rods before the Lord in the tabernacle of witness. And it came to pass, that on the morrow Moses went to the tabernacle of witness; and behold, the rod of Aaron for the house of Levi was budded, and brought forth buds, and bloomed blossoms, and yielded almonds" (Num. 17:22–23).

The origin of the cherry is lost in the distant past, but the previous generic name of the wild cherry, *Cerasus vulgaris*, is derived from the Turkish province of Kirasun (mod. Girasun). It was from here that Lucullus first introduced cherries into Italy, and eventually they spread throughout Europe. It is also thought that the Romans introduced cherries into Great Britain, but there is no mention of the fruits being sold commercially in England until 1415. In mythology the cherry and the cuckoo are frequently associated. One German proverb states that "the cuckoo never calls until he has thrice eaten his fill of cherries." In England there is an old children's game in which they dance around a cherry tree and sing:

> Cuckoo, cherry tree,
> Come down and tell me
> How many years I have to live, to live.

Each child then, in turn, shakes the tree, and the number of cherries that fall indicates the number of years that each will live.

The genus *Prunus* comprises at least one hundred species of mostly hardy deciduous or evergreen trees and shrubs. They are distinguished by their property of possessing a single seed—in contrast to the genus *Malus* (apple), whose fruits are many-seeded. Those prunus cultivated in gardens for their flowers do not produce the large fruits so characteristic of the genus, although the fruits of some of the flowering species and varieties are quite agreeable. As flowering trees and shrubs there are certainly few more beautiful subjects, particularly in the case of the Japanese cherries. The natural habitat of the genus is spread over the greater part of the world, particularly in temperate zones.

Apart from the economic value of its fruits, and the ornamental value of its flowers, the genus has considerable importance as a source of supply of medicinal substances. One of the most important is obtained from *Prunus Amygdalus*, oil of almonds, which contains benzaldehyde and hydrocyanic acid. There is also a sedative produced from the leaves of *Prunus Laurocerasus*, a tonic and astringent

Prunus triloba var, *plena*

Prunus nana
From *Curtis's Botanical Magazine*,
1791, plate 161

obtained from the fruits and stalks of *Prunus avium*, a laxative obtained from the fruits of *Prunus communis*, a sedative, diuretic, and expectorant prepared from an infusion of the bark and leaves of *Prunus Persica*, and a tonic for convalescence from fevers prepared from the bark of *Prunus serotina*. The fruits of *Prunus spinosa* are used to make sloe gin and also in making jam.
Cultivation. The number of prunus is so vast that it is not easy to generalize about their cultivation. All those grown in European and American gardens are hardy and not difficult to grow. The least hardy are peaches and almonds, which are not advisable for the colder, northernmost gardens. The majority are more tolerant of heat and sun than the closely related genus *Malus* and should always be planted in an open, warm, sunny position in well-drained soil. They are equally successful in acid or alkaline (calcareous) soils. Some species and their varieties (such as *Prunus mume*) are also tolerant of shade, while the evergreen types give excellent results in partial shade. All prunus require a deep fertile soil that is never allowed to become excessively dry. The majority do not require pruning, but where this is necessary it is so stated in the individual descriptions. The best planting season for the deciduous types is autumn and spring for the evergreen types. Practically all prunus can be raised from seed sown outside as soon as the fruits are ripe, but germination will probably not take place until the following spring. Prunus also propagate well from hard-wooded cuttings which, in the case of the deciduous varieties, should be taken as soon as the leaves have fallen and placed outside in coldframes or even in sheltered nursery beds. Cuttings of the evergreen varieties are best taken from half-ripened wood in June–July and placed outside in closed frames, where they will generally root before late autumn. They should not be planted out, however, until the following spring, although they can be potted individually and given the winter protection of an unheated greenhouse. Commercially, the majority of flowering and fruiting prunus are grafted onto stock of the more common species which can be easily raised from seed on a vast scale. It is worth noting that those prunus raised from seed or obtained from cuttings are generally longer-lived than the grafted plants.
The nomenclature of the genus *Prunus* is probably more confused and complicated than that of any other similar group of plants, and there is inevitably considerable lack of agreement on this point, even among the best authorities. In accordance with modern nomenclature and classification the genus *Prunus* now includes all of the one-time separate genera of
    Amygdalus (Almond)
    Armeniaca (Apricot)
    Cerasus (Flowering Cherry)
    Laurocerasus (Cherry Laurel)

Lusitanica (Portuguese Laurel)
Padus (Bird Cherry)
Persica (Peach)
Prunus (Plum)

Prunus americana Marshall (Wild or Yellow Plum)
Native to eastern North America. A graceful deciduous tree with tapering obovate leaves up to 4 ins. long and 1½ ins. wide. Extremities of the branches pendulous. Flowers white, 1 in. in diameter, in clusters of 2–5. Fruits globose, 1 in. in diameter, yellow at first, becoming red when ripe; pulp yellow. Little-known in Europe but selected varieties are widely grown in the eastern United States. Very attractive, with the yellow and red fruits appearing simultaneously on the branches. A true, edible plum.

Deciduous tree
Flowering period: Mar.–Apr.
Height: up to 30 ft.
Zone 3 southwards

Prunus Amygdalus Batsch. (syn. *Amygdalus communis* L.) (Almond)
Naturalized in Southern Europe, North Africa, and the Middle East, but some doubt exists as to its original native habitat. A deciduous tree with an erect much-branching habit. In its young state has the appearance of a large shrub. Leaves lanceolate, 3–6 ins. long, 1–2 ins. wide, pointed. The magnificent single flowers, very pale pink or white, appear in February–March according to the district and climate. If flowering branches are cut while the buds are still closed they will soon bloom when placed in water indoors. Apart from its economic value, the almond is without doubt one of the most beautiful of all flowering trees, and one of the earliest-flowering as well. The individual blooms are 1½–2 ins. in diameter, generally in pairs, borne on the previous season's growths. Fruits are 1½–2½ ins. long and slightly less wide, with a velvet-like surface, and contain the typical almond nut with its conspicuously pitted husk. There are several interesting varieties:

Deciduous tree
Flowering period: Feb.–Mar.
Height: up to 30 ft.
Zone 6 southwards

> var. *amara*, the so-called bitter almond, with larger flowers darker-coloured in the centre
> var. *dulcis*, the so-called sweet almond, distinguishable by its more glaucous-green foliage
> var. *macrocarpa*, with larger flowers and fruits, individual blooms up to 2½ ins. in diameter
> var. *pendula*, with pendulous branches
> var. *praecox*, a particularly early-flowering form
> var. *rosea-plena*, double-flowered pink

Prunus angustifolia Marshall (syn. *Prunus chicasa*) (Chickasaw Plum)
Native to, or at least naturalized in, the southeastern United States, but there is some doubt as to its true habitat. Forms a much-branched twiggy shrub with lanceolate leaves up to 2 ins. long, dentated,

Deciduous shrub
Flowering period: Mar.–Apr.
Height: up to 12 ft.
Zone 3 southwards

pointed, tapering at the base. Leaf stalk and young bark glabrous, reddish brown. Flowers in groups of 2–4, white, ½ in. wide. Fruit globose, shiny red, ½ in. in diameter. Several varieties of this plum are grown in the United States for eating, but it is scantily cultivated in Europe, probably because the summers are neither long enough nor warm enough to ensure a regular crop of fruits, which are of greater ornamental value than the blooms.

(Apricot)
Deciduous tree
Flowering period: Mar.–Apr.
Height: up to 25 ft.
Zone 5 southwards

Prunus Armeniaca L. (syn. *Armeniaca vulgaris* L.)
Native to northern China. Its flowers do not compare in beauty with those of the almond or peach, but it is of botanical interest as the parent of the modern fruiting apricot. Leaves ovate, 2½–3½ ins. long, pointed, dark green. Flowers very pale pink or white, 1 in. wide, borne singly on the previous season's growth. Fruit globose, 1¼ ins. in diameter (generally larger when cultivated in gardens), yellowish red, with a pleasant flavour.

(Common Sweet Cherry or Wild Cherry)
Deciduous tree
Flowering period: April
Height: up to 60 ft.
Zone 3 southwards

Prunus avium L. (syn. *Cerasus sylvestris* Loud.)
Native to Europe. The wild cherry frequently found in woodlands and throughout the countryside. A deciduous tree with conspicuous, shiny, peeling bark. Leaves oval, pointed, 3–5 ins. long, 1½–2 ins. wide, dentated. Flowers white, 1 in. in diameter, borne on the previous season's growths. Fruits globose, red-black, ¾ in. in diameter; sweet when dead ripe. In April, a large tree in full bloom is a lovely sight, and the autumn colouring of the foliage is also excellent. One of the parents of the cultivated edible cherry, in particular the black-fruited varieties. There are several good varieties of *Prunus avium*:

> var. *asplenifolia* (syn. var. *laciniata*), with deeply and irregularly dentated leaves
> var. *decumana* Koch (syn. *Prunus macrophylla* Poir.), with larger flowers and leaves up to 10 ins. long
> var. *pleno* Schn., one of the most beautiful of all flowering trees with masses of pure-white blooms, 1½ ins. in diameter; each flower with 30–40 petals and of long duration

Prunus avium is sometimes confused with *Prunus Cerasus* and *Prunus acida*, but it differs from these two species because it has a tree-like habit, while the other two are shrub-like; also the leaves of *P. avium* are more dentated and the ripe fruit is not acid.

(Sand Cherry or Hansen Bush Cherry)
Deciduous shrub
Flowering period: March
Height: up to 5 ft.
Zone 2 southwards

Prunus besseyi Bailey
Native to the central United States. A dwarf cherry with grey-green oval-lanceolate foliage up to 2½ ins. long. Flowers in clusters of 2–4, white, ⅝ in. in diameter. Fruits rounded or slightly oval, ¾ in. long, black but covered with purple bloom, edible, sweet. As it is so very hardy it is frequently used as a stock for grafting. In locales with

Prunus subhirtella
From *Curtis's Botanical Magazine*,
1896, plate 7508

relatively brief, cool summers (such as Europe), the cherries are not freely borne; but in Colorado it has been recorded that eighty fruits have been picked from a single 1-ft.-long branch of a three-year-old plant.

Large deciduous shrub
Flowering period: Mar.–Apr.
Height: up to 15 ft.
Zone 3 southwards

Prunus x *blireiana* André (syn. *Prunus cerasifera* var. *blireiana*)
Of hybrid origin. At one time it was believed to be a variety of *Prunus cerasifera* but now it is considered to be a hybrid between *Prunus cerasifera* var. *pissardii* and *Prunus mume*. One of the most attractive of the reddish-purple small-leaved prunus belonging to the plums, with masses of very double small pink flowers in spring. With its compact, much-branched habit, it is one of the most effective flowering plums for the smaller garden. The plants bloom at the same time as daffodils and if the bulbs of these are naturalized around the base of the prunus a beautiful effect can be obtained. Because the flowers are so completely double, the smooth-skinned, round, 1-in. fruits are rarely produced. The var. *nigra* has much darker foliage.

Deciduous tree
Flowering period: Mar.–Apr.
Height: up to 30 ft.
Zone 7 southwards

Prunus campanulata Maxim.
Native to Taiwan. A deciduous cherry-type prunus which reaches a height of 30 ft. in its natural habitat, but in gardens it generally has the proportions of a very large shrub. A plant of remarkable beauty, quite unlike any other prunus and certainly the most brilliantly coloured. Its general habit is particularly graceful, with obovate leaves $2\frac{1}{2}$–4 ins. long and 1–2 ins. wide. The exquisite pendulous bell-shaped flowers are borne in clusters of 2–6 on the previous season's growths in March–April, before the leaves. They are $1\frac{1}{4}$ ins. long and $\frac{2}{3}$ in. wide, each on a stalk $1\frac{1}{4}$ ins. long. Their colour is rich ruby-crimson and the tip of each petal is conspicuously notched. The stamens are attractive for their bright-yellow anthers, while the calyx tube is several shades darker in colour than the petals. The small conical fruits are red. This lovely species was originally introduced into Europe in 1899, but after a few years was lost to cultivation until it was reintroduced in 1915. Numerous young plants I planted in 1938 have now developed into superb specimens, surviving even severe frost.

(Cherry Plum
or Myrobalan Plum)
Deciduous tree
Flowering period: Mar.–Apr.
Height: up to 20 ft.
Zone 3 southwards

Prunus cerasifera Ehrhart
Native to the Caucasus. A round-headed deciduous tree up to 30 ft. in the wild, but in gardens it assumes the form of a very large shrub. Leaves ovate, $1\frac{1}{2}$–$2\frac{1}{2}$ ins. long, dentated. Flowers white, 1 in. in diameter, in clusters of 1–3 on the previous season's growths. Fruits red, globose, $1\frac{1}{2}$ ins. in diameter, edible, smooth-skinned. Belongs to the plums, and is of the greatest value for its prolific early flowering (March). Perhaps even better known than the original species is the var. *pissardii* Carr. (syn. var. *atropurpurea*), which is

widely planted for its pale-pink flowers and beautifully coloured foliage which is ruby-red when young, later changing to reddish purple. Generally planted to form a vista or for bordering a road, but can be effectively used to make a large hedge. Seen to best effect, however, grown on the lawn as a large isolated specimen with a ground cover of naturalized muscari (grape hyacinths). The var. *nigra* has darker almost purple-black foliage; while the var. *diversifolia* has narrow deeply incised leaves.

Prunus Cerasus L. (syn. *Cerasus vulgaris* Mill.)
Native to Europe. A small deciduous tree (or large shrub) of rounded habit producing an abundance of basal growths that eventually form a dense mass of vegetation. Leaves oval, pointed, $1\frac{1}{4}$–$3\frac{1}{4}$ ins. long and $\frac{2}{3}$–$1\frac{3}{4}$ ins. wide. Flowers white, 1 in. in diameter, borne in clusters on the previous season's growths. Fruits reddish black, globose, very acid, about $\frac{3}{4}$ in. in diameter, juicy. One of the parents of the cultivated cherry, in particular the black-fruited varieties, but not of great ornamental value. But the var. *flore pleno* (syn. var. *rhexii*) is a plant of the greatest beauty with a profusion of double white flowers $1\frac{1}{4}$ ins. in diameter and of long duration. Another interesting variety is var. *marasca*, the fruits and pits of which are used in the distillation of the famous Dalmatian maraschino liqueur.

(Sour Cherry or Dwarf Wild Cherry)
Deciduous tree
Flowering period: Mar.–Apr.
Height: up to 35 ft.
Zone 3 southwards

Prunus communis Hud. (syn. *Prunus domestica* L.)
Although found growing wild in many parts of Europe, the true native habitat of this wild plum is uncertain. A small deciduous tree up to 20 ft. or more; in gardens generally a large shrub with many basal growths. Leaves elliptical, $1\frac{1}{2}$–3 ins. long, half as wide, dull green, dentated. Flowers white, $1\frac{1}{4}$ ins. in diameter, generally borne in pairs on the previous season's growths. Fruits blue-black, egg-shaped, $1\frac{1}{4}$ ins. long. Of no particular ornamental value in the garden, but interesting as one of the parents of cultivated plums. Strangely enough there are no garden hybrids of floral interest, although the double-flowered var. *flore pleno* is attractive. The species is also of interest for its medicinal value. The dried fruits provide one of the ingredients in the preparation of certain laxatives and are also used for flavouring other less palatable medicines.

(Plum)
Deciduous tree
Flowering period: March
Height: up to 20 ft.
Zone 3 southwards

Prunus davidiana Franch.
Native to China. First introduced into Europe by Père David, who sent seeds to Paris in 1865. A small deciduous tree up to 30 ft. high in the wild, but in gardens a very large shrub. It is a peach, and one of the first to bloom, often in February. Thus, although a hardy plant, in northern gardens the flowers are liable to be damaged by frost. Leaves elongated, 3–5 ins. long, 1–$1\frac{3}{4}$ ins. wide, pointed, dentated. Flowers white, 1 in. in diameter, borne singly on the previous season's

Deciduous tree
Flowering period: Feb.–May
Height: up to 30 ft.
Zone 3 southwards

growths. Fruit globose, 1¼ ins. in diameter, yellow. The var. *rubra* has beautiful reddish-pink flowers.

Prunus domestica (see *Prunus communis*)

(Flowering Almond)
Deciduous shrub
Flowering period: Mar.–Apr.
Height: up to 5 ft.
Zone 6 southwards

Prunus glandulosa Thunb.
Native to China and Japan. A deciduous shrub with ovate-lanceolate leaves 1–2½ ins. long, ¾–1¼ ins. wide, pointed, finely dentated. Flowers white or very pale pink, 1¼ ins. in diameter. Fruits red, ⅓ in. wide. Although attractive the true species is much less important than its two magnificent varieties; var. *alba*, white, and var. *rosea*, pink. These are two of the most beautiful of all the dwarf prunus. They make excellent pot plants and are widely used commercially for forcing into out-of-season bloom. The individual blooms are borne on long erect slender stems and are 1¼ ins. in diameter, with many petals. The leaves are also larger (often 4 ins. long) than those of the species. These varieties have been cultivated in Europe since 1774 but originated in Japan and China many years previously. They are among the very few prunus that require pruning, and both the single- and double-flowered varieties should be severely pruned immediately after they have flowered. They are sometimes sold commercially as *Prunus sinensis*, and belong to the almonds.

(Hortulan Plum)
Deciduous tree
Flowering period: Mar.–Apr.
Height: up to 30 ft.
Zone 5 southwards

Prunus hortulana Bailey
Native to the southern and central United States. A large deciduous tree in the wild, but in gardens generally has the proportions of a large shrub. Leaves ovate-lanceolate, up to 6 ins. long, and 1½ ins. wide, dentated. Flowers white, 1 in. in diameter, borne in clusters of 2–6 on the previous season's growths. Belongs to the plums and bears yellowish-red fruits 1 in. in diameter. Numerous varieties are grown for their edible fruits.

(Islay or Evergreen Cherry)
Evergreen tree
Flowering period: April
Height: up to 30 ft.
Zone 8 southwards

Prunus ilicifolia Walpers (syn. *Laurocerasus ilicifolia* Roemer)
Native to California. One of the less hardy evergreen prunus belonging to the cherry section of the genus. Habit neat and compact with holly-like leaves, ovate, up to 2 ins. long, 1¼ ins. wide, rounded at the base, dentated, and a dark shiny green. Inflorescence a raceme up to 3 ins. long; individual flowers white, ⅓ in. in diameter. Fruits globose, pointed, ½ in. wide, purple-black, edible.

Deciduous tree
Flowering period: March
Height: up to 20 ft.
Zone 6 southwards

Prunus incisa Thunb. (syn. *Cerasus incisa* Lois.)
Native to Japan. Cherry section of the genus *Prunus*. A small deciduous tree or large shrub with slender branches and an elegant habit. Young foliage slightly red, later becoming green, obovate, 1–2½ ins. long, ¾–1¼ ins. wide, pointed, dentated. Flowers white or pale pink, ⅔–1 in. in diameter, borne in groups of 2–4 on the previous season's

growths. Each petal notched at the tip. Unopened flower buds reddish pink. Fruits egg-shaped, ⅓ in. long, purple-black. Originally discovered in 1776 by Carl Peter Thunberg. A special interest is attached to this species because it is the prunus generally used in the Bonsai method of cultivation and will survive and even bloom when artificially dwarfed and restricted to small pots. It is a prunus of great beauty and has also produced some excellent varieties; var. *February Pink*, with pink flowers appearing in February, and var. *moerheimii*, a pendulous form with profuse pink flowers.

Prunus lannesiana Wilson (syn. *Cerasus lannesiana* Carr.)
(Japanese Flowering Cherry)
Deciduous tree
Flowering period: April
Height: up to 30 ft.
Zone 5 southwards

Native to Japan. The garden hybrids of this wild cherry species are much confused with the garden hybrids of *Prunus serrulata*, also native to Japan. These wild cherry hybrids are known collectively as Japanese Flowering Cherries and, in each case, are more widely cultivated than either of the original species. Some authorities even combine *Prunus lannesiana* and *Prunus serrulata* into one single species. For the average gardener this involved question of botanical nomenclature is best left to the botanist, but for the sake of the record the following are the distinctions between the two species as defined by E. H. Wilson, one of the chief authorities on the subject, in *Trees and Shrubs Hardy in the British Isles* by W. J. Bean (vol. 2, p. 556): "*Prunus lannesiana*—leaves unfolding green or slightly reddish, pale green beneath, the marginal teeth like long bristles; bark pale grey; flowers fragrant. *Prunus serrulata*—leaves more or less glaucous beneath, marginal teeth shorter, bark dark chestnut-brown; flowers not fragrant." There are, however, several varieties so intermediate between these two definitions that it is practically impossible to decide to which species they belong. The twelve best hybrid Japanese Flowering Cherries are given below:

> Amanogawa, a remarkable variety with an erect, closely compact form like a Lombardy poplar. Semi-double, reddish-pink flowers
> Fugenzo (syn. J. H. Veitch), large double rich pink flowers
> Gyoi-Ko, large semi-double greenish-yellow flowers
> Hata-Zakura, large double pink flowers
> Hizakura (syn. Kanzan), double dark-pink flowers
> Shirotae (syn. Mt. Fuji), very wide white flowers in pendulous groups
> Tai-Haku, enormous double white flowers
> Oku-Miyako (syn. Longipes), large white flowers
> Shidare-Zakura, pendulous branches, double pink flowers
> Shiro-Fugen, double carmine-pink flowers
> Ukon, semi-double yellow-green flowers
> Yoshino, large white flowers suffused pink

Prunus lannesiana

(Cherry Laurel)
Evergreen shrub
Flowering period: April
Height: up to 20 ft.
Zone 6 southwards

Prunus Laurocerasus L. (syn. *Laurocerasus officinalis* Roem.)
Native to Eastern Europe and Asia Minor. Introduced into European gardens in 1629. A hardy evergreen shrub of rapid development with a wide-spreading habit making it excellent for the formation of large hedges. Height up to 20 ft., and, if cultivated as an isolated specimen, twice that in diameter. Belongs to the Laurocerasus section of the genus. Leaves leathery textured, dark shiny green, oblong, 4–6 ins. in length, $1\frac{1}{2}$–2 ins. wide. Flowers borne in terminal and axillary racemes up to 5 ins. long and $\frac{3}{4}$ in. in diameter, dull white. Fruits purple-black, conical, $\frac{2}{3}$ in. long. Particularly useful for its tolerance to semi-shade. There are many varieties whose principal differences are in the shape of the leaves.

> var. *caucasica*, with dark-green leaves 7 ins. long and $4\frac{1}{2}$ ins. wide
> var. *magnoliaefolia*, the variety with the largest foliage, up to 12 ins. long and 5 ins. wide
> var. *otinii*, with large, broad leaves of such a dark green that they appear to be black

Prunus Laurocerasus leaves are used in the preparation of certain sedatives and a decoction from the foliage has been of medicinal value in the treatment of coughs, asthma, and whooping cough.

(Portuguese Laurel)
Evergreen shrub
Flowering period: June
Height: up to 15 ft.
Zone 6 southwards

Prunus lusitanica L. (syn. *Laurocerasus lusitanica* Roem.)
Native to Spain and Portugal. Laurocerasus section of the genus. A hardy evergreen shrub with wide-spreading development that makes it ideal for the formation of large informal hedges or for use as a windbreak. Individual isolated specimens will develop into really enormous plants with a pleasing, rounded habit. The branches are retained down to ground level. Leaves ovate, 3–6 ins. long, $2\frac{1}{2}$–3 ins. wide, very dark glossy green. Flowers borne in racemes from the ends of the previous season's growth. The inflorescence is 6–10 ins. long and $1\frac{1}{4}$ ins. in diameter and is borne erect. Individual flowers $\frac{1}{3}$ in. in diameter, white, with a hawthorn-like fragrance. Fruits dark purple, cone-shaped, $\frac{1}{3}$ in. long. Introduced into European gardens in 1648 by William Aiton. It is one of the most effective of all evergreen shrubs, useful for many purposes, and also tolerant of shade. Although hardy, it is not suitable for high altitudes or for areas subject to continuous icy and violent winds which can spoil the beauty of the handsome lustrous foliage. There are several varieties:

> var. *azorica*, the variety with the biggest leaves and of exceptional vigour
> var. *myrtifolia* (syn. var. *pyramidalis*), with much smaller leaves and with a more rigid, stiff, compact, conical habit
> var. *variegata*, leaves margined with white and very attractive

Prunus lusitanica

Prunus maritima Wang.   (Beach Plum)
Deciduous shrub
Flowering period: April
Height: up to 6 ft.
Zone 3 southwards

Native to the eastern United States. Found mostly in sandy soil along coastal districts, particularly in the Cape Cod area. A low-growing, compact shrub belonging to the plums. Leaves obovate, 1½–3 ins. long, half as wide, dentated. Flowers ½ in. in diameter, white, axillary, in groups of 2–3 on the previous season's growths. Fruit dark reddish to purple-black, globose, up to 1 in. in diameter, edible, and best employed for jellies or jams. The var. *flava* has yellow fruits. One of the most decorative of the dwarf plums and one of the easiest to cultivate.

Prunus mume Sieb. & Zucc. (syn. *Armeniaca mume* Sieb.)   (Japanese Apricot)
Deciduous small tree
Flowering period: Feb.–Mar.
Height: up to 10 ft.
Zone 6 southwards

Native to Korea and China, but widely cultivated in Japan, from where it was introduced into Europe in 1878 and offered commercially under the name *Prunus myrobalana flore pleno*, a name still sometimes used. The plants develop into large deciduous shrubs, sometimes with the appearance of a small tree, with a close, compact, rounded habit. Belongs to the Armeniaca section of the genus. This is a plant of exceptional beauty and with so many good qualities that one wonders why it is not cultivated in every garden. It will even tolerate complete shade as I have been able to demonstrate over a period of many years, even flowering and fruiting in such a position. Leaves 2½–4 ins. long, broadly ovate, pointed, dentated. Flowers pink, 1¼ ins. in diameter, borne singly or in pairs in the greatest profusion on the previous season's growths in February–March; deliciously scented and excellent for cutting. Fruits yellow, globose, 1¼ ins. in diameter, with the typical apricot appearance and with an exquisite flavour. There are several varieties, the double-flowered forms being particularly attractive:

    var. *alba*, white
    var. *alba plena*, double white
    var. *plena*, double pink

Prunus nana Stokes (syn. *Prunus tenella, Amygdalus nana* L.)   (Dwarf Russian Almond)
Deciduous shrub
Flowering period: Mar.–Apr.
Height: up to 5 ft.
Zone 2 southwards

Native to southern Russia and Southeastern Europe. Amygdalus section of the genus. This Dwarf Russian Almond is a very hardy dwarf deciduous shrub of bushy habit. Leaves obovate, 1½–3¼ ins. long, ⅔–1¼ ins. wide, dentated, dark glossy green above, paler beneath. Flowers in groups of 1–3, borne on the previous season's growths, reddish pink, ⅔ in. in diameter. Fruit with the form of a miniature almond, 1 in. long. A beautiful little shrub and ideal for the smaller garden. In cultivation since 1683. There are some interesting varieties:

    var. *alba,* white-flowered

var. *Fire Hill*, a magnificent dwarf almond with crimson flowers

var. *Trailblazer*, purple-green foliage and white flowers

(Canada Plum)
Deciduous tree
Flowering period: Mar.–Apr.
Height: up to 30 ft.
Zone 2 southwards

Prunus nigra Aiton

Native to the eastern United States and Canada. Belongs to the plum section and as a parent has played a part in the development of cultivated plums. A deciduous tree with an erect narrow form. Leaves obovate, long-pointed, heart-shaped at the base, 4 ins. long and half as wide, dentated, surface covered with fine down. Flowers borne in groups of 3–4 on the previous season's growths, white, $1\frac{1}{2}$ ins. wide, stalks red. Fruits oval, $1\frac{1}{4}$ ins. long, reddish yellow. Introduced into European gardens in 1773. As they fade, the pleasantly fragrant flowers become reddish.

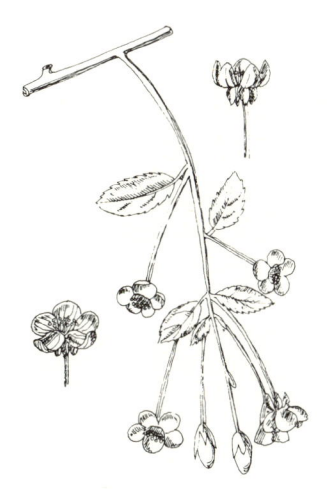

Prunus Cerasus

A Japanese aprocot: the fruit of *Prunus mume*

(Bird Cherry)
Deciduous tree
Flowering period: Apr.–May
Height: up to 40 ft.
Zone 3 southwards

Prunus Padus L. (syn. *Padus racemosa* Lam.)

Native to many of the northern parts of the Old World and, in one or another of its geographical forms and varieties, extending to Japan. A member of the Padus section of the genus. A very hardy small deciduous tree with an open habit; general appearance somewhat gaunt when without its foliage. Leaves obovate, 3–7 ins. long, about half as wide, pointed, dentated, dark green above, paler and glabrous beneath. Flowers fragrant, white, $\frac{1}{2}$ in. in diameter, borne in semi-pendulous racemes up to 6 ins. long on the previous season's growths. The entire inflorescence resembles a small spike of buddleia. Fruit globose, black, $\frac{1}{3}$ in. in diameter, with a bitter and unpleasant taste. The bark has a strong, pungent odour. A very easy subject which appears to be happy in almost any position or soil; excellent for semi-wild areas and for woodlands. Some of the varieties are much more decorative than the original species:

> var. *commutata,* a variety from Manchuria which begins to bloom a month before the others. Individual flowers up to ½ in. wide.
> var. *plena,* a magnificent double-flowered form with a longer flowering season
> var. *watereri,* the best of the single-flowered hybrids with inflorescences often 10 ins. long

Prunus pennsylvanica L. f. (syn. *Cerasus pennsylvanica* Lois.)
Native to the northern United States. A deciduous tree belonging to the Cerasus section of the genus. Leaves ovate, up to 5 ins. long and 1½ ins. wide, long-pointed, glabrous, brilliant green, dentated with incurved teeth. Bark shiny red and aromatic. Flowers white, ¾ in. in diameter, borne in groups of 4–10 in umbels on short racemes. Fruits red, globose, ⅓ in. wide. A beautiful small tree with the flowers appearing when the foliage is young and still not fully developed.

(Wild Red Cherry)
Deciduous tree
Flowering period: Mar.–Apr.
Height: up to 30 ft.
Zone 3 southwards

Prunus Persica Batsch. (syn. *Persica vulgaris, Amygdalus Persica* L.)
Original habitat doubtful, but believed to have been China. Belonging to the Persica section of the genus. The ornamental flowering varieties of *Prunus Persica* (peach) are among the most beautiful of all flowering shrubs; while the original species is a parent of our modern edible peaches. A small deciduous tree with a bushy, branched habit. Leaves lanceolate, 4–6 ins. long, about half as wide, pointed, dentated. Flowers generally solitary, borne on the previous season's growths, pale pink, up to 1½ ins. in diameter. Fruits fleshy, globose, with a velvet-like outer covering, up to 3 ins. in diameter, yellowish red. In the case of the cultivated varieties (of which there are many), the fruits are, of course, much larger, but here we are not concerned with the peach as an edible fruit. Flowering peaches have been cultivated in gardens for hundreds of years and the double forms are particularly effective. They form large shrubs or small trees and are hardy in all but exceptionally cold localities, but are not indicated for high altitudes. Occasionally these flowering peaches also produce edible fruits. *Prunus Persica* has certain medicinal properties, a preparation from the bark and the leaves sometimes being used as a sedative, diuretic, and expectorant. Some of the best varieties are:

(Peach)
Deciduous tree
Flowering period: April
Height: up to 20 ft.
Zone 6 southwards

> var. *alba,* single white flowers
> var. *alba plena,* double white
> var. *foliis rubris,* pinkish-white flowers and purple-red leaves and fruit

var. *magnifica*, double crimson flowers 2 ins. wide
var. *pendula*, pendulous branches and pink flowers
var. *rosea plena*, double pink
var. *Russell's Red*, one of the best with double crimson flowers
var. *sanguineo-plena*, double crimson

Prunus pissardii (see *Prunus cerasifera* var. *pissardii*)

Large deciduous shrub or small tree
Flowering period: Apr.–May
Height: up to 15 ft.
Zone 6 southwards

Prunus x *pollardii* Hort. (syn. *Prunus Amygdalo-Persica pollardii*)
Of hybrid origin. The most spectacular of all the peach/almond group of the genus and extensively cultivated for the sale of its flowering branches in flower shops. The plant has a similar habit and appearance to the almond, but with more dentated leaves. It is generally believed to be the result of a cross between *Prunus Amygdalus* and *Prunus Persica* (that is, between the peach and almond). It was originally raised in 1904 by Mr. Pollard of Ballarat, Australia. The beautiful vivid pink flowers are 2 ins. in diameter and it is a variety easily forced into bloom out of season. As a garden plant it is superb, and, where space permits the cultivation of only one flowering peach, this is the variety to choose.

(Sand Cherry)
Deciduous shrub
Flowering period: Apr.–May
Height: up to 6 ft.
Zone 2 southwards

Prunus pumila L.
Native to the northeastern United States. Grown in European gardens since 1756. Cerasus section of the genus. A smallish shrub of erect habit with very dark bark. Leaves narrowly obovate, up to 2 ins. long, $\frac{3}{4}$ in. wide, grey-green. Flowers white, $\frac{1}{2}$ in. in diameter in umbels of 2–4. Fruit bitter tasting, purple-black, $\frac{1}{2}$ in. in diameter, globose. The var. *depressa* is almost prostrate, rarely more than 12 ins. high, and useful for planting on steep banks, etc. *Prunus pumila* is a modest little plant but quite attractive and it can be satisfactorily used where the soil is very loose and sandy.

Deciduous tree
Flowering period: Apr.–May
Height: up to 60 ft.
Zone 5 southwards

Prunus sargentii Rehd. (syn. *Prunus serrulata sachalinensis* Wilson)
Native to Japan. Introduced into Kew by Sargent in 1893. Cerasus section. A large tree with a trunk 2–3 ft. in diameter. (Since it is a true tree, it is really beyond the scope of this work.) Leaves oval, long-pointed, up to 4 ins. long, reddish in their juvenile state. Flowers $1\frac{1}{2}$ ins. wide, of a beautiful rich pink, borne 2–6 together in umbels. Fruit globose, black, $\frac{1}{3}$ in. in diameter. A remarkably beautiful tree for its flowers and fruits and for the fine autumn colouring of its foliage. Also greatly esteemed as a timber tree.

(Wild Black Cherry or Choke Berry)
Deciduous tree
Flowering period: Mar.–Arp.
Height: up to 60 ft. or more
Zone 2 southwards

Prunus serotina Ehrhart (syn. *Padus serotina*)
Native to eastern North America. A handsome, very large wild cherry of the Padus section (a full discussion of this section is also beyond the scope of the present work). Leaves oval-lanceolate, up to

6 ins. long. Flowers white, $\frac{1}{3}$ in. in diameter, borne in cylindrical $\frac{3}{4}$-in.-wide racemes. Fruits black, globose, $\frac{1}{2}$ in. wide, and used for flavouring rum. The leaves are reputed to contain a very poisonous substance which is particularly toxic when the foliage is withered.

Prunus serrulata Lindl. (see *Prunus lannesiana*)

Prunus spinosa L.

(Sloe or Blackthorn)
Deciduous shrub
Flowering period: Mar.–Apr.
Height: up to 15 ft. or more
Zone 4 southwards

Native to Europe and Northern Asia. A hardy very spiny deciduous shrub with a dense, much-branched habit. Belongs to the plum section of the genus. Sometimes reaches the dimensions of a small tree. Leaves oval, up to 4 ins. long and half as wide, dentated. Flowers produced before the leaves, on the previous year's growths; white, $\frac{2}{3}$ in. in diameter. Fruits globose, $\frac{2}{3}$ in. in diameter, at first blue, becoming black; used in the preparation of sloe gin. An excellent plant for hedge-making. There are two attractive varieties: var. *plena,* with smaller but very double flowers, and var. *purpurea,* foliage reddish purple, pink flowers (one of the elite among small shrubs with coloured leaves).

Prunus subhirtella Miq.

(Rosebud Cherry)
Deciduous tree
Flowering period: Mar.–Apr.
Height: up to 30 ft.
Zone 4 southwards

Native to Japan. Cerasus section of the genus. A small deciduous tree or very large shrub with a much-branched graceful habit. Leaves $1\frac{1}{2}$–3 ins. long and half as wide, ovate, pointed, dentated. Flowers in groups of 2–5, pale pink, $\frac{2}{3}$ in. in diameter, borne on the previous season's growths. Fruit round, black, $\frac{2}{3}$ in. in diameter. First introduced into Kew in 1895, it is one of the most beautiful of the small-flowered prunus. Of particularly easy cultivation, abundant in its flowering, very hardy and long-lived, with a long flowering period. There are two varieties of special merit:

> var. *autumnalis,* with a more open, looser habit and semi-double flowers which begin to bloom in late September and continue to flower intermittently until the following spring
> var. *pendula,* completely pendulous branches which in spring are covered with small pale-pink flowers making a cascade of bloom

Prunus triloba Lindl.

Deciduous shrub
Flowering period: Mar.–Apr.
Height: up to 12 ft.
Zone 4 southwards

Native to China. Amygdalus section of the genus. An erect deciduous shrub. Leaves obovate, $1\frac{1}{2}$–$2\frac{1}{2}$ ins. long, $\frac{2}{3}$–$1\frac{1}{4}$ ins. wide, pointed at both ends, dentated. Flowers pinkish white, 1 in. in diameter, borne several together on the previous year's growths. Fruits globose, red, $\frac{1}{2}$ in. in diameter with the typical almondy velvety outer covering. One of the best known and most widely cultivated of the smaller prunus. Ideal for growing in pots, and the double-flowered forms are well adapted to forcing into bloom, as frequently seen in flower shops in winter and early spring. This is one of the few prunus that require annual pruning; the flowering branches should be severely cut back immediately after the flowers have fallen. New growths will then appear (often 2–2½ ft. long), which will bear next season's flowers along their entire length. The most frequently cultivated form is the var. *plena,* which was introduced by R. F. Fortune in 1855. It flowers most profusely, with very double pink blooms 1½ ins. in diameter. The leaves of this form are three-lobed at the apex and it is for this characteristic that Lindley gave the species its specific name. The species and its varieties are ideal for the smaller garden. An unusual and attractive method of cultivation is to plant them against a wall and train the branches in the form of a fan over the wall surface.

Pulsatilla

(ANEMONE PULSATILLA, PASQUE FLOWER, WIND FLOWER, OR ANEMONE)
(*Also see* ANEMONE)
Family: Ranunculaceae
Hardy herbaceous perennials
Position: sun in the north, partial shade in the south
Propagation: seed or division
Cultivation not always easy, especially in the south

Pulsatilla vulgaris

Until relatively recently the genus *Pulsatilla* was classified under the genus *Anemone*, and for the purpose of nomenclature it is still often necessary to use that name. Modern botanists, however, preferred to create a separate genus for the graceful pasque flower. This new genus comprises thirteen species, all of which have a typical characteristic appearance which easily distinguishes and separates them from the popular true anemone.

Pulsatillas are essentially European alpine plants native to the Alps, Dolomites, and Apennines, where the spring or early-summer spectacle of mountain meadows full of these exquisitely beautiful flowers is a sight not likely to be forgotten. They are plants that love the cool fresh mountain air, and no matter how well they survive in lowland gardens they always remain unwilling captives if taken too far from their native environment. The most difficult to transport is *Pulsatilla alpina*; while the other two species discussed here, *P. vernalis* and *P. vulgaris*, will survive if given proper treatment. These plants are so lovely—with their violet-coloured blooms, golden stamens, and pendulous form on silky-haired stems—that some extra trouble is well worthwhile.

Pulsatilla leaves and flowers have some medicinal value, but are poisonous. They contain an alkaloid whose action can be described as nervine, antispasmodic, and alterative, and which in ancient times was esteemed as a remedy in cases of nervous exhaustion and catarrh.

Cultivation. This varies slightly according to the species, and it is here dealt with specifically. Pulsatilla seed is very slow to germinate. It can be sown in flats or pans or in frames at any time between April and July, using a soil rich in humus and organic matter. The flats or pans must be kept shaded and moderately moist. Pricking out should be done as soon as the seedlings are large enough to handle; the young plants can be planted out in their permanent positions the following spring. A quicker method of propagation is by division of established plants, and this can be done in either autumn or spring before the plants begin to produce growth.

Pulsatilla alpina

Pulsatilla alpina Schrank
Native to the mountains of Europe and the Caucasus Mountains. Generally a hairy tomentose plant but occasionally glabrous. Leaves stalked, triangular in outline, three times divided into three; leaflets stalked and feathery. The stems bear three slightly stalked leaflets similar to the basal foliage. Flowers solitary, at first erect, later inclining downwards, hairy outside, white or pinkish white inside, suffused violet outside. The var. *sulphurea*—sometimes considered a sub-species—has sulphur-yellow blooms. *Pulsatilla alpina* requires a semi-shady position in peaty sandy soil and is never really happy at low altitudes.

Flowering period: Mar.–Apr.
Height: 4–5 ins.

Pulsatilla vernalis Mill.
Native to Europe and western Siberia; found mostly in alpine meadows. Roots rhizomatous, thick, blackish, and branched. The entire plant covered with long silky hairs. Leaves small, leathery, hairy, rosette-forming, and made up of two pairs of rounded-oval evergreen leaflets. Stem leaves sessile and linear. Buds and flowers at first inclined, later becoming upright, with the six petals initially forming a bell-shaped bloom which eventually opens wide; internally white, later becoming a delicate violet, externally covered with thick golden-bronze down or felt-like hairs. Not easily cultivated in gardens; requires an acid soil which is peaty, very porous, cool, and fresh and a shady, fresh situation. Sometimes gives better results if over-wintered in pots placed in an unheated greenhouse.

Flowering period: May–June
Height: 8 ins.

Flowering period: Mar.–Apr.
Height: 6–8 ins.

Pulsatilla vulgaris Mill.
Native to Europe. Found in rather dry alpine meadows in alkaline (calcareous) soils. Has long branched black tap-roots; stems hairy, furnished towards the top with a collar of 10–15 linear leaflets and bearing a large solitary terminal flower that is at first erect, later becoming pendulous. Leaves stalked, much-divided, feathery-like and covered with scattered silky hairs. The corolla is covered with silky wool and consists of six oval-lanceolate petals forming a bell-like shape; colour violet, or lilac if seen against the light; stamens with yellow anthers, style violet, pointed. When the flowers have finished, a small feathery ball-like mass of filaments develops around the seeds and forms one of the main characteristics of the plant. At high altitudes *Pulsatilla vulgaris* loves the sun—as it does in any cool, fresh climate—but in the south the plants require at least partial shade. They like alkaline (calcareous) soil in an exposed, windy position and will also thrive in a fibrous, loamy soil that is alkaline (calcareous). The typical type has reddish-violet blooms and, although widespread and even common in its natural habitat, it is rarely found at low altitudes. The sub-species *P. grandis* Wender. has much larger flowers; the sub-species *P. slavica* Reuss. is very early-flowering. The var. *halleri* Willd. has erect pinkish petals; var. *montana* Hpe. has blackish-violet perpetually semi-pendent flowers.

Punica

(POMEGRANATE)
Family: Punicaceae
Half-hardy deciduous shrubs or small trees
Position: sun
Propagation: seed, cuttings, or grafting
Cultivation easy

The pomegranate is so beautiful in all its aspects—the fruit, the leaves, the shape of the plant—that it has given rise to countless legends and has become the theme of dream, fantasy, and story, entering into religion as well as mythology, symbology, and folklore. In the arts, too, pomegranates have been apostrophized in poetry, depicted on ceramics, woven into fine fabrics, reproduced in precious metals, and carved in wood.
Before delving into the pomegranate's legendary and historical past it would be well to mention that it is a plant of great antiquity,

traceable back to the Pliocene period. It seems to have originated in what is now Iran and is still found growing wild there, flourishing in the rocky Persian terrain.

The plant and its fruit are depicted in Egyptian tomb reliefs dating back as early as 2500 B.C.; and the fruit is mentioned in papyri from the time of Thutmosis I (1525–1512 B.C.) and Akhenaten (1379–1362 B.C.). In the burial chamber of the tomb of Ramesses IV (1166–1160 B.C.) actual dried pomegranates were found. The pomegranate also loomed large in Sumerian, Phoenician, and other ancient Near Eastern religions. In one of her Asian aspects, the goddess Rhea (or Cybele) was invoked as Agditis, and was often represented as a hermaphroditic deity; and a certain myth concerning this vegetation-cult divinity relates that Agditis was tied to a pomegranate tree and robbed of her/his male attributes. This is an extremely early instance of the connexion between pomegranates and blood and fertility.

The Old Testament contains a number of references to the pomegranate; some of the most evocative may be found in the Song of Songs: "Thy temples are like a piece of pomegranate within thy locks" (4:3); "Thy plants are an orchard of pomegranates with pleasant fruits" (4:13); "I would cause thee to drink of spiced wine of the juice of my pomegranate" (8:2). The Hebrews held the pomegranate in great esteem as one of the characteristic plants of the land of Israel: "A land of wheat and barley, and vines, and fig trees, and pomegranates" (Deut. 8:8). Pomegranates *(rimmonim)* ornamented the robes of the High Priest and were also employed in the decorations of Solomon's Temple. Originally, the ornaments that topped the rollers of the Scrolls of the Law were silver or gold pomegranates, and to this day these elements are called *rimmonim* whether they resemble pomegranates or not. The rabbis made frequent metaphorical use of the pomegranate; the many-seeded fruit was a symbol of the Torah with its 613 precepts, and even the most worthless of men was "as full of good deeds as is the pomegranate full of seeds".

The story of Persephone (which has been frequently mentioned in this book) is perhaps the best-known example of the importance of the pomegranate in Classical mythology. After Persephone's abduction by Hades, her mother, Demeter, sought for her throughout the world. On discovering that her daughter had been spirited off to the nether regions, she appealed to Zeus for aid. The god told Demeter that Persephone could be liberated on one condition: that during her sojourn in the Underworld she must not have partaken of any food. But it was revealed that she had eaten a few pomegranate seeds from the fruit that Hades offered her, and this prevented her release. A compromise was reached, however, and Persephone was allowed to return to earth for a certain period each year, but she must return to the Underworld and pass as many months there as the seeds she had eaten. Thus were the seasons differentiated: during Persephone's months in the Underworld all green and blooming things withered and died, and they did not return to life and growth until she herself emerged from the bowels of the earth to bring fruitfulness and life to the sere and desolate landscape.

Christian symbolism thus drew not only upon the Hebraic tradition in its espousal of the pomegranate, but upon the pagan as well. The pomegranate is the symbol of Christ's Resurrection, a symbol of fertility, and, because of the countless seeds found within a single fruit, a symbol of the inner unity of the Church.

The Greeks believed that Aphrodite planted the first pomegranates on the island of Cyprus. In the *Odyssey,* Homer writes of the "gods' glorious gifts in the palace of Alcinoös", King of the Phaiacians, where there were "tall trees in full luxuriance, pears and pomegranates and apple-trees with glorious fruit" that "never fails or comes to an end all the year round". In the lore of some parts of the Middle East, it was a pomegranate, not an apple, that Eve offered to Adam in the Garden of Eden. There is also a tradition that it was a pomegranate that Paris awarded to Aphrodite (thereby setting in motion the circumstances that finally precipitated the Trojan War). In some of the Oedipus myths pomegranates are figured. One version has it that the pomegranate planted over the tomb of Eteocles, Antigone's cruel brother, bore fruit that dripped blood; another states that a pomegranate sprang from the blood of their cousin Meneocles when he killed himself. This association with blood is only natural, because of the blood-red juice of the fruit and its deep blood-red rind with its almost lacquer-like sheen.

One of the Hindu myths about the legendary Emperor Vikramaditya tells of a young princess whose parents locked her within a walled garden guarded so closely that entry was impossible. They then proclaimed that they would give her in marriage to any man who could penetrate the garden and secretly remove the three pomegranates concealed beneath the couch where the princess slept surrounded by her serving-maids. (This peculiar story seems to contain within it the seeds of many well-known European fairy tales: among them, that of the sleeping beauty and the princess and the pea.)

Even today, the pomegranate with its ruby-red interior bursting with glistening seeds is a symbol of fecundity among Mediterranean peoples. In areas like Sicily it is popularly assumed that whenever "pomo" is mentioned, it is a pomegranate rather than an apple that is referred to. In Turkey, the old custom (probably Greek in origin) still obtains of the bride throwing a ripe pomegranate to the ground, the number of seeds that fall out of the split fruit indicating the number of children she will bear. The co-author of this book recalls that his father, the noted Italian composer Ildebrando Pizzetti, a man of extraordinary sensitivity and sensibility, like the ancients considered the pomegranate as sacred. Every autumn, a selection of the fruits was bought, and in his exquisite and orderly calligraphy Maestro Pizzetti inscribed the date on the shiny red skin of each fruit. They were then placed in tall glass jars or vases, where, even when dry, they made a brave display throughout the winter months. They never rotted or shrivelled, which is a characteristic peculiar to this fruit when properly stored.

Here, then, is a plant fabulously rich in lore and legend, ancient and beautiful, yet, paradoxically, common enough for its fruits to be available at almost every vegetable market and even supermarket. For all its background, it can be widely grown by anyone who lives in a locality where the winters are not too severe; and when dwarfed it can even be grown as a house plant or trained as a Bonsai.

The name pomegranate derives from the Latin *pomum* (apple) and *granatus* (having many seeds). The name of the genus derives from *Punicus*, the Latin adjective for Carthage; and Pliny the Elder wrote that the choicest pomegranates came from that city.

Those readers who live in Southern Europe, or in those parts of the United States where the plants can be grown, should certainly cultivate the pomegranate. If you are superstitious, you may believe that the fruits will bring good luck; if not, you will still have in your garden one of the most beautiful of plants, whose attractive form and richly brilliant colouring will give long-lasting pleasure.

The most attractive pomegranate fruits are borne by the fruiting varieties in their various forms. The purely flowering pomegranates with double blooms do not produce fruits, while several other varieties that are cultivated exclusively for their flowers produce less spectacular fruits. It should be noted, however, that numerous types produce quite good fruits and superb flowers, including the lovely little dwarf pomegranate *Punica granatum* var. *nana*, a perfect pot plant producing an abundance of brilliantly coloured flowers and fruits while only 8–10 ins. high.

Of the two species that comprise the genus, *Punica protopunica* is native to the island of Socotra; while *Punica granatum* is diffused throughout the Mediterranean region—its cultivation normally being possible wherever fig trees are grown.

We do not know for certain when pomegranates were first cultivated in European gardens. We know from William Turner that in 1548 the plant was cultivated in the Duke of Somerset's garden at Syon House, near Kew, but it is very probable that the plant was grown before that date in some monastery or convent garden for its medicinal properties. Prior to 1618 John Tradescant introduced from the Continent a double-flowered variety with crimson blooms, "as big as a double Provence rose". At the beginning of the same century there were also numerous garden varieties in cultivation.

The medicinal virtues of *Punica granatum* have been known since

Punica granatum var. *nana*
From *Curtis's Botanical Magazine*,
1803, plate 634

Antiquity. Cato spoke of its properties as a vermifuge, and it is one of the oldest of drugs used in the removal of tapeworm. The active principle is contained in the root bark. The bark has a slight odour and an astringent acid flavour, and when chewed turns the saliva yellow. It contains various alkaloids, and resinous and peptic substances. The bark and the skin of the fruit have similar properties but to a lesser degree. The pulp-coated seeds are used in flavouring certain syrups of which the best-known is grenadine. Curiously enough, Bryant's *Flora Diaetetica* (1783) notes that pomegranates should "be eaten in moderation because they can putrify the blood". Pomegranate rind is rich in tannin and was often used to manufacture a red dye that was chiefly employed in the tanning of morocco leather, and an excellent ink was once extracted from the pericarp of the fruits.

The fruit and flowers of the pomegranate, *Punica granatum*

Cultivation. This is very easy. *Punica granatum* can tolerate temperatures as low as 15°F. if protected from strong and continuous wind. It is much hardier than orange, lemon, or olive trees. It thrives in any type of soil, even tolerating that near the sea, and it does not mind drought. In the north it is often grown in large tubs or pots and it is excellent for such purposes, especially the dwarf form. The plants develop a dense mass of interlacing branches; in spring these should be thinned to allow light and air to reach the centre and also to keep the plant a good shape. Pot-grown plants will benefit from periodic applications of a liquid organic fertilizer, but only during their growing season; in winter they are completely dormant and require very little water. Well-coloured but not dead-ripe fruits should be harvested in September–October, and they will continue to ripen after they have been picked.

Propagation can be effected from seed or by cuttings. The dwarf pomegranate is best raised from seed sown as soon as it is ripe in a warm greenhouse; the seedlings should be grown on in pots. They will flower and fruit within 3–4 years. For the large normal types, propagation from seed would be too slow and they should be raised from cuttings or, in the case of special varieties, by grafting onto seedlings of the type plant. Cuttings can be taken in March, before the leaves appear, and rooted in a warm greenhouse in pure sand. Propagation can also be effected by air layering in July, or, in the case of large specimens, by detaching the young growths that generally appear around the base of the parent plant. Normal pomegranate plants are reasonably fast-growing if situated in a warm sunny position; the dwarf form is incredibly slow-growing in both height and width, but when grown in pots this is an advantage (especially for *bonsai* enthusiasts), as they have such a neat, compact habit and will flower when only a few inches high.

(Pomegranate)
Flowering period: June–Aug.
Height: up to 18 ft.
Zone 8 southwards

Punica granatum L.

Native to an area extending from Iran to northwestern India. A large half-hardy deciduous shrub or small tree with a few scattered spines on its branches. Leaves oblong or ovate, opposite, obtuse, entire, glabrous, and generally shiny-surfaced. Flowers axillary, five-petalled, single, $1-1\frac{1}{2}$ ins. in diameter, brilliant orange-red; calyx tubular, divided into 5–9 laciniated coral-red triangular sections. Fruit apple-like, 2–3 ins. in diameter, containing numerous reddish juicy sweet seeds which are the edible part of the fruit. When ripe, the rind assumes magnificent tints of orange and scarlet, and, before they fall, the leaves turn rich golden-yellow, making the plants of considerable value for autumn colouring in the garden. The flowering types have more spectacular blooms and, in the case of the double varieties, do not fruit; and the fruiting varieties have less conspicuous flowers. The following is a brief list giving the best varieties of each type:

For fruiting

> var. *acida* or var. *selvatica*, flavour acid, fruits very large, often 4 ins. in diameter, skin brilliantly coloured
>
> var. *Dolce*, similar to var. *acida* but with smaller fruits and darker skin
>
> var. *nana*, a dwarf form of var. *acida*, with single flowers, and fruits up to 2 ins. in diameter
>
> var. *Paper Shell*, a very thin-skinned variety, pale yellow with crimson markings; fruits very large, juicy, and very sweet
>
> var. *Rhoda*, large crimson fruits with thin but hard skins; sweetly flavoured and fragrant
>
> var. *Spanish Ruby*, large vividly coloured fruits with rich crimson pulp
>
> var. *subacida*, fruits with acid-flavoured pulp
>
> var. *Wonderful*, brilliant crimson fruits up to 5 ins. in diameter; skin vivid crimson; pulp surrounding the seeds brightly coloured, fragrant, and juicy

For flowering
> var. *Double Red*, pompon-like flowers, very large, with vivid scarlet petals; larger-flowered than the single type
> var. *Double Yellow*, similar to the preceding but with pale-yellow variegated petals
> var. *Double White*, similar to var. *Double Red* but with pure-white flowers
> var. *legrellei*, double flowers with the petals variegated yellow and scarlet; the same plant sometimes also bears scarlet flowers irregularly variegated
> var. *nana doppia* (syn. *Punica granatum nanum*), double scarlet flowers in groups, very free-flowering and excellent for pot culture; dwarf, compact habit, and very slow-growing

Pyracantha

(FIRE THORN)
Family: Rosaceae
Hardy evergreen shrubs
Position: sun or partial shade
Propagation: seed or cuttings
Cultivation easy

There are few plants whose nomenclature has been so confused as the various species of the genus *Pyracantha*. Different authorities—botanists, nurserymen, and gardeners—have classified these shrubs into the genera *Cotoneaster*, *Mespilus*, and *Crataegus*; in spite of the fact that plants of genus *Pyracantha* have definite characteristics that distinguish them from those of any other genera. Pyracanthas' most important characteristics show that they are evergreen, with entire leaves (never lobed), spiny, with alternate foliage, have white flowers, plus various minute purely botanical variations in the construction of these flowers. Plants of the genus *Crataegus*, with which pyracanthas are most frequently confused, are deciduous, have lobed foliage, and the double or single flowers can be either white, pink, or red. Cotoneasters never have spines and have leaves that are entire. This confusion is particularly common on the Continent, where the name pyracantha is sometimes not even included in the index of catalogues published by otherwise reputable nurserymen. The genus *Pyracantha* comprises about half a dozen species—

Berries of
Pyracantha coccinea

slightly more according to the classification of some botanists—with a wide area of distribution including Southern Europe, Asia Minor, the Himalayas, and China. They are extremely useful and versatile garden plants which, according to the manner in which they are cultivated, can be used in several different ways. They are excellent for forming magnificent hedges, attractive at all seasons, with their white flowers, their evergreen habit, and colourful berries. If left to develop naturally in positions where there is an abundance of space, pyracanthas will form enormous individual specimens of surpassing beauty. They are ideal for cultivating as wall plants, either in the garden or against the walls of buildings. Trained in the form of pyramids, etc., they create splashes of flame with their orange-scarlet berries. The name is of Greek origin and does, in fact, correspond to the common name of Fire Thorn—*pyr* (fire) and *acantha* (thorn).

Cultivation. Very easy, but although the plants are hardy they are not to be recommended for high altitudes or for localities where prolonged very severe frosts are regularly experienced. They prefer a not-too-heavy soil, in either sun or partial shade, which is always well-drained and deep. Propagation can be effected from seed sown in the open in autumn or spring, or by means of cuttings taken from half-ripened wood in July and inserted in sandy soil in frames or in a sheltered position outside. Seed is freely available when the globose yellow, red, orange, or scarlet fruits ripen in late summer and autumn; although these are always a great temptation to birds. If not eaten by the birds, these brightly coloured decorative berries persist well into the winter.

Flowering period: May–June
Fruiting period:
early fall–early spring
Height: up to 12 ft.
Zone 7 southwards

Pyracantha angustifolia C. K. Schneider
Native to China. Forms a dense spreading shrub of bushy habit with rigid branches which when young are covered with a downy grey felt. Leaves narrow, oblong, up to 2 ins. in length, glabrous, dark green. Small white flowers of little ornamental value. Fruits brilliant orange-yellow when ripe, covered with grey down when young, globose with a flattened top. First introduced into Kew by a Lieutenant Jones in 1899. Valuable because it retains its prolific berries until March, long after those of other species have fallen.

Flowering period: May–June
Fruiting period: Sept.–Oct.
Height: up to 20 ft.
Zone 6 southwards

Pyracantha atalantioides Staff. (syn. *Pyracantha gibbsii*)
Native to China. First discovered by General Mesny in 1880 but not introduced into European gardens until 1907. Habit erect and rigid. One of the least spiny species and one of the most vigorous. Small white flowers in early summer, followed by vivid scarlet berries in autumn. Originally named *Pyracantha gibbsii* in honour of the Honourable Vicary Gibbs, in whose famous garden at Aldenham

one of the finest specimens was cultivated; later it was discovered that the same species had many years previously been identified and named *Pyracantha atalantioides*. Consequently, and in accordance with the International Code of Nomenclature, the older specific name had to be given precedence.

Pyracantha coccinea Roem. (Everlasting Thorn)
Flowering period: May–June
Fruiting period: Sept.–Oct.
Height: up to 20 ft.
Zone 5 southwards

Native to Southern Europe and Asia Minor. A species with a very dense close-growing abundantly leaved habit. The white flowers are profusely produced and have a certain ornamental value. Fruits brilliant coral-red. This is the most suitable pyracantha for growing against walls, where the plants will produce a really impressive quantity of berries which, unfortunately, are greatly favoured by blackbirds. This species is, in fact, one of the best of all evergreen wall plants. A particularly good form is the var. *lalandei* Diepell., raised from seed by M. Lalande of Angers, in 1874. This variety has larger leaves, obovate in shape, up to $3\frac{1}{4}$ ins. long, dark shiny green above, lighter green beneath, with a more vigorous habit and larger orange-red berries $\frac{1}{3}$ in. in diameter. There is also a rarely seen white-berried form, var. *fructu-albo*.

Pyracantha crenulata Roem.
Flowering period: May–June
Fruiting period: Sept.–Oct.
Height: up to 15 ft.
Zone 7 southwards

Native to the warmer regions of the Himalayas. A variable species closely resembling *Pyracantha coccinea*, but less vigorous and less tolerant of cold. It has rounded leaves (instead of pointed as in *P. coccinea*), with smaller flowers and smaller fruits, the latter varying in colour from orange-yellow to red. It forms a large spiny shrub but is slower growing than *Pyracantha coccinea*. For a restricted space in a mild climate *Pyracantha crenulata* can be more useful than the bigger *Pyracantha coccinea*. By some authorities it is considered to be only a form of the latter.

Pyracantha rogersiana Chitt.
Flowering period: May–June
Fruiting period: Sept.–Oct.
Height: up to 10 ft.
Zone 7 southwards

Native to China. A very spiny shrub of dense habit and with the typical small white flowers, but the leaves are much smaller than in other species, not exceeding $1\frac{1}{2}$ ins. in length, oblanceolate, glabrous, bright or even vivid green. Very distinct for its beautiful golden-yellow berries, $\frac{1}{4}$ in. in diameter. Several attractive varieties are also available, such as var. *flava*, with bright yellow berries, and var. *aurantiaca*, with reddish-orange berries. A graceful and elegant group of pyracanthas easily distinguished by their small foliage.

Pyracantha yunnanensis Chitt. (syn. *Pyracantha crenatoserrata*)
Flowering period: May–June
Fruiting period: Oct.–Nov.
Height: up to 18 ft.
Zone 6 southwards

Native to the Yunnan province of China. Similar to the species *P. atalantioides* but more spiny and with smaller coral-red fruits which mature later. Also distinguished by its larger leaves, often $2\frac{1}{2}$ ins.

long and half as wide. Originally introduced into France in 1906. Birds permitting, it retains its fruits all the winter and even until spring, a fact that makes it a particularly welcome species in the garden.

Quamoclit

(STAR GLORY OR CYPRESS VINE)
Family: Convolvulaceae
Tender perennial or annual climbers
Position: sun
Propagation: seed
Cultivation easy

The derivation of the name *Quamoclit* is uncertain, although some sources state it is Aztec in origin. The quamoclits are a genus of delightfully elegant and graceful climbers, mostly grown as annuals although in their native tropical habitat many are perennials. There are about a dozen species diffused throughout tropical America, among which is an attractive and curious climber more frequently known as *Mina lobata*, with red and yellow flowers.

Although their cultivation is as easy as that of their near relatives, the convolvulus, seed germination is sometimes capricious and erratic; a small annoyance easily rectified by successive sowings and amply compensated by the pleasure provided by the very attractive flowers and foliage. Quamoclits are not hardy and will not tolerate frost. They are also rather fussy about soil and give best results in a mixture of:

    2 parts fibrous loam
    2 parts leafsoil
    1 part sand

Propagation is from seed, which should be sown in February–March in a warm greenhouse, preferably in fibre pots with a diameter of $2\frac{1}{2}$–3 ins. Plant 2–3 seeds per pot, and allow the seedlings to develop to a height of 4–6 ins. before planting them out in their flowering positions when all danger of frost has passed. It will be necessary to provide some small stakes as supports while the seedlings are still in their pots.

Quamoclits require a warm, sunny position and, if not supplied with supports on which to climb, are suitable for planting against wire or plastic netting or a wooden trellis. They give good results on terraces and balconies, where they can be grown in large pots, but where, because of the limited supply of soil, it is necessary to give them periodic applications of liquid fertilizer. In southern gardens where the weather is always mild, *Quamoclit coccinea* and *Quamoclit pennata* can be sown outside in March in their flowering position. I have, in fact, found that these two species will often reproduce year after year from self-sown seed that is always produced in abundance.

Quamoclit coccinea Moench (syn. *Ipomoea coccinea*)
Native to tropical America. Leaves heart-shaped, long-pointed. Stems slender, up to 18 ft. long under the most favourable conditions. Flowers solitary, three or more on branching axillary longish stems. Flowers trumpet-shaped, 1 in. long, corolla tube narrow, but with the mouth up to $\frac{3}{4}$ in. wide; colour brilliant crimson-scarlet. The var. *luteola* (syn. *Ipomoea luteola*) has yellow or yellowish-orange flowers; while the var. *hederifolia* (syn. *Ipomoea hederifolia*, *Mina sanguinea*) has darker green ivy-like foliage divided into 3–5 narrow lobes, with considerably larger flowers.

(Star Ipomoea)
Annual
Flowering period: July–Oct.
Height: up to 18 ft.

Quamoclit lobata

Quamoclit coccinea

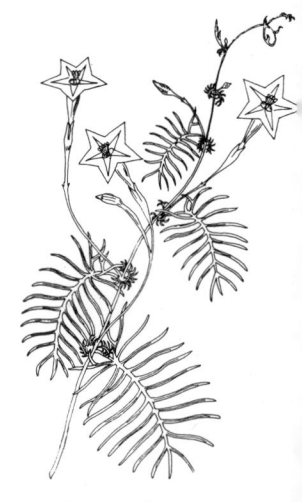

Quamoclit pennata

Quamoclit lobata House (syn. *Mina lobata*, *Ipomoea versicolor*, *Quamoclit mina*)
Native to Mexico. Leaves three-lobed, heart-shaped at the base, dark green. Stems vigorous, twining, with reddish surfaces. Inflorescences borne at the ends of branching stalks and composed of numerous cylindrical flowers arranged in a slender spike, with up to twelve individual blooms per spike; each flower 1–1$\frac{1}{2}$ ins. long. Initially the flowers are crimson-red, changing to yellow as they become fully

Perennial
Flowering period: July–Sept.
Height: up to 18 ft.

expanded, when the mouth opens to expose the prominent stamens. All the flowers face in the same direction. Each flower spike can be up to 10–12 ins. long, with all the red flowers at the base, half-red and half-yellow flowers in the centre, and the yellow flowers at the top, producing an attractive, fascinating effect.

(Cypress Vine)
Annual
Flowering period: July–Aug.
Height: up to 10 ft.

Quamoclit pennata Bojer. (syn. *Ipomoea quamoclit, Convolvulus pinnatus*)
Native to tropical America. An unusually graceful and decorative annual climber with the most beautiful finely dissected dark-green foliage with the numerous linear segments deeply cut down to the central vein. Stems slender, twining. Flowers rich scarlet, $1\frac{1}{2}$ ins. long, with the corolla tube narrow and the mouth broadly star-like. These solitary but freely produced flowers are long-stalked and stand up vertically, giving the impression of tiny red parasols.

Ranunculus

(BUTTERCUP OR CROWFOOT)
Family: Ranunculaceae
Hardy or half-hardy herbaceous or tuberous-rooted perennials
Position: sun or partial shade
Propagation: seed or division
Cultivation easy
Poisonous

Ranunculus Ficaria

The name *Ranunculus* derives from the Latin word *rana* (frog). The plant was so-named since ranunculuses frequently grow in marshy places inhabited by frogs. They also flourish not only by ponds and stagnant water, but also along the banks of streams and brooks, and in cool, moist fields and meadowlands. They grow side by side with white field daisies and blue hepaticas; the shiny petals of *Ranunculus Ficaria* are one of the first signs of spring, even before the sun's rays have any real warmth and before the cuckoo begins to call. As the season advances, other ranunculuses open their equally attractive flowers: *Ranunculus Thora, Ranunculus aquatilis, Ranunculus divaricatus*. Weeds though they may be, they are an essential and beautiful part of European flora. Those lucky enough to have a stream or a pond in their garden, or even a very damp patch of grassland nearby, would do well to offer hospitality to a collection of native European ranunculuses, which can hold their own in the company of many exotic semi-aquatic bog plants.

Apart from the European species, and apart from other beautiful but difficult species such as *Ranunculus glacialis*—which is almost impossible to cultivate in the average garden—the one most frequently referred to is the species *R. asiaticus*. History confirms that *Ranunculus asiaticus* was first imported into Europe by the Crusaders in the twelfth and thirteenth centuries, and in particular by King Louis IX of France (1214–1270), on his return from the Fifth Crusade. The results, however, were unfortunate and the plants soon disappeared, either because of ignorance on the part of the cultivators, or because they did not find favour with our ancestors. It was not until the reign of Sultan Mohammed IV (1648–1687) that ranunculuses became really fashionable and widely grown throughout Europe. This ruler of the Ottoman Empire was a genuine fanatic about flowers and a true ranunculus enthusiast; he procured the most beautiful varieties from Crete, Rhodes, Cyprus, and Damascus for the gardens of his seraglio, guarding them with the same jealousy with which he guarded his wives. Eventually, however, through bribery and corruption, some of his plants were stolen and passed into the hands of ambassadors and foreign dealers. The first commercial centre for the sale of ranunculus corms (or claws, as they are known in the trade) was Marseilles; later the trade passed to the Dutch, like the trade of most other bulbous plants. Father Agostino del Riccio has left written confirmation of their culture in Italy in 1592.

The genus comprises 280 or more species with a world-wide distribution, the number depending on how they are classified by various authorities. About fifty species are native to Southern Europe. In the majority of cases they prefer a rather arid soil, and are found wild at considerable altitudes. The 6-in.-high, white- or pink-flowered *Ranunculus glacialis* is indigenous up to 12,000 ft. or more in Arctic regions.

Nearly all of the ranunculuses are poisonous, and even the most hare-brained folk-medicine prescriptions have rarely suggested them for internal use, with the possible exception of minute doses prepared from *Ranunculus sceleratus* for use as a pain-killer. All parts of the plant are poisonous, containing an acrid, volatile substance. As fodder, when dried and mixed with grass and other herbs, they are not poisonous to animals. Apuleius gave the name Horror Plant to the ranunculus because at one time beggars rubbed their legs with the foliage, thereby creating horrible sores and blisters to arouse compassion. Ranunculus poisoning, caused by chewing any green part of the plant, is characterized by vomiting, gastric pains, diarrhoea, dizziness, cramps, loss of consciousness, difficulty in breathing, and palpitations. If a stomach pump is not used quickly the victim can die within a day or two. Some of the most poisonous species are *R.*

Ranunculus acris

Peony-flowered
Ranunculus asiaticus hybr

aquatilis, R. aconitifolius, R. Flammula, R. Lingua, R. repens, and *R. acris*. The only non-poisonous species is the gay little *Ranunculus Ficaria*, whose fleshy roots are even reputed to be edible.

Cultivation. The cultivation of *Ranunculus asiaticus* has now become an important large-scale industry for the production of cut bloom; the original species having been transformed into many lovely single and double types and varieties by the hybridist. The original red and yellow colours have also been extended to many other tints including green and bicoloured and tricoloured varieties; however, the colour blue has still to be developed. *Ranunculus asiaticus* are easy to cultivate, requiring a light, deeply dug, well-drained soil rich in humus. They should never be fertilized with fresh manure, although well-rotted and totally composted manure gives excellent results. They like an open, airy position in full sun, and while hardy in mild climates, in northern gardens it is better to remove the fang-shaped corms from the soil in autumn when the foliage begins to die down prior to their entering the dormant winter period, and replanting each spring. The corms or claws are very fragile and should be handled with care, planting them with the eye uppermost, at a distance of 4–5 ins. apart and at a depth of 2–3 ins., according to their size. When the corms have started active growth, periodic applications of a liquid organic fertilizer will be beneficial. When flowering has finished, the leaves and any remaining flower stems should not be cut off until they have turned yellow and died down. When removed from the soil the claws should be stored in sand or dry peat, in a frost-free, dry, well-aired place until the following spring. Although the corms can be left in the ground in mild localities, or removed from the soil and replanted the following spring, flowering gradually degenerates in successive years and better flowers will always be obtained from fresh, new stock. Propagation is by division of the corms or from seed sown in late summer in pots, pans, or flats in a coldframe or an unheated greenhouse, using a soil mixture of sand and peat. Seedlings should be planted out in spring. The herbaceous perennial ranunculuses can be propagated by division in autumn or spring, or from seed sown in coldframes in spring.

Ranunculus aconitifolius

Herbaceous perennial
Flowering period: May–June
Height: up to 2 ft.

Ranunculus aconitifolius L.
Native to Europe. A hardy herbaceous perennial up to 2 ft. high mainly found in mountain pastures. An excellent garden plant for its masses of small button-like white flowers. Leaves shiny, palmately divided, dark green, with the segments conspicuously dentated. There is a double-flowered form with small rosette-like blooms.

(Tuberous, Persian, or French Ranunculus)
Tuberous-rooted herbaceous perennial
Flowering period: July–Sept.
Height: up to 15 ins.
Useful for cutting

Ranunculus asiaticus L. (syn. *Ranunculus orientalis*)
Native to Southeastern Europe, Greece, and Asia Minor. Moderately hardy tuberous-rooted perennials, with the small, black corms shaped like claws or fangs. It is the best known of all the ranunculuses in its

Ranunculus gramineus
From *Curtis's Botanical Magazine*,
1791, plate 164

various hybrid forms, and is widely cultivated for its beautiful multi-coloured flowers. Basal leaves cuneate-oval; stem leaves divided into numerous ovate segments, light green in colour. The many types are known commercially as Peony-flowered, Turban, Persian, French, etc., all of which are semi-double or very double geometrically formed compact flowers with a diameter of 1–2 ins., in a remarkable colour range including all shades of pink, red, yellow, mauve, orange, and white. The original species is now rarely cultivated and some of the best of each group are:

Persian: Barbaroux, orange-scarlet
Fireball, scarlet
Jaune Suprême, golden-yellow
Jupiter, brick-red
Montblanc, pure white
Pink Perfection, pink

French: Count Aehrenthal, yellow
Mahogany, dark maroon
Mathilde Christine, white
Orange Queen, orange-red
Primrose Beauty, pale yellow
Veronica, carmine-red

Peony: Brilliant Star, scarlet
Edelweiss, cream-white
Golden Ball, orange-yellow
Scarlet Glow, scarlet
Triumphator, dark pink

Turban: Canarybird, sulphur-yellow
Grand Duke, carmine-red
Hercules, white
Rosalie, pink
Romano, scarlet
Turban Orange, orange

(Buttercup)
Herbaceous perennial
Flowering period: June–Sept.
Height: up to 18 ins.

Ranunculus bulbosus L.
Native to Europe. A hardy herbaceous perennial which can be a troublesome weed in gardens. In late spring, however, it is one of our most beautifully coloured wild flowers; its intense butter-yellow has earned it the name of Buttercup. The flowers are single and internally the petals have a shiny, enamelled appearance. There is a less invasive double-flowered form var. *speciousus plenus* with very attractive foliage and beautiful yellow flowers 2 ins. in diameter.

Herbaceous perennial
Flowering period: Apr.–June
Height: 12 ins.

Ranunculus gramineus L.
Native to Southwestern Europe. A hardy herbaceous perennial with narrow, lanceolate, grass-like, blue-grey leaves 12 ins. high. Small golden-yellow single flowers in great profusion on graceful erect stems.

Reseda

(MIGNONETTE)
Family: Resedaceae
Herbaceous perennials generally cultivated as annuals

A modest little plant cultivated since ancient times; the species *R. luteola* was grown for the production of a valuable yellow dye, now, of course, replaced by some synthetic product. In literature, the intense fragrance of *Reseda odorata* has often been called divine, and the English poet William Cowper dedicated some lines to the mignonette in his poem "The Task", describing it as "the fragrant weed, the Frenchman's darling". It is Cowper who is supposed to have given the plant its common name.

Reseda odorata has also been credited with certain medicinal virtues, and in the past it was used externally for the relief of arthritis and some forms of dermatitis. The genus consists of fifty-five species, three of which are native to Europe (*R. alba*, *R. lutea*, and *R. luteola*) while the strongly scented *Reseda odorata* is native to North Africa; the remainder are indigenous to the Mediterranean regions and the Red Sea area. However, only *Reseda odorata* has any real garden value.

Cultivation. The cultivation of mignonette is relatively easy. It is a herbaceous perennial, normally grown as an annual, and suitable for beds, borders, balconies, terraces, window boxes, and pot culture. It prefers an acid, moist, but well-drained soil rich in humus (such as well-rotted leafsoil). In the north it thrives in a sunny open position, but in the south it is more successful in partial shade. Seed is generally sown in a warm greenhouse in spring, preferably only a few seeds in individual pots, eliminating the weakest seedlings and then growing on the remainder in successively larger pots (without separating them, because mignonette resents root disturbance and does not easily transplant). The resulting plants can be planted out in their flowering positions in May, or used as flowering plants in pots (pots should be at least 6 ins. in diameter). In warm southern climates seed can also be sown directly into its flowering position in March–April, thinning out the seedlings to about 6 ins. apart, but where heavy spring rains or storms are experienced the young plants inevitably suffer. At no time should the plants be coddled or cultivated in a high temperature.

Reseda luteola

Reseda lutea

Reseda odorata L.

Native to North Africa. Introduced into European gardens in 1752. Leaves alternate, oblong, either entire or three-lobed; flowers intensely fragrant. Inflorescence an erect spike with minute cream-

Flowering period: May–July
Height: 6–18 ins.
Position: sun or partial shade
Propagation: seed
Cultivation fairly easy
Very fragrant

white individual blooms in the original species, but more colourful flowers in the hybrids. Few flowers possess a fragrance so delightful and distinctive, thus its popularity never diminishes, although without its powerful fragrance the plant would probably never have attracted the attention of hybridists. During the past 150 years many new hybrids have been introduced with greatly enlarged flower spikes the colours of which now include shades of yellow, white, and red. Some of the best are:

> Bismark, red
> Cloth of Gold, yellow
> Golden Queen, yellow
> Matchet, red
> Parson's White, white

Reseda odorata

Rhododendron

(INCLUDING AZALEA)
Family: Ericaceae
Hardy and half-hardy evergreen or deciduous trees or shrubs
Flowering period: early spring, spring, or summer
Position: partial shade, or sun at high altitudes
Propagation: seed, cuttings, grafting, or layering
Cultivation easy
In some cases scented, and useful for cutting

On the Continent it is an old joke to ask which arrived first, the British or the rhododendrons. That is, was it the acid, peaty soil and perpetually moist atmosphere of certain areas—such as the Italian Lake District—which intuitively attracted the British as a suitable rhododendron climate; or did the British simply take advantage of the existing natural conditions in an area they found so agreeable and so satisfying to their passion for growing rhododendrons? Whatever the answer may be, it is well known that many of Europe's oldest and most beautiful gardens owe their origin to British residents or British influence; and wherever climate and soil were suitable, rhododendrons were planted.

The rhododendron is a very ancient plant, and fossil remains show that certain species date back to the Miocene Era. The first rhododendrons mentioned in old texts are *Rhododendron ferrugineum* and *Rhododendron hirsutum*, both indigenous to Europe. During the sixteenth century, botanists use numerous other names to describe rhododendrons, such as *Ledum* or *Cistus*; and *Chamaecistus* was

Rhododendron luteum
From *Curtis's Botanical Magazine*,
1799, plate 433

used by Clusius. The name *Rhododendron* appears to have been given to the genus by Andrea Cesalpino in 1583. In his *De Plantis* (Vol. XV, Ch. XVII), he described *Rhododendron ferrugineum* as a shrub with oleander-like flowers. In Alpine mythology, the rhododendron is the most frequently mentioned plant. As favourite flower of the god Donner (Thor of Nordic mythology) it was known as Flower of the Giants, and in the Tyrol it was believed that a thunderbolt thrown by Donner was more likely to strike anyone wearing or carrying a flower of *Rhododendron ferrugineum*. From the Apennines comes the following legend: Near Mount Termino, where the roses of death (Alpine Rose or *Rhododendron ferrugineum*) now grow in solitude, a young man committed suicide by throwing himself from a high ridge of the mountainside because he suspected his sweetheart was unfaithful to him. On the contrary, the girl had been true to her beloved and she descended into the valley to shed desperate tears over his pitiful, broken body. And from the place where she had knelt gazing at the dear face of the one who had loved her so much, and now moistened with his blood and her tears, there sprang a quantity of roses of death which bloom in May in frightful solitude near the giant of the Apennines.

The genus name was officially recognized by Linnaeus in 1753, and at the same time he created another genus, *Azalea*. Later, botanists united azaleas with rhododendrons, thus creating a certain confusion in the minds of gardeners and commercial growers, but for present-day botanists the genus *Rhododendron* now includes azaleas, and the genus *Azalea* officially no longer exists. The most important differences that had previously divided the two for Linnaeus was that rhododendrons have ten stamens and are mostly evergreen, while the so-called azaleas have five stamens and are mostly deciduous; but there are several species of both genera where these characteristics are so intermingled that it now seems more logical to place them all in the genus *Rhododendron*. Their cultural requirements are broadly similar also, except in the case of certain species which require particular treatment.

The first species grown in European gardens was *Rhododendron hirsutum*, established before 1656 in the garden of John Tradescant; but this was evidently an exception because, like *Rhododendron ferrugineum*, it is a difficult plant to grow in gardens and neither of these species gives really successful results when removed from its native habitat. In 1736 John Bartram sent Collinson the first evergreen species, *Rhododendron maximum*, from the American Colonies. Probably because of an error in cultivation the plant was not provided with an acid soil and it did not bloom until 1756. *Rhododendron ponticum*, one of the most famous species and the parent of many hybrids, was not introduced into England until 1763. It was discovered by Tournefort during his travels to the

Near East (1700–1702) and so named because it was growing near the shores of the Black Sea, which was once part of the ancient Near Eastern kingdom of Pontus. Its European introduction was via Gibraltar apparently, and it became so well established in Great Britain that it soon escaped from cultivation and naturalized itself over large areas. During the first decade of the nineteenth century, *Rhododendron caucasicum* and *Rhododendron catawbiense* arrived. The first was discovered on the summits of the Caucasus Mountains, nearly at the timberline, and a specimen was presented to Sir Joseph Banks by the Russian traveller Count Apollos Apollosovitch Mussim-Pushkin (after whom, fortunately, the plant was not named). *Rhododendron caucasicum* was soon crossed with *Rhododendron chrysanthum*, which had been introduced from Siberia in 1796, to obtain yellow flowers and to provide hybrids with a yellow base that could be further exploited. *Rhododendron catawbiense* was discovered in North America by John Fraser and his son in 1799 while they were collecting plants for Tsar Paul I of Russia. The lucky discovery took place high in the Roanoke Mountains. The plant was brought to England by the two explorers in 1809.

Rhododendron
Ascot Brilliant

The first garden hybrids were obtained from crosses between *Rhododendron maximum*, *R. ponticum*, *R. caucasicum*, and *R. catawbiense*. These, however, produced only rather pale pink and mauvish blooms. To give colour to this new generation, the first Himalayan species made its welcome appearance. *Rhododendron arboreum* was discovered by Capt. Harwick in 1796, although flowering specimens did not reach Great Britain until 1825. In 1847–1851 Sir Dalton Hooker organized an expedition to the Himalayas and succeeded in collecting forty-three species, many of which were unknown. He also sent home to England seeds, descriptions, and drawings so that it was possible for his father, William Jackson Hooker, to publish the famous *Rhododendrons of the Sikkim Himalayas* (1849); the first monograph of its kind. A few years later, in 1855, *Rhododendron fortunei* was found in China by Robert Fortune.

Even before Hooker's expedition hybridists had already taken giant strides, but when all these new species became available they redoubled their efforts and soon flooded the market with new hybrids. The firm of Waterer, for instance, specialized in rhododendrons and azaleas for four successive generations. Among the Chinese species introduced during the twentieth century, *Rhododendron griersonianum*, discovered by Forrest in 1917, merits special attention. By 1952 this species had already produced 122 different hybrids and its possibilities have probably not yet been exhausted.

So much for the original rhododendrons. Among the plants previously known as azaleas, the first to be introduced into England was *Rhododendron viscosum*, part of a group of plants that Bishop Compton received from the Rev. John Banister. It was described by Plunkenet in 1691, died soon afterwards, and was reintroduced by Collinson in 1734, together with *Rhododendron nudiflorum*. *Rhododendron luteum* was introduced between 1793 and 1803. A furious programme of hybridization was also initiated with these plants, both in England and on the Continent. P. Mortier, a Ghent baker, forced the late-flowering varieties into bloom and retarded those which were precocious so as to have a wider range of material with which to work. Others followed his example and a real azalea industry was begun at Ghent; an industry that still thrives today. In 1850 there were already five hundred varieties of these Ghent azaleas, and then *Rhododendron molle* arrived from Japan to give the cultivation of hybrids a still greater impetus. In 1851 William Lobb sent the white *Rhododendron occidentale* from California to Veitch at Chelsea; this late-bloomer was then used by Anthony Waterer to give his hybrids the fragrance lacking in so many hybrids. Another group that was rapidly gaining favour was the dwarf evergreen types which originated from *Rhododendron simsii*. The popular Kurume types derive mainly from *Rhododendron obtusum* var. *kiusianum*, introduced into England in 1914 by E. H. Wilson, who also sent a collection of them to America from Japan in 1917. In 1918 Wilson made a special trip to Kurume—on the island of Kyushu, Japan—where he chose the fifty best varieties from the collection of 250 of Kijiro Akashi and had them sent to the Arnold Arboretum.

Nowadays, specialist catalogues offer a choice of more than 1,100 rhododendron species and varieties and, choosing with discernment, it is possible to have rhododendrons in flower in the garden from December to September, as specified in the flowering calendar that follows. According to the *Rhododendron Handbook* (1952), the genus *Rhododendron* comprises 750 species, but in the view of Capt. Kingdon-Ward this is not complete as there are still over one hundred species yet to be discovered in unexplored valleys of China and Tibet. If these valleys were not so remote, and if political conditions were better, such an assertion would cause considerable unrest in the minds of many would-be explorers and collectors.

The genus *Rhododendron* is very varied, and it includes little creeping shrubs only a few inches in height, as well as trees that reach a height of nearly 100 ft. The species are distributed over a vast area of the world and can be found growing under the most diverse conditions. *Rhododendron nivale* lives for eight months of the year buried in snow; while there are epiphytic species that thrive in tropical forests. Many are high alpine plants, and the zones richest in rhododendron species are the Himalayas and central and western China. Some are also indigenous to the Philippines and the Americas; North America having about twenty species. Many rhododendrons are deliciously scented, with a fragrance reminiscent of carnations, honeysuckle, and a suggestion of honey, and these are not so well known as they

Rhododendron ferrugineum

should be as shrubs with scented flowers. The Kurume and Kaempferi types are scentless, while many of the American species are fragrant.

Apart from their decorative value, European rhododendrons have little pharmacopoeial importance, although leaves of the species *R. ferrugineum* and *R. hirsutum* contain ericoline and arbutine, substances reputed to be effective in treating muscular rheumatism and certain kidney complaints. A more energetic reaction has been obtained from the species *R. chrysanthum*, *R. punctatum*, and *R. maximum*, which contain andromedotoxin, which is absent from the European species. Rhododendrons are, however, not entirely innocuous, although stories about the poisonous honey being made from certain species are probably exaggerated. Most reference books refer to the comments made by Pliny on a passage in Xenophon's *Anabasis*, where it is told that when Cyrus's victorious army reached Trebizond the famished soldiers began eating some honeycombs and were immediately taken ill, exhibiting such symptoms as vomiting, diarrhoea, delirium, and, finally, coma. Pliny was of the opinion that the honey was derived from oleander flowers, which at that time were called rhododendrons; but Tournefort, basing his information on local knowledge collected during his travels, asserts that the honey originated from flowers of *Rhododendron ponticum*. In 1796, while Anthony Hove was travelling in southern Russia, he wrote that along the Dnieper's southern reaches *Rhododendron ponticum* was known as "the stupefying shrub" and was considered by local people as a poison, although useful for treating certain maladies. In the Caucasus, cases of fatal poisoning have been verified when honeycombs are gathered; but it appears that as the honey matures its toxic properties diminish. Certain rhododendrons indigenous to Central Asia—we do not know for sure which species—are reputed to give off toxic smoke when their wood is burned, poisoning local people who have used the twigs to light their hearth fires. There is, however, another side to the story: many rhododendron flowers are particularly rich in nectar and even plants of *Rhododendron ponticum* grown in a greenhouse have been known to produce a large drop of nectar in each bloom which, as the flower fades, crystallizes into a substance resembling pure sugar. In Tibet candied rhododendron flowers were a much-sought-after delicacy. The foliage of certain species is poisonous to animals that graze on them; Alice M. Coats recalls that two shoots of *Rhododendron ciliatum* eaten by a baker's horse almost caused the death of the unfortunate beast.

Calendar of Flowering Periods (*month by month*)
The following is a selection of rhododendrons with their respective flowering periods. These dates refer to plants growing in northern Italy near the Swiss frontier (similar in climate to Zone 5 in North

Rhododendron thomsonii
From *Curtis's Botanical Magazine*,
1857, plate 4997

America). In milder climates the flowering period may start earlier, while at higher altitudes the flowering period will be a little later. More detailed descriptions are given in the specific discussions. (Hybrid types are printed in roman type, species in italic.)

January	Christmas Cheer	*lutescens*
	Praecox	Nobleanum
	mucronulatum	*dauricum*
February	*lutescens*	Praecox
	mucronulatum	Christmas Cheer
	Nobleanum	*dauricum*
March	Ascot Beauty	Jacksonii
	Broughtonii	*arboreum*
	lutescens	
April	*campylocarpum*	Broughtonii
	Cynthia	*arboreum*
	Ascot Beauty	Purple Splendour
	Britannia	Betty Wormold
	Jacksonii	Cunningham's White
	Zuider Zee	
May	Alice	Britannia
	Cynthia	*arboreum*
	Purple Splendour	*dichroanthum*
	Mme. de Bruin	Garibaldi
	Zuider Zee	*fortunei*
	Betty Wormold	Cunningham's White
	cinnabarinum	*insigne*
	ponticum	*campylocarpum*
	catawbiense	*molle*
	amoenum	*indicum*
	simsii	
June	Garibaldi	Mme. de Bruin
	cinnabarinum	Kluis Sensation
	dichroanthum	Azaleoides
	fortunei	Goldsworth Orange
	Concessum	*griersonianum*
	indicum	*caucasicum*
	simsii	*catawbiense*
	ponticum	*maximum*
July	*griersonianum*	Concessum
	Kluis Sensation	Polar Bear
	discolor	Albatross
	auriculatum	Goldsworth Orange
	diaprepes	Azaleoides
	Hesperides	Argosy
	maximum	

August	*auriculatum*	*diaprepes*
	serotinum	
September	*auriculatum*	*serotinum*
October	———	
November	———	
December	*mucronulatum*	Praecox
	Christmas Cheer	

Cultivation. Rhododendrons are not difficult to cultivate. In general, no pruning is necessary, but the plants do require a certain amount of care and attention at nearly every season. There are no half measures with rhododendrons: they either thrive, or they rapidly degenerate and die. Nearly all require similar cultural treatment and they prefer coolness to excessive heat. There are, however, certain exceptions such as the few tropical rhododendrons and the epiphytic species that live on the trunks of trees, but we are not concerned with those in this work. The successful cultivation of hardy rhododendrons can, therefore, be summarized in the following four fundamental, basic rules:

1. They must have an acid soil completely free from alkaline (calcareous) matter, and be watered exclusively with non-alkaline (non-calcareous) water.
2. They require a cool, light, moist, and well-drained soil, which must also be rich in organic matter such as peat, leafsoil, and humus.
3. The atmosphere where they are planted must be moist; and during spring, summer, and early autumn the plants must be abundantly and regularly watered unless there is a more or less constant rainfall. During very hot dry weather it is also necessary to spray the foliage.
4. Unless the plants are growing at high altitudes (where the sun may be brilliant, but its rays are not scorching), rhododendrons should have semi-shade; preferably that provided by such trees as birch, conifers, or sweet-chestnut—all trees that I have found ideal for associating with large plantings of rhododendrons.

In amplification of the above essential requirements, and regarding some other factors governing successful rhododendron cultivation, the following points should always be borne in mind. The plants are so generous and prolific with their flowers, and so abundant in seed production, that they are sometimes liable to exhaust themselves. Therefore, when practical, it is advisable to remove the flower heads as soon as they fade, thus sparing the plant from expending the energy of developing unwanted seed. From an altitude of approximately 700–2,000 ft., semi-shade is generally sufficient, but at lower altitudes

Rhododendron indicum

the shade should be much more dense; above 2,000 ft. shade is not necessary, although semi-shade will not be harmful. A practical confirmation of these figures can be seen in the superb Felice Piacenza Park, La Burcina, near Biella in northern Italy; here Europe's largest and finest collection of rhododendrons is thriving in full sun at an altitude of about 2,400 ft., in a completely natural, informal manner. (However, in the United States, especially north of Zone 7, the majority of nursery-raised rhododendrons are field-grown in full sun. Much of this field-grown stock will not bloom after the first year if planted in full shade. However, after ten years or so, the plants will acclimatise and produce blooms. There are exceptions to this, of course, and many native varieties do well in shade or sun.)

Rhododendron Praecox

Rhododendron roots are always shallow and the periodic application of a top dressing or mulch preferably in early spring or in autumn is very beneficial. Such top dressing can consist of well-composted manure mixed with leafsoil and peat. It is imperative, however, that the soil level should never be raised in the vicinity of the roots, and even an extra 2–3 ins. of soil or compost on top of the root ball can ruin a plant. An excellent fertilizer for rhododendrons is dried blood or cottonseed meal. The ideal pH for rhododendrons is a reading between 4 and 5.

Since rhododendrons dislike a bare soil surface above their shallow roots, a suitable ground cover for associating with hybrid and species rhododendrons can be formed with any of the following plants, all of which require the same cultural conditions as rhododendrons: primulas, vinca, ferns, lily of the valley, epimediums, tradescantias, trilliums, gaultherias, and shortias.

As we have said, rhododendrons, if properly treated, are not difficult to cultivate. As in the case of all other garden plants, however, some are easier than others, and the following is a brief selection of the easiest species and hybrids:

Species:

arboreum	*catawbiense*	*ponticum*	*caucasicum*
simsii	*indicum*	*amoena*	*molle*
lutescens	*insigne*	*dauricum*	*obtusum*
			maximum

Hybrids:

Alice	Bagshot Ruby	Betty Wormold	Caucasicum Album
Corona	Kate Waterer	Old Port	Cunningham's White
Zuider Zee	Britannia	Unknown Warrior	Goldsworth Yellow
Ascot Brilliant		Baron de Bruin	Gomer Waterer

1100

| Concessum | Doncaster | Pink Pearl | Mme. de Bruin |
| Cynthia | Countess of Athlone | | |

Rhododendrons may be propagated by seed, cuttings, grafting, or air layering. Propagation from seed is not generally advisable—except for the young—as it is very slow and it will take many years to obtain a flowering plant. However, this is the method employed when new hybrid seedlings are being raised. Seed should be sown in an unheated greenhouse in January–February, or in coldframes in March–April, preferably in shallow terra-cotta pans, or trays, using a finely sifted soil mixture composed of peat, shredded sphagnum moss, leafsoil, and sand, all in equal proportions. This same compost may be used later when pricking out into flats, boxes, or pans, or into nursery beds outside, where the seedlings should be allowed to grow and develop to a reasonable size before being planted out in their growing positions. Cuttings can be made in June–July from the current season's growth, which generally appears immediately after flowering has finished. They should be treated with one of the root-forming hormone preparations and then inserted in a mixture of peat and sand in equal proportions and kept in a warm, shaded greenhouse or under transparent plastic or a glass bell-jar. Rooting will take place in 4–8 weeks, after which the plants should be gradually hardened-off with an increasingly lower temperature and more ventilation. After this they may be planted outside in nursery beds until large enough for their final planting. Air layering is best done in June–July, but it is a slow process, often taking up to a year. Propagation by division is rarely done, although in the case of very common particularly robust species such as *R. ponticum* it is effective and quick. Propagation by grafting is the method normally used by commercial growers. This is done in spring, using young plants of *Rhododendron ponticum* or *Rhododendron catawbiense* that have been raised from seed as stock onto which the variety to be propagated is grafted.

Rhododendron maximum

Rhododendron arboreum Smith
Native to the Himalayas. The most important of the tree-like rhododendrons but not the largest (*Rhododendron giganteum* is bigger). Near Chakatra, in the western Himalayas, I have seen many superb specimens, including one giant with a trunk $2\frac{1}{2}$ ft. in diameter. In European gardens there are also numerous fine specimens of tree-like proportions that retain their branches down to ground level—a large specimen in full bloom is a spectacular sight. Leaves are leathery, oblong, up to 7 ins. long and 2 ins. wide; pointed, glabrous above and in some forms rust-coloured beneath. Inflorescence a compact globose terminal cluster up to 6 ins. in diameter, composed of many individual bell-shaped flowers each 2 ins. wide, in shades

(Tree Rhododendron)
Large evergreen shrub or small tree
Flowering period: Mar.–Apr.
Height: up to 45 ft.
Zone 7

ranging from pale pink to blood-red. Introduced into European gardens in 1815, flowering for the first time in England in 1825. The variation in the colour of the flowers and undersurface of the leaves has resulted in several named forms:

> var. *album*, flowers white, undersurface of leaves rust-red
> var. *campbelliae*, flowers purple-pink, undersurface of leaves red-brown
> var. *cinnamomeum*, flowers pale pink, undersurface of leaves reddish
> var. *limbatum*, flowers purple-red, undersurface of leaves silver

Rhododendron arboreum has been widely used as a parent to modern hybrid rhododendrons, in particular those with red flowers. The following deserve special mention:

> Altaclerense (*R. arboreum* x *R. ponticum*) dark reddish-pink-flowers
> Nobleanum album (*R. arboreum album* x *R. caucasicum*) white-flowered
> Nobleanum (*R. arboreum* x *R. caucasicum*) flowers rich vivid pink, 2 ins. in diameter; leaves brown on the undersurface
> Russellianum (*R. arboreum* x *R. catawbiense*) crimson
> Venustum (*R. arboreum* x *R. caucasium*) flowers pink suffused purple

Rhododendron catawbien.

Rhododendron augustinii Hemsl.
Native to China. One of the most beautiful species for its lovely and unusual rich blue flowers. There are numerous forms on the market with inferiorly coloured flowers which have been raised from seed, but the true blue form can be propagated only from cuttings. One of the smaller rhododendrons but fast-growing, beginning to bloom when quite small. Compact bushy habit; leaves lanceolate, 2–4 ins. long, $\frac{1}{3}$–1 in. wide; pointed, dark green, thin-textured. Flowers in groups of 3–4; 2–2$\frac{1}{4}$ ins. in diameter, funnel-shaped, with ruffled petals, and produced in the greatest profusion. Discovered by Augustine Henry and given his Christian name.

Evergreen shrub
Flowering period: May
Height: up to 12 ft.
Zone 7

Rhododendron auriculatum Hemsl.
Native to China. Almost a small tree in its natural habitat, but in gardens generally a wide-spreading shrub with a stiff, open habit. If my choice of rhododendrons should be limited to six, this would certainly be included because it has many good qualities: very late-flowering, beautiful blooms with a fragrance that always reminds me of ripe apples, handsome foliage, and rapid growth. It was given an award of merit by the Royal Horticultural Society in 1922. Leaves light green, oblong, leathery, up to 12 ins. long and 7 ins. wide, bearing two "ears" (auricles) at the base which provide an easy

Evergreen shrub
Flowering period: July–Aug.
Height: up to 25–30 ft.
Scented
Zone 8

method of identification when the plant is not in bloom, and which explains the specific name. Inflorescence is an enormous head bearing eight white or very pale pinkish loosely arranged widely funnel-shaped individual flowers 4 ins. long and deliciously fragrant. Discovered by Augustine Henry and introduced by E. H. Wilson in 1900 and generally recognized as one of the most beautiful of all Chinese rhododendrons.

Evergreen shrub
Flowering period: Mar.–Apr.
Height: up to 15 ft.
Scented
Zone 7

Rhododendron campylocarpum Hook. fil.
Native to the Himalayas. One of the most attractive yellow-flowered evergreen rhododendrons. Inflorescence a loose terminal group of 6–8 individual bell-shaped flowers each $2\frac{3}{4}$ ins. in diameter; primrose-yellow, fragrant. Leaves heart-shaped, $2\frac{1}{2}$–4 ins. long and $1\frac{1}{4}$–2 ins. wide, pointed; dark shiny green above, glaucous white beneath.

(Carolina Rhododendron)
Evergreen shrub
Flowering period: May–June
Height: up to 6 ft.
Zone 4

Rhododendron carolinianum Rehd.
Native to North Carolina. Originally considered to be a variety of *Rhododendron minus,* until Dr. Rehder reclassified it as a true species in 1912. Originally introduced into England in 1810 by John Fraser, then lost, and subsequently reintroduced in 1895 from a Carolina nursery. Close, compact habit; leaves elliptic, up to $3\frac{1}{2}$ ins. long and $1\frac{3}{4}$ ins. wide, blunt-pointed. Flowers 4–10 in terminal trusses, each $1\frac{1}{2}$ ins. in diameter, light pinkish purple, sometimes spotted. There is also a white-flowered var. *album.*

(Mountain Rose-Bay)
Evergreen shrub
Flowering period: May–June
Height: up to 18 ft.
Zone 4

Rhododendron catawbiense Michx.
Native to the southeastern United States. A large dense shrub often wider than it is high, with an abundance of foliage and much-branched. Introduced to European gardens in 1809 by John Fraser and one of the most important of all rhododendrons as a parent in the evolution and development of modern hybrid rhododendrons. Its progeny are distinguished by their hardiness, relatively wide leaves (wider than the equally important and similar *Rhododendron ponticum),* vigour, and ease of cultivation, and their flowering period of May–June. It is also much used as a stock plant onto which hybrids are grafted. The original species is also a fine garden plant, with oblong leaves 3–6 ins. long and $1\frac{1}{2}$–$2\frac{3}{4}$ ins. wide, dark shiny green, glabrous. Inflorescence 6 ins. in diameter, composed of a large group of individual broadly bell-shaped flowers, $2\frac{1}{2}$ ins. wide, and a delightful lilac-purple colour.

Evergreen shrub
Flowering period: May–June
Height: up to 3 ft.
Zone 5

Rhododendron caucasicum Pall.
Native to the Caucasus. Another species that has played a major part in the development of modern rhododendron hybrids. Forms a dense, compact dwarf shrub; slow-growing, with dark-green leathery obovate leaves 2–4 ins. long and 1–$1\frac{3}{4}$ ins. wide, with the undersurface

Rhododendron obtusum
From *Curtis's Botanical Magazine*,
1853, plate 4728

covered with red-brown hairy down. Inflorescence a terminal truss of cream-white flattish bell-shaped flowers suffused lilac, each 2 ins. in diameter. A characteristic of several of its progeny is a yellow marking on a light background on the petals. Some of the more important of its hybrids are:

    Cunningham's White (*R. caucasicum* x *R. ponticum album*)
    Rosa Mundi (*R. caucasicum* x *?*)
    Sulphureum (*R. caucasicum* x *R. arboreum album*)
    Venustum (*R. caucasicum* x *R. arboreum*)

Evergreen shrub
Flowering period: May–June
Height: up to 12 ft.
Zone 6

Rhododendron cinnabarinum Hook. fil.
Native to Sikkim. Distinct from many other rhododendrons for the long tubular funnel-shaped flowers which have almost the exact size and shape of that lovely climber lapargeria (Chilean Bellflower). The leaves, too, are distinct and unusual; oval in shape, 2–4 ins. long, 1–1½ ins. wide, pointed at both ends; grey-green on the upper surface; glaucous or reddish glaucous beneath. In colour the flowers vary from red to reddish yellow or greenish orange; semi-pendulous, borne in terminal, flattish groups of 3–5.

Deciduous shrub
Flowering period: Jan.–Feb.
Height: up to 6 ft.
Zone 6

Rhododendron dauricum L.
Native to Siberia. One of the oldest of all garden rhododendrons; in continuous cultivation since 1780. Also one of the earliest to bloom. Flattish saucer-shaped flowers vivid purple-pink, 1¼–1½ ins. in diameter, solitary, terminal. Leaves oval, 1½ ins. long, ¾ in. wide, dark shiny green. In spring, when there is so much competition from other flowers, this species would not be particularly significant, but flowering as it does in winter it is of great value, giving a lovely effect: the plants in full bloom with the snow-covered ground beneath them. There is an evergreen form, var. *sempervirens* Sims. (syn. *Rhododendron atrovirens*).

Evergreen shrub
Flowering period: May–June
Height: up to 10 ft.
Scented
Zone 6

Rhododendron decorum Franch.
Native to western China. A fine species related to the eastern Chinese *Rhododendron fortunei*. Leaves grey-green, oblong, up to 6 ins. long, thick-textured. Flowers in trusses of 8–10, very large, scented, white or pale pink, funnel-shaped. A particularly delightful form is the var. *minor,* of neat, compact habit and with all the attraction of *R. decorum* but on a smaller scale.

Evergreen shrub
Flowering period: May–June
Height: up to 6 ft.
Zone 7

Rhododendron dichroanthum Diels.
Native to China. Discovered by Thomas Forrest in 1906. Habit rounded and compact, and a species of particular beauty for the unusual colour of its flowers. Leaves obovate, pointed, 2–4 ins. long, up to 1½ ins. wide; dark green and glabrous above, glaucous white beneath. Inflorescence a terminal group of 6–8, long, bell-shaped orange-pink flowers, each 2 ins. long with waxy petals.

Rhododendron discolor Franch.
Native to China. A very fine late-flowering species. Leaves narrowly oval, up to 7 ins. long and 2½ ins. wide; dark green above, paler green beneath. Terminal inflorescence composed of numerous pale blue-pink funnel-shaped fragrant flowers, each 3¼ ins. long with the petals lobed at the mouth.

Evergreen shrub
Flowering period: July
Height: up to 20 ft.
Scented
Zone 7

Rhododendron ferrugineum L.
Native to the European Alps. A very hardy small evergreen shrub with a rather flat semi-prostrate compact habit emphasized by the plant's windswept natural habitat. Probably the most beautiful flowering shrub of the European flora but—as far as my experience is concerned—almost impossible to cultivate in gardens in a warm or temperate climate at low altitudes. The vast expanses of these rhododendrons growing in their natural solitude at the very top of the Simplon Pass linking Italy to Switzerland are a great sight in June, but they must be left in their cold, windswept, sunny environment where there is an abundance of light without excessive heat. Flowers small, crimson-pink, borne many together in compact terminal clusters; each flower ¾ in. long. There is some variation in the colour, ranging from pale pink to scarlet-pink. I have also seen a rare white-flowered form and a form with variegated foliage. Leaves oval, narrow, pointed, 1–1¾ ins. long; dark shiny green above, rust-red on the undersurface.

(Alpine Rose)
Evergreen shrub
Flowering period: June–July
Height: up to 3 ft.
Zone 5

Rhododendron fortunei Lindl.
Native to eastern China. Discovered by Robert Fortune in 1855. A beautiful species which certainly merits a place in the garden, but its chief importance is that of parent to some of the most attractive of all modern rhododendron hybrids, to which it has given the fragrance of its flowers, its habit of blooming earlier than many of the other hybrids, and its elegant but never gaudy colour. Inflorescence a loose, open terminal truss of up to twelve bell-shaped flowers, each 3½ ins. in diameter and of a most delicate shade of pink. Leaves oblong, pointed, 4–8 ins. in length, 2–2½ ins. wide; glabrous, light green above, glaucous beneath.

Evergreen shrub
Flowering period: May
Height: up to 12 ft.
Scented
Zone 6

Rhododendron giganteum Forr. & Tagg.
Native to the Yunnan province of China. Discovered by Forrest in 1919 at an altitude of 10,000 ft. The largest of all rhododendrons; a real tree eventually forming a trunk 7½ ft. in circumference. Inflorescence a large cluster of up to twenty-five bell-shaped flowers, each 3 ins. long, crimson-pink with a darker crimson mark at the base of the petals. Leaves oval, 9–16 ins. long, 3–5 ins. wide; glabrous, vivid green above, reddish green beneath.

Evergreen tree
Flowering period: May–June
Height: up to 80 ft.
Zone 7

Rhododendron arboreum var. *album*
From *Curtis's Botanical Magazine*,
1834, plate 3290

Rhododendron griersonianum Balf. & Forr.
Native to China. Discovered by Forrest in 1917 at a height of about 10,000 ft. Completely different from all other rhododendrons and one of the most beautiful species. Also the parent of a race of superb hybrids with flower colours such as geranium-red. They are late-flowering, blooming when the majority of other rhododendrons are finishing. A shrub with a loose, graceful and elegant open habit. Inflorescence a truss of up to twelve loosely arranged individual trumpet-shaped scarlet-pink or vermilion flowers, each $2\frac{3}{4}$ ins. long and $2\frac{1}{4}$ ins. wide. Leaves lanceolate, pointed, 4–7 ins. long, 1–2 ins. wide, an unusual shade of brownish golden green above, covered with grey-brown down beneath.

Evergreen shrub
Flowering period: June–July
Height: up to 10 ft.
Zone 6

Rhododendron hirsutum L.
Native to the Swiss and Italian Alps. A very hardy small shrub with a similar habit to the other Alpine species, *R. ferrugineum*. Distinguished by its hairy leaves, which are narrow, oval, 1 in. long, half as wide, brilliant green; the margins bearing conspicuous bristles almost like eyelashes. Flowers pinkish scarlet, $\frac{3}{4}$ in. in diameter, borne several together in terminal groups. Of special interest as one of the very few rhododendrons that actually require an alkaline (calcareous) soil similar to that found in its native habitat among limestone rocks. There is also a white-flowered var. *albiflorum*.

Evergreen shrub
Flowering period: June
Height: up to 3 ft.
Zone 5

Rhododendron indicum Sweet (syn. *Azalea indica* L.)
Native to Japan. A name which is generally, but incorrectly, applied to the so-called Florist's Azalea, Belgian Azalea, or Indian Azalea (also sometimes known as *Azalea macranthum*): all of which are really some form of *Rhododendron simsii* (which see). The true *Rhododendron indicum* is now a rare plant not often found in cultivation outside botanic gardens. From 1850 onwards it was gradually replaced by *Rhododendron simsii* Planch.; although prior to that date it was widely cultivated in gardens. *Rhododendron indicum* has a wide-spreading habit and is parent of many hybrids of diverse colours. Leaves lanceolate, pointed, $1-1\frac{3}{4}$ ins. long; dark shiny green. Flowers solitary or in pairs, terminal and borne on almost every branch over the entire surface of the plant; in form broadly funnel-shaped, $1\frac{1}{2}-2$ ins. wide, reddish pink, with 5 stamens. Introduced in 1833 by McKilligan and cultivated widely until the introduction of the species *R. simsii*. *Rhododendron simsii* and *Rhododendron indicum* have been much confused and the confusion will probably continue, but the following are the chief differences. *Rhododendron indicum* is only indigenous to Japan, has 5 stamens, and is more tolerant of frost than *R. simsii* but of less vigorous growth. *Rhododendron simsii* is native to China and Taiwan, has 8–10 stamens, and is less hardy than *R. indicum* but of more vigorous growth.

Evergreen shrub
Flowering period: May–June
Height: up to 6 ft.
Zone 6

Evergreen shrub
Flowering period: May
Height: up to 18 ft.
Zone 7

Rhododendron insigne Hemsl. & Wilson
Native to China. Introduced into Europe by E. H. Wilson in 1908. Valuable for the fact that plants only 1 ft. high will flower. Inflorescence a rounded terminal head 5½ ins. in diameter composed of 15–20 individual bell-shaped dark-pink flowers, each 2 ins. wide, and with each petal marked with maroon spots. Leaves leathery, lanceolate, pointed, dark shiny green above, silvery brown beneath; 2–5 ins. long, ⅔–2 ins. wide and very decorative.

Semi-evergreen or deciduous shrub
Flowering period: May
Height: up to 10 ft.
Zone 7

Rhododendron kaempferi Planch. (syn. *Rhododendron obtusum kaempferi* Wilson, *Azalea indica kaempferi* Rehd.)
Native to Japan. First introduced into America by Prof. C. S. Sargent and sent to Kew in 1894. A hardy semi-evergreen or sometimes deciduous shrub of medium size. Although a good garden plant, it has been largely replaced by the many superb hybrids of which it is parent. Leaves 1–2½ ins. long, ¾–1 in. wide, oval, dark shiny green. Flowers terminal in small clusters, each flower ⅔ in. in diameter, bell-shaped, variable in colour from purple to pinkish red.

Evergreen shrub
Flowering period: Jan.–Feb.
Height: up to 8 ft.
Zone 6

Rhododendron lutescens Franch.
Native to China and Tibet. Discovered by Père David and introduced by E. H. Wilson in 1904. An ideal pale-yellow-flowered companion for the more vivid *Rhododendron dauricum* and *Rhododendron mucronulatum* which bloom simultaneously. *Rhododendron lutescens* is a much-branched shrub of open habit, with the flowers borne in terminal and axillary groups, opening a few at a time, thus prolonging the flowering period; colour sulphur-yellow, broadly bell-shaped, 1 in. in diameter. Leaves lanceolate, pointed, reddish green when young; eventually dark green; 1½–3½ ins. long, ½–1½ ins. wide.

Deciduous shrub
Flowering period: May
Height: up to 12 ft.
Scented
Zone 6

Rhododendron luteum Sweet (syn. *Rhododendron flavum* G. Don, *Azalea pontica* L.)
Native to the Caucasus and Asia Minor. One of the most beautiful and easiest to cultivate of all yellow-flowered rhododendrons, giving a brilliant display of bloom in May. Introduced into European gardens in 1793 and, apart from its decorative value, widely used as a stock onto which other rhododendrons are grafted, in particular the hybrids of *Rhododendron molle (Azalea mollis)*. This explains why so many fine specimens of *Rhododendron luteum* are to be seen in old gardens, where originally some choice grafted hybrid was planted but, through neglect, the graft died back and the stock remained and flourished. This was not a bad exchange, and I personally find *Rhododendron luteum* as attractive as any of the hybrids, with its profuse rich vivid-yellow fragrant blooms. The inflorescence is a terminal group of individual flowers borne before the leaves, each flower up

to 2 ins. in diameter, with the flower stalk characteristically sticky. Leaves oblong, glaucous, 2½–5 ins. in length, 1–1½ ins. wide.

Rhododendron maximum L. (Great Laurel or Rose Bay)
Evergreen shrub or small tree
Flowering period: June–July
Height: up to 30 ft.
Slightly fragrant
Zone 3

Native to the eastern United States. A useful species with two characteristics that distinguish it from most other garden rhododendrons. It is unusually late-flowering (and interesting for that reason), but is of greater value as a foliage plant than as a flowering shrub. In their native habitat plants will reach a height of up to 30 ft., forming a definite trunk 1 ft. in diameter; but in gardens the plants more often have the form of dense compact shrubs ideal for screening because of their attractive and profuse leaves. It will thrive and blossom in full shade, but the flowers are certainly not among the most spectacular of this brilliant genus. They vary in colour from pale to deep purple-pink, with greenish-yellow spots on the upper surface of the corolla. The 4-in.-wide inflorescence is a cluster of individual bell-shaped blooms each 1½ ins. in diameter, but the flowers are liable to be smothered by the mass of foliage. The leaves are narrowly obovate; 4–10 ins. long; dark green above, paler beneath; and strong in texture. The species was introduced into European gardens in 1736, but is not widely cultivated there. On young plants the bark of the stems is reddish in colour and inclined to be rough-textured. The var. *album,* with smaller white flowers, was at one time known as *R. purshii* Don.

Rhododendron molle G. Don. (syn. *Azalea mollis*) (Azalea mollis)
Deciduous shrub
Flowering period: Apr.–May
Height: up to 9 ft.
Zone 6

Native to Japan. Much crossed with *Rhododendron sinense* to produce the popular vividly coloured beautiful race of *Azalea mollis* hybrids so widely grown commercially for forcing into bloom in winter for sale as pot plants (particularly in Holland). They range in colour from shades of yellow to white, orange, pink, salmon, or orange-red. They are also superb garden plants and give best results when cultivated in a mixture of pure peat, leafsoil, and sand. The flowers appear before the leaves. The true species *Rhododendron molle* has a rounded compact habit with erect generally reddish-brown growths. Leaves oval, 2–4 ins. long, ⅓–1¼ ins. wide, dark green, mat-surfaced. Inflorescence a globose terminal group of about ten individual flowers 2½–4 ins. in diameter. Blooms appear in late April, before the leaves. Colour variable from pink to orange-red.

Rhododendron mucronulatum Turez.
Deciduous shrub
Flowering period: Jan.–Feb.
Height: up to 9 ft.
Zone 6

Native to China, Manchuria, and Japan. Flowers solitary, terminal, purple-pink, 1½ ins. wide, and profusely borne. Leaves oblong, 2¾ ins. long, half as wide, not leathery in texture, pointed. Introduced in 1907 and allied to *Rhododendron dauricum*. One of the most beautiful

Rhododendron schlippenbachii
From *Curtis's Botanical Magazine*,
1894, plate 7373

winter-flowering shrubs that can also be effectively used as a temporary pot plant indoors.

Rhododendron obtusum Planch. (syn. *Azalea amoena, Azalea obtusa*) Native to Japan, where its habitat is reputed to be restricted to Mount Kirishima on the island of Kyushu. A slow-growing shrub excellent for cultivating in receptacles as well as for planting in the garden. Habit very dense and compact, with many interlacing branches retained down to ground level. Foliage and flowers among the smallest of all rhododendrons, but the colour of the flowers is one of the most vivid. Leaves very dark, shiny green, obovate, $\frac{2}{3}$ in. long, half as wide, and so prolific that they completely cover the plant and hide the stems. Flowers profusely produced in May, intense purple-red (the colour of cooked beetroots or red cabbage), about $\frac{3}{4}$ in. in diameter. Excellent for massing where a slow-growing flowering evergreen shrub is required. The var. *amoenum* has semi-double flowers. Two particularly good but very distinct forms of *Rhododendron obtusum* are the well-known Hinodegiri, red, and Hinomayo, pink. There are also many magnificent hybrids of *Rhododendron obtusum* commercially known as Kurume Hybrids.

Evergreen shrub
Flowering period: May
Height: up to 10 ft.
Zone 6

Rhododendron ponticum L.
Native to Spain and Portugal, now naturalized in many other parts of Europe. Introduced into British gardens in 1763. One of the most important species, easily raised from seed and of rapid vigorous and even rampant growth, thus making it an ideal stock plant onto which hybrids and varieties are grafted in enormous quantities every year by commercial growers. As in the case of *Rhododendron luteum*, there are many fine specimens in old gardens that are the results of grafted plants after the graft has died. *Rhododendron ponticum*, although so attractive, increases rapidly, and in zones it finds agreeable it can even become invasive. Some large hunting preserves in England find it a useful cover for pheasants. It resembles the American *Rhododendron catawbiense* but has longer, narrower leaves and is more rampant. It has also been used for hybridization and its influence can be seen in numerous hybrids. Forms a dense, much-branched, many-leafed compact shrub often greater in width than in height. Leaves oblong, 4–8 ins. long, 1–2$\frac{1}{2}$ ins. wide, dark shiny green above, paler beneath, glabrous. Inflorescence 6 ins. in diameter forming a terminal globose group of individual widely bell-shaped flowers of a pleasing purple-pink and 2 ins. in diameter.

Evergreen shrub
Flowering period: May–June
Height: up to 15 ft.
Zone 6

Rhododendron quinquefolium Bisset & Moore
Native to Japan. Discovered by Bisset in 1876. Included here because it possesses so many unusual characteristics that help to demonstrate the variability of this vast genus. Forms a compact, erect, much-

Deciduous shrub
Flowering period: Mar.
Height: up to 15 ft.
Zone 7

branched bushy shrub with slender growths. Deciduous, and as its specific name suggests, the leaves are borne in terminal whorls of five at the end of each small branch, thus giving the leaf clusters the appearance of a miniature parasol. They are pale apple-green, not hard or leathery, and edged with a purple-green zone. Each leaf is obovate, up to 2 ins. long and half as wide. Flowers either solitary or in groups of 2–3, terminal, bell-shaped, $1\frac{1}{2}$ ins. in diameter, of an exquisite pale pink, and borne simultaneously with the leaves in March. Much more tolerant of sun than the majority of rhododendrons.

Evergreen shrub
Flowering period: May
Height: up to 4 ins.
Zone 6

Rhododendron radicans Balf. & Forr.
Native to Tibet at an altitude of 15,000 ft. This is the baby of the rhododendrons, and like all babies a real treasure, but in this case difficult to raise. In most gardens it misses the cool atmosphere of its natural habitat high in the mountains. Forms an almost prostrate carpet of dense vegetation with dark vivid-green miniature oval leaves, $\frac{1}{4}-\frac{1}{2}$ in. long. The flowers are very large in proportion, up to $\frac{3}{4}$ in. wide, solitary, flattish bell-shaped, purple. Another similar and equally lovely little species, also from Tibet, is *Rhododendron repens*, with scarlet flowers.

Deciduous shrub
Flowering period: Mar.–Apr.
Height: up to 15 ft.
Scented
Zone 7

Rhododendron schlippenbachii Maxim.
Native to Manchuria and Korea. Originally discovered by Baron Schlippenbach in 1863. A much-branched slender-stemmed deciduous shrub with the leaves in terminal groups of 3–7; pale green, in the young stage suffused reddish purple, obovate, glabrous. Flowers light pink with the upper petals bearing brownish marks, $3\frac{1}{3}$ ins. in diameter, in groups of 3–6, fragrant.

Evergreen shrub
Flowering period: Sept.
Height: up to 6 ft. or more
Scented
Zone 7

Rhododendron serotinum Hutch.
Native to China. Introduced to European gardens in 1889. Particularly interesting for its late flowering, and a first-class species for its flowers and foliage. Forms a robust shrub with a loose, open habit with growths up to 15 ft. long; if trained and tied, these can be induced to assume a climbing form. Leaves oblong, 3–7 ins. long, $1\frac{1}{4}$–$2\frac{1}{2}$ ins. wide, dark green above, glaucous beneath. Inflorescence a terminal cluster 10 ins. wide composed of eight pure-white bell-shaped fragrant flowers 4 ins. in diameter.

(Indian Azalea
or Florist's Azalea)
Evergreen shrub
Flowering period: May–June
Height: up to 6 ft.
Zone 6

Rhododendron simsii Planch. (syn. *Rhododendron indicum* Hort., *Azalea indica* Sins. not L.)
Native to China and Taiwan Much confused with *Rhododendron indicum*. The so-called Belgian Azalea, Florist's Azalea, or Indian Azalea which is sometimes referred to as *Azalea macranthus*. A large shrub with a wide-spreading but close-growing habit often with a width in excess of its height. Has a dense, stiff, much-branched form

Rhododendron x *norbitonense broughtonianum*
From *Paxton's Magazine of Botany*,
1842, plate 179

with a great number of leaves. Old specimens form a complete wall of vegetation from the top of the plant to ground level. Begins to bloom when still very small. Much cultivated in pots and of great commercial value for forcing into bloom from November onwards. Remarkably floriferous and vigorous and of the easiest cultivation. (See also observations under *R. indicum*.) Leaves lanceolate, $1\frac{1}{2}$–$3\frac{1}{2}$ ins. long, up to 1 in. wide; dark green. Flowers borne in terminal groups of two or more; broadly funnel-shaped, up to 3 ins. wide, stamens generally 10, occasionally 8; colour reddish pink. The parent of an enormous number of single- and double-flowered hybrids with a range of colours from white to orange-scarlet and from pink to brick-red.

Evergreen shrub
Flowering period: May
Height: up to 30 ft.
Zone 8

Rhododendron sinograndy Balf. & W. W. Sm.

Native to the Yunnan province of China, Burma, Tibet. Discovered by Forrest in 1912. If this species did not bloom it would still be worth cultivating for its magnificent leaves, which, if not the biggest, are certainly the most handsome of all rhododendron leaves. Each leaf is up to 18 ins. long and 5–8 ins. wide, oval, glabrous, rounded at both ends, dark green above, silver-grey beneath. Inflorescence a large terminal head 10 ins. in diameter, composed of up to thirty individual bell-shaped flowers, each 2 ins. long; pale yellow or ivory, with red marks at the base of each petal. A remarkable plant, but easy to raise.

Evergreen shrub
Flowering period: Apr.–May
Height: up to 15 ft.
Zone 8

Rhododendron thomsonii Hook. fil.

Native to Nepal and Sikkim, found at altitudes of up to 12,000 ft. Introduced into Europe in 1849. A magnificent shrub with a compact habit, often with a width in excess of its height. Leaves oval, dark green above, bluish white beneath. Flowers an intense blood-red, 3 ins. in diameter, bell-shaped, borne 6–7 together in a large globose inflorescence. Parent of numerous rich and brilliantly coloured hybrids.

Evergreen shrub
Flowering period: Mar.–Apr.
Height: up to $4\frac{1}{2}$ ft.
Zone 7

Rhododendron williamsianum Rehd. & Wilson

Native to China. Discovered by E. H. Wilson in 1908. One of the most beautiful of the smaller species rhododendrons. A shrub of rounded, very compact globose habit, with a width much in excess of its height. Many small interlacing branches and an abundance of foliage, giving the plant the appearance of a huge flattish green ball, frequently only 2 ft. high and possibly with a width of $4\frac{1}{2}$ ft. Leaves orbicular, $\frac{2}{3}$–2 ins. wide, bronze-green when young, eventually dark shiny green. Flowers terminal, in pairs, freely produced, bell-shaped, $2\frac{1}{2}$ ins. wide, reddish pink, and relatively large for so small a plant.

Rhododendron yunnanense Franch.
Native to western China. Introduced into France in 1889 by the Abbé Delavay. An evergreen or semi-evergreen shrub somewhat sparsely branched. Leaves obovate, up to 3 ins. long and ¾ in. wide, pointed at either end; bright green on the upper surface, paler beneath. Inflorescence in the form of terminal clusters of 4–5 individual blooms, each up to 2 ins. in diameter, light pink with dark crimson spots on the upper petals.

Evergreen shrub
Flowering period: May
Height: up to 20 ft.
Zone 7

Rhododendron Hybrids
Certain species rhododendrons have played a major part in the development of hybrid garden rhododendrons. These include the species *R. arboreum, R. catawbiense, R. caucasicum, R. fortunei, R. molle, R. griersonianum, R. indicum, R. simsii, R. luteum, R. obtusum,* and *R. ponticum.* The hybrids resulting from these species are some of the most beautiful of all cultivated rhododendrons and for the sake of convenience they are generally divided into groups. There are, of course, so many that it is impossible to enumerate them, but some of the best from each group are listed below.

Hybrids Derived from Chinese and Other Asiatic Species. The hybrids of this group represent the highest development in the evolution of hybrid rhododendrons for general use in the garden. All are evergreen and their flowering periods are approximately those of their parents (which see).

Loderi (*R. griffithianum* x *R. fortunei*) is generally considered to be one of the finest of all rhododendron hybrids. Forms a large wide shrub that needs plenty of space. Inflorescence enormous, often the size of a football, and composed of numerous individual blooms up to 6 ins. in diameter; strongly scented, white. At least twenty-five different varieties of this hybrid have been given separate names. The best are:

Pink Diamond, Pink Topaz, and Sir Edmund, pinkish white
Sir Joseph Hooker, white veined with pink
Venus, dark pink
White Diamond, pure white

Albatross (*R.* x *loderi* x *R. discolor*) is a tall, vigorous large-leafed shrub bearing fragrant funnel-shaped flowers 5 ins. in diameter, white flushed with pink.
Arthur Osborn (*R. didymum* x *R. griersonianum*) is a small shrub with the characteristics of *R. griersonianum*. Rich ruby-red flowers.
Blue Tit (*R. impeditum* x *R. augustinii*) is a small shrub with the colouring and general appearance of *R. augustinii*. Flowers lavender-blue.
Bow Bells (*R. williamsianum* x hyb. Corona) is a semi-dwarf plant of rounded, bushy habit. Pink flowers.

Cornish Cross (*R. thomsonii* x *R. griffithianum*) is a large shrub of loose, open habit up to 12 ft. high. Huge pink flowers.

C. P. Raffill (*R. griersonianum* x hyb. Britannia) has the general form of *R. griersonianum,* with blood-red flowers. Named after a former assistant curator at Kew Gardens, who was one of England's great gardeners and my greatest friend.

Lady Chamberlain (*R. cinnabarinum* x hyb. Royal Flush) is one of the most beautiful of all rhododendrons. Forms a large stiffly branched shrub with inflorescences of pendulous bell-shaped flowers, mandarin-red shading to orange. The following forms are of special merit:

> Chelsea, apricot-orange
> Etna, orange
> Gleam, orange-yellow
> Salmon Trout, salmon-pink

Naomi (hyb. Aurora x *R. fortunei*) is of medium size with magnificent inflorescences of fragrant flowers; lilac-pink suffused greenish yellow. The following forms are of special merit:

> Astarte, pink shading to yellow
> Exbury, lilac tinted yellow
> Pink Beauty, dark pink
> Nereid, lavender and yellow

Polar Bear (*R. auriculatum* x *R. diaprepes*) is a tall superb late-summer-flowering hybrid with all the good qualities of *R. auriculatum*. Pure-white flowers with a green throat. Fragrant.

Praecox (*R. ciliatum* x *R. dauricum*) is a very popular hybrid giving a fine show of lavender-pink flowers in early spring.

Hybrids Derived from European, American, and Himalayan Species. The hybrids in this group also include some of the older varieties that are crosses between one hybrid and another hybrid, which since 1825 have proved to be some of the finest of all rhododendrons for general use in the garden. They are characterized by great hardiness, abundant foliage, a good compact form, close and full trusses of bloom, and tolerance to bad weather. All are evergreen:

> Alice, pink inflorescence with a paler centre, tall conical trusses
> Ascot Brilliant, blood-red, early-flowering, compact habit
> Bagshot Ruby, particularly vigorous, ruby-red
> Baron de Bruin, later-flowering, large trusses of dark-scarlet flowers
> Betty Wormold, lilac-pink flowers marked with darker zones
> Britannia, gloxinia-shaped crimson flowers; one of the best
> Caucasicum album (*R. caucasicum* x *R. ponticum album*), white, of great merit
> Christmas Cheer, pink in bud, opening white
> Concessum, pink with a paler centre

Rhododendron kaempferi

Corona, coral-pink, compact growth
Countess of Athlone, mauve with a greenish-yellow mark on the petals
Cunningham's White, beautiful, compact, white-flowered
Cynthia, one of the oldest and best pink hybrids
Doncaster, crimson-scarlet, a slow-growing dome-shaped shrub
Earl of Athlone, a fine red-flowered hybrid
Garibaldi, one of the best scarlet-red hybrids
Goldsworth Orange, large trusses of pale-orange flowers
Gomer Waterer, late-flowering, pale pink, popular since 1906
Jacksonii, one of the smaller hybrids, with miniature pink flowers
Kate Waterer, late, with large pink flowers with a yellow centre
Kluis Sensation, late-flowering, vivid scarlet
Lee's Dark Purple, a fine and very old hybrid, dark-purple flowers
Mme. de Bruin, cherry-red flowers
Nobleanum, winter- and early-spring-flowering, scarlet-pink flowers
Old Port, dark plum-purple flowers
Pink Pearl, the most popular hybrid ever raised, famous since 1897, large pink flowers in very large conical inflorescences
Purple Splendour, dark purple with black marks on the petals
Souv. de Anthony Waterer, salmon-pink with yellow mark on each petal
Unknown Warrior, bright red flowers
Zuider Zee, cream-white flowers with crimson markings

Rhododendron hirsutum

Hybrid Evergreen Azalea-type of Rhododendron Resulting from Crosses of Rhododendron Kaempferi. A few of these originated in Europe, but the majority are of Japanese origin. They are very hardy, of close, compact habit with small dark-green leaves. The flowers are also relatively small, and frequently double. They are produced in such profusion that they completely hide the branches during the flowering period in late April–May. The majority are of modest height, 3–4½ ft., and they are more tolerant of sun than most other rhododendrons. They are not suitable for planting at high altitudes or in positions subject to very cold winds. For general garden purposes, however, they are among the most effective and most beautiful of all small evergreen rhododendrons and also make excellent pot plants. Some of the best are:

Alice, salmon-red with a darker mark on the petals
Anny, orange-red
Arendsii, purple-crimson
Atalantum, pale lilac
Bengal Fire, flame-red
Betty, salmon-pink with a darker centre
Carmen, pink with red and brown markings on the petals

Favourite, dark pink
Fedora, rich pink
Jeanette, reddish pink
John Bock, magenta-mauve
John Cairns, dark orange-red
Leo, pale orange
Orange Beauty, salmon-orange
Yachiyo, lavender

Deciduous Hybrid Rhododendrons Commercially Known as Ghent Azaleas. These beautiful hybrids are distinguished by their fragrant blooms, which resemble honeysuckle flowers. They are taller and more branched than the Mollis-type Hybrids and their flowering season is later, from the end of May onwards. Some of the best are:

Bouquet de Flore, vivid pink
Gloria mundi, orange-red
Guelder Rose, white and orange
Ignea nova, carmine-red and yellow
Nancy Waterer, golden yellow
Pallas, red and orange
Pucella (syn. Fanny), magenta-pink
Sang de Gentbrugge, blood-red
Unique, orange-yellow
Willem III, orange

Hardy Deciduous Rhododendrons Commercially Known as Rothschild Hybrids, Exbury Hybrid Azaleas, or Knap Hill Hybrid Azaleas. The Exbury strain was raised by the late Lionel de Rothschild (of the famous banking family) in his garden near Southampton. The Knap Hill strain was raised by the well-known nursery of the same name. The same parents were used in each case, mostly varieties of *Rhododendron molle* and *Rhododendron lutescens*. They are both superior strains of great beauty, generally propagated by vegetative means to perpetuate some particularly good colour. The flower colours have a range extending through shades of yellow, cream, apricot, orange, pink, flame, and crimson; many have petals marked with a different colour. Their autumn colouring is superb, the foliage providing a double season of colour. Some of the best are:

Exbury Strain

Aurora, pink and gold
Ballerina, white
Basilisk, pale yellow and orange
Beaulieu, pink shaded orange
Brazil, tangerine-red
Caprice, dark pink
Firefly, dark red

George Reynolds, butter-yellow
Nancy Buchanan, white and yellow

Knap Hill Strain
Fireglow, orange-vermilion
Harvest Moon, pale yellow
H. H. Hunnewell, dark crimson
Homebush, pink
Persil, white and yellow
Pink Delight, peach-pink
Satan, blood-red
Seville, intense orange
Westminster, almond-pink
Whitethroat, white

Many of these hybrids have been given the prestigious award of merit by the Royal Horticultural Society.

Hybrid Evergreen Azalea-type of Rhododendron Known as Kurume Azaleas. During recent years this relatively new strain of rhododendrons has received much publicity and its origin is interesting. The plants are hardy, evergreen, small-leafed, small-flowered, compact in habit, and resemble the *R. obtusum* type of rhododendron. Kurume is a city on the island of Kyushu, Japan, and is the habitat of *Rhododendron obtusum,* its var. *album,* and *Rhododendron kaempferi,* all of which have been cultivated by the Japanese for over one hundred years. They have been crossed and recrossed, and the resulting hybrids and number of individual forms is reputed to be more than two hundred. In 1919 that tireless collector E. H. Wilson succeeded in introducing fifty of the best forms into the United States, with colours ranging through cream, white, pink, carmine, crimson, and scarlet. Apparently Kurume had not previously been in horticultural contact with the rest of the world and these remarkable hybrids proved to be a novelty. They are now available commercially in America and Europe. Some of the best are:

Addy Werry, vermilion-red
Aya-kammuri, pink, salmon, and white
Azuma-kagami, dark pink, double
Benegiri, vivid crimson
Daphne, white, double
Esmeralda, pink, double
Hatsugiri, crimson-purple
Ima-shojo, red, double
Iro-hayama, lavender-pink
Kimigaya, mauve-pink
Mizu-no-yamabuki, ivory-cream
Sakata, fire-red
Ukamuse, vermilion and pink, double

Kurume azaleas

1120

Nearly every one of these has also been given an award of merit by the Royal Horticultural Society.

Hybrids Derived from the Deciduous Rhododendron japonicum *and* Rhododendron molle *Commercially Known as Mollis Hybrids.* This group includes the varieties of the original species *R. japonicum* and *R. molle,* and the hybrids that have been raised from crossing them with each other. Their large scentless flowers are borne in beautiful terminal trusses in late April–May, before the leaves. Their normal height is about $4\frac{1}{2}$ ft., but they begin to bloom when less than 18 ins. high and are widely used for forcing and for sale as pot plants in winter. (See also *Rhododendron molle* in the list of species.) Some of the best are:

Anthony Koster, yellow flushed orange
Chevalier de Reali, cream-white and orange
Christopher Wren, orange-yellow
Comte de Gomer, pink
Comte de Papadopoli, pink and orange
Dr. M. Oosthoek, dark orange-red
Floradora, orange-red with spotted petals
Hollandia, orange-yellow
Hugo Hardyzer, rich scarlet
Lemonora, apricot-yellow
Mrs. A. E. Endtz, dark yellow
Nicholas Beets, bronze-yellow

Mollis hybrid azaleas

Miscellaneous Hybrids (including some that are not hardy)
Rhododendron x *altaclarense* is a very fragrant hybrid of *R. luteum* with orange-yellow flowers.
Rhododendron x *broughtonii aureum* (see *Rhododendron norbitonense broughtonianum*).
Rhododendron x *norbitonense broughtonianum* (syn. *Rhododendron smithii aureum*) is a beautiful evergreen shrub 3 ft. high with glaucous foliage and primrose-yellow flowers in May.
Rhododendron x *Raphael de Smet* is a double-flowered mollis type with beautiful white flowers flushed pink and foliage with superb autumn colouring.
Rhododendron x *graciosum* is a magnificent hybrid of *R. occidentalis* with cream-pink flowers marked yellow. Deciduous.
Rhododendron x *azaleoides* (syn. *Rhododendron odoratum, Rhododendron fragrans*) is of interest as being the first recorded of the hybrid rhododendrons, initially raised in 1820. There are doubts about its parentage, but it is believed to be a cross between *R. ponticum* and *R. viscosum*. Sometimes called "Azaleadendron" because it unites the two groups, *Rhododendron* and *Azalea*. A hardy evergreen shrub which may be semi-deciduous in very cold localities. Height $4\frac{1}{2}$–6 ft., with a much-branched habit. Leaves

Rhododendron simsii
From *Curtis's Botanical Magazine*,
1812, plate 1480

oblanceolate, 2–4 ins. long, $\frac{2}{3}$–$1\frac{1}{2}$ ins. wide, pointed, dark green above, glaucous beneath. Flowers white irregularly suffused lilac, in terminal groups of 15–20 individual, funnel-shaped blooms each $1\frac{1}{4}$ ins. wide, strongly scented. One of the most beautiful flowering shrubs in June–July.

Rhododendron x *scottianum* Hutch. is a non-hardy evergreen shrub from the Himalayas, height up to 10 ft. White flowers suffused pink with a yellow mark internally at the base of the petals. Scented. Summer-flowering.

Rhododendron x *sesterianum* is an evergreen shrub of hybrid origin and the most strongly fragrant of all rhododendrons. The flowers have a perfume like that of lilies, and quite as strong. Hardy in mild climates but not tolerant of hard frost. Flowering period, summer. Excellent for pot culture. Individual flowers 3 ins. in diameter, broadly bell-shaped, borne several together in loose terminal clusters; cream-white suffused greenish yellow in the centre. The plant has a loose, open habit with leaves dark green, narrow, shiny, 5 ins. long.

Rhodotypos kerriodes

(JET BEAD)
Family: Rosaceae
Deciduous shrub
Flowering period: May–July
Height: up to 6 ft.
Position: sun or partial shade
Propagation: seed or cuttings
Cultivation very easy
Zone 4 southwards

A monotypic genus of only one species and no varieties. A very attractive hardy deciduous shrub which would appear to offer excellent opportunities to the hybridist. It is often appropriately referred to as a white-flowered *Kerria japonica*; although it has a rather less compact and more open habit. *Rhodotypos kerrioides* (*kerrioides* meaning kerria-like) is native to China and Japan and was introduced to European gardens in 1866, but strangely enough it has never achieved the popularity of kerria or forsythia; a pity in view of its elegance, grace, and charm. It is a shrub which can be planted in almost any position, except in dense shade, and it makes no special demands about soil. No pruning is necessary. Apart from the attractive white flowers, the shiny black fruits are also decorative.

Some particularly pleasing effects can be obtained by planting *Rhodotypos kerrioides* in association with blue violas or pansies.

Rhodotypos kerrioides Sieb. & Zucc. (syn. *Rhodotypos scandens*)
Native to China and Japan. Leaves opposite, $2\frac{1}{2}$–4 ins. long, $1\frac{1}{4}$–2 ins. wide, dentated, long-pointed. On the larger leaves the dentation is deep and very irregular. Upper surface dark green, undersurface paler green. Flowers solitary, terminal on the secondary branchlets, pure white, four-petalled, $1\frac{1}{4}$–2 ins. in diameter and somewhat similar to a small single rose. In autumn the shiny black fruits are freely borne in clusters; each fruit is about the size of a small pea and thus the common name of Jet Bead is most appropriate. Propagation is easy by means of seed sown outside in spring, either in pots or in seed beds, or by means of cuttings taken from half-ripened wood in July, inserted in frames or in a sheltered nursery bed. Soft-wood cuttings also root quite easily if taken in spring and inserted in sand in a warm greenhouse.

Rhodotypos kerrioides

Romneya

(CALIFORNIA TREE POPPY)
Family: Papaveraceae
Tender herbaceous perennials or sub-shrubs
Position: full sun
Propagation: seed or root cuttings
Cultivation often difficult

Romneyas are as beautiful as they are capricious, sometimes prospering and spreading like rampant weeds, but frequently proving to be obstinately difficult to establish. They were introduced into European gardens in the mid-nineteenth century. The genus was named after the Rev. T. Romney Robinson, an Irish astronomer. There are only two species.

There can be no question about their beauty, with their spectacular, pure-white large poppy-like flowers and lovely foliage. The plants require a deep fertile soil in a very sunny relatively dry position. Their worst enemy is root disturbance, a characteristic of many plants belonging to the family Papaveraceae. The roots like to establish themselves at the base of a wall, under the paving of a terrace or courtyard, or on steps, where it is impossible to weed or hoe. For this same reason it is necessary to exercise the greatest care when planting, always using pot-grown plants, and taking care not to break the root ball. Better results are generally obtained when the plants are grown in alkaline (calcareous) soil. Generally, the plants have a typical habit of herbaceous perennials and die back to ground level in autumn. In warm climates, however, the stems will sometimes remain, allowing the plant to develop a semi-shrubby character. Although tolerant of a certain amount of frost, the plants will not survive if the soil freezes to the depth of the roots.

Propagation by means of root cuttings is relatively easy in spring, but such a disturbance will often result in the death of the parent plant. Romneyas can also be propagated from seed sown in a warm greenhouse in spring, growing on the seedlings in small pots until ready for planting.

Romneya coulteri

(California or Matilija Poppy)
Flowering period: June–Sept.
Height: up to 8 ft.

Romneya coulteri Harv.
Native to California. Herbaceous perennial or semi-shrubby plant with attractive sea-green or grey-green broadly-lanceolate deeply-lobed leaves up to 4 ins. long. Flowers solitary, terminal, single, snow-white, 6 ins. in diameter, with a conspicuous mass of golden-yellow stamens in the centre, giving the appearance of a large paper-textured white poppy. Pleasantly fragrant, and so attractive to bees that these insects can often be seen in an apparent state of inebriation in the vicinity of the flowers. The plants have an erect, wide-spreading branching habit. Discovered by and named after Dr. Coulter in 1844.

Flowering period: June–Sept.
Height: up to 5–6 ft.

Romneya trichocalyx Eastw.
Native to California and Mexico. Very similar in general appearance to *Romneya coulteri*, but of smaller habit, without its agreeable perfume, and with a hairy calyx. It often proves to be a hardier plant.

Rosa

(ROSE)
Family: *Rosaceae*
Half-hardy and hardy deciduous or evergreen shrubs or climbers
Position: sun
Propagation: seed, cuttings, grafting, budding, or layering
Cultivation easy
Fragrant
Useful for cutting

> That which we call a rose
> By any other name would smell as sweet.
> (*Romeo and Juliet*, Act II, sc. 2)

It was in the 1920s that Gertrude Stein wrote "Rose is a rose is a rose is a rose", and probably she had nothing else in mind but the flower; it is indeed the only thing to be said about a rose, apart from writing an entire poem about it. The quintessence of a rose is unattainable, mysterious, and even more than a mystery, something that makes adjectives useless and futile and that can never be adequately described. Roses are romantic, steeped in sentiment, true flowers of the Victorian era. Experts tell us that even the fragrance of roses can be elusive, varying according to the environment, the temperature, and general conditions of cultivation. (This, no doubt, is true, and perhaps under certain conditions even the famous variety *Baccara* did, at some time in some place, have an agreeable perfume, but certainly not in flower shops.) Also, we often forget that originally roses were almost exclusively climbers or large, spreading shrubs with a loose, open habit; now many of them are dwarfed, tortured, stunted, or grown into unsightly standards with 4–6 ft. of bare, ugly pole-like stems.

Before beginning to grow roses one should—ideally—make a firm decision to have nothing whatever to do with roses which do not have a rose-like scent. Many rose experts blandly and ingenuously tell us that modern roses are just as fragrant as the older roses (although not all were scented), and we must agree that some modern varieties do have at least some perfume; but the older roses had such fragrance that the characteristic was accepted and taken for granted as an essential prerequisite of the flower. But let us see what Sacheverell Sitwell has to say on the subject: "It is sufficient to order a few shrubs of such old roses as *Stanwell Perpetual*, *Tricolor de Flandre*, and *Madame Pierre Oger*, and wait for summer. Nobody who acquires this modest collection will have any further interest in modern roses. They will prefer the old ones."

Rosa rugosa
From *Curtis's Botanical Magazine*,
1832, plate 3149

The value of roses does not entirely depend on the actual flowers. In a great many cases the foliage, fruits, and even the thorns have the maximum decorative value, especially in autumn, when the plants are no longer in bloom. Taken collectively, and planting them in the multifarious ways their natural forms suggest, roses can form the true basis of a garden. There is practically no limit to their potential uses and Sacheverell Sitwell is absolutely right when he quotes Franz Liszt: "It would still be possible to have an idea of the pleasure of music if all instruments except the piano were abolished [the only instrument—with the possible exception of the organ—to which such an assertion is applicable], and in the same way the rose is the universal flower of all gardens."

To trace the complete history and diffusion of roses would involve a discussion much too long for this volume, and only a brief summary can be given. In the little Rose Museum in the Rose Garden at Hayles-Roses, near Paris, there are preserved fossilized roses, found in the Baltic provinces, that date back to the Miocene Era. Other fossil roses have been found in Colorado and Oregon that date back to the Oligocene Era. These fossils thus are from sixty million to one million years old. Genetic studies have revealed that the rose is a plant of northern origin, and in the course of millennia has been moving southwards, adjusting itself periodically to new climatic conditions. In the genus *Rosa* the number of chromosomes is nearly always a multiple of 7. A diploid species has 2 series (that is, 14) in each cell, a triploid has 21, a tetraploid has 28, and so on. The difference between the number of chromosomes is generally linked to the climatic conditions; northern species as a rule have a higher number of chromosomes in comparison to subtropical species. Experience has shown that mutations resulting in a loss of chromosomes are much more frequent than those resulting in an increase. This permits us to argue that the original rose was probably a decaploid (with 70 chromosomes) from which all other existing species have derived, and these, on their way to the south, have relieved themselves of chromosomes just as we discard our jackets and woolen pullovers when we travel to hotter countries.

The genus *Rosa* is distributed throughout the Northern Hemisphere from just below the Arctic Circle to North Africa, Mexico, and India. Botanists are not yet in agreement about the exact number of species and the following comment made by Linnaeus in 1753 has not lost its significance even today: "*Rosa* species are very difficult to classify, and those who have seen only a few are better able to distinguish one from another than those who have examined many." Roy E. Shepherd, in *The History of the Rose* (Macmillan, New York, 1954), suggests an indeterminate number of less than two hundred.

According to some philologists the name rose derives from the Celtic word *rhodd* or *rhudd*, meaning red; from which the Greek

Hybrid tea rose Samurai

word *rhodon* also was derived. Varrone asserts that the Latin word *rosa* derives from the Greek *rhodon* and that, at least in root, it remains unchanged in nearly every European language. The first historical testimony we have of the rose dates back to ancient Mesopotamia. Sargon I, king of the Akkadians—who lived from 2684–2630 B.C.—brought to Ur "vines, figs and rose trees" on his way back from a military expedition beyond the River Tigris. Thus, at least 5,000 years ago people knew roses. In Homer's *Iliad* (ninth century B.C.), Achilles's shield is decorated with roses, and it is also written that the ointments used by Aphrodite to embalm Hector's body were mixed with roses. Passing from the ninth century to the sixth we learn from Anacreon that roses originated from the sea foam that bore Aphrodite, and therefore they must have been white. In the same century, Sappho called the rose the queen of flowers. According to Herodotus, the rose was introduced to Greece by the mythical King Midas of Phrygia (he of the "golden touch"), who was supposed to have lived in Asia Minor about 700 B.C. History specifies that Midas's rose was strongly scented and had about sixty petals, indicating that the rose in question was a variety of horticultural origin. In any case, prior to 300 B.C., Theophrastus could already speak of roses with five to one hundred petals; possibly *Rosa centifolia* was already known at that time. Roses were figured on the coinage of Rhodes minted in 325 B.C. Even if we are not sure of their origin, it is certain that roses entered Greece by way of the Orient. From Confucius we know that during his life (551–479 B.C.), the Emperor of China already had in his library six hundred books concerning the culture of roses. The Chinese of the fifth century B.C. also had cognisance of the oil of roses extracted from the plants grown in the Emperor's garden. Its use was only permitted the nobles and dignitaries of the court; if a commoner were found in possession of even the smallest quantity of this oil he was condemned to death.

Egyptian wall paintings and objects representing roses and garlands of *Rosa richardii* (an Abyssinian form of *Rosa gallica*) have been found in tombs dating from the fifth century B.C. to Cleopatra's time. The famous queen herself had a passion for everything Roman, and her mania for roses was picked up from her allies; she even used roses to replace the ancient Egyptian lotus. The first roses appeared in Rome, from Greece, a few decades before Cleopatra's time, and they rapidly caught on among the highly cultured Romans. Virgil, in the *Georgics*, sings of the rose of Preneste (*Rosa damascena*); Pliny the Elder gives detailed descriptions of *Rosa centifolia, Rosa alba* (in his words, "rose of the Campagna"), *Rosa spinosissima* var. *myriacantha, Rosa moschata,* and *Rosa sempervirens.* The Romans were also familiar with *Rosa gallica* var. *officinalis.*

Horace in the *Odes* wrote that it was customary to adorn head,

Hybrid rose
Elizabeth of Glamis

shoulders, and breast with roses at a banquet when the time came to "enjoy the choicest and rarest wines"; and to strew rose petals over the couches on which guests would recline. The statues of Venus, Hebe, Flora, Juno, and Hymen were crowned and adorned with roses, and during the feasts in Athens young people of both sexes, crowned with roses, danced naked in the shadow of the temple of Hymen to symbolize the innocence of the Golden Age. During the public games all the streets of Rome were strewn with rose petals. One of Martial's epigrams mocks a great political *faux-pas* made by the Egyptians who, believing that they were doing something very special, sent roses in mid-winter to the Emperor Domitian. Whereupon the Latin poet replied to the *gaffe* by saying: "In every road one inhales the scent of spring, one sees the blazing splendour of garlands of flowers. Send us corn O Egyptians, we will cover you with roses." The Romans believed that by decorating their tombs with roses they would placate the Manes (spirits of the dead); and the rich specified in their wills that entire rose gardens should be maintained to provide flowers for their graves.

Nero, of course, overdid things even with roses. According to the testimony of chroniclers, during lavish dinner parties rose petals rained down from the ceiling of his banqueting hall; indeed, it is said, they fell in such profusion that some imprudent diners, evidently intoxicated, were buried and suffocated. Seneca related that special localities were built in Rome for rose cultivation, these complete with a hot-water heating system for forcing the plants into early bloom. Theophrastus wrote on the cultivation of roses from seeds and by cuttings; while Pliny describes propagation by budding (that is, inserting an "eye" or vegetative bud into the bark). During Rome's golden age, rose cultivation became a real industry; not only in Rome and Egypt, but in all the colonies where the climate was suitable. The strictures of Seneca and of other Stoic philosophers regarding the excessive use of roses were mild and bland in comparison to the furious and angry attacks of the early Christians who saw in the rose a symbol of paganism, orgy, and lust. Tertullian wrote an entire volume against the flower, and about A.D. 202, Clement of Alexandria forbade Christians to adorn themselves with roses. Nevertheless, it seems that the early Christians did not pay much attention to their theologians in this matter, and they continued to cultivate roses, even taking the blooms into church for various ceremonies. Slowly the Church realised that it was better to absorb some aspects of paganism by changing them into Christian symbols instead of drastically rejecting them. One of the earliest legends reflecting the Church's tolerance towards roses concerns the fourth-century martyr Saint Dorothy. Persecuted for her adherance to Christianity, Dorothy was cast into prison before her execution. A lawyer named Theophilus mockingly asked her to send him some roses from the garden

Rosa spinosissima var. *lutea*
From *Curtis's Botanical Magazine*,
1813, plate 1570

(Paradise) where she said she was going. That night an angel brought a spray of roses to Dorothy's cell. In the morning she gave them to the astounded Theophilus, who was converted on the spot.

In Catholic litanies, the Virgin Mary is called "Rosa mystica" and in many hymns she is invoked as the "rose without thorns". Before the rose was consecrated by Pope Leo IX in the eleventh century, it had regained its status as an ornamental plant, at least among royalty. In 550 King Childebert I had a rose garden planted for the queen in Paris. Charlemagne even ordered the cultivation of rose bushes in the castles where he held diets or assemblies. But after Leo IX was elected pope in 1084 he instituted the ceremony of the Golden Rose, which was consecrated every year on Laetare Sunday (the fourth Sunday in Lent). The Golden Rose was sent to favoured monarchs as a particular token of papal esteem, and many of these roses still extant are masterpieces of the goldsmith's art. The ceremony was continued for many centuries and was still held in the early decades of the twentieth century.

Many rose varieties were lost during the years between the fall of the Roman Empire and the Moslem invasion of Europe. After the conquest of Persia in the seventh century, the Moslems manifested a particular fondness for the rose, and as their empire was extended from India to Spain, Asiatic species and varieties of rose were introduced into Europe, and vice-versa, often escaping from cultivation and naturalizing themselves. Thus it was due to the Moslems that such species as *Rosa hemisphaerica*, *Rosa foetida*, and *Rosa foetida bicolor* reached the West.

During the Dark Ages roses found refuge in the gardens of the monasteries, where many species and varieties which would otherwise have been lost to cultivation were saved. It was a rule that at least one monk in each community should be versed in botany and familiar with the medicinal and healing virtues of plants. To our great fortune, not a few of those intelligent, contemplative friars also smuggled into their monastery gardens certain species and varieties whose only curative properties were to soothe the eye and please the nose. To one of these monks, the theologian, botanist, and alchemist St. Albertus Magnus (c. 1206–1280), we owe the most accurate descriptions of the rose species *R. arvensis*, *R. canina*, *R. eglanteria*, and *R. centifolia*.

It is recorded that on his return from the Seventh Crusade, Thibaut IV, Count of Brie and Champagne and King of Navarre (1201–1253), brought back to his wife a gift of rose bushes from Syria. During the years following, the cultivation of roses was above all a prerogative of the French and the town of Rouen was particularly distinguished; in 1435 new varieties of *Rosa gallica* var. *officinalis*, the famous *Rose de Provence*, were developed and diffused.

In England the rose acquired importance as a heraldic emblem

Rosa spinosissima hybrid Frühlingsmorge

during the reign of Edward I (1272–1307), the first British king to choose the rose for his banner. Its heraldic role reached major significance in 1460, at the time of the War of the Roses, fought between the House of York and the House of Lancaster, the first choosing a white rose, presumably *Rosa* x *alba* var. *incarnata*, and the second, a red rose, *Rosa gallica* var. *Red Damask*.

Not until the second half of the sixteenth century were there sources able to give us any scientifically reliable information about roses. Following the classical monastic custom, these books dealt with the rose as a medicinal plant, but with precise observations and descriptions that provide very accurate pictures. The most widely cultivated roses at that time were the species *R. canina*, *R. gallica*, and *R. damascena*. Also during this time, several new roses were introduced into cultivation: *Rosa majalis* (*R. cinnamonea plena*) and *Rosa marginata*, called *Rosa trachyphylla* or Calvary Rose, Rose of St. Francis, or *Rosa centifolia parvifolia*. Towards the end of the sixteenth century and the beginning of the seventeenth century, the Dutch began to show interest in rose cultivation. In particular, they developed *Rosa centifolia*, and obtained innumerable varieties, of which the most important is *Rosa centifolia* var. *muscosa*. From *Rosa muscosa* and *Rosa centifolia* the Dutch produced more than 2,000 varieties. The most accurate descriptions of roses cultivated in Europe towards the end of the sixteenth century was given by Matthias L'Obel in his *Icones* (1581), where he described the species *R. centifolia*, *R. gallica*, *R. canina*, *R. cinnamonea*, *R. eglanteria*, *R. spinosissima*, *R. foetida*, and three types of *Rosa moschata*. The sixteenth-century German botanist Johann Teodor Tabernaemontanus and John Gerard filled the gaps of this list; the first in 1590 described *Rosa alba*; the second in 1597 described *Rosa damascena*. During the next one hundred years the following roses were introduced and described: *Rosa centifolia* var. *parviflora*, *R. francofurtana*, *R. hemisphaerica*, *R. arvensis*, *R. pomifera*, *R. sempervirens*, *R. damascena* var. *versicolor*, and, finally, *R. virginiana*, the first American rose to be introduced into Europe, and drawn by Parkinson in 1640. In 1696 Plunkenet named *Rosa multiflora cathayensis* and *Rosa laevigata*, and in 1704 Petiver named *Rosa microcarpa*.

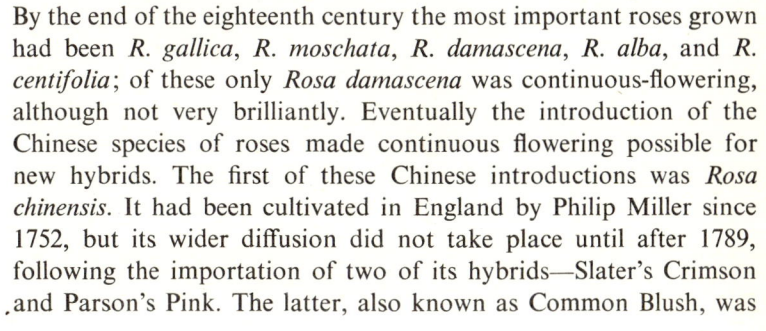

By the end of the eighteenth century the most important roses grown had been *R. gallica*, *R. moschata*, *R. damascena*, *R. alba*, and *R. centifolia*; of these only *Rosa damascena* was continuous-flowering, although not very brilliantly. Eventually the introduction of the Chinese species of roses made continuous flowering possible for new hybrids. The first of these Chinese introductions was *Rosa chinensis*. It had been cultivated in England by Philip Miller since 1752, but its wider diffusion did not take place until after 1789, following the importation of two of its hybrids—Slater's Crimson and Parson's Pink. The latter, also known as Common Blush, was

Rosa rubiginosa

Rosa gallica var. *versicolor*
From *Curtis's Botanical Magazine*,
1816, plate 1794

to be found in every cottage garden in England by the year 1823. Next the first tea rose was imported into England in 1808 from a nursery near Canton. This plant, *Rosa odorata*, was thought to be the result of a cross between *Rosa chinensis* and *Rosa gigantea*, and it was believed that the fragrance of tea attributed to it was due to fresh tea leaves with which the flowers had been in contact. It is now no longer in cultivation, nor is the yellow tea rose imported in 1824.

All the principal roses of the nineteenth century derived from these four Chinese plants. But *Rosa rugosa* from Japan also had great importance in the formation of modern roses. This plant was originally introduced into England in 1796, but it did not become diffused until later when it was reintroduced by Siebold about the year 1845. *Rosa banksiae* was well known during the nineteenth century to those English visitors who started making gardens in Italy, particularly in Florence and on the Italian Riviera. The sepia-yellow *Rosa banksiae* was sent to England in 1871 by way of the Florence Botanic Garden and the Hanbury Botanic Garden at La Mortola, on the Ligurian Riviera. The double-flowered form, *Rosa banksiae* var. *lutea*, was imported into England direct from Calcutta in 1824, and the double white form, var. *albo-plena*, was the first to arrive, reaching Kew Gardens in 1807. One of the most fragrant roses is the single, white-flowered *R. banksiae*, which "drove Farrer mad with rapture" when he discovered it by chance in Great Britain in 1905. The collector had stumbled on a plant more than a hundred years old, in the garden of Megginch Castle, Strathay. It had originally been imported from China by Robert Drummond in 1796 and, ironically, while they searched for it in vain in China, it was growing hidden and forgotten in Scotland.

Other important Asiatic roses imported into England were *Rosa bracteata*, introduced from China in 1793, and *Rosa multiflora*, in 1804. *Rosa wichuraiana* was discovered in 1861 in Japan by the German botanist Max Ernst Wichura, but the plants he introduced into Germany died; the species was reintroduced in 1886 to Monaco and Brussels, when it was given the discoverer's name. These roses were, of course, not the only ones used to create our modern hybrid roses. There are many others whose mention would make the story too long for these pages, and the complete story is extraordinarily complicated. However, the reader who can become familiar with the species here mentioned, identify them, and possibly grow them, certainly deserves much praise. Those who wish to know more can consult *History of the Rose* by Roy E. Shepherd (Macmillan, New York, 1954), and *Collins' Guide to Roses*, by Bertram Park (Collins, London, 1956); and for those who read German, the excellent *Rosen in Garten* by Fritz Glasau (Parey, Berlin, 1961). On the other hand, those who like Alice consider the only worthwhile books to be those with illustrations, should visit the antiquarian book shops. The first European book devoted exclusively to roses was written by a Miss Lawrence and published in 1799 with ninety coloured plates. In 1802–1820 there was published in Germany a book called *Die Rosen*, by C. G. Roessig, with 121 plates; while the *Rosarum Monographia* by John Lindley was published in 1821. The most complete (and sumptuously magnificent) work on roses published in the nineteenth century is one by Thory, containing 172 hand-colored engravings by Pierre Joseph Redouté, and issued in Paris in three volumes between 1817 and 1824. The most important twentieth-century book on roses is *The Genus Rosa* by Ellen Wilmott, in two volumes, published by Murray in London between 1911 and 1914.

The primacy for roses in the nineteenth century was held by the French, and was due mainly to the Empress Joséphine, who started her collection at Malmaison in 1804. Within ten years, in 1814, the garden contained every species then known. There were 167 *R. gallica*, 9 *R. damascena*, 22 Chinese species, 4 *R. spinosissima*, 8 *R. alba*, 3 *R. foetida*, and 1 *R. moschata* in various types, forms, and varieties. Among the true species were included *Rosa alpina*, *Rosa arvensis*, *Rosa banksiae*, *Rosa carolina*, *Rosa cinnamonea*, *Rosa clinophylla*, *Rosa laevigata*, *Rosa rubrifolia*, *Rosa rugosa*, *Rosa sempervirens*, and *Rosa setigera*. Indeed, the impulse given to rose cultivation by the Empress was so enormous that a catalogue published in 1829 by Desportes listed 2,562 different roses, while a catalogue published only thirty-eight years previously by Fillassier, in 1791, listed only twenty-five. This passion for roses spread rapidly from France to the British Isles, throughout Western Europe to America and Australia. Since Napoleon's time the rose has undergone a long and exciting evolution. The *R. damascena* has been supplanted by the *R. bourbon*; these were followed by the Hybrid Tea roses (H. T.) and Hybrid Polyantha roses, which today constitute the major part of cultivated roses.

The modern history of roses is of such importance that it seems only right that we should remember some of the best-known rose growers (whose names appear in italics) who have dedicated themselves to the creation of new hybrids:

France: *Meilland*: Peace, 1945, Baccara, 1954, Grace de Monaco, 1956, Grisbi, 1956, Belle Blonde, 1957, Champs Élysées, 1957, Sarabande, 1967, Christian Dior, 1958, Pink Peace, 1959, Marella, 1961, New Style, 1962, Allegro, 1962, Papa Meilland, 1963, Maria Callas, 1965

Germany: *Kordes*: Golden Rapture, 1933, Crimson Glory, 1935, World's Fair, 1936, Pinocchio, 1940, Sammetglut, 1943, Independence, 1950, Feurio, 1956, Meteor, 1959, Heinz Erhard, 1962, Vienna Charm, 1962

Hybrid Tea Roses, Papa Meilland and Belle Blonde
From an original watercolour by Giovanna Casartelli, 1968

Italy: *Aicardi*: Saturnia, 1933, Gloria di Roma, 1937, Eterna Giovinezza, 1939, Elettra, 1939, Papilio, 1955, Cristoforo Colombo, 1955, Radiosa, 1956

Giacomasso: Chiarastella, 1949, Diamantina, 1951, Antonelliana, 1952, Maristella, 1952, Monterosa, 1952, Quo Vadis, 1959

Cazzaniga: Cetonia, 1943, Abbondanza, 1951, Armonia, 1951, Nigritella, 1952, Cingallegra, 1957, Lodovico, 1960, Olympia, 1960, Paeonia, 1963

England: *S. MacGredy*: Mrs. H. Stevens, 1910, Golden Emblem, 1917, Mrs. S. MacGredy, 1929, Flamengo, 1960, Daily Sketch, 1961, Mischief, 1961, Evelyn Fison, 1962, Elizabeth of Glamis, 1964

Wheatcroft: Josephine Wheatcroft, 1951, My Fair Lady, 1959, Alison Wheatcroft, 1959

United States: *Armstrong*: First Love, 1951, Baghdad, 1954, Circus, 1955, Duet, 1960, Eiffel Tower, 1963, Lilac Dawn, 1964, Gaytime, 1965

The Meilland hybrid Sarabande (France, 1967)

If we have lingered perhaps too long over certain plants' medicinal virtues and healing properties, the temptation becomes even more difficult and more involved in the case of roses, chiefly because medical or pseudo-medical literature on the subject is so vast that our book could risk becoming a volume of prescriptions. It was John Lindley who suggested that the rose could form the sole basis for the entire pharmacopoeia. Even if he were exaggerating, he was not entirely wrong, and modern medicine has demonstrated how great is the importance of vitamin C. Generally this vitamin is obtained from citrus fruits. Oranges, however, contain only 49 mg. of vitamin C per 100 g. of pulp, whereas the fruits (known as rose hips) of *Rosa rugosa* contain from 2,275 to 6,977 mg. of vitamin C per 100 g. of pulp. In past centuries, therefore, rose hips were correctly used for the prevention of scurvy. The floral buds of *Rosa gallica*, stripped of calyx and stamens, and air dried in the shade, were used in ancient times in the preparation of a gargle solution for curing mouth and throat infections, and as an internal astringent. The majority of other rose fruits (or hips) have laxative properties. The fresh fruits of *Rosa canina* make an excellent conserve and have been used in the preparation of various pills; an infusion prepared from the petals of *Rosa gallica* has been used as a tonic, a flavouring agent for other medicines, and as an ophthalmic lotion. Because of their fragrance, the petals of *Rosa centifolia* are used for distillation of rosewater.

The famous attar of roses is generally obtained from *Rosa damascena*, widely cultivated for this purpose in Bulgaria, Turkey, Tunisia, Egypt, India, and to lesser extent in some European countries. The flowers are picked in May, during the early morning, and subjected to a double distillation. Initially 10,000 roses produce one gallon of a greenish yellow liquid of a scent "not very pleasing and strong when in bulk, but most pleasing when diluted". The yield of bushes from their third year onwards and during a life span of about ten years provides an average of about 6,000 lbs. of petals per $2\frac{1}{2}$ acres, which is equivalent to three million flowers. In the Near East and the Orient, the rose perfumes are prepared from half-opened buds dried in the shade and stored in barrels. In Bulgaria and Greece there are types of very sweet confection known as *Oka ghulu* and *Labat loukoum* prepared from rose essence, but they not indicated for those who suffer from toothache. For those who appreciate and enjoy such sweet delicacies we offer the following recipes.

Note: In all the recipes listed below, the following precautions should be kept in mind—Do *not* use roses that have been freshly sprayed with insecticide or treated with any of the commonly used rose dusts. (If roses have been so sprayed or dusted, wait at least a week; or two weeks, if no rain has fallen during the first week.)

Do *not* use any blossoms that have passed their prime; gather only the newly opened blooms.

Discard the calyces and sepals (they are bitter), as well as any whitish portions at the base of the petals.

Gather the blossoms early in the morning, before the sun has struck them and while they are still moist with dew (or pick them on a cloudy morning). Examine the petals carefully for insects. Do *not*, however, wash the petals, since this causes them to lose their perfume.

Use only your most strongly perfumed, sweetest roses, such as *Rosa centifolia* or *Rosa damascena* (or any of the varieties and hybrids listed on page 1143).

ROSE HONEY (an old German recipe)

  1 part chopped fresh rose petals, packed down
  $\frac{1}{2}$ part grain alcohol (or use 100-proof vodka)
  1 part glycerine
  9 parts strained honey

Place the rose petals in a large screw-top glass jar. Add the alcohol, and marinate for three days, shaking the container thoroughly at least three times a day. Strain through a triple thickness of cheesecloth or muslin, squeezing gently to extract all of the liquid. Stir in the glycerine and honey. Place the mixture in loosely capped jars and allow to stand in a dark place for two weeks. Then screw on the caps tightly and store in a closet or pantry. Use on toast, to sweeten fresh fruit compotes, to flavor drinks, etc.

ROSE PETAL PRESERVES

2 quarts fresh rose petals
$3\frac{1}{2}$ cups water
$\frac{1}{4}$ cup rosewater
3 tablespoons lemon juice
4 cups granulated (caster) sugar

Place all the ingredients except the rose petals into a large stainless-steel or enamel saucepan or pot. Bring to a full, rolling boil. Stir in the rose petals, and cook at as high a temperature as possible (without allowing the mixture to foam up and boil over), stirring every now and then until the jelly point is reached (two drops form on the edge of a metal spoon, and then flow together). Pour into sterilized half-pint jars and seal. *Makes about 1 quart.*

ROSE PETAL SUGAR

3 pounds granulated (caster) sugar
$1\frac{1}{4}$ pounds fresh rose petals

Place petals and sugar in a large mixing bowl and stir, fold, and turn with your hands, crushing the petals into the sugar every now and then. Continue this process for 5 to 10 minutes, or until the petals are crushed and limp and almost transparent. Pour the petals and sugar into a large screw-top jar, seal tightly, and expose jar to the sun for about 1 month. Turn the jar every few days and shake it, to give all the ingredients full exposure. After a month, sift through a fine sieve and pack into pint jars. Seal well and store in a dark place. *Makes about 3 pounds.*
Note: This sugar may be used in cakes, pastries, drinks, and is delicious for sweetening Turkish or espresso coffee. It is also excellent for sprinkling on fresh fruit compotes.

ROSE OIL

3 quarts fresh rose petals
1 pint neutral-tasting vegetable oil

Place petals and oil in an enamel or stainless-steel saucepan and mix well. Place over the *lowest* possible heat on the top of the stove, cover, and let the mixture "cook" for $\frac{3}{4}$ hour. Remove from heat and allow to cool. Pour into a large screw-top glass jar and expose to the sun for 4 days. Strain through a triple thickness of cheesecloth or muslin, squeezing out every drop of oil. Bottle in small bottles, corking well. Store in a dark, cool place. *Makes 1 pint.*
Note: This exotic and unorthodox-sounding preparation may be used in Near Eastern and Oriental recipes (both sweet and savoury), or a few drops may be added to the dressing for a fruit salad. It is very concentrated, so caution must prevail when using it. It also makes an unusual sun-tan oil with an exquisite and penetrating fragrance.

CANDIED ROSE PETALS (A dainty confection adapted from William Rabisha's *The Whole Body of Cookery Dissected*, published in 1675)

Select the best petals from *Rosa damascena* and sprinkle them lightly with water. Arrange them in a single layer on a large sheet (or sheets) of white paper, making sure that the petals do not touch one another. Gently sift a thin coating of superfine (*not* confectioner's) sugar over the petals and place the petals in direct sunshine. Every hour or so, sift another thin coating of sugar over the petals until the heat of the sun has candied their surface. Turn each petal over and repeat the process. If desired, the whole procedure may be repeated during the course of several days. (However, the petal-covered paper must be brought into the house at night if this course is followed.) When all the petals are beautifully candied, and quite dry, carefully store them in an airtight container or jar. They *must* be completely dry before storing, otherwise the sugar will dissolve and a gluey mess will result.

ROSE HIP EXTRACT

2 cups rose hips (from *Rosa rugosa*)
3 cups water
2 tablespoons lemon juice

Wash the hips and remove the calices and stem-ends with a stainless-steel paring knife (any other metal tends to act negatively on the vitamin C content of the fruit). Cut the hips in half and place them in a stainless-steel or enamelware saucepan or pot and add the water and lemon juice. Bring to a boil over low heat and boil gently for 15 minutes, stirring frequently. Remove from stove, cover pan, and let it stand overnight. The next day, strain the liquid through a triple thickness of cheesecloth or muslin, pressing well to extract all the juices. Pour into sterile jars or bottles and seal well. This extract is not sweet, and may be used to enrich vegetable soups, fruit juices, or, sweetened to taste and diluted with icewater to make a delicious drink. A spoonful taken each day provides an excellent source of natural vitamin C. *Makes about 1 quart.*

The Aicardi hybrid Gloria di Roma (Italy, 1937)

ROSE HIP PURÉE

2 pounds rose hips (from *Rosa rugosa*)
4 cups water

Prepare hips as directed in previous recipe. Bring to a slow boil, and cook, stirring frequently, until fruit has softened to a mush. Press through a fine stainless-steel or plastic sieve to remove the skins and seeds, and pour the purée into half-pint sterilized jars and seal. This purée may be added to vegetable soup (1 part purée to 3 parts soup), to curries, or to cooked vegetable mélanges, providing a tasty vitamin C supplement. It can even serve as a sauce (a similar sauce, called "Eglantine Rose Sauce", was a favourite of Queen Victoria's) with the addition of lemon juice to taste. The sauce could be a flavoursome (and healthful) condiment for cold fish, meat, or game.

ROSE HIP JAM

> 3 cups dead-ripe rose hips (from *Rosa rugosa*)
> 1 orange
> 1 lemon
> 1 cup water
> 1½ cups sugar

Prepare the hips as directed for Rose Hip Extract, but scrape out the seeds with a small spoon. Wash seeded hips well, and drain thoroughly. Cut the peel from the orange and the lemon, using a rotary vegetable peeler (make sure you only cut the "zest" and do not include any of the white part). Cut the peel into small slivers. Place the water and the peel in a large stainless-steel or enamelware pot or saucepan, bring to a boil, and cook for 5 minutes. Squeeze the juice from the orange and the lemon, strain it, and add the juice to the peel together with the seeded rose hips and the sugar. Stir well, cover pan, lower the heat, and simmer gently for 15 minutes. Remove cover, raise heat, and cook rapidly, stirring every so often, until the hips are transparent and the jam has thickened. Pour into half-pint sterilized jars and seal. *Makes about 1 pint.*
Note: If you wish to make more than 1 pint, do so in small batches as directed above. Doubling this recipe will also double the cooking time, and the resulting jam will not have so delicate a flavour.

ROSEWATER

Rosewater is usually imported from France or from the Near East, and is available at a chemist's (drugstore) or at specialty food shops. Used in cookery it can add an exquisite and elusive flavour to sponge cakes or angel cakes, to custards, cookies, and soufflés. It should be used in place of any flavour extract (such as vanilla) at about twice the amount called for in the recipe (for instance, if the recipe calls for 1 teaspoon vanilla extract, use 1 tablespoon of rosewater).

Even if the complaint that modern roses—particularly the large-flowered, perpetual- or continuous-flowering hybrids—have lost their fragrance is true, not all modern roses are scentless. We believe it may be useful to offer the following list of the most fragrant roses. To this list of hybrids we have also added a selection of old rose species and varieties which we advise growing for scent.

Hybrid minature rose
Perle de Montserrat

Large-flowered Hybrid Tea Continuous-flowering Roses

American Home	Diorama	Liberty Bell
Arlene Francis	Eden Rose	Liebeszauber
Bacchus	Elsa Arnot	Mme. Butterfly
Bajazzo	Ena Harkness	Monique
Betty Uprichard	Ernest H. Morse	Ophelia
Blue Moon	Fragrant Cloud	Papa Meilland
Bond Street	Golden Melody	Pink Peace
Buccaneer	Grace de Monaco	President Hoover
Charles Mallerin	Hector Deane	Prima Ballerina
Christopher Stone	Hugh Dickson	Shot Silk
Chrysler Imperial	Josephine Bruce	Signora
Cleopatra	June Park	Sutter's Gold
Crimson Glory	Konrad Adenauer	Vienna Charm
Dame Edith Helen	Lady Seton	Vogue
Diamond Jubilee	Lady Sylvia	Wendy Cussons

Rosa polyantha and Rosa floribunda (multiflora)

Angela	Daily Sketch	Ivory Fashion
Apricot Nectar	Elizabeth of Glamis	Lilac Charm
Arthus Bell	Florida von Scharbeutz	Masquerade
Castanet	Fragrant Cloud	Orange Sensation
Charm of Paris	Gold Marie	Paddy McGredy
Cognac	Golden Delight	Sweet Repose

Species and Varieties

Rosa centifolia
Rosa moschata
    var. *Blanc Double de Coubert*
    var. *Cardinal de Richelieu*
    var. *Conrad Ferdinand*
    var. *Grüss an Teplitz*
    var. *Mme. Alfred Carrière*
    var. *Reine des Violettes*
Rosa helenae
    var. *Tour de Malakoff*
Rosa damascena
    var. *Belle de Crécy*   var. *Königin von Danemark*
    var. *Boule de Neige*   var. *Old Blush*
    var. *Comte de Chambord*   var. *Parfum de l'Hay*
    var. *Gloire de Dijon*
Rosa wichuraiana
    var. *White Bath*

Rosa canina

Cultivation. The cultivation of roses is not particularly difficult, although it must be admitted that roses are liable to be attacked by a formidable number of diseases, the majority of which are easier prevented than cured. Some of these diseases are zonal—for instance, black spot, the worst of all, is less prevalent in urban areas than in the country. More than anything else, roses require an open, sunny position. They thrive in heavy, compact, clayey soils that are moderately alkaline (calcareous), fertile, and well manured. One of the best rose fertilizers still remains well-composted manure, applied in generous quantities round the base of each plant in late autumn, so that during the cold winter months it will give protection against severe frost exactly at the most delicate point: where the plant was grafted or budded, just below the soil surface. In early spring before new growth begins the manure should be forked and cultivated into the soil. The modern continuous-flowering large-flowered hybrid roses, with their abundant and vigorous growth and profuse blooms, require constant fertilizing from early summer until autumn; monthly applications of some organic fertilizer such as dried blood are ideal for this purpose. The best planting time for roses is late autumn or in mild localities even as late as December; otherwise plant in early spring. Roses have only a few deeply penetrating roots and the soil should be prepared and well spaded to a depth of at least 18–20 ins. The individual planting holes should also be deep and wide. After planting new roses the soil should be heaped up for a few inches round the collar of the plant (that is, the point at ground level). With few exceptions modern roses are completely hardy, actually preferring coolness to excessive heat. In areas above Zone 6 (and even in certain parts of that zone) winter protection becomes a necessity. In those areas where the temperature falls below 10°F., rose bushes should be cut back in the fall to about 12 ins. high, and earth should be mounded up to completely cover the pruned-back bush (if one is lazy one can get away with pruning the bush to 7–8 ins. before mounding over—but one should keep in mind that the more wood surviving the winter, the better the plant the following spring). The mounded earth (which may be mixed with half its volume of well-composted manure) should be removed in early spring when all danger of severe frost has passed (the exposed new growth will not be harmed by light frosts or even a late snowfall). In even colder areas (Zones 3 and 4), the mound should be additionally protected by a heavy layer of salt hay or pine branches. In these locations, climbing roses will also have to be protected by removing them from their support, laying them flat on the ground, and protecting them with heavy paper or plastic and covering this with at least 6 ins. of straw, salt hay, earth, or pine branches.

Roses do not suffer from moderate drought, but during periods of very hot, dry weather frequent watering is necessary; however, the foliage should not be wetted. The hybrids, particularly, require severe pruning in early spring or fall (see above), while the true species require much less pruning. There should be some variation in

Polyantha Hybrid Zambra and Hybrid Climber Mermaid
From an original watercolour by Giovanna Casartelli, 1968

the pruning method for different types, and more complete details are given under the separate headings. Only by personal, practical experience can the precise details of pruning be understood; this is also true of the removal of dead, badly formed, weak, and unwanted growths. In every case, when pruning is done, the cut should be made with very sharp clippers (ones not used for any other purpose), about $\frac{1}{3}$ in. above an eye, or node, and always in an oblique direction, away from the eye.

The hardiness of Hybrid Tea (H.T.) roses. Modern H.T. roses are of hybrid origin, descendants from many crosses between less hardy species. To give them greater hardiness in our gardens, they are therefore budded (or grafted) onto hardier frost-resistant roses raised from seed. The most suitable species for this purpose have for many years proved to be the very hardy *Rosa canina* (in one of its thirty-odd forms) and *Rosa multiflora*. It thus follows that our modern garden roses are as hardy as the root stock onto which they are budded, and no hardier. Unfortunately—mainly due to economic considerations and for reasons of convenience—less-hardy root stock is sometimes used; which although giving good results in warm climates, makes the plants less resistant to severe frost. In very cold localities, one should therefore insist on plants which have been budded or grafted onto *Rosa canina*. (Although this factor is most important, it is frequently ignored by commercial rose growers when compiling their catalogues, and it is not always referred to in gardening books. In other words, commercial growers are liable to employ root stocks which are convenient for them, without considering under what climatic conditions the budded plants are ultimately to be grown. It does not automatically follow that the stock used for hybrid roses in the south is suitable for the same hybrid grown in the north, or vice-versa, and probably no commercial grower could afford to offer roses budded onto the type of stock best suited to individual localities; although this would be the ideal solution. Thus, whenever possible, it is best to obtain H.T. roses from a local grower or firm: plants raised in the same climate that prevails in the grower's fields will be perfectly hardy in gardens located in the same zones.)

Pests and Diseases. There are, unfortunately, many pests and diseases that attack roses; some are zonal, some can be carried over from one season to another, and many are easier to prevent than to cure. A few are of fungus origin, others are caused by viruses, while insect pests can be introduced via the soil or by air. Some of these annoyances are easy to combat, others are extremely difficult to eliminate. Several chemical firms in England, on the Continent, and in the United States have, in recent years, produced many aids to help the rose grower (a few of these are highly toxic and need the most careful handling). There are also many excellent, generally free, advisory services provided by government departments, rose societies, and the chemical manufacturers themselves. This service is given by experts with a specialized knowledge of local climates, conditions, temperatures, soils, etc., all factors that have considerable bearing on the type of pest or disease likely to be encountered in various zones. In all cases there is now available on the market a variety of products —under many different trade names—suitable for combatting any pest or disease likely to be encountered in any garden. Some of the more common pests and diseases of roses are listed here.

Mildew. This is a fungus disease that is very common and easy to control; it is also most visibly obvious and active at any season during which the roses are in leaf. Not particularly harmful in its initial stages, it can be serious if neglected, spreading with great rapidity and causing the young growths to become dwarfed and misshapen. It appears as a white, powder-like substance covering the young foliage and stems. Treatment calls for dusting with powdered sulphur early in the morning while the leaves are still damp with dew, or spraying with a colloidal copper white-oil emulsion or one of the many specialized products available on the market under various trade names.

Black spot. This is a fungus disease which in certain localities assumes almost epidemic proportions, and when firmly established on a rose is almost impossible to eliminate. It is less common in cities, where the polluted atmosphere seems to act as a natural preventive. It is, however, zonal, and some localities remain completely free. The spores can winter-over in the soil and infect the plants again the following season, so all diseased leaves should be collected and burned. This fungus is easier to prevent than to cure and is rarely active when the temperature is below 55–60°F. It appears as a number of small black spots on the leaf surface. These rapidly expand and become surrounded with a yellowish maroon halo and eventually cause defoliation which seriously weakens the plant. Many different fungicides have been used to combat this enemy, so far without much success. The most promising is a relatively new compound marketed under the trade name Captan and sold under various proprietary names. In areas likely to be affected, used as a preventive at bimonthly intervals before any attacks become visible, it has given good results. Many growers are, however, convinced that the best solution is to breed resistant or immune varieties of roses.

Rust. This is a fungus disease as dangerous as the above-mentioned black spot, but not so frequent. It is worse in some years than others and, when severe, it can rapidly kill a small plant through complete defoliation. It first appears as small rust-coloured spots scattered on the undersurface of the leaves (black spot is seen on the upper surface) which rapidly spread, unite, and cause the leaf to fall. It can winter-over in soil, so all affected foliage should be burned. It is as difficult to cure as black spot and, like that disease, it is easier to pre-

Rosa banksiae var. *albo-plena*
From *The Botanical Register*,
1819, plate 397

vent than to cure. Apart from affecting the foliage, rust can also extend to all other green parts of the plant, causing distortion and wounds. Treatment should be similiar to that for black spot, taking care to spray the undersurface of the foliage as well as the stems, but no really satisfactory cure is yet known.

Chlorosis. This is not a true disease but a physiological condition caused by an excess of alkaline (calcareous) matter and a deficiency of iron in the soil. With roses in particular, and with most other garden plants in general, chlorosis manifests itself as a yellowing of the foliage. Such discoloration can also be caused by excessive watering, bad drainage, or acute shortage of some particular nutrient; but in many cases it can be attributed to an excess of alkaline (calcareous) matter in the soil. The complicated chain of chemical actions by which plants in alkaline (calcareous) soils are deprived of their essential quota of iron is well understood, but until recently there was no really satisfactory method of improving matters, although massive doses of iron sulphate added to the soil did give temporary relief. Now, however, the application of powdered iron chelates dissolved in water and watered into the soil (in very small doses and according to the manufacturer's directions) provides a rapid and effective treatment. A plant with unhealthy, weak, yellowish foliage and young growths will reassume its natural green colour within a matter of a week or so. A plant suffering from chlorosis is unable to manufacture the essential chlorophyl that keeps it green and healthy. In simple words, a chlorotic plant eventually dies of starvation.

Aphid and green fly. These are the most common pests that affect roses. These insects are generally green, but can also be grey or black, and they are readily visible to the naked eye and can be easily controlled. They are active from April to November, or even longer in mild climates, and are found on the young growths and shoots, often in great quantities. They feed on the sap by a process of sucking, eventually greatly weakening the plant. They can be treated by spraying with one of the many products now available which have a nicotine or pyrethrum base.

Thrips. These are much smaller than the green fly and thus not easily visible, although their harmful effects are very obvious. They cause discolouration, distortion, and weakening of young growths, leaves, buds, and flowers; sometimes to a serious degree. They are dark brown or black in colour. They damage the plants by destroying the surface tissue in order to reach the sap on which they feed. Thrips appear to be particularly active during spells of hot, dry weather. Treat as for green fly, although thrips are much more difficult to destroy and more energetic action is necessary, even spraying every day or so. At the present time much work is being done to produce a systemic insecticide for killing sap-sucking insects. Excellent results are being obtained and there are several products already on the market.

They are applied to the foliage, or to the roots (in liquid form), and enter the sap itself, killing the insect that feeds on the sap without harming the plant.

Scale. These are found mostly on the older, mature growths in the form of numerous small but easily visible brownish scales closely attached to the back of leaves and stems. In some cases the scales are a dirty white colour and are particularly common on the old stems of climbing roses and standards. When only a few plants are affected, scales can be removed by hand with a small wire brush, or painted with a solution of 50 percent methylated spirits and 50 percent water. Large plantings should be sprayed with one of the white-oil-and-nicotine emulsions readily available on the market. Scale does not cause rapid, immediate damage, but if neglected it can lead to serious harm since some scales represent the nymphal or larval stage of mealybugs. In the case of very severe infestations it is best to remove and burn the affected growths.

Caterpillars. These are so large and so obvious that in a small garden the most effective control is to remove by hand. Otherwise spray with one of the products containing pyrethrum or nicotine.

Japanese beetles. During the past 35 years these pests have become a serious problem to gardeners in the United States. Although certain areas are no longer as thickly infested as they were a decade or so ago, the beetle still represents a considerable nuisance as a voracious feeder on both blooms and foliage. Certain bacterial preparations (marketed under the name of Doom, etc.) have been successful in killing the underground grubs, but the adult beetles are almost immune to a large majority of the safely administered pesticides. Apart from certain patented traps that can be set up around the garden, the only effective measure seems to be a daily tour of the garden armed with a can of kerosene (paraffin), plucking the beetles off the flowers by hand, drowning them in the kerosene.

NOTE: For the benefit of gardeners who are fanatic in their avoidance of synthetic and chemical insecticides, it might be instructive and helpful to mention that the pyrethrins, or pyrethrum-based preparations, are extracted from the dried flower-heads of *Chrysanthemum coccineum*. For those who are opposed to the use of any insecticide whatsoever, the following suggestion might prove useful: there seems to be some efficacy in introducing ladybugs and praying mantises into the garden. The ladybugs make a specialty of feeding on aphids, and the mantises are voracious insect predators. Ladybugs can be ordered shipped live in lots of one hundred and more, and the mantises are procured in egg cases, which must be left in the garden to hatch (one egg case produces hundreds of mantises, but it is best to obtain at least three or four cases). Do not expect, however, that these insect "watchdogs" will all obediently settle in *your* garden exclusively. They won't. But a certain percentage will remain to feed, if there are enough insects around to satisfy their appetites.

Roses may be propagated from seed, by means of cuttings, or by budding. Species roses are best propagated from seed, although they can also be increased by means of cuttings. Hybrid roses are only propagated from seed when raising new varieties. On a commercial scale the propagation of hybrid garden roses is done almost exclusively by budding, using seedlings of the species *R. indica, R. polyantha,* or *R. canina* as the stock onto which the desired hybrid is to be budded. Many climbing roses can also be propagated by layering during the summer months.

Seed should be sown as soon as it is ripe, outside in seed beds, flats, pans, frames, pots, or boxes. Germination will generally take place the following spring. Cuttings are best taken from half-ripened wood in July–August, and inserted in sandy soil either in a sheltered position outside, or in pots or frames. Some roses root with greater ease than others, but in all cases it is advisable to treat the cuttings with one of the root-forming hormone preparations now available on the market. Plants raised from cuttings are frequently less vigorous than those propagated from seed or by budding. Budding is best done during June–July—using vegetative buds, not flower buds.

The classification and nomenclature of roses presents certain difficulties, and, in fact, few other plants have been so carelessly classified. Through an excess of zeal, certain botanists have created more species than is justified and there is much difference of opinion concerning the actual number of species. A few years ago some authorities gave seventy as the approximate number, but many new introductions, especially from China, legitimately increased the number to about one hundred. Other botanists have classified the wild roses into three hundred species, and one fanatic so divided his species that as a result of minute and scarcely discernible variations two alleged species could be observed on the same plant. Apart from the species, which also have their forms and varieties, which are variously known as Botanical Roses, Old-fashioned Roses, etc., there are also a great number of hybrid roses whose classification and nomenclature becomes more difficult every year as more and more are produced. Formerly, it was the custom to separate garden roses into various classes according to their pedigree, but in recent years this has become increasingly difficult, if not impossible, because of the constant crossing and recrossing between the hybrids, so that certain classes merge one into another. Certain hybrids now have less similarity to their parents than they have to roses from another group of parents. Therefore, it is now more convenient to group garden hybrids according to their appearance and not according to their parentage. (For details of roses in each group see lists of hybrids.) Many of the roses in these groups also have a variety of forms so that, for instance, a Hybrid Tea type is available as a bush, a standard, or

Rosa hugonis
From *Curtis's Botanical Magazine*,
1905, plate 8004

a climber. These various groups of hybrid roses are given here after the list of species.

The following wild rose species are plants of the greatest beauty and of enormous garden value. In general they are easier to cultivate than the modern hybrid roses, being less subject to disease, requiring practically no pruning, and useful for many different purposes, such as creating large groups of individual specimens, while several are ideal for use as climbers on summer-houses, walls, etc. They are also early-flowering (from March to July). It is true that they are not all continuous-flowering like the modern hybrids, but in recompense many produce autumn displays of beautifully coloured and often attractively shaped fruits. Some have ornamental thorns or spines; while several are first-class subjects in autumn when their leaves turn beautiful shades of red, yellow, gold, and crimson. In the majority of cases they require an abundance of space, although some are of modest proportions. Their native habitat is very wide and includes Europe, the Middle East, Asia, the Americas, and Northern Africa. The majority are deciduous and practically all are completely hardy. Many have a strong and delicious fragrance.

Deciduous shrub
Flowering period: June–July
Height: up to 10 ft.
Zone 4 southwards

Rosa x *alba* L.

Naturalized in certain parts of Europe, but believed to be a natural hybrid between *Rosa gallica* and *Rosa canina* var. *dumetorum*. A deciduous shrub of vigorous, almost rampant growth. Large hooked thorns or spines. Flowers nearly 3 ins. in diameter, white, single, with conspicuous stamens, produced in groups, fragrant. Fruits red, oblong, $\frac{3}{4}$ in. in length. Leaves composed of 5–7 leaflets, grey-green, rugose-surfaced, ovate, dentated; each leaflet $1-2\frac{1}{2}$ ins. long. There are several very beautiful forms:

> var. *celestial,* semi-double, pink; grey-green foliage, Royal Horticultural Society's award of merit, 1948
>
> var. *Maiden's Blush* (syn. *carnea*), double pink flowers; strong perfume
>
> var. *maxima,* very double flat white flowers
>
> var. *suaveolens,* flowers white or very pale pink. Widely cultivated for the extraction of the essence, attar of roses.

(Lady Bank's Rose)
Semi-evergreen climber
Flowering period: Apr.–June
Height: up to 40 ft.
Zone 7 southwards

Rosa banksiae R. Br.

Native to China. Introduced in 1807. A very vigorous evergreen or semi-evergreen climber that can reach a height of up to 40 ft. Not hardy in very cold zones, but one of the best-known and most widely planted climbing roses in southern gardens. It is a lover of sun and warmth and many very old, very large specimens can be seen in Riviera gardens and gardens of the southern United States. It is a "rose without thorns", with long slender branches which love to climb through the branches of a tree, over a summer-house, or on a sunny wall. Leaves composed of 3–5 leaflets each 1–2½ ins. long and ⅓–1 in. wide; oblong-lanceolate, pointed, dentated, glabrous. Flowers slightly scented and produced in profusion, 1–1½ ins. wide, in clusters. Fruits dark red, but rarely produced, the size and shape of a pea. There are four forms:

>   var. *alba,* single white and strongly fragrant
>   var. *albo-plena,* double white flowers
>   var. *lutea,* double yellow flowers, Royal Horticultural Society's award of merit, 1960
>   var. *lutescens,* single yellow

Rosa blanda Ait.

Deciduous shrub
Flowering period: May–June
Height: up to 6 ft.
Zone 3 southwards

Native to the United States and Canada. One of the largest-flowered species, with pink single blooms up to 3 ins. in diameter. This, too, is a rose without thorns. A deciduous shrub of medium proportions with leaves 2–2¾ ins. long composed of 5–7 obovate leaflets each ¾–1½ ins. long, dentated. The flowers can be either solitary or in groups of 3–7. Fruits red, pear-shaped, ⅓ in. wide.

Rosa bracteata Wendl.

(Macartney Rose)
Evergreen climber
Flowering period: June–July
Height: up to 20 ft.
Zone 8 southwards

Native to China. Introduced into Europe by Lord Macartney in 1793. Only hardy in mild localities. A very vigorous evergreen climber. Leaves composed of 5–11 obovate, dentated leaflets, each ¾–2 ins. long and ¾–1 in. wide. Flowers 1½–2¾ ins. in diameter; solitary, white, scented, and very beautiful. Fruits globose, orange-red, 1¼–1½ ins. wide and highly decorative. Certainly one of the most attractive of the evergreen species.

Rosa canina L.

(Dog Rose)
Deciduous climber
Flowering period: Apr.–May
Height: up to 15 ft.
Zone 4 southwards

Native to Europe, Western Asia, and naturalized in North America. Widely diffused in its natural state, and always much admired, but relatively rare in gardens. Grown from seed on a commercial basis for use as a stock onto which hybrid roses are grafted; a practise about which Shakespeare wrote (*The Winter's Tale,* Act IV, sc. 3):

> You see, sweet maid, we marry
> A gentler scion to the wildest stock,
> And make conceive a bark of baser kind
> By bud of nobler race; this is an art
> Which does mend nature, change it rather, but
> The art itself is nature.

Rosa canina—commonly known as the Dog Rose—is a vigorous hardy climber. Leaves composed of 5 or 7 ovate dentated leaflets varying greatly in size. The five sepals are also of various sizes and

Rosa moysii
From *Curtis's Botanical Magazine*,
1910, plate 8338

forms, some hairy and some glabrous—a fact that inspired the following riddle, at one time popular in England:

What Are We?

Five brothers of one house are we,
All in one little family.
Two have beards, and two have none,
And only half a beard has one.

This great diversity of form and habit, which is so characteristic of *Rosa canina*, makes the species more of a group than a single type. Indeed, some authorities have classified the forms as subspecies, but the matter is not of great garden interest, although the following variety is sufficiently different to merit special mention:

> var. *dumetorum* Baker (syn. *Rosa dumetorum* Thuill., *Rosa corymbifera* Bork.), one of the parents of the natural hybrid *Rosa* x *alba*, with grey-green, downy leaves.

The flowers of *Rosa canina* are a lovely shade of pale pink. There is much variation in the size and shape of the red fruits, which have a medicinal value because of their content of a form of sugar, citric acid, and malic acid.

Rosa carolina L.
Native to Eastern North America. Introduced into Europe in 1726. A delightful little species of modest proportions, forming a dense, compact, deciduous shrub. Leaves up to 4 ins. long, composed of 5–7, obovate leaflets $1\frac{1}{2}$ ins. long, dentated, green on the upper surface, grey-green beneath. Flowers dark purple-pink, $2\frac{1}{2}$ ins. wide, scented, in clusters. Fruits globose, $\frac{1}{3}$ in. wide, red.

(Pasture Rose)
Deciduous shrub
Flowering period: June–July
Height: up to 3 ft.
Zone 4 southwards

Rosa centifolia L. (syn. *Rosa gallica centifolia* Regel)
Origin unknown but of great age and referred to by Pliny. Also called *Rose des Peintres* because of its frequent depiction by the old Dutch painters. A hardy shrub-like deciduous species with a compact, erect habit. Leaves composed of 5 oval, leathery, dentated leaflets each $\frac{2}{3}$–1 in. long and half as wide. Flowers red, borne in clusters, strongly scented, very double, with many erect petals that overlap like the leaves of a cabbage—hence the common English name of Cabbage Rose. Fruits oblong, $\frac{3}{4}$ in. long, and of a certain medicinal value as an aperient. The flowers are also used for the distillation of rosewater.

(Cabbage Rose
or Hundred-leaved Rose)
Deciduous shrub
Flowering period: June–July
Height: up to 6 ft.
Zone 4 southwards

> var. *cristata*, has curiously crested petals
> var. *muscosa* (syn. *Rosa muscosa*), called moss rose, has the sepals, flower stalk, and leaf stalk covered with what appears to be green moss but is actually a glandular formation

(Damask Rose)
Deciduous shrub
Flowering period: May–July
Height: up to 7 ft.
Zone 5 southwards

Rosa damascena
var. *variegata*

Rosa damascena Mil.
Of hybrid origin and of doubtful parentage but one of the oldest roses in cultivation, the Damask Rose has played an important part in the development of hybrid garden roses. Its progeny, when crossed with varieties of *Rosa indica,* resulted in the race known as Hybrid Perpetuals (H.P.), the most famous of which is Frau Karl Druschki, a hybrid of vigorous habit and superb double white flowers produced continuously from late spring until autumn (given an award of merit by the Royal Horticultural Society in 1902). Another marvellous old rose belonging to this strain is Souvenir du Docteur Jamain, intensely fragrant, continuous-flowering, with wine-coloured flowers suffused purple (award of merit from the Royal Horticultural Society in 1963). These H.P. roses have now been largely superseded by the more modern Hybrid Tea (H.T.) strain which have flowers of a better form, with a wider range of colours, but with less fragrance and often with less robustness (except in the case of the exuberant Peace). The original *Rosa damascena* is a hardy deciduous shrub with an upright, rigid habit and many large spines. Flowers strongly fragrant, borne in clusters of up to 12, white suffused pink or red, long-stalked. Fruits pear-shaped, red, hairy, 1 in. long. Leaves composed of 5 oval dentated leaflets each $\frac{3}{4}$–2 ins. long and half as wide.

> var. *Madame Hardy,* flowers cream-white changing to pure white; flat and very double with the central petals incurved
>
> var. *Quatre Saisons Blanc Mousseux,* blush-white, perpetual-blooming
>
> var. *trigintipetala,* important as one of the sources of supply for attar of roses
>
> var. *variegata,* petals striped pink and white (the York and Lancaster Rose)

Deciduous shrub
Flowering period: May
Height: up to 5 ft.
Zone 6 southwards

Rosa ecae Ait. (syn. *Rosa xanthina* Hook. f., not Lindl.)
Native to Afghanistan. Introduced to Kew in 1880 by Dr. Aitchison, who named it with an adaptation of his wife's initials. One of the smallest, most graceful species, it is a small, hardy deciduous shrub with slender, arching, spiny branches. Flowers solitary, of an unusually vivid yellow, 1 in. in diameter, single. Leaves 1 in. long, composed of 5, 7, or 9 minute oval dentate leaflets. A beautiful little plant ideal for warm, sunny positions.

(Threepenny-Bit Rose)
Deciduous shrub
Flowering period: May–June
Height: up to 6 ft.
Zone 5 southwards

Rosa farreri Stapf.
Native to China. The Threepenny-Bit Rose, so-called because its minute flowers are the smallest of all roses, like the threepenny bit, the smallest of English coins before the introduction of decimal coinage. Introduced by R. Farrer in 1915. A vigorous, much-branched, hardy deciduous shrub forming a dense mass of slender, interlacing branches. Leaves graceful and fern-like, composed of 7–9 leaflets,

oval, dentated, less than $\frac{1}{4}$ in. long, with the entire leaf $2\frac{1}{4}$ ins. long. Fruits oval, coral-red, $\frac{1}{3}$ in. long. Flowers dark red in bud, pink when fully open, $\frac{1}{2}$ in. in diameter and borne in the greatest profusion. The foliage assumes a good autumn colour.

Rosa gallica L. *(Provence or French Rose)*
Deciduous shrub
Flowering period: June–July
Height: up to 4 ft.
Zone 4 southwards

Native to Central and Southern Europe. Cultivated in gardens from the most remote times and a parent of a vast number of hybrids. It can, in fact, be described as one of the most important species in the development of modern roses. In particular it has been crossed with *Rosa moschata, Rosa setigera, Rosa indica, Rosa arvensis,* and *Rosa canina.* A hardy deciduous shrub with an erect, compact habit; rapidly increases by means of underground growths which send up new vegetation all around the parent plant. Flowers generally solitary, $2–2\frac{1}{2}$ ins. in diameter, dark red. Fruits globose or pear-shaped, dark red, $\frac{1}{2}$ in. wide. Leaves composed of 3, 5, or 7 oval leaflets each $\frac{2}{3}–2\frac{3}{4}$ ins. long and $\frac{1}{2}–1\frac{1}{2}$ ins. wide. dentated, glabrous, dark green. A very handsome species in flower and fruit and of the greatest botanical interest for the progeny it has produced. Some of the more important hybrids are:

> Complicata, a deciduous flowering shrub of exceptional beauty (Royal Horticultural Society's award of merit, 1951). Forms a vigorous rounded bush bearing masses of very large single flowers of a clear, exquisite rich pink. Scented.
> Conditorum (syn. Crimson Damask), very large, semi-double flowers, vivid crimson-purple and richly fragrant. Forms a wide, spreading, dome-shaped dwarf bush.
> Officinalis, semi-double, crimson-pink, with prominent yellow stamens. Also called the Apothecary's Rose because an infusion made from the petals has been used for flavouring medicines.
> Violacea, fragrant semi-double flowers with velvet-like petals. Crimson-black in bud, dark wine-purple when expanded, with a contrasting disc of golden anthers in the centre.

Rosa hugonis Hemsl. *(Father Hugo's Rose)*
Deciduous shrub
Flowering period: Apr.–May
Height: up to 8 ft.
Zone 4 southwards

Native to China. Sent to Kew in 1899 by Father Hugo Scallon, a missionary in China. The earliest-flowering species, often in April. A very hardy deciduous bush of graceful rounded form with arching branches literally covered with bright yellow flowers, 2 ins. in diameter, single, solitary, with conspicuous masses of stamens in the centre. Fruits globose, reddish black, $\frac{1}{2}$ in. wide. Leaves fern-like, vivid green but bronze-green in autumn; 2–4 ins. long, composed of 5–11 oval leaflets $\frac{3}{4}$ in. long. A beautiful shrub ornamental in leaf, flower, and fruit.

Deciduous shrub
Flowering period: May–Sept.
Height: 12–15 ft.
Zone 8 southwards

Rosa indica Lindl. (syn. *Rosa chinensis* Jacq.)
Native to China. An important, beautiful species that has played a significant part in the evolution of numerous races of hybrid roses. A plant of variable habit, and different forms have been discovered by botanical collectors. Probably the most typical form is that found by Professor A. Henry in 1890 in central China. A large shrub of loose, open habit often with the character of a semi-climber. Not tolerant of severe or prolonged frost. Both the species and its progeny are characterized by their long-flowering habit, from May to September or even later. Blooms are generally produced intermittently and not in simultaneous masses. Leaves composed of 3–5 leaflets, shiny green above, glabrous and glaucous beneath; each leaflet oval, $1\frac{1}{2}$–3 ins. long, pointed, dentated. Flowers solitary, single, 2 ins. in diameter with slightly ruffled petals. Colour pinkish brick-red. Fruits top-shaped, $\frac{3}{4}$ in. long, scarlet. Among the numerous varieties the following are of special interest:

> var. *Chinensis mutabilis,* a remarkable rose at one time widely planted in Southern European gardens. One is tempted to make many guesses as to who planted them and from where they came. In old gardens at least one plant is invariably to be seen, often abandoned and neglected, often growing over a balustrade, pillar, or wall. From May until the end of the year there are always a few blooms. It forms a small upright shrub with single flowers $2\frac{3}{4}$–4 ins. in diameter, fragrant; pinkish yellow suffused copper-red in bud, apricot-pink shaded carmine as it opens, and finally crimson when the flowers are old. On a large specimen it is possible to see flowers of all these different gradations of colours at once. Award of merit from the Royal Horticultural Society in 1957.

> var. *fragrans* (syn. *Rosa fragrans* Thory.), tea-scented and one of the most deliciously fragrant of all roses. Introduced in 1810 and founder of the modern strain of Hybrid Tea roses. Also parent of those two superb climbers, the yellow Maréchal Niel, and the yellow-and-orange Gloire de Dijon, two of the most fragrant, most beautiful of all climbing roses (sometimes referred to as Noisette roses). Unfortunately Maréchal Niel is not hardy in cold zones and has to be grown in an unheated greenhouse.

> var. *viridiflora* (syn. *Rosa monstrosa*), a true green rose, where the petals are transformed into leaf-like organs. Curious rather than beautiful, but of great botanical interest and certainly not monstrous as one of its names suggests. Discovered in 1855 in a Paris garden owned by a M. Verdier, who received the plant from America.

Rosa laevigata Michx. (syn. *Rosa sinica* Ait.) (Cherokee Rose)
Native to China. (Official state flower of Georgia.) This white-flowered climber, together with its pink-flowered variety var. *Anemone,* are two of the glories of many southern gardens in Europe and the United States where they find conditions to their liking, but they are not hardy in very cold zones. They make a perfect companion to the equally beautiful and hardier yellow-flowered climber Mermaid. *Rosa laevigata* is a large vigorous evergreen climber with leathery, trifoliate, shiny bright-green leaves, each segment oval, $1\frac{1}{2}$–4 ins. long, $\frac{3}{4}$–2 ins. wide, dentated. Flowers single, white, up to 5 ins. in diameter, solitary, and fragrant. Fruits oval, $\frac{3}{4}$ in. wide, red. Introduced into Europe in 1803 from America, where it has been cultivated since 1780. Certainly one of the most spectacular species and given an award of merit by the Royal Horticultural Society in 1951.

Evergreen climber
Flowering period: June–Aug.
Height: up to 15 ft.
Zone 8 southwards

Rosa lutea Mill. (syn. *Rosa eglanteria* Mill., *Rosa foetida* Herm.)
Native to Asia Minor, Afghanistan, and the Himalayas. Cultivated in European gardens since 1650. A moderately hardy semi-climbing deciduous shrub with arching branches. Requires alkaline (calcareous) soil. Leaves composed of 5, 7, or 9 oval leaflets each $\frac{3}{4}$–$1\frac{1}{2}$ ins. long, $\frac{1}{3}$–$\frac{2}{3}$ in. wide, dentated, dark green, glabrous. Flowers solitary, 2–$2\frac{3}{4}$ ins. long, and of a most intense clear vivid yellow. Needs an abundance of sun and warmth in a fairly dry position to ensure good flowering. Fruits red, globose, $\frac{1}{2}$ in. in diameter. The var. *punicea* (syn. *Rosa punicea* Mills., *Rosa lutea bicolor*) is of remarkable beauty with copper-red flowers. Occasionally a plant will bear both yellow and copper-red blooms. Some particularly fine specimens can be seen in the Rome Rose Garden, and when I go there as a member of the international jury that awards the Rome prize for the best new rose, I often think this old rose is more beautiful than some of the newer modern hybrids to be judged. *Rosa lutea* and its varieties have also been used in the development of modern hybrid roses. Two of the most beautiful of its progeny are:

Deciduous semi-climber
Flowering period: Apr.–May
Height: up to 12 ft.
Zone 4 southwards

Rosa lutea

> Harisonii, semi-double, vivid yellow; with black fruits. This originated in 1825 in the garden of the Rev. Harrison of Trinity Church in New York City
>
> Persian Yellow, with magnificent golden-yellow double blooms

Rosa moschata Herrman (syn. *Rosa brunonii* Lindl.) (Musk Rose)
Native to Southern Europe, northern India, and China. A moderately hardy deciduous climber. Leaves composed of 5–9 oval, dentated, glabrous leaflets each 1–3 ins. long and $\frac{1}{3}$–1 in. wide. Entire leaf 7–8 ins. long. Flowers pale yellow in bud, white when fully open, single, $1\frac{1}{2}$ ins. in diameter, with a mass of conspicuous yellow stamens. The flowers are in groups of corymbs forming a magnificent composite inflorescence up to 12–15 ins. in diameter, with a slight perfume of

Deciduous climber
Flowering period: June–July
Height: up to 30 ft.
Zone 7 southwards

musk. Fruits red, oval, $\frac{1}{3}$ in. in diameter. Known in gardens since 1656. Seen to best effect when allowed to develop naturally as a wide-spreading large shrub. One of the parents of numerous modern hybrid roses. There are several varieties of the original species:

>   var. *La Mortola,* with larger more fragrant flowers and larger silver-grey foliage
>   var. *nepalensis* (syn. *Rosa nepalensis*), with pale-yellow blooms
>   var. *pissardii* (syn. *Rosa pissardii* Carr.), white flowers suffused pink
>   var. *plena,* double flowers with smaller leaves

Deciduous shrub
Flowering period: June–July
Height: up to 12 ft.
Zone 4 southwards

Rosa moysii Hemsl. & Wilson

Native to China, found at an altitude of up to nearly 10,000 ft. near the frontier of Tibet. Discovered in 1890 by A. E. Pratt and introduced into Western gardens by E. H. Wilson in 1903. The name commemorates the Rev. J. Moyes, a missionary in China. A hardy deciduous shrub with large single flowers that are probably the most vividly coloured and certainly among the most beautiful of all rose species. Parent of several superb hybrids, all of which are magnificent garden plants of great vigour and very free flowering. The original species has 7–13 dentated ovate leaflets, $1\frac{1}{4}$–$1\frac{1}{2}$ ins. long and half as wide. Entire leaf is 3–6 ins. in length; dark green above, glaucous beneath. Fruits red, 2–$2\frac{1}{2}$ ins. long, of a fascinating bottle- or gourd-like shape, often persisting after the leaves have fallen. Flowers single, $2\frac{1}{2}$–$2\frac{3}{4}$ ins. in diameter; solitary or in pairs, intense blood-crimson. Some of the best varieties are:

>   var. *fargesi,* identical to the proginal species but with carmine-red flowers. Royal Horticultural Society's award of merit, 1922
>   var. *Geranium,* habit more compact, flowers geranium-red. Award of merit, 1950
>   var. *highdownensis,* velvet-crimson. Award of merit, 1928
>   var. *Nevada,* pale pink in bud, cream-white when open. Award of merit, 1949

Rosa multiflora

(Multiflora Rose)
Deciduous shrub
Flowering period: July–Aug.
Height: up to 15 ft.
Zone 4 southwards

Rosa multiflora Thunb. (syn. Rosa polyantha Sieb. & Zucc.)

Native to China, Korea, and Japan. Introduced to gardens in 1875. Not only is this one of the most beautiful of all wild roses, it is also the dominant parent of the modern race of Hybrid Polyantha roses that are now so popular. It forms a hardy, gracefully spreading deciduous bush up to 15 ft. high with curving branches up to 6 ft. long. Leaves composed of 7–9 leaflets, oval, dentated, each $\frac{3}{4}$–2 ins. long. Entire leaf $3\frac{1}{2}$–6 ins. long. Flowers white, 1 in. in diameter, with conspicuous golden stamens, borne many together in branching panicles up to 6 ins. wide. Fruits oval, red, $\frac{1}{4}$ in. in diameter. The var. *plena* has double flowers.

Hybrid Tea Rose Bettina
From an original watercolour by Giovanna Casartelli, 1968

Deciduous shrub
Flowering period: May–July
Height: 1½ ft.
Zone 3 southwards

Rosa nitida Willd.

Native to Eastern North America. Introduced into Europe in 1807. Conspicuous among the smaller species for its very spiny stems, brilliantly coloured flowers, and narrow shiny leaflets. Forms a low-growing shrub with erect very spiny reddish growths. Leaves composed of 5–9 oblong leaflets, $\frac{1}{3}$–$1\frac{1}{4}$ ins. long, dentated, shiny green. Entire leaf 2–3 ins. in length and most attractive in autumn when it assumes a reddish purple tint. Flowers $2\frac{1}{4}$–$2\frac{3}{4}$ ins. in diameter, brilliant pinkish red, either solitary or in groups of 2–3. Fruits globose, scarlet, hairy, $\frac{1}{3}$ in. in diameter.

(Nootka Rose)
Deciduous shrub
Flowering period: June–July
Height: up to 5 ft.
Zone 7 southwards

Rosa nutkana Presl.

Native to the coastal areas of Western North America, and first found in 1793 on Vancouver Island by A. Menzies. Generally regarded as one of the most attractive of the American rose species, forming a vigorous spiny shrub. Leaves composed of 5–9 ovate leaflets 1–2 ins. long, dentated, downy on the undersurface. Entire leaf 3–5 ins. long. Flowers can be either solitary or in groups of 2–3, vivid red, $2\frac{1}{2}$ ins. in diameter, single. Fruits spherical, $\frac{1}{2}$ in. in diameter, scarlet-red, with erect long sepals at their tips.

Deciduous shrub
Flowering period: June–July
Height: up to 15 ft.
Zone 6 southwards

Rosa omeiensis Rolfe

Native to China. Discovered by the Rev. E. Faber in 1886 and introduced into Western gardens by E. H. Wilson in 1901. A large dense-growing hardy deciduous shrub. Flowers solitary, white, 1–$1\frac{1}{2}$ ins. wide, with four petals arranged in the shape of a Maltese cross. Fruits pear-shaped, $\frac{3}{4}$ in. long, red with a yellow stalk. Leaves fern-like, $1\frac{1}{2}$–4 ins., long and divided into 11–19 minute, dark-green, oblong glabrous leaflets sometimes with spines on the undersurface veins. One of its varieties has the most beautiful spines to be found among roses:

> var. *pteracantha* Rehd. & Wils. Similar in form to the original species but with smaller flowers and only 9–13 leaflets. The thorns, however, are remarkable on the young growths. These thorns (or spines) are translucent, $1\frac{1}{2}$ ins. wide at the base, flat, thin, 1–$1\frac{1}{4}$ ins. long, and brilliant blood-red. They extend along the entire length of the branches and almost have the appearance of miniature wings. To encourage the production of the young basal growths with their conspicuous thorns, the plants should be severely pruned in winter or very early spring. On the older branches the thorns lose their vivid colour.

Deciduous shrub
Flowering period: June–July
Height: up to 6 ft.
Zone 6 southwards

Rosa pendulina L. (syn. *Rosa alpina*)

Native to Europe. A vigorous hardy deciduous shrub without thorns. Flowers single, solitary, dark pink, $1\frac{1}{2}$ ins. in diameter with stalks

1½ ins. long. Fruits red, pear-shaped 1 in. long. Leaves composed of 5–9 leaflets, each 1–2 ins. long, glabrous, dentated. Entire leaf 2–6 ins. long. Cultivated in gardens for at least three hundred years. Attractive for its flowers, foliage, and fruits. Generally found in mountainous regions. The var. *pyrenaica* (syn. *Rosa pyrenaica*) has numerous glands on the fruits and flower stalks, which when touched emit an odour of turpentine. There is also a rare double-flowered form, var. *flore-pleno* with silver-pink flowers.

Rosa pomifera Herm. (Apple Rose)
Deciduous shrub
Flowering period: June
Height: up to 6 ft.
Zone 6 southwards

Native to Europe. Often called the Apple Rose because its large round fruits are bigger than those of any other rose. Fruits are bright scarlet, up to 1¾ ins. in diameter, and with the appearance of small apples. A vigorous hardy deciduous shrub with dark-pink flowers 2½–3¼ ins. in diameter borne in clusters of 3. Leaves 7 ins. long, composed of 5 or 7 oval leaflets 1–2½ ins. long and ¾–1½ ins. wide, bright green. Can be effectively used to create an informal hedge.

Rosa roulettii Correvon
Evergreen shrub
Flowering period: May–Sept.
Height: 6–8 ins.
Zone 6 southwards

Native habitat unknown, but for a great many years cultivated as a pot plant in the village of Mauborget in Switzerland. An evergreen or semi-evergreen hardy shrub only 6–8 ins. high with a compact, dense form. Leaves composed of 3–5 oval, pointed, dentated, minute green leaflets, with a slight purple-green tinge. Flowers double, 1 in. wide, bright pink, borne in clusters. This is one of the smallest-flowered species, although there are hybrids with even smaller blooms. The history of this delightful little plant is remarkable. It was first recorded in 1922 by H. Correvon of Geneva, to whom it was shown by his friend, Dr. Roulet, after whom Correvon named it. Dr. Roulet first found it growing in a pot on a windowsill at Mauborget, near Grandon. Mauborget was later completely destroyed by fire, and the plant was also consumed in the holocaust, but eventually one other plant was discovered in a nearby village. From this all the specimens now in cultivation have been raised. I have cultivated it outdoors, where it remains in bloom from May until the autumn. Grown in a pot the plant remains more dwarf.

Rosa rubiginosa L. (syn. *Rosa eglanteria* L.) (Sweet Briar)
Deciduous shrub
Flowering period: May–June
Height: up to 10 ft.
Zone 3 southwards

Native to Europe. One of the most treasured of British flora, the English having a truly sentimental attachment to this rose, which they call Sweet Briar. Generally resembles the equally attractive *Rosa canina*, although it is distinguished by its smaller leaves and by the delicious fragrance of its foliage, a fragrance particularly strong after rain and similar to that of apples or sweet peas. The plant is a hardy deciduous shrub with long arching branches. Leaves composed of 5,

7, or 9 ovate, dentated leaflets, the undersurface bearing glands that contain the characteristic fragrance. Flowers single, pale pink, solitary or in groups, 1½ ins. in diameter. Fruits egg-shaped, red, 1¼ ins. long. Can be effectively used as an informal hedge if severely pruned in late winter. The var. *plena* has double flowers. *Rosa rubiginosa* and *Rosa lutea* are the parents of a strain of hybrids known as the Penzance Roses raised about 1884 by Lord Penzance. These lovely hybrids have combined the fragrant leaves of *Rosa rubiginosa* with the yellow-orange flowers of *Rosa lutea*. Some of the best are:

    Amy Robsart, dark pink
    Anne of Gierstein, crimson
    Flora McIvor, white suffused pink
    Green Mantle, crimson and white
    Lady Penzance, yellow and copper
    Lord Penzance, yellow and pink

Fruits of *Rosa rubrifolia*

Deciduous shrub
Flowering period: June
Height: up to 8 ft.
Zone 3 southwards

Rosa rubrifolia Vill. (syn *Rosa ferruginea* Déség.)
Native to the Alps and Pyrenees and in the mountainous zones of Central Europe. Closely related botanically to *Rosa canina*, differing completely in the fascinating colouring of its leaves and stems. One of the most conspicuous and most attractive of all wild roses. A hardy deciduous shrub with purple-red stems. Leaves composed of 5–7 oval leaflets 1–1½ ins. long and half as wide, dentated, glabrous, of an exquisite glaucous purple-crimson. Foliage contrasts beautifully with the clusters of dark-red single flowers 1½ ins. in diameter. Fruits red, globose, ⅔ in. in diameter. (The name should not be confused with *Rosa rubifolia*, a synonym of *Rosa setigera*.)

Deciduous shrub
Flowering period: May–June
Height: up to 6 ft.
Zone 3 southwards

Rosa rugosa Thunb. (syn. *Rosa ferox* Lawrence, not Bieb.)
Native to China, Japan, and Korea. One of the most robust and vigorous hardy species forming a dense deciduous shrub with an abundance of thorns up to ¾ in. long. Leaves composed of 5–9 oblong leaflets ½–2 ins. long and half as wide, dentated, with the entire leaf 3–7 ins. long with a rugose surface. Single flowers purple-pink, strongly scented, 3½ ins. in diameter, borne in groups or alone. Fruits bright red, tomato-shaped, 1 in. in diameter. Introduced by Siebold in 1845. Reputed to have been cultivated in China (where the petals have been used to make potpourri) for at least eight hundred years. Parent of a vast number of progeny which are attractive for their flowers, fragrance, edible fruits, and robust habit. Some good forms are:

    var. *alba*, white
    var. *albo-plena*, double white
    var. *plena*, double, purple-red

Rosa setigera Mich. (syn. *Rosa rubifolia* R. Br.)
Native to Eastern and Central North America. Introduced into Europe in 1800. Probably the most beautiful of the North American rose species and late-flowering, thus making it of greater value in the garden. A hardy deciduous shrub so vigorous that growth of up to 7–8 ft. is made in a single season. Leaves trifoliate, leaflets 3 ins. long, 2 ins. wide, ovate, dentated, dark green, glabrous. Flowers dark pink, borne in corymbs 6 ins. in diameter; each flower 2–2½ ins. wide. Fruits globose, orange-red, ⅓ in. in diameter.

(Prairie Rose)
Deciduous climber
Flowering period: June–Aug.
Height: up to 15 ft.
Zone 4 southwards

Rosa soulieana Crépin
Native to China. First grown in Europe by Maurice de Vilmorin in 1896 and sent by him to Kew in 1899. A magnificent free-flowering deciduous species suitable for planting where a large area has to be covered. One of the most rampant of all roses and ideal for trellises or summer-houses, steep banks, or the wild garden. It is much too vigorous for a restricted space, and should be established and then left completely alone for many years. The cream-white flowers, 1¾ ins. in diameter, are borne in corymbs 6 ins. in diameter in such abundance that the entire plant is completely hidden. If trained over a summer-house, 15-ft.-long pendulous branches will be produced, and from a distance a well-developed specimen looks like a waterfall. The flowers have a strong, delicious scent. The foliage is an attractive grey-green, each leaf composed of 7–9 oval leaflets, 1–1½ ins. in length, glabrous, dentated. The plant is also of great decorative value in October–November when the branches are covered with vivid orange-red fruits ⅔ in. in diameter. An ideal species for hot, sunny positions. Although hardy, it flowers better in southern gardens.

Deciduous climber
Flowering period: July
Height: up to 25 ft.
Zone 6 southwards

Rosa spinosissima L. (syn. *Rosa pimpinellifolia* L., *Rosa scotica* Mill.)
Native to Europe and Northern Asia. A semi-dwarf hardy deciduous shrub and parent of a valuable group of at least ninety hybrids, all of which are collectively known as Scotch or Burnet roses. Erect rigid growth with new stems continuously produced from below ground level all around the parent plant. Leaves composed of 5, 7, or 9 oval leaflets, each ⅛–¼ in. long, dentated. Entire leaf 1–2½ ins. long; dark green, glabrous. Flowers white or pink, solitary, single, 1½–2 ins. in diameter. Fruits black, globose, ⅔ in. in diameter. Among the various forms, var. *lutea* is outstandingly beautiful, with bright vivid-yellow flowers 2 ins. in diameter.

(Scots Rose or Burnet Rose)
Deciduous shrub
Flowering period: June–Aug.
Height: 2–3 ft.
Zone 4 southwards

Rosa virginiana Mill. (syn. *Rosa humilis* Marsh., *Rosa lucida* Ehrh.)
Native to Eastern North America and reputed to be the first American rose to reach Great Britain. Habit very dense with a mass of erect spiny stems. Leaves 3–5 ins. long, shiny green, composed of 7 or 9

Deciduous shrub
Flowering period: June–July
Height: 4–5 ft.
Zone 3 southwards

ovate leaflets up to 2 ins. long; dentated, glabrous. Flowers pink $2\frac{1}{2}$ ins. in diameter, solitary or in groups of 3, single. Fruits globose, red, $\frac{1}{2}$ in. in diameter. There are several varieties:

> var. *alba,* white
> var. *grandiflora,* a fine variety with larger dark-pink flowers
> var. *plena,* double pink and very attractive

Very hardy and of value for the excellence of its autumn colouring.

(Memorial Rose)
Semi-evergreen shrub
Flowering period: June–Sept.
Height: 1 ft.
Zone 4 southwards

Rosa wichuraiana Crépin (syn. *Rosa luciae*)
Native to Japan. Introduced into Kew in 1891. A nearly prostrate semi-evergreen hardy shrub with long horizontal growths. Leaves composed of 5, 7, or 9 leaflets, oval, $\frac{1}{4}$ in. long, dentated, bright shiny green. Entire leaf 2–4 ins. long. Individual flowers 2 ins. in diameter, white, borne in panicles of 6–10 carried on erect stems 6 ins. above the prostrate mass of vegetation. Fragrant. Fruits dark red, globose, $\frac{1}{3}$ in. in diameter. An ideal rose for planting on slopes or for training over trunks of old trees. Parent of many of the most famous old so-called rambler-type roses such as Dorothy Perkins, Alberic Barbier, Lady Gay, Jersey Beauty.

Deciduous shrub
Flowering period: June–July
Height: 4–6 ft.
Zone 3 southwards

Rosa woodsii Lindl.
Native to central North America. Leaves composed of 5–7 oblong leaflets up to $1\frac{1}{2}$ ins. long, dentated, and an attractive shade of blue-green. Flowers $1\frac{1}{2}$–$2\frac{1}{2}$ ins. in diameter, single, generally pink but occasionally white; either solitary or in groups of 3. The var. *fendleri* is less tall and the leaf stalks are sticky to the touch.

Deciduous shrub
Flowering period: Apr.–May
Height: 5–6 ft.
Zone 4 southwards

Rosa xanthina Lindl.
Native to China. Introduced into the West at the Arnold Arboretum in 1907 by F. N. Meyer. An elegant deciduous shrub with arching growths. Leaves $1\frac{3}{4}$–$3\frac{1}{4}$ ins. long and composed of 7–13 ovate leaflets $\frac{1}{3}$–$\frac{2}{3}$ in. long. Flowers yellow, double, solitary, $1\frac{3}{4}$ ins. in diameter. A most delightful very hardy yellow-flowered species of modest proportions. The var. *spontanea* is single-flowered, with dark-red, globose fruits $\frac{1}{2}$ in. in diameter, and by some authorities suspected of being the true species, while the double-flowered type is more likely to be of hybrid origin.

Rosa Hybrids
NOTE: A selection of the hybrids of *R. lutea,* the Penzance hybrids of *R. rubiginosa,* the hybrids of *R. indica (chinensis),* and the hybrids of *R. moysii* has been given with the descriptions of those species.

Hybrid Tea Roses (H.T.). Large-flowered shrubs with a continuous-flowering period from May to autumn. Indicated for beds, borders, and for cut bloom. Very hardy. Prune severely in February or March, leaving only 4–5 eyes. Remove weak, badly formed, and dead branches. Some varieties of this type are also available as standards or climbers; see catalogues of various rose nurseries.

Red and reddish

Pharaon	Samurai	Papa Meilland
Champs Élysées	Suspense	Christian Dior
Baccara	New Style	Soraya
Super Star	Tally-Ho	Gloria di Roma
Grazia	Marella	Texas Centennial

Pink

Dr. F. Debat	Michèlle Meilland	Suzon Lotthe
Maria Callas	Pink Peace	Carina
Grace de Monaco	Versailles	Mignonne
Dame Edith Helen	Kordes Perfection	Ballet
Eden Rose	Rendez-vous	Confidence

White

Alaska	Marcia Stanhope	Neige Parfum
Virgo	Yuki San	Message
White Swan	Ninfea	Pascali

Apricot, orange, and salmon

Provence	Beauté	Comtesse Vandal
Helen Traubel	Antheôr	Topaz Orientale
Grand Mogul	Vienna Charm	Eve
Bettina	Femina	Silva

Yellow

Buccaneer	Sutter's Gold	Mme. Kriloff
Speck's Yellow	Grisbi	Tahiti
Belle Blonde	Eclipse	Barbara
Emeraude d'Or		Golden Masterpiece

Mauve and violet

Saint-Exupéry	Prelude	Souvenance
Blue Moon	Saphir	Eminence
Intermezzo	Sterling Silver	Clair de Lune

Bicoloured

Amoreuse, ivory suffused yellow
Onyx Flamboyant, yellow suffused coral
Tourmaline, white and pink
Peace, yellow tinged pink
Voeux de Bonheur, pink and carmine
Sultane, red and yellow
Melrose, cream, carmine, and red
Kordes Perfecta, golden-pink
Charleston, scarlet and yellow
Rose Gaujard, red and copper
Daily Sketch, ivory and red

Hybrid Perpetual Roses (H.P.). Older varieties with the same characteristics as the Hybrid Tea roses but with flowers of an inferior shape

Rosa centifolia var. *muscosa*

and with a smaller range of colours. In some cases also less continuous-flowering, but frequently with a better perfume. Now largely superseded by the Hybrid Tea type. Very hardy. Prune as for the H.T. roses. Some of these are also available as standards or climbers.

>Baron Girod de L'Ainé, crimson petals edged white, rich perfume
>Frau Karl Druschki, white, R.H.S. award of merit, 1902
>General Jacqueminot, scarlet-crimson, very fragrant
>Mrs. John Laing, pink, very fragrant
>Prince Camille de Rohan, red shaded purple
>Reine des Violettes, violet-pink, very fragrant
>Roger Lambelin, dark purple-crimson, very fragrant
>Souvenir du Dr. Jamain, wine-coloured shaded purple, very fragrant, R.H.S. award of merit, 1963
>Ulrich Brunner, cherry-red

Miniature Roses (Lilliput). Small sisters of the larger roses. These bloom continuously from May to November. Very hardy, height 10–12 ins. Available as shrubs or standards. Indicated for beds, borders, the rock-garden, pots, etc. Minute leaves. No pruning is necessary, but in March remove any dead or badly formed branches and lightly clip the plant to give it a good shape.

Baby Masquerade, yellow, pink, red, and orange flowers on the same plant simultaneously
Coralin, coral-red
Little Buckaroo, red
Perle de Alcanada, carmine-crimson
Baby Gold, yellow
Joseph Wheatcroft, pale yellow
Scarlet Gem, scarlet
Sweet Fairy, lilac
Pixie Gold, golden-yellow
Red Elf, crimson-red, scented
Pour Toi, white
Zwerghoenigin, pink
Mimi, dark red
Perle de Montserrat, pink, scented
Oakington Ruby, crimson, R.H.S. award of merit, 1934

Hybrid Polyantha (multiflora) and Hybrid Floribunda. These groups are now so mixed with each other that practically none of the commercial growers attempt to offer them separately. In almost all catalogues they are listed together, so the same system is followed here (but giving the characteristics of each variety). Continuous-flowering shrubs with large or small blooms in sprays. Indicated for beds, borders, etc. Completely hardy. Flowering period May until late autumn. Inflorescence a corymb. Prune as for the H.T. types but less severely.

>Tamagno, vivid dark red, double, $2–2\frac{3}{4}$ ft.
>Polka, dark pink suffused pale pink, double, $1\frac{1}{2}–1\frac{3}{4}$ ft.
>Charleston, scarlet and orange, double, $1\frac{1}{2}–2$ ft.
>Sarabande, scarlet-red, enormous flowers, single, 15–18 ins.
>Fidelio, geranium-red, double, $2–2\frac{3}{4}$ ft.

Zambra, vivid orange, double, 1½–1¾ ft.
Rimosa, yellow, single, 15–24 ins.
Concerto, dark red, double, 18–24 ins.
Ivory Fashion, ivory-white, double, 1½–2 ft.
Cinquantenario di Fatima, salmon suffused pink and yellow, double, 1½–2 ft.
Ahoy, fire-red, double, 2–2½ ft.
Hymne, pink, double, 15–18 ins.
Tutu Mauve, reddish mauve and pink, double, 1½–2 ft.
Border King, strawberry-red and orange, double, 15–18 ins.
Jean de la Lune, yellow, double, 15–18 ins.

Hybrids of Rosa rugosa (see also list of species). Compact and symmetrical bushes with dark green, glossy foliage; very spiny. Average height 4½–5 ft., flowering period from June onwards. Very hardy. Remove dead and weak growths and also those that are badly formed or very old.

Agnes, amber-yellow, double, fragrant, 6 ft., R.H.S. award of merit, 1951
Blanc Double de Coubert, semi-double, white, fragrant, 4½ ft.
Conrad F. Meyer, double, silver-pink, fragrant, 4½ ft., R.H.S. award of merit, 1901
Fimbriata, semi-double, pale pink, 3½ ft., R.H.S. award of merit, 1896
Frau Dagmar Hastrop, single, pink, R.H.S. award of merit, 1958
Max Graf, dark pink, 12–15 ins., fragrant, R.H.S. award of merit, 1964
Nova Zembla, cream-white, semi-double, fragrant, 4½ ft.
Pink Grootendorst, double pink, 4½ ft., R.H.S. award of merit, 1953
Rubra, dark red, single, fragrant, 4¾ ft., R.H.S. award of merit, 1955
Sarah van Fleet, semi-double, pale pink, fragrant, 4½ ft., R.H.S. award of merit, 1962
Schneezwerg, white, semi-double, 4½ ft., R.H.S. award of merit, 1948

Hybrids of Rosa spinosissima (see also list of species). Compact deciduous shrubs with a dense habit. Maximum height 4 ft. Flowering period from May onwards. Very hardy. Prune as for *Rosa rugosa*.

Frühlingsanfang, ivory-white, single flowers on long, arching branches; very fragrant, 5 ft., R.H.S. award of merit, 1964
Frühlingsgold, semi-double, yellow, 4½ ft., R.H.S. award of merit, 1950
Frühlingsmorgen, single, pink and cream, 4½ ft., R.H.S. award of merit, 1951

Frühlingszauber, semi-double, pink, 4½ ft.
Ormiston Roy, single, yellow, 4½ ft., R.H.S. award of merit, 1955
Stanwell Perpetual, semi-double, pink, 4 ft.
William III, magenta-crimson semi-double flowers, grey-green foliage, black fruits, 2½ ft.

Hybrid Moschata Roses. Hardy deciduous shrubs of a compact, bushy habit. More or less continuous-flowering. Height 4½–6 ft. Flowers borne in clusters, slightly musk-scented. Flowering period from May onwards. Prune as for *Rosa rugosa*.

Buff Beauty, apricot-yellow, double, fragrant
Cornelia, strawberry flushed yellow, double, very fragrant
Danäe, cream-yellow, semi-double, R.H.S. award of merit, 1912
Daybreak, golden-yellow, semi-double, dark-green foliage
Felicia, pink, double, very fragrant, abundant autumn flowering
Moonlight, white suffused yellowish lemon, semi-double, scented, R.H.S. award of merit, 1911
Robin Hood, crimson
Vanity, pink, semi-double, R.H.S. award of merit, 1956
Will Scarlet, crimson-scarlet, semi-double, R.H.S. award of merit, 1954

Hybrids of Climbing Type. Large-flowered climbers. In many cases these are climbing forms of the H.T. type of rose (which see). There are also many others of a different origin. Remove dead or badly formed growths; also those exhausted by continuous flowering in previous years. Prune the small growths which produced blooms the previous season, leaving only 2–3 eyes. Do not prune the new growths which develop during the summer because these will bear flowers the following spring. Flowering period from May onwards.

Blaze, vivid scarlet, semi-double
Chaplain's Pink, pink, semi-double, R.H.S. award of merit, 1928
Danse du Feu, orange-red, semi-double
La Follette, pink and carmine, double
Clair Matin, semi-double, scented, pink
Mermaid, single, sulphur-yellow, evergreen, not tolerant of severe cold
Lady Waterglow, salmon-pink, double
Benvenuto, red, semi-double
Cocktail, single, red with yellow centre

Also includes many of the H.T. types already described but in the form of climbers. Several of the polyantha/floribunda types are also available as climbers.

Hybrid rose
Zephyrine Drouhin

Hybrids of Rambler Type (not continuous-flowering). Small- or large-flowered ramblers with the blooms in sprays. Very vigorous and hardy. Spring-flowering for 4–6 weeks with the greatest abundance (see also *R. Wichuraiana*). Prune immediately after flowering. Cut off the growths which have produced blooms to a point 2–3 ins. from the position where they depart from the main stem. The new growths produced in summer will bear the following season's flowers.

> Alberic Barbier, cream-white, buds yellow, semi-evergreen, double
> American Pillar, single, dark pink with white centre, R.H.S. award of merit, 1909
> Crimson Conquest, crimson-scarlet, semi-double
> Dorothy Perkins, double pink, R.H.S. award of merit, 1902
> Eastleas Golden Rambler, semi-double, yellow tinted crimson, fragrant
> Hiawatha, single, dark crimson, R.H.S. award of merit, 1906
> Sanders White, semi-double, white, scented
> Veilchenblau, semi-double, deep lilac

Miscellaneous Hybrids

> Souvenir de la Princesse de Lamballe, double, pale pink striped carmine. Forms a dense shrub up to 10–11 ft. with the blooms in enormous inflorescences from May onwards. Decorative scarlet fruits.
> Variegata di Bologna, semi-rambler, fragrant, double flowers white spotted carmine in May/June.
> Zephyrine Drouhin, vivid pink, semi-rambler, scented, double.
> *Rosa* x *hardii*, single yellow flowers with an orange spot at the base of each petal. Requires a warm, sunny position. Semi-rambler, June flowering.
> *Rosa* x *odorata gigantea* var. *Cooper*, rambler, stems shiny red, fragrant white flowers, 3 ins. in diam. in May/June.

Rosa moschata

Rosa centifolia

Rudbeckia

(BLACK-EYED SUSAN OR CONE FLOWER)
(*Also see* ECHINACEA)
Family: Compositae
Hardy herbaceous perennials or biennials, or annuals
Position: sun or partial shade
Propagation: division or seed
Cultivation easy
Useful for cutting

Once enthusiasm has been kindled for garden plants belonging to the Compositae family, one develops an urge to aquire more and more species of the various genera. They are, in fact, among the most satisfactory of all herbaceous perennials and annuals, with rudbeckias high on the list of popular favourites. They are of the easiest cultivation, completely hardy, and resistant to inclement weather even when in bloom.

The not very euphonic name of the genus derives from Olaf Rudbeck, a seventeenth-century Swedish botanist, to whom Linnaeus dedicated the plant. The genus comprises about twenty-five species, all native to North America, mostly found in the northern districts. The natural environment varies, but they are generally found in sandy meadows and damp soils of practically any type. They are, therefore, plants with few special requirements, very hardy, and tolerant of at least temporarily adverse conditions. Drought may cause them to wilt and wither, but the first rain shower will restore them immediately to their customary vigour. Even in late summer, when other flowers are beginning to manifest signs of end-of-the-season tiredness, rudbeckias are still full of life, vigour, and colour, gamely carrying on their display of golden-yellow blooms until October.

Cultivation. The cultivation of both perennial and annual rudbeckias is very easy, and here we give details of propagation for each species separately. Rudbeckias are practically indifferent to the type of soil, although they prefer alkaline (calcareous) soil which is well drained but moist and deep. If grown in full sun they need abundant watering during the summer; if planted in partial shade they grow quite as well but need less water. The most suitable species for a dry locality is *Rudbeckia hirta*, while an excellent species for naturalizing in meadow grasses is *Rudbeckia speciosa*.

Annual or biennial
Flowering period: June–Oct.
Height: 3–5 ft.

Rudbeckia amplexicaulis L.
Native to an area extending from Missouri to Kansas and as far south as Mississippi and Texas. Stems grey-green, glabrous, much-

branched. Leaves alternate, oval-oblong, stalkless and with the base clasping the stem. The calyx is composed of 6–8 very small acuminate-linear scales; the petals (ligules) are nearly ½ in. long, yellow, often with the base purple-maroon, at first widely spread, eventually curving downwards. The central disc is maroon, and when fully developed assumes a conical form. This is an annual or biennial species and seed can be sown in seed beds in August–September, transplanting the seedlings to their flowering position in spring and planting them 1½–2 ft. apart. Seed can also be sown in frames from February to April, planting out the seedlings in April–May. In localities where spring is mild and early, seed can also be sown directly into the flowering position in April.

Rudbeckia bicolor Nutt. (Thimble Flower)
Annual or biennial
Flowering period: Aug.–Sept.
Height: 2 ft.

Native to Arkansas, Texas, and Georgia. An annual or biennial species covered with silky hairs. Leaves elongated-lanceolate, those at the base obovate, generally obtuse, up to 2½ ins. long, mostly stalkless. Flowers 2–3 ins. in diameter; petals (ligules) 1 in. long, yellow with a purple-maroon mark at the base. Central disc dark purple. There are numerous varieties:

    var. *Herbstwald*, variable in colour from yellow to maroon and bronze, with either self-coloured blooms or bi- or tricoloured

    var. *Sonnenuntergang*, 2 ft. 4 ins. high, yellow-flowered with maroon-black central disc

    var. *superba*, flowers 2 ins. wide, petals yellow on the upper surface, purplish maroon beneath

Cultivation from seed the same as for *Rudbeckia amplexicaulis*.

Rudbeckia fulgida Ait. (syn. *Rudbeckia aspera, Rudbeckia scabra*) (Orange Cone Flower)
Herbaceous perennial
Flowering period: Aug.–Oct.
Height: 1½–1¾ ft.

Native to the United States; in the northeast from Michigan to Pennsylvania, south to Virginia and Florida, and west to Missouri and Texas. Mostly found in dry river beds, light woodlands, and in the vicinity of swamps. Stems covered with fine silky hairs. Leaves variable in size and shape, either heart-shaped, lanceolate, or linear and long-stalked, but with the upper foliage almost clasping the stem. Flowers one or more together, long-stemmed, axillary, petals (ligules) about twenty, up to 1½ ins. long, central disc blackish maroon, calyx green and hairy. There are several good varieties:

    var. *compacta*, dwarf and very compact in form

    var. *fulgida variegata*, leaves marked yellow, must be propagated by division

    var. *Goldsturm*, very beautiful and even better than the species *R. speciosa* var. *sullivantii*, common from Michigan to Missouri and as far east as West Virginia; in moist positions; with larger irregularly dentated foliage, sometimes hairy, and petals up to 1¾ ins. long

var. *variabilis*, up to 3 ft. high with many rigid stems bearing yellowish-maroon flowers with dark-purple discs

Rudbeckia fulgida is a very easy plant that does not require any special attention; it tolerates drier and sunnier positions than most rudbeckias. Propagation is by division in spring or autumn or from seed sown outside in spring in seed beds, frames, or boxes. In the south it can be sown outside in late summer. Escaping gardens, it often naturalizes. Perennial.

(Black-Eyed Susan or Yellow Daisy)
Annual or biennial
Flowering period: July–Aug.
Height: 1¾–2 ft.

Rudbeckia hirta L. (syn. *Rudbeckia flava*)
Widely diffused throughout North America, where it has even become an invasive weed; also freely naturalized in many European gardens. Stems erect, rough-surfaced with short silky bristles. Basal leaves spatulate, upper leaves elongated or lanceolate, entire, stalkless. Flowers long-stalked, solitary, petals golden-yellow, up to 2 ins. long, often darker in colour at the base; centre disc at first nearly black, later becoming dark maroon. Suitable for growing in arid localities. The var. *vomerensis* has larger flowers and petals varying from golden-yellow to canary-yellow. Propagation and cultivation as for *Rudbeckia amplexicaulis*.

(Cone Flower)
Herbaceous perennial
Flowering period: July–Oct.
Height: 6–8 ft.

Rudbeckia laciniata L.
A perennial species native to North America, from Quebec to Florida, west to Montana, Idaho, and Arizona, in moist positions. Requires a damper soil and more water in summer than most of the other species. Roots rhizomatous, spreading. Stems glabrous, the upper part branching. Leaves alternate, divided into 3–5 elongated pointed segments of unequal size. Flowers very large, 4–5 ins. in diameter, with oval-lanceolate petals (ligules), entire or dentated at the tips, yellow, drooping. There are numerous interesting and lovely varieties:

var. *foliis variegatis*, leaves marked yellowish white, can only be propagated by division and the variegation is irregular and not constant

var. *Golden Glow*, a double-flowered variety recorded by Bailey as being discovered in 1894, and now widely naturalized in cultivated land throughout Europe. Useful for massing but has the defect of having pendulous flowers. It can become an invasive pest, however, and many American gardeners consider it anything but "lovely".

Rudbeckia laciniata
From *Curtis's Botanical Magazine*,
1822, plate 2310

var. *Goldquelle*, a fine variety introduced in 1951 and obtained by crossing *Rudbeckia nitida* var. *Herbstonne* with *Rudbeckia laciniata* var. *Goldball*. Of the easiest cultivation, requiring no attention, thriving in sun or shade. Propagation by division. If planted 18 ins. apart will create a hedge-like effect.

var. *humilis*, native to the mountains of Kentucky and Virginia, 3 ft. high, leaves divided into 3 segments but rounded

Propagation of the original species can be effected from seed sown outside or in frames in July–August or in spring. The varieties must be propagated by division, either in spring or autumn, as for *R. fulgida*.

Herbaceous perennial
Flowering period: July–Oct.
Height: 6 ft.

Rudbeckia nitida Nutt.

A perennial species native to North America from Georgia to Texas and Florida, found in moist semi-shady positions. Stems glabrous, upper part branching. Leaves mostly lanceolate, but the lower ones ovate, rarely divided, shiny light green, slightly leathery, dentated; upper ones stalkless. Flowers large, petals (ligules) 8–12, yellow, elongated-ovate; central disc greenish yellow; segments of the calyx green, oval-acuminate. The best variety is var. *Herbstsonne*, 6–7 ft. high, with golden-yellow flowers. Propagation as for *Rudbeckia fulgida*.

Herbaceous perennial
Flowering period: July–Oct.
Height: 2 ft.

Rudbeckia speciosa Wenderoth (syn. *Rudbeckia Newmanii*)

Native to North America, from Pennsylvania to Michigan and from Arkansas to Alabama. A perennial species found in moist positions. Stems covered with silky bristles, branched in the upper parts, slightly marked red. Roots rhizomatous, spreading. Leaves generally lanceolate, long-stalked, irregularly dentated, with those on the upper stem stalkless and stem-clasping. Petals yellow, greenish on the undersurface, about $1\frac{1}{4}$ ins. long; central disc maroon-black. The segments of the calyx are borne in a double row and are green, hairy, and lanceolate. A species that requires a humus-rich soil in a sunny or semi-shady position. Propagation as for *R. fulgida*.

(Sweet Cone Flower)
Herbaceous perennial
Flowering period: July–Sept.
Height: 6 ft.

Rudbeckia subtomentosa Pursh.

Native to the midwestern United States. A perennial with the entire plant covered with grey-green hairs. Leaves ovate, occasionally three-lobed, dentated, about 5 ins. long. Flowers yellow, with the petals (ligules or ray-florets) darker in colour at their base. Centre disc dark brown.

Annual or biennial
Flowering period: July–Sept.
Height: up to $1\frac{3}{4}$ ft.

Rudbeckia triloba L.

Native to the United States from New York to Michigan, Iowa, and Kansas, south to Florida, Louisiana, and Oklahoma. Found in damp soils in light woodlands. A much-branched hairy annual. Leaves thin-textured, oval-lanceolate, the upper ones slightly dentated, basal leaves three-lobed, coarsely dentated, narrowing at the base. Flowers small but profuse, 8–10 petals, intense yellow, occasionally maroon or purple-maroon at their base, $\frac{3}{4}$ in. long. Central disc purple-black. Propagation as for *Rudbeckia amplexicaulis*.

Rudbeckia Hybrids (Gloriosa Daisy)
In the United States in recent years, Dr. A. F. Blankeslee has created a remarkable and beautiful race of new rudbeckia hybrids. Although perennial, they are generally cultivated in gardens as annuals, and seed sown in early spring produces plants that bloom the same season. They are among the most interesting of recent garden introductions, with spectacular and brilliantly coloured enormous flowers in shades varying from vivid yellow to mahogany, with bicoloured variations of orange, red, and gold. The blooms, with long and wide petals (ligules), are up to 7 ins. in diameter, generally with a darker central eye, and are borne on rigid stems up to $2\frac{3}{4}$ ft. high. The plants are vigorous and robust, thriving in practically any soil, in sun or partial shade, and I have noted that both the plants and the flowers are resistant to the most adverse weather. In very windy localities, however, they may require some support. The flowering period is remarkably long, from early summer until autumn, and the blooms are excellent for cutting. A batch of seedlings produces both single and semi-double flowers. Propagation and cultural requirements are the same as for other annual rudbeckias, but if some particular form or colour is especially desirable, the parent plant must be propagated by division to ensure faithful reproduction of the desired characteristic.

Rudbeckia bicolor

Salpiglossis sinuata

(PAINTED TONGUE)
Family: Solanaceae
Tender annuals

Salpiglossis sinuata

The name of the genus *Salpiglossis* is Greek in origin, *salpinx* (trumpet) and *glōssa* (tongue), and refers to the form of the corolla and style. This plant is another of those beautiful annuals belonging to the family Solanaceae, cousins of the petunia and nicotiana, but is much less frequently grown in our gardens than those two favourites.

The genus is native to Chile, where 7–8 species are indigenous. The first examples were probably introduced into Europe between 1820 and 1830. The plants have an elegant appearance, with elongated sticky foliage and tapering funnel-shaped flowers. They are particularly interesting for their variety and combinations of colours, which include every shade and gradation of yellow, scarlet, pink, and blue, superimposed on a basic colour of cream, mahogany, chestnut, carmine, crimson, violet, purple, or black. The petals are also covered with a longitudinal network of blue, yellow, maroon, and red veins. As the flowers develop and mature the intensity of the colours increases.

Cultivation. Salpiglossis will not thrive equally well in every position, and their cultivation is not the easiest. They require a warm sheltered position in a not-too-heavy moderately alkaline (calcareous) soil. They dislike fresh manure, excessive moisture, and dry, sandy, arid soils. The best food for these fascinating but fastidious beauties is some organic fertilizer, such as dried blood dissolved in water. Seed should be sown in a warm greenhouse in March–April, barely covering the seed with a dusting of fine soil. The seedlings can be pricked out into trays, flats, or boxes, and when large enough potted individually, growing them on until ready for planting in their flowering positions outdoors. They are not easy to transplant, and in warm southern gardens better results will be obtained if the seed is sown directly into its flowering position in April, thinning out the seedlings to about 6–9 ins. apart. They are also excellent subjects for growing and flowering in pots.

Flowering period: June–Sept.
Height: 15 ins.–3 ft.
Position: sun
Propagation: seed
Cultivation not always easy
Useful for cutting

Salpiglossis sinuata Ruiz & Pav. (syn. *Salpiglossis variabilis*)
Native to Chile. The only species in general cultivation, of which there are several horticultural varieties:

var. *grandiflora,* $2-2\frac{1}{2}$ ft.
var. *grandiflora nana,* 15–16 ins.

var. *superbissima* (syn. var. *imperiale*), the best variety, 2–2½ ft. high with very large flowers and characteristic for its large central stem at the top of which are borne the individual flowers

Leaves broadly lanceolate, alternate, margins slightly undulated or occasionally deeply dentated. Flowers in terminal clusters, funnel-shaped, wide-mouthed, and produced from the leaf axils.

Salvia

(SAGE)
Family: Labiatae
Hardy or half-hardy annuals, biennials, and herbaceous perennials, or tender small shrubs
Position: sun or partial shade
Propagation: seed, division, or cuttings
Cultivation easy

The genus *Salvia* comprises at least five hundred species diffused throughout the temperate zones of the world. It takes its name from the Latin *salvare* (save) because of the curative properties attributed to *Salvia officinalis* by the Romans. It includes the culinary sage, which—like many wild salvias found growing in fields and meadows—deserves a place in the flower garden for its attractive foliage and beautifully coloured flowers. Unfortunately, to many people salvia has only one connotation: the summer-bedding *Salvia splendens*, which is often used to excess, although it is a fine plant with many useful qualities, which in recent years has become less monotonous through the introduction of new colours and forms. On the Continent, in particular, *Salvia splendens* has been so exploited that it is often referred to as the "railway-station plant" (station-masters, following the line of least resistance, plant it *ad nauseam* as something easy, sure, and long-lasting). Nonetheless, the many blue-flowered perennial salvias and the lovely shrubby species (often with aromatic foliage) are largely ignored, although they include several plants of surpassing beauty.

As mentioned above, the medicinal virtues of *Salvia officinalis* (sage) were known in Roman times. The leaves were brewed into an infusion as a gargle for sore throats, quinsy, and laryngitis, and also used for treating ulcers of the mouth. The aromatic properties of the foliage are also much appreciated in the kitchen. *Salvia Sclarea* (Clary) has also been used for its antispasmodic and balsamic prop-

Salvia officinalis

Salvia splendens
From *The Botanical Register*,
1823, plate 687

erties. Old-time herbalists favoured a decoction of the leaves for the treatment of ophthalmic disorders. *Salvia horminum* has been used in the treatment of stomach and digestive disorders.

Cultivation. On the whole, salvias are easy to cultivate, although many are not tolerant of severe cold. They thrive in any fertile soil, including that which is strongly alkaline (calcareous), in either sun or partial shade, but each species has its own preferences. Contrary to general belief, *Salvia splendens* will also grow well in shade, although in such a position it begins to flower much later. Cultural details and methods of propagation are here given separately for each species.

Salvia azurea Lam.

Native to the central United States. A herbaceous perennial of considerable beauty and of value for its late-flowering habit—which extends into autumn—and for the magnificent colour of its flower spikes. Hardy in all but exceptionally cold localities. Leaves, opposite, narrow, lanceolate, entire or irregularly dentated, and of an attractive glaucous green making a pleasing contrast with the tall, rigid spikes of brilliant sky-blue flowers. Excellent for the mixed border or for growing in isolated groups. Thrives in any normal fertile soil in a sunny or semi-shady position. Propagation by division in spring as seed is rarely produced, although when available it should be sown in pots or frames in August, or when ripe. The var. *grandiflora* (syn. *Salvia pitcheri*) has slightly hairy grey-green foliage and larger flowers; var. *angustifolia* has very narrow leaves.

Herbaceous perennial
Flowering period: Aug.–Sept.
Height: 4½ ft.

Salvia farinacea Benth.

Native to Texas. A moderately hardy herbaceous perennial with a graceful elegant habit and slender, elongated flexible stems. Leaves narrowly oval, slightly glaucous, 4 ins. long, dentated, aromatic. Inflorescences in the form of long graceful spikes bearing numerous violet-blue flowers 1 in. long that somewhat resemble a spike of lavender, although much larger. Excellent for cutting. Thrives in any normal fertile soil in sun or partial shade. Propagation can be effected by division in spring or from seed sown in a greenhouse in spring. The seedlings should be planted out when all risk of frost has passed. As the specific name suggests, the entire plant has a somewhat farinaceous appearance due to its covering of minute whitish hairs and its mealy-surfaced stems.

Herbaceous perennial
Flowering period: June–Aug.
Height: 3 ft.

Salvia glutinosa L.

Native to Southern Europe and to Asia. A not very hardy sticky-leaved erect herbaceous perennial with 6–8-in.-long dark-green oblong foliage. Flowers borne in loose racemes, light yellow, 1½ ins. long, and very attractive in summer.

Herbaceous perennial
Flowering period: July–Aug.
Height: up to 3 ft.

Evergreen shrub
Flowering period: June–Oct.
Height: 3–4½ ft.
Zone 8 southwards

Salvia grahamii Benth.
Native to Mexico. Discovered in 1830 by J. G. Graham, who sent specimens to the Royal Horticultural Society. A small evergreen shrub hardy only in warm climates. Habit erect, rather open and loose, with many slender branches. Leaves opposite, ovate, dentated, opaque green, 1–3 ins. long and ½–1½ ins. wide. Flowers mostly in pairs, borne in terminal 6-in.-long racemes, each flower 1 in. in length and of a beautiful ruby-red. Flowering period from June to October. When crushed, the foliage has a most pleasing black-currant fragrance, and the plant as a whole is most recommendable. It requires a warm, sunny position in a rather dry, not-too-rich soil. Can be propagated by means of soft cuttings taken in spring and rooted in a warm greenhouse or from seed sown in a warm greenhouse in spring.

Evergreen shrub
Flowering period: June–Oct.
Height: 3–4½ ft.
Zone 8 southwards

Salvia greggii A. Grey
Native to Mexico. Discovered by J. Gregg in 1848. A small shrub hardy only in warm climates, and requiring the same cultural treatment as *Salvia grahamii* and the same methods of propagation. Wide-spreading habit with slightly arching branches. Leaves oblong-lanceolate, dark green, 1–1½ ins. long. Inflorescences in the form of terminal racemes up to 6 ins. long and 1 in. wide composed of groups of carmine-red flowers in groups of 2–3. A delightful companion to *S. grahamii,* and another highly desirable little shrub.

Herbaceous perennial usually grown as an annual or biennial
Flowering period: June–Sept.
Height: 4½ ft.

Salvia haematodes L.
Native to Greece. A herbaceous perennial species hardy in all but exceptionally cold localities, but nearly always cultivated as a summer-flowering annual or as a biennial. Even if grown as a perennial it is not long-lived. A most interesting plant worthy of being used in isolated groups or in individual beds. The large brilliant green heart-shaped leaves are mostly basal and rosette-forming, up to 9 ins. long and 6 ins. wide, with a deeply wrinkled surface covered with silvery hairs. The robust erect 3-ft. flower stems bear panicles made up of whorls of many funnel-shaped violet-blue flowers. Requires a not-too-rich soil in a warm, sunny position. As a biennial, seed can be sown in July in coldframes, pricked out and kept in the frames, or in an unheated greenhouse during the winter and planted out in spring. As an annual in warm localities, it can be sown in March in coldframes and planted out in spring.

Annual or biennial
Flowering period: May–June
Height: 18 ins.

Salvia horminum L.
Native to Southern Europe. Generally found in rather dry pasture land. Cultivated in gardens since 1596. A most attractive annual or biennial species with oval-oblong soft-surfaced hairy leaves, rounded at the base. Inflorescence a rigid erect spike bearing numer-

ous purple, lilac, or violet-coloured flowers, each 1 in. long and surrounded by a bright purple bract. The several varieties have different-coloured bracts:

>   var. *alba,* white
>   var. *purpurea,* purple-red
>   var. *violacea,* violet-blue

Salvia horminum requires a warm, sunny position in a not-too-rich soil. Propagation is by means of seed sown in March, in an unheated greenhouse or coldframe (planting out the seedlings in May), or by sowing directly into the flowering position in March–April.

Salvia leucantha Cav.
Native to Mexico and consequently not hardy in cold localities. A small shrubby species with lanceolate leaves up to 6 ins. long densely covered with white hairs on the undersurface, dentated. The $\frac{3}{4}$-in.-long white flowers are borne in whorls on terminal racemes. The calyx is covered with lavender-coloured hairs and is very attractive.

(Mexican Bush Sage)
Evergreen shrub
Flowering period: June–July
Height: 2 ft.
Zone 7 southwards

Salvia nemorosa Crantz (syn. *Salvia* x *superba, Salvia virgata* var. *nemorosa*)
A very widely cultivated hardy herbaceous perennial whose original habitat is obscure and uncertain. It is particularly colourful, and excellent for planting in the mixed border or in individual beds. The violet-red bracts which surround the violet-blue flowers persist after the flowers themselves have finished, thus providing a long, colourful blooming season. The plants have a compact erect habit, with slender stems bearing a profusion of blooms which are excellent for cutting and also for drying for winter use indoors. Leaves small, glaucous-green, aromatic. Thrives in any normal garden soil in a sunny position. Seed can be sown in June–July in seed beds or in coldframes, planting out the seedlings in autumn (or the following spring in cold localities, after over-wintering the seedlings in frames).

(Violet Sage)
Herbaceous perennial
Flowering period: June–Sept.
Height: 2–2½ ft.

Salvia officinalis L.
Native to Southern Europe. A moderately hardy evergreen shrubby species generally found in rather arid, dry, stony localities in open, warm, sunny positions. It is generally confined to the vegetable or herb garden, where its characteristic and agreeably fragrant foliage is much appreciated for culinary purposes. It also deserves a place in the flower garden. It has an attractive, modestly proportioned compact habit. Its pleasing silvery grey-green, oval-lanceolate, opposite, slightly dentated rough-surfaced foliage, and the lovely purple-mauve flowers borne in erect terminal racemes—each flower 1 in. long, tubular and long lasting—make it an excellent plant. Unfortunately, when the plants are grown in the vegetable garden, the inflorescences are generally eliminated before they develop so

(Sage)
Evergreen shrub
Flowering period: May–July
Height: up to 5 ft.
Zone 8 southwards

Salvia azurea
From *Curtis's Botanical Magazine*,
1815, plate 1728

as to encourage the production of foliage. A very easy plant to cultivate in any type of soil, but it is not tolerant of severe frost. Can be propagated by division in spring, by means of cuttings taken from half-ripened wood at any time during the summer, or from seed sown in spring. There are several very attractive varieties:

    var. *alba,* white-flowered
    var. *icterina,* ornamental leaves variegated yellow and green
    var. *purpurascens,* purple-leaved
    var. *tricolor,* compact habit with leaves variegated green, pink, and white

Salvia patens Cav.

Herbaceous perennial
Flowering period: July–Sept.
Height: up to 2 ft.

Native to Mexico. A tuberous-rooted herbaceous perennial of great beauty but suitable for permanent outdoor planting only in frost-free localities. Where the summers are long and warm, this lovely plant can also be grown outside as a temporary summer-flowering subject, lifting the tubers in late autumn in the same manner as for dahlias and replanting them the following spring when all risk of frost has passed. In frost-free districts the plants may be left undisturbed for many years, unless propagation by division is done in spring. The common English name, Gentian Salvia, refers to the spectacular blue 2-in.-long flowers, borne in groups on tall, erect stems. The leaves are ovate, pointed, dentated, not very prolific, and dark green. The var. *alba* is white-flowered, while the var. *Cambridge Blue* has light-blue flowers. Requires a deep, rich, rather moist non-alkaline (non-calcareous) soil.

Salvia Sclarea L.

(Clary)
Biennia
Flowering period: June–July
Height: 3 ft.

Native to Europe. A hardy biennial species with an intense, penetrating, characteristic but not unpleasant odour. Leaves oval or heart-shaped, dentated, and covered with silver-white hairs. Inflorescences in the form of branched panicles consisting of many bluish-white $1\frac{1}{4}$-in.-long flowers surrounded by pink or white bracts. A most effective plant for growing in isolated groups or in the mixed border. Requires a warm, sunny position in a well-drained fertile soil. Easily raised from seed sown in seed beds in June, with the seedlings planted out in September for flowering the following season. The var. *turkestanica,* with white flowers suffused pink, is particularly effective.

Salvia splendens Ker-Gawl. (syn. *Salvia brasiliensis*)

(Scarlet Sage)
Non-hardy shrub invariably grown as an annual
Flowering period: May–Oct.
Height: up to $2\frac{1}{2}$ ft.

Native to Brazil. The best-known salvia, and one of the most popular of all garden plants for summer bedding. A bushy plant of compact habit with bright-green dentated 3–4-in.-long ovate foliage that is pointed and somewhat wrinkled on the upper surface. Inflorescence an erect terminal spike bearing 1½-in.-long "flowers". However, the true flowers are insignificant and the spectacular scarlet colouring is provided by the vividly coloured bracts surrounding the true flower. The fact that they are bracts and not actual flowers explains why they are so long-lasting. During recent years numerous new forms and colours have been introduced with purple, pink, or white "flowers", making a pleasant change from the usual reds and scarlets. All are of the easiest cultivation and the following varieties deserve special mention:

    var. *Calypso,* pink
    var. *Royal Purple,* purple
    var. *Tom Thumb,* scarlet and only 6 ins. high

Although perennial in their natural state, *Salvia splendens* plants are invariably grown as annuals in the garden. Seed can be sown in a warm greenhouse in January–February, or in an unheated greenhouse in March. Seedlings should be grown on either in boxes or in small individual fibre pots prior to planting out in late spring, or when all danger of frost has passed. If grown as a perennial in southern climates, propagation can also be effected by means of soft cuttings taken in late summer and rooted in a warm greenhouse. *Salvia splendens* will thrive in either sun or shade in any normal fertile garden soil.

Salvia Sclarea

Herbaceous perennial
Flowering period: July–Oct.
Height: 4½ ft.

Salvia uliginosa L.
Native to Eastern North America. A beautiful herbaceous perennial but not hardy in severely cold localities. Slender, graceful habit with oblong deeply dentated dark-green leaves. Inflorescences in the form of erect branched spikes bearing numerous flowers of a rich intense blue. Requires a very damp position in a hot, sunny locality, and a non-alkaline (non-calcareous) soil with an abundance of organic matter. Propagation by division in spring, or from seed sown in a warm greenhouse in January–February.

Herbaceous perennial
Flowering period: June–Aug.
Height: up to 2 ft.

Salvia virgata Ait.
Native to the Mediterranean regions. Generally found in rather dry, arid meadows. Leaves nettle-like and pleasantly fragrant when touched. Inflorescence a large branched terminal panicle borne on an erect stem, and composed of numerous intensely blue small funnel-shaped flowers arranged in groups. A very common but attractive weed particularly suitable for massing in semi-wild parts of the garden. A hardy herbaceous perennial easily propagated by divi-

sion in spring, or from seed sown in frames or seed beds in spring. If plants are required for early flowering they can be sown in July, planting out the seedlings in autumn.

Sanvitalia

Family: Compositae
Tender annual or perennial herbaceous plants

There is some uncertainty as to whether the name of the genus *Sanvitalia* derives from the noble Italian family Sanvitale, or from the Italian botanist Sanvitali, who died in 1787. Sanvitalias are small, attractive, unassuming members of the vast Compositae family, and *Sanvitalia procumbens* is worthy of wide cultivation. The genus comprises 7–8 species of herbaceous perennials and annuals with an area of distribution extending from Arizona to Mexico. They are all of modest proportions, much-branched, often trailing, easy to grow, and very long-flowering. The only species in general cultivation is the one described here.

Cultivation. This is easy, although sanvitalias are tender and will not tolerate frost. The plants prefer a light sandy soil which is moderately moist (although I have had excellent results growing them in heavy, almost clayey alkaline—calcareous—soil). Seed can be sown in pots, flats, trays, or boxes in an unheated greenhouse or coldframe in March–April, or in a sheltered position outside in April, or as soon as all danger of frost has passed. If sown in a heated greenhouse in February–March the resulting plants will begin to flower earlier. The seed should not be covered at the time of sowing; it is sufficient to press it lightly into the soil surface. Germination is rapid, a matter of 5–6 days at a temperature of 60°–65°F. Although generally treated as an annual, an occasional plant may survive a second year when grown in a frost-free locality.

Sanvitalia procumbens Lam.
Native to Mexico. An easily grown little annual (rarely perennial) with a spreading trailing habit and a height of 6 ins. or less. Suitable for sun or partial shade, remaining more dwarf in a sunny position. Stems slender, slightly hairy. Leaves ovate, 1 in. long. Flowers like a miniature rudbeckia or zinnia, very prolific, yellow-petalled, with a dark purple or almost black central disc; $\frac{2}{3}$–1 in. in diameter. An excellent subject for the rock-garden, small beds, edging, or as a ground cover.

Annual
Flowering period: June–Sept.
Height: 3–6 ins.
Position: sun or partial shade
Propagation: seed
Cultivation easy

Sanvitalia procumbens
From *The Botanical Register*,
1823, plate 707

Saponaria

(SOAPWORT OR BOUNCING BET)
Family: Caryophyllaceae
Hardy herbaceous perennials or annuals
Flowering period: spring–summer
Position: sun
Propagation: seed or division
Cultivation easy

Many years ago—before we became "clever" enough to use the modern detergents that are efficiently polluting our rivers, lakes, and even the sea—*Saponaria officinalis* was an honoured denizen in our gardens because the roots were employed for washing clothes. The plant provided a type of soap valued by those who loved nature, simplicity, and all things genuine; from home-grown vegetables and salads to local honey, garden potatoes, sun-ripened fruit, and barnyard chickens. It is not necessary to go back to Virgil's time to find a civilization without the weed-killers, detergents, insecticides, chemical fertilizers, hormones, etc., that make our life more agreeable and ruin our health and food.

No longer cultivated for domestic purpose, *Saponaria officinalis* is now much less grown even for its ornamental value. The name of the genus *Saponaria* derives from the Latin *sapo* (soap), and it comprises about thirty species distributed between the Mediterranean basin and temperate Asia. Saponarias contain the glucoside saponine, which when extracted from the dried roots yields a suds-producing substance particularly effective for dissolving fats, oils, grease, and resins. (It has even been used for producing a head on beer.) In the past, folk medicine made use of practically every part of *Saponaria officinalis* in the treatment of such ailments as rheumatism, angina, gout, and for giving relief in cases of urinary complaints, skin diseases, and liver disturbances. Used indiscriminately, however, the plant can be harmful and even dangerous.

Saponaria officinalis

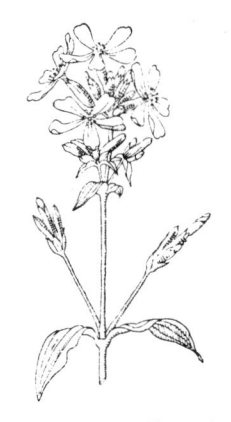

Cultivation. This does not present any difficulty as saponarias will grow in almost any soil, wet or dry, providing the plants receive an abundance of sun. Seed can be sown in the flowering position at any time in spring. In warm climates sow in autumn to produce earlier-flowering plants. From a spring sowing the annual varieties may be expected to bloom within ten weeks. Sowing directly into the flowering position is advisable whenever possible, because saponarias resent both transplantation and root disturbance. If it is desired to raise young plants of such species as *S. pumila* and *S. caespitosa* for planting in dry walls—a use for which they are well suited—a few seeds can be sown in small fibre pots. The resulting seedlings can be placed in the pockets of the wall, complete with their pot, which will eventually dissolve.

Herbaceous perennial
Flowering period: May–July
Height: 3–4 ins.

Saponaria caespitosa L.
A typical alpine species native to the mountains of Spain, where it is found at an altitude of between 5,000 and 7,500 ft. The small linear-lanceolate leaves are grass-green and cushion-forming. Flowers minute, pink, borne in closely formed umbels almost on the surface of tuft-like little plants. This plant is well-suited to the rock-garden, gardens at high altitudes, or for planting in the fissures of dry walls where the little tufted cushions of vegetation will unite to form a dense mat. Requires a heavy, gritty, well-drained soil.

Herbaceous perennial
Flowering period: May–July
Height: 8–15 ins.

Saponaria ocymoides L.
Native to the mountains of Western and Central Europe, particularly among alkaline (calcareous) rocks. Found at altitudes up to 6,000 ft. A lovely little plant, which the Swiss nurseryman Correvon noted on one of his springtime walks in the Alps. He wrote that "it is found everywhere: on railway embankments, on the walls which sustain the terraces of vineyards, at the side of paths and lanes. It spreads and expands; rich, prolific, joyous, and cheerful, equally happy under contorted pines, among junipers and wild blackberries." Concluding, he notes that, "no matter how black our thoughts may be, and however troubled our minds, the pink flowers of this saponaria banish all gloomy forebodings and fill our hearts with joy." Perhaps Correvon exaggerates through sheer enthusiasm, but, nevertheless, *Saponaria ocymoides* is certainly one of the most cheerful plants in the springtime garden. Its slender stems are prostrate, extending 10–12 ins. from the centre of the plant to form a wide rounded mat of dense vegetation with small lanceolate or elliptic leaves, which eventually are almost hidden by the loose clusters of bright pink star-like flowers. There are several varieties:

> var. *alba,* pure white
> var. *Karminkönigin,* carmine-pink
> var. *splendens,* with darker, pinkish red flowers

(Bouncing Bet)
Herbaceous perennial
Flowering period: July–Sept.
Height: 2–3 ft.
Scented

Saponaria officinalis L.
Native to Southern and Central Europe and found as far eastwards as Asia Minor, Siberia, Central Asia, and Japan. A vigorous perennial with broadly lanceolate leaves up to 3 ins. long. Flowers 1 in. in diameter, white or pink, borne in dense compact clusters. Roots somewhat fleshy and wide-spreading. It has been cultivated in gardens for centuries and is now naturalized in many parts of the

Saponaria ocymoides
From *Curtis's Botanical Magazine*,
1791, plate 154

United States. The double-flowered forms are those mostly grown today:

>var. *alba plena,* double white
>var. *plena,* double pink

Herbaceous perennial
Flowering period: July–Sept.
Height: 3 ins.

Saponaria pumila L. (syn. *Silene pumilo*)
Native to the eastern Alps at an altitude of 5,500–7,500 ft. A minute little plant forming a dense cushion of prostrate vegetation almost at soil level. Leaves minute, linear, slightly wider at the tips. The bright pink solitary flowers are conspicuous and relatively large in proportion to the size of the plant. Generally found in alpine meadows, it requires an acid soil that is cool, moist, and rich in humus. These conditions are often difficult to reproduce in the garden, especially in the south. Propagation is from seed sown in pots outside in spring. An exquisite little plant that often gives better results when grown in pots.

Saxifraga

(ROCKFOIL OR SAXIFRAGE)
Family: *Saxifragaceae*
Hardy herbaceous perennials, either evergreen or deciduous, annuals or biennials
Position: generally sunny at high altitudes and in the north, shade or partial shade in the south, but always according to the species
Propagation: seed, cuttings, or division
Cultivation: many species very easy, others difficult

Saxifraga Hirculus

The name of this interesting and fascinating genus derives from the Latin, *saxum* (stone) and *frangere* (break or fragment), and demonstrates the stubborn tenacity of the plant which, in the case of many species, appears to live and root entirely on rocks and stones, even splitting them during the roots' search for food and moisture and for fissures into which they can penetrate to ensure a secure foothold. The genus is vast, comprising at least three hundred species and probably as many hybrids. Many are alpine plants found growing at heights of up to 12,000 ft. or more. The majority of species are native to Europe, while others are distributed throughout the northern and southern temperate zones and in the Arctic regions of Asia.

Saxifrages are fascinating little plants with the most exquisite perfection of form and flower. Close examination will reveal that the leaves and blooms are veritable gems in their design. Except for a few notable exceptions, their use in gardens is somewhat restricted. They are best employed in rock-gardens, stone troughs, dry walls, stone steps, and paving. For the true saxifrage enthusiast, they do well grown individually in terra-cotta pans with rock or stone fragments. These "dish-gardens" are placed in a specially constructed alpine house, such as can be seen in the botanic gardens at Kew and Edinburgh, at Wisley Gardens, and also in the gardens of enthusiastic amateurs in the United States and in Europe. Under these special conditions the plants can be seen (frequently in mid-winter) to perfection, and their relatively large, often brilliantly coloured, but always exquisite flowers can be enjoyed at eye level. Planted thus, it is also possible to provide the saxifrages with the correct type of soil, moisture, and appropriate temperature. The last factor is especially important, as the majority of saxifrages demand a cool, fresh environment.

Saxifraga oppositifolia

As there are so many species, we cannot give the detailed attention they deserve within the limits of this work. (Also, many are not pertinent or relative to a book on flowers.) To provide some idea of the genus's complexity, however, we shall give brief descriptions and the cultural requirements of the sixteen groups into which *Saxifraga* is divided. These will be followed by a selected list of species and varieties from each group which are of greatest use in the garden and which merit special attention and more general cultivation. The flowering periods given are of necessity approximate, and they depend largely on position and altitude. There can, in fact, be a difference of several weeks between the plants' flowering period in their natural habitat high in the mountains and their flowering period in gardens. We must also remind the reader that the popular evergreen large-leaved pink-flowered "saxifrage" common to many gardens—which begins to bloom in February–March—does not belong to the genus *Saxifraga,* and its correct name is bergenia (syn. megasea).

Cultivation. With a few notable exceptions, saxifrages are not difficult to cultivate, providing they are given the appropriate environment and correct treatment. They prefer cold to heat; in fact, excessively high temperatures are their greatest enemy, and they give better results in northern gardens than in southern. The majority require a cool, moist, but well-drained soil, although some will thrive under the most arid conditions, while others require almost bog or swamp conditions.

Propagation is easy by division in spring or autumn, and can also be effected from seed sown in pots and placed in coldframes in spring, or by means of cuttings taken in spring and rooted in an unheated greenhouse or coldframe.

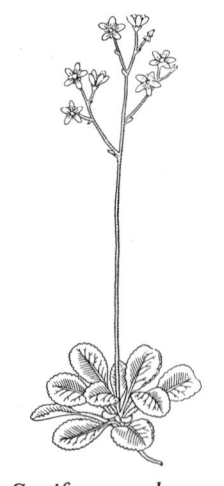

Saxifraga umbrosa

Group 1. Boraphila. Leaves basal, rosette-forming. Flowers in spikes, white or spotted. Require a cool damp position in an acid soil.

Group 2. Hirculus. Leaves deciduous, entire, oval, with a mat-forming habit. Flowers yellow or orange on leafy stems. Require a wet position in a gritty soil.

Group 3. Robertsonia. Leaves spoon-shaped, leathery, entire, but dentated at the margins, generally in basal rosettes. Flowers small, white, pink, or spotted, borne in loose open inflorescences. Of particularly easy cultivation in shady, slightly moist positions.

Group 4. Miscopetalum. Plants with a tufted habit and leathery rounded leaves; stalked, with irregular dentation at the edges. Stems upright and leafy. Inflorescence an open panicle of small mostly white and sometimes spotted flowers, frequently with an uneven number of petals. The plants are shade-lovers.

Group 5. Cymbalaria. Small freely branched annuals with ivy-shaped leaves and golden or white star-shaped flowers. Prefer a cool shady position.

Group 6. Tridactylites. Unimportant annuals or biennials with basal rosettes of flimsy three-pointed entire leaves. Leafy branching stems and small white flowers. Prefer poor sandy soil in sun or shade.

Group 7. Nephrophyllum. Deciduous plants sometimes bearing bulbils at the base or in the leaf axils of the flowering stems. Leaves mostly kidney-shaped, of soft tissue, with variously dentated edges. Flowers mostly white. Cool position.

Group 8. Dactyloides. All the so-called mossy saxifrages belong to this section. Plants form a dense mat of small rosettes. Freely produced flowers in shades of white, pink, or red. Not tolerant of hot sun or drought.

Group 9. Trachyphyllum. Small mat-forming species with small entire narrow-pointed leaves. Flowers on branching stems. White or pale yellow. Prefer an acid soil.

Group 10. Xanthizoon. Plants form loose mats of vegetation with narrow leaves and loose open rosettes. Leaves entire but dentated at the edges. Flowers single or in loose cymes; yellow, orange, purple, or red. Prefer a stony soil in a damp position.

Group 11. Euaizoonia. Broad silver-leaved plants forming rosettes which are surrounded by smaller juvenile rosettes, thus forming a dense cushion of vegetation. Tall branching flower stems bearing loose inflorescences of bloom in summer. Flowers white but often heavily spotted with pink, red, or purple. Sometimes an individual flower will be completely red or pink. Rosettes die after flowering. Require alkaline (calcareous) soil and a sunny but not hot position.

Group 12. Kabschia. Includes the elite of the genus. Small, dense, compact, cushion-forming. Minute sharply pointed leaves. Flowers produced singly or on branching stems; white, yellow, lilac, pink, or red. Never spotted. Thirty-six known species and more than one hundred garden varieties. Require a well-drained gritty soil in a sunny but not hot position.

Group 13. Engleria. Rosette-forming leafy flower stems terminating in spikes or branched racemes of minute flowers enveloped in highly coloured calyces. The stems of the leaves are also frequently brightly coloured. Moderately dry position in semi-shade.

Group 14. Porphyrion. Creeping mat-forming plants generally with purple flowers, but a few white and bicoloured forms are known. Leaves opposite. Gritty porous soil in a cool moist but sunny position.

Saxifraga sarmentosa
From *Curtis's Botanical Magazine*,
1789, plate 92

Group 15. Tetrameridum. Only one species of this section is in cultivation. Differs from all other saxifrages in having no petals and only four sepals. Flowers solitary on short stems. Dense tufted habit and short branching stems densely covered with overlapping opposite minute narrow leaves. Require a dry position.

Group 16. Diptera. Tufts of broad leaves of leathery texture from which in autumn arise branches bearing curiously shaped flowers with one or two of the petals elongated; white, sometimes spotted. Require a cool position in a soil rich in humus.

Following is a selected list of the best species and varieties now in general cultivation. The numbers in parentheses indicate the group to which each plant belongs. See above groups for fuller descriptions as well as cultural details.

Saxifraga aizoides L. (Group 10)
Native to Europe. Yellow-flowered. Height 3–4 ins. Var. *atrorubens*, red; var. *aurantia*, orange; var. *autumnalis*, orange. Late-summer- and early-autumn-flowering.

Evergreen herbaceous perennial
Flowering period: July–Sept.
Height: 3–4 ins.

Saxifraga Aizoon Jacq. (Group 11)
Native to Europe. Leaves leathery, up to 3 ins. long, but variable in shape according to variety. Height 6 ins. Innumerable varieties: var. *balcana*, flowers white spotted red; var. *lutea*, yellow; var. *minor*, a miniature form with white flowers; var. *rosea*, pink. Summer-flowering.

Evergreen herbaceous perennial
Flowering period: June–July
Height: 6 ins.

Saxifraga x *apiculata* (Group 12)
Of hybrid origin. Height 4 ins. Flowers yellow. Spring-flowering. Var. *alba*, white.

Evergreen herbaceous perennial
Flowering period: Apr.–May
Height: 4 ins.

Saxifraga aspera L. (Group 9)
Native to Europe. Height 2½ ins. Yellow flowers marked with orange. Summer-flowering.

Evergreen herbaceous perennia
Flowering period: June–July
Height: 2½ ins.

Saxifraga x *borisii* (Group 12)
Of hybrid origin. Height 2½ ins. Yellow flowers in spring.

Evergreen herbaceous perennia
Flowering period: Apr.–May
Height: 2½ ins.

Saxifraga x *boydii* (Group 12)
Of hybrid origin. Height 2½ ins. Citron-yellow flowers in spring, with red flower stems.

Evergreen herbaceous perennia
Flowering period: Apr.–May
Height: 2½ ins.

Evergreen herbaceous perennial
Flowering period: May–June
Height: 2½ ins.

Saxifraga burseriana L. (Group 12)
Native to the eastern Alps. Height 2½ ins. White flowers in early summer. Many superb varieties: var. *Gloria,* white flowers on red stems; var. *major,* large white flowers; var. *sulphurea,* pale yellow.

Evergreen herbaceous perennial
Flowering period: June–July
Height: 6 ins.

Saxifraga cochlearis L. (Group 11)
Native to the Maritime Alps. Height 6 ins. White flowers in summer. The var. *minor* forms a minute silver cushion of vegetation.

Evergreen herbaceous perennial
Flowering period: June–July
Height: 5–8 ins. (2 ft. in flower)

Saxifraga Cotyledon L. (Group 11)
Native to the western and central Alps. White flowers in summer. The flower stems can exceed 2 ft. in length. Numerous beautiful varieties: var. *caterhamensis,* white flowers spotted red; var. *pyramidalis,* with very large rosettes and enormous plumes of white flowers in June–July.

Annual
Flowering period: June–July
Height: 2 ins.

Saxifraga Cymbalaria L. (Group 5)
Native to the Caucasus and Asia Minor. Height 2 ins. An annual species with yellow flowers in summer.

Evergreen herbaceous perennial
Flowering period: Apr.–May
Height: 4 ins.

Saxifraga ferdinandi-coburgii L. (Group 12)
Native to Bulgaria. Height 4 ins. Yellow flowers in spring.

Herbaceous perennial
Flowering period: Sept.–Oct.
Height: 12–15 ins.

Saxifraga fortunei L. (Group 16)
Native to Asia. Height 12–15 ins. Deciduous. White flowers in autumn.

Evergreen herbaceous perennial
Flowering period: June–July
Height: 4–5 ins.

Saxifraga Geum L. (Group 3)
Native to Europe. Height 4–5 ins. White flowers in summer.

Herbaceous perennial
Flowering period: June–July
Height: up to 12 ins. in flower

Saxifraga granulata L. (Group 7)
Native to Europe. Height up to 12 ins. White flowers in summer. Deciduous, small, kidney-shaped foliage.

Evergreen herbaceous perennial
Flowering period: June–July
Height: 6–8 ins.

Saxifraga grisebachii L. (Group 13)
Native to Greece. Height 6–8 ins. Crimson flowers in summer. The var. *Wisley* has red flowers with crimson bracts.

Evergreen herbaceous perennial
Flowering period: Apr.–May
Height: 2¾ ins.

Saxifraga x haagii (Group 12)
Of hybrid origin. Particularly attractive, with dark-green rosettes of vegetation and small star-like yellow flowers in spring. Height 2¾ ins.

Herbaceous perennial
Flowering period: June–July
Height: 4 ins.

Saxifraga Hirculus L. (Group 2)
Native to Europe. Height 4 ins. Yellow flowers in summer. Deciduous.

Saxifraga hypnoides All. (Group 8)
Native to Europe. Height 4 ins. White flowers in summer. There are many fine garden varieties.

Evergreen herbaceous perennial
Flowering period: June–July
Height: 4 ins.

Saxifraga x *irvingii* (Group 12)
Of hybrid origin. One of the most beautiful, forming tiny grey hummocks of vegetation with masses of pale-pink flowers in February–March. Height 1½ ins.

Evergreen herbaceous perennial
Flowering period: Feb.–Mar.
Height: 1½ ins.

Saxifraga latepetiolata L. (Group 7)
Native to Spain. A biennial species 10–12 ins. high. White flowers in summer.

Biennial
Flowering period: June–July
Height: 10–12 ins.

Saxifraga lilacina L. (Group 12)
Native to the Himalayas. Height ¾ in. Lilac-coloured flowers in spring.

Evergreen herbaceous perennial
Flowering period: Apr.–May
Height: ¾ in.

Saxifraga longifolia var. *Tumbling Waters* (Group 11)
Of hybrid origin. A superb hybrid with enormous plumes of white flowers in summer up to 2½ ft. long. The central rosette of silvery leaves dies after flowering.

Evergreen herbaceous perennial
Flowering period: June–July
Height: up to 2½ ft. in bloom

Saxifraga x *macnabiana* (Group 11)
Of hybrid origin. Height 6–8 ins. Produces broad-leaved rosettes in summer which bear sprays of white flowers spotted red on stems up to 1½ ft. long.

Evergreen herbaceous perennial
Flowering period: June–July
Height: up to 1½ ft. in bloom

Saxifraga marginata L. (Group 12)
Native to Italy and the Balkans. Height 3 ins. Forms a grey-green cushion of compact vegetation with white flowers in early summer.

Evergreen herbaceous perennial
Flowering period: June
Height: 3 ins.

Saxifraga oppositifolia L. (Group 14)
Native to Europe. Up to 1¼ ins. high. A most valuable garden plant for its prostrate trailing habit. Pink flowers in spring. There are numerous excellent varieties such as var. *alba*, white; var. *coccinea*, crimson; var. *latina*, pink flowers and foliage tipped with silver.

(Mountain Saxifrage)
Evergreen herbaceous perennial
Flowering period: Apr.–May
Height: ¾–1¼ ins.

Saxifraga x *paulinae* (Group 8)
Of hybrid origin. Height 4 ins. Yellow flowers in spring.

Evergreen herbaceous perennial
Flowering period: Apr.–May
Height: 4 ins.

Saxifraga pedemontana All. (Group 8)
Native to Europe. Height 4 ins. White flowers in summer.

Evergreen herbaceous perennial
Flowering period: June–July
Height: 4 ins.

Saxifraga pensylvanica L. (Group 1)
Native to North America. Height 4–6 ins. Long sprays of yellow-white flowers in summer on stems up to 2½ ft. long.

Evergreen herbaceous perennial
Flowering period: June–July
Height: up to 2½ ft. in bloom

Evergreen herbaceous perennial
Flowering period: June–July
Height: 1¼ ins.

Saxifraga retusa L. (Group 14)
Native to the Alps. Height 1¼ ins. Red flowers in summer.

Evergreen herbaceous perennial
Flowering period: Mar.
Height: up to 15–18 ins.

Saxifraga rotundifolia L. (Group 4)
Native to Europe. One of the largest species, with long-stalked kidney-shaped fleshy leaves and conspicuous sprays of white flowers speckled with pink in early spring. Height up to 18 ins.

Saxifraga rotundifolia   *Saxifraga granulata*   *Saxifraga Aizoon*   *Saxifraga burseriana*

Evergreen herbaceous perennial
Flowering period: June–July
Height: 3 ins.

Saxifraga sancta L. (Group 12)
Native to Asia Minor. Height 3 ins. Mossy rosettes of vegetation, and yellow flowers in summer.

(Strawberry Geranium,
Aaron's Beard,
Beefsteak Saxifrage,
or Mother of Thousands)
Evergreen herbaceous perennial
Flowering period: June–July
Height: 5–6 ins.

Saxifraga sarmentosa L. (Group 16)
Native to Asia. Height up to 6 ins. Pink-spotted white flowers in summer. Commonly known as Mother of Thousands because of the habit of producing numerous young plants around the parent plant.

(London Pride)
Evergreen herbaceous perennial
Flowering period: June–July
Height: 10–12 ins. in bloom
Useful for cutting

Saxifraga umbrosa L. (Group 3)
Native to Europe. The true species is rarely found in cultivation, but for many years its name has been wrongly used for a saxifrage of hybrid origin, *Saxifraga* x *urbium,* actually a cross between *Saxifraga spathularis* and *Saxifraga umbrosa.* This hybrid is one of the most popular plants in England; especially so in cities, where it bravely tolerates adverse atmospheric conditions, hence the common English name of London Pride. (In the United States it is also known as St. Patrick's Cabbage.) It is an attractive plant of the easiest cultivation. Height 10–12 ins. Pink flowers in loose sprays in summer. Excellent for cutting.

Scabiosa

(SCABIOUS)
Family: Dipsaceae
Annuals or hardy herbaceous perennials
Position: sun
Propagation: seed or division
Cultivation easy

If flowers were chosen for their names, scabiosas would surely be as rare in gardens as orchids. It is undoubtedly among the least inviting and least attractive names that could be selected for any flower. There is, however, a valid reason for this unhappy choice. Originally the plant was grown for its virtue of curing scabies, and not for its decorative value. It is still sometimes used for this curative property, although fortunately the disease is now rare in the Western world.

Wild scabiosas are delightfully fragrant attractive flowers found growing in European fields and meadows. They are worthy of introduction into our gardens for their fragrance, form, pleasing colours, and long-flowering habit. In many respects, they have greater appeal than the modern hybrid types now so widely sold as cut bloom. We do not know when scabiosas first became appreciated for their medicinal properties, although we find an old reference in a poem by an unknown author written around 1099, during the pontificate of Pope Urban II:

> Urbanus pro se nescit pretium Scabiosae
> nam purgat pectus
> quod comprimit aegra senectus
> lenit pulmonem, purgat laterum regionem
> abscessus frangit,
> si locum bibita tangit
> Tribus uncta foris, anthracem liberat oris.

(Urban does not know the virtues of the scabiosa/ It is a balsam to relieve infirmities of old age/ To sustain the lungs and treat abscesses/ If swallowed it reaches the point of infection/ And spread three times on the mouth eliminates carbuncles.) Actually, the plant here referred to is *Succisa pratensis* Moench, a species at one time included in the genus *Scabiosa* and by some botanists still called *Scabiosa Succisa* L. (Its common name is Devil's Bite because the roots are praemorse—that is, their blunted base has the appearance of having been abruptly bitten off, and, in those distant times any phenomenon

Scabiosa Succisa

Scabiosa atropurpurea

a little out of the ordinary was automatically attributed to the devil.) The name *Succisa* has, in fact, the same derivation as the word succinct, that is, short, or brief. The medicinal properties of the plant are found in the roots, which contain the glucoside scabiosine.

The genus *Scabiosa* was introduced into European gardens many years after Urban's time. In 1596 the British imported *Scabiosa stellata* from Spain, followed by *Scabiosa atropurpurea* in 1629, which eventually was to be developed as one of the most important of the annual horticultural forms. Other species followed at intervals: as late as 1803 the famous *Scabiosa caucasica* appeared, the parent of the superb modern large-flowered herbaceous perennial scabiosas (which were produced after much patient hybridization and crossing by J. C. House of Bristol, who some forty years ago obtained a magnificent race of hybrids which are still popular today).

There are many species of scabiosa, the actual number varying from 70–90 according to the classification of different botanists. Their area of distribution extends through Europe, Asia, and Africa, with the major concentration of species in the Mediterranean regions. In England they are often referred to as Pincushion Flowers because of the characteristic form of the blooms, particularly apparent in the case of the annual varieties.

Cultivation. Scabiosas are not difficult to cultivate. *Scabiosa atropurpurea* and its hybrids are grown as annuals or biennials, and are thus propagated from seed. This should be sown in June–July in seed beds outside or in frames, pricking out the seedlings into nursery beds and then planting out in flowering positions in spring. Otherwise seed can be sown in April–May (even in March in warm localities), planting out the seedlings in May–June. Another method is to sow directly in the flowering positions in April–May, then thinning out the seedlings to 15–18 ins. apart. The perennial species can be propagated from seed sown in May–June in seed beds or frames, pricking out the seedlings into nursery beds and planting out in their permanent positions in autumn or spring. Perennial scabiosas can also be propagated by division in autumn or spring, the only method in the case of named varieties.

Annual
Flowering period: June–Oct.
Height: up to 2½ ft.

Scabiosa atropurpurea L. (syn. *Scabiosa major*, *Scabiosa calyptocarpa*) Native to Southern Europe. A hardy annual species with deliciously fragrant flowers whose perfume has also been transmitted to the many beautiful garden hybrids which are its progeny. The leaves form an almost prostrate compact basal rosette and are deeply lobed or divided. The flower stems bear numerous small leaves, and are erect, rigid, up to 2½ ft. high. At their summit they bear the typical pincushion-like rounded inflorescences, dark crimson in colour and up to 2 ins. in diameter. Cultivated in gardens since 1629. There are

Scabiosa caucasica Vincent Hybrid
From *Curtis's Botanical Magazine*,
1805, plate 886

now many attractive hybrid varieties and forms with a wide range of colours. Some of the best of these are:

> Blue Moon, height 2½ ft., with very large, conical inflorescences of lavender-blue on long, wiry stems
>
> Coral Moon, similar to the above but with coral-red flowers
>
> Dobie's Giant Hybrids, height 2½ ft., with very large double flowers in shades of pink, scarlet, lavender, blue, maroon, white. Excellent for cutting
>
> Dwarf Double Mixed, height 18 ins., with a compact habit and flowers in shades of pink, scarlet, mauve, blue, and maroon. An excellent annual for windy positions

Herbaceous perennial
Flowering period: May–July
Height: 12–15 ins.

Scabiosa caucasica Bieb.

Native to the Caucasus. A hardy herbaceous perennial but not suitable for outdoor cultivation in exceptionally cold zones. Excellent for alkaline (calcareous) soils. The most important of the perennial scabiosas, and, together with its hybrids, the perennial species of greatest garden value. Apart from its beauty when cultivated in beds or borders, it is one of the finest of all herbaceous perennials for providing cut bloom, and it is widely grown on a commercial scale for that purpose. The original species, introduced into European gardens in 1803, has lavender-blue flowers up to 2 ins. in diameter on erect slender stems. The leaves are dentated, lobed or pinnate, up to 8 ins. long, but not profuse. Although still grown, it has now largely been replaced by the many continuous-flowering hybrids with rigid stems up to 2 ft. high. The size of the flowers can vary from 2–3½ ins. in diameter, with larger and more conspicuous external petals than the species and the annual types, and sometimes with a less conspicuous pincushion centre to the flowers. These hybrids are the results of many years' work by J. C. House, and the hybrid Mrs. Isaac House, one of the first, is still the best white form. Other excellent hybrids are:

> Cannon Andrews, rich purple
> Clive Greaves, dark mauve
> Imperial Purple, dark lavender-mauve with frilled petals
> Sally, grey-blue with pink stamens
> Silver King, silvery white
> Souters Violet, dark violet
> Vincent, cobalt-blue
> Wanda, rich blue

Herbaceous perennial
Flowering period: June–July
Height: 8–10 ins.

Scabiosa graminifolia L.

Native to Southern Europe. A hardy herbaceous perennial. As its specific name suggests, the foliage is slender, grass-like, almost prostrate, and of an attractive silver-grey colour. Flowers pale mauve, of the typical pincushion type, borne on rigid stems 10 ins. high.

Scabiosa ochroleuca L.
Native to Southern Europe and Asia. A herbaceous perennial with greenish-white hairy foliage; leaves at the base elongated-lobate, while the stem leaves are divided into many narrow segments. Flowers bright yellow, of the pincushion type, borne on long rigid stems.

Herbaceous perennial
Flowering period: July–Oct.
Height: 12–18 ins.

Scabiosa prolifera L.
Native to Asia Minor. A hardy annual species with narrowly oblong pointed foliage up to $2\frac{1}{2}$ ins. in length. Flowers round, flattish, cream or ivory-white, on rigid stems. A species of considerable beauty but too rarely seen in gardens. Flowering period exceptionally long if dead blooms are regularly removed.

Annual
Flowering period: June–Aug.
Height: 2–2½ ft.

Scabiosa stellata L.
Native to Southern Europe. A charming little annual species up to 15–18 ins. high when in flower. Basal leaves oblong-oval, dentated, stem leaves deeply lobed. The slender graceful flower stalks bear rounded flattish terminal inflorescences 1 in. in diameter and of a lovely shade of blue.

Annual
Flowering period: June–Aug.
Height: 12–18 ins.

Schizanthus

(BUTTERFLY FLOWER)
Family: Solanaceae
Annuals
Position: sun
Propagation: seed
Cultivation fairly easy

It would be difficult to find a more appropriate name than Butterfly Flower, which British and American gardeners have christened this lovely Chilean annual with its tropical-butterfly-like flowers. The more prosaic Germans give it the name Poor Man's Orchid, a description not unapt, as the blooms do somewhat resemble miniature orchids.
As L. H. Bailey rightly notes, superb schizanthus plants can be cultivated in pots. In fact, they are sometimes more satisfactory when grown as pot plants in an unheated greenhouse, particularly in the north where the summer weather is uncertain. In southern gardens schizanthus are perfectly satisfactory as summer bedding plants in a

warm, sunny position. It must be admitted, however, that they do have a rather delicate constitution and are liable to be damaged by bad weather, the stems being brittle and fragile; but they are remarkably graceful and elegant plants, with an extraordinary range of colours.

The genus comprises about eleven species, all native to Chile. The name given to them by the botanists Ruiz and Pavon derives from the Greek *skhizo* (to cut) and *anthos* (flower)—thus, cut flower—as so clearly indicated by the deeply incised corolla of *Schizanthus pinnatus,* the first species to be introduced into Europe in 1822. This was followed by *Schizanthus retusus* in 1829—but what a learned scientific name for such a delicate and graceful flower.

Although schizanthus like warmth and sunshine, they do not enjoy great heat, their native habitat being on the slopes of the Andes. For summer-flowering purposes seed should be sown in a warm greenhouse in February–March, using sand-and-peat soil. When the seedlings have 3–4 leaves they should be pricked out individually into 2-in. pots, replanting into 4-in. pots when well-developed, and then soon afterwards transferred to an unheated greenhouse or coldframe for a few weeks until planting-out time in May–June. Planting out should be done only when all risk of frost has passed. During their period in the larger pots—and in the case of plants destined to flower in pots—periodic applications of a liquid, organic fertilizer are necessary, and eventually the plants will have to be potted-on again. For winter or spring flowering, seed should be sown in a warm greenhouse in August, pricking out the seedlings into trays, flats, or boxes. When well-developed they can be potted individually into 3 in. pots, later repotting them into larger 4–5-in. pots, and finally into 6-in. pots, where the plants will bloom. During this growing period the plants should be kept at a temperature of 50–55°F., either in an unheated greenhouse or in coldframes. A judicious topping or pinching out of the terminal and lateral growths will ensure vigorous, robust, well-branched plants. An appropriate soil mixture for pot-grown schizanthus is:

    2 parts fibrous loam
    1 part leafsoil
    1 part peat
    1 part coarse sand
    1 part dried manure

For general garden purposes, and for pot-grown plants, the best type of schizanthus are the hybrids known as the Wisetonensis strain.

Flowering period: June–July
Height: up to 4 ft.

Schizanthus pinnatus Ruiz & Pav.
Native to Chile. A rather sticky-surfaced non-hardy annual with pale-green foliage cut and divided into many fern-like segments

Schizanthus pinnatus
From *Paxton's Magazine of Botany*,
1835, plate 198

which can be either bipinnate or tripinnate. Flowers very prolific; the lower lip rather dark violet- or lilac-coloured, the upper lip lighter coloured, suffused yellow at the base and spotted (but very variable in colour). Entire flower $1\frac{1}{2}$ ins. in diameter, with conspicuous stamens. The hybrid forms, however, are those that are mostly grown.

Flowering period: June–July
Height: 2–2½ ft.

Schizanthus retusus Hook.

Native to the Chilean Andes. A much-branched erect annual with opposite, glabrous, pinnatified leaves 8–10 ins. long, with the segments irregularly dentated. Flowers borne in large axillary racemes, each bloom up to $1\frac{1}{2}$ ins. wide, divided into two lips, the upper one three-lobed with the two lateral lobes again divided into 2–4 parts; colour light pink, with the longer central lobe incurved and marked with yellow. The lower lip is divided into three parts, the central section often recurved and hooded or merely divided into three parts. There are many lovely varieties:

> var. *albomaculatus,* flowers marked with white
> var. *albus,* white, with the central segments of the upper lip marked yellow
> var. *lilacinus,* with lilac-coloured flowers
> var. *trimaculatus,* crimson-purple flowers bearing three golden-yellow marks and margined intense purple

Flowering period: June–July
Height: up to 4 ft.

Schizanthus x wisetonensis

A lovely strain of hybrid origin (*Schizanthus pinnatus* x *Schizanthus grahami*), with pink, blue, white, maroon, lilac, purple, or carmine flowers marked with yellow. Many are obtainable as separate named varieties. It is these hybrids that are the most widely cultivated for both garden and pot culture.

Schizanthus retusus

Scilla

(SQUILL OR BLUEBELL)
Family: Liliaceae
Hardy or tender perennial bulbs
Position: sun or partial shade
Propagation: seed or division
Cultivation: very easy
Useful for cutting
Poisonous

Together with muscari (grape hyacinths) and narcissus, scillas are among the most beautiful flowering bulbs for naturalizing in grassland and on lawns. Those species normally grown in European and American gardens are very hardy, easy, and vigorous; they will increase rapidly and are perfect plants for the gardener who has little time. They can be left undisturbed for many years, requiring no attention.

The genus is very large and comprises about one hundred species, not all of which are hardy. Indeed, some are only suitable for greenhouse cultivation, and although these are extremely interesting for their often colourfully marked foliage, they are generally difficult to procure. The hardy species, however, are well known and widely cultivated, one of the most common being the lovely English Bluebell, whose beautiful blue is also the dominating colour of the genus, with many fascinating gradations of that shade. There are, however, white- and pink-flowered varieties. The majority are spring-flowering but some species bloom in summer and autumn.

Scillas have an area of distribution extending from Europe to China, with an offshoot into Algeria. At least ten species are indigenous to Europe, including *S. non-scripta, S. peruviana,* and *S. autumnalis,* all of which are of particular garden value.

The name of the genus *Scilla* is a Greek word used by Hippocrates. It means "to wound" or "harm", and alludes to the toxic properties of some species. Even some of those recognized as medicinally valuable, such as *Scilla maritima* (syn. *Urginea maritima* Steinth.), native to Southern Europe, are poisonous.

Scillas like a soil rich in humus and they thrive in partial shade. Bluebells and several other species are, in fact, woodland plants found growing in veritable carpets of leafsoil. In southern gardens, or in very hot and dry localities, they should be planted in the shade (unless at high altitudes); in the north they can be planted in more sunny positions. As with other hardy bulbs, propagation is by

Scilla siberica

division when the bulbs are dormant. They may also be propagated from seed sown in an unheated greenhouse or coldframe in spring, but this process is very slow.

Flowering period: Aug.–Sept.
Height: 6 ins.

Scilla autumnalis L.
Native to Europe. A charming little bulb with lilac-pink flowers in August–September. Excellent for naturalizing in a shady position between shrubs or underneath trees. The bulbs are relatively large, oval, whitish; the foliage is semi-cylindrical, grooved, and darkish green.

(Spanish Bluebell)
Flowering period: May
Height: 12 ins.

Scilla hispanica Mill. (syn. *Endymion hispanicus*)
Native to Spain. Leaves up to 1 in. in diameter. Flowers borne in clusters of 12–15 on erect 1-ft.-high stems. Each flower 1 in. in diameter; blue in the typical species, but there are also pink and white forms. Some of the best named varieties are:

>   var. *Excelsior,* very large dark blue flowers
>   var. *Mount Everest,* white
>   var. *Queen of the Blues,* purple-blue
>   var. *Queen of the Pinks,* dark lilac-pink

This species is very similar to the English Bluebell (*Scilla non-scripta*), although it is scentless, with larger inflorescences and bigger individual blooms. Some authorities include it in the genus *Scilla,* while others have reclassified this as well as other scillas into the genus *Endymion*. To make the confusion complete, nature hybridized the two genera, producing intermediate forms.

(Bluebell)
Flowering period: Mar.–Apr.
Height: 12–15 ins.
Scented

Scilla non-scripta Hoff. & Link (syn. *Scilla festalis, Scilla nutans, Endymion non-scriptus*)
Native to Europe. The typical English Bluebell and one of Europe's most beautiful wild flowers in spring. Usually found in woods where it forms vast blue carpets over large areas. Used with great effect in gardens, especially when naturalized in grass underneath clumps of silver birches, where the combination of white bark and blue flowers creates a lovely picture. Leaves slender, long, pale green, slightly arching. Flowers pendulous, bell-shaped, freely borne on rigid stems up to 12–15 ins. long. Excellent for picking. There are also white- and pink-flowered forms, all of the easiest cultivation.

(Cuban Lily)
Flowering period: Apr.–May
Height: 8–10 ins.

Scilla peruviana L.
Native to the Mediterranean regions, notwithstanding its specific name. Generally found in arid, stony soils, and of the easiest cultivation. Inflorescences in the form of small spikes bearing star-shaped lilac-pink flowers. Leaves lanceolate and rather fleshy. There is also a white-flowered form.

Scilla siberica Andr.   (Siberian Squill)
Flowering period: Feb.–Mar.
Height: 4–6 ins.

Native to Asia Minor. Cultivated in European gardens since 1700. A beautiful little bulb for planting permanently in the rock-garden, or among shrubs where it will provide a welcome mass of blue flowers before the shrubs begin to bloom. Also an excellent subject for cultivating in pots for temporary use indoors at the beginning of the year. Leaves ½ in. wide, not more than 4–6 ins. long, bright green. Flowers pendulous, borne in groups of 3–5, widely star-shaped. There are numerous good hybrids such as:

    Alba, white
    Spring Beauty, large dark-blue flowers on taller stems
    Taurica, vivid blue flowers and very early-blooming

Scilla tubergeniana Hort.
Flowering period: Feb.–Mar.
Height: 6–8 ins.

Native to Iran. Introduced into European gardens by the famous Dutch bulb firm of C. G. Van Tubergen. One of the most attractive early-spring-flowering bulbs. The blooms are pale blue with dark-blue stripes on each petal. Each bulb produces several flowering stems. Ideal for naturalizing or for pot culture.

Sedum

(STONECROP)
Family: *Crassulaceae*
Hardy or half-hardy herbaceous perennials, annuals, or biennials
Position: sun
Propagation: seed, cuttings, or division
Cultivation easy

Within the scope of this work it is difficult to give a true picture of the genus *Sedum*. It is very vast and has a distribution extending throughout the major part of the world, including Europe, North and South America, the Mediterranean regions, China, Japan, Siberia, and the Himalayas. There are at least 250 species, ranging from those that are semi-tropical to those tolerant of severe frost; from prostrate mat-forming species to those with a height of up to 2 ft.; from troublesome weed-like species to species that are extremely rare and difficult to cultivate; from annuals to perennials that can reach a great age; from species with conspicuous spectacular flowers to those whose inflorescences are insignificant. Several species and

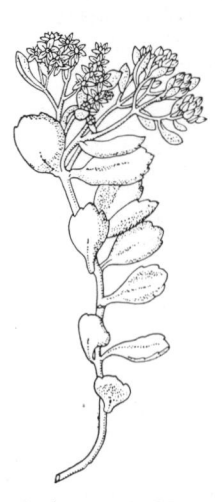

Sedum sieboldii

varieties are more attractive for their foliage than for their bloom, while some are little more than botanical curiosities. There are, however, certain species and varieties of outstanding garden value, the most important of which are described here.

The name of the genus *Sedum* has a curious origin, and dates back to the time of the Romans, who used to establish the plants on the roofs of their houses, believing that sedums would keep away lightning. The name comes from the Latin *sedo* (to calm or allay). Regarding cultivation, there is little to say. Sedums thrive in any normal, porous garden soil that is well-drained. They are sun-lovers, although some species such as *Sedum acre* will grow well in partial shade. They are excellent subjects for dry positions, and many are ideal for the rock-garden, dry walls, paving, stone steps, etc.

Propagation is easily done by division, preferably in spring, or it may be done by means of seed sown in an unheated greenhouse or coldframe in spring. The plants can also be increased by means of cuttings taken in June–July and inserted in sandy soil in frames.

Sedum acre

Sedum acre L.

(Wall Paper, Mossy Stonecrop, Golden Moss, Gold Dust, or Love Entangle)
Evergreen perennial
Flowering period: May–June
Height: up to 3 ins.

Native to Europe and Asia. Completely prostrate and carpet-forming. One of the easiest and most useful plants for forming a dense, compact mat-like covering in a dry position in poor soil, either in sun or partial shade. From a distance it gives the appearance of a normal lawn, but because of the minute fleshy foliage it cannot be walked on. In late spring the plants are covered with masses of small bright-yellow flowers. Also useful for the rock-garden and for pot culture.

(Worm Grass)
Evergreen perennial
Flowering period: July
Height: 8 ins.

Sedum album L.

Native to Europe, Asia, and North Africa. A nearly prostrate creeping evergreen species with $\frac{1}{2}$-in.-long fleshy cylindrical foliage. Flowers borne in terminal branching inflorescences about 1 in. wide; individual blooms white, $\frac{1}{4}$ in. in diameter. The attractive var. *murale* has purple-green foliage and pale-pink flowers.

Annual
Flowering period: July–Aug.
Height: 3–4 ins.

Sedum caeruleum L.

Native to Southern Europe. An annual species only 3–4 ins. high—a little gem for small beds, the rock-garden, or for pots. In its natural habitat it grows in dry, stony localities and in walls. It has a close, compact habit with minute fleshy, cylindrical, linear foliage and forms a dense covering over the soil. During the summer months the plants are covered with masses of minute pale-blue flowers. Easily grown from seed, which should be sown either in its flowering position in April in a dry, warm, sunny position; or in pots in March in an unheated greenhouse or coldframe, planting out the seedlings in May.

Sedum dasyphyllum L.
Native to Europe. A slender-branched dwarf evergreen species with a tufted habit. Leaves $\frac{1}{8}$ in. long, fleshy, cylindrical. Flowers pinkish yellow, $\frac{1}{4}$ in. in diameter. A delightful little plant for the rock-garden, where its June-flowering habit is much appreciated after the spring-flowering alpines have finished.

Evergreen perennial
Flowering period: June
Height: 2 ins.

Sedum kamtschaticum Fish & Mey.
Native to eastern Siberia and northern China. A 9-in.-high erect perennial with opposite or alternate oval leaves 2 ins. long, margins slightly dentated. Flowers $\frac{3}{4}$ in. wide, orange-yellow, and produced late in the season when few other plants of this type are in bloom.

Herbaceous perennial
Flowering period: July–Aug.
Height: 9 ins.

Sedum sieboldii Sweet
Native to Japan. A particularly interesting and colourful plant with small rounded fleshy leaves, blue-green in summer changing to bright carmine-pink in autumn. Flowers small, pink, borne on much-branched densely formed inflorescences. An excellent plant for cultivating in pots on terraces, etc.

Herbaceous perennial
Flowering period: Sept.–Oct.
Height: up to 12 ins.

Sedum spathulifolium L.
Native to Western North America. Exceptionally attractive for its dwarf compact habit and its fleshy rounded 1-in.-wide reddish-green foliage with a metallic sheen. Flowers yellow, $\frac{1}{2}$ in. in diameter, borne in flattish cymes. Even more attractive is the var. *purpureum*, with dark-purple foliage.

Evergreen herbaceous perennial
Flowering period: May–June
Height: up to 4 ins.

Sedum spectabile Bor.
Native to Japan. One of the most popular garden plants, with several fine varieties. A handsome species with an erect rigid habit and broad glaucous-green oval foliage. The blooms are among the most showy of the species, with masses of minute individual bright-pink flowers massed together in large flat saucer-like inflorescences. The flowers have a remarkable attraction for butterflies, and on a sunny day it is rare to see a flowering plant without its attendant group of these gaily coloured insects. There are several improved hybrid forms such as:

Evergreen herbaceous perennial
Flowering period: July–Aug.
Height: up to 2 ft.

  var. *Album,* a plant of exceptional beauty with white flowers
  var. *Atropurpureum,* with darker pink flowers
  var. *Brilliant,* flowers of a more intense pink
  var. *Meteor,* with red flowers

Sedum caeruleum

Sedum spurium Bieb.
Native to the Caucasus. A very vigorous creeping evergreen species up to 4–6 ins. high with oval 1-in.-wide fleshy opposite leaves.

Evergreen herbaceous perennial
Flowering period: July–Aug.
Height: 6 ins.

Flowers pink, ½ in. in diameter freely borne in loosely formed cymes slightly above the level of the foliage. There is a var. *album* with white flowers and a var. *splendens* with larger deeper pink flowers. All are excellent plants for covering slopes and banks where soil is poor and dry.

Sempervivum

(HOUSELEEK)
Family: Crassulaceae
Hardy or half-hardy evergreen prostrate herbaceous perennials
Position: sun
Propagation: seed or division
Cultivation very easy

This genus—typified by lovely green or red rosette-forming curious and attractive little plants—has a most appropriate name: *Sempervivum* (ever-living), meaning the plants are beyond the control or influence of seasons (their fresh, succulent, fleshy appearance is the same at any time of the year). They are plants with an exquisite geometric form, with dwarf rosettes spreading such a perfect mat of dense vegetation over the soil surface that they almost appear artificial. They are all plants from stony, rocky regions and are therefore ideal for the rock-garden or for growing in shallow receptacles. The majority are so similar in appearance that individual detailed descriptions would be superfluous, the only differences being in the size and colour of the rosette. Some are conspicuous for the dense cobweb-like white threads which cover their leaves. The genus comprises almost exclusively hardy perennial species; those not hardy that at one time belonged to the genus *Sempervivum* have been transferred to other genera such as *Aeonium*. There are also a few sub-shrubby tender species.

The native habitat of the hardy sempervivums comprises Europe, the Mediterranean regions, and Asia. Apart from their use in the rock-garden, they are excellent for dry walls, stone steps, paved terraces, etc. Some fascinating effects also can be obtained by planting sempervivums in crevices or holes in large stones or boulders or in old stone troughs or tubs, thereby creating a miniature portable garden. The plants require very little soil, but it should be sandy, porous, well-drained, and in an open, sunny position. Large colonies

Sempervivum tectorum

Sempervivum arachnoideum
From *Curtis's Botanical Magazine*,
1788, plate 68

of *Sempervivum tectorum* can often be seen growing on the roofs of old houses, especially in rural mountainous areas in Europe. Although their main attraction is in their foliage, nearly all the rosette-forming sempervivums flower quite freely in early summer. The inflorescences are quite spectacular and—in proportion to the size of the plant—exceptionally large, often borne on tall, stout, rigid stems up to 6 ins. high, but in many cases much shorter. After producing its inflorescence, the central rosette dies, but it is replaced by many new rosettes, thus offering an easy method of propagation. New plants can also be raised in spring from seed sown outdoors in pots.

Flowering period: July
Height: 1–2 ins.

Sempervivum allionii Nym.
Native to the Alps. The rosettes are 1 in. in diameter, pale green, with the leaves slightly hairy and tipped with red. Flowers yellow.

(Cobweb Houseleek)
Flowering period: July
Height: 1 in.

Sempervivum arachnoideum L.
Native to the mountains of Southern Europe. Small reddish $\frac{3}{4}$-in.-wide rosettes covered with white cobweb-like threads. Flowers reddish pink.

Flowering period: July
Height: 1 in.

Sempervivum ciliosum L.
Native to Bulgaria. Grey-green 2-in.-wide rosettes with incurved leaves. Flowers yellow.

Flowering period: Aug.
Height: up to 1 in.

Sempervivum pittonii Schott
Native to Syria. Very hairy, $1\frac{1}{2}$-in.-wide rosettes with dull green leaves. Flowers yellow.

Flowering period: July
Height: 2–3 ins.

Sempervivum ruthenicum L.
Native to Europe. Rosettes $1\frac{1}{2}$ ins. wide with relatively long slightly hairy leaves; green shading to purple-brown towards the tips. Flowers yellow with crimson filaments.

(Hen-and-Chickens)
Flowering period: July
Height: 2–3 ins.

Sempervivum soboliferum L.
Native to Austria. The Hen and Chickens sempervivum, so called because the central rosette is generally surrounded by numerous small young rosettes coloured green shaded copper-red. Rosette $1\frac{1}{4}$–$1\frac{1}{2}$ ins. wide. Flowers yellow.

(Common Houseleek)
Flowering period: July
Height: up to 2 ins.

Sempervivum tectorum L.
Native to Europe. Frequently found on the roofs of old houses and in walls. Rosettes 3–4 ins. wide. Flowers reddish purple. The var. *calcareum* has glaucous green leaves tipped with purple.

Sempervivum zeleborii Schott *Flowering period: July*
One of the most attractive Asiatic species with 3-in.-wide grey-green *Height: up to 2 ins.*
rosettes shaded purple. Flowers crimson and purple.

Senecio

(RAGWORT OR GROUNDSEL)
Family: Compositae
Hardy or half-hardy herbaceous perennials and annuals and half-hardy or tender shrubs and climbers
Position: sun or shade according to the species
Propagation: seed, division, or cuttings
Cultivation easy

The genus *Senecio* is one of the largest in the vegetable kingdom—some authorities consider it to be *the* largest—comprising more than 1,300 species distributed throughout the entire world. With a few notable exceptions it is also one of the least interesting for garden purposes; however, these exceptions represent plants of enormous ornamental value and include some of our best garden and greenhouse plants. Senecios vary so much in habit and in every other respect that it is strange the genus has not been divided by the ever-active botanists, who are generally so ready to create new genera.
To the ordinary gardener it seems inconceivable that the beautiful florists' cineraria *(Senecio cruentus)*, the obnoxious weed *Senecio vulgaris*, Groundsel (so loved by canaries), the lovely yellow-flowered non-hardy climber *Senecio angulatus*, the popular silver-leaved *Senecio Cineraria* (syn. *Cineraria maritima*), and the tree-like *Senecio johnstonii*—which grows at an altitude of 12,000 ft. on Mt. Kilimanjaro—should all belong to the same genus. A few years ago the genus was even larger and included plants now classified as *Ligularia* and *Jacobaea* (which for simplicity are here referred to as senecios with the newer name given as a synonym).
Although so large, the genus *Senecio* has remarkably few associations in history, mythology, literature, or legend; and none of the species have ever made headlines as sensational new introductions discovered by famous botanical explorers. It is also significant that the Museum of Economic Botany at the Royal Botanic Gardens at Kew does not catalogue a single example of any species having economic value. The genus has, however, had considerable medicinal importance in both the official materia medica and in folk medicine. In ancient times *Senecio aureus* was used in treating consumption in

Senecio cruentus (Cineraria hybrida)
From an original watercolour by Giovanna Casartelli, 1968

its early stages, and it has also been used as a tonic. Preparations from *Senecio jacobaea* have been prescribed to relieve coughs, influenza, catarrh, sciatic and rheumatic pains, and ophthalmic inflammation. The common *Senecio vulgaris* has been employed in the preparation of a purgative and emetic. The silver-leaved *Senecio maritima* has been used in the preparation of eye drops for treating cataracts.

The name of genus *Senecio* is derived from the Latin *senex* (old man), and refers to the white or grey hair-like appendages (pappus) attached to the seeds. Among the true senecio species, the dominant colour of the flowers is yellow. Cultural directions will be given separately for each species.

Senecio clivorum Maxim. (syn. *Ligularia clivorum*)

Herbaceous perennial
Flowering period: June–Aug.
Height: up to 3 ft.
Position: shade or partial shade

Native to Japan and China. A very hardy herbaceous perennial up to about 3 ft. high when in bloom. The more modern generic name, *Ligularia,* derives from the Latin *ligula* (strap) and refers to the shape of the external ray flowers—commonly referred to as petals, although they are actually ligules—found around the circumference of the flower head. These, along with the central tubular disc flowers, make up the complete inflorescence. This is a magnificent plant of large proportions and rapid development; it is most effective when planted in big informal masses. Requires semi- or complete indirect shade in a deep, cool, moderately moist fertile soil. Leaves heart-shaped, dark green, very robust, up to 1 ft. in diameter. The profuse flowers are carried on tall rigid vigorous stems well above the level of the foliage. The individual flowers are up to 3 ins. in diameter, single, daisy-like, orange with a brownish centre. The var. *Othello* has greenish-purple foliage, and var. *hessei* has yellow flowers borne on branching stems up to $5\frac{1}{2}$ ft. high. Propagation is by division in autumn or spring, or from seed sown in March–April in pots, flats, or boxes in coldframes or in an unheated greenhouse.

Senecio cruentus L. (syn. *Cineraria cruenta*)

(Cineraria)
Annual
Flowering period: May–July
Height: up to 18 ins. or more
Position: partial shade

Native to the Canary Islands. A non-hardy annual in the case of the modern hybrid cineraria, although the original species is sometimes perennial (occasionally a hybrid can be induced to live for several years—although the best flowers are produced the first year from plants raised from seed). *Senecio cruentus* is the parent of the florists' hybrid cinerarias, of which there are numerous forms. It is doubtful, however, if the true species is now in cultivation, and the present-day hybrids are often collectively referred to as *Cineraria hybrida*. The true species is an attractive plant up to $1\frac{1}{2}$ ft. high when in flower. Leaves triangular or heart-shaped, up to 8 ins. long, dentated, with undulated edges. Inflorescence large, wide, loosely formed, and composed of numerous clusters of small reddish purple single daisy-like

flowers 1 in. in diameter in May–July. It is, however, a species variable in its flower colours and in the shape and size of its foliage.
The popular garden cinerarias are the results of crosses between the various forms of the species and between the hybrids themselves. The present-day types in cultivation are:

> var. *grandiflorus,* height 12–15 ins. with a dwarf compact habit and large closely borne together flowers up to 2 ins. in diameter carried only slightly above the foliage. This variety is available in almost every colour
>
> var. *intermedius,* a strain intermediate in height and size of flower between the two other types. Available in the same wide range of colours
>
> var. *stellatus,* up to nearly 3 ft. high with an upright open habit and small star-like flowers $1-1\frac{1}{2}$ ins. in diameter, in an almost unlimited range of colours

Seed of all the above is available in a mixture or in separate colours. In the case of the *grandiflorus* and *intermedius* types there are also bicoloured flowers. In all these varieties, the leaves are dark green, triangular or heart-shaped, with a length varying from 6–12 ins. The foliage of the *stellatus* type is smaller than that of the other forms.

Cultivation. Florists' cinerarias are normally cultivated as non-hardy annuals. They are certainly not tropical plants, and they should be grown under temperate conditions since excessive heat weakens them. Seed can be sown at any time between May and July, according to when the plants are required to bloom. Seed is generally sown in flats, pots, pans, or boxes in a moderately heated greenhouse and germination takes about ten days. When large enough to handle conveniently—generally when the seedlings have 2–3 minute leaves—they can be potted individually into pots with a diameter of 2 ins. and kept in a lightly shaded greenhouse. When root action is well established, transfer the pots to a shaded frame outdoors, where they can remain until autumn (or even later in mild localities, but they must never be subjected to frost). During this period the frames should be covered when there is any bad weather. It is essential, however, that the plants have an abundance of air and indirect light. While in frames, it will be necessary to repot the plants as they develop (probably 2–3 times) until the final repotting into pots with a diameter of 6–7 ins. When the outside temperature becomes too low, and when the plants begin to produce flowers, they can be removed to a warm greenhouse where the blooms will develop, but at no time should the temperature exceed 60°–65°F. External temperature permitting, it is best to leave the plants in frames for as long as possible to ensure healthy, robust, vigorous specimens. The best moment to move the plants to a greenhouse is when the flower buds

Senecio maritima

are actually showing signs of colour. From seed sown in May, flowering plants can be expected in December–January. Seed sown later will produce flowering plants from late winter until spring according to the date of sowing. A normal interval between sowing and flowering is about 7–8 months, which means that if flowering plants are required for bedding out in the garden in April the seed should be sown in July–August. The flowering date can, of course, also be controlled by the date the plants are taken into the greenhouse. A suitable soil mixture for pot-grown cinerarias is:

  5 parts fibrous loam
  2 parts well-decomposed leafsoil
  1 part peat
  1 part fairly coarse sand

To each pailful of compost add a 5-in.-diameter potful of bone meal. As the plants develop they should be fertilized periodically with an organic liquid plant-food, such as manure-water or dried blood dissolved in water, or a commercial preparation, following the manufacturer's instructions. These applications should cease when the plants begin to bloom.

Senecio elegans L. (syn. *Senecio purpureus, Jacobaea elegans*)
Native to South Africa. A non-hardy annual with a compact bushy habit. Leaves oblong, dentated, and deeply lobed; $4\frac{3}{4}$ ins. long, $2\frac{1}{2}$ ins. wide, dark green, sticky surfaced. Inflorescence borne on a tall erect stem well above the foliage with a loose, open form and composed of numerous reddish-purple daisy-like flowers with yellow central discs. The petals are arranged in a somewhat irregular and uneven manner, sometimes close together and sometimes wide apart. Each flower is about $1\frac{1}{2}$ ins. in diameter. A very attractive plant which has been in cultivation since 1700 and one of the easiest summer-flowering annuals. Requires a warm sunny position in a fertile soil that is moderately dry. There are also several good forms:

  var. *albus,* white
  var. *purpureus,* dark purple
  var. *roseus,* pink

All are excellent for cutting. There are also double-flowered forms in each colour. For the most effective display, it is better to grow this senecio in a mixture of colours. Seed may be sown directly into the flowering position in April, or in pots, pans, or flats in coldframes or in an unheated greenhouse in March. The young plants should be planted into their flowering positions in April–May.

Senecio greyii Hook. f.
Native to New Zealand. An evergreen shrub, 9–10 ft. high in its native habitat but in gardens generally about $3-4\frac{1}{2}$ ft. high. Loose,

(Purple Ragwort)
Annual
Flowering period: July–Sept.
Height: up to 2 ft.
Position: sun

Senecio greyii

Evergreen shrub
Flowering period: June–Sept.
Height: up to 10 ft.
Position: sun
Zone 8 southwards

open, rounded habit with a diameter of up to 12–15 ft. in the case of old specimens. Hardy in all except very cold zones. The entire plant—with the exception of the upper surface of the leaves—is covered with a soft white felty down. Leaves oblong-ovate, 2–4 ins. long, $1\frac{1}{4}$–$2\frac{1}{4}$ ins. wide; dark green on the upper surface with the margins white. Inflorescence a terminal panicle up to 6 ins. long and $4\frac{1}{2}$ ins. wide composed of many individual daisy-like blooms 1 in. in diameter, vivid yellow in colour. A remarkably beautiful plant which from June to September makes a lovely display with its yellow and white colouring. Particularly indicated for seaside localities in a hot, sunny, moderately dry position in any normal garden soil. Seed should be sown in a temperate greenhouse in March–April, or cuttings may be taken of half-ripened wood and inserted in frames in July–August.

Evergreen shrub
Flowering period: June–July
Height: up to 9 ft.
Position: sun
Zone 9 southwards

Senecio hectori Buch.–Ham.
Native to New Zealand. Introduced into Europe in 1910. A beautiful evergreen shrub hardy only in mild localities. Habit loose, open, somewhat disorderly. Leaves very irregular in size and shape, narrowly oval or lanceolate, lobed at the base, dentated, 3–9 ins. long, $1\frac{1}{2}$–$4\frac{1}{2}$ ins. wide, grey-green on the upper surface, undersurface covered with silky white hairs. The young vegetation also has a wool-like silky covering. Inflorescence a flat rounded terminal corymb up to 10 ins. in diameter composed of masses of white daisy-like flowers 2 ins. wide. Conspicuous among shrubby senecios for its large irregularly shaped leaves. Requires a hot, sunny position in a moderately dry, not-too-rich soil. Excellent for seaside localities. Propagation as for *Senecio greyii*.

Herbaceous perennial
Flowering period: July–Sept.
Height: up to 5 ft.
Position: partial shade

Senecio japonicus L. (syn. *Ligularia japonica*)
Native to Japan. A hardy herbaceous perennial up to 5 ft. high when in bloom. Leaves rounded-oval, 12 ins. in diameter, and divided into about eleven segments. Inflorescence and general aspect similar to *Senecio clivorum,* but differing in its divided foliage and later flowering, the orange-yellow blooms appearing from July to September. Requires an abundance of moisture at its roots, even thriving in almost boggy positions, and prefers at least partial shade. Propagation as for *Senecio clivorum*.

Herbaceous perennial
or sub-shrub
Flowering period: July–Sept.
Height: up to 3 ft.
Position: sun

Senecio maritima L. (syn. *Senecio Cineraria, Cineraria maritima*)
Native to the Mediterranean regions. A non-hardy herbaceous perennial often grown as an annual. This is the popular silvery-white-leaved senecio widely used for summer bedding. It is a beautiful plant by itself, and is also good when associated with vividly coloured flowers such as geraniums (pelargoniums) or *Salvia splendens*.

In a mild climate the plants can be left permanently outside, and they will then eventually assume almost shrub-like proportions with a woody stem. Where winters are cold—more than a few degrees below 32°F.—it is necessary to replant every spring. The inflorescence is composed of typical daisy-like single flowers about $\frac{1}{2}$ in. in diameter, brilliant vivid yellow, borne up to twelve together in the form of a corymb on a tall rigid leafless stem. When the plants are cultivated for their beautiful foliage, however, the flowers should not be allowed to form and should be removed as soon as they appear. This will give the plant a more compact form and ensure more of the silvery leaves. The foliage is 6 ins. long, 2 ins. wide, and so deeply cut and divided that each of the 10–12 segments have the appearance of separate leaflets. The leaf is more cut at the base than at the top, and the lower segments are smaller. Both leaves and stems are completely covered with a beautiful silver-white film which is present on both the upper and lower surfaces of the foliage and is more conspicuous when the leaves are dry. This is a plant that requires full sun in a moderately dry position, but it is not particular about soil so long as there is a good supply of organic material available. Excellent for seaside localities and for very alkaline (calcareous) soils. Propagation is from seed sown in a warm greenhouse in January–February, growing on the young plants in pots for planting outside in April–May; or by means of cuttings from soft or slightly mature growths taken in September and inserted in pots of sand in a coldframe or greenhouse. An interesting new introduction which can be raised from seed and treated as an annual is a dwarf form var. *Dwarf Silver,* which has all the characteristics of the typical form but is only 9 ins. high and has more finely divided foliage.

Senecio multibracteatus L.
Native to South Africa. A non-hardy annual species up to $2\frac{1}{2}$ ft. high when in flower. A plant of exceptional beauty, elegance, grace and charm, which, although cultivated in gardens since 1872, has never become widely known. I remember that many years ago it was extensively grown at the La Mortola Botanic Gardens, Ventimiglia, Italy, in beds and as pot plants, and it remained in bloom from June to September. The leaves are small, lanceolate, 2–3 ins. long, narrow, and deeply lobed. Inflorescences borne on tall erect branching stems and composed of masses of small daisy-like flowers bright mauve-pink in colour with a yellow central disc; each flower is $3\frac{1}{2}$ ins. wide. Propagation is from seed sown in pots in a warm greenhouse in March. Seedlings should be grown on in individual pots and planted out in their flowering positions in April–May. In warm climates they can also be sown directly into their flowering positions in March–April. Requires a warm sunny position in deep, fertile, moderately alkaline (calcareous) soil.

Annual
Flowering period: June–Sept.
Height: $2\frac{1}{2}$ ft.
Position: sun

Evergreen climber
Flowering period: Oct.–Nov.
Height: up to 20 ft.
Position: sun

Senecio scandens Don (syn. *Senecio angulatus*)
Native to the Far East. A non-hardy, vigorous, rampant climbing shrub. Evergreen in a warm climate, but in colder districts it will lose its leaves in winter and may even die down to ground level, revegetating again in spring if the roots have not been frozen. A beautiful climber widely used in Riviera gardens—for training over walls, summer-houses, etc.—where it remains in bloom from October to April. In slightly cooler locales the flowering period is October–November. It is, in fact, one of the most conspicuous of flowering plants during the late autumn. Leaves small, bright apple-green, dentated, $2\frac{1}{2}$–3 ins. long. Flowers are produced in the greatest profusion; they are vivid yellow, daisy-like, single, 1 in. in diameter, and borne in compact panicles that cover the entire plant. Seed should be sown in a warm greenhouse in February–March, and grown on in pots until large enough for planting out in a permanent position; may also be propagated by cuttings of half-ripened wood taken in July–August and rooted in a warm greenhouse.

Herbaceous perennial
Flowering period: June–Aug.
Height: up to 6 ft.
Position: shade

Senecio veitchianus Hemsl. (syn. *Ligularia veitchiana*)
Native to China. A hardy herbaceous perennial up to 6 ft. high when in flower. Leaves heart-shaped, up to 2 ft. in diameter. Flowers golden-yellow. Apart from its larger proportions, it has all the characteristics of *Senecio clivorum,* requiring the same cultural treatment and propagated in the same manner. It is a truly noble plant, almost monumental in size, and it is ideal for naturalizing where there is an abundance of space for its development. Most effective when grown in individual isolated groups and not mixed with other herbaceous perennials.

Silene

(CATCHFLY OR CAMPION)
(*Also see* LYCHNIS)
Family: Caryophyllaceae
Hardy herbaceous perennials and biennials, or annuals
Position: sun or partial shade
Propagation: seed or division
Cultivation very easy

This is a vast and variable genus of 320 species with comparatively few of garden value, although some are among the most popular of all garden plants. Certain species exude a sticky substance from the

Silene pendula var. *rosea*
From *Curtis's Botanical Magazine*,
1790, plate 114

stems wherein flies are often caught, hence the common English name Catchfly. In gardens the best-known silenes are the varieties of *Silene pendula,* annuals widely used for planting in beds as a background for tulips and other spring-flowering bulbs, where they form a dwarf, compact, free-flowering ground cover. Annual silenes are also excellent as summer-flowering plants in beds, borders, the rock-garden, in large receptacles, or for edging. All are of the easiest cultivation in any soil, but object to excessive moisture. They are distributed throughout the temperate zones of Europe and North America. Propagation is generally by means of seed or division—fuller details are here given under each species.

(Cushion Pink)
Herbaceous perennial
Flowering period: May–June
Height: 1–1½ ins.

Silene acaulis L.
Native to the northern temperate zones. A minute little plant ideal for the rock-garden or for cultivation in pans, pots, flats, etc. Forms a compact moss-like cushion of bright green vegetation, which in May–June is covered with masses of tiny pink flowers. There is also a white-flowered form var. *alba.* Requires a well-drained sandy soil in a sunny position. Propagation is by means of seed sown in pots, outside or in frames, in spring; prick out the seedlings before planting them in their permanent positions.

(Sweet William Catchfly or None-So-Pretty)
Annual
Flowering period: June–Aug.
Height: 18–24 ins.

Silene Armeria L.
Native to Southern Europe. A most attractive summer-flowering annual species which has been a favourite in gardens for many years. Masses of dark pink ½-in.-wide flowers are borne in terminal clusters on stems 18–24 ins. high. Leaves up to 3 ins. long, broadly lanceolate, glaucous green. Most effective when massed in beds or borders. Often found naturalized in the United States. There is also a white-flowered var. *alba.* Seed may be sown directly in the flowering position in spring.

(Wild Pink)
Herbaceous perennial
Flowering period: May–June
Height: 6–12 ins.

Silene caroliniana L.
Native to the eastern United States. A herbaceous perennial species with a slender erect habit. Leaves up to 5 ins. long, broadly lanceolate. Flowers ¾ in. in diameter, pink or white, borne in rather sparse terminal clusters. Can be propagated by division in autumn or spring, or from seed sown outside in frames or seed beds in July. Of easy cultivation but prefers partial shade in a deep, well-drained, fertile, humus-rich soil.

Annual
Flowering period: Apr.–July
Height: 6–8 ins.

Silene pendula L. (syn. *Silene rosea*)
Native to the Mediterranean regions. The many annual hybrids and varieties of this species are widely used as dwarf compact free-flowering bedding plants for spring and summer display. If required for early-spring flowering, seed should be sown in July in frames or seed

beds. Prick out the seedlings into nursery beds a few weeks prior to planting out in their flowering positions in autumn. Some very lovely effects can be obtained by associating the pink-flowered silene with white- or purple-flowered tulips (in the same way that blue forget-me-nots combine so beautifully with yellow- or pink-flowered tulips). The silene must, of course, be planted before the bulbs. If these annual silenes are required for summer-flowering, seed should be sown in an unheated greenhouse or coldframe in early spring. Leaves broadly lanceolate, dark green. Flowers about $\frac{1}{2}$ in. in diameter borne in loose pendulous clusters. Numerous attractive varieties are available, such as:

    var. *alba*, pure white
    var. *alba flora plena*, double white
    var. *bijou*, double-flowered salmon-pink
    var. *Bonnettii*, magenta-pink
    var. *carnea*, pale pink
    var. *rosea*, pink
    var. *rosea flora plena*, double pink
    var. *ruberrima*, purple-pink

Silene schafta L.
Native to the Caucasus. A handsome perennial species of particular value for its later-flowering habit, remaining in bloom until October. This is a dense, spreading 6-in.-high plant excellent for edging or for the rock-garden. Flowers are a lovely shade of purple-pink. Propagation by division in autumn or spring, or from seed sown in frames in July, growing the seedlings on until they are ready for planting out in the autumn.

(Moss Campion)
Herbaceous perennial
Flowering period: July–Oct.
Height: 6 ins.

Sinningia

(GLOXINIA)
Family: Gesneriaceae
Tender perennial tubers
Position: partial shade
Propagation: seed or cuttings
Cultivation rather difficult

The best-known sinningia is the species *Sinningia speciosa* (syn. *Gloxinia speciosa*). In the past it was widely grown as a pot plant,

Sinningia speciosa

but now it is superseded by the strain of magnificent hybrids—popularly known as gloxinias—which are widely cultivated in greenhouses, as temporary house plants, and, to a lesser extent, as summer-flowering subjects for beds in the garden. The flowers are delicate, however, and not resistant to bad weather, their general cultural requirements in the garden being the same as those indicated for tuberous begonias. During recent years gloxinias have been increasingly exploited commercially, and in flower shops they are often as common as cyclamens. They are native to Brazil and Burma, and therefore not hardy.

The propagation of gloxinias from seed is a fascinating operation, and the young plants can be expected to bloom within 7–8 months from the date of sowing. Seed should be sown in a greenhouse in January, at a temperature of not less than 68°F. An excellent soil mixture for seed-sowing, and for subsequent potting on of the young plants, can be prepared with equal parts of peat, leafsoil, and sand. The seedlings should be potted on when their first leaves are 1 in. long, using pots with a diameter of $2-2\frac{1}{2}$ ins. When a quantity of vigorous roots have been formed—generally after about two months—the plants can be repotted into larger pots with a diameter of 5–6 ins. After the flowering has finished the leaves will gradually begin to turn yellow, indicating the approach of the dormant period, and the water supply should be gradually and progressively reduced and eventually stopped as the tubers become dormant. They must then be kept dry until March (leaving them in the pots), when they should be repotted and watered, lightly at first but gradually increasing as growth develops. When facilities are not available for raising gloxinias from seed, tubers of flowering size may be bought in early spring and started into growth as explained above. These will flower earlier than plants raised from seed. At all times gloxinias require a warm, moist, semi-shady position. During their growing period they should be given fortnightly doses of an organic liquid fertilizer such as dried blood dissolved in water.

Two interesting and beautiful plants occasionally offered in bulb catalogues are:

> *Gloxinia maculata insignis,* a non-hardy tuberous-rooted perennial excellent for greenhouse cultivation or for use as a temporary house plant. It has very decorative large bronze-green leaves, and in autumn produces big sky-blue sweetly scented tubular flowers. Height $2\frac{1}{2}$ ft.
>
> *Gloxinia tubiflora* (syn. *Achimenes tubiflora*), a tuberous-rooted herbaceous perennial; non-hardy, but excellent for the greenhouse or for use in the garden during the summer months. Flowers elongated-tubular, fragrant, white with a wax-like texture, and borne on erect stems up to 3 ft. high.

Sinningia hybrida
From *Paxton's Magazine of Botany*,
1838, plate 219

Flowering period: July–Sept.
Height: 8–12 ins

Sinningia speciosa Benth. & Hook. (syn. *Gloxinia speciosa*)
Native to Brazil. Introduced into Europe in 1817. A non-hardy tuberous-rooted plant with semi-pendulous narrow tubular flowers, violet-purple in colour and produced in late summer. Height 8–12 ins. Leaves rather fleshy, dark green, dentated, ovate, up to 6 ins. long and 4 ins. wide. Apart from being raised from seed, as explained above for the hybrids, it may also be propagated by means of leaf cuttings taken at any time during the vegetation period and inserted in sand in a warm greenhouse.

Sinningia Hybrids
Spectacular plants with wide, oval, velvety, rich green foliage, bearing very large flowers up to 4 ins. in diameter at the mouth. Flowers are tubular shaped but with wide, opened mouths and velvet texture. They have an extensive range of colours, red, purple, pink, and white, and some have beautiful colour combinations in the same flower. These are all the results of a long series of crosses and repeated hybridization that have evolved from the original species. A brief selection of the best includes: Blanche de Meru, purple-pink and white; Emperor Frederick, scarlet and white; Emperor William, blue and white; Étoile de Feu, carmine-red; Montblanc, white.

Solanum

Family: Solanaceae
Tender shrubs, climbers, herbaceous perennials, or annuals
Position: sun or partial shade
Propagation: seed
Cultivation mostly easy

This vast and variable genus of more than 1,000 species is perhaps of greater interest to the vegetable garden than to the flower garden. About twenty species are of ornamental value for their flowers, fruits, and foliage (but they cannot compete in importance with plants such as the potato—one of the world's most important food crops and a plant that has even changed history—whose botanical name is *Solanum tuberosum,* and the eggplant or aubergine, *Solanum Melongena*). Some species such as *Solanum dulcamara* and *Solanum carolinense* are of medicinal value, while many are weeds of no horticultural interest. In many species, some part of the plant is poisonous while other parts are edible or possess medicinal properties as indicated by the generic name, which is of Latin origin, *solari* (to give relief), indicating that the substances they contain have narcotic and sedative action.

Because of the number and diversity of the species, cultural details and methods of propagation are given here separately for each species. In general, most species are of only limited hardiness, and as can be inferred from their various places of origin, many do not tolerate even the slightest frost. Here, we confine our observations to those species of major importance to flower gardens in warm climates. All of those discussed below can be considered as some of the most beautiful plants to cultivate in such localities.

Solanum Capsicastrum Link

(Winter Cherry or Star Capsicum)
Evergreen shrub
Flowering period: Aug.–Sept.
Height: 18 ins.
Zone 10

Native to Brazil. For winter decoration indoors this is one of the most popular of all pot-grown plants, especially at Christmas, when the masses of scarlet berries borne in such abundance among the small dark grey-green leaves are so welcome. The plants form miniature evergreen shrubs which in warm localities can also be grown outside, although they will not survive frost. The flowering period is August–September and the small white blooms also have considerable attraction. The plants detest a hot, dry atmosphere, particularly when in fruit, and this is one of the reasons why indoors the plants often shed their berries and foliage prematurely. Dryness at the roots is also very harmful. During the summer, pot-grown plants are happier placed outside in a semi-shady position. To ensure a good crop of berries moderate pruning is necessary in spring, which is also the best time for repotting, in a soil mixture rich in humus and well-decomposed organic material. Propagation is from seed sown in a warm greenhouse in February.

Solanum Capsicastrum

Solanum crispum

Evergreen shrub
Flowering period: July–Aug.
Height: up to 15 ft.
Scented
Zone 10

Solanum crispum Ruiz & Pav.

Native to Chile. Introduced into Europe in 1830. One of the most beautiful and graceful of all large shrubs for the frost-free garden. Plants develop rapidly into large specimens with an open, spreading habit, and, if planted against a wall, they can be trained as a climber. Evergreen or semi-evergreen according to the winter temperature. The large alternate foliage is ovate, tapering to a point. The individual purple-blue fragrant flowers with yellow centres are abundantly produced throughout the summer in long-stalked corymbs. The var. *autumnale* is later-flowering and remains in bloom until October or even later. Moderately severe pruning is advisable in early spring to encourage vigorous young growths that will bear the flowers. *Solanum crispum* will thrive in a poor but well-drained soil, but it requires an abundance of sun in a warm position. Propagation is from seed sown in a warm greenhouse in spring, or by means of cuttings taken in July and rooted in sand in a heated greenhouse.

Evergreen climber
Flowering period: June–Sept.
Height: up to 35 ft.
Zone 9 southwards

Solanum jasminoides Paxt.

Native to Brazil. A fast-growing evergreen or semi-evergreen slender climber of great elegance and charm which, in localities such as the Riviera, Florida, and California—where it is known as the Potato Vine—is widely used to train on the walls of houses and over summer-houses. The clusters of very pale blue flowers are abundantly and continuously produced from early summer until autumn. Plants will thrive in almost any fertile soil—even that which is very alkaline (calcareous)—in a hot, moderately dry, sunny position. The foliage is dark green, up to 2 ins. long, and $1\frac{1}{4}$ ins. wide. Propagation is by means of seed sown in a warm greenhouse in spring, or from cuttings of half-ripened wood taken in July–August and rooted in an unheated greenhouse or in a closed coldframe. It is the least tender of all the garden solanums and will withstand occasional very light frost.

(Jerusalem Cherry)
Evergreen shrub
Flowering period: Aug.–Sept.
Height: up to 2 ft.
Zone 10

Solanum Pseudocapsicum L.

Native to tropical and semi-tropical regions. In general appearance very similar to *Solanum Capsicastrum,* requiring the same cultural treatment, and even more widely used as a temporary house plant for its decorative winter-borne orange-scarlet berries, but with shiny dark-green foliage. Fruits rounded, $\frac{1}{2}$ in. wide; flowers white, $\frac{1}{2}$ in. in diameter. Propagation as for *Solanum Capsicastrum.*

Deciduous shrub
Flowering period: Aug.–Oct.
Height: up to 12 ft.
Zone 10

Solanum rantonnettii Carr.

Native to Argentina. When I first saw this graceful deciduous shrub about forty years ago in the Hanbury Botanic Garden in Ventimiglia, Italy, it so impressed me with its beauty that I have never forgotten it, and I have never ceased to wonder why it is not more widely cultivated in gardens with a Riviera-type climate. The plant was literally covered with violet-purple flowers, $\frac{3}{4}$–1 in. in diameter, each with a conspicuous orange-yellow eye. Leaves light green, up to 3 ins. long and half as wide. Can be grown outdoors only in a mild climate, but it is very easy and not particular about soil, even thriving in that which is very alkaline (calcareous), but it requires warmth and sun. Propagation is from seed sown in a warm greenhouse in spring, by means of soft cuttings in May rooted in a warm greenhouse, or from cuttings of half-ripened growths taken in June–July and rooted in a closed frame.

Solanum seaforthianum Andr.
Native to Barbados. A spectacular semi-evergreen or evergreen climber with large clusters of 1-in.-wide purple-blue flowers borne in cymes from June to November. Leaves divided into segments of unequal size, entire leaf up to 7 ins. long. Fruits scarlet, about the size of a pea. Suitable only for a hot, dry, sunny position preferably against a wall. Widely grown in Riviera gardens and in gardens of tropical and sub-tropical America. Propagation from seed sown in a warm greenhouse in spring, or by means of soft cuttings taken in spring and rooted in a greenhouse.

Evergreen climber
Flowering period: June–Nov.
Height: up to 15 ft.
Zone 10

Solanum wendlandii Hook. f.
Native to Costa Rica. A vigorous evergreen or semi-evergreen climber with attractive clusters of 2-in.-wide lilac-blue flowers throughout the summer and autumn. Leaves compound, the central segment the largest; entire leaf up to 8–9 ins. long. Stems slightly spiny. In a warm climate there are few flowering climbers more spectacular for so long a period. Cultural requirements and method of propagation as for *Solanum seaforthianum*.

(Costa Rica Nightshade)
Evergreen climber
Flowering period: June–Oct.
Height: up to 20 ft.
Zone 10

Solanum jasminoides

Solanum seaforthianum

Solidago

(GOLDENROD OR AARON'S ROD)
Family: Compositae
Hardy herbaceous perennials
Position: sun or shade
Propagation: seed or division
Cultivation very easy
Useful for cutting

Only two species of genus *Solidago* are indigenous to Europe: *S. Virgaurea* L., and *S. serotina* Ait. The remainder are all native to North America. The name *Solidago* derives from the Latin *solido* (to make whole), because it was thought that the plant had the virtue to rejuvenate and heal. *Solidago Virgaurea*, a handsome perennial found in thin woodlands and alpine meadows, has been widely used in folk medicine; the yellow flowers were gathered to make an infusion for the treatment of kidney inflammation, and a decoction was also used in poultices applied to festering wounds—all very useful properties, but as a flowering plant for the garden the species is not worth much.

For many years *Solidago Virgaurea* and its American counterparts were neglected or forgotten by hybridists and florists. This oblivion was partly justified by the fact that the majority of goldenrods were looked upon as little more than weeds; in some cases even as invasive pests. One day, however, the hybridist H. Walkden took an interest in goldenrod and became convinced that attempts to improve the genus would be crowned with success. He dedicated the next twenty years of his career to realizing his conviction. The final results were a selection of hybrids worthy of serious attention, and today, under the name of *Solidago* x *hybrida*, they are considered excellent perennials for the garden (see below).

It is interesting to note that a goldenrod has also been crossed with a perennial aster, and the resulting intergeneric group of hybrids has been given the name of *Solidaster*. The best of these is *Solidaster luteus*, a really good garden plant with narrow aster-like leaves and graceful yellow flowers in September–October. Height $2\frac{1}{2}$ ft., and an excellent subject for the herbaceous border.

Cultivation. Goldenrods and solidasters are of the easiest cultivation, and flourish in sun or shade and in any type of soil. The flowers of all the varieties are excellent for cutting, and because of their light feathery character are ideal for mixing with larger heavy flowers such as dahlias. Propagation is by seed sown outside in spring, or by division either in spring or autumn.

Solidago hybrid

Solidago caesia L. (Wreath Goldenrod)
Native to the eastern United States and extending westwards to Texas. Leaves lanceolate, up to 5 ins. long, dentated. Stems smooth, blue-green in colour. Inflorescences borne in the leaf axils and composed of clusters of small yellow flowers.

Flowering period: July–Sept.
Height: up to 3 ft.

Solidago sempervirens L. (Beach or Seaside Goldenrod)
Native to the eastern United States, westwards to Texas. Found in coastal or swampy localities, even tolerating salty sandy soils near the sea. Leaves elongated ovate, up to 10 ins. long, rather thick and fleshy, not dentated; stems stout and rigid. Inflorescence a large branched terminal panicle composed of many small individual yellow flowers. A somewhat coarse plant but an excellent herbaceous perennial for seaside gardens.

Flowering period: June–Sept.
Height: up to 8 ft.

Solidago Virgaurea L. (European Goldenrod)
Native to Europe. A very vigorous, even rampant herbaceous perennial somewhat variable in form and habit. Inflorescence a flat plate-like raceme of small yellow flowers; better known and more widely grown in its dwarf form var. *nana,* which is 12 ins. or less high with a rosette of basal foliage and terminal heads of yellow flowers. An excellent little plant for small beds or for the front of a herbaceous border.

Flowering period: July–Sept.
Height: 3 ft.

Solidago Hybrids
A group of garden hybrids which includes the best of the genus and comprises numerous really excellent hardy herbaceous perennials such as:

> Ballardii, 2 ft. high, with much-branched sprays of vivid golden-yellow flowers in August–October
>
> Goldenmosa, up to 3 ft., with fluffy mimosa-like bright yellow flowers from August onwards, foliage yellowish-green
>
> Golden Wings, up to 6 ft., with branching sprays of rich yellow flowers
>
> Lesale, $2\frac{1}{2}$–3 ft., of very erect habit and excellent for cutting; flowers light yellow

Sophora

Family: *Leguminosae*
Hardy or half-hardy evergreen or deciduous shrubs or small trees
Position: sun
Propagation: seed or cuttings
Cultivation easy

A genus of shrubs and small trees with elegant pinnate foliage and blooms which, in some cases, recall the inflorescences of wisteria on a smaller scale. Some species also have very decorative fruits with long capsules contracted between one seed and another to form a necklace-like chain. (Certain of the fruits also appear to have medicinal value. Some years ago the Lister Institute of Preventive Medicine in London requested that I send them large quantities for experimental purposes; the pulp surrounding the seeds contains the alkaloid known as sophoria, a substance believed to be of use for treating diabetes.)

Sophoras are native to Southern Asia, New Zealand, Chile, and North America. *Sophora tetraptera* is indigenous to both New Zealand and Chile, a factor of considerable significance in the study of world plant distribution.

Cultivation. Sophoras are plants of easy cultivation, thriving mostly in all but very cold localities. They require a deep, moderately dry, not-too-heavy well-drained soil in a sunny position. The shrubby species can be propagated from seed sown in a cool greenhouse in

Sophora tetraptera
From *Curtis's Botanical Magazine*,
1791, plate 167

spring, or by means of cuttings taken from half-ripened wood in July and inserted in sandy soil in frames. The tree-like species are propagated from seed sown outside in spring or autumn.

Deciduous shrub or small tree
Flowering period: June
Height: up to 20 ft.
Zone 5 southwards

Sophora affinis Torr. & Gray

Native to Texas and Arkansas. A small deciduous tree with a compact rounded head. Leaves pinnate, composed of 13–19 leaflets. Flowers white suffused with pale rose and borne in slender racemes. Fruit an elongated pod, each seed in its own compartment (which is formed by the constriction along the length of the pod between one seed and another). At one time a type of ink was made from the resin exuded from the ripe black fruits. An interesting and attractive small tree worthy of wider use.

(Japanese Pagoda Tree)
Deciduous tree
Flowering period: July–Aug.
Height: up to 60 ft. or more
Zone 4 southwards

Sophora japonica L.

Native to China and not to Japan as the specific name suggests. A deciduous tree of generous proportions. In gardens cultivated more often as a large shrub, particularly in the case of the weeping form, var. *pendula,* one of the most beautiful of all leguminous trees. Rich green pinnate leaves up to 10 ins. long composed of 9–15 leaflets. Inflorescence in the form of a miniature wisteria-like pendulous raceme 8–10 ins. long and composed of numerous cream-white flowers. A superb long-lived tree excellent for planting as an isolated individual specimen, when it can attain really vast proportions. The fruits are also ornamental, and of medicinal value as mentioned above. The weeping form is obtained by grafting pendulous growths onto the normal erect form, and when fully developed the resulting plants make a most attractive arbour.

(Mescal Bean)
Evergreen shrub or small tree
Flowering period: June–July
Height: up to 20 ft.
Scented
Zone 8 southwards

Sophora secundiflora Lagasca.

Native to Texas and Mexico. A large evergreen shrub or small tree. Leaves up to 6 ins. long, pinnate, with seven or nine obovate 1–2-in.-long leaflets. Flowers violet or violet-blue, 1 in. long, borne in 3-in.-long racemes on the new season's growths; strongly fragrant with a violet-like perfume. A most desirable plant, but not hardy in non-tropical climates, although it flowered in Madrid in 1797.

(Kowhai)
Evergreen shrub
Flowering period: June–July
Height: up to 18 ft.
Zone 8 southwards

Sophora tetraptera Mill.

Native to New Zealand and Chile. A large beautiful erect shrub, evergreen in a mild climate. The growth of the branches has a curious contorted zigzag habit, and the small elegant fern-like foliage is most attractive. The 2-in.-long very beautiful golden-yellow tubular flowers are borne in pendulous clusters. Requires a hot, sunny position in a light, well-drained soil. Introduced into Europe in 1772 from New Zealand.

Sophora viciifolia Hance.
Native to China. An attractive deciduous shrub of rounded habit and modest proportions, rarely more than 10 ft. high, with slightly spiny branches. Fern-like pinnate foliage with 7–10 pairs of leaflets. Flowers blue and white, with the shape of miniature Sweet Pea blooms, borne in racemes in early summer. A small shrub of great elegance, charm, and floral beauty. Requires a hot, moderately dry, sunny position.

Deciduous shrub
Flowering period: June–July
Height: up to 10 ft.
Zone 4 southwards

Spartium junceum

(SPANISH BROOM OR WEAVER'S BROOM)
Family: Leguminosae
Half-hardy deciduous shrub
Flowering period: June–Sept.
Height: 5–10 ft.
Position: sun
Propagation: seed
Cultivation very easy
Fragrant
Zone 7 southwards

The genus *Spartium* is monotypic, with only a single species and one variety. It is often confused with the genera *Cytisus* and *Genista*, to which it is related; but it is a much later-flowering plant. The single species, *Spartium junceum* L., is a large deciduous shrub of tall, erect, rather gaunt habit with glabrous dark green stems which—in the almost complete absence of foliage—fulfil the functions of leaves. The few leaves produced are small, simple, and linear. Flowers 1 in. long, of the typical leguminous pea shape, rich vibrant yellow, fragrant, and disposed in terminal racemes up to 12–16 ins. long on the current season's growths, making it one of the most strikingly beautiful flowering shrubs during the period June–September. It is native to Southern Europe and very widely planted in California, where it blooms almost continuously throughout the year. *Spartium junceum* is an ideal subject for planting in hot, dry, sunny positions in poor soils—including those which are alkaline (calcareous)—and fine effects may be obtained by associating it with dwarfer flowering shrubs such as cistus or ulex, which hide the less attractive basal parts of the spartium. There is also a double-flowered form, var. *plenum* (which has to be propagated by grafting on to the original species), introduced into England in 1746 by Peter Collinson, who purchased it in Nuremberg, noting that "it cost me a golden ducat." A particularly strong and resistant fibre is sometimes obtained from the stems, and is used in the manufacture of rope. Propagation is by seed sown either directly into the flowering position or in small pots in spring. (See page 1242 for colorplate.)

Specularia

(VENUS'S LOOKING GLASS)
Family: Campanulaceae
Annuals
Position: sun or partial shade
Propagation: seed
Cultivation easy

Making a garden is, in a certain sense, creating a work of art. A work of art which can be created by anyone possessed with a sense of observation and patience. On more than one occasion we have attempted to call our readers' attention to the close ties that should link our gardens to the surrounding woods, fields, and countryside, and to illustrate that the end of a garden should mark the beginning of its blending into its surroundings. Those environs ought to serve as an extension to, or prolongation of, the garden proper. In other words, a garden should not compete with nature but should give emphasis to certain aspects of nature. For this transition it is necessary to observe carefully nature's methods and to note the spontaneous association of plants in nature. Geraniums, dahlias, and zinnias would certainly not harmonize or help link the garden to its surrounding environment, but there are numerous plants that seem to completely fit in a spontaneous, natural manner, and that are equally appropriate to the garden and to rural and informal settings. They include subjects such as yellow *Linaria vulgaris,* blue nigella, red field poppies, white daisies, pink digitalis, and the lovely purple-flowered *Specularia Speculum Veneris*.

The genus *Specularia* was created by Heister in 1748 and by some authorities is now referred to as *Legousia,* after Legouz de Gerland. It comprises about a dozen species, six of which are indigenous to the Mediterranean regions, and five to North America. They are modest little plants closely resembling campanulas, and ideal for the rock-garden, small beds and borders, for cultivation in pots, and for naturalizing in the semi-wild garden. The most attractive is *Specularia Speculum Veneris,* the so-called Venus's Looking Glass.

Cultivation. Specularias are easy and simple plants to cultivate. Seed

Spartium junceum
From *Curtis's Botanical Magazine*,
1789, plate 85

may be sown outside in pans, flats, pots, or boxes in September, or in frames or seed beds. The seedlings will be ready for planting out in March and will then bloom in May or June. September-sown seedlings produce strong, bushy, compact plants. Seed can also be sown directly into the flowering position, or into pots, in March, and flowering will then begin in June. Seed sown between mid-June and mid-July will produce flowering plants for the autumn. Specularias are not fussy about soil, but they prefer a semi-shady, cool, moist position (in the north they can also be grown in full sun).

Flowering period: summer–autumn
Height: 8–12 ins.

Specularia Speculum Veneris D.C. (syn. *Legousia Speculum Veneris, Campanula Speculum*) (See page 1247 for colorplate)
Native to Central and Southern Europe, North Africa, and Western Asia. Mostly found in fields or meadows and in cultivated land, where it will increase so rapidly that it may even become invasive. Stems erect, occasionally prostrate, smooth, branching, and generally angled. Basal leaves ovate, wider at the tip; upper leaves elongated or lanceolate. Flowers borne in terminal racemes and short-stalked. Individual blooms up to 1 in. in diameter, dark violet and paler externally; some are occasionally white or lilac-coloured. Unlike most of the Campanulaceae, the flowers are flat instead of bell-shaped. The shape of the corolla has been likened to that of a hand mirror complete with handle, thus giving rise to both its common and specific names. This attractive little plant has been cultivated in European gardens since the sixteenth century, possibly even longer. There are several popular varieties: var. *alba,* white-flowered; var. *flora plena,* double-flowered; var. *procumbens,* with a trailing habit.

Spiraea

(*Also see* ASTILBE)
Family: Rosaceae
Hardy deciduous shrubs
Flowering period: spring–autumn
Position: sun or partial shade
Propagation: seed or cuttings
Cultivation very easy

Spiraea, from the Greek *speira* (a coil), was the name used by the ancients for a plant whose branches were used to make garlands and crowns. Clusius wished to identify *Spiraea salicifolia* with this name.

It had been sent to Vienna from Silesia by a certain Sibesius, apothecary to the Duke of Brieg. The plant was not cultivated in England before 1640, but it was that year in which John Parkinson described "the salix spikes of Theophrastus and of Clusius" from hearsay, without ever having seen it. Twenty-five years later *Spiraea salicifolia* was widely diffused throughout the British Isles, where it was commonly known as *Spiraea frutex*. Today it is naturalized in many places.

The nineteenth-century botanical author (*Flora Historica*) Henry Phillips gave an affecting and magniloquent description of *Spiraea salicifolia,* noting that the plant grows "spontaneous in the desert to console the Moscovite lawbreakers, whom a tyrannical, despotic government sent to waste the flower of their youth in the desolate regions of Siberia". *Spiraea salicifolia* is native to Eastern Europe and Asiatic Russia, and is a somewhat rampant 6-ft.-high plant with pinkish-white flowers borne in 4-in.-high, 2-in.-wide terminal panicles. But this Asiatic species was soon neglected in favour of the newer and more intensely colourful American introductions. A bad exchange, comments Alice M. Coats, "because the pink and red hues of the genus were thus extended to the flaming tints of aniline dyes".

The first pink-flowered American species to be introduced to Europe was *Spiraea tomentosa,* in 1736. Then *Spiraea menziesii* arrived from America in 1838, and it is suspected by some authorities to be a natural hybrid (*Spiraea douglasii* x *Spiraea salicifolia*) and not a true species. In 1870 *Spiraea japonica* was introduced from Japan, and it eventually gave rise to the var. *Anthony Waterer,* which has remained one of the most popular forms since its introduction in 1890. In 1864 Karl Johann Maximowicz introduced the dwarf species *Spiraea bullata* from Japan. The first white-flowered species to be brought to Europe was *Spiraea hypericifolia,* so called because it has perforated foliage similar to that of *Hypericum perforatum.* It appears to have been cultivated prior to 1640, and various improved varieties have been derived from it. In the middle of the sixteenth century, *Spiraea chamaedryfolia* appeared in European gardens, and it is believed that in Kamchatka Peninsula in the Soviet Union its leaves were used as a substitute for tea. In 1845, Robert Fortune introduced *Spiraea prunifolia flore pleno,* which enjoyed great popularity in China and was frequently planted on tombs. Around 1863 the Chinese species *Spiraea thunbergii* was introduced (the species *S. henryi* and *S. veitchii* are also of Chinese origin).

The history of spiraeas ends here. They have not ever made headline news, and have never had much to say for themselves. However, they were and still are a problem to botanists, who apparently cannot decide whether there are 50, 54, 70, or 75 species. Nearly all are mountain plants, native mostly to the cool, fresh climates of the

Northern Hemisphere: Asia, reaching as far west as the Himalayas, North Africa as far south as the Sahara, and North America as far south as Mexico.

Cultivation. The cultivation of spiraeas is child's play. They are completely hardy and will tolerate the most polluted atmosphere of cities, with their smog and exhaust fumes. The plants will succeed in full sun, although in a hot, dry climate they prefer partial shade. They do not spurn good living and fully repay a place in soil which is fresh, deep, and rich in humus. Seed can be sown outside in spring; however, as a method of cultivation this is not to be advised since it is tedious and the seedlings can be a disappointment. Propagation should be effected by dividing the basal growths or suckers which generally appear freely round the parent plants, or by means of soft cuttings taken in spring and rooted under glass, or from cuttings of half-ripened wood taken in July and inserted in frames. Early-flowering species, such as the double-flowered form of *S. prunifolia plena* and *Spiraea thunbergii,* can be cultivated in pots and forced into bloom early in the year. A nineteenth-century account of this method explains how it is done: "For this type of culture all that is necessary is to choose some good, well-formed plants in autumn; pot them in a light soil, taking care to firmly press the soil round the roots. Place the potted plants in a heated greenhouse at a temperature of about 65°F., when growth and an abundant flowering will soon occur. By repeating this procedure it is possible to have plants in flower all the winter." Some varieties flower on the new season's wood and some on the old growths, so the necessary indications for pruning are given separately for each species.

Flowering period: June–July
Height: up to 12 ft.
Zone 5 southwards

Spiraea aitchisonii Hemsl. (syn. *Sorbaria angustifolia* Zabel)
Native to Afghanistan and Kashmir. Discovered by Dr. Aitchison in 1879. A vigorous erect shrub with an open, expanding habit. The bark of new growths is reddish. Leaves are pinnate, 10–16 ins. long, composed of up to twenty narrow pointed leaflets 2–4 ins. long and $\frac{1}{4}$–$\frac{1}{2}$ in. wide, dentated, glabrous, and opaque green. Inflorescences branched pyramidal panicles 12–18 ins. long, 10–12 ins. wide, composed of great quantities of small white flowers. A species to be recommended for the beauty of its foliage and for its spectacular blooms. Pruning necessary only if it is desired to keep the plants to a limited size, in which case this should be done at the end of winter or in early spring.

(Garland Spiraea)
Flowering period: Mar.–Apr.
Height: up to 7½ ft.
Zone 4 southwards

Spiraea arborea Bean (syn. *Sorbaria arborea* C.K.S.)
Native to China. A vigorous shrub; in its native state it will reach a height of up to 30 ft., but in gardens it is generally about half that height. Leaves pinnate, 12–18 ins. long, composed of up to seventeen oblong-ovate dentated pointed leaflets 2–4 ins. long, $\frac{1}{2}$–$\frac{3}{4}$ in. wide.

Inflorescence a pyramidal panicle 12–16 ins. long, formed of a great many minute white flowers. A most effective almost monumental plant seen to best effect when massed and allowed to develop completely naturally in a semi-wild condition. This is essentially a plant for large gardens or parks. It prefers deep, fresh, fertile soil. Can be pruned at the end of winter.

Spiraea x *arguta* Zabel
Believed to be of hybrid origin, a result of crosses between the species *S. thunbergii, S. crenata,* and *S. hypericifolia.* A shrub with a rounded much-branched compact habit. Branches slender and erect, leaves oblong-lanceolate, slightly dentated, $\frac{3}{4}$–$1\frac{1}{2}$ ins. long, $\frac{1}{4}$–$\frac{1}{2}$ in. wide, bright green, and glabrous. Flowers white, $\frac{1}{3}$ in. in diameter, with slender $\frac{1}{2}$-in.-long stalks, borne in groups of 4–8 along the entire length of the previous season's growths, always on the upper surface, forming a spray of blooms up to 12 ins. long. Certainly one of the most beautiful, if not the most beautiful, of all spiraeas. Pruning may be necessary to keep the plant to a certain size or to ensure a good shape and should be done immediately after flowering.

Flowering period: June–July
Height: up to 15 ft.
Zone 5 southwards

Spiraea assurgens Bean (syn. *Sorbaria assurgens*)
Native to China. Introduced into Europe in 1900 by Vilmorin. An erect shrub of symmetrical form. Leaves pinnate, 12–15 ins. long, composed of up to seventeen lanceolate dentated pointed leaflets 2–3 ins. long. Inflorescences in the form of narrow pyramidal terminal panicles up to 1 ft. in length. Individual flowers minute, white, with conspicuous stamens. Pruning should be done at the end of winter or in early spring.

Flowering period: June–July
Height: up to 12 ft.
Zone 5 southwards

Spiraea bullata Maxim. (syn. *Spiraea crispifolia*)
Native to Japan. One of the smallest of the spiraeas, and very different from most others, with a maximum height of about 18 ins., in contrast to the almost tree-like proportions of the Sorbaria section of the genus *Spiraea*. It is a compact dwarf shrub of erect rounded habit with widely ovate dentated leaves up to $\frac{3}{4}$ in. long and half as wide; dark green in colour. The inflorescences are flat branched corymbs $2\frac{3}{4}$ ins. in diameter, borne at the ends of the current season's growths. Individual flowers are minute, pinkish red, and produced so freely that they completely cover the entire plant. No pruning is necessary. This charming little shrub is well-suited to the larger rock-garden, for small beds, or for massing in front of a mixed border. The specific name *crispifolia* refers to the crinkled crenated leaf surface.

Flowering period: June–July
Height: 12–18 ins.
Zone 6 southwards

Spiraea canescens Don (syn. *Spiraea flagelliformis*)
Native to the Himalayas. Introduced into European gardens in 1837. In its native habitat it reaches a height of up to 15 ft., but in gardens

Flowering period: June
Height: up to 15 ft.
Zone 5 southwards

Specularia Speculum Veneris
From *Curtis's Botanical Magazine*,
1789, plate 102

it is generally of more modest proportions. Leaves small, oval, dentated, tapering towards the base, $\frac{1}{2}$–2 ins. long, $\frac{1}{3}$–$\frac{1}{2}$ in. wide; opaque grey-green on the upper surface, grey and woolly beneath. Inflorescences terminal corymbs up to 2 ins. in diameter composed of a great many minute cream-white flowers. Long, slender, flexible growths up to 3 ft. in length are produced each year, and the following season they bear the lateral short-stalked inflorescences along their entire length, making this one of the most distinctive and attractive species. Prune after flowering. The specific name *flagelliformis* refers to the whip-like branches.

Spiraea chamaedryfolia L.
Native to Southern Europe, Siberia, Manchuria, and Japan. Like many other plants with such a vast area of distribution, this species has numerous geographical forms and varieties with individual characteristics. In general, however, the plant forms a much-branched erect shrub, somewhat disorderly in appearance, with the twigs and branches interlacing. Leaves ovate, dentated, 1$\frac{1}{2}$–3 ins. long and about half as wide; dark green above and glaucous beneath. Inflorescences 1$\frac{1}{2}$-in.-wide corymbs composed of many small white flowers with conspicuous stamens. Suitable for sunny or shady positions but prefers a rather moist soil. Flowers produced on the previous season's growths, so pruning should be done after flowering.

Flowering period: June–July
Height: up to 6 ft.
Zone 4 southwards

Spiraea henryi Hemsl.
Native to China. Named in honour of Professor Henry who discovered it in 1885. It was given a high award by the Royal Horticultural Society in 1934. A shrub with a rather loose, open habit, developing as much in width as in height, with conspicuous red stems. Leaves narrowly oblong, dentated, 2$\frac{1}{2}$–3$\frac{1}{2}$ ins. long, $\frac{2}{3}$–1$\frac{1}{4}$ ins. wide, smaller on the lower branches. The small white flowers are borne in terminal corymbs 2 ins. in diameter on the previous season's growths. To appreciate the full beauty of this species it should be grown as a single isolated specimen with an abundance of space. No pruning is necessary; but if this has to be done to keep the plant to a certain size or to improve its shape, the correct time is after flowering.

Flowering period: May–June
Height: up to 9 ft.
Zone 6 southwards

Spiraea japonica L.f. (syn. *Spiraea callosa, Spiraea fortunei*)
Native to China and Japan and naturalized in Europe and several other temperate regions. An erect-growing shrub of rigid, not very compact habit. Leaves narrowly oval, 2$\frac{3}{4}$–4 ins. long, 1–1$\frac{3}{4}$ ins. wide, dark green, undersurface glaucous. Bark of the stems and branches shiny. Inflorescences dense compact branched flat corymbs—actually several corymbs united together—borne on the current season's growths and composed of many intensely reddish pink

Flowering period: May–June
Height: up to 9 ft.
Zone 4 southwards

minute flowers. Prefers a moderately moist soil and will also thrive in shade. Prune in early spring. There are several excellent varieties:

> var. *alba,* with white flowers
>
> var. *Anthony Waterer,* the best variety, up to $2\frac{1}{2}$–3 ft. with intensely carmine-pink flowers. If removed as they fade the plant will remain in bloom until September or later. A curious characteristic of the plant is that it sometimes produces leaves variegated green and cream-white or completely white
>
> var. *bumalda* (syn. *Spiraea bumalda*), dwarf, 18–20 ins. high, with carmine-pink flowers

Spiraea menziesii    *Spiraea* x *arguta*

Flowering period: July–Aug.
Height: up to 5½ ft.
Zone 6 southwards

Spiraea menziesii Hook.
Naturalized in many parts of North America but of uncertain origin. Some authorities believe it is a natural hybrid between *Spiraea douglasii* and *Spiraea salicifolia*. A beautiful plant with a rigid, erect habit and of great garden value for its late flowering in July–August. Stems maroon-coloured. Leaves widely ovate, dentated at the tips, $1\frac{1}{2}$–$3\frac{3}{4}$ ins. long, 1–2 ins. wide, opaque greyish green. Very conspicuous inflorescences in the form of erect, branched terminal panicles, 4–8 ins. high and borne on the current season's growths. Each inflorescence is composed of a closely packed mass of minute purple-pink flowers. Requires severe pruning at the end of winter or in early spring. The var. *triumphans* is an improvement on the type, with larger and more richly coloured blooms.

(Bridal Wreath)
Flowering period: Mar.–Apr.
Height: up to 6 ft.
Zone 4 southwards

Spiraea prunifolia Sieb. & Zucc.
Native to China. Discovered by E. H. Wilson in the Hupeh province of central China, and introduced into Europe via Japan by Dr. Sie-

Spiraea japonica
From *Curtis's Botanical Magazine*,
1860, plate 5164

Spiraea assurgens
From *The Botanical Register*,
1845, plate 33

bold in 1845. The original species is now rarely grown, having given place to the double-flowered variety *Spiraea prunifolia plena,* which when in bloom is truly spectacular. Forms a close-growing compact shrub with slender arching branches. Leaves ovate, dentated, hairy on the undersurface; 1–2 ins. long, $\frac{2}{3}$–nearly 1 in. wide. Flowers borne in groups of 3–6 on $\frac{3}{4}$-in.-long stalks, packed so close together that they have the appearance of a bachelor's-button-like white flower $\frac{1}{2}$ in. in diameter. The flowering occurs on the previous season's growths, so pruning should be done immediately after flowering has finished.

Spiraea reevesiana Lindl. (syn. *Spiraea cantoniensis*)

Flowering period: June
Height: up to 5 ft.
Zone 5 southwards

Native to China and Japan. The original species with single flowers is rarely seen in gardens today, preference being given to the more attractive double-flowered var. *plena*. Habit expansive and graceful with many slender arching branches. Leaves 1–2$\frac{1}{2}$ ins. long, $\frac{1}{2}$–$\frac{3}{4}$ ins. wide, so deeply dentated that they sometimes appear to be lobed; green above with the undersurface glaucous. The $\frac{1}{3}$-in.-wide white flowers are borne in 2-in.-wide corymbs with stalks up to 2 ins. long. The double-flowered form has flowers $\frac{1}{2}$ in. in diameter. This is certainly one of the best of the spring-flowering spiraeas, its long arching branches of bloom giving a beautiful effect. Prune after flowering.

Spiraea thunbergii Sieb.

Flowering period: Mar.–Apr.
Height: up to 5$\frac{1}{2}$ ft.
Zone 4 southwards

Native to China. An exceptionally hardy easily grown shrub with a much-branched graceful habit and many slender almost cord-like growths. Often greater in width than in height. One of the best-known and most widely planted species, it is spectacular in spring when covered with masses of pure-white flowers. It is the earliest-flowering spiraea, but unfortunately the flowers are of very brief duration. Leaves linear, light green, pointed, 1–1$\frac{3}{4}$ ins. long, less than $\frac{1}{4}$ in. wide. Before the leaves appear, the small flowers are borne in corymbs on the previous season's growths. The plant has a naturally pleasing compact habit and pruning is not necessary. If this has to be done for the sake of space, the operation should be carried out immediately after flowering.

Spiraea x *vanhouttei* Zabel

Flowering period: Apr.–May
Height: up to 6 ft.
Zone 4 southwards

Of hybrid origin (*Spiraea trilobata* x *Spiraea cantoniensis*), raised in 1862 in the nursery of Billiard at Fontenay-aux-Roses near Paris. A slender-branched graceful shrub with arching stems. Leaves obovate, occasionally three-lobed, dentated, $\frac{3}{4}$–2 ins. long, $\frac{1}{3}$–1 in. wide, dark green above, glaucous beneath. Inflorescence a 2-in.-wide umbel composed of many small white flowers, borne towards the tips of the previous season's growths. Pruning is not necessary, but if because of space it must be done, it should be done immediately after flowering.

Flowering period: June–July
Height: up to 12 ft.
Zone 6 southwards

Spiraea veitchii Hemsl.
Native to China. Discovered by E. H. Wilson in 1900. A vigorous shrub with arching graceful stems which in a single season can reach a length of over 3 ft. Leaves obovate, $\frac{2}{3}$–2 ins. long, $\frac{1}{3}$–$\frac{2}{3}$ in. wide. Inflorescences dense corymbs $2\frac{1}{2}$–$2\frac{3}{4}$ ins. wide composed of a mass of small white flowers borne along the entire length of the previous season's growths. Prune after flowering.

Staphylea

(BLADDER NUT)
Family: Staphyleaceae
Hardy deciduous shrubs
Position: sun or partial shade
Propagation: seed or cuttings
Cultivation easy

Among the many shrubs that bloom in late spring, the staphyleas should not be forgotten. They are plants recommendable for their profuse flowers borne in dense cream-white racemes, and for their elegant pinnate foliage, which is also attractive for its autumn-colouring. Another interesting characteristic of the genus is the fruit; a swollen membranous capsule containing 2–3 seeds.

The name of the genus *Staphylea* is derived from the Greek word *staphylē* (bunch). The genus is indigenous to most of the northern temperate zones. *Staphylea pinnata* can be found wild in Europe and Asia Minor, the species *S. colchica* is found in the Caucasus, *S. emodi* in the Himalayas and Afghanistan, and in China can be found *Staphylea holocarpa,* one of the few species with pink flowers, while *Staphylea bumalda* is native to Japan. Crossing the Pacific we find the species *S. bolandieri* in Western North America, and *Staphylea trifolia* is native to the Atlantic Coast of the United States.

Staphyleas are of the easiest cultivation, resistant to severe cold, and with few demands about soil. In the north they will thrive in full sun, but in the south they give better results in partial light shade. Propagation is by means of seed sown outside in spring or autumn, or from cuttings of half-ripened wood inserted in coldframes in July.

Staphylea pinnata

Staphylea colchica Stev.
Native to the Caucasus. The most handsome species, with stiff erect branches. The white flowers are borne in erect panicles often 6 ins. long. The large inflated seed capsules can be up to 4 ins. in length, and are most decorative in late summer. Often cultivated in large containers so that it can be forced into bloom early in the year. Sometimes referred to as False Pistachio. The attractive leaves are composed of 3–5 elongated-ovate leaflets up to $3\frac{1}{2}$ ins. long with only the terminal leaflet stalked.

Flowering period: May–June
Height: up to 9 ft.
Zone 4 southwards

Staphylea pinnata L.
Native to Europe and Asia Minor. Leaves pinnate, with up to seven leaflets. The white flowers are borne in pendulous terminal panicles up to 4 ins. long, and the $1\frac{1}{2}$-in.-long, rounded seed capsule in the form of a bladder contains one or two pea-sized seeds. It is recorded that in 1596 the plant grew wild in the centre of London in the Strand. The white pendulous inflorescences composed of $\frac{1}{2}$-in.-long individual flowers have given rise to the common name, Job's Tears.

Flowering period: May–June
Height: up to 12 ft.
Zone 4 southwards

Staphylea trifolia L.
Native to the eastern United States. Leaves invariably composed of three ovate leaflets up to 4 ins. long, with the terminal leaflet stalked. Inflorescences in the form of 2-in.-long pendulous panicles bearing white bell-shaped flowers. Seed capsules up to $1\frac{1}{2}$ ins. long with one or frequently no seeds.

Flowering period: May–June
Height: up to 12 ft.
Zone 3 southwards

Sternbergia lutea

(YELLOW STAR FLOWER, LILY OF THE FIELD, OR WINTER DAFFODIL)
Family: Amarylliadaceae
Hardy perennial bulbs

The only species we include from this genus is a small bulbous plant with flowers similar to a crocus. Sternbergias are another of those bulbs so suitable for naturalizing in grass, for those who love a semi-wild garden. The genus consists of only four species, with a distribution confined to the European Mediterranean zones and Asia. The name commemorates Count Moritz von Sternberg, a botanist who lived in Prague in the sixteenth century.

Sternbergia lutea
From *Curtis's Botanical Magazine*,
1795, plate 290

Sternbergia cultivation is very easy. They prefer a rather moist soil in partial or complete shade, and once planted may be left undisturbed indefinitely, unless one desires to propagate them by division. The bulbs should be planted during their dormant period in July. This month is also the correct time for lifting, dividing, and replanting. They are hardy in all but the coldest localities.

Sternbergia lutea L.
Native to Asia Minor, but naturalized in various parts of Central and Southern Europe and in the Mediterranean regions. One of the most beautiful of all autumn-flowering bulbs. The vivid yellow crocus-like flowers appear in September–October, while the narrow shiny dark-green leaves are produced in spring. The bulbs remain completely dormant during the summer, when they should be planted or replanted and established in positions where they may remain undisturbed for many years. They are particularly effective arranged at the base of big trees. Another delightful effect can be obtained by planting the bulbs underneath trees of *Prunus subhirtella autumnalis,* whose pale-pink flowers open when the sternbergia is in bloom.

Flowering period: autumn
Height: 6 ins.
Position: shade
Propagation: division
Cultivation very easy

Styrax

(SNOWBELL)
Family: Styracaceae
Hardy deciduous shrubs
Position: sun or partial shade
Propagation: seed or cuttings
Cultivation easy
Fragrant

Like rhododendrons, styrax are shrubs or small trees that require an acid soil rich in organic matter and not too much sun. They also do not require any pruning and they naturally have a most pleasing form. Many of the numerous species are completely hardy and of the easiest cultivation. Their area of distribution includes North America, China, Japan, Korea, Greece, Italy, and Asia Minor. Although they are such attractive plants, relatively few species are widely cultivated either in English or American gardens. Economically, *Styrax Benzoin* is a species well-known for the resin it produces, variously known as gum benzoin, gum benjamin, benzoin, Sumatra benzoin, Siam

Styrax japonica

benzoin, Palembang benzoin. In ancient times it was used as an incense, and later entered the official materia medica as a stimulant and expectorant. It forms part of the ingredients of several popular "balsams" that in Europe are highly esteemed in the treatment of coughs and bronchitis. The gum contains benzoic acid.

Propagation is often prodigally spontaneous, especially in the case of *Styrax japonica,* which flowers so profusely and produces such an abundance of seed that I have frequently seen hundreds of seedlings beneath the branches of large specimens. The seed can, of course, be sown in the open either in spring or autumn. Propagation can also be effected from cuttings taken from half-ripened wood in July and inserted in frames.

Flowering period: May–June
Height: up to 10 ft.
Zone 5 southwards

Styrax americana Lam.

Native to the southeastern United States. Introduced into Europe in 1765. A deciduous shrub with narrowly obovate leaves $1\frac{1}{2}$–4 ins. long, $\frac{1}{2}$–$1\frac{1}{4}$ ins. wide, pointed, with a wedge-shaped base; dark green on the upper surface, paler beneath, and minutely dentated. Flowers white, up to $1\frac{1}{4}$ ins. in diameter, pendulous, generally in groups of four. Fruits oval, $\frac{1}{4}$ in. wide, and covered with grey down. Somewhat similar to *S. japonica,* but rather less hardy and not so attractive as a garden plant.

Flowering period: May–June
Height: up to 15 ft.
Zone 4 southwards

Styrax japonica Sieb. & Zucc.

Native to Japan and Korea. Introduced into Europe in 1862. A large deciduous shrub of elegant form with a close, dense habit and small oval leaves up to $3\frac{1}{2}$ ins. long. The pure-white $\frac{3}{4}$-in.-wide flowers are borne in clusters along the entire length of the slender horizontal branches. The small egg-shaped fruits are $\frac{1}{2}$ in. long, and each contains one seed. These fruits are produced in the greatest profusion, often remaining on the branches long after the leaves have fallen, and frequently germinating spontaneously around the parent plant. Many competent authorities consider this plant one of the most desirable of all hardy shrubs.

Flowering period: May–June
Height: up to 25 ft.
Zone 4 southwards

Styrax Obassia Sieb. & Zucc.

Native to Japan. Introduced to European gardens in 1879. This is one of the most beautiful and striking of all Japanese flowering shrubs or small trees which can be cultivated in European or North American gardens. It has a somewhat narrow, rigidly erect habit with most unusual foliage. On the same plant, and even on the same branch, the leaves can assume a diversity of shapes and sizes—from oval to round, from palmate to lobate—with an average length of 4–8 ins. They are glabrous and green on the upper surface, grey-green and velvety beneath. The delicately fragrant flowers are pure white, 1 in. long, and borne in terminal pendulous racemes 6–8 ins. long.

Syringa

(LILAC)
(*Also see* PHILADELPHUS)
Family: Oleaceae
Hardy deciduous shrubs
Position: sun
Propagation: seed, cuttings, division, or grafting
Cultivation easy
Fragrant
Useful for cutting

To paraphrase François Villon, where are the lilacs of yesteryear? Those superbly colored, exquisitely fragrant flowers were nothing like the pale, insipid forced lilacs one sees in flower shops today. The "lilacs of yesteryear" were enormous almost tree-like specimens weighed down with masses of smallish but intensely scented blossoms. And until about forty years ago they were one of the glories of most old-fashioned English gardens. Now, their very mention is evocative of golden early-summer days which many long to recapture, like the past so beloved by Marcel Proust; times when it seemed that even the most modest garden was graced with a fine old lilac bush, and when during May and June every open window facing the garden invited the characteristic lilac fragrance to fill the room. Not only were lilacs much beloved in English gardens, they were also cherished in France (which produced many of the best hybrid forms) and in Germany as well. The German name for lilac is *Flieder,* a word that to the music-lover immediately brings to mind the second act of Wagner's *Meistersinger* and the famous *Fliedermonolog* of Hans Sachs (or, to the more sentimental-minded, the sweetly sad melodies of Franz Schubert adapted for that perennial operetta favourite, *Lilac Time*).

At one time the name syringa was used for shrubs we now call philadelphus, but Linnaeus changed the nomenclature and chose syringa as the generic name for lilacs. The genus *Syringa* belongs to the same family as the olive and privet (Oleaceae) and comprises about thirty species. Unfortunately, syringa is still used by some people to denote philadelphus, a situation that causes much needless confusion.

Perhaps because of their dominant shade of mauve, purple, or violet blossoms lilacs have often been associated with mourning, melancholy, and death. In some countries it is considered unlucky to introduce branches of lilac blooms into the house. In ancient Persia, lilacs signified desertion or abandonment, and a branch was given by

Syringa Josikaea
From *Curtis's Botanical Magazine*,
1833, plate 3278

lovers to their mistresses when they intended to leave them. An old American and English superstition had it that a girl who wore lilac flowers would never find a husband; while a bunch of lilacs sent to one's betrothed indicated that the engagement was terminated. However, in the language of flowers, the lilac is reputed to have the happier meaning that first love coincides with the spring, when lilacs begin to bloom.

Syringa vulgaris was the first species to be introduced into Europe, arriving from Turkey in the sixteenth century, and was described for the first time by Pierre Bélon, a French naturalist who travelled throughout Europe and the Near East for Cardinal de Tournon, and who published his observations in 1553. The plant was introduced to Vienna in 1562 by Ogier de Busbecq when he returned from his post as Habsburg ambassador to the court of Suleiman the Magnificent. It was also illustrated in the fifth edition (1565) of Matthiolus' *Commentarii,* where the Latin name for lilac made its first appearance. Later, Clusius succeeded in raising some plants from seed sent to him by a certain Dr. Von Ungnad, Busbecq's successor at Constantinople. It is recorded that in England Gerard had a garden full of lilac plants in 1597. *Syringa vulgaris* rapidly naturalized in many parts of Europe, but its true native habitat remained unknown until 1828, when the naturalist Anton Rocher found the plant growing wild in the province of Banat in western Rumania; later it was also found to be indigenous to the Balkans. Some researchers suggest that the plant was found and subsequently cultivated by the Turks when they invaded Greece in 1453. In 1613 white lilac was named for the first time in *Hortus Eystettensis,* but it was not a true white; Parkinson described it in 1640 as "milky-silver with a dash of blue", and observed that at that time it had not yet been introduced into England. In 1659, however, Sir Thomas Hanmer was growing blue and white lilacs, as well as the very rare red variety. A red variety is also mentioned in the catalogue of Edinburgh Physic Garden dated 1683, and the plant was later called Scotch Lilac or var. *purpurea.*

Syringa persica was grown in Persian and Indian gardens in ancient times. If the opinion of sixteenth-century botanists is correct, and if this plant is that identified as blue jasmine by the Arabic physician Serapio, it was first cultivated around 800 B.C. Prior to 1614, the species was introduced into Europe by way of Constantinople by the ambassador of the Venetian Serenissima. We know it was grown in England by John Tradescant, in 1640.

For his classification, Linnaeus chose the form with entire leaves, which is sterile and probably of garden origin. The fertile form, var. *laciniata* (which had been in cultivation since 1672, the date of introduction of the entire-leaved form), was not found in the wild state until as late as 1915, when it was discovered by F. N. Meyer near Kungchow in southwest Kansu province, a region traversed by the ancient trade route between China and Persia, and over which had passed many other botanic introductions from China, such as the peach, apricot, rhubarb, as well as goods such as silk. Until the nineteenth century, the two species *S. Vulgaris* and *S. persica* and their varieties were the only syringas known. In 1827, the species *Syringa Josikaea* was introduced into Europe. This species was named in honour of a Hungarian baroness, Rosalie von Josika, as it was she who informed botanists that the species grew wild in certain parts of Hungary. In 1840, Dr. Royle introduced into Europe the species *Syringa emodi* from the Himalayas; and in 1856, the first Chinese species, *Syringa oblata,* was introduced into England by Robert Fortune.

During the Franco-Prussian War—while Nancy was occupied by the Germans—Lemoine initiated his experiments with the genus, trying to create a double-flowered lilac, which would certainly have been a novelty at that time. As one of the parents he selected the var. *azurea plena,* which had double flowers that were very small and widely spaced. The flowers had no stamens and only a few abortive pistils. As Victor Lemoine was very nearsighted, he was obliged to send Madame Lemoine up a ladder to rummage about among the flower spikes in order to find some properly developed pistils so that she could apply the pollen that he had collected from garden varieties and the Chinese species *Syringa oblata.* The first year husband and wife were rewarded with seven seeds; in 1872 about thirty. Three of the resulting seedlings flowered for the first time in 1876. The cross with *Syringa oblata* was named *hyacinthiflora,* while several double varieties were obtained as a result of further crosses and recrosses. The Lemoine firm produced no less than 153 new registered varieties between 1876 and 1927, several of which are still among the most popular lilac varieties. The fact that lilacs withstand cold climates so well has largely contributed to their popularity in Canada; so much so that even in 1833 there was rarely a Canadian garden without a lilac bush. The position occupied in the nineteenth century in Nancy by Lemoine, was taken over during the twentieth century by Canadian nurseries, in particular by the work of Isabella Preston of the Division of Horticulture at Ottawa. In 1920 she crossed *Syringa villosa* with *Syringa reflexa,* obtaining nearly three hundred seedlings that flowered in 1924, creating the race now known as Prestoniae hybrids.

Between the end of the eighteenth century and the beginning of the nineteenth, the importation of Chinese species had become increasingly frequent, and, among others, the following species were introduced by E. H. Wilson for the firm of Veitch and for the Arnold Arboretum: *S. tomentella, S. reflexa,* and *S. sweginzowii,* all of the greatest beauty. According to the opinion of the experts of the time, the possibilities of these Chinese species as parents of garden varieties were scarcely explored.

During 1890–1900 Parisian greenhouses raised vast quantities of white lilac, and a single florist in Paris employed eighty people and eight strong horses and made a profit of over one million francs each season. During those hectic years, the French capital supplied the major cities of Europe with lilacs, and it was possible to buy forced branches at every month of the year. Next to France, the most important producers of forced lilacs on an industrial scale were Germany, the Netherlands, and Denmark. The forcing methods employed at that time were far from simple, and often even dangerous, especially the Danish method that used chloroform and ether. Today, the Netherlands remains the largest producer; in 1957 Dutch lilac cultivation occupied over 275 acres of land at Aalsmeer, on the so-called Lilac Island, with a harvest of about eight and a half million branches annually. However, with the increasingly wide cultivation of other flowers such as tulips, freesias, carnations—which are much less expensive to produce and therefore cheaper to market—the lilac demand is falling off.

At one time, and on a minor scale even today, lilac oil and essence were extracted from the most strongly fragrant species for use in the perfume industry. The wood has no particular value, except for the manufacture of rather poor-quality pipes. The bark and seed capsules of *Syringa vulgaris* contain syringin, a substance once used in folk medicine to combat intermittent fever. The bitter leaves have been used in a tonic and in a liniment for rheumatism.

The most strongly scented species is said to be *Syringa sweginzowii*, and it certainly has a delightful fragrance (which reminds me of a typical English country lane in midsummer, with a trace of new-mown hay). *Syringa vulgaris, Syringa oblata*, and *Syringa pubescens* have a sweeter, more typical "perfume" rather than "fragrance". *Syringa villosa* and *Syringa Josikaea* are almost scentless. Unfortunately, the majority of the large-flowered disease-resistant brilliantly coloured modern hybrids have little or no fragrance; and one should seek out a wild shrub of *Syringa vulgaris* if one wishes to have a scented lilac for one's garden. The flowers may not be spectacular, but their perfume fully compensates for what the eye loses. Bailey wisely suggests that different varieties should not be cultivated near one another, and recommends planting them in isolated groups of individual species and varieties. Those who have a sufficiently large garden are also advised to choose their lilacs in such a way that their combined collective flowering period will be as long as possible.

Cultivation. Syringas will grow in any normal garden soil but they prefer heavy soils rather than those which are very light. The plants like a moderately moist but well-drained position in full sun in the north; in the south they may also be grown in partial shade. To ensure an abundance of bloom the plants should be well fertilized in spring with some well-rotted manure or compost. Otherwise the

Syringa vulgaris
From *Curtis's Botanical Magazine*,
1792, plate 183

plants do not require any special attention, although it is beneficial to remove the old inflorescences before they begin to form seed. Syringas can be planted in autumn or spring.

Propagation of the species can easily be effected from seed sown outside in spring; while both the varieties and the species can be propagated by means of cuttings taken from half-ripened wood in July and inserted in sandy soil in frames, or by means of soft cuttings taken in June and rooted in a greenhouse or under transparent plastic, a glass bell-jar, or in a small propagating case. Many of the species can also be increased by means of the suckers that appear so freely round the parent plant. Commercially, however, the modern lilac hybrids are propagated by grafting in May onto stocks of seed-raised *Syringa vulgaris* or *Ligustrum*. Of the five hundred or so hybrid lilacs which have been grown at one time or another, less than half now remain in cultivation; those with small flower spikes or uncertain colours have gradually been discarded. The most important European collections at present are at Aalsmeer, where two hundred varieties are still grown, and in the botanic garden at Dortmund in Germany. Few nurserymen, however, can now offer more than about thirty.

Syringa emodi Wallich.
Native to the Himalayas. A hardy deciduous shrub with conspicuous greenish-brown bark covered with pale markings. Leaves ovate or oval, 5–8 ins. long, 3–4 ins. wide, pointed at both ends; dark green above, almost white on the undersurface. Inflorescence a branched terminal columnar panicle up to 6 ins. long and 4 ins. wide. Flowers very pale purple or whitish purple, $\frac{1}{3}$ in. long. Blooms produced on the current season's growth. A useful species in the garden for its late-flowering habit.

Flowering period: May–June
Height: up to 12 ft.
Zone 5 southwards

Syringa x *hyacinthiflora* Lemoine
Of hybrid origin. A group of hybrids created in 1911 by Émile Lemoine in his nursery at Nancy. They are early-flowering hardy deciduous shrubs of great beauty, with a height of up to about 15 ft. Their parents were *Syringa oblata* crossed with various forms of *Syringa vulgaris:* some of the best hybrids are Lamartine, Descartes, Necker, Villar, Vuaban, and Claude Bernard.

Flowering period: Apr.–May
Height: up to 15 ft.
Zone 4 southwards

Syringa Josikaea Jacq.
Native to Hungary. A hardy deciduous shrub with glossy oval or obovate leaves 2–5 ins. long, $1\frac{1}{4}$–$2\frac{1}{2}$ ins. wide; dark green above, whitish on the undersurface. Inflorescence an erect terminal panicle up to 8 ins. high and 4 ins. wide composed of many dark lilac-coloured flowers closely and compactly arranged. Individual flowers $\frac{1}{2}$ in. long. Blooms produced on the current season's growth. An

(Hungarian Lilac)
Flowering period: May–June
Height: up to 12 ft.
Zone 4 southwards

interesting and beautiful hybrid of Canadian origin is *Syringa* x *josiflex* Pres. *(Syringa reflexa* x *Syringa Josikaea)*, 10 ft. high, with fragrant pink flowers.

Flowering period: Apr.–May
Height: up to 12 ft.
Zone 4 southwards

Syringa oblata Lindl.
Native to China. A hardy deciduous shrub with conspicuous purple leaf buds. Leaves heart-shaped, greater in width than length, 1½–3 ins. long, 1½–4 ins. wide. Inflorescence a wide branched terminal panicle, generally borne two together on the previous season's growth. Individual flowers pale mauve-lilac, ½ in. long. Botanically allied to *Syringa vulgaris,* but distinguished by its wider foliage and earlier flowering. In autumn the leaves assume a magnificent red tint. There is also a white-flowered form var. *alba.*

Syringa persica

(Persian Lilac)
Flowering period: Apr.–May
Height: up to 8 ft.
Zone 4 southwards

Syringa persica L.
Native to an area extending from Iran to China. A hardy deciduous shrub with a rounded, much-branched, and very dense habit. A shrub of exceptional beauty and one of the most desirable of all spring-flowering shrubs. Old plants develop an overall diameter of up to 12 ft. Leaves narrowly ovate, pointed, green and glabrous above and on the undersurface, 1–2½ ins. long, ⅔–1 in. wide. Inflorescence small branching axillary and terminal 3-in.-long panicles borne on the previous season's growth and completely covering the plant in late April or early May. Individual flowers typical lilac colour, deliciously fragrant, ¼ in. long.

Flowering period: Apr.–May
Height: up to 15 ft.
Zone 4 southwards

Syringa pubescens Turcz.
Native to China. A hardy deciduous shrub often with the proportions of a small tree and a definite head of branches. Leaves ovate,

1–2½ ins. long, ¾–1½ ins. wide, pointed; dark green above, glaucous beneath. Inflorescence a terminal panicle, generally two together, borne on the previous season's growth; 5 ins. high, 3 ins. wide. Individual flowers ½ in. long, pale mauve or almost white, fragrant.

Syringa reflexa Schneid.
Native to China. A hardy deciduous shrub with oblong pointed leaves 4–8 ins. long, 1½–4 ins. wide; dark green above, pale green beneath. Conspicuous grey bark on the older branches. A very distinct species for its pendulous inflorescences in the form of drooping terminal panicles borne on the current season's growth; 10 ins. long and 4 ins. wide. Individual flowers tubular, ⅔ in. long, purple-pink externally, pale pink or white internally; petals reflexed at the mouth, giving a diameter of ⅓ in. Completely different from all other species because of its pendulous inflorescences. Discovered in 1889 by Henry, but not introduced to European gardens until 1910 by Wilson.

Flowering period: May–June
Height: up to 15 ft.
Zone 4 southwards

Syringa sweginzowii Koehne & Lingelsh.
Native to China. A hardy deciduous shrub with the flowers strongly fragrant, and of so unusual and pleasing a scent that it should be planted in every garden. Excellent for cutting. Habit spreading, open, with slender erect branches; bark on the young growths purple-grey. Leaves light green, thin-textured, lanceolate, pointed, 2–4 ins. long, 1–2 ins. wide. Inflorescences borne on the current season's growth in the form of branching erect terminal panicles 8 ins. long and half as wide. Individual flowers mauve-pink externally, pinkish white internally, ⅔–1 in. long.

Flowering period: Apr.–May
Height: up to 12 ft.
Zone 4 southwards

Syringa tomentella Bureau & Franch.
Native to China. A hardy deciduous shrub with oval pointed leaves 3–6 ins. long, 1½–2½ ins. wide; dark green above, glaucous beneath. Inflorescences produced on the current season's growth in the form of loosely formed erect terminal panicles up to 8 ins. long and 5 ins. wide. Individual flowers ⅔ in. long, pale lilac-pink externally and white internally; fragrant. Originally collected in its native habitat in 1891 by Prince Henri d'Orléans.

Flowering period: May–June
Height: up to 15 ft.
Zone 4 southwards

Syringa villosa Vahl.
Native to China. Introduced in 1885 and discovered by the Jesuit priest D'Incarville. A hardy deciduous shrub with a vigorous erect, stiff habit. Leaves elongated oval, pointed at the tips, rounded at the base; 3–6 ins. long, 2–3 ins. wide, dark green above, glaucous beneath. Inflorescences terminal and axillary panicles borne on the current season's growth, generally three together; 6–10 ins. long, 3–5 ins. wide. Individual flowers pinkish lilac, ⅔ in. long. One of the most

Flowering period: May–June
Height: up to 12 ft.
Zone 4 southwards

beautiful and vigorous of species, and one of the most attractive of all flowering shrubs. It has also produced a very lovely race of hybrids known as *Syringa* x *prestoniae (Syringa villosa* x *Syringa reflexa)*. These are of Canadian origin and are the results of many years of devoted work by Isabella Preston. They are notable for their hardiness, vigour, elegant growth, and large inflorescences. Some of the best are:

> Audrey, dark lilac with inflorescences up to 7 ins. long and 6–7 ins. wide, award of merit, R.H.S., 1939
> Hiawatha, reddish purple
> Royalty, violet-purple

(Common Lilac)
Flowering period: Apr.–May
Height: up to 20 ft.
Zone 3 southwards

Syringa vulgaris L.
Native to Europe. A hardy deciduous shrub or even a small tree; much-branched in the case of old specimens, with a woody central trunk up to 2 ft. in circumference. Leaves heart-shaped, 2–6 ins. long, 3–4½ ins. wide; those on the lower branches larger than those on the higher branches. Inflorescences in the form of terminal pyramidal panicles, borne in pairs on the previous season's growth; 6–8 ins. long and half as wide. Individual flowers ⅔ in. long, typically lilac-coloured and strongly scented. A beautiful shrub but now largely replaced by the many superb single- or double-flowered hybrids which are its progeny. Some of the best are:

Single-flowered Hybrids:
> Clarke's Giant, a new American variety, with large lilac-blue flowers in pyramidal inflorescences 12 ins. high. Award of merit, R.H.S., 1958
> Glory of Horstenstein, rich lilac-red changing to dark lilac
> Maréchal Foch, massive panicles and large individual flowers, dark carmine changing to carmine-pink. Award of merit, R.H.S., 1935
> Souvenir di Louis Spath, dark red, one of the best varieties
> Purple Heart, a new American variety with dark-purple flowers (individual flowers up to 1¼ ins. in diameter)
> Jan van Tol, white. Award of merit, R.H.S., 1924
> Reaumur, large dark-crimson inflorescences. Award of merit, R.H.S., 1916
> Primrose, primrose-yellow flowers. Award of merit, R.H.S., 1950
> Madame Francisque Morel, violet-pink
> Massena, dark purple-red. Award of merit, R.H.S., 1928

Double-flowered Hybrids:
> Katherine Havemeyer, purple-lavender. Award of merit, R.H.S., 1933
> Edith Cavell, cream changing to milk-white

Belle de Nancy, purple-red changing to pink
Condorset, lavender-lilac flowers
Madame Antoine Buchner, carmine-pink suffused mauve
Madame Lemoine, white. Award of merit, R.H.S., 1891
President Poincaré, wine-red mauve
President Grevy, lilac-blue. Award of merit, R.H.S., 1892
Miss Ellen Wilmott, white. Award of merit, R.H.S., 1917
Monique Lemoine, white. Award of merit, R.H.S., 1958

Tagetes

(MARIGOLD)
Family: Compositae
Annuals or tender perennials
Position: sun
Propagation: seed or cuttings
Cultivation very easy
Useful for cutting

Searching for the derivation of plant names is far from an easy undertaking. Occasionally even authoritative textbooks are inexact, and some writers simply declare the origins unknown, or they completely ignore the problem. Even when an origin or a source has been discovered, it is often impossible to arrive at any logical conclusion about why the plant was given a particular name, or to decipher the connection between the plant's name and its origin.
Tagetes, for example, is derived from Tages, the boy-god with the wisdom of age who arose from a freshly ploughed field to instruct the Etruscans in the art of haruspicy (divination through the examination of entrails). But to establish the connection between a Mexican flower and an Etruscan deity, one would have to resuscitate Tournefort, who named the genus. Some obscure motive, superstition, or popular legend must exist to unite the flower with this god of divination; especially since in the language of flowers the tagetes (which we will now call marigold—its familiar name) represents divination. We are equally in the dark concerning the origin of the German name for marigolds, *Studentenblumen* (student's flower). It is easier to understand the origin of the common Italian name of *Puzzola* or *Puzzalina,* meaning smelly or malodorous; although I must confess that I am not in agreement with that definition, and personally find the

Tagetes lucida
From *Curtis's Botanical Magazine*,
1804, plate 740

odour of marigolds quite pleasing; it has a robust wildness about it which while possibly offensive indoors, is almost invigorating in the garden. Its odour is revolting, however, when the stalks have become water-soaked and have begun to decompose; then the marigold fully merits one of its common names, the Flower of the Dead.

Throughout the nineteenth century and at the beginning of the twentieth, marigolds were in fashion, no doubt because of their ease of cultivation and the profusion of their flowering. Between the two world wars they fell into disrepute and were mostly used in formal and carpet bedding. During recent years, though, they have staged a spectacular and welcome comeback with the introduction of many superb new forms, types, sizes, and colours, with a flowering season extending from July to December, and (in the case of the smaller varieties) a resistance to bad weather equalled by few other annuals. Their popularity is now so great that for several years one of the major seed firms in the United States has annually offered a reward of 10,000 dollars for a pure-white-flowered form of *Tagetes erecta*, a colour that persistently eludes the hybridists' most skilful efforts. Many gardeners are also discovering how effective the smaller marigolds can be when naturalized or grown in a haphazard informal manner, their bright colours creating unexpected effects when planted at random in semi-wild parts of the garden. As bedding subjects they certainly have no equal; apart from watering, they need little attention to keep them blooming throughout the summer and autumn.

According to Robert Sweet in his *Hortus britannicus*, marigolds were originally imported into Europe in the sixteenth century; from Cibo we have confirmation that they were growing in Italy in 1532. Before the genus was officially named *Tagetes*, the botanist Matthiolus (Pierandrea Mattioli) called them *Caryophyllus indicus*, Indian Pink, because at that time they were thought to be of East Indian origin. All the marigolds now grown in gardens are of Mexican origin. The genus comprises about thirty species, mostly annuals, diffused throughout the warmer regions of the New World from New Mexico and Arizona to Argentina.

Carnation-flowered marigold a hybrid of *Tagetes erecta*

Cultivation. Marigold cultivation is very easy. The plants thrive in any normal garden soil that is reasonably fertile, although if fertilized excessively they produce more foliage than flowers. Above all they require a sunny open position, similiar to their warm, sunny native habitat. A certain amount of water is necessary during hot dry weather, but this should always be in moderation, as marigolds are tolerant of dry conditions. Excess moisture can be harmful to the dwarf very compact types, and can cause them to rot.

Seed should be sown from February to April, according to local climatic conditions, but marigolds are not tolerant of frost. The most convenient method is to sow the seed in pots, boxes, or flats in either a heated or unheated greenhouse or in a frame; plant the seedlings out into their flowering positions as soon as they are large enough to handle. At no time should the seedlings be forced, or subjected to high temperatures, otherwise they will become leggy, weak, and delicate. Germination generally takes place within 8–15 days. Under favourable conditions, marigolds will reproduce naturally from self-sown seed (although hybrids tend to revert to type), and the seed can be sown directly into the open ground in spring after all danger of frost is passed. Also advantageous is that large plants can be transplanted with the greatest ease, even when in bloom. The taller forms are excellent for providing cut bloom and, if their foliage is stripped off and the water is changed daily, they will last up to 12–15 days. The flowers can also be successfully dried for winter use indoors.

Tagetes erecta L.

(African Marigold, Aztec Marigold, or Big Marigold)
Annual
Flowering period: July–Oct.
Height: 8 ins.–3½ ft.

Native to Mexico. An annual with strong, vigorous erect stems, bushy and branching towards the apex. Leaves profuse, brilliant green, elegantly divided into dentated lanceolate segments. Inflorescences 2–4 ins. in diameter, double and voluminous with many petals (ligules), pompon-like, in various shades of yellow, orange, and bronze. The flower buds are conspicuous, bell-shaped, and with longitudinal grooves. The numerous hybrids and forms extend the colour range through many shades of gold, lemon-yellow, and reddish orange. Variously shaped blooms are offered in seed catalogues as Carnation-flowered, Chrysanthemum-flowered, Peony-flowered, etc. The tall varieties are often very bushy and require an abundance of space, and they are sometimes even used to form a type of annual hedge; they can also be most effectively employed in large masses in the mixed border. There are also dwarfer forms only 8–9 ins. high with an excellent compact habit and an exceptionally long flowering period; these are ideal for beds and for edging.

(Mexican or Sweet-scented Marigold)
Perennial normally cultivated as an annual
Flowering period: Aug.–Nov.
Height: 1–1½ ft.

Tagetes lucida Cav.

Native to Mexico. A late-flowering herbaceous perennial generally grown as an annual, and more suited to southern gardens than to the north where summers are of briefer duration. Stems erect, straight, compactly borne to produce bushy plants that are branched at their summit. Leaves either opposite or alternate, lanceolate, entire, evenly dentated and, when crushed, agreeably fragrant with a perfume not at all like the typical marigold odour. Flowers small, only about ½ in. in diameter, with few widely spaced petals (ligules), golden-yellow or orange-yellow, borne in dense terminal corymbs, scented. An easy, free-flowering plant, but not hardy; weather permitting, it remains in bloom until November or later. The most widely cultivated form in gardens is the var. *floridus,* with larger

Tagetes patula
From *Curtis's Botanical Magazine*,
1791, plate 150

flowers bearing only three petals (ligules), and excellent for cutting. The true species is also used for culinary purposes, the young foliage being substituted for tarragon or other aromatic herbs in salads and for flavouring vinegar.

(French Marigold)
Annual
Flowering period: July–Oct.
Height: up to 2¾ ft.

Tagetes patula L.
Native to Mexico. An annual species bearing many glands which if rubbed or crushed give off an unpleasant odour. Stems profusely and widely branched from the base to form dense, shrubby little compact plants with stems often veined in dark violet or reddish brown. Leaves either alternate or opposite, smooth, much cut and divided into linear segments. Flowers solitary, terminal. The unopened buds swollen and grooved, $2\frac{1}{2}$ ins. long. Flowers $1\frac{1}{2}$–$2\frac{1}{2}$ ins. wide with the external petals (ligules) wide-spreading, those of the central disc tubular and small. Unlike the double- and very double-flowered *Tagetes erecta,* it is the single-flowered forms of *Tagetes patula* that are so popular. There are many forms and varieties with a considerable range of size and colour, including bicoloured or even tricoloured forms, mostly in shades of yellow, orange, bronze, mahogany, red, maroon, etc.; some are only a few inches high with either single, double, or crested flowers with an exceptionally long flowering period. Some especially recommendable modern forms are:

    Bolero (bronze medal, All-America Selections 1970)
    Boy Scout (bronze medal, All-Britain Trials 1971)
    Red Glow (silver medal, All-Britain Trials 1970)
    Giant Crested
    Yellow Nugget
    Sparky
    Petite Gold
    Naughty Marietta

(Climbing Marigold)
Annual
Flowering period: Sept.–Dec.
Height: up to 10 ft.

Tagetes sarmentosa
Sarmentosa (literally meaning "climbing" marigold) is a name of convenience used to describe a mystery marigold not available commercially but which periodically makes its appearance in European gardens, and which apparently has never been properly classified. It really does exist, and although I have grown it off and on for about forty years, it has never been given official recognition, some authorities even doubting its existence. That monumental work *Encyclopedia of Annual and Biennial Garden Plants* by C. P. Booth (Faber & Faber, London) does not mention it among the 1,200 plants described. It is an annual, possibly a form of *Tagetes lacera*. Height up to 10 ft., but very tall rather than actually climbing; exceptionally late-flowering, the first blooms produced in mid-September, and continuing until December if not killed by frost—a factor that makes it

more suited to southern than to northern gardens. Width of a single plant up to 3 ft. The habit is loose, open, erect. Flowers not unpleasantly scented, single, $1\frac{1}{2}$ ins. wide; colour rich, vivid golden-yellow with reddish-orange markings but variable; flower stems 10 ins. long, each bearing a solitary bloom. Foliage aromatic. The plant can be used in many ways, but it is particularly effective when it is allowed to intertwine over a tall wooden or plastic trellis, and it is of great value for prolonging autumn colour in the garden.

Tagetes tenuifolia Bartl. (syn. *Tagetes signata*)

(Bush Marigold)
Annual
Flowering period: July–Oct.
Height: $1\frac{3}{4}$–$2\frac{1}{2}$ ft.
Scented

Native to Mexico. An annual marigold forming much-branched bushy compact plants with side growths produced from the ground upwards, and of a graceful, elegant appearance. Leaves either alternate or opposite, small, finely cut, and divided into very narrow delicate segments. Flowers terminal, up to $1\frac{1}{4}$ ins. wide, single, profuse, with 4–5 external petals (ligules) $\frac{1}{2}$ in. long, oval, yellowish marked with orange or dark purple. Nowadays, the original species is rarely grown, its place having been taken by the many hybrid forms of the dwarf form *Tagetes signata* var. *pumila,* some of the most useful of all dwarf annuals, 8–9 ins. high with small single orange, yellow, or lemon-yellow flowers so freely produced that they completely hide the plants. Two of the best are Lemon Gem and Ursula.

Tamarix

(TAMARISK)
Family: Tamaricaceae
Hardy deciduous or evergreen shrubs or small trees
Position: sun
Propagation: seed or cuttings
Cultivation easy

Along the Riviera many visitors often see large, somewhat untidy shrubs or small trees that at first sight might be mistaken for junipers or some other conifer; shrubs with disorderly, grey-green stems bearing minute erica- or scale-like foliage and, at the appropriate season, attractive plumes of pinkish flowers. These belong to the genus *Tamarix,* shrubby trees that thrive in positions where one would least expect a plant to survive, often on cliffs and slopes and among rocks and stones where there is only the shallowest of poor, arid, salty soil. And apparently quite happy to expose their branches to the salt-filled sea breezes.

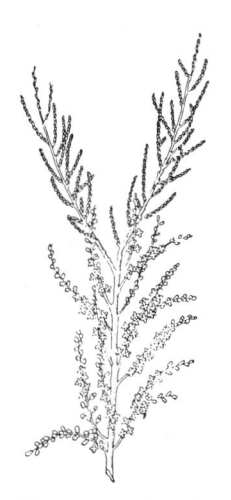

Tamarix tetrandra

When cultivated in gardens, however, tamarisks become rather demanding and require more care and more water. There is an interesting reason for this: some species are native to hot, dry, arid regions where the soil is rich in saline substances. In such places, these salts are absorbed by the plant and prevent excessive transpiration; when these substances are absent from the soil (such as in a garden), and nature's safeguard against too great a loss of moisture no longer exists, a more generous and regular supply of water at the roots becomes necessary. No shrubs are more easily propagated than tamarisks (with the possible exception of willows and forsythias). Cuttings should be made in late autumn of the previous summer's growths, each about the thickness of a pencil, and placed in the soil in a vertical position to a depth of about a third their length. Excellent hedges are often made of *Tamarix anglica* by the simple process of cutting branches about the size of a walking stick from existing plants, sharpening them at the bottom, and pushing them into the ground where the hedge is to be formed. After a reasonable time they sprout and flourish.

The genus *Tamarix* is native to Continental Europe, the Mediterranean regions, and Asia, China in particular. About half a dozen species are grown in gardens, all distinguished by the light, feathery character of the foliage and branches, with very small flowers crowded on short racemes. There are few shrubs whose nomenclature is more obscure and involved; many of the species need microscopic examination in order for their identification to be determined.

(English Tamarisk)
Evergreen shrub
Flowering period: Aug.–Sept.
Height: 5–10 ft.
Zone 5 southwards

Tamarix anglica Webb

Native to the seaside localities of Great Britain and northern France. An evergreen shrub of erect habit and with young wood of a reddish-brown colour. Leaves minute, bright green. Flowers borne in slender racemes, white tinted pink in late summer and autumn. A magnificent shrub for planting in large informal masses.

(French Tamarisk or Salt Cedar)
Evergreen
or semi-deciduous shrub
Flowering period: July–Sept.
Height: 10–15 ft.
Zone 4 southwards

Tamarix gallica L.

Native to northern France and parts of Italy, always found in coastal districts or growing near streams or rivers. In gardens generally 10–15 ft. high, but in hot climates it can reach a height of up to 30 ft. Evergreen or semi-evergreen according to the mildness of the region where it is growing. Habit erect, young growths with a smooth reddish-purple bark. Minute glaucous foliage. Racemes of pink flowers.

(Kashgar Tamarisk)
Deciduous shrub
Flowering period: Aug.–Sept.
Height: 3–4½ ft.
Zone 6 southwards

Tamarix hispida Willd.

Native to Western Asia and the desert areas east of the Caspian Sea. A deciduous shrub distinct from all other cultivated species for the downiness of its young branches and leaves. Habit erect, compact, with small, very glaucous foliage. Flowers bright pink borne in erect racemes. Introduced into cultivation by the Russian traveller and explorer Roborowsky, who originally collected seed near Kashgar in western China and sent them to the famous Lemoine nursery of Nancy. It was first placed on the market in 1893. Its glaucous-white colour, attractive flowers, and late-blooming habit make it a valuable species for the garden.

Tamarix pentandra Pall.
Native to Southeastern Europe and Asia Minor. A large deciduous shrub with long slender plumose branches. Leaves minute, pointed. Flowers densely arranged in slender sometimes branching racemes borne along the entire terminal part of the current season's growths, which during August–September are transformed into huge plume-like panicles of bloom often a yard in length. To obtain a really good crop of bloom, the plants should be severely pruned at the beginning of winter, after flowering has finished. The individual flowers have five stamens.

Deciduous shrub
Flowering period: Aug.–Sept.
Height: 12–15 ft.
Zone 4 southwards

Tamarix tetrandra Pall.
Native to the eastern Mediterranean regions. A deciduous shrub with glabrous, dark-barked, arching branches and minute scale-like leaves. Flowers pink, very small, arranged on slender cylindrical racemes in May on the previous season's growths, and with only four stamens. This is the most common species grown in gardens and is often sold commercially under such names as *Africana, Caspica, Algeriensis, Indica,* and *Parviflora,* names which, in some cases, rightly belong to other species. Among cultivated tamarisks it is distinguished for its early-flowering on the old wood, and for bearing flowers with only four stamens. Introduced in 1821.

Deciduous shrub
Flowering period: May–June
Height: 10–15 ft.
Fragrant
Zone 4 southwards

Tecoma

(Trumpet Creeper)
(*Also see* Campsis *and* Bignonia)
Family: Bignoniaceae
Tender deciduous shrubs
Position: sun
Propagation: seed or cuttings
Cultivation easy

The genus was named *Tecoma* by A. L. Jussieu, who extracted it from *tecomaxochitl,* an Aztec name that means "rose-flower". According to the opinions of different botanists, the genus can also be referred

Tecoma stans
From *Curtis's Botanical Magazine*,
1832, plate 3191

to by several other names, *Pandorea, Tecomaria, Campsis, Podronea, Stenolobium.* All these names are given as synonyms in *Hortus Mortolensis,* the catalogue of plants cultivated in the Hanbury Botanic Gardens, La Mortola, Italy, where, in a lovely Riviera setting, the best European collection of tecomas can be found.

Tecomas are very similar to bignonias, but they have a shrubby, erect habit instead of being climbers. They have pinnate foliage and long-lasting bell-shaped flowers in shades of yellow and orange. The genus comprises five species diffused throughout the West Indies, Mexico, Argentina, Peru, Guatemala, Colombia, and Chile, and in the United States are found in Florida and Texas. The most widely cultivated species, *Tecoma stans,* was introduced into Europe in 1730 by Linnaeus, who named it *Bignonia stans.*

None of the tecomas are hardy, and they can only be grown outside in a frost-free, Florida or southern California type of climate; in such an environment *Tecoma stans* reaches a height of up to 20 ft. and it is one of the most decorative shrubs or small trees for the autumn garden. Because of its rapid development, it is often used for screening, and the flowers are fragrant. Tecomas thrive in a heavy soil containing a percentage of sand to ensure good drainage. They are also excellent subjects for alkaline (calcareous) soils and respond well to generous fertilizing. Propagation can be effected from seed sown in a warm greenhouse in spring, or by means of soft cuttings taken in spring and rooted in a warm greenhouse.

Tecoma mollis L.

Native to Mexico, Chile, and Peru. In many respects similar to the better-known *Tecoma stans,* but covered with fine hairs. Leaves divided into 5–9 leaflets that are oblong-ovate, pointed, only slightly dentated, pubescent on either surface; 2–4 ins. long. Flowers pale yellow, similar to those of *Tecoma stans* but smaller and not scented; all these features tend to make it a less valuable garden plant, although it has the advantage of a long flowering period and it is excellent for cutting, a use not usually indicated for tecomas and similar plants.

Flowering period: Sept.–Nov.
Height: 10–20 ft.
Zone 9 southwards

Tecoma smithii Hort.

Originally introduced into the United States from Australia and believed to be a hybrid raised from *Tecoma mollis* by E. Smith. An attractive erect shrub with irregularly pinnate foliage composed of 11–17 blunt-tipped or pointed oblong leaflets 1–2 ins. long. Flowers borne in large compact racemes up to 8 ins. long and 8 ins. wide; the individual blooms are tubular, funnel-shaped, brilliant yellow suffused orange, with five rounded recurved lobes; each flower up to 5 ins. long. Suitable for outdoor cultivation only in frost-free locali-

Flowering period: Oct.–Jan.
Height: 10–20 ft.
Zone 9 southwards

ties, but it is excellent for use as a pot-grown plant in the greenhouse, where specimens only one year old will bloom in autumn.

Tecoma stans L.
(Yellow Elder)
Flowering period: Sept.–Nov.
Height: up to 20 ft.
Fragrant
Zone 8 southwards

Native to southern Florida, the West Indies, and South America, where it is often known as yellow bignonia. A large erect shrub with irregularly pinnate rather glabrous foliage divided into 5–11, bright green elongated-ovate or lanceolate pointed leaflets 2–5 ins. long. Flowers borne in terminal racemes or panicles; corolla funnel-shaped, bell-shaped at the mouth, rich yellow, up to nearly 2 ins. long, fragrant. The var. *angustata,* native to Texas, Arizona, and Mexico, has foliage divided into 7–11 lanceolate or linear-lanceolate leaflets $1\frac{1}{2}$–3 ins. long and is hardier than the type.

Teucrium

(GERMANDER)
Family: Labiatae
Hardy herbaceous perennials or half-hardy evergreen shrubs
Position: sun
Propagation: division, seed, or cuttings
Cultivation easy

A large genus consisting mainly of herbaceous perennials, plus a few shrubby species; the latter are of major importance as garden plants, but considering their large number (generally believed to be about one hundred) few of the remaining species are of significant decorative or ornamental value. The shrubby *Teucrium fruticans,* in particular, deserves to be much more extensively planted, as it is attractive and useful for many different purposes. Teucrium is closely related to such widely grown herbs as rosemary and lavender; it has opposite leaves and flowers with a corolla tubular at the base but expanding at the mouth into two lips—a characteristic typical of the Labiatae family. Some have aromatic foliage.

The genus *Teucrium* has an area of diffusion that includes Continental Europe and the Mediterranean regions. The name is derived from Teucer, the first king of Troy, who, according to legend, discovered the medicinal virtues of the plants. From the stalks and young foliage of *Teucrium chamaedrys* (germander), a bitter aromatic tea can be prepared which has proved effective in folk medicine in the treatment of rheumatism, intermittent fevers, and scrofula and certain other skin diseases. The plant has also been used for its stimulant, tonic,

Teucrium fruticans
From *Curtis's Botanical Magazine*,
1793, plate 245

diaphoretic, and diuretic actions. In eighteenth-century England, *Teucrium chamaedrys* was an important ingredient in the popular medicine known as Portland Powder, a name acquired because the preparation cured the Duke of Portland of gout. The plant has a pleasing, slightly aromatic fragrance when crushed. *Teucrium scorodonia* was at one time used as an antiseptic, diaphoretic, and stimulant, and it had a reputation as an excellent remedy in all inflammatory ailments. An infusion prepared from the leaves of *Teucrium scorodonia* has been used for its astringent, tonic, and emmenagogic properties.

Teucriums do not require any special care, and they thrive in normal fertile garden soil which is warm but not too rich, well drained, and only slightly alkaline (calcareous) in the case of the herbaceous species. The shrubby *Teucrium fruticans* thrives in even very alkaline (calcareous) or completely acid soil. In the north they need full sun but in the south they can also be planted in light shade. The herbaceous teucriums are hardy, but the shrubby species are less tolerant of long spells of severe frost. Herbaceous teucriums can be propagated by division in spring or autumn, or from seed sown outside in spring. The shrubby species can also be propagated from seed sown in a greenhouse in spring or by means of cuttings taken from half-ripened growths in July and inserted in sandy soil in frames.

(Wall Germander)
Evergreen shrub
Flowering period: June–Sept.
Height: 10–12 ins.
Zone 7 southwards
Aromatic

Teucrium chamaedrys L.
Native to Southern Europe. An easily grown, slightly aromatic, semi-shrubby evergreen with bright-green hairy leaves elongated-oval in shape, dentated, ¾ in. long. The pretty little purple-pink ¾-in.-long flowers are borne in short spikes throughout the summer. Of rapid growth and useful as a ground-cover plant in a sunny dry position in light, porous soil.

Evergreen shrub
Flowering period: July–Oct.
Height: up to 9 ft.
Zone 8 southwards

Teucrium fruticans L.
Native to Southern Europe and North Africa. A beautiful, easily cultivated shrub with attractive 1-in.-long silvery grey-green oval leaves slightly curled at the edges. A first-class plant introduced into European gardens in 1714 by the Duchess of Beaufort; but it has not achieved the popularity it deserves, possibly because of its limited hardiness, although in localities where the summers are sufficiently dry and warm to thoroughly ripen and mature the wood, the plants can withstand a considerable amount of frost. It is, however, more suited to southern than to northern gardens. Forms a dense much-branched shrub ideal for hedge-making, or it can be left to develop in an informal natural manner or clipped to any desired size or form. The pale-blue rosemary-like flowers are borne in loose racemes 1–2 ins. long throughout the summer and autumn. Requires a position

in full sun in a moderately dry soil and, like so many plants with silvery, grey, or glaucous foliage, it will thrive in alkaline (calcareous) soils.

Teucrium subspinosum L.
Native to the Mediterranean regions. A minute, spiny little grey-leaved, shrub which always attracts attention for its neat, compact dwarf habit. Leaves tiny, linear, pointed. An abundance of small mauve-pink flowers are produced in mid-summer, making the plant an ideal subject for the rock-garden in a hot dry sunny position in rather poor well-drained soil.

Evergreen shrub
Flowering period: June–Sept.
Height: 3 ins.
Zone 7 southwards

Thalictrum

(MEADOW RUE)
Family: Ranunculaceae
Hardy herbaceous perennials
Position: sun or partial shade
Propagation: seed or division
Cultivation easy
Useful for cutting

Thalictrums are popular hardy herbaceous perennials useful for their effective appearance in the garden and also for cutting and drying for use indoors in winter. The foliage is beautiful when cut and is sometimes likened to that of the maidenhair fern. The genus includes about 120 species and has a vast area of diffusion, extending from the Arctic regions to Continental Europe, as well as the Himalayas, China, Japan, and North America. The Asiatic species are the most decorative and most widely used as garden plants, although the North American and European species *Thalictrum aquilegiifolium* is attractive. Several of the species often classed as weeds in the United States are useful in the wild garden, particularly the species *Thalictrum dioicum* and *Thalictrum polyganum*.

Thalictrum angustifolium, native to the damp meadowlands of Southern Europe, has certain uses in folk medicine as a febrifuge. The minute *Thalictrum kiusianum,* native to Japan and only 4–5 ins. high, is frequently employed by the Japanese in Bonsai culture, being used as a background or ground cover in the receptacles in which the dwarf trees are grown. It also makes a charming little pot plant for temporary use indoors.

Thalictrums are of the easiest cultivation. The plants thrive in any normal fertile garden soil that is not excessively heavy or compact. As predominantly woodland plants, they appreciate partial shade. In the south, they like complete shade and a cool, moderately moist position; in the north and at high altitudes they can be grown in full sun. Propagation can be effected by seed sown in a greenhouse or frame in spring, or by division of well-developed old specimens in autumn.

Thalictrum aquilegiifolium

Flowering period: May–June
Height: up to 6 ft.

Thalictrum aquilegiifolium L.
Native to Europe and North America. A hardy herbaceous perennial up to 5–6 ft. high with alternate glaucous foliage divided into three segmented, often lobed oval segments and similar in appearance to the foliage of aquilegia (columbine). A very ornamental plant with wide panicles of soft pinkish-purple minute flowers. This is the earliest-flowering thalictrum normally grown in gardens. At one time, a yellow dye for wool was extracted from the foliage. The var. *alba* has white flowers, the var. *Bee's Purple* has darker purple-pink flowers.

Flowering period: June–Aug.
Height: up to 5 ft.

Thalictrum dipterocarpum Frank.
Native to China. The most attractive species, with divided foliage and branching panicles of mauve-pink flowers with conspicuous stamens. Excellent for cutting, adding grace and elegance to heavier blooms in vases. The var. *Hewitt's Double* has completely double mauve flowers like little peas borne on long, slender stems with a tendency to intertwine. Leaves apple-green.

Thalictrum speciosissimum L. (syn. *Thalictrum glaucum*)
Native to Southern Europe and North Africa. Beautifully cut and divided glaucous foliage. The flowers are pale yellow with very prominent stamens, and are borne in large pyramidal panicles. The var. *illuminator* is an improved form with lemon-yellow flowers and glaucous blue-green foliage.

Flowering period: June–Aug.
Height: up to 4 ft.

Thunbergia

Family: Acanthaceae
Tender annual or perennial climbers
Position: sun
Propagation: seed or cuttings
Cultivation easy

One day while in Munich, walking along the Maximilianstrasse, I noticed a plant of unusual aspect and considerable beauty in a flower-shop window. It was growing in a rather small pot, and its elegant, graceful growths were trained over an arched wire trellis. The plant had attractive green leaves, yellow flowers bearing a black mark in the center, and was obviously being offered for sale as a temporary house plant; a use for *Thunbergia alata* which is rarely employed but for which it is well suited, although in frost-free areas it is widely used as a garden climber.
The genus *Thunbergia* takes its name from Carl Peter Thunberg, professor of botany at Uppsala University, and successor to Rudbeck and Linnaeus. Thunbergias are mostly climbers, but a few of them are shrubs. The genus is diffused through most tropical regions, especially South Africa, Madagascar, and Asia. There are about one hundred species, but those of a shrubby nature such as the species *T. erecta, T. natalensis,* and *T. vogeliana,* or those of a woody, climbing character such as *T. affinis, T. coccinea, T. laurifolia,* and *T. mysorensis* do not concern us here, as they can only be grown in a heated greenhouse where there is enough space for their somewhat voluminous development. Here we will be concerned only with the herbaceous perennial climbers generally grown as annuals, such as *Thunbergia alata, Thunbergia fragrans,* and *Thunbergia gibbsonii;* although mention will also be made of *Thunbergia grandiflora* because, although a greenhouse plant, it can be cultivated outside in warm localities, or even as an annual in cooler zones, because of its rapid, vigorous development.

Cultivation. In gardens, thunbergias are mainly cultivated as annuals, although if (like *Cobaea scandens*) the plants can be held over during the winter or transferred to a cool greenhouse for the winter and then replanted the following season, far better results will be obtained the second year. They cannot, however, withstand even a minimum of frost. If planted in a heated greenhouse, or if grown for use as temporary house plants in pots, or cultivated in hanging baskets, they will continue to bloom practically throughout the year. As house plants, thunbergias require lots of light with a warm, humid atmosphere and adequate support for the trailing twining growths to develop and expand. In the garden they are ideal for training over wire netting, trellis-work, or for training on walls, columns, pillars, summer-houses, etc. They can also be encouraged to trail over the soil surface, and grown thus, they are particularly effective on slopes and banks.

Seed should be sown in a warm greenhouse as early as possible to obtain early-flowering plants; they should be grown individually in pots for planting outside as soon as the warm late-spring or early-summer weather arrives. Thunbergias need a sheltered, warm, sunny position in a rich, preferably alkaline (calcareous), very well-drained soil which is not too compact or heavy. Outdoors, they are more suited to southern gardens than to those in cold, damp, northern climates.

Thunbergia alata Bojer

(Clock Vine or Black-eyed Susan)
Perennial climber generally cultivated as an annual
Flowering period: July–Sept.
Height: up to 15 ft.

Native to Southeast Africa but now diffused throughout the tropics through garden escapes. In some areas it has even become an invasive weed. It was first introduced into England in 1823 from Zanzibar, and it is a vigorous climber with foliage resembling that of ivy. The type plant has yellow flowers with a black centre, and the calyx surrounded by two conspicuous characteristic green bracts; there are also forms with yellow-maroon or cream flowers. The petals are five in number, the width of the flowers is $1\frac{1}{2}$ ins. There are numerous lovely garden varieties, all of which can be grown as annuals and, if sown in a greenhouse in spring, will flower profusely that summer:

> var. *alba,* white, with a dark eye
> var. *aurantiaca,* orange, with a reddish-black centre
> var. *bakeri,* pure white
> var. *dodsii,* brownish orange, with a chestnut centre, the 3-in.-long foliage variegated green and white
> var. *fryeri,* pale yellow, with a white eye
> var. *lutea,* pure yellow

(Mountain Creeper)
Perennial climber
Flowering period: July–Sept.
Height: up to 10 ft.
Fragrant

Thunbergia fragrans Roxbg.

Native to India, from where it was imported into England in the eighteenth century. A tender evergreen climber with triangular foliage

Thunbergia grandiflora
From *Curtis's Botanical Magazine*,
1822, plate 2366

Thunbergia alata var. *alba*
From *Paxton's Magazine of Botany*,
1836, plate 28

similar to that of *Thunbergia alata,* 2–3 ins. long, but more pointed. The fragrant flowers are white, axillary, tubular, wide-mouthed, and 1½ ins. long. The varieties *T. laevis* and *T. vestita* are both inferior and scentless.

Thunbergia gibbsonii Moore

Perennial climber generally cultivated as an annual
Flowering period: July–Sept.
Height: up to 15 ft.

Native to tropical Africa. A tender perennial climber generally grown as an annual from seed sown in a greenhouse in spring, the seedlings being grown on in small pots and planted out in their flowering positions in May, when they will bloom throughout the summer. Requires an abundance of sunshine and a long, hot summer season. Leaves ovate, 2–3 ins. long. Flowers tubular, 1⅓ ins. long, wide-mouthed; brilliant orange with a dark central eye. A very beautiful plant and ideal for growing on a hot, sunny wall.

Thunbergia grandiflora L.

(Sky Flower)
Perennial climber
Flowering period: July–Oct.
Height: up to 10 ft.

Native to eastern India, where during the rainy season it can be found in full bloom in the vicinity of Calcutta, its shining blue flowers providing a spectacular display, surpassing in beauty any of the other thunbergias. Leaves opposite, oval-cordate, evergreen, 6–8 ins. long, dentated. Flowers periwinkle-blue with the throat yellowish and veined, 3 ins. long, borne singly or in clusters of up to fifteen in the leaf axils, and slightly pendent. Widely grown in the warmer parts of Florida and California, but in less-favoured localities it needs the protection of a greenhouse unless a particularly warm, sunny, sheltered position can be provided outside. Although a perennial, it can, under favourable conditions, be grown as an annual if seed is sown early in a warm greenhouse. Can also be propagated from soft cuttings taken in early summer and rooted in a greenhouse. Requires a reasonably rich soil made up of fibrous loam, peat, leafsoil, and sand. Although not normally exceeding about 10 ft. in height, it is of rapid growth and requires plenty of space to develop. As in the case of *Thunbergia alata,* it is excellent for growing on a trellis. Requires abundant watering in summer.

Tibouchina semidecandra

(Brazilian Spider Flower or Glory Bush)
Family: Melastomataceae
Tender evergreen shrubs

Only one species of genus *Tibouchina* is in general cultivation, *Tibouchina semidecandra,* a spectacular tender evergreen Brazilian shrub, with the lush and vigorous growth typical to the vegetation of that country. It has large rich-green foliage and striking violet-purple flowers. The blossoms' long conspicuous twisted stamens have inspired the common name of Brazilian Spider Flower. Considering their place of origin it is not surprising that the plants cannot be grown outdoors in Europe or in the United States, except perhaps in the warmest corners of California and Florida or in favoured spots on the Riviera. Nevertheless, it is widely used in northern gardens as a seasonal summer-flowering plant in the same manner as bougainvilleas, *Hibiscus Rosa-sinensis,* lantanas, etc. It is cultivated in large pots or tubs kept in a greenhouse between October and April, and placed outside during the summer season. The plants can, of course, be planted permanently in a heated greenhouse—preferably against a wall—where well-cared-for specimens will cover large areas, and if carefully trained and tied will reach a height of up to 15 ft. or more, flowering almost continuously. The genus is, however, a difficult one. It comprises 3–4 species of which *T. elegans* and *T. holosericea* are also sometimes grown as pot plants. Tibouchinas require an abundance of hot sunshine and a rich non-alkaline (non-calcareous) soil containing a high percentage of humus and other well-decomposed organic matter. Propagation is by means of soft cuttings taken from young growths in early summer and rooted in a warm greenhouse.

Tibouchina semidecandra

Flowering period: June–Sept.
Height: up to 8 ft.
Position: sun
Propagation: cuttings
Cultivation not easy
Zone 10

Tibouchina semidecandra Cogn. (syn. *Lasiandra macrantha*)
Native to Brazil. A non-hardy evergreen shrub which grown as a pot plant maintains a height of about 6–8 ft.—although plants only 18 ins. high also flower quite well. Habit erect and rigid. Leaves 2–4 ins. long, dark green, ovate-oblong, alternate, densely hairy on the upper surface, paler beneath. The beautiful 5-in.-wide intense-violet-purple flowers are either solitary or borne in clusters. They are flattish, five-

petalled, and have ten conspicuous stamens of unequal length. Beneath each flower there are two conspicuous rounded sepals. The flowering period lasts throughout the summer, and when grown in pots or tubs the plants make fine subjects for a sunny terrace or courtyard. In a Florentine courtyard I once saw a wonderful effect created by big pot-grown plants of *Datura arborea* associated with equally large pot-grown plants of *Tibouchina semidecandra,* the white flowers of the datura making a striking contrast to the rich colouring of the tibouchina blossoms. There is also an attractive light-pink-flowered variety.

Tigridia

(TIGER FLOWER OR IRIS SHELL FLOWER)
Family: Iridaceae
Tender perennial corms
Position: sun
Propagation: seed or division
Cultivation easy

The name of this genus comes from *tigris* (tiger) because its markings are vaguely tiger-like. Some prefer to liken its gaudy and varied colouring to the plumage of a peacock, and the specific name of the most widely grown species is *Tigridia pavonia* (from *pavo,* peacock). The flowers of genus *Tigridia* are unusual, more curious than beautiful, but undoubtedly spectacular; unfortunately the blossoms are ephemeral, lasting for only one day, a characteristic that necessitates growing the plants in massed groups so that the abundance and frequency of flowers will compensate for their brevity.

There are thirteen species distributed throughout Mexico, Central America, Peru, and Chile; they are not hardy in European or North American gardens, although they can be treated as summer-flowering bulbs. Tigridias were known in Europe in the sixteenth century and were described by Matthias L'Obel in 1576.

Cultivation. Tigridia cultivation is identical to that of gladioli, although they can be planted much closer together. They should be planted in April, at a distance of about 4 ins. apart, in a fertile, warm, well-drained soil, preferably not too heavy, and in a hot, sunny position. Propagation is by means of the freely produced young bulbs that develop around the parent bulb and which bloom when two years old. They can also be propagated from seed sown in

March–April in a warm greenhouse, but flowering-sized bulbs cannot be expected until after 3–4 years. During the intervening years the young bulbs must be planted every spring and lifted from the soil in autumn (the same procedure being followed for flowering-sized bulbs), and stored in a frost-free place during the winter in the same manner as gladioli. In warm climates where frost is not experienced, the corms can be left permanently in the ground.

Tigridia pavonia

Flowering period: July–Aug.
Height: up to 2½ ft.

Tigridia pavonia Ker.
Native to Mexico and Guatemala. This is semi-rare in European gardens, or at least an uncommon exotic bulb; in Mexico it is much prized for its edible properties and high starch content. Stems erect, rarely branched, smooth. Leaves sword-shaped, up to 18 ins. long, grooved, and pointed. Flowers borne on tall, erect rigid stems; many together but opening one or two at a time in succession, each bloom lasting for only one day; up to 5 ins. in diameter; red, conspicuously spotted and spectacular; the centre is cup-shaped and divided into three smallish segments, surrounded by three outer much larger segments with the central part of the flower yellowish, marked purple. There are many lovely varieties:

    var. *alba*, white, spotted red towards the centre
    var. *alba immaculata*, pure-white
    var. *canariensis*, yellow
    var. *conchiflora*, brilliant yellow
    var. *flava*, pale yellow, centre marked red
    var. *grandiflora*, very large flowers similar to the type
    var. *liliacea*, lilac-coloured spotted flowers
    var. *lutea immaculata*, pure yellow without marks
    var. *rosea*, pink flowers variegated yellow in the centre
    var. *speciosa*, a more dwarf variety with brilliant red flowers
    var. *watkinsonii* (syn. *aurea*), hybrid, *T. pavonia* x *T. conchiflora*
    var. *wheeleri*, scarlet

Tigridia pringlei Wats.
Native to Mexico. Similar to *Tigridia pavonia* but distinguished by its smaller, kidney-shaped petals. The colour of the flowers is orange suffused scarlet, with crimson marks at the base of each petal and the marks much larger than found on the flowers of the species *T. speciosa*. Leaves erect, glabrous, sword-shaped, $1\frac{1}{2}$ ins. wide.

Flowering period: June–Aug.
Height: up to 2 ft.

Tithonia

Family: Compositae
Tender woody perennials, generally grown as annuals
Position: sun
Propagation: seed
Cultivation easy
Useful for cutting

Tithonia rotundifolia

This member of the Compositae family, with a name of mythological origin—Titonus was the favourite lover of Aurora—owes its appellation perhaps to the sun-like appearance of its flowers and to the fact that it is such a sun-lover. The genus includes about ten species native to Mexico, Central America, and the West Indies. They are robust, fast-growing, very handsome wood-based shrubby perennials. Because of their non-hardy character they are invariably grown in gardens as annuals for late-summer flowering. The plants will not tolerate any frost and are more suited to southern than to northern gardens. The flowers are of considerable beauty, vividly coloured and excellent for cutting. Their general appearance is that of a large single zinnia or daisy. They are among the largest of all annuals—or plants grown as annuals—with a height of up to 8 ft., each plant occupying a space of one square yard in the case of well-grown specimens, and are therefore not suitable for small beds. Tithonias do, however, make excellent subjects for the back of a mixed or herbaceous border, and they are of particular value for their late-flowering habit, another factor that precludes their cultivation in the north where summers are of short duration.

There is no difficulty about cultivation. Tithonias require a rich fibrous soil that is warm, not too heavy, and well-drained, in a hot, sheltered sunny position. To obtain really well-developed specimens periodic applications of a liquid organic fertilizer are necessary during the maximum growing period, while an abundance of water is necessary during very hot, dry weather.

Seed can be sown in a greenhouse or frame in March–April, planting out the seedlings in May. Seed can also be sown in February–March in a warm greenhouse and the seedlings planted out in April, or when all danger of frost has passed. Germination takes from 8–14 days.

Flowering period: July–Sept.
Height: up to 8 ft.
Zone 9 southwards

Tithonia diversifolia Blake
Native to Mexico and Guatemala. In general appearance similar to the more widely cultivated species *T. rotundifolia,* but with orange-yellow flowers. Leaves rounded-ovate, entire or 3–5-lobed, 6–8 ins. long. Stems covered with fine hairs. Flowers solitary, long-stalked, up to 3 ins. in diameter.

Flowering period: July–Sept.
Height: up to 8 ft.
Zone 9 southwards

Tithonia rotundifolia Blake (syn. *Tithonia speciosa, Tithonia tagetiflora, Helianthus speciosus*)
Native to Mexico. Introduced into British gardens before 1713. Erect bushy habit with beautiful scarlet-orange single dahlia- or sunflower-like blooms up to $3\frac{1}{2}$ ins. in diameter borne on long stems (and excellent for cutting), with the reverse of the petals orange. Stems reddish, hairy. Leaves alternate, heart-shaped, or widely ovate, up to 10 ins. long; 3-lobed, dentated, rough-surfaced. The var. *fackel* has flowers of a more intense colour.

Torenia

(WISHBONE FLOWER)
Family: Scrophulariaceae
Tender annuals
Position: partial shade
Propagation: seed
Cultivation easy

The genus *Torenia*, native to tropical regions of Asia and Africa, includes annual and perennial species, none of which are hardy. They are much-branched plants with opposite, entire, or dentated leaves and axillary flowers borne either singly or in small racemes. Their colour range is confined to blue, purple, and white with yellow markings, often with two or three different colours in the same flower. The curious common name of Wishbone Flower comes from the shape of the stamens. They are of the easiest cultivation, but although there are about forty species, only *Torenia fournieri*, together with its varieties, is in general cultivation, generally as a summer-flowering annual. In northern countries it is not always successful when grown outside, and it is certainly not hardy. In the south, however, it makes

Torenia fournieri
From *Curtis's Botanical Magazine*,
1884, plate 6747

a charming massed-bedding plant for a semi-shady position and it can also be effectively grown in pots or hanging baskets.

The plants require a warm, reasonably moist soil and a long, hot summer season, and they will remain in bloom until October. Pot-grown specimens can be used as temporary house plants or for decorating an unheated greenhouse.

Propagation is by means of seed sown in a warm greenhouse in spring. The genus was named in honour of Olaf Torén, a Swedish botanist. A curious characteristic of the leaves is that during a period of unseasonably cold weather they assume a reddish-green colour.

Annual
Flowering period: June–Oct.
Height: 12–15 ins.

Torenia fournieri Lindl.
Native to South Vietnam. An annual of loose, almost semi-pendent habit up to 12–15 ins. high, not hardy. Leaves $1\frac{1}{2}$–2 ins. long and half as wide, oval, pointed, dentated, light green. The curious, attractive flowers are somewhat similar to a small snapdragon and are tricoloured, with the upper petals pale sky-blue and the lower petals dark purple or violet, with the centre yellow. They are axillary, either solitary or in small racemes. The varieties var. *grandiflora* and var. *speciosa* are an improvement on the original species. Sometimes the var. *bicolor compacta* is offered in seed catalogues; it has a more compact habit with blue-and-white flowers. Other varieties are var. *alba*, with white flowers and var. *nana compacta Gefion*, only 4 ins. high, with pale blue flowers marked darker blue and with a white throat.

Trachelospermum

(STAR JASMINE OR CONFEDERATE JASMINE)
Family: Apocynaceae
Half-hardy evergreen climbing shrubs
Position: sun
Propagation: seed or cuttings
Cultivation easy
Very fragrant

This genus of moderately hardy intensely fragrant evergreen climbers belongs to the same family as such widely different genera as *Vinca* (periwinkle) and *Nerium* (oleander), and, like the latter, it exudes a sticky, milky sap when cut. Its shiny, rather leathery foliage is not unlike that of a vinca. The name of genus *Trachelospermum* is of Greek origin: *trachelos* (neck) and *sperma* (seed), that is, seed with a neck.

The genus comprises about twenty species of vigorous evergreen climbers indigenous to eastern India and Japan. In cold northern localities they must be treated as cool greenhouse plants, unless a particularly warm, sheltered sunny position is available. But in the south they thrive outdoors on sunny walls, often being used as ivy would be in the north for covering houses. Their intense and delicious fragrance can then be fully appreciated. They are, however, not self-attaching, and some support must be provided, such as wire netting or trellis-work through which the long slender growths can twine and climb.

Cultivation. This is not difficult so long as the plants have an abundance of warmth and sunshine in a warm well-drained soil. Among authorities there is some difference of opinion about the type of soil preferred by trachelospermums; some recommend a heavy soil, others advocate a sand-and-peat soil. Probably both are right, and, personally, I have found that the plants will flourish in any type of soil that is fertile, deep, well-drained, and even alkaline (calcareous). Generous fertilizing will be amply repaid by more vigorous growth and profuse flowering.

Trachelospermum jasminoide

Propagation is by means of cuttings taken from lateral growths of half-ripened wood—preferably with a heel—in July, inserted in pots with a sand-and-peat soil, and placed in a greenhouse or closed frame. They can also be propagated from seed sown in a warm greenhouse in spring, the seed requiring about four weeks to germinate. When planting young specimens raised from cuttings or from seed, it is advisable to add a little sand and peat in the vicinity of the roots.

Trachelospermum asiaticum Nakai (syn. *Trachelospermum divaricatum* Kan.)

Flowering period: July–Aug.
Height: up to 15 ft.
Zone 8 southwards

Native to Korea and Japan. A somewhat more hardy species than *T. jasminoides*, even being grown in sheltered spots in England—a fine specimen has been growing on a wall at Kew for the past thirty-five years. Leaves leathery, oval, up to $1\frac{1}{4}$ ins. long. Flowers yellowish white, 1 in. in diameter, similar in form to vinca flowers, and borne in terminal racemes up to $2\frac{1}{2}$ ins. long, sweetly scented. A vigorous evergreen climber that appears to thrive in any type of soil. Easily distinguished from the other species grown in gardens by its smaller foliage and yellowish flowers.

Trachelospermum jasminoides Lem. (syn. *Rhyncospermum jasminoides*)

Flowering period: June–July
Height: up to 30 ft.
Zone 7 southwards

Native to China and the sub-tropical Himalayas. Introduced into England in 1844 by the Scottish botanist Robert Fortune. A moderately hardy climbing evergreen shrub. Leaves short-stalked, ovate-lanceolate, shiny surfaced. Flowers white, $\frac{3}{4}$ in. in diameter, star-like, intensely and sweetly fragrant, and completely covering the plant during June–July. The var. *variegatum* has its foliage marked and edged with cream-white but is less free-flowering. The var. *japonicum* is even more vigorous than the type, with wider leaves which in autumn are suffused with crimson and bronze. The var. *wilsonii* is smaller-leaved, and this, too, assumes an autumn tint.

Tritonia

(MONTBRETIA OR BLAZING STAR)
Family: Iridaceae
Half-hardy or tender perennial corms
Position: sun
Propagation: division or seed
Cultivation easy

The nomenclature of the genus *Tritonia* is confused enough to make one dizzy, and is another example of the apparent confusion that occasionally exists in certain genera of garden plants, although in this case the confusion is the result of revision and correction of earlier mistakes caused by arbitrary classifications which further research proved to be incorrect. The common Montbretia of gardens is frequently referred to as *Tritonia* x *crocosmaeflora,* but it should actually be called *Crocosmia* x *crocosmiiflora* N. E. Br., being a hybrid between *Crocosmia aurea* and *Crocosmia pottsii*. For the sake of convenience and clarity, however, it is included here in the genus *Tritonia* since that is the name by which so many gardeners know it, although some Dutch bulb firms refer to it as *Montbretia crocosmiiflora*. It is pertinent to note that the reason for the use of *Crocus* in these various names is because the flowers have a slight saffron fragrance, and a crocus is the origin of saffron.

Tritonias are bulbous plants; that is, they are corms. In the case of the popular tritonia (Montbretia), they are generally considered hardy, although even these are not suitable for permanent planting outside where the ground freezes in depth for long periods. The other tritonias are much less hardy, even tender, as is expected of plants native to South Africa. They require a rather light, fairly dry, well-drained soil in a hot, sunny position.

Tritonia crocosmiiflora Princess Beatrix Hybrid
From *Paxton's Magazine of Botany*,
1849, plate 3

Cultivation. Tritonias are easy enough to cultivate and will rapidly increase. The common Montbretias may be planted outside permanently in March in any well-drained light soil where there is no danger of winter frost reaching down to the level of the corms. Otherwise, they should be treated in the same manner as the non-hardy species and grown as gladioli—that is, planted in spring, removed from the soil in autumn, dried and stored in a frost-free place (preferably packed in sand) during the winter, and replanted the following season either in the open ground or in large pots. Montbretias should be planted at a depth of 2 ins., the others a little less deep. Propagation is very easy by division, or by seed sown in a warm greenhouse in spring, but 3–4 years are necessary to produce flowering-size corms.

Flowering period: July–Aug.
Height: 10–12 ins.

Tritonia crocata Ker-Gawl.
Native to South Africa. A fascinating little plant with thin graceful foliage and attractive brilliant orange-red flowers 2 ins. in diameter. Flowers flattish with a minute transparent zone at the base of each petal like a miniature window. Ideal for pot culture; I recall the superb effect made when a hundred pots in full bloom were placed in a large courtyard in front of an old Riviera palace with reddish-pink walls. Requires a hot, dry, sunny position in a light soil. The corms are not hardy, and in cold localities must be treated like gladioli.

(Montbretia)
Flowering period: July–Aug.
Height: up to 3–4 ft.

Tritonia x *crocosmiiflora* N. E. Br.
The official name of this is now *Crocosmia* x *crocosmiiflora*. A cormous plant of hybrid origin, widely used in gardens. Hardy in all but exceptionally cold zones. Increases rapidly through the multiplication of the small corms. There are many modern hybrids with large flowers in shades of yellow, crimson, and orange. The graceful flower spikes appear in mid-summer among the abundant light green, long, narrow foliage. They are excellent for cutting, and the flowers are long-lasting in water. The flower stems are branching, 3–4 ft. high, individual blooms up to 2 ins. in diameter. Some of the best named hybrids are Vesuvius, Emily MacKenzie, Comet, His Majesty, James Coey, Rheingold, and Princess Beatrix.

Flowering period: July–Aug.
Height: up to 2–3 ft.

Tritonia pottsii (Baker) Benth. (syn. *Crocosmia pottsii* N. E. Br.)
Native to South Africa. Leaves not prolific, but linear, narrow, light green. Flower stems branching, up to 3 ft. high; individual flowers funnel-shaped, 1 in. long, with an elongated tube. Yellow suffused red. One of the parents of the common Montbretia; the true species is only infrequently grown in gardens.

Trollius

(GLOBE FLOWER)
Family: Ranunculaceae
Hardy herbaceous perennials
Position: sun or partial shade
Propagation: division or seed
Cultivation easy
Useful for cutting
Poisonous

The origin of the name of this beautiful genus is open to discussion. It is first mentioned in writing by the Swiss botanist Conrad Gesner, who affirmed that the flowers on Mount Pilatus, near Lucerne, were known in German as *Trollblumen*—that is, Globe Flowers. Other commentators believe that *troll* refers to the Scandinavian troll, a type of malefic monster or goblin. There is also a school of thought which suggests that the *troll* of *Trollius* refers to its evil character as a poisonous plant. However, the fictional troll is a humorously grotesque creature and trollius flowers, too, are slightly ridiculous, with their rounded, paunchy, somewhat puffed-up, and rather impudent cheerfulness. (Nobody has apparently attempted to link the *troll* of *Trollius* with the diminutive of the old English word trollop!)

Trollius are not flowers to be put in just any casual position in the garden. They are splendid in the right locality, especially on a green lawn, or better still in slightly marshy grassland, or on the banks of a stream or pond.

The genus comprises about twenty-nine species distributed throughout the cold and temperate regions of the northern hemisphere. Only one species is native to Europe, *Trollius europaeus,* which is found in swampy alpine localities at a height of up to 10,000 ft., mostly in alkaline (calcareous) soils, and less frequently below an altitude of 2,500 ft. It is poisonous, like most of the Ranunculaceae, and has apparently never been used in folk medicine.

Cultivation. Trollius does not present any great difficulty. Seed is not always easy to obtain since the plants are very parsimonious in their seed production. Trollius love a cool, damp, fresh, fertile soil, and although they can be grown in full sun in the north and at high altitudes, they prefer partial shade in the south and are certainly not plants for dry and arid localities. Seed may be sown from April to June, in pans, flats, pots, or boxes, in a cool shady position; planting out the seedlings the following spring. Germination is often very

Trollius europaeus

slow. Otherwise, propagation is by division in autumn or spring, which is the only method in the case of named hybrid varieties.

(Asiatic Globe Flower)
Flowering period: May–June
Height: up to 2 ft.

Trollius asiaticus L.
Native to Siberia. Cultivated in gardens since 1759. A hardy herbaceous perennial of vigorous habit. Leaves finely segmented, bronze-green. Flowers solitary, globose, but more expanded than in most species, with generally ten petal-like sepals and ten petals, all of which are orange. The var. *albus* has pale yellow flowers.

(Chinese Globe Flower)
Flowering period: July–Aug.
Height: up to 3 ft.

Trollius chinensis Bunge (syn. *Trollius ledebourii*)
Native to northeast China. First introduced into European gardens in 1827 and subsequently reintroduced in 1913. Foliage deeply divided into 5–7 segments, each segment again divided and dentated. A hardy herbaceous perennial with golden-yellow flowers, each with five sepals and 10–12 short petals.

(European Globe Flower)
Flowering period: May–Aug.
Height: 1–1½ ft.
Fragrant

Trollius europaeus L.
Native to most of Europe, especially alpine meadows and thin woodlands. Roots fibrous, black; stems branched towards the summit, erect and rigid. Leaves alternate, mostly basal, dark green above, pale green beneath; palmate, five-lobed, dentated, and deeply cut. Flowers $\frac{3}{4}$–1 in. in diameter; single, solitary, rounded, scented, and with 10–15 petal-like concave sepals which surround a mass of conspicuous stamens. The colour of the flowers is golden-yellow, more intense internally—in Germany the colour inspired the common name *Butterblume* (butter-flower). The var. *roddigesii* has flowers of a darker yellow and is of garden origin; while a natural variety, var. *altissima,* has branching flower stems bearing several flowers. There is also a var. *napellifolius* with 5–7-lobed foliage, and a pale-yellow-flowered var. *albidus*.

(American Globe Flower)
Flowering period: May
Height: 2 ft.

Trollius laxus L.
Native to the United States. A somewhat straggly herbaceous perennial that is quite hardy in European gardens. Leaves long-stalked, 5–7-lobed, each lobe segmented and dentated. Flowers up to 2 ins. in diameter, solitary, globose but wide-spreading; with 5–7 greenish-yellow petal-like sepals and 5–15 short narrow yellowish petals. Requires a really wet position.

(Dwarf Globe Flower)
Flowering period: June–July
Height: 8–10 ins.

Trollius pumilus D. Don
Native to the Himalayas. A hardy herbaceous perennial with small short-stalked crinkled leaves about 1–2 ins. wide, 5-lobed, each lobe divided into three segments. Flowers solitary, 1 in. wide, yellow, with 5–6 spreading sepals notched at their tips and 10–12 short petals.

Tropaeolum

(NASTURTIUM)
Family: Tropaeolaceae
Tender herbaceous perennials and climbers, tuberous-rooted perennials, or annuals
Position: sun or partial shade
Propagation: seed, division, or cuttings
Cultivation fairly easy

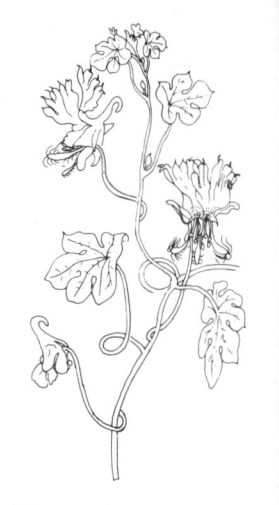

Tropaeolum peregrinum

This genus is frequently called "nasturtium", a common name invariably applied to the many hybrid forms of the best-known species, *Tropaeolum majus*. This name, however, should not be used for *Tropaeolum* because it is actually the correct generic name for watercress (*Nasturtium officinale,* a synonym of which is *Rorippa Nasturtium-aquaticum*). This practise of using a common name which quite often is the correct name for another genus presents many dangers and inconveniences. In this case, both plants are edible, with an agreeable, piquant flavour; otherwise they have nothing in common.

The genus was named *Tropaeolum* by Linnaeus, and the name is derived from the Greek *tropaion* (trophy); a trophy in ancient times was a tree trunk on which victors hung the shields and helmets of the vanquished. Linnaeus, who, as is well known, possessed a picturesque mind and an imagination not far removed from the baroque, no doubt wished to identify the plant's most remarkable leaves with old-fashioned shields, and the generally red or orange flowers with the gilded helmets spattered with blood and pierced by lances.

By whatever name they are known, tropaeolums, nasturtiums, or the French *capucines*, these plants have not achieved any lasting fame. They were introduced into cultivation in Europe in 1684. After being held in esteem for two centuries, they lost favour early in the twentieth century. Now they are frequently looked upon as common, even vulgar plants, too easy to cultivate, too popular, and disdained by the serious gardener as not worthy of his skill. In reality, the truly successful culture of "nasturtiums" is not so easy as one might believe at first sight. Certainly, it is easy enough to buy a packet of mixed seed, sow it in a haphazard, casual manner, and obtain plants that produce leaves and flowers. In many cases, however, the resulting plants bear too much foliage and too few blooms, or the blooms are small, badly shaped, and of poor colour, resembling a jellyfish out of water. Grown as annuals, so-called nasturtiums give their best only when planted in the right position, and the beautiful, rather

Tropaeolum azureum
From *Paxton's Magazine of Botany*,
1842, plate 247

fleshy intense-green leaves should remind the gardener that he is dealing with plants that need a moist position, preferably near water, and partial shade in southern localities with a hot dry atmosphere (or when cultivated in pots on excessively hot, dry, sunny terraces or balconies). The plants will not flower with their characteristic freedom if grown in excessive shade, especially in the north. Above all, it is vital to buy seed in named varieties or strains from reliable sources; there is a superb selection offered under the names *Tropaeolum majus* or *Tropaeolum minus* annual hybrids; the latter is the popular garden "nasturtium", by some authorities grouped together under the name *Tropaeolum cultorum*. Several other species are very difficult to establish in gardens, in particular the spectacular but capricious perennial climbing species *Tropaeolum speciosum*.

Although normally grown as annuals, "nasturtiums" are really perennials, but they are not tolerant of even the slightest frost; in autumn they are the first plants to show effects from the earliest touch of frost. The other species are either herbaceous perennials or tuberous-rooted perennials. Some have delicately scented blooms. The foliage and flowers of *Tropaeolum majus* are edible, with a pleasing, piquantly peppery flavour, and often used in salads or sandwiches; the fresh, green seeds can be preserved in vinegar in the same manner as capers. There are also types with coloured foliage and single or double flowers, varying in size from minute to enormous, in a vast range of colours. In the past, tropaeolums have been used in folk medicine, especially for the treatment of scabies.

The genus comprises about fifty species of American origin, with an area of diffusion particularly wide in the moist, humid, mountainous areas of Mexico and Chile. They are plants with elongated growths, often climbers, generally with sappy, fleshy stems and mostly lobate or shield-shaped leaves, and with conspicuous axillary flowers. The popular garden "nasturtiums" grown as annuals are hybrids resulting from crosses between the species *T. majus, T. minus*, and *T. peltophorum*.

Cultivation. As mentioned above, the hybrid forms of *Tropaeolum* are easy to cultivate, but they should not be entirely neglected or sown in poor, hungry soil. Just as there are no animals that can survive without food, there are no plants that can prosper without a supply of suitable nourishment. In the case of "nasturtiums", fertilizers with a high percentage of nitrogen should be avoided as these tend to encourage an excess of foliage with few flowers. To obtain a real abundance of bloom, it is advisable to use fertilizers with a high percentage of phosphorus. The soil should also contain a good proportion of sand to ensure adequate aeration and loose texture. The smaller types of annual tropaeolums are excellent for cultivating in large receptacles on terraces, etc., and an appropriate soil mixture for this purpose should be made up of 2 parts ordinary

Tropaeolum majus

Tropaeolum tuberosum

Tuberous-rooted
herbaceous perennial climber
Flowering period: July–Aug.
Height: up to 6–7 ft.
Slightly fragrant

(Indian Cress or Nasturtium)
Herbaceous perennial climber
generally grown as an annual
Flowering period: July–Oct.
Height: 1–10 ft.
according to variety
Fragrant flowers
and piquant-flavoured foliage

garden soil, 1 part peat, and ½ part sand. Where necessary, details of particular cultural requirements are given for each species.

The annual garden "nasturtiums" are mostly raised from seed sown directly into the flowering positions from March to May, according to climate and locality but in any case after all risk of frost has passed. In warm, frost-free localities many "nasturtiums" can also be grown as perennials. The plants can also be propagated from cuttings (the only method in the case of certain double-flowered, sterile forms) taken at any time during the summer and rooted in a warm greenhouse. The perennial species can be propagated by division in spring or from seed sown in a warm greenhouse in spring. The tuberous-rooted species are only moderately hardy; in localities where the soil surface is liable to freeze in depth, they should be treated in the same manner as dahlia tubers—lifted in late autumn, stored in sand or peat in a frost-free place during winter, and replanted in late spring when all risk of frost has passed. In warm localities, the tubers can be left undisturbed for many years. None of the climbing tropaeolums are self-attaching, and adequate supports should be provided as soon as growth begins.

For those species grown from seed, it is a good practise to soak the seed for 24 hours in warm water before planting them in the soil. Also, as these plants seem to attract aphids and other sucking insects, some gardeners bury a mothball (camphor-ball) or two with every seed. This seems to act as a systemic, and the insects tend to give the seedlings a wide berth. "Nasturtiums" are also excellent subjects for gardens in districts that are plagued by rabbits, ground-hogs, and such: their spicy flavour obviously has little gastronomic attraction for these rodents.

Tropaeolum azureum Miers
Native to Chile. A tuberous-rooted species and the least hardy; in the north suitable only for greenhouse cultivation. Stems slender, much-branched, leafless; foliage long-stalked, divided into 5–7 linear-lanceolate segments. Flowers slightly scented, calyx green and short-spurred, petals of equal size, dark lilac or a lovely violet-blue, egg-shaped, with a yellowish-white zone at the base. The var. *grandiflora* has somewhat larger flowers up to $1\frac{1}{4}$ ins. wide, with a white centre.

Tropaeolum majus L.
Native to an area extending from Peru to Columbia. Habit trailing or climbing, with smooth, branched stems. Leaves shield-shaped to rounded, slightly lobed; stalks long and often twisted. Spurs of the flowers are often recurved. Large seeds are cork-like in texture. Flowers orange or golden-yellow, plus many other tints among the hybrids. The hybrid forms, which constitute the popular garden "nasturtiums", are the results of hybridization and crosses between

the species *T. majus, T. minus,* and *T. peltophorum* (sometimes grouped together under the name of *Tropaeolum cultorum*). There are many forms. For the sake of convenience, seedsmen have divided them into several groups:

Tropaeolum majus Tall Hybrids. These will extend for a distance of up to 10 ft.; with single flowers in crimson, scarlet, orange, or yellow, and many intermediate shades.

Tropaeolum majus Nanum Hybrids. These are found under such names as Compact varieties, Tom Thumb varieties, Tom Pouce varieties, and Dwarf varieties; all 9–10 ins. high with semi-double or single, often scented, blooms in a range of colours including salmon-pink, scarlet, cherry-red, primrose-yellow, orange, mahogany-red, etc., and often with bluish-green or reddish-green leaves.

Tropaeolum Gleam Hybrids. These form robust, vigorous, bushy plants up to 1 ft. high, with semi-double fragrant blooms in shades of salmon, golden-yellow, orange-scarlet, cherry-red, primrose-yellow, orange, crimson, etc.

Tropaeolum peltophorum

Among the best of the named hybrids of each group the following are worthy of special mention:

Tall Hybrids:
- Atropurpureum, dark red
- Atropurpureum foliis aureis, dark red flowers and golden-yellow foliage
- Coccineum, scarlet
- Coccineum foliis aureis, scarlet flowers, golden-yellow foliage
- Hemisphericum, light yellow
- Heinemannii, chocolate-coloured flowers
- Luteum, yellow
- Regelianum, violet-purple
- Scheurianum coccineum, striped red
- Schillingii, yellow marked maroon
- Schulzii, scarlet flowers and dark foliage
- Lucifer, dark scarlet flowers and dark foliage
- Flore pleno, double flowers in various colours
- Scharlachglanz, scarlet
- Goldglanz, golden-yellow

Dwarf or Tom Thumb Hybrids:
- Atrococcineum, vivid scarlet
- Atrococcineum, vivid scarlet
- Atropurpureum, dark scarlet-red
- Goldkönig, golden-yellow flowers, dark foliage
- Goldkugel, double golden-yellow flowers
- Orangekugel, double orange flowers
- Scharlachkugel, double scarlet flowers

Tropaeolum polyphyllum

Tropaeolum majus Schillingii Hybrid
From *Paxton's Magazine of Botany*,
1835, plate 193

        Atrosanguineum dark blood-red
        Coccineum, scarlet
        Nanum coccineum foliis aureis, scarlet flowers and golden-yellow leaves
        Coeruleo-roseum, dark pink
        Luteum, clear yellow
        Regelianum, violet-purple
        Tom Pouceblanche, very pale yellow
        King of Tom Thumbs, intense, velvety, dark-scarlet-red flowers, stems and leaves glaucous green, slightly bronzed

Gleam Hybrids: Golden Gleam, golden-yellow
                Orange Gleam, orange
                Scarlet Gleam, scarlet

Tropaeolum minus

Tropaeolum minus L.   (Dwarf Nasturtium)
Native to Peru. Earlier flowering than *Tropaeolum majus* and, like that species, one of the parents of modern garden "nasturtiums". A dwarf trailing or semi-trailing plant with smooth stems. Small flowers rounded to shield-shaped. Flowers somewhat variable in colour with a dominant shade of orange-yellow striped carmine. Petals narrow and pointed, the lower petal more marked or striped than the others.

Perennial semi-climber generally grown as an annual
Flowering period: July–Sept.
Height: up to 2 ft.

Tropaeolum peltophorum Benth. (syn. *Tropaeolum lobbianum* Hook.)
Native to the mountains of Colombia and Ecuador. Another of the species from which the modern hybrids have evolved. A very vigorous plant with shield-shaped or rounded petals that are occasionally slightly lobed; velvet-textured on the upper surface, the undersurface covered with greyish-white down; calyx and stalks also downy. Flowers typical nasturtium-like, brilliant red with a scarlet-red spur that becomes light green at its tip. The var. *fimbriata* has fringed petals; var. *hederifolium* has ivy-shaped leaves; var. *compactum* has a more compact habit; var. *regina* has salmon-orange flowers; the flowers of var. *atropurpureum* are dark purple; var. *aureum* are golden-yellow; var. *fulgens* are dark scarlet.

Perennial semi-climber
Flowering period: nearly perpetual in a mild climate
Height: up to 12–13 ft.

*(Canary Creeper
or Canary Bird Flower)*
Annual climber
Flowering period: July–Sept.
Height: up to 12 ft.

Tropaeolum peregrinum Jacq. (syn. *Tropaeolum canariensis*)
Native to Peru and Ecuador. A smooth-stemmed much-branched climber. Leaves divided into 5–7 lobes or segments, brilliant green on the upper surface, pale grey-green beneath. The lobes are egg-shaped, with the apex downwards. Flowers very numerous, graceful, lemon-yellow, the three lower petals small, narrow, fringed at the tips; the two upper petals much larger, frilled, and spotted red. The spur is curved and hook-shaped. A late summer- and autumn-flowering plant that thrives in partial shade and should be grown away from other more vigorous rampant climbers that could easily overgrow and suffocate this graceful, elegant species.

*Perennial climber or trailer
with rhizomatous roots*
Flowering period: June–Sept.
Height: up to 3–4 ft.

Tropaeolum polyphyllum Cav.
Native to Chile and Argentina. A plant with trailing or climbing succulent stems and fleshy rhizomatous root stock. Leaves shield-shaped, prolific, greyish blue, deeply cut to the centre in narrow segments. The shape of the flowers is similar to those of *Tropaeolum majus*, but much smaller, with yellow petals and long spurs, the two upper petals striped red. Not hardy in very cold localities, where the rhizomes should be protected in winter with a mulch of peat, salt hay, or straw, or lifted from the soil and stored in the same manner as dahlia tubers.

(Flame Flower)
Perennial climber
Flowering period: Aug.–Sept.
Height: up to 10 ft.

Tropaeolum speciosum Poepp. & Endl.
Native to central and southern Chile, where it is a semi-woodland plant found climbing over shrubs and small trees. Hardy in all but exceptionally cold localities (above Zone 7) and widely grown in British gardens. The base of the plant likes a cool, fresh, moist position, while the long slender growths love to ramble through the branches of a shrub or a conifer, where the brilliant scarlet flowers thrive in full sun. Roots in the form of long thin rhizomes. Leaves graceful and elegant, divided into 5–6 elongated segments; bright green above, undersurface covered with fine hairs. Flowers exceptionally attractive but the plant is often extremely difficult, occasionally impossible, to establish, requiring an acid, lime-free soil rich in humus. The ground should never be disturbed, hoed, or even roughly weeded in the vicinity of the roots. Some authorities give excellent advice when they suggest it be associated with rhododendrons and hydrangeas.

*Tuberous-rooted
herbaceous perennial*
Flowering period: Aug.–Oct.
Height: up to 10 ft.

Tropaeolum tuberosum Ruiz & Pav.
Native to Peru and Bolivia. Cultivated in Chile and Colombia (under such names as *Maca, Mashua, Mayua,* or *Maxua*) for its edible roots that are of considerable economic importance. The tubers are 2–3 ins. long, yellow marbled red. Stems and branches flattish, reddish.

Leaves deeply cut almost to the centre, forming five lobes. Flowers long-stemmed, small, long-spurred, calyx and spurs reddish, petals yellow, small, almost erect. Requires a warm, sunny position and is not tolerant of frost.

Tulipa

(TULIP)
Family: Liliaceæ
Hardy perennial bulbs
Position: sun
Propagation: division or seed
Cultivation easy
Useful for cutting

The tulip is one of the few popular flowers that have not been spoiled by commercial cultivation. Even if those varieties have disappeared for which such follies were committed in the sixteen hundreds, there is still no lack of tulips of every form and colour, early- or late-flowering, hybrids and species. Each autumn the amateur and professional gardener is deluged with catalogues offering tulips of every kind. If among flowers the rose has the longest and most complicated history—rich in episodes and adventure, with an incredible literature dedicated to it—the tulip is not far behind, with a kaleidoscopic history packed with exciting events.

We do not know for certain when the garden cultivation of tulips really began. It is a flower of Oriental origin and in the East its cultivation was initiated about a thousand years ago. In Persia it grew wild, and near Kabul the Great Mogul Baber counted thirty-three different species. According to a Persian legend, the first tulips sprang up from the drops of blood shed by a lover; for a long time the tulip was the symbol of avowed love. Poets sang its praises and artists drew and painted it so frequently that when imported into Europe it was considered to be the symbol of the Ottoman Empire. For its exportation from Constantinople we are indebted to the famous Ambassador of the Holy Roman Empire, Ogier de Busbecq, whose acquaintance we have already made in connection with lilacs. He sent and also personally took tulip seeds and bulbs which he gave to Clusius in Vienna, who was embarrassed by the gift and did not know what to do with such curiosities. Eventually he planted the bulbs in a heap. As the horticulturists of those days were more con-

Tulipa gesneriana
From Gaetano Savi's *Flora italiana* . . .
(plate 62), Pisa, 1818

cerned with practical matters and often more interested in the alimentary possibilities of new introductions than in ornamental value, Clusius gave a hundred bulbs to his grocer in Vienna, who preserved them in sugar. Even worse, an Antwerp trader fried his tulip bulbs and ate them dressed with oil and vinegar. Fortunately, however, these culinary experiments did not engender wide practise; although, to be quite honest, they were not so absurd as they seem, since in Baluchistan the local people still eat *Tulipa montana* bulbs, while in some parts of Japan a type of flour is made from *Tulipa edulis* bulbs; in times of famine, even the Dutch have eaten tulip bulbs when nothing else was available. These few cases are, however, exceptional and not sufficient justification for classifying the tulip as an edible crop. Nevertheless, the economic value of tulips has probably made them more important than any other ornamental plant. After Clusius' unfortunate mistake, tulips finally came to be known in Vienna. Conrad Gesner gave the plant its name and made the first drawings of it, prior to 1559, after seeing a specimen in bloom at Augsburg in the garden of Counsellor Herwath. The word "tulip" is believed to be a corruption of the name used by the Turks for the headgear of the Slavonians, from the Turkish *tülbend* or *turban*, although the etymology is not certain or clear.

The very earliest known tulip was called *Tulipa gesneriana* in honour of Gesner. It was also Gesner who, in 1561, first mentioned *Tulipa suaveolens*, native to southern Russia; this species, through succeeding crosses, imparted something of its perfume to subsequent hybrids. In 1596, Clusius saw a new tulip, *Tulipa oculus-solis,* in the garden of Joseph de Jonge, at Middelburg. In 1598, *Tulipa biflora,* native to the Caucasus, flowered for the first time in Clusius' garden. Wealthy people soon began to purchase the bulbs that were being brought back from Turkey by Venetian merchants. In 1577, Clusius sent to England bulbs of *Tulipa claremont,* a parent of the early-flowering tulips; this was followed in 1582 by a straw-coloured example and a white tulip suffused pink. But strangely enough, the British did not appear to fully appreciate the treasure that had fallen into their hands. At the beginning of the seventeenth century, France also began to show an interest in tulips. In 1610, fashionable French ladies were already wearing corsages of tulips. It was the seventeenth century that saw the commencement of the real tulipomania, with the most extravagant follies and exaggerations. Tulip values increased day by day and the fever spread throughout Europe from France to the Low Countries, where the bulb achieved its real triumph. It was probably Clusius who also introduced the tulip into Holland, since in 1593 he left Vienna to take the chair of professor of botany at Leiden, and although there is no documentary proof, it seems very probable that his luggage also included a sack of tulip bulbs. In the course of the next few years, Dutchmen were seized by tulipomania. Even

Peony-flowered hybrid tulip Scarlet Cardinal

Parrot tulip Blue Parrot

at Lille an innkeeper exchanged his alehouse for a tulip bulb and the establishment was renamed *Brasserie Tulipe* to commemorate the episode. Early in the seventeenth century, a small bed of tulips was valued at 15,000–20,000 francs. But the lust for tulips had nothing whatever to do with enthusiasm for the flowers, and, as it has been accurately recorded, the bulbs became a type of currency, or articles of exchange, their value varying from day to day and quoted like stocks and shares. During the period 1634–1637, people abandoned jobs, businesses, wives, homes, and lovers to become tulip growers. For a bulb of the variety *Vice-Roi* one Dutchman paid thirty-six bushels of wheat, seventy-two of rice, four oxen, twelve sheep, eight pigs, two barrels of wine and four of beer, two tons of butter, a thousand pounds of cheese, a bed, clothes, and a silver cup; altogether making a total value of 2,500 Dutch florins. For a single bulb another gave a new carriage and twelve horses; while another gave twelve acres of land. In 1636 the sum of 30,000 florins was paid for three bulbs of the variety *Semper Augustus*. Bulbs of the var. *Admiral Enkhuiszen* were quoted at a price of 11,500 florins. In time the mania became a type of fanaticism; a certain man who had paid for a bulb with its weight in gold learned that a cobbler of Haarlem possessed the same variety. Thereupon he bought that one for 15,000 florins and, before the cobbler's eyes, crushed it underfoot so that his would remain the only existing specimen. He sadistically told the cobbler that he would have been prepared to pay ten times as much for the bulb, whereupon the cobbler, without a word, went up into his loft and hanged himself on the first beam. Naturally, this frenzy also influenced fashion, and many fabrics, materials, and lace were decorated with tulip-flower patterns. No artist painted a still life without tulips. According to one Dutch historian, "Nabobs and labourers, workmen and noblemen, peasants and shipbuilders, servants and lackeys, ladies and dressmakers, fishmongers and children, frequented the market and speculated in tulip shares. It is even believed that the actual word *bourse* [stock exchange] derives from that period, because those who speculated in the tulip market held their meetings in the house of the noble family Van Bourse, at Bruges."

In the beginning, the bulbs arrived at the market from Lille, in Flanders, where they were grown by monks. Later, it was enough to exhibit a piece of paper attesting to ownership of a bulb to sell it at a higher price, without even producing the actual bulb. The number of bulbs on the market was believed to be in the region of ten million. Inevitably, however, the craze for tulips began to wane, and eventually the bubble burst and prices fell in the same spectacular manner as they had risen. On April 27, 1637, a decree was issued declaring that the purchase and sale of tulip bulbs was to be conducted in the same manner as any other business. Speculation

Tulipa silvestris
From *Curtis's Botanical Magazine*,
1809, plate 1202

ceased and many people were ruined. An operator who had amassed an income of 60,000 florins a year was within four years reduced to beggary. Although prices fell to reasonable proportions, tulips never did become really cheap, and even today they are still relatively expensive.

After its European adventure, the tulip continued its career of folly in Turkey, where, although it had been grown there for centuries, it found in the eighteenth century the ideal historical and social conditions for further exploitation and triumph. An eighteenth-century manuscript in Berlin notes that the Sheik Mohammed Lalizare, official tulip grower to the Grand Vizier, counted 1,323 varieties. Under the reign of Ahmed III (1703–1730) annual tulip festivals were held, and during one of these occasions the Grand Vizier invited the Sultan and his court to be his guests. Judging from the descriptions of contemporary travellers, the event must have been an expensive one: bulbs were ordered fifty thousand at a time, and the garden contained half a million blooms. Even in Turkey such excesses eventually diminished, but tulips remained popular and in great favour for many more years. In the nineteenth century tulips took another step forward and gained more modest but more valid honours in England; a diarist recorded that they "became popular with shopkeepers and workmen", and a great many varieties were grown.

Modern tulips are often very different from those cultivated in past centuries. If one observes the tulips represented in seventeenth-century Dutch paintings, it is immediately apparent that few of those old varieties have survived, and that the form, shape, line, and general aspect of the plants have changed. As recorded by Sacheverell Sitwell, prominence was given to the ability of tulips to vary and transform their appearance. After several years of normal growth cultivated bulbs can undergo an evolution and develop a "break" or colour transformation, with the corolla becoming "feathered" or "flamed"; the bulb is then referred to as a "breeder". In feathered flowers the tips of the petals have a different color or colour variation, while in flamed flowers the entire length of the petals is striped. The descendants of these bulbs retain the characteristics of their parents. The process is due to a virus infection which has no other effect than to cause the colour mutation and does not harm the bulb. The old variety, *Sir Joseph Paxton,* exhibits all three stages—breeder, feathered, and flamed.

Between 1830 and 1870 was the golden age of tulips in England. Sometime after 1873 and after Russia had conquered Central Asia, numerous exotic species were found in European gardens; *Tulipa kaufmanniana* and *Tulipa greigii* in 1898, *Tulipa fosteriana* in 1904. As to European varieties, the first parrot tulip was not raised by hybridists, but appeared spontaneously in 1665. Subsequent attempts to create new parrot tulips failed, even when a Dutch grower cultivated one hundred thousand seedlings which he thought would produce at least a percentage of the desired results. This proved that parrot tulips cannot be propagated from seed, and all subsequent new varieties of this type have occurred by chance. The lily-flowered tulip was obtained at the beginning of the twentieth century by crossing *Tulipa retroflexa* with a cottage tulip; it was first marketed in 1914. In 1886, Jules Lenglart created the first Darwin tulip; while in 1909 the firm of Kreelage offered the first Mendel tulip. At the present time the most widely grown tulips are all hybrids of the types: Darwin, Mendel, triumph, parrot, lily- and peony-flowered.

According to the botanist Parey, the genus *Tulipa* comprises about one hundred and fifty species, diffused throughout Eastern and Central Asia, North Africa, and Europe. According to the *Index Kewensis,* however, there are three hundred species, while other sources place the number at far less than one hundred and fifty, a number that should help reassure the reader. A century ago one could trust and believe in nomenclature and in taxonomy, but more recently the science of genetics has taught us that the boundaries between species are very uncertain and, even more important, the fact that the genus is still developing and evolving. At the beginning of the twentieth century, *Tulipa* species were found in northern Italy, the south of France, and in Greece, where they had not been seen previously. Cytology has included these new tulips in a group called neo-tulips, among which there are *Tulipa marjoletti, Tulipa billietiana, Tulipa praecox,* and others. The process is a simple one to follow: since the beginning of the seventeenth century, garden-grown species and hybrids have escaped from gardens; first to all nearby cultivated land, and later throughout the countryside by means of seed, small bulbs, and stolon-borne bulbils together with stem bulbils. The situation is best explained by K. H. Meyer in his *Gefahrten des Gartenjahres* (Parey, Berlin, 1960). Here it is shown that genetic examination confirms that *Tulipa silvestris* is a tetraploid form (that is, with four series of chromosomes in each cell) of the diploid *Tulipa australis; Tulipa turkestanica* is a tetraploid form of the diploid *Tulipa biflora,* and *Tulipa praecox* is a triploid form of the diploid *Tulipa oculus-solis,* and so on.

Scented Tulips. Scented tulips are few in number. Recommended among the early-flowering varieties are:

> Bellona, light yellow
> De Wet, orange and scarlet striped
> Doctor Plesman and Prince of Austria, vermilion
> Prince Carnival, striped red and yellow
> Princess Irene, orange-bronze

Lily-flowered tulip
Queen of Sheba

Single early tulip Prince Carnival

Breeder tulip Dillenburg

All of these have a fragrance similar to that of freesias. The species *T. clusiana, T. marjoletti,* and the late-flowering *T. patens* (or *persica*) are slightly scented. The most strongly and sweetly scented of all is *Tulipa silvestris,* with a perfume similar to violets. Other scented tulips are: Black Parrot and Cherbourg, with a lily-of-the-valley scent; Crown Imperial, carnation-scented; Demeter, Fred Moore, with a sweet fragrance; Golden Age, cherry-scented; Mrs. Moon, almond-scented; Schoonoord, honey-scented; and Grenadier and Bruno Walter.

Cultivation. Tulips are perhaps one of the easiest flowers to cultivate, at least in the case of those bulbs bought for planting in pots or beds for a temporary spring display. The matter becomes more complicated, however, if the bulbs are considered permanent, increasing and flowering again in successive years. In that case it is necessary to prepare and fertilize the soil so that the bulbs do not completely exhaust themselves the first year and will gain enough strength to recoup the energy they use in flower and foliage production. Many of the wild tulip species are native to the steppes of Eastern Europe and Western Asia; there they live in a heavy, compact, clayey soil that dries out completely in summer, becoming parched and hard. These conditions subject the bulbs to considerable lateral pressure, against which their form, consistency, and hard outer involucre are adequate safeguards (completely different from the loosely formed construction of relatively soft lily bulbs which require a soft, loose soil). Thus, tulips prefer a rather heavy soil that is at the same time rich in humus and well fertilized, but not with animal manure. The site should be dug to a depth of at least 12–15 ins., cleaned of stones, and enriched with peat or leafsoil. For the cultivation of tulips in pots or other containers the following mixture is advised: 1 part ordinary garden soil, 1 part leafsoil, 1 part peat, and 1 part sand. It should be borne in mind, however, that it is not possible to obtain a second (still less a third) flowering from tulip bulbs grown in unnatural conditions such as pots or boxes. After the first flowering the bulbs should be planted in a garden where they can gradually regain their lost vigour. The planting season for tulip bulbs extends from the end of August until December; the end of August at high altitudes and in the far north, December in warm localities such as the Riviera and the southern parts of the United States. The most suitable, average planting time is late September to mid-October.

Tulips planted in straight rows are not attractive, and even in relatively small formal beds they look better when in bloom if planted in a zig-zag, alternate manner. One of the best ways to grow tulips is to naturalize them in permanent positions (hybrid garden-variety tulips are not suitable for naturalizing). The best way to naturalize them is to broadcast them over the site and then plant the bulbs in the positions where they fall; numerous authors suggest walking over the site with a bag of bulbs and throwing handfuls here and there, planting them where they fall. As a general rule, it can be assumed that the species tulips will increase and flourish for many years when naturalized in grass, among deciduous shrubs, or even in borders and the rock-garden; whereas the modern large-flowered hybrid tulips gradually degenerate if left in the soil permanently, although they are quite hardy.

When planting, it is necessary to bear in mind the date of flowering, height, and colour; all factors that vary greatly. In a big garden with plenty of space, the most interesting species for naturalizing are *T. clusiana, T. kaufmanniana, T. sprengeri, T. tarda,* and *T. acuminata*; all can be left undisturbed for many years. Where little space is available, some people prefer to concentrate on quality rather than on quantity, collecting the curious little-known unusual tulips of bygone days, cultivating them in pots arranged on small benches or hung on walls or other supports as was the fashion in Turkey at one time.

The planting distance between bulbs varies from 5–10 ins. according to the species or variety; 6–8 ins. being an average distance, except in the case of naturalized bulbs where the distances are completely irregular and haphazard. (Tulips grown in pots, etc., for temporary indoor use can be planted much closer together; for instance three bulbs in a pot 3–4 ins. in diameter; or 7–8 bulbs in a window box 18 ins. x 6 ins.) There should be 4–6 ins. of soil above the point of the bulb; plant slightly higher in heavy cold soils, and deeper in dry light soils. Some of the species produce very small bulbs, and these should not be planted so deeply. After flowering, the flower stem (*not* the foliage) should be cut off to spare the bulb from the unnecessary effort of producing seed, a process that greatly exhausts the bulbs; in the case of pot-grown bulbs, watering should be progressively reduced after flowering, and the foliage will turn yellow and eventually die down prior to the bulbs' dormant period. When the foliage of bedding tulips has almost completely died down the bulbs can be removed from the soil, but the operation should not be delayed until the foliage has entirely disappeared, otherwise the bulb will have so dried and matured that the outer skin or involucre will have detached, and it is better that this should remain around the bulb during its dormant period. After removing the bulbs from the soil, the young bulblets around the parent can be removed. Dry both in a well-ventilated shady position. When completely dry they can be stored until planting time comes around again. The best place for storage is a cool, dark, well-ventilated location where there is no risk of rats or mice eating the bulbs. They can be arranged in wooden trays, cardboard boxes, or any other non-metal container. At planting time the young bulbs can be planted in rows in nursery beds, where

Tulipa fosteriana hybrid Red Emperor

they will develop into normal-sized bulbs. Until they reach their full size they should not be allowed to bloom. Bulbs of species tulips not permanently naturalized that show signs of exhaustion will also benefit if grown in richer soil in nursery beds, and if not allowed to produce flowers for one season; after this they can be used again in the garden. Tulips can also be propagated from seed, although probably few people have sufficient time, patience, and enthusiasm for this method, unless they are prepared to pass the seedlings on to their children. The seed should be sown in September–October, in pots or pans, at a depth of $\frac{1}{3}$ in. and placed in frames. Germination will take place the following spring and flowering-sized bulbs will reach maturity within about five years; but before any particular characteristic can be isolated and perpetuated, at least 15–20 years are necessary. Propagation is best, therefore, by division and multiplication of the bulbs.

To force tulip bulbs for winter display indoors, planting should be done between Sept.–Nov., according to climate. Employ the soil mixture mentioned above; however, do not bury the bulbs deeply, but place them so that the top quarter of the bulb protrudes above the soil surface. For maximum effect, bulbs should be planted in groups of three or more per pot (a 6-in. pot will hold three or four bulbs, an 8-in. pot five or six, etc.) with the flattish side of each bulb facing outwards (this is the side that produces the largest leaf and thus all the large leaves will face outwards, giving a pleasing appearance to the arrangement). The best pots for forcing are known commercially as bulb "pans", and they are wider than they are deep. But any pot may be used, such as terra-cotta, plastic, and even glazed earthenware; however, whatever type is chosen, it is vital that it possess a drainage hole at the bottom.

After planting the bulbs, water the pots well (if terra-cotta pots have been employed they should be well scrubbed and then soaked for 24 hours before the bulbs are planted in them), making sure the soil is thoroughly and deeply soaked, but not soggy. The potted bulbs must now be stored in a dark place where the temperature can be maintained at between 40°F. and 50°F. (In areas where winter temperatures rarely fall this low for extended periods, the potted bulbs should be stored in an extra refrigerator.)

A temperature of 40°F. is essential for root production, and it takes from twelve to fourteen weeks for the bulbs to fill the pots with roots. These factors should be kept in mind when planting. In areas where September and October are warm months, some authorities suggest that prior to planting the unpotted bulbs be given a week's sojourn in the refrigerator, stored in the vegetable "crisper" section (do *not* put them in the freezer or in the section immediately beneath the freezer).

The method most often used for the storage of potted bulbs is to place them in a shallow trench, which may be dug in a sheltered, out-of-the-way place in the garden. The trench should be about 15–18 ins. deep, and once the pots have been placed in it, it should be filled with a loose, friable mulch consisting of dead leaves, straw, salt hay, peat moss, etc., using enough mulch to cover the pots. Then, place a piece of wire netting over the trench and, finally, cover this with a layer of loose earth (about 2 ins. deep). One may also cover each pot with an upside-down pot of a similar size (this method is neater, makes for less danger to the new growth when the pots are dug up, and eliminates the protection suggested in the following sentence). If bulb-hungry rodents such as mice or squirrels tend to be a problem, a generous sprinkling of mothballs (camphor-balls) can be distributed around the pots before they are covered, or each individual pot can be protected by a wire "cage".

An alternate method of storing the bulbs is to place the pots in a sheltered location such as an unheated, or cool, basement, garage, or attic. Keep the pots in total darkness (they can be placed in covered cartons or they could be covered with opaque plastic sheeting), and check at least once a week to see whether they need to be watered. The potted bulbs may even be packed into very large cartons and well-insulated with amply packed, slightly damp autumn leaves (or even peat moss—a procedure that might be practical for city-dwellers with large terraces who would have a hard time finding enough leaves to fill the cartons); the cartons should then be sealed with tape to prevent the moisture from escaping. Whichever method is employed, it is vital that the temperature should remain at an approximate constant of 40°F., as too high or too low a temperature will retard root growth.

After twelve weeks, the potted bulbs should be examined for root and top growth. (If they were planted in the trench, just dig out one pot.) If the roots have filled the pot and the top growth is about $1\frac{1}{2}$ ins. high, then remove all the pots to a dimly lighted room (or a similarly dim place in an unheated greenhouse) with a temperature no higher than 65°F. for a week or ten days. This "hardens" the growths and allows them to adjust to the new environment and thus expand slowly but surely. After the pots have been removed from the trench (or from the leaf-stuffed cartons), they should be carefully washed clean. Sometimes a greyish mould will have formed; and although this mould is harmless while the pots have been buried, it should be removed at once after they are brought into contact with the air. To prevent the formation of mould, the pots may be sprinkled with a fungicide prior to their being buried or packed away (the fungicide—usually a powder—should be washed off also, but mainly for aesthetic reasons).

After the week-long hardening-off period, the pots may be brought into a well-lighted room in the house, and placed near a window

Tulipa Mendel
Orange Wonder

where they can receive full light but no direct sunlight. Normal foliage and flower development will follow. Once the flowers have faded, the bulbs are usually discarded, as the forcing will have exhausted them. However, if one wishes to keep them to plant in the garden the following fall, their complete growth cycle must be maintained until the foliage withers and yellows. Thus, after flowering, cut the flower stems off at the base, give the plants weekly applications of a very dilute liquid fertilizer, and keep the pots in a sunny location. When replanting these forced bulbs, it should be remembered that they will not produce vigorous flowers the following spring, and any flower stems produced should be cut off at the base.

(Horned Tulip)
Flowering period: Apr.
Height: 12–15 ins.

Tulipa acuminata
A very distinct and curious tulip, at one time believed to be a true species but now thought to be of hybrid origin and classified into the *Neo-Tulipae* group together with others of doubtful origin. (These tulips are rather an embarrassment to botanists, having at one time or another been given specific names, but lacking an authentic natural habitat.) The flowers have a certain fascination but are more curious than attractive, having long, thin, horned petals; variable in colour, sometimes bicoloured and often twisted.

Flowering period: Apr.
Height: up to 10 ins.

Tulipa australis Link
Native to the Mediterranean regions and North Africa. Leaves ribbon-shaped, channelled, up to 4 ins. long. Flowers yellow suffused red outside, scented, generally solitary but occasionally in pairs; petal tips pointed, up to 2 ins. long. Has much in common with *Tulipa silvestris* (both of which freely spread by stolons), but generally found at higher altitudes. Flower stalk up to 10 ins. high.

Flowering period: May
Height: 5–6 ins.

Tulipa batalini Regel
Native to Bukhara. A dwarf species not more than 6 ins. high even when in bloom. Leaves narrow, almost grass-like. Flowers yellow marked with greyish yellow or glaucous yellow, petal tips blunted and often notched, $1\frac{1}{2}$ ins. long. One of the most beautiful of the smaller species, excellent for the rock-garden or for cultivating in pans in the unheated greenhouse. Has been crossed with *Tulipa linifolia* and *Tulipa maximowiczii* to produce some lovely pink and apricot-yellow hybrids.

(Lady Tulip)
Flowering period: Apr.
Height: 8–10 ins.

Tulipa clusiana D.C.
Originally native to Persia, Afghanistan, and Kashmir, but now naturalized throughout the Mediterranean regions. One of the most beautiful bulbs found growing spontaneously in Southern Europe, and one of the most graceful of all wild tulips; superb for naturalizing. Flowers small, slender, and graceful, about 2 ins. long, pointed

when closed or in the bud stage. Petals elliptic-lanceolate, white with a longitudinal crimson-red stripe on the outside, and pure white inside with a dark purple, almost black centre. Flower stems flexible and slender. Leaves narrow, linear lanceolate, glaucous green often margined with red, both basal and stem-borne. Length of flower stalk up to 8–10 ins. Suitable for sun or partial shade and completely hardy. Few of the modern hybrid tulips have the grace and charm of this species.

Tulipa eichleri Regel   *Flowering period: Apr.*
Native to Bukhara, Turkestan, and Iran. A beautiful large-flowered *Height: 12–15 ins.*
species, with blooms up to 5 ins. in diameter when fully expanded, borne on stems up to 15 ins. high. Petals pointed, of an intense scarlet, with a black mark edged yellow at their base. Anthers violet-black. Leaves wide, bluish glaucous green. Not very hardy but excellent for naturalizing in temperate climates.

Tulipa fosteriana Hoog.   *Flowering period: Mar.–Apr.*
Native to Central Asia. Without doubt one of the most spectacular *Height: up to 18 ins.*
and largest-flowered of all species tulips. Has been much exploited by hybridists to produce a great many beautiful hybrids. The original species has vermilion-scarlet external petals, and internally the petals are crimson-red with an irregular purple-black mark at the base. When fully expanded the blooms have a diameter of 9 ins., with a shiny, silky sheen. The anthers are purple-black. Leaves glaucous, wide, non-rigid. The globose reddish-brown bulbs are proportionately large. Thrives in any soil in a hot, sunny position; it is hardy but not suited to excessively cold localities. Gives better results if lifted and dried after the leaves have died down and replanted each autumn. Some of the best forms are:

    Canopus, brilliant red
    Czardas, orange-scarlet
    Gold Beater, golden-yellow
    Pinkeen, pinkish orange
    Red Emperor (syn. Mme. Lefeber), the best variety, vermilion
    White Emperor (syn. *purissima*), the only pure-white variety

Tulipa gesneriana L.   *Flowering period: Apr.–May*
Native to Turkey and Asia Minor, but naturalized in Southern *Height: 12–15 ins.*
Europe. Cup-shaped flowers generally vermilion-red or crimson-scarlet, variably marked or striped white, yellow, or dark violet. Petals not all of the same size. Only 3–4 leaves, glaucous. A very variable species, generally with a dark yellow-edged mark at the base of each petal. Its right to species status is doubted by some botanists. There are several fine hybrid forms.

Tulipa clusiana
From *Curtis's Botanical Magazine*,
1811, plate 1390

Tulipa greigii L.
Flowering period: Mar.–Apr.
Height: up to 2 ft.

Native to Turkestan. Another magnificent large-flowered species which can be compared to even the best of the modern hybrid tulips. Somewhat similar in appearance to *Tulipa fosteriana* and moderately hardy. The foliage is characteristic of the species; the leaves are wide, glaucous, and copiously marked with irregularly shaped dark-purple zones. Flowers very big, widely cup-shaped with the tips of the petals recurved and borne on stems up to 2 ft. high. Colour variable, always intense, and generally some shade of vermilion-scarlet or reddish orange, with a black mark at the base of the petals and the interior of the throat greenish black. Anthers black and very conspicuous. Requires the same cultural treatment as *Tulipa fosteriana*. There are many fine forms:

>   Fatima, scarlet-orange
>   Margaret Herbst, vermilion-red
>   Oratorio, pinkish red
>   Pandour, yellow and red
>   Pride of the Caucasus, orange
>   Red Riding Hood, scarlet

All of these have the foliage marbled in the same manner as the species.

Tulipa kaufmanniana Regel
(Water-Lily Tulip)
Flowering period: Apr.–May
Height: 10–12 ins.

Native to Central Asia. Called the water-lily tulip because the shape of the blooms resembles those flowers. Petals narrow, variable in colour from white to cream or pale yellow, sometimes marked with red; of medium size and carried on stems 10–12 ins. high. Leaves broad, glaucous. Of the easiest cultivation and excellent for permanent naturalizing, completely hardy. There are many lovely forms:

>   Alfred Cortot, scarlet and black
>   Berlioz, red and lemon-yellow
>   Gaiety, cream-white and orange
>   Shakespeare, salmon and apricot
>   Solanus, golden-yellow and orange
>   Vivaldi, cream-yellow

Tulipa praecox Tenore
Flowering period: Mar.–Apr.
Height: 18 ins.

Native to Iran, but naturalized throughout most of the Mediterranean regions. Another beautiful species with medium-sized flowers. Petals scarlet, pointed, the external ones larger than the internal ones, each marked at the base with a black patch edged greenish yellow but variable in colour. Leaves wide, glaucous; flower stems glabrous, up to 18 ins. high. One of the best for naturalizing in any type of soil in a hot, sunny site.

Flowering period: Mar.
Height: 4–6 ins.

Tulipa pulchella Fenzl.
Native to Asia Minor. Although given species rank by Sir Daniel Hall in his monograph *The Tulip* (Martin Hopkinson, London, 1929), there is some confusion; the closely related species *Tulipa aucheriana, Tulipa violacea*, and *Tulipa pulchella*, by some authorities are all thought to be geographical forms of *Tulipa humilis*. By whatever name it may be known, *Tulipa pulchella* is a lovely little plant, only 4–6 ins. high even when in bloom. Its flowers are urn-shaped, the outer petals violet-green on the outside, brilliant violet inside; the insides of the petals vary in colour from mauve to vivid carmine-purple; each petal with a basal dark blue, white, or yellowish mark at the edges. Foliage glaucous green, narrowly strap-shaped, channelled and nearly prostrate; 4–6 ins. long, only 2–3 per bulb. It is the variety *Violet Queen* that is mostly cultivated in gardens.

Flowering period: Mar.
Height: 12 ins.

Tulipa saxatilis Sieber
Native to Crete, naturalized in and perhaps indigenous to Italy. An unusual hardy species with cup-shaped pinkish-magenta flowers marked with vivid yellow at the base of the petals and in the internal zone of the throat. Petals obovate-spatulate. Leaves a conspicuous brilliant green, wide, and produced some weeks in advance of the blooms. Excellent for naturalizing in a sunny position in any type of soil. This is a sterile species and can be propagated only by bulb division. The flower stems are up to 12 ins. high and generally bear only one 2-in.-long flower, although sometimes two are produced.

Flowering period: Mar.–May
Height: 12–15 ins.

Tulipa silvestris L.
Native to Europe and an area extending from Iraq west to North Africa. This is the most common and vigorous of the European species; variable in form and colour but generally yellow suffused green outside and occasionally marked with red. Hardy. Height when in bloom 12–15 ins., often with two flowers per stem. Flower petals ovate-lanceolate. Leaves weak, fragile, long and narrow, glaucous green. Requires a warm, sunny position. The best of several varieties is *Tabriz*, with large yellow flowers.

Flowering period: May
Height: up to 1½ ft.

Tulipa sprengeri Baker
Native to Asia Minor. In its native state it reaches a height of up to $2\frac{1}{2}$ ft., but in gardens rarely exceeds 18 ins. One of the latest tulips to bloom, in certain localities often not until the end of May. Leaves narrow, bright green; flowers globose, dark red. Hardy and excellent for naturalizing in almost any soil; more tolerant of shade than most tulips.

Flowering period: Mar.–Apr.
Height: 5–6 ins.

Tulipa tarda Stapf (syn. *Tulipa dasystemon*)
Native to Turkestan. A dwarf only 5–6 ins. high, elegant and graceful in habit, and different from all other tulips. The stems bear 4–6

Tulipa acuminata
From *The Botanical Register*,
1816, plate 127

small yellow or yellow-and-white blooms, star-shaped when fully expanded. Leaves long, narrow, green, and almost prostrate. Hardy, of the easiest cultivation, excellent for naturalizing in any soil in a sunny position and ideal for the rock-garden.

Tulipa Hybrids

The popular hybrid garden tulips are divided into many different classes, each class with its own particular characteristics concerning flowering period, form, size, etc. The following is a representative selection of the most widely grown classes together with a number of the most recommendable varieties in each class.

Single Early Tulips. Semi-dwarf; rather small flowers in March–April. Suitable for bedding and excellent for pot culture.

    Bellona, golden-yellow
    De Wet, orange-red
    Keizerskroon, carmine-red and yellow, one of the best, large flowers
    Mainau, dark red
    Pink Perfection, carmine-pink
    Prince Carnival, scarlet striped yellow
    Silver Standard, pink, red, white
    White Beauty, white

Double Early or Peony-flowered Tulips. Large, long-lasting peony-like blooms in April. Excellent for pot culture and also useful for bedding, although those with very large flowers—up to $4\frac{1}{2}$ ins. in diameter—are liable to be damaged by bad weather.

    Caliph of Baghdad, dark yellow
    Dante, blood-red
    Goya, orange-red
    Murillo maxima, pink suffused white
    Peach Blossom, pink
    Scarlet Cardinal, scarlet
    Schoonoord, white

Mendel Tulips. Single-flowered of medium height (18 ins.). Flowering period early April, intermediate between Darwin tulips and single early tulips. Excellent for forcing and bedding.

    Athlete, white
    Emmy Peeck, lilac-pink
    Her Grace, white and pink
    Krelage's Triumph, geranium-red
    Mimosa, yellow
    Mirjoran, carmine-red
    Orange Wonder, orange-bronze and scarlet
    Sulphur Triumph, primrose-yellow

Triumph Tulips. Large flowers about mid-April. Height up to 20 ins. Excellent for bedding, with strong stems and robust flowers. Earlier than the popular Darwin tulips and less tall.

Adorno, salmon-orange
Bandoeng, dark red
Elmus, cherry-red
Merry Widow, red and white
Nova, lilac
Purple Star, purple-black
Sulphur Glory, yellow
Sweet Seventeen, pink

Darwin Tulips. The most beautiful and most popular of all garden hybrid tulips. Tall erect stems up to 2–2½ ft. high; superb for bedding and magnificent for cutting. Flowers large, with the tip of the petals rounded. May flowering.

Ace of Spades, purple-black
Bishop, dark lavender
Bleu Aimable, lavender-mauve
Breitner, blood-red
Charles Needham, brilliant red
Clara Butt, bright rose-pink
Dorrie Overall, petunia-violet
Eclipse, scarlet-crimson
Giant, reddish violet
Glacier, cream
Golden Age, dark yellow
Golden Hind, dark golden-yellow
Joan of Arc, ivory
Mimosa, buttercup-yellow
Mark Antony, purple and bronze
Niphetos, lemon-yellow
Nobel, dark red
Paul Richter, geranium-red
Queen of Bartigons, salmon-pink
Queen of Night, almost black
Smiling Queen, pink
Zwanenburg, white

Darwin tulip

Darwin Hybrid Tulips. This relatively new class is even better than the original Darwin tulips. Flowers enormous, globose, and with brilliant colours inherited from one of the parents, *Tulipa fosteriana*. Slightly earlier-flowering than the normal Darwin type. Magnificent for bedding and cutting, with vigorous 2–2½-ft.-high stems.

Apeldoorn, orange-red
Dover, scarlet
General Eisenhower, orange-red, yellow base
Gudoshnik, cream splashed red
Holland's Glory, intense scarlet
Oxford, scarlet-red
Parade, scarlet-red
Red Matador, scarlet

Breeder Tulips. May-flowering, single, 2 ft. high; enormous oval blooms in a vast range of colours, marked or stained with another tint.

Astrakhan, magenta and gold
Bacchus, royal purple and violet
Kathleen Truxton, shades of coffee-brown
Louis XIV, purple and bronze

Chappaqua, cherry-red and orange-red
Dillenburg, salmon-orange and terra-cotta
Papageno, reddish brown and scarlet
Southern Cross, cherry-red and orange-red

Lily-flowered Tulips. A class much appreciated for its elegant, graceful flowers with long pointed petals that recurve when fully expanded. Flowering period at the same time as the Darwin hybrid tulips. Of relatively recent introduction, and superb for bedding and cutting. Flowers single, in lovely colours, borne on stems 18 ins. high.

Astor, bronze and pink
China Pink, pink
Dyanito, brilliant red
Leica, cream-white
Mariette, salmon
Queen of Sheba, rust-red
White Triumphator, white
Yellow Marvel, dark yellow

Cottage Tulips. A vigorous, robust, very old class of tulips. Unlike the majority of the garden hybrid tulips, these can be naturalized and left undisturbed for many years. Flowers single, elongated egg-shaped, and of good size. Flowering period late April–early May. Height up to 18 ins. Good colours. Excellent for bedding and cutting.

Belle Jaune, dark yellow
Beverley, orange-flame
Henry Ford, dark pink
Marshal Haig, scarlet
Mount Shasta, white
Pandion, purple
Queen of Spain, cream-yellow

Rembrandt Tulips. This is a class comprising Darwin tulips with the so-called broken flowers—that is, instead of being one uniform colour, the petals are variegated, striped, or marbled in diverse colours.

American Flag, red marbled white
Cordell Hull, red and white
Montgomery, white and pink
Paljas, scarlet variegated white

Parrot Tulips. A class with very large single flowers with fringed or slashed petals. Flower stems up to 18–24 ins. high but often too weak for the size and weight of the flowers. Flowering period late April–May. Curious more than beautiful, but can be used to great effect in cut-flower arrangements.

Blue Parrot, steel-blue
Doorman, cherry-red
Double Fantasy, double, pink
Faraday, white
Gadelan, dark violet-mauve
Orange Parrot, orange
Red Parrot, scarlet
Van Dijk, pink
Violet Queen, lavender-blue

Double Late Tulips. Like the double early tulips, these too are often called peony-flowered tulips because of the peony-like aspect of the blooms. May-flowering. Rigid stems, beautiful colours. Excellent for bedding and cutting. Will tolerate partial shade better than most tulips. Height up to 18 ins.

    Blue Flag, violet-blue   Mount Tacoma, white
    Gerbrandt Kieft, carmine-red   Rocket, scarlet-orange
    Lilac Perfection, lilac-blue   Symphonia, cherry-red
    May Wonder, pink   Uncle Tom, maroon-red

Multiflora tulip    Triumph tulip    *Tulipa kauffmannia*

Multiflora Tulips. A very interesting class with branched flower stems which are very rigid and produce from 3–6 blooms from a single bulb. Height up to 18 ins. May-flowering. Flowers smallish, but graceful and elegant. Useful for bedding and cutting.

    Claudette, white, petals margined red
    Emir, brilliant red
    Georgette, yellow
    Rainbow, pink
    Rose Mist, white suffused pink
    Wallflower, mahogany-red

Green-flowered Tulips. A group of tulips rather than an actual class, and the answer to the often-asked question "Is there a tulip with a green flower?" They are much appreciated for flower arrangements and are always interesting in the garden. Height 15–18 ins. May-flowering.

    Artist, at first terra-cotta and green, later green
    Chérie, yellow and green

Formosa, yellowish green
Greenland, green, dark red, and mother-of-pearl
Viridiflora, green and yellow with undulated petals

The hybrid forms of *Tulipa kaufmanniana, Tulipa greigii*, and *Tulipa fosteriana* are mentioned under those names in the list of species tulips.

Ulex

(Furze, Gorse, or Whin)
Family: Leguminosae
Hardy evergreen
and semi-evergreen shrubs
Position: sun
Propagation: seed or cuttings
Cultivation easy

If *Ulex* plants were rare and costly, they would be more esteemed by gardeners and more frequently used by landscape architects, particularly in seaside localities and rural areas where informally planted they can transform a modest country or seaside garden into a blazing mass of bloom for many months of the year. Being so common, however, they are almost despised and the so-called whin, furze, or gorse is only infrequently included in official planting schemes. They are very attractive with their contorted, intricate, curiously formed evergreen stems, almost without foliage, and with the few small sparse leaves that are often lost among the somewhat formidable spines. Planted along with those varieties of erica that bloom at the same time, gorse can provide surprisingly beautiful yellow and reddish-pink effects in an informal or semi-wild setting. Other advantages of gorse include its exceptionally long flowering period and its adaptability to poor stony soils of any type which at first glance give the impression of being unsuitable for the cultivation of any plant.
The genus is native to Europe and very widely dispersed, often covering vast tracts in its wild state. It can even become invasive; when very dry it can also present a fire hazard. Although its uses are manifold, it is much neglected as a garden plant.
Cultivation. Gorses are strong, vigorous, robust, hardy shrubs tolerant of wind and frost. They will thrive in poor arid soils where few other plants could survive, such as sand dunes, but they are difficult to establish and detest being moved or transplanted. It is

Ulex europaeus

practically a waste of time to attempt the transplanting of wild specimens to the garden, and seed should be sown directly in the flowering position in autumn or spring. Another method is to sow 1–2 seeds in small fibre pots, outside or in frames, and then plant the seedlings out in their permanent position without removing them from the pots. Propagation can also be effected by cuttings taken from half-ripened wood in July and inserted in frames; but the problem of transplanting remains. The gorses require no special treatment, no pruning, and no fertilizing, but they should not be planted in shade nor in positions where the soil is shallow or excessively alkaline (calcareous).

Ulex europaeus L.
Native to Europe. A spiny evergreen shrub with a maximum flowering period in April–May, but at least some flowers are produced throughout the year, the first appearing in January–February. An old English proverb says, "When gorse is out of flower, then kissing is out of fashion". The blooms are single, rich yellow, and resemble the flowers of cytisus, or broom. The plants give best results in a poor, hungry soil in full sun. Both the leaves and bark contain the alkaloid ulexine, which has been used in folk medicine in the same manner as cytisine, which is obtained from *Cytisus scoparius*. The leaves are minute and prickly, often reduced to mere spines, and the plant is classified as evergreen because of its green spines and branches. One of its best uses is in the formation of impenetrable hedges, and it is also effective when planted in large informal groups or cultivated as a single isolated specimen. The var. *plenus* is even more attractive than the species, with a very compact habit, longer and freer flowering, and double. The stamens are transformed into petals and the plant is thus not productive of seed; this quality eliminates the risk of the plant becoming invasive, but necessitates propagation by cuttings.

Flowering period: maximum Apr.–May, but practically continuous
Height: up to 6 ft.
Zone 5 southwards

Ulex gallii Planch.
Native to Europe. A compact semi-evergreen spiny shrub with its maximum flowering period in August–September. Colour bright yellow. Beautiful autumn effects can be obtained by associating this species with *Erica cinerea* and *Erica tetralix*.

Flowering period: Aug.–Sept.
Height: up to 2 ft.
Zone 6 southwards

Ulex nanus Forst.
Native to Europe. A dwarf evergreen spiny shrub of very compact close habit that is excellent for the smaller garden. In some very windy and exposed positions almost prostrate. In general appearance this is like a miniature form of *Ulex europaeus*, with golden-yellow flowers borne in late autumn when the other species are producing fewer blooms.

Flowering period: Sept.–Nov.
Height: 12–18 ins.
Zone 6 southwards

Ursinia

(Jewel of the Veldt)
Family: Compositae
Tender herbaceous perennials, annuals, or sub-shrubs
Flowering period: summer
Height: 8 ins.–2 ft. according to the species
Position: sun
Propagation: seed
Cultivation easy
Aromatic

The genus *Ursinia* owes its name to Johannes H. Ursinus of Regensburg, Germany (1608–1666), author of *Arboretum Biblicum*. It comprises about sixty species native to South Africa, including herbaceous perennials, annuals, or sub-shrubs, with leaves that emit strongly aromatic fragrance when bruised. They have finely divided flexible foliage and large flowers, mostly in delicate shades of yellow, buff, and orange. The species most frequently cultivated in gardens are *Ursinia anethoides* and *Ursinia anthemoides, Ursinia speciosa,* and *Ursinia versicolor*, together with their hybrids. The species have all been known since 1836, but it is only relatively recently that they have become really popular and widely used in gardens. They are quite as attractive as gazanias, with which they can be effectively associated, and they are generally cultivated as summer-flowering annuals. Their modest proportions make them excellent for the larger rock-garden, for small beds, or for use as a ground cover in a sunny position.

Cultivation. Ursinias require a fertile not-too-light soil and do not give good results in damp or rainy localities. They need an abundance of light, warmth, and sunshine; the same environment enjoyed by gazanias. The seed is minute, and in warm districts is best sown directly into its flowering position in April. Otherwise, seed can be sown in a greenhouse in February–March, the seedlings grown on in pots, flats, or boxes, and planted out in May. The roots are very delicate and the greatest care is necessary when transplanting or potting. Excess watering should be avoided.

Herbaceous perennial or sub-shrub
Flowering period: June–Sept.
Height: 12–15 ins.

Ursinia anethoides Gaertn. (syn. *Sphenogyne anethoides*)
Native to South Africa. A sub-shrubby or herbaceous perennial plant with smooth or slightly hairy branches and stems. Leaves 1–1¼ ins. long, light green, finely and much divided. Flowers terminal,

solitary, borne on long wiry stems, and up to 2 ins. in diameter. Their colour is a rich orange-yellow with a ring of dark purple-red at the base of the petals (ligules). The flower shape is typically daisy-like and, unlike so many other plants of this type, they remain open even if there is not bright sunshine but only an abundance of strong, indirect light. The var. *Sunstar* has larger flowers.

Ursinia anthemoides Poir. (syn. *Arctotis anthemoides, Sphenogyne anthemoides*)

Annual
Flowering period: July–Sept.
Height: 8–10 ins.

Native to South Africa. An annual species 8–10 ins. high with slightly hairy or smooth stems. Leaves finely divided into narrow linear segments; the daisy-like 1½-in.-wide flowers, yellow or yellowish orange, are distinct from those of the species *Ursinia anethoides* by the violet-purple colouring of the undersurface of their petals (ligules). It also begins to flower slightly later than *U. anethoides*.

Ursinia speciosa D.C.

Annual
Flowering period: July–Sept.
Height: 12–15 ins.

Native to South Africa. An annual species with a bushy compact habit. The erect stems are without hairs. Flowers terminal, solitary, borne on stems 3–3½ ins. high which are slightly curved before the blooms expand. Flowers daisy-like, yellow, the central disc dark and surrounded by a crimson-red ring at the base of the petals (ligules). Flowers violet-mauve outside. General habit rather disorderly, but it is profuse in its flowering and requires an abundance of strong sunshine. The var. *albida* has an almost white central disc.

Ursinia versicolor D.C. (syn. *Ursinia pulchra, Sphenogyne versicolor*)

Annual
Flowering period: July–Sept.
Height: 12–14 ins.

Native to Namaqualand in Southern Africa. An annual species up to 12–15 ins. high. Flowers terminal, long-stemmed, up to 2 ins. in diameter; yellow with a purple-maroon mark at the base of each petal (ligule), and the central disc is still darker. A characteristic of this very attractive plant is that it bears yellow flowers and orange flowers simultaneously.

Ursinia Hybrids
There are numerous decorative hybrid forms available commercially, such as Aurora (probably a cross between *U. versicolor* and *U. anethoides*), with orange flowers bearing a bronze circle in the centre; Pygmaea is another, only 4 ins. high, with masses of small brilliant-orange flowers without a coloured ring at the base of the petals (ligules).

Ursinia versicolor
From *Paxton's Magazine of Botany*,
1839, plate 77

Valeriana

(VALERIAN)
Family: *Valerianaceae*
Hardy herbaceous perennials
Position: sun or partial shade
Propagation: seed or division
Cultivation very easy

As in the name of the genus *Solidago*, *Valeriana* is derived from the Latin *valere* (keep well), in recognition of the medicinal properties of the most common species, *Valeriana officinalis*, which is diffused in thin woodlands and shady meadows throughout Europe. (It is also thought to commemorate the Roman Emperor Valerianus.) Until a few years ago, before the discovery of synthetic tranquilizers, valerian root was valued for its efficacy in treating cases of nervous debility and hysterical afflictions. It allays pain, promotes sleep, and lacks harmful narcotic side-effects. The leaves of another European species, *Valeriana olitoria*, are edible and sometimes used in salads, and they also have antiscorbutic properties. The chief value of valerian is to be found in its medicinal virtues, and many of the species are of little ornamental value for the garden. Others, however, are not to be neglected, even if their attraction is modest and unassuming. With their graceful foliage and pleasing flowers, they possess a certain appeal, especially in the case of the dwarf forms. Apart from those native to continental Europe, other species are indigenous to the Mediterranean regions, the Caucasus, and North America. The genus consists of about two hundred species.

Valerian will thrive in almost any soil, in sun or partial shade. Propagation is from seed sown in an unheated greenhouse or cold-frame in spring, or by division of established plants in autumn.

Valeriana officinalis

Valeriana officinalis L.
Native to Europe. A hardy herbaceous perennial, with graceful leaves composed of many pairs of leaflets. Flowers borne in terminal corymbs, pale pink in the bud stage but white when fully expanded, and possessing only three stamens.

(Common Valerian or Garden Heliotrope)
Flowering period: Apr.–July
Height: up to 3 ft.

Valeriana phu L.
Native to the Caucasus. A hardy species up to 2 ft. high, often planted in gardens for its attractive foliage, especially the var. *aurea*, which has beautiful golden leaves. The small white flowers appear in midsummer.

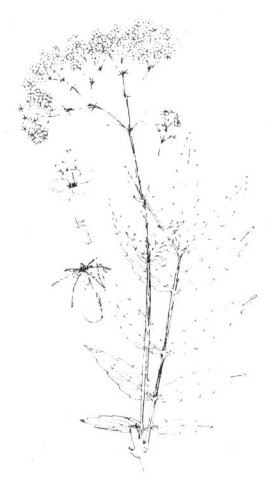

(Cretan Spikenard)
Flowering period: July–Sept.
Height: up to 2 ft.

Flowering period: July–Aug.
Height: up to 4 ft.

Valeriana sambucifolia L.
Native to Europe. A hardy herbaceous perennial up to nearly 4 ft. high with foliage similar to that of *Sambucus* (elder). Inflorescences borne in July–August in the form of large umbels bearing hundreds of minute flesh-pink flowers of considerable attraction.

Venidium

(NAMAQUALAND DAISY OR MONARCH OF THE VELDT)
(*Also see* DIMORPHOTHECA)
Family: Compositae
Tender herbaceous perennials or annuals
Position: sun
Propagation: seed
Cultivation easy

Venidium fastuosum

Like those other glorious South African plants of the genera *Ursinia, Arctotis, Dimorphotheca,* and *Gazania*—all members of the Compositae family and widely cultivated for their brilliant summer display in gardens—venidiums can also be considered one of the most beautiful subjects which can be grown either as an annual or as a perennial according to the climate. None of the plants composing this lovely quintet are hardy and all are sun-lovers. There are eighteen species of *Venidium*. The name is of Latin origin, *vena*, alluding to the prominent veins of the stems.

We are often told that venidiums must have a light soil, and it is true that they thrive in such a medium; but there are often too many preconceived ideas in gardening that prevent our trying alternate methods that often give equally good results. Only recently, I have had great success growing venidiums in a hard, compact, heavy, alkaline (calcareous) soil; I obtained fine vigorous plants which bloomed profusely throughout the summer. Furthermore, I have seen them growing wild in South Africa in a soil that would certainly not be considered good in American or European gardens. Venidiums must, however, be given a well-drained warm position in full sun.

Although there are many species, only two are really widely grown in gardens, *Venidium fastuosum* and *Venidium decurrens*; both are generally cultivated as annuals and raised from seed sown in a warm greenhouse in February–March, the seedlings being grown on in individual pots and planted out in their flowering positions in April.

Seed can also be sown in frames in April and the plants placed outside at the end of May.

Venidium decurrens Less. (syn. *Venidium calendulaceum*)
Native to South Africa. Slightly less tall than the species *V. fastuosum*. A lovely non-hardy perennial easily cultivated as an annual. Large deeply lobed greenish-grey foliage. Flowers 2½ ins. wide, golden-yellow with a black circle in the centre. The var. *calendulaceum* is an even better plant for beds and borders.

Herbaceous perennial generally grown as an annual
Flowering period: July–Sept.
Height: up to 2 ft.

Venidium fastuosum Stapf
Native to South Africa. This is the best species for use as a summer-flowering annual and certainly the most spectacular. The foliage is irregularly lobed and covered with downy white hairs. The flowers are up to 5 ins. in diameter; the centre is a shiny black and purple, making a vivid contrast with the long deep-orange petals, each of which has a brown mark as its base. The blooms close at dusk. There are also numerous hybrids of South African origin with white, yellow, and orange flowers.

Annual
Flowering period: July–Sept.
Height: up to 3 ft.

Verbascum

(MULLEIN)
Family: Scrophulariaceae
Hardy herbaceous biennials or annuals
Position: sun
Propagation: seed or division
Cultivation easy

Verbascum thapsus

Verbascums are among the oldest of cultivated garden plants; they are elegant and imposing hardy biennials or annuals, with a noble erect habit, notable for their beautiful tall conspicuous spikes of yellow, pink, or mauve flowers. In many cases, the foliage, too, is highly decorative; generally basal and rosette-forming, often white or silvery surfaced with a covering of downy hairs. There are also numerous exceptionally attractive hybrids of a perennial nature. Verbascums are diffused throughout the Mediterranean regions, Europe, and Asia Minor, and they naturalize freely. There are about 250 species, but only a small proportion are used in gardens. The fact that so many are biennials has, no doubt, played a negative part in their greater exploitation and wider employment. The name *Verbascum* is of Latin origin and was used by Pliny the Elder.

Verbascum olympicum

Verbascum phoeniceum
from *Curtis's Botanical Magazine*,
1805, plate 885

Seed can be sown in frames from April to July, pricking out the seedlings into nursery beds or frames, and then planting out in their flowering positions either in autumn or the following spring. The perennial species can also be propagated by division in autumn or spring. Verbascums like a moderately dry sunny position in a well-drained soil—either acid or alkaline (calcareous)—which contains a good proportion of organic matter; otherwise, they have no particular likes or dislikes, although fully grown plants are not easy to move.

Verbascum blattaria L. (Moth Mullein)
Native to Europe. A tall, stately biennial with greyish-green, dentated, 3-in.-long oval leaves. Inflorescences in the form of erect rigid spikes up to 6 ft. high bearing masses of yellow flowers with conspicuous purple stamens. A fine plant for the herbaceous border.

Biennial
Flowering period: July–Aug.
Height: up to 6 ft.

Verbascum bombyciferum L.
Native to Asia Minor. A biennial of remarkable beauty; the entire plant—stem, foliage, and inflorescence—covered with a dense layer of felt-like silvery hairs creating an effective setting for the 5-ft.-high spikes of yellow flowers.

Biennial
Flowering period: July–Aug.
Height: up to 5 ft.

Verbascum olympicum Boiss.
Native to Southern Europe. A handsome plant with vivid golden flowers and white stamens borne on tall erect 6-ft.-high inflorescences with a branching, candelabra-like form. The 12-in.-long, down-covered grey leaves are arranged in large rosettes around the base of the plant, and are most decorative.

Biennial
Flowering period: July–Aug.
Height: up to 5–6 ft.

Verbascum phoeniceum L. (Purple Mullein)
Native to Europe. A species of moderate size forming basal rosettes of dark green leaves from which rise branching inflorescences bearing racemes of violet, pink, or purple flowers. This is one of the parents of the many lovely forms included below in the group called Verbascum Hybrids. The few scattered stem leaves are alternate and stalkless.

Biennial
Flowering period: June–Aug.
Height: up to 5 ft.

Verbascum thapsus L. (Velvet Plant, Candlewick, or Flannel Wick)
Native to Europe and Asia. A woolly-leaved species with rigid erect stems bearing pale yellow flowers. The whole plant is densely hairy and most attractive, but perhaps better known for its medicinal properties. A preparation made from the leaves, flowers, and roots is used in the treatment of pulmonary diseases and for preparing a tisane, or herb tea.

Biennial
Flowering period: July–Aug.
Height: up to 6 ft.

Verbascum Hybrids
A name of convenience used to describe a group of lovely perennial hybrids which have in part originated from *Verbascum phoeniceus,* and which are sometimes listed in catalogues under that name. They are remarkably beautiful plants with a wide range of exquisite colours, 3–4½ ft. high, and seen to best effect when planted in groups of not less than a dozen. They can also be treated as annuals and if sown in February–March will bloom the first year. Some of the best named varieties are:

    C. L. Adams, deep yellow flowers and silver foliage
    Cotswold Beauty, pale bronze
    Cotswold Queen, apricot
    Gainsborough, sulphur-yellow
    Lilac Domino, mauve
    Miss Wilmott, white
    Pink Domino, pale pink

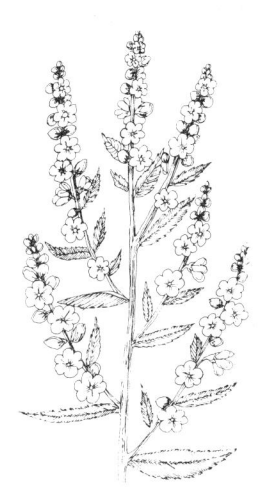

Verbascum blattaria

Verbena

(VERVAIN)
Family: Verbenaceae
Half-hardy herbaceous perennials or annuals
Position: sun
Propagation: seed, division, or cuttings
Cultivation easy

It is a mystery why some people take great pains to cultivate difficult, complicated, and often temperamental plants in windowboxes, on terraces, in small beds or borders, or in the rock-garden, when they could be assured of a continuous display of blooms from late spring until autumn by using the brilliantly coloured, easily grown, attractive forms of verbena. The only criticism to be made of verbenas is their lack of scent, and therein lies another paradox. It seems to have been forgotten that these plants were at one time strongly fragrant; even by authors who are generally so punctilious about recording the fragrance of the plants they describe (neither Plenzat nor Wilson and Bell include the plants). Only Fletcher dedicates a few lines to the subject of verbena perfume, noting that at one time the plants had such strong fragrance that a perfume was extracted from them; today this fragrance has been lost largely through se-

Verbena canadensis
From *Curtis's Botanical Magazine*,
1820, plate 2200

lection, crossing, and hybridization to procure better colours and larger flowers. Fletcher further observes that although some of the bedding verbenas still possess some scent it often varies greatly from plant to plant, and some have a much stronger perfume than others. Thus there remains only one solution if one desires to regain the traditional characteristic fragrance of verbena: sow many different varieties and then select only the most strongly scented for future propagation.

Verbenas have been known since the most ancient times. The Druids had the greatest veneration for the sweetly scented plant, and before gathering it offered a sacrifice to the soil. They also held bunches of verbena between their hands during their devotions. When the Romans sent messengers of peace to other nations they adorned their apparel with sprays of verbena. Images of Venus Victrix were often crowned with wreaths of verbena and myrtle. The peoples of Antiquity also attributed verbenas with certain medicinal properties. Pliny the Elder was familiar with two species, *Verbena officinalis* and *Verbena supina* (both native to Italy), which he designated "male" and "female" respectively. He noted also that much of the fame attached to the plants was mainly attributable to magical practises performed with the herbs. The Romans credited powers of rekindling the flames of dying love to the plant, and gave it the name *Herba Veneris* (plant of Venus). During the Middle Ages and the Renaissance, it became an instrumental component in the rites of witches and sorcerers.

In folk medicine, a decoction of verbena leaves boiled in vinegar was used to treat rheumatic pains, lumbago, and pleurisy. It also provided a potion for aiding digestion. The flowering tips of young growths and the leaves of *Verbena officinalis* dried in the sun have an aromatic fragrance and bitter taste and, among other substances, contain the glucoside verbenaline which, if incorrectly used, can cause paralysis. Verbena is, therefore, not entirely harmless in its medical properties. Leclerc, who experimented with practically all plants of medicinal value, claims to have achieved positive results in treating trigeminal neuralgia by using a liquid extract of verbena. Finally, the root of *Verbena officinalis* has been used since the last century as a bitter tonic, nervine, emetic, and sudorific.

Verbena rigida

Until the eighteenth century the European species had certain practical uses but little horticultural value. The introduction of exotic species came later: *Verbena bonariensis* in 1732, *Verbena canadensis* in 1774, *Verbena pulchella* in 1827, *Verbena teucrioides* in 1837, *Verbena rigida* in 1863, and so on with all the others. Today, only a few of these species are grown in gardens (although *V. peruviana*, *V. pulchella*, and *V. rigida* are popular); their place has been taken by the more spectacular hybrids mostly raised from crosses between the species *V. peruviana*, *V. phlogifera*, *V. incana*, *V. teucrioides*, and *V. platensis*. It was the Peruvian species which introduced the colour red; *V. phlogiflora* gave pink and purple; *V. platensis* provided white and fragrance; and a cross between *V. phlogiflora* and *V. platensis* brought about the white eye. The taller verbenas have a mostly erect habit, while the dwarfer forms are mostly spreading, trailing, or prostrate. Regarding colour, verbena flowers include almost every tint except yellow.

The genus comprises about 200 species, although, as usual, some dissenting botanists place the number at 80, 100, or 250. Their area of diffusion is particularly wide in the New World, mostly in tropical and subtropical areas. *Verbena officinalis* is truly cosmopolitan, being indigenous to the whole of Europe; another species, *V. supina,* has a habitat restricted to the Mediterranean regions, the Caucasus, and the Canary Islands; there is a single species in Australia. The name *Verbena* has given much labour to the philologist: the French link it to an ancient Celtic word *ferfaon*; the Italians believe it was derived from the Latin *herbena* (green). Others maintain that the word comes from a Sanskrit root with the significance of "becoming larger, growing, prospering". In this respect one might well ask if it was the origin of the word that inspired belief in the magical properties of the plant to make love grow and prosper, or if it was the supposed magical virtues of the plant that inspired the name.

Cultivation. Verbenas thrive in all well-drained light soils. If cultivated in receptacles, they prefer a medium composed of equal parts of leafsoil, peat, and sand. They love a sunny but well-ventilated position and flower poorly in partial shade. They do not require a particularly rich soil in the garden, but periodic applications of liquid fertilizer are beneficial during the growing season; this is also applicable to plants grown in receptacles. In the case of plants which have borne an abundance of bloom and then show signs of exhaustion, a light pruning will produce another crop of flowers within 15–20 days. The dwarf, trailing, or prostrate species are excellent for the rock-garden, as a ground cover, for dry walls, stone steps, the interstices between paving stones, and for growing in large pots, boxes, stone troughs, etc., but they are not very hardy and will tolerate only light frost (*Verbena peruviana* none at all). The taller species are useful in the herbaceous border, beds, for edging, or for the mixed border. The annual verbena hybrids are superb for bedding or for growing in receptacles, for a ground cover, or for edging.

During recent years, there have been numerous reports of annual verbenas being attacked by a minute, worm-like pest which bores into the stem of the plant—either at ground level or by way of the roots—and causes apparently healthy plants to collapse and die in a few hours. The name of this pest is *Anguillulina dipsaci* Kuhn., and if its presence is suspected, the soil should be dusted with a product marketed for the purpose of destroying such pests.

Propagation of the perennial species is by seed, cuttings, or division.

Verbena teucrioides

Verbena phlogiflora

Seed can be sown in spring as explained below for the propagation of the hybrid verbenas grown as annuals. Division is best done in spring, while cuttings can be taken at any time during late spring and early summer and rooted under a glass bell-jar, transparent plastic, or in a closed frame. In the case of the prostrate forms, the lateral growths form roots every few inches where the nodes touch the soil, and all that is necessary is to remove some of these rooted nodes from the parent plant and pot or replant them in any desired position. As previously mentioned, the popular large-flowered modern verbena hybrids are invariably grown as annuals from seed, either as a mixture or in separate colours. Seed should be sown in a warm greenhouse in February–March and the seedlings grown on individually in small pots so that they will be ready for planting out in their flowering positions in May. Otherwise, seed can be sown in an unheated greenhouse or frame in March–April, potting the seedlings, and then planting them out in early June. Seed can also be sown directly into the position where the plants are to bloom; but unless one is gardening in a mild, favoured climate this cannot be done until May, thinning out the seedlings to about 6–8 ins. apart. Where only small quantities are required, it is sometimes more convenient to sow 2–3 seeds directly into small fibre pots that can be planted out when all risk of frost has passed. In the case of any particular hybrid producing flowers of an unusual or specially desired colour, or with a more than average fragrance, the plant can also be propagated from cuttings.

Perennial
Flowering period: June–Sept.
Height: up to 4½ ft.

Verbena bonariensis L.

Native to Brazil. A tall herbaceous perennial hardy in all but very cold localities (best treated as an annual above Zone 8), with a loose open habit and slender, graceful, branching square stems bearing at their extremities and in the leaf axils small globose inflorescences of violet-lavender flowers. Leaves dark green, small, sparse, linear-oblong, and deeply dentated. In a warm sunny position, the plants bloom with such abundance and produce such quantities of seed that they tend to exhaust themselves. This can be avoided by regularly removing the dead flowers. They can also be treated as annuals, the plants flowering the first year from seed. Unless grown in very large masses, this species is too loose and too open in habit to make a spectacular display, but if interplanted with dwarfer contrasting subjects such as ground ivy (*Nepeta*), *Cineraria maritima,* ageratums, etc., delightful effects can be obtained.

Perennial
Flowering period: June–Sept.
Height: 12–15 ins.

Verbena canadensis L.

Native to the central and southern United States. A wide-spreading hardy herbaceous perennial. Stems very hairy and branching. Leaves ovate, small, sometimes three-lobed, dentated, basal, and stem-borne. Flowers variable in colour from purple-red to violet and pinkish white, small, numerous, and borne in terminal inflorescences.

Verbena corymbosa L.
Native to South America. Hardy in areas that experience only light frosts (below Zone 8). Develops into a very leafy compact plant and requires full sun in a soil containing an abundance of organic matter. Leaves dark green, much-divided, 2–3 ins. long. Inflorescences borne on tall, rigid, leafy stems and composed of terminal and axillary rounded heads of minute lavender-blue flowers. Given an award of merit by the Royal Horticultural Society in 1929.

Perennial
Flowering period: June–Sept.
Height: up to 2½ ft.

Verbena erinoides Lam. (syn. *Verbena laciniata*)
Native to Chile and Argentina. A lovely little herbaceous perennial, hardy and evergreen in almost frost-free climates. In areas where the winters are cold, it can be propagated and cultivated as an annual, sowing the seed in a warm greenhouse in February–March. Also very easy to propagate by means of the lateral growths that root readily where they come into contact with the soil surface; a few of these can be potted in autumn and wintered over in a sheltered place. This little species is appropriately called the Moss Vervain because of its dense, prostrate habit and minute, finely divided vivid-green foliage which forms a flat, compact, moss-like covering over the soil surface by means of its slender trailing lateral growths. It is sometimes used to form a type of unorthodox lawn (but not suitable for walking upon). From May until September it bears masses of lilac-coloured flowers in small rounded inflorescences borne on minute stems 3–4 ins. high. Requires a hot, moderately dry sunny position in a light soil. Excellent for planting in the interstices of paving, on dry walls, in the rock-garden, etc.

(Moss Vervain)
Perennial
Flowering period: May–Sept.
Height: 3–5 ins.

Verbena peruviana Druce. (syn. *Verbena chamaedryfolia*)
Native to Brazil and Peru. A non-hardy evergreen herbaceous perennial of prostrate spreading habit, up to 3–5 ins. high when in bloom. Leaves small, dark green, deeply dentated, forming a carpet of vegetation from which arise rigid little stems bearing flattish, rounded inflorescences composed of masses of minute individual flowers of a scarlet so intense that it is equalled by few other plants. It remains in bloom from June to October; although not hardy, it can be used as a summer-flowering bedding annual. The prostrate spreading growths readily produce roots when they come in contact with the soil, thus providing an easy method of propagation. Requires a hot, moderately dry, sunny position.

Perennial
Flowering period: June–Oct.
Height: 6–8 ins.

Perennial
Flowering period: June–Sept.
Height: 6–7 ins.

Perennial
Flowering period: July–Oct.
Height: up to 1½ ft.

Verbena peruviana

Verbena Hybrid

Verbena pulchella Sweet
Native to South America, and sometimes known as *Verbena tenera*. Of almost prostrate, trailing habit and similar to *Verbena erinoides,* but develops into a larger plant. Hardy in mild, almost frost-free districts. Small, dark-green, much-divided foliage. Masses of small lilac-blue flowers borne in rounded terminal inflorescences on slender stems 6–7 ins. high. Requires full sun in a moderately dry light soil. Propagation as for *Verbena erinoides*.

Verbena rigida Spreng. (syn. *Verbena venosa*)
Native to Brazil and Argentina. A vigorous wide-spreading herbaceous perennial hardy only in frost-free climates, although it may be cultivated in districts experiencing light frosts if given winter protection. Otherwise, it should be replanted every spring or grown as an annual from seed. Leaves narrow, dark green, dentated, pointed, 2–4 ins. long. Inflorescence a spike up to 6 ins. high composed of a mass of small intensely vivid violet-purple flowers from July to October. Requires a hot, moderately dry, sunny position in a porous not too compact soil. Magnificent for beds and borders.

Verbena Hybrids (*Verbena hortensis*)
Of hybrids origin. Both the above names are terms of convenience including the numerous large-flowered verbenas cultivated as summer-flowering annuals. They are beautiful plants, widely used in beds, borders, windowboxes, large pots, etc. They are notable for their vivid colouring and long-flowering habit, which extends from May to October. These verbenas are among the easiest of summer annuals but less successful during a wet summer or in rainy districts, where the foliage is liable to attacks of mildew. The plants should be placed in a hot, dry, sunny, well-ventilated position in a light, porous soil. These hybrids have originated from crosses between such species as *Verbena peruviana*, *Verbena phlogiflora*, *Verbena incana*, and *Verbena teucrioides*; only *V. peruviana* is now in general cultivation in gardens. They are mostly bushy compact plants, 4½–15 ins. high; some have a semi-trailing habit. Leaves soft-textured, oval, pointed, dentated. Inflorescence a wide flat rounded mass up to 3 ins. in diameter composed of many small closely packed individual flowers. Some of the best forms are:

> Rainbow Mixture, 10–12 ins., early-flowering, compact habit, includes many shades of apricot, lavender, mauve, pink, salmon, crimson, scarlet
> Blaze, 8–10 ins., neat compact habit with inflorescences up to 3½ ins. wide, colour vivid scarlet, leaves dark green, very similar to the species *V. peruviana*
> Hybrida Nanissima, 4½–6½ ins., very compact

Sweet Lavender, 15 ins., globe-shaped inflorescences, soft lavender in colour; graceful, elegant, much-divided fern-like foliage; a really lovely plant

Amethyst, 10–12 ins., spreading habit, very tolerant of bad weather, violet-blue flowers with white eye

Rose Vervain, 12–14 ins. A compact-growing form of *Verbena aubletia* with masses of vivid pink flowers and very long-lasting

Delight, 6 ins., miniature little plants particularly suitable for windowboxes, coral-pink flowers suffused salmon

Seed is available in named varieties such as Dazzler, red; Delight, coral-pink; Sparkle, scarlet with white eye; Crystal, white; and Splendour, purple.

Veronica

(SPEEDWELL)
Family: Scrophulariaceae
Hardy herbaceous perennials
Position: sun or partial shade
Propagation: seed or division
Cultivation easy

A genus of about two hundred widely differing species; thirty are indigenous to Europe and all are herbaceous perennials. At one time the genus also included many shrubby, woody plants but these have now been placed in the separate genus *Hebe,* although some authorities still do not recognize the division. The shrubby hebes are of New Zealand origin and are not so hardy as the herbaceous perennial veronicas. The name *Veronica* is Latin in origin and honors Saint Veronica. All are of pleasing, elegant, graceful appearance, with some lovely shades of blue as the dominant colour of their modest but conspicuous blooms. There are, however, also white- and pink-flowered forms. The veronica's flowering period is long, and the plants are of the easiest cultivation if established in a fertile soil rich in humus and moderately moist. They are sun-lovers, but do not do well in great heat, so in the south it is advisable to plant in partial shade. They are hardy and prefer cold to heat.

The propagation of veronicas is easily effected by division in autumn or spring, or from seed sown in frames in spring, growing on the young plants in pots or in nursery beds until large enough for planting out in their permanent positions in the autumn.

(Birds' Eyes)
Flowering period: May–June
Height: up to 18 ins.

Veronica chamaedrys L.
Native to Europe and Asia. An erect plant up to 18 ins. high with small ovate dentated leaves rounded at the base. The $\frac{1}{4}$-in.-long bright-blue flowers are borne in compact, attractive terminal spikes up to 6 ins. long. This species is widely naturalized in Eastern North America.

Flowering period: July–Aug.
Height: up to 2 ft.

Veronica gentianoides Vahl.
Native to Southeastern Europe and Asia Minor. A hardy herbaceous perennial up to 2 ft. high when in bloom with narrowly oblong leaves up to 3 ins. in length. Inflorescence a loose terminal raceme of blue flowers conspicuously veined with darker blue.

Flowering period: June–July
Height: 15–18 ins.

Veronica incana L.
Native to Asia Minor. A beautiful plant with oblong slightly dentated silver-grey foliage which makes a lovely contrast to the terminal spikes of pale-blue flowers. The var. *glauca* and the var. *argentea* are silver in all their parts and have darker-blue flowers. There is also a lovely pink-flowered form, var. *rosea*. All are excellent subjects for small beds or for the herbaceous border.

Flowering period: July–Sept.
Height: up to 3 ft.

Veronica longifolia L.
Native to Central Europe and Northern Asia. An attractive plant with the leaves either opposite or in groups of three arranged in whorls and conspicuously dentated at the edges. Each leaf narrowly oblong, tapering, up to 4 ins. in length. Long, erect inflorescence in the form of a spike of closely packed lilac-blue flowers. There are several attractive garden varieties, including:

    var. *albiflora,* white-flowered
    var. *rosea,* pink
    var. *subsessilis,* purple-blue, with branched flower spikes; a much superior plant to the true species

Flowering period: May–June
Height: 6 ins.

Veronica pectinata L.
Native to the Caucasus. A beautiful little species only 6 ins. high with a spreading habit. Ideal for the rock-garden, dry walls, or steps. Masses of small rich-blue flowers with a white eye are borne in miniature racemes. Leaves oval, dentated, and covered in white hairs.

Flowering period: May–July
Height: prostrate

Veronica repens L.
Native to Corsica. Probably the most attractive of the mat-forming prostrate species. Of very rapid growth and excellent for creating

Veronica Teucrium
From *Curtis's Botanical Magazine*,
1838, plate 3683

a ground cover, for the rock-garden or planting in dry walls and stone steps or in paving. Intensely blue minute flowers borne in late spring and early summer. Prefers partial shade in hot sunny localities.

(Cat's-Tail Speedwell)
Flowering period: July–Sept.
Height: up to 2 ft.

Veronica spicata L.
Native to Europe. A particularly desirable herbaceous perennial which, together with its numerous hybrids, is the most popular of the taller veronicas; all are excellent subjects for beds, borders, and the large rock-garden. Leaves lanceolate, dentated, up to 2 ins. long. Bright-blue flowers in dense branching spikes. There are also white- and pink-flowered forms—var. *alba* and var. *rosea*—together with numerous very fine forms, including:

> Barcarole, dark pink, 12 ins.
> Blue Peter, dark-blue flowers in very compact spikes, 15 ins.
> Minuet, grey-green foliage and pink flowers, 12 ins.
> Romily Purple, dark violet, very rigid spikes, 18 ins.
> Well's Variety, bright blue flowers and evergreen foliage, 15 ins.
> Wendy, pale blue flowers and silvery foliage, 15 ins.

(Germander Speedwell)
Flowering period: June–Aug.
Height: up to 18 ins.

Veronica Teucrium L. (syn. *Veronica latifolia*)
Native to Central Europe. One of the most beautiful veronicas of medium height. A most conspicuous plant when in bloom, with long slender stems clothed with narrowly oblong dark-green dentated leaves and bearing slender spikes of lavender-blue flowers. Among the excellent garden forms, the following merit particular mention:

> Trehane, golden-yellow foliage and pale-blue flowers, 8 ins.
> Royal Blue, gentian-blue flowers, 18 ins.
> Shirley Blue, sky-blue flowers, 18 ins.

Veronica spicata   *Veronica repens*   *Veronica longifolia*

Viburnum

Family: Caprifoliaceae
Hardy deciduous or half-hardy evergreen shrubs
Position: sun or partial shade
Propagation: seed, cuttings, layering, or division
Cultivation easy

The genus *Viburnum* is of great importance in American and European gardens; sometimes for its beautiful, often deliciously fragrant flowers, sometimes for the lovely autumn tints assumed by the deciduous varieties, and sometimes for the brilliant colours of the so-freely produced fruits. In some cases, these three attractions are combined in a single species or variety, while others are esteemed for their attractive evergreen foliage. During relatively recent years (in the gardening world "recent" indicates a period of 30–40 years), the importance of viburnums has increased still further because of the recent botanical exploration of northern China, the natural habitat of the majority of viburnum species. Dr. Rehder includes sixty-five species from that area which, with others from India, North America, and Europe, brings the total to more than one hundred, apart from the many hybrids and varieties. Not all are sold commercially, however, although specialist firms in Great Britain catalogue at least fifty species. Some years ago I established a collection of forty species in the Villa Taranto Botanic Gardens at Pallanza, Italy.

The genus is composed of deciduous or evergreen shrubs or even small trees; the leaves are opposite, simple or lobed, while the flowers are small, white or pinkish, and generally borne in rounded cymose clusters or pyramidal terminal panicles, the inflorescence close and compact. Corolla is five-lobed, bell-shaped, with five stamens. Fruit is a drupe, either red, blue, or black, containing one seed. The most distinctive characteristic of all, however, is that in several species there are two distinct types of flower borne on the same inflorescence—one sterile and decorative. The sterile flower is without stamens or pistil, and its function is to attract pollinating insects; the other is smaller, less decorative, but completely fertile, and its function is to produce seeds. It is an interesting example of division of labour in the vegetable kingdom, where the two functions are frequently combined in one flower. The same division also may be found in the genus *Hydrangea*. The gardener, always ready to "improve" nature's work, has profited by this phenomenon and, in the cases of such species as *Viburnum opulus, Viburnum macrocephalum*, and *Viburnum tomentosum*, has succeeded in developing

Viburnum Lantana

very showy varieties whose inflorescence consists almost entirely of the spectacular sterile blooms.

The origins of the somewhat curious names of two European species are interesting. Guelder Rose (*Viburnum opulus*) is thought to derive from *rose de Gueldre*, or Guelders (Gelderland), the Dutch province; in his *English Flora*, Sir J. E. Smith suggests that the name may be a corruption of "elder rose": both elder (*Sambucus*) and *Viburnum* belong to the same family and, in the case of certain species, have inflorescences of a similar shape. One species, Wayfaring Tree (*Viburnum Lantana*), is mentioned by W. Howitt in the following poem:

> Wayfaring Tree! What ancient claim
> Hast thou to that right pleasant name?
> Was it that some faint pilgrim came
> Unhopedly to thee,
> In the brown desert's weary way,
> 'Midst thirst and toil's consuming sway,
> And there, as 'neath thy shade he lay,
> Blessed the Wayfaring Tree?

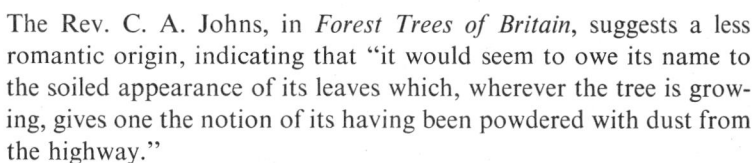

Viburnum tinus

The Rev. C. A. Johns, in *Forest Trees of Britain*, suggests a less romantic origin, indicating that "it would seem to owe its name to the soiled appearance of its leaves which, wherever the tree is growing, gives one the notion of its having been powdered with dust from the highway."

Considering the size of the genus, viburnums have not been used much in either folk medicine or official materia medica. Two species, however, have had considerable importance. *Viburnum prunifolium*, native to Eastern North America where it is known as Black Haw, is not one of the most popular garden species, although its dark-blue fruits are handsome and edible and the white flowers borne in July are not without attraction. The bark of the roots, either in powdered form or in a fluid extract, has been used as a uterine tonic, sedative, and antispasmodic. It has been widely employed for preventing miscarriages and as a remedy for dysmenorrhoea. *Viburnum opulus* (sometimes known as Cramp Bark) has been very effectively used in cases of cramps, convulsions, and spasms; it was generally administered in a tincture prepared from the bark, and at one time it was held in high esteem.

Cultivation. Viburnums are easy to cultivate, although it should be remembered that many species are native to woodlands, thriving in partial shade in deep, cool, fairly moist soils rich in humus. My personal experience fully confirms the widely accepted view that in very hot, very sunny, dry places, the plants quickly exhaust themselves and, even under more favourable conditions, they have a relatively short life-span (15–20 years). Apart from cool soil, they also like moist atmosphere and are best suited to northern gardens. They

Viburnum macrocephalum var. *sterile*
From *The Botanical Register,*
1834, plate 1650

must, however, have really good drainage. Several species will thrive in complete shade, especially the so-useful evergreen *Viburnum tinus*, which remains in bloom for nearly twelve months of the year and often carries flowers and fruits simultaneously. The most suitable species for warm, sunny positions are *Viburnum carlesii, Viburnum x burkwoodii* (of hybrid origin), *Viburnum tomentosum, Viburnum suspensum, Viburnum rhytidophyllum*, and *Viburnum odoratissimum*. All those mentioned here are hardy, although the evergreen species *Viburnum tinus, Viburnum davidi*, and *Viburnum macrocephalum* are liable to suffer if exposed to continuous very cold winter winds. Propagation can easily be effected from seed sown in pots, flats, or boxes, in frames in spring, or even in seed beds in the open in mild climates. Viburnums also root quite easily from cuttings made from half-ripened wood taken in July and inserted in sandy soil in frames. The choicer hybrid varieties are often propagated by grafting onto the more common species raised from seed, but this system is not recommended since it involves the constant removal of basal suckers. Deciduous species such as *Viburnum tomentosum* and *Viburnum opulus* are very easy to propagate by layering; in fact, the lower branches will often layer spontaneously when they come into contact with the soil surface. No regular pruning is necessary, except for keeping the plants a good shape and removing weak or dead growths. The flowers are borne on the previous season's vegetation.

(Dockmackie)
Deciduous
Flowering period: June
Height: up to 6 ft.
Zone 4 southwards

Viburnum acerifolium L.
Native to North America. One of the first American viburnums to be introduced into Europe, in 1736. A deciduous shrub of modest proportions with maple-like, three-lobed, 2–4-in.-long leaves, 2–4 ins. wide. Flowers white, borne in long-stalked terminal cymes of little ornamental value. The plant is well worth growing for the beauty of its foliage in autumn, when it assumes the most superb crimson shades. The fruits are at first red, and with maturity become purple-black.

Deciduous
Flowering period: Aug.–Sept.
Height: up to 12 ft.
Zone 5 southwards

Viburnum betulifolium Batal.
Native to China, where it is found in the provinces of Hupeh and Szechwan. Discovered by Potanin in 1885 and introduced into Europe by E. H. Wilson in 1901. Leaves ovate, 2–4 ins. long, $1\frac{1}{4}$–$2\frac{1}{4}$ ins. wide, wedge-shaped at the base; dark green above, paler beneath. Flowers white in 4-in.-wide cymes; fruits red. Worth cultivating for its spectacular masses of red fruits in autumn, which are produced in such abundance that their weight bends the branches.

Deciduous
Flowering period: Apr.–May
Height: up to 10 ft.
Fragrant
Zone 4 southwards

Viburnum bitchiuense Makino
Native to Japan, and introduced into Europe in 1911 with the incorrect name *Viburnum carlesii*, from which it greatly differs in its

taller, less compact habit and smaller inflorescences. It is, however, a beautiful shrub of very easy culture with a loose open habit. Leaves ovate, 1½–2½ ins. long, less than half as wide; pointed, rounded at the base. Flowers sweetly scented, borne in flattish rounded corymbs 2½ ins. in diameter; pink in the bud stage, opening white. Fruits black.

Viburnum x burkwoodii

Of hybrid origin, raised by the English firm of Burkwood & Skipwith in 1924 by crossing *Viburnum utile* with *Viburnum carlesii*. An evergreen shrub of modest proportions; the most attractive of all the evergreen viburnums, and especially valuable for its compact habit which renders it eminently suitable for the smaller garden. Leaves ovate, pointed, 1¼–3½ ins. long, ¾–2 ins. wide; dark green, shiny above, covered with pale brownish down on the undersurface. Deliciously fragrant. Inflorescence a rounded globose terminal cluster up to 3 ins. in diameter; individual flowers pinkish in the bud stage, white when fully open.

Evergreen
Flowering period: Apr.–May
Height: up to 10 ft.
Very fragrant
Zone 5 southwards

Viburnum carlesii Hemsl.

Native to Korea, introduced into Japan in 1885, and from Japan to England (Kew) in 1902. The most fragrant of all viburnums and among the elite of the genus. Widely used as a pot plant for forcing into bloom during the winter. The inflorescence is formed in late autumn and can remain exposed to all weathers throughout the winter without suffering any damage. Has been given every possible award by the Royal Horticultural Society. A deciduous shrub of rounded, compact, rigid habit. Leaves broadly ovate, ¾–2¾ ins. long, ¾–1½ ins. wide, dull green above, greyish beneath. Inflorescence a globose terminal cluster up to 3 ins. in diameter composed of closely packed, intensely and deliciously fragrant white flowers. Fruits black. Easily propagated from seed or by means of cuttings. The commercially available specimens are generally grafted onto more common seedling viburnums.

Deciduous
Flowering period: Apr.–May
Height: up to 8 ft.
Very fragrant
Zone 4 southwards

Viburnum cassinoides

Viburnum cassinoides L.

Native to Eastern North America. A deciduous shrub with a shapely rounded bushy appearance. Leaves ovate oval, 2–4 ins. long, 1–2 ins. wide, with dentated undulated margins; dark green and thick-textured. Flowers yellowish white, borne in cymes up to 3 ins. in diameter. Fruits blue-black. Introduced into Europe in 1761 and often confused with *Viburnum nudum* L., which it resembles, although it does not have the glossy foliage of the latter or the long stalk to the inflorescence. An excellent species for the autumn colouring of its leaves.

(Witherod or Appalachian Tea)
Deciduous
Flowering period: June
Height: up to 7 ft.
Zone 3 southwards

Evergreen
Flowering period: July–Aug.
Height: up to 12 ft.
Zone 7 southwards

Viburnum cylindricum Hamilton. (syn. *Viburnum coriaceum*)
Native to China and the Himalayas. Introduced into Kew, via India, in 1881. A large evergreen shrub which in gardens generally has a maximum height of about 12 ft., but in its native habitat reaches a height of up to 30 ft. Leaves oval, 3–8 ins. long, $1\frac{1}{2}$–4 ins. wide; upper surface dark green and covered with a thin invisible film of wax which when scratched or rubbed becomes white. I remember that one day I foolishly demonstrated this to a group of tourists who immediately detached many of the leaves and with pointed matchsticks incised their names on the waxy covering, taking the leaves home as souvenirs. Flowers greenish white, minute, arranged in flattish cymes 5 ins. in diameter, with conspicuous attractive lilac-coloured anthers. Fruits black. An interesting and curious species that requires an abundance of space.

Evergreen
Flowering period: May–June
Height: up to 3–4 ft.
Zone 7 southwards

Viburnum davidi Franch.
Native to China. Introduced into Europe by E. H. Wilson in 1904. A species completely different from all other viburnums, excellent for semi- or complete shade, but also thrives in sunny positions in a temperate climate. An evergreen shrub of low compact rounded habit. Leaves leathery, oval, 2–5 ins. long and $\frac{3}{4}$–$2\frac{1}{4}$ ins. wide, very conspicuously veined; dark green above, paler beneath, glabrous on either surface. Flowers minute, cream-white, borne in densely crowded cymes up to $3\frac{1}{2}$ ins. wide. Fruits vivid blue, globose, shiny, and prolific. When a good crop of these lovely blue berries is produced on a well-developed specimen, possibly only 15–18 ins. high, the effect is stupendous. Since some plants bear only male flowers and others only female flowers, it is essential that both forms should be planted in close proximity to ensure pollination and subsequent fruits.

Deciduous
Flowering period: Nov.–Mar.
Height: up to 10 ft.
Fragrant
Zone 5 southwards

Viburnum fragrans Bunge
Native to China. Introduced into England by W. Purdon for the famous nursery firm of Veitch. A deciduous shrub with an erect, rigid, but wide-spreading habit; often with a width equal to its height. Leaves obovate, pointed, conspicuously dentated, 2–$3\frac{1}{3}$ ins. long, 1–$2\frac{1}{2}$ ins. wide. Flowers borne in globose corymbs 2 ins. in diameter; pink in bud, opening white. Very early-flowering, in mild localities often in November–December; deliciously and strongly fragrant. Fruits red. Both the plant and the flowers—which appear before the leaves—are very hardy, and their greatest enemies are excessive heat and drought. The botanical explorer Reginald Farrer, in his famous book *On the Eaves of the World*, refers to *Viburnum fragrans* as "this most glorious of shrubs", and his praise is not an exaggeration.

Viburnum Lantana L.
Native to Europe. A vigorous, almost rampant deciduous shrub. In the young stage, all parts of it are covered with pale down. Leaves ovate, heart-shaped at the base; 2–nearly 5 ins. long, $1\frac{1}{2}$–4 ins. wide, upper surface velvety. Flowers white, borne in cymes up to 4 ins. in diameter. Fruits at first red, changing to black. An attractive shrub for a semi-wild position and valuable for the autumn colouring of its foliage. The var. *aureus variegatus* (*punctatus*) has green leaves marked yellow.

(Wayfaring Tree)
Deciduous
Flowering period: May–June
Height: up to 15 ft.
Zone 4 southwards

Viburnum Lentago L.
Native to Eastern North America from Canada to Georgia. A large, robust shrub or even a small tree. Leaves obovate, rounded at the base; long-pointed, dentated, 2–4 ins. long and half as wide, dark shiny green. Individual flowers $\frac{1}{4}$ in. wide, cream-white, fragrant, borne in terminal cymes up to $4\frac{1}{2}$ ins. in diameter. Fruits blue-black, oval, $\frac{1}{2}$ in. long and very attractive. A free-flowering small tree excellent for its many fragrant flowers.

(Nannyberry or Sheepberry)
Deciduous
Flowering period: May–June
Height: up to 25–30 ft.
Zone 3 southwards

Viburnum macrocephalum Fortune (syn. *Viburnum keteleeri* Carr., *Viburnum arborescens* Hemsley)
Native to China. The true species is rarely cultivated in gardens as it bears small inconspicuous flowers in 5-in.-wide cymes. The more decorative garden form—which should be referred to as *Viburnum macrocephalum* var. *sterile*—is one of the most imposing of the viburnums, with inflorescences larger than any of the other species or varieties, often up to 6 ins. in diameter. It is a deciduous or partially evergreen shrub with a large, rounded habit. Leaves ovate, 2–4 ins. long, $1\frac{1}{2}$–$2\frac{1}{2}$ ins. wide, dull green. Flowers white, all sterile, each $1\frac{1}{2}$ ins. in diameter, forming a large globose truss 4–6 ins. wide. It was introduced from China by Fortune in 1844 and is, of course, a garden type.

(Chinese Snowball Tree)
Deciduous or semi-evergreen
Flowering period: May
Height: up to 15 ft.
Zone 6 southwards

Viburnum nudum L.
Native to Eastern North America. An attractive deciduous shrub of modest proportions and very free flowering. Introduced into Europe in 1752. Leaves oval-lanceolate, 2–$4\frac{1}{2}$ ins. long, 1–$2\frac{1}{2}$ ins. wide; dark shiny green and glabrous on the upper surface. Flowers yellowish white, minute, borne in cymes 4 ins. in diameter and long-stalked. Fruits blue-black.

(Possum Haw)
Deciduous
Flowering period: June–July
Height: up to 12 ft.
Zone 4 southwards

Viburnum odoratissimum Ker-Gawl.
Native to China, India, and Japan. Introduced into Europe in 1818. Occasionally confused with *Viburnum japonicum*, another evergreen species that it resembles. (Neither can be included among the most hardy of viburnums.) Leaves leathery, obovate, 3–8 ins. long, $1\frac{1}{2}$–4

Evergreen
Flowering period: June–Aug.
Height: up to 15 ft.
Fragrant
Zone 7 southwards

ins. wide; wedge-shaped at the base, glossy-green above, paler beneath, and very decorative. Flowers white, borne in broadly pyramidal panicles up to 6 ins. high and 4½ ins. in diameter at the base. Although pleasantly fragrant, the flowers do not really merit the specific name *odoratissimum* as there are other species and varieties with much stronger perfume.

(Guelder Rose or Cranberry Tree)
Deciduous
Flowering period: May–June
Height: up to 18 ft.
Zone 3 southwards

Viburnum opulus

Viburnum opulus L.
Native to Europe. Probably the best-known of all viburnums. A large deciduous shrub forming a dense mass of erect vegetation. Leaves lobed, maple-like, 2–4 ins. long, and of a similar width; dark green above. Inflorescence a cyme up to 3¼ ins. wide with a border of sterile white flowers. Fruits red, translucent, very decorative, prolific, and persistent. In autumn the foliage assumes beautiful colouring. However, it is the various forms and varieties of this species that are so widely planted in gardens, particularly:

> var. *nanum*, only 2½–3 ft. high
> var. *sterile*, with all the flowers sterile and the inflorescence in the form of a "snowball" 2½ ins. in diameter. One of the most spectacular and best-known deciduous shrubs but, of course, does not bear seeds.
> var. *xanthocarpum*, fruits yellow instead of red

The American form of *Viburnum opulus* (syn. *Viburnum americanum* Miller.) differs very little from the Old World type, although its growth is more vigorous; some authorities suggest that it is not a separate, American species but a naturalized form of the European species.

Evergreen
Flowering period: May–June
Height: up to 15 ft.
Zone 5 southwards

Viburnum rhytidophyllum Hemsl.
Native to China. Introduced into Europe in 1900 by E. H. Wilson. A robust, vigorous, even rampant evergreen shrub which, although handsome, often creates a somewhat coarse effect through its exuberance. Often greater in width than in height; leaves ovate-oblong, up to 9 ins. long and 3 ins. wide, with the upper surface deeply and conspicuously wrinkled; the undersurface greyish with a thick layer of felt-like down. Flowers borne in large flattish umbels often 8 ins. in diameter; dull yellowish white and not very attractive. Fruits oval, at first red and then black. One of the chief attractions of this somewhat gross and cumbersome plant is that the fruits, produced in abundance in large flat heads, do not all ripen simultaneously and thus present a contrasting mixture of scarlet and black over a period of many weeks.

Evergreen
Flowering period: July
Height: up to 12 ft.
Scented
Zone 7 southwards

Viburnum suspensum Lindl. (syn. *Viburnum sandankwa*)
Native to southern Japan. Introduced into Europe in 1850. One of the less hardy evergreen viburnums and a species that appreciates

warmth and sunshine. Of modest proportions; leaves leathery, ovate, pointed, rounded at the base, up to 5 ins. long and 3 ins. wide; shiny green, glabrous. Flowers agreeably scented, white flushed pink, cylindrical, $\frac{1}{3}$ in. wide at the mouth; borne in panicles up to 4 ins. long and 3 ins. in diameter. Fruits globose, red.

Viburnum tinus L. (Laurustinus)
Native to the Mediterranean regions and to Southeastern Europe. A very dense much-branched evergreen shrub widely used for the formation of hedges, and a fine plant when cultivated as an individual specimen or against a wall. Together with the deciduous *Viburnum opulus*, probably the best-known and most widely cultivated of all viburnums. Normal height up to about 12–15 ft., but it can be constantly cut to any desired height. A pleasing feature of the plant is that it retains all its branches down to ground level, thus forming a mass of vegetation from its base upwards. No other viburnum produces such a mass of foliage. Leaves narrowly ovate, $1\frac{1}{2}$–$2\frac{1}{2}$ ins. long and $\frac{3}{4}$–$1\frac{1}{2}$ ins. wide, dark shiny green above, paler beneath. Flowers pinkish in the bud stage, later white, and produced almost throughout the year, although the maximum flowering period is late winter and spring. Inflorescences in the form of terminal cymes $1\frac{1}{2}$–3 ins. in diameter. Fruits a beautiful shade of blue, often produced simultaneously with the flowers. A garden plant of the greatest value, thriving in almost any position, including sun and complete shade. As it is a Mediterranean plant, it will not tolerate excessive cold. There are several varieties:

Evergreen
Flowering period: intermittent from autumn to spring
Height: up to 12–15 ft.
Zone 7 southwards

    var. *Eve Price*, smaller foliage, carmine buds and pink flowers
    var. *French White*, a white-flowered form
    var. *purpureum*, leaves with a dark-purple tinge
    var. *variegatum*, leaves irregularly variegated with yellow

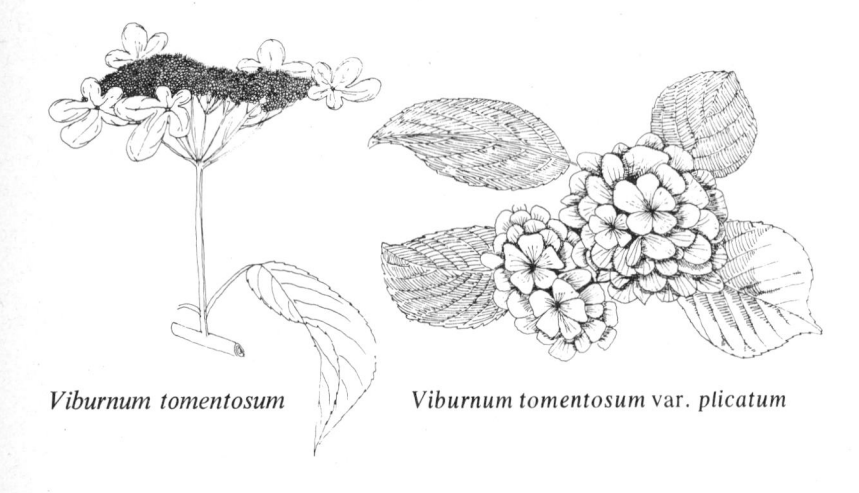

Viburnum tomentosum

Viburnum tomentosum var. plicatum

Deciduous
Flowering period: May–June
Height: up to 10 ft.
Zone 4 southwards

Viburnum tomentosum Thunb.
Native to China and Japan. Introduced into Europe in 1865. This species, together with its varieties, is not only one of the finest of all the viburnums, but it is also one of the best flowering shrubs that can be grown in American and European gardens. The plants are attractive in flower and fruit, and notable for their autumn colouring, particularly the var. *mariesii*. There are, in fact, few shrubs with so many good qualities. The species forms a wide-spreading deciduous shrub with horizontal branches. Leaves oval, pointed, 2–4 ins. long and half as wide; dull green above, pale grey-green beneath. Inflorescence a flat umbel up to 4 ins. in diameter borne at the ends of short branches. The individual outer flowers are of the large showy sterile type, while the central flowers are normal; colour cream-white. Fruits coral-red, becoming black. The var. *mariesii* is a great improvement and so free-flowering that with its flattish horizontal growths it gives the appearance of a large table of bloom. The var. *plicatum* (syn. *Viburnum plicatum* Thunb.) has only sterile flowers arranged in a ball-like inflorescence $3\frac{1}{2}$ ins. in diameter.

Vinca

(MYRTLE OR PERIWINKLE)
Family: Apocynaceae
Hardy, half-hardy, evergreen herbaceous perennials
or tender annuals
Position: shade or semi-shade
Propagation: seed, cuttings, or division
Cultivation easy

Vinca rosea

Periwinkle is not a plant to be grown just anywhere, without due regard to its particular demands. It is a light-woodland plant, ideal for forming an evergreen ground cover underneath trees in a semi-shady position similar to its natural habitat. It also thrives at the sides of ditches, at the base of hedges, among shrubs, and even trailing over rocks or in the fissures of old walls. It is a humble little plant, but greedy for humus, and it loves to hug the soil surface, spreading and trailing, forming roots at each node, passing underneath fallen branches, small heaps of dead leaves, or logs, and reappearing 8–10 ins. farther along. In spring the lovely blue flowers form a carpet of bloom. It is not scented, although it is automatically associated with woodland fragrance, and it is often hardy. One often speaks of periwinkle blue, but this is not an accurate description since the flower colour varies considerably, with gradations ranging from dark violet-blue to pale sky-blue and further extending in either direction to almost wine-red or pure white. This colour variation is something of a mystery and, according to Correvon, is not constant and does not depend on the nature of the soil. The city of Geneva has adopted the flower as its emblem. In the language of flowers it is considered the symbol of friendship and fidelity. For the Belgians, periwinkle constitutes the sign of virginity, and in country districts the flowers were strewn in the path of bridal couples. The ancients entwined sprays of vinca in funeral wreaths, seeing in the vigour and evergreen habit of the plant a sign of immortality. The Celts believed it was a plant sacred to witches; for this reason it is still known as Witches' Violet in certain parts of France and in the Celtic regions of England. Recalling the plant's use at weddings, there is an old French love song that begins *Aux quatre coins du lit/Quatres bouquets de pervinches* (At the four corners of the marriage bed/Four bouquets of periwinkle raise their head).

Some authorities believe that "periwinkle" is derived from an old Slavic word, *pervinka,* which in turn is derived from *pervi,* signifying "first". This theory is not too far-fetched, as the periwinkle is one of the first flowers to appear in the spring (it was aptly described by one author as "the swallow among flowers"). Other authorities believe that the word derives from the Latin *pervinca* (conquers all).

Apart from their value as a garden plant, vincas are also of considerable importance as medicinal herbs. *Vinca major,* or greater periwinkle, has been used as an astringent and tonic and is reported to be of use for treating haemorrhages in general. The non-hardy South African *Vinca rosea* has been used in folk medicine as a cure for diabetes, supposedly more efficacious than insulin, and in *Potter's Cyclopaedia of Botanical Drugs and Preparations* (Potter & Clarke, London), the following is recorded: "A registration officer in Durban was declared cured after two months' treatment and considerable notice appeared in the South African and London Press as to its virtues." In 1960, doctors at the University of Western Ontario extracted two alkaloids from *Vinca rosea;* one, vincristine, caused remission in cases of lymphocytic leukemia.

The genus comprises about twelve species that are distributed throughout Europe, the Mediterranean regions, the Far East, and the tropics. Propagation of the prostrate species is easiest by means of the trailing, spreading growths that root so freely at every node; the non-hardy pink-flowered *Vinca rosea* can be propagated from seed sown in a warm greenhouse in spring for use as a summer-flowering annual for bedding or as a pot plant.

Vinca difformis Pourr.
Native to Southern Europe. A trailing evergreen herbaceous perennial very similar to the better-known *Vinca minor,* but distinctive

Half-hardy evergreen herbaceous perennial
Flowering period: Apr.–June
Height: 10–12 ins.

Vinca herbacea
From *The Botanical Register*,
1818, plate 301

because the petals are cut obliquely, like the small celluloid pinwheels on a stick so loved by small children.

Vinca herbacea Waldst. & Kit.
Native to Southeastern Europe and southern Russia. This annual species, like the perennial vinca, loves moist, cool, fresh woodland conditions, where its pretty little pale blue flowers make a most pleasing effect. Excellent for naturalizing in semi-wild conditions.

Annual
Flowering period: Apr.–May
Height: 5–7 ins.

Vinca major L.
Native to Europe. A slender-stemmed trailing tender evergreen perennial almost identical to the more common *Vinca minor* but much larger, with fine blue flowers up to 2 ins. in diameter and shiny, dark-green, large oval foliage. Of very rapid growth and excellent for use as a ground cover, or as a trailing plant on shady slopes, or in damp, shady walls. The var. *variegata* is probably better known than the type plant; its attractive green-and-cream-white foliage makes it an excellent subject for growing in pots or windowboxes. However, it is not tolerant of severe frost. Two other interesting forms with variegated leaves are var. *elegantissima* and var. *reticulata*.

Tender evergreen herbaceous perennial
Flowering period: Apr.–May, earlier in mild climates
Height: prostrate to 6 ins.

Vinca minor L.
Native to Europe. A hardy trailing herbaceous perennial with small, oval, opposite, dark green, shiny, and almost coriaceous evergreen foliage. The lovely little five-petalled flowers are borne on short stems, while the long slender growths spread rapidly over the soil surface, rooting at every node to form new plants. The individual flowers are about $\frac{3}{4}$ in. in diameter and are somewhat variable in colour, but always in some lovely shade of blue. The following varieties offer some exceptions:

(Common Periwinkle, Creeping Myrtle, or Running Myrtle)
Hardy evergreen herbaceous perennial
Flowering period: Apr.–May, earlier in mild climates
Height: prostrate to 4 ins.

- var. *alba,* white-flowered
- var. *alba plena,* with double white flowers
- var. *alba variegata,* single white flowers, variegated foliage
- var. *argentea variegata,* pale-blue flowers, foliage variegated silver
- var. *atropurpurea compacta,* dark-purple flowers
- var. *aurea,* pale-blue flowers and golden foliage
- var. *coerulea,* single sky-blue flowers
- var. *coerulea argentea marginata,* leaves margined silver-white
- var. *elegantissima* (syn. *The Bride*), white flowers with a pink eye
- var. *flore pleno,* double blue flowers
- var. *purpurea plena,* double purplish flowers
- var. *rosea,* pink-flowered
- var. *rosea flore pleno,* double pink

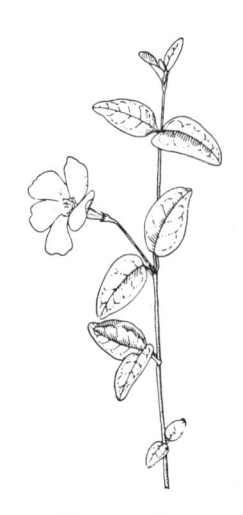

Vinca minor

(Cape Periwinkle, Old Maid, or Madagascar Periwinkle)
Tender evergreen herbaceous perennial generally grown as an annual
Flowering period: June–Sept.
Height: 12 ins.

Vinca rosea L. (syn. *Ammocallis rosea, Lochnera rosea*)

The only species native to the tropics and, of course, not hardy. A beautiful plant, prolific in its flowering, and remaining in bloom from June to September. Although it can be treated as a perennial in warm climates, it is nearly always grown as an annual in gardens from seed sown in a warm greenhouse in early spring, and it is used either for summer bedding or as a pot plant. Unlike the hardy trailing species, it has an erect almost rigid habit with a height of about 1 ft., forming a compact bushy plant which, in the case of really well-grown specimens, can reach a diameter of up to $2\frac{1}{2}$ ft. It is more tolerant of sun than other vincas, and the branches are particularly brittle. Leaves opposite, lanceolate, dark shiny green. Flowers $1\frac{1}{2}$ ins. in diameter and variable in colour from white with a red eye to pink marked with red. There are several excellent varieties:

    var. *Creeping Carpet,* similar to the type but prostrate and trailing
    var. *Little Bright Eye,* white flowers with a pink centre
    var. *Little Pinkie,* dwarfer and more compact in habit

Viola

(Violet, Pansy, or Viola)
Family: Violaceae
Hardy or half-hardy herbaceous perennials
Position: shade, semi-shade, or sun according to the species
Propagation: seed, division, or cuttings
Cultivation easy

One of the most ancient legends surrounding the genus *Viola* relates that it sprang up by divine command to serve as fodder for Io, daughter of the river god Inachus (Io had been transformed into a heifer by Zeus to shield her from the jealous wrath of his spouse, Hera: possibly, Zeus thought that any woman so honoured by his love should, when translated into bovine form, be nourished by something more dainty than common grass). Since the genus *Viola* includes both the pansy and the violet, pedants in Classical times used to engage in scholarly disputes (as vain and as time-consuming as those fruitless arguments that raged over the sex of angels) as to whether Io-as-heifer grazed upon the flowers of *Viola odorata* (violets), *Viola tricolor* (pansies), or both.

The pansy flower also figured in Christian lore, and it was seen as a symbol of the Trinity because of its similarity with a motif often employed to represent the triune aspect of God: an all-seeing eye in the centre of a triangle (the three sides symbolizing the Father, the Son, and the Holy Spirit) surrounded by a nimbus or glory (a similar motif may be seen on the back of the dollar bill—the origin of both signs is probably Gnostic). In the pansy flower the divine eye could be discerned in the stigma, the triangle in the general contour delimited by the petals, and the nimbus in the streaks of colour radiating from the flower's centre. Because of these elements, as well as the three-colour aspect of the flower, the Elizabethans called it Herb Trinity, the medieval Italians termed it *Herba Sancta Trinitas* (a similar name is still used in Tuscany today), and possibly because of its spiritual association it was often called Heartsease in England. Other popular names include Mother-in-Law-and-Daughter-in-Law (because of the different contrasting colours present in the same flower), and the charming German *Stiefmütterchen,* or Little Step-Mother, which was probably given to the flower because of its resemblance to a cross little face.

Even though *Viola tricolor* was commonly found throughout Europe and was easy to grow and generally appealing as a garden flower, little was done to develop it, and the really triumphant period of pansy cultivation and hybridization did not begin until relatively late, horticulturally speaking. According to some authorities, the garden cultivation of *Viola tricolor* began after the first quarter of the sixteenth century. Yet even by the seventeenth and eighteenth centuries all the known varieties still belonged to *Viola tricolor* var. *hortensis* (the still-grown and much-beloved Johnny-jump-up, the original Heartsease and Herb Trinity). Further development did not take place until the beginning of the nineteenth century.

There are two different accounts as to who actually introduced the pansy flower as we know it today. According to John Claudius Loudon, "about 1810 Lady Bennett had a small private garden on the estate of her father Lord Tankerville, at Walton, and in this little garden there was a heart-shaped bed where the amiable lady used to plant all the varieties of pansy she happened to find in her father's garden. With the zeal and industrious support of Mr. Richardson, the gardener, numerous beautiful varieties were discovered and planted in that little flower bed, so that by 1813 no less than 14 different and excellent forms had been obtained." Other gardeners and pansy enthusiasts also showed interest in Lady Bennett's activity, helping her to raise the total number of varieties to twenty. Contemporaneously, Lord Gambier had apparently collected various wild forms of *Viola tricolor* which his gardener, Thomson, carefully cultivated. Eventually the gardener started a small business of his own, which earned him the well-merited title Father of the Heartsease.

Viola cornuta
From *Curtis's Botanical Magazine*,
1804, plate 791

By about 1850 German, English, and French gardeners took a keen interest in the flower. In France, Vilmorin distinguished himself in this field; while in Germany, Benary, Heinemann, and others specialized in pansy development. Glenny defined the characteristics ideal pansy flowers should possess: they should be round, flat, with very rounded corners, and whatever the colour, that of the three inferior petals had to be of the same colour, either white, yellow, or straw-coloured. Whether these three petals were smooth, undulated, or spotted, there could not be even a shade of difference or variation in colour among them.

The road from then on was long and arduous. The small multiflora types of 1850 gave way to other strains, always a little better, with more robust stems and larger blooms. Later, C. Engelmann of England took the lead; then, after 1945, the primacy passed to the Netherlands with the development of the Giant Aalsmeer strain.

Another viola, perhaps more important than the pansy, even if the latter is the more widely cultivated, is *Viola odorata,* the Sweet Violet of gardens. Theophrastus called it *Viola oscura,* while Dioscorides and Pliny referred to it as *Viola purpurea.* In the Fifth Book of the *Odyssey,* Homer states that sweet-smelling violets were among the flowers and plants that grew on the fair island of the seductive nymph Calypso. *Viola odorata* is often mentioned as one of the flowers (together with poppies and narcissus) gathered by Persephone at the moment she was abducted by Hades. And, as mentioned above, it appears in the myth of Io. The violet was the emblematic flower of ancient Athens through its connection with Ion (son of Creusa and Apollo), eponymous leader of the Ionians and the legendary founder of Athens. As Ion was leading his followers to Attica, the naiads who inhabited the shores of Cythera offered him violets as homage. The Athenians took pride in their descent from the Ionians and bore a special affection for the violet. All of the statues in Athens were crowned with violet wreaths, and no house was without violets, either in the garden or on the domestic altar. According to Aristophanes, the people of Athens took great pride in being referred to as the "violet-crowned Athenians".

Viola calcarata

Even though they were familiar to the ancient Greeks, it is not known when violets were first cultivated. They were familiar to the Romans too, who used masses of violets for decorating their banqueting tables (as did the Greeks before them), as they believed the flowers had the power to prevent drunkenness; and violets were scattered over children's graves as a symbol of purity and modesty.

In pre-Revolutionary France, the violet cultivation became quite a mania; a gentleman of the eighteenth century who was a great admirer of a famous actress spent his entire life cultivating violets, and daily for thirty years he presented her with a bunch of freshly picked scented blooms. The lady, not wishing to lose one iota of her lover's floral token, made an infusion of the petals which she drank every evening. Later in French history *Viola odorata* took on political significance as well, and became the floral emblem of the Bonapartists, since Napoleon had promised, on his way to Elba, that he would return when the violets were in bloom. Thus, the loyal Bonapartists were wont to refer to him as "Monsieur Violette" in their secret plans for his eventual (though brief) restoration.

The city of Parma, of Parma Violet fame, adopted the violet as its emblem, and tourists visiting that old Italian city invariably acquire a bottle of the famous Parma Violet perfume as a souvenir.

The genus *Viola* comprises about four hundred species, mostly herbaceous perennials; among these there are also some of a shrubby nature, diffused over the temperate zones of the Southern Hemisphere: the mountains of South America, tropical and subtropical Africa, Australia, and New Zealand. Like their northern cousins, they generally grow in shady positions in woods, along the banks of streams, and in some cases among rocks. There are fourteen species indigenous to Europe, including one of the most beautiful, *Viola calcarata,* and, of course, the common violet.

The scent of various species calls for at least a brief comment. Many pansies are not scented; and if they do have perfume it is the residue of an inheritance left by *Viola cornuta* of the Pyrenees which has long been used for hybridization. The most fragrant pansies—with a perfume similar to that of primulas—are the warm-coloured yellow and apricot-orange types and those with a reddish tinge. The smaller-flowered types are also generally stronger scented. Among the large-flowered pansies, the only one that is really strongly scented is Read's New Century Scented. The queen of scented violets is, of course, *Viola odorata,* together with the many forms and hybrids of present-day violets; the scent cannot be noted for lengthy consecutive periods, as it has a soporific effect on our olfactory nerves. The following are still among the best violets for fragrance: Rosina, Rochelle, White Czar. Wilson and Bell also particularly recommend the variety El Duende for use as ground cover where bulbs have been planted and as a good companion to the early-flowering dwarf narcissus, Trumpet Major. The var. *Double Russian* blooms only in spring and is the sole double-flowered American form. Among the Parma Violets (the original of which is *Viola odorata* var. *pallida plena*), the following are particularly recommended: Swanley, white; Napolitana, lavender-blue shading to white in the centre; Marie Louise, intense lavender-blue. All three are the most strongly scented of all violets. In a frost-free greenhouse it is possible to have Parma Violets in bloom for six months of the year. Other particularly good forms are Princess of Wales, Bournemouth Gem, Triumph, Red Charm, and Königin Charlotte.

In both folk medicine and the official materia medica, *Viola odorata,*

Viola canina

Viola tricolor Giant Swiss Hybrids
From an original watercolour by Giovanna Casartelli, 1968

Viola hirta, Viola canina, and *Viola tricolor* have been used since ancient times. All parts of the plant contain, among other substances, a bitter alkaloid, violine, and a glucoside. The flowers also contain a blue pigment used for certain chemical reactions, salicylic acid, and sugar. Various preparations containing these substances have been used as antiseptics and expectorants, in blood disorders and in catarrhal affections. Most interesting of all, however, is an old report concerning the use of *Viola odorata* given in *Potter's Cyclopaedia of Botanical Drugs and Preparations* (Potter & Clarke, London): "*Viola odorata* leaves contain certain glucosidal principles, not yet fully investigated, but of distinct antiseptic properties. It has lately been recommended and used with benefit to allay pain of cancerous growths—some say even to cure cancer."

Cultivation. Almost all members of the genus *Viola* prefer to be grown under semi-wild woodland conditions in semi-shade, thriving in a cool, fresh humus-rich soil. They associate particularly well with anemones and other woodland plants, and are often used with success in shady corners of the rock-garden. *Viola odorata* is also frequently used for edging, where its abundant foliage is effective. The plants are mostly quite hardy and like to be fertilized with horse or cow manure; they also thrive in even very alkaline (calcareous) soils. For general garden purposes, the single-flowered types are more satisfactory than the double-flowered. Propagation is easy by division. Regarding the propagation of the other viola species, many can be increased by division in spring or autumn, and they can also be raised from seed sown in pots in spring and placed in coldframes. The popular garden violets and pansies are mostly propagated from seed sown in frames or in nursery beds in June–July, the seedlings pricked out into other nursery beds and grown on until autumn or the following spring, when the young plants can be planted in their flowering positions. They can also be propagated from soft cuttings taken at any time during the late spring or early summer and rooted in sandy soil in frames. Although both violets and pansies are actually perennials, better results are generally obtained by treating them as annuals and raising new plants each season. In all cases, the flowering period can be much prolonged by the regular removal of dead blooms. Where necessary, further details of cultivation are given under the species.

Flowering period: Mar.–May
Height: 4–5 ins.
Semi-shade

Viola bosniaca L. (syn. *Viola elegantula*)

Native to Southwest Europe. A small herbaceous perennial species more satisfactorily grown as an annual or biennial to ensure a more compact habit and better flowering. Semi-trailing, with delicate oval, pointed leaves with undulated margins. Flowers small, pinkish purple, with a yellow mark at the base of the lower petal.

Viola canina L.
Flowering period: Apr.–June
Height: 8–9 ins.
Shade

Native to Europe. A hardy herbaceous perennial with all the characteristics of the typical Sweet Violet but of larger proportions, with bigger leaves and completely without perfume. The flowering period is also considerably later. Leaves dark green, pointed, dentated. Flowers large, violet-blue or, in the case of the white-flowered form, pure white. A curious characteristic of the plant is that the leaves, 3 ins. in diameter and carried on stems 5 ins. long, grow to double that size, with stems up to 10 ins. long, after flowering has finished. Propagation by division.

Viola cornuta L.
(Horned Violet or Viola)
Flowering period: May–Aug.
Height: 6–8 ins.
Semi-shade

Native to the Pyrenees. Foliage small, oval, pointed, dentated, forming a compact tuft of vegetation. A graceful, somewhat fragile little hardy herbaceous perennial easily increased from seed or by cuttings; one of the chief parents of the popular modern garden violets. Flowers intense violet, $\frac{3}{4}$ in. in diameter, long-stalked, and prolific for several months if the dead blooms are regularly removed. Requires a semi-shady position in the south (can take more sun in northern climates) in a moderately moist soil. Effective in small beds and for edging. The hybrids derived from this species crossed with *Viola tricolor* have little in common with either parent, and are too well known to require detailed description. They vary in height from 4–8 ins. and generally have flowers of only one colour; much larger in size than *Viola cornuta,* but smaller than garden hybrid pansies. If dead flowers are constantly removed, the flowering period extends from early spring until summer. Some of the best forms are:

    Admiration, violet-blue
    Arkwright Ruby, crimson shaded and suffused terra-cotta
    Campanula Blue, clear sky-blue
    Chantreyland, apricot suffused orange
    Purple Perfection, wine-red
    White Lady, white
    White Perfection, cream-white
    Yellow Bedder, golden-yellow

Another hybrid strain of recent introduction is Funny Face, in a mixture of contrasting colours causing the flowers to resemble little faces. Height 6–7 ins.

Viola cucullata L. (syn. *Viola papilionacea* Pursh.)
Flowering period: Apr.–June
Height: 6 ins.
Semi-shade

Native to Eastern North America. A small but vigorous herbaceous perennial with heart-shaped, dentated basal foliage. Flowers borne on stems up to 5–6 ins. long, violet-blue with a greenish-white eye. Requires a cool, fresh, fairly moist position. Propagation from seed sown in pots in frames in spring.

Flowering period: Apr.–July
Height: 4 ins.
Sun

Viola gracilis Sibth. & Smith
Native to the Balkans. A graceful, elegant, somewhat fragile little herbaceous perennial easily raised from seed or propagated from cuttings. Foliage abundant, dark green, minute, Flowers small, violet-blue, velvety, and very prolific. Must have partial shade in the south, but of the easiest cultivation. There are some excellent varieties, such as:

> var. *alba,* white
> var. *Black Knight,* purple-black
> var. *lutea,* golden-yellow
> var. *major,* intense dark violet

(Sweet Violet or Garden Violet)
Flowering period: Mar.–Apr.
Height: 4–5 ins.
Shade
Fragrant

Viola odorata L.
Native to Europe, the common Sweet Violet. Leaves heart-shaped, 2–3 ins. in diameter, bright green. The normal flowering period is in March, but during a mild winter (or in mild climates) flowering plants can often be found in sheltered positions in January–February, and I have even found a few scattered blooms at the end of December. For the size of the plant, the flowers are relatively large, about 1 in. in diameter; they are generally of a rich bright violet but somewhat variable in colour, a pure-white form occasionally being found. The many hybrid forms have larger variously coloured single or double blooms and are widely grown commercially, often out of season, for sale as cut bloom. They generally have some fragrance but can rarely compare with the exquisite perfume of the true wild violets. The hybrid types are also cultivated commercially for the extraction of their scent, and the flower colours include shades of white, pink, lavender, violet, purple, and cream-yellow. One of the most famous is the previously mentioned Parma Violet, with very large pale lavender intensely fragrant double blooms. Other good varieties are:

Viola odorata

> var. *Coeur d'Alsace,* pink, strongly fragrant, 4 ins.
> var. *Czar,* large blue flowers, 4 ins.
> var. *Marie Louise,* double mauve-pink flowers, strongly fragrant, the flowering period beginning in autumn, 4 ins.
> var. *Princess of Wales,* large dark-violet flowers on 6-in. stems
> var. *sulphurea,* small cream-yellow flowers, 4 ins.
> var. *White Czar,* the best white-flowered form, 5 ins.

(Bird's-Foot Viola)
Flowering period: Apr.–May
Height: 3–4 ins.
Semi-shade

Viola pedata Torr. & Gray
Native to the eastern and midwestern United States. A very small hardy herbaceous perennial of tufted habit. Leaves basal, and as indicated by the common name, divided into segments like a bird's foot. Flowers with the three lower petals a lovely delicate lilac, the two upper petals dark violet. Unlike most violas, it thrives in a dry,

sunny, open position, although in the hotter south some shade is necessary. Propagation is from seed sown outside in pots.

Viola pedunculata Torr. & Gray
Native to California. A herbaceous perennial species especially suitable for the rock-garden because of its modest development and ability to tolerate much drier conditions than most of the other species. Leaves widely oval, dentated; flowers a warm rich yellow.

Flowering period: May–July
Height: 6–8 ins.
Semi-shade

Viola tricolor L.
Native to Europe. Although as a wild plant it is very common and quite attractive, its place in the garden has been taken by the many hybrid forms derived from a long series of crosses among *Viola tricolor, Viola lutea,* and *Viola altaica,* often referred to as *Viola hortensis.* The original *Viola tricolor* is a hardy herbaceous perennial with long trailing stems up to 12–15 ins. in length; it is not long-lived, but it easily reproduces from self-sown seed. The stems are square and bear small heart-shaped leaves. Flowers tricoloured, solitary, small, blue, white, and yellow. Among the modern hybrid pansies, the following are some of the most interesting:

(Pansy)
Flowering period: according to variety
Height: 4–6 ins.
Sun

> Swiss Giants, enormous flowers up to 3 ins. in diameter on erect stems borne well above the foliage. Habit orderly and compact, and the range of colours and combination of colours is almost without limit. Flowering period from early spring to mid-summer.
>
> Early-Flowering Dutch Giants, a fairly new early-flowering strain available as a mixture or in separate colours of almost every hue.
>
> Majestic Giants, enormous flowers up to 4 ins. in diameter on long stems which are excellent for cutting. Available as a mixture or in separate colours.
>
> Gay Jester, often referred to as Winter-Flowering Pansies, since they begin to bloom in September–October and, weather permitting, continue throughout the winter until the following spring. Very large flowers in a wide range of colours.
>
> Jumbo Giants, an American strain, early-flowering, and remaining in bloom for up to six months. Colours in a good selection of apricot, bronze, pink, purple, and red shades.

Other particularly good forms are Oxford Blue, dark blue; Raspberry Rose, carmine-pink; Snow White, white with a yellow eye; and Ullswater, light and dark blue.

Viola tricolor

Viola pedunculata
From *Curtis's Botanical Magazine*,
1857, plate 5004

Vitex

(TREE OF CHASTITY, CHASTE TREE, HEMP TREE, OR MONK'S PEPPER TREE)
Family: Verbenaceae
Half-hardy deciduous shrubs
Position: sun
Propagation: seed or cuttings
Cultivation easy
Flowers fragrant
Foliage aromatic

The best-known species of this genus is *Vitex agnus-castus*. Everything concerning the history of the plant is relevant to chastity. The name, *agnus-castus*, is of Greek origin in part, *agonos* (without descent), and part Latin, *castus* (chaste). The common English names, Chaste Tree and Tree of Chastity, recall the Greek custom of scattering the plants' fragrant foliage on the beds of virgins during feasts held in honour of Ceres. It is believed that the seed of *Vitex agnus-castus* (often known as Nun's Pepper or Monk's Pepper) contains a glucoside possessing anaphrodisiac properties. The plant seems to have been in cultivation since ancient times, and it is certainly very long-lived. In the Padua Botanic Garden there is a fine vigorous specimen which was planted in 1561.

The genus is native to the warmer regions of the Old World and comprises about one hundred species. Regarding cultivation, the plants have no particular demands. The two described here are hardy and will thrive in any normal fertile garden soil, acid or alkaline (calcareous), in a warm, moderately dry, sunny position. They do, however, require severe pruning in early spring; all the previous season's very long growths should be removed to within 2–3 eyes of the main stem, as flowers are produced on the new season's vegetation. Propagation can be effected by means of seed sown in a warm greenhouse in spring, or from soft cuttings rooted in a warm greenhouse in early summer. The basal growths also freely layer themselves.

About the only problem vitex poses to North American gardeners is its tendency to winter-kill if exposed to cold winds and lengthy periods of temperatures below 15°F. Above Zone 6—and even in less sheltered positions within that zone—a heavy mulching of straw, salt hay, or even dead leaves will prove beneficial to *V. agnus-castus*. Even if the plant does winter-kill if not sufficiently protected (or because of an excessively severe winter), it will usually produce new basal growth in the spring. For largish specimens, a burlap windscreen will often prevent winter damage to the branches.

Vitex agnus-castus

(Chaste Tree)
Flowering period: July–Aug.
Height: up to 10–12 ft.
or more
Zone 6 southwards

Vitex agnus-castus L.
Native to the Mediterranean regions, frequently in seaside localities, and often in the vicinity of tamarisks. It is a wide-spreading shrub of loose habit with opposite leaves composed of five digitate segments widely spread, rather like an open-fingered hand. The fragrant flowers are borne in slender erect racemes; the entire inflorescence up to 6 ins. long and occasionally branched, always on the new growths, thus making severe pruning necessary in February–March to induce new vegetation. The flowers are very long-lasting, rich violet in colour, although there are also white- and pink-flowered forms. The seeds resemble dried peppercorns. The entire plant has a very strong, though not unpleasant, pungent aroma.

Flowering period: July–Aug.
Height: up to 10–12 ft.
Zone 6 southwards

Vitex negundo Lam. (syn. *Vitex incisa*)
Native to China. A wide-spreading shrub with digitate foliage; similar in general aspect to *Vitex agnus-castus* but of smaller proportions and with a less rigid, more graceful habit, and paler-green foliage. The inflorescences are looser in form and less brightly coloured, but they are also borne on the current season's growths, thus necessitating the same method of severe pruning.

Weigela

(*Also see* DIERVILLA)
Family: Caprifoliaceae
Hardy deciduous shrubs
Position: sun or partial shade
Propagation: seed or cuttings
Cultivation easy

When the lilacs, Japanese flowering cherries, flowering crab apples, and quinces begin to fade, the first flower buds of the weigela show signs of opening. Their flowering period lasts for at least a month or even longer, the earliest beginning to bloom in May, while others carry on their flowering period through June, thus perfectly filling what is often a colourless, flowerless gap in the garden at a time that is neither spring nor summer.

The earliest weigela known to the West, and parent of the majority of present-day hybrid forms, was the Chinese *Weigela florida,* sent to England by Robert Fortune in 1841, after he had discovered it in a mandarin's garden at Chushan. Describing details of his discovery,

Fortune noted that the garden, known as the "Grotto" because of its beautiful, rock-like architecture, was frequently visited by officers of the regiments quartered at a nearby garrison, and all the visitors especially went to see and admire this beautiful weigela, which was one of the favourite plants of the garden's owner. Fortune considered it one of the most beautiful shrubs of northern China and he enthusiastically sent home specimens by every ship until he received news that one had arrived safely in good condition. His consignments were planted in Kew Gardens, where they immediately became acclimatized and thrived; and Fortune had the satisfaction of being able to inform the Chinese who had procured the plants for him that they had even "attracted the attention of Her Majesty the Queen". During succeeding years, other species were introduced into English gardens: *Weigela coraeensis* sometime prior to 1856; *Weigela floribunda* in 1860; *Weigela japonica* in 1892; *Weigela praecox* in 1894. The least hardy, *Weigela middendorfiana,* was introduced in 1850 and is the only yellow-flowered species.

Thunberg named the genus in honour of Christian Ehrenfried von Weigel (1748–1831), a professor at Greifswald and author of *Flora Pomerana-Rugica*, published in 1769. In China the plants have been given more poetic names: Flower of the Embroidered Girdle or Flower of the Silken Ribbon. The genus includes about a dozen species, all native to the Far East. They are included by some authorities in the genus *Diervilla*.

Cultivation. Weigela cultivation is very easy; the plants have no particular demands about soil, but they prefer a sunny, airy position in a fertile soil that never becomes excessively dry. Propagation is generally effected by means of hard-wood cuttings taken in late summer and inserted in sandy soil in frames; or from seed sown in an unheated greenhouse or in coldframes in spring. They do not require a lot of severe pruning since the flowers are produced on short growths from the previous season's vegetation. If pruning is done for size or good shape, it should be accomplished immediately after flowering.

Weigela coraeensis Thunb. (syn. *Diervilla coraeensis*)

Flowering period: May–June
Height: up to 15 ft.
Zone 4 southwards

Native to Japan. A much-branched glabrous shrub with rigid stems. Leaves obovate to widely elliptic, 3–5 ins. long, dentated, pointed. Inflorescence composed of numerous individual blooms variable in colour from white to pink or carmine-red. The corolla is $1-1\frac{1}{2}$ ins. long, tubular at the base, gradually widening towards the mouth. The var. *alba* has yellowish-white flowers that fade to pink.

Weigela floribunda K. Koch (syn. *Diervilla floribunda*)

Flowering period: May–June
Height: up to 9 ft.
Zone 4 southwards

Native to the mountains of Japan. Slender hairy branches; leaves ovate to elongated-ovate, pointed, dentated, rounded or wedge-

Weigela florida
From *Curtis's Botanical Magazine*
1848, plate 4396

shaped at the base, 2¾–4 ins. long, hairy on the undersurface. Flowers stalkless, axillary, borne singly or in groups of 2–3. The corolla base is tubular, gradually widening towards the mouth, dark purple, hairy on the outside 1–1¼ ins. long. This is a shrub of vigorous growth, with a profusion of numerous small flowers. The var. *grandiflora* has larger almost reddish-brown flowers; the var. *versicolor* has flowers at first greenish white changing to red.

Weigela florida D.C. (syn. *Diervilla pauciflora, Diervilla florida*)
Native to northern China and Korea. A much-branched robust shrub with two parallel lines of hairs along the length of the young stems. Leaves very short-stalked; elliptic or elongated-ovate, pointed, dentated along the entire margin except at the base, glabrous above, the veins more or less tomentose on the undersurface, 2–4 ins. long. Flowers axillary, in groups; the corolla bell-shaped at the mouth, narrowing towards the base, 1¼ ins. long; pink or dark pink, pale pink or nearly white at the base inside, rather hairy outside. One of the most widely planted varieties in gardens, var. *venusta* from Korea, has smaller elongated-elliptic foliage and flowers borne in dense compact little masses along the branches, with the corolla purple-pink margined lighter pink. The var. *alba* has flowers at first white, changing to pinkish; the var. *purpurea* (named *Java Red* in the United States) is dwarf with reddish-brown foliage and dark-pink flowers; while the var. *variegata* has the leaves margined yellowish white and dark-pink flowers, a combination of colours that makes this an outstandingly beautiful flowering shrub. *Weigela florida* is also one of the main parents (together with the species *W. coraeensis* and *W. floribunda*) of the many lovely garden hybrids which are better known and more widely planted than the actual species.

Flowering period: May–June
Height: up to 10 ft. or more
Zone 4 southwards

Weigela japonica Thunb. (syn. *Diervilla japonica*)
Native to Japan. Young growths glabrous and bearing hairy stripes. Leaves short-stalked, elliptic or ovate, dentated, slightly pointed, 3–4 ins. long, hairy along the veins on the undersurface. Flowers generally in groups of three; corolla funnel-shaped, 1 in. long, widening to bell-shaped at the mouth, very hairy outside; at first greenish white, later becoming light carmine-red. The var. *hortensis* has leaves with the upper surface almost glabrous while the undersurface is covered with a dense grey felt; the corymbs of blooms are long-stalked, and the flowers are carmine. Var. *sinica* has small slender leaf stalks and the undersurface of the foliage covered with soft hairs; the pale-pink flowers are bell-shaped with the corolla abruptly contracted into a narrow tube about half-way along its length. The var. *alba* is identical to the var. *hortensis* but with white flowers.

Flowering period: May–June
Height: up to 9 ft.
Zone 4 southwards

Flowering period: May–June
Height: 2–4½ ft.
Zone 4 southwards

Weigela middendorfiana Lem. (syn. *Diervilla middendorfiana*)
Native to northern China, Manchuria, and Japan. Stems greyish yellow, in their young stage bearing two hairy stripes. Leaves almost stalkless, ovate-lanceolate, 2–3¼ ins. long, finely dentated, slightly corrugated, with the veins covered with short hairs on either surface. Flowers in groups of 1–3, terminal or axillary. Corolla yellowish white with the lower segments of the lobe marked orange; funnel-shaped, 1½ ins. long. Particularly suited to cool, moist, but protected positions.

Weigela Hybrids
Until a few years ago there were at least 150 garden hybrids. The first were put into circulation by Van Houtte in 1860, more by Lemoine in 1867, and by 1930 the total was about sixty. In the meanwhile, Billiard and Rathke were also busy producing their hybrids and seedlings. At the present time, some of the most interesting hybrids are of American origin. The following is a selection of the most popular.

White- or Nearly White-flowered

> Candida *(W. florida* x *W. coraeensis)*, white flowers throughout entire blooming period, foliage light green
> Dame Blanche *(W. coraeensis* x *W. japonica)*, large white flowers slightly suffused pink outside, yellowish white in bud
> Madame Lemoine Billiard *(W. florida* x *W. coraeensis)*, pinkish white
> Madame Tellier Billiard *(W. florida* x *W. coraeensis)*, large white flowers suffused pink
> Montblanc Lemoine *(W. florida* x *W. japonica)*, white flowers, greenish white in bud; tendency to fade to pinkish with age

Pink- or Carmine-flowered

> Abel Carrière Lemoine *(W. florida* x *W. japonica)*, early, with large flowers, vivid pink-reddish-carmine, throat marked yellow
> Conquête Lemoine *(W. florida* x *W. japonica)*, large pale pink flowers
> Espérance Lemoine. Large pinkish-white flowers suffused salmon-red, buds pale salmon, early
> Floreal Lemoine. Early, very free-flowering, large carmine-pink blooms margined pinkish white, throat carmine-red
> Fraicheur Lemoine. Early flowering, large, corolla pink margined white, internally yellowish white
> Gustave Mallet Billiard *(W. florida* x *W. coraeensis)*, pink margined white

Othello *(W. florida* x *W. floribunda)*, carmine, darker externally

Séduction Lemoine. Carmine-red–wine-red, margined paler red, early and prolific in flowering, buds carmine

Stelzneri Van Houtte *(W. florida* x *W. coraeensis)*, dark red

Styriaca Klenert *(W. florida* x *W. floribunda)*, medium-sized carmine-pink flowers passing to carmine-red, free-flowering, early

Van Houttei *(W. florida* x *W. japonica)*, carmine

Weigela hybrid Eva Rathke

Crimson- or Dark Crimson-flowered

Bristol Ruby Cumming. Carmine-red, less brilliant in colour but similar to and more robust than Eva Rathke

Congo *(W. coraeensis* x *W. floribunda)*, large crimson-purple flowers

Eva Rathke *(W. floribunda* x *W. coraeensis)*, intense carmine-pink, erect habit, very free-flowering

Incarnata *(W. coraeensis* x *W. floribunda)*, dark red

Lavallei *(W. coraeensis* x *W. floribunda)*, vivid crimson

Majesteux Lemoine. Amaranth-red, corolla margins paler

Newport Red U.S.A. Violet-red, conspicuous in winter for its green stems

Hendersonii *(W. florida* x *W. floribunda)*, light crimson, crimson in bud

Varieties with Coloured Foliage

var. *kosteriana variegata,* leaves margined yellow, pink flowers, dwarf

var. *luteo-marginata,* leaves margined yellow

var. *nana variegata,* leaves variegated white, flowers nearly white, dwarf

var. *sieboldii argenteo marginata (W. florida* x *W. japonica),* leaves margined white, flowers pink

Wistaria

(WISTERIA)
Family: Leguminosae
Hardy deciduous climber
Position: sun
Propagation: seed, cuttings, layers, or grafting
Cultivation easy
Fragrant

Thomas Nuttall named the genus *Wistaria* in 1818 in memory of a German professor at the University of Pennsylvania, Caspar Wistar, whom he described in Pickwickian terms as "a philanthropist of simple aspect and modest bearing, but a very active promoter of the sciences". There has, however, always been some doubt if the name should be spelled *Wistaria* or *Wisteria,* and apparently Nuttall himself could not make up his mind on this point. The problem arose because the professor's original German name was Wüster and one branch of his family had anglicized it to Wister, while another branch chose Wistar. Thus Nuttall used both spellings for the genus so as not to offend either branch. Prior to Nuttall, botanists attributed *Wistaria* to the genus *Glycinia* (from the Greek *glykys*—sweet), and in some Continental countries the plant is still known as *Glicine* or *Glycine.* Wisteria blooms automatically suggest an association with the Orient, but few realize that there are also American species. These latter were the first of the genus to be introduced into Europe, where they had a brief moment of glory prior to being soon overshadowed by the arrival of their Asiatic cousins.

The genus comprises two species of Eastern North American origin and four species native to the Far East. The first to be discovered was the North American *Wistaria frutescens,* introduced into England in 1724 by Mark Catesby under the curious name of Carolina Kidney Bean. It was a vigorous robust species, but it could not compare in beauty and magnificence of bloom with the Asiatic species. *Wistaria sinensis* was first described in a letter written by a French

Jesuit missionary in 1723, but nothing more was heard of the plant until about 1812. Then John Reeves saw it in the garden of a Cantonese merchant, whose anglicized Chinese name was Consequa and who was one of the eleven Hong agents in Canton authorized to trade with foreigners. Reeves persuaded him to propagate his plant, promising to buy all he could produce. In May of 1816, the first plants of *Wistaria sinensis* arrived in Great Britain, transported by two East India Company captains who had earned the distinction of carrying home other important introductions. The owner of one of these new plants was Mr. C. H. Turner, of Rooksnest Park, Surrey, who apparently did everything in his power to kill his treasured possession; first roasting it in a hothouse and then freezing it in a cold dark corner. But the courageous wisteria survived, flowered the following spring, and was written up and illustrated in the *Botanical Magazine*. In the meanwhile, Reeves had despatched another plant to the Royal Horticultural Society, while yet another reached Kew only a few years later (if the curious reader wishes to see the Kew specimen, it is still there).

Wistaria floribunda was introduced into Europe from Japan in 1830, by Philipp Franz von Siebold; for general garden planting it is (for several reasons) to be less recommended than *Wistaria sinensis*. In the first place, *Wistaria sinensis* is a much faster grower, in a few years covering walls, summer-houses, old trees, etc., while *Wistaria floribunda* has nothing like the same rapid development. Furthermore, *Wistaria sinensis* is far more fragrant. In recompense, *Wistaria floribunda* is more robust and will tolerate lower temperatures. It blooms 2–3 weeks later than *W. sinensis* and it has smaller, more widely spaced flowers that open progressively, beginning at the base of the cluster (a raceme) of bloom, while the flowers of *W. sinensis* all open at once. Another curious feature distinguishing the two plants is that the Chinese species twines around its supports in a clockwise manner, while the Japanese *Wistaria floribunda* twines in a counterclockwise direction. Many European and American gardeners prefer to grow their wisterias as standards, training the plants up to a height of about 8 ft., with a single trunk robust enough to stand without support, and then allowing the terminal head of branches to hang downwards, producing a weeping, pendulous mass of bloom that is most effective. The best wisteria for this purpose is *W. floribunda* var. *macrobotrys*; although it bears fewer individual flowers than the species, it is capable of producing racemes up to $4\frac{1}{2}$ ft. long. Collingwood recalls that in 1920, near Kasukabe, Japan, he saw a specimen he judged to be some hundreds of years old; its trunk was nearly 9 ft. in circumference, and it bore 80,000 racemes of bloom (imagine the patience needed to count them).

Wistaria japonica, introduced from Japan in 1878 by Charles Maries for the firm of Veitch, is much less grown. It has the great virtue of blooming in July–August, bearing whitish-yellow branching racemes 12–15 ins. long, and it is worthy of much wider cultivation if only for its late flowering. The individual blooms are the smallest of all the wisterias, only ½ in. long and very attractive. Wilson and Bell describe the scent of *Wistaria sinensis* as "unique and indescribable", possessing "something of lilac and something of honey . . . but with a characteristic of its own". The white-flowered *Wistaria sinensis* has a slightly different fragrance, "rather pungent, like cinnamon". *Wistaria floribunda* is not one of the most strongly scented, and its vars. *Naki-Naga* and *macrobotrys* both have the typical "sugary and pungent odour" of wisteria. It is significant to note that all the authorities consulted unanimously refer to the double-flowered forms with diffidence.

Cultivation. Wisterias can be grown and used in many different ways. The Japanese even employ them for Bonsai culture. *Wistaria sinensis* can easily climb to a height of 80 ft. or extend along a wall or balustrade for a length of 200 ft. On their traditionally low houses, the Japanese train wisterias along the eaves of the roof so that the foliage remains uppermost, with the racemes of bloom all hanging downwards in an uninterrupted row. Brigadier C. E. Lucas Phillips quite rightly advises a certain caution and prudence in the use of wisteria, noting that if a plant is restricted to a too-confined space it can cause considerable structural damage to its support. The plant is difficult to train or guide and not infrequently the roots have split drains and sewers open, and even penetrated or distorted metal pipes. If the growths penetrate beneath the slates or shingles of a roof they will raise them, while the stems seem almost to enjoy forcing apart the bricks or stones of terraces and walls. The enormously strong trunks can wrap themselves around stout metal supports and, over a period of years, actually distort or even break them. Thus, wisterias should be rigorously controlled through systematic and energetic pruning and constant surveillance. Pruning is necessary twice a year, first in August and then in late winter or very early spring. The summer pruning consists of shortening the new growths to within about 12 ins. from their branches; in winter prune right back to the second bud, node, or eye, from which the new season's inflorescences will be produced. Wisteria will readily adapt itself to its environment, although when planted in a rich soil the plants will obviously develop more rapidly and flower with greater profusion. They are real sun-lovers and, unlike many other climbers, they do not object to strong hot sunshine on the soil surface immediately above their roots. The plants do, however, require lots of water during hot weather and if not supplied by rain or by artificial means the roots will extend great distances searching for water.

Wisterias are bad movers, and if they survive being transplanted they take a long time to recover. New plants should, therefore, always be bought in pots. The most frequent method of propagation is by layering during summer (preferably into pots), thus providing well-rooted plants for the following season. A long vigorous branch can provide a number of new plants. Layer alternate nodes to form roots (the nodes not layered develop new vegetation) and cut the branch into sections when the various nodes have all rooted. Wisterias are also easy to raise from seed, although in the case of hybrids and varieties it is unlikely that they will breed true, but the seedlings are often useful as stock onto which the choicer varieties can be grafted. Other methods of propagation are effected by hard-wooded cuttings inserted in frames in July–August, or by root cuttings placed in sand in a greenhouse or under a glass bell-jar or transparent plastic.

Wistaria floribunda D.C.

(Japanese Wisteria)
Flowering period: May–June
Height: up to 25 ft. or more
Zone 4 southwards

Native to Japan. A woody climber with pinnate leaves up to 15 ins. long composed of 13–19 ovate-elliptic, or elongated-ovate, pointed leaflets $1\frac{1}{2}$–3 ins. long, at first slightly downy, later almost glabrous. Flowers blue or violet-blue, $\frac{1}{2}$–$\frac{3}{4}$ in. long in relatively short racemes 5–10 ins. in length which bloom gradually from the base upwards. Easily distinguished from *Wistaria sinensis* for its greater hardiness, for the fact that it sheds its foliage earlier in autumn, and because it flowers 2–3 weeks later. There are several varieties: var. *alba*, with white flowers in racemes up to 2 ft. long; var. *rosea*, pink with the wings and keel of the flowers pointed with purple; var. *variegata*, with variegated foliage; var. *violaceo plena*, double; var. *macrobotrys*, the finest form, with leaflets up to 4 ins. long and the racemes attaining a remarkable length of up to 5 ft.; var. *russelliana*, flowers a darker violet and marked cream-white.

Wistaria frutescens D.C. (*Glycine frutescens* L.)

Flowering period: June–July
Height: up to 30 ft.
Zone 5 southwards

Native to the southeastern United States. Leaves pinnate, up to 12 ins. long, composed of 9–15 ovate $1\frac{1}{2}$–$2\frac{1}{2}$-in.-long leaflets slightly downy when young. Inflorescences in terminal racemes up to 6 ins. long, borne on the current season's growths, erect in the case of the shorter racemes. Individual flowers $\frac{3}{4}$ in. long, lilac-purple with a yellow spot. The var. *alba* is white.

Wistaria macrostachya Nutt.

Flowering period: June–July
Height: 25 ft.
Zone 5 southwards

Native to Tennessee, Missouri, Arkansas, and other areas of the south central United States. In general aspect very similar to the American *Wistaria frutescens*, but a superior plant with larger foliage. Racemes up to 1 ft. in length or even longer, very compact, and bearing as many as ninety individual flowers. Not so well known or so widely planted as it deserves to be.

Wistaria sinensis
From *Paxton's Magazine of Botany*,
1840, plate 127

Wistaria sinensis Sweet (syn. *Wistaria consequana, Kraunhia sinensis, Glycine sinensis*)

(Chinese Wisteria)
Flowering period: Apr.–May
Height: up to 30 ft. or more
Zone 5 southwards

Native to China. A woody climber that often blooms before the leaves appear. Leaves pinnate, composed of 7–13 elongated-ovate, or ovate-lanceolate, pointed leaflets $1\frac{1}{2}$–3 ins. long; at first covered with silky hairs, later glabrous. Flowers violet-blue, 1 in. long, slightly fragrant, in dense racemes up to 12–15 ins. in length. The var. *alba* has white flowers in still denser but shorter racemes. Fruits similar to large bean pods, up to 6 ins. long, velvet-textured, and containing 2–3 seeds. After its first flowering in late April or May, this species generally produces a few more flowers in August. There is also a double-flowered form var. *plena*.

Wistaria venusta Rehd. & Wils.

(Silky Wisteria)
Flowering period: June–July
Height: up to 30 ft. or more
Zone 6 southwards

Native to Japan. The plant cultivated there in gardens generally is not the same as the wild form found in the hills around Nagasaki. Its closest relative is *Wistaria sinensis*, but it has larger white flowers, while the true wild species is violet-blue. Leaves 8–14 ins. long composed of 9–13 ovate $1\frac{1}{2}$–$3\frac{1}{2}$-in.-long pointed leaflets that are rounded at the base. Racemes 4–6 ins. long, 3–4 ins. wide, scented.

Zantedeschia

(Calla or Arum Lily)
Family: *Araceae*
Tender rhizomatous-rooted herbaceous perennials
Position: sun or partial shade
Propagation: division or seed
Cultivation fairly easy
Fragrant
Useful for cutting

Few know the lovely African calla or arum lily by its genus name *Zantedeschia*; but after many vicissitudes of nomenclature, and much discussion, the genus appears to be definitely and finally correctly named. The poor plant, deprived of its original name *Calla*, which was given to a European, swamp-loving species *Calla palustris* to form the monotypic genus *Calla*, was next assigned the name *Richardia*. Later that name was thrown out to avoid confusion with a completely different *Richardia* genus, belonging to the family

Rubiaceae. The name *Zantedeschia* was finally chosen to honour Francesco Zantedeschi, an Italian physician and botanist who lived from 1773 to 1846.

Not everybody has an enthusiasm for arum lilies, not surprising in view of the wide use made of the flower at memorial ceremonies and funerals. This aversion is also intensified by the rigid, deathly white, waxy blooms that make them unpopular for indoor decoration. Also, the types generally found for sale are completely without scent (although some of the original species are pleasantly fragrant). But *Zantedeschia* manifests its real beauty only when grown under conditions similar to its natural habitat: near water, at the edge of a pool, stream, or river bank, either in large masses alone or associated with other aquatic or bog plants, or even grown in shallow water where it forms islands of lush green vegetation.

According to Robert Sweet in his *Hortus Britannicus*, *Zantedeschia aethiopica* was first introduced into Europe in 1731, and *Zantedeschia albomaculata* in 1860, but not much else of their story or history has been recorded. A. Engler, in his monograph on the genus *Zantedeschia*, confirms that there are eight species and, for once, this number appears to be definite. They are all native to Africa, with an area of distribution extending southwards from the equator to the Cape, Natal, the Transvaal, and Basutoland.

Cultivation. If its natural requirements are observed, the calla is very easy to cultivate, and in frost-free areas even naturalizing itself and growing wild if planted near water. It must, however, have a semi-dormant rest period, when the underground rhizomes are left alone to live on the food and moisture they have stored during their growing period; this dormant period also serves to start the new season's growth and subsequent flowering. Cultural requirements do vary, however, according to the species and to how the plants are grown. *Zantedeschia aethiopica* grown outside in localities where severe frost is not experienced can be left in the ground permanently. In late summer, the foliage will die down naturally, even if the rhizomes are in a moist soil, and the plants will remain semi-dormant throughout autumn and winter. Grown in pots—a purpose for which they are eminently suited—for indoor or greenhouse decoration, the rhizomes must be given a period of rest when water is withheld. This should come after flowering has finished and after the production of new leaves has ended. In September, the plants can be divided, removing the young rhizomes; for if these are left around the parent the result will be an excess of foliage with few flowers the following season. (These young rhizomes provide an easy method of propagation, and can be grown on until they reach flowering size.) The plants can then, as explained above, be watered less until they become dormant, losing all foliage; then watering should be suspended until early spring, when the rhizomes can be repotted prior to the emergence of new growth, and normal watering commenced once more. During their dormant period the rhizomes should be kept in slightly damp sand in a frost-free place. In areas where there is no danger of the water freezing in winter, pot-grown *Zantedeschia aethiopica* can even be wintered over in receptacles of water, at a depth of about 18 ins., a system often practised in Southern Europe. If the plants are to be cultivated in a greenhouse for early flowering in pots, they should be repotted and watering started in December; keep them at a temperature of 50°F., gradually raising to 60°F. as growth develops. By February, the plants will have produced an abundance of foliage and the first flowers will appear. They can also be used as temporary house plants, giving them an abundance of moisture preferably by standing the pots in saucers of water. An appropriate soil mixture for the pot cultivation of *Zantedeschia aethiopica* can be prepared as follows: 1 part fibrous loam, $\frac{1}{2}$ part of well-decomposed manure, $\frac{1}{4}$ part sand, and $\frac{1}{4}$ part leafsoil. During the period of active vigorous growth the plants should periodically be given doses of liquid organic fertilizer. All the other species, with yellow or pink spathes (the so-called flowers), definitely require a completely dormant period between October and February before beginning their new season's growth. The initial drying-off stage can be conducted in the same manner as for the white *Zantedeschia aethiopica*, but the rhizomes should be left in the pots and allowed to dry in the soil, repotting them in early spring and restarting the growth as explained for the white callas. If cultivated in the open ground, the rhizomes should be lifted after growth has finished and stored in very slightly moist sand. The coloured callas are not semi-aquatic plants like the white *Zantedeschia aethiopica* and are also not hardy. Apart from propagation by division as explained above, the plants can also be propagated from seed sown as soon as it is ripe in pans in a warm greenhouse, keeping the soil moderately moist; grow on the seedlings either in boxes or in small individual pots. Flowering-sized rhizomes can be expected within 3–4 years.

Zantedeschia aethiopica Spreng. (syn. *Richardia africana*) (Arum Lily or Calla Lily)
Native to tropical and South Africa. Rhizome robust, fleshy, blackish; roots fibrous, white. Leaves all produced from the base, long-stalked, elongated heart-shaped, pointed, rich green, shiny. The flower stem can be up to nearly 3 ft. high, terminating in an inflorescence held well above the foliage. The white spathe is up to 9 ins. long, tapering to a long point, vase-shaped, curled at the base, and generally curved at the apex, with the interior cream-white. Rising from the base of the spathe there is the yellow or yellowish-orange spadix, bearing the true but insignificant flowers, here consisting only of the actual organs of reproduction. The var. *minor* (Little Gem) is identical to the species but in miniature, with a height

Flowering period: June–Sept.
Height: up to 3 ft.

Zantedeschia aethiopica
From *Curtis's Botanical Magazine*,
1805, plate 832

of only 12–15 ins. The var. *devoniensis* is more profusely flowering and more fragrant. Other dwarf varieties, excellent for pot culture, are var. *Perle von Stuttgart*, var. *gedesfreyana,* and var. *childsiana.* There are also forms with double and triple spathes but they are more curious than attractive. Varieties with particularly large spathes are var. *Weisser Hercules*, var. *gigantea*, and var. *grandiflora*

Zantedeschia albo maculata

Zantedeschia albo maculata Baill. (syn. *Richardia albo-maculata*)
Native to South Africa. A bushy, compact species found growing in grassy slopes. Leaves elongated-lanceolate, pointed, 6–15 ins. long, with numerous transparent white marks over their surface. Spathe cream-coloured with a dark mark at its base.

(Spotted Calla)
Flowering period: May–Aug.
Height: up to 2½ ft.

Zantedeschia elliottiana Engl. (syn. *Richardia elliottiana*)
Native to southeast Africa; found growing in grassy highlands. Leaves oval or heart-shaped, brilliant green with numerous transparent white marks on their surface. Spathe 6 ins. long, dark yellow without any mark at the base, externally greenish yellow, margins undulated.

(Golden Calla)
Flowering period: June–Aug.
Height: up to 2½ ft.

Zantedeschia melanoleuca Engl. (syn. *Richardia melanoleuca*)
Native to Natal. Foliage and stems silky. Leaves elongated-lanceolate, pointed, 5–7 ins. long, their surface covered with whitish marks. Spathe very open, straw-yellow, marked purple at the base.

(Black-throated Calla)
Flowering period: June–Aug.
Height: up to 18 ins.

Zantedeschia rehmannii Engl. (syn. *Richardia rehmannii*)
Native to Natal, where it is found growing in stony soil in hilly localities. Leaves of irregular elongated-lanceolate form, 8–14 ins. long, only 1¼ ins. wide, and covered with transparent whitish marks. Spathe pink suffused violet at the edges; spadix short. The var. *speciosa* is dwarfer and of a more robust habit.

(Pink Calla or Rose Calla)
Flowering period: June–Aug.
Height: up to 16 ins.

Zinnia

Family: Compositae
Annuals
Position: sun
Propagation: seed
Cultivation easy
Useful for cutting

Typical single- and double-flowered zinnias

The genus *Zinnia* is last in alphabetical order in this book but first in importance among annuals. Those who have only grown zinnias in northern gardens, far from their native habitat in Central and South America, can have no idea of the true magnificence of these superb plants when cultivated under hot, sunny conditions with a temperature of about 80°F. or more for several months, and a summer season that lasts from June to October. Except for fragrance, zinnias have many good qualities: a limitless range of colours; ideal for cutting; individual flowers very long-lasting, with a flowering season that extends from July to October; a fascinating variety of shapes, sizes, forms, and heights making them useful for such diverse purposes as the rock-garden, edging, bedding, borders, or naturalizing; ease of cultivation; minimum maintenance (except in the case of the very tall types that need support, and the periodic removal of dead flowers); resistance to bad weather, particularly in the case of the dwarfer forms; brilliant, attractive, and spectacular appearance and lovely, often unusual colours. In return for so much, zinnias ask for an abundance of sun, and a hot, moderately dry position in a warm, rich, deep soil, either acid or alkaline (calcareous). They are mostly native to Mexico, although their area of diffusion extends as far north as Texas and Colorado, and as far south as Chile. There are about fifteen species; only three, together with their varieties, are normally cultivated in gardens.

The first zinnias reached Europe about the second half of the eighteenth century: *Zinnia pauciflora* in 1750, and *Zinnia multiflora* in 1770. Neither of these is now in general cultivation, although together with *Zinnia elegans* they have played a large part in the development of the modern zinnia hybrids. In fact, apart from the incredible *Zinnia linearis*, practically every garden zinnia today is of hybrid origin.

The genus was named by Linnaeus in honour of his disciple Johann Gottfried Zinn (1727–1759), professor of botany at the University of Göttingen. It is ironic that a genus that is now so involved and complicated, with its many types, forms, and varieties, should

Zinnia elegans
From *Curtis's Botanical Magazine*,
1801, plate 527

Zinnia elegans
Lilliput hybrid

Flowering period: June–Oct.
Height: 12–15 ins.

(Youth and Old Age)
Flowering period: July–Oct.
Height: 3 ins.–4 ft.
according to variety

signify "simplicity" in the language of flowers. Actually, the form of the flowers of the original species was extremely simple, and in spite of the vast changes that have taken place in the plant's form, the actual flowers still retain much of their original symmetrical simplicity (only the petals of certain varieties have had their shape changed).

Cultivation. The cultivation of zinnias does not present any difficulties, although they dislike a close, stagnant environment and an excessively wet soil. They thrive in almost any type of soil, having a preference for alkaline (calcareous); as fast growers they require plenty of plant food, preferably one rich in phosphorous since an excess of nitrogen is liable to favour leaf growth at the expense of flower production. Before planting, the soil should be deeply dug and enriched with well-rotted manure. Seed can be sown during April–May in seed beds or in frames, in a light soil, and in a warm, sheltered position. Germination is very rapid, often in twenty-four hours, and the seedlings can be transplanted into their flowering positions when only a few inches high. In the case of the large-flowered tall varieties, the young plants should be topped when they have produced three pairs of leaves, as this will encourage basal branching and bushy plants. It should be remembered that zinnias are not hardy and in northern localities both sowing and planting may have to be retarded if late-spring frosts are likely.

Zinnia angustifolia H.B.K. (syn. *Zinnia haageana, Zinnia mexicana, Zinnia ghiesbreghtii, Zinnia aurea, Sanvitalia mexicana*)
Native to Mexico. One of the small-flowered species, with spreading, erect, much-branched hairy stems marked with red. Leaves opposite, stalkless, hairy; those at the base oval-lanceolate, the remainder much narrower, $3\frac{1}{2}$ ins. long and half as wide.

Zinnia elegans Jacq.
Native to Mexico. A large, robust annual with rigid, erect, much-branched hairy stems. Leaves opposite, rough-surfaced, large, light green, oval or heart-shaped, pointed. This is, in its many hybrid forms, the most popular zinnia in gardens. The original species has purple or lilac-pink flowers that are single, terminal, and about 2 ins. wide. They are solitary and borne on rigid stalks swollen at the summit. The varieties have an almost limitless range of colours, and are generally double flowered. The so-called flowers are actually a complete inflorescence composed of external ray flowers (ligules, or petals) and disc flowers in the centre. The ray flowers have the most brilliant colouring; the small tubular disc flowers are yellow or orange, and in the case of hybrid forms are nearly completely absent. In the early stages, the centre of the flower is a small cylindrical cone. As the flower develops and later fades, this becomes

much enlarged. This cone is composed of many imbricated bracts, among which the seeds develop; when the flowers are completely finished it remains at the end of the stalk until the seeds are ripe. To ensure a continuity of bloom, however, the dead blooms should be removed before this cone develops. In the case of large-flowered double hybrid zinnias this central cone is inconspicuous or even invisible until the flower is old, being covered and surrounded by the ligules (petals) which are up to $\frac{1}{3}$ in. wide and $1\frac{1}{2}$ ins. long and arranged in a spiral, symmetrical, uniform manner.

For garden purposes, these *Zinnia elegans* hybrids are divided into numerous types or classes, each containing a great many varieties and different colours. The most important are:

- Double, $2\frac{1}{2}$ ft. high, with flowers 3–4 ins. in diameter
- Lilliput or Pompon, $1\frac{1}{2}$ ft. high, with flowers $1\frac{1}{2}$–2 ins. wide and bushy compact plants
- Dahlia-flowered, $2\frac{1}{2}$–3 ft. high, flowers 4–6 ins. wide with outward-curving petals
- Californian Giant, 3 ft. or more in height, flowers 6 ins. or more in diameter, the largest of hybrid zinnias
- Scabiosa-flowered, $2\frac{3}{4}$ ft. high, flowers $3\frac{1}{4}$ ins. wide and of a typical scabiosa flower form
- Cactus-flowered, $2\frac{1}{2}$–3 ft. high, flowers up to 4 ins. wide with slightly recurved, reflexed petals
- Pumila, up to 18 ins. high and very compact habit, flowers $2\frac{3}{4}$ ins. wide, very double, flowering period rather shorter than that of the Lilliput type, which continues to bloom until the first frost
- Thumbelina, a relatively new strain only 4–6 ins. high forming dwarf, compact, cushion-like little plants of great fascination and charm, with double or semi-double flowers $1\frac{1}{2}$ ins. in diameter, excellent for the rock-garden and for small beds
- Sombrero, also of recent introduction, single flowers $2\frac{1}{2}$ ins. wide, petals crimson-scarlet tipped with bright yellow, height 15–18 ins., excellent for cutting

Zinnia linearis

Zinnia linearis Benth.

Native to Mexico. A species not generally known in gardens but worthy of much wider cultivation because of its brilliant colouring and remarkably long flowering period. A dwarf, wide-spreading, compact plant 8–10 ins. high with many slender semi-trailing stems. Flowers single, 2 ins. in diameter, borne on slender erect stems in such profusion that they completely hide the plants. Requires a long hot summer and should be planted in masses in full sun. Excellent for small beds, edging, dry walls, the rock-garden, and for use as a temporary ground cover, when it will form a dense carpet of bloom. There is also a lovely but rare white-flowered form.

Flowering period: June–Nov.
Height: 8–10 ins.

SEED, BULB, & PLANT SOURCES, A SELECTIVE LISTING

The following represent some of the best-known North American firms. The majority issue extensive catalogues, and many of these can be obtained free on request; for others a small charge is made, often deductible with the first order.

When ordering shrubs or trees, deciduous or evergreen, it is best to select a firm located as close to one's own hardiness zone as possible. Since most nursery stock is field-grown, specimens raised in a warmer area may prove less hardy in colder, more northerly localities. However, if one is obliged to order material from a nursery located in a warmer climatic zone, it is wise to inquire whether the desired specimen can tolerate the climate in one's own zone or if it should be given winter protection until it becomes acclimatized to colder conditions.

Note: When ordering from foreign sources, U.S. Department of Agriculture regulations must be kept in mind. Although most seeds and some bulbs may be imported with no restrictions, plants and certain seeds and bulbs cannot be imported at all, and certain others can be imported only if the order is accompanied by a special permit issued by the Department (PQ. Form 687). Applications for permits and full information on all seeds and/or plants which are forbidden importation may be obtained from the Plant Quarantine Division, U.S. Department of Agriculture, 209 River Street, Hoboken, New Jersey 07030. The catalogues of many British seedsmen (Thompson & Morgan, in particular) usually specify non-importable species.

PERENNIALS
(Specialist)

Chrysanthemums

HUFF'S GARDENS
Burlington, Kan. 66839

NORVELL GREENHOUSES
318 South Greenacres Rd.
Greenacres, Wash. 99016

STAR MUMS
West Grove, Pa. 19390

SUNNYSLOPE GARDENS
8638 Huntington Dr.
San Gabriel, Cal. 91775

THON'S
4815 Oak St.
Crystal Lake, Ill. 60014

Daylilies (Hemerocallis)

SCHREINER'S
3625 Quinaby Rd. N.E.
Salem, Ore. 97303

GILBERT H. WILD & SON
Sarcoxie, Mo. 64862

Hosta

SAVORY'S GREENHOUSES
5300 Whiting Ave.
Edina, Minn. 55435

Iris

COOLEY'S GARDENS
Silverton, Ore. 97381

EDEN ROAD IRIS GARDENS
P.O. Box 117
Wenatchee, Wash. 98801

MELROSE GARDENS
Best Rd. South
Stockton, Cal. 95206

SCHREINER'S
3625 Quinaby Rd. N.E.
Salem, Ore. 97303

GILBERT H. WILD & SON
Sarcoxie, Mo. 64862

PERENNIALS
(General)

W. ATLEE BURPEE CO.
P.O. Box 6929,
Philadelphia, Pa. 19132
P.O. Box B 2001,
Clinton, Iowa 52732

(*Seeds*)P.O. Box 748,
Riverside, Cal. 92502

INTER-STATE
NURSERIES
Hamburg, Iowa

LAMB NURSERIES
E. 101 Sharp
Spokane, Wash. 99202

GEORGE W. PARK SEED CO.
Greenwood, S.C. 29646

SKINNER'S
NURSERY LTD.
Dropmore, Manitoba,
Canada

SPRING HILL
NURSERIES
Tipp City, Ohio 45366

WAYSIDE GARDENS CO.
Mentor Ave.
Mentor, Ohio 44060

WHITE FLOWER FARM
Litchfield, Conn. 06759

TREES, SHRUBS, & VINES
(Specialist)

"Azaleas"

WARREN BALDSIEFEN
Box 88
Bellvale, N.Y. 10912

COMERFORD'S
Box 100
Marion, Ore. 97359

NUCCIO'S NURSERIES
3555 Chaney Trail
Altadena, Cal. 91001

Camellias

NUCCIO'S NURSERIES
3555 Chaney Trail
Altadena, Cal. 91001

ORINDA NURSERY
Bridgeville, Del. 19933

Clematis

ARNOLD'S CLEMATIS
NURSERY
2005 S.E. Park Ave.
Milwaukie, Ore. 97222

THE D.S. GEORGE
NURSERIES
2491 Penfield Rd.
Fairport, N.Y. 14450

Heathers, Heaths

MAYFAIR NURSERIES
RD #2, Box 68
Nichols, N.Y. 13812

"Lilacs" (Syringa)

J. HERBERT
ALEXANDER
1224 Wareham St.
Middleboro, Mass. 02346

MABEL FRANKLIN
9225 S. Penn Ave.
Minneapolis, Minn. 55431

Rhododendrons

WARREN BALDSIEFEN
Box 88
Bellvale, N.Y. 10912

COMERFORD'S
Box 100
Marion, Ore. 97359

LABARS'
RHODODENDRON
NURSERY
Box 111
Bryant St.
Stroudsburg, Pa. 18360

NUCCIO'S NURSERIES
3555 Chaney Trail
Altadena, Cal. 91001

ORINDA NURSERY
Bridgeville, Del. 19933

A. SHAMMARELLO
& SON NURSERY
4590 Monticello Blvd.
South Euclid, Ohio 44143

Unusual

BRIMFIELD GARDENS
NURSERY
245 Brimfield Rd.
Wethersfield, Conn. 06109

TREES, SHRUBS, & VINES
(General)

ACKERMAN
NURSERIES
Lake Street
Bridgman, Mich. 49106

BURGESS SEED
& PLANT CO.
Box 218
Galesburg, Mich. 49053

1398

CALIFORNIA NURSERY
CO.
36501 Niles Blvd.
Fremont, Cal. 94536

FARMER SEED &
NURSERY CO.
Rt. 60
Faribault, Minn. 55021

EARL FERRIS NURSERY
Bridge St.
Hampton, Iowa 50441

HENRY FIELD SEED &
NURSERY CO.
407 Sycamore St.
Shenandoah, Iowa 51601

GIRARD NURSERIES
RD #4, North Ridge East
Geneva, Ohio 44041

GURNEY SEED
& PLANT CO.
Yankton, S.D. 57078

H.G. HASTINGS CO.
Box 4088
Atlanta, Ga. 30302

INTER-STATE
NURSERIES, INC.
Hamburg, Iowa 51640

KELLY BROS.
NURSERIES, INC.
Dansville, N.Y. 14437

MELLINGER'S
North Lima, Ohio 44452

MUSSER FORESTS, INC.
Box 7D
Indiana, Pa. 15701

SHERIDAN NURSERIES
LTD.
100 Sherway Dr.
Etobicoke, Ontario, Canada

STARK BROS.
Louisiana, Mo. 63353

STERN'S NURSERIES
Geneva, N.Y. 14456

WAYSIDE GARDENS
CO., INC.
Mentor Ave.
Mentor, Ohio 44060

WESTERN MAINE
FOREST
NURSERY CO.
Fryeburg, Me. 04037

WHITE FLOWER FARM
Litchfield, Conn. 06759

ROSES

ARMSTRONG
NURSERIES, INC.
1239 S. Palmetto
Ontario, Cal. 91761

JACKSON
& PERKINS CO.
Medford, Ore. 97501

STAR ROSES
West Grove, Pa. 19390

Old and New

JOSEPH J. KERN
ROSE NURSERY
Box 33, Jackson St. &
Heisley Rd.
Mentor, Ohio 44060

TILLOTSON'S ROSES
241 Brown's Valley Road
Watsonville, Cal. 95076

MELVIN E. WYANT
200 Johnny Cake Ridge
Mentor, Ohio 44060

BULBS

W. ATLEE BURPEE CO.
P.O. Box 6929,
Philadelphia, Pa. 19132

P.O. Box B 2001,
Clinton, Iowa 52732
P.O. Box 748,
Riverside, Cal. 92502

INTERNATIONAL
GROWERS
EXCHANGE
Box 397A
Farmington, Mich. 48024

P. DE JAGER & SONS,
INC.
South Hamilton, Mass.
01982

JOHN MESSELAAR
BULB CO.
Box 269A
Ipswich, Mass. 01938

JOHN SCHEEPERS, INC.
63 Wall St.
New York, N.Y. 10005

VAN BOURGONDIEN
BROTHERS
Box A
Babylon, N.Y. 11702

THE WAYSIDE
GARDENS CO.
Mentor Ave.
Mentor, Ohio 44060

WHITE FLOWER FARM
Litchfield, Conn. 06759

Begonias

ANTONELLI
BROTHERS
2545 Capitola Rd.
Santa Cruz, Cal. 95060

Dahlias

DAHLIADEL IN THE
MOUNTAINS
Box 990
Waynesville, N.C. 28786

DOUGLAS DAHLIAS
Myrtle Creek, Ore. 97457

Gladiolus

CHAMPLAIN VIEW GARDENS
South Hamilton, Mass. 01982

NOWETA GARDENS
Box 100
St. Charles, Minn. 55972

Lilies

REX BULB FARMS
Box 145-K
Newberg, Ore. 97132

WILDFLOWERS

GARDENS OF THE BLUE RIDGE
Ashford (McDowell County),
North Carolina 28603

RUTH HARDY'S WILDFLOWER NURSERY
Rt. 7, South Canaan Road
Falls Village, Conn. 06031

PUTNEY NURSERY
Putney, Vermont 05346

SISKIYOU RARE PLANTS NURSERY
522 Franquette Street
Medford, Oregon 97501

THREE LAURELS
Marshall,
North Carolina 28753

WOODLAND ACRES NURSERY
Rt. 2
Crivitz, Wisconsin 54114

ANNUALS (General)

W. ATLEE BURPEE CO.
P.O. Box 6929,
Philadelphia, Pa. 19132
P.O. Box B 2001,
Clinton, Iowa 52732
(*Seeds*) P.O. Box 748,
Riverside, Cal. 92502

HENRY FIELD SEED & NURSERY CO.
Shenandoah, Iowa 51601

GURNEY SEED & NURSERY CO.
Yankton, S.D. 57078

JOSEPH HARRIS CO., INC.
Moreton Farm
Rochester, N.Y. 14624

J.W. JUNG SEED CO.
Randolph, Wis. 53956

EARL MAY SEED & NURSERY CO.
Shenandoah, Iowa 51601

OLDS SEED CO.
Box 1069
Madison, Wis. 53701

GEORGE W. PARK SEED CO.
Greenwood, S.C. 29646

R.H. SHUMWAY
Rockford, Ill. 61101

STOKES SEEDS INC.
1102 Stokes Bldg.
Buffalo, N.Y. 14240

ANNUALS (Specialist)

"Geraniums" (Pelargoniums)

MERRY GARDENS
Camden, Me. 04843

WILSON BROTHERS
Roachdale, Ind. 46172

ANNUALS (English Sources)

SAMUEL DOBIE & SONS LTD.
Llangollen
North Wales, England

SUTTONS SEEDS LTD.
Reading
Berks, RG 6, 1AB, England

THOMPSON & MORGAN LTD.
London Rd.
Ipswich, 1P2, OBA,
England

SELECTED BOOKS FOR FURTHER READING

Compiled by Elizabeth Cornelia Hall

It has been the aim of the bibliographer to list currently available books. In certain instances, however, an out-of-print title has been included because of its outstanding importance as a reference work.

CLASSICAL WORKS

BLUNT, WILFRID. *The Compleat Naturalist: The Life and Work of Linnaeus.* London: Collins; New York: Viking; 1971.

Curtis's Botanical Magazine: containing coloured figures with descriptions and observations on the botany, history and culture of choice plants (present ed. David R. Hunt). Richmond, Surrey: Royal Botanic Gardens, Kew, 1787–date.

DIOSCORIDES, PEDANIOS. *The Greek Herbal of Dioscorides.* Illustrated by a Byzantine, A.D. 512, Englished by John Goodyer, A.D. 1655, ed. and first printed A.D. 1933 by Robert T. Gunther. New York: Hafner, 1968. (Translation of *De Materia Medica.* Venice: Stagnino, 1538.)

GERARD, JOHN. *Leaves from Gerard's Herball.* Arranged for Garden Lovers by Marcus Woodward. London: Constable; New York: Dover, 1969. (Based on *The Herball.* London: A. Islip, 1633.)

Magazine of Botany and Register of Flowering Plants (ed. Joseph Paxton). 16 vols. London: Orr, 1834–1849.

MILLER, PHILIP. *The Gardener's Dictionary.* 2 vols. in 1. New York: Hafner, 1969. (Reprint of abridged edition. London: Rivington, 1754.)

PARKINSON, JOHN. *Paradisi in Sole Paradisus Terrestris.* London: Methuen, 1904. (Reprint of London: H. Lownes, 1629.)

PLINY (Gaius Plinius Secundus). *Natural History* (trans. W. H. S. Jones). London: Heinemann; Cambridge, Mass.: Harvard University Press, 1963. (From *Naturalis Historiae.* Venetiis: P. Manutium, 1559.)

STRABO WALAHFRID. *Hortulus* [*The Little Garden*] (trans. Raef Payne). New York: Hafner, 1966. (Facsimile of a 9th-century manuscript.)

THEOPHRASTOS, ERESIOS. *Enquiry into Plants and Minor Works on Odours and Weather Signs* (trans. Sir Arthur Hort). 2 vols. London: Heinemann; New York: Putnam, 1916. (From *Historia Plantarum.* Amsterdam: H. Laurentium, 1644.)

VILMORIN-ANDRIEUX & CIE. *Les Fleurs de Pleine Terre.* Paris: (5th ed.), 1909.

GENERAL GARDENING: Encyclopedias, Etc.

BAILEY, LIBERTY HYDE. *The Standard Cyclopedia of Horticulture.* 3 vols. London and New York: Macmillan (3rd rev. ed.), 1942.

BAILEY, LIBERTY HYDE, and BAILEY, ETHEL ZOE, comp. *Hortus Second; A Concise Dictionary of Gardening, General Horticulture and Cultivated Plants in North America.* London and New York: Macmillan, 1941.

EVERETT, THOMAS H. *The New Illustrated Encyclopedia of Gardening.* 26 vols. London and New York: Greystone (rev. ed.), 1972.

FLETCHER, H. L. V. *Popular Flowering Plants.* London: Pelham, 1970; New York: Drake, 1972.

FOLEY, DANIEL J. *Gardening for Beginners.* London: Vision Press; New York: Funk & Wagnalls (rev. ed.), 1972.

HARING, ELDA. *Colour for Your Yard and Garden.* London: Hawthorn, 1971. American edition: *Color for You and Your Garden.* New York: Hawthorn, 1971.

HAY, ROY, and SYNGE, PATRICK M. *The Dictionary of Garden Plants in Colour.* London: Ebury, 1969. American edition: *The Color Dictionary of Flowers and Plants for Home and Garden.* New York: Crown, 1969.

HELLYER, A. G. L. *The Amateur Gardener.* London: Collingridge; Levittown, N.Y.: Transatlantic (3rd ed.), 1973.

HUXLEY, ANTHONY. *Garden Flowers in Color.* 2 vols. London and New York: Macmillan, 1971.

PHILLIPS, GEORGE A. *The Observer's Book of Garden Flowers.* London and New York: Warne, 1957.

Royal Horticultural Society. *Dictionary of Gardening: A Practical and Scientific Encyclopedia of Horticulture* (ed. Fred J. Chittenden). London and New York: Oxford University Press (2nd ed.), 1965. *Supplement* (ed. Patrick M. Synge). London and New York: Oxford University Press (2nd ed.), 1969.

SANDERS, T. W. *Encyclopaedia of Gardening* (ed. A. G. L. Hellyer). London: Collingridge (rev. ed.), 1971; Levittown, N.Y.: Transatlantic, 1972.

TAYLOR, NORMAN. *Taylor's Encyclopedia of Gardening, Horticulture and Landscape Design.* Boston: Houghton Mifflin (4th ed.), 1961.

WILSON, JAMES W. *Flower Gardening: A Primer.* London: Van Nostrand Reinhold, 1970. American edition: *Flower Gardening for Beginners.* New York: Van Nostrand Reinhold, 1970.

WYMAN, DONALD. *Wyman's Gardening Encyclopedia.* London and New York: Macmillan, 1972.

BOTANY AND NATIVE PLANTS

CRONQUIST, ARTHUR. *Basic Botany.* London and New York: Harper & Row, 1973.

HUTCHINSON, JOHN. *British Wild Flowers.* 2 vols. Newton Abbot: David & Charles; Cranbury, N. J.: Fairleigh Dickinson (rev. ed.), 1972.

MANNING, A. S. *Systematic Guide to Flowering Plants of the World.* London: Butler & Tanner; New York: Taplinger, 1965.

PETERSON, ROGER TORY, and McKENNY, MARGARET. *Field Guide to Wildflowers of Northeastern and North-Central North America.* Boston: Houghton Mifflin, 1968.

POLUNIN, OLEG, and HUXLEY, ANTHONY. *Flowers of the Mediterranean.* London: Chatto & Windus, 1965; Boston: Houghton Mifflin, 1966.

SMITH, A. W. *A Gardener's Dictionary of Plant Names: A Handbook on the Origin and Meaning of Some Plant Names* (revised and enlarged by W. T. Stearn and I. L. L. Smith). London: Cassell; New York: St. Martin, 1972.

STOKOE, WILLIAM J. *The Observer's Book of Wild Flowers.* London and New York: Warne, 1963.

TAYLOR, KATHRYN S., and HAMBLIN, STEPHEN F. *Handbook of Wild Flower Cultivation.* London and New York: Macmillan, 1963.

POPULAR GARDEN FLOWERS

Begonias

LANGDON, BRIAN. *The Tuberous Begonia.* London: Cassell, 1969; New York: International Publications Service, 1971.

Chrysanthemums

GOSLING, STANLEY. *Pocket Encyclopedia of Chrysanthemums in Colour.* London: Blandford; New York: International Publications Service, 1971.

MACHIN, B. J., and SEARLE, S. A. *Chrysanthemums the Year Round.* London: Blandford; New York: International Publications Service (3rd ed.), 1968.

Dahlias

LEBAR, T. R. *Dahlias for Everyone.* London: Blandford; New York: St. Martin (rev. ed.), 1961.

Delphiniums

OGG, STUART. *Delphiniums for Everyone.* London: Blandford; Newton Centre, Mass.: Branford, 1961.

Fuchsias

GOULDING, EDWIN J. *Fuchsias: A Guide to Cultivation and Identification.* New York: Arco, 1973.

WILSON, STANLEY J. *Fuchsias: A Complete Guide to Their Propagation and Cultivation for House and Garden.* London: Faber & Faber (2nd ed.), 1972.

Geraniums (Pelargoniums)

CLIFFORD, DEREK. *Pelargoniums; Including the Popular 'Geranium.'* London: Blandford; New York: Fernhill (2nd ed.), 1970.

WILSON, HELEN VAN PELT. *The Joy of Geraniums.* New York: Morrow, 1972.

Iris

PRICE, MOLLY. *The Iris Book.* London: Constable; New York: Dover (2nd ed.), 1973.

RANDALL, HARRY. *Irises.* London: Batsford; New York: Taplinger, 1969.

Lilies

DE GRAFF, JAN, and HYAMS, EDWARD. *Lilies.* London: Nelson, 1967; New York: Funk & Wagnalls, 1971.

FELDMAIER, CARL. *Lilies* (trans. Matt Templeton). London: Batsford; New York: Arco, 1970.

Primroses

CLAPHAM, SIDNEY. *Primulas.* London: Yoseloff; South Brunswick, N. J.: Barnes, 1972.

KLABER, DORETTA. *Primulas and Spring.* New York: Morrow, 1966.

ANNUALS AND PERENNIALS

Annuals

CROCKETT, JAMES U. *Annuals.* (The

Time-Life Encyclopedia of Gardening.) New York: Time-Life, 1971.

FOGG, H. G. WITHAM. *Dictionary of Annual Plants.* Newton Abbot: David & Charles; New York: Drake (rev. ed.), 1972.

Perennials

BLOOM, ALAN. *Perennials for Trouble-Free Gardening.* London: Faber & Faber; Levittown, N. Y.: Transatlantic, 1960.

CROCKETT, JAMES U. *Perennials. (The Time-Life Encyclopedia of Gardening.)* New York: Time-Life, 1972.

CUMMING, RODERICK W. *Contemporary Perennials.* London and New York: Macmillan, 1960.

BULBS

CROCKETT, JAMES U. *Bulbs. (The Time-Life Encyclopedia of Gardening.)* New York: Time-Life, 1971.

GENDERS, ROY. *Bulbs: A Complete Handbook.* London: Blackwell; Indianapolis: Bobbs-Merrill, 1973.

JEFFERSON-BROWN, MICHAEL J. *Daffodils, Tulips and Other Hardy Bulbs.* London: Faber & Faber; Newton Centre, Mass.: Branford, 1966.

WISTER, GERTRUDE. *Hardy Garden Bulbs.* London: Dent; New York: Dutton, 1964.

FLOWERING SHRUBS AND TREES

General

BEAN, W. J. *Trees and Shrubs Hardy in the British Isles* (ed. Sir George Taylor). 3 vols. London: Murray; Levittown, N. Y.: Transatlantic (8th ed.), 1970–1974.

CROCKETT, JAMES U. *Flowering Shrubs. (The Time-Life Encyclopedia of Gardening.)* New York: Time-Life, 1972.

———. *Trees. (The Time-Life Encyclopedia of Gardening.)* New York: Time-Life, 1972.

FLETCHER, H. L. V. *Popular Flowering Shrubs.* London: Pelham; New York: Drake, 1972.

HILLIER, H. G., and others. *Hilliers Manual of Trees and Shrubs.* Newton Abbott: David & Charles; Cranbury, N. J.: Barnes, 1971.

SHEWELL-COOPER, W. E. *The A.B.C. of Flowering Shrubs.* London: English Universities Press; New York: International Publications Service, 1967.

STOKOE, W. J. *The Observer's Book of Trees and Shrubs.* London and New York: Warne (5th ed.), 1964.

WHITEHEAD, S. B. *The Observer's Book of Flowering Trees and Shrubs.* London and New York: Warne, 1972.

WYMAN, DONALD. *Shrubs and Vines for American Gardens.* London and New York: Macmillan (rev. ed.), 1969.

———. *Trees for American Gardens.* London and New York: Macmillan (rev. ed.), 1965.

Camellias

ANDERSON, EDWARD B. *Camellias.* London: Blandford; Newton Centre, Mass.: Branford, 1963.

Sunset Magazine, Eds. *How to Grow and Use Camellias.* Menlo Park, Calif.: Lane (rev. ed.), 1968.

Cherries

CHADBUND, GEOFFREY. *Flowering Cherries.* London and New York: Collins, 1972.

Magnolias

MILLAIS, J. G. *Magnolias*. London: Minerva Press, 1972. (Reprint of London: Longmans, Green, 1927.)

Rhododendrons

LEACH, DAVID G. *Rhododendrons of the World*. London and New York: Scribner, 1961.

Roses

CROCKETT, JAMES U. *Roses. (The Time-Life Encyclopedia of Gardening.)* New York: Time-Life, 1971.

GAULT, S. MILLER, and SYNGE, PATRICK M. *The Dictionary of Roses in Color*. London: Ebury Press; New York: Grosset & Dunlap, 1971.

HOLLIS, LEONARD. *Collingridge Standard Guide to Roses*. London: Collingridge; Levittown, N. Y.: Transatlantic, 1970.

THOMAS, GRAHAM S. *Old Shrub Roses*. Newton Centre, Mass.: Branford, 1972.

YOUNG, NORMAN. *The Complete Rosarian: The Development, Cultivation and Reproduction of Roses*. London: Hodder & Stoughton; New York: International Publications Service, 1971.

TYPES OF PLANTING

Container

TALOUMIS, GEORGE. *Container Gardening Outdoors*. New York: Simon & Schuster, 1972.

Moisture-loving

BLOOM, ALAN. *Moisture Gardening: Hardy Perennials in Their Natural Environment*. London: Faber & Faber; Newton Centre, Mass.: Branford, 1966.

Rock

FOSTER, H. LINCOLN. *Rock Gardening*. Boston: Houghton Mifflin, 1968.

HEATH, ROYSTON E. *Rock Plants for Small Gardens*. London: Collingridge, 1969; Levittown, N. Y.: Transatlantic, 1970.

Seaside

FOLEY, DANIEL J. *Gardening by the Sea*. London and Radnor, Pa.: Chilton, 1965.

KELWAY, CHRISTINE. *Gardening on the Coast*. Newton Abbott, Devonshire, and North Pomfret, Vt.: David & Charles, 1971.

Shade

MORSE, HARRIET K. *Gardening in the Shade*. London and New York: Scribner (rev. ed.), 1962.

ECOLOGY GARDENING

CARSON, RACHEL. *Silent Spring*. London: Hamish Hamilton; Boston: Houghton Mifflin, 1962.

HUNTER, BEATRICE T. *Gardening Without Poisons*. London: Hamish Hamilton; Boston: Houghton Mifflin (2nd ed.), 1972.

Sunset Magazine, Eds. *Sunset Guide to Organic Gardening*. Menlo Park, Calif.: Lane, 1971.

SOILS AND FERTILIZERS

DONAHUE, ROY L., and others. *Soils: An Introduction to Soils and Plant Growth*. Hemel Hempstead, Herts., and Englewood Cliffs, N.J.: Prentice-Hall (3rd ed.), 1971.

TISDALE, SAMUEL L., and NELSON, WERNER L. *Soil Fertility and Fertilizers*.

London and New York: Macmillan (2nd ed.), 1966.

INSECTS AND DISEASES

PIRONE, PASCAL P. *Diseases and Pests of Ornamental Plants.* New York: Ronald (4th ed.), 1970.

———. *Plant Disease Handbook.* London and New York: Van Nostrand Reinhold (3rd abridged ed.), 1971.

WESTCOTT, CYNTHIA. *The Gardener's Bugbook.* New York: Doubleday (4th ed.), 1973.

HERBS, HERBALS, PHARMACOPOEIAS, Etc.

ARBER, AGNES. *Herbals: Their Origin and Evolution.* Cambridge University Press, 1953; New York: Hafner, 1970. (Reprint of 1953 edition.)

BAIRACLI-LEVY, JULIETTE DE. *Herbal Handbook for Everyone.* London: Faber & Faber; Newton Centre, Mass.: Branford, 1966.

CLARKSON, ROSETTA E. *Herbs: Their Culture and Uses.* London and New York: Macmillan, 1942.

GRIEVE, MAUD. *A Modern Herbal: The Medicinal, Culinary, Cosmetic and Economic Properties, Cultivation and Folk-Lore of Herbs, Grasses, Fungi, Shrubs and Trees, with All Their Modern Scientific Uses.* 2 vols. London and New York: Hafner, 1971. (Reprint of London: J. Cape, 1931.)

LOEWENFELD, CLAIRE. *Herb Gardening: Why and How to Grow Herbs.* London: Faber & Faber; Newton Centre, Mass.: Branford, 1965.

NORTHCOTE, ROSALIND. *Book of Herb Lore.* New York: Dover, 1971. (Reprint of *The Book of Herbs.* London: Constable, 1912.)

OSOL, ARTHUR, and PRATT, ROBERTSON. *The U.S. Dispensatory.* Philadelphia: Lippincott (27th ed.), 1973.

Pharmaceutical Society of Great Britain. *British Pharmacopoeia.* London: Pharmaceutical Press, 1973. Available through: Rittenhouse Book Store, Philadelphia.

SMITH, LEONA WOODRING. *The Forgotten Art of Flower Cookery.* London and New York: Harper & Row, 1973.

STEVENSON, VIOLET. *Dried Flowers for Decoration.* New York: Drake (rev. ed.), 1972.

WHEELWRIGHT, EDITH G. *Physick Garden: Medicinal Plants and Their History.* Clifton, N.J.: Kelley, 1972. (Reprint of London: Jonathan Cape, 1934.)

WREN, R. C. *Potter's New Cyclopedia of Medicinal Herbs and Preparations* (re-edited and enlarged by R. W. Wren). New York and London: Harper & Row, 1972. English edition: *Potter's New Cyclopaedia of Botanical Drugs and Preparations.* London: Potter & Clarke (7th ed.), 1956.

PROPAGATION AND BREEDING

ADRIANCE, GUY W., and BRISON, F. R. *Propagation of Horticultural Plants.* London and New York: McGraw-Hill (2nd ed.), 1955.

BAILEY, LIBERTY HYDE. *Nursery Manual.* London and New York: Macmillan (rev. ed.), 1967.

FREE, MONTAGUE. *Plant Propagation in Pictures.* New York: Doubleday, 1957.

GORER, RICHARD. *Development of Garden Flowers.* London: Eyre & Spottiswoode; Newton Centre, Mass.: Branford, 1970.

HARTMANN, HUDSON T., and KESTER, DALE E. *Plant Propagation: Principles and Practices.* London and Englewood Cliffs, N.J.: Prentice-Hall (2nd ed.), 1969.

LAWRENCE, WILLIAM J. C. *Plant Breeding.* London: Arnold; New York: St. Martin, 1971.

MAHLSTEDE, J. P., and HABER, E. S. *Plant Propagation.* London and New York: Wiley, 1962.

WELLS, JAMES S. *Plant Propagation Practices.* London and New York: Macmillan, 1955.

LANDSCAPE DESIGN

BRETT, WILLIAM S. *Planning Your Garden: How to Design and Construct It.* London: Ward Lock; New Rochelle, N.Y.: Soccer, 1973. (Reprint of 1957 edition.)

CROCKETT, JAMES U. *Landscape Gardening.* (The Time-Life Encyclopedia of Gardening.) New York: Time-Life, 1971.

ECKBO, GARRETT. *The Art of Home Landscaping.* London and New York: McGraw-Hill, 1956.

IREYS, ALICE R. *How to Plan and Plant Your Own Property.* New York: Morrow, 1967.

JEFFERSON-BROWN, M. J. *Small Garden Design.* London: Gifford & Foyle; Newton Centre, Mass.: Branford, 1969.

PHILLIPS, C. E. LUCAS. *The Design of Small Gardens.* London: Heinemann; New York: International Publications Service, 1969.

FLOWERS AND GARDENS OF THE WORLD

COATS, PETER. *Great Gardens of the Western World.* London: Weidenfeld & Nicolson; New York: Putnam, 1963.

McEACHARN, NEIL. *Catalogue of the Plants in the Gardens of the Villa Taranto.* Milan: R. Scotti, 1963.

McFADDEN, DOROTHY L. *Touring the Gardens of Europe.* New York: McKay, 1965.

PERRY, FRANCES. *Flowers of the World.* London: Hamlyn; New York: Crown, 1972.

WIT, H. C. D. DE. *Plants of the World* (trans. A. J. Pomerans). 3 vols. London: Thames & Hudson; New York: Dutton, 1966–1969.

FLOWER LORE AND HISTORY

ANDERSON, ALEXANDER W. *How We Got Our Flowers.* New York: Dover, 1966. (Reprint of *The Coming of the Flowers.* London: Williams & Norgate, 1950.)

BAKER, MARGARET. *The Folklore of Plants.* Tring: Shire; New York: International Publications Service, 1969.

CARRUTHERS, MISS. *Flower Lore: The Teachings of Flowers, Historical, Legendary, Poetical and Symbolical.* Detroit: Singing Tree Press, 1972. (Reprint of London: McCaw, 1879.)

COATS, ALICE M. *The Book of Flowers: Four Centuries of Flower Illustration.* London and New York: McGraw-Hill, 1974.

——. *Flowers and Their Histories.* London and New York: McGraw-Hill, 1970.

ELLACOMBE, HENRY N. *The Plant-Lore and Garden-Craft of Shakespeare.* New York: AMS Press, 1972. (Reprint of London: Satchell, 1884.)

FOLKARD, RICHARD. *Plant Lore, Legends and Lyrics.* Ann Arbor, Mich.: Finch Press, 1972. (Reprint of London: Low, 1884.)

FRIEND, HILDERIC. *Flowers and Flower*

1407

Lore. 2 vols. Detroit, Mich.: Gale, 1971. (Reprint of London: Sonnenschein, 1884.)

JACOB, DOROTHY. *Witch's Guide to Gardening.* New York: Taplinger, 1965.

PERRY, VINCENT. *The Language of Flowers.* Norwalk, Conn.: Gibson, 1973.

ROHDE, ELEANOUR S. *Shakespeare's Wild Flowers.* New York: AMS Press, 1973. (Reprint of London: Medici Society, 1935.)

THISELTON-DYER, THOMAS F. *The Folk-lore of Plants.* Detroit, Mich.: Singing Tree Press, 1968. (Reprint of London: Chatto & Windus, 1889.)

TYAS, ROBERT. *Flowers and Heraldry; or Floral Emblems and Heraldic Figures.* Ann Arbor, Mich.: Finch Press, 1972. (Reprint of London: Houlston & Stoneman, 1851.)

BIOGRAPHICAL PARTICULARS OF THE BOTANICAL AUTHORITIES MOST FREQUENTLY LISTED IN THE TEXT

The most accurate scientific listing of a botanical species should, ideally, include the name of the authority who proposed it. According to the standard practise of botanical nomenclature (which is international), the authority's name follows the name of the species and is usually abbreviated for convenience. Thus, *Physalis Peruviana* L. means that Linnaeus was responsible for placing this species into the genus *Physalis*, and for giving it the specific name of *peruviana* (which indicates that he believed it to be native to Peru), while *Physalis pruinosa* Jacq. reveals that Nicolaus Joseph Jacquin was the authority. As the majority of general garden books and encyclopaedias do not include authorities in their species listings, it was felt that it would be of interest if brief biographical sketches of the authorities most frequently listed in these volumes were included. For readers who wish to gain detailed information on nomenclature and taxonomy, it is suggested that they consult *Hortus Kewensis*. Current Codes of Nomenclature may be obtained from the International Bureau for Plant Taxonomy and Nomenclature, 106 Lange Nieuwstraat, Utrecht, The Netherlands.

Adans.: ADANSON, MICHEL (1727–1806). France.
Spent five years in Senegal, whose flora and fauna he described in *Histoire naturelle du Sénégal* (1753). He also wrote *Les familles naturelles des plantes* (1763).

Ait.: AITON, WILLIAM (1731–1793). Scotland.
Director of the Royal Botanic Gardens, Kew, and an editor of *Hortus Kewensis* (1789), which contains records of all the plants cultivated at Kew.

All.: ALLIONI, CARLO (1728–1804). Italy.
Physician to Vittorio Amadeo III of Savoy. He was known as the "Piedmontese Linnaeus" because of his dedication to natural history. Author of *Flora Pedemontana* (1785).

Anders.: ANDERSON, THOMAS (1832–1870). Scotland.
Superintendent of the Calcutta Botanic Gardens. Author of *Florula Adenensis, A Systematic List of the Plants of Aden* (1860), and *Catalogue of Plants Cultivated in the Royal Botanical Gardens, Calcutta, from April, 1861 to September, 1864* (1865).

André.; ANDRÉ, EDOUARD (1840–1911). France.
Editor of the journals *L'Illustration horticole* and *La Revue horticole* and author of numerous monographs.

Andr.: ANDREWS, HENRY C. (fl. 1799–1830). England.
Author of the 10-volume *Botanists' Repository* (1797–1811).

Ant.: ANTOINE, FRANZ (1815–1886). Austria.
Director of the Imperial Gardens at Schönbrunn. Author of several studies on coniferous plants.

Aschers.: ASCHERSON, PAUL FRIEDRICH (1834–1913). Germany.
Professor of botany at the University of

Berlin, whose principal works include *Flora der provinz Brandenburg* (1864) and (with Paul Graebner) the 14-volume *Synopsis der mitteleuropäischen flora* (1896–1913).

Aubl.: AUBLET, JEAN-BAPTISTE CHRISTOPHORE FUSÉE (1720–1778). France.
The first western explorer to penetrate the forests of Guiana. Author of *Histoire des plantes de la Guiane françoise* (1775), which mentions about 400 new species.

Bailey: BAILEY, LIBERTY HYDE (1858–1954). United States.
Botanist. Author and editor of numerous botanical works, including the monumental 3-volume *Standard Cyclopedia of Horticulture* (5th ed., 1958). Known for research on North American sedges, blackberries, raspberries, and New World palms.

Baill.: BAILLON, HENRI-ERNEST (1827–1895). France.
Professor of botany at the University of Paris. Author of the 13-volume *Histoire des plantes* (1866–1894) and the 4-volume *Dictionnaire de botanique* (1876–1892), both considered to be among the most important publications on natural history.

Baker: BAKER, JOHN GILBERT (1834–1920). England.
Director of the Herbarium at the Royal Botanic Gardens, Kew, and author of over a dozen important books.

Banks: BANKS, SIR JOSEPH (1743–1820). England.
Botanical collector who accompanied Captain Cook on his voyages around the world. Author of several volumes including the *Journal During Captain Cook's First Voyage* (posthumously published under the editorship of Sir Joseph Hooker—q.v.—in 1896)

Bartr.: BARTRAM, WILLIAM (1739–1823). United States.
Explorer and naturalist who recorded his experiences in *Travels through North and South Carolina, Georgia, east and west Florida . . .* (1791).

Bean: BEAN, W. J. (1863–1947). England.
For many years curator of the Royal Botanic Gardens, Kew. Author of many books, including the monumental *Trees and Shrubs Hardy in the British Isles* (8th ed., 1970).

Becc.: BECCARI, ODOARDO (1843–1920). Italy.
Explorer who made long journeys through New Guinea, the East Indies, and East Africa collecting valuable scientific material. Among his books are the 3-volume *Malesia* (1877–90), and *Nelle Foreste di Borneo . . . (In the Forests of Borneo, Travels and Researches of a Naturalist)* (1902).

Beissn.: BEISSNER, LUDWIG (1853–1927). Germany.
Inspector of Bonn Botanic Gardens, author of a number of works on German and Asian conifers including the *Handbuch der Nadelholzkunde* (1891).

Benth.: BENTHAM, GEORGE (1800–1884). England.
Author of various books on systematic botany including the famous 3-volume *Genera Plantarum* (1862–83), in collaboration with Sir Joseph Hooker, (q.v.) and *Handbook of the British Flora* (1858, 2nd ed., with illustrations, 1865).

Berg. A.: BERGER, ALWIN (1871–1931). Germany.
Botanist. Director of the Royal Gardens of Württemberg and curator of the Hanbury Botanic Gardens, La Mortola, Ventimiglia, Italy. Author of several books on cacti.

Bert.: BERTERO, CARLO GIUSEPPE (1789–1831). Italy.
Botanist who made a special study of the flora of Italy, particularly that of Piedmont and Sardinia.

Bier.: BIERBERSTEIN, BARON FRIEDRICH AUGUST, MARSCHALL VON (1768–1827). Germany.
Botanist and traveller who for many years lived in Russia.

Blume: BLUME, KARL LUDWIG VON (1796–1862). Germany.
Professor of botany at the University of Leyden. Carried out important botanical research in the Dutch East Indies.

Boiss.: BOISSIER, PIERRE EDMOND (1810–1885). Switzerland.

Botanist. In his 5-volume *Flora Orientalis* (1867–84) he collected the results of his botanical findings in Asia Minor and in the Mediterranean area.

Bojer: BOJER, W. (1800–1856). Austria.
Author of *Hortus Mauritianus* (1837).

Bonpl.: BONPLAND, AIMÉ JACQUES ALEXANDRE (1773–1858). France.
Botanist, whose real name was Goujaud. Accompanied Von Humboldt (q.v.) during his five-year journey through Central and South America, collecting many important details of the local flora. Collaborated with Von Humboldt on several major works, and the author of the magnificent illustrated *Déscription des plantes rares cultivées à Malmaison et à Navarre* (1813).

Brongn.: BRONGNIART, ADOLPHE THÉODORE (1801–1876). France.
Botanist on the staff of the Musée d'Histoire Naturelle in Paris. Author of *Histoire des végétaux fossiles, ou recherches botaniques et géologiques* (1828–47), an authoritative multivolume work on palaeobotany still considered a standard reference work.

Br. N. E.: BROWN, N. E. (1849–1934). England.
Botanist at the Royal Botanic Gardens, Kew. His speciality was the study of cacti and the succulents. Did extensive revision on the genus *Mesembryanthemum*.

Br. R.: BROWN, ROBERT (1773–1858). Scotland.
Naturalist who accompanied one of the Flinders expeditions that was sent to Australia in the late eighteenth century by the Royal Society. Discovered the irregular oscillatory movement of molecules, which was called the Brownian Movement in his honour. Two of his more important books are *Prodromus florae Novae Hollandiae* (1810) and *General Remarks, Geographical and Systematical, on . . . Terra Australis* (1814).

Buch.-Ham.: BUCHANAN, FRANCIS (later LORD HAMILTON) (1762–1820). Scotland.
Superintendent of the Calcutta Botanic Gardens and author of many books on Indian flora.

Bull.: BULLIARD, PIERRE (1742–1793). France.
Author of *Herbier de la France* (1780–95), a work in 12 folio volumes illustrated with 600 hand-coloured plates.

Bunge: BUNGE, ALEXANDER VON (1803–1890). Russia.
Botanist and traveller in Siberia, North China, the Altai, Central Russia, and Central Asia. Author of numerous studies on the flora of those regions.

Burm.: BURMAN, JOHANNES (1706-1779). The Netherlands.
Professor of botany at the University of Amsterdam who described the flora of Ceylon, Africa, and Malabar in a series of major studies.

Carr.: CARRIÈRE, ELIE ABEL (1816–1896). France.
Noted botanist who was editor of the *Revue Horticole* and the author of dozens of monographs and treatises.

Casp.: CASPARY, ROBERT (1818–1887). Germany.
Professor of botany at the University of Königsberg. Author of many studies on German flora.

Cass.: CASSINI, ALEXANDRE HENRI GABRIEL, VICOMTE DE (1784–1832). France.
Magistrate and councillor of the Court of Cassation of France. He was also a student of botany and recorded his findings in the 3-volume *Opuscules phytologiques* (1826–34).

Cav.: CAVANILLES, ANTONIO JOSÉ (1745–1804). Spain.
Botanist and director of the Madrid Botanical Gardens. Author of the 6-volume *Icones et descriptiones plantarum... Hispaná* (1791–1801)....

Cham.: CHAMISSO, ADALBERT VON (1781–1838). Germany.
Poet and naturalist who became the curator of the Berlin Botanic Gardens. Journeyed as botanist to the Pacific with Otto von Kotzebue, and recorded his experiences in several important publications. His poetry is equally noteworthy.

Chapm.: CHAPMAN, ALVAN WENTWORTH (1809–1899). United States.
Author of *Flora of the Southern United States* (1860).

Chois.: CHOISY, JACQUES DENYS (1799–1859). Switzerland.
Botanist for whom the genus *Choisia* is named.

Clusius Carolus: See L'Ecl.: L'ECLUSE, CHARLES, DE

Cogn.: COGNIAUX, CÉLESTIN ALFRED (1841–1916). Belgium.
Director of the Royal Botanical Museum in Brussels. Author of many monographs devoted to tropical genera, as well as studies on the Belgian flora.

Colla: COLLA, LUIGI (1766–1848). Italy.
Lawyer and senator. An enthusiastic botanist to whom credit is due for the creation of the famous gardens at the Villa Medici in Rivoli. Among his many books the following deserve special mention: *Hortus Ripulensis* (1824–28), richly illustrated with hand-coloured plates of the rare plants found in the gardens of Rivoli and the 8-volume *Herbarium Pedemontanum* (1833–37).

Coulter: COULTER, JOHN MERLE (1851–1928). United States.
Professor of botany at the University of Indiana until 1893, then head of the Department of Botany at the University of Chicago from 1896 to 1925. Specialized in plant genetics and systematic botany. In 1875, he founded the *Botanical Gazette*, still considered the most important botanical periodical in the United States. Author of numerous books, including the *Textbook of Botany* (1906), *Plant Genetics* (1918), *Plant Relations* (1899), and *Manual of the Botany of the Rocky Mountain Region* (1885).

Cunn.: CUNNINGHAM, RICHARD (1793–1835). England.
Botanist who spent much of his life in Australia.

Cunn. A.: CUNNINGHAM, ALLAN (1791–1839). England.
Botanist. Brother of Richard; traveller and plant collector.

Curt.: CURTIS, WILLIAM (1746–1799). England.
A London chemist who was the author of a great many books on botany and entomology. His name is permanently linked with the famous and beautiful periodical *The Botanical Magazine* (first issued in 1777), which describes and illustrates in colour many garden and greenhouse plants. The work is still published monthly. Books by Curtis include *Flora Londinensis* (1777) and the 3-volume *Lectures on Botany* (1805).

Dalech.: DALECHAMPS (DALECHAMPSIUS—JACQUES D'ALECHAMPS) (1513–1588). France.
Noted physician and botanist. Author of *Historia generalis Plantarum* (1587).

Darwin: DARWIN, SIR CHARLES ROBERT (1809–1882). England.
Physician who sailed as naturalist on the H.M.S. *Beagle* on a surveying expedition to South America and Australasia (Dec. 1831–Oct. 1836). Among his many important books are *Zoology of the Voyage of the Beagle* (1840), *On the Origin of the Species By Means of Natural Selection* (1859), *The Variation of Animals and Plants under Domestication* (1868), and (his best-known work) *The Descent of Man* (1871), in which his theory of evolution was presented, and in which he attempted to prove that man was descended from an animal of the anthropoid group.

Daws.: DAWSON, SIR JOHN WILLIAM (1820–1899). Canada.
Naturalist and geologist. An opponent of the Darwinian theory of the origin of life forms.

D. C.: DE CANDOLLE, AUGUSTIN PYRAME (1778–1841). Switzerland.
Professor at the universities of Geneva and Montpellier. Created and documented a new natural system for the classification of species in his 7-volume *Prodromus systematis regni vegetabilis* (1824–74) and the 2-volume *Regni vegetabilis systema naturale* (1818–21).

Decne.: DECAISNE, JOSEPH (1807–1882). France.
French botanist for whom the genus

Decaisnea is named. Author of over 100 monographs and studies.

Desf.: DESFONTAINES, RÉNÉ LOUICHE (1750–1833). France.
Professor of botany and attached to the staff of the Jardin des Plantes in Paris; elected to the French Academy of Sciences in 1783. Travelled extensively in North Africa, from where he brought home much valuable material, which was included in the posthumous publication *Voyage dans les régences de Tunis et d'Alger* (1835). Other of his works include *Flora Atlantica* (1798–1800) and *Catalogue des plantes du jardin de roi* (1801).

Diels.: DIELS, LUDWIG (1874–1921). Germany.
Professor of botany at the University of Marburg. In 1921 he became director of the Berlin Botanic Gardens. Travelled in Asia and Australia. Among his published works are *Zentralchina* (1901), *Jugendformen und Blütenreife...* (1906), *Droseraceae* (1906), and *Menispermaceae* (1910).

Dill.: DILLEN (OR DILLENIUS), JOHANN JAKOB (1687–1747). Germany.
Following a curious family tradition, this botanist lengthened his name to Dillenius, just as his father had extended the family name of Dill to Dillen. Studied botany in England, specializing in the field of generic classification. His system served as a basis for the work of Linnaeus. Prior to his tenure as the first Sherardian professor of botany at Oxford University, he wrote his great work *Hortus Elthamensis* (1719), which contained descriptions of hundreds of plants, as well as more than 300 of his own illustrations. Linnaeus named the genus *Dillenia* in his honour; his name also gave rise to the name of the family dilleniaceae.

Dipp.: DIPPEL, DR. L. (1827–1914). Germany.
Botanist. Author of several important works, including the 3-volume *Handbuch der Laubholzkunde* (1889–93).

Dodoens: DODOENS (OR DODONAEUS OR DODONEO), REMBERT (1517–1585).
The Netherlands.
Physician to Emperor Maximilian II, whose court he was obliged to leave. He then dedicated himself to travel. Among his works are *De frugum historia* (1552), *De stirpium historiae* (1583), and *Medicinalium observationum exempla rara* (1521).

Don D.: DON, DAVID (1799–1841). Scotland.
Botanist, brother of George Don. Author of many monographs and studies on native and exotic genera and species. Professor of botany at King's College.

Don G.: DON, GEORGE (1798–1856). Scotland.
Botanist. Collected for the Royal Horticultural Society in Brazil, the West Indies, and Sierra Leone. Edited Sweet's *Hortus Britannicus* (3rd ed.) and prepared the first supplement to Loudon's *Encyclopaedia*.

Donn: DONN, JAMES (1758–1813). England.
Author of the important *Hortus cantabrigiensis* (1796). Curator of Cambridge Garden.

Douglas: DOUGLAS, DAVID (1799–1834). Scotland.
Botanist and collector of American plants of California and the Northwest. Discovered the Douglas fir in 1825.

Drude: DRUDE, KARL GEORG OSKAR 1852–1933). Germany.
Director of the Dresden Botanic Gardens, and professor at Technische Hochschule. His published works include *Die Florenreiche der erde* (1884) and *Handbuch der Pflanzengeographie* (1890).

Duchesne: DUCHÈSNE, ANTOINE NICOLAS (1747–1827). France.
Professor of natural history at the Academy of Saint-Cyr and at the Lycée de Versailles. Author of many books, notably *Manuel de botanique* (1764), which included descriptions of both ornamental and medicinal species.

Dumort.: DUMORTIER, CHARLES BARTHÉLEMY (1797–1878). Belgium.
Politician and naturalist. Among his books is *Florula Belgica* (1827), which earned him membership in the Brussels Academy of Sciences, and *Analyse des familles des plantes* (1829).

Dunal: DUNAL, MICHEL FELIX (1789–1856). France.
Studied botany under De Candolle (q.v.): later was appointed to the faculty of botany at the University of Montpellier, and in 1816 he filled his former teacher's position as full professor there.

Dunn: DUNN, STEPHEN TROYTE (1868–1938). England.
Botanist. Wrote *Alien flora of Britain* (1905), and several studies (with W. J. Tutcher) on the flora of China for the *Kew Bulletin*.

Dyer: THISTLETON-DYER, SIR WILLIAM TURNER (1843–1928). England.
Assistant director and later director of the Royal Botanic Gardens, Kew, and editor of *Flora of Tropical Africa*. Founded the *Kew Bulletin* (1887).

Eaton: EATON, AMOS (1776–1842). United States.
This student of natural science wrote *A Manual of Botany for the Northern States* (1817), the first popular work on this subject to be published in the United States.

Ehrh.: EHRHART, FRIEDRICH (1742–1795). Germany.
Botanist. Author of the 2-volume *Beiträge zur Naturkunde* (1787–92).

Ellis: ELLIS, JOHN (1711–1776). Ireland.
A natural science enthusiast who carried out important research on corals. Among his botanical works are *De dionola muscipula* (1760), *Direction for Transporting Seeds and Plants* (1770), and *An Historical Account of Coffee* (1774), which contains illustrations and full botanical descriptions of the plant.

Endl.: ENDLICHER, STEPHAN LADISLAUS (1804–1849). Hungary.
Professor at the University of Vienna and director of the Imperial Botanic Gardens at Schönbrunn. Largely instrumental in the founding of the Vienna Academy of Sciences in 1846. Among his many works are *Flora Posoniensis* (1830), *Atakta botanika* (1833), and *Iconographia generum plantarum* (1838).

Engelm.: ENGELMANN, GEORGE (1809–1884). Germany.
After completing his studies in Germany, he moved to the United States in 1832, where he studied indigenous flora, in particular the cacti. Wrote numerous studies and monographs on North American genera.

Engler: ENGLER, ADOLF (1844–1930). Germany.
Professor at the University of Berlin and co-author (with Karl Prantl) of the 11-volume *Naturlichen Pflanzenfamilien* (1897–1909). Worked out a natural system of classification of plants.

Fee: FÉE, ANTOINE LAURENT APOLLINAIRE (1789–1874). France.
Physician, and professor of natural sciences at the University of Strasbourg, director of the Jardin des Plantes in Paris, and a member of the French Academy of Sciences. His publications include *Catalogue méthodique des plantes et histoire du Jardin Botanique de la Faculté de médecine de Strasbourg* (1836), *Mémoires lichenographiques* (1838), and a biography of Linnaeus (1832).

Fisch.: FISCHER, FRIEDRICH ERNST LUDWIG VON (FEODOR BOGDANOVICH FISER) (1782–1854). Russia.
Professor of botany at the University of St. Petersburg and director of the Imperial Botanic Gardens in St. Petersburg. His book, *Sertum Petropolitanum seu icones et descriptiones plantarum* (1844), described the many plants there.

Forb.: FORBES, JAMES (1773–1861). England.
Gardener and collector of plants at Woburn Abbey, residence of the Duke of Bedford. Author of several works, including *Pinetum Woburnense* (1839).

Forst.: FORSTER, JOHANN REINHOLD (1729–1798). Germany.
Protestant pastor from Danzig who abandoned his ecclesiastical career to devote himself to travel and scientific research. He explored parts of Russia for Catherine the Great, and was naturalist on Captain Cook's second voyage through the South Seas. Through the offices of Frederick the Great he became director of the Halle Botanic Gar-

dens. A few years later, he was appointed professor of botany at the University of Halle. Published *Florae Americae septentrionalis* (1771) with Georg Forster, the *Characteres generum plantarum, quas in itinere ad insulas maris australis* (1772–75), and *Observations Made During a Voyage Round the World* (1779).

Fortune: FORTUNE, ROBERT (1813–1880). Scotland.
Botanist, traveller, and plant collector. In 1843 he was commissioned by the Royal Horticultural Society to collect plants in China. His experiences are recorded in *Wanderings in China* (1847). He made several other expeditions in search of botanical species of economic value, in particular tea plants.

Franch.: FRANCHET, ADRIEN (1834–1900). France.
Botanist on the staff of the Jardin des Plantes, Paris. Wrote many books devoted to French and Chinese flora.

Fraser: FRASER, JOHN (1750–1811). England.
A hosier by profession, who was a noted collector and hunter of plants, chiefly in North America. He established a nursery in Sloane Square in London in 1795. He was appointed plant collector to the Czar of Russia in 1798.

Gaertn.: GAERTNER, JOSEPH (1732–1791). Germany.
Teacher of medicine, anatomy, and botany at the universities of Tübingen and St. Petersburg; he was also director of the Imperial Botanic Gardens in St. Petersburg. Carried out important studies describing the differences between phaenogams and cryptogams. His most important work was the 3-volume *De fructibus et seminibus plantarum* (1788–1807), illustrated with 225 engraved plates.

Gagnep.: GAGNEPAIN, FRANÇOIS (1866–1952). France.
Botanist who wrote many studies on Asiatic flora.

Gaud.: GAUDICHAUD-BEAUPRÉ, CHARLES (1789–1854). France.
Studied chemistry in Paris. In 1817 was appointed naturalist to the South American expedition of Captain Louis de Freycinet. In 1836 he made a voyage around the world and collected much valuable material. He was a member of the French Academy of Sciences and became professor of natural sciences, a post made available by the death of De Jussieu (q.v.). Among his books are *Recherches générales sur l'organographie . . . des végétaux* (1841) and two volumes on his voyages, published in 1836 and 1849.

Gerard: GERARD, JOHN (1545–1612). England.
Physician and herbalist. His most important works are the *Herball* (1597) and his adaptation of Dodoens's *De stirpium historiae* (1583). The genus *Gerardia* is named for him.

Gmel.: GMELIN, SAMUEL GOTTLIEB (1743–1774). Germany.
Botanist and teacher at the St. Petersburg Imperial Academy of Sciences. By order of Catherine the Great he explored the regions between Persia and the Caspian Sea (he died during this expedition). Wrote the 3-volume *Reise durch Russland . . . (Travels across Russia for the Study of the Three Kingdoms of Nature)*, the last volume of which was posthumously published in 1784.

Goepp.: GOEPPERT, HEINRICH ROBERT (1800–1884). Germany.
Professor of natural science at the University of Breslau. Famous for his studies of plant physiology and palaeobotany. Among his vast number of books are *Ueber die Wärme-Entwickelung in den Pflänzen (Production of Heat in Plants)* (1830), *De floribus in statu fossili Commentatio botanica* (1837), *De coniferarum structura anatomica* (1841), and a monograph on fossils of the Coniferae, published in 1850.

Gord.: GORDON, GEORGE (1806–1879). England.
Author of *The pinetum* (1st ed., 1858), a highly important study on all the coniferous plants then known.

Graebn.: GRAEBNER, PAUL (1871–1933). Germany.
Professor of botany at the University of Berlin. Author of several major studies on German flora.

Gray: GRAY, ASA (1819–1888). United States.
As professor of natural sciences at Harvard University from 1842, he helped make Cambridge a center of botanical study in the United States. Travelled widely throughout America and Europe collecting material for such books as *Elements of Botany* (1836), *Manual of the Botany of the Northern United States* (1848), *Genera Florae Americae bore-ali-orientalis illustrata* (1848), *How Plants Grow* (1858), *How Plants Behave* (1872), and many articles and studies on Charles Darwin, including *Darwiniana* (1876).

Griff.: GRIFFITH, WILLIAM (1810–1845). England.
Surgeon who lived in India where he studied tea cultivation, and made numerous journeys through the unexplored regions of India and Afghanistan. His voluminous posthumous publications include *Icones plantarum asiaticarum* (1847–54) and *Notulae ad plantas asiaticas* (1847–54).

Griseb.: GRISEBACH, HEINRICH R. A. (1814–1879). Germany.
Botanist who wrote extensively on tropical New World flora, especially that of Cuba.

Harms: HARMS, HERMANN AUGUST THEODOR (1870–1942). Germany.
Professor of botany at the University of Berlin, and director of the Botanical Museum, Berlin. Wrote extensively on tropical flora.

Harv.: HARVEY, WILLIAM HENRY (1811–1866). Ireland.
Botanist (who specialized in marine botany). Author of many works, including *The Genera of South African Plants* (1838).

Haw.: HAWORTH, ADRIAN HARDY (1772–1833). England.
Botanist and entomologist. Author of several important works, including *Observations on the Genus Mesembryanthemum* (1794), *Synopsis plantarum succulentarum cum descriptionibus synonymis locis* (1812), and *Saxifragearum enumeratio* (1821).

Hayne: HAYNE, FRIEDRICH GOTTLOB (1763–1832). Germany.
Chemist, and professor at the University of Berlin from 1814. Author of many works, including *Termini botanici iconibus illustrati* (1807) and *Descriptions of Plants Used in Medicine* (1802–1831), which contains 600 illustrations by the author.

H.B.K.: HUMBOLDT, BARON ALEXANDER VON; BONPLAND, AIMÉ JACQUES ALEXANDRE; and KUNTH, KARL SIGMUND
For specifics, see Bonpl., Humb., and Kunth.

Hemsl.: HEMSLEY, WILLIAM BOTTING (1843–1924). England.
Botanist on the H.M.S. *Challenger* expedition in 1873–76. Director of the Herbarium at the Royal Botanic Gardens, Kew, from 1899. Author of several studies on Chinese and Himalayan flora, as well as those of his native land.

Henfr.: HENFREY, ARTHUR (1819–1859). Scotland.
Professor of botany at Kings College, London. Author of *Outlines of Structural and Physiological Botany* (1847), *The Rudiments of Botany* (1849), and *Outlines of the Natural History of Europe* (1852).

Henry: HENRY, AUGUSTINE (1857–1930). Ireland.
Botanist. Reader in Forestry at Cambridge, professor of forestry at University College, Dublin, and collector of many Chinese plants (he introduced *Lilium henryi*). Author of many books, notably those on forestry.

Herb.: HERBERT, HON. & REV. WILLIAM (1778–1847). England.
Dean of Manchester, and notable botanist and botanical artist. His books include *Amaryllidaceae* (1837), illustrated with his own plates, and other works.

Hochst.: HOCHSTETTER, CHRISTIAN FRIEDRICH (1787–1860). Germany.
Specialist in the study of African flora as well as those of Northern Europe. Noted for *Enumeratio plantarum Germaniae Helvetiaeque indigenarum* (with Ernst Steudel, 1826).

Hoffm.: HOFFMANN, GEORG FRANZ (1761–1826). Germany.
Botanist and author of the 2-part *Deutschlands Flora* (1791 and 1795).

Hook.: HOOKER, SIR WILLIAM JACKSON (1785–1865). England.
Professor of botany at Glasgow University and director of the Royal Botanic Gardens, Kew. Among his works are *Exotic Flora* (1823–27), *Icones Filicum* (1829–31), and *British Flora* (1830 and 1850). He was editor of *The Botanical Magazine* and *The London Journal of Botany*.

Hook. J.: HOOKER, SIR JOSEPH DALTON (1817–1911). England.
Physician, son of Sir William Hooker, and a close friend of Charles Darwin (q.v.). He was a member of Sir James Ross's expedition to the Antarctic. In 1847, he published the 2-volume *Flora Antarctica*. He also travelled throughout India and Tibet searching for botanical specimens. He succeeded his father as director of the Royal Botanic Gardens, Kew. Among his many publications are *The Rhododendrons of Sikkim–Himalaya* (1849), *Illustrations of Himalayan Plants* (1855), and the first volume of *Flora indica* (with T. Thompson, 1855), a systematic study of native Indian flora. With George Bentham (q.v.), Hooker wrote an important work on systematic botany, *Genera plantarum ad exemplaria imprimis in Herbariis Kewensibus servata definita* (1862–83).

Host: HOST, NICOLAUS THOMAS (1761–1834). Austria.
Chief medical advisor to the Emperor of Austria, and for forty years director of the Imperial Botanic Gardens at Schönbrunn. Author of numerous books, including *Synopsis plantarum in Austria* (1797), *Icones et descriptiones graminum austriacorum* (1801), and *Flora austriaca* (1827). The genus *Hosta* is named in his honour.

Humb.: HUMBOLDT, FRIEDRICH HEINRICH ALEXANDER, BARON VON (1769–1859). Germany.
Naturalist, traveller; friend and companion to Georg Forster on his travels through Belgium, Holland, England, and France (1790), and to Captain Cook on his voyages through the South Seas. Accompanied by Aimé Bonpland (q.v.), he made a scientific expedition to South America, Mexico, and Cuba. In the course of this expedition many botanical specimens were collected, especially flora of the Amazon. Author of numerous books, the most important of which are accounts of his travels.

Jacq.: JACQUIN, NICOLAUS JOSEPH, BARON VON (1727–1817). The Netherlands.
After studying under Bernard de Jussieu (q.v.) in Paris, Jacquin made an expedition to South America, as a result of which he was able to enrich the botanic gardens of Vienna and Schönbrunn with over 50 new genera. His works include *Enumeratio systematica plantarum quas in insulis Caribaeis* (1760), *Selectarum stirpium Americanarum historia* (1788), the 3-volume *Hortus botanicus Vindobonensis* (1770–76), illustrated with 300 plates, and the 5-volume *Florae Austriacae* (1773–78), illustrated with 450 plates.

Jaub.: JAUBERT, HIPPOLYTE FRANÇOIS, COMTE DE (1798–1884). France.
Politician, who was successively a member of the Legislative Assembly, the Senate, the Tribunate, and Privy Council. Jaubert was also an enthusiastic amateur botanist and wrote several important works, including *Illustrationes plantarum Orientalium* (1842–46), written after a journey to the Orient (from whence he brought an extensive collection of botanical specimens), *La botanique à l'Exposition Universelle de 1855* (1855), and *Sur l'enseignement de la botanique* (1855).

Juss.: JUSSIEU, ANTOINE LAURENT DE (1748–1836). France.
Botanist and nephew of Bernard. Member of the staff of the Jardin des Plantes, Paris. In his *Genera plantarum* (1789), he elaborated on the plant classification system founded by Bernard. Author of numerous monographs on several genera.

Juss.: JUSSIEU, BERNARD DE (1699–1777). France.
Botanist at the Jardin des Plantes, Paris; later established a botanical garden at Versailles for Louis XV. There, he arranged the plants according to their natural groups, laying the foundation for a natural system of classification of plants.

Kaemp.: KAEMPFER, ENGELBERT (1651–1716). Sweden.
Physicist and secretary to Charles XI of

1417

Sweden. Travelled widely in Russia and Persia. He also visited Java, making a study of the flora, and Japan, where he remained for two years. Among his posthumously published botanical works is the richly illustrated *Icones selectae plantarum, quas in Japonia collegit et delineavit* (1791).

Karsten: KARSTEN, HERMANN G. K. W. (1817–1908). Germany.
Studied chemistry and botany in Berlin. Journeyed to Venezuela; on his return home taught botany at the University of Berlin. Among his books are *Die vegetationsorgane der Palmen* (1847) and the 2-volume *Flora Columbiae* (1858–69), with 200 hand-coloured plates.

Karw.: KARWINSK VON KARWIN, WILHELM FRIEDRICH, FREIHERR VON (1780–1855). Hungary.
Botanist who collected plants in Brazil and Mexico.

Ker., Ker-Gawl.: BELLENDEN, KER (1765–1871). England.
Botanist, whose real name was John Gawler: in 1804 he changed it to Ker Bellenden. Editor of the *Botanical Register* from 1815 to 1824. Wrote extensively on the Irideae.

Klotzsch: KLOTZSCH, JOHANN FRIEDRICH (1805–1860). Germany.
Director of the Royal Herbarium in Berlin. Among his many works is a monograph on the Begoniaceae, published in 1854, which includes 12 beautiful hand-coloured plates.

Koch: KOCH, KARL (1809–1879). Germany.
Made several trips to the Orient and Russia; founded the Academy of Rural Economy in Berlin. Among his books are *Monographia generis Veronicae* (1838), the 2-volume *Hortus dendrologicus* (1853), and *Die botanische Gärten* (1860).

Koehne: KOEHNE, EMIL (1848–1918). Germany.
Professor of botany at the University of Berlin. Among his published works is *Deutsche dendrologie* (1893).

Kotschy: KOTSCHY, KARL GEORG THEODOR (1813–1866). Austria.
Botanist. Travelled in Egypt and Asia and was the first to systematically describe the flora of the Upper Nile in detail. Member of the Vienna Academy of Sciences and director of the Botanical Museum in Vienna. Among his numerous works are *Abbildungen und Beschreibungen . . . (Figures and Descriptions of Rare Plants and Animals Collected During Travels in Syria)* (1843), and *Plantae Tinneanae* (1868), which describes the plants collected in the course of the Nile expedition.

Kunth: KUNTH, KARL SIGISMUND (1788–1850). Germany.
Botanist. Author of many major works, including the monumental 5-volume *Enumeratio plantarum* (1833–50) and several studies on Von Humboldt's and Bonpland's discoveries.

Kuntze: KUNTZE, OTTO (1843–1907). Germany.
Botanist who specialized in plant nomenclature and wrote innumerable treatises on this subject.

L.: LINNAEUS, CAROLUS (CARL VON LINNÉ) (1707–1778). Sweden.
The father and master of systematic botany, Linnaeus dedicated his career to the problem of the classification of the three kingdoms of nature (animal, vegetable, mineral). In his *Systema Naturae* (1737), he introduced the method of Latin nomenclature still in use today. He wrote extensively, and among his important works are *Fundamenta botanica* (1736), *Genera plantarum* (1737), and *Classes plantarum* (1738).

Lag.: LAGASCA, MARIANO (1776–1839). Spain.
Studied medicine at Saragossa, later moving to Madrid, where he became a friend of Antonio Cavanilles (q.v.). In 1803 he was commissioned to explore the Iberian peninsula to collect necessary material for a proposed book on the Spanish flora, but unfortunately his studies were lost. From 1834 he was director of the Madrid Botanic Gardens. Among his major works are *Elenchus plantarum quae in Horto regio botanico Matritensi colebantur anno 1815* (1816) and *Genera et species plantarum quae aut novae sunt aut nondum recte cognoscuntur* (1816).

Lam.: LAMARCK, JEAN BAPTISTE ANTOINE DE MONET (1744–1829). France.
Botanist. Friend of Bernard de Jussieu (q.v.). Became well-known for his adoption of a new method of classification, the so-called Dichotomy Key, which eliminated extraneous particulars and details, thus arriving at a precise determination of a species. His 8-volume *Encyclopédie méthodique* (1783–1808) and *Flore françoise* (1778) incorporate and embody practical applications of this system. Among his other works may be mentioned the 3-volume *Tableau encyclopédique et méthodique des trois règnes de la nature* (1791–1823).

Langs.: LANGSDORF, GEORG HEINRICH VON (1774–1852). Germany.
A laureate in medicine who was personal physician to the Prince of Waldeck. In 1803 Langsdorf participated in expeditions to Kamchatka and Siberia. Later, as Russian consul in Brazil, he acquired a valuable collection of plants which he presented to the Imperial Botanic Gardens in St. Petersburg. Among his works is the 2 part *Plantes recueillies pendant le voyage des Russes . . . (Plants Collected by Russians During Their Voyage Around the World)* (1810 and 1818).

Lauth: LAUTH, THOMAS (1758–1826). Germany.
Botanist. Author of an important monograph on the genus *Acer, De Acere* (1781).

L'Ecl.: L'ECLUSE, CHARLES DE, Latinized to *Carolus Clusius* (1526–1609). France.
Botanist who collected and described many then-new and little-known plants of Europe and Asia. Clusius is considered to be one of the founders of descriptive botany and is credited with introducing the potato into Europe. Author of several major early studies on botany.

Lecq.: LECOQ, HENRI (1802–1871). France.
Studied chemistry and medicine in Paris; established himself at Clermont-Ferrand, where in 1828 he founded the *Annales scientifiques, litteraires et industrielles de l'Auvergne*. He was a professor of natural history, director of the Botanic Gardens of Clermont-Ferrand, and a member of the French Academy of Sciences. Among his numerous works are *Principes élementaires de botanique et de physiologie végétale* (1828) and *Recherches sur la reproduction des végétaux* (1827).

Ledeb.: LEDEBOUR, KARL FRIEDRICH VON (1785–1851). Germany.
Laureate in natural history. Director of Botanic Gardens in Greifswalde (Prussian Pomerania). Later, he taught at the University of Dorpat (present-day Tartu) in Estonia, a post he held until 1836. Among his works are *Flora Altaica* (1829) and the richly illustrated *Icones plantarum novarum vel imperfecte cognitarum Floram rossicam, imprimis Altaicam* (1822).

Lehm.: LEHMANN, JOHANN GEORG CHRISTIAN (1792–1860). Germany.
Professor at the Johanneum in Hamburg and director of that city's Botanic Gardens. Author of several monographs describing many new species.

Lehm. F. C.: LEHMANN, FRIEDRICH CARL (1850–1903). Germany.
German botanist who collected in South America (he died in Colombia while on a collecting expedition). Among his works is the important *Systematische Bearbeitung der Pyrenomycetengattung Lophiostima, etc.* (1886).

Lem.: LEMAIRE, CHARLES (1800–1871). Belgium.
Botanist who carried out extensive research on cacti and on plants of horticultural value.

Lemoine: LEMOINE, VICTOR (1823–1911) and ÉMILE (1862–1942). France.
Famous nurserymen at Nancy. Both father and son were horticulturists of considerable importance. Numerous hybrids and varieties were created in their nursery. The firm Lemoine is still extant.

Less.: LESSING, CHRISTIAN FRIEDRICH (1810–1862). Germany.
A physician who produced an important work dealing with the family Compositae, *Synopsis generum Compositarum . . .* (1832).

1419

L'Her.: L'HÉRITIER DE LA BRUTELLE, CHARLES LOUIS (1746–1800). France.
An amateur botanist, whose endeavours were highly regarded by the naturalists of his day. His botanical library was considered to be among the most important in Europe. Among his writings are *Geraniologia; seu Erodii, Pelargonii, Geranii, Monsoniae et Grieli historia iconibus illustrata* (1787–88) and *Cornus specimen botanicum* . . . (1788).

Liebm.: LIEBMANN, FREDERIK MICHAEL (1813–1856). Denmark.
Finnish-born botanist who lived in Denmark. His works are mainly devoted to the flora of Mexico and Central America.

Lind.: LINDEN, JEAN JULES (1817–1898). Belgium.
Botanist, for many years director of the Royal Botanic Gardens in Brussels. Also editor of *L'Illustration Horticole*.

Lindl.: LINDLEY, JOHN (1799–1865). England.
One of the most illustrious botanists and horticulturists. Lindley was equally interested in both the theoretical and practical branches of botany. Among his vast body of works is one of special importance (which he edited with Thomas Moore—q.v.): *The Treasury of Botany, A Popular Dictionary of the Vegetable Kingdom* (1866), a remarkable synthesis of what was known about plants at that time.

Link: LINK, HEINRICH FRIEDRICH (1769–1851). Germany.
Professor of natural sciences and botany at the universities of Rostock, Breslau, and Berlin. He was also director of the Berlin Botanic Gardens. He is noteworthy for his studies on the microscopic structure of plants and botanical anatomy. Among his many works are *Philosophiae botanicae novae* . . . (1798) and *Enumeratio plantarum Horti regii botanici: Berolinensis altera* (1821).

Linn. J.: LINNÉ, CARL VON (1741–1783). Sweden.
Botanist and son of the great Linnaeus.

Lobelio: L'OBEL (or LOBEL), MATTHIAS DE (LOBELIUS) (1538–1616). Belgium.
A Flemish botanist who travelled widely throughout Europe, particularly France and Italy, collecting plants for his descriptive botanical works. Invited to England by King James I, he became court botanist, physician, and artist. Among his works are *Stirpium illustrationes* (1570), and a famous study written in collaboration with Pierre Pena titled *Stirpium adversaria nova* (1576). Other works are *Plantarum seu stirpium historia* (1576) and *Plantarum seu stirpium icones* (1581 and 1591). The genus *Lobelia* is named in his honour.

Lodd.: LODDIGES, CONRAD (1738–1826). England.
German-born English gardener and nurseryman. His son George (1784–1846) was responsible for the 20-volume catalogue, *Loddiges Botanical Cabinet* (1817–33), which is illustrated with 2,000 hand-coloured plates.

Loisel.: LOISELEUR-DESLONGCHAMPS, JEAN LOUIS AUGUSTE (1774–1849). France.
Botanical enthusiast who made a scientific exploration of the South of France, searching out indigenous flora with an eye to their potential employment as substitutes for the rarer or exotic medicinal plants then in use. Among his works are the 2-part *Flora gallica* (1806–07), the 8-volume *Herbier général de l'amateur, contenant la description, l'histoire, les propriétés et la culture des végétaux utiles et agréables* (1816–27), and *Flore générale de France* (1828). The genus *Loiseleuria* is named in his honour.

Loud.: LOUDON, JOHN CLAUDIUS (1783–1843). Scotland.
A botanist and famous expert on gardens and gardening. His writings include several treatises on garden layout and design, on hothouse management, and on general garden management. His *Hortus Britannicus* (first ed. 1830) lists all indigenous British plants. Other notable works include the *Encyclopaedia of Gardening* (first ed., 1822), *Arboretum et fruticetum britannicum* (1838), and the *Encyclopaedia of Trees and Shrubs* (1842). He was also editor of the *Gardener's Magazine* from 1826 until his death.

Lour.: LOUREIRO, JUÃO DE (1715–1794). Portugal.
A Jesuit missionary in southern China who collected much valuable information on Asiatic flora. His best-known work is *Flora cochinchinensis* (1790).

Makino: MAKINO, TOMITARO (1862–1957). Japan.
Noted botanist, and author of numerous books on Japanese flora.

Mart.: MARTIUS, CARL FRIEDRICH PHILIPP VON (1794–1868). Germany.
A chemist and natural scientist. In 1817, at the request of the Austrian government, he participated in a 3-year scientific expedition to Brazil, recording his findings in the 3-volume *Nova genera et species plantarum, quas in itinere Brasiliam 1817–20* (1824–32). He was professor of botany at the University of Munich and director of the Munich Botanic Gardens. Among his other notable works are *Palmarum familia* (1824) and *Herbarium florae Brasiliensis* (1833). He was editor of the monumental *Flora Brasiliensis*, published in 15 volumes (1840–96).

Mast.: MASTERS, MAXWELL TYLDEN (1833–1907). England.
An early editor of *The Gardener's Chronicle*. Author of *Vegetable Teratology* (1869) and several studies on vegetable morphology, as well as numerous books and articles describing new plants of ornamental value.

Mat.: MATTIOLI, PIETRO ANDREA MATTHIOLUS (1500–1577). Italy.
Physician and naturalist who dedicated himself to the study of botany. Collecting all the information available at the time concerning medicinal botany, he published it in *Commentarii in libros sex Pedacii Dioscoridis De medica materia* (1544). This commentary on Dioscorides's works soon ran through numerous well-illustrated editions in Latin, Italian, French, and German. The genus *Matthiola* is named in his honour.

Maxim.: MAXIMOWICZ, KARL JOHANN (1827–1891). Russia.
One of the most important Russian botanists. He dedicated himself particularly to systematic botany and also wrote many important books devoted to Asiatic flora.

Med.: MEDIKUS, FRIEDRICH KASIMIR (1736–1808). Germany.
Director of the Mannheim Botanic Gardens. Author of one of the first books published in Germany dealing with American trees and plants (collected in Mannheim during his tenure) *Über nordamerikanische Bäume und Sträucher . . .* (1792).

Meisn.: MEISNER, KARL FRIEDRICH (1800–1874). Switzerland.
Botanist. Author of several studies on botany including one on the family Leguminosae (1844–45).

Mey. C. A.: MEYER, CARL ANTON (1795–1855). Germany.
Director of the St. Petersburg Botanic Gardens. Author of several studies on Russian flora.

Mey. E.: MEYER, ERNST HEINRICH FRIEDRICH (1791–1858). Germany.
Botanist. Noted for his thorough history of botany, the 4-volume *Geschichte der Botanik* (1854–57), as well as studies devoted to the flora of Surinam and Labrador.

Michx.: MICHAUX, ANDRÉ (1746–1802). France.
Botanist and explorer. Famous for his travels in North America, as well as several collecting journeys in England and Spain and a notable series of explorations in Persia and India. Celebrated for his works on North American flora, including: *Histoire des Chênes de l'Amérique Septentrionale* (1801), *Flora Boreali-Americana* (1803). His 8-volume *Journal* (posthumously pub. 1888) is also of major importance.

Mill.: MILLER, PHILIP (1691–1771). England.
Botanist and author of the celebrated *Gardener's Dictionary* (1731), which ran through numerous editions (9th ed., 2 vols. in 4, 1807). He was curator of the Chelsea Physic Garden from 1722 to 1770.

Miq.: MIQUEL, FRIEDRICH ANTON WILHELM (1811–1871). The Netherlands.
Professor of botany at the universities of

Rotterdam, Amsterdam, and Utrecht. Author of important works on cacti and the flora of Japan and Indonesia.

Moench: MOENCH, KONRAD (1744–1805). Germany.
Botanist. Professor at the University of Marburg. Author of several studies on medicinal plants and horticulture.

Moore: MOORE, THOMAS (1821–1887). England.
Curator of the Chelsea Botanic Garden. Author of *Index Filicum* (1857–63) and many works on British flora, as well as a study (written with George Jackman) on the clematis (pub. 1880).

Muell. Arg.: MUELLER, JEAN (MÜLLER-ARGOVIENSIS) (1828–1896). Switzerland.
Collaborator on the work on plant classification by De Candolle (q.v.), and author of several monographs.

Muell. F. M.: MUELLER, SIR FERDINAND JAKOB HEINRICH VON (1825–1896). Germany.
Famous author and botanist who served in the post of Government Botanist in Melbourne. Wrote a vast number of books devoted to the economic botany of Australia. He was knighted for his services to the Empire in 1879.

Murr. A.: MURRAY, ANDREW (1812–1878). Scotland.
Entomologist. Author of *The Pines and Firs of Japan* (1863) and other works.

Nees: NEES VON ESENBECK, CHRISTIAN GOTTFRIED DANIEL (1776–1858). Germany.
Botanist and naturalist. Noted for his studies on fungi and mosses.

Nichols.: NICHOLSON, GEORGE (1847–1908). England.
Director of the Royal Botanic Gardens, Kew, from 1873 to 1901. Author of the 4-volume *Illustrated Dictionary of Gardening* (1884–1902) and other works.

Nutt.: NUTTALL, THOMAS (1786–1859). England.
Botanist. Came to the United States in 1808. Curator of Harvard University Botanical Gardens, professor of botany at Harvard from 1822 to 1834. Author of *Genera of North American Plants* (1818). Turned his attention to ornithology in the 1830s, and made lasting contributions to bird study in North America.

Ort.: ORTEGA, CASIMIRO GÓMEZ (1740–1818). Spain.
Botanist. Author of *Tabulae botanicae* . . . (1783) and *Continuacion de* [Quer y Martinez's] *la Flora Española* (1784).

Otto: OTTO, FRIEDRICH (1783–1856). Germany.
Botanist. Author of *Plantae rariores quae in Horto Regio Berolinensi* (1820) and editor of *Allgemeine Gartenzeitung* from 1853 to 1856.

Pall.: PALLAS, PETER SIMON (1741–1811). Germany.
Naturalist. Noted for his travels in Russia, Siberia, and Crimea, Pallas's explorations made invaluable contributions to almost all areas of the natural sciences, as well as to ethnology and archaeology.

Park.: PARKINSON, JOHN (1567–1650). England.
Apothecary. Author of the famous *Paradisi in Sole Paradisus Terrestris* (1629), a highly important (and delightfully readable) treatise on gardening in England.

Paxt.: PAXTON, SIR JOSEPH (1803–1865). England.
Horticulturist and architect. Created the beautiful Conservatory of Chatsworth (1836–40) for the Duke of Devonshire. Famed for the construction of the Crystal Palace (the first iron-and-glass construction of great size) for the Great Exhibition of 1851 in London. Author of numerous botanical-horticultural works. Edited the *Magazine of Botany* from 1834 to 1849. This periodical is richly illustrated with many unique hand-coloured plates.

Pers.: PERSOON, CHRISTIAN HENDRIK (1755–1837). South Africa.
Botanist. Author of *Synopsis Plantarum* (1805–07) and other distinguished works, including several on mycology. The genus *Persoonia* is named in his honour.

Phil.: PHILIPPI, RUDOLF AMANDUS (1808–1904). Germany.
Botanist. Lived most of his life in Chile. Wrote numerous studies on the flora of the Cordillera.

Planch.: PLANCHON, JULES ÉMILE (1833–1900). France.
Professor of botany at the University of Montpellier. Wrote extensively on the flora of Montpellier, especially on its medicinal plants.

Poir.: POIRET, JEAN LOUIS MARIE (1755–1834). France.
Botanist. Wrote the 7-volume *Histoire philosophique, littéraire, économique des Plantes de l'Europe* (1825–29) and collaborated with Lamarck (q.v.) on his *Encyclopédie*.

Prain: PRAIN, SIR DAVID (1857–1944). England.
Botanist. Director of the Royal Botanic Gardens, Kew, from 1905 to 1922. Had a distinguished career in India and England. Author of numerous botanical monographs.

Presl.: PRESL, KAREL BOŘIWOG (1794–1852). Bohemia.
Botanist. Author of numerous books, including several studies on the flora of Bohemia.

Pursh: PURSH, FRIEDRICH TRAUGOTT (1774–1820). Germany.
Botanist. Travelled in North America between 1799 and 1811, studying the local flora. Settled in Canada in 1815. Wrote several important surveys on North American plant life.

Regel: REGEL, EDUARD AUGUST VON (1815–1892). Germany.
Botanist. Founder of the periodical *Gartenflora*. Superintendent of the Imperial Botanic Gardens at St. Petersburg. Wrote many studies on Russian flora. The genus *Regelia* is named in his honour.

Rehd.: REHDER, ALFRED (1863–1949). United States.
An expert dendrologist who was attached to the Arnold Arboretum at Harvard University from 1898 to 1940. Author of many distinguished and useful books, including the well-known *Manual of Cultivated Trees and Shrubs* (1940).

Reichb.: REICHENBACH, HEINRICH GOTTLIEB LUDWIG (1793–1879). Germany.
Botanist and zoologist. Professor at the University of Dresden. Author of several monumental works, including the *Iconographia botanica; seu Plantae Criticae* . . . (1823–32), illustrated with 1,000 hand-coloured plates, and *Flora Germanica* (1830–32).

Riddell: RIDDELL, JOHN LEONARD (1807–1865). United States.
Chemist and botanist. Author of several works, including *Catalogus florae Ludovicianae* (1852), a study on the flora of Louisiana, and *A Synopsis of the Flora of the Western States* (1835).

Roem.: ROEMER, JOHANN JAKOB (1763–1819). Switzerland.
Botanist. Professor of botany at the University of Zurich. Edited Linnaeus's *Systema Vegetabilium* (1820). The genus *Roemeria* is named in his honour.

Roscoe: ROSCOE, WILLIAM (1753–1831). England.
Botanist. Founded the Liverpool Botanic Gardens in 1802. Author of several notable monographs.

Rose: ROSE, JOSEPH NELSON (1862–1928). United States.
Vice-director of the National Herbarium of the Smithsonian Institution, and a noted authority on Mexican flora. Author (with N. L. Britton) of the 4-volume *The Cactaceae* (1919–23).

Roth: ROTH, ALBRECHT WILHELM (1757–1834). Germany.
Physician and botanist. Author of several works on indigenous and exotic flora.

Roxb.: ROXBURGH, WILLIAM (1759–1815). England.
Botanist. Superintendent of the Calcutta Botanic Gardens from 1793 to 1814. As an expert on Indian flora, his posthumously published 3-volume *Flora Indica* (1820–32) is a celebrated work.

Royle: ROYLE, JOHN FORBES (1800–1858). India.
Surgeon and botanist. An expert on the flora of India and the Himalayas. Author of several fine works, including *Manual of Materia Medica* (1847), and *Botany of the Himalayas* (1834–38).

Ruiz and Pav.: RUIZ LOPEZ HIPOLITO (1764–1815). Spain. PAVÓN, JOSÉ (1754–1844). Spain.
Botanists and authors of the well-known 3-volume *Flora Peruviana et Chilensis* (1798–1802). The genus *Pavonia* was named in Pavon's honour.

Rupr.: RUPRECHT, FRANZ JOSEPH IVANOVICH (1814–1870). Bohemia.
Botanist. Custodian of the Herbarium at the Imperial Academy of St. Petersburg. Author of many works devoted to Russian and exotic flora.

Sabine: SABINE, JOSEPH (1770–1837). England.
Botanist. Noted for his books on Chinese chrysanthemums as well as those on peonies. He was one of the founders of the Royal Horticultural Society, and its Secretary from 1816 to 1823. The genus *Sabinea* is named in his honour.

Salisb.: SALISBURY, RICHARD ANTHONY (1761–1829). England.
Botanist. Author of *Paradisus Londinensis* (1805–08). Secretary of the Royal Horticultural Society from 1805 to 1816.

Salm-Dyck: SALM-REIFFERSCHEID-DYCK, PRINCE JOSEPH FRANZ MARIA (1773–1861). Germany.
One of the leading authorities on succulents. Author of many monographs on these plants. The genus *Dyckia* is named in his honour.

Sarg.: SARGENT, CHARLES SPRAGUE (1841–1927). United States.
Dendrologist. First director of the Arnold Arboretum of Harvard University. Author of the 14-volume *The Silva of North America* (1891–1902) and *Manual of the Trees of North America* (1905). The genus *Sargentia* is named in his honour.

Savi: SAVI, GAETANO (1769–1844). Italy.
Botanist. Director of the Pisa Botanic Garden. Author of the 2-volume *Flora pisana* (1798) and *Materia medica vegetabile Toscana* (1805).

Scheidw.: SCHEIDWEILER, MICHEL JOSEPH FRANÇOIS (1799–1861). Germany.
Professor of botany at the Ghent Horticultural Institute.

Schlecht.: SCHLECHTENDAL, DIEDRICH LEONHARD VON (1794–1866). Germany.
Professor of botany at the University of Halle. Author of many important volumes on trees and shrubs, both native and exotic, and *Zu Flora Croatiens* (1861–62).

Schneider C.K.: SCHNEIDER, CAMILLO KARL (1876–1951). Germany.
Dendrologist. Author of *Die Nadelhölzer in der Architektonischen Anlage im Garten* (1913), and *Illustriertes Handbuch der Laubholzkunde* (1904–12).

Schult.: SCHULTES, JOSEF AUGUST (1773–1831). Austria.
Botanist. Wrote the catalogue of the Botanic Garden of the University of Cracow in 1806, author of *Österreichs Flora* (1814).

Schum.: SCHUMACHER, HEINRICH CHRISTIAN FRIEDRICH (1757–1830). Denmark.
Botanist. Author of a number of works on the flora of Denmark, notably *Den Kjøbenhavnske flora* (1804).

Schumann: SCHUMANN, KARL MORITZ (1851–1904). Germany.
Professor of botany at the University of Berlin. Author of many important books on cacti.

Sibth.: SIBTHORP, JOHN (1758–1796). England.
Professor of botany at Oxford from 1783 to 1795. Author of *Flora Oxoniensis*, and—published posthumously—the magnificent 10-volume *Flora Graeca* (1806–40), which contains 966 hand-coloured plates.

Sieb.: SIEBOLD, PHILIPP FRANZ VON (1796–1866). Germany.
Botanist. Many species have been named in

his honour. He is celebrated for his writings on the flora and fauna of Japan, especially the multi-volume *Flora Japonica* (1835–70). During his six years in Japan with the Dutch East India Company's colony at Nagasaki he collected and discovered many native plants.

Sims: SIMS, JOHN (1792–1838). England.
Botanist. Succeeded William Curtis (q.v.) as editor of *Curtis's Botanical Magazine* (1801–26).

Sm.: SMITH, SIR JAMES EDWARD (1759–1828). England.
In 1784, Smith purchased the herbarium and library of Linnaeus for 1,000 guineas and brought it to London. He founded the Linnean Society in 1788. Author of many books on botany.

Soland.: SOLANDER, DANIEL CARL (1736–1782). Sweden.
Botanist. A pupil of Linnaeus (q.v.). Accompanied Sir Joseph Banks (q.v.) as botanist on Captain Cook's first voyage (1768–71). Keeper of the Natural History Department at the British Museum from 1773 until his death. The genus *Solandra* is named in his honour.

Spach: SPACH, EDOUARD (1801–1879). Alsace.
Botanist. Author of the 14-volume *Histoire naturelle des végétaux* (1834–48) and numerous other works. A curator at the Musée d'Histoire Naturelle in Paris for many years.

Speg.: SPEGAZZINI, CARLO (1858–1926). Italy.
Botanist. Author of many notable studies on South American flora and fungi.

Sprague: SPRAGUE, THOMAS (1877–1958). Scotland.
Botanist. Assistant director of the Herbarium at the Royal Botanic Gardens, Kew, for many years.

Spreng.: SPRENGEL, KURT (1766–1833). Germany.
Botanist and physician. Author of histories of medicine, surgery, and botany, as well as a vast number of treatises and monographs of horticultural value.

Stapf: STAPF, OTTO (1857–1933). Austria.
Botanist. Keeper of the Herbarium, Royal Botanic Gardens, Kew, from 1909 to 1921. Editor of the *Botanical Magazine* (1922–33).

St. Hil.: SAINT-HILAIRE, AUGUSTE FRANÇOIS CÉSAR PROUVENÇAL DE (1779–1853). France.
Botanist. Notable for his explorations in Brazil, and for the 3-volume *Flora Brasiliae* (1825–33), and for many other works on tropical American flora.

Sweet: SWEET, ROBERT (1783–1835). England.
Nurseryman. Author of several well-known books including *Geraniaceae* (1820–30), *The British Flower Garden* (1822–31), and *Hortus Britannicus* (1826). The first two are multi-volume works and are richly illustrated.

Tausch: TAUSCH, IGNAZ FRIEDRICH (1793–1848). Austria.
Botanist. Author of *Catalog der Flora Böhmens* (1851), a systematic study of the flora of Bohemia.

Tenore: TENORE, MICHELE (1780–1861). Italy.
Professor of botany at the University of Naples and director of the Naples Botanic Gardens. The discovery of many species are due to his efforts; his most important book is the 5-volume *Flora Napolitana* (1811–38).

Thore: THORE, JEAN (1762–1822). France.
Physician and amateur botanist. Author of *Essai d'une Chloris du département des Landes* (1803).

Thunb.: THUNBERG, CARL PETER (1743–1828). Sweden.
One of the most famous Swedish botanists; as a physician employed by the Dutch East India Company, he travelled extensively. In 1781 he became professor of botany at Uppsala University. Author of numerous celebrated works, including *Flora Japonica* (1784), *Nova genera Plantarum* (1781–1801), and hundreds of dissertations on various genera. The genus *Thunbergia* is named in his honour.

Torr.: TORREY, JOHN (1796–1873). United States.
One of America's great botanists. Collaborated with Asa Gray (q.v.) in preparation of the

1425

first two volumes of the *Flora of North America*. The genus *Torreya* is named in his honour.

Tourn.: TOURNEFORT, JOSEPH PITTON DE (1656–1708). France.
Travelled extensively in Europe and Africa on behalf of Louis XIV. A precursor of Linnaeus, he was the originator of an artificial system of plant classification based on the characteristics of the plant's corolla. He was also the first to group plants into genera. Author of the 3-volume *Eléméns de botanique, ou Méthode pour Connôitre les Plantes* (1700) illustrated with 476 engraved plates. The genus *Tournefortia* is named in his honour.

Underw.: UNDERWOOD, LUCIEN MARCUS (1853–1907). United States.
Professor at Columbia University, New York. Author of *Our Native Ferns and How to Study Them* (1881), and *Moulds, Mildews, and Mushrooms* (1899).

Vahl: VAHL, MARTIN (1749–1804). Norway.
Botanist. Wrote several books on American flora and one on the flora of Madeira.

Van Houtte: VAN HOUTTE, LOUIS BENOÎT (1810–1876). Belgium.
Founder and co-editor of the periodical *Flore des Serres . . . en Europe* (1845–55).

Veitch: VEITCH, JOHN GOULD (1839–1867). England.
One of the most famous of British nurserymen, who imported a great number of then-new and now well-known plants and created many new hybrids. The genus *Veitchia* is named in honour of him and of his father, James Veitch (1815–1869).

Vent.: VENTENAT, ÉTIENNE PIERRE (1757–1808). France.
Botanist. Author of several important works, most notable of which is possibly the spectacular *Jardin de la Malmaison* (1803), which is illustrated with 120 hand-coloured plates.

Versch.: VERSCHAFFELT, AMBROISE COLETTE ALEXANDRE (1825–1886). Belgium.
Founder and publisher of *L'Illustration Horticole* in 1854. Also wrote the notable 6-volume *Nouvelle iconographie des Caméllias* (1848–60), which is illustrated with 624 hand-coloured plates. The genus *Verschaffelia* is named in his honour.

Vilm.: VILMORIN, PIERRE PHILIPPE ANDRÉ LÉVÊQUE DE (1746–1804); VILMORIN, PIERRE (1816–1860); and VILMORIN, HENRY L. DE (1843–1899). France.
Famous family of horticulturists, who for generations were proprietors of one of the most famous nurseries and seed warehouses, with headquarters in Paris (Vilmorin-Andrieux et cie.). Several famous gardening books have been issued by their firm: especially notable is *Les fleurs de pleine terre* (1863), and in an English translation *The Vegetable Garden* (3rd ed., 1920), is still considered to be the most practical book ever written on the subject. The firm is still extant.

Voss: VOSS, ANDREAS (1857–1924). Germany.
Botanist. Author of several books on taxonomy, and editor of the German edition of Vilmorin's *Les fleurs de pleine terre* (q.v.): *Vilmorin's Blumengärtnerei* (1896).

Wahl.: WAHLENBERG, GÖRAN (1781–1851). Sweden.
Botanist. Professor at Uppsala University. Author of many works, notably *Flora Lapponica* (1812). The genus *Wahlenbergia* is named in his honour.

Wall.: WALLICH, NATHANIEL (1786–1854). Denmark.
Botanist. Superintendent of the Calcutta Botanic Gardens from 1814 to 1841. Author of several books dealing with plants of India and Asia. The genus *Wallichia* is named in his honour.

Walt.: WALTER, THOMAS (1740–1788). England.
Planter. Author of *Flora Caroliniana* (1788).

Ward.: KINGDON-WARD, CAPT. FRANCIS (1885–1958). England.
One of the most famous botanical collectors and explorers who wrote several fascinating books describing his experiences in the mountains of eastern Asia. The last of these

was the posthumously published *Pilgrimage for Plants* (1960).

Web.: WEBER, FRIEDRICH (1781–1823). Germany.
Botanist. Professor at the University of Kiel. Author of many textbooks on botany and natural history.

Wendl.: WENDLAND, HERMANN (1823–1903). Germany.
Curator of the Royal Botanic Garden at Herrenhausen. Author of several monographs on palms.

Willd.: WILLDENOW, KARL LUDWIG (1765–1812). Germany.
Professor of botany at the University of Berlin. Author of several important works dealing with systematic botany.

Wilson: WILSON, ERNEST H. (1876–1930). England.
A famous botanist, botanical collector, and explorer. Travelled extensively throughout China. From there he introduced more than 1,000 new species to the gardens of England and the United States—many of which now bear his name. Eventually he moved to the United States, where he filled an important position at the Arnold Arboretum at Harvard University. During his distinguished career (cut short by his death in an automobile accident) he made over eight expeditions to China and Japan. His *China, Mother of Gardens* (1929) is but one of his many important—and highly readable—books. The genus *Sinowilsonia* is named in his honour.

Wittm.: WITTMACK, MAX KARL LUDWIG (1839–1929). Germany.
Professor of botany at the University of Berlin. Editor of the journal *Gartenflora* from 1886 until the time of his death.

Wood: WOOD, ALPHONSO (1810–1881). United States.
Botanist. Author of horticultural and botanical books. His *Class-Book of Botany* (1845) attained extraordinary popularity, and by 1875 had gone through 41 editions.

Zabel: ZABEL, HERMANN (1832–1912). Germany.
Dendrologist. Author of many important treatises on deciduous trees.

Zucc.: ZUCCARINI, JOSEPH GERHARD (1797–1848). Germany.
Professor of botany at the University of Munich. Author of many works devoted to the flora of Bavaria.

GLOSSARY

ACHENE: a small, brittle, dry indehiscent (non-splitting) fruit

ACID: term used in garden parlance to denote a soil with a preponderance of humus and with a pH value below 7; the opposite to alkaline or calcareous

ACUMINATE: (leaf) having a gradually tapering thin point

ACUTE: (leaf) sharply pointed

ALKALINE: term used in garden parlance to denote a soil derived from calcareous matter, with a pH value above 7; the opposite to an acid soil

ALTERNATE: (leaves) spaced singly, on opposite sides of the stem, at different heights

ANNUAL: a plant that completes its life cycle within a year

ANTHER: the pollen-bearing organ at the end of a stamen (*see* Flower, structure of)

APETALOUS: (flower) without petals

APEX: tip or growing point of a leaf or other organ

APICULATE: tips of leaves or petals terminating in a short point

ARBORESCENT: tree-like

ARTICULATE: jointed

ASEXUAL: sexless flowers; without stamens, pistils, or ovules, and therefore sterile. Asexual propagation indicates vegetative propagation rather than propagation from seed (cuttings, budding, grafting, division, or layering)

ASYMMETRICAL: of irregular, non-symmetrical, non-proportional shape

AURICULATE: eared (auricles), frequently used to define the two lobes at the base of a leaf

AXIL: the angle between leaf or leaf-stalk and stem

AXILLARY: growing in or from the axil

BACCATE: berry-like

BASAL: at the base

BERRY: many seeded fleshy or pulpy fruit

BIENNIAL: a plant which completes its life cycle in two years, or in two growing seasons, generally not blooming until the second year

BILABIATE: two-lipped

BIPINNATE: (leaf) twice pinnately cut, or divided, with the leaflets or segments arranged in a feather-like manner

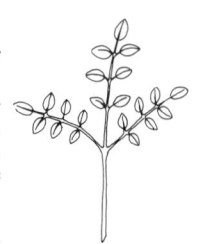

BISEXUAL: (flower) having both stamens and pistils

BLADE: the expanded portion of a leaf (*see* Leaf, structure of)

BRACT: modified, often coloured leaf, frequently assuming the appearance of a petal

BUDDING: propagation by a form of grafting, used mostly in the multiplication of roses, in which a vegetative bud of some chosen variety is budded onto a more common stock. In typical grafting a small growth is used in place of a bud

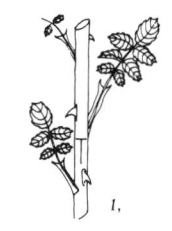

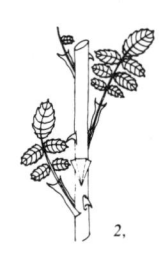

BULB: an underground, generally rounded, fleshy storage organ derived from the modified base of a stem and bearing modified, scale-like leaves

BULBIL: small bulb frequently stem-borne

CALCAREOUS: (soil) *see* Alkaline

CALYX: the outer, external whorl of floral organs, composed of sepals. These are usually green and serve as protection for the petals (*see* Flower, structure of)

CAMPANULATE: bell-shaped

CANDELABRA: flowers of an inflorescence arranged in tiers up the stem

CAPILLARY: hair-like

CAPITATE: inflorescence or single flower in a terminal head

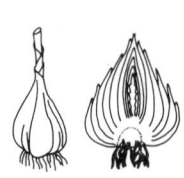

CAPSULE: a dry fruit often consisting of several compartments, that generally splits open lengthwise when ripe

CARPEL: a simple pistil or one

Acuminate

Acute

Bipinnate

1,

2,

3

Budding

Lily bulb *Cross-section Tulip bulb*

member of a compound pistil, which develops into an ovary

CHLOROPHYLL: the basic green colouring matter of plants

CILIATE: fringed with hairs

COMPOUND: refers to an organ (compound leaf) that is made up of many similar parts

CONIFEROUS: cone-bearing

CORDATE: (leaf) heart-shaped at the base, with two rounded lobes

CORIACEOUS: leathery

CORM: swollen base of a stem that stores food material below the soil surface, as in a bulb

COROLLA: that part of a flower composed of petals (*see* Flower, structure of)

CORONA: inner appendage to a petal or to the throat of a corolla

CORYMB: broad, wide, flat-topped inflorescence or cluster of flowers; those at the perimeter open first

COTYLEDON: the primary or seed leaf appearing immediately after germination

CRENATE: (leaf) dentated at the edge with rounded teeth or with a scalloped edge

CUNEATE: wedge-shaped

CYME: inflorescence arranged as a broad, flattened flower cluster

DECIDUOUS: (foliage) not persistent or evergreen; generally falling in autumn

DEHISCENT: (seed pods, capsules, etc.) the spontaneous opening of seed when ripe

DENTATE: toothed, dentated at the edges

DICOTYLEDON: a plant having two primary seed leaves when germination takes place

DIGITATE: (leaf) compound, with the leaflets arising from one central point at the apex of the stalk

DIOECIOUS: indicating male and female flowers on separate plants

DISCOID: disk-like

DISK: the central part of flowers such as daisies

DISSECTED: divided into numerous segments

ELLIPTIC: (leaf) oval but narrowing towards each of the rounded ends

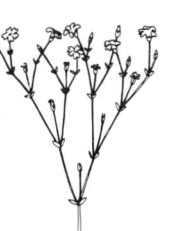

EMARGINATE: (leaf or petal) having a notched tip

EMBRYO: the rudimentary plantlet within the seed

ENDEMIC: confined to a particular region

ENTIRE: (leaf) not divided or segmented, and with margins not toothed or dentated or lobed

EPIPHYTE: a plant that grows on another plant, particularly in the case of certain orchids; in a wider sense, plants growing on some other support such as a pole, telegraph wire, or rock, etc., but not parasitic

F1, F2: symbols used to indicate first or second generations from a deliberate cross

FALL: the lower or pendulous petal of an iris bloom

FAMILY: a group of plants with common botanical characteristics, generally containing a number of genera

FARINA: flour-like substance occasionally present on the surface of leaves or fruit

FERTILE: able to produce fruit; in the case of stamens, pollen-bearing

FILAMENT: the thread-like stalk of a stamen

FIMBRIATE: fringed

FLORET: a small, individual flower; generally one of a group or cluster

FLOWER: structure of ⟶

FOLIACEOUS: leaf-like in appearance or texture

FRUIT: the seed-bearing organ of a plant

FUSIFORM: spindle-shaped

GAMOPETALOUS: having the petals of the corolla united

GAMOSEPALOUS: having the sepals united

GENUS: a group of species with common characters, which collectively form a family. Each species of a genus bears the same generic name (*Prunus sevalata*, *Prunus pissardi*, etc.)

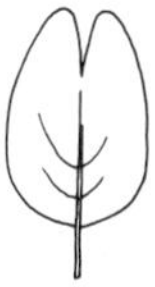

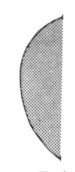

GLABROUS: smooth, not rough or hairy

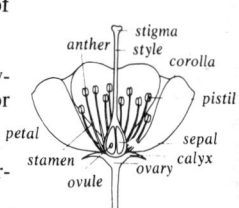

GLAND: a secreting surface or structure, either embedded in the surface or as a protuberance or bulge often containing some kind of oil or perfume
GLANDULAR: bearing glands
GLAUCOUS: greyish in colour and often covered with a waxy "bloom". Used to describe the colour of certain leaves
GLOBOSE: ball-shaped
GRAFTING: a method of multiplication widely used in shrub and tree propagation, where a small growth of some chosen variety is grafted onto a common stock
GYMNOSPERMOUS: bearing naked seeds (as in the cone of a pine or head of a sunflower)

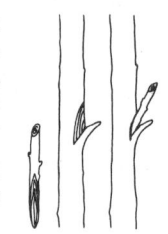

Two methods of grafting

HABITAT: district or geographical area where a plant is found growing in the wild (the plant's natural habitat)
HASTATE: spear-like; generally used to describe those leaves whose base has two equal, triangular lobes pointed outwards
HERBACEOUS (HERB): a plant with no persistent woody stem above ground, although the foliage may be either evergreen or deciduous
HERMAPHRODITE: flowers furnished with both stamens and pistils
HIRSUTE: pubescent, with coarse or stiff hairs
HISPID: covered with bristle-like hairs
HYBRID: the offspring of crosses between two plants of the same variety or race, between different varieties, species, or even genera

IMBRICATED: overlapping in regular order, like tiles on a roof; applicable to scales, petals, leaves, etc. An excellent example is the monkey-puzzle tree, *Araucaria Imbricata*, whose leaves are arranged in an imbricated fashion
INCISED: having the leaves or petals deeply cut at the margins, generally in an irregular manner
INDEHISCENT: fruit or seed pod, etc., that is self-opening for the dispersal of the seeds
INFLATED: bladdery; frequently used to describe a type of fruit or seed vessel
INFLORESCENCE: a term used in gardening to refer to a group or cluster or spike of individual flowers on a stem or branch (i.e., lilac, rhododendron, Michelmas Daisy), as opposed to a single bloom such as a dahlia or tulip (see Corymb, Cyme, Panicle, Raceme, Spike)
INTERNODE: the area of a stem between two nodes (joints)
INVOLUCRATE: having an involucre
INVOLUCRE: a number of bracts or small leaves surrounding a cluster of flowers on a single bloom

Hastate

KEEL: a central, dorsal ridge—like the keel of a boat—that occurs with the union of two petals, as in sweet peas, lupines, etc. The longitudinal ridge on the foliage of certain Red-hot Pokers (kniphofia) causes them to be referred to as keeled foliage

LACINIATE: petals or leaves cut or slashed
LAMINA: (leaf blade) the extended part of a leaf (see below)
LANCEOLATE: (leaf) lance-shaped; much greater in length than width
LEAF: structure of ⟶ *Basic leaf*
LIGULAR: like a ligule
LIGULE: strap-shaped, as in certain petals or leaves
LINEAR: (leaf or petal) narrow, with mostly parallel margins; much greater in length than in width
LOBED: (leaf or petal) a segment generally rounded and extending deeply towards the center
LONGITUDINALLY: along the length
LYRATE: pinnatified (*see* Pinnate) with a large, rounded terminal lobe (as in *Ficus lyrate*)

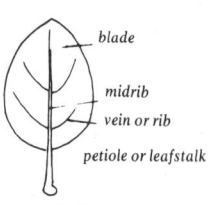

Lanceolate

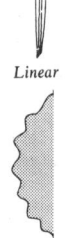

blade
midrib
vein or rib
petiole or leafstalk

Linear

Lobed

MEMBRANOUS: thin, soft, more or less translucent

MONADELPHOUS: with the filaments of the stamens joined together

MONOCOTYLEDON: having only one cotyledon or seed leaf at germination

MONOECIOUS: male and female flowers borne on the same plant, with the sexual organs in separate flowers

MUTATION: term used to denote a sudden change in the character of a plant; a tendency to revert

NECTAR: a sweet fluid secreted by certain glands

NODE: the point on a stem where the leaf is attached (joint)

OBOVATE: (leaf) egg-shaped, with the widest end above the middle

OBTUSE: (leaf) blunt at the end, or bluntly rounded

OFFSET: a lateral growth used for propagating

ORBICULAR: circular

OVARY: the usually swollen base of a pistil, containing one or more ovules, which, after fertilization, become the seeds (see Flower, structure of)

OVATE: (leaf) egg-shaped, with the widest part below the middle

OVULE: see Ovary

PALMATE: (leaf) divided or lobed like the palm and fingers of a hand

PANICLE: inflorescence in the form of a branched or compound raceme

PARASITIC: a plant growing on and deriving nourishment from another plant

PARTHENOGENETIC: developing without fertilization

PELTATE: (leaf) shield-shaped, with the stalk attached to the lower surface

PERENNIAL: plant lasting for an indefinite number of years

PERFOLIATE: a leaf whose base clasps the stem, as in *Papaver somniferum*

PERIANTH: the calyx and corolla together

PETAL: one of the sections which form the corolla (see Flower, structure of)

PETIOLE: the stalk of a leaf

pH: symbol followed by a number that indicates the degree of acidity or alkalinity of the soil

PINNATE: a compound leaf with the leaflets arranged on both sides of a common stalk

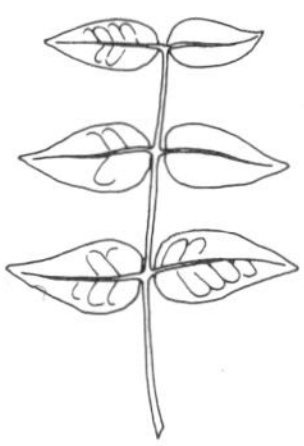

PISTIL: female, seed-bearing organ made up of ovary, style, and stigma (see Flower, structure of)

PLUMOSE: having feathery hairs

PUBESCENT: covered with silky or downy hairs

PUNCTATE: marked with glands or dots

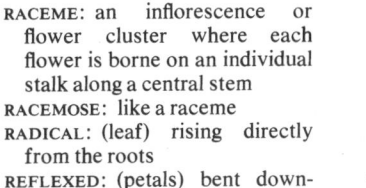

RACEME: an inflorescence or flower cluster where each flower is borne on an individual stalk along a central stem

RACEMOSE: like a raceme

RADICAL: (leaf) rising directly from the roots

REFLEXED: (petals) bent downwards or backwards

RENIFORM: (leaf) kidney-shaped

RETICULATE: net-veined

REVOLUTE: (leaf) with the margins rolled backwards

RHIZOME: a horizontal stem usually growing under the ground (sometimes partially above the ground), producing roots from its underside and sending up growing shoots from its upper side

ROSETTE: a circular cluster or arrangement of leaves

RUGOSE: wrinkled

SAGITTATE: (leaf) pointed like an arrow

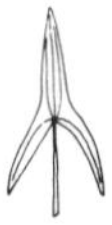

SCABROUS: rough

SEGMENT: one of the parts of a compound leaf or other divided organ

SEPAL: one of the separate parts of the calyx (see Flower, structure of)

SERRATE: toothed along the margins

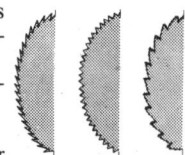

SESSILE: not having a stalk

SIMPLE: (leaf) not compound or divided; in one piece

SINUATE: with undulated or wavy margins
SPATULATE: shaped like a spatula, the narrow end at the base
SPICATE: in the form of a spike
STAMEN: anther and filament, constituting the male, pollen-bearing part of the flower (*see* Flower, structure of)
STELLATE: star-shaped
STERILE: unproductive of seed
STIGMA: that part of the pistil which is receptive when pollen is deposited upon it (*see* Flower, structure of)
STIPULE: an appendage resembling a tiny leaf, sometimes occurring in pairs, at the base of the petiole (*see* Flower, structure of)
STOLON: a runner or any basal growth disposed to spread and form new roots
STRIATE: with fine parallel lines or stripes on the surface
STYLE: the area of the pistil between stigma and ovary (*see* Flower, structure of)
SUCCULENT: fleshy, juicy; as in the case of many succulent plants or cacti

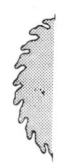

TENDRIL: a slender, twining organ that enables a plant to climb
TERMINAL: at the top
TOMENTOSE: covered with soft woolly hairs on the surface
TOOTHED: dentated; bearing small teeth on the edges (*see* Dentate)
TRIFOLIATE: with three leaves or leaflets (like clover)

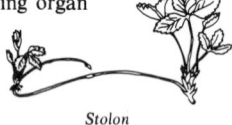

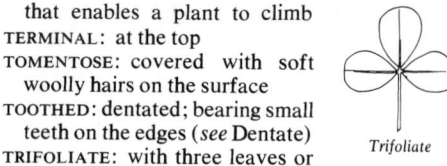

UMBEL: inflorescence with stalked flowers arising from one point (as in agapanthus)

VERTICULATE: arranged in a whorl or in a series of whorls
VESICLE: a small bladder or blister-like organ
VISCID: sticky, glutinous

WHORL: a circular arrangement of foliage or flowers round an axis, at a node, such as the leaves round the stems of some lilies
WOOLLY: (generally leaves or stems) covered with long, soft hairs that are usually white or grey in colour

Sinuate

Spatulate

Spike

Stolon

Trifoliate

Umbel

Verticulate

INDEX

This index includes families (roman type), genera (in CAPITALS), and species (*italic* type); named hybrids and varieties have not been indexed. Page numbers for illustrations appear in *italics*. Volume I (A–J) includes pages 1–694, Volume II (K–Z) includes pages 695–1396. Page numbers in roman numerals refer to the Introduction in Volume I.

Aaron's Beard, see *Hypericum calycinum; Linaria Cymbalaria; Saxifraga sarmentosa*
Aaron's Rod, see *Solidago*
Abel, Dr. Clarke, 1, 164
ABELIA [a-BEE-leeya] 2–3
 chinensis (syn. *A. rupestris*) 1
 floribunda 1; *1*
 grandiflora 1
 rupestris (syn. *A. chinensis*) 1
Abelmoschus esculentus, see *Hibiscus esculentus*
Abelmoschus moschatus, see *Hibiscus Abelmoschus*
ABUTILON [ab-YEW-till-on] 2–4
 megapotamicum (syn. *A. vexillarium*) 2
 vitifolium 2; *3*
ACACIA [ack-AY-sha] (Mimosa, Wattle) 4–12
 armata (syn. *A. paradoxa;* Kangaroo Thorn) 6, 8
 baileyana (Cootamundra Wattle, Bailey's Mimosa) 8
 cultriformis (Knife Acacia) 8
 dealbata 9; *9*
 farnesiana (syn. *A. leptophylla;* Gaggia, Opinac) 9
 hybrida (Clair de Lune) 12
 longifolia (Golden Wattle) 9; *4*
 melanoxylon (Lightwood, Blackwood) 9
 pulchella 11; *7*
 retinoides (syns. *A. Semperflorens, A. Floribunda;* Monthly Mimosa) 11
 riceana 11; *10*
 verticillata (Star Acacia, Prickly Mimosa, Whorl-leaved Acacia) 12; *7*
Acanthaceae (family)
 Thunbergia 1284–1288

ACHILLEA [ack-ill-EE-ya] (Yarrow) 12–19
 atrata (Black Yarrow) 14
 clavenae (syns. *A. clavennae, A. argentea*) 14; *15*
 filipendulina (syn. *A. eupatorium*) 16
 Millefolium (Milfoil) 13, 14, 17
 moschata (syn. *A. genipi*) 14, *18*
 nobilis (syn. *A. camphorata*) 14, 18
 ptarmica (Sneezewort) 13, 18
 tomentosa (syn. *A. aurea*) 18; *15*
Achilles 13
Achimenes tubiflora, see *Gloxinia tubiflora*
ACIDANTHERA [a-seed-AN-thera] 19–20
 bicolor 19; *20*
acidity of soil xxv–xxvii
Aconite, see *Aconitum*
ACONITUM [acko-NYT-um] (Monkshood, Aconite) 20–25
 Anthora (syn. *A. pyrenaicum*) 23; *21*
 autumnale 23
 ferox 23
 japonicum 23, 24
 lycoctonum (Wolf's Bane) 22, 23, 24
 napellus (True Monkshood) 22, 23, 24; *22*
 paniculatum 23
 volubile (syn. *A. uncinatum*) 25
Acqua Angelica 878
Actinidiaceae (family)
 Actinidia (?) 25–27
ACTINIDIA [ack-tinn-IDD-eeya] 25–27
 chinensis (Chinese Gooseberry, Yangtao) 25
 Kolomikta (Kolomikta Vine) 26; *26*
 polygama (Silver Vine) 26; *26*
Adonis 27

ADONIS [ad-DOE-niss] 27–30
 aestivalis (syns. *A. autumnalis, A. annua;* Pheasant's-eye) 28
 flammeus 27, 28; *28*
 vernalis 28; *29*
Aduseton saxatile, see *Alyssum saxatile*
Aegle sepiara, see *Poncirus trifoliata*
Aesculapius, the Greek god of medicine 87
AESCULUS [ESS-kew-lus] (Horse-Chestnut) 30–31
 hippocastanum 30
 parviflora (syns. *A. macrostachya, Pavia macrostachya;* Dwarf Buckeye) 30; *31*
African Corn Lily, see *Ixia*
African Daisy, see *Arctotis stoechadifolia; Dimorphotheca; Gazania; Gerbera*
African Lily, see *Agapanthus*
African Marigold, see *Tagetes erecta*
AGAPANTHUS [aga-PAN-thus] (African Lily, Lily-of-the-Nile) 31–34
 africanus 34
 campanulatus 34
 caulescens 34
 minor 34
 mooreanus 34
 orientalis 34; *32*
 umbellatus 34
 weillighii (syn. *A. inapertus*) 34
Agathaea amelloides, see *Felicia amelloides*
Agathaea coelestris, see *Felicia amelloides*
Agathaea hispida, see *Felicia hispida*
AGERATUM [ajer-AY-tum] (Floss Flower) 35–36

houstonianum (syn. *A. mexicanum*) 35; *35*
Agrostemma Coeli-rosa, see *Lychnis Coeli-rosa*
Agrostemma coronaria, see *Lychnis coronaria*
Agrostemma Flos-cuculi, see *Lychnis Flos-cuculi*
Agrostemma Flos-Jovis, see *Lychnis Flos-Jovis*
Aitchison, Dr. James Edward Tierney, work with *Rosa ecae* 1157; discovers *Spiraea aitchisonii* 1245
Aiton, William, on *Malus prunifolia* 834; work with *Prunus lusitanica* 1065
Aizoaceae (family) *Mesembryanthemum* 854–858
Albertus Magnus, Saint, 1132
Alder, Dwarf, see *Fothergilla gardenei*
Alder, Witch, see *Fothergilla*
alkalinity of soil xxv–xxvii
Alkanet, see *Anchusa*
ALLIUM [ALLY-yum] 36–39
  albopilosum 37
  caeruleum (syn. *A. azureum*) 37
  giganteum (Giant Garlic) 37
  karataviense 37; *38*
  Moly (Lily Leek) 36, 37, 39; *36*
  ostrowskianum (syn. *A. oreophilum* var. *ostrowskianum*) 39
  siculum 39
  stellatum 39
  validum 39
Almond, see *Prunus Amygdalus*
Almond, Dwarf Russian, see *Prunus nana*
Almond, Flowering, see *Prunus glandulosa*
ALONSOA [al-lon-ZOH-a] (Mask-Flower) 39–40
  acutifolia (syn. *A. myrtifolia*) 40
  caulialata 40
  incisifolia 40; *40*
  warscewiczii 40
Alstroemer, Baron Clas, 41
ALSTROEMERIA [al-stre-MEER-eeya] (Peruvian Lily) 41–43
  aurantiaca 41
  Pelegrina 41, 43; *42*
Alstroemeriaceae (family), see *Alstroemeria*
ALTHAEA [al-THEE-a] (Hollyhock, Rose-Mallow) 43–48

ficifolia 46; *46*
frutex, see *Hibiscus syriacus*
rosea 44, 48; *47*
Alum root (Alumroot), see *Geranium maculatum; Heuchera*
ALYSSUM [a-LISS-um] (Madwort) 48–51
  argenteum (Yellow Tuft) 49
  montanum 49; *50*
  saxatile (syns. *Aduseton saxatile, Alyssum petraeum, Aurinia saxatilis;* Gold-Dust, Golden Turf, Basket-of-Gold) 49, 51; *50*
  Also see *Lobularia*
Alyssum, Sweet, see *Lobularia*
Amaranth, Globe, see *Gomphrena*
Amaranthaceae (family)
  Amaranthus 51–52; *Celosia argentea* 203–204; *Gomphrena* 542
Amaranths, see *Amaranthus*
AMARANTHUS [am-a-RANTH-us] (Amaranths) 51–52
  caudatus (syns. *A. paniculatus, A. sanguineus;* Love-Lies-Bleeding) 51–52; *51*
  gangeticus 52
  hypochondriacus (Prince's Feather) 52
  salicifolius (Fountain-Plant) 52
Amaryllidaceae (family)
  Alstroemeria 41–43; *Amaryllis* 52–54; *Galanthus* 494–495; *Hippeastrum* 601–605; *Leucojum* 745–746; *Narcissus* 880–891; *Polyanthes tuberosa* 1026–1028; *Sternbergia lutea* 1254–1256
AMARYLLIS [am-ar-ILL-iss] (Belladonna Lily) 52–54
  Amaryllis belladonna 54
  Also see *Hippeastrum*
Amberboa moschata, see *Centaurea moschata*
Amblyolepsis setigera, see *Helenium setigerum*
American Globe Flower, see *Trollius laxus*
American Hemerocallis Society 586
Amherst, Lady, 263
Amherst, Lord, 1
Ammocallis rosea, see *Vinca rosea*
Amygdalus communis, see *Prunus Amygdalus*

Amygdalus nana, see *Prunus tenella*
Amygdalus Persica, see *Prunus Persica*
Anacreon, on roses 1129
ANCHUSA [an-KOOS-a] (Bugloss, Alkanet) 54–56
  azurea (syn. *A. italica*) 55; *56*
  caespitosa 55
  capensis 55
  myosotidiflora (syn. *Brunnera macrophylla*) 56; *56*
  officinalis 56
Anderson-Henry, Isaac, cultivates *Clematis* 256
André, Edouard, work with *Cytisus* 349
Andrews, H. C., *Coloured Engravings of Heaths* 442
Andromeda, see *Pieris japonica*
Andromeda campanulata, see *Enkianthus campanulatus*
Andromeda floribunda, see *Pieris floribunda*
Andromeda formosa, see *Pieris formosa*
Andromeda japonica, see *Pieris japonica*
Andromeda perulata, see *Enkianthus perulatus*
Anemone, see *Pulsatilla*
ANEMONE [an-EM-mo-nee] (Windflower) 56–66
  apennina (syn. *A. pygmaea*) 58; *58*
  blanda 58
  coronaria (Poppy Anemone) 58, 60–61; *63*
  x *fulgens* 61
  hepatica, see *Hepatica triloba*
  hortensis (syn. *A. stellata*) 61; 65
  x *hybrida* 64
  japonica (syn. *A. hupehensis;* Japanese Anemone) 62; *64*
  narcissiflora 64
  nemorosa (Wood Anemone) 64
  pavonina (Peacock Anemone) 64
  ranunculoides 64
  sylvestris (Snowdrop Windflower) 64, 66; *59*
  Also see *Pulsatilla* and *Hepatica*
Anemone, Blue, see *Hepatica americana*
Anemone Pulsatilla, see *Pulsatilla*
Angel's Tears, see *Narcissus triandus* var. *albus*

Angel's Trumpet, see *Datura arborea; Datura suaveolens*
Anisostichus capreolatus, see *Bignonia capreolata*
Annunciation Lily, see *Lilium candidum*
ANTHEMIS [AN-thee-miss] (Camomile, Chamomile) 66–67
  nobilis 66
  Sancti-Johannis 67
  tinctoria (Golden Marguerite) 67; *66*
ANTIRRHINUM [anti-RY-num] (Snapdragon) 67–72
  asarina (syn. *Asarina procumbens*) 71; *69*
  glutinosum 71
  majus (Snapdragon) 71–72; *70*
aphids 1149
Apocynaceae (family)
  Mandevilla 838–840; *Nerium* 898–904; *Trachelospermum* 1295–1297; *Vinca* 1361–1365
Appalachian Tea, see *Viburnum cassinoides*
Apple, Crab, see *Malus*
Apple, May, see *Passiflora incarnata*
Apple, Wild, see *Malus pumila*
Apple Rose, see *Rosa pomifera*
Apricot, see *Prunus Armeniaca*
Apricot, Japanese, see *Prunus mume*
Apuleius, on oleander 901; on peony 934
AQUILEGIA [ack-will-EEJ-jeeya] (Columbine) 72–79
  alpina 76
  caerulea 76; *73*
  canadensis 76; *78*
  chrysantha 78; *77*
  pyrenaica (syn. *A. einseleana*) 78
  skinneri 78
  vulgaris 78–79; *75*
ARABIS [AR-ra-biss] (Rock Cress) 79–82
  alpina (syn. *A. verna*) 80; *81*
  x *arendsii* (syn. *A. aubrietioides* x *A. caucasica*) 80
  blepharophylla 80
  caucasica (syn. *A. albida;* Wall Cress) 80, 82
Araceae (family)
  Zantedeschia 1388–1392
ARCTOTIS [ARK-toe-tiss] 82–85
  acaulis (syn. *A. scapigera*) 83; *84*
  anthemoides, see *Ursinia anthemoides*
  breviscapa (syn. *A. leptorhiza* var. *breviscapa*) 83
  stoechadifolia (African Daisy) 83, 86
Ardoino, H., work with *Cytisus* 351
Arends, Georg, 99
Argyocytisus, see *Cytisus battandieri*
Aristophanes 1368
Armeniaca mume, see *Prunus mume*
Armeniaca vulgaris, see *Prunus Armeniaca*
ARMERIA [ar-MEER-eeya] (Thrift, Sea Pink) 85–87
  caespitosa 86
  maritima (syns. *A. vulgaris, Statice maritima, Statice pubescens*) 86
  plantaginea (syns. *A. alliacea, Statice alliacea, Statice dianthoides*) 87
  pseudoarmeria (syns. *A. plantaginea, A. montana, A. latifolia, Statice pseudoarmeria*) 87
Art Nouveau 942
Athens, violet as emblem of 1368
Artichoke, Jerusalem, see *Helianthus tuberosus*
Arum Lily, see *Zantedeschia aethiopica*
Asclepiadaceae (family)
  Asclepias 87–90
ASCLEPIAS [ask-KLEE-peeyus] (Milkweed) 87–90
  curassavica (Blood Flower) 88
  incarnata (Swamp Milkweed, Rose Milkweed) 89
  speciosa (syn. *A. douglasii*) 89
  syriaca (syn. *A. cornuti;* Silk Plant) 89
  tuberosa (Butterfly Weed) 90; *88*
Asiatic Globe Flower, see *Trollius asiaticus*
ASTER [ass-TERR] 90–98
  alpinus (Rock Aster) 92; *93*
  amellus (Italian Aster) 94; *94*
  bergerianus, see *Felicia bergeriana*
  capensis, see *Felicia amelloides*
  ericoides (Heath Aster) 94
  x *frikartii* 95
  novae-angliae (New England Aster) 95
  novi-belgii (New York Aster, Michaelmas Daisy) 95; *97*
  rotundifolius, see *Felicia amelloides*
  sinensis, see *Callistephus chinensis*
  staticifolius 96; *96*
  tenellus, see *Felicia tenella*
  tradescantii 98
  yunnanensis 98
  Also see *Callistephus*
Aster, Annual, see *Callistephus chinensis*
Aster, China, see *Callistephus chinensis*
Aster, Heath, see *Aster ericoides*
Aster, Italian, see *Aster amellus*
Aster, Mexican, see *Cosmos*
Aster, New England, see *Aster novae-angliae*
Aster, New York, see *Aster novi-belgii*
ASTILBE [as-TILL-bee] (Florist's Spirea) 98–102
  x *arendsii* 99–100
  astilboides (syn. *Spiraea astilboides*) 100
  davidi (syn. *A. chinensis* var. *davidi*) 100
  japonica (syn. *Spiraea japonica*) 100; *101*
  lemoinei 100
  rosea 102
  thunbergii 102
Atragene alpina, see *Clematis alpina*
Atragene macropetala, see *Clematis macropetala*
aubergine 1231
Aubriet, Claude, 102
AUBRIETIA [aw-BREE-shah] (Purple Rock Cress) 102; *102*
Auricula, see *Primula*
Aurinia saxatile, see *Alyssum saxatile*
Australian Pea, see *Dolichos lignosus*
Avens, see *Geum*
Azalea, see *Rhododendron*
Azalea, Belgian, see *Rhododendron simsii*
Azalea, Exbury Hybrid, 1119
Azalea, Florist's, see *Rhododendron simsii*
Azalea, Ghent, 1119
Azalea, Indian, see *Rhododendron simsii*
Azalea, Knap Hill Hybrid, 1119
Azalea, Kurume, 1120; *1121*
Azalea, Rothschild Hybrids, 1119
Azalea mollis, see *Rhododendron molle*
Aztec Marigold, see *Tagetes erecta*

1435

Baby Blue Eyes, see *Nemophila*
Baby's Breath, see *Gypsophila*
Bachelor's Button, see
  *Chrysanthemum
  Parthenium; Centaurea
  Cyanus*
Bailey, L. H., on *Berberis* 118; on
  Daphne 366; on *Hibiscus*
  591; on *Schizanthus* 1206; on
  Syringa 1262
Bailey's Mimosa, see *Acacia
  baileyana*
Baker, John Gilbert, on *Paeonia*
  930
Balloon Flower, see *Platycodon
  grandiflorus*
Balm, Bee, see *Monarda didyma*
Balm, Red, see *Monarda didyma*
Balsam, see *Impatiens*
Balsaminaceae (family)
  Impatiens 643–651
Banister, Rev. John, work with
  Magnolia 819;
  Rhododendron 1094
Banks, Sir Joseph, work with
  Acacia verticillata 12;
  Chaenomeles 216;
  Hydrangea 623; *Magnolia*
  819; peonies 932;
  Rhododendron 1094
Barbados Lily, see *Hippeastrum*
Barberini, Cardinal, garden of
  784
Barberry, see *Berberis*
Barberry, Japanese, see *Berberis
  thunbergii*
Barberry, Magellan, see *Berberis
  buxifolia*
Barberton Daisy, see *Gerbera*
Barrenwort, see *Epimedium*
Bartonia, see *Mentzelia*
Bartram, John, work with
  Rhododendron 1093
Bartram, William, work with
  Magnolia 823
Basket Flower, see *Centaurea*
Basket-of-Gold, see *Alyssum
  saxatile*
Battandier, Jules Aimé, 353
Bauhin, Gaspard, 13
Bay, Swamp, see *Magnolia
  virginiana*
Bay, Sweet, see *Magnolia
  virginiana*
Bay, White, see *Magnolia
  virginiana*
Beach Goldenrod, see *Solidago
  sempervirens*
Bean, W. J., on *Clematis* 256;
  species named for 353; names
  Erica 447; on *Magnolia* 818,

824; on *Malus niedzwetzkyana*
  834; on *Malus prunifolia* 834;
  on *Poncirus trifoliata* 1029;
  on *Prunus lannesiana* 1064
Bean Tree, see *Laburnum*
Beard Tongue, see *Penstemon*
Beaufort, Duchess of, introduces
  Teucrium fruticans 1281
Beauty Bush, see *Kolkwitzia
  amabilis*
Beaver Tree, see *Magnolia
  virginiana*
Bedinghaus (gardener to the Duc
  d'Aremberg), work with
  Gladiolus 530
Bee Balm, see *Monarda*
Bee Plant, see *Cleome serrulata*
Beefsteak Saxifrage, see
  Saxifraga sarmentosa
beetles, Japanese, 1150
Beggar Lice, see *Desmodium
  canadense*
Beggar Ticks, see *Desmodium
  canadense*
Beggarweed, see *Desmodium
  purpureum*
Bégon, Michel, 104
BEGONIA [begg-OH-neeya]
  103–112
  evansiana 106
  rex 103–104; *105*
  semperflorens (syn. *B.
  semperflorens-cultorum;*
  Wax Begonia) 104, 106–108;
  109
  socotrana 104; *104*
  tuberosa (syn. *B.
  tuberhybrida;* Tuberous
  Begonia) 104, 108, 110–112;
  107; 110; 111
Begonia, Tuberous, see *Begonia
  tuberosa*
Begonia, Wax, see *Begonia
  semperflorens*
Begoniaceae (family)
  Begonia 103–112
Bell, Léonie, see Wilson and Bell
Belladonna Lily, see *Amaryllis*
Bellevalia romana, see *Hyacinthus
  romanus*
Bellflower, Chinese, see
  Platycodon grandiflorus
Bellflower, Japanese, see
  Platycodon grandiflorus
BELLIS [BELL-iss] 112–117
  perennis (Daisy, English Daisy)
  113–117; *113; 115*
  rotundifolia 117
Bélon, Pierre, describes lilacs 1260
Benary (German gardener), work
  with pansies 1368

Bentham, George, work with
  Nemophila 894
Benthamia fragifera, see *Cornus
  capitata*
Bentinok, William, work with
  Genista 507
Berberidaceae (family)
  Berberis 117–126; *Epimedium*
  434–437
BERBERIS [BUR-berr-iss]
  (Barberry) 117–126
  aristata 121
  buxifolia (syn. *B. dulcis;*
  Magellan Barberry) 124; *118*
  candidula 124–125
  darwinii 125; *122*
  gagnepainii 125; *120*
  linearifolia 125
  lologensis 125
  polyantha 121, 123
  rubrostilla 123; *121*
  stenophylla 125–126
  thunbergii 123; *119*
  vulgaris 118, 123; *117*
  wilsoniae 124
Bergamot, see *Monarda*
Bergamot, Wild, see *Monarda
  fistulosa*
Bergenia [berr-JEAN-eeya]
  ("saxifrage") 1194
Bermuda Buttercup, see *Oxalis
  cernua*
Bernet, Edouard, work with
  Cistus 246
Bethlehem, Star of, see
  Ornithogalum nutans
Bidens atrosanguinea, see
  Cosmos atrosanguineus
Bidens dahlioides, see *Cosmos
  diversifolius*
Bidens diversifolia, see *Cosmos
  diversifolius*
Big Marigold, see *Tagetes erecta*
Bignon, Abbé Paul, species
  named for 126
BIGNONIA [big-NO-neeya]
  capreolata (syns.
  *Anisostichus capreolatus,
  Doxantha capreolata;*
  Trumpet Flower, Cross-Vine,
  Quarter Vine) 126–129; *127*
Bignonia chinensis, see *Campsis
  grandiflora*
Bignonia radicans, see *Campsis
  radicans*
Bignoniaceae (family)
  Bignonia capreolata 126–129;
  Campsis 182–186; *Incarvillea*
  651–654; *Tecoma* 1276–1279
bignonias 1278
Bindweed, see *Convolvulus*

Birds' Eyes, see *Veronica chamaedrys*
Bird's-Foot Viola, see *Viola pedata*
Bisset, work with *Rhododendron* 1112
Bitterwort, see *Gentiana lutea*
Bivena-Bernardi, Baron Antonio, work with *Genista* 507
Black Cosmos, see *Cosmos diversifolius*
Black-Eyed Susan, see *Rudbeckia hirta; Thunbergia alata*
Black Haw *(Viburnum prunifolium)* 1353
Black Sampson, see *Echinacea purpurea*
black spot (fungus disease) 1147
Blackthorn, see *Prunus spinosa*
Black-throated Calla, see *Zantedeschia melanoleuca*
Blackwood, see *Acacia melanoxylon*
Black Yarrow, see *Achillea atrata*
Bladder Cherry, see *Physalis alkekengi*
Bladder Nut, see *Staphylea*
Blankeslee, Dr. A. F., work with *Rudbeckia* 1178
Blanket Flower, see *Gaillardia*
Blazing Star, see *Tritonia; Liatris; Mentzelia laevicaulis*
Bleeding Heart, see *Dicentra*
Bletia, see *Bletilla*
BLETILLA [blet-TILL-a] (Bletia) 129–130
   hyacinthina (syns. *B. striata, Bletia hyacinthina*; Hardy Chinese Orchid) 129–130; *129*
Blister Cresses, see *Cheiranthus*
Blood-Flower, see *Asclepias curassavica*
Blossom, Blue, see *Ceanothus thyrsiflorus*
Bluebeard, see *Caryopteris*
Bluebell, see *Clematis crispa; Scilla*
Bluebell, Californian, see *Phacelia viscida*
Bluebell, English, see *Scilla non-scripta*
Bluebell, Spanish, see *Scilla Hispanica*
Blue Blazing Star, see *Liatris scariosa*
Blue Blossom, see *Ceanothus thyrsiflorus*

Bluebottle, see *Centaurea Cyanus*
Blue Daisy, see *Felicia amelloides*
Blue Dawn Flower, see *Ipomoea mutabilis*
Bock, Hieronymus, 13, 43, 1010
Boerner, Eugene, on *Crataegus* 322; on *Daphne* 366
Bolboxalis cernuus, see *Oxalis cernua*
Bonavist, see *Dolichos Lablab*
Bonnet, Blue, see *Centaurea Cyanus*
Bonsai method of cultivation 1064, 1385
Book of Changes (I Ching) 13
Booth, C. P. *(Encyclopedia of Annual and Biennial Garden Plants)* 1273
Boraginaceae (family)
   Anchusa 54–56; *Echium* 427–428; *Heliotropium* 572–575; *Lithospermum* 781–784; *Myosotis* 873–877
Borzot (French gardener), work with *Impatiens Balsamina* 646
Bosio, Giacomo, on *Passiflora* 953
Bossin *(Les plantes bulbeuses),* on *Hyacinthus* 616
Bottle-Brush Flower, see *Callistemon*
Bougainville, Louis Antoine de, genus named for 130
BOUGAINVILLEA [boo-gehn-VILL-eeya] 130–132
   glabra 131
   hybrida 132
   spectabilis 131; *130*
Bouncing Bet, see *Saponaria officinalis*
Bowers, Faubion, on chrysanthemums 228
Bowles, E. A., work with *Hamamelis* 549
Boxwood, see *Cornus florida*
Brazilian Morning Glory, see *Ipomoea stans*
Brazilian Spider Flower, see *Tibouchina semidecandra*
Breeder Tulips 1328
Breynius, Jacob, describes chrysanthemums in his *Prodromus* 228
Bridal Wreath, see *Spiraea prunifolia*
Brimeura amethystina, see *Hyacinthus amethystinus*

Brimeura fastigiata, see *Hyacinthus fastigiatus*
broccoli 582
Brontë, Emily (heather in *Wuthering Heights*) 153–154
Broom, see *Cytisus; Genista*
Broom, Spanish, see *Spartium junceum*
Broom, Weaver's, see *Spartium junceum*
"Broomfield Hill" (Scottish ballad) 348
Brunfels, Otto, 120
Brunnera macrophylla, see *Anchusa myosotidiflora*
Bryant, Charles *(Flora Diatetica* and pomegranates) 1078
Buckbrush, see *Ceanothus*
Buckeye, Dwarf, see *Aesculus parviflora*
Buddle, Rev. Adam, genus named for 133
BUDDLEIA [BUDD-leeya] (Butterfly Bush) 132–139
   alternifolia 136; *133*
   asiatica 136
   auriculata 136–137
   colvilei 137
   davidii (syn. *B. variabilis; Summer Lilac*) 137–138; *135*
   globosa 138; *134*
   madagascariensis 138–139
Bugloss, see *Anchusa*
Bull Bay, see *Magnolia grandiflora*
Bunchberry, see *Cornus canadensis*
Bunge, Dr. Alexander von, covers *Caryopteris* 191; work with *Ceratostigma* 211; *Jasminum* 689
Burchell, W. J., 136
Burman, Johannes *(Rariarum Africanorum Plantarium)* 960
Burnet Rose, see *Rosa spinosissima*
Burns, Robert, on daisies 112
Busbecq, Ogier de, 992; work with lilacs 1260; tulips 1310
Bush, F. A., on *Daphne* 366
Bush Marigold, see *Tagetes tenuifolia*
Bush Moonflower, see *Ipomoea leptophylla*
Bush Trefoil, see *Desmodium canadense*
Busy Lizzie, see *Impatiens*
Butter-and-Eggs, see *Linaria vulgaris*
Buttercup, see *Ranunculus bulbosus*

Buttercup, Bermuda, see *Oxalis cernua*
Butterfly Bush, see *Buddleia*
Butterfly Flower, see *Schizanthus*
Butterfly Weed, see *Asclepias tuberosa*
Button Snakeroot, see *Eryngium yuccaefolium*

Cabbage, Saint Patrick's, see *Saxifraga umbrosa*
CALCEOLARIA [kal-see-o-LAIR-eeya] (Slipperwort, Pouch Flower) 139–143
 amplexicaulis 141; *142*
 biflora (syn. *C. plantaginea*) 141
 darwinii 141
 fuchsiaefolia 140
 herbeohybrida 143; *139*
 integrifolia (syn. *C. rugosa*) 140
 polyrrhiza (syn. *C. acutifolia*) 141
 violacea 140
CALENDULA [kal-END-yew-la] (Marigold) 144–146
 arvensis 145
 chrysanthemifolia, see *Dimorphotheca chrysanthemifolia*
 officinalis 144; *144*
Calico Bush, see *Kalmia*
California Poppy, see *Eschscholzia; Romneya coulteri*
California Windbreak, see *Lavatera assurgentiflora*
Californian Bluebell, see *Phacelia viscida*
Calla, Black-throated, see *Zantedeschia melanoleuca*
Calla, Golden, see *Zantedeschia elliottiana*
Calla, Pink, see *Zantedeschia rehmannii*
Calla, Rose, see *Zantedeschia rehmannii*
Calla, Spotted, see *Zantedeschia albomaculata*
Calla Lily, see *Zantedeschia aethiopica*
Calliopsis, see *Coreopsis*
CALLISTEMON [kal-iss-TEE-mon] (Bottle-Brush Flower) 146–148
 citrinus (syn. *C. lanceolatus*) 148; *147*

hortensis, see *Callistephus chinensis*
 salignus 148
 speciosus (syn. *Metrosideros speciosus*) 148
CALLISTEPHUS [kal-ISS-tee-fuss] *chinensis* (syns. *Aster sinensis, Callistemon hortensis, Callistephus hortensis;* Annual Aster, China Aster) 148–153; *149; 151; 153;* Also see *Aster*
CALLUNA [kal-LOON-ah] *vulgaris* (syn. *Erica vulgaris;* Scotch Heather, Heath, Ling) 153–156; *155*
CALONYCTION [kal-o-NIK-teeyon] (Moonflower) 157–159
 aculeatum (syns. *C. speciosum, Ipomoea latiflora, I. bona-nox, I. childsii, I. noctiflora, I. mexicana, I. grandiflora* var. *alba;* Moonflower) 159; *158*
 muricatum (syns. *C. speciosum* var. *muricatum, Convolvulus muricatus, Convolvulus petiolaris, Ipomoea muricata;* Moonflower) 159
Calystegia pubescens, see *Convolvulus japonicus*
Calystegia sepium, see *Convolvulus sepium*
CAMELLIA [kam-EEL-ya] 159–173, 495
 japonica (syn. *Thea japonica;* Common Camellia) 170, 172; *162; 167*
 maliflora (McCaskill Camellia) 172; *171*
 reticulata (syn. *Thea reticulata*) 172
 saluenensis 173
 sasanqua (sanangua) 160, 165, 173; *164*
 sinensis (syn. *Camellia thea*) 173; *161*
Camellia, Common, see *Camellia japonica*
Camellia, McCaskill, see *Camellia maliflora*
Camomile, 13; also see *Anthemis*
CAMPANULA [kam-PAN-new-la] 174–183
 carpatica 176; *176*
 cochlearifolia (syn. *C. pulsilla*) 176; *174*
 fragilis 176; *174*
 garganica 176

 glomerata 178; *174*
 isophylla 178
 lactiflora 178
 latifolia 178
 medium (Canterbury Bells) 179; *179*
 mollis 179; *181*
 persicifolia 179–180; *177*
 portenschlagiana (syn. *C. muralis*) 180
 pyramidalis 175, 180; *175*
 rapunculus 180; *180*
 rotundifolia 182; *175*
 speculum, see *Specularia speculum*
 Trachelium 182
 x *van houttei* (syn. *C. punctata*) 182
Campanulaceae (family) 1243
 Campanula 174–182; *Lobelia* 784–790; *Platycodon grandiflorus* 1017–1020; *Specularia* 1241–1243
Campion, see *Lychnis; Silene*
Campion, Moss, see *Silene schafta*
CAMPSIS [KAMP-sis] (Trumpet Vine, Trumpet Creeper) 182–186, 1278
 grandiflora (syns. *Tecoma grandiflora, Tecoma chinensis, Bignonia chinensis, Campsis adrepens, Campsis chinensis;* Trumpet Vine, Trumpet Creeper) 185
 radicans (syns. *Bignonia radicans, Tecoma radicans;* Chinese Trumpet Creeper) 183, 185; *184*
 x *tagliabuana* (syns. *Tecoma radicans* var. *grandiflora-purpurea, Tecoma grandiflora* var. *rubra; Campsis* Hybrids) 185–186
Canada Potato, see *Helianthus tuberosus*
Canary Bird Flower, see *Tropaeolum peregrinum*
Canary Creeper, see *Tropaeolum peregrinum*
Candied Rose Petals, recipe for 1141
Candle Wick, see *Verbascum thapsus*
Candolle, Augustin de, on *Hibiscus* 591; on *Kerria japonica* 700; work with *Lavandula* 736; *Platycodon* 1017
Candytuft, see *Iberis*
CANNA [KAN-na] 186–188

indica 187–188; *187*
Cannaceae (family)
  Canna 186–188
Canterbury Bells, see *Campanula medium*
Cape Figwort, see *Phygelius*
Cape Fuchsia, see *Phygelius*
Cape Gooseberry, see *Physalis peruviana*
Cape Jasmine, see *Gardenia jasminoides*
Cape Marguerite, see *Dimorphotheca*
Cape Marigold, see *Dimorphotheca*
Caper, see *Capparis*
Capparidaceae (family)
  Capparis 188–190; *Cleome* 270–271
CAPPARIS [KAP-par-iss] (Caper) 188–190
  spinosa 190; *189*
Caprifoliaceae (family)
  Abelia 1–2; *Diervilla* 409–410; *Kolkwitzia amabilis* 710–712; *Lonicera* 792–805; *Viburnum* 1352–1361; *Weigela* 1377–1383
Cardinal Flower, see *Lobelia cardinalis*
Cardiocrinum giganteum, see *Lilium giganteum*
Carnation, see *Dianthus*
Carolina Kidney Bean, see *Wistaria frutescens*
Carpobrotus acinaciformis, see *Mesembryanthemum acinaciforme*
Carpobrotus edulis, see *Mesembryanthemum edule*
Caryophyllaceae (family)
  Cerastium 209–210; *Dianthus* 394–405; *Gypsophila* 543–546; *Lychnis* 813–818; *Saponaria* 1190–1193; *Silene* 1225–1228
CARYOPTERIS [kar-ry-OP-ter-iss] (Blue Spirea, Bluebeard) 191–193
  x *clandonensis* (syn. *C. Mastacanthus* x *Caryopteris mongholica*) 192–193
  Mastacanthus (syn. *C. incana*) 192; *191*
  mongholica 192
CASSIA [KASS-eeya] (Senna) 193–195
  artemisioides 193
  corymbosa 195; *194*
  marilandica (Wild Senna, American Senna) 195
  tomentosa 195
Castalis tragus, see *Dimorphotheca aurantiaca*
Catchfly, see *Lychnis; Silene*
Catchfly, Sweet William, see *Silene Armeria*
caterpillars 1150
Catesby, Mark, on *Campsis* 183; on *Magnolia* 819; work with *Kalmia* 695; work with *Wistaria* 1383
Cathcartia integrifolia, see *Meconopsis integrifolia*
Catmint, see *Nepeta*
Catnip, see *Nepeta*
cats, plants attractive to, see *Actinidia polygama* and *Nepeta cataria*
Cat's-tail Speedwell, see *Veronica spicata*
cauliflower 582
Cavanilles, Abbé, work with *Dahlia* 356, 359
CEANOTHUS [see-an-O-thuss] (Wild Lilac, Buckbrush) 195–203
  americanus (New Jersey Tea, Indian Tea, Walpole Tea, Redroot) 198
  x *burkwoodii* 200
  coeruleus (syn. *C. azureus*) 198; *199*
  cyaneus 200–201
  x *delilianus* 198
  dentatus 201
  fendleri 200
  Hybrids 202–203
  papillosus 201
  prostratus (Mahala Mat) 201
  rigidus 201–202
  thyrsiflorus (Blue Blossom, Blue Myrtle, California Lilac) 202
  x *veitchianus* 202
CELOSIA [sell-O-seeya]
  argentea (Cockscomb) 203–204; *203*
CENTAUREA [senn-TORR-eeya] (Knapweed, Centaury, Basket Flower) 204–209
  americana (Basket Flower) 207
  babylonica 207
  candidissima (syns. *C. rutifolia, C. Cineraria;* Dusty Miller) 207–208
  Cyanus (syn. *C. arvensis;* Bachelor's Button, Cornflower, Bluebonnet, Ragged Sailor, Blue Bonnet) 208; *205*
  gymnocarpa 208
  macrocephala 208
  montana (Mountain Blue) 208–209; *206*
  moschata (syns. *C. odorata, Amberboa moschata;* Sweet Sultan) 209; *205*
  nigra (Knapweed, Hardhead, Spanish Button) 209
Centaury, see *Centaurea*
Centranthus rubra 1336, 1337
Cephalophora aromatica, see *Helenium aromaticum*
CERASTIUM [serr-ASS-teeyum] (Snow in Summer) 209–210
  tomentosum 210; *210*
Cerasus incisa, see *Prunus incisa*
Cerasus lannesiana, see *Prunus lannesiana*
Cerasus pennsylvanica, see *Prunus pennsylvanica*
Cerasus sylvestris, see *Prunus avium*
Cerasus vulgaris, see *Prunus Cerasus*
CERATOSTIGMA [serr-at-OSS-tigma] (Plumbago, Leadwort, Moustache Plant) 210–214
  griffithii 212
  plumbaginoides (syns. *Valoradia plumbaginoides, Plumbago larpentae*) 212; *213*
  willmottianum 212, 214
  Also see *Plumbago*
Ceres, hyacinth consecrated to 616
Cesalpino, Andrea, work with *Rhododendron* 1093
CESTRUM [SESS-trum] 214–215
  aurantiacum 215
  diurnum (Day Jasmine) 215
  elegans (syns. *C. purpureum, Habrothamnum elegans;* Coral Jasmine, Purple Cestrum) 215; *214*
  newellii 215
  nocturnum (Night Jasmine, Queen of the Night) 215
  parqui (Willow-leaved Jasmine) 215
Cestrum, Purple, see *Cestrum elegans*
CHAENOMELES [kee-NOM-eh-leez] (Flowering Quince) 216–221
  x *Californica* 219
  cathayensis 219
  Hybrids 221
  japonica (Japanese Quince, Japanese Dwarf Quince,

1439

Japonica) 219–220; *217*
sinensis (Chinese Quince) 220
speciosa (syn. *C. lagenaria*)
220; *218*
x *superba* 221
Chain, Golden, see *Laburnum*
Chalk Plant, see *Gypsophila paniculata*
Chamaecerasus nitida, see *Lonicera nitida*
Chamaecerasus pileata, see *Lonicera pileata*
Chamomile, see *Anthemis*
Chaparral Lily, see *Lilium rubescens*
Char de Venus, see *Aconitum*
Charlemagne 668, 751, 910, 1132
Chaste Tree, see *Vitex*
Chastity, Tree of, see *Vitex*
Chaucer, Geoffrey, writing on *Cornus sanguinea* 301
CHEIRANTHUS [ky-RAN-thuss] (Wallflower, Blister Cresses) 221–224
   x *allionii* (syns. *Erysimum allionii, Erysimum asperum;* Siberian Wallflower) 223–224
   Cheiri (Wallflower) 224; *222*
   linifolius (syn. *Erysimum linifolium;* Alpine Wallflower) 224
Chelone barbata, see *Penstemon barbatus*
chemical fertilizers xxxi–xxxiv
Cherokee Rose, see *Rosa laevigata*
Cherry, Bird, see *Prunus Padus*
Cherry, Bladder, see *Physalis alkekengi*
Cherry, Common Sweet, see *Prunus avium*
Cherry, Cornelian, see *Cornus Mas*
Cherry, Evergreen, see *Prunus ilicifolia*
Cherry, Flowering, see *Prunus lannesiana*
Cherry, Ground, see *Physalis pubescens*
Cherry, Hansen Bush, see *Prunus besseyi*
Cherry, Islay, see *Prunus ilicifolia*
Cherry, Jerusalem, see *Solanum Pseudocapsicum*
Cherry, Rosebud, see *Prunus subhirtella*
Cherry, Sand, see *Prunus besseyi; Prunus pumila*
Cherry, Sour, see *Prunus Cerasus*

Cherry, Wild, see *Prunus avium*
Cherry, Wild Black, see *Prunus serotina*
Cherry, Wild Red, see *Prunus pennsylvanica*
Cherry, Winter, see *Physalis alkekengi; Solanum Capsicastrum*
Cherry Pie, see *Heliotropium*
Chickasaw Plum, see *Prunus angustifolia*
Childebert I, King, 1132
Chilean Guava, see *Myrtus ugni*
China Aster, see *Callistephus*
Chincherinchee, see *Ornithogalum thyrsoides*
Chinese Bellflower, see *Abutilon; Platycodon grandiflorus*
Chinese (Globe) Flower, see *Trollius chinensis*
Chinese Gooseberry, see *Actinidia chinensis*
Chinese Lantern, see *Physalis alkekengi*
Chinese Snowball Tree, see *Viburnum macrocephalum*
Chinese Trumpet Creeper, see *Campsis radicans; Incarvillea*
Chinese Wisteria, see *Wistaria sinensis*
CHIONODOXA [ky-on-o-DOCKS-a] (Glory of the Snow) 224–225
   luciliae 225; *225*
   sardensis 225
chlorosis 499, 1149
Chocolate Flower, see *Geranium maculatum*
Choke Berry, see *Prunus serotina*
Christmas Rose, see *Helleborus*
CHRYSANTHEMUM [kriss-ANTH-em-mum] 225–244
   argenteum (syn. *Tanacetum argenteum*) 236
   carinatum (syns. *C. atrococcineum, C. tricolor*) 232, 242; *230*
   coccineum (syn. *Pyrethrum roseum;* Pyrethrum, Painted Lady, Painted Daisy) 232, 236; *235*
   coreanum (syn. *C. sibericum*) 232, 236–237; *232; 233*
   coronarium (Crown Daisy) 232, 242, 244
   frutescens (Paris Daisy, Marguerite) 232, 242; *242*
   x *hortorum* (Florist's Chrysanthemum) 233, 234, 237–238; *237; 239*

indicum 238, 240
Leucanthemum (Common Daisy, Ox-Eye Daisy, White Daisy) 233, 240; *241*
mawii 240; *243*
maximum (Shasta Daisy) 232, 240; *238*
Parthenium (syn. *Matricaria eximia;* Feverfew, Bachelor's Button) 232, 240–241
rubellum (syn. *C. erubescens*) 232, 241
segetum (Corn Marigold) 232, 244
sinense (syn. *C. morifolium*) 241; *227*
uliginosum (Moon Daisy, Giant Daisy) 232, 241
viscosum (syn. *C. viscidi-hirtum*) 232, 244
Chrysanthemum, Florist's, see *Chrysanthemum* x *hortorum*
Cibo (sixteenth-century Italian), on Tagetes 1270
Cigar Flower, see *Cuphea*
Cineraria, see *Senecio cruentus*
Cineraria cruenta, see *Senecio cruentus*
Cineraria maritima, see *Senecio maritimus*
Cinquefoil, see *Potentilla*
Cistaceae (family)
   Cistus 244–251; *Helianthemum* 555–557
CISTUS [SISS-tuss] (Rock Rose) 244–251
   albidus 249
   crispus 249
   x *cyprius* 249
   ladaniferus (Gum Cistus) 249; *251*
   laurifolius 249
   monspeliensis 250
   populifolius (syns. *C. cordifolius, C. cupanius*) 250
   x *purpureus* 250
   salvifolius 250; *245*
   villosus (syn. *C. incanus*) 250; *247*
Citrange 1029
Citrus trifoliata, see *Poncirus trifoliata*
Clarici, Paolo Bartolomeo, on *Digitalis* 411–412
Clark, Captain William, genus named for 252
CLARKIA [KLARK-eeya] 252–253
   elegans 252–253
   pulchella 253; *252*

classification of plant names xxxvi (also see nomenclature)
CLEMATIS [KLEMM-at-tiss] 253–270
  alpina (syn. *Atragene alpina*) 261; *254*
  armandii 267
  balearica (syn. *C. calycina*; Fern-leaved Clematis) 267
  chrysocoma 261
  cirrhosa (syn. *C. balearica*) 267–268
  crispa (Blue Jasmine, Bluebell, Curly Clematis) 261
  davidiana 261–262
  flammula 262
  florida 262
  Hybrids 268–270
  x *jackmanii* (Japanese Clematis) 262
  lanuginosa 263
  macropetala (syn. *Atragene macropetala*) 263
  montana 263–264
  paniculata 264
  patens (syn. *C. coerulea*) 264; *260*
  spooneri (syns. *C. montana serieea, C. chrysocoma* var. *sericea*) 264
  tangutica (syn. *C. orientalis* var. *tangutica;* Golden Clematis) 264, 266; *269*
  texensis (syn. *C. coccinea;* Scarlet Clematis) 266; *265*
  virginiana (Woodbine, Love Vine) 266
  Vitalba (Traveller's Joy, Withywind, Old Man's Beard) 266; *257*
  viticella (Virgin's Bower, Vine Bower) 266–267; *253*
Clematis, Curly, see *Clematis crispa*
Clematis, Fern-leaved, see *Clematis balearica*
Clematis, Golden, see *Clematis tangutica*
Clematis, Japanese, see *Clematis* x *jackmanii*
Clematis, Scarlet, see *Clematis texensis*
Clement of Alexandria 1130
CLEOME [klee-O-mee] 270–271
  serrulata (syn. *C. integrifolia;* Bee Plant, Stinking Clover) 271
  spinosa (syn. *C. pungens;* Spider Flower) 271; *270*
Cleopatra 1129

CLERODENDRUM [klair-o-DENN-drum] (syn. *Clerodendron*) 272–275
  bungei (syn. *C. foetidum;* Red Mexican Hydrangea, French Hydrangea) 274; *275*
  fragrans (syns. *C. coronaria, Volkameria fragrans;* Glory Tree)
  thomsonae (syn. *C. balfourii*) 275; *274*
  trichotomum (syns. *C. serotinum, Volkameria japonica;* Harlequin Glory-Bower) 275; *273*
Clifford, Derek, *Pelargoniums, Including Popular Geraniums* 961
Climbing Marigold, see *Tagetes sarmentosa*
Climbing Sailor, see *Linaria Cymbalaria*
Clock Vine, see *Thunbergia alata*
Cloth of Gold, see *Crocus susianus*
Clove, see *Dianthus*
Clusius, Carolus, work with *Clematis* 267; *Ipomoea* 659; on *Iris* 670; work with *Rhododendron* 1093; *Spiraea* 1243, 1244; raises *Syringa* 1260; *Tulipa* 1310, 1312
Coats, Alice M., on *Berberis* 120; *Buddleia* 132; *Camellia* 164, 165; *Ceratostigma* 211; *Cytisus* 349; *Lonicera* 794; *Paeonia* 929; *Rhododendron* 1096; *Spiraea* 1244
Cobbett, on *Magnolia* 819
Cobo, Barnabos, genus named for 276
COBAEA [koh-BEE-ya] (Cup and Saucer Vine, Mexican Ivy Plant) 276–278
  scandens 276, 278; *277*
Cobweb Houseleek, see *Sempervivum arachnoideum*
Cockerell, Mrs. T. D. A., work with *Helianthus* 560
Cockscomb, see *Celosia argentea*
Cockspur Thorn, see *Crataegus crus-galli*
colchicine (poisonous alkaloid found in colchicums) 279–280
COLCHICUM [KOLL-chee-kum] (Autumn Crocus, Naked Ladies, Meadow Saffron) 278–283

  agrippinum 281
  autumnale 281; *280*
  byzantinum 282
  decaisnei 282
  luteum (syn. *Synsiphon luteum*) 282
  speciosum 282–283; *279*
  variegatum 283
  Also see *Crocus*
COLEUS [KO-leeyus] 283–284
  blumei (Flame Nettle, Foliage Plant) 283–284
  thyrsoides 284
Colicroot, see *Liatris squarrosa*
Collingwood, on *Wistaria* 1384
Collinson, Peter, work with *Ceanothus* 196; *Cornus* 308; *Hamamelis* 549; *Hydrangea* 623; *Kalmia* 695; *Rhododendron* 1093, 1095; *Spartium junceum* 1241
cologne, lavender, recipe for 732
Colosseum (Rome) 616
Columbine, see *Aquilegia*
Colvile, Sir James, 133
Colville and Company (nursery of Chelsea) 530, 961
Comber, H. F., 120, 125, 918
Commerson, P., work with *Hydrangea* 623; discovers *Nicotiana* 982
complete fertilizers xxxiii
Compositae (family)
  Achillea 12–19; Ageratum 35–36; Anthemus 66–67; Arctotis 82–85; Aster 90–98; Bellis 112–117; Calendula 144–146; Callistephus chinensis 148–153; Centaurea 204–209; Chrysanthemum 225–244; Coreopsis (Calliopsis) 295–300; Cosmos 309–312; Dahlia 355–364; Dimorphotheca 415–419; Doronicum 421–422; Echinacea 422–425; Felicia 459–462; Gaillardia 491–493; Gazania 502–506; Gerbera 524–526; Helenium 551–555; Helianthus 557–565; Helichrysum 565–569; Heliopsis 569–572; Leontopodium 740–742; Liatris 746–749; Olearia 917–919; Rudbeckia 1173–1178; Sanvitalia 1188–1189; Senecio 1218–1225; Solidago 1235–1237; Tagetes 1268–1274; Tithonia 1292–1293; Ursinia 1333–

1441

1335; *Venidium* 1337–1338;
   Zinnia 1393–1396
Compton, Bishop, cultivates
   Ceanothus 196; cultivates
   Rhododendron 1094
Cone Flower, see *Echinacea;
   Rudbeckia laciniata*
Cone Flower, Orange, see
   Rudbeckia fulgida
Cone Flower, Sweet, see
   Rudbeckia subtomentosa
Confederate Jasmine, see
   Trachelospermum
Confucius 1129
CONVALLARIA [kon-val-AIR-
   eeya] 285–287
   japonica (syn. *Ophiopogon
      japonicus;* Lily Turf, Mondo)
      285–286; *286*
   majalis (Lily of the Valley)
      286–287; *286*
Convolvulaceae (family)
   Calonyction 157–159;
   Convolvulus 287–295;
   Ipomoea 656–667;
   Quamoclit 1083–1085
CONVOLVULUS [kon-VOLL-
   view-lus] (Morning Glory,
   Bindweed) 287–295
   althaeoides 289; *288*
   arvensis (Lesser Bindweed,
      Field Bindweed) 289;
      293
   cneorum (syn. *C. argenteus*)
      289, 291
   floridus 291
   hederaceus, see *Ipomoea
      hederacea*
   japonicus (syn. *Calystegia
      pubescens;* California Rose)
      291
   majus, see *Ipomoea purpurea*
   mauritanicus 292
   muricatus, see *Calonyction
      muricatum*
   mutabilis, see *Ipomoea
      purpurea*
   Nil, see *Ipomoea Nil*
   pentapetaloides (Five-flowered
      Bindweed) 292; *294*
   petiolaris, see *Calonyction
      muricatum*
   pinnatus, see *Quamoclit
      pennata*
   purpureus, see *Ipomoea
      purpurea*
   sepium (syn. *Calystegia
      sepium;* Rutland Beauty,
      Hedge Bindweed) 292
   soldanella (Sea Convolvulus)
      292–293; *293*

   tricolor (Dwarf Morning Glory)
      293, 295; *290*
   Also see *Ipomoea*
Convolvulus, Sea, see
   Convolvulus soldanella
Cootamundra Wattle, see *Acacia
   baileyana*
Coral Bells, see *Heuchera*
Corchorus japonicus, see *Kerria
   japonica*
COREOPSIS [kore-ee-YOP-siss]
   (syn. *Calliopsis;* Tick-Seed)
   295–300
   auriculata 297
   bigelovii (syn. *Leptosyne
      bigelovii*) 298
   delphinifolia 297
   douglasii (syn. *Leptosyne
      bigelovii*) 298
   drummondii (syn. *C.
      diversifolia;* Golden Wave)
      298
   grandiflora 297
   lanceolata 297; *296*
   maritima (syn. *Leptosyne
      maritima;* Sea Dahlia) 297
   nuecensis 298
   rosea (Swamp Tick-Seed) 298
   stillmanii (syn. *Leptosyne
      stillmanii*) 300
   tinctoria (syns. *C. bicolor, C.
      elegans;* Golden Coreopsis)
      300; *299*
   verticillata 298
Coreopsis, Golden, see *Coreopsis
   tinctoria*
Corn, Squirrel, see *Dicentra
   canadensis*
Corn, Turkey, see *Dicentra
   canadensis*
Cornaceae (family)
   Cornus 300–308
Cornel, see *Cornus*
Cornflag, see *Gladiolus segetum*
Cornflower, see *Centaurea
   Cyanus*
CORNUS [KOR-nus] (Dogwood,
   Cornel) 300–308
   alba (Tartarian Dogwood) 306
   canadensis (Bunchberry,
      Crackerberry) 308; *307*
   capitata (syn. *Benthamia
      fragifera;* Bentham's Cornel)
      304
   florida (Flowering Dogwood,
      Boxwood) 304; *302*
   Kousa (Japanese Dogwood)
      305
   Mas (Cornelian Cherry) 303–
      304; *303*
   nuttallii (Pacific Dogwood) 305

   sanguinea (Red Dogwood,
      Common Dogwood) 306
   stolonifera (Red Osier
      Dogwood) 306
Correns, Carl Erich, uses
   Mirabilis 866
Correvon, Henry, writing on
   Clematis 255; on
   Lithospermum 781; on poppies
   944; work with *Rosa roulettii*
   1164; on *Saponaria
   ocymoides* 1191; on *Vinca*
   1362
CORYLOPSIS [kore-ee-LOPP-
   siss] (Winter Hazel) 308–309
   glabrescens (syn. *C. gotoana*)
      309
   pauciflora 309
   spicata 309; *308*
COSMOS [KOS-mose] (Mexican
   Aster) 309–312
   atrosanguineus (syns. *C.
      diversifolius* var.
      *atrosanguinea, Bidens
      atrosanguinea, Dahlia
      zimapanii*) 310
   bipinnatus 310, 312; *309*
   diversifolius (syns. *Bidens
      diversifolia, Bidens
      dahlioides;* Black Cosmos)
      312; *311*
   sulphureus 312
Cosmos, Black, see *Cosmos
   diversifolius*
Costa Rica Nightshade, see
   Solanum wendlandii
COTONEASTER [ko-tohn-ee-
   ASS-ter] 312–322, 1080
   adpressa 313
   bullata 315
   buxifolia 318
   conspicua 318
   x *cornubia* 318
   dammeri 320
   dielsiana (syn. *C. applanta*)
      315
   divaricata 315
   foveolata 315
   franchetii 320
   frigida 316
   glaucophylla 316
   henryana 320
   horizontalis 316; *313*
   hupehensis 316
   lactea 320
   lucida 316
   microphylla 320; *319*
   moupinensis 317
   multiflora 317
   nitens 317
   pannosa 321; *314*

racemiflora 317
rhytidophylla 321
rotundifolia 317
salicifolia 321
simonsii 318
watereri 321
zabelii 318
Cottage Tulips 1329
Cottingham, Captain, 2
Cotton Rose, see *Hibiscus mutabilis*
Coulter, Dr. T., work with *Romneya coulteri* 1125
Cowper, William, mignonette in poem of 1090
Cowslip, see *Primula*
Crab, American, see *Malus coronaria*
Crab, Eley, see *Malus* x *eleyi*
Crab, Garland, see *Malus coronaria*
Crab, Iowa, see *Malus ionensis*
Crab, Oregon, see *Malus rivularis*
Crab, Prairie, see *Malus ionensis*
Crab, Showy, see *Malus floribunda*
Crab, Siberian, see *Malus baccata*
Crab, Sweet, see *Malus coronaria*
Crab, Toringo, see *Malus sieboldii*
Crab Apple, see *Malus*
Crackerberry, see *Cornus canadensis*
Cramp Bark, see *Viburnum opulus* 1353
Cranberry Tree, see *Viburnum opulus*
Cranesbill, see *Geranium*
Crape Myrtle, see *Lagerstroemia*
Crassulaceae (family)
  Sedum 1212–1215;
  Sempervivum 1215–1218
CRATAEGUS [krat-EE-gus] (Hawthorn, Quick, May, Thorn, Thornapple) 322–330, 1080
  azarolus (syn. *C. Aronia*) 325
  x *Carrierei* 326
  coccinea (Scarlet Haw) 326; *325*
  crus-galli (Cockspur Thorn) 326, 328; *324*
  heterophylla 328; *327*
  mollis (Red Haw) 328
  monogyna (Quick, May, Hawthorn) 328–329
  nitida 329
  Oxyacantha (syn. *C.*

  oxyacanthoides; Hawthorn) 322, 329; *323*
  phaenopyrum (syn. *C. cordata;* Washington Thorn) 329
  prunifolia 330
Creeper, Trumpet, see *Tecoma*
Crepe Myrtle, see *Lagerstroemia*
Cress, Purple Rock, see *Aubrietia*
Cretan Spikenard, see *Valeriana phu*
Crete, villa at Amnisos 750
Crocosmia x *crocosmiiflora* 1297
Crocosmia pottsii, see *Tritonia pottsii*
CROCUS [KRO-kuss] 330–338, 1297
  aureus (Dutch Yellow Crocus) 335; *334*
  biflorus 335; *331*
  byzantinus 336
  chrysanthus 335
  Hybrids 337–338
  imperati 335
  korolkowi 336
  kotschyanus (syn. *C. zonatus*) 336–337
  longiflorus 337
  sativus (Saffron) 337
  sieberi 336
  speciosus 337; *337*
  susianus (Cloth of Gold) 336
  tomasinianus 336
  vernus 336; *337*
  Also see *Colchicum*
Crocus, Autumn, see *Colchicum*
Crocus, Dutch Yellow, see *Crocus aureus*
Cross-Vine, see *Bignonia capreolata*
Crowfoot, see *Ranunculus*
Crown Daisy, see *Chrysanthemum coronarium*
Crown Imperial, see *Fritillaria imperialis*
Cruciferae (family)
  Alyssum 48–51; *Arabis* 79–82; *Aubrietia* 102–103; *Cheiranthus* 221–224; *Iberis* 638–643; *Lobularia* 790–792; *Lunaria* 805–844; *Matthiola* 840–844
Crusades, the, 1086
Cryophytum crystallinum, see *Mesembryanthemum crystallinum*
Cuban Lily, see *Scilla peruviana*
Cuckoo Flower, see *Lychnis Flos-cuculi*
Cucumber Tree, see *Magnolia acuminata*

Culpeper, Thomas, on *Berberis* 118
Cup, Golden, see *Hunnemannia fumariifolia*
Cup and Saucer Vine, see *Cobaea*
Cupani, Father Francisco, work with *Lathyrus* 724
CUPHEA [KEW-feeya] (Cigar Flower) 338–339
  ignea (syn. *C. platycentra*) 338–339; *338*
  Llavea (syn. *C. miniata*) 339
Curtis, Samuel, writes first book on camellias 161
Cushion Pink, see *Silene acaulis*
CYCLAMEN [SICK-lam-enn] (Sowbread) 339–346
  europaeum 342; *344*
  neapolitanum 342–343; *344*
  orbiculatum 343; *340*
  persicum 344; *345*
  repandum (syn. *C. hederaefolium*) 344, 346
CYDONIA [sy-DOE-neeya]
  oblonga (syns. *C. vulgaris, Pyrus cydonia;* Quince) 346–348; *347*
  Also see *Chaenomeles*
Cymbalaria muralis, see *Linaria Cymbalaria*
Cypress Vine, see *Quamoclit pennata*
CYTISUS [SIT-iss-sus] (Broom) 348–355, 506, 1240
  albus (White Spanish Broom) 351; *351*
  ardoinii 351
  austriacus 353
  battandieri 353; *353*
  x *beanii* 353
  canariensis (Genista of Florists) 353
  x *dallimorei* 354
  glabrescens, see *Genista glabrescens*
  x *kewensis* 354
  monspessulanus 354
  nigricans 354
  x *praecox* (Warminster Broom) 354
  purgans 355; *352*
  radiatus, see *Genista glabrescens*
  scoparius 355; *348; 349*

Daffodil, see *Narcissus*
Daffodil, Winter, see *Sternbergia lutea*

1443

Dahl, Andreas, genus named for 358, 359
DAHLIA [DAH-leeya] 355–364
 coccinea 362
 excelsa 362
 imperialis 362–363; *361*
 Hybrids 363–364; *355; 357; 358; 359*
 juarezii 363
 merckii (syn. *D. glabrata*) 363
 zimapanii, see *Cosmos atrosanguineus*
Daisy, see *Bellis perennis; Chrysanthemum Leucanthemum*
Daisy, African, see *Arctotis; Dimorphotheca; Gerbera; Gazania*
Daisy, Barberton, see *Gerbera*
Daisy, Common, see *Chrysanthemum Leucanthemum*
Daisy, Crown, see *Chrysanthemum coronarium*
Daisy, English, see *Bellis perennis*
Daisy, Giant, see *Chrysanthemum uliginosum*
Daisy, Gloriosa, see *Rudbeckia* Hybrids
Daisy, Kingfisher, see *Felicia bergeriana*
Daisy, Livingstone, see *Mesembryanthemum criniflorum*
Daisy, Moon, see *Chrysanthemum uliginosum*
Daisy, Namaqualand, see *Dimorphotheca aurantiaca; Venidium*
Daisy, Ox-Eye, see *Chrysanthemum Leucanthemum*
Daisy, Painted, see *Chrysanthemum coccineum*
Daisy, Paris, see *Chrysanthemum frutescens*
Daisy, Purple, see *Echinacea angustifolia*
Daisy, Rain, see *Dimorphotheca pluvialis*
Daisy, Shasta, see *Chrysanthemum maximum*
Daisy, White, see *Chrysanthemum Leucanthemum*
Daisy, Yellow, see *Rudbeckia hirta*
Daisy Bush, see *Olearia*
Daisy Tree, see *Olearia*

Dallimore, W., work with *Cytisus* 350
Damask Rose, see *Rosa damascena*
D'Annunzio, Gabriele, 20
DAPHNE [DAFF-nee] 364–369
 x *burkwoodii* 367
 chrysantha, see *Edgeworthia papyrifera*
 Cneorum 367
 collina 367; *365*
 Genkwa 368
 Laureola (Spurge Laurel) 368
 Mezereum 368; *366*
 odora (syns. *D. sinensis, D. indica*) 368–369
 petraea 369
Darwin, Charles, 125, 793
Darwin, Erasmus, on *Lonicera* 792; on *Mimosa* 858
Darwin Tulips 1328; *1328*
DATURA [du-TOOR-uh, *or* day-TOOR-a] 369–376
 arborea (Angel's Trumpet) 373
 ceratocaula (syns. *D. cornigera, Solandra herbacea*) 373; *375*
 chlorantha 373
 metel (syns. *D. fastuosa, Stramonium fastuosum*) 373–374; *370*
 sanguinea 374
 Stramonium (Jimson Weed, Thorn Apple, Stramonium) 369, 371, 372, 374, 376; *374*
 suaveolens (Angel's Trumpet) 376; *369*
David, Père Armand, species named for 133, 261; work with *Caryopteris mongholica* 191; and *Lilium davidii* 760; introduces *Prunus davidiana* 1062; work with *Rhododendron* 1109
Daylily, see *Hemerocallis*
De Bey, work with *Iris* hybrids 670
Decadents, the, 942
Delavay, Père Jean-Marie, discovers species of *Clematis* 261; work with *Cotoneaster* 316, 320, 321; *Deutzia* 390; *Jasminum* 689; *Osmanthus* 923–924; *Paeonia* 933
Delibes, Leo, *Datura Stramonium* in plot of the opera *Lakmé* 371
DELPHINIUM [del-FINN-eeyum] 376–387

 Ajacis (Larkspur, Rocket Larkspur) 384
 cardinale (Scarlet Larkspur) 384; *383*
 Consolida (Field Larkspur, Knight's Larkspur) 384–385; *377*
 elatum (Bee Larkspur, Candle Larkspur) 383; *378*
 formosum (Garland Larkspur) 386
 grandiflorum (Siberian Larkspur, Bouquet Larkspur) 386; *379*
 nudicaule (Red Larkspur) 386–387
 Zalil 387; *381*
Desert Candle, see *Eremurus*
Desfontaines, R. L., work with *Dahlia* 359
Deslongchamps, Loiseleur, on *Nerium* 902
DESMODIUM [dez-MOE-deeyum] 387–389
 canadense (Bush Trefoil, Beggar Lice, Beggar Ticks) 387–388
 motorium (syn. *D. gyrans;* Telegraph Plant) 388
 penduliflorum (syn. *Lespedeza thunbergii*) 388; *389*
 purpureum (Beggarweed) 388
 tiliifolium 389; *389*
Despertes, list of roses 1136
Deutz, Johann van der, genus named for 390
DEUTZIA [DEWT-zeeya, *or* DOYT-zeeya] 389–394
 discolor 391
 gracilis 391, 393; *391*
 x *lemoinei* 393; *390*
 longifolia 393
 pulchra 393
 scabra (syn. *D. crenata;* Pride of Rochester) 393–394; *392*
Devil-in-a-Bush, see *Nigella*
Devil's Bit, see *Liatris spicata*
Devil Wood, see *Osmanthus americanus*
De Vries, Hugo, work with *Oenothera* 913
DIANTHUS [dy-ANN-thus] (Carnation, Pink, Clove, Gillyflower) 394–405
 alpinus 397–398; *402*
 barbatus (Sweet William, Bunch Pink) 398
 carthusianorum (Clusterhead Pink) 398; *403*
 Caryophyllus (Carnation) 399–400; *396; 402*

chinensis (syns. *D. sinensis*, *D. fischeri*; China Pink, Indian Pink) 400; *403*
deltoides (Maiden Pink) 400, 402; *403*
knappii 402
neglectus 402–403
plumarius (Grass Pink) 403; *402*
superbus 405; *404*
DICENTRA [dy-SENT-ra] 405–409
canadensis (Squirrel Corn, Turkey Corn) 406; *407*
chrysantha (Golden Eardrops) 406
cucullaria (Dutchman's Breeches, White Eardrops) 407
eximia (Wild Bleeding Heart) 407
formosa (California Bleeding Heart) 407
spectabilis (syn. *Dielytra spectabilis*; Bleeding Heart, Lock and Keys) 407, 409; *407*
Dick, Sleepy, see *Ornithogalum umbellatum*
Diech, work with *Malus niedzwetzkyana* 834
Dielytra spectabilis, see *Dicentra spectabilis*
Diem, Robert, work with *Gerbera* 525
DIERVILLA [dyer-VILL-a] 409–410
coraeensis, see *Weigela coraeensis*
floribunda, see *Weigela floribunda*
florida, see *Weigela florida*
japonica, see *Weigela japonica*
Lonicera (syn. *D. canadensis*; Gravel Weed) 410; *409*
middendorfiana, see *Weigela middendorfiana*
pauciflora, see *Weigela florida*
rivularis 410
sessilifolia 410
x *splendens* 410
Also see *Weigela*
DIGITALIS [diji-TAL-iss, *or* diji-TAIL-iss] (Foxglove) 411–415
ambigua (syn. *D. grandiflora*; Yellow Foxglove) 414; *413*
purpurea (syn. *D. tomentosa*; Common Foxglove, Fairy Glove, Finger Flower) 414–415; *414*
Dilleniaceae (family)
Actinidia (?) 25–27

Dillenius, John James, *Hortus Elthamensis* 960, 1010
DIMORPHOTHECA [dy-mor-foh-THEE-ka] (Star of the Veldt, Cape Marguerite, Cape Marigold, African Daisy) 415–419
aurantiaca (syn. *Castalis tragus*; Namaqualand Daisy) 416–417
barberiae (syns. *D. lilacina*, *Osteospermum barberiae*) 417
calendulacea 417
chrysanthemifolia (syn. *Calendula chrysanthemifolia*) 417
ecklonis (*Osteospermum ecklonis*) 417; *418*
pluvialis (syn. *D. annua*; Rain Daisy) 417, 419
sinuata 419
Dioscorides, on *Nerium* 901; *Nigella* 910; *Viola* 1368
Diplacus glutinosus, see *Mimulus glutinosus*
Dipsaceae (family)
Scabiosa 1202–1206
Dockmackie, see *Viburnum acerifolium*
Dodoens, Rembert, work with *Campanula* 174; writes on *Helianthus* 558
Dogwood, see *Cornus*
Dogwood, English, see *Philadelphus inodorus*
DOLICHOS [DOLL-eek-os] 419–421
Lablab (syns. *D. cultratus*, *D. purpureus*, *Lablab cultratus*; Hyacinth Bean, Bonavist, Lablab) 420; *420*
lignosus (Australian Pea) 420
Don, David, 99
DORONICUM [doh-RONN-eek-um] (Leopard's Bane) 421–422
austriacum 421
caucasicum 421–422
Plantagineum 422; *421*
Dorotheanthus bellidiflorus, see *Mesembryanthemum criniflorum*
Dorotheanthus gramineus, see *Mesembryanthemum tricolor*
Dorothy, Saint, 1130, 1132
Dorrien-Smith, Major A. A., work with *Olearia* 918
Douglas, David, work with *Penstemon cordifolius* 978

Doxantha capreolata, see *Bignonia capreolata*
Dracocephalum virginianum, see *Physostegia virginiana*
Dragonhead, False, see *Physostegia virginiana*
Drake, Sir Francis, 904
Drummond, Robert, work with *Rosa* 1135
Drummond Phlox, see *Phlox drummondii*
Dumas *(fils)*, Alexandre, 163
Dusty Miller, see *Centaurea candidissima*; *Lychnis coronaria*
Dutchman's Breeches, see *Dicentra cucullaria*
Dwarf Alder, see *Fothergilla gardenei*
Dwarf Globe Flower, see *Trollius pumilus*
Dwarf Nasturtium, see *Tropaeolum minus*
Dyer's Greenweed, see *Genista tinctoria*
Dyke, W. R., *The Genus Iris* 670

Easter Lily, see *Lilium longiflorum*
Ebony, False, see *Laburnum*
ECHINACEA [eck-in-AY-seeya] (Cone Flower) 422–425
angustifolia (syn. *Rudbeckia angustifolia*; Purple Daisy) 422, 424
Hybrids 424–425
purpurea (syn. *Rudbeckia purpurea*; Hedgehog Cone Flower, Black Cone Flower, Black Sampson, Purple Cone Flower) 424; *423*
Also see *Rudbeckia*
ECHINOPS [ECK-in-ops] (Globe Thistle) 425–426
ritro 425–426
ECHIUM [ECK-eeyum] (Viper's Bugloss) 427–428
fastuosum 427
plantagineum 428
wildpretii 428; *428*
Eckford, Henry, work with *Lathyrus* 724
Edelweiss, see *Leontopodium*
EDGEWORTHIA [edj-WURR-theeya] *papyrifera* (syns. *E. chrysantha*, *Daphne chrysantha*; Paper Tree, Paper Bush) 429–430; *429*
Edward I, King of England, 1133

eggplant 1231
Eglantine, Twisted, see *Lonicera periclymenum*
Elder, Yellow, see *Tecoma stans*
Elijah 507
Ellis, John, work with *Gardenia* 496
ELSHOLTZIA [ell-SHOLT-zeeya] 430–431
  cristata 430
  polystachya 430
  stauntonii 431; *430*
Elwes, Henry, on *Chionodoxa* 225
Endymion hispanicus, see *Scilla hispanica*
Endymion non-scriptus, see *Scilla non-scripta*
Engelmann, C., work with *Viola* 1368
Engler, A., on *Zantedeschia* 1389
English Bluebell, see *Scilla non-scripta*
English Dogwood, see *Philadelphus inodorus*
English Tamarisk, see *Tamarix anglica*
ENKIANTHUS [en-kee-ANTH-us] 431–434
  campanulatus (syn. *Andromeda campanulata*) 432; *431*
  perulatus (syns. *E. japonicus*, *Andromeda perulata*) 434; *433*
  quinqueflorus (syn. *E. reticulatus*) 434
EPIMEDIUM [eppi-MEE-deeyum] (Barrenwort) 434–437
  alpinum 435; *435*
  grandiflorum (syn. *E. macranthum*) 435; *436*
  macranthum, see *E. grandiflorum*
  perralderianum 435
  pinnatum 435
  x *rubrum* (syn. *E. alpinum* var. *rubrum*) 437
  versicolor var. *sulphureum* 437
  x *youngianum* 437
Epiphany Tree, see *Hamamelis mollis*
ERANTHIS [eh-RANN-thiss] (Winter Aconite, New Year's Gift) 437–438
  hyemalis 438; *440*
  siberica 438
  x *tubergenii* var. Guinea Gold 438

EREMURUS [eh-ree-MEW-riss] (Foxtail Lily, Desert Candle) 438–439
  Bungei 439; *438*
  elwesii 439
  himalaicus 439
  robustus 439
Erepsia mutabilis, see *Mesembryanthemum tricolor*
ERICA [EH-ree-ka, *or* eh-RY-ka] (Heath, Heather) 441–451
  arborea (Tree Heath) 444; *441*
  australis (Spanish Heath) 444
  carnea 446; *445*
  ciliaris (Fringed Heath, Dorset Heath) 446–447; *448*
  x *darleyensis* (syn. *E. mediterranea* hybrids) 447
  gracilis 447
  Hybrida 449
  mediterranea (Irish Heath) 449
  pageana (syn. *E. campanulata*) 449
  scoparia (Besom Heath) 450
  terminalis (syns. *E. corsica*, *E. stricta*; Corsican Heath) 450
  tetralix (Cross-leaved Heath) 450; *442*
  vagans (Cornish Heath) 450; *443*
  vulgaris, see *Calluna vulgaris*
  Also see *Calluna*
Ericaceae (family)
  Calluna vulgaris 153–157;
  Enkianthus 431–434; *Erica* 441–451; *Kalmia* 694–700; *Pieris* 1015–1017; *Rhododendron* 1091–1123
ERINUS [eh-RY-nus] *alpinus* 451–452; *451*
Eriolobus trilobata, see *Malus triloba*
ERYNGIUM [eh-RINJ-eeyum] (Sea Holly, Eryngo) 452–455
  agavifolium 454
  alpinum 454; *453*
  amethystinum 454
  bourgati 454
  giganteum 454
  x *olivierianum* 454
  planum 455; *452*
  yuccaefolium (Button Snakeroot, Rattlesnake Master) 455
Eryngo, see *Eryngium*
Erysimum allionii, see *Cheiranthus* x *allionii*
Erysimum asperum, see *Cheiranthus* x *allionii*
Erysimum linifolium, see *Cheiranthus linifolius*

Eschscholz, Johann Friedrich, genus named for 455; work with *Ceanothus* 197
ESCHSCHOLZIA [esh-SHOLTZ-eeya] (California Poppy) 455–458
  californica 458; *456*
  Also see *Papaver*
Eugenia ugni, see *Myrtus ugni*
European Globe Flower, see *Trollius europaeus*
European Goldenrod, see *Solidago virgaurea*
Eurybia semidentata, see *Olearia semidentata*
Eutoca viscida, see *Phacelia viscida*
Evening Primrose, see *Oenothera*
Everlasting Flower, see *Helichrysum*
Everlasting Thorn, see *Pyracantha coccinea*
EXOCHORDA [ekso-KORD-a] (Pearl Bush) 458–459
  giraldii 459
  korolkowii (syn. *E. alberti*) 459
  racemosa (syn. *E. grandiflora*) 459; *460*
Exogonium Purga, see *Ipomoea Purga*
Extract, Rose Hip, recipe for 1141

Faassen (Dutch nurseryman), work with *Nepeta* 896
Fabbroni, Marchese Pelli, on *Iris* 668
Fairy Glove, see *Digitalis purpurea*
False Dragonhead, see *Physostegia virginiana*
False Ebony, see *Laburnum*
False Pistachio, see *Staphylea colchica*
False Sunflower, see *Helenium autumnale*
Farewell to Spring, see *Godetia amoena*
Farges, Père Paul, 124
Farrer, Reginald, comments on *Buddleia* 133; work with *Forsythia* 464; discovers *Lilium leucanthum* 764; on *Lonicera* 794; work with peonies 934; work with *Rosa farreri* 1157; on *Viburnum fragrans* 1357
Father Hugo's Rose, see *Rosa hugonis*

Feathers, David L., writing on camellias 166
FELICIA [feh-LISH-ihya, *or* feh-LISS-eeya] 459–462
 amelloides (syns. *Agathaea coelestris, Agathaea amelloides, Aster rotundifolius, Aster capensis;* Blue Daisy, Blue Marguerite) 461–462; *459*
 bergeriana (syn. *Aster bergerianus;* Kingfisher Daisy) 462; *462*
 hispida (syn. *Agathaea hispida*) 462
 tenella (syns. *F. fragilis, Aster tenellus*) 462
Felix, Herr, *Felicia* named for 459
Fennel Flower, see *Nigella*
Ferrari, Father, writing on *Hibiscus* 590
fertilizers and manures xxvii–xxxv
Feverfew, see *Chrysanthemum Parthenium*
Fiddleneck, see *Phacelia tanacetifolia*
Fig, Hottentot, see *Mesembryanthemum edule*
Fig Marigold, see *Mesembryanthemum*
Figwort, Cape, see *Phygelius*
Fillassier, Jean Jacques, list of roses 1136
Finger Flower, see *Digitalis purpurea*
Fire Thorn, see *Pyracantha*
Fish Geranium, see *Pelargonium zonale*
Flag, Blue, see *Iris versicolor*
Flag, Water, see *Iris Pseudacorus*
Flag, Yellow, see *Iris Pseudacorus*
Flag Iris, see *Iris germanica*
Flame Flower, see *Kniphofia; Tropaeolum speciosum*
Flame Nettle, see *Coleus blumei*
Flannelwick, see *Verbascum thapsus*
Flax, see *Linum*
Fleming, Alexander, 23
Fletcher, H. L. V., on *Heliotropium* 572; *Lathyrus* 724; *Lavandula* 733; *Narcissus* 883; *Verbena* 1341, 1342
Florence, Italy, iris as the emblem of 668
Floridus, M., on peonies 934
Floss Flower, see *Ageratum*

Flower of an Hour, see *Hibiscus Trionium*
Flower of Jove, see *Lychnis Flos-Jovis*
Flueckiger, F. A., work with *Hibiscus* 591
Foerster, Karl, work with *Delphinium* 378
Foliage Plant, see *Coleus blumei*
Forget-Me-Not, see *Myosotis*
Forrest, George, discovers species of *Camellia* 165; work with *Jasminum* 689
Forrest, Thomas, work with *Rhododendron* 1094, 1105, 1106, 1108, 1115
Forsyth, William, genus named for 463
FORSYTHIA [for-SITH-eeya] (Golden Bells) 463–467
 giraldiana 464–465
 Hybrids 467
 intermedia (syn. *F. suspensa* x *F. viridissima*) 465
 ovata (Early Forsythia) 465
 suspensa (Weeping Golden Bell, Weeping Forsythia) 465, 467; *464*
 viridissima 467; *466*
Forsythia, Early, see *Forsythia ovata*
Forsythia, Weeping, see *Forsythia suspensa*
Fortune, Robert, work with *Actinidia* 25; *Caryopteris Mastacanthus* 191; *Ceratostigma* 211; *Chrysanthemum* 229; *Clematis* 263; *Deutzia* 390; *Dicentra* 405; *Exochorda* 459; *Forsythia* 464; *Jasminum* 689; *Lonicera* 793, 794, 798, 803; *Paeonia* 932, 933, 937; *Rhododendron* 1094, 1106; *Spiraea* 1244; *Syringa* 1261
Fothergill, John, cultivates *Clematis* 256; *Fothergilla* named for 468; cultivates *Malus spectabilis* 837
FOTHERGILLA [fother-GILL-la] (Witch Alder, American Witch Alder) 468–469
 gardeni (Dwarf Alder) 468
 major 469; *468*
 monticola 469
Fountain-Plant, see *Amaranthus salicifolius*
Four-O'Clock, see *Mirabilis*
Fox Geranium, see *Geranium robertianum*

Foxglove, see *Digitalis*
Foxtail Lady, see *Eremurus*
Fraser, John, introduces *Aesculus parviflora* 30; work with *Magnolia* 823; *Rhododendron* 1094, 1103
FREESIA [FREE-zeeya] 469–471
 alba 471
 corymbosa (syn. *F. odorata*) 471
 Hybrids 471; *470*
 refracta 471; *470*
French Marigold, see *Tagetes patula*
French Tamarisk, see *Tamarix gallica*
FRITILLARIA [fritt-ill-LAY-reeya, *or* fritt-ill-AIR-reeya] (Fritillary) 471–473
 imperialis (Crown Imperial) 472; *471*
 karadaghensis 472
 lanceolata (Checkered Lily) 472
 meleagris (Toad Lily, Snake's Head Lily, Guinea Hen Flower) 472; *471*
 pallidiflora 473
 pluriflora (Adobe Lily, Pink Fritillary) 473
 pudica (Yellow Fritillary) 473
 recurva (Scarlet Fritillary) 473
Fritillary, see *Fritillaria*
Frost, Robert (quoted) 1038
Frostweed, see *Helianthemum*
Fuchs, Leonhart, work with *Digitalis* 412; *Fuchsia* named for 474
FUCHSIA [FEW-sha, popular: but properly FEWKS-eeya] (Ladies Eardrops) 473–491
 arborescens (syn. *F. syringaeflora*) 483; *489*
 boliviana 484
 corymbiflora 484; *482*
 excorticata 484
 fulgens 485; *481*
 gracilis, see *Fuchsia magellanica* var. *gracilis*
 Hybrids (*Fuchsia Speciosa*) 489–491
 macrantha 485
 magellanica (syn. *F. macrostemma*) 485; *479; 485; 487*
 microphylla 488
 procumbens 488; *489*
 riccartonii, see *Fuchsia gracilis* var. *riccartonii*

1447

splendens 488
triphylla 489; *475*
Fuchsia, Cape, see *Phygelius*
Fuchsia, Tree, see *Fuchsia arborescens*
Fumariaceae (family) *Dicentra* 405–409
Funkia, see *Hosta*
Furze, see *Ulex*

Gaggia, see *Acacia farnesiana*
GAILLARDIA [gay-LARD-eeya] (Blanket Flower) 491–493
  amblyodon 492
  aristata (syns. *G. grandiflora, G. lutea, G. maxima, G. perennis*) 492–493
  pulchella (syns. *G. bicolor, G. drummondii*) 493; *493*
GALANTHUS [gay-LAN-thus, *or* guh-LAN-thus] (Snowdrop) 494–495
  byzantinus 494
  elwesii 494
  nivalis 495; *494*
Galen, on *Paeonia* 934
Garbo, Greta, 163
Garden, Dr. Alexander, work with *Fothergilla* 468; *Gardenia* named for 496
Garden Heliotrope, see *Valeriana officinalis*
Garden Violet, see *Viola odorata*
GARDENIA [gar-DEEN-eeya, *or* gar-DIN-eeya] 495–502
  amoena 499; *500*
  globosa 499; *501*
  grandiflora 499
  jasminoides (syns. *G. florida, G. radicans;* Cape Jasmine) 496, 499, 501; *497*
  lucida 501
  rothmannia 502; *501*
  thunbergia 502; *501*
gardening, general rules xix–xxxix
Garland Spiraea, see *Spiraea* x *arguta*
Garlic, Giant, see *Allium giganteum*
Gay Feather, see *Liatris spicata*
GAZANIA [guh-ZAY-neeya] (African Daisy) 502–506
  Hybrids 506; *505*
  longiscapa 504
  pavonia 504
  rigens (syn. *G. splendens*) 504
Geneva (Switzerland), *Vinca* as the emblem of 1362

GENISTA [jeh-NISS-ta] (Broom) 506–512, 1240
  aetnensis (syn. *Spartium aetnensis*) 508; *509*
  cinerea 510
  germanica 510
  glabrescens (syn. *Cytisus glabrescens*) 510
  hispanica (Spanish Broom) 510; *506*
  horrida 510
  monosperma (syn. *Retama monosperma*) 511
  pilosa 511
  radiata (syn. *Cytisus radiatus*) 511; *509*
  sagittalis 511
  tinctoria (Dyer's Greenweed, Waxen Woad) 512; *507*
  villarsii 512
Genista (of Florists), see *Cytisus canariensis*
Gentian, see *Gentiana*
GENTIANA [jen-shee-AY-na, *or* jen-shee-AH-na] 512–519
  acaulis 514; *513*
  andrewsii (Closed Gentian, Bottle Gentian) 515
  asclepiadea 515; *512*
  bavarica 515; *515*
  calycosa 515
  ciliata 516
  crinita (Fringed Gentian) 516
  cruciata 516
  farreri 516
  linearis 516
  lutea (Yellow Gentian, Bitterwort) 516; *515*
  menziesii 518
  Pneumonanthe 518
  porphyrio 518
  purpurea 518; *514*
  septemfida 518; *517*
  sino-ornato 518
  tibetica 518
  verna 518; *515*
  walujewi 519
Gentianaceae (family) *Gentiana* 512–519
genus, defined xxxvi–xxxvii
Geoffrey the Handsome 507
Georgi (botanist), *Dahlia* species named for 358
Georgia, *Rosa laevigata* as state flower of, 1160
Geraniaceae (family) *Geranium* 519–524; *Pelargonium* 959–976
GERANIUM [jer-AY-neeyum] (Cranesbill) 519–524
  argenteum 520; *521*

  endressii 520
  grandiflorum 520; *519*
  ibericum 520
  incisum 522
  macrorrhizum 522
  maculatum (Alum root, Chocolate Flower) 522
  nepalense 522
  peltatum, see *Pelargonium peltatum*
  pratense (Meadow Cranesbill) 522
  psilostemon (syn. *G. armenum*) 522
  pylzowianum 522
  robertianum (syn. *Robertiella robertianum;* Herb Robert, Red Shanks, Fox Geranium) 523; *523*
  sanguineum (Streaked Cranesbill) 523; *520*
  tuberosum 523
  wallichianum 523
  zonale, see *Pelargonium zonale*
  Also see *Pelargonium*
Geranium, Fancy, see *Pelargonium domesticum*
Geranium, Fish, see *Pelargonium zonale*
Geranium, Horseshoe, see *Pelargonium zonale*
Geranium, Ivy-leaved, see *Pelargonium peltatum*
Geranium, Lady Washington, see *Pelargonium domesticum*
Geranium, Oak-leaved, see *Pelargonium quercifolium*
Geranium, Show, see *Pelargonium domesticum*
Geranium, Stork's Bill, see *Pelargonium*
Geranium, Strawberry, see *Saxifraga sarmentosa*
Geranium, Sweetheart, see *Pelargonium echinatum*
Geranium, Zonal, see *Pelargonium zonale*
Gerard, John, on aconite 22; on campanulas 174; cultivates *Cistus* 246; cultivates *Clematis* 256; describes species of *Crocus* 332; on *Cytisus* 348; cultivates *Hibiscus* 590; cultivates *Lonicera* 794; cultivates *Nerium* 900; on *Philadelphus* 992; work with *Rosa* 1133; raises *Syringa* 1260; *Herball* of 1597

Gerber, Traugott, *Gerbera* named for 524
GERBERA [JURR-burr-a] (Barberton Daisy, African Daisy) 524–526
  jamesonii 526
  viridifolia 526
German Catchfly, see *Lychnis Viscaria*
Germander, see *Teucrium*
Germander, Wall, see *Teucrium Chamaedrys*
Germander Speedwell, see *Veronica Teucrium*
Gesner, Conrad, writes on *Trollius* 1300; work with *Tulipa* 1312
Gesneriaceae (family) *Sinningia* 1228–1231
GEUM [JEE-um](Avens, Herb Bennett) 526–529
  x *borisii* 527; *527*
  bulgaricum 527
  chiloense, see *Geum coccineum*
  coccineum (syn. *G. chiloense*) 527; *528*
  montanum 529
  reptans 529; *526*
  triflorum (Prairie Smoke, Johnny Smoker) 529
Gibbs, Hon. Vicary, raises *Malus* x *eleyi* 831
Gibraltar Candytuft, see *Iberis gibraltarica*
Gillyflower, see *Dianthus; Matthiola incana*
Gladiola, see *Gladiolus*
GLADIOLUS [glad-EYE-oh-lus, or glad-ee-OH-lus] 529–538
  byzantinus 534
  cardinalis 534; *532*
  x *colvillii* 534
  x *gandavensis* 535
  grandis (syns. *G. liliaceus, G. versicolor*) 535
  Hybrids and varieties 536–538
  illyricus 535
  primulinus 535; *535*
  psittacinus (Parrot Gladiola) 535
  segetum (Cornflag) 536
  tristis 536; *536*
Gladwin, see *Iris foetidissima*
Glasau, Fritz *(Rosen in Garten)* 1135
Glenny, George, work with pansies 1368
Globe Amaranth, see *Gomphrena*
Globe Flower, see *Kerria japonica; Trollius*

Globe Flower, American, see *Trollius laxus*
Globe Flower, Asiatic, see *Trollius asiaticus*
Globe Flower, Dwarf, see *Trollius pumilus*
Globe Flower, European, see *Trollius europaeus*
Globe Thistle, see *Echinops*
GLORIOSA [glow-ree-OH-sa] (Glory Flower, Gloriosa Lily, Glory Lily) 538–539
  rothschildiana 539
  superba 539; *538*
Gloriosa Daisy, see *Rudbeckia* Hybrids
Glory Bush, see *Tibouchina semidecandra*
Glory Flower, see *Gloriosa*
Glory of the Snow, see *Chionodoxa*
Glory Tree, see *Clerodendrum fragrans*
Gloxinia, see *Sinningia*
Gloxinia, Hardy, see *Incarvillea*
Gloxinia maculata insignis 1229
Gloxinia speciosa, see *Sinningia speciosa*
Gloxinia tubiflora (syn. *Achimenes tubiflora*) 1229
Glycine frutescens, see *Wistaria frutescens*
Glycine sinensis, see *Wistaria sinensis*
Glycinia 1383
Gnaphalium Stoechas, see *Helichrysum Stoechas*
Godet, C. H., *Godetia* named for 540
GODETIA [go-DEE-sheeya] 539–542
  amoena (Farewell to Spring) 540; *539*
  grandiflora (syns. *G. whitneyi, Oenothera whitneyi*) 542; *541*
  viminea 542
Goes, Hugo van der, columbine in *Portinari Altarpiece* of 72
Goethe, Johann Wolfgang von, and hollyhocks 43; collection of dahlias 356, 358
Gold Dust, see *Alyssum saxatile; Sedum acre*
Golden Bells, see *Forsythia*
Golden Calla, see *Zantedeschia elliottiana*
Golden Chain, see *Laburnum*
Golden Cup, see *Hunnemannia fumariifolia*
Golden Eardrops, see *Dicentra chrysantha*

Golden Marguerite, see *Anthemis tinctoria*
Golden Moss, see *Sedum acre*
Golden Rain, see *Laburnum*
Goldenrod, see *Solidago*
Goldenrod, Beach, see *Solidago sempervirens*
Goldenrod, European, see *Solidago Virgaurea*
Goldenrod, Seaside, see *Solidago sempervirens*
Goldenrod, Wreath, see *Solidago caesia*
Golden Tuft, see *Alyssum saxatile*
Golden Wattle, see *Acacia longifolia*
Golden Wave, see *Coreopsis drummondii*
GOMPHRENA [gom-FREE-na] (Globe Amaranth) 542–543
  globosa 543; *542*
Goodnight at Noon, see *Hibiscus Trionum*
Gooseberry, Cape, see *Physalis peruviana*
Gordon, James, cultivates *Cytisus* 350
Gori (Italian botanist), on China asters 149
Gorse, see *Ulex*
Graaff, Jan de, work with *Lilium* 756
Graham, J. G., discovers species of *Salvia* 1183
Granadilla, see *Passiflora*
Grape Hyacinth, see *Muscari*
Grasse (France), jasmine industry in 687
Gravel Weed, see *Diervilla Lonicera*
Grayson, Esther C., *Book of Lilies* 756
Greek Valerian, see *Polemonium*
Green-flowered Tulips 1330
green fly (insect pest) 1149
Gregg, J., discovers species of *Salvia* 1183
Gromwell, see *Lithospermum*
Ground Cherry, see *Physalis pubescens*
Ground Pink, see *Phlox subulata*
Groundsel, see *Senecio*
Guava, Chilean, see *Myrtus ugni*
Guelder Rose, see *Viburnum opulus*
Guinea Hen Flower, see *Fritillaria meleagris*
Gum Cistus, see *Cistus ladaniferus*
Gumbo, see *Hibiscus esculentus*

GYPSOPHILA [jip-SOFF-illa]
    (Baby's Breath) 543–546
  cerastioides 544
  elegans (Annual Baby's
    Breath) 544; *544*
  muralis 545
  paniculata (Chalk Plant,
    Gypsum Pink, Baby's
    Breath, Mist) 545
  repens 545; *543*
Gypsum Pink, see *Gypsophila paniculata*

Habranthus advenus, see
    Hippeastrum advenum
Habranthus pratensis, see
    Hippeastrum pratense
Hadden, Norman G., work with
    Cytisus 354
Hales, Stephen, *Halesia* named
    for 546
HALESIA [ha-LEEZ-eeya]
    (Snowdrop Tree) 546–548
  carolina (Silver Bell Tree,
    Snowdrop Tree) 546
  diptera 546
  monticola (Tisswood) 548
Hall, Dr. G. R., work with *Malus halliana* 833
Hall, Sir Daniel, *The Tulip* 1325
Hamamelidaceae (family)
    Corylopsis 308–309;
    Fothergilla 468–469;
    Hamamelis 548–551
HAMAMELIS [hamma-MEE-liss] (Witch Hazel, Winter Bloom) 548–551
  japonica 550
  mollis (Epiphany Tree) 550
  vernalis 551
  virginiana (Witch Hazel) 551
Hamilton, Lord, 99
Hanbury, Daniel, work with
    Hibiscus 591
Hanmer, Sir Thomas, work with
    Hibiscus 590; cultivates lilacs 1260
Hansen Bush Cherry, see *Prunus besseyi*
Hardhead, see *Centaurea nigra*
hardiness xix–xxii
Harlequin Glory-Bower, see
    Clerodendrum trichotomum
Hartmannia rosea, see
    Oenothera rosea
Harwick, Captain, work with
    Rhododendron 1094
Haw, Red, see *Crataegus mollis*

Haw, Scarlet, see *Crataegus coccinea*
Hawker, Rev. W., work with
    Cytisus 351
Haworth-Booth, Sir Michael, 366, 463, 623, 625, 626
Hawthorn, see *Crataegus*
Hazel, Winter, see *Corylopsis*
Heath, see *Calluna vulgaris; Erica*
Heather, see *Erica*
Heather, Scotch, see *Calluna vulgaris; Erica cinerea*
Hebe 1348
Heinemann, work with pansies 1368
Heister, Lorenz, work with
    Specularia 1241
HELENIUM [hell-EE-neeyum]
    (Sneezeweed) 551–555
  aromaticum (syn.
    Cephalophora aromatica) 552
  autumnale (syn. *H. grandiflorum;* Yellow Star, False Sunflower) 552–553; *554*
  bigelovii 553
  bolanderi 553
  hoopesii 553; *553*
  setigerum (syn. *Amblyolepsis setigera*) 553
  tenuifolium (Sneezeweed) 555; *551*
HELIANTHEMUM [helli-ANthem-mum] (Rock Rose, Sun Rose, Frostweed) 555–557
  apenninum (syn. *H. polifolium*) 556
  Chamaecistus (syns. *H. vulgare, H. nummularium*) 556; *555*
  glaucum 556
  Hybrids 557
  nummularium, see *H. Chamaecistus*
  Tuberaria 556
  vulgare, see *H. Chamaecistus*
HELIANTHUS [hee-lee-ANTHus] (Sunflower) 557–565
  angustifolius (Swamp Sunflower) 559
  annuus (syn. *H. lenticularis;* Common Sunflower) 559–561; *558*
  atrorubens (syn. *H. sparsifolius*) 561
  cucumerifolius (syn. *H. debilis*) 561, 563; *560*
  decapetalus (River Sunflower) 563; *562*

  laetiflorus (syns. *H. rigidus, H. scaberrimus*) 564
  mollis 564
  salicifolius (syn. *H. orgyalis*) 564; *561*
  speciosus, see *Tithonia rotundifolia*
  tuberosus (Jerusalem Artichoke, Canada Potato) 564–565; *563*
HELICHRYSUM [helli-KRYsum] (Strawflower, Everlasting Flower) 565–569
  bellidioides 568
  bracteatum (Straw Flower) 568; *566; 567*
  petiolatum 568
  Stoechas (syn. *Gnaphalium Stoechas*) 569
HELIOPSIS [hee-lee-OP-sis]
    (Orange Sunflower) 569–572
  buphtalmoides 570
  laevis (syn. *Heliopsis helianthoides;* False Sunflower) 570; *571*
  scabra (Rough Heliopsis) 570
Heliotrope, see *Heliotropium*
Heliotrope, Garden, see
    Valeriana officinalis
Heliotrope, Wild, see *Phacelia tanacetifolia*
HELIOTROPIUM [hee-lee-oTRO-peeyum](Heliotrope, Vanilla, Cherry Pie) 572–575
  aborescens (syns. *H. peruvianum, H. corymbosum*) 575; *572*
Hellebore, see *Helleborus*
HELLEBORUS [hell-eh-BORus] (Hellebore, Christmas Rose, Lenten Rose) 575–580
  corsicus (Stinking Hellebore, Bear's Foot) 578
  foetidus 578
  guttatus (syns. *H. macranthus, H. caucasicus* var. *guttatus;* Christmas Rose) 578
  niger 575, 579; *576*
  odorus 579
  orientalis (Lenten Rose) 579–580
HEMEROCALLIS [hem-ehr-oKAL-is] (Daylily) 580–586
  altissima 583
  aurantiaca 583
  citrina 583
  dumortieri 583
  flava (syn. *H. lilio-asphodelus*) 583; *582*
  fulva 583; *581*
  Hybrids 584–586

middendorffi 584
minor (syn. *H. graminea*) 584
thunbergii 584
Hemp Tree, see *Vitex*
Hen and Chickens, see
  Sempervivum soboliferum
Henderson, work with *Clematis* 256
Henry, Dr. Augustine, collects *Buddleia* 133; work with *Kerria japonica* 700; work with *Lilium henryi* 763; work with *Lilium leucanthum* 764; imports *Lonicera pileata* 801; work with *Rhododendron* 1102, 1103; work with *Rosa* 1159; species of *Spiraea* honors 1248; discovers *Syringa reflexa* 1266
HEPATICA [heh-PAT-ik-a] (Liverwort) 586–589
  americana (Mayflower, Blue Anemone) 587
  triloba (syn. *H. nobilis*) 587; *588*
Hera, association with the lily 751
Herb Bennett, see *Geum*
Herb Robert, see *Geranium robertianum*
Herbe d'amour 573
Herbert, William, work with *Erica* 442
Hernandez, Francisco, *Dahlia* in *Thesaurus* of 356, 904
Herodotus, on roses 1129
heroin 944
Heucher, Johann Heinrich von, genus named for 589
HEUCHERA [HEW-kerr-uh] (Coral Bells, Alumroot) 589–590
  sanguinea 589–590; *589*
Hibber, G., work with *Hosta* 610
HIBISCUS [hy-BISS-cuss] (Mallow) 590–601
  Abelmoschus (syn. *Abelmoschus moschatus*) 594
  coccineus (syn. *H. speciosus*) 596
  esculentus (syn. *Abelmoschus esculentus;* Okra, Gumbo) 596
  Manihot 596–597; *599*
  militaris 597
  Moscheutos (syn. *H. palustris;* Rose Mallow) 597
  mutabilis (Cotton Rose) 598
  rosa-sinensis (syn. *H. sinensis;* Rose of China) 598; *592*

  Sabdariffa (syn. *H. rosella;* Roselle, Red Sorrel, Jamaica Sorrel) 598
  schizopetalus 598; *591*
  syriacus (syn. *Althaea frutex;* Rose of Sharon) 600; *595*
  Trionum (syns. *H. versicarius, H. africanus;* Flower of an Hour, Goodnight at Noon) 601
Hildegard of Bingen, Saint, on *Calendula* 144; on *Physalis* 1010
Hill, Sir John, 13
Hill, Thomas *(Family Herbal)* 1039
HIPPEASTRUM [hippi-AST-rum] (Barbados Lily, Amaryllis) 601–605
  advenum (syn. *Habranthus advenus*) 604
  equestre 605; *602*
  Hybrids 605; *601*
  pratense (syn. *Habranthus pratensis*) 605
  reginae 605
  vittatum 605
  Also see *Amaryllis*
Hippocrates 1210; on *Paeonia* 934
HOHERIA [ho-HEER-eeya] 605–607
  glabra (syn. *Plagianthus lyallii*) 606; *607*
  lyallii (syn. *Plagianthus lyallii* var. *ribifolia*) 606
  populnea (syn. *H. sinclairii*) 606
Hollyhock, see *Althaea*
Homer, on pomegranates 1075; roses in *Iliad* 1129; violets in *Odyssey* 1368
Honesty, see *Lunaria*
Honey, Rose, recipe for 1139
Honeysuckle, see *Lonicera*
Honeysuckle, Jamaica, see *Passiflora laurifolia*
Hooker, Sir Joseph Dalton, on *Acacia riceana* 11; collects *Rhododendron* 1094; discovers *Buddleia colvilei* 133; work with *Fuchsia* 474
Hooker, William Jackson *(Flora of the British Isles)* 174; names *Valoradia plumbaginoides* 211; names *Impatiens sultani* 648; on *Portulaca* 1031; book on *Rhododendron* 1094
Horace *(Odes),* on myrtle 877; roses 1130

Horned Tulip, see *Tulipa acuminata*
Horned Violet, see *Viola cornuta*
Horse-Chestnut, see *Aesculus*
Horsemint, see *Monarda*
Horseshoe Geranium, see *Pelargonium zonale*
Hortense de Nassau 623
Hortensia, see *Hydrangea*
Hortensia opuloides, see *Hydrangea Hortensis*
Hortus Mortolensis (catalogue of plants) 1278
Host, Nicolaus Thomas, genus named for 609
HOSTA [HOSS-tah] (Funkia, Plantain Lily, Niobe) 608–611
  albomarginata 610
  crispula 610
  fortunei 611
  glauca (syn. *Funkia sieboldiana*) 611; *609*
  lancifolia 611; *609*
  plantaginea (Funkia *subcordata*) 611; *610*
  tardiflora 611
  undulata 611
  ventricosa (syn. *H. coerulea*) 611; *610*
Hottentot Fig, see *Mesembryanthemum edule*
House, J. C., work with *Scabiosa* 1205
Houseleek, see *Sempervivum*
Houseleek, Cobweb, see *Sempervivum arachnoideum*
Houston, Dr. William, 133
Hove, Anthony, on *Rhododendron ponticum* 1096
Howitt, W., poem mentioning Wayfaring Tree 1353
Humble Plant, see *Mimosa pudica*
Humboldt, F. A. von, writes on *Ipomoea* 659
humus xxx
Hundred-leaved Rose, see *Rosa centifolia*
Hungarian Lilac, see *Syringa Josikaea*
Hunneman, John, genus named for 612
HUNNEMANNIA [hunn-emm-MAN-eeya] *fumariifolia* (Mexican Poppy, Tulip Poppy, Golden Cup) 612; *613*
Husk Tomato, see *Physalis*
Hyacinth, Grape, see *Muscari*
Hyacinth, Starch, see *Muscari*

1451

botryoides
Hyacinth, Yellow Grape, see
  Muscari macrocarpum
Hyacinth Bean, see *Dolichos Lablab*
Hyacinthella azurea, see
  Hyacinthus azureus
HYACINTHUS [hya-SINN-thus] 614–622
  amethystinus (syn. *Brimeura amethystina*) 620
  azureus (syn. *Hyacinthella azurea*) 620
  fastigiatus (syns. *H. Pouzolzii, Brimeura fastigiata*) 621
  orientalis 621; *617; 621*
  romanus (syn. *Bellevalia romana*) 621; *621*
  Also see *Muscari*
hybrid, defined xxxix
HYDRANGEA [hy-DRAIN-jah, or hy-DRAIN-jee-uh]
  (Hortensia) 622–633, 1352
  arborescens 629; *627*
  bretschneideri (syns. *H. pekinensis, H. vestita pubescens*) 629
  Hortensis (syns. *H. macrophylla, H. Hortensia, H. opuloides, Hortensia opuloides*) 629–630; *624*
  macrophylla, see *H. Hortensis opuloides,* see *H. Hortensis*
  paniculata 631; *631*
  petiolaris (syn. *H. scandens*) 631; *631*
  quercifolia 632
  sargentiana 632
  serrata (syns. *H. cyanea, H. thunbergii*) 632–633
  villosa 633
Hydrangea, French, see
  Clerodendrum bungei
Hydrangea, Red Mexican, see
  Clerodendrum bungei
Hydrophyllaceae (family)
  Nemophila 893–896; *Phacelia* 988–991
Hypericaceae (family)
  Hypericum 633–637
HYPERICUM [hy-PERR-ih-kum] (St. John's-Wort, Rose of Sharon) 633–637
  androsaemum (syn.
    Androsaemum officinale;
    Tutsan) 634; *637*
  calycinum (Rose of Sharon, Aaron's Beard) 636; *635*
  leschenaultii 636
  x *moserianum* (syn. *H. patulum* x *Hypericum*

calycinum) 636; *637*
olympicum 636
patulum 637; *637*
reptans 637

IBERIS [eye-BEER-iss] (Candytuft) 638–643
  amara (syn. *I. coronaria;* Rocket Candytuft) 640
  gibraltarica (Gibraltar Candytuft) 640; *639*
  pinnata 641
  saxatilis 641
  semperflorens (Winter Candytuft) 641
  sempervirens (Perennial Candytuft) 642
  umbellata (Common Annual Candytuft) 642; *642*
Ice Plant, see
  Mesembryanthemum crystallinum
I Ching (The Book of Changes) 13
Impatience, see *Impatiens*
IMPATIENS [im-PAY-shens, or im-PAY-shee-ens]
  (Impatience, Touch-Me-Not, Quick-in-Hand, Balsam, Busy Lizzie, Snapweed) 643–651
  balfourii 644
  Balsamina (Balsam) 646; *649*
  glandulifera (syn. *I. roylei*) 647
  holstii 647; *645*
  Hybrids 649–651
  Noli-tangere (Touch-Me-Not) 648; *649*
  sultani (Busy Lizzie) 648; *649*
Incarville, Le Cheron d', Pierre, work with *Clematis* 263; *Dicentra* 405; *Syringa* 1266; genus named for 651
INCARVILLEA [in-car-VILL-eeya] (Chinese Trumpet Creeper, Hardy Gloxinia) 651–654
  compacta 653
  delavayi 653; *651*
  grandiflora, see *I. compacta* var. *grandiflora*
  olgae 654; *652*
  variabilis 654
Index Kewensis 1316
Indian Cress, see *Tropaeolum majus*
Indian Tobacco, see *Lobelia inflata*
Indigo, see *Indigofera*

INDIGOFERA [in-dih-GOFF-er-ah] (Indigo) 654–656
  amblyantha 655
  decora 655
  gerardiana (syn. *I. dosua*) 655; *654*
  pendula 655
  potaninii 656
inorganic (chemical) fertilizers xxxi–xxxv
Io, mythological association with *Viola* 1365, 1368
Ionoxalis deppei, see *Oxalis deppei*
IPOMOEA [ippo-MEE-uh, or eye-po-MEE-ya] (Morning Glory) 157, 287, 656–667
  bona-nox, see *Calonyction aculeatum*
  childsii, see *Calonyction aculeatum*
  coccinea, see *Quamoclit coccinea*
  digitata (syns. *I. paniculata, I. palmata*) 660
  fistulosa (syn. *I. texana*) 660
  grandiflora var. *alba,* see *Calonyction aculeatum*
  hederacea (syns. *Convolvulus hederaceus, Pharbitis hederacea*) 662
  horsfalliae 662
  latiflora, see *Calonyction aculeatum*
  learii, see *I. mutabilis*
  leptophylla (Bush Moonflower) 662
  mexicana, see *Calonyction aculeatum*
  muricata, see *Calonyction muricatum*
  mutabilis (syns. *I. dealbata, I. learii;* Blue Dawn Flower) 662; *661*
  Nil (syns. *I. imperialis, Convolvulus Nil, Pharbitis Nil*) 663
  noctiflora, see *Calonyction aculeatum*
  pandurata (syn. *I. fastigiata;* Wild Potato Vine) 663
  Purga (syns. *I. Jalapa, Exogonium Purga*) 665; *659*
  purpurea (syns. *Convolvulus majus, Convolvulus purpureus, Convolvulus mutabilis, Ipomoea ispida, Pharbitis ispida*) 665; *665*
  quamoclit, see *Quamoclit pennata*

setosa 667
stans (Brazilian Morning Glory) 666
tricolor (syns. *I. rubro-caerulea, Pharbitis rubrocaerulea*) 667; *657*
tuberosa 667
versicolor, see *Quamoclit lobata*
Also see *Calonyction; Convolvulus*
Ipomoea, Star, see *Quamoclit coccinea*
Iridaceae (family)
  Acidanthera 19–20; *Crocus* 330–338; *Freesia* 469–471; *Gladiolus* 529–538; *Iris* 669–682; *Ixia* 683–684; *Tigridia* 1290–1292; *Tritonia* 1297–1299
IRIS [EYE-riss] 669–682
  aurea, see *Iris crocea*
  barbata, see *Iris germanica*
  Chamaeiris 672; *672*
  cristata (Crested Iris) 672
  crocea (syn. *I. aurea*) 674
  dichotoma 674
  fimbriata, see *Iris japonica*
  florentina 674
  foetidissima (Gladwin, Stinking Gladwin) 674; *670*
  germanica (syn. *Iris barbata;* Purple Iris, Flag Iris) 674–676; *676*
  germanica nana 676
  japonica (syn. *Iris fimbriata*) 676–677; *669*
  Kaempferi (Japanese Iris) 677; *677*
  laevigata 678; *677*
  pallida 678; *671*
  Pseudacorus (syn. *Iris aquatica;* Water Flag, Yellow Flag) 678; *688*
  pumila (Dwarf Iris) 678
  reticulata 681; *681*
  siberica 679; *673*
  stylosa, see *Iris unguicularis*
  susiana (Mourning Iris) 679; *680*
  tectorum (Roof Iris) 679
  unguicularis (syn. *Iris stylosa*) 679; *682*
  versicolor (Blue Flag) 681; *682*
  xiphioides (syn. *Iris anglica;* English Iris) 681; *682*
  xiphium (Spanish Iris) 681
  xiphium var. *praecox* x *tingitana* (Dutch Iris) 682; *682*
Iris, Crested, see *Iris cristata*

Iris, Dutch, see *Iris xiphium* var. *praecox* x *Iris tingitana*
Iris, Dwarf, see *Iris pumila*
Iris, English, see *Iris xiphioides*
Iris, Flag, see *Iris germanica*
Iris, Japanese, see *Iris Kaempferi*
Iris, Purple, see *Iris germanica*
Iris, Roof, see *Iris tectorum*
Iris, Spanish, see *Iris xiphium*
Iris Shell Flower, see *Tigridia*
Iron Helmet, see *Aconitum*
Islay Cherry, see *Prunus ilicifolia*
Ivy, Colosseum, see *Linaria Cymbalaria*
Ivy, Kenilworth, see *Linaria Cymbalaria*
Ivy-leaved Gèranium, see *Pelargonium peltatum*
IXIA [IKS-eeya] (African Corn Lily) 683–684
  flexuosa 683; *683*
  Hybrids 684
  maculata 684
  speciosa (syn. *I. campanulata*) 684
  viridiflora 684

Jacobaea elegans, see *Senecio elegans*
Jack-in-Prison, see *Nigella*
Jack-in-the-Green, see *Nigella*
Jackman, George, cultivates *Clematis* 256, 262
Jacob's Ladder, see *Polemonium*
Jacquin, Nicholaus J., 1017
Jalap, Mexican, see *Mirabilis longiflora*
Jam, Rose Hip, recipe for 1142
Jamaica Honeysuckle, see *Passiflora laurifolia*
Jamaica Sorrel, see *Hibiscus Sabdariffa*
Jameson, William, work with *Gerbera* 525
Japanese Anemone, see *Anemone japonica*
Japanese beetles 1150
Japanese Bellflower, see *Platycodon grandiflorus*
Japanese Pagoda Tree, see *Sophora japonica*
Japanese Wisteria, see *Wistaria floribunda*
Japonica, see *Chaenomeles japonica*
Jasmine, see *Jasminum*
Jasmine, Arabian, see *Jasminum sambac*

Jasmine, Blue, see *Clematis crispa*
Jasmine, Cape, see *Gardenia jasminoides*
Jasmine, Catalonian, see *Jasminum grandiflorum*
Jasmine, Chilean, see *Mandevilla*
Jasmine, Common, see *Jasminum officinale*
Jasmine, Confederate, see *Trachelospermum*
Jasmine, Coral, see *Cestrum elegans*
Jasmine, Day, see *Cestrum diurnum*
Jasmine, Italian, see *Jasminum revolutum*
Jasmine, Night, see *Cestrum nocturnum*
Jasmine, Primrose, see *Jasminum primulinum*
Jasmine, Spanish, see *Jasminum grandiflorum*
Jasmine, Star, see *Trachelospermum*
Jasmine, Sweet, see *Jasminum officinale*
Jasmine, White, see *Jasminum officinale*
Jasmine, Willow-leaved, see *Cestrum parqui*
Jasmine, Winter, see *Jasminum nudiflorum*
JASMINUM [JAZ-min-um] (Jasmine) 684–694
  azoricum 691; *686*
  beesianum 691
  grandiflorum (Spanish Jasmine, Catalonian Jasmine) 691
  mesnyi, see *J. primulinum*
  nudiflorum (syn. *J. sieboldianum;* Winter Jasmine) 692; *689*
  officinale (Sweet Jasmine, White Jasmine, Common Jasmine) 692; *685*
  parkeri 692
  polyanthum 693; *693*
  primulinum (syn. *J. mesnyi;* Primrose Jasmine) 693
  sambac (Arabian Jasmine) 694
  x *stephanense* 694
Jerusalem Artichoke, see *Helianthus tuberosus*
Jerusalem Cherry, see *Solanum Pseudocapsicum*
Jerusalem Cross, see *Lychnis chalcedonica*
Jerusalem Sage, see *Phlomis fruticosa*

Jet Bead, see *Rhodotypos kerrioides*
Jewel of the Veldt, see *Ursinia*
Jew's Mallow, see *Kerria japonica*
Jimson Weed, see *Datura Stramonium*
Johnny Smoker, see *Geum triflorum*
Johns, Rev. C. A., on *Viburnum* 1353
Johnston, Major Lawrence, cultivates *Jasminum* 689
Jonquil, see *Narcissus*
Josephine, Empress, collection of *Erica* 442; *Rosa* 1136
Josika, Rosalie von, species of *Syringa* named for 1261
Jussieu, Antoine Laurent de, raises *Callistephus* 149; names *Incarvillea* 651; names *Petunia* 982; names *Tecoma* 1275

Kaempfer, Engelbert, describes *Camellia japonica* 160; *History of Japan* 164; finds *Campsis grandiflora* 183; on *Deutzia* 390, on *Hydrangea* 623; on *Kerria japonica* 700
Kalm, Peter, work with *Kalmia* 695
KALMIA [KAL-meeya] (Mountain Laurel, Sheep Laurel, Lambkill, Swamp Laurel, Calico Bush) 695–700
  angustifolia (Sheep Laurel, Lambkill, Dwarf Laurel, Wicky) 698–699; *699*
  cuneata 698
  hirsuta (syn. *Kalmiella hirsuta*) 698
  latifolia (Mountain Laurel, American Laurel, Calico Bush) 698–699; *696*
  polifolia (syn. *Kalmia glauca*) 699–700; *699*
Kalmiella hirsuta, see *Kalmia hirsuta*
Kamel, Georg Josef, *Camellia* named for 161
Kenilworth Ivy, see *Linaria Cymbalaria*
Kerr, William, work with *Kerria japonica* 700; *Lonicera* 793; *Paeonia* 932
KERRIA [KEHR-reeya] *japonica* (syn. *Corchorus japonicus;* Japanese Rose,

Globe Flower, Jew's Mallow) 700–704; *701; 703*
  "white-flowered," see *Rhodotypos kerrioides*
Kingdon-Ward, Captain, work with *Meconopsis betonicifolia* 848; discovers *Primula florindae* 1046; work with *Rhododendron* 1095
Kingfisher Daisy, see *Felicia bergeriana*
KIRENGSHOMA [kirrings-HO-muh] *palmata* (Yellow Waxbells) 704–705; *706*
Knapweed, see *Centaurea*
Knife Acacia, see *Acacia cultriformis*
Kniphof, Johann Hieronymus, genus named for 705
KNIPHOFIA [nip-HO-feeya, *or* ny-FOE-feeya] (Red-hot Poker, Tritoma, Flame Flower, Torch Lily, Poker Plant) 705–710
  burchellii 707
  caulescens (syn. *Tritoma caulescens*) 708; *709*
  foliosa (syn. *Tritoma foliosa*) 708; *709*
  galpinii (syn. *Tritoma galpinii*) 708
  Hybrids 709–710
  macowanii (syns. *Tritoma rigidissima, Tritoma maroccana*) 708
  rufa 708
  tuckii 708
  uvaria (syns. *K. aloides, K. hybrida, Tritoma uvaria*) 709; *709*
Kolkwitz, R., genus named for 712
KOLKWITZIA [kohl-KWITZ-eeya] *amabilis* (Beauty Bush) 710–712; *711*
Kolomikta Vine, see *Actinidia Kolomikta*
Kowhai, see *Sophora tetraptera*
Kraunhia sinensis, see *Wistaria sinensis*

labdanum (resinous substance from *Cistus ladaniferus*) 245–246
Labiatae (family)
  Coleus 283–284; *Elsholtzia* 430–431; *Lavandula* 730–736; *Leonotis* 739–740;

Monarda 868–870; *Nepeta* 896–898; *Phlomis* 998–999; *Physostegia virginiana* 1013–1015; *Salvia* 1180–1188; *Teucrium* 1279–1282
Lablab, see *Dolichos Lablab*
Lablab cultratus, see *Dolichos Lablab*
Laburnocytisus x *adami,* see *Laburnum* x *adami*
LABURNUM [lab-URN-um] (Golden Chain, Golden Rain, Bean Tree) 712–716
  x *adami* (syn. *Laburnocytisus* x *adami;* Purple Laburnum) 715
  alpinum (Scotch Laburnum) 715; *714*
  anagyroides (syn. *L. vulgare;* Common Laburnum) 716
  x *vossii,* see *Laburnum* x *watereri*
  x *watereri* (syn. *L.* x *vossii*) 716
Lace Cup 625, 630; also see *Hydrangea Hortensia*
Ladies Eardrops, see *Fuchsia*
Lady Bank's Rose, see *Rosa banksiae*
ladybugs 1150
Lady-in-the-Bower, see *Nigella*
Lady Tulip, see *Tulipa clusiana*
Lady Washington Geranium, see *Pelargonium domesticum*
La Fontaine, Jean de, on *Iris* 671
Lagerstroem, Magnus von, genus named for, 717
LAGERSTROEMIA [lay-gurr-STREEM-eeya] (Crape Myrtle, Crepe Myrtle) 716–720
  flos-reginae, see *L. speciosa*
  indica (Crape Myrtle) 718; *719*
  speciosa (syns. *Munchausia speciosa, Lagerstroemia flos-reginae;* Queen's Flower) 720
  subcostata 720
Lalizare, Sheik Mohammed, grows *Tulipa* 1315
Lamarck, Jean Baptiste Antoine Pierre Monnet de, work with *Hosta* 610
Lambkill, see *Kalmia*
Lamp-Brush Flower, see *Callistemon*
Lampshade Meconopsis, see *Meconopsis integrifolia*
Langdon, Charles F., work with *Delphinium* 377, 378
LANTANA [lan-TANN-na] (Red Sage, Yellow Sage) 720–723

Camara (syn. *L. aculeata;* Mountain Sage of Jamaica) 722; *721*
delicatissima, see *L. sellowiana*
montevidensis, see *L. sellowiana*
sellowiana (syns. *L. delicatissima, L. montevidensis;* Weeping Lantana, Trailing Lantana) 723
Lantern, Chinese, see *Physalis alkekengi*
Larkspur, see *Delphinium*
Lasiandra macrantha, see *Tibouchina semidecandra*
LATHYRUS [LATH-ih-russ] (Sweet Pea) 723–730
grandiflorus (Everlasting Pea) 728
latifolius (Perennial Pea, Everlasting Pea) 728; *728*
luteus (syn. *Orobus luteus*) 729
odoratus (Sweet Pea) 729; *726; 729*
splendens (Pride of California, Campo Pea) 729
tingitanus (Tangier Scarlet Pea) 729; *724*
tuberosus (Tuberous Pea) 730; *725*
Laurel, American, see *Kalmia latifolia*
Laurel, Cherry, see *Prunus Laurocerasus*
Laurel, Dwarf, see *Kalmia angustifolia*
Laurel, Great, see *Rhododendron maximum*
Laurel, Mountain, see *Kalmia*
Laurel, Pale, see *Kalmia polifolia*
Laurel, Portuguese, see *Prunus lusitanica*
Laurel, Sheep, see *Kalmia*
Laurel, Spurge, see *Daphne Laureola*
Laurel, Swamp, see *Kalmia; Magnolia virginiana*
Laurocerasus ilicifolia, see *Prunus ilicifolia*
Laurocerasus lusitanica, see *Prunus lusitanica*
Laurocerasus officinalis, see *Prunus Laurocerasus*
Laurustinus, see *Viburnum tinus*
Lavallée, A., work with *Lonicera korolkowii* 800
LAVANDULA [lav-ANN-dew-la] (Lavender) 730–736
dentata 733; *731*
latifolia 734
multifida (syn. *L. pinnata*) 734; *735*
officinalis, see *L. spica*
spica (syn. *L. officinalis;* Common Lavender) 734; *734*
stoechas (French Lavender) 736; *732*
vera 736
Lavater, see *Lavatera*
LAVATERA [lav-at-TEE-ra] (Lavater, Mallow) 736–739
arborea (Tree Mallow) 738
assurgentiflora (California Windbreak) 738
thuringiaca 739
trimestris (syn. *L. rosea*) 739; *737*
Lavender, see *Lavandula*
Lavender, Sea, see *Limonium*
Lawrence, D. H., 4
Lawrence, Miss, book on *Rosa* 1136
Lawrence, Sir William, work with *Lonicera* x *Tellemanniana* 804
Leadwort, see *Ceratostigma; Plumbago*
Leclerc, work with *Verbena* 1343
Lee, James, work with *Fuchsia* 474
Legentil de la Galaisière, G.J.H.J.-B., 623
Legousia 1241
Legousia Speculum Veneris, see *Specularia speculum Veneris*
Legouz de Gerland, genus named for 1241
Legrand *(Manuel du cultivateur des Dahlias)* 358
Leguminosae (family)
Acacia 4–12; *Cassia* 193–195; *Cytisus* 348–355; *Desmodium* 387–389; *Dolichos* 419–421; *Genista* 506–512; *Indigofera* 654–656; *Laburnum* 712–716; *Lathyrus* 723–730; *Lupinus* 806–813; *Mimosa* 858–860; *Sophora* 1237–1240; *Spartium junceum* 1240–1241; *Ulex* 1331–1332; *Wistaria* 1383–1388
Leichtlin, Max, work with *Clematis* 257
Lemoine, nursery of (Nancy, France), work with *Gladiolus* 530; *Hydrangea* 625; *Paeonia* 933, 934; *Pelargonium* 961; *Syringa* 1261, 1264; *Tamarix* 1276
Lemon, Water, see *Passiflora laurifolia*
Lemon Mint, see *Monarda citriodora*
Lenglart, Jules, work with *Tulipa* 1316
Lent Lily, see *Narcissus Pseudo-narcissus*
Lenten Rose, see *Helleborus orientalis*
Leo IX, Pope, 1132
LEONOTIS [lee-o-NO-tiss] (Lion's Ear, Lion's Tail) 739–740
leonurus (Lion's Tail) 740; *740*
LEONTOPODIUM [lee-on-to-PO-deeyum] (Edelweiss) 740–742
alpinum (Edelweiss) 742; *741*
haplophylloides (syn. *L. aloysiodorum*) 742
nivale 742
Leopard's Bane, see *Doronicum*
Lepeaute, Madame, species of *Hydrangea* named for 623
LEPTOSPERMUM [lepto-SPERM-um] (South Sea Myrtle, Tea Tree) 742–745
flavescens 743; *744*
laevigatum 743
scoparium 743, 745
Leptosyne bigelovii, see *Coreopsis bigelovii; Coreopsis dongasii*
Leptosyne maritima, see *Coreopsis maritima*
Leptosyne stillmanii, see *Coreopsis stillmanii*
Lespedeza thunbergii, see *Desmodium penduliflorum*
LEUCOJUM [lew-KO-jum] (Snowflake) 745–746
aestivum 746
autumnale 746
vernum 746; *748*
Leucothoe 1015
LIATRIS [ly-AY-tris] (Snakeroot, Blazing Star, Kansas Feather) 746–749
graminifolia (Grass-leaved Liatris) 747
pycnostachya (Prairie Button Snakeroot, Kansas Gay-Feather) 747
scariosa (Rattlesnake Master, Blue Blazing Star) 749
spicata (Gay Feather, Prairie Pine, Devil's Bit) 749; *747*
squarrosa (Blazing Star, Colicroot) 749

1455

Liberty Tea 196; also see
    Ceanothus coeruleus
Lice, Beggar, see *Desmodium canadense*
light, see shade
Lightwood, see *Acacia melanoxylon*
Ligularia clivorum, see *Senecio clivorum*
Ligularia japonica, see *Senecio japonicus*
Ligularia veitchiana, see *Senecio veitchianus*
Lilac, see *Syringa*
Lilac, California, see *Ceanothus thyrsiflorus*
Lilac, Common, see *Syringa vulgaris*
Lilac, Hungarian, see *Syringa Josikaea*
Lilac, Persian, see *Syringa persica*
Lilac, Summer, see *Buddleia davidii*
Lilac, Wild, see *Ceanothus*
Liliaceae (family)
    Agapanthus 31–34; *Allium* 36–39; *Chionodoxa* 224–225; *Colchicum* 278–283; *Convallaria* 285–287; *Eremurus* 438–439; *Fritillaria* 471–473; *Gloriosa* 538–539; *Hemerocallis* 580–586; *Hosta* 608–611; *Hyacinthus* 614–622; *Kniphofia* 705–710; *Lilium* 749–770; *Muscari* 870–873; *Ornithogalum* 919–922; *Scilla* 1210–1212; *Tulipa* 1311–1331
LILIUM [LILY-um] (Lily) 749–770
    amabile 758
    auratum (Golden-rayed Lily of Japan) 758–759
    bolanderi 759
    brownii 759
    bulbiferum 759; *759*
    candidum (Madonna Lily, Annunciation Lily) 760; *760*
    chalcedonicum 760; *750*
    croceum, see *L. bulbiferum* var. *croceum*
    dauricum 760
    davidii 760, 762
    x *elegans*, see *L. hollandicum*
    formosanum 762
    giganteum (syn. *Cardiocrinum giganteum*) 762
    henryi 763
    x *hollandicum* 763

humboldtii 763
Hybrids 755–758
japonicum 764
kelloggii 764
leucanthum 764
longiflorum (Easter Lily) 764–765
Martagon (Turk's Cap Lily) 765; *765*
michauxi (Carolina Lily) 766
nepalense 766
ochraceum (syn. *L. primulinum*) 766
pardalinum (Leopard Lily) 766
parvum (Sierra Lily) 766
pumilum (Coral Lily) 767
pyrenaicum 767
regale (Royal Lily) 767; *757*
rubescens (Chaparral Lily) 767
sargentiae 768
speciosum 768; *761*
sulphureum (syn. *L. myriophyllum*) 768
superbum (Turk's Cap Lily of America, Swamp Lily, Wild Tiger Lily) 769
tenuifolium, see *L. pumilum*
x *testaceum* (Nankin Lily) 769
tigrinum (Tiger Lily) 769–770
umbellatum, see *L.* x *hollandicum*
washingtonianum (Washington Lily) 770
Lily, see *Lilium*
Lily, Adobe, see *Fritillaria pluriflora*
Lily, African, see *Agapanthus*
Lily, African Corn, see *Ixia*
Lily, Annunciation, see *Lilium candidum*
Lily, Arum, see *Zantedeschia*
Lily, Barbados, see *Hippeastrum*
Lily, Calla, see *Zantedeschia*
Lily, Carolina, see *Lilium michauxi*
Lily, Chaparral, see *Lilium rubescens*
Lily, Checkered, see *Fritillaria lanceolata*
Lily, Coral, see *Lilium pumilum*
Lily, Cuban, see *Scilla peruviana*
Lily, Easter, see *Lilium longiflorum*
Lily, Foxtail, see *Eremurus*
Lily, Gloriosa, see *Gloriosa*
Lily, Glory, see *Gloriosa*
Lily, Gumbo, see *Mentzelia decapetala*
Lily, Lent, see *Narcissus Pseudo-narcissus*

Lily, Leopard, see *Lilium pardalinum*
Lily, Madonna, see *Lilium candidum*
Lily, Nankin, see *Lilium* x *testaceum*
Lily, Peruvian, see *Alstroemeria*
Lily, Plantain, see *Hosta*
Lily, Prairie, see *Mentzelia decapetala*
Lily, Rothschild, see *Gloriosa rothschildiana*
Lily, Royal, see *Lilium regale*
Lily, Sierra, see *Lilium parvum*
Lily, Snake's Head, see *Fritillaria meleagris*
Lily, Swamp, see *Lilium superbum*
Lily, Tiger, see *Lilium tigrinum*
Lily, Toad, see *Fritillaria meleagris*
Lily, Torch, see *Kniphofia*
Lily, Turk's Cap, see *Lilium Martagon*
Lily, Washington, see *Lilium washingtonianum*
Lily, Wild Tiger, see *Lilium superbum*
Lily-flowered Tulips 1329; *1316*
Lily Leek, see *Allium Moly*
Lily of the Field, see *Sternbergia lutea*
Lily-of-the-Nile, see *Agapanthus*
Lily of the Valley, see *Convallaria majalis*
Lily Tree, see *Magnolia* x *soulangiana*
Lily Turf, see *Convallaria japonica*
LIMONIUM [ly-MO-neeyum] (Statice, Sea Lavender) 770–772
    latifolium (syn. *Statice latifolia*) 771
    sinuatum (syn. *Statice sinuata*) 771; *770*
    suworowii (syn. *Statice suworowii*) 771
    tataricum (syn. *Statice tatarica*) 771
    vulgare (syn. *Statice limonium*) 771–772
Linaceae (family)
    Linum 776–781
LINARIA [ly-NAY-reeya, *or* lih-NAY-reeya] (Toadflax) 772–776
    alpina 774; *773*
    bipartita 774
    Cymbalaria (syn. *Cymbalaria muralis;* Kenilworth Ivy,

Colosseum Ivy, Aaron's Beard, Climbing Sailor) 774; *774*
dalmatica 774
maroccana 775
purpurea 775; *773*
repens 775
vulgaris (Butter-and-Eggs, Wild Toadflax) 775
Lincoln, Earl of, cultivates *Lonicera* 793
Lindley, John, describes camellias 165; proposes genus *Chaenomeles* 216; names *Mandevilla* 838; *Rosarum Monographia* 1136, 1138
Ling, see *Calluna vulgaris*
Linnaeus, Carolus, classifies or names *Aconitum lycoctonum* 22; *Antirrhinum* 68; *Asclepias* 88; *Aster* 91; *Begonia* 104; *Bignonia capreolata* 126; *Buddleia* 133; *Calluna* (as *Erica vulgaris*) 154; *Camellia* 161; *Ceanothus* 196; *Centaurea* 204; *Cheiranthus* 222; *Chrysanthemum* 228; *Colchicum* 281; *Coreopsis* 295; *Cornus* 300; *Cytisus* 350; *Daphne* 364; *Epimedium* 434; *Fuchsia* 474; *Halesia* 546; *Hibiscus* 591; *Hyacinthus* 616; *Iris* 668; *Kalmia* 694; *Lantana* 722; *Limonium* 770; *Lobelia* 785; *Lonicera* 794; *Mirabilis* 864; *Nerium* 900; *Oenothera* 913; *Passiflora* 955; *Philadelphus* 991; *Rhododendron* 1093; *Rosa* 1128; *Rudbeckia* 1173; *Syringa* 1258, 1260; *Tecoma stans* 1278; *Tropaeolum* 1302; *Zinnia* 1393
LINUM [LY-num] (Flax) 776–781
alpinum 778; *778*
austriacum 779; *780*
campanulatum 779
flavum (Golden Flax) 779
grandiflorum (syn. *L. rubrum;* Flowering Flax) 779; *777*
narbonense 779
perenne 779
usitatissimum (Common Flax) 781
Lion's Ear, see *Leonotis*
Lion's Tail, see *Leonotis*
Liszt, Franz, 1128

LITHOSPERMUM [litho-SPERM-um] (Gromwell, Puccoon) 781–784
canescens (Orange Puccoon) 782
diffusum (syn. *L. prostratum*) 782
incisum (Yellow Puccoon) 783
purpureo-caeruleum 783; *783*
rosmarinifolium 783–784
Liverwort, see *Hepatica*
Livingstone, Dr. David, species named for 857
Livingstone Daisy, see *Mesembryanthemum criniflorum*
Loasaceae (family) *Mentzelia* 852–854
Lobb, William, work with *Rhododendron* 1095
Lobel, Matthias (Matthias de l'Obel), genus named for 784; on *Rosa* 1133; *Tigridia* described by 1290
LOBELIA [lo-BEE-leeya] 784–790
cardinalis (Cardinal Flower) 787; *787*
Erinus (syns. *L. heterophylla, L. gracilis, L. bicolor;* "Edging Lobelia") 788
fulgens 788–789
inflata (Indian Tobacco) 785, 789
laxiflora 789
syphilitica 789
tenuior (syn. *L. ramosa*) 789; *786*
tupa 789
Lobeliaceae (family) *Lobelia* 784–790
LOBULARIA [lo-bew-LAY-reeya] (Sweet Alyssum, Snowdrift) 790–792
maritima (syn. *Alyssum maritimum*) 791; *791*
Also see *Alyssum*
Lochnera rosea, see *Vinca rosea*
Lock and Keys, see *Dicentra spectabilis*
Loganiaceae (family) *Buddleia* 132–139
London Pride, see *Saxifraga umbrosa*
LONICERA [lon-ISS-er-a] (Honeysuckle) 792–805
alseuosmoides 797
x *bella* 797
caprifolium (Common Woodbine, Italian Honeysuckle) 797

chrysantha 797
dioica (Small Honeysuckle, Small Woodbine) 798
etrusca 798
flava (Yellow Honeysuckle) 798
fragrantissima 798; *792*
hildebrandiana 799
hirsuta (Rough Woodbine) 799
involucrata (Twinberry) 799
japonica 799–800; *802*
korolkowii 800
maackii 800
morrowii 800
nitida (syn. *Chamaecerasus nitida*) 801
periclymenum (Woodbine, Twisted Eglantine, Honeysuckle) 801; *793*
pileata (syn. *Chamaecerasus pileata*) 801, 803
sempervirens (Trumpet Honeysuckle, Coral Honeysuckle) 803; *795*
standishii 803
tatarica (Tartarian Honeysuckle, Bush Honeysuckle, Garden Fly Honeysuckle) 803–804
x *Tellemanniana* 804; *796*
thibetica 804
xylosteum (European Fly Honeysuckle) 804
yunnanensis 805
Lonitzer, Adam, genus named for 794
Lophospermum erubescens, see *Maurandia erubescens*
Loudon, John Claudius, work with *Berberis* 120; on *Chaenomeles* 216; on *Cytisus* 349; on *Fuchsia* 476; on *Hibiscus* 590; on *Magnolia* 819; work with *Malus rivularis* 836; on *Viola* 1366
Louis IX, King of France, 1086
Loureiro, Juan, uses name *Campsis* 183; work with *Enkianthus* 431
Love Entangle, see *Sedum acre*
Love-in-a-Mist, see *Nigella*
Love-Lies-Bleeding, see *Amaranthus caudatus*
Love Vine, see *Clematis virginiana*
LUNARIA [loo-NAY-reeya, *or* lun-NAH-reeya] (Honesty, Satin Flower, Moon Wort, Silver Shilling, St. Peter's Pence) 805–806

annua (syn. *L. biennis*) 806; 805
rediviva 806
Lupine, see *Lupinus*
LUPINUS [loo-PY-nus] (Lupine) 806–813
arboreus (Tree Lupine) 811; 807
hartwegii 811
luteus 811
mutabilis 811–812; *810*
nanus 812
perennis (Quaker Bonnet) 812
polyphyllus 812; *809*
Russell Hybrids 812–813
LYCHNIS [LIK-niss] (Campion, Catchfly) 813–818
chalcedonica (Scarlet Lychnis, Jerusalem Cross, Maltese Cross, Scarlet Lightning) 814; *816*
Coeli-rosa (syn. *Agrostemma Coeli-rosa;* Rose of Heaven) 814
coronaria (syn. *Agrostemma coronaria;* Mullein Pink, Dusty Miller, Rose Campion) 814; *815*
coronata (syns. *L. grandiflora, L. bungeana*) 814; *816*
Flos-cuculi (syn. *Agrostemma Flos-cuculi;* Cuckoo Flower, Ragged Robin) 816
Flos-Jovis (syn. *Agrostemma Flos-Jovis;* Flower of Jove) 816; *817*
x *Haageana* 816
pyrenaica 818
Viscaria (syn. *Viscaria viscosa;* German Catchfly) 818; *816*
Also see *Silene*
Lynch, Irwin, work with *Gerbera* 525
Lythraceae (family)
Cuphea 338–339;
Lagerstroemia 716–720

Macartney Rose, see *Rosa bracteata*
Madame Bovary (association with lilies) 751
Madonna Lily, see *Lilium candidum*
Madwort, see *Alyssum*
Magellan Barberry, see *Berberis buxifolia*
Magnol, Pierre, genus named for 819

MAGNOLIA [mag-NO-leeya] 818–829
acuminata (Cucumber Tree) 820
campbellii 822
dawsoniana 822
delavayi 822
denudata (syns. *M. conspicua, M. Yulan;* Yulan) 822; *821*
fraseri (syn. *M. auriculata*) 823
glauca, see *M. virginiana*
grandiflora (syn. *M. foetida;* Bull Bay, Evergreen Magnolia, Big-leaved Magnolia) 823; *823*
kobus 823
x *lennei* 824
liliflora (syn. *M. purpurea*) 824; *825*
macrophylla 824; *818*
obovata (syn. *M. hypoleuca*) 826; *826*
parviflora, see *M. sieboldii*
rustica rubra, see *M.* x *soulangiana* var. *rustica rubra*
salicifolia 826
sieboldii (syn. *M. parviflora;* Oyama Magnolia) 827; *826*
x *soulangiana* (Lily Tree) 827
stellata (syn. *M. halleana;* Star Magnolia) 827; *826*
thompsoniana 828
tripetala (syn. *M. umbrella;* Umbrella Tree) 828
x *veitchii* 828
virginiana (syn. *M. glauca;* Sweet Bay, Beaver Tree, White Bay, Swamp Bay, Swamp Laurel) 828
wilsonii 829
Magnolia, Big-leaved, see *Magnolia grandiflora*
Magnolia, Evergreen, see *Magnolia grandiflora*
Magnolia, Oyama, see *Magnolia sieboldii*
Magnolia, Star, see *Magnolia stellata*
Magnoliaceae (family)
Magnolia 818–829
Mahala Mat, see *Ceanothus prostratus*
Malvaceae (family)
Abutilon 2–4; *Althaea* 43–48; *Hibiscus* 590–601; *Hoheria* 605–607; *Lavatera* 736–739
Mallow, see *Hibiscus; Lavatera*
Maltese Cross, see *Lychnis chalcedonica*

MALUS [MAHL-uss] (Crab Apple) 829–838, 1055
angustifolia (syn. *Pyrus angustifolia;* Southern Crab-Apple) 830
x *arnoldiana* 831
x *atrosanguinea,* see *M. floribunda* var. *atrosanguinea*
baccata (syn. *Pyrus baccata;* Siberian Crab) 831; *830*
communis, see *M. pumila*
coronaria (syn. *Pyrus coronaria;* American Crab, Sweet Crab, Garland Crab) 831
x *eleyi* (syn. *Pyrus* x *eleyi;* Eley Crab) 831
florentina. (syn. *Pyrus crataegifolia*) 833; *832*
floribunda (syn. *Pyrus floribunda;* Showy Crab) 833
fusca, see *M. rivularis*
halliana (syn. *Pyrus halliana*) 833
hupehensis, see *M. theifera*
ionensis (syn. *Pyrus coronaria ionensis;* Prairie Crab, Iowa Crab) 833
niedzwetzkyana 834
prunifolia (syn. *Pyrus prunifolia*) 834
pumila (syns. *M. communis, Pyrus malus;* Wild Apple) 836
x *purpurea* (syn. *Pyrus purpurea*) 836
rivularis (syns. *M. fusca, Pyrus fusca;* Oregon Crab) 836
sargentii (syn. *Pyrus sargentii*) 836
x *scheideckeri* (syn. *Pyrus* x *scheideckeri*) 837
sieboldii (syn. *Pyrus sieboldii;* Toringo Crab) 837
spectabilis (syn. *Pyrus spectabilis*) 837; *835*
theifera (syns. *M. hupehensis, Pyrus theifera*) 837
toringoides (syn. *Pyrus toringoides*) 837
trilobata (syns. *Eriolobus trilobata, Pyrus triloba*) 838
zumi (syn. *Pyrus sumi*) 838
MANDEVILLA [mand-VIL-la] 838–840
suaveolens (Chilean Jasmine) 838; *839*
Mandeville, Sir John, 120
manures, fertilizers and xxvii–xxxv

1458

Maple, Flowering, see *Abutilon*
Marentonneau, Gaillard de, genus named for 491
Marguerite, see *Chrysanthemum frutescens*
Marguerite, Blue, see *Felicia amelloides*
Marguerite, Golden, see *Anthemis tinctoria*
Maries, Charles, work with *Actinidia chinensis* 25; camellias 164; *Caryopteris* 191; *Enkianthus* 432; *Hamamelis* 549; *Hydrangea* 625; *Wistaria* 1384
Marigold, see *Calendula; Tagetes*
Marigold, African, see *Tagetes erecta*
Marigold, Aztec, see *Tagetes erecta*
Marigold, Big, see *Tagetes erecta*
Marigold, Bush, see *Tagetes tenuifolia*
Marigold, Cape, see *Dimorphotheca*
Marigold, Climbing, see *Tagetes sarmentosa*
Marigold, Corn, see *Chrysanthemum segetum*
Marigold, Fig, see *Mesembryanthemum*
Marigold, French, see *Tagetes patula*
Marigold, Mexican, see *Tagetes lucida*
Marigold, Sweet-scented, see *Tagetes lucida*
Martial (Roman poet), on roses 1130
Marvel of Peru, see *Mirabilis*
Mask-Flower, see *Alonsoa*
Masson, Francis, work with *Erica* 441
Matilija Poppy, see *Romneya coulteri*
Matriciaria eximia, see *Chrysanthemum Parthenium*
MATTHIOLA [ma-THY-oh-la] (Stock) 840–844
  bicornis (Night-Scented Stock, Evening Stock) 843
  incana (Gillyflower, Brompton Stock) 843
  sinuata (Sea Stock) 844; *842*
Matthiolus (Mattioli), Pietro Andrea, genus named for 841; on lilacs *(Syringa)* 1260; names *Tagetes* 1270
MAURANDIA [mor-AND-eeya] 844–847
  barclaiana 845; *845*

  erubescens (syn. *Lophospermum erubescens*) 847
  scandens (syn. *M. semperflorens*) 847; *846*
Maw, George, on *Chionodoxa* 224
Maximowicz, Karl Johann, work with *Spiraea* 1244
May, see *Crataegus*
May Apple, see *Passiflora incarnata*
Mayflower, see *Hepatica americana*
May Pop, see *Passiflora incarnata*
Mazarin, Cardinal, cultivates carnations 395
McCaskill Camellia, see *Camellia maliflora*
McEacharn, Captain Neil, 762, 766
McKilligan, work with *Rhododendron* 1108
Meadow Rue, see *Thalictrum*
Meckel, work with Cyclamen 341
MECONOPSIS [meck-on-OPP-sis] (Poppywort) 847–852
  aculeata 848
  baileyi, see *M. betonicifolia*
  betonicifolia (syn. *M. baileyi*; Himalayan Blue Poppy) 848
  cambrica (Welsh Poppy) 850
  dhwojii 850
  grandis 850
  heterophylla (syns. *Papaver heterophyllum, Stylomecon heterophylla*; Wind Poppy) 850
  horridula (syns. *M. prattii, M. rudis, M. racemosa, M. rigidiuscula*) 851
  integrifolia (syn. *Cathcartia integrifolia*; Lampshade Meconopsis) 851
  napaulensis (syns. *M. wallichii, M. nepalensis*; Satin Poppy) 851
  prattii, see *M. horridula*
  quintuplinervia 851
  regia 851
  x *sheldonii* 851
  simplicifolia 851; *849*
  superba 852
  wallichii, see *M. napaulensis*
  Also see *Papaver*
Medici, Cosimo de' 616; jasmine collection of 687
Megasia (syn. for *bergenia*; "saxifrage") 1194

Melastomataceae (family) *Tibouchina* 1288–1290
Memorial Rose, see *Rosa wichuraiana*
Mendel, Father Gregor, work with *Lathyrus* 725
Mendel Tulips 1327; *1320*
Mentzel, Christian, 852
MENTZELIA [ment-ZEE-leeya] (Bartonia) 852–854
  bartonioides 852
  decapetala (syns. *Bartonia decapetala, M. ornata*; Prairie Lily, Gumbo Lily) 854
  laevicaulis (Blazing Star) 854
  lindleyi (syns. *Bartonia aurea, M. aurea*) 854; *853*
Menzies, A., work with *Rosa nutkana* 1163
Mescal Bean, see *Sophora secundiflora*
Mesembryanthemaceae (family) *Mesembryanthemum* 854–858
MESEMBRYANTHEMUM [meh-sem-bree-ANTH-eh-mum] (Fig Marigold) 854–858
  acinaciforme (syn. *Carpobrotus acinaciformis*) 855; *854*
  aurantiacum 855
  criniflorum (syn. *Dorotheanthus bellidiflorus*; Livingstone Daisy) 857
  crystallinum (syn. *Cryophytum crystallinum*; Ice Plant) 857
  edule (syn. *Carpobrotus edulis*; Hottentot Fig) 857
  tricolor (syns. *Erepsia mutabilis, Mesembryanthemum pyropaeum, Dorotheanthus gramineus*) 858; *856*
Mespilus 1080
Metrosideros speciosus, see *Callistemon speciosus*
Mexican Aster, see *Cosmos*
Mexican Bush Sage, see *Salvia leucantha*
Mexican Ivy Plant, see *Cobaea*
Mexican Jalap, see *Mirabilis longiflora*
Mexican Marigold, see *Tagetes lucida*
Mexican Poppy, see *Hunnemannia fumariifolia*
Meyer, F. N., discovers *Syringa* 1260
Meyer, K. H., on *Tulipa* 1316
Mezeray, Latour ("l'homme aux camélias") 163

1459

Michaelmas Daisy, see *Aster novi-belgii*
Mignonette, see *Reseda*
mildew 1147
Milfoil, see *Achillea Millefolium*
Milkweed, see *Asclepias*
Miller, Philip, work with *Callistephus* 149; *Cytisus* 350; *Diervilla* 409; *Erica* 441; *Hibiscus* 590; *Rosa* 1133
MIMOSA [mim-O-sah] 858–860
  pudica (Sensitive Plant, Humble Plant) 859; *858*
  spegazzinii 860
Mimosa, see *Acacia*
Mimosaceae (family) *Mimosa* 858–860
MIMULUS [MIM-yew-lus] (Monkey Flower, Musk) 860–864
  brevipes 862
  cardinalis 862; *861*
  cupreus 862
  glutinosus (syn. *Diplacus glutinosus*) 862
  guttatus, see *M. luteus* var. *guttatus*
  langsdorfii, see *M. luteus* var. *guttatus*
  lewisii 863
  luteus 863
  moschatus (Musk) 863
  primuloides 864
  ringens 864
Mina lobata, see *Quamoclit lobata*
Mint, Lemon, see *Monarda citriodora*
MIRABILIS [mih-RABB-il-iss, or my-RABB-il-iss] (Four-O'Clock, Marvel of Peru) 864–868
  Jalapa (syns. *Nyctago Jalapa*, *Nyctago hortensis;* Four-O'Clock, Marvel of Peru) 867; *865*
  longiflora (syn. *Nyctago longiflora;* Mexican Jalap) 868
Mist, see *Gypsophila paniculata*
Mitchell, classifies *Penstemon* 976
Mock Orange, see *Philadelphus*
Moench, Konrad, names *Kniphofia* 705
Mohammed IV, Sultan, 1086
Mollis, Azalea, see *Rhododendron molle*
Mollis Hybrids (*Rhododendron*) 1121

Monarch of the Veldt, see *Venidium*
MONARDA [mo-NARD-a] (Bee Balm, Oswego Tea, Horsemint, Bergamot) 868–870
  citriodora (Lemon Mint) 870
  didyma (Oswego Tea, Bee Balm, Red Balm) 870; *869*
  fistulosa (Wild Bergamot) 870
Monardes, Nicholas, 868
Mondo, see *Convallaria japonica*
Monkey Flower, see *Mimulus*
Monk's Pepper Tree, see *Vitex*
Monkshood, see *Aconitum*
Montbretia, see *Tritonia*
Monthly Mimosa, see *Acacia retinoides*
Moon Daisy, see *Chrysanthemum uliginosum*
Moon Wort, see *Lunaria*
Moonflower, see *Calonyction*
Moonflower, Bush, see *Ipomoea leptophylla*
Morgan, Hugh, cultivates *Clematis* 255
Morison, Robert, describes *Physalis* 1010
Morning Glory, see *Convolvulus; Ipomoea*
Morning Glory, Dwarf, see *Convolvulus tricolor*
Mortier, P., work with *Rhododendron* 1095
Moss, Golden, see *Sedum acre*
Moss, Rose, see *Portulaca*
Moss, Sun, see *Portulaca grandiflora*
Moss Campion, see *Silene schafta*
Moss Pink, see *Phlox subulata*
Moss Vervain, see *Verbena erinoides*
Mossy Stonecrop, see *Sedum acre*
Moth Mullein, see *Verbascum blattaria*
Mother of Thousands, see *Saxifraga sarmentosa*
Mountain Blue, see *Centaurea montana*
Mountain Creeper, see *Thunbergia fragrans*
Mountain Fetter Bush, see *Pieris formosa*
Mountain Laurel, see *Kalmia*
Mountain Sage of Jamaica, see *Lantana Camara*
Mountain Saxifrage, see *Saxifraga oppositifolia*
Mourning Iris, see *Iris susiana*

Moustache Plant, see *Ceratostigma*
Moyes, Rev. J., species of *Rosa* named for 1161
Muchle, Arpad, lists varieties of *Canna* 187
mulching xxxii, xxxiv
Mullein, see *Verbascum*
Mullein, Moth, see *Verbascum blattaria*
Mullein, Purple, see *Verbascum phoeniceum*
Mullein Pink, see *Lychnis coronaria*
MUSCARI [muss-KAY-ree] (Grape Hyacinth) 870–873
  armeniacum 871
  botryoides (Starch Hyacinth) 871; *872*
  macrocarpum (Yellow Grape Hyacinth) 873
  moschatum (Musk-scented Muscari) 873
  racemosum 873; *871*
Musk, see *Mimulus*
Musk Rose, see *Rosa moschata*
Musk-scented Muscari, see *Muscari moschatum*
Mussim-Pushkin, Count Apollos Apollosovitch, 1094
Mussolini 593
MYOSOTIS [my-o-SO-tiss] (Forget-Me-Not) 873–877
  alpestris (syn. *M. rupicola*) 874; *874*
  arvensis (Field Forget-Me-Not) 875
  azorica 875
  caespitosa 875
  dissitiflora 875; *876*
  palustris (syn. *M. scorpioides;* Water Forget-Me-Not) 875
  sylvatica (syns. *M. alpina, M. oblonga*) 875, 877
Myrtaceae (family) *Callistemon* 146–148; *Leptospermum* 742–745; *Myrtus* 877–879
Myrtle, see *Myrtus; Vinca*
Myrtle, Blue, see *Ceanothus thyrsiflorus*
Myrtle, Crape (or Crepe), see *Lagerstroemia*
Myrtle, South Sea, see *Leptospermum*
MYRTUS [MIR-tuss] (Myrtle) 877–879
  bullata 878
  communis (True Myrtle) 878; *879*
  nummularia 879

ugni (syns. *Eugenia ugni, Ugni molinae;* Chilean Guava) 879

Naked Ladies, see *Colchicum*
Namaqualand Daisy, see *Dimorphotheca aurantiaca; Venidium*
Nankin Lily, see *Lilium* x *testaceum*
Nannyberry, see *Viburnum Lentago*
Napoleon ("Monsieur Violette") 1369
NARCISSUS [nahr-SISS-us] (Daffodil, Jonquil, Narcissus) 880–891
 asturiensis 885
 bulbocodium (Petticoat Narcissus, Hoop Petticoat) 885; *886*
 caniculatus 885
 cantabricus 885
 cyclamineus 885, 887; *884*
 elegans (syn. *N. autumnalis*) 887
 Jonquilla (Jonquil, Daffodil) 887; *882*
 poeticus (Poet's Narcissus) 887; *886*
 Pseudo-narcissus (Trumpet Narcissus, Daffodil, Lent Lily) 887–889; *890*
 rupicola 889
 tazetta (Polyanthus Narcissus, Paper White Narcissus) 889; *880*
 triandrus var. *albus* (Angel's Tears) 889; *881*
 Watieri 891
Narcissus, Hoop Petticoat, see *Narcissus bulbocodium*
Narcissus, Paper White, see *Narcissus tazetta*
Narcissus, Petticoat, see *Narcissus bulbocodium*
Narcissus, Poet's, see *Narcissus poeticus*
Narcissus, Polyanthus, see *Narcissus tazetta*
Narcissus, Trumpet, see *Narcissus Pseudo-narcissus*
Nasturtium, see *Tropaeolum; Tropaeolum majus*
Nasturtium, Dwarf, see *Tropaeolum minus*
Nees von Esenbeck, Christian Gottfried, 149
Negri, Giovanni, on *Cornus* 301; *Helleborus* 577

NEMESIA [nem-EE-shee-a, *or* nem-EE-seeya] 891–893
 floribunda (syn. *N. affinis*) 892
 lilacina 892
 strumosa 893; *891*
NEMOPHILA [nem-OFF-illa] (Baby Blue Eyes) 893–896
 aurita (syn. *Pholistoma auritum*) 894
 maculata 894
 menziesii (syns. *N. insignis, N. atomaria, N. modesta, N. pedunculata*) 894, 896; *895*
NEPETA [NEPP-et-a] (Catmint, Catnip) 896–898
 cataria 897; *896*
 x *faassenii* 897
 mussinii, see *N.* x *faassenii*
 nervosa 897
NERIUM [NEE-reeyum] (Oleander, Rose Bay) 898–904
 indicum, see *N. odorum*
 odorum (syn. *N. indicum;* Sweet Oleander) 903
 oleander (syn. *N. laurifolium;* Common Oleander) 903; *899; 902*
Nero 1130
New Year's Gift, see *Eranthus*
Nicot, Jean, genus named for 904
NICOTIANA [nikk-o-shee-AY-na] 904–910, 982
 affinis, see *N. alata*
 alata (syn. *N. affinis*) 906; *909*
 axillaris, see *Petunia axillaris*
 glauca 906
 langsdorfii 908
 longiflora 908
 noctiflora 908; *907*
 x *sanderae* 908; *909*
 suaveolens 908
 sylvestris 909
 tabacum (Tobacco Plant) 909; *905*
 tomentosa 909–910
nicotine 905
NIGELLA [ny-JELL-a] (Love-in-a-Mist, Fennel Flower, Devil-in-a-Bush, Jack-in-Prison, Jack-in-the-Green, Lady-in-the-Bower) 910–912
 damascena 911; *911*
Nightshade, Costa Rica, see *Solanum wendlandii*
Niobe, see *Hosta*
nomenclature xxxv–xxxix
None-so-Pretty, see *Silene Armeria*
Nootka Rose, see *Rosa nutkana*
Nut, Bladder, see *Staphylea*

Nuttall, Thomas, work with *Nemophila* 894; names *Wistaria* 1383
Nyctaginaceae (family) *Bougainvillea* 130–132; *Mirabilis* 864–868
Nyctago hortensis, see *Mirabilis hortensis*
Nyctago Jalapa, see *Mirabilis Jalapa*
Nyctago longiflora, see *Mirabilis longiflora*

Oak-leaved Geranium, see *Pelargonium quercifolium*
Obedient Plant, see *Physostegia virginiana*
Odin's Helmet, see *Aconitum*
OENOTHERA [ee-noh-THEE-ra, *or* ee-NOTH-erah] (Evening Primrose, Sundrops) 912–917
 biennis (syn. *Onagra biennis;* Evening Primrose) 914; *912*
 bistoria 914
 caespitosa (syn. *Pachylophus caespitosa*) 914
 fruticosa 914; *912*
 hookeri 914
 lamarckiana 915
 missourensis (Missouri Primrose) 915; *916*
 perennis (syns. *O. pumila, O. pusilla*) 915
 rosea (syn. *Hartmannia rosea*) 915; *913*
 speciosa 917
 tetragona (syn. *O. youngii*) 917
 trichocalyx (syn. *Onagra trichocalyx*) 917
 whitneyi, see *Godetia grandiflora*
Oil, Rose, recipe for 1140
Ointment No. 36 (Jasmine ointment) 687
Okra, see *Hibiscus esculentus*
Oldham, Richard, work with *Magnolia* 819
Old Man's Beard, see *Clematis Vitalba*
Oleaceae (family) 1258
 Forsythia 463–467; *Jasminum* 684–694; *Osmanthus* 922–924; *Syringa* 1258–1268
Olea fragrans, see *Osmanthus fragrans*
Oleander, see *Nerium*
OLEARIA [o-lee-RAY-a] (Daisy Bush, Daisy Tree) 917–919

1461

gunniana 918; *917*
haastii 918–919
semidentata (syn. *Eurybia semidentata*) 919
Olearius, J. G., association with *Olearia* 917
olive 1258
Olive, Fragrant, see *Osmanthus*
Olive, Sweet, see *Osmanthus*
Olive, Tea, see *Osmanthus*
Onagra biennis, see *Oenothera biennis*
Onagra trichocalyx, see *Oenothera trichocalyx*
Onagraceae (family)
 Clarkia 252–253; *Fuchsia* 473–491; *Godetia* 539–542; *Oenothera* 912–917
Onussen *(Speculum rerum botanicum)*, on *Digitalis* 411
Ophiopogon japonicus, see *Convallaria japonica*
Opinac, see *Acacia farnesiana*
opium 944, 947
Opium Poppy, see *Papaver somniferum*
Orange, Hardy, see *Poncirus trifoliata*
Orange, Mock, see *Philadelphus*
Orange, Trifoliata, see *Poncirus trifoliata*
Orange Sunflower, see *Heliopsis*
Orchid, Hardy Chinese, see *Bletilla hyacinthina*
Orchidaceae (family)
 Bletilla 129–130
organic fertilizers xxxi–xxxv
Orléans, Prince Henri d', work with *Syringa* 1266
ORNITHOGALUM [or-nith-OGG-alum](Chincherinchee, Star of Bethlehem) 919–922
 arabicum 921; *920*
 nutans (Star of Bethlehem) 921; *919*
 thyrsoides (Chincherinchee) 921
 umbellatum (Summer Snowflake, Sleepy Dick) 921–922; *919*
Orobus luteus, see *Lathyrus luteus*
OSMANTHUS [oz-MANN-thuss](Sweet Olive, Fragrant Olive, Tea Olive) 922–924
 americanus (Devil Wood) 923
 Aquifolium (syn. *O. ilicifolius*) 923
 delavayi (syn. *Siphonosmanthus delavayi*) 923–924

forrestii 924
fragrans (syn. *Olea fragrans*) 924; *922*
ilicifolius, see *O. Aquifolium*
Osteospermum barberiae, see *Dimorphotheca barberiae*
Osteospermum ecklonis, see *Dimorphotheca ecklonis*
Oswego Tea, see *Monarda*
Ovid *(Metamorphoses)*, *Digitalis* in 411; Hyacinth in 614–615
Oxalidaceae (family)
 Oxalis 924–929
OXALIS [OKS-al-iss, *or* OKS-sallis](Wood Sorrel, Rose Shamrock) 924–929
 adenophylla (syn. *O. bustillosii*) 926
 cernua (syn. *Bolboxalis cernuus*; Bermuda Buttercup) 927
 deppei (syn. *Ionoxalis deppei*) 927; *927*
 enneaphylla 927; *927*
 floribunda (syn. *O. lasiandra*) 928
 rosea 928; *925*
 variabilis (syn. *O. grandiflora*) 928
 violacea (Purple Wood Sorrel) 928
Ox-Eye Daisy, see *Chrysanthemum Leucanthemum*
Oxlip, see *Primula*

Pachylophus caespitosa, see *Oenothera caespitosa*
Padus racemosa, see *Prunus Padus*
Padus serotina, see *Prunus serotina*
PAEONIA [pee-OH-neeya] (Peony, Paeony) 929–941
 albiflora, see *P. lactiflora*
 delavayi 939; *940*
 lactiflora (syns. *P. albiflora*, *P. sinensis*) 939–940
 lutea (syn. *P. delavayi* var. *lutea*) 940; *940*
 mlokosewitschi 940
 moutan, see *P. suffruticosa*
 officinalis (syn. *P. fulgida*) 940; *936; 937*
 peregrina 941; *929*
 russi 941
 sinensis, see *P. lactiflora*
 suffruticosa (syns. *P. moutan*, *P. arborea*; Tree Peony,

Moutan Peony) 941; *931; 935*
 tenuifolia (Fringed Peony) 941; *938*
Paeony, see *Paeonia*
Pagoda Tree, Japanese, see *Sophora japonica*
Painted Daisy, see *Chrysanthemum coccineum*
Painted Lady, see *Chrysanthemum coccineum*
Painted Tongue, see *Salpiglossis sinuata*
Pallas, Peter Simon, work with *Paeonia* 930
Pandorea, syn. for *Tecoma* 1278
Pansy, see *Viola*; *Viola tricolor*
PAPAVER [pah-PAY-ver] (Poppy) 942–952
 alpinum (Alpine Poppy) 949
 bracteatum 949
 californicum 949
 glaucum (Tulip Poppy) 950
 heterophyllum, see *Meconopsis heterophylla*
 nudicaule (Iceland Poppy) 950; *946*
 orientale (Oriental Poppy) 950; *943*
 rhoeas (Corn Poppy, Common Red Poppy, "Flanders Poppy") 952; *951*
 somniferum 944, 947, 948; *944; 951*
Also see *Eschscholzia*; *Meconopsis*
Papaveraceae (family)
 Eschscholzia 455–458; *Hunnemannia fumariifolia* 612–613; *Meconopsis* 847–852; *Papaver* 942–952; *Romneya* 1124–1125
Paper Bush, see *Edgeworthia papyrifera*
Paper Tree, see *Edgeworthia papyrifera*
Parey, on *Daphne* 366; *Helleborus* 577; *Paeonia* 929
Paris Daisy, see *Chrysanthemum frutescens*
Park, Bertram *(Collins Guide to Roses)* 1135
Parker, R. N., work with *Jasminum* 690
Parkinson, John, on *Campsis* 183; on *Cistus* 246; cultivates *Clematis* 256; work with *Crocus* 332; work with *Hibiscus* 590; cultivates *Lonicera* 794; on *Narcissus* 881; grows *Nerium* 900; on *Primula* 1039; draws *Rosa*

virginiana 1133; describes
  Spiraea 1244; *Syringa* 1260
Parma (Italy), violet as emblem
  of 1369
Parrett, Ronald *(Delphiniums)*
  376
Parrot Gladiola, see *Gladiolus
  psittacinus*
Parrot Tulips, 1329; *1313*
Pasque Flower, see *Pulsatilla*
PASSIFLORA [passi-FLOH-rah]
  (Passion Flower, Granadilla)
  952–959
  x *allardii* 956
  caerulea (Blue Passion Flower)
    956; *954*
  coccinea 956; *955*
  edulis (Purple Granadilla,
    Passion Fruit) 956; *956*
  incarnata (May Pop, May
    Apple) 957; *953*
  laurifolia (Yellow Granadilla,
    Water Lemon, Jamaica
    Honeysuckle) 957
  manicata 957
  mollissima (syn. *Tacsonia
    mollissima*) 957
  pinnatistipula (syn. *Tacsonia
    pinnatistipula*) 957; *958*
  quadrangularis (Granadilla)
    959; *953*
  racemosa (syn. *P. princeps*)
    959; *955*
  van-volxemii (syn. *P.
    antioquiensis*) 959; *952*
Passifloraceae (family)
  Passiflora 952–959
Passion Flower, see *Passiflora*
Passion Fruit, see *Passiflora
  edulis*
Pausanias, on *Hyacinth* 616
Pavia macrostachya, see
  Aesculus parviflora
Pea, Australian, see *Dolichos
  lignosus*
Pea, Campo, see *Lathyrus
  splendens*
Pea, Everlasting, see *Lathyrus
  grandiflorus; Lathyrus
  latifolius*
Pea, Perennial, see *Lathyrus
  latifolius*
Pea, Sweet, see *Lathyrus*
Pea, Tangier Scarlet, see
  Lathyrus tingitanus
Pea, Tuberous, see *Lathyrus
  tuberosus*
Peach, see *Prunus Persica*
Peacock Anemone, see *Anemone
  pavonia*
Pearl Bush, see *Exochorda*

Peers, Ralph, work with camellias
  164
Peerson, names *Heliopsis* 569
PELARGONIUM [pell-ar-GO-
  neeyum] (Pelargonium,
  Geranium, Stork's Bill
  Geranium) 956–976
  acetosum 967
  domesticum (syns. *P.* x
    *macranthum, P.
    grandiflorum, P. regale;*
    Pelargonium, Royal
    Pelargonium, Lady
    Washington Geranium, Show
    Geranium, Fancy Geranium,
    Butterfly Pelargonium) 967–
    968; *963*
  echinatum (Sweetheart
    Geranium) 968; *975*
  grandiflorum, see *Pelargonium
    domesticum*
  x *hortorum,* see *P. zonale*
  x *macranthum,* see *P.
    domesticum*
  peltatum (syn. *Geranium
    peltatum;* Ivy-leaved
    Geranium) 968; *964; 966*
  quercifolium (Oak-leaved
    Geranium) 969
  quinquelobatum 969
  regale, see *P. domesticum*
  Species and Varieties with
    Scented Foliage 973–976
  stipulatum 969
  tricolor 970; *970*
  triste 969
  zonale (Zonal Geranium,
    Horseshoe Geranium, Fish
    Geranium) 970–973; *961; 972*
  Also see *Geranium*
Pelargonium, Butterfly, see
  Pelargonium domesticum
Pelargonium, Royal, see
  Pelargonium domesticum
PENSTEMON [pen-STEE-mon,
  or pent-STEE-mon] (syn.
  Pentstemon; Beard Tongue)
  976–982
  barbatus (syn. *Chelone
    barbata*) 978
  Cobaea 978; *979*
  cordifolius 978
  gloxinioides 980
  hartwegii 980; *980*
  heterophyllus 981
  isophyllus 981
  menziesii 981
  scouleri (syn. *P. menziesii* var.
    scouleri) 982
  utahensis 982
Peony, see *Paeonia*

Peony, Fringed, see *Paeonia
  tenuifolia*
Peony, Moutan, see *Paeonia
  suffruticosa*
Peony, Tree, see *Paeonia
  suffruticosa*
Periwinkle, see *Vinca*
Persephone, and the pomegranate
  1074; and *Viola* 1368
Persian Lilac, see *Syringa persica*
Persica vulgaris, see *Prunus
  Persica*
Peru, Marvel of, see *Mirabilis*
Petiver, James, describes
  Camellia japonica 160;
  names species of *Rosa* 1133
Petre, Lord, raises camellias 161
Petticoat Narcissus, see
  Narcissus bulbocodium
PETUNIA [peh-TOO-neeya, or
  peh-TEWN-eeya] 982–988
  axillaris (syns. *Nicotiana
    axillaris, P. nyctaginiflora*)
    986
  Hybrids 987–988; *985–987*
  inflata 986
  integrifolia, see *P. violacea*
  nyctaginiflora, see *P. axillaris*
  parviflora 987
  violacea 987
Peyerimhoff, work with *Cytisus*
  353
Pfitzer, Ernst, work with
  Gladiolus 530
pH factor xxv
PHACELIA [fah-SEE-leeya]
  988–991
  campanularia 989; *990*
  tanacetifolia (syn. *P.
    tripinnata;* Wild Heliotrope,
    Fiddleneck) 989
  viscida (syn. *Eutoca viscida;*
    Californian Bluebell) 991
  Whitlavia (syns. *Whitlavia
    grandiflora, P. grandiflora*)
    989
Pharbitis hederacea, see
  Ipomoea hederacea
Pharbitis ispida, see *Ipomoea
  purpurea*
Pharbitis Nil, see *Convolvulus
  Nil*
Pharbitis rubrocaerulea, see
  Ipomoea tricolor
Pheasant's-eye, see *Adonis
  aestivalis*
PHILADELPHUS [filla-DEL-
  fus] (Syringa, Mock Orange)
  991–998
  argyrocalyx 995
  coronarius (Common Mock

Orange) 991, 992, 995; *993*
gordonianus 995
grandiflorus, see *P. inodorus*
   var. *grandiflorus*
hirsutus 995
Hybrids 997–998; *997*
inodorus (English Dogwood) 996
lewisii 996
microphyllus 996
pekinensis 996
pubescens 996
Also see *Syringa*
Phillips, Brigadier E. Lucas, *Climbing Plants for Walls and Gardens* 796; on *Wistaria* 1385
Phillips, Henry, describes *Spiraea* 1244
PHLOMIS [FLO-miss] (Jerusalem Sage) 998–999
cashmeriana 999
fruticosa (Jerusalem Sage) 999
tuberosa 999; *998*
PHLOX [flocks] 999–1007
adsurgens 1002
amoena (syns. *P. walteri, P. involucrata, P.* x *procumbens*) 1002
bifida (Sand Phlox) 1003
divaricata (syn. *P. canadensis;* Wild Sweet William, Blue Phlox) 1003; *999*
drummondii (Annual Phlox, Texan Pride, Drummond Phlox) 1003; *1003; 1004*
maculata (syn. *P. pyramidalis*) 1003
paniculata (syn. *P. decussata;* Summer Perennial Phlox, Garden Phlox) 1006; *1000*
pilosa (Prairie Phlox) 1006
x *procumbens,* see *P. amoena*
stolonifera (syn. *P. reptans*) 1007
subulata (syn. *P. setacea;* Ground Pink, Moss Pink) 1007; *1005*
Phlox, Annual, see *Phlox drummondii*
Phlox, Blue, see *Phlox divaricata*
Phlox, Garden, see *Phlox paniculata*
Phlox, Prairie, see *Phlox pilosa*
Phlox, Sand, see *Phlox bifida*
Phlox, Summer Perennial, see *Phlox paniculata*
Pholistoma auritum, see *Nemophila aurita*
PHYGELIUS [fy-JEE-leeyus] (Cape Fuchsia, Cape

Figwort) 1007–1009
aequalis 1008
capensis 1009; *1008*
PHYSALIS [FISS-allis] (Chinese Lantern, Cape Gooseberry, Husk Tomato) 1009–1013
alkekengi (Bladder Cherry, Winter Cherry, Chinese Lantern) 1011; *1011*
edulis, see *P. peruviana*
franchetii, see *P. alkekengi* var. *franchetii*
ixocarpa (Tomatello) 1012
peruviana (syn. *P. edulis;* Cape Gooseberry) 1012
pruinosa (Strawberry Tomato) 1012
pubescens (Ground Cherry) 1012
PHYSOSTEGIA [fy-so-STEE-jeeya] *virginiana* (Obedient Plant, False Dragonhead) 1013–1015; *1014*
Piasetski, Pavel Jakovlevich, 133
PIERIS [py-EER-iss] (Andromeda) 1015–1017
floribunda (syn. *Andromeda floribunda*) 1016; *1016*
formosa (syn. *Andromeda formosa,* Mountain Fetter Bush) 1016
forrestii (syn. *P. formosa* var. *forrestii*) 1016
japonica (syn. *Andromeda japonica;* Andromeda) 1017; *1016*
taiwanensis 1017
pinching back, operation of ("stopping") 234, 236
Pine, Prairie, see *Liatris spicata*
Pink, see *Dianthus*
Pink, Cushion, see *Silene acaulis*
Pink, Ground, see *Phlox subulata*
Pink, Moss, see *Phlox subulata*
Pink, Wax, see *Portulaca*
Pink, Wild, see *Silene caroliniana*
Pink Calla, see *Zantedeschia rehmannii*
Pisanello (columbine in his *Portrait of a Lady*) 72
Pison, William, discovers *Lantana Camara* 722
Pistachio, False, see *Staphylea colchica*
Pistorius, Verkerk, work with *Forsythia* 464
Plagianthus lyallii, see *Hoheria glabra*
Plagianthus lyallii var. *ribifolia,* see *Hoheria lyallii*

Plantagenet, origin of the name of 507
Plantain Lily, see *Hosta*
PLATYCODON [plat-ee-KO-don] *grandiflorus* (Balloon Flower, Chinese Bellflower, Japanese Bellflower) 1017–1020; *1019*
Plenzat, *Clematis* perfume 258; on *Hydrangea* 622; 1341
Pliny the Elder, on *Achillea* 13; *Anemone* 56; *Bellis* 113; cornflowers 204; *Iris* 668; myrtle 878; *Nerium* 901; *Paeonia* 934; *Polemonium* 1024; origins of honey 1096; *Rosa* 1129, 1130; *Verbascum* 1338; *Verbena* 1343; *Viola* 1368
Plum, Beach, see *Prunus maritima*
Plum, Canada, see *Prunus nigra*
Plum, Cherry, see *Prunus cerasifera*
Plum, Chickasaw, see *Prunus angustifolia*
Plum, Hortulan, see *Prunus hortulana*
Plum, Myrobalan, see *Prunus cerasifera*
Plum, Wild, see *Prunus americana*
Plum, Yellow, see *Prunus americana*
Plumbaginaceae (family) *Armeria* 85–87; *Ceratostigma* 210–214; *Limonium* 770–772; *Plumbago* 1020–1024
Plumbago, see *Ceratostigma*
PLUMBAGO [plum-BAY-go] (Leadwort) 1020–1024
caerulea 1022
capensis (Leadwort) 1022; *1023*
indica, see *P. rosea*
larpentae, see *Ceratostigma plumbaginoides*
rosea (syns. *P. indica, P. sanguinea*) 1022; *1021*
zeylanica 1022
Also see *Ceratostigma*
Plumier, Father Charles, names *Begonia* 104; work with *Fuchsia* 474; names *Lobelia* 784; *Magnolia* 819
Plunkenet, Leonard, work with *Rhododendron* 1045; names species of *Rosa* 1133
Po Chi-i, poem quoted describing sale of peonies 929

Podronea, as synonym for
 Tecoma 1278
Poker Plant, see *Kniphofia*
Polemoniaceae (family)
 Cobaea 276–278; *Phlox* 999–1007; *Polemonium* 1024–1026
POLEMONIUM [po-lee-MO-neeyum] (Jacob's Ladder, Greek Valerian) 1024–1026
 carneum 1024
 coeruleum 1026; *1025*
 confertum (Skunkweed) 1026
 pauciflorum 1026
Pollard, work with *Prunus* x *pollardii* 1069
POLYANTHES [polly-ANTH-eez—*or* pole-ee-ANTH-eez] *tuberosa* (Tuberose) 1026–1028; *1026*
Polyanthus, see *Primula Polyantha*
Pomegranate, association with Persephone 1074; also see *Punica*
PONCIRUS [pon-SY-russ] *trifoliata* (syns. *Aegle sepiara, Citrus trifoliata;* Hardy Orange, Trifoliate Orange) 1028–1029; *1029*
Poppy, see *Papaver*
Poppy, California, see *Eschscholzia; Romneya coulteri*
Poppy, California Tree, see *Romneya*
Poppy, Himalayan Blue, see *Meconopsis betonicifolia*
Poppy, Matilija, see *Romneya coulteri*
Poppy, Mexican, see *Hunnemannia fumariifolia*
Poppy, Satin, see *Meconopsis napaulensis*
Poppy, Shirley, see *Papaver rhoeas*
Poppy, Tulip, see *Hunnemannia fumariifolia*
Poppy, Welsh, see *Meconopsis cambrica*
Poppy, Wind, see *Meconopsis heterophylla*
Poppy Anemone, see *Anemone coronaria*
Poppywort, see *Meconopsis*
Porcher, Felix, on *Fuchsia* 474
Portland powder 1281
PORTULACA [por-tew-LACK-a, *or* por-tew-LAKE-a] (Sun Plant, Rose Moss, Wax Pink, Sun Moss) 1030–1033
 grandiflora (Garden Portulaca, Sun Moss) 1031; *1030; 1032*
 oleracea (Purslane, Pussley) 1033
Portulaca, Garden, see *Portulaca grandiflora*
Portulaceae (family)
 Portulaca 1030–1033
Possum Haw, see *Viburnum nudum*
Potanin, Grigori N., work with *Indigofera* 656; *Viburnum betulifolium* 1355
Potato, Canada, see *Helianthus tuberosus*
Potato Vine, see *Solanum jasminoides*
Potato Vine, Wild, see *Ipomoea pandurata*
POTENTILLA [po-ten-TILL-a] (Cinquefoil) 1033–1037
 atrosanguinea 1034
 x *davurica* (syn. *P. glabra*) 1035
 fruticosa 1035, 1037; *1034*
 nepalensis (syn. *P. formosa*) 1037
 nitida 1037
 recta 1037
 reptans 1037; *1036*
Potter's Cyclopedia of Botanical Drugs and Preparations 514, 785, 1362
Pouch Flower, see *Calceolaria*
Prairie Pine, see *Liatris spicata*
Prairie Rose, see *Rosa setigera*
Prairie Smoke, see *Geum triflorum*
Pratt, A. E., work with *Rosa* 1161
praying mantises 1150
Preserves, Rose Petal, recipe for 1140
Preston, Isabella, work with *Syringa* 1261
Prickly Mimosa, see *Acacia verticillata*
Pride of California, see *Lathyrus splendens*
Pride of Rochester, see *Deutzia scabra*
Primrose, see *Primula*
Primrose, Bird's Eye, see *Primula farinosa*
Primrose, Chinese, see *Primula sinensis*
Primrose, Common, see *Primula vulgaris*
Primrose, English, see *Primula vulgaris*
Primrose, Evening, see *Oenothera*
Primrose, Fairy, see *Primula malacoides*
Primrose, Missouri, see *Oenothera missourensis*
PRIMULA [PRIM-yew-la] (Primrose, Auricula, Cowslip, Oxlip, Polyanthus) 1038–1054
 acaulis, see *P. vulgaris*
 aurantiaca 1042
 Auricula (Auricula) 1042–1043
 auriculata 1043; *1042*
 beesiana 1043
 bulleyana 1043; *1038*
 cachmiriana, see *P. denticulata* var. *cachmiriana*
 capitata 1043
 chionantha 1044
 classification of 1052, 1054
 clusiana 1044
 cortusoides 1044; *1045*
 denticulata 1044; *1044*
 elatior (Oxlip) 1044; *1039*
 farinosa (Bird's Eye Primrose) 1046
 florindae 1046
 frondosa 1046
 helodoxa 1046
 japonica 1046; *1041*
 juliae 1047
 malacoides (Fairy Primrose) 1047
 marginata 1048; *1041*
 obconica 1048; *1048*
 palinuri 1049; *1040*
 parryi 1049
 Polyantha (Polyanthus) 1049
 pulverulenta 1049
 rosea 1049
 secundiflora 1049
 sieboldii 1050
 sikkimensis 1050
 sinensis (syns. *P. chinensis, P. stellata;* Chinese Primrose) 1050; *1053*
 stellata, see *P. sinensis*
 veitchi (syn. *P. polyneura*) 1051
 veris (syn. *P. officinalis*) 1051; *1054*
 viscosa (syn. *P. lactifolia*) 1051
 vulgaris (syn. *P. acaulis;* Common Primrose, English Primrose) 1051; *1051*
 winteri (syn. *P. edgeworthii*) 1052
Primulaceae (family)
 Cyclamen 339–346; *Primula* 1038–1054

Prince's Feather, see
    *Amaranthus
    hypochondriacus*
privet 1258
Proust, Marcel, 1258
Provence Rose, see *Rosa gallica*
PRUNUS [PROO-nus] 1054–1071
    americana (Wild Plum, Yellow
        Plum) 1058
    Amygdalus (syn. *Amygdalus
        communis*; Almond) 1058
    angustifolia (syn. *P. chicasa*;
        Chickasaw Plum) 1058
    Armeniaca (syn. *Armeniaca
        vulgaris*; Apricot) 1059
    avium (syn. *Cerasus sylvestris*;
        Common Sweet Cherry, Wild
        Cherry) 1059
    besseyi (Sand Cherry, Hansen
        Bush Cherry) 1059
    x *blireiana* (syn. *P. cerasifera*
        var. *blireiana*) 1061
    campanulata 1061
    cerasifera (Cherry Plum,
        Myrobalan Plum) 1061
    Cerasus (syn. *Cerasus
        vulgaris*; Sour Cherry, Dwarf
        Wild Cherry) 1062; *1067*
    communis (syn. *P. domestica*;
        Plum) 1062
    glandulosa (Flowering
        Almond) 1063
    hortulana (Hortulan Plum)
        1063
    ilicifolia (syn. *Laurocerasus
        ilicifolia*; Islay Cherry,
        Evergreen Cherry) 1063
    incisa (syn. *Cerasus incisa*)
        1063
    lannesiana (syn. *Cerasus
        lannesiana*; Flowering
        Cherry) 1064
    Laurocerasus (syn.
        Laurocerasus officinalis;
        Cherry Laurel) 1065
    lusitanica (syn. *Laurocerasus
        lusitanica*; Portuguese
        Laurel) 1065; *1065*
    maritima (Beach Plum) 1066
    mume (syn. *Armeniaca mume*;
        Japanese Apricot) 1066; *1067*
    nana (syns. *Amygdalus nana*,
        P. tenella; Dwarf Russian
        Almond) 1066; *1056*
    nigra (Canada Plum) 1067
    Padus (syn. *Padus racemosa*;
        Bird Cherry) 1067
    pennsylvanica (syn. *Cerasus
        pennsylvanica*; Wild Red
        Cherry) 1068
    Persica (syns. *Amygdalus*

Persica, Persica vulgaris;
    Peach) 1068
pissardii, see *P. cerasifera* var.
    pissardii
x *pollardii* (syn. *P. Amygdalo-
    Persica pollardii*) 1069
pumila (Sand Cherry) 1069
sargentii (syn. *P. serrulata
    sachalinensis*) 1069
serotina (syn. *Padus serotina*;
    Wild Black Cherry, Choke
    Berry) 1069
serrulata, see *P. lannesiana*
spinosa (Sloe, Blackthorn) 1070
subhirtella (Rosebud Cherry)
    1070; *1060*
triloba 1070; *1055*
Puccoon, see *Lithospermum*
PULSATILLA [pulsa-TILL-a]
    1071–1073
alpina 1072; *1072*
vernalis 1072
vulgaris 1073; *1071*
Also see *Anemone*
PUNICA [PEW-nik-a]
    (Pomegranate) 1073–1080
granatum 1079–1080; *1077;
    1078*
Punicaceae (family)
    Punica 1073–1080
Purdom, William, work with
    Clematis 257, 263; peonies
    934; *Viburnum* 1357
Purée, Rose Hip, recipe for 1141
Purple Mullein, see *Verbascum
    phoeniceum*
Purple Ragwort, see *Senecio
    elegans*
Purple Rock Cress, see *Aubrietia*
Purslane, see *Portulaca oleracea*
Pussley, see *Portulaca oleracea*
PYRACANTHA [pyra-KAN-tha]
    (Fire Thorn) 1080–1083
angustifolia 1081
atalantioides (syn. *P. gibbsii*)
    1081
coccinea (Everlasting Thorn)
    1082; *1081*
crenatoserrata, see *P.
    yunnanensis*
crenulata 1082
rogersiana 1082
yunnanensis (syn. *P.
    crenatoserrata*) 1082
Pyrethrum (*Chrysanthemum
    cinerariifolium*) 231; also see
    Chrysanthemum coccineum
Pyrethrum roseum, see
    Chrysanthemum coccineum
Pyrus (distinguished from *Malus*)
    829, 830

Pyrus angustifolia, see *Malus
    angustifolia*
Pyrus baccata, see *Malus
    baccata*
Pyrus coronaria, see *Malus
    coronaria*
Pyrus coronaria ionensis, see
    Malus ionensis
Pyrus crataegifolia, see *Malus
    florentina*
Pyrus cydonia, see *Cydonia
    oblonga*
Pyrus x *eleyi*, see *Malus* x *eleyi*
Pyrus floribunda, see *Malus
    floribunda*
Pyrus fusca, see *Malus rivularis*
Pyrus halliana, see *Malus
    halliana*
Pyrus malus, see *Malus pumila*
Pyrus prunifolia, see *Malus
    prunifolia*
Pyrus purpurea, see *Malus* x
    purpurea
Pyrus sargentii, see *Malus
    sargentii*
Pyrus x *scheideckeri*, see *Malus*
    x *scheideckeri*
Pyrus sieboldii, see *Malus
    sieboldii*
Pyrus spectabilis, see *Malus
    spectabilis*
Pyrus sumi, see *Malus zumi*
Pyrus theifera, see *Malus
    theifera*
Pyrus toringoides, see *Malus
    toringoides*
Pyrus triloba, see *Malus triloba*

Quaker Bonnet, see *Lupinus
    perennis*
Quamoclit [KWOM-ok-lit] (Star
    Glory, Cypress Vine) 1083–
    1085
coccinea (syn. *Ipomoea
    coccinea*; Star Ipomoea)
    1084; *1084*
lobata (syns. *Ipomoea
    versicolor, Mina lobata, Q.
    mina*) 1084; *1084*
pennata (syns. *Ipomoea
    quamoclit, Convolvulus
    pinnatus*; Cypress Vine)
    1085; *1084*
Quarter Vine, see *Bignonia
    capreolata*
Queen of the Night, see *Cestrum
    nocturnum*
Queen's Flower, see
    Lagerstroemia speciosa

Quick, see *Crataegus*
Quick-in-Hand, see *Impatiens*
Quince, see *Cydonia oblonga*
Quince, Chinese, see
 Chaenomeles sinensis
Quince, Flowering, see
 Chaenomeles
Quince, Japanese, see
 Chaenomeles japonica

Rabisha, William, *The Whole Body of Cookery Dissected* 1141
Ragged Robin, see *Lychnis Flos-cuculi*
Ragwort, see *Senecio*
Ragwort, Purple, see *Senecio elegans*
Rain, Golden, see *Laburnum*
Rain Daisy, see *Dimorphotheca pluvialis*
Raleigh, Sir Walter, 904
Ranunculaceae (family) 936
 Aconitum 20–25; *Adonis* 27–30; *Anemone* 56–66; *Aquilegia* 72–79; *Clematis* 253–270; *Delphinium* 376–387; *Eranthus* 437–438; *Helleborus* 575–580; *Hepatica* 586–589; *Nigella* 910–912; *Paeonia* 929–941; *Pulsatilla* 1071–1073; *Ranunculus* 1085–1089; *Thalictrum* 1282–1284; *Trollius* 1300–1301
RANUNCULUS [ra-NUN-kew-lus] (Buttercup, Crowfoot) 1085–1089
 aconitifolius 1087; *1087*
 asiaticus (syn. *R. orientalis;* Tuberous Ranunculus, Persian Ranunculus, French Ranunculus) 1087, 1089; *1086*
 bulbosus (Buttercup) 1089
 gramineus 1089; *1088*
Rattlesnake Master, see
 Eryngium yuccaefolium; Liatris scariosa
recipes: Candied Rose Petals 1141; lavender cologne 732; Rose Hip Extract 1141; Rose Honey 1139; Rose Hip Jam 1142; Rose Oil 1140; Rose Petal Preserves 1140; Rose Hip Purée 1141
Redgrave, H. Stanley, *Scent and All About It* 246
Red Haw, see *Crataegus mollis*
Red-hot Poker, see *Kniphofia*

Redouté, Pierre Joseph, painting of *Lilium superbum* 769; engravings of roses 1136
Redroot, see *Ceanothus americanus*
Red Shanks, see *Geranium robertianum*
Red Sorrel, see *Hibiscus Sabdariffa*
Reeves, John, work with *Wistaria* 1384
Regel, E., work with *Exochorda* 459
Rehder, Alfred, work with *Rhododendron* 1103; on *Viburnum* 1352
Reinelt, F., work with *Delphinium* 378
Rembrandt Tulips 1329
René of Anjou, cultivates carnations 395
RESEDA [reh-SEED-a] (Mignonette) 1090–1091
 odorata 1090–1091; *1091*
Resedaceae (family)
 Reseda 1090–1091
Retama monosperma, see *Genista monosperma*
Rhamnaceae (family)
 Ceanothus 195–203
RHODODENDRON [ro-doe-DEN-dron] (including AZALEA) 1091–1123
 amoenum, see *R. obtusum* var. *amoenum*
 arboreum (Tree Rhododendron) 1101–1102; *1107*
 augustinii 1102
 auriculatum 1102
 campylocarpum 1103
 carolinianum (Carolina Rhododendron) 1103
 catawbiense (Mountain Rose-Bay) 1103; *1102*
 caucasicum 1103
 cinnabarinum 1105
 dauricum 1105
 decorum 1105
 dichroanthum 1105
 discolor 1106
 ferrugineum (Alpine Rose) 1106; *1095*
 fortunei 1106
 giganteum 1106
 griersonianum 1108
 hirsutum 1108; *1118*
 Hybrids 1116–1123
  from Chinese and Other Asiatic Species 1116–1117; *1100*
  from European, American and Himalayan Species, 1117–1118; *1094*
  Evergreen Azalea-type Resulting from Crosses of Rhododendron Kaempferi 1118–1119
  Ghent Azaleas 1119
  Rothschild Hybrids, Exbury Hybrid Azaleas, or Knap Hill Hybrid Azaleas 1119–1120
  Kurume Azalea 1120–1121; *1121*
  Mollis Hybrids 1121; *1120*
  Miscellaneous Hybrids 1121, 1123
 indicum (syn. *Azalea indica*) 1108; *1099*
 insigne 1109
 kaempferi (syns. *R. obtusum kaempferi, Azalea indica kaempferi*) 1109; *1117*
 lutescens 1109
 luteum (syns. *R. flavum, Azalea pontica*) 1109; *1092*
 maximum (Great Laurel, Rose Bay) 1110; *1101*
 molle (syn. *Azalea mollis*) 1110
 mucronulatum 1110
 obtusum (syns. *Azalea amoena, Azalea obtusa*) 1112; *1104*
 ponticum 1112
 quinquefolium 1112
 radicans 1113
 schlippenbachii 1113; *1111*
 serotinum 1113
 simsii (syns. *R. indicum, Azalea indica;* Indian Azalea, Florist's Azalea, Belgian Azalea) 1113
 sinogrande 1115
 thomsonii 1115; *1097*
 williamsianum 1115
 yunnanense 1116
 Calendar of Flowering Periods 1096–1099
Rhododendron, Carolina, see *Rhododendron carolinianum*
Rhododendron, Tree, see *Rhododendron arboreum*
RHODOTYPOS [ro-doe-TY-pos]
 kerrioides (syn. *R. scandens;* Jet Bead) 1123–1124; *1124*
Rhynchospermum, see *Trachelospermum*
Rhynchospermum jasminoides, see *Trachelospermum jasminoides*

Riccio, Father Agostino del, 1086
Richardia 1388; also see
 Zantedeschia
Richardia africana, see
 Zantedeschia aethiopica
Rino *(Liber de simplicilius),*
 describes *Jasminum* 686
Robertiella robertianum, see
 Geranium robertianum
Robinson, Rev. T. Romney,
 Romneya named for 1124
Robinson, William, on *Clematis*
 256
Roborowsky (Russian explorer),
 introduces *Tamarix hispida*
 1276
Rocher, Anton, work with
 Syringa 1260
Rock, Dr. J. F., work with
 peonies 934
Rock Cress, see *Arabis*
Rock Rose, see *Cistus;*
 Helianthemum
Rockfoil, see *Saxifraga*
Rockwell, F. F., *Book of Lilies*
 756
Roessig, C. G., *Die Rosen* 1136
Romani, Abbé, on *Kerria*
 japonica 702
ROMNEYA [rom-NEE-ya]
 (California Tree Poppy)
 1124–1125
 coulteri (California Poppy,
 Matilija Poppy) 1125; *1125*
 trichocalyx 1125
Romulus (legend of cornus-wood)
 301
Roof Iris, see *Iris tectorum*
ROSA [RO-zah] (Rose) 1126–
 1172
 x *alba* 1153
 banksiae (Lady Bank's Rose)
 1153; *1148*
 blanda 1154
 bracteata (Macartney Rose)
 1154
 canina (Dog Rose) 1154; *1143*
 carolina (Pasture Rose) 1156
 centifolia (syn. *R. gallica*
 centifolia; Cabbage Rose,
 Hundred-leaved Rose) 1156;
 1168; 1172
 chinensis, see *R. indica*
 damascena (Damask Rose)
 1157; *1157*
 ecae (syn. *R. xanthina*) 1157
 eglanteria, see *R. rubiginosa;*
 R. lutea
 farreri (Threepenny-Bit Rose)
 1157
 foetida, see *R. lutea*

gallica (Provence Rose, French
 Rose) 1158; *1134*
harisonii, see *R. lutea* var.
 harisonii
hugonis (Father Hugo's Rose)
 1158; *1152*
Hybrids 1136, 1138, 1167–1172
 Hybrid Moschata Roses 1171
 Hybrid Perpetual Roses
 1168–1169
 Hybrid Polyantha
 (multiflora) and Hybrid
 Floribunda 1169–1170;
 1138; 1145
 Hybrid Tea Roses 1167–
 1168; *1128; 1137; 1141;*
 1162
 Hybrids of *Rosa rugosa* 1170
 Hybrids of *Rosa*
 spinosissima 1170; *1132*
 Hybrids of Climbing Type
 1171; *1145*
 Hybrids of Rambler Type
 1172
 Miniature Roses (Lilliput)
 1169; *1143*
 Miscellaneous Hybrids 1172;
 1171
indica (syn. *R. chinensis*) 1159
laevigata (Cherokee Rose)
 1160
lutea (syns. *R. eglanteria, R.*
 foetida) 1160; *1160*
moschata (syn. *R. brunonii;*
 Musk Rose) 1160; *1172*
multiflora (syn. *R. polyantha;*
 Multiflora Rose) 1161; *1161*
nitida 1163
nutkana (Nootka Rose) 1163
omeiensis 1163
pendulina (syn. *R. alpina*) 1163
polyantha, see *Hybrid*
 polyantha
pomifera (Apple Rose) 1164
roulettii 1164
rubiginosa (syn. *R. eglanteria;*
 Sweet Briar) 1164
rubrifolia (syn. *R. ferruginea*)
 1165; *1165*
rugosa (syn. *R. ferox*) 1165;
 1127
setigera (syn. *R. rubrifolia;*
 Prairie Rose) 1166
soulieana 1166
spinosissima (syns. *R.*
 pimpinellifolia, R. scotica;
 Scotch Rose, Burnet Rose)
 1166; *1131*
virginiana (syns. *R. humilis, R.*
 lucida) 1166
wichuraiana (syn. *R. luciae;*

 Memorial Rose) 1167
woodsii 1167
xanthina 1167
Rosaceae (family)
 Chaenomeles 216–221;
 Cotoneaster 312–322;
 Crataegus 322–330; *Cydonia*
 oblonga 346–348; *Exochorda*
 458–459; *Geum* 526–529;
 Kerria japonica 700–704;
 Malus 829–838; *Potentilla*
 1033–1037; *Prunus* 1054–
 1071; *Pyracantha* 1080–
 1083; *Rhodotypos kerrioides*
 1123–1124; *Rosa* 1126–1172;
 Spiraea 1243–1253
Rose, Alpine, see *Rhododendron*
 ferrugineum
Rose, Apple, see *Rosa pomifera*
Rose, Burnet, see *Rosa*
 spinosissima
Rose, Cabbage, see *Rosa*
 centifolia
Rose, California, see *Convolvulus*
 japonicus
Rose, Cherokee, see *Rosa*
 laevigata
Rose, Christmas, see *Helleborus*
Rose, Cotton, see *Hibiscus*
 mutabilis
Rose, Damask, see *Rosa*
 damascena
Rose, Dog, see *Rosa canina*
Rose, Father Hugo's, see *Rosa*
 hugonis
Rose, French, see *Rosa gallica*
Rose, Guelder, see *Viburnum*
 opulus
Rose, Hundred-leaved, see *Rosa*
 centifolia
Rose, Japanese, see *Kerria*
 japonica
Rose, Lady Bank's, see *Rosa*
 banksiae
Rose, Lenten, see *Helleborus*
Rose, Macartney, see *Rosa*
 bracteata
Rose, Multiflora, see *Rosa*
 multiflora
Rose, Musk, see *Rosa moschata*
Rose, Nootka, see *Rosa nutkana*
Rose, Pasture, see *Rosa carolina*
Rose, Prairie, see *Rosa setigera*
Rose, Provence, see *Rosa gallica*
Rose, Rock, see *Helianthemum*
Rose, Scotch, see *Rosa*
 spinosissima
Rose, Sun, see *Helianthemum*
Rose, Threepenny-Bit, see *Rosa*
 farreri
Rose Bay, see *Nerium;*

Rhododendron maximum
Rose-Bay, Mountain, see
  Rhododendron catawbiense
Rose Calla, see *Zantedeschia rehmannii*
Rose Campion, see *Lychnis coronaria*
Rose Hip Extract, recipe for 1141
Rose Hip Jam, recipe for 1142
Rose Hip Purée, recipe for 1141
Rose Honey, recipe for 1139
Rose Mallow, see *Hibiscus Moscheutos; Althaea*
Rose Moss, see *Portulaca*
Rose Museum (Hay-les-Roses, near Paris) 1128
Rose of China, see *Hibiscus rosa-sinensis*
Rose of Heaven, see *Lychnis Coeli-rosa*
Rose of Sharon, see *Hibiscus syriacus; Hypericum*
Rose Oil, recipe for 1140
Rose Petal Preserves, recipe for 1140
Rose Petal Sugar, recipe for 1140
Rose Petals, Candied, recipe for 1141
Rose Shamrock, see *Oxalis*
Rosebud Cherry, see *Prunus subhirtella*
Roselle, see *Hibiscus Sabdariffa*
Rosenbergia, see *Cobaea*
Rosewater, recipe for 1142
Rothschild Lily, see *Gloriosa rothschildiana*
Roulet, Dr., work with *Rosa roulettii* 1164
Royle, Dr., work with *Syringa* 1261
Rubiaceae (family)
  Gardenia 495–502
Rudbeck, Olaf, genus named for 1173
RUDBECKIA [rood-BEK-eeya] (Black-eyed Susan, Cone Flower) 1173–1178
  amplexicaulis 1173
  angustifolia, see *Echinacea angustifolia*
  bicolor (Thimble Flower) 1174; *1178*
  fulgida (syns. *R. aspera, R. scabra;* Orange Cone Flower) 1174
  hirta (syn. *R. flava;* Black-eyed Susan, Yellow Daisy) 1173, 1175
  Hybrids (Gloriosa Daisy) 1178
  laciniata (Cone Flower) 1175; *1176*

newmanii, see *R. speciosa*
nitida 1177
purpurea, see *Echinacea purpurea*
speciosa (syn. *R. newmanii*) 1173, 1177
subtomentosa (Sweet Cone Flower) 1177
triloba 1177
Also see *Echinacea*
Rugged Sailor, see *Centaurea Cyanus*
Ruskin, John, on *Kalmia* 695
Russell, George, work with *Lupinus* 808, 812
Rust, fungus disease of, 1147
Rutaceae (family)
  Poncirus trifoliata 1028–1029
Rutland Beauty, see *Convolvulus sepium*

sachets, lavender, preparation of 732
Sachs, Hans, 1258
Saffron, see *Crocus sativus*
Saffron, Meadow, see *Colchicum*
Sage, see *Salvia*
Sage, Jerusalem, see *Phlomis fruticosa*
Sage, Mexican Bush, see *Salvia leucantha*
Sage, Red, see *Lantana*
Sage, Violet, see *Salvia nemorosa*
Sage, Yellow, see *Lantana*
Saint Agnes, Flower of, see *Helleborus*
Saint Albertus Magnus 1132
Saint Dorothy 1130, 1132
Saint John's-Wort, see *Hypericum*
Saint Patrick's Cabbage, see *Saxifraga umbrosa*
Saint Peter's Pence, see *Lunaria*
Saint Veronica 1348
Salisbury, Richard Anthony, 154
SALPIGLOSSIS [sal-pih-GLOSS-sis] *sinuata* (syn. *S. variabilis;* Painted Tongue) 1179–1180; *1179*
Salt Cedar, see *Tamarix gallica*
SALVIA [SAL-veeya] (Sage) 1180–1188
  azurea 1182; *1185*
  farinacea 1182
  glutinosa 1182
  grahamii 1183
  greggii 1183
  haematodes 1183

  horminum 1183
  leucantha (Mexican Bush Sage) 1184
  nemorosa (syns. *S.* x *superba, S. virgata* var. *nemorosa;* Violet Sage) 1184
  officinalis (Sage) 1184; *1180*
  patens 1186
  Sclarea 1186; *1187*
  splendens 1186; *1181*
  uliginosa 1187
  virgata 1187
Sampson, Black, see *Echinacea purpurea*
SANVITALIA [san-vit-TAY-leeya] 1188–1189
  mexicana, see *Zinnia angustifolia*
  procumbens 1188; *1189*
Sapindaceae (family)
  Aesculus 30–31
SAPONARIA [sap-o-NAIR-eeya] (Soapwort, Bouncing Bet) 1190–1193
  caespitosa 1191
  ocymoides 1191; *1192*
  officinalis (Bouncing Bet) 1191
  pumila (syn. *Silene pumilo*) 1193
Sappho (on roses) 1129
Sargent, Charles, work with *Malus* 837, 838; *Prunus sargentii* 1069; *Rhododendron* 1109
Sargon I, King, 1129
Satin Flower, see *Lunaria*
SAXIFRAGA [sax-IFF-ra-ga] (Rockfoil, Saxifrage) 1193–1201
  aizoides 1198
  Aizoon 1198; *1201*
  x *apiculata* 1198
  aspera 1198
  borisii 1198
  boydii 1198
  burseriana 1199; *1201*
  cochlearis 1199
  Cotyledon 1199
  Cymbalaria 1199
  ferdinandi-coburgii 1199
  fortunei 1199
  Geum 1199
  granulata 1199; *1201*
  griesbachii 1199
  x *haaggii* 1199
  Hirculus 1200; *1193*
  hypnoides 1199
  x *irvingii* 1200
  latepetiolata 1200
  lilacina 1200
  longifolia var. *Tumbling*

1469

Waters 1200
x *macnabiana* 1200
marginata 1200
oppositifolia (Mountain Saxifrage) 1200; *1194*
x *paulinae* 1200
pedemontana 1200
pennsylvanica 1200
retusa 1201
rotundifolia 1201; *1201*
sancta 1201
sarmentosa (Strawberry Geranium, Aaron's Beard, Beefsteak Saxifrage, Mother of Thousands) 1201; *1197*
umbrosa (St. Patrick's Cabbage, London Pride) 1201; *1194*
Saxifragaceae (family)
Astilbe 98–102; *Deutzia* 389–394; *Heuchera* 589–590; *Hydrangea* 622–633; *Kirengshoma palmata* 704–705; *Philadelphus* 991–998; *Saxifraga* 1193–1201
Saxifrage, see *Saxifraga*
Saxifrage, Beefsteak, see *Saxifraga sarmentosa*
Saxifrage, Mountain, see *Saxifraga oppositifolia*
SCABIOSA [skab-ee-O-sah] (Scabious) 1202–1206
atropurpurea (syns. *S. major, S. calyprocarpa*) 1204; *1204*
caucasica 1205; *1203*
graminifolia 1205
ochroleuca 1206
prolifera 1206
stellata 1206
Succisa (Devil's Bite) 1202; *1202*
Scabious, see *Scabiosa*
scale, control of 1150
Scallon, Father Hugo, work with roses 1158
Scarlet Haw, see *Crataegus coccinea*
Scarlet Lightning, see *Lychnis chalcedonica*
SCHIZANTHUS [sky-ZANthuss] (Butterfly Flower) 1206–1209
pinnatus 1208; *1207*
retusus 1209; *1209*
x *wisetonensis* 1209
Schrader, Heinrich Adolph, 1017
Schubert, Franz, 1258
SCILLA [SILL-a] (Squill, Bluebell) 1210–1212
autumnalis 1211
hispanica (syn. *Endymion hispanicus*; Spanish Bluebell) 1211
non-scripta (syns. *S. festalis, S. nutans, Endymion non-scriptus*; English Bluebell) 1211
peruviana (Cuban Lily) 1211
siberica (Siberian Squill) 1212; *1210*
tubergeniana 1212
Scotch Rose, see *Rosa spinosissima*
Scrophulariaceae (family)
Alonsoa 39–40; *Antirrhinum* 67–72; *Calceolaria* 139–143; *Digitalis* 411–415; *Erinus alpinus* 451–452; *Linaria* 772–776; *Maurandia* 844–847; *Mimulus* 860–864; *Nemesia* 891–893; *Penstemon (Pentstemon)* 976–982; *Phygelius* 1007–1009; *Torenia* 1293–1295; *Verbascum* 1338–1341; *Veronica* 1348–1351
Sea Dahlia, see *Coreopsis maritima*
Sea Holly, see *Eryngium*
Sea Lavender, see *Limonium*
Sea Pink, see *Armeria*
Seaside Goldenrod, see *Solidago sempervirens*
SEDUM [SEE-dum] (Stonecrop) 1212–1215
acre (Wall Pepper, Mossy Stonecrop, Golden Moss, Gold Dust, Love Entangle) 1213; *1213*
album (Worm Grass) 1213
caeruleum 1213; *1214*
dasyphyllum 1214
kamtschaticum 1214
sieboldii 1214; *1212*
spathulifolium 1214
spectabile 1214
spurium 1214
SEMPERVIVUM [semper-VYvum] (Houseleek) 1215–1218
allionii 1217
arachnoideum (Cobweb Houseleek) 1217; *1216*
ciliosum 1217
pittonii 1217
ruthenicum 1217
soboliferum (Hen and Chickens) 1217
tectorum (Common Houseleek) 1217; *1215*
zeleborii 1218
Seneca 1130

SENECIO (Ragwort, Groundsel) 1218–1225
Cineraria, see *S. maritima*
clivorum (syn. *Ligularia clivorum*) 1220
cruentus (syn. *Cineraria cruenta*; Cineraria) 1220; *1219*
elegans (syns. *S. purpureus, Jacobaea elegans*; Purple Ragwort) 1222
greyii 1222; *1222*
hectori 1223
japonicus (syn. *Ligularia japonica*) 1223
maritima (syns. *S. cineraria, Cineraria maritima*) 1223
multibracteatus 1224
scandens (syn. *S. angulata*) 1225
veitchianus (syn. *Ligularia veitchiana*) 1225
Senna, see *Cassia*
Sensitive Plant, see *Mimosa pudica*
Serres, Olivier de, on carnations 395
shade xxii–xxiv
Shakespeare, William, on lilies 754; on *Malus* 830; on "gillyvors" (*Matthiola*) 841; on daffodils 880; on primroses 1051; on roses 1126
Shamrock, Rose, see *Oxalis*
Sharon, Rose of, see *Hibiscus syriacus*
Shasta Daisy, see *Chrysanthemum maximum*
Sheep Laurel, see *Kalmia*
Sheepberry, see *Viburnum Lentago*
Shelley, Percy Bysshe, 858
Shepherd, Roy E., *The History of the Rose* 1128, 1135
Shewell-Cooper, W. E., on *Daphne* 366
Shirley Poppy, 945; also see *Papaver rhoeas*
Siberian Squill, see *Scilla siberica*
Siebold, Franz Philipp von, on *Camellia* 161; work with *Clematis* 264; *Desmodium* 388; *Epimedium* 434; *Malus prunifolia* 834; peonies 933; *Rosa* 1135, 1165; *Spiraea* 1249; *Wistaria* 1384
SILENE [sy-LEE-nee] (Catchfly, Campion) 1225–1228
acaulis (Cushion Pink) 1227
Armeria (Sweet William

Catchfly, None-so-Pretty) 1227
caroliniana (Wild Pink) 1227
pendula (syn. *S. rosea*) 1227; *1226*
pumilo, see *Saponaria pumila*
schafta (Moss Campion) 1228
Also see *Lychnis*
Silk Plant, see *Asclepias syriaca*
Silky Wisteria, see *Wistaria venusta*
Silver Bell Tree, see *Halesia carolina*
Silver Shilling, see *Lunaria*
Silver Vine, see *Actinidia polygama*
Simmonds, A., work with *Caryopteris* 191
Sims, John, on *Physalis* 1010
SINNINGIA [sin-INN-jeeya] (Gloxinia) 1228–1231
Hybrids 1231; *1230*
speciosa (syn. *Gloxinia speciosa*) 1231; *1228*
Siphonosmanthus delavayi, see *Osmanthus delavayi*
Sitwell, Sacheverell, on *Fuchsia* 473; on *Pelargonium* 962; on *Rosa* 1126, 1128; on *Tulipa* 1315
Skunkweed, see *Polemonium confertum*
Sky Flower, see *Thunbergia grandiflora*
Slade, John, work with camellias 161
Sleepy Dick, see *Ornithogalum umbellatum*
Slipperwort, see *Calceolaria*
Sloe, see *Prunus spinosa*
Smith, Erwin Frink, work with *Tecoma* 1278
Smith, James Edward, work with *Hydrangea* 623; on *Viburnum* 1353
Snakeroot, see *Liatris*
Snapdragon, see *Antirrhinum; Antirrhinum majus*
Snapweed, see *Impatiens*
Sneezeweed, see *Helenium*
Sneezewort, see *Achillea ptarmica*
Snow in Summer, see *Cerastium*
Snowbell, see *Styrax*
Snowdrift, see *Lobularia*
Snowdrop, see *Galanthus*
Snowdrop Tree, see *Halesia*
Snowdrop Windflower, see *Anemone sylvestris*
Snowflake, see *Leucojum*
Snowflake, Summer, see *Ornithogalum umbellatum*
snuff 14, 364
soap, *Saponaria officinalis* used as 1190
Soapwort, see *Saponaria*
Socialism, carnation as symbol of 395
soil and soils xxiv–xxvii
soil, acid xxv
soil, alkaline xxv
Solanaceae (family)
Cestrum 214–215; *Datura* 369–376; *Nicotiana* 904–910; *Petunia* 982–988; *Physalis* 1009–1013; *Salpiglossis sinuata* 1179–1180; *Schizanthus* 1206–1209; *Solanum* 1231–1234
Solandra herbacea, see *Datura ceratocaula*
SOLANUM [so-LAY-num] 1231–1234
Capsicastrum (Winter Cherry, Star Capsicum) 1232; *1232*
crispum 1233; *1232*
dulcamara 1232
jasminoides (Potato Vine) 1233; *1234*
Pseudocapsicum (Jerusalem Cherry) 1233
rantonnettii 1233
seaforthianum 1234; *1234*
wendlandii (Costa Rica Nightshade) 1234
SOLIDAGO [soli-DAY-go] (Goldenrod, Aaron's Rod) 1235–1237
caesia (Wreath Goldenrod) 1236
Hybrids 1237; *1236*
sempervirens (Beach Goldenrod, Seaside Goldenrod) 1236
Virgaurea (European Goldenrod) 1236
Solidaster 1235
SOPHORA [SOF-orr-a] 1237–1240
affinis 1239
japonica (Japanese Pagoda Tree) 1239
secundiflora (Mescal Bean) 1239
tetraptera (Kowhai) 1239; *1238*
Vicifolia 1240
Sorbaria angustifolia, see *Spiraea aitchisonii*
Sorbaria arborea, see *Spiraea arborea*
Sorbaria assurgens, see *Spiraea assurgens*
Sorrel, Jamaica, see *Hibiscus Sabdariffa*
Sorrel, Red, see *Hibiscus Sabdariffa*
Sorrel, Wood, see *Oxalis*
Soulange-Bodin, Étienne, work with *Magnolia* 819, 827
South Sea Myrtle, see *Leptospermum*
"Southern Cranberry," see *Hibiscus Sabdariffa*
Sowbread, see *Cyclamen*
Spanish Bluebell, see *Scilla hispanica*
Spanish Broom, see *Spartium junceum*
Spanish Button, see *Centaurea nigra*
Spanish Iris, see *Iris xiphium*
sparteine 349
Spartium 506
Spartium aetnensis, see *Genista aetnensis*
SPARTIUM [SPAR-shee-um]
junceum (Spanish Broom, Weaver's Broom) 1240–1241; *1242*
species, defined xxxvi–xxxvii
SPECULARIA [spek-yew-LAIR-eeya] (Venus's Looking Glass) 1241–1243; *1247*
speculum veneris (syns. *Legousia Speculum Veneris, Campanula Speculum*) 1243; *1247*
Speedwell, see *Veronica*
Speedwell, Cat's-tail, see *Veronica spicata*
Speedwell, Germander, see *Veronica Teucrium*
Sphenogyne anethioides, see *Ursinia anethioides*
Sphenogyne anthemoides, see *Ursinia anthemoides*
Sphenogyne versicolor, see *Ursinia versicolor*
Spider Flower, see *Cleome spinosa*
Spider Flower, Brazilian, see *Tibouchina semidecandra*
SPIRAEA [spy-REE-ya] 1243–1253
aitchisonii (syn. *Sorbaria angustifolia*) 1245
arborea (syn. *Sorbaria arborea*) 1245
x *arguta* (Garland Spiraea) 1246; *1245; 1249*
assurgens (syn. *Sorbaria*

assurgens) 1246; *1251*
bullata (syn. *S. crispifolia*) 1246
canescens (syn. *S. flagelliformis*) 1246
chamaedryfolia 1248
henryi 1248
japonica (syns. *S. callosa, S. fortunei*) 1248; *1250*
menziesii 1249; *1249*
prunifolia (Bridal Wreath) 1249
reevesiana (syn. *S. cantoniensis*) 1252
thunbergii 1252
x *vanhouttei* 1252
veitchii 1253
Also see *Astilbe*
Spirea, Blue, see *Caryopteris*
Spirea, Florist's, see *Astilbe*
Spotted Calla, see *Zantedeschia albomaculata*
Spring-Rice, T., 11
Spurge Laurel, see *Daphne Laureola*
Squill, see *Scilla*
Squill, Siberian, see *Scilla siberica*
Squirrel Corn, see *Dicentra canadensis*
STAPHYLEA [staff-ill-EE-ya] (Bladder Nut) 1253–1254
colchica (False Pistachio) 1254
pinnata 1254; *1253*
trifolia 1254
Staphyleaceae (family) *Staphylea* 1253–1254
Star, Yellow, see *Helenium autumnale*
Star Acacia, see *Acacia verticillata*
Star Capsicum, see *Solanum Capsicastrum*
Star Flower, Yellow, see *Sternbergia lutea*
Star Glory, see *Quamoclit*
Star Ipomoea, see *Quamoclit coccinea*
Star Jasmine, see *Trachelospermum*
Star of Bethlehem, see *Ornithogalum nutans*
Star of the Veldt, see *Dimorphotheca*
Starch Hyacinth, see *Muscari botryoides*
Statice, see *Limonium*
Statice *alliacea*, see *Armeria plantaginea*
Statice *dianthoides*, see *Armeria plantaginea*

Statice maritima, see *Armeria maritima*
Statice pseudoarmeria, see *Armeria pseudoarmeria*
Statice pubescens, see *Armeria maritima*
Stein, Gertrude, 1126
Stenolobium, synonym for *Tecoma* 1278
Sternberg, Count Moritz von, 1254
STERNBERGIA [stern-BURR-jeeya] *lutea* (Yellow Star Flower, Lily of the Field, Winter Daffodil) 1254–1256; *1255*
Stinking Clover, see *Cleome serrulata*
Stock, see *Matthiola*
Stoerck, Anton, 23
Stonecrop, see *Sedum*
Stonecrop, Mossy, see *Sedum acre*
stopping, operation of 234, 236
Stork's Bill Geranium, see *Pelargonium*
Stramonium, see *Datura Stramonium*
Stramonium fastuosum, see *Datura metel*
stratification 313
Strawberry Geranium, see *Saxifraga sarmentosa*
Strawberry Tomato, see *Physalis pruinosa*
Strawflower, see *Helichrysum*
Struve, work with *Cyclamen* 341
Stylomecon heterophylla, see *Meconopsis heterophylla*
Styracaceae (family) *Halesia* 546–548; *Styrax* 1256–1257
STYRAX [STY-racks](Snowbell) 1256–1257
americanum 1257
japonica 1257; *1256*
obassia 1257
Succisa pratensis (syn. *Scabiosa Succisa*; Devil's Bite) 1202
Sugar, Rose Petal, recipe for 1140
Sundrops, see *Oenothera*
Sunflower, see *Helianthus*
Sunflower, False, see *Helenium autumnale; Heliopsis laevis*
Sunflower, Orange, see *Heliopsis*
Sun Moss, see *Portulaca grandiflora*
Sun Plant, see *Portulaca*
Sun Rose, see *Helianthemum*

Swamp Bay, see *Magnolia virginiana*
Swamp Laurel, see *Kalmia; Magnolia virginiana*
Sweet, Robert, on *Cistus* 246; *Geranium* 519, 961; *Leptospermum flavescens* 743; *Tagetes* 1270; *Zantedeschia* 1389
Sweet Alyssum, see *Lobularia*
Sweet Bay, see *Magnolia virginiana*
Sweet Briar, see *Rosa rubiginosa*
Sweetheart Geranium, see *Pelargonium echinatum*
Sweet Olive, see *Osmanthus*
Sweet Pea, see *Lathyrus*
Sweet-scented Marigold, see *Tagetes lucida*
Sweet Sultan, see *Centaurea moschata*
Sweet Violet, see *Viola odorata*
Sweet William, see *Dianthus barbarus*
Sweet William, Wild, see *Phlox divaricata*
Sweet William Catchfly, see *Silene Armeria*
Symbolists 942
Synge, Patrick M., *Collins Guide to Bulbs* 224
Synsiphon luteum, see *Colchicum luteum*
SYRINGA [sih-RING-ga] (Lilac) 1258–1268
emodi 1264
x *hyacinthiflora* 1264
Josikaea (Hungarian Lilac) 1264; *1259*
oblata 1265
persica (Persian Lilac) 1265; *1265*
x *prestoniae*, see *S. villosa*
pubescens 1265
reflexa 1266
sweginzowii 1266
tomentella 1266
villosa 1266
vulgaris (Common Lilac) 1267; *1263*
Also see *Philadelphus*

Tabernaemontanus, Johann Teodor, 1133
Tacsonia mollissima, see *Passiflora mollissima*
Tacsonia pinnatistipula, see *Passiflora pinnatistipula*
Tages, *Tagetes* named for 1268

TAGETES [ta-JEE-teez]
    (Marigold) 1268–1274
  erecta (African Marigold,
    Aztec Marigold, Big
    Marigold) 1271; *1270*
  lucida (Mexican Marigold,
    Sweet-scented Marigold)
    1271; *1269*
  patula (French Marigold) 1273;
    1272
  sarmentosa (Climbing
    Marigold) 1273
  tenuifolia (syn. *T. Signata*;
    Bush Marigold) 1274
Tamaricaceae (family)
  Tamarix 1274–1276
Tamarisk, see *Tamarix*
Tamarisk, English, see *Tamarix
    anglica*
Tamarisk, French, see *Tamarix
    gallica*
Tamarisk, Kashgar, see *Tamarix
    hispida*
TAMARIX [TAM-aricks]
    (Tamarisk) 1274–1276
  anglica (English Tamarisk)
    1275
  gallica (French Tamarisk, Salt
    Cedar) 1275
  hispida (Kashgar Tamarisk)
    1275
  pentandra 1276
  tetrandra 1276; *1275*
Tanacetum argenteum, see
    Chrysanthemum argenteum
Tangier Scarlet Pea, see *Lathyrus
    tingitanus*
taxonomy (nomenclature) xxxvii
Tea, Indian, see *Ceanothus
    americanus*
Tea, Liberty, see *Ceanothus
    coeruleus*
Tea, New Jersey, see *Ceanothus
    americanus*
Tea, Oswego, see *Monarda*
Tea, Walpole, see *Ceanothus
    americanus*
Tea Olive, see *Osmanthus*
Tea Tree, see *Leptospermum*
TECOMA [teh-KO-ma] (Trumpet
    Creeper) 1276–1279
  chinensis, see *Campsis
    grandiflora*
  grandiflora, see *Campsis
    grandiflora*
  grandiflora var. *rubra*, see
    Campsis x *tagliabuana*
  mollis 1278
  radicans var. *grandiflora-
    purpurea*, see *Campsis* x
    tagliabuana

  smithii 1278
  stans (Yellow Elder) 1279; *1277*
  Also see *Bignonia; Campsis*
Tecomaria, synonym for
    Tecoma 1278
Telegraph Plant, see *Desmodium
    motorium*
Tennyson, Alfred, verse on Thorn
    324
Ternstroemiaceae (family)
    Actinidia 25–27; *Camellia* 159–
    173
Tertullian 1130
Teucer, first king of Troy,
    Teucrium named for 1279
TEUCRIUM [TU-kree-um]
    (Germander) 1279–1282
  chamaedrys (Wall Germander)
    1281
  fruticans 1281; *1280*
  subspinosum 1282
Texan Pride, see *Phlox
    drummondii*
THALICTRUM [tha-LICK-trum]
    (Meadow Rue) 1282–1284
  aquilegiifolium 1283; *1283*
  dipterocarpum 1283
  glaucum, see *T. speciosissimum*
  speciosissimum (syn. *T.
    glaucum*) 1284
Theaceae (family)
  Camellia 159–173
Thea japonica, see *Camellia
    japonica*
Thea reticulata, see *Camellia
    reticulata*
Theocritus (on *Anemone*) 56
Theodorus of Gaza, *Gazania*
    named for 502
Theophrastus, on stramonium
    372; on *Iris* 668; describes
    oleander 901; mentions
    Nigella 910; associated with
    Oenothera 912; on *Paeonia*
    934; on *Rosa* 1129, 1130; on
    Viola 1368
Thibaut IV, Count of Brie and
    Champagne and King of
    Navarre, 1132
Thimble Flower, see *Rudbeckia
    bicolor*
Thorn, see *Crataegus*
Thorn, Everlasting, see
    Pyracantha coccinea
Thornapple, see *Crataegus*
Thorn Apple, see *Datura
    Stramonium*
Thorne, T., on *Fuchsia* 481
Thor's Hat, see *Aconitum*
Thory, Claude Antoine, book on
    roses 1136

Thrift, see *Armeria*
thrips (insect pests) 1149
Thunberg, Carl Peter, work with
    Berberis 123; *Chaenomeles*
    216; *Clematis* 262, 264;
    Deutzia 390; *Forsythia* 464;
    Hosta 609; *Hydrangea* 623;
    Kerria japonica 700;
    Magnolia 819; *Prunus* 1064;
    genus named for 1284;
    names *Weigela* 1378
THUNBERGIA [thun-BER-
    jeeya] 1284–1288
  alata (Clock Vine, Black-eyed
    Susan) 1285; *1287*
  fragrans (Mountain Creeper)
    1285
  gibbsonii 1288
  grandiflora (Sky Flower) 1288;
    1286
Thymelaceaceae (family)
    Daphne 364–369; *Edgeworthia
    papyrifera* 429–430
TIBOUCHINA [tib-ook-KY-na]
  semidecandra (syn.
    Lasiandra macrantha;
    Brazilian Spider Flower,
    Glory Bush) 1288–1290;
    1289
Tick-Seed, see *Coreopsis*
Ticks, Beggar, see *Desmodium
    canadense*
Tiger Flower, see *Tigridia*
TIGRIDIA [ty-GRID-eeya] (Tiger
    Flower, Iris Shell Flower)
    1290–1292
  pavonia 1291; *1291*
  pringlei 1292
Tisswood, see *Halesia monticola*
TITHONIA [ty-THO-neeya]
    1292–1293
  diversifolia 1293
  rotundifolia (syns. *T. speciosa*,
    *T. tagetiflora, Helianthus
    speciosus*) 1293; *1292*
Toadflax, see *Linaria*
Tobacco Plant, see *Nicotiana
    tabacum*
Tomatello, see *Physalis ixocarpa*
Tomato, Husk, see *Physalis*
Tomato, Strawberry, see
    Physalis pruinosa
Tongue, Painted, see *Salpiglossis
    sinuata*
Torch Lily, see *Kniphofia*
Toren, Olaf, genus named for
    1295
TORENIA [toh-RENN-eeya]
    (Wishbone Flower) 1293–
    1295
  fournieri 1295; *1294*

1473

Touch-Me-Not, see *Impatiens*
Tournefort, J. P. de, describes *Achillea* 13; and generic name *Antirrhinum* 68; names *Bignonia capreolata* 126; names *Chrysanthemum* 226; names *Cornus* as genus 300; names variety of *Cyclamen* 341; names *Diervilla* 409; names *Hyacinthus* 616; names *Iris* 668; names *Lupinus* 809; work with *Rhododendron* 1093; theory of origins of honey 1096; names *Tagetes* 1268
trace elements xxxiii
TRACHELOSPERMUM [tra-KELL-o-SPERM-um] (syn. *Rhyncospermum;* Star Jasmine, Confederate Jasmine) 1295–1297
  asiaticum (syn. *T. divaricatum*) 1296
  jasminoides (syn. *Rhyncospermum jasminoides*) 1296; *1296*
Tradescant, John, work with *Jasminum* 689; *Lonicera* 794; *Punica* 1076; *Rhododendron* 1093; grows *Syringa* 1260
Traveller's Joy, see *Clematis Vitalba*
Tree, Chinese Snowball, see *Viburnum macrocephalum*
Tree, Cranberry, see *Viburnum opulus*
Tree, Daisy, see *Olearia*
Tree, Hemp, see *Vitex*
Tree, Monk's Pepper, see *Vitex*
Tree, Wayfaring, see *Viburnum Lantana*
Tree of Chastity, see *Vitex*
Trefoil, Bush, see *Desmodium canadense*
Trinity, pansy symbolic of the, 1366
Tritoma, see *Kniphofia*
Tritoma caulescens, see *Kniphofia caulescens*
Tritoma foliosa, see *Kniphofia foliosa*
Tritoma galpinii, see *Kniphofia galpinii*
Tritoma maroccana, see *Kniphofia macowanii*
Tritoma rigidissima, see *Kniphofia macowanii*
Tritoma uvaria, see *Kniphofia uvaria*

TRITONIA [try-TOE-neeya] (Montbretia, Blazing Star) 1297–1299
  crocata 1299
  x *crocosmiiflora* 1299; *1298*
  pottsii (syn. *Crocosmia pottsii*) 1299
Triumph Tulips 1328; *1330*
TROLLIUS [TROL-eeyus] (Globe Flower) 1300–1301
  asiaticus (Asiatic Globe Flower) 1301
  chinensis (syn. *T. ledebourii;* Chinese Globe Flower) 1301
  europaeus (European Globe Flower) 1301; *1300*
  laxus (American Globe Flower) 1301
  pumilus (Dwarf Globe Flower) 1301
Tropaeolaceae (family) *Tropaeolum* 1302–1310
TROPAEOLUM [tro-PEE-o-lum] (Nasturtium) 1302–1310
  azureum 1305; *1303*
  lobbianum, see *T. peltophorum*
  majus (Indian Cress, Nasturtium) 1305–1308; *1304; 1307*
  minus (Dwarf Nasturtium) 1308; *1308*
  peltophorum (syn. *T. lobbianum*) 1308; *1306*
  peregrinum (syn. *T. Canariensis;* Canary Creeper, Canary Bird Flower) 1309; *1302*
  polyphyllum 1309; *1306*
  speciosum (Flame Flower) 1309
  tuberosum 1309; *1305*
True Monkshood, see *Aconitum napellus*
Trumpet Creeper, see *Campsis; Tecoma*
Trumpet Flower, see *Bignonia capreolata*
Trumpet Vine, see *Campsis*
Tuberose, see *Polyanthes tuberosa*
Tulip, see *Tulipa*
Tulip, Horned, see *Tulipa acuminata*
Tulip, Lady, see *Tulipa clusiana*
Tulip, Water-lily, see *Tulipa kaufmanniana*
TULIPA [TEW-lip-a, *or* TOO-lip-a] (Tulip) 1310–1331
  acuminata (Horned Tulip) 1321; *1326*
  australis 1321

batalini 1321
clusiana (Lady Tulip) 1321; *1323*
dasystemon, see *T. tarda*
eichleri 1322
fosteriana 1322; *1318*
gesneriana 1322; *1311*
greigii 1324
Hybrids 1327–1331
kaufmanniana (Water-lily Tulip) 1324; *1330*
praecox 1324
pulchella 1325
saxatilis 1325
silvestris 1325; *1314*
sprengeri 1325
tarda (syn. *T. dasystemon*) 1325
Tulip Poppy, see *Hunnemannia fumariifolia*
Tulips, Breeder, 1328
Tulips, Cottage, 1329
Tulips, Darwin, 1328; *1328*
Tulips, Double Early or Peony-flowered, 1327; *1312*
Tulips, Double Late, 1330
Tulips, Green-flowered, 1330
Tulips, Lily-flowered, 1329; *1316*
Tulips, Mendel, 1327; *1320*
Tulips, Multiflora, 1330; *1330*
Tulips, Parrot, 1329; *1313*
Tulips, Rembrandt, 1329
Tulips, scented, 1316
Tulips, Single Early, 1327; *1317*
Tulips, Triumph, 1328; *1330*
Turkey Corn, see *Dicentra canadensis*
Turk's Cap Lily, see *Lilium Martagon; Lilium superbum*
Turnball, A., work with *Erica* 442
Turner, C. H., work with *Wistaria* 1384
Turner, William, names *Clematis* 255; on *Nerium* 901; on *Punica* 1076
Tutsan, see *Hypericum androsaemum*
Twinberry, see *Lonicera involucrata*
Twisted Eglantine, see *Lonicera periclymenum*
Tyr's Helmet, see *Aconitum*

Ugni molinae, see *Myrtus ugni*
ULEX [YEW-lex] (Furze, Gorse, Whin) 506, 1331–1332
  europaeus 1332; *1331*
  gallii 1332
  nanus 1332

Umbelliferae (family)
　Eryngium 452–455
Umbrella Tree, see *Magnolia tripetala*
Unwin, Charles, work with *Lathyrus* 724
Urban III, Pope, mentioned in poem about *Scabiosa* 1202
URSINIA [er-SINN-eeya] (Jewel of the Veldt) 1333–1335
　anethoides (syn. *Sphenogyne anethoides*) 1333
　anthemoides (syns. *Arctotis anthemoides, Sphenogyne anthemoides*) 1334
　Hybrids 1334
　pulchra, see *U. versicolor speciosa* 1334
　versicolor (syns. *U. pulchra, Sphenogyne versicolor*) 1334; *1335*
Ursinus, Johannes H., 1333
Uvedale, Doctor (gardener near London) 724

Vahl, Marin, names *Forsythia* 463
Vaillant, Sébastien, names *Helichrysum* 566
Valerian, see *Valeriana*
VALERIANA [va-leer-ee-AY-na] (Valerian) 1336–1337
　coccinea, see *Centranthus rubra*
　officinalis (Common Valerian, Garden Heliotrope) 1336; *1336*
　phu (Cretan Spikenard) 1336
　rubra, see *Centranthus rubra*
　sambucifolia 1337
Valerianaceae (family)
　Valeriana 1336–1337
Valoradia plumbaginoides, see *Ceratostigma plumbaginoides*
Vanilla, see *Heliotropium*
variety, defined xxxviii
Vasco da Gama 686
Veitch, John Gould, work with *Hamamelis* 549; *Jasminum* 689; *Kolkwitzia amabilis* 712; *Magnolia* 819; *Rhododendron* 1095
Velvet Plant, see *Verbascum thapsus*
VENIDIUM [veh-NID-eeyum] (Namaqualand Daisy, Monarch of the Veldt) 1337–1338

decurrens (syn. *V. calendulaceum*) 1338
fastuosum 1338; *1337*
　Also see *Dimorphotheca*
Ventenat, Étienne-Pierre, work with *Nemesia* 891
Venus, and the lily 751; and myrtle 877
Venus's Looking Glass, see *Specularia*
Venus Victrix, images of 1343
VERBASCUM [ver-BASS-kum] (Mullein) 1338–1341
　blattaria (Moth Mullein) 1340; *1341*
　bombyciferum 1340
　Hybrids 1341
　olympicum 1340
　phoeniceum (Purple Mullein) 1340; *1339*
　thapsus (Velvet Plant, Candle Wick, Flannel Wick) 1340; *1338*
VERBENA [ver-BEE-na] (Vervain) 1341–1348
　bonariensis 1345
　canadensis 1345; *1342*
　corymbosa 1346
　erinoides (syn. *V. laciniata*; Moss Vervain) 1346
　Hybrids (*Verbena hortensis*) 1347; *1347*
　peruviana (syn. *V. chamaedryfolia*) 1346; *1347*
　phlogiflora 1343; *1344*
　pulchella 1347
　rigida (syn. *V. venosa*) 1347; *1343*
　teucrioides 1343; *1344*
　venosa, see *V. rigida*
Verbenaceae (family)
　Caryopteris 191–193; *Clerodendrum* 272–275; *Lantana* 720–723; *Verbena* 1341–1348; *Vitex* 1376–1377
Verdi, Giuseppe, camellias in *La Traviata* 163
VERONICA [ver-ON-ik-ka] (Speedwell) 1348–1351
　chamaedrys (Birds' Eyes) 1349
　gentianoides 1349
　incana 1349
　longifolia 1349; *1351*
　pectinata 1349
　repens 1349; *1351*
　spicata (Cat's-tail Speedwell) 1351; *1351*
　Teucrium (syn. *V. latifolia*; Germander Speedwell) 1351; *1350*
Veronica, Saint, 1348

Vervain, see *Verbena*
Vervain, Moss, see *Verbena erinoides*
VIBURNUM [vy-BURR-num] 1352–1361
　acerifolium (Dockmackie) 1355
　betulifolium 1355
　bitchiuense 1355
　x *burkwoodii* 1356
　carlesii 1356
　cassinoides (Witherod, Appalachian Tea) 1356; *1360*
　cylindricum (syn. *V. coriaceum*) 1357
　davidi 1357
　fragrans 1357
　Lantana (Wayfaring Tree) 1358; *1352*
　Lentago (Nannyberry, Sheepberry) 1358
　macrocephalum (syns. *V. Keteleeri, V. arborescens*; Chinese Snowball Tree) 1358; *1354*
　nudum (Possum Haw) 1358
　odoratissimum 1358
　opulus (Guelder Rose, Cranberry Tree) 1359; *1359*
　rhytidophyllum 1359
　suspensum (syn. *V. Sandankwa*) 1359
　tinus (Laurustinus) 1360; *1353*
　tomentosum 1361; *1360*
Villon, François, 1258
Vilmorin, Maurice de, on cultivation of *Althaea* 43; work with *Berberis candidula* 124; cultivates *Buddleia davidii* 137; on *Campanula pyramidalis* 175; work with *Clematis* 261; cultivates *Cotoneaster* 313; work with carnations 395; *Heliotropium* 572; on *Iberis* 638; work with *Impatiens* 646; on *Iris* 670; on *Lupinus* 806; grows *Osmanthus delavayi* 923; *Rosa soulieana* 1166; work with *Spiraea* 1246; *Viola* 1368
VINCA [VIN-ka] (Myrtle, Periwinkle) 1361–1365
　difformis 1362
　herbacea 1364; *1363*
　major 1364
　minor 1364; *1364*
　rosea (syns. *Ammocallis rosea, Lochnera rosea*) 1365; *1361*
Vine Bower, see *Clematis viticella*

1475

VIOLA [vy-OH-la] (Violet, Pansy, Viola) 1365–1375
  bosniaca (syn. *V. elegantula*) 1371
  canina 1372; *1369*
  cornuta (Horned Violet, Viola) 1372; *1367*
  cucullata (syn. *V. papilionacea*) 1372
  gracilis 1373
  odorata (Sweet Violet, Garden Violet) 1373; *1373*
  papilionacea, see *V. cucullata*
  pedata (Bird's-Foot Viola) 1373
  pedunculata 1374; *1375*
  tricolor (Pansy) 1374; *1370; 1374*
Viola, Bird's-Foot, see *Viola pedata*
Violaceae (family) *Viola* 1365–1375
Violet, see *Viola*
Violet, Garden, see *Viola odorata*
Violet, Horned, see *Viola cornuta*
Violet, Sweet, see *Viola odorata*
Violet Sage, see *Salvia nemorosa*
Viper's Bugloss, see *Echium*
Virgil, on asters 90–91, *Cornus* in *The Aeneid* 300; myrtle 877; roses in *The Georgics* 1129
Virgin's Bower, see *Clematis viticella*
Viscaria viscosa, see *Lychnis Viscaria*
VITEX [VY-tecks] (Tree of Chastity, Chaste Tree, Hemp Tree, Monk's Pepper Tree) 1376–1377
  agnus-castus (Chaste Tree) 1377; *1376*
  negundo (syn. *V. incisa*) 1377
Volkameria fragrans, see *Clerodendrum fragrans*
Volkameria japonica, see *Clerodendrum trichotomum*
Von Ungnad, Dr., 1260

Wagner, Richard, 1258
Wahlenbergia 1017
Walkden, H., work with *Solidago* 1235
Wall Cress, see *Arabis*
Wallflower, see *Cheiranthus*
Wallflower, Alpine, see *Cheiranthus linifolius*
Wallflower, Siberian, see *Cheiranthus* x *allionii*
Wall Germander, see *Teucrium chamaedrys*
Wall Pepper, see *Sedum acre*
Warburg, Sir Oscar, comments on *Cistus* 246
War Helmet, see *Aconitum*
War of Roses 1133
Washington Lily, see *Lilium washingtonianum*
watercress 1302
Waterer, Anthony, work with *Rhododendron* 1095
Water Flag, see *Iris Pseudacorus*
Water Lemon, see *Passiflora laurifolia*
Water-lily Tulip, see *Tulipa kaufmanniana*
Watson, W., comments on *Jasminum* 686
Wattle, see *Acacia*
Waxbells, Yellow, see *Kirengshoma palmata*
Waxen Woad, see *Genista tinctoria*
Wax Pink, see *Portulaca*
Wayfaring Tree, 1353; also see *Viburnum Lantana*
Weaver's Broom, see *Spartium junceum*
Weeping Forsythia, see *Forsythia suspensa*
Weeping Golden Bell, see *Forsythia suspensa*
Weigel, Christian Ehrenfried von, 1378
WEIGELA [wy-JEE-la] 1377–1383
  coraeensis (syn. *Diervilla coraeensis*) 1378
  floribunda (syn. *Diervilla floribunda*) 1378
  florida (syns. *Diervilla pauciflora, Diervilla florida*) 1380; *1379*
  Hybrids 1381–1383; *1382*
  japonica (syn. *Diervilla japonica*) 1380
  middendorfiana (syn. *Diervilla middendorfiana*) 1381
  Also see *Diervilla*
Wendland, Joseph Christian, collection of *Erica* 442
Whin, see *Ulex*
White Eardrops, see *Dicentra cucullaria*
Whitlavia grandiflora, see *Phacelia Whitlavia*
Whorl-leaved Acacia, see *Acacia verticillata*
Wichura, Max Ernst, work with *Rosa* 1135
Wicky, see *Kalmia angustifolia*
Wild Pink, see *Silene caroliniana*
Wild Potato Vine, see *Ipomoea pandurata*
Wild Sweet William, see *Phlox divaricata*
Wilks, Reverend W., on *Papaver* 945
Williams, J. C., experiments with camellias 165
Williams, Lt. Robert, work with *Erica* 444
Willmott, Ellen, species named for 212; *The Genus Rosa* 1136
Wilson, Ernest H., work with *Actinidia chinensis* 25; *Berberis polyantha* 121; discovers *Berberis wilsoniae* 124; work with camellias 164, 165; discovers *Ceratostigma willmottianum* 212; work with *Clematis* 264, 267; *Cotoneaster* 315, 316, 317, 318, 320, 321; *Deutzia* 391, 393; *Hydrangea* 633; *Malus* 834, 837, 838; *Jasminum* 689; *Kerria japonica* 700; *Kolkwitzia amabilis* 712; *Lilium* 767, 768; *Lonicera* 794; *Magnolia* 822, 829; introduces *Pieris taiwanensis* 1017; on *Prunus* 1064; work with *Rhododendron* 1095, 1102, 1109, 1115; *Rosa* 1161, 1163; discovers *Spiraea prunifolia* 1249; *Spiraea veitchii* 1253; introduces species of *Syringa* 1261, 1266; work with *Viburnum* 1355, 1357, 1359
Wilson, Helen Van Pelt; and Bell, Léonie, on *Narcissus* 883; *Oenothera* 913; *Paeonia* 936; *Pelargonium* 962; *Verbena* 1341; *Viola* 1369
Windbreak, California, see *Lavatera assurgentiflora*
Windflower, see *Anemone*
Wind Flower, see *Pulsatilla*
Winter Bloom, see *Hamamelis*
Winter Cherry, see *Solanum Capsicastrum*
Winter Daffodil, see *Sternbergia lutea*
Wishbone Flower, see *Torenia*
Wistar, Caspar, genus named for 1383

WISTARIA [wis-TAIR-eeya, *or* wis-TEER-eeya](Wisteria) 1383–1388
  floribunda (Japanese Wisteria) 1386
  frutescens (syn. *Glycine frutescens*) 1386
  macrostachya 1386
  multijuga, see *W. floribunda* var. *macrobotrys*
  sinensis (syns. *W. consequana, Kraunhia sinensis, Glycine sinensis;* Chinese Wisteria) 1388; *1387*
  venusta (Silky Wisteria) 1388
Wisteria, see *Wistaria*
Wisteria, Chinese, see *Wistaria sinensis*
Wisteria, Japanese, see *Wistaria floribunda*
Wisteria, Silky, see *Wistaria venusta*
Witch Alder, see *Fothergilla*
Witch Hazel, see *Hamamelis*
Witherod, see *Viburnum cassinoides*
Withywind, see *Clematis Vitalba*
Wolf's Bane, see *Aconitum lycoctonum*
Wood, Devil, see *Osmanthus americanus*
Wood Anemone, see *Anemone nemorosa*
Woodbine, see *Clematis virginiana; Lonicera periclymenum*

Woodbine, Common, see *Lonicera caprifolium*
Woodbine, Rough, see *Lonicera hirsuta*
Woodbine, Small, see *Lonicera dioica*
Wood Sorrel, see *Oxalis*
Worm Grass, see *Sedum acre*
Wreath, Bridal, see *Spiraea prunifolia*
Wreath Goldenrod, see *Solidago caesia*
Wright, Richardson, on *Paeonia* 929

Yangtao, see *Actinidia chinensis*
Yarrow, see *Achillea*
Yellow Elder, see *Tecoma stans*
Yellow Flag, see *Iris Pseudacorus*
Yellow Star, see *Helenium autumnale*
Yellow Star Flower, see *Sternbergia lutea*
Yellow Tuft, see *Alyssum argenteum*
Youth and Old Age, see *Zinnia elegans*
Yulan, see *Magnolia denudata*
Yung-Lo, Emperor, and *Paeonia* 930

Zanoni, Alonzo, 40
Zantedeschi, Francesco, *Zantedeschia* named for 1389
ZANTEDESCHIA [zan-tee-DESK-eeya](Calla or Arum Lily) 1388–1392
  aethiopica (syn. *Richardia africana;* Arum Lily, Calla Lily) 1390; *1391*
  albomaculata (syn. *Richardia albomaculata;* Spotted Calla) 1392; *1392*
  elliottiana (syn. *Richardia elliottiana;* Golden Calla) 1392
  melanoleuca (syn. *Richardia melanoleuca;* Black-throated Calla) 1392
  rehmannii (syn. *Richardia rehmannii;* Pink Calla, Rose Calla) 1392
Zenobia 1015
Zinn, Johann Gottfried, genus named for 1393
ZINNIA [ZIN-eeya] 1393–1396
  angustifolia (syns. *Z. haageana, Z. mexicana, Z. ghiesbreghtii, Z. aurea, Sanvitalia mexicana*) 1395
  elegans (Youth and Old Age) 1395; *1394; 1395*
  linearis 1396; *1396*
Zonal Geranium, see *Pelargonium zonale*
zucchini 582

1477